2008
Gun Digest®

**Edited by
Ken Ramage**

Gun Digest® Books
An imprint of F+W Publications
700 East State Street • Iola, WI 54990-0001
715-445-2214 • 888-457-2873
www.gundigestbooks.com

Our toll-free number to place an order or obtain
a free catalog is (800) 258-0929.

Manuscripts, contributions and inquiries, including first class return postage, should be sent to the GUN DIGEST Editorial Offices, Gun Digest Books, 700 E. State Street, Iola, WI 54990-0001. All materials recieved will receive reasonable care, but we will not be responsible for their safe return. Material accepted is subject to our requirements for editing and revisions. Author payment covers all rights and title to the accepted material, including photos, drawings and other illustrations. Payment is at our current rates.

CAUTION: Technical data presented here, particularly technical data on handloading and on firearms adjustment and alteration, inevitably reflects individual experience with particular equipment and components under specific circumstances the reader cannot duplicate exactly. Such data presentations therefore should be used for guidance only and with caution. Gun Digest Books accepts no responsibility for results obtained using these data.

ISSN 0072-9043

ISBN 13: 978-0-89689-499-0
ISBN 10: 0-89689-499-1

Designed by Patsy Howell & Tom Nelsen

Edited by Ken Ramage

Printed in the United States of America

TWENTY-SIXTH ANNUAL
JOHN T. AMBER LITERARY AWARD
Terry Wieland

Terry Wieland on top of Mount Burko, overlooking the Great Rift Valley in Tanzania, in November 2006.

Terry Wieland is Shooting Editor of *Gray's Sporting Journal*. A full-time freelance writer since 1985, Wieland is also a columnist for *African Sporting Gazette*, *Safari Times* and *Petersen's RifleShooter*, and a frequent contributor to *Shooting Sportsman*, the *American Rifleman*, and GUN DIGEST.

Wieland has hunted extensively in America, Europe, and Africa. He made his first visit to Africa, as a freelance journalist, in 1971, to cover the civil war in the Sudan, returning in 1972 to cover the Asian exodus from Uganda and again in 1976 to see the bush war in Rhodesia. Since 1990, he has made 11 hunting safaris in Tanzania, Botswana, Zimbabwe and South Africa.

Wieland's books include *Spanish Best*, *Spiral-Horn Dreams*, *The Magic of Big Game*, and *A View From A Tall Hill – Robert Ruark in Africa*. His latest book is *Dangerous-Game Rifles* (Countrysport Press).

In 1999, Terry Wieland was named Leupold "Writer of the Year."

"My fascination with nitro-express cartridges dates from an Elmer Keith article on Westley Richards double rifles in a GUN DIGEST from the 1960s," Wieland says. "I bought a book by John Taylor, and then another. I was hooked, and I've stayed hooked." Wieland's own big double is a 500 Nitro Express, built in 2000 by John Rigby & Co. of California.

He is the winner of this 26th annual John T. Amber Award for his article "Nitro Express!", which appeared in GUN DIGEST 2007.

The only juried literary award in the firearms field, the John T. Amber Award replaced the Townsend Whelen Award originated by the late John T. Amber and later re-named in his honor. Now, a $1000 prize goes to the winner of this annual award.

Nominations for the competition are made by GUN DIGEST editor Ken Ramage and are judged by a distinguished panel of editors experienced in the firearms field. Entries are evaluated for felicity of expression and illustration, originality and scholarship, and subject importance to the firearms field.

This year's Amber Award nominees, in addition to Wieland, were:

Clarence M. Anderson,
"The Winchester Telescopic Sights of 1909"
Jim Foral,
"The Genesis of the Lyman #48 Sight"
James E. House,
"Winchester's Last Rimfire?"
George J. Layman,
"Military Rolling Blocks of the Rarest Kind"
John Malloy,
"Six Decades of Automatic Pistols"
Tom Osborne,
"A Tale of Three Outdoorsmen"
Harvey L. Pennington,
"An Americanized 450 3 ¼-in. Blackpowder Express"
J. M. Ramos,
"The AuVer System: 21st Century Combat Revolver"
Layne Simpson,
"Dean Grennell's 45 Super"

Serving as judges were John D. Acquilino, editor of *Inside Gun News*; Bob Bell, former editor-in-chief of *Pennsylvania Game News*; James W. Bequette, editorial director of Intermedia's outdoor group; David Brennan, editor of *Precision Shooting*; Sharon Cunningham, director of Dixie Gunworks' Pioneer Press; Pete Dickey, former technical editor of the *American Rifleman*; Jack Lewis, former editor and publisher of *Gun World*; Mark Keefe IV, editor of the *American Rifleman* and Dave Petzal, deputy editor of *Field & Stream*.

This year, there is a change in the ranks of our judges. Bill Parkerson has stepped away after years of service, and we are very pleased to welcome Mark Keefe IV to the John T. Amber Award jury in his stead. Parkerson, himself a former editor of the *American Rifleman* magazine, and today the director of research and information for the NRA, has provided keen insight and journalistic sensibility over the years, and we are all the better for it. Thank you, Bill.

INTRODUCTION

It has been another active year in the shooting sports. More companies have changed hands – or are in the process of doing so as this is written – and we have many new products to consider.

Smith & Wesson has acquired Thompson/Center Arms, and early indications are the two are a good fit. T/C introduced its first bolt-action rifle, the ICON, at the SHOT Show. Later, during the 2007 NRA Show, S&W introduced its new bolt-action rifle, the first in many years.

As this book goes to press, the purchase of Remington Arms by Cerberus Capital Management is in process. Cerberus, you may know, recently bought Bushmaster Firearms, and is also in the process of buying the automaker Chrysler.

In the publishing realm, *Outdoor Life* and *Field & Stream* magazines are under new ownership as of March. Our friends at *Guns & Ammo, Shooting Times*, etc., are also under new ownership. Early indications are that the transfers went smoothly, and that the publications we have enjoyed for years are unaffected.

Product development is always a good sign, indicative of a vital manufacturing sector and consumer market. The annual SHOT Show is typically when most new product announcements are made. This year's show in Orlando was no exception. Major new items were being introduced as late as the mid-April NRA Show. Read the Contributing Editors' reports for a complete recap; here are just a few to pique your interest.

Bushmaster has a new AR-15 model chambered for the new Hornady-loaded cartridge, the 450 Bushmaster. I had the opportunity to fire this combination in January and came away impressed. Sturm, Ruger & Company has a number of new rifles and pistols for 2007. The Model 77 is now available in the new Hawkeye rifle format. On our front cover are the Hawkeye Alaskan (synthetic stock) and the Hawkeye African. Both are chambered for the new 375 Ruger round, a new cartridge factory-loaded by Hornady. Ruger also has a target version of their Mini-14 – the Mini-14 Target Rifle – featuring two stock options and other refinements, including a hammer-forged barrel fitted with a harmonic dampener

to fine-tune the accuracy of whichever flavor of 223 ammunition you are using.

Handgunners are not forgotten. S&W brought their new compact M&P9 to a pre-SHOT Show range day, and I had the opportunity to fire it. The little 9mm worked perfectly, and was very accurate. S&W also introduced a line of classic models, to include the Model 1917, the Model 29 and several others. Colt announced a compact 1911 called the Concealed Carry. Iver Johnson enters the 1911 arena with two models, chambered in 45 ACP and 22 LR, that are promised later in 2007. An upcoming introduction I'll be watching for is USFA's reintroduction of the (Colt) Woodsman 22 autopistol. I spotted a partially-machined frame in the company's SHOT Show display and had the opportunity to visit with the company's president. He says there are more to come, after the Woodsman. Taurus has also been busy, and their recently-introduced 1911 is becoming available in the blued version; stainless comes later this year. Cimarron adds to their line of cartridge conversion single-action revolvers with models slightly enlarged to accept the 45 Colt cartridge. I like the looks of the converted.Remington New Model Army. Ruger has two interesting revolvers, both derived from well-established models. These are a pair of 44 Magnum "snubbies," one the 4-inch Redhawk and the other the 2¾-inch Alaskan.

Handloaders have new die sets, accessories and bullet moulds in 2007, thanks to all the "old" and new cartridge introductions. Hornady, Lyman and Redding have numerous new reloading die sets, and Lyman and Redding announced several new mould designs, primarily for the cowboy action shooter. RCBS has a number of new items. One that caught my eye is the Shell Holder Rack, a great way to organize and store a bunch of loose shellholders.

In this edition we have several articles that are – in a fundamental way – of great relevance to America's shooting sports activity. Common threads that run through them are the 22 rifle and cartridge, youth shooting experiences, national shooting programs, and personal involvement and dedication. I refer to "You, Me and the CMP," by Chuck Karwan, "22 Dreamin'," by Jesse "Wolf" Hardin, "Winchester 22-Caliber Rifles...," by Hollis M. Flint and "Fifty Years in Boy Scout Shooting," by John Malloy.

We consider ourselves a nation of riflemen, and in the not-too-distant past we pretty much were. We can continue to be, despite recent shifts in our society. Nearby is a rather unique photograph of former President Harry Truman presenting a shooting award to a high school JROTC rifle team in 1958, just five years after leaving office. Back then, many schools had JROTC units and many had rifle teams, often several to accommodate student interest. Girls' teams were common, and the young ladies found their gender was anything but a handicap, as their scores often rivaled or exceeded those of their male counterparts. The point is that sport shooting was wide-spread, and many people were introduced to it early in life. The shooting sports scene is different today, but certainly still active and vital. With organizations like the CMP, the Boy Scouts, the NRA, and dedicated individuals like our John Malloy and others like him, America's shooting sports heritage will continue to evolve. Young men and women, once pleasantly introduced to recreational shooting, may well stay with it throughout their lives.

This is the eighth edition of this annual book that I have had the pleasure of editing. I have enjoyed each one, and learned a lot along the way. Corresponding with readers and working with new authors has been a particular pleasure, and my appreciation of our shooting sports heritage has only deepened. I wish you a good year.

In 1958, former President Harry Truman (out of office just five years) presented awards at an invitational smallbore rifle match held in Independence, Missouri. Here, receiving their team trophy, are the members of the Leavenworth High School (Leavenworth, Kansas) JROTC rifle team (l/r): Bill Drake, Bob Aufdemberge, President Truman, Ken Ramage (your editor), Tom Boots and team coach U. S. Army MSgt. Eugene W. McConiga.

Ken Ramage, Editor
GUN DIGEST

GUN DIGEST Staff

EDITOR
Ken Ramage

CONTRIBUTING EDITORS

Holt Bodinson – Ammunition, Ballistics & Components; Web Directory
Raymond Caranta – The Guns of Europe
J. W. "Doc" Carlson – Blackpowder Review
John Campbell – Single-Shot Rifles
John Haviland – Shotgun Review

John Malloy – Handguns Today: Autoloaders
Layne Simpson – Rifle Review
John Taffin – Handguns Today: Six-guns & Others
Tom Turpin – Engraved & Custom Guns
Wayne Van Zwoll – Scopes & Mounts

ABOUT THE COVERS

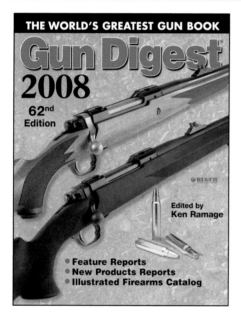

FRONT COVER

The new Ruger M77 Hawkeye Alaskan and the Hawkeye African are both chambered for the new 375 Ruger cartridge. This new rifle and cartridge combination provides shooters with a standard length action, shorter bolt stroke and an easier-feeding rifle, while producing better ballistics than the 375 H&H Magnum. These powerful new rifles are approximately half the price of a comparable 375 H&H Magnum rifle.

The M77 Hawkeye African features a slim American walnut stock with a red rubber recoil pad, rugged V-notch sights, a 23-inch hammer-forged barrel and an overall matte blue finish. The African carries standard M77 Hawkeye features including the new LC6 trigger, Mauser-type controlled feed extractor, positive floor plate latch, three-position safety, integral scope mount and free scope rings.

The new Ruger M77 Hawkeye Alaskan is also chambered for the powerful new 375 Ruger cartridge and is now available in matte-finish stainless steel. The Alaskan version has iron sights on its 20-inch barrel, is available only in 375 Ruger and is fitted with a synthetic stock. Like the African, it is fitted with the new LC6 trigger, Mauser-type controlled feed extractor, positive floor plate latch, three-position safety, integral scope mount and free scope rings.

BACK COVER

The Ruger 4-Inch Redhawk –
New this year from Ruger is a Redhawk 44 Magnum revolver with a 4-inch barrel, fitted with stocks that handle the recoil better than the standard factory grips. It is all stainless steel with a massive six-shot cylinder, and a solid frame with no sideplate.

There are two major changes to the original Redhawk besides the obvious shorter barrel. Instead of the interchangeable front sight system, the 4-inch Redhawk has a pinned-in ramp front sight with a red insert, and a white outline rear blade.

The stocks, instead of the standard factory wood grips, are hand-filling finger-grooved Hogue rubber grips, which are much more comfortable when firing heavy 44 Magnum loads. The surface of these Hogue grips also offers a more secure hold, thanks to their pebble-grained but non-punishing surface, than provided by the original smooth wood grips. The result? A perfect revolver for hard outdoor use.

The Ruger Mini-14 Target Rifle –
Ruger's new Mini-14 Target Rifle, chambered for the 223 Remington cartridge, is designed for rapid-fire action shooting competition and comes in two versions: one wearing a gray laminated target stock and the other fitted with a Hogue overmolded stock. Both include the following features: Heavy, hammer-forged stainless steel barrel with recessed target crown. Adjustable harmonic dampener to tune rifle for maximum accuracy. Non-slip grooved rubber recoil pad. Simple, rugged Garand-style breechbolt locking system, with a fixed-piston gas system and a self-cleaning gas cylinder. Stainless steel scope rings are included with both versions.

CONTENTS

PAGE 42   PAGE 43   PAGE 58   PAGE 59

CATALOG OF ARMS AND ACCESSORIES

A military instructor assists a young Scout in firing from the standing position at Camp Emerald Bay, CA, in 1958.
(BSA Archives)

FIFTY YEARS IN
BOY SCOUT SHOOTING

by John Malloy

Sadly, there are forces in our country that do not like this sort of activity. They would like to see the shooting sports abolished. They would like to see private ownership and use of firearms ended. Preventing young people from shooting is a goal with such people, and opposition reportedly has been raised against Boy Scout shooting. I think that the Boy Scout shooting programs are a force to keep the shooting sports alive in this country. I would encourage individuals and gun clubs to contact their local Boy Scout councils and offer to work with them on shooting opportunities.

Below: *A Scout tries prone position rifle shooting in this 1989 photo from the National Capital Area Council.* (BSA Archives)

I remember reading somewhere that the Boy Scouts of America (BSA) is the organization that uses the greatest quantity of 22-caliber rimfire ammunition each year. I cannot remember the source, and such a statement might be difficult to verify. However, there is no denying that the eager young Scouts in the BSA's shooting programs like to shoot up a lot of ammunition. I know this first-hand.

I have been fortunate to be involved in coordinating and running Boy Scout shooting programs for a period spanning over half a century. I ran my first BSA summer-camp shooting program back in 1956 and celebrated my 50th anniversary by running a BSA summer-camp shooting program in 2006.

Ever since its formation in 1910, the BSA has involved boys in a variety of shooting sports. The benefits of a shooting program to the Boy Scout organization are obvious. Boys want to shoot. The two most popular areas of a summer camp are Shooting Sports and Aquatics. The chance to shoot is a factor that draws many boys into the Scout program and keeps them involved.

In return, the Scout shooting program benefits the shooting sports in general. School-age boys who are given a safe exposure to the fun of the shooting sports are less likely to be influenced by anti-gun rhetoric. Many young Scouts are introduced to shooting, become interested, and grow to become responsible hunters, recreational shooters or competitive shooters. Some become instructors who will train other young people.

In like fashion, the benefits of a shooting program to the boys themselves are many. Shooting helps a boy to develop self-discipline and responsibility. Shooting is a good safe sport, actually a number of sports, with many variations of guns, targets and ranges. Unlike some sports, interest and participation in shooting can last a lifetime. Boys of small stature or those with health problems may not do well in many team sports. However, just about any boy who learns the fundamentals and then practices can become a good shooter.

Through the Scout program, many boys who have never shot before are introduced to the shooting sports. In some cases, the family has never developed an interest in shooting, and is glad to have the certified instruction that the Scout program provides. Other parents may actually tend to be anti-gun, but because shooting is done as a Scout activity, they allow their sons to participate. There are many reasons parents support the Boy Scout shooting programs.

However, most boys like to shoot simply because it is fun!

What can Scouts shoot? The Scout Standards, set by the national office in Irving, Texas, are very specific.

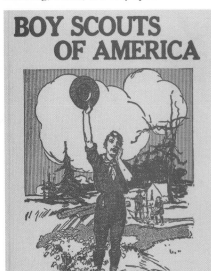

BOY SCOUTS OF AMERICA

HANDBOOK FOR BOYS

Cub Scouts, those below age 11, can shoot BB guns in a supervised camp environment.

Boy Scouts, ages 11 through 17, can shoot 22-caliber rifles, shotguns and muzzleloading caplock rifles in a variety of programs. Boy Scouts can also shoot airguns under the same conditions as Cub Scouts.

Venture Scouts (formerly Explorer Scouts) to age 20 can shoot all the guns the Cubs and Boy Scouts can. They have also recently been approved to shoot modern pistols and revolvers. As an aside, the Venture program is now also open to girls, and the shooting program can be a draw for many young ladies.

The opportunities for shooting within the programs of the BSA are better now than in times past.

When I was a Cub Scout during the 1945-1948 period, Cubs had no shooting program at all. Of course, at that time, at the end of World War II and the immediate post-war period, it seemed that all boys of all ages were interested in guns. I could hardly wait to become a Boy Scout, in part so that I could get into the shooting program, which at that time consisted of 22 rifle marksmanship.

My timing was poor. In 1949, the year in which I turned 12, the BSA changed the starting age for Scouts to 11. I was instantly cheated out of a year of Scouting!

Shooting was gaining importance as a part of BSA summer camp programs. After the end of World War II in 1945, 133 camps received permits to provide rifle marksmanship

Left: The first Boy Scout handbook (here shown as a reprint) was published in 1911. Among the original merit badges included in it was the Marksmanship merit badge. Boy Scout shooting has been with us since the first days of the Boy Scouts of America.

Tallahassee Rifle & Pistol Club member Steve McClain, in period dress, instructs a Scout at the muzzleloading rifle event of the TRPC's annual Boy Scout Fun Shoot in 1999.

programs. When I entered Scouting a few years later, our local camp, Camp Soule, near Safety Harbor, Florida, had started building a rifle range. Unfortunately, I never got a chance to use it. Pending the rifle range completion, the camp substituted the Mo-Skeet-O program of shooting miniature clay targets with 22-caliber shotguns using the tiny 22 LR Shot cartridges. I don't remember ever breaking one of those tiny clays (everybody waited too long to shoot) but I was always there when the shooting started.

Marksmanship - 1911

The Boy Scouts of America had been incorporated in 1910, and the shooting program was among the first programs that rated a merit badge in the new organization. The first Boy Scouts of America publication, *Handbook for Boys*, (offered the next year, in 1911), listed the Marksmanship Merit Badge among

Right: *Malloy's first Boy Scout handbook was this 1948 edition. Marksmanship was an integral and important part of BSA's program in the post-WWII years.*

❧ ● ❧ ● ❧ ● ❧ ● ❧ ● ❧

the first merit badges. The new youth organization had a relationship with the National Rifle Association (NRA), an organization that had been formed four decades before, in 1871. The requirements for the Marksmanship badge simply stated, "To obtain a merit badge for Marksmanship a scout must...qualify as a marksman in accordance with the regulations of the National Rifle Association."

In 1903, the National Rifle Association (at that time only 32 years old), had begun planning toward organizing a youth shooting program. By 1908, a boy in an NRA program could earn a Junior Marksman award for either indoor

Malloy officiates as Webelos Cub Scouts shoot BB guns from the standing position. The scene was the Summer 1987 Cub Scout Day Camp, in Houston, TX.

This 1953 edition of the Marksmanship merit badge pamphlet was used by the writer when he ran his first BSA summer camp shooting program back in 1956.

❦ ● ❦ ● ❦ ● ❦ ● ❦ ● ❦

or outdoor shooting. This program is apparently the one by which a Scout could earn the early Marksmanship merit badge. The Indoor award required 10 shots standing and 10

shots prone, fired at 50 feet. I have no information as to what targets were used or what scores were required.

However, the close relationship between BSA and NRA in determining the principles to be covered in Scout instruction and shooting remained with time, and it continues to this day.

That first *Handbook for Boys* included advertising in the back section, a practice that continued into the 1960s. Ads for axes, knives, first-aid kits and other related items were included. Guns and shooting accessories were included in every *Handbook* that carried advertising. The 1911 handbook featured a full-page ad from Remington-UMC that described two Remington 22-caliber rifles. The first was a long single-shot rolling-block 22 called the "Boy's Scout Special," at $5. (Note that this rifle is often listed in some modern publications as the "Boy Scout Special." The name was close to, but not quite that. Remington possibly intended to imply, but not to state, that the rifle was approved by the BSA.) Also shown was the new Remington slide-action 22 repeater, listing for $12.65.

After the first handbook in 1911, the BOY SCOUTS OF AMERICA worked

with the National Rifle Association in formulating a new qualification course to be used for earning the Marksmanship Merit Badge. The new standards required shooting a 22-caliber rifle at 50 feet and scoring 80 or better out of a possible 100 points. Using a special bullseye target with "5" as its highest score, a Scout had to fire 10 shots standing and 10 shots prone. The standing score had to be at least 38 out of 50, and the prone score 42 or better.

A revised new edition of the *Handbook for Boys* was printed in 1914, and that edition covered the revised Marksmanship requirements. Later, new editions of the *Handbook* were subsequently published in 1927 and in 1940. The covers of those two books featured paintings by a promising young artist, Norman Rockwell.

Marksmanship - 1948

By the time I became a Scout in 1949, the next offering, the 1948 edition, was the current handbook. By then, the requirements for the Marksmanship Merit Badge specified that shooting be done at 50 feet with a 22-caliber rifle. Iron sights were required, and the target was the official NRA 50-foot Junior target (same as the current NRA A-1 target), with 10 as the highest scoring ring. Five shots were fired at each target, for a possible score of 50.

- From the standing position, a Scout had to shoot four targets with a score of 30 or better.

- From the prone position, six targets with a score of 40 or better were needed.

- In addition to shooting skills, the knowledge of safety rules, cleaning a rifle, sight adjustment and other requirements were listed.

❦ ● ❦ ● ❦ ● ❦ ● ❦ ● ❦

A rifle range at the Philmont Scout ranch in New Mexico was the scene many years ago when this picture was posed, of Scouts shooting 22 rifles from the standing position.

(BSA Archives)

Ads in my 1948 handbook included Peters High-Velocity 22 ammunition, and Iver Johnson 22-caliber rifles. Remington (by then affiliated with DuPont) had a two-page ad showing the company's new Model 521T "Junior Special" 22 target rifle. An interesting "Indoor Target Rifle" that used rubber tubing for power and shot BBs was advertised by Johnson Automatics, with a picture of young Melvin M. Johnson III saying, "My Dad invented a gun for us!" "Dad" was, of course, Melvin M. Johnson II, the inventor of the Johnson rifles and light machineguns used by the Marines during World War II.

The next *Handbook for Boys* was introduced in 1949, only a year after the 1948 edition. Apparently the primary reason for the new handbook was to document the change in the minimum age requirement from 12 to 11. The requirements for the Marksmanship Merit Badge remained exactly the same.

Ten years would pass before another edition of the handbook came out in 1959. The cover was again a painting by Norman Rockwell. The name of the publication had changed from *Handbook for Boys* to *Boy Scout Handbook*. Inside, other changes had been made, and the requirements for the merit badges were no longer listed. Scouts looking for more information about a particular merit badge needed to refer to the Merit Badge Pamphlet specific to that award. Ads relating to guns and shooting were prevalent in this handbook. Several printings were made. A 1963 printing of the 1959 edition contained ads for Colt 22 rifles and bows, Browning 22 autoloading rifles and bows, Remington ammunition and the Model 521 rifle, Weaver riflescopes, Winchester's new lever, pump and semiautomatic 22 rifles, the Daisy Model 99 Target Special BB gun, the Mossberg Model 320B and 340B 22 rifles, and the Savage Model 63 22 rifle.

⊗ ● ⊗ ● ⊗ ● ⊗ ● ⊗ ● ⊗

Unidentified Boy Scouts from some decade long past fire 22-caliber rifles from the kneeling position at a rustic shooting range. (BSA Archives)

Another edition appeared in 1965. Then, in 1972, the eighth edition, then simply called *Scout Handbook*, reinstated the listing of requirements for all the merit badges. By that time, the Marksmanship Merit Badge had been replaced (in 1967) by the Rifle and Shotgun Shooting merit Badge. Although the name was new, the badge itself still had the same appearance, with concentric red and white rings forming a stylized bullseye target. Now, however, two options were offered for earning the award—rifle shooting or shotgun shooting. That meant that either rifle shooting or shotgun shooting—but not both—could be chosen. This situation would change before long, however.

A new edition, with a name change back to *Boy Scout Handbook*, appeared in 1979. Norman Rockwell again provided the cover, marking over half a century since his first 1927 *Handbook for Boys* cover. In this edition, the merit badges were pictured with a brief description, but the requirements were not listed.

Subsequent editions of 1990 and 1998 (the 1998 version is the one in use at the time of this writing) listed all merit badges available to Scouts, and, after 1989, two shooting merit badges—now separated into Rifle Shooting and Shotgun Shooting—have been available to Scouts. The late handbooks did not give the requirements, at least not for badges that are not required for the rank of Eagle Scout. The shooting merit badges are elective badges, and are not required for Eagle. However, Rifle Shooting and Shotgun Shooting still remain two separate merit badges. Scouts of today who are interested in shooting have twice the opportunity to earn shooting merit badges than in earlier times.

For all practical purposes, the evolution of the Boy Scout shooting programs is best seen through the merit badge pamphlets themselves. The first one I acquired was the 1953 edition, and that was the one I used when I was chosen to run that first Boy Scout summer camp program back in 1956.

Looking back, it is hard to remember exactly how I got that position. I had been interested in guns and shooting ever since I was a young boy. This interest seemed universal to almost all male "Depression Babies" who grew up during and after World War II. All my friends were interested in what kinds of firearms were being used in the war, how they worked, and how to shoot them. It

Malloy, left, checks the sign-in sheets with volunteer David Hamilton for the October 2002 Boy Scout Fun Shoot in Tallahassee, FL. Malloy started the program in 1991, and it soon became an annual event.

≈◉≈◉≈◉≈◉≈◉≈

seemed every boy wanted to shoot anything he could get his hands on. After the war, ammunition became available for civilian use again, and shooting programs seemed to grow up everywhere. I attended a shooting program put on by the St. Petersburg Police Department, and joined an NRA-affiliated junior rifle club sponsored by the AMVETS. My enthusiasm for shooting was perhaps more important to me because of my chronic asthma, which kept me out of normal team sports. Shooting, however, was something I could do well. In 1948, at age 11, I bought my first rifle, a manually-cocked single-shot Winchester 67. I bought that wonderful 22 rifle second-hand with nine dollars of my lawn-mowing money. By the early 1950s, I had begun working on the NRA Junior Division 50-foot rifle program awards.

I graduated from St. Petersburg High School in 1955 and went to college at Emory University in Atlanta. One of the first things I checked out was the existence of a school rifle team. I joined and in 1956 had become captain of the team. With a real target rifle to use, I completed the Junior Division course, earning the highest rank of Distinguished Rifleman. The rifle team made a number of road trips, and we were invited to shoot against the United States Marine Corps smallbore team at Parris Island, SC. One of the great moments of my young life came when I outscored the last man on the Marine team! While we were at Parris Island, the Marines allowed us to shoot the full long-range National Match course with the M-1 Garand (I qualified as Expert), and to also shoot Browning Automatic Rifles (BARs) over a short-range course. To say that my life interests were beginning to revolve around guns and shooting may have been an understatement.

Again, I do not remember exactly how I heard about the rifle instructor position at Boy Scout Camp Bert Adams near Atlanta, at Vinings, Ga. (Camp Bert Adams still exists, but it is now in Covington, Ga. Atlanta grew outward in subsequent years and overwhelmed the original Vinings location.)

When I learned about the camp rifle instructor position, it was another aspect of shooting, and I jumped at the chance. Shooting was becoming an ever-larger part of the Boy Scout program. At the 3rd Boy Scout National Jamboree, held in July 1953, over 11,000 Scouts had participated in the rifle shooting event. (That number would double at the next Jamboree, four years later.) The 1953 Jamboree was held near Los Angeles (California was not anti-gun back in those days), and a temporary 50-position rifle range had been constructed. The event was so popular that Scouts lined up for hours to get a chance to shoot.

My 1956 camp, the original Camp Bert Adams, had just a small, four-position rifle range, but I loved it. I was in my element. Beside the Marksmanship Merit Badge, the camp program awarded the NRA Junior Division marksmanship awards as well. I was very familiar with that program, having just completed it.

All was not smooth. Before camp opened, a break-in occurred, and the camp rifles were stolen. For the first week, I ran the course with my Winchester 67 and two borrowed rifles, using only three of the four shooting bays at the range. In a way, it gave me a chance to upgrade the camp equipment, as I was able to order 22-caliber rifles with aperture rear sights, instead of the open sights previously used. We received Remington Model 510P rifles, sturdy single shots with Remington's simple friction-locked adjustable "Point-crometer" receiver sight.

Marksmanship - 1953

The Bert Adams camp, as did most others, used 22-caliber rifles. However, by 1953, the options for earning the Marksmanship merit badge had grown, as indicated in the new merit badge pamphlet issued that year.

- The score requirements remained the same as in 1948—30 points out of a possible 50 points for 5 shots standing, and 40 of a possible 50 points for 5 shots prone. Four qualifying targets were required in the standing position, and six were needed for prone position.

- Thus, ten qualifying targets with a minimum total score of 360 points had to be fired.

However, perhaps because of the problem of finding suitable 50-foot range space (I remembered the unfinished range at the camp I had attended as a young Scout) other options using airguns were now available:

- A 15-foot course could be fired using spring-powered BB gun-type air rifles, fired at the appropriate 15-foot official BSA or NRA target.

- A 25-foot course could be fired with pneumatic or gas-type air rifles (not larger than 22-caliber), or with spring-type air rifles with barrels rifled for pellets.

- An interesting variation for the 25-foot course—used for only a short time—was to use a standard 22-caliber rifle, but use 22 BB Cap or 22 CB Cap rimfire cartridges. (BB Cap and CB Cap ammunition was readily available in the 1950s, but eventually lost popularity. In the 1960s, the BB/CB Cap option was omitted from the merit badge pamphlet.)

Along with the merit badge program, the Bert Adams camp also let the Scouts shoot to earn the NRA Junior Division marksmanship awards. Showing the close relationship between the BSA and the NRA, the complete requirements for the NRA Junior Rifle Awards were incorporated into the merit badge pamphlet.

The NRA qualification program had an interesting history. It was an essential part of organized youth shooting.

The predecessor of the NRA qualification awards had been the awards used by the Winchester Junior Rifle Corps. This program had been initiated by the Winchester Repeating Arms Company in 1918, at the end of World War I. The program was a qualification course in which a young shooter could earn a number of medals for progressively better shooting. The program was popular. By 1925, only seven years later, 55,000 medals had been awarded. Winchester carried on until the next year, 1926, when the program was taken over by the National Rifle Association. The resulting NRA program combined the best points of the previous Winchester and NRA programs, and became the NRA's Junior Marksmanship Qualification program, with specific targets and awards.

The first award was the Pro-Marksman award, earned by shooting 10 targets with a score of 20 or better per target, fired from any position. The qualification course then continued through Marksman, Marksman First Class, Sharpshooter, nine additional "bar"

Malloy, a BSA and NRA Instructor, here explains the parts of a rifle, circa 1992. His "75" Scout bolo was offered during the year 1985, which was the 75th anniversary of BSA's founding in 1910. The organization will soon reach its 100th anniversary in 2010.

stages of Sharpshooter, Expert and Distinguished Rifleman. Higher scores and more difficult positions—sitting, kneeling and standing—were required as the shooter progressed. The program was open to all young shooters through the age of 18. The program continues today, little changed, except that in the 1960s it was opened to shooters of all ages, not just juniors. The highest award was changed from Distinguished Rifleman to Distinguished Expert. This change allowed the award to be earned in areas other than rifle shooting. Many other qualification programs—for several types of rifle, pistol and shotgun shooting—were added.

The NRA Junior qualification awards added a lot of record keeping and paperwork to the duties of my 1956 summer camp shooting program. I worked out a system for keeping track of the Scouts and what awards they had earned. Then, at the end of the first week, it was time to organize

the award presentations. The medals were sorted out, and the certificates were set out in order. I remember asking camp management who was in charge of doing all the lettering on all those certificates. Being a staff of one, I soon realized I was that person. Another new skill—I learned how to block letter neatly and quickly.

The Marksmanship program of that 1956 camp was a high point in my life. I was involved with shooting all day, every day, and I loved it. I learned a lot about how boys relate to shooting and I developed some skills toward being a satisfactory rifle instructor.

After that 1956 summer camp was over, for a short time I was involved as a leader with a Boy Scout troop in the Atlanta area. However, finishing my studies eventually took precedence, and I phased out of Scouting, but not shooting, for a while. I had always been interested in the outdoors, and finished in

RIFLE AND SHOTGUN SHOOTING

MERIT BADGE SERIES

BOY SCOUTS OF AMERICA

In 1967, the Marksmanship merit badge was renamed Rifle and Shotgun Shooting, and an option to use shotguns was offered, in addition to the original rifle program. Twenty-two years later, two separate merit badges would be offered.

1959 with a degree in Geology. Later that same year, I returned to Florida and began postgraduate work at Florida State University.

By 1963, I had acquired another Geology degree and hired on with a major oil company in New Orleans. I soon joined a local shooting club and helped set up some competition programs, and started trying to get more young people involved in shooting. In 1973, I found time to get married, and two sons came along in 1976 and 1978.

However, even before these life changes, I was again involved with Boy Scout shooting. I had been looking for an opportunity to initiate some sort of youth shooting program. Coincidentally, the New Orleans Area Council of the Boy Scouts had been thinking about creating a new Explorer Post as a Marksmanship specialty post. I became the Post Advisor. A geologist friend of mine, a

shooter and former Navy officer, made arrangements with Tulane University to use their Navy ROTC rifle range on specified nights. The Explorers shot for the NRA Qualification awards.

The Post also was occasionally invited to the nearby St. Bernard Pistol & Rifle Range, the club I had joined, for special shooting events. The Explorers decided to challenge the St. Bernard club to a rifle competition. The course of fire would be fired at 50 feet, on the NRA 50-foot targets, from four positions. This, of course, was the exact course of fire with which the Post members were familiar! It was a heady experience for the boys to come out on top.

Working with the Marksmanship Post, I became familiar with the new requirements for Boy Scout shooting programs.

Rifle and Shotgun Shooting - 1967

In 1967, the shooting program had been changed. The 1967 merit badge pamphlet was titled *"Rifle and Shotgun Shooting"* at that time. A Scout could earn the merit badge by shooting either a rifle course or a shotgun course. If a Scout desired to shoot both rifle and shotgun, he could. However, he could only earn the merit badge one time.

The 1967 *rifle-shooting* requirements were somewhat similar to the 1953 requirements, but changes had been made. Previously, prone and standing positions had to be used. For 1967,

- Targets now had to be fired from three positions: prone, kneeling and standing.

- Four 5-shot targets were to be shot from each position, for a total of twelve qualifying targets instead of the previous ten targets.

- From prone, the required minimum score was 35. For kneeling, 25. For standing, 20.

This would seem to be an easier course in the prone and standing positions, as the previous required scores had been 40 and

30, respectively. However, the new requirements also stated that the scores of the 12 targets must add to a total score of at least 380 points. It was noted in the pamphlet that "it will be necessary to make more than the minimum score on some targets to make the required total of 380 points." A bit of an understatement! The minimum scores added up to only 320 points, leaving 60 additional points to be made up with the 12 targets—an average of 5 points per target!

- The three rifle courses of fire remained 50 feet with 22-caliber rifles, 25 feet with rifled airguns and 15 feet with smoothbore BB guns.

The new 1967 *shotgun-shooting* option required the Scout to:

- Break at least 13 clay birds out of 25 in each of five separate 25-bird events. This amounted to a substantial amount of shooting—125 birds—and was probably difficult to accomplish with a large class of Scouts shooting only an hour or so a day during a week of summer camp.

An optional course of fire was offered in an apparent attempt to make things somewhat easier and less expensive. Along with the standard gauges and standard clay targets, a second, 22-caliber shotgun option, was offered. It was to be fired with 22-caliber smooth bore shotguns using 22-caliber rimfire shot cartridges. The Mo-Skeet-O targets, about two inches in diameter, were to be used.

Swinging on those tiny targets and sending that tiny pinch of Number 12 shot after them quick enough to break them was, in a word, challenging. Remembering my own experiences with 22-caliber shotgun shooting, I still wonder if any Scout, anywhere, ever qualified for the merit badge using that option.

Still, the 22-caliber shotgun option remained in effect until the shooting program was changed in 1989, 22 years later.

A Scout shooting for the Rifle and Shotgun Shooting merit badge

Some Scout camps have shotgun shooting stations with wings to limit the movement of the gun. (BSA Archives)

under the 1967 requirements was also required to understand and demonstrate gun safety, proper shooting fundamentals and care of firearms. In addition, a Scout had to understand the role of guns and hunting in conservation, and to know the laws for owning and using guns *in his town*. Because the requirements were written before the passage of the Gun Control Act of 1968 (GCA68), federal laws were not a factor. This situation would be addressed in the next revisions of the shooting merit badge program.

I continued with the Marksmanship Explorer Post until I was transferred to Houston, Texas in 1978. Our sons were pre-school age, so I had a short hiatus until the older boy reached Cub Scout age in 1982. Then, I was recycled back into the Scout program and became involved in a big way. I never again had a time in my life without involvement in Scout shooting.

The Cub Scout BB gun program had been initiated, and it seemed a natural thing to set up BB gun shooting for our Cub units. I eventually became the BB Gun Director for the Mustang District of the Sam Houston Area Council. The Sam Houston Area Council was a large council, and some summer day camp programs ran for two solid weeks, with BB gun shooting every day.

As my sons grew into Boy Scout age, I became a merit badge counselor for several merit badges, including the Rifle and Shotgun Shooting merit badge. In 1989, the Rifle and Shotgun Shooting merit badge was replaced by two separate new shooting badges, called, logically enough, the Rifle Shooting merit badge and the Shotgun shooting merit badge.

Rifle Shooting - 1989

The 1989 Rifle Shooting merit badge required knowledge of gun safety, laws regarding hunting, and the ownership and use of guns.

- The federal GCA68 law, restricting both ownership and use throughout the country, now influenced the requirements for understanding gun laws.

- The need for eye and ear protection while shooting, not really understood during earlier decades, was now emphasized.

⬥⬥●⬥⬥●⬥⬥●⬥⬥●⬥⬥●⬥⬥

A simple manual trap mounted on a sturdy bench served adequately for Shotgun Shooting merit badge classes at the 2006 Wallwood camp.

- Cleaning, types of ammunition, parts and operation of different types of rifles, and the fundamentals of rifle shooting were still requirements.

- The positions—prone, sitting, kneeling and standing—had to be demonstrated, but all shooting was now to be done from the supported benchrest position. *This was a major change in the requirements.* The new shooting requirement apparently was decided on to help speed up the merit badge course at summer camps by concentrating on the fundamentals of sight alignment and trigger control, instead of position steadiness, during actual shooting.

Three options were now available. Option A used 22-caliber rifles, Option B used air rifles, and—a new innovation—Option C used muzzleloading rifles.

For Option A, standard 22 rifles and the traditional NRA 50-foot targets were used.

※ ● ※ ● ※ ● ※ ● ※ ● ※

Malloy uses cardboard cutouts to explain the proper sight picture to Cub Scouts at a Cub Family Weekend BB gun range in 2001.

- In initial shooting, a 3-shot group must be fired that can be covered by a quarter. Five such groups were fired.

- Then, when the sights had been adjusted to center the group, five more groups—5-shot groups this time—must be fired in which each shot scores 8 or better. (Other targets could be used, with slightly different score requirements.)

For Option B, using a BB gun at 15 feet, or a pellet air rifle at 25 feet,

- Five 3-shot groups must be covered by a quarter,

- Then five 5-shot groups must score 8 or better on the appropriate targets. If an air rifle was used at 33 feet, each shot must score 6 or better on the standard 10-meter target.

For the new Option C, a caplock (percussion) muzzleloader of any caliber may be used.

- The shooter must fire three 3-shot groups that can be covered by the base of a standard soft drink can.

- Then, with the sights adjusted, and shooting at 25-yards on the 50-yard muzzleloading target, three 5-shot groups with a score of 8 or better per shot were required. For those camps with a 50-yard range, a 100-yard target could be used.

The muzzleloading option created new interest in the BSA shooting programs, but it had some special conditions. The slow loading of the muzzleloading rifles meant that fewer shots could be fired during a specific time period. Because of the possibility of loading problems with inexperienced shooters, one instructor per Scout shooter was required. Running a muzzleloading program meant that these factors had to be taken into consideration.

Use of common items such as a coin or a drink shortened the time to determine if targets qualified,

and was easily understood and remembered by the Scouts.

The new 1989 Rifle Shooting merit badge itself took on a new look. The traditional stylized red-and-white bullseye badge (which had been worn by Scouts since 1911) was replaced by a cloth badge that showed a powder flask and two centerfire rifle cartridges.

The 1989 merit badge pamphlet had some problems with text and illustrations. The next year, 1990, saw a revision of the Rifle Shooting pamphlet. The requirements remained the same.

Shotgun Shooting - 1989

The 1989 Shotgun Shooting merit badge requirements had many of the same points as found in the Rifle Shooting pamphlet, namely safety, cleaning, laws for hunting, owning and using guns, and the need for eye and ear protection. Two shooting options were available:

Option A used modern cartridge shotguns.

- A Scout was required to hit at least 24 of 50 clay targets thrown, in two 25-target rounds. Clays could be thrown by a hand trap, manual mechanical trap, or on any trap or skeet field.

Option B allowed muzzleloading shotguns.

- A Scout needed hits on at least 5 of 15 thrown targets. The small number of targets theoretically allowed the course with the slower-loading muzzleloaders to be run in about the same amount of time as the cartridge option.

The new 1989 Shotgun Shooting merit badge award depicted a powder flask and two modern shotgun shells.

1989—that year of the new Shotgun Shooting and Rifle Shooting merit badges—was a year of big changes in my life. Toward the end of that year, my family moved from Houston, Texas, back to Florida.

With the downturn of the oil industry in the mid-1980s,

the industry and I had parted company. I had written as a hobby for some shooting and outdoor publications before. After leaving the petroleum industry, I began writing seriously for a number of publications, primarily about guns and shooting. I met with some success, and eventually, I found myself becoming something of a chronicler of the firearms industry. Because writing can be done from almost anywhere, we had decided to move back to Florida.

By late 1989, we had moved to Tallahassee, Florida's capital city, and had joined a Boy Scout troop and the Tallahassee Rifle & Pistol Club. I was immediately back into Boy Scout shooting. I again phased into Cub Scout BB gun shooting at Cub Family Weekends and Cub Day Camps, and have continued working with these programs.

By 1990, I was the Scoutmaster of my sons' troop, and extended my training. *Woodbadge* is considered the BSA's highest adult training course. Part of the Woodbadge program involves a "ticket," a series of projects to be completed within two years of the initial course. I saw the need for a new program that would give Boy Scouts a safe

introduction to the fun of a variety of different shooting events, and added that to my ticket. The members of the Tallahassee Rifle & Pistol Club (TRPC) were enthusiastic about the project, and the first presentation was held at the club's range in 1991.

This first event was attended by just a few Scout troops, and the actual participation by the Scouts consisted of shooting 22-caliber rifles. Demonstrations of shotgun shooting and muzzleloading rifle shooting were offered, but the Scouts did not get to shoot these other guns. This event was well-received by both the Scouts and the TRPC members, who voted to put on a similar event the next year. Soon, everyone got tired of voting on it each year, and it became an annual event. Now, it is always on the calendars of both the Scout Council and shooting club as the annual Boy Scout Fun Shoot, on the first Saturday in October.

The Scouts in the early "Fun Shoot" years had watched the demonstrations of shotgun shooting and black powder shooting with great interest. Soon, a clamor arose that they be allowed to shoot those guns also, along with the 22 rifles. We responded by adding trapshooting and muzzleloading rifle shooting

to the Fun Shoot activities. After a while, the club got a Sporting Clays tower, and we added Sporting Clays also. By the end of the 1990s, the club had an active 22-caliber metallic silhouette program, and we added rifle silhouette shooting.

The program grew. We hit a high point of 160 Scouts and over 100 leaders one year. Most years, we average something under 100 Scouts and 40 to 50 adult Scout leaders each time we run a Boy Scout Fun Shoot. The first stop for each troop is a session on safety and marksmanship, after which they can shoot—in any order—the five shooting events we offer. 2006, my 50th anniversary in Boy Scout shooting, was also the 16th offering of the Boy Scout Fun Shoot.

The club was also enthusiastic about other programs. Because Scout summer camp programs come only once a year, we occasionally offered interim intensive single-day merit badge programs for both Rifle Shooting and Shotgun shooting at TRPC. We also have a monthly youth shooting program—Scouts who receive a partial completion for a merit badge at summer camp can attend this program to complete the requirements.

After the turn of the century, I realized how close my 50th anniversary was, and applied for the position of Shooting Sports Director at our local Scout council for the 2006 summer camp. 2006 was also a significant year for the local camp, Wallwood, as it was the 40th anniversary of the 1966 opening of the camp.

I admit I had a little concern about committing for the entire summer camp program. After all, I was *half a century older* than when I had run my first course!

Boy Scout shooting activities generally must be supervised by a

At a Cub Family Weekend in March 2001, Malloy goes over safety rules prior to allowing Cub Scouts to enter the BB gun range at Wallwood camp in North Florida.

Malloy coaches Scout Daniel Harrell as he shoots for qualification for his Rifle Shooting merit badge at Wallwood summer camp in 2006. (Pamela Harrell photo)

currently-certified NRA Instructor. In addition, an Instructor must have additional training at a BSA National Camping School to become certified as a Scout camp's Shooting Sports Director. My 5-year BSA certification was coming up for renewal, so I took a recertification course at a camp in May 2006, prior to the summer. There had been some changes to the Rifle Shooting program in 2001 and to the Shotgun Shooting program in 2005.

Rifle Shooting – 2001

A number of changes had been made to the requirements for the Rifle Shooting merit badge in 2001. Much of the material remained the same for safety, hunting laws, laws for the ownership and use of guns, and understanding of eye and ear protection. A Scout in 2001 also had to explain how he could join shooting sports activities—a factor that could get a boy thinking about continuing his interest in shooting beyond acquiring a merit badge.

One interesting new requirement was an understanding of the importance of hygiene in shooting. Basically, a Scout had to understand that he should thoroughly wash up after shooting, or after handling ammunition or cleaning materials, before eating or drinking.

The shooting options were still three, but with some changes.

- Option A (modern 22-caliber cartridge rifle) requirements were basically the same as in 1989, but the scoring of targets became slightly easier. Each shot of a 5-shot qualifying group now had to score only 7 instead of 8 of a possible 10. In addition, it was noted that "It is not always practical to adjust the sights (i.e., when using a borrowed fixed-sight rifle)". In such cases, the alternative requirement was that a 5-shot group must be small enough that all shots can be covered by, or touch, a quarter coin. This change allowed qualifying by group instead of score and saved time during the scoring process—a quarter was simply placed on the target over the group. This procedure had been used for the 3-shot group requirements previously, and could now be used with the 5-

shot groups. Groups could be fired from benchrest or from supported prone positions.

- Option B (air rifle) shooting requirements stayed basically the same. Use of a quarter for scoring continued for the initial 3-shot groups, but the 5-shot groups still had to be scored as in the 1989 requirements.

- Option C (muzzleloading rifle) requirements also required scoring the final 5-shot groups, but, as with the 22-caliber option, the required per-shot score was lowered from 8 to 7.

Shotgun Shooting – 2005

Most of the requirements of 1989 remained the same for the 2005 Shotgun Shooting merit badge. In several cases, items were made clearer or more specific.

- Option A (modern shotshell-type shotgun) requirements for 1989 had specified that clay targets should be thrown at "reasonable speed and in the same direction." The new requirements added that, when using a regulation trap field, the trap should be set to throw straightaway targets, and station 3 should be used. On a Skeet field, station 7 low-house birds should be shot. In addition, the shooting requirements specified hitting at least 12 out of 25 targets (48 percent) in two 25-target groups. The percentage was thus the same as before, but it was now clear that the two groups need not be shot in consecutive order.

- Option B (muzzleloading shotgun). The basic requirements stayed the same, but also added the same allowable use of trap and skeet field stations as in Option A.

These were the requirements that were in effect for the summer 2006 camp at Wallwood in North Florida, when I arrived to take over as Shooting Sports Director.

The summer camp session ran one month in this council, essentially the four weeks of June. I had accumulated props and instructional material over the years, and it was nice to be able to move it all to one place, ready to use.

The NRA Qualification awards had never been offered at Wallwood before. Prior to the opening of the camp, I met with the camp director and we planned to offer the NRA program for 50-foot rifle shooting. The program would be in addition to the traditional camp activities, such as merit badge classes, free-time shoots, Scoutmaster shoots and firearms demonstrations. Alas, an office communications problem prevented our getting the materials we needed in time to offer the NRA Qualification program. Next year, for sure. We did offer the National Shooting Sports Foundation (NSSF) "Take Your Best Shot" program, in which the Scouts (or their leaders) could send in qualifying targets to receive free "Junior Shooting Team" patches. NRA and NSSF patches and medals are not official Boy Scout awards, but may be worn on the Scout uniform as temporary awards.

My assistant was 19-year-old Henry Miller, who had assisted in Wallwood summer camp shooting programs for the past five years. I was fortunate to have him. Not only was he an excellent instructor who had good rapport with the Scouts, but he was very familiar with the camp routine outside the Shooting Sports area.

It was coincidence that he was the same age I had been when I ran my first program. That meant, of course, that there was a 50-year difference in our ages. Our varying viewpoints worked well together, and our program was an effective one.

Our rifle program used a covered 50-foot range with eight stable shooting benchrests. Eight shooters is the maximum number of Scouts that can shoot at one time under the supervision of a certified Instructor. Our bolt-action 22-caliber rifles were of several different makes and models, but most had good micrometer receiver sights, and were suited to shooting the scores necessary to qualify for the merit badge. Rifles

of the same model are preferable, as instruction about operation is easier when the rifles are uniform. However, the ones we had available, with their precision sights, served well.

On the other hand, the additional simple open-sighted rifles we had were primarily of one manufacturer. This uniform model served well in a separate niche for free-time shooting and Scoutmaster shoots, where a very short instruction course had to be presented at each session prior to shooting.

My day at camp started before breakfast, getting the equipment ready for the rifle range. Fifty-minute Rifle Shooting merit badge classes ran from 9 AM until just before noon. Archery classes ran on the same morning schedule, but on an adjacent range that served for both archery and shotgun shooting. After lunch, the shotgun classes took over on that combined range and ran until just before 4 pm. Then, free-time shooting, the weekly Scoutmaster competition, additional practice for those working on merit badges and any special events filled up the time until supper. Thus, rifles and shotguns were shot every day, but at different times.

The camp had several different types of 20-gauge shotguns—semiautomatic, pump and hinged single-shot. Included were smaller "youth" guns in pump and single-shot models. Our trap was a simple manually-operated swing-arm trap that we mounted to a heavy bench. For shotgun shooting, an instructor must be at hand for each shooter, so the single trap was adequate. We used commercial shotshells loaded with number 7-½ or number 8 shot, and our downrange safety zone was adequate for this ammunition.

Eye and ear protection, not even considered at the time of my long-ago 1956 camp, were required for shooting both rifles and shotguns. Eye protection alone was used for archery.

The shooting merit badges cover a lot of "book" material and require substantial shooting. Thus, they take a lot of time, and sometimes they are difficult to earn in a week of camp. We devoted extra periods, when we could, to help some Scouts finish their

shooting. Almost everyone who started the classes earned their awards.

Not strangely, I was working with a staff much younger than I. Most Scout camps seem to be staffed predominantly by young men in their late teens and twenties.

Strangely, I soon lost track of the age difference, and subconsciously felt I was that age also. (Someone once said that Scouting keeps a person young—perhaps it is so.) At any rate, the only time I was disillusioned was when shaving each morning—I wondered who that old guy in the mirror was!

A special moment came when one of my former Scouts—now married and with a family—introduced his son to me as the boy was entering the shooting program at the camp. All the Scouts had fun, and I had a wonderful time.

Sadly, there are forces in our country that do not like this sort of activity. They would like to see the shooting sports abolished. They would like to see private ownership and use of firearms ended. Preventing young people from shooting is a goal with such people, and opposition reportedly has been raised against Boy Scout shooting. I think that the Boy Scout shooting programs are a force to keep the shooting sports alive in this country. I would encourage individuals and gun clubs to contact their local Boy Scout councils and offer to work with them on shooting opportunities.

Just a few years down the road, in 2010, the Boy Scout organization will reach its centennial—its 100th anniversary. The basic principles on which the organization was founded have never changed. The Scout program encourages character, good citizenship and leadership in young men. It uses a wholesome outdoor program of camping, hiking, swimming, climbing, canoeing, and other activities that interest boys. The program includes, and has always included, the shooting sports.

Shooting has been a part of the Boy Scouts of America since its formation almost a century ago. I am glad, and more than a little proud, that I have been able to be involved with Boy Scout shooting for a period spanning over half that time. ✦

Above: *The author's young friend Harvey likes nothing better than to shoot, and the boy seldom misses. The Ithaca he carries is a single-shot with a Martini-type action made to resemble a lever-action cowboy rifle.*

Right: *Imagine a passel of kids with their noses pressed against the display window of their local hardware store getting their first look at the svelte new Remington Model 1912.*

22 DREAMIN':
KIDS, RIMFIRE RIFLES, & THE WILD WEST

by Jesse L. Wolf Hardin

Picking up any old rifle or replica in this modern age is like a ticket to the past. For the youngster, a 22 is often a symbol of growing up: tasks to accomplish, great deeds to do, struggles to win. And for the adult, it's a chance to feel young once again.

Generations of kids grew up with the Winchester 1890 22 pump repeater and subsequent variations.

Courtesy Old Town Station, Ltd.

Before Bill Hickok earned his reputation as "Wild," he was a hook-lipped tyke whose buddies liked to tease and call "Duckbill." There was a time when a young Jesse James had to lean the family's heavy, muzzle loading smoke pole on tree limbs if he hoped to get a grouse 'fore dark.... when little Annie Oakley was still Phoebe Ann and Billy really was a kid!

Name any one of the frontier's leading historical characters and more likely than not, they developed their quick reactions and unerring aim long before growing their first beard or downing their first stomach churning drink. Their motor skills and heightened instincts were initially honed not in the process of staving off outlaw bands or Indian attacks, but in the course of hunting for a high-protein meal. Small ranchers could seldom afford the luxury of butchering their own stock, and tree squirrels, rabbits and birds were far more plentiful around settlements than large mammals like deer. It thus became the responsibility of a homesteader's children to provide much of the meat that made it into the family pot, a job they often liked a lot. Girls vied with the boys in trying to "knock the eyes out" of wood grouse and ground-squirrel "picket-pins" – an old expression meaning a clean head shot that would spare the animal unnecessary pain, and keep young Johnny from spoiling half the meat again.

Kids with dogs would use them to chase a fuzz-tail around to their side of the tree, to flush quail from the thickets and run jacks through a clearing where they could be seen. Those without this kind of four-legged advantage would wait patiently above a water hole or well-worn route... or walk the ridges and fence lines ready for a snap shot on whatever popped out. They'd often get home well after dark, a bounty of food tucked into their "possibles" bags or hanging from their belts. The smile on their faces came not from the taking of life, but from the glow of pride... proud

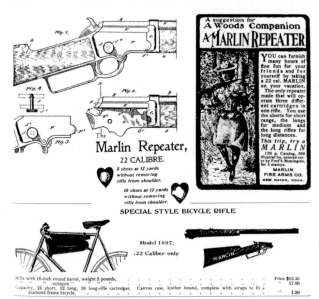

A patent drawing for Hepburn's takedown feature on the Marlin 1897 22 rifle. Inset: A 1903 ad extolling its virtues as a Woods Companion." Bottom: A catalog listing promoting this first-ever lever-action 22 as the perfect "bicycle rifle." The standard model cost $15.35, and the octagon barrel option was an extra $1.65. Those were the days.

to have done their part to provide.

Sometimes the only arm dad had for them to use was an old musket that was longer – and nearly as heavy – as the kid carrying it. And given the prohibitive cost of blackpowder, and especially of those newfangled "cah-tridges," there were practical reasons for the parental admonition of "one shot, one kill." Snaking through sagebrush or peeking from behind Ponderosa pines, a fellow might imagine himself saving innocent ladies from harm, repelling bad-guy ambushes or recapturing a fallen flag. And a little girl so dispensed, might picture herself one day performing trick shots in front of a worldwide audience!

Kids shot whatever was available and most affordable, but from around the time of the Civil War until today the proverbial gun of youth has been the rimfire 22. Its introduction in 1857 coincided with the unveiling of the first ever bored-through cartridge revolver, the S&W "tip-up," chambered for the first U.S. manufactured metallic cartridge. The 22 Short, as it later came to be called, was derived from the 1845 Flobert BB Cap, designed for use in the then-popular shooting galleries of Europe. But whereas the BB ("bullet breech") projectile was propelled by the power of the priming charge alone, the new Short packed 4 grains of extra fine black powder, pushing the same 29-grain bullet muzzle velocity up to a velocity of 800 fps or more. It was followed in 1871 by the 22 Long,

featuring a longer case, an extra grain of powder, and a 100 fps boost. And then in 1880, by the 22 Extra Long, burning 6 grains and launching a heavier hitting 40-grain slug. It was Stevens Arms Co., in 1887, that first brought to the world what has become the most versatile and popular-selling cartridge of all time, the extremely accurate 22 Long Rifle, driving a 40-grain round nosed bullet to around 1,000 fps. Its immediate and continuous widespread acceptance would in time make all the previous 22 rounds essentially obsolete.

While proving less than ideal for personal defense, the Lilliputian 22s quickly proved themselves as a cheap, accurate and quiet harvester of small game, and the rifles that chambered it were often scaled down with shorter stocks just right for the arm span of a lucky girl or boy. Many is the youngster who has stood in front of a hardware store window, fantasizing what it would be like to hold a certain model in their hands for all to see, one guaranteed "made just for me."

With the advent of periodicals like *Forest & Stream* and *Outdoor Life*, pictorial ads started appearing that were targeted at children. Promotions

෨෨ ● ෨෨ ● ෨෨ ● ෨෨ ● ෨෨ ● ෨෨

An ad for Stevens rifles features a young fellow holding what appears to be one of their 22 single-shot takedown models. Accompanying are some antique toys and such.

for the 22s of the day appealed not to any practical duties, but rather to more primitive instincts. They promised that a two-hour foray into the oaks in the back wood lot could be as exciting as any safari into darkest Africa. The heroic illustrations harkened back not only to the idyllic game fields of the past, but to the never-never land of castles, damsels and dragons... of danger and the good fight, determination and delight.

Most often this dream rifle was a single-shot falling block design, usually the inexpensive and elegant little Stevens models including the appropriately named "Marksman" and "Favorite," as well as the even cheaper "knock-off" copies that were rushed into the stores. Winchester, however, also marketed modest numbers of the Browning designed Model 1885 single-shot falling-block rifle in 22, the most common being the military styled Winder issued for marksmanship classes and competitive matches by shooting clubs and (pre-Columbine!) public schools. In the West as in the East, the single-shot had the advantage of contributing to a code of sportsmanship, forcing the sometimes novice hunters to aim extra carefully since by the time a second round could be chambered one's quarry was likely to have already gotten away. This had the added benefit of less rounds being fired altogether, in times and places where every precious penny had to be carefully spent.

Fast follow-up shots on running game, however, only became practical with the introduction of repeaters. The first American made 22-caliber repeating rifle was, coincidentally, the long arm most often associated with the Wild West, the Winchester 1873 lever action. Only about 20,000 were ordered in this chambering, however, beginning in 1884. Being both considerably heavier than the same model in 44 WCF, and comparatively expensive, it is likely that few if any ever ended up in youngsters' hands.

Then, beginning in 1884, the Colt company had considerably more success with a unique new slide (or pump) action rifle they called the Lightning. Winchester responded with the release of a similar but considerably improved design, again from John Browning's workbench, the trim and racy Model 1890. It sold 850,000 units and was followed by other exposed hammer, trombone variants, including the Models 1906, '61 and '62, in competition with other popular pump guns like Remington's lithe Model 1912.

The first lever-action rifle scaled down for the 22 cartridge was a svelte takedown model with buckhorn sights and a sexy octagon barrel designed by an engineer named Hepburn for Marlin in 1891, and perfected as the Model 1897. By the time self-loading, gas-operated rifles appeared in 1903, historians like Frederick Turner had already penned their sad obituaries for the American frontier, and the once Wild West had admittedly been largely altered and tamed.

Tame, it should be noted, is a quality that darn few kids care to either encourage or emulate. To a child, *tame* is a stallion gelded and bridled, a land robbed of excitement and risk, earth girdled with fences and roads, a little girl forced to wear restrictive hoop skirts at a picnic, a boy suffering too-tight brogans and Sunday go-to-meetin' tie. On the other hand, *wild* is the force that breaks out of the best-built corrals at the first peal of mountain thunder, insistent seeds sprouting beneath pavement and pushing up through the cracks towards the sun. Wild is the boy staring out the window from a line of school chairs, anxious to get outside

and kick off his shoes. And wild the girl who can't wait to get out of sight of her parents in order to chuck her wired skirt, skinny dip in the creek, or get her bloomers good and dirty while playing in the grass on her knees.

The gift of a 22 has long been a way for a parent to show that they could relate to and support this intrinsic wildness, while investing their offspring with the weight of responsibility. Cleverly wrapped inside the back pages of a Harper's Weekly, or dressed up with rare red ribbon tied in a bow about its stock – it was a way of telling them they could be trusted with a tool that could both cause death, and sustain life. It was thus a way of acknowledging their ability to be careful, as well as to make appropriate moral choices. The bicycle gun with a child's name roughly scratched onto its receiver, was not only a rifle unsheathed... but a magic wand empowering the young warrior princess, and a sword with which each worthy knight is bequeathed.

The catalog section in a recent edition of GUN DIGEST featured over a dozen pages listing 22 rifles, proof that the little rimfires are more popular than ever. And of these, a number are either exact reproductions of venerated Old West designs, or else designed to evoke the spirit and history of the past. These include the Marlin, Browning and Henry lever-action 22s. Taurus makes the Model 62R, a copy of the pump-action Winchester 1890. Browning continues to manufacture the bottom-ejecting semi-auto 22 Browning developed at the start of the 20th century, and Savage still makes a single-shot Stevens "Favorite" they call the Model 30 or 30G (the latter is the take-down version).

Nothing new. Buffalo Bill made his fortune on it when the buffalo business dried up. As a kid, I listened to the good-natured advice of Roy Rogers and Hopalong Cassidy on a small black and white picture tube, usually with a silly blue felt cowboy hat on my head. The Gunsmoke radio and TV dramas began with the narrator announcing, "Welcome to those thrilling days of yesteryear!" Yesteryear, for us, was not only a moment lost in time, but an actual place we could

Marlin's Model 1897 was the perfected version of Hepburn's Model 1891 – the first lever-action rifle to be both chambered and proportioned for the 22 rimfire cartridge. The Five Happy Weeks book, to many children of the time, meant a summer spent rifle in hand – exploring secretive canyons and wooded mountain trails.

❧ ● ❧ ● ❧ ● ❧ ● ❧ ● ❧

saddle up and ride to, a magic place where the cost of admission was an old 22, a couple boxes of ammo, and an indomitable spark in the eye!

Picking up any old rifle or replica in this modern age is like a ticket to the past. Firing an early design has the power to transport us back to the innocence, enthusiasm and delight of our youth. Gazing over the flat top of an octagon barrel, we sight in on not only the squirrel up in the crotch of the tree, but on a simpler and more aware way of living, and an opportunity for difficult tests and wild adventures. For the youngster, a 22 is often a symbol of growing up: tasks to accomplish, great deeds to do, struggles to win. And for the adult, it's a chance to feel young once again. ✹

(Derived by permission from a chapter in *Old Guns & Whispering Ghosts: Tales & Twists Of The Old West*, © Shoot! Pub. 2006, www.shootmagazine.com. For more information or to contact the author, go to www.oldgunsbook.com)

RIMFIRES FROM
CZ USA
PERFORMANCE, LOOKS AND VALUE

by James & Kathleen House

What do you want to do with a rimfire rifle? If the answer is informal target shooting and small game hunting, it is difficult to imagine a more suitable tool than the CZ 452 in 22 LR. If the answer is to shoot smaller varmints out to around the 150-yard mark, the 17 HMR version will serve you well. Although we have not tested the 17 Mach 2 or 22 WMR versions, they should give excellent performance, and the 22 WMR would be suitable for use on somewhat larger varmints. Whatever the task to be handled by a rimfire rifle, the CZ 452 merits serious consideration.

Although there have been many rimfire sporters, one of the most famous rifles of all time is the Winchester Model 52. Vivid memories remain also of the trim, elegant little Winchester Model 75 sporter that a cousin toted through the woods back in the 1950s. With a Weaver K4 mounted, that rifle was a pleasure to carry, and the accuracy it delivered was impressive. A nephew now has a Remington Model 541S that is equally capable and elegant if not quite as trim as the Winchester 75. Recognizing that many rimfire shooters prefer a bolt-action rifle led to the introduction of several other models over the years, most notably the lower priced Winchester 69A

and Remington 513. Eventually, all of these models disappeared so that throughout a rather large segment of the last few decades of the 1900s only inexpensive bolt actions such as those made by Marlin and Savage and a few expensive imported models were available. Many rimfire shooters yearned for something between these extremes.

In 1983, Ruger introduced the Model 77/22, a bolt-action sporter with a checkered walnut stock of classic sporter design. The Model 77/22 utilizes a rotary 10-round magazine that is legendary for its reliability. Being available in several versions and in a 22 WMR chambering, the Ruger 77/22 became a popular rimfire

Opposite: *For roaming the hills in search of small varmints, the CZ 452 in 17 HMR, with a good scope attached, is an ideal companion.*

Right: *The compact action of the CZ 452 features a trigger that is adjustable for length of travel. Note the metal magazine box.*

CZ 452 rifles utilize a wing-type safety that is located on the right hand side at the rear of the bolt.

sporter. In addition, Kimber, Cooper and Anschutz rimfires are justifiably held in high regard. For many rimfire shooters, their only drawback is related to their cost. Remington joined the rimfire fray in 2004 with the Model 504, which has received a lot of attention. More recently, the Remington Model 5 was introduced. Produced in Serbia but carrying the Remington name, the Model 5 is an entry-level bolt-action sporter.

It is with this backdrop of how we got where we are that attention is directed to yet another rimfire sporting rifle of classic design. At issue here is a line of rifles produced in the Czech Republic. CZ stands for Ceska Zbrojovka, the parent company that is located at Uhersky Brod. Today, most rimfire bolt-action rifles are available not only in the traditional 22 LR but also in 17 Mach 2. Magnum versions of most models are available in 22 WMR and the latest sensation, the 17 HMR. The fine rifles produced by CZ are no exception. Eight different versions of the CZ 452 bolt-action rimfire repeater are available that differ primarily in stock material and style, barrel length and sight options. The recently introduced members of the series are left-hand models that are available in 22 LR and 17 Mach 2. Even more recently announced is the Model 453, which has a set trigger. A heavy-barreled version known as the Varmint Model is also available in all four popular rimfire chamberings.

For many rimfire shooters, cost is a factor, and a rifle that sells for around $1,000 or more is simply beyond the available means if not the dreams. While not at that price point, the MSRP for the Remington 504 is $775 and that of the Ruger 77/22 is $690. The Cooper, Kimber, Sako and Anschutz rifles go upward from there. For the budget-minded shopper, the CZ has a lot to offer at a price that will allow you to add a good scope and still not break the bank. The MSRP for the CZ Model 452 in 22 LR and 17 Mach 2 is $409 with the magnum and left-hand models being slightly higher. Even the standard model has such features as a trigger that is adjustable for weight of pull and checkered Turkish or American walnut stock.

The 452 American comes with a receiver having the 3/8-inch width that is standard in the U.S. In most European countries, the dovetail grooves on rimfire rifles have a width of 11mm. Therefore, the CZ rifles that are not directed primarily at the American market have receivers with that width. In keeping with the modern trend, the Model 452 rifles have no iron sights. We believe that this is a mistake because there are times when the trim, unadorned rifle is a welcome companion, and scopes (or mounts) do sometimes go astray. Iron sights are found on almost all rifles in our safe. Although a large number of scope mounts can be used, CZ markets a set of steel rings with a retail price of $42.

Almost unique among rimfire rifles produced today, the CZ has the barrel threaded into the receiver in the classic manner. The hammer-forged, lapped barrel has a large diameter at the breech and the action has a receiver ring of generous diameter. The resulting bearing surface where the barrel mates to the action is large, which results in a very robust unit. This is undoubtedly one factor that contributes to outstanding accuracy, which will be discussed later. In addition, metal parts are highly polished and blued for a fit and finish that belies the price tag of the 452. The Model 452 has a two-position wing type safety that is located on the right side of the bolt at the rear. The elegant appearance of the 452 is enhanced by the walnut stock that is nicely checkered and fitted with swivel studs. The standard magazine holds 5 rounds but 10-round versions are also available. A single-shot adapter that replaces the 5-round magazine is available for the rifles in 22 LR.

For many rimfire shooters it is accuracy that makes a rifle interesting. Although the 22 LR and 17 HMR rifles were evaluated, the CZ 452 is also available in 22 WMR and 17 Mach 2. All of the Model 452 rifles are almost identical in appearance except for the flush-fitting magazine of the 22 LR and 17 Mach 2 rifles and the protruding magazine of those in 22 WMR and 17 HMR. For accuracy testing, a Redfield 3-12 x 44 scope was mounted on the 17 HMR rifle, and a Tasco Mag IV 6-24 x 40 AO scope was mounted on the 22 LR rifle. During the tests, the scopes were set on the highest magnification. The usual companion for the 22 LR version is a superb Weaver Classic 3-9 x 32 AO rimfire scope that is shown in the photos, and it was also used in some tests.

Being intended for use on centerfire rifles, the Redfield scope is free of parallax at 100 yards, rather than the usual distance of 50 yards like most scopes intended for use on rimfire rifles. Because the 17 HMR is suitable for use on small varmints at ranges over 100 yards, such a scope is appropriate. To evaluate the accuracy of the rifles, five 5-shot groups were fired at a range of 50 yards so that a direct comparison of the 22 LR and 17 HMR rifles could be made. Six types of 17 HMR ammunition were tested. With an enormous range of loads available in 22 LR, the tests included some standard and target velocity loads as well as some high velocity types. The CZ 452 has a very tight match-type chamber, and it was found that the CCI SGB cartridges were very difficult to seat fully. The results obtained from the accuracy testing of the CZ rifles are shown in the accompanying tables.

How accurate is accurate? An average group size of an inch or less is generally considered to be adequate for untuned sporters. Certainly that level of accuracy enables shots to be taken at animate objects about as far as the 22 LR cartridge would justify. The requirements for rifles in 17 HMR are generally somewhat more stringent in keeping with their intended use on small varmints at ranges up to perhaps 150 yards or so. The data shown in the tables leave no doubt that the rifles tested meet all reasonable expectations in terms of accuracy.

The CZ 452 is available in calibers (top) 17 Mach 2, 22 LR, 17 HMR and 22 WMR.

CZ 452 American 17 HMR with Redfield 3-12X Scope

Ammunition	Group size, inches		
	Largest	Smallest	Average
CCI Game Point (20 gr. HP)	0.84	0.23	0.61
CCI TNT (17-gr. HP)	0.72	0.54	0.62
Federal V-Shok	0.56	0.35	0.48
Hornady V-Max	0.66	0.39	0.56
Hornady XTP (20 gr. HP)	0.78	0.27	0.61
Remington Premier	0.72	0.54	0.68
		Overall Avg.	0.59

Accuracy with CZ 452 American 22 LR and Tasco Mag IV 6-24X or Weaver 3-9X Rimfire Scope.

Ammunition	Group size, inches		
	Average	Largest	Smallest
CCI Green Tag	1.15	0.60	0.79
CCI Mini Mag	0.99	0.61	0.91
CCI SGB	1.09	0.80	0.95
CCI Standard Velocity	1.53	0.55	0.94
CCI Velocitor	1.43	0.86	1.13
Eley Target	0.61	0.32	0.51
Federal High Velocity H.P.	1.12	0.56	0.81
Federal Target (711B)	1.26	0.90	1.07
Federal Ultra Match	0.67	0.39	0.54
PMC Match Rifle	1.14	0.64	0.76
Remington Game Load	0.84	0.46	0.66
Remington Target	1.40	0.77	1.08
RWS Rifle Match	0.94	0.31	0.69
Winchester Power Point	0.94	0.68	0.83
Winchester Super-X H.P.	1.05	0.62	0.82
Winchester Supreme	0.96	0.51	0.67
Winchester T-22	1.00	0.44	0.67
Wolf Match Target	0.68	0.32	0.55
		Overall Avg.	0.80

With the 17 HMR ammunition being produced by CCI using essentially premium components, there is little difference in accuracy regardless of the color of the tip on the bullet or the printing on the label. All of the loads tested gave composite group sizes of less than 0.7-inch, and the overall average group size was only 0.59-inch. Some of the testing was conducted on ranges where there was a strong breeze. On one occasion, groups were fired at 100 yards on a range in Montana where there was a significant wind. Under those conditions, the groups averaged around 1.5 inches, but this rifle is capable of much better performance. With the very small bore of a 17-caliber rifle, even a barrel of sporter weight has thick walls and is capable of performance equal to that of a heavier barrel in a larger caliber. The CZ 452 in 17 HMR makes an excellent rifle for taking pests of appropriate

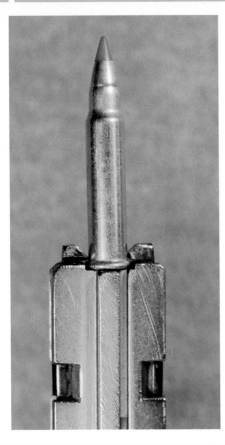

size out to at least 150 yards, but at that distance the remaining energy is only about 125 ft-lbs so the pests should be small ones.

The CZ 452 in 22 LR performed admirably. A sporter-weight rifle that produces groups in the half-inch range at 50 yards is quite accurate. The 452 did that with Eley Target, Federal Ultra Match and Wolf Match Target, which gave average group sizes of 0.51-, 0.54-, and 0.55-inch, respectively. Of the 18 types of ammunition for which data are shown, only three gave average group sizes of just over an inch. A composite group size of only 0.80-inch for that number of loads is outstanding. There are rifles that will consistently group in one-half inch or less, but not in the price range of the CZ 452. A Ruger 77/22 belonging to

※ ● ※ ● ※ ● ※ ● ※ ● ※

Dual extractors used on the 452 assure positive extraction.

one of the authors has been tested extensively, and the composite group size is almost exactly the same as that obtained with the CZ 452. With an actual selling price that is usually a bit less than $400, it represents an outstanding value. The Ruger 77/22 is furnished with a set of rings, but they are not included with the CZ rifle.

What do you want to do with a rimfire rifle? If the answer is informal target shooting and small game hunting, it is difficult to imagine a more suitable tool than the CZ 452 in 22 LR. If the answer is to shoot smaller varmints out to around the 150-yard mark, the 17 HMR version will serve you well. Although we have not tested the 17 Mach 2 or 22 WMR versions, they should give excellent performance, and the 22 WMR would be suitable for use on somewhat larger varmints. Whatever the task to be handled by a rimfire rifle, the CZ 452 merits serious consideration. ✿

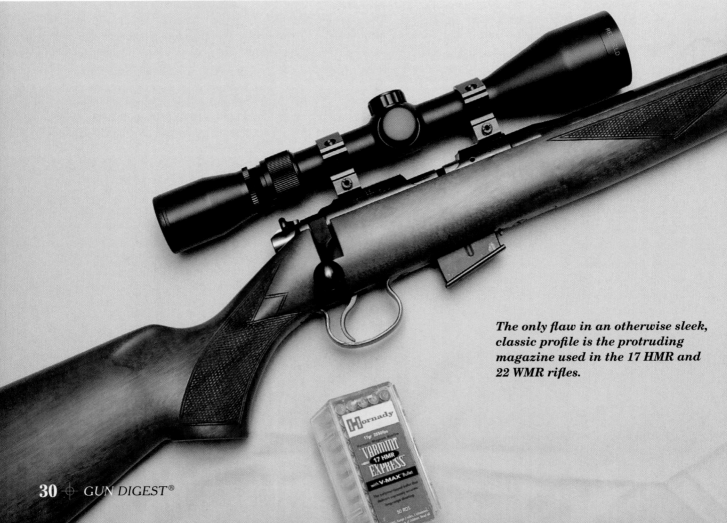

The only flaw in an otherwise sleek, classic profile is the protruding magazine used in the 17 HMR and 22 WMR rifles.

SEVENTY YEARS OF THE
MODEL 70

by Wayne Van Zwoll

Model 70 magic owes much to history. This was by any measure the best affordable production rifle available in the late 1930s. The Model 70 also looks right – clean, lean, sleek, balanced. As with a 911 Porsche roadster or a vintage Harley-Davidson motorcycle, there's something about this rifle's profile that distinguishes it from others of its type and tells your eye that "this is better." The wood and steel have been properly married and contoured. Its graceful but functional lines and a predatory heft take the Model 70 out of the tool category. It marks a high point in the design and manufacture of bolt rifles. The 70 has become an archetype, the measure of its kind, a classic by the purist definition of that over-used word.

Night had brought sharp cold. The crust was barely thick enough to hold a housecat. Only where wind had scoured the mountain was I allowed a few silent steps. But the elk had wandered north into the lodgepoles, where snow had sifted deep before melting and then re-freezing. I almost quit.

But nothing guarantees failure like quitting.

Perhaps the wind or the trees swallowed my step. Maybe I just got lucky. But suddenly they came clear of the timber, their thick winter coats rippling in gusts sweeping in from the Pintlars. Two bulls, then three. The Winchester eased to my shoulder. Alas, the elk stopped moving just as the striker fell; the bullet flew by in front! Elk dashed in all directions. The forest drained them before I could fire again.

A good hunt doesn't always include a kill. But missing turns a good hunt sour. Wearily, I took the track. Slim odds had just grown slimmer. Now the elk would be alert, watching their back-trails, listening.

Moving fast along the hoof-gashes, I kept close watch ahead. Presently an opening appeared in the lodgepoles. I stopped short of it to glass the other side. Sometimes elk pause after crossing such a meadow, to watch for a trailing hunter. A

spot of color caught my eye. The rifle stole to my shoulder again, stealthy in its movement, like a thing alive. Then, as if no gift were too good for me this morning, an antler tip came clear. I sifted pieces of elk to assemble a sight picture. Offhand, I let the rifle vent its nervous energy. When it settled, I locked my lungs and pressed the trigger.

I didn't need the blood, because the crosswire had stayed spot-on until recoil had ripped it away. But there was plenty of blood – bright, bubbly blood staining the crust several feet either side of the hoof gouges. It hadn't leaked but was blown onto the snow in a spray that told me the trail would be short.

Model 70 Winchesters don't always bring me such luck. In another season, on another mountain, the going was quieter in fresh, cottony snow. The two bulls were not at all alarmed. But on that steep face, snow-laded Douglas-firs limited my vision. Suddenly, grenade-blasts of snow and limbs erupted behind the tight screen of conifers. I could do nothing but watch snow cascade gently from bobbing limbs just a few feet away. It continued to sift long after they were gone.

I was too deeply invested to break off the track now. Cinching my pack tighter, I climbed. The two furrows

An apron appeared above the tang around 1950. It hid an inletting gap that prevented stock splits.

❧ ● ❧ ● ❧ ● ❧ ● ❧ ● ❧

split eventually. The bull taking the steeper route held more promise. He would crest. And at the crest he would throttle back before picking his way down through rocky rims above the Lostine. The snow got deeper as slowly I reeled in the mountain. Within rifle-shot of the top I was pushing powder with my shins. Then, movement! I dropped to a knee. Slivers of brown winked behind the dark web of firs

and their heavy load of snow. The report came as a dull "putt." The elk churned noiselessly away.

I found a tiny blood-hole in the snow and great wads of gray-and-tawny hair strung out beyond the animal's prints. My bullet had grazed the brisket, in front. Still, I took the track. The elk had plunged back down into timber. Blood was glaringly absent. Once the elk had lost its footing, to skid headlong into a tree. It had no trouble after that, though the slope was so steep I had to hold myself to it with one hand. We went until dark, the elk and I, and the elk never slowed.

Both those Model 70s are gone now, the 300 Holland and the 300 Winchester. I'd buy them back for double what I took for them, because I've never sold a Model 70 that I *didn't* eventually want back. But when early Model 70s were just beginning to climb in price, I was fresh out of college and newly married. Keen to prove myself responsible, I relinquished rifles in ill-fated trades. I let a fine 30-06 go for $185, a 257 for $285. I declined a 35 Remington in mint condition because $400 seemed too high a price.

Decades later, those decisions haunt me. Sure, the used market offered other great rifles – Savage 99s and commercial Mausers, early Mannlicher-Schoenauers and Winchester lever guns. Perhaps the

Model 70 seemed special because it defined the archetypal hunting rifle for my generation. Still clear in my memory is the 1961 Winchester catalog that showed the Model 70 Westerner and Alaskan, then only three years old. Like the 30-06 straddling moose antlers at the local hardware store, they listed for $154. Meanwhile, Jack O'Connor wrote of long expeditions into sheep country with his Biesen-stocked Model 70 270 Featherweight.

The Model 70 was not a revolutionary rifle. It was matter-of-fact in design, a practical marriage of ideas already proven successful in other bolt rifles. But it also had an eerie elegance. Something about the profile of an early Model 70 made you want to look longer, to handle it and aim it. It felt *gunny*. Countless Saturdays squandered at gun shows have convinced me that old Model 70s even have a compelling scent. It is that of walnut and oil and old steel worn bright in callused hands. It is saddle leather and linseed oil, the lodgepoles of western Montana, the sagebrush of eastern Oregon. You can never really separate a Model 70 from its travels and exploits in game country.

Model 70 Origins

Winchester's most famous bolt rifle has deep roots. You might trace them to Paul Mauser's 1888 Commission Rifle and its progeny, the 1898 Mauser. Among the first rifles chambered for smokeless, high-velocity cartridges, the '98 was strong and reliable. In short order it became the first choice of most of the world's armies, and you can clearly see Mauser ancestry in every modern bolt rifle.

Lever guns are 50 years older. During the 1840s inventor Walter Hunt developed a tube-fed rifle with outside priming and a finger loop to operate the mechanism. In 1849 he earned a patent for a breech-loading "Volitional" repeating rifle. Fellow New Yorker George Arrowsmith helped with cash and business acumen. Lewis Jennings improved the magazine, then assigned patent

The controlled-feed bolt face (left) is partly rimless, so cartridges can slide up into the extractor.

Above: *The early Model 70 barrel had a coned breech and extractor cut (right).*

Left: *Winchester's Model 70 trigger is stout, simple – one of the best ever for a hunting rifle.*

rights to Arrowsmith, who sold all rights for $100,000 to Courtlandt Palmer – who brought Horace Smith, Daniel Wesson and B. Tyler Henry into the project. This partnership was bought by a group of New York financiers. Its president: shirt-maker Oliver F. Winchester.

"...It may revolutionize the whole science of war. Where is the military genius . . . (to) so modify the science of war as to best develop the capacities of this terrible engine – the exclusive use of which would enable any government. . . to rule the world?" This could once have been written of the horse. Perhaps now the atomic bomb comes to mind. But the words were Oliver Winchester's, in an appeal for military adoption of the Henry rifle. Confederate soldiers would call it "that damned Yankee rifle you loaded on Sunday and fired all week."

Oliver Winchester was a descendant of 17th-century immigrants. He married in 1834 and that year opened a retail store of men's furnishings in Baltimore. Despite a financial panic in 1837, Oliver expanded his business. A prosperous decade and three children later, he decided the world could use a better shirt. A curved seam reduced the "pull of the neckband." He patented it, sold his Baltimore

business and moved to State Street in New Haven to make shirts. The following year Oliver Winchester teamed up with John M. Davies, a leading New York importer. Their partnership, Winchester & Davies, built a factory. By 1860 it had 40 men and 1,500 women on the payroll, with 500 foot-pedal machines producing 480,000 shirts – and $600,000 – a year.

By 1855, when Oliver Fisher Winchester invested in Volcanic Repeating Arms, he was living well.

That company didn't last long. In February, 1857, it folded. Winchester bought all assets for $40,000 and reorganized the firm into the New Haven Arms Company. He charged B. Tyler Henry with improvements to the Hunt lever rifle. Henry earned a patent for a repeater with a two-pronged firing pin. The 44-caliber 216-grain bullet, launched by 26 grains of blackpowder, clocked 1,025 fps. In 1866 Henry's successor Nelson King redesigned the rifle's magazine by adding a spring-loaded port in the receiver. The resulting Model 1866 would anchor a lever-action dynasty. During the late 1870s, however, Oliver Winchester fixed his hopes on the bolt-action rifle his company had acquired from B.B. Hotchkiss. Ordnance tests in 1878 favored the Hotchkiss, but

problems delayed production. Oliver Winchester died December 10, 1880 at age 70. His son-in-law, Thomas G. Bennett, would guide the firm through its most rapid growth.

That growth came by way of an unlikely alliance between the nation's premier rifle manufacturer and the son of a pioneer. In July, 1847, as Walter Hunt pondered breech-loading mechanisms, Brigham Young's beleaguered band of Mormons arrived at the Great Salt Lake. Gunmaker Jonathan Browning, who had stayed behind to produce firearms for the group, arrived five years later. Jonathan's family included 11 children. By a second wife, he would father 11 more, one of them John Moses.

John was just 10 when he built a flintlock musket from a scrapped barrel and a board shaped with a hatchet. He was well-placed to design rifles. The transcontinental railway had just been finished at Promontory Point, 50 miles from Ogden. Soon John was running Jonathan's gunshop.

In 1878 John Browning turned 23. With no drafting tools, he sketched a single-shot rifle action, then hand-forged the parts, shaping them with file and chisel and a foot-lathe. The rifle worked perfectly. Its massive parts and simple construction suited it to the frontier. John filed for a patent May 12, 1879. While he waited for the papers, his father died, leaving him head of two households. With help from brothers Ed, Sam and George, and gunmaker Frank Rushton, John and Matt erected a small factory. A week after pricing John's new rifle at $25 a copy, Matt sold all the rifles they'd finished in three months!

Even before he received a patent for his first rifle, John had designed another dropping-block action. By 1882 he'd built a repeating rifle. The following year Winchester salesman Andrew McAusland picked up a used Browning single-shot rifle and showed it to Winchester's president. Thomas Bennett left right away for what was billed as the biggest gun store between Omaha and the Pacific. He found half a dozen men barely out of their teens in an Ogden shop smaller than a livery. But Bennett was no fool. He found John Browning, then came straight to the point: "How much will you take for your rifle?"

❦ ● ❦ ● ❦ ● ❦ ● ❦ ● ❦

Lower Left: *This fine whitetail dropped to Wayne's 270 Model 70, in a pine thicket at close range.*

Lower Right: *A long shot with a Model 70 to the top of an Oregon rim dropped this deer for Wayne long ago.*

One rifle? No, *the* rifle. All rights.

"Ten thousand dollars," said John coolly. It was an enormous sum in 1883.

"Eight thousand, plus jobbing grants."

The rifle next appeared as Winchester's Model 1885. John followed up with a powerful lever-action, which Bennett bought for $50,000 – "more money than there was in Ogden," according to Browning. But an astute friend called the rifle Winchester's future. It became the Winchester 1886.

Thomas Bennett kept John busy. During their 20-year association, Winchester bought 44 Browning patents, apparently for asking price but with no royalties. Only 10 were manufactured as Winchesters. Bennett paid for designs he couldn't use, just to keep them from competitors.

By 1900 three of every four guns used by American sportsmen were of Browning design. They were all Winchesters. When he died in 1926, at age 71, John Browning had garnered 128 patents for 80 distinct firearms. Browning's work established Winchester as the industry titan during the last decades of the 19th century, arguably the most prolific period in firearms history. His were among the first successful repeating rifles designed for smokeless powder.

But Winchester's first high-power bolt rifles came by another path.

Hail and Farewell

In 1920 Thomas Bennett and other patriarchs reorganized the firm. The Winchester Repeating Arms Company made guns and ammunition, while its sister firm, the Winchester Company, manufactured cutlery, gas refrigerators, skates, flashlights, fishing gear, hand tools, washing machines, baseball bats, skis, batteries, paints and household brushes. This diversification failed to reduce debt; ironically, the gun division prospered.

For some time after armistice, Winchester gun designers had almost no budget. Still, they fashioned two fine rifles: the Model 52 bolt-action rimfire in 1919 and the Model 54 centerfire in 1924. The 54 was the firm's first successful bolt-action centerfire rifle, though the company had tried to enter that field for 30 years. The 45-70 Hotchkiss was discontinued in 1900; the Lee Straight Pull lasted from 1897 to 1903. Engineers working on the Model 54 borrowed the 1903 Springfield's coned breech. The ejector was of Newton design. A Mauser-style bolt cocked on opening and wore a beefy extractor and safety. The 54 stock was patterned after popular Sedgely sporting rifles of that period. A nickel-steel barrel screwed to a cyanide-hardened receiver bottled pressures from the new 270 WCF

cartridge, whose 130-grain bullet clocking 3,000 fps awed hunters used to 30-30s. The 54 cost more than a surplus military rifle, but much less than a custom sporter. Though it never earned the accolades given the earlier Model 94 or the Model 70, Winchester's M54 appeared at a pivotal time. The Springfield had introduced shooters to the potential of bolt rifles and powerful cartridges. The 54 was delightfully nimble; the 270 shot flatter than anything most deer hunters had ever seen.

When the Depression hit, Winchester was too weak to stand. In February, 1929 the old organization was dissolved, and the Winchester Repeating Arms Company of Delaware took its place. The company went bankrupt January 22, 1931, the year its Model 21 shotgun would come to market. In December Winchester was acquired by Western Cartridge Company. Western paid $3 million cash and $4.8 million (par value) of Western stock. The firm entered the Depression under Franklin Olin's son, John, who had a keen interest in firearms. In the next decade 23 new Winchester guns would appear.

The decision to replace the Model 54 with another rifle was prompted largely by a desire for a better centerfire target rifle. Since its introduction in 1919, the Model 52 had built an unassailable record on smallbore ranges, and Winchester wanted centerfire laurels as well. Western had kept the Model 54 alive, allowing T.C. Johnson and his staff to refine the rifle they'd engineered. Ten configurations followed, in 10 chamberings. Prices (in 1936) ranged from $59.75 for the basic Model 54 to $111.00 for the Sniper's Match. The Model 54's main weakness was its trigger. Fashioned after military triggers of the day, it also served as a bolt stop. Competitive shooters grumbled. Hunters content to fight a mushy trigger balked at the high-swing safety, which precluded low

◈ ● ◈ ● ◈ ● ◈ ● ◈ ● ◈

Controlled-round-feed under a Mauser-type extractor is standard on Dakota 76 rifles.

The Model 70 trigger is adjustable for weight of pull but not sear engagement.

scope mounting. Bill Weaver's Model 330 scope had shown what optical sights could do; rifles that wouldn't accommodate them had a dim future.

The Winchester Model 54 was cataloged and available through 1941,

but production diminished to a trickle during the last five years. Beginning December 29, 1934, Winchester started work on a stronger, better-looking rifle – the Model 70. It came to market slowly. The 54 still had a

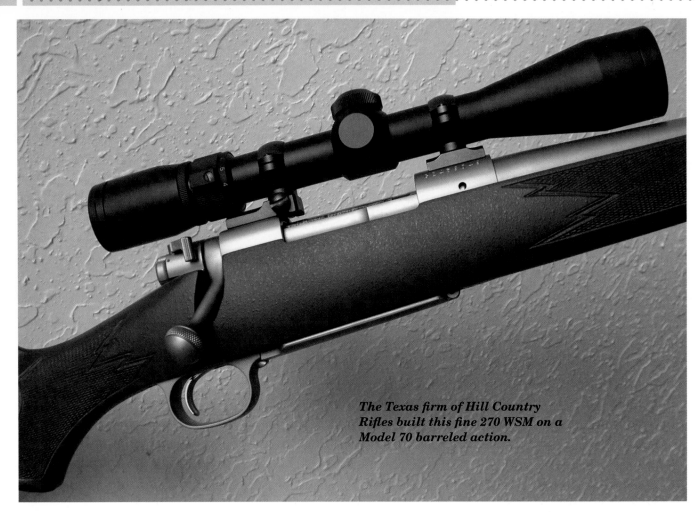

The Texas firm of Hill Country Rifles built this fine 270 WSM on a Model 70 barreled action.

following. Also, the legions of jobless men at soup kitchens were hardly in the market for a new hunting rifle. On January 20, 1936 the first Model 70s got serial numbers. On the official release date (January 1, 1937), 2,238 rifles awaited shipment.

Barrel and receiver on the first Model 70s looked a lot like the Model 54's. But the trigger was much better, a separate sear allowing for adjustment in take-up, weight and over-travel. The bolt stop was also separate. To eliminate misfires – too common with the 54's speed lock – striker travel on the Model 70 was increased 1/16 inch. To replace the awkward M54 safety, engineers came up with a tab on top of the bolt shroud. It swung horizontally. Four years later it would be redesigned as a side-swing tab, a middle detent blocking the striker while permitting bolt manipulation. Like the Model 54, the Model 70 had three guard screws, but instead of a stamped, fixed

magazine cover and guard, the 70 wore a hinged floorplate secured by a spring-loaded plunger in the separate trigger guard. A low bolt handle acted as a safety lug. The square bolt shoulder precluded low scope mounting and was later eliminated.

Model 70 barrels had the same contours and threads as Model 54 barrels. They were drop-forged, straightened by hand with a 15-pound hammer, then turned true on a lathe. After boring by deep-hole drill, they were straightened again. Next, each bore was reamed to proper diameter and hook-rifled by a cutter slicing progressively deeper on several passes, one groove at a time. Rifling took roughly 11 minutes per barrel. After lapping, barrels were threaded and slotted for rear sights and front sight hoods. Forged, hand-stippled ramps appeared on the first Model 70s; later ramps were soldered on and machine-matted. Before chambering, each barrel was inspected, then

stamped underneath with caliber designation and the last two digits of the year of manufacture. The last of four reamers left the chamber undersize for headspacing. The barrel then was roll-marked, given a caliber stamping, polished and blued.

The first Model 70 receivers were machined from solid bar stock, each beginning as a 7 1/2-pound chrome-moly billet. After 75 machinings, a finished receiver weighed 19.3 ounces. It was 8.77 inches long, 1.357 inches through the receiver ring. Spot-hardening the extraction cam behind the bridge preceded a full heat treatment. Next, each receiver spent 24 hours in a 1,200-degree salt bath, to bring Rockwell hardness to 47C. The test left a dimple in the tang. Most small parts were drop-forged, then machined. The extractor was fashioned from 1095 spring steel.

The Model 70's stock was more substantial than the 54's, though it looked like the late Model 54 version.

Standard stocks were roughed by bandsaw from 2x36-inch American black walnut; then they went eight at a time to the duplicator for contouring. Workers finished the inletting by hand, and fitted each butt-plate. Next, the stock was drum-sanded, then hand-sanded. Stick shellac or a glue-and-wood paste repaired minor flaws. The first stocks got a clear nitrocellulose lacquer finish over an alcohol-based stain. Because these lacquers contained carnauba wax, they produced a soft, oil-like finish. After the war, when carnauba wax became scarce, harder lacquers appeared. Hand checkering with carbide-tipped cutters followed.

Hill Country Rifles builds sleek, accurate hunting rifles on Model 70 actions.

Wayne takes aim with a 30-06 custom-built on an Model 70 action by Rick Freudenberg of Seattle.

Headspacing preceded assembly. Bolt parts were matched and fitted, the trigger and sear honed. A function check followed. The Winchester Proof (WP) stamp signified firing of one "blue pill" cartridge that generated pressure of about 70,000 psi. After its serial number was etched on the bolt, each rifle was zeroed at 50 yards. List price in 1937: $61.25. Early Model 70s were offered in 22 Hornet, 220 Swift, 250-3000 Savage, 257 Roberts, 270 WCF, 7mm Mauser and 30-06 – plus 300 and 375 H&H Magnums. Between 1941 and 1963, nine more chamberings were added; oddly, the 300 Savage was never cataloged. The rest of the stable of "pre-64" Model 70 cartridges (all from Winchester) appeared in the 1950s and early 1960s: the 243, 264 Magnum, 308, 300 Magnum, 338 Magnum, 358 and 458 Magnum. Before 1964, Model 70s appeared in 29 basic styles and 48 sub-configurations – not including special orders. Deer hunters kept sales of standard-weight 30-06 and 270 rifles at the top of the charts.

So successful that it earned the title of "the rifleman's rifle," Winchester's Model 70 became less and less profitable as labor costs escalated. In August, 1954, Olin was swallowed by the Mattheson Chemical Corporation. In 1960 company accountants urged reducing production costs. Two years later, engineers had identified 50 changes. These were implemented in 1963. The most visible drew public outrage. The stock wore crude, pressed checkering; the barrel "floated" free of its channel between unsightly gaps. A recessed bolt face featured a tiny hook extractor instead of the beefy Mauser claw. Machined steel bottom metal was supplanted by aluminum, solid action pins by roll-pins, the bolt stop's original coil spring by music-wire. A painted red cocking indicator stuck out like a flat tongue from under the bolt shroud. The overall effect was depressing. Prices of pre-64 Model 70s shot through the ceiling; new rifles languished on dealer racks.

The company scrambled to correct its blunder. In relatively short order it was offering rifles with the traditional

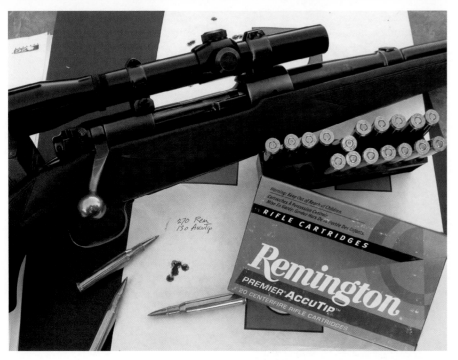

This old 270 still shoots very well, here with Remington AccuTip ammunition.

David Miller of Tucson builds his Marksman hunting rifles on Winchester 70 actions.

features most hunters wanted, but without the hand-work that had become prohibitively expensive.

Winchester improved the "new Model 70" with an anti-bind device for the bolt in 1966, a classier stock in 1972, a Featherweight rifle that looked and handled much better

in 1980. A short-action Model 70 arrived in 1984. Three years later, Winchester reintroduced the Mauser claw extractor on custom-shop 70s, and three years after that, a "Classic" version with controlled-round feed entered the catalog. The ensuing two decades brought myriad versions

of the Model 70 to market. Most were cosmetic variations. Stocks of various designs and increasingly of synthetic materials were married to barrels of heavy and light contour, stainless and chrome-moly. When Olin-Mattheson sold the Winchester Sporting Arms business in July, 1981, the new firm, U.S. Repeating Arms, continued improving its products. But in 1984 USRAC filed for Chapter 11 bankruptcy. In 1987 five investors bought the company. Among them: Fabrique Nationale (FN), a Belgian company that already owned Browning. FN is itself owned by Societe Generale, which controls 70 percent of Belgium's GNP. Early in 1991 a French conglomerate bought FN and, with it, USRAC. You'll often hear "Use-rack" in talk about guns of New Haven lineage post-1981. They're still Winchesters.

In the late 1990s, Winchester Short Magnum and Super Short Magnum cartridges challenged the Model 70's dimensions. Winchester accommodated both and continued to offer the push-feed bolt, with front-mounted claw extractor, and a "Classic" action with Mauser claw. A hybrid bolt called "controlled-round push-feed" appeared later. It combined the open underside of the original bolt face with an up-front hook extractor. The hook caught rising rims like the claw but permitted easy straight-in feeding of single rounds.

While the cachet of pre-64 Model 70s keeps prices high, there's no practical advantage to the early rifles. You won't see hand finishing on late guns. But then, checkering machines produce better results than are evident on many Model 70s built when gasoline cost 28 cents a gallon. The only thing wrong about the most recent Model 70s is that they're almost surely the last you'll see from New Haven.

Winchester's plant shut its doors in March, 2006, probably for good. Production costs – primarily labor – had risen to the point of erasing the factory's net return. In fact, one reliable source from inside the Browning/Winchester consortium told me that annual losses before closure were running to seven figures. Sadly, the Model 70 died 70 years after its introduction. Rumors of a resurrection followed quickly, but the New Haven Winchester is gone; any new manufacturing will most likely take place off-shore.

Winchester's 2006 catalog, the last to feature Model 70s from the Connecticut plant, listed 21 versions of the rifle, in four action sizes and 23 chamberings. Wood, synthetic and laminated stocks were married to stainless and chrome-moly steel, in various combinations with controlled-round feed and controlled-round push-feed bolt-face types. Starting price for the last of the Rifleman's Rifle: $525.

Model 70 Clones

Is the pre-64 Model 70 the best production-line rifle ever made? Some shooters say so, though on average it was not the most accurate. The Model 70 had a strong action that handled many cartridges well. But magnum-length actions are common now, and short receivers make better sense for short cartridges. Many rifles now wear the vaunted Mauser-style extractor. There's no more rugged hunting trigger than the 70's; still, affordable replacements from Timney give you easier adjustments and as light a pull as you'd wish.

Model 70 magic owes much to history. This was by any measure the best *affordable production rifle* available in the late 1930s. The Model 70 also looks right – clean, lean, sleek, balanced. As with a 911 Porsche roadster or a vintage Harley-Davidson motorcycle, there's something about this rifle's profile that distinguishes it from others of its type and tells your eye that "this is better." The wood and steel have been properly married and contoured. Its graceful but functional lines and a predatory heft take the Model 70 out of the tool category. It marks a high point in the design and manufacture of bolt rifles. The 70 has become an archetype, the measure of its kind, a classic by the purist definition of that over-used word.

"It's good enough," the late Don Allen told me, "that we designed the Dakota 76 as a modern pre-war Model 70 – with better wood and

David Miller (left) and Curt Crum examine their handiwork, a Marks-man rifle on a 70 action.

Wayne's Montana/Serengeti rifle (a Model 70 clone, better finished) shot this tight group.

more attention to detail. The primary mechanical change is our flush-mounted swing-arm bolt release." Dakota 76s afield are surely superior to the Model 70 in fit and finish. Stocks of figured walnut are finely checkered, with crisp edges. The metal's flawless

polish shows off a satin blue. The 76 is bored for popular hunting rounds, including rimless Dakota magnums on the 404 Jeffery case.

Dakota rifles afford you many options. So do the Model 70-style rifles from Montana Rifle Company and Serengeti Rifles. The two Kalispell firms offer metal and wood, respectively. Montana Rifles got its start in 1990 and was soon making barrels. Brian Sipe and Rod Rogers then designed the Model 1999 bolt action, patterned after the early Model 70 Winchester. Rod eventually left to found Serengeti Rifles.

The Model 1999 action comes in short and long versions, right-hand or left, stainless or chrome-moly steel. Montana bottom metal mimics the Model 70's. It is, however, of one-piece design, an improvement. The 3.15-inch magazine box on the short action suits the 7x57 and derivatives, and the 284. Short boxes on other rifles are typically proportioned for the 308, forcing deep bullet seating with mid-length rounds.

The bolt face and claw extractor of Montana's 1999 are pure Model 70. So is the trigger, but with a smooth, not a grooved, finger piece. The coned breech has been modified. There's no extractor cut in the barrel; instead, the 1999 features a collar inside its receiver ring to accept the extractor nose. The Montana action sports a dovetail-shaped guide lug on the extractor clip to reduce bolt bind. The ejector and three-position safety are vintage Model 70, but not the bolt release. Instead of a tab at the rear of the receiver wall, Montana's 1999 rifle employs a spring-loaded latch on the receiver's left flank. It's like the Sako release, almost as bulky as an 1898 Mauser gate. Montana Rifle Company's button-rifled barrels are hand-lapped.

Serengeti is a first-stop source if you want to custom-stock a Montana 1999. The company offers many choices, in wood grade and furniture, checkering and special features like crossbolts. "You pick your own combinations on computer," said Serengeti president Larry Tahler.

Given my limited computer skills, that sounded more ambitious than carving a stock from a log.

"We make it easy," said Larry. He showed me several fetching, slim-wristed stocks. One had an unusual comb. "It actually slopes *up* to the heel to take recoil away from your face. This is also a laminated stock, what we call an ACRA-Bond." It didn't look laminated from the side, but a closer look showed three strips of walnut in an almost seamless sandwich.

A couple of months later, at my home computer, I keyed in the requisite w's and back-slashes and corrected the typos. Had it been an inletting chisel, my computer would have ruined a $700 stick of English walnut. But it wasn't. Click. Click. Click. Up popped Serengeti's web-site, then images of wood, showing color, figure and layout. After scrolling through dozens of blanks, I e-mailed my top four choices to Larry, and specified dimensions, checkering and fittings. The average Serengeti stock costs $1,500.

I kept abreast of the 257's progress on the computer screen. Larry sent notes, photos, and, at last, a target with a 3/4-inch group. A couple of weeks later, the rifle arrived. It looked good and pointed easily. The slim, open grip and slender forend were just to my taste, with beautifully cut checkering. Crisp on the edges, and flat on the surfaces, with obvious attention to detail – that description applied to every surface. The steel grip cap, Talley swivel bases and Decelerator pad fit as if grown with the stock. Metal profiling from the Montana Rifle Company matched the

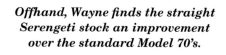

Offhand, Wayne finds the straight Serengeti stock an improvement over the standard Model 70's.

woodwork. The Montana action fed with smooth authority. The trigger broke cleanly. Hornady ammo with 117-grain SSTs printed inside 5/8 inch.

Before Winchester's assembly line snared the last Model 70 actions, a few went to FNH USA, the U.S. subsidiary of FN Herstal. This huge firm, partly controlled by the government, owns U.S. Repeating Arms, which for years has used the Winchester name under license from Olin. FN owns Browning too.

FN no longer turns out the lovely Mausers that Browning marketed as its High Power line when I was young. But FN bolt guns still make news. An SPR, or Special Police Rifle, came along in 2000. Four years later it was adopted by the FBI. That year FN modified the SPR to fashion the PBR, or Precision Bolt Rifle. Both these firearms are built on the Model 70 action. Finished receivers differ from those of the Model 70 only in the size of their scope mount holes. The big 8-40s are an improvement over traditional 6-48s. All SPR and PBR receivers are proportioned for WSM rounds. So a 308 gets extra beef in ring and rails. The SPR features a Mauser-type extractor. The lower-priced PBR has Winchester's controlled-round push-feed bolt. The XP (Extreme Performance) rendition of the PBR wears the SPR's extractor and a fluted barrel. SPR and both PBRs feature hammer-forged barrels that, like the receiver, have a distinctive nitride metal finish (the SPR A3 is Parkerized). SPR bores are chrome plated – and accurate! After one SPR was fired 15,000 times during a 100-hour FBI endurance trial, it punched an 0.64-inch group!

According to Dave Golladay, who represents FN to the press, Hogue fashions the black stocks for the PBR. McMillan supplies SPR stocks, in OD green. Some feature competition-type adjustments.

The PBR lists for about $900, the XP version $1,000. An FNH SPR costs from $1,300 to $2,400.

Model 70s to Remember

The few Winchester 70s in my rack are remnants: a 375 with a repaired stock and receiver sight, a post-war 30-06 I've promised to shoot but haven't in the 30 years I've owned it, an early 270 with Lyman Alaskan scope – the 2-1/2x that, with Weaver's K4, introduced many hunters to optical sights....

I have a favorite 270 Model 70. Unlike Jack O'Connor's famous Biesen-stocked Featherweights, this is a heavy rifle. The stock has all the figure of a railroad tie, and is thick through the wrist. Nearly all its finish has been worn off, with half the metal's blue. Of my modest assortment of Model 70s, this is by any measure the ugliest. Yet I like it. The bolt slides as smoothly as a Mannlicher's; the trigger wilts when you want it to. Most importantly, this 270 shoots to the same spot, year after year. Equipped with a 2.5x Lyman All American in Tilden mounts, it is in many respects a quintessential Model 70.

I made my longest shot at big game with a different Model 70, a 30-06. It was at a mule deer so far away that I'd not consider the shot now....

It is just after dawn on an alpine ridge many Octobers ago. Benches cascading to the Lostine River below bear the black stubble of a three-year-old burn. I'm minutes into the 7x35 Bausch & Lomb before spotting the buck. He's too far, but there is no time to approach. He's moving toward a bed I will not find.

And I am young enough to see a shot too long as simply a long shot.

Prone, I snug the sling. My left hand cushions the 30-06 on the rock. The antlers glint in the sun, but without the sun I'd not see them. He is beetle-size in the 4x Leupold, and facing me. Wind rumbles in from 8 o'clock. It will pull the Core-Lokt at least a foot. The crosswire nudges a rock windward of the deer.

The bullet strikes near the deer's foot. Cycling the bolt, I aim higher. The bullet slides by a knee. There is one more round in the Winchester. Holding 20 inches left and 30 high, I crush the trigger.

The hit is audible after the empty bounces on the rock. The buck sprints. Yellow dust hangs in the sun, over blackened pine carcasses and brilliant green grass. The descent will be long. But the buck is dead.

That rifle, a Model 70 made three years before I was born, had the scalloped safety and cloverleaf tang of "transition"-era rifles built in the late Forties. I sold it too cheap, when I was broke from college and driving log trucks for a living. Then you could buy sound, lightly used pre-1964 Model 70s for $200.

I replaced the 30-06 with a Model 70 in 300 Winchester, its stock a riot of tigertail. An unusual rifle that, because it came off the line in

The Dakota 76 is an elegant rifle, designed by Don Allen after the pre-64 Winchester 70.

⁑ ● ⁑ ● ⁑ ● ⁑ ● ⁑ ● ⁑

1963. By that time, wood quality and workmanship had begun to slide. Coarse, shabby checkering in reduced panels hinted at the cost-cutting that would gut the Model 70 in 1964 and draw howls of rage from shooters. But this 300 had superb wood. The bolt moved as if on buttered rails, and 180-grain Nosler Partitions, pushed by 75 grains of H4831, nipped tiny groups. I killed several elk with that rifle, including a bull running across a hillside at 250 yards. He tumbled like a shot hare. I have no idea why I sold that Model 70, but I recall getting a note from the buyer, who delighted in the walnut and vowed never to part with the rifle and to take good care of it. He accepted it as if I'd given him my first-born.

Model 70 aficionados are like that.

Wayne shot this Alaskan mountain goat with a Winchester 70 in .325 WSM.

Robert L. Hillberg during gunnery practice with a Lewis machinegun, Duluth, Minnesota, 1937. U.S. Navy Squadron VN11 RD9 Curtiss O2C1.

Original prototype for the Wildey pistol, produced by Bellmore Johnson Tool Co., 1980. Original design by Hillberg.

ROBERT L. HILLBERG:
PROFILE OF A
FIREARMS DESIGNER

by Don Findley

Over his many years of designing firearms, everything from machineguns to sporting pistols, shotguns and rifles, when asked of all his accomplishments, what he is most proud of; Bob replied "The Whitney pistol." History will surely remember Robert L. Hillberg as one of the foremost firearms designers of the 20th century.

You may remember Robert L. Hillberg as the man who designed and manufactured the Whitney Wolverine 22 pistol in the mid-1950s. The Whitney's space-age profile "grabbed" the attention of firearms enthusiasts everywhere. Unless you are employed in the firearms industry and are actually involved in the production of firearms, you may never have heard of Robert L. Hillberg at all. Bob is one of the men who design and test the guns, working in the background, and often leaving others to receive the

accolades for their achievements. Bob Hillberg is far from a one-dimensional gun designer and his career in the firearms industry spans over 60 years.

Bob was born in Anamosa, Iowa on August 27, 1917. As a young boy he accompanied his father, an avid outdoorsman, on hunting trips in Minnesota and South Dakota. Starting at a young age, he was interested in anything mechanical, especially guns. His first gun was a 12-gauge Browning Auto Five shotgun. He was intrigued by the number of mechanical events that

Opposite Bottom: *Old Friends. L/R: The late Harry H. Sefried II (Harry worked with Bob at High Standard and later for Bob at Whitney Firearms, Inc., from Whitney to Ruger where he retired in 1980), Robert A. Greenleaf Sr. (product engineer from 1964 to 1988, Savage Arms), and Robert L. Hillberg at Hillberg's home in Cheshire, Conn., June 2005.*

Right: *First production model of the C.O.P. (Compact Off-Duty Police) 4-barrel handgun in 357 Magnum, designed by Robert L. Hillberg.*

had to occur in a semi-automatic firearm to fire, extract, eject, reload, re-cock and be ready to fire the next round in a split second. Bob was not formally trained in firearms design. His engineering skills were "picked up" from odd jobs, after school and summers, in machine shops. He read everything available on firearms. He did, however, attend the University of Minnesota.

Hillberg became an avid firearms collector. After several years of collecting guns and studying their design, he designed a 357 Magnum submachine gun in 1937, and built a working prototype at the U.S. Naval Air Base, Wold Chamberlin Field, where he was a reserve member of Squadron VN11 RD-9.

Hillberg took his prototype to Colt Firearms in Hartford, Connecticut in 1938 and demonstrated his gun, hoping to sell the design. Colt wasn't interested in the submachine gun, but they were interested in Bob and offered Hillberg a job, which he accepted. This was his first employment in the firearms industry. While at Colt, he worked in engineering, assembly, inspection and manufacturing. Hillberg also designed a short action for their revolver and developed a 7/8-scale 22 version of Colt's Frontier Single Action that went into production years later.

In 1940 Hillberg accepted employment at Pratt & Whitney Aircraft, located in East Hartford, Connecticut and worked in the engineering department where he was involved with the design of engine components and experimental engine installations in test aircraft. While at Pratt & Whitney he began the development of a 30-caliber carbine, as well as a 20mm aircraft cannon.

Hillberg moved to Burlington, Vermont in 1942 to take a position with the Ordnance Division of Bell Aircraft, where he worked as project engineer. He worked on numerous other projects including the B-17 turret, bomb racks and rocket releases. During his stay at Bell, Bob designed a 20mm continuous belt-fed mechanism for submarines and anti-aircraft. The 30-caliber carbine, started at Pratt & Whitney, was activated and prototypes were built at Bell. The design was completed late in the U.S. carbine competition, which was won by Winchester. Hillberg's carbine was radical in concept, in that it did not employ a moving breech block. The barrel moved forward with each shot. The rifle fed automatically, loading on the rearward stroke of the barrel. Since the magazine was located forward of the standing breech face, the cartridges fed forward in the magazine. This required a special crimp between the bullet and the cartridge case. The advantage in this unorthodox design was the rifle was two inches shorter than a conventional rifle with the same length barrel. It met the 5-pound criteria for carbines and was tested successfully at Bell and then sent to Canada for evaluation. World War II ended just as the carbine was finalized, and it never entered production.

After the war, 1947, Bob accepted a job with Republic Aviation, Armament Division, in Farmingdale, Long Island, NY. He worked on the F-84 gun deck and later was appointed F-91 armament unit leader and also worked in the "secret room" as an armament consultant for advanced fighter aircraft. He designed the gun mounts and feed systems for the F-84, as well as rocket systems and bomb racks for the F-84. While at Republic, Hillberg designed a series of semi-automatic weapons.

With each move Hillberg gained experience and knowledge. By 1951 he had left the aircraft industry and returned to designing firearms. He took a job with High Standard Manufacturing Company in 1951. After a few months, he accepted the position as head of research and development. Hillberg had gained a great deal of knowledge in the use of high strength aluminum alloy while working in the aircraft industry, and applied this expertise to firearms design. Hillberg should be given a great deal of credit for the commercial use of aluminum in firearms production. With Bob as head of R&D, High Standard was one of the first firearms manufacturers to make use of aluminum. High Standard's inventory included a complete line of sporting arms, shotguns, rifles and handguns.

High Standard was also involved in the manufacture of military weapons. Hillberg designed the T-152 tank machinegun for the Springfield Armory and the Detroit Tank Arsenal. This gun was later put into production as the M-37. He also designed the 9mm T-3 double-action pistol, a 22 semi-auto sporting rifle and the world's first commercial gas-operated semi-auto shotgun, originally called the Model 60. This shotgun was marketed by High Standard and was a huge commercial success.

Original 4-barrel Winchester Liberator combat shotgun in 16-gauge, designed by Hillberg.

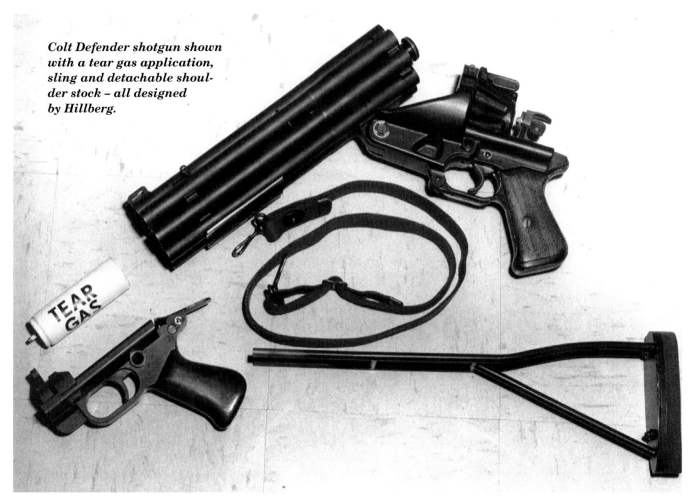

Colt Defender shotgun shown with a tear gas application, sling and detachable shoulder stock – all designed by Hillberg.

Hillberg had an idea for a 22 sporting pistol, an all-new design that could be manufactured at a low cost without sacrificing quality, a pistol he believed could compete in a market dominated by Colt, High Standard and, more recently, Ruger. While at High Standard, he became acquainted with Howard "Howie" Johnson of the Bellmore Johnson Tool Company of Hamden, Connecticut. Bob was convinced, by his good friend (Johnson) to retire from High Standard and develop and manufacture the new pistol on his own.

Subsequently, Hillberg left High Standard and co-founded Whitney Firearms, Inc., of North Haven, Connecticut in 1954. Howard Johnson was president, Robert Hillberg, vice president and chief engineer. Employees included the top machinists and gunsmiths in the business and the two partners had high hopes for the new company.

After the 22 pistol was established as the company cornerstone, other models were to be introduced. Whitney Firearms had the necessary motivation and the right people in place — the possibilities seemed unlimited. After almost two years of designing and testing, production began in 1956. The new pistol, with its space-age profile, was called the Whitney Wolverine; "Tomorrow's Pistol Today." Ten thousand pistols were produced and shipped the first year.

Whitney Firearms, Inc. was set up to design and produce firearms, and needed distribution and marketing savvy. A deal was struck with J. L. Galef, a firearms broker from New York, to market the guns. That exclusive marketing contract ultimately led to the demise and closing of Whitney Firearms in May of 1957.

From mid-1957 to 1980 Hillberg was employed as Chief Engineer

for Bellmore Johnson Tool Company. From his office, located in Cheshire, Connecticut, he ran a firearm consultant and design service. Customers included about every major firearms company in the U.S., plus several Pentagon agencies (confidential firearms projects). His designs while at Bellmore Johnson ranged from shotguns — both combat and sporting — to rifles and handguns.

Hillberg designed double-action revolvers for Browning and Winchester. His work on the Winchester Liberator, Colt Defender and the Model J brought the combat shotgun to a new level of refinement. The Liberator was a four-barrel repeating combat shotgun with the firepower of a semi-automatic without the mechanical complexity.

The Defender is a 20-gauge 3-inch Magnum combat shotgun designed to appeal to law enforcement agencies. The Defender featured eight

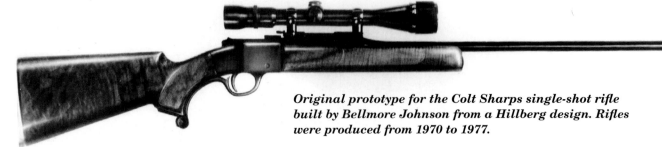

Original prototype for the Colt Sharps single-shot rifle built by Bellmore Johnson from a Hillberg design. Rifles were produced from 1970 to 1977.

selective-fire 12-inch independent barrels — all arranged in a circular cluster around a hollow axis — and an investment cast aluminum alloy receiver. Two machinegun-type grips are employed to control and fire the gun, from the shoulder or the hip. During independent testing conducted by a police expert at Colt Firearms' request, the expert's post-evaluation report stated, in part: "In no instance did the gun fail to function, to be absolutely correct, the gun could not be made to malfunction."

The Model J is a box-fed pump-action shotgun with an ejection port on both sides. A switch determines from which direction the spent shells are ejected for left or right-handed shooters. One of the first shotguns equipped with a folding stock, the Model J was tested in Vietnam by the U.S. military.

Robert L. Hillberg Designs

Production and experimental prototypes of civilian & military weapons, and accessories.

T-152 Tank machine gun (Tank Arsenal/Springfield Armory). 9mm submachine gun. 223 M-1 carbine (CIA). 22 L.R. conversion for the M-16 rifle. 12-gauge police/riot pump shotgun. 4-barrel military & police riot shotgun. 8-barrel military & police combination tear gas/riot shotgun. 38 cal. revolver, pocket size (Colt). 4-shot tear gas & 22 cal. pocket pistol (Colt). 22 sporting pistol (Colt). Low-cost 22 pistol (High Standard). Single-shot 22 western-style revolver (Savage). Single-shot 22 Winchester M-94-style youth rifle (Ithaca). Single-shot shotgun (Ithaca). Single-shot shotgun (Savage). Semi-automatic shotgun (Savage). 357 & 22 revolver (Browning). Over & under centerfire rifle (Browning). Pump shotgun (Browning Model BPS). 357 & 22 revolver (Winchester). Cattle stun gun (Winchester). 45-70 Lever-action rifle (Marlin). 30-30 lever-action rifle (Mossberg). Sharps centerfire single-shot rifle (Colt). 12-gauge semi-automatic shotgun (Marlin). 357 COP, 4-barrel handgun (Compact-Off-duty Police). Ring airfoil missile launcher (U. S. government). 22 semi-automatic pistol (Whitney Firearms, Inc.). 10-round 22 pistol magazine (Whitney Firearms,

Savage 101 22 single-shot pistol, designed by Hillberg. Produced from 1960 to 1968.

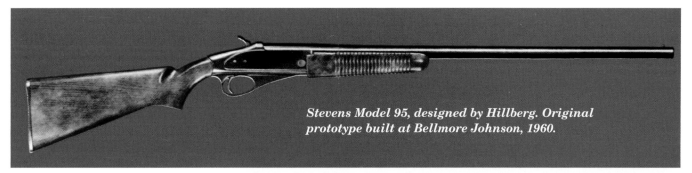

Stevens Model 95, designed by Hillberg. Original prototype built at Bellmore Johnson, 1960.

Inc.). Folding stock for riot shotgun (Remington). Wildey 45-caliber semi-automatic pistol (Wildey Firearms) and the 22 Mini COP pistol.

From 1980 to the present Hillberg has served as an independent expert witness — for both plaintiff and defendant — in court cases relating to firearms, with special interest in cases that involve design, testing, safety and prior art. Also, he is a retired deputy sheriff and a member of the following police organizations: New England Association of Chiefs of Police; International Association of Chiefs of Police; American Law Enforcement Officers Association; New Haven County Sheriff's Association National Sheriff's Association and the Connecticut Chiefs of Police Association (firearms committee).

Robert Hillberg has been granted over 36 patents — foreign and domestic — pertaining to firearms. The American National Standard, an industry performance standard established to provide the firearms designer and manufacturer with recommendations for test procedures to evaluate new designs as defined under the Federal Gun Control Act of 1968, lists Hillberg as an "independent expert."

If you seek a career in the firearms industry, find a copy of the June 1966 *American Rifleman* magazine, and refer to page 95. You may take some advice from that article offered by a man who has "been there and done that." Highlights from that article titled "Gun Designers," by Robert L. Hillberg: "The golden era of firearms design was at the turn of the century. Men like von Mannlicher, Paul Mauser, Andreas Schwarzlose, John

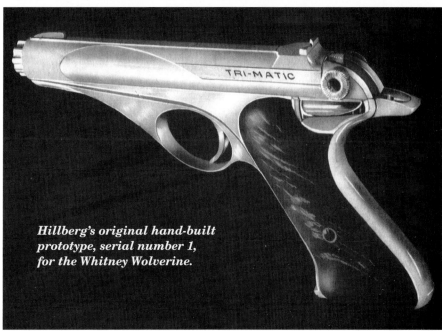

Hillberg's original hand-built prototype, serial number 1, for the Whitney Wolverine.

Browning, and others pioneered the art so thoroughly that virtually nothing new in basic firearms design has been developed since. The heritage of every modern design, both military and commercial, can be traced back to the creative genius of a small group of designers some 60 years ago." The article concludes "Today's firearms industry needs top technical help in all other phases. If giving the public a better gun for the same money or the same gun for less money is your destiny, the gun industry will welcome you with open arms. If being a part of a team to produce this gun or to merchandise it is your aim, there is a place for you in the industry. If your burning ambition is to design a new gun and get rich---forget it."

Over his many years of designing firearms, everything from machineguns to sporting pistols, shotguns and rifles, when asked

of all his accomplishments, what he is most proud of Bob replied "The Whitney pistol." History will surely remember Robert L. Hillberg as one of the foremost firearms designers of the 20th century.

The next time you reach for that favorite deer rifle or old reliable shotgun, or perhaps the 22 pistol your dad left you, take a minute to remember the people who designed and perfected those cherished pieces; the men and women who labor behind the scenes to guarantee a dependable and reliable product, a product that will withstand the test of time and man. Every great firearms design, from the early matchlock to today's newest military assault weapon, began with one man's idea. ✸

Acknowledgments:
Robert L. Hillberg for his assistance and the loan of documents and photographs from his personal collection. Robert A. Greenleaf, Sr. for background information and photographs from his personal collection.

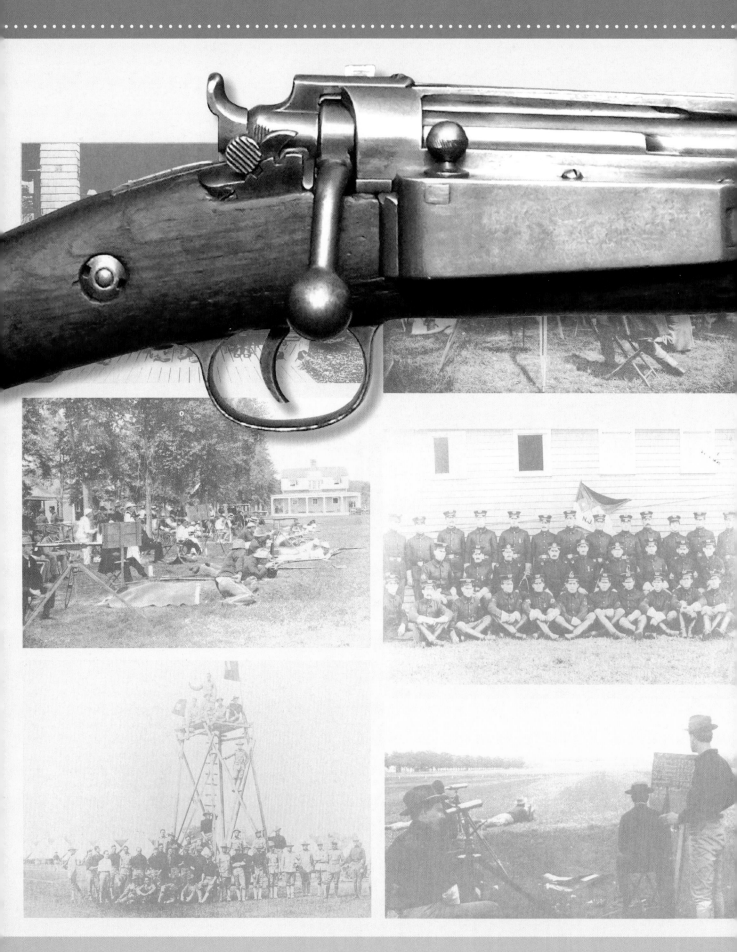

WALTER HUDSON–
KRAG SPECIALIST

by Jim Foral

A hundred years ago, Dr. Walter Hudson's experiences with the competition Krag rifle ran the entire spectrum of levels. For as long as the craze lasted, he was the talented, self-appointed guiding spirit behind the perfection of the ammunition, and repeatedly demonstrated his mastery of both the rifle and himself. At the same time, he skillfully imparted his knowledge to a nation of fellow riflemen. Almost single-handedly, he took military rifle shooting out of the Dark Ages, and emerged as a star player in one of the more interesting chapters in the history of arms and ammunition.

Right: *Author's copy of Hudson's book was formerly in the library of E. C. Crossman, prolific gunwriter and firearms authority of the period. It is a toss-up whether he or his esteemed peer, Townsend Whelen, was more lastingly influential.*

*I*t is the nature of those who shoot the rifle competitively, particularly those accomplished in a particular discipline of another, to become attracted to an offshoot branch of the same sport. A deliberation to sample the other activity logically follows. The rational first instinct of many is to resist the impulse. Energy, time, and resources may be already too thinly spread, and their division is not conducive to the necessary focus for successful dual interests.

Another camp insists that one more iron in the fire is not excessive

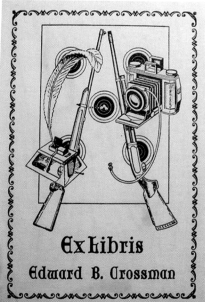

Ex Libris
Edward B. Crossman

– for a while. Genuinely zealous in the beginning, they are wholly sidetracked for a time. They fire a couple of matches and finish mid-pack. The interest is lost and the undertaking abandoned. The specialized rifle that just last year they were so keen on is forgotten and sold at a loss. We have then the sort of person that is determined to succeed in a new pursuit. In the main, this man possesses the ability, the self-discipline to educate himself and practice diligently, and the inborn drive to make more than a cursory go of it. He seems to feel at home on any range. To compete and win occasionally is one thing, to continually excel in multiple aspects of the rifle games, and remain foreseeably and invariably triumphant is quite another. To have mastered and dominated one rifle sport, extended into others with the same overwhelming superiority over the competition establishes an ultra-rare specimen: the naturally born talent with the rifle.

To single out and hold up one individual as an ideal, there could be no better example than Dr. Walter Hudson.

Hudson's background in competitive shooting of any sort is not entirely clear. His name isn't included in any competitor's roster in the overly

New Jersey National Guard Signal Corps, 1902. This was Hudson's unit, but he's not in this picture.

extensive coverage of match results that *Forest and Stream* magazine reported until January of 1898, and it is presumed that he got his start shortly prior to this date. In the main, his interests and proficiencies were in the rifles sport. He excelled at gallery small bore but was best known across the East as a Schuetzen standout, generally regarded as one of the two or three men to beat. He was a skilled, but seemingly under-enthusiastic revolver shot, and there is some indication that he was an occasional contestant in live bird tournaments.

It is generally believed that once Dr. Hudson was smitten with the competition Krag when military rifle shooting became fashionable after the Spanish American War, he abandoned entirely the more traditional and conventional shooting disciplines. Notwithstanding his apparent preference for the military style marksmanship in its season, Hudson remained vitally active in both gallery and Schuetzen competitions, and was a championship-level contender in each. The more snobbish of his elitist single-shot peers sneered at the "unnatural" exercise of lying on one's stomach while aiming a rifle to be beneath the dignity of

a crack offhand shot. Others were critical of his division of attentions.

Hudson didn't neglect his beloved Schuetzen shooting during the peak of his Krag years. Indeed, *Forest and Stream* magazine considered him to be the "Champion of our Eastern 200-yard riflemen." E.C. Crossman, whose opinion is worthy of respect, once wrote that Dr. Hudson was the "finest off-hand shot I'd seen perform." At the 1902 NRA Meetings at Sea Girt,

Walter Hudson, known familiarly as "The Human Machine Rest," easily won the Schuetzen segment of the program. Billed as an Individual Rifle Championship of Greater New York, the annual Election Day match, shot at Armbruster's Shooting Park in Greenville, New Jersey, was just about the most important event on the eastern competitor's dance card. The first prize was the Hayes Trophy. At the 1903 contest, Dr. Hudson, shooting a Stevens-Pope iron-sighted 33-caliber against a field of recently allowable telescope-sighted match rifles, fired a record-breaking score of 2301, an astonishing 76 points in front of the second-place finisher. Heralded as a remarkable achievement then, Hudson's record remains a milestone in twentieth-century rifle competition. He won the Election Day Match once again in 1905, took third in 1900, fourth in 1906 and was high on the winners' list in other years.

1904 was a good year for the "gun doctor," as he was called. Breaking the previous record by twenty points, Hudson was awarded the King's Medal and crowned Schuetzen King after finishing first at the National Schuetzenfest at Union Hill, New Jersey. Hudson used a "New Remington Schuetzen Rifle" to win, and this became a rather marketable point for Remington Arms. In June, he out-pointed second-place Harry Pope

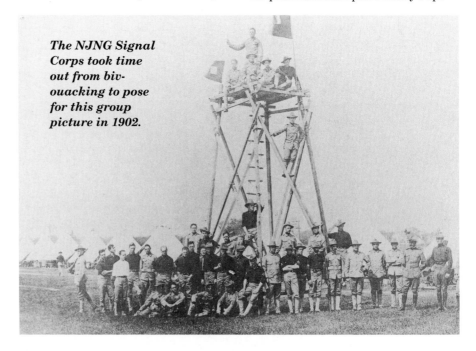

The NJNG Signal Corps took time out from biv-ouacking to pose for this group picture in 1902.

and the rest of the field at the fourth National Bundfest. And for the second year in a row, Hudson bested perennial nemesis Michael Dorrier, the three-time winner of the Hayes prize, in a well publicized one-on-one challenge match. The Doctor, who decisively handled this same individual opponent in 1903, finished 52 points ahead of his exceptionally talented rival.

Each March, at Armbruster's park, Hudson routinely did very well in the hundred-shot American Record Match. He won in 1905. He also posted the high score with rifle and revolver in the International match between the Manhattan Rifle and Revolver Assn. and the Cercle des Carabiners of Paris in June of 1907, when he broke the French and world's record at 200 yards on the French target. In addition to these major victories, Dr. Hudson picked up prizes in all manner of lesser Schuetzen contests.

His wintertime passion and his strong point was gallery shooting. A *Forest and Stream* journalist conceded that the doctor was "a hard man to beat in any shooting game", and he was a formidable contestant at the various New York City indoor ranges. He was a fixture at the famed Zettler gallery. Representing the Manhattan Rifle and Revolver Assn., where he happened to be president, or himself individually, Hudson shot a Remington Hepburn Schuetzen rimfire to bring home prize badges uncountable. At Zettler's 1902 100-shot match "open to the world", Hudson came in second to L.P. Itel by two points, and was awarded a prize of unspecified description. In 1906, Hudson fired an unprecedented five possible at the Zettler Club's Open Tournament. That same year, he placed first in the New York Open Rifle Tournament using U.M.C. Shorts. Hudson favored U.M.C. rimfire ammunition, and the Bridgeport concern had a flair for bragging the fact in their advertising. In an important match held in conjunction with the Annual Sportsman's Expo at Madison Square Garden, Hudson placed third against a huge field. Through his Pope-

Ballard he shot both Peters and U.M.C. 22 cartridges. Throughout the off-season of the 1900-1907 Krag era, seeing Walter Hudson's name near the head of the winner's list in an important gallery match was the usual and expected thing.

Dr. Hudson's intensely focused involvement with the Krag Jorgensen rifle falls into three distinct but occasionally overlapping areas: competition, ammunition improvement and public education.

As a twenty-nine year old physician, Walter Hudson joined the New Jersey National Guard for a five-year enlistment in August of 1899. His home residence is recorded as Jersey City, and he was assigned to Company E, Fourth Regiment. Clearly, Dr, Hudson was a thoroughly non-traditional recruit. The only satisfactory explanation why a professional man would strap himself with a time-consuming military obligation was the opportunity to compete with the Krag rifle.

His record with the New Jersey Guard is somewhat less than stable. In February of 1900, he transferred to Company C, where he is thought to have had some shooting buddies. Gallery and big-bore standouts Sgt. William A. Tewes and Pvt. Patrick J. O'Hare (P.J. O'Hare) were both in C Company. Hudson dropped out entirely in December of 1900, but was reinstated in June of 1901, and transferred to the Signal and Telegraph Corp by special order from HQ in September. With his mind on the firing line and his heart on the competition the Guard afforded, Pvt. Hudson wigwagged the flags with the other enlisted and semaphored the drill time away.

He dropped out again in October of 1902. In August of 1903, he was again reinstated. Apparently he didn't like his assignment and transferred back to Company C. In January of 1904, he voluntarily terminated his enlistment. Curiously, Hudson spent almost three years with the New York National Guard. In August of 1903, Pvt. Hudson, the doctor who ran the hospital at Number 9 Chambers Street, signed

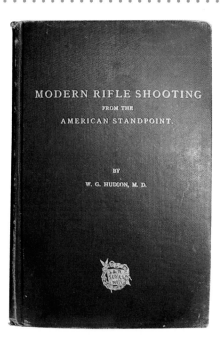

Hudson's little blue book, the bible of the hopefully proficient and competitive Krag rifleman.

❧ • ❧ • ❧ • ❧ • ❧ • ❧

on as a lowly hospital corpsman with the 9th Regiment. He accepted a Captaincy that December and served as the 9th's assistant surgeon. He mustered out with an honorable discharge in February of 1905.

The transition from Schuetzen offhand match rifle to military rifle was a smooth one for a natural like Guardsman Walter Hudson. At the annual meeting of the New Jersey Rifle Assn., fired at Sea Girt in 1899, Hudson placed second in the 30-shot Wimbledon Cup Match. At the 1900 New Jersey State shoot, he and his Krag again placed second, thirty-seven points ahead of the third-place finisher. Civilian William De V. Foulke of Philadelphia won the Wimbledon that year and Hudson may have fired as a civilian as well. He is listed on one roster as Doctor, and Private in another. Pvt. Hudson helped the New Jersey Guard team capture the 500- and 600-yard Hilton Trophy. The New Jersey team kept the Hilton Trophy in 1901, with Pvt. Hudson as high point man in the match, as he was when the NJ Guard team won the Short Range Interstate Military Match.

1902 Palma Team group photo. There's Hudson standing center row extreme right, justifiably proud.

The annual Sea Girt meeting was the main event of the yearly shooting calendar of many eastern military marksmen. This was the occasion when the 30-shot, 1,000 yard Wimbledon Cup was contested. A military or match rifle was legal. Of the thirty-three competitors for the prize, thirty-one shot Krag magazine rifles or the finely sighted Remington-Lee match guns. Hudson and one other fellow came up on line with outdated large-caliber blackpowder Creedmoor-style target rifles. Dr. Hudson finished last man in the race with a piddling score of eight out of 150 points possible. Equipment failure is the speculated alibi. When one considers that the doctor was high man at the inter-Club Match for the Schuetzen team championship of the U.S. that same afternoon of the last day in August 1901, bad form or bad luck can be logically ruled out.

The hoped-for Palma contest of 1901 almost didn't happen. The American NRA elected to host a shoot and invited seventeen nations to send teams. In April of that year, the British NRA sent word that the English reason for not supplying a team was that there were "not enough skilled men for the contest." The project was almost abandoned. Finally, Canada agreed to make the September trip to Sea Girt and took the trophy home with them. Strangely, Ireland sent over

eight men from Ulster County who passed over the main event. Rather, they had come to shoot against an American team consisting of shooters from three states, to include Walter Hudson. This was a match following the Palma as to distances. Though the rules allowed the use of any rifle (with a maximum caliber of .315-in.) the Americans shot their issue Krags. Various press accounts of the proceedings do not jibe, and names, ranks, or individual scores from any source are not to be swallowed as gospel. The *Forest and Stream* reporter listed W.G. Madson for Dr. Hudson. In any event, the Irish, who "shot very well" actually narrowly defeated Hudson and his "poorly shooting teammates." Dr. Hudson and his Krag, as expected, kept their end up.

Of the total strength of the New Jersey Guard and Naval Reserve who reported to the Sea Girt Range in the Spring of 1902, only ninety-one qualified as Expert. Of these, Dr. Hudson fired a perfect 35 x 35, one of eleven troopers to do so. At the New Jersey State Rifle Assn. Matches, he finished third in the Wimbledon Cup Match using, as most firers did, a straight military Krag and government-issued ball ammo. In the other individual matches, he placed first in the Hayes Medal Match and the General E.P. Meany Match, and a

very decisive first place in the Laflin and Rand Aggregate A and third in Aggregate B. Both were awarded for best scores in several matches. Some bad luck at the thousand-yard stage put him out of the running for the President's Match, and he finished fifth. In the Hilton Trophy Match, a team competition, Walter Hudson shot the highest point total of anyone on the range that day, but he alone could not carry the New Jersey team to victory. The team fielded by the New York Guard won by a small margin. Again in 1902, the Interstate Medal Match went to the team from New Jersey.

Hudson tried out for the eight-man 1902 Palma Team and easily made the cut, one of two New Jersey Guardsmen representing the U.S. The '02 contest, hosted by the Canadians, was held at the Rockcliffe Range near Ottawa.

September 13 dawned dull and gloomy. A twenty miles-per-hour wind blew a light stinging rain into the faces of the firers lying prostrate at the 80-yard line. Despite the horrendous conditions, the Americans commanded the lead at the end of this segment. The sun broke through and a fluky 25 mph wind broke loose during the post-luncheon 90-yard stage, and here the match was lost. The British pulled ahead far enough that the Americans couldn't catch up, despite a heroic effort at a thousand yards. In the end, the British narrowly defeated the Americans and the Canadian squad more decisively. Pvt. Hudson wasn't the team's top man, but apart from several dropped points at 90, made a very respectable showing.

At the Sea Girt shoot in 1903, Hudson went home with the All-Comer's, Hayes, General E.P. Meany, and the Trophy Match Cups, as well as the Laflin and Rand Aggregate A special prize. Reportedly, he used a rifle (Krag) equipped with a barrel fitted by Remington Arms.

Even though Dr. Hudson knew that he wouldn't be able to take the necessary time away from his medical practice for the 1903 Palma tour at Bisley, England, he nonetheless tried out for the team. He attended the May 18-20 1903 Sea Girt qualifier just for the practice and camaraderie. Thirty-seven firers competed for a position, each prospective team member bringing his own rifle and providing his own ammunition. The fact that the NJ Signal Corp. private fired four bullseyes on the wrong target notwithstanding, Hudson still posted a respectable score of 563, good enough for a spot on the squad. This didn't end his involvement with the team however. He avidly followed the progress of his fellow Krag competitors, and was certainly there with them in spirit. And, as part of the select committee representing the American NRA, he was there to greet his victorious comrades when they arrived home on the steamer Lucania the first Saturday in August, 1903.

In the 1904 contests, Hudson again came away winner of the All-Comer's Short and Mid-Range matches, and came out on top in the Thurston Match. He was a regular participant in and winner of many of the New York State championship-level matches conducted at Creedmoor by the New York State Rifle Assn. Here he successfully contested either as an individual civilian or a representative of the Manhattan Rifle and Revolver Assn. He won the Roger's Match, a prone seven-shot Krag event, in '04, '06, '07 and '09. The 200-yard seven-shot Wingate Match was shot from standing – Dr. Hudson's strong position – with a military rifle. Hudson put his name on it every year from 1904 to 1907, and several times thereafter with the Springfield rifle. Between 1904 and 1914, he won the historic Wingate prize on seven occasions.

With U.M.C. cartridges, Dr. Hudson placed first in the 800- and 900-yard match at the 1906 Sea Girt tournament. The winning target was impressive enough to merit reproduction in U.M.C. ads, together with some sly words about U.M.C. ammunition and the wisdom and ability of competitors who made it their preference: "The experts do not shoot Government-loaded cartridges unless the conditions require it." Both the 200-yard All-Comer's Short Range and 600-yard Mid-Range matches went to Hudson in '06 too.

Despite nine consecutive bullseyes at eight hundred, Hudson was outgunned by Capt. J. Semon for the Leech Cup in 1907. Second place in the Wimbledon seemed to be the eternal destiny of the shooting doctor; it happened again in 1907.

After the Bisley debacle of 1903, the next Palma meeting wasn't held for four years. The 1907 match marked Hudson's second and final participation and, appropriately, the final international contest to be fired with the infantry Krag. The Canadians put on the show that year on September 7th. Dr. Hudson won a position on the American team, competing as a civilian representative of his Manhattan Rifle and Revolver Assn. Dropping just one point at 800, he was low man at 900, but redeemed himself with the team's second best at the 1,000 yard line. Individually, Ohio's Maj. C.B. Winder posted a 219 x 225 with Hudson four points behind, a remarkable performance, all things considered. The Americans fired a world record score of 1,712. Canada followed distantly with 1,671, and Australia and Great Britain were not even in the race. Our President Roosevelt received the victors at Sagamore Hill the following week.

Most of us are familiar with someone with a personality similar to Dr. Hudson's. He was a private, reserved man who seemed to have preferred his own company to that of others. Those that knew him, few could have said they knew him well. Consequently, it was said, perhaps unfairly, that he had an odd or eccentric nature. Evidently he shunned photographers. I, or someone else, can generally rustle up a portrait-type photo of any of his much less notable peers, but a close-up of Dr. Hudson hasn't turned up yet. Dutifully, we must suppose, he sat still for Palma Team pictures, each time erect and proud.

Walter Hudson, more so than anyone else during this period was active in the desperate need to improve the Krag's ammunition. Issue 220-grain arsenal loadings would be relied upon to be reasonably accurate, though borderline for match work, out to 800 yards. But the consensus

seemed to be that past this range the best shooters were not getting all that they were holding for. The impact of unaccountable rounds ranged from near misses, to frequently as much as 30-40 feet in any direction of the target. Attributed at first to inexperience or pulled shots, the trouble was too widespread for these excuses to be acceptable for very long. The wobbly, corkscrewy flight of the Krag bullets was unmistakably observable through powerful range telescopes, and elliptical holes in the paper pointed to tipping bullets, verifying a suspected stability problem. It needs to be borne in mind that the average National Guardsman was not a diehard rifle crank, and most had but a rudimentary knowledge of how a bullet behaved on its way to the target. Generally, though, this person was not interested in – or qualified to access – the difficulties cropping up with his ammunition. He just wanted to shoot the gun and hit what was aimed at. In the late 1890s, both military thought and rifle marksmanship were undergoing a metamorphosis. For the first few years after its adoption the range performance of the Krag was a source of frustration and old school veteran guardsmen of the Trapdoor Springfield era discovered that the old 45-70 lead bullet refinements simply wouldn't transfer to the new bolt action and its ammunition. Understanding the fine points of the smokeless/jacketed concept required a revision in thinking and approach, but historically, the powers at Army ordnance had not demonstrated an interest or expertise in this area. Civilian riflemen, on the other hand, puzzled over the poor scores, and sensed that the rifle was handicapped in some not easily seen way. The ammunition became the leading suspect. Given the apparent indifference at the War Department, getting the Krag to shoot straight remained a civilian undertaking, and Walter Hudson was the self-appointed conductor of the mission. He possessed the necessary qualifications. A determined analyst and trained diagnostician, he was also well-connected within the arms industry. Just as importantly, he had an analytical turn of mind and a tremendous level of self-application. In addition, he not only had been responsible for publicly broadcasting the ammunition's deficiencies, he had displayed the most interest in the project. Moreover, this was the sort of thing that was expected of him. As things turned out, the military rifle shooting fraternity couldn't have hoped for an investigator more dedicated to the task.

There was little that could be done with the ordinary primer. It was best to use one of the non-mercuric primers obtainable, the U.M.C. 9-1/2 or the Hudson preferred Frankford Arsenal H-48. "The best shells to use are those of the Government make," he wrote, settling this minor question.

It was very easy to eliminate any smokeless powder other than Laflin and Rand's W.A. 30 Cal. And 36.1 grains of it gave the Krag 220-grainer the standard velocity of 1,960-2,000 fps with sane pressures. In 1903. Hudson summarized everyone's opinion with these words, "The powder that was found best in the beginning still remains far in the lead, and appears to be as nearly perfect as anyone could reasonably ask." Good as it was, W.A. wasn't

❧ ● ❧ ● ❧ ● ❧ ● ❧ ● ❧

The Hudson-Thomas 220-grain bullet (left) and the Winchester-Hudson 1904 tapered 200-grain bullet.

perfect. The nitro powder was very erosive and hard on chamber throats.

Hudson knew instinctively the trouble was with the bullet and endeavored to take the needed steps towards a remedy. He theorized that the 220-grain bullet simply didn't have enough rotational speed to keep it point foremost past 800 yards, and deduced that there were two reasonable approaches to handle the bullet's instability. Quickening the rifle's 1-10 inch twist could certainly solve the problem and it was proven that it did with experimental eight-inch twist rifles. But to remain in compliance with international competition rules, the standard government rifling pitch could not be altered. Shortening the bullet by reducing its weight or length was another way. Increasing the diameter of the 220-grain bullet from .307- to .309-inch would have helped with two problems at once. Hudson found that the issue Krag appearing to be turning in the best long-range scores were those slugging .309-.3095-inch. Dramatically decreasing the weight and corresponding length of the bullet would be far more beneficial.

In 1902, Dr. Hudson contacted William Morgan ("UMC") Thomas, the affable ballistician with Union Metallic Cartridge Company, and told him of his woes and the urgency to get suitably accurate bullets in time for the September Palma. Their collaboration resulted in a 200-grain square edge, flat-based bullet which had a slightly different nose than the government projectile. To better fit the bulk of Krags with slightly oversized bores, it was uniformly swaged to .3085-inch. The Hudson-Thomas bullet did not have the customary arsenal crimping or lubrication grooves. The smooth bullet was probably Hudson's idea. The three cannelures of the typical Krag bullet held a mixture of Japan wax and graphite, which functioned as a waterproofing as much as a lubricant. Hudson observed its effects through the critical eyes of a chemist, and determined what was going on upon ignition. The compound was broken down into hydrogen and carbon, its constituent elements.

The hydrogen escaped as a gas, and the carbon built up in the bore, contributing to fouling troubles.

Hudson's experiments conducted in the early summer of 1902 proved conclusively that the 200-grain bullet reasoned out with Mr. Thomas, and produced by U.M.C., grouped far more closely at 900 and 1,000 yards than the issue 220-grainers of any diameter. In July of 1902, Thomas visited Sea Girt with this new smooth bullet and watched Lt. Leizeas (8th Penn.) shoot a startling 72 x 75 at a thousand yards, the best 15-shot score made up to that time with the issue Krag rifle. Hudson himself shot a 70. Thomas made doubly sure that the project was completed in time for the 1902 International Match, and U.M.C. provided contract ammunition for the tournament. Not only did Hudson fire for the American Palma team that year, he designed and perfected the ammunition for the event. Though the American team didn't carry home the Palma trophy, it was no fault of the bullet. The 1903 Palma was shot with the same superb ammunition.

Still, the twisted flight of the government bullet persisted. A clue to the real cause of the trouble resulted from a study of a number of recovered bullets fired into a water tank. Rifling engravature clearly showed that the bullet was entering the throat in a slightly slanted position. Upon firing, the bullet tended to hug on land or groove, and exited the muzzle microscopically unsupported. The effects around 800 yards were still visible in flight and from the obliquely-printed holes in the thousand-yard target.

Dr. Hudson was inspired by the fruitful results obtained by a co-experimenter in the cause. L.N. Walker was an old Creedmoor standout and knew what he was doing. As an experienced designer for Remington Arms, he had the resources of the entire Ilion facility at his disposal. In early 1903, Walker swaged a blunted nose 220-grain bullet that for the greater part of its length was a perfect cylinder. The special 13-inch twist Remington barrel had to be throated to accept the new bullet. During range tests in August of 1903,

Walker shot a 15-shot possible with them. Hudson misjudged the wind that day and wound up with a 71 x 75. More importantly, each bullet left a nice round 30-caliber hole in the target. The disadvantage to the Walker system was an excessively long bearing surface which generated unwanted friction, together with the required special throating, made it impractical for Krag fixed ammunition.

Its merits were plain to see, however, and Hudson figured Walker may be on the right track. During the winter of 1903-'04, Hudson acquired a quantity of common three-groove government 220-grain jacketed bullets and reshaped them in a swage. The .3085-inch rear section was secured in the case neck, from which point the bullet abruptly tapered to .3065-inch. The .300-inch forward portion rode on and was centrally supported by the tops of the lands. Hudson felt that a slightly more pronounced point was better than Walker's nearly hemispherical version, and ingenious experiments with a gyrostat proved him right. The swaging process made the bullets somewhat shorter, and due to the lead core extruded from the constricted jacket, a few grains lighter. Reports regarding accuracy lack essential details, but Hudson recorded in April of 1904 that these reworked bullets did "remarkably fine work." Winchester was persuaded to put this bullet into limited scale production, and a quantity of these tapered grooveless Winchester-Hudson bullets and factory-loaded cartridges were ready for the 1904 annual Sea Girt competition.

In October of that year, Winchester was able to make an advertisable point of its many successes. The 220-grain W-H bullets allowed Dr. Hudson to run a string of seventeen consecutive bullseyes at 800 yards on his way to claiming the 800-900 yard Thurston match. With the same Winchester ammunition, Corp. "Doc" Short perforated the 800-yard bull sixteen times in succession to place second. John Barlow of Ideal considered that a handload of 36 grains of W.A., metered into a H-48 primed F.A. shell, with the W-H bullet seated to be the

"best combination in the world for a full high-power cartridge." In 1904, Barlow went on to write: "When all the manufacturers all make as good shells and primers as Frankford Arsenal makes and when they all use the Winchester-Hudson bullet, there will be no military or sporting ammunition in the world to beat them."

Hudson teamed up with veteran rifleman William Hayes to co-design another bullet, about which little is known. After the Sea Girt and Fort Riley National meetings of 1904, John Barlow, the Ideal Man, wrote in the December number of *Recreation* that the Hayes and Hudson 220-grain HH bullet was the second move in the direction towards perfection in the Krag bullet. The Hudson-Thomas bullet was first, in Barlow's opinion. New Jersey Guardsman Howard Gensch won the President's match at Sea Girt in 1904, using the "H&H" bullets and 36 grains of W.A. President Roosevelt called Gensch with a personal message of congratulations.

By 1905, the quality of government ball ammunition, in terms of uniformity and accuracy, was noticeably improved over that of only a few years prior. Arsenals began to realize the pointlessness of the inside-cannelured jacketed bullet, the importance of a slightly greater bore diameter and getting powder charges metered more consistently. Civilians Hudson, Walker, Hayes, et al were instrumental in guiding the way to this betterment.

Motivated by the need for better ranging characteristics, Hudson and Thomas again collaborated in 1906 in the final step towards perfecting the Krag bullet. The resulting Hudson-Thomas bullet was a spire point, profiled very much like the point of a sharpened pencil. In fact, these were familiarly known as "pencil point" bullets, and were available in 150, 172, 180 and 190-grain weights. The 1907 Palma team used a special Hudson-Thomas pointed projectile in its victory in Ottawa. Accounts vary considerably, but the more reliable data suggests that the Palma bullet weighed 203.5 grains and was propelled by 36.2 grains of W.A. for a velocity of 2,160

The Hudson-Thomas bullets (l-r): 172-grain pencil point loaded by UMC; 150-grain pencil point in a later commercial loading by Remington-UMC; last, the break-through H-T 200-grain loading of 1902.

fps. U.M.C. again won the contract to supply the team's cartridges, and that fall the firm's ads boasted unabashedly that it was their cartridges that "again upheld America's honor." The extreme accuracy potential of the pointed bullet was established beyond question and as its merits became better known, it became the standard for target shooting thereafter.

Bob Kane, the editor of *Outers Book*, recognized the significance of Dr. Hudson's role as the Krag ammunition's investigator/innovator. He wrote in February of 1910: "I feel that we who now enjoy the pleasures of military rifle shooting with a perfect arm, do not fully appreciate how much of the credit is due him (Hudson) for the present high standard of accuracy to which our military rifle and ammunition have been brought. The way to good scores, especially at long range, has been made comparatively easy by his persistent efforts towards this goal."

Proficiency with the Krag required range time and practice firing. In 1900, the War Department underestimated the value of rifle marksmanship and dispensed training ammunition in a miserly fashion. The need for a cheap mid-range practice load became increasingly evident. Barrel conservation was a prime concern here, too. Lt. Townsend Whelen recorded the useful life of a Krag bore, shooting service cartridges, at 1,400 rounds. A cast-bulleted handload, which could be assembled by unit armorers or the troopers themselves, seemed to be the logical route, and civilian Dr. Hudson applied himself to devising a suitable cartridge for this purpose. Once again, the principle obstacle was the bullet. Fundamentally, Hudson intended to design a simple plain-based cast bullet that would be accurate out to 600 yards. The existing 200-grain #3081 could potentially be adapted to the need, Hudson reasoned in 1900. Shooting these bullets through a 30-40 Winchester High Wall held in a machine rest showed keyholing in varying degrees with mediocre accuracy. The Horace Kephart designed, dirt scraper-equipped 175-grain #308206 was tried next, but didn't group or feed well from the magazine. Loaded to the proper 30-40 cartridge length left a grease groove exposed, another distinct disadvantage, it was felt. In

the summer of 1901, Hudson convinced John Barlow at Ideal to shape for him a cherry for a bullet that looked very much like the Krag service bullet. The resultant #308223 was available in 150-, 175- and 200-grain weights. With 9 grains of Sharpshooter, the 175-grain #308223 made a good 200-yard bullet, but 1,200 fps was its practical limit before accuracy-destroying gas-cutting occurred. Both more velocity and a bullet capable of withstanding it were needed. Ideal #s 308256, 308259 and 308268 were developed in 1903. Each had a greatly oversized breech-corking front band and gas-sealing rear band, which helped to reduce, but not eliminate the pesky gas-cutting. Accuracy out to 500 yards was good, but not quite acceptable. Finally on the right track, Dr. Hudson again recognized the need for a muzzle speed of 1,500 fps and a survivable bullet.

1904 was the year that Hudson and the crew at Ideal came up with the 195-grain dome-pointed 208279 with its bore-riding nose and inordinately wide base band. This bullet was the most accurate of Hudson's bunch, but 1,300 fps was the upper limit. Still, 14-15 grains of Marksman and #308279

became the standard practice load for some time, and the eastern Guard units shot these in Krag handloads by the thousands. Hudson invested a lot of range time experimenting with cereal fillers, wads, and metallic wafers to firewall the soft bullet base from the searing powder gases, and these trials culminated in the co-development of the copper gas check cup. John Barlow had a hand in this too. The still familiar Hudson-designed #308284 was the first gas-checked lead alloy bullet, and 23 grains of Lightning gave the 207-grain projectile 1,700 fps with wonderful 600-yard accuracy, and this Hudson-recommended handload was used extensively with every success. A fully detailed report on the evolution of the Hudson/Krag cast bullets was published in Gun Digest 2004.

National Guard troops liked to practice with their Krags at the indoor armory ranges, but the government-provided gallery cartridges were substandard even for very close range work. In New Jersey, Hudson's unit used chamber bushings, the Winchester type of cartridge adapter, to fire 32-caliber centerfire pistol cartridges. This

Depending on what year it was, one of these bullets found the thousand-yard bullseye. Hudson's jacketed match bullets delivered a significant improvement over the pedestrian government-issue ball.

approach involved a two-inch freebored leap into the rifling, considerable gas leakage and a loss of accuracy.

Dr. Hudson devised an implement to hold the shell in the front of the chamber, putting the bullet much closer to the rifle's throat. With this adaptor, the pistol cartridge "shot very well," but the drawback was the high cost of the ammunition. Disregarding the profit angle, Hudson donated the idea to an entrepreneur by the name of Brayton, who tired of it and sold it to the Marble Safety Axe Co. To put that another way, the old Marble's Cartridge Adaptor was another of Hudson's innovations.

A cast bullet load was called for in the indoor shooting too, and about 1901 Hudson developed it. Ideal #303252, the 32 Colt Auto cast bullet that shot almost noiselessly and accurately with 2.5 grains of Laflin and Rand's Unique, immediately became the popular handloaded alternative to the second-rate government gallery loads.

In 1899, Laflin and Rand Powder Company commissioned Hudson to author the definitive book on the subject of military 30-caliber rifle shooting. *Modern Rifle Shooting from the American Standpoint*, released in the Spring of 1903, contained thirteen chapters, scholarly treating the subjects of rifle selection, ammunition, shooting positions, targets and the rifleman himself. *Forest and Stream* magazine considered "Hudson's little Blue Book" important enough that it was reviewed three times across the pages of their bi-weekly. The June 13, 1903 issue was America's first exposure to the information-saturated 154-page volume. To its vast readership, the magazine writer professed it to be "The latest and soundest contribution to the literature of the rifle, both concerning its theory and practice, which has appeared in many months." Hudson's work also included practical information on shell cleaning and preparation, lubrication and powder measures. Two methods of improving the Krag trigger pull were also included. In addition there were valuable recipes for the formulation of Hudson's famous nitro solvent and preservative, sight black, and anti-rust grease.

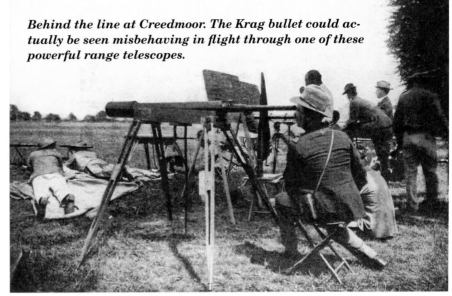

Behind the line at Creedmoor. The Krag bullet could actually be seen misbehaving in flight through one of these powerful range telescopes.

In a May 1904 issue, the *Forest and Stream* staffer editorialized the following: " probably no one in the United States writes with more authority than Dr. Hudson, and yet his writing is so straightforward and readable that it holds one like a good novel." The *Forest and Stream* publishers so thoroughly believed that "the peace and prosperity of this country are conserved by encouraging long-range rifle practice" that they felt compelled to fulfill their patriotic obligation by offering the book to subscribers at the one dollar regular price.

Every National Guardsman who aspired to squeezing the Krag trigger in competition bought a copy of Hudson's book. Significantly, it was so highly regarded that it was for years used as a manual of marksmanship by military schools and organizations.

So widespread was the popularity and interest in military match shooting that *Forest and Stream* invited Hudson to contribute a series of essays covering the fundamentals of rifle mastery, a simple explanation of basic ballistic principles, and other allied subjects. Hudson's articles were printed in late 1904 and early 1905. In the first of these, the doctor expresses and explains the public's, and presumably his own, attraction to the military match rifle: "There is a large number of civilian riflemen who confine themselves almost entirely

to this kind of shooting (Schuetzen), and who are, nevertheless very well posted and skilled riflemen able to take up other branches of rifle shooting on short notice; and their skill and holding and intimate knowledge of many of the technicalities of the rifle, learned by long and careful practice with their own weapons, certainly puts them far in the lead of the novice, no matter what branch of rifle shooting they adopt. But it is in long-range shooting undoubtedly that the rifleman finds the highest development of the sport. And in later years, since the advent of the modern smokeless powder rifle of high power and small caliber, it is gratifying to note, that the military and match (Schuetzen) rifle have approached very near to each other."

A hundred years ago, Dr. Walter Hudson's experiences with the competition Krag rifle ran the entire spectrum of levels. For as long as the craze lasted, he was the talented, self-appointed guiding spirit behind the perfection of the ammunition, and repeatedly demonstrated his mastery of both the rifle and himself. At the same time, he skillfully imparted his knowledge to a nation of fellow riflemen. Almost single-handedly, he took military rifle shooting out of the Dark Ages, and emerged as a star player in one of the more interesting chapters in the history of arms and ammunition. ✸

Ruger's Alaskan offers 454 punch in a short barrel. The Freedom Arms 83 legitimized the Casull.

FILL YOUR HAND!

...THE BEST OF THE BIGGEST REVOLVERS EVER MADE

by Wayne Van Zwoll

During the mid-1950s, other handgunners were busy boosting horsepower in Colt's iconic 1873. Dick Casull loaded the 45 Colt to pressures higher than were safe in early SAs, and from his shop came the 454 Casull (acknowledged by P.O. Ackley in 1959). That year Ruger announced its Super Blackhawk in 44 Magnum and Blackhawks in 45 Colt. The stout Blackhawk was perfect for the 454 Casull. Dick replaced its six-shot cylinder with a five-round version to increase chamber wall thickness. Meanwhile, the 44 Magnum went to Hollywood. When Clint Eastwood raised his Model 29 and rasped, "Go ahead, make my day," he sold more 44 Magnum pistols than Smith and Wesson could have by including a trip to Tahiti with each one. Dirty Harry reminded people who'd never heard of Elmer Keith that the raw-boned bronc-buster's brainchild was still, after four decades, the most powerful handgun in the world.

"With improvements, I think they can be rendered the most perfect weapon in the world for light mounted troops...." In 1846 Texas Ranger Captain Samuel H. Walker praised Colt's Paterson revolver but suggested changes. Pushed by the Ordnance Department's order for 1000 of the new pistols, Walker and Sam Colt collaborated on a massive 44-caliber revolver. The prototype, from the New York City gunshop Blunt & Syms, weighed 4 pounds, 9 ounces. Eli Whitney, Jr. won the production contract, including a run of 100 revolvers for public sale.

Just a few months later, at the battle of Juamantla, Captain Walker was killed by a Mexican lance.

Impressive in the hand and lethal on target, the Walker Colt did not ignite a trend to bigger pistols. Colt's 1873 Single Action Army, a smaller gun in 45 Colt, struck fear into bandits and lawmen alike. Development of smokeless powder in the 1890s made these revolvers even more effective; but not until 1955 would a pistol round hit significantly harder than the 45 and its contemporary heavy-weight, the 44-40. Their 255-grain and 200-grain bullets clocked 900 fps and 1100 fps, respectively.

Ironically, the modern hunting revolver has rimfire roots. During the late 1920s, Smith & Wesson designed a beautiful 22 double-action. In 1930 the six-shot, 35-ounce K-22 Outdoorsman featured a 6-inch barrel, checkered grips of Circassian walnut and target sights. Shortly a centerfire counterpart appeared, a 38 Special with the heavy "N" frame used on 44-caliber revolvers. Like its smallbore sibling, the 38/44 Outdoorsman had a fine trigger. Gun writer Phil Sharpe urged Smith & Wesson to develop a more potent round for the pistol. Winchester Repeating Arms assisted with that project, coming up with a case 1/8 inch longer than the 38 Special's. It debuted as the 357 Magnum, spitting 158-grain bullets at over 1500 fps. The first N-frame revolvers so chambered appeared during the Depression at $60, roughly $15 more than S&W charged for any other revolver. The company's own market gurus predicted limited demand, so they advertised the first 357 Magnums as custom guns, available with many sight and barrel options. Each gun would be zeroed by the factory *at 200 yards*, and each owner would get a registration certificate.

Demand for the powerful new gun far exceeded expectations. In 1938, after 5,500 revolvers, S&W dropped the registration certificate. At 120 guns a month, it could barely keep up with orders! Exhibition shooter Ed McGivern had demonstrated the round's great reach by hitting deer-size targets at 600 yards. If shooters hadn't thought of the K-22 Masterpiece or 38/44 Outdoorsman as hunting guns, many now saw the 357 Magnum as having potential beyond law enforcement, defense and target shooting.

In 1946, under the stewardship of Carl Hellstrom, Smith & Wesson began a vigorous push to hike civilian sales. Four years later they paid for a new 270,000-square-foot plant. About this time Elmer Keith appeared; a short cowboy in a tall Stetson, complete with tales of life in Idaho's wild canyons. But despite his rough-hewn demeanor, he had extraordinary gun-savvy. Keith's 44 Special handloads in the 1950 N-frame Target revolver made factory ammunition look anemic. He advocated a super-velocity 44 cartridge

in a longer case. Remington's R.H. Coleman took Keith's notion to heart and in 1954 brought to Smith & Wesson a new 44 (the hull ⅛-inch taller than the 44 Special) chambered in a modified Model 1950. The S&W Model 29 revolver weighed 7 ounces more than its forebear – and became an immediate hit. More than 3,100 Model 29s sold the first year. An obvious sequel: single-action revolvers bored for this powerful round. But Smith & Wesson wasn't in the single-action business.

During the mid-1950s, other handgunners were busy boosting horsepower in Colt's iconic 1873. Dick Casull loaded the 45 Colt to pressures higher than were safe in early SAs, and from his shop came the 454 Casull

(acknowledged by P.O. Ackley in 1959). That year Ruger announced its Super Blackhawk in 44 Magnum and Blackhawks in 45 Colt. The stout Blackhawk was perfect for the 454 Casull. Dick replaced its six-shot cylinder with a five-round version to increase chamber wall thickness. Meanwhile, the 44 Magnum went to Hollywood. When Clint Eastwood raised his Model 29 and rasped, "Go ahead, make my day," he sold more 44 Magnum pistols than Smith and Wesson could have by including a

❦ ● ❦ ● ❦ ● ❦

Bill Booth examines a revolver from the S&W Performance Center. Here, anything is possible!

trip to Tahiti with each one. Dirty Harry reminded people who'd never heard of Elmer Keith that the raw-boned bronc-buster's brainchild was still, after four decades, the most powerful handgun in the world.

But in the early 1980s the mighty 29 lost that title to a tightly fitted single-action revolver built in the small town of Freedom, Wyoming, and chambered to the 454 Casull. The 454 uses a Small Rifle primer to light the fire under its .451-inch bullet, which was bigger than the 44 Magnum's .429-inch bullet. The Casull pushes a 260-grain bullet at 1800 fps, and a 300-grain at 1625. Pressures can exceed 50,000 CUP. Loaded by Winchester with 260-grain Partition Golds and Platinum Tips, a 250-grain JHP and a 300-grain JFP, the Casull was once listed with 300-grain Core-Lokt Ultra bullets by Remington. Federal still loads a 250-grain Barnes Expander, Hornady 240- and 300-grain XTPs.

Ruger's first handgun round, the 480 Ruger, appeared in the company's revolvers about 20 years after the Casull. The 480's 325-grain bullet (.476-inch in diameter) is heavier than any commonly loaded in the Casull; but factory loads develop less pressure, so muzzle energy won't match the 454's.

Arguably, hunters didn't need more power than provided by the Casull and company. But they got more in the 475 Linebaugh, initially a handloading proposition but chambered in Freedom Arms revolvers. It came about in 1988, when Missouri shooter John Linebaugh trimmed a 45-70 case and installed a five-round cylinder and a 5 ½-inch .475 barrel on a Ruger Bisley. With a 370-grain bullet at nearly 1500 fps, a 400-grain at 1400 and a 440-grain at 1360, the Linebaugh develops 1800 foot-pounds at the muzzle.

Of course, no revolver can equal the performance of stout, fixed-breech handguns chambered for rifle rounds – like the Thompson/Center Contender. In 1965, shortly after Warren Center joined the K.W. Thompson Tool Company of Rochester, New Hampshire, Thompson agreed to manufacture an odd pistol that Center had designed in his basement. The Contender appeared in 1967, with switchable barrels and a good trigger. It fired proven deer rounds like the 30-30, accommodating pointed bullets and scopes. It sold briskly and still does. Barrels on new G2 pistols interchange with old Contender barrels, but not with those of the beefier Encore. Bolt-action pistols from Remington, Weatherby and H-S Precision, and the recent 5-pound Savage Striker with muzzle brake and magnum chamberings, have nothing on the Contender. But neither a hinged breech nor a bolt action delivers the heft, lines, balance and fast repeat shots of a revolver. Consequently, Smith & Wesson never felt threatened by them. But it chafed under the growing popularity of the 454 Casull in Freedom Arms revolvers. Not that either could compete with the Model 29 in sales, but Eastwood's iron was no longer heralded as the world's most powerful. S&W Product Manager Herb Belin wanted to trump the Casull. In early 2002, he and engineer Brett Curry started work on a super-size handgun, while engaging Cor-Bon's Peter Pi and Terry Murback to design its cartridge. The Cor-Bon team came up with a 50-caliber bullet in a case 1.625 inches long, with three loads under a pressure lid of 48,000 psi (20 percent lower than the Casull's). A 275-grain Barnes X launched at 1675 fps, a 400-grain Hawk JSP at 1650, and a 440-grain hard cast bullet from Cast Performance at 1625. The Barnes X, though lighter than the other bullets, is also harder and has a long bearing surface. So at any pressure, velocity can lag what's possible with lead bullets of similar heft. But it does not lack for penetration! Smith & Wesson's 500 develops 700 foot-pounds more energy than a 454 Casull and twice as much as a 44 Magnum.

The "X-Frame" revolver for the 500 S&W has a five-shot cylinder 2-¼ inches long. Its sleeved barrel has a frame-to-yoke cylinder latch and a muzzle cap with top porting to reduce climb. At 72 ounces, the S&W 500 is more than a pound heavier

than a Model 629 44 Magnum with the same-length (8 ⅜-inch) barrel.

"Seventy years ago the 357 Magnum made headlines with a 158-grain bullet at 1200 fps," mused Bill Booth, as he thumbed the hammer slowly to ready his 500 S&W for the shot. The big revolver stayed under control as it lifted from the sandbag. Not a jump or a hop; this was a muscular launch that not even veteran handgunners with ham-size hands could deny. Thin white smoke swirled as the big Smith's thunder echoed through the canyon. Double ear protection had been a good idea.

I peered through the spotting scope. A hundred yards downrange, Bill's second bullet had landed an inch and a half from the first. Many shooters cannot milk that consistency from rifles!

"We had trouble with your gun," said Bill. A career in law enforcement has given Bill an inside track on revolver mechanics. "In fact, all four of these 500s for the hunt needed attention."

"Huh?" I'd been one of the first to take the S&W 500 afield (the model name is the cartridge name minus the preceding period). "Problems?" On a Florida pig hunt I had found the 500 accurate and reliable.

"Well, it wasn't really the gun. The cantilevered scope base was actually flexing in recoil, so the forward end contacted the barrel. Warne got to work and provided a base with a reinforcing block. Problem solved." Bill had subsequently installed the Warne base and Bushnell 2-6x scopes on all the guns for this hunt: mine, his, Frank Miniter's and Tom Taylor's. Frank works as an editor at American Hunter magazine; Tom is vice-president for marketing at S&W.

We'd met in Buffalo, Wyoming at Pete Dube's Bear Track Outfitters camp. Wind and light rain had

Top-break revolvers of the 19th century could handle big cartridge, but not high pressures.

followed us to the range, where Bill and Tom drilled tight groups in the centers of their paper targets. "Good bullets," said Bill of Cor-Bon's sleek 385-grain hollowpoints. Cor-Bon had recently added the load to its three initial offerings. Hornady had weighed in with a 300-grain poly-tipped Evolution bullet at 1950 fps, a 350-grain XTP at 1900 and a 500-grain XTP at 1425.

The 500 Smith & Wesson's recoil depends mainly on bullet weight and speed. The 440-grain lead bullets in full-power loads make your hands tingle. However, Cor-Bon's other ammunition was surprisingly manageable in the heavy pistol. The 385 HP has a long ogive for flat flight. It is, to my mind, the best game bullet of the bunch – heavy enough to drive deep, with the legs for easy hits to 200 yards. Not that I shoot that long. My confidence with a handgun reaches about as far as I can hurl a medicine ball.

"One secret to good shooting with this gun is a high grip," said Bill. "You'll absorb recoil better with the web of your hand well up toward the hammer. And you'll find the revolver easier to steady." My first bullet landed at 6 o'clock, the next at 3. Of the next three, only one landed in the middle. I felt like a rookie. Then, as Bill banged a steel chicken at 160 yards with his pistol, I slunk to the far end of the line, and squeezed off 10 more rounds. My last four shots printed a 2-inch group, well centered.

In the morning, guide Mark Kirby took Bill and me into a series of hills creased with coulees and studded with deciduous brush and the occasional pine. I spied a buck and circled to get the wind. In a classic display of sixth sense, the buck stopped feeding my way and paused, lost in thought. Then he turned and ambled into a draw. Illogical behavior helps deer grow old.

Our binoculars found many other deer that morning, but few mature bucks. Presently I found pieces of mule deer in my 8x32 Pentax. Does. Then Mark whispered, "Buck!" The animal had risen from its bed, but all I could make out were antler tips. Though a crosswind favored us, a doe had zeroed in on my scope lens; we didn't have much time. Mark rolled aside as I squirmed to his spot and pushed my pack under the extended 500. When the reticle quivered to a near standstill on a front rib, I pressed the trigger.

Recoil jerked the revolver up, obscuring my view and then I heard the sharp "thwack" of a hit. Does squirted from the pines. I saw the great buck lunge, recover, then tumble down the steep grade, trailing dust and rubble. He kicked weakly, and then lay still. The Cor-Bon hollowpoint had struck exactly where I had aimed, scrambled the lungs and exited. No rifle bullet would have killed better. Mark's Bushnell rangefinder pegged the shot distance at 94 yards.

Pete Dube drew Bill and me the next morning. We glassed diligently but without effect. Our luck turned, though, when Pete spied an outstanding buck at the hem of a deep draw. We moved slowly up the draw, confident the big deer was still ahead of us. The thump of hooves signaled an end to our game, and Pete saw the buck only as it rocketed away.

Tired and despondent, we shuffled to the truck. "Let's find some pronghorns," said Pete. A couple of hours later, with a red sun at my back, I bellied to a small bush 150 yards from a loose group of antelope. Now, with the 'Smith steadied in a fork of sage, I sighted through a small gap in the bush as the buck angled toward me. I crushed the last ounce from the trigger, heard the explosion and felt the big gun lift

through a shower of sage leaves.

The buck crumpled without a twitch, the bullet having smashed its spine ahead of the shoulder. We photographed and field-dressed the pronghorn, then fetched the pickup and loaded it into the back.

Motoring slowly out of the valley between two bluffs, we spotted a fine mule deer buck, statue-still, at the base of a bluff. "He's about 200 yards," said Bill. "I can make that shot if he'll give me a moment." The animal watched us with interest but not alarm as Bill lowered himself to a sit on the prairie, bracing his shoulder against the pickup tire and – at last – fired. The sound of the strike followed close after the blast, and the deer collapsed into the grass. A marvelous shot, it demonstrated not only the 500's reach and power, but Booth's skill with a handgun.

Smith & Wesson now markets a 500 with a 4-inch barrel. You can get other barrel lengths from the company's Performance Center. A caveat: the muzzle porting that keeps long pistols manageable in recoil accentuates noise even more with a short tube, and the front of the pistol lifts faster and farther at the shot. My preference in the 500 is for a 7 ½-inch barrel. Whatever your barrel preference, accurate shooting with the 500 S&W requires concentration and steady nerves.

A second X-frame gun, chambered for a new, faster cartridge, appeared in mid-2004. With a case even longer than the 500's, the 460 XVR spits 200-grain Hornady SST bullets at 2211 fps, while 250 Cor-Bons fly at 2291, 325s at 1591 and 395s at 1511. Zeroed 3 inches high at 100 yards, pointed Hornady bullets strike 3.8 inches low at 200, where they deliver 837 fpe – nearly twice the energy of the 45 Colt at the muzzle! Smith & Wesson's 460 revolver has gain-twist rifling, increasing from a throat pitch of 1-in-100 to 1-in-20 at the muzzle. The slow initial spin keeps a lid on pressures and reduces bullet deformation.

Tom Kelly tells me that Performance Center 460s do not have gain twist. "But guns from

A 400-grain bullet at 1250 fps leaves with some violence, but drills tight groups.

both shops give us outstanding accuracy." My range time with a PC 460 left me mightily impressed. The revolver showed the fit and finish you'd expect in a best-quality British grouse gun. It shot with the precision of a bolt-action hunting rifle. Its accuracy and downrange energy make it a 200-yard elk gun!

Many shooters accept – some even relish – the length and weight of specialty handguns, and the added bulk of powerful scopes. Indeed, portability and speed don't count for much if you're in deer blind or toting a handgun on a sling as you would a rifle. But if convenient carry matters, if you must back up a rifle with multiple shots at dangerous game in tight quarters, or if you favor the lines and handling qualities of traditional double-action revolvers, you'll stay with Smith & Wesson's 29 or a Colt Anaconda or a Ruger Redhawk. The 44 Magnum may not match the latest artillery for reach and smash, but it's still a powerful round, with more authority than delivered by many rifle cartridges of the 19th century! If single-actions turn your crank, Ruger's Blackhawk and Vaquero series, along with Colt and Uberti 45s, give you affordable options.

Packaging the smash of a S&W 500 or 460 in a backup revolver is a daunting job for engineers. Such a handgun would deliver fearsome recoil – enough to discourage even infrequent

Hornady's pointed bullets extend the effective range of S&W's potent 460 cartridge.

practice and to deny you control for a quick second shot in an emergency. A useful compromise came along 50 years ago, when Dick Casull and Jack Fulmer built their first 50-ounce single-action for a 45 wildcat that would hurl 240-grain bullets 1900 fps. The 454 came within 300 fps and 200 foot-pounds of matching the mighty 460!

The Freedom Arms Model 83 revolver in 454 Casull and 475 Linebaugh yields explosive power in a portable package renowned for its fine fit and finish. I've stopped several times at the FA shop on the Salt River. Not far from Olympic gold-medal wrestler Rulon Gardner's home, Freedom, Wyoming hardly merits a dot on the map. But it's a celebrated hunting destination. Last autumn, returning from a hunt where permits were more plentiful, I pulled into Freedom Arms again, for an update from company chief Bob Baker.

"I'll give you the tour," he said. "Won't take long."

He did and it didn't. I was impressed by Bob's willingness to host a drop-in shooter – and by the shop's capabilities. Freedom revolvers are made from scratch here. Almost, you might say, by hand. Not only

⟨⟩⊕⟨⟩⊕⟨⟩⊕⟨⟩⊕⟨⟩⊕⟨⟩

Grizzly-loaded 370-grain cast bullets shot very well; so did the others Wayne tried in his M83.

are all the major parts machined to incredibly close tolerances; they're hand-fitted, and then kept together by number and bin during production. Sure, the parts are interchangeable. But to ensure the snug fit and glass-smooth operation and extraordinary accuracy that have earned Freedom its reputation, Bob insists that each pistol come together as a single unit.

There aren't many models. Freedom's flagship is its large-frame, five-shot Model 83, cataloged now for 20 years. Beside 454 Casull and 475 Linebaugh, it also comes in 44, 41 and 357 Magnum, even 22 LR. "Or 500 Wyoming Express," said Bob. "It's new, a straight-walled *belted* revolver cartridge." He explained that it offers more bullet weight than a 454 and hits about as hard, but doesn't recoil as sharply. He picked a revolver from the finishing station, and a perforated target from a box nearby. The target's two five-shot groups could each be covered with half a business card. One of them showed four shots cutting one hole, the fifth less than ¾ inch away. Proofed at 50 yards, this Model 83 did not measure up and was going back through the line! "We don't release pistols that we would not choose for ourselves," Bob said simply. "We demand a lot of our products; that's why they cost more."

He said when prospective buyers balk about the price, he just refers them to customers. "The gist of their

Wayne found extended range sessions comfortable. He used Grizzly loads for the 500 WE.

❧ • ❧ • ❧ • ❧ • ❧ • ❧

message is the same I'd deliver: Hunting is expensive; it just makes sense to take all the accuracy and power you can get. If you're a silhouette shooter, you might as well buy a Freedom revolver, because you'll have to shoot against one." Indeed, over the last decade, Freedom has dominated silhouette matches. Bob chuckled. "I'm not kidding when I say that at some matches you have to look hard to find a revolver that *didn't* come from this shop. Shooters who demand top performance buy our guns."

I asked about the new 500 Wyoming Express.

"It's actually about a year old," replied Bob. "We designed it as a big-bore alternative to the 454, one that would outperform the rimless 500 Action Express and approach the 500 Linebaugh in a standard revolver cylinder." (The 500 AE, you'll recall, is a rimless round developed in 1991 for the massive Desert Eagle Mk VII autoloading pistol. The 500 Linebaugh predated the 475 Linebaugh and was based on the 348 Winchester case.) "The belt made sense because a rim on a 50-caliber case would have been too small if we sized it to fit our current Model 83 cylinder. Also, a belt strengthens the case head, and since forming the belt is part of the heading operation, it can be made more uniform than a machined rim."

The 500 WE case is 1.37 inches long, for an overall cartridge length of about 1.76. The head is designed for Large Rifle primers and fits a standard Number 41 RCBS shellholder. Bob told me Freedom is supplying dies, which should be adjusted to size the case down to within about 0.10-inch of the belt. "Seat and crimp in separate operations," he added. Freedom's own tests show the 500 Wyoming Express cases are long-lived when loads are kept to recommended pressure levels. "We typically get 10 loads per case," said Bob. "Belt expansion of 0.002-inch on the first firing is common, but the belt should never be sized. Subsequent expansion up to 0.003-inch has no effect on chambering."

Designed for bullets scaling between 350 and 450 grains, the 500 WE is well served by Hodgdon Lil' Gun, H4227 and H110 powders. Here are starting and maximum loads for four bullet weights:

Factory-loaded ammunition is available from Grizzly Cartridge Company, POB 1466, Rainier OR 97048. After wresting a Freedom Arms Premier revolver in 500 AE from Bob, I used Grizzly's 370-, 400- and 440-grain loads in range work. All bullets were hardcast flatnose. Loaded to 950 fps, all were pleasant to shoot and accurate. At 1300 and 1250 and 1200 fps, respectively, they were noticeably more frisky but still very accurate. The bullets were beautifully made and would make the short list of missiles I'd choose for hunting. That saucer-size flat would blast a huge hole through vitals; bones of game as big as elk would give way.

While a Ransom Rest or Caldwell HAMMR Machine Pistol Rest would have better tested the 83's inherent accuracy, I chose to shoot this revolver over sandbags. I wanted to *feel* the 500 WE, and to learn how the grip, trigger, sights – and recoil affect my ability to shoot it accurately. Bob had sent me a Premier model, with impregnated hardwood grips. Standard versions feature Pachmayr Presentation grips. Other differences: The Premier has a satin finish, standard models a low-luster matte; the Premier's rear sight is screw-adjustable for windage and elevation, while standard models have a screw for elevation only and must be drifted to change windage. Both grades are of stainless steel (except sights), the parts seamlessly fitted and the actions so finely tuned that revolvers of other makes seem loose in comparison. Nothing slips or rattles on a Freedom Arms revolver. The cylinder rotates like the hand of a Rolex. Every click is solid, purposeful – and somewhat muted by the weight and snug fit of each part.

A single-action revolver, especially one chambered for potent rounds, should be allowed to rotate in your hand during recoil. I found the 83's grip allowed for that slippage

Starting load				Maximum load			
POWDER	BULLET	PRESS/VEL.		POWDER	BULLET	PRESS/VEL.	
29.0 Lil' Gun	350 XTP	34,500	1467	32.0 Lil' Gun	350 XTP	42,700	1617
31.0 H4227	350 XTP	32,400	1378	35.0 H4227	350 XTP	44,200	1584
32.0 H-110	350 XTP	34,600	1486	35.0 H-110	350 XTP	43,100	1629
29.0 Lil' Gun	370 WFNGC	34,200	1460	31.0 Lil' Gun	370 WFNGC	37,100	1528
31.0 H4227	370 WFNGC	33,600	1382	34.0 H4227	370 WFNGC	43,300	1535
34.0 H-110	370 WFNGC	37,500	1527	36.0 H-110	370 WFNGC	41,800	1607
28.0 Lil' Gun	400 WFNGC	38,600	1454	31.0 Lil' Gun	400 WFNGC	45,700	1565
30.0 H4227	400 WFNGC	39,900	1390	33.0 H4227	400 WFNGC	46,700	1509
32.0 H-110	400 WFNGC	39,800	1497	34.5 H-110	400 WFNGC	47,900	1589
26.0 Lil'Gun	440 WFNGC	38,100	1355	28.0 Lil' Gun	440 WFNGC	46,300	1450
26.0 H4227	440 WFNGC	34,400	1220	30.0 H4227	440 WFNGC	48,300	1413
27.0 H-110	440 WFNGC	34,000	1302	29.5 H-110	440 WFNGC	44,200	1415

Fully adjustable iron sights take advantage of the Model 83's accuracy. They're of blued steel.

without compromising control. After 25 rounds, my hand was not at all sore, nor was blast objectionable. The 7 ½-inch barrel not only gives this revolver good looks and balance but limits muzzle flip with heavy loads and mitigates recoil.

With all three bullets, I was able to print five-shot groups of about 2-½ inches at 25 yards – about as tight as I can expect with iron sights. Every group had holes touching. Predictably, the 440-grain bullets struck highest on the target, as they spent more time than the lighter bullets in the barrel during recoil and muzzle lift. The 370- and 400-grain bullets hit lower but right in line. Switching to a more ambitious 400-grain load, I punched holes directly below the 370-grain cluster, confirming that barrel time, not gravity, determines shot placement from pistol barrels up close.

The 83's trigger broke crisply and consistently at 3 pounds 1 ounce. This revolver is easy to shoot!

The 500 Wyoming Express is no threat, ballistically, to the 500 Smith & Wesson. Herb Belin and company can still say that no handgun round is more powerful. Double-action fans can still claim Smith & Wessons as the best such revolvers in the world. But if you prefer the lines and feel of a single-action, in a package that's closer to 50 ounces than 70, there's nothing to compare with a gun from Freedom Arms. The 454 Casull and 475 Linebaugh remain potent options in the Model 83 line. Now, however, you have a 50-caliber alternative. The 500 Wyoming Express offers great flexibility in loading, long case life, and enough power to flatten any North American big game.

An elegant gun with a terrific punch – you might have also said that about S&W's first 357 in 1935, or about the Keith-inspired 44 Magnum revolver two decades following. You could have repeated it 30 years later at the debut of the Freedom Arms Model 83 in 454 Casull. In my view, the current M83 Premier in 500 Wyoming Express merits the accolade now.

This pronghorn buck fell to one shot from Wayne's 500 S&W at just over 90 yards.

This squirrel fell to a scoped Smith & Wesson 22. Good revolvers aren't all big-bores!

Wayne killed this Wyoming buck at 95 yards with one of the first S&W 500s, a Cor-Bon bullet.

ver ●

Oostende

Brugge

FLANDERS

Dunkerque

2 U.S. Army divisions
added this Belgian offensive

Albert (Belgian) (Fal

Passchendaele
1917

Ypres

Messiness 1917

Lys
1918

Rupprecht
[April 1918]

Lille

Béthune

Loos

Lens

Douai

Vimy

Arras
1917

Quéant

Cambrai
1917

Le

Haig (British)
(Fall 1918)

Perrone

Crown Prince

St. Quent

Rupprecht & [Spring 1918]

Cantigny 1918

Roye

Montdidier

Barisi

Noyon

Laon

1914

1918

A VETERAN'S STORY

by the Veteran, with George Creed

The discerning reader will become aware that some liberties were taken in this article, however all historical and technical information is correct.

I was born in 1905 at Enfield, England. I am a #1 MK 1 Short Magazine, Lee Enfield. There are those who say that I must have started life as a long rifle, but that was so long ago I can't really remember. I know in my early life I was back to the arsenal for many changes and revisions. I have been a #1 MK 1 for a long time. My right-hand charger guide is mounted on my bolt with no bridge over my receiver. My rear sight guards are mounted on my lower handguard and my front sight guards bend inward and would make a complete circle if they joined. At first it seemed like no one wanted me, for a while I belonged to the Royal Navy. They put some very good sights on me, similar to those that later came out on the # 1 MK 3s, with finer adjustment than the MK 3s.

The War, WWI, started and the navy gave me to the army. I finally had an owner. I knew that Tommy and I would get along fine. I could tell by the way he held me. We went across the channel to the continent, and before we were there very long we got into a really big fight. Tommy was shooting me so fast that I was afraid my forearm would catch on fire. And, he wasn't just making noise; he was aiming every shot. Our mates along the line were shooting just the same as us. We were able to hold against a vastly superior force and to retreat, in an orderly fashion, into a defensive position. Later we heard that they thought we had a whole bunch of machineguns against them.

We dug in and tried to outflank them and they did the same to us. We each dug trenches until we had two parallel ditches three hundred yards apart right across Europe, from Switzerland to the North Sea. There, both sides remained for years, hardly gaining on the other anywhere. The conditions were terrible, with mud and dirt everywhere, but Tommy took as good a care of me as he could, wiping me off and cleaning my bore every chance he got. A few times Tommy put on my bayonet and we attacked the enemy just at dawn. Sometimes we'd go out and poke around between the trenches in the middle of the night; once we even did a full-scale attack at night. We never seemed to get anywhere.

Finally, in 1918, the German army started to deteriorate and the U.S. had come over to help. At 10:59 a.m. on November 11 the Yanks fired off every field piece they could unlimber with a terrible roar. Then, there was silence. The war was over! Tommy went back to being a civilian and I got cleaned up, more or less, and put into storage. There I stayed for just over twenty years

War started again! This time the military thought I was enough different from the #1 MK 3s and #4s that I didn't go to the front lines. I stayed home and was issued to one of Tommy's mates from *The War* for home defense. Those were dark days indeed. We thought that Hitler's forces would be coming across the channel at any time. Everything was in short supply. In the beginning we had only enough ammunition to fill my magazine once. We finally won that war without me ever having fired a shot.

A few years after the war, the British government decided that I was just too old and too outdated to serve in the army. Along with a lot of other rifles similar to me, I was sold to an enterprising U.S. arms dealer who resold me to a man in northern Idaho. I didn't mind when I heard I was going to the States because I remembered the Yanks as being pretty good guys, and fine shots. I was disappointed. My new owner just seemed to want the pride of owning me. He shot me only a couple times, cleaned up my bore, wiped me off, and put me in a closet where I stayed most of the time

for a number of years until he died.

Things changed! His widow sold me to a man in northeast Washington. The first thing he did was to tear me apart, completely. He started to clean me up. I actually still had dirt in me from the trenches. Part of this was a little scary—like getting all my wood parts cleaned with oven cleaner. When everything that was stamped into my wood started appearing, my new owner said that even though I was full of dings and scratches, he would never touch me with sandpaper. After all the old oil was washed out of my wood, he rubbed me down well with boiled linseed oil. When he started pushing patches through my bore, he discovered that even though it was somewhat dark, my rifling was sharp and smooth. When I think about it, I probably hadn't been fired more than about five hundred times and most of that in that first big fight in World War I. He dressed up all my screw heads, brushed all of my metal parts clean with a brass-bristled brush, and put me back together again, checking everything as he went. My forearm bore tight around my action, and under

the Knox form of my barrel. It then floated free until one inch either side of my inner band. My inner band cleared my barrel by ten thousandths of an inch. It floated free again all the way to the muzzle; the nose cap cleared the barrel by ten thousandths of an inch. My handguards never touched my barrel, except for the clips on the lower hand guard being held away by the sides of the forearm. There was a little dimple in my cocking piece from it constantly striking on the sear when the bolt was closed. That was carefully stoned out. I was finally back together again! And I'll tell you I didn't look bad for being one hundred years old.

My new owner said that I would never again be fired at man or beast, only paper targets. We would use only cast bullets. Since my five-grooved barrel is so hard to measure we dispensed with slugging the barrel and just started with bullets sized .313-inch hoping for the best. By pushing a bullet in from my chamber end it was discovered that any bullet we had available, when seated so it would feed through my magazine, still had a little bit of free bore. The

Lee-Enfield #1 Mk. III (top), compared to Lee-Enfield #1 Mk. I.

The Veteran with recently-won medals.

Lyman #314299 and #311467 seemed to make the closest fit. Both bullets were loaded for trial with IMR 4227 and IMR 4895, eighteen grains for the 4227 and twenty-eight grains for the 4895. CCI Large Rifle primers were used throughout. The bullets were cast from straight wheel weights using a ladle. Bullets were lubed with NRA formula ALOX. Both of the loads previously performed well in other 303s, with twenty-eight grains of 4895, and #311467 having a slight edge in rifles that shot well.

So, off to the range we went. At one hundred yards I was consistently shooting just under three inches for five-shot groups. The #311467 seemed to have a slight edge.

For several weeks, we were shooting every day or so trying various powders: 2400, Reloader #7, and 3031. We were using 4895, bullet #311467 as a control load for comparison. We

also tried Lyman bullet #311413 and a Lee mould #90371. Nothing seemed to shoot quite as good as the #311467 with 28 grains of 4895. It couldn't seem to get much better than three inches at one hundred yards.

After every trip to the range when my bore was cleaned, it got just a little shinier. The fired cases coming out of my chamber showed that I had a rather tight chamber with very little relief at the shoulder, and no bulging at the base.

In these shooting sessions, my owner would use up the left-over test rounds, shooting offhand, at a twelve-inch, one hundred-yard gong. That's went I got to really show my stuff! I hardly ever missed. When he finally realized that I shot as good—if not better—offhand as I did off the bench, he quit all the foolishness and went back to the original #311467 load.

We went to our first rifle match. It was for manually-operated military weapons, as issued, from any country. First we shot twenty rounds at one hundred yards prone, then we shot ten shots starting with five in the magazine, in seventy seconds, going from standing to prone, then we did the same thing from standing to sitting and, last, we shot ten shots offhand. I wound up with the third place medal in that match! It just so happened that a Garand Match, having the same

❧ ● ❧ ● ❧ ● ❧ ● ❧ ● ❧

Ammunition for the Veteran: (L/R) the Mk. VII cartridge, a Winchester 180-grain softpoint cartridge, and the cast bullet load used in the matches.

course of fire, except the time limit was sixty seconds for ten shots, was being fired at the same time. In the last relay there was just an M-1 and me. The range officer decided he would blow two whistles, one at sixty seconds for the M-1 and one at seventy seconds for me. My owner said that really wasn't necessary. In the rapid-fire matches the second whistle was never blown because we were always done, with my owner holding me up to show I was empty, before the M-1 fired his last shot. It was almost like being back with Tommy. Of course, no one will ever be able to shoot me like Tommy did.

We went to a match that was open to rifles in the 303 British chambering only and put on by the Nelson, B.C., Rod and Gun club. I thought that would be just fine, and a lot of fun. I remembered the Canadians from *the War* as being a pretty good bunch. I met a lot of old veterans from World War I, World War II, and even Korea. There were a couple Ross and P-14s; #1s and #4s were well represented. There was one Model '95 Winchester. I was the oldest rifle there! The shooting was prone at one hundred, two hundred and three hundred yards aggregated together; we took the third-place medal again. It looked like we were destined to be third place.

In November of 2004 another manually-operated military match was held to coincide with Armistice Day; it was the same course of fire as before. This time we took the second place medal. There is another match coming up in May and my owner and I will be there shooting for first place. ✿

THE ART OF
ENGRAVED &
CUSTOM GUNS

by Tom Turpin

A factory Ruger No. 1 chambered for the 300 H&H
cartridge was the raw material provided to Gary Goudy.
He fitted the Kepplinger trigger to the rifle and did
all the metal polishing. He then crafted
the stock from a superb stick of
English walnut, finished off by
one of his trademark exquisite
checkering jobs. The pattern he
used is reminiscent of patterns
used on high-grade Winchester
guns in the past.

Photo by Gary Bolster

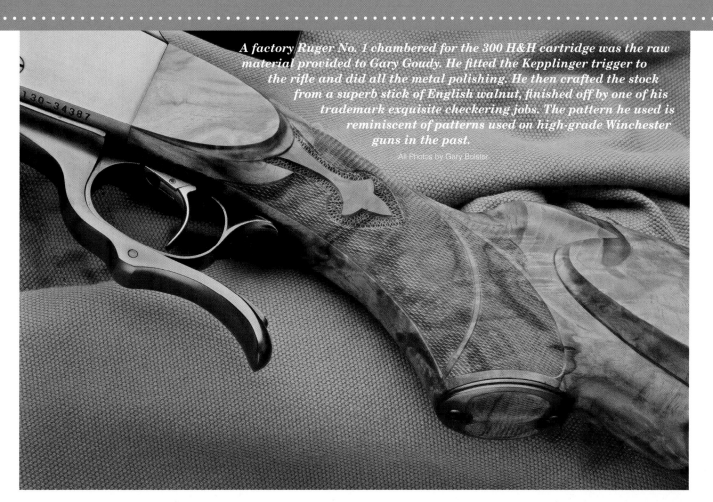

A factory Ruger No. 1 chambered for the 300 H&H cartridge was the raw material provided to Gary Goudy. He fitted the Kepplinger trigger to the rifle and did all the metal polishing. He then crafted the stock from a superb stick of English walnut, finished off by one of his trademark exquisite checkering jobs. The pattern he used is reminiscent of patterns used on high-grade Winchester guns in the past.

All Photos by Gary Bolster

Herman Waldron started with a small ring VZ-33 Mauser action for this rifle. He did all the metalsmithing chores necessary to convert the military action to a wonderful sporting rifle, including stippling the bolt knob. He fitted the barrel and chambered it for the 25-06 cartridge. Fisher/Blackburn rounded bottom metal was used for the rifle as well. Gary Goudy fashioned the lovely custom stock from a nice stick of California English walnut, and executed one of his renowned checkering patterns on it. This rifle is ready for the field.

This Remington Model 700 Left Hand rifle came from the shop of the Williams Gun Sight Company. The detail photos show various examples of the work. The factory action was "blueprinted" and the barrel-mounted recoil lug removed. A new recoil lug was pinned and soldered in place. New England Custom Gun sights and EAW scope mounts were installed. The custom Bastogne walnut stock features a Dakota skeleton grip cap and buttplate, and is extensively checkered with a 26-panel pattern with fine ribbons throughout. All metalwork was accomplished by Williams metalsmith Rob Canze, and the stock and checkering executed by Williams stockmaker Kevin Wigton.

Photo by Terry Tremewan

Gunmaker Hughes was looking for
a suitable sidelock barreled action
around which to craft a superb duck
gun for one of his clients. He found what
he was looking for when a Belgian exhibitor at
the SCI Convention displayed an in-the-white barreled action. It had been made
in Belgium by Britte Armes En Blanc, which ceased making sporting gun parts in
1936. That barreled action had been sitting in the basement of the former company for nearly seventy years!
Hughes did much of the metalwork, rust-bluing the gun, and nitre-bluing the screws and small parts. E.L.
"Larry" Peters executed the wonderful layout and engraving, Doug Turnbull Restorations did the color case-
hardening, and J. Peter "Pete" Mazur charcoal-blacked the furniture and gold-plated the lock parts.

Photo by Steven Dodd Hughes

A lightweight 270 Improved from the shop of Lee
Helgeland, weighing in at six pounds, twelve ounces,
with scope and mounts. It features a G33/40 Mauser
action and a 26-inch Krieger barrel. The stock was crafted
from a stick of tiger-tail California English walnut. Jerome
Glimm did the screw head engraving, George Komadina did the rust blue,
and Larry Baer did the color case on the trigger guard, rings and bases.
Lee did everything else, in-house.

Photos by Steven Dodd Hughes

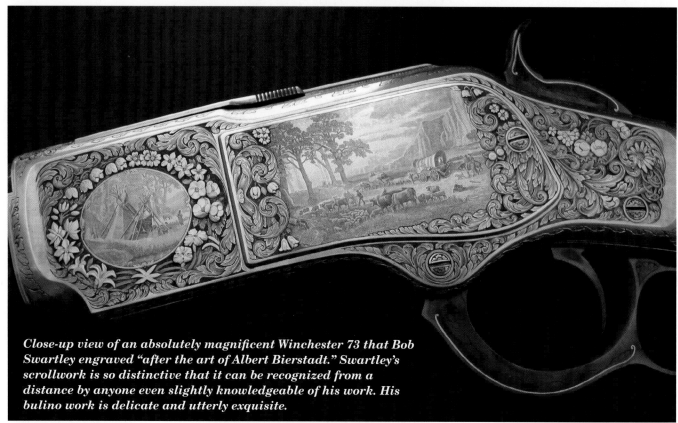

Close-up view of an absolutely magnificent Winchester 73 that Bob Swartley engraved "after the art of Albert Bierstadt." Swartley's scrollwork is so distinctive that it can be recognized from a distance by anyone even slightly knowledgeable of his work. His bulino work is delicate and utterly exquisite.

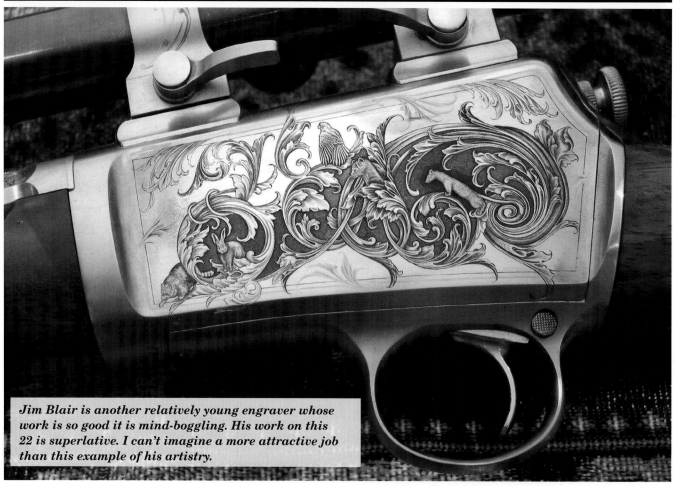

Jim Blair is another relatively young engraver whose work is so good it is mind-boggling. His work on this 22 is superlative. I can't imagine a more attractive job than this example of his artistry.

*A right side and left-side view of
a lovely rifle which exhibits a little
of the California influence on maker Ray Riganian. The diamond-
shaped ivory inlays are somewhat reminiscent of the Roy Weatherby rifle.
Ray started with a Winchester Model 70 Classic action, and he applied
all the bells and whistles to it. Surface grinding, truing all surfaces concentric with the bore, fitting
Blackburn bottom metal, making custom bases for modified Talley rings, building up and checkering the bolt
release, and thinning the trigger to a shotgun-type trigger, are just some of the refinements to the action. He
fitted a Krieger barrel and chambered it for the 7mm Weatherby Magnum cartridge.
He then crafted the stock from a very nice stick of California English walnut, and pillar-bedded the barreled
action into the wood. This rifle is a tack-driver, according to Riganian.*

Photo courtesy of Ray Riganian

*The Springfield action 400 Whelen rifle from the shop of N.L.
Heineke is shown here without the case and accessories. Styled
after the pre-war Griffin & Howe sporters so favored by Col.
Whelen, it is a superb rifle. The rifle is chambered for the
400 Whelen cartridge, and is fitted with two scopes,
a Burris 4x scope and a Lyman Alaskan
2.5x scope, but mounted in G&H side
mounts.*

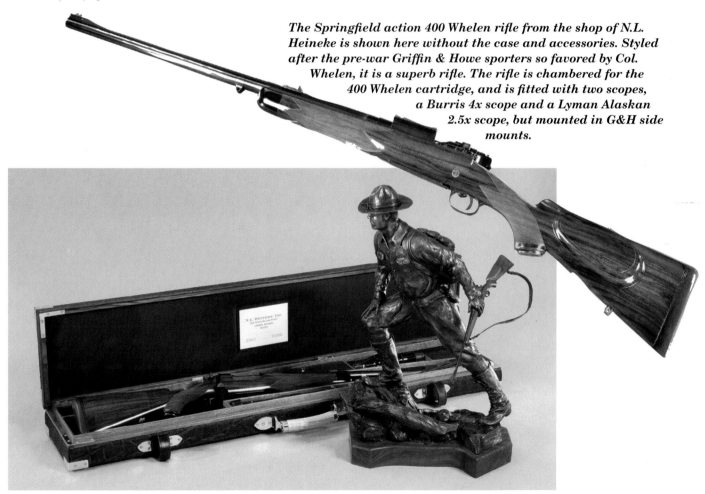

*Two images of the cased set commemorating Col. Townsend Whelen. Mike Halterman
sculpted the wonderful bronze statuette, called simply "The Colonel." James Wear made the
elephant hide-covered oak and leather trunk case to house the rifle and accessories. The
carrying handle was fabricated from a hippo tusk. Finally, the rifle had tasteful engraving
added by engraver Mark Hoechst.*

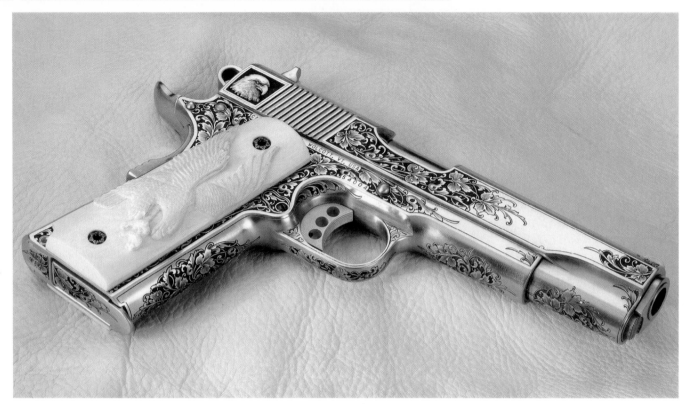

A magnificent Terry Tussey custom 45 auto fabricated from a Caspian Arms frame and slide. When finished, master engraver Eric Gold, who also carved the superb ivory grips, marvelously engraved the gun. This gun is a superb example of the engraver's art.

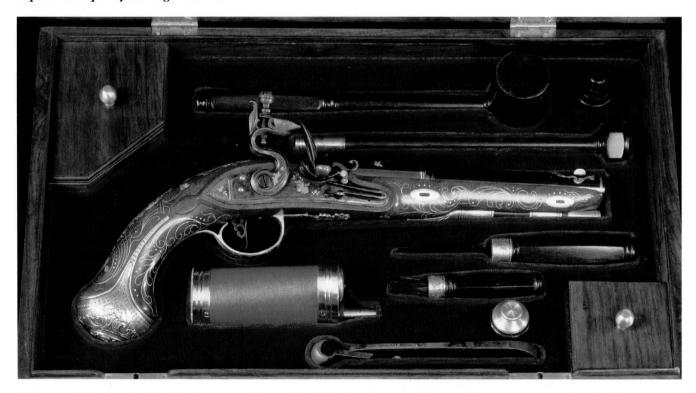

This cased flintlock pistol is the work of Jerry Huddleston. Jerry made every item and every piece in this set, including the case, with the exception of the commercially acquired lock. Even there, he completely redid the lock to meet his requirements. He even cast all the silver accoutrements, and made the barrel. He also did all the engraving and inlay work.

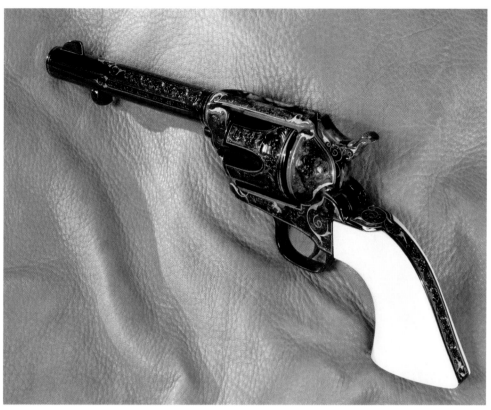

A nice side view of a lovely Colt Single Action Army revolver. The revolver is a 5 1/2-inch barrel 357 Magnum 3rd Generation Colt. Ron engraved the gun in what Colt calls tight American scroll, 3/4 coverage or "C" coverage. The gold inlay work is in the fashion of Leonard Francolini. Dan Chesnak did the ivory grips, and the case colors and bluing are by Dewey Vicknair.

Two images of a glorious rifle put together by a team of superb craftsmen. The action is a "baby" Farquharson that was made by Clayton Nelson, probably twenty or so years ago. Fine rifle connoisseur Jack Lilliendahl somehow ended up with the action and another superb project was begun. Steve Heilmann did the metalwork on the rifle, and barreled and chambered it for the 17 HMR cartridge. Stockmaker James Tucker crafted the extraordinary stock from an exceptional stick of walnut. Sam Welch executed the engraving in a theme suitable to the caliber of the rifle, and dubbed the rifle the "Rabbit Rifle," or sometimes "Thumper." The finishing chores were turned over to Pete Mazur, a master of the alchemy of metal finishing. The finished rifle was awarded the Award of Excellence, presented annually by the Firearms Marketing Group, at the 2007 combined ACGG and FEGA Exhibition in Reno.

RESTORED TO LIFE

by Terry Wieland

At that point, you look at this chunk of scrap which is a potential piece of history and ask yourself what it is worth, to you, to salvage that piece of history for posterity, whether you personally profit by it or not. If you count as profit the feeling of having saved something valuable that otherwise would have been lost, and presenting it to lovers of fine guns to treasure forevermore, then you might become hooked as I have.

The shabby old Winchester Model 1886, when it came into my possession, was almost indescribable.

It could have been a good one: Chambered for the highly desirable 40-65, with an octagonal barrel, fine bore and clean internal mechanism, the rifle should have commanded a premium price. Instead, it was going for less than half of "book." There was no need to ask why.

At some point during its century on this earth, the hapless firearm had fallen into the hands of a man with a jack-knife, artistic pretensions and far too many long winter evenings. The result was, well, almost indescribable.

"Thirteen hundred and it's yours," Jeff said. "Sad, isn't it?"

"Maybe," I replied, studying the sacrilegious carvings and the pitted frame. "But then again, maybe not."

As I wrapped up the old warrior and carried it gently from the shop, I could have sworn I heard a whimper of relief.

To my mind, Winchester Model 1886 #121321 was a prime candidate, not just for some cosmetic repairs, but

Right: *The amazing thing about this Model 1886 is that it was so good inside, but looked like this on the outside. Since it left New Haven in 1900, it had obviously led an active life, even without falling into the hands of a would-be wood carver.*

Far Right: *The rich colors of a fine case-hardening job are truly a thing of beauty.*

for a full-scale restoration as only Doug Turnbull can do. Not refinishing, not even what is called refurbishment, but complete, historically accurate and authentic restoration: Returning the rifle to the exact condition in which it proudly left New Haven in May, 1900.

Restoration! I can hear the gasps as Winchester collectors from coast to coast start dialing the nearest exorcist. You mean...you mean...alter an original '86? A collector's item? Yes, and no. Yes we'll alter it, and no, it's not a collector's item — at least not one worth preserving.

Right there is the key phrase: "worth preserving."

At what point does a gun stop having serious collector value, and become more valuable as a candidate for restoration? A look at any book of suggested gun values shows how the value drops off quickly, from new-in-the-box, to mint, to 98 percent, and on down. When a rifle is judged to be about 75 percent condition, with the bluing gone, collector value (except in the rarest cases) is really little more than you might pay to get a gun for hunting, shooting, or cowboy matches.

Is that condition worth preserving for posterity? I think not.

All of us have seen rifles that have been "refinished" (and often refinished poorly.) These sell at a discount even to an original rifle in poorer

condition, and rightly so. The lettering is faint and uneven, sharp corners are rounded off, and the bluing is modern and nondescript. Often, stocks are sanded so much the buttplate protrudes on all sides. But that is refinishing by amateurs. It is not restoration, and authentic restoration of firearms is the subject here.

Americans as a people are preoccupied with collector value, not just in firearms, but also in many other fields. The fear that any kind of repair will damage collector value has relegated many a fine gun to a reluctant home over the fireplace, or resulted in its being traded for something more modern. Giving up the pleasure of using a fine old rifle to hunt deer in exchange for a new contraption with a shiny barrel, a plastic stock, and no character, all in the name of collector's value, strikes me as a very poor bargain.

The key question is whether this abhorrence of alteration is legitimate. After all, there are areas of equally obsessive collection (and much bigger money) where restoration is not only accepted but, when properly done, actually adds value.

Antique automobiles are the prime example. Any car that was ever used cannot be "factory original." Oil gets changed, tires wear out, and carburetors, windshields, and

headlamps are replaced. This is normal maintenance. The key to auto restoration is to restore it to original condition, meaning that everything is as it once was or might have been. Tires must be authentic, and even the paint color, enamel, and application method must be historically correct. The result, when done properly by experts, is a car that is letter-perfect in both condition and features.

These restored automobiles win jet-set competitions, change hands for millions, and grace the most exclusive collections. The critical consideration is authenticity. So if this is true of vintage Ferraris, and accepted without question, why not vintage Winchesters?

Robert M. Lee is a prominent collector of both firearms and automobiles, one of a handful of men on the planet who is a genuine expert in both fields at the highest level.

"To a serious gun collector, condition is everything," he told me. "The difference between cars and guns is that there are many more guns in fine to pristine condition, even guns hundreds of years old, than there are automobiles. Automobile collectors really do not have a choice, because mint original specimens are so rare.

"When it comes to gun restoration, there are two principles. If a piece is in fine condition it should not be touched; and, if a piece is extremely rare or one of kind, it should not be touched regardless of condition.

"If you have a gun that is in shabby condition, and there are thousands of them around — the Winchester 94 is a perfect example — then proper restoration will give you a really nice example of a rifle you otherwise could not afford."

Bob Lee says he has "great respect" for a gunmaker who is capable of restoring antique firearms. Most of them are in Europe, and they

❦ ● ❦ ● ❦ ● ❦ ● ❦ ● ❦

Far Left: *The action floor of the Winchester 1886 as I found it: A pitted gray mess.*

Left: *The action floor after Turnbull's restoration, returned to case-hardened glory.*

ply their trade for museums and collectors, like Lee, who operate in the stratosphere of collecting. Lee ranks Doug Turnbull in that group.

"I have seen his work. His case-hardening is excellent, excellent. There are so few people who know how to do that, and most are in Europe."

Although he avoids restored firearms in his own collection except for a few special circumstances, Lee says it represents another class of collecting, and one that is growing.

In the case of my Winchester 1886, such concerns simply did not matter. To me, the rifle was an abused puppy to be rescued. The anguished howls of the local Winchester aficionados rang in my ears as I settled down to do something about the execrable condition of poor old #121321.

The first step was a call to Doug Turnbull, followed by photos of the rifle, close-up and from all angles.

"Sure we can do something," Doug said. "What about the stock, though...?"

"We'll re-stock it. Nothing can save the existing one."

"Yes, it's too bad," he replied. "It was a nice piece of walnut."

"Yes. Was. I'll get you a blank."

The goal was to return the rifle to the look it had when it left New Haven. That means a piece of walnut typical of the period. Although black walnut was standard on American rifles of the time, it was not absolute. What was important was avoiding a piece so showy as to be out of place. Gorgeous walnut looks at home on a Holland & Holland, but simply wrong on an old lever action.

Bill Dowtin is a dealer in stock blanks and a stockmaker of more than 30 years experience. Now an importer of walnut from central Asia, Bill prides himself on being able, not just to judge a blank, but to match the character of a piece of wood to the intended gun. I explained the situation.

"Don't worry," Bill said, "I'll get you a suitable blank. On those rifles, they liked walnut that was very red. Some were feather-crotch, but most were cut one or two slabs away. It is hard to describe the figure. Almost an irregular anomaly type of figure. Mottled is about the best term for it."

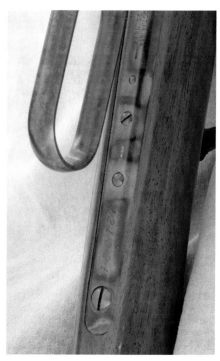

Top Left: *Could anything look worse? As if the amateur carving was not bad enough, the screw heads had been butchered and the tang was scratched and gouged.*

Top Right: *The tang as it is now, polished, serial number re-cut, case-hardened, with Winchester factory original replacement screws, properly aligned.*

Top Left: *A rifle's muzzle takes a beating.*

Top Right: *The muzzle was squared and re-crowned, and the magazine cap and front sight replaced.*

His description meant little to me at the time, but the finished product certainly did when I saw it several months later. But all that was to come.

I sent the rifle to Turnbull Restoration where operations manager Jason Barden logged it in and began a thorough assessment of its condition. The first step was to determine exactly what it had been when it left the Winchester factory in May 1900. A letter to the Cody Firearms Museum in Wyoming (custodian of the Winchester records) gave us a slight shock.

"When the rifle left the factory it was not a 40-65," Doug told me, "It was a 38-56. It is not even factory original now, and there's no way of knowing when it was rebarreled, or by whom. He did a good job, though. It has a good bore. And it is a Winchester barrel."

There was really nothing to be decided. I liked the rifle as it was, and 40-65 brass is easy to come by these days compared to the arcane 38-56. To my mind it all just added to the rifle's charm and mystery.

"We'll get a letter from the museum but leave the rifle as it is." I said. "Whoever owns it 50 years from now will appreciate it."

So, ironically, the rifle had no real collector's value when I bought it because it was not factory original even then and had not been for a long time. It is generally accepted that alterations carried out by the original maker count as "factory original" for collecting purposes, but you need proof. The replacement barrel is a Winchester, but that is all we will ever know.

Mechanically, Turnbull found the rifle to be quite sound, but cosmetics were another thing entirely. The barrel was bad enough, with rust, pitting, and the odd dent and ding, but the receiver was a grey, splotchy mess. The magazine tube showed the usual signs of wear, and both the sharply curved rifle buttplate and steel forend cap were scratched, dinged and rusted. Every screw head in the rifle had, it seemed, been worked on with a hatchet. If any of the owners ever possessed a proper screwdriver, there was no evidence of it.

In a drawer I had an original Lyman receiver sight for an 1886, itself a valuable collector's item, and I sent it to Doug with a request that it be installed to match the rifle. The '86 was going to be put back to work, as a hunting rifle, once it was all put to rights.

The old 1886 was a full-scale restoration project with the straightforward goal of making the rifle "as new."

But I had a Winchester 94 of comparable vintage (1910, actually) that also needed attention. Here, the problem was quite different. The rifle was a 32 Special with a 26-inch octagonal barrel that had been well used but well looked after throughout its life.

From end to end, the 94 was aging gracefully as a century-old rifle should. The only problem was a large brown blemish on the left side of the receiver — a patch two inches square that reproached me every time I looked at it. At some point, the rifle had come in contact with something corrosive. Mercifully, its previous owners had not taken a wire wheel to it, so there was no real damage.

The challenge to Doug Turnbull's team of vintage-rifle experts: Refinish the receiver of the 94 but make it look at home, gently aged like the rest of the rifle.

The 94 and the 1886, although manufactured only 10 years apart, display a marked difference in the way Winchester made rifles.

"Receivers on all the early lever actions were case-hardened," Doug said. "This was the process that hardened the exterior of the steel, and made it rust resistant, after it had been completely machined. The colors, beautiful though they were, were a by-product of an essential industrial process."

A word of explanation: Frequently today we see reference to "case-coloring" — modern chemical processes which impart rippling blue and amber colors to steel, without

---

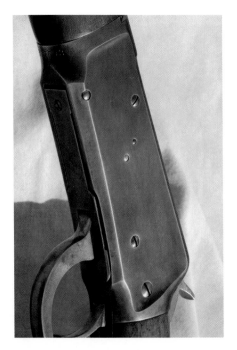
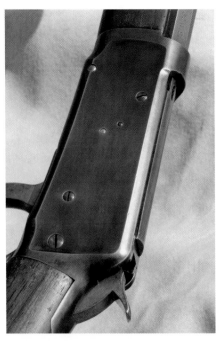

Far Left: *The Winchester 94, made in 1910, left the factory with a blued receiver. It was well used but well cared for, except for one disfiguring blotch on the receiver where it came in contact with something corrosive. The challenge for Turnbull was to correct the problem, but give the receiver an appearance in keeping with the graceful aging of the rest of the rifle.*

Left: *Turnbull's skillful craftsmen gave the receiver an "aged blue" look, and left just enough aging marks on the 94's receiver that it is very difficult to tell that it has even been touched.*

changing the composition of the metal. Case-hardening, the original process, baked carbon into the skin of the steel, hardening it almost like glass, while leaving the steel beneath softer but tougher. Case-hardening was the final step, applied after the steel had been completely machined, polished and engraved.

As the quality of steel in firearms evolved, so did the final treatment applied.

"Around 1900, Winchester began using harder alloy steels for its receivers. They phased out case-hardening and began bluing the receivers instead, because the new steel was tougher and harder to begin with." Turnbull said. "Your 1886 was made in 1900, so it was right on the cusp of that change, although it was case-hardened originally. The shell was hard as glass, as you would have found if you'd tried a file on it.

"Your 94, on the other hand, had been blued rather than case-hardened, so the challenge was to reblue it but make it appear the bluing was done many years ago."

If much of this seems like black magic and alchemy, it is because it is. Gunmaking is an ancient craft, and many of the processes date back to a time of coal forges and leather aprons. Skills were passed from father to son. When a man was renowned for imparting a beautiful finish to a gunstock or case-hardening a frame to exquisite colors, the technique was jealously guarded within the family.

In many cases, alas, this led to arcane knowledge being lost. the making of damascus gun barrels, for example, is a lost art. No one today knows how to do it.

Today, many processes are standardized and a gun from one maker looks much like a gun from another. A century ago, however, each maker had his own techniques and the differences were highly prized.

Parker was famous for its case

colors. In fact, Turnbull says, in terms of colors there were two types in America: Parker, and everyone else. Case-hardening is the most mysterious of all the gunmaking arts, since it involves baking steel in a mixture of charcoal and animal parts like bone or leather. It is the animal carbon that imparts the colors, and the secrets revolve around this type of bone, or that type of leather.

Doug Turnbull came by his interest in the old techniques through his father, who opened a small retail business in upstate New York in 1958. Doug was born three years later, and grew up in his father's shop, watching as he experimented with different techniques of metal finishing, and talking with customers and enthusiasts who came in with antique firearms in need of work.

Although he did not train formally as a gunsmith, Doug went into the business when he finished school, and took a special interest in restoration.

"My father had been experimenting with case-hardening and metal preparation," Turnbull said, "And I took over that side of it. It turned into years of trial and error. Some of these processes are literally lost arts. There are no books about it. Very little was written down, but in the 1960s, a few of the old craftsmen were still alive and were eager to pass on

what they knew, if anyone asked.

"My father learned from them, and I learned from him."

Just like the old way, when you think about it.

Another aspect of authentic restoration is matching the level of original workmanship. Over the years, as manufacturing methods changed and different pressures — usually economic — were brought to bear, gunmakers reduced the attention they gave to certain details. This is easiest to see on a rifle like the Winchester 94, which was manufactured during the entire span of 20th century industrial history.

Loosely — and this applies to all firearms — there was the golden age of craftsmanship which lasted from the late 1800s until 1914, when the world went to war. When commercial production resumed after 1918, many of the practices learned (and bad habits acquired) during the war years were applied. Pearl Harbor was the next great watershed, and by 1950, the whole philosophy of mass-production gunmaking had changed.

Put a 1900-vintage Model 94 beside one made in 1912 and you'll see a slight difference; add one from 1921 and the difference is striking. And after 1945, it was all downhill.

Doug Turnbull and his specialists have studied this aspect of restoration

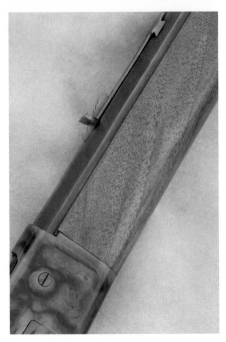

Far Left: **What can one say?**

Left: **Better. Much better.**

and can return a rifle or handgun to the original level of workmanship. Amateur refinishers usually rush the polishing so they can get to the bluing, which is totally wrong.

"Time spent in preparation is all-important," Turnbull said. "Take your 1886. We knew from the hardness that it had been case-hardened originally. It was right at the end of that era — the switch over to bluing the 1886 took place around serial number 120,000.

"We dismantled the rifle completely, cleaned it, annealed the receiver (to eliminate the hardness), polished it, re-cut the lettering and factory markings, then case-hardened it using the original Winchester process."

It sounds simple, but it is painstaking indeed. Polishing requires extreme care, a light touch, and exquisite attention to detail. Pitting almost always looks worse than it is. A shotgun bore with pits like the craters of Mars can often be polished and not even go out of proof. The essential thing is never to remove more metal than is absolutely necessary.

A square, flat surface like a lever-action receiver requires special care in order to come out the other end looking square, flat, and even, with sharp corners. To the naked eye it looks factory original; only a sensitive caliper reveals the dimensional difference.

Proper metal polishing is an under-appreciated art. It was the key to the seductive smoothness of guns from the golden age. The parts were polished inside and out. Look at the internal bits of a Holland & Holland, made then or made now, and you will see every little bit polished to perfection. This gives smooth, effortless operation. As industrial processes deteriorated after 1914, polishing was steadily reduced.

"Proper polishing requires time, and time is money," Doug Turnbull says. "If you can eliminate ten hours of polishing, that is a substantial reduction in costs. Internal parts can often be left unpolished without materially affecting the operation of the gun, at least in the short term, so they let them go.

"Over the years, less and less polishing was applied, and it shows in both the operation and the external finish on these guns."

Turnbull's favorite example is the venerated Colt single-action revolver. "A Colt from before 1913 was given 35 to 45 hours of preparation to get the finish ready for bluing and case-hardening," he says, "While one from later years was given only 25 to 30 hours." Therefore, in restoring one, you want to restore only to the level of finish appropriate for that era. Turnbull said he could make a post-1918 Colt as good as a pre-1913 one, but then it wouldn't be authentic."

No production Winchester was ever made to the level of finish of an H&H Royal, but even so the difference between an old and new 94 is readily apparent. An action that starts off slick gets slicker with use; one that starts off rough only gets rickety. The 1886 has a reputation as the smoothest lever gun Winchester ever made; part of that is the design, but part is the level of internal finish.

Bluing is an art in itself, and one that requires knowledge of both metallurgy and chemistry.

Like case-hardening, bluing served a number of purposes. Not only did it impart a surface finish that would reduce reflection, resist rust, or simply make the gun more attractive, but the method of bluing sometimes changed the qualities of the metal itself.

Old Winchesters require three different types of bluing to duplicate factory condition: nitre, carbona (or charcoal), and rust bluing. Each has its own use.

Nitre blue imparts that deep, iridescent, midnight blue that one sees on gun springs, screws, and the door of a lever-action loading gate. It requires glassy polishing and surgical cleanliness. It is used where temper and hardness are critical.

Carbona is a heat blue, used on small parts as well as the receiver of the rifle. It draws some of the hardness out of the metal, so one must be careful in its use, but it is easier than nitre and less labor-intensive than rust bluing. It imparts a deep, lustrous finish.

Rust bluing is used on barrels and magazine tubes, and has more of a matte appearance. It is applied by immersing the barrel in the solution, letting it rust, carding it off, re-dipping and re-carding ad infinitum until the desired shade and depth of blue has been achieved.

Since these processes look different from the start, they age differently, which is why old Winchester receivers age to grey, while the barrels go brownish. It is an attractive look that makers of new guns now spend time and money trying to reproduce.

A critical change for barrel bluing took place in the early 1900s during the switch from blackpowder to smokeless. Gunmakers needed harder, tougher steels to resist the greater pressures and intense heat of smokeless powder, and abrasion from jacketed bullets. For Winchester, the star cartridge of the dawning smokeless era was not the 30-30, as one might suppose, but the later 32 Special. It was introduced only after they had perfected the use of nickel-steel barrels, and my 32 wears a barrel that has imprinted on it "NICKEL STEEL BARREL — ESPECIALLY FOR SMOKELESS POWDER." Nickel steel is stainless steel of an early type, and naturally resists rust, so it requires a different bluing process. This is one reason two barrels from the same general era might age differently.

After 1940, black oxide became the standard commercial bluing method. It is a water-based chemical blue that is easy and fast but cannot match the beauty of either rust or carbona bluing.

The barrel and magazine tube on the 1886 were rust blued and its loading gate nitre blued. The receiver on the Winchester 94 was carbona blued. The differences are deliciously apparent.

Finally, the stock on the 1886. The carving and scratching carried out by the previous owner, perhaps as long as a hundred years ago, rendered the stock not only ugly but unsalvageable. Bill Dowtin came through with a piece of Central Asian English walnut that looked as if Jove intended it for a vintage Winchester.

It had that prized natural red hue, whisperings of feather-crotch grain all the way to the toe of the stock, several layers of figure that glowed subtly through the oil finish, and straight, extremely strong grain through the wrist. The forend matched the color and rippled gently.

Turnbull put the blank on the pantograph with the original stock, and then turned the semi-finished product over to his stocker for fitting. The final touch was an authentic glossy Winchester finish.

At the center of any collector's concern is monetary value. Some years ago, Doug Turnbull told me about another restored Winchester 1886, as an example of how restoration can affect value.

The Winchester 1886 is a highly desirable collector's item. Only 159,994 were made, compared to more than a million 1892s and close to six million 94s. Turnbull took an '86 that was worth, in its rather shabby, unrestored condition, about $3,000. Had it been in 98 percent original condition, it would have been worth as much as $20,000. Once restored to like-new condition, that $3,000 rifle sold at auction for $9,750. Not the equal of the collector's prize original, but still considerably more than it had been.

Steve Fjestad is editor of the *Blue Book of Gun Values*, the indispensable bible of gun dealers everywhere. Does he think collectors will ever accept restored firearms?

"The answer for most guns is 'no,' except for factory reconditioned English shotguns and rifles by famous makers," he said. "The English have never looked down on properly restored long arms, because they've sent their guns back to the factories for reconditioning for decades."

(Also, it should be pointed out, it is very hard to define "factory original" when the vast majority of guns by companies like Holland & Holland were custom guns, made to the client's specifications. There simply are no standards by which to measure originality.)

I then asked Fjestad about restoring a rifle that has seen a lot of use, with most of the bluing gone, dings on the stock and no finish left. Is that a collector's item that should be preserved, or would it be better going to someone like Doug Turnbull to be restored?

"In that situation, you can't win either way," Fjestad said, "And here's why: It's already not much of a collector's item because of its lower condition, unless it's a rare major-trademark model. And by the time you pay for a professional restoration, you may or may not get all your money back when selling."

Fair enough. If money is the only consideration, then restoration may not be a rock-solid financial investment. After all, if you buy an 1886 for $3,000, have it restored for $4,000, and then sell it for $6500, you've lost money. But to a serious lover of fine firearms, there is far more to it than mere dollars.

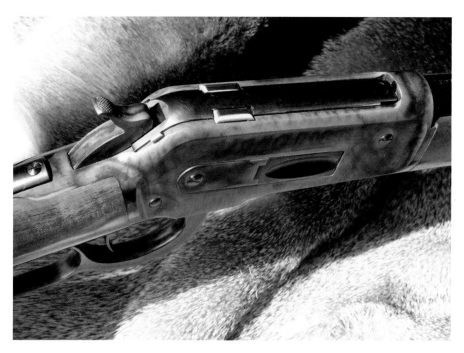

The Winchester 1886 – considered by many to be the greatest lever-action Winchester ever made. It is certainly the handsomest.

Winchester Model 1886, #121321, was shipped from New Haven in May 1900. After an adventurous life that saw its barrel changed from 38-56 to 40-65, here it is after Doug Turnbull's complete restoration, ready to go hunting once again in formal dress.

Over the past decade or so, I have had several shotguns and rifles restored or (to use the British term) refurbished. In England, a "refurb" is completely respectable and its effect on value depends only on how well it is carried out. The economics became plain to me when it was explained that an unusable H. Holland 50-caliber muzzleloading double rifle could be returned to excellent shootable condition for $5,000 — after which I would have a rifle that might be worth $5,000.

At that point, you look at this chunk of scrap which is a potential piece of history and ask yourself what it is worth, to you, to salvage that piece of history for posterity, whether you personally profit by it or not. If you count as profit the feeling of having saved something valuable that otherwise would have been lost, and presenting it to lovers of fine

guns to treasure forevermore, then you might become hooked as I have.

Among my pack of rescued puppies I have a 28-gauge James Erskine hammer gun from the 1880s that saw hard service in Africa; an 1890 E.M. Reilly boxlock that was owned by a Scottish gamekeeper, brought to the new world, and spent 30 years in the rafters of a henhouse; a Savage 1899 (1916), and an Ithaca trap gun (1921). All are in excellent working order, and each gets used.

Bob Lee pointed out that, with automobiles, restoration is almost always necessary just to get them to run "unless you want a pile of junk that just sits there." For many rifles and shotguns, the same is true. Under the British proof system, to be used a gun must be in proof, and putting an old gun in proof often takes a complete refurb.

Looking at these fine old guns, all of them leaning casually against

my bookshelf, and now with the Model 1886 proudly among them, I know that at some point I could get my investment back.

But there is something else. It is a truth universally acknowledged that more really fine guns survive through the years in really fine condition because when a buyer pays big money he tends to look after his investment, and his heirs do as well. A gun made as a tool gets treated like a tool.

The guns I have had restored are now firmly in the former category and a hundred years from now, with any luck, they will reside in the collection of someone who cares deeply about guns and workmanship. At that point, I sincerely doubt he will really care that they were restored or refurbished, unless it is to silently give thanks that people like Doug Turnbull existed.

For that matter, a hundred years from now, the imprimatur "Restored by Turnbull" on a Winchester 1886 might well carry as much cachet as the Winchester name itself. ❀

YOU, ME AND THE
CMP

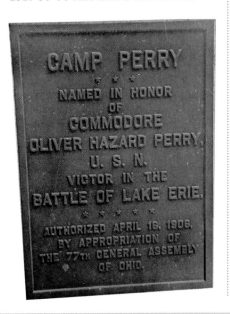

by Charles W. Karwan

They wrote legislation that established the Corporation for the Promotion of Rifle Practice and Firearms Safety. This non-profit federally chartered corporation was given the responsibility for the supervision, oversight, and control of the U.S. Civilian Marksmanship Program. The law forming this corporation mandates that the mission of the CMP is the "Instruction of the citizens of the United States in marksmanship....." with the highest priority going to training juniors. The CMP supplies firearms safety and marksmanship training through a nationwide network of affiliated shooting clubs, state shooting associations, and other organizations such as the Boy Scouts and school shooting teams.

The official United States government-sponsored Civilian Marksmanship Program (CMP) is known to only a small fraction of American gun owners, even though it is of incredibly high importance to our country and the future of firearms use in general—for ourselves and our descendants.

My family has a long history with the Civilian Marksmanship Program, going back over 70 years. Indeed, I personally owe a great deal of who and what I am to my participation in various CMP programs since I was a young lad. I still own an M-1917 30-06 rifle and a Colt M-1917

45 ACP revolver that my late father purchased in the early 1930s from the CMP's predecessor—the Director of Civilian Marksmanship (DCM).

Did you know that even today most Gun Digest readers can buy military surplus M-1 Garand rifles, M-1903 Springfield rifles, M-1917 rifles, surplus military 22 LR target rifles, ammunition, and gun parts taken directly from surplus U.S. government stocks—at excellent prices? Did you know that gun clubs affiliated with the CMP can qualify to do the same at even better prices, and get substantial other support from the CMP? Even better, the proceeds of the sale of all these items goes to fund the operation of the CMP and its many programs.

For the last 100 years the Civilian Marksmanship Program has trained millions of American youths and adults to shoot in a safe and proper manner. In addition, the CMP sustains the operation of the U.S. National Rifle and Pistol Matches, supports the marksmanship programs of all the state shooting associations, and has made sure that our country always has a substantial number of our population who know how to shoot well. My own extensive experience in the military bears out the significance and importance of my personal CMP background and training.

The CMP program can trace

The author's late father near the firing line at Camp Perry in the mid-1950s when the M-1 Garand was king of the service rifles.

its roots clear back to 1903, when Congress first passed legislation to establish the formation of the National Board for the Promotion of Rifle Practice (NBPRP). This legislation was passed with the full support of President Theodore Roosevelt and the National Rifle Association (NRA). At the same time it also established the U.S. National Rifle and Pistol Matches, as well as appropriations to transport teams of marksmen from the various branches of the U.S. military to attend the National Matches. The main objective of these laws was to promote better rifle marksmanship in our armed forces.

In 1905 Congress passed further legislation, again with the strong support of President Roosevelt and the NRA, that authorized the sale (at cost) of surplus military rifles, ammunition, and other military equipment to civilian shooting clubs meeting requirements laid down by the NBPRP. This was the beginning of a century-old U.S. government-sponsored national program that continues to this day to supply obsolete military rifles to qualified civilians for the purpose of promoting and developing marksmanship in the civilian population. Right from the beginning, the primary objective has been to build and maintain a

reserve of trained marksmen among the civilian population that could be called upon for military service in time of war, either as soldiers or marksmanship instructors.

In the summer of 1916, with Europe already at war, Congress passed the National Defense Act. That law earmarked money specifically to promote civilian marksmanship training and authorized the distribution of appropriate arms and ammunition to organized civilian shooting clubs for the same purpose. In addition, it set aside funding for the operation of military rifle ranges and the transportation of military shooting instructors to assist civilian clubs in marksmanship training and allowed civilian shooters access to most military rifle ranges. In addition, it created the office of the Director of Civilian Marksmanship (DCM) to oversee these activities. Finally, it authorized funds to transport civilian teams from across the country to the National Matches to compete with the standard military rifles and pistols of the day. Much to the embarrassment of the military teams, in 1916, in the first of the National Matches open to civilians, both the individual national service rifle and pistol champions were civilians.

The aftermath of World War I found the U.S. military awash with a huge surplus of military rifles and handguns. These included 280,000 Russian M91 7.62x54Rmm Mosin-Nagant rifles originally made by Remington and New England Westinghouse for the Russian government. These had been rendered undeliverable by the Russian revolution so the U.S. government purchased them from their manufacturers, ostensibly for training purposes, but more likely to help the manufacturers out of a financial bind since they were already doing

❧ ● ❧ ● ❧ ● ❧ ● ❧ ● ❧

This certificate is proof the author attended the Small Arms Firing School at Camp Perry some 45 years ago. He still has fond memories of the experience and still uses the knowledge gained there.

DEPARTMENT OF THE ARMY
NATIONAL BOARD FOR THE PROMOTION OF RIFLE PRACTICE
WASHINGTON

SMALL ARMS FIRING SCHOOL

Certificate

This Certificate is Awarded to ___ CHARLES W. KARWAN JR. ___

As Evidence of Having Attended a Regular Course in

Rifle Marksmanship

Conducted in Conjunction with the 1960 National Matches at Camp Perry, Ohio

In Witness Whereof are Affixed the Signatures of the Executive Officer of the National Matches and the Director of the School.

Colonel, Infantry
Weapons Department
United States Army Infantry School
Director

Colonel, Ordnance Corps
Executive Officer, National Matches

Author's service-grade M-1, shown here with a WWII ammo belt, a clip of ball ammo and a clip of black-tipped armor piercing (AP) ammo. He recalls that when his club drew its allocation of 30-06 ammo from the DCM, they were delighted if it was AP because it invariably shot much better than the standard 150-grain ball bullet.

substantial work on other important U.S. government contracts. I cannot find any record that the M91 Mosins were ever actually used for training purposes. However, some of these M91 Mosin rifles were issued to–and carried by–U.S. troops assigned to the international expeditions to Russia to protect Allied interests from the Bolshevik revolution, during and shortly after WWI.

Also on hand were 20,000 Canadian Ross Mark II 303 straight-pull rifles procured from Canada during WWI, ostensibly for use as training rifles. In addition, there were over 100,000 obsolete U.S. Krag 30-40 rifles and carbines, thousands of old 45-70 Springfield "Trapdoor" carbines and rifles, over 200,000 M-1917 S&W and Colt 45 ACP revolvers, and a couple million M-1917 "Enfield" 30-06 rifles. There were also large quantities of M-1903 30-06 rifles and M-1911 45 ACP

Typical competitors' quarters at Camp Perry in the 1950s and '60s. They had a cement floor and the furnishings consisted primarily of Army cots. The author's family would occupy one of these semi-tents for the duration of the matches his father shot in.

pistols that were, during the post-WWI period, the standard service arms of the U.S. armed services.

Since the U.S. government trusted its citizens with firearms in those days, the above-mentioned rifles and pistols were all made available for civilian purchase through the DCM, often at incredibly low prices. For example, brand new Russian M91 Mosin-Nagant rifles sold for as low as $3.24 with 7.62x54Rmm ammunition at $4.00 per thousand rounds. The Ross rifles went for about $5, with about the same amount for a thousand rounds of 303 ammo. Krag rifles went for as little as $1.50 and Trapdoor Springfield 45-70 rifles for only $1.25. The M-1917 30-06 rifle, the primary rifle used by U.S. forces in WWI and easily one of the very best military rifles of its day, could be bought for the grand sum of $7.50.

During this period, civilians could also purchase M-1903 Springfield rifles through the DCM in a wide variety of variations: used and new service rifles, service rifles with star-gauge barrels, National Match variations, the NRA Sporter, Springfield M-1 and M-2 22 LR training rifles and many more model variations.

Between the world wars, all of the Mosin-Nagant, Ross, Krag, and Trapdoor Springfield rifles were sold off, either through the DCM or through surplus disposal channels. However, large quantities of M-1917 rifles, M-1903 rifles and M-1917 revolvers were still on hand when WWII broke out. These arms were quickly put back into U.S. military service, usually in a secondary role, or supplied to our allies. Over a million M-1917 rifles were sent to England, and they were also widely used by both our Chinese and Free French allies.

Shortly after WWII, the civilian marksmanship programs restarted. Again the DCM made large quantities of surplus rifles and handguns available to qualified buyers at bargain prices, including large quantities of M-1903A3 rifles introduced and produced during the war. Eventually, surplus M-1 Garands and M-1 Carbines, as well as M-1911 and M-1911A1 pistols, were also made available.

After WWII, the M-1 Garand was eventually refined and accurized at Springfield Arsenal for use in service rifle competition. When the military teams began to win the National Service Rifle Matches with these match-grade M-1 Garands, civilian competitors clamored for match-grade M-1 rifles as well. Subsequently, new M-1 National Match rifles assembled at Springfield Arsenal were made available by the DCM for purchase by qualified civilian competitors. I still own my father's National Match M-1 that he purchased at the National Matches at Camp Perry, Ohio in 1960.

The same thing happened in the Service Pistol category with military shooters using arsenal- and custom-accurized M-1911A1 pistols. For a short period the DCM offered for sale to civilian shooters National Match M-1911A1 pistols that had been hand-assembled at Springfield Arsenal. However, the demand for such pistols was soon filled by the commercial firearms community and the sale of DCM National Match 45 pistols soon ended.

Unfortunately, the days of inexpensive surplus guns being available directly from the government at bargain prices were numbered. By the end of the '60s, anti-gun congressmen managed to close down DCM sales of firearms and remove much of the DCM's funding in spite of the fact that huge numbers of surplus guns were still in military stocks, and criminal use of such guns was virtually unknown. Incredibly, these anti-gun congressmen preferred to waste money destroying these guns rather than selling them to the very citizens that paid for them in the first place and who, in many cases, had risked their lives using them in service to their country. Unfortunately, during this period hundreds of thousands such guns were destroyed at considerable cost to the government, turning a substantial financial asset into a financial liability that subsequently poured precious tax dollars down the drain.

During this same period Congress commissioned a formal study of the DCM program by an independent firm to determine whether or not it justified its cost. Much to the chagrin of the anti-gun members of Congress, this study came back with findings that strongly supported the program.

❦ ● ❦ ● ❦ ● ❦ ● ❦ ● ❦

The M-1917 Colt 45 ACP revolver the author's late father purchased from the DCM in the early 1930's. Note the carving on the grips he did before WWII, and the grip adapter later added by the author.

The investigators found it an extremely cost-effective recruiting aid to get high-caliber American youth to enlist into the armed forces. It also reported that servicemen active in the DCM marksmanship programs prior to their service required less training to become proficient marksmen and were—as a group—better prepared for combat than recruits that had not been in the program. In other words, the original intention for the civilian marksmanship program was being accomplished and the existence of the program was completely validated. Needless to say, the anti-gun members of Congress totally ignored the findings of this study.

During those dark days, the DCM continued to support the National Matches, as well as many youth and club marksmanship programs. Eventually, it was able to get permission to sell some surplus M-1 Garand rifles to individuals, but the requirements for qualification to make a purchase were greatly increased. The person had to be over eighteen, a U.S. citizen, and a member of a DCM-affiliated club or association (formerly NRA membership was sufficient). They also had to show proof of recent participation in rifle competition, they could never have purchased an M-1 from the government before, and they had to submit to an FBI fingerprint check. At that time the cost of service-grade DCM M-1 Garand rifles was $94.30, but the price went up steadily over time.

The DCM programs continued to be attacked by anti-gun congressmen for decades and, eventually, their fiscal allocations for operation were completely lost. In 1996 Congress abolished the NBPRP. To save the CMP and the tremendous amount of good work it does, an innovative approach was taken by some clever members of Congress.

They wrote legislation that established the Corporation for the Promotion of Rifle Practice and Firearms Safety. This non-profit federally chartered corporation was given the responsibility for the supervision, oversight, and control of the U.S. Civilian Marksmanship Program. The law forming this corporation mandates that the mission of the CMP is the "Instruction of the citizens of the United States in marksmanship....." with the highest priority going to training juniors. The CMP supplies firearms safety and marksmanship training through a nationwide network of affiliated shooting clubs, state shooting associations, and other organizations such as the Boy Scouts and school shooting teams.

To fund these activities the CMP is authorized to sell government surplus 22- and 30-caliber rifles, ammunition, repair parts, equipment and other related supplies. The proceeds from these sales are mandated to be spent to support the CMP programs. Indeed, the entire funding of the CMP operation is strictly from match entry fees and the sales of these items. Consequently, the near-giveaway prices of the old DCM days are, by necessity, gone.

Since this reorganization of the CMP, its leadership has taken a very wise long term approach to its funding. They place $100 from the sale of each M-1 rifle—and the entire proceeds of any special sales—into a "Permanent Investment Account." The idea behind this is to accumulate enough funds in this account so that, by the time all the M-1 Garands on hand are sold off, the CMP will be able to continue operating for a long time afterward. Hopefully it will be able to run just off the interest on the account. In effect, the surplus stocks of M-1 Garand rifles are the CMP's cash cow. When they are gone the CMP does not want to go away as well.

Some of the special sales of surplus rifles conducted in recent years include lotteries and sealed bid auctions of small quantities of various particularly desirable rifles such as M-1D and M-1C sniper rifles, and others. Periodically such "goodies" turn up in some government storage facility and the CMP is quick to acquire them for their program.

Currently, regular M-1 Garand rifle sales include M-1 service rifles in a variety of variations and grades running from rack grade to collector grade, priced from $295 to $1400. These include rifles supplied to Denmark and Greece that have been repatriated to the U.S. Thankfully, none have importer markings. While these M-1 Garands are not being sold at giveaway prices, they are being sold at low-end market value and represent excellent buys. In my experience, the vast majority of service-grade M-1 Garands sold would rate NRA Very Good condition and the rack-grade rifles would rate NRA Good+ to Very Good - condition.

The "Collector Grade" M-1s include: any M-1 of any manufacturer that has all its original parts, any pre-WWII M-1 with most of its original parts, any Winchester M-1 "dash-13" variation, any

International Harvester M-1 with original barrel and most of its original parts—as well as those bearing unusual logos on the receiver and any H&R M-1 with a serial number over 6 million, among others.

It is hard to believe, but some M-1903, M-1903A3, and M-1917 rifles are still available after all these years. Their prices run in the $350 to $400 range. Some of these had been loaned to veterans' organizations for ceremonial use and then returned to government stocks, while others have just been sitting in a government warehouse all these years.

The recent sales of surplus military 22 LR target rifles have included these models: Mossberg M44, Remington 541X, Remington 40X, and Winchester M52C and D target rifles. As this is written, the only surplus small-bore rifles available are new Kimber Model 82 Government Model 22 LR single-shot target rifles at $600, used H&R M-12 22 target rifles at $225, Mossberg 144US 22 target rifles at $229, and some incomplete Winchester M52 rifles.

To qualify to purchase an M-1 or other firearm through the CMP you must be a U.S. citizen, at least eighteen years old, a member of a CMP-affiliated club or association, and have proof of some kind of marksmanship activity. The sale

must also comply with all federal, state, and local laws, so you must also pass a National Instant Check System background check. Once this is accomplished and the rifle paid for, it is shipped right to your door.

If you are not already a member of a CMP-affiliated club or association, the simplest way to meet that requirement is to join your CMP-affiliated state shooting association. Every state has one. The CMP can supply you with the appropriate contacts and the cost is minimal. The proof of participation can be a match bulletin that lists you as a competitor in virtually any kind of shooting competition.

Interestingly, the competition requirement is waived if you can document that you are in any of the following categories: have current or past honorable military service, are a certified law enforcement officer, have proof of completion of a marksmanship clinic or hunter's safety course that includes live-fire training, have NRA Distinguished, Instructor or Coach status, have a state-issued concealed-carry license or firearms identification card, have certification of shooting activity by a shooting range or club official, or are over 60 years of age. There is even a method for a parent or guardian to procure a rifle for a qualified junior shooter who is under the age of 18. There is a limitation on the number of rifles an individual can purchase per year once you qualify, but it is liberal.

Beside the normal service rifle and pistol matches, the CMP also holds and sponsors a variety of special matches that are conducted at the National Matches and by affiliated clubs. The most fun and interesting are the John C. Garand

❈ ● ❈ ● ❈ ● ❈ ● ❈ ● ❈

The author with his late father's old DCM M-1917 Colt 45 ACP revolver. This was the very first firearm he remembers ever seeing, and it was his father's primary utility and defensive handgun for most of his life. It, and his dad's M-1, are two of the author's most prized possessions.

Match, the Springfield Match and the Vintage Military Rifle Match.

All are shot at 200 yards. The shooter fires ten shots prone slow fire, ten shots standing to sitting rapid fire, and ten shots standing slow fire. For the Garand Match the rifles are limited to standard "as-issued" service rifle specimens of the M-1 Garand (30-06 only), M-1903 in all service rifle variations, M-1 Carbine, M-1941 Johnson and M-1917 "Enfield", in other words the U.S. service rifles used to some degree in WWII. The Springfield Match is open to any bolt-action U.S. service rifle in as-issued condition, including those listed above, and U.S. Krags. The Vintage Military Rifle Match is open to foreign bolt-action military service rifles, also in as-issued condition. No military match rifles, match parts, glass bedding, or other changes from "as-issued" are allowed in any of these categories. The idea of these matches is to increase interest and participation in military rifle shooting without the technological arms race that seems to accompany most other competitive shooting sports. It is entirely possible to acquire an accurate foreign military surplus rifle to compete in this match for under $100.

These matches are a lot of fun and are the most popular matches at the National Matches. In 2004 there were 816 entries in the Springfield and Vintage Military Match and a staggering 1401 entries in the Garand Match. Shooters often show up wearing uniforms of the period their rifle was made or, in the case of foreign military rifles, in the uniform of the country the rifle was issued. This adds to the color and fun of these matches. In the 2004 Vintage Military Match at Camp Perry, the variety of foreign countries and rifles represented included the Swedish Mausers, Swiss Schmidt Rubins, Persian Mausers, Italian Carcanos, British Enfields, and more.

The current standard U.S. service rifle is the M-16. Accurized versions of semiautomatic commercial equivalents of the M-16 are currently dominating national-level service

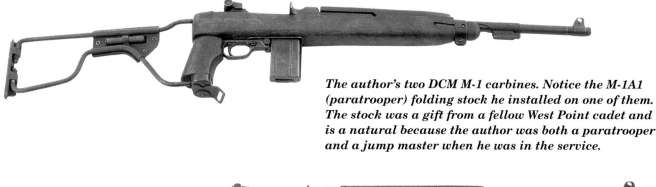

The author's two DCM M-1 carbines. Notice the M-1A1 (paratrooper) folding stock he installed on one of them. The stock was a gift from a fellow West Point cadet and is a natural because the author was both a paratrooper and a jump master when he was in the service.

rifle competition. At the National Matches, there is also a special M-16 Match where the shooter is issued a genuine military-issue M-16 service rifle to shoot the match. This match is proving particularly popular with new shooters.

During the National Matches, the CMP sponsors a Small Arms Firing School, a program that has been in place since shortly after WWII. Rifles and ammunition are supplied and the shooting instruction is absolutely top-notch. I highly recommend that anyone interested in rifle shooting attend this school, particularly teenagers and young adults. It can quite literally change your life— it did for me when I went through it back in 1960.

The CMP also conducts many other junior and senior marksmanship programs, including programs in conjunction with 4-H clubs, the Boy Scouts, ROTC, college shooting teams, and a wide variety of other clubs and associations. They also sponsor an extensive youth air rifle competition program. In the past, they made lightweight low-recoiling M-1 Carbines available to clubs for junior-level centerfire rifle training, and may do so again in the near future. They also sell surplus ammunition, as well as a variety of M-1 Garand and other rifle parts to clubs and

individuals at quite reasonable prices.

While my father introduced me to guns and shooting at an early age, it was the CMP programs at our local gun club that probably had the most influence on my shooting ability. As a teenager, I often placed near the top in our club among the high-power rifle shooters.

It is notable that the guns my dad purchased from the DCM are among my first memories of firearms of any kind. As I said earlier, my father purchased his first guns from the DCM in the early 1930s: an M-1917 Enfield rifle and an M-1917 Colt revolver, both veterans of WWI. I once asked him why he purchased a Colt M-1917 rather than the also-available S&W M-1917. He told me the latter cost a few dollars more and that, since money was in such short supply during the Great Depression, he simply bought the cheapest one.

My father was working in California when the Japanese attacked Pearl Harbor. He told me that shortly after the attack it was impossible to find any firearms or ammunition for sale because everybody was arming themselves against a possible Japanese invasion of the West Coast. He recalled being very glad that he was already well armed, by the standards of the day, with his DCM M-1917 rifle and M-1917

Colt revolver. It was learned after the war that the Japanese were aware of the large numbers of well-armed American civilians, like my father, which contributed to discouraging any invasion plans. Yet again the CMP's mission was vindicated.

My dad's DCM M-1917 Colt was his primary utility and home defense handgun for most of his life, in spite of his subsequent acquisition of many more handguns. That old Colt was the gun he always used to dispatch sick or injured animals, as well as farm animals that were being butchered. It was the gun he grabbed to investigate things that went bump in the night. When, in his final years, he finally gave me the old beast, it had been kept loaded almost continuously for about fifty years. In honor of my late father, I still keep it loaded with modern high-performance hollowpoints; it now resides in a locked cabinet and has been loaded for over 70 years.

I was with my dad when he bought his National Match M-1 from the DCM in 1960 while he attended the National Matches at Camp Perry. As a teenager I usually competed with a surplus M-1903 Springfield because that was all that I could afford with my paper route income. Later, as my shooting improved, he often loaned me that superbly accurate M-1 to shoot in our club matches. That National

Match M-1 is now one of my most prized possessions and I still break it out on occasion for a local rifle match.

As a youngster I was active in our local DCM-affiliated shooting club's youth program. We shot DCM-supplied Remington 513T 22 target rifles in the basement of the local YMCA. Thanks to good instruction, good equipment, and plentiful ammunition, I became a reasonably good small-bore rifle shooter.

At the unusually young age of 13 I attended the DCM's Small Arms Firing School at Camp Perry, along with two of my cousins and my late uncle Joe Karwan, while my late father was shooting in matches. There was no particular minimum age requirement to attend the school as long as you were big and strong enough to properly handle a 10-pound M-1 Garand rifle. Since I was already just under six feet tall, and nearly 200 pounds at 13, I qualified easily.

My uncle, who was in the Army in Hawaii when the Japanese attacked Pearl Harbor, and later served in Europe as a Combat Engineer from D-Day until the end of the war, was along mostly just to ride herd on the youngsters. He knew how to shoot an M-1 rifle very well already. He told us that when he was an NCO, which was for most of the war, even though he could have carried an M-1

The author in younger days holding his late father's National Match M-1 rifle bought in 1960 at Camp Perry from the DCM.

Carbine or a submachine gun as his personal weapon, he always chose to carry an M-1 Garand because it was so reliable and effective.

It was quite a heady experience for me and my cousins to have a brand new National Match M-1 Garand issued to us for the duration of the Small Arms Firing School, and any matches we wanted to enter. We were told to keep our M-1s clean and to keep the bolt locked back at all times, except when actually shooting. Indeed, if any competitor was caught off the firing line with his rifle bolt forward he would–at a minimum–get severely scolded. While we were there, one match competitor was caught in a common area with his M-1's bolt forward with rounds in the magazine; why, no one can say. He was unceremoniously packed up and escorted off the Camp Perry installation with instructions never to return.

Not only were we supplied with match-grade rifles at no cost, high-quality National Match 30-06 ammunition was even supplied—free! It was issued to us right on the firing line. We all had a great time, learned a lot about rifle shooting, and enjoyed the experience tremendously, including my Uncle who acquitted himself very well with an old and dear friend, the M-1 Garand. When we finally left Camp Perry, I could not afford to buy the National Match M-1 I had been issued, but I sure wanted to! My father bought his, though.

At the Small Arms Firing School we were instructed and coached by members of the various armed services teams, some of whom were national champions and record-holders. There is no doubt that my positive experience there with those outstanding military NCOs and officers was instrumental in my choosing to go to West Point a few years later. As an infantry officer in Vietnam, and later a Special Forces officer, the knowledge and

skills in marksmanship acquired at Camp Perry and through other DCM programs were extremely useful to me and to the troops I commanded and worked with.

There are many examples. When I was an upper-class cadet at West Point I was detailed to help train underclassmen on shooting the M-14, and then get them "qualified," The instruction I received from the CMP helped me immensely. Indeed, when any cadet failed to qualify, that knowledge allowed me to identify the problem with his rifle or technique and, with my help, most qualified the second time around. The same held true later as a junior officer in the Army. My CMP-acquired knowledge was passed on to others and employed to help my troops on numerous occasions.

My experiences in the CMP were also of tremendous value when I served in Vietnam. When I took over my rifle platoon in the 1st Cavalry Division, their idea of cleaning an M-16 was to fire a few tracers through it! Fortunately I knew better and soon had my platoon cleaning, maintaining, and zeroing their M-16 rifles properly. My background in precision marksmanship in the CMP also helped me a great deal in supporting and using snipers effectively and made me a strong proponent of the use of precision marksmanship in combat. Even though I was an officer and usually occupied with commanding my unit, for about half my tour I carried an accurized M-14 or an XM21 sniper rifle as my personal weapon.

After Vietnam I served in both the 10th and 5th Special Forces Groups. At that time (mid-'70s) the Army had no active sniper program, and Special Forces never did have one. I took a shot at changing that and made a presentation to some staff members at the Special Warfare Center at Ft. Bragg, advocating the issuance of an M21 sniper rifle to each Special Forces A Detachment. I used my personal Springfield Armory M-1A (M-14 type) match rifle that I used for service rifle competition and fitted it with a borrowed ART sniper scope and mount to simulate an M21 sniper rifle for the presentation since there was not a single M21 on Ft. Bragg at the time.

In the presentation I outlined the many capabilities of the M21 sniper rifle and emphasized the effectiveness it offered a Special Forces detachment, especially with regard to economy of force and cost-effectiveness. There is no question in my mind that, without my CMP training and experiences, I could never have made that presentation. Evidently I was convincing because, after my proposal was run up the flag pole, it was adopted and, ever since, every Special Forces Detachment Alpha (A-team) has been issued a sniper rifle.

Not only that but General Emerson, the 18th Airborne Corps Commander at Ft. Bragg at the time, liked the idea so much he initiated a sniper program for his major units (the 82nd and 101st Airborne Divisions) as well. The history books credit General Emerson with reviving the Army's sniper program after it was dropped after Vietnam, but it was lowly Captain Karwan in the 5th Special Forces that actually started that revival. My experience with the CMP deserves a lot of the credit as well. One of my buddies who knows the above story insists on calling me "The Father of U.S. Special Forces Sniping." I don't know about that, but I admit I am proud of the fact that today both the U.S. Special Forces and regular Army have an ongoing permanent sniper program and I had a significant role in making it happen.

While I have been out of the Army for a long time, there are still many soldiers out there that have had the benefit of the CMP to help prepare them for combat service. Just recently an Army unit that was about to deploy to Iraq was issued optically-sighted M-14 rifles for use as Squad Designated Marksman (SDM) rifles. An SDM is a sort of low-level sniper that is under the control of the rifle platoon leader and supports that unit with precision rifle fire,

⚜ ● ⚜ ● ⚜ ● ⚜ ● ⚜ ● ⚜

The author's son Jake enjoys shooting his father's and grandfather's DCM M-1s and will eventually inherit them.

particularly at distances beyond the capability of a normal rifleman.

The problem was that nobody in the unit knew very much about the M-14 rifle or its capabilities in the SDM role. As a consequence, they turned to the CMP-affiliated Texas Rifle and Pistol Association which supplied some top-level civilian marksmen highly familiar with the M-14 to provide the necessary training on these rifles before the unit deployed. Yet again, the CMP accomplished precisely the mission it was originally developed for. I was just old enough in the '60s to get in on the tail-end of the period where the DCM was able to sell surplus guns to NRA members without much hassle, and at really low prices. During that period, my father and I both purchased M-1911 45-caliber pistols and M-1 Carbines from the DCM. One of my cousins and I also purchased M-1903A3 30-06 rifles. As I recall the price of each of the above, with packing and shipping, was right around $20 apiece. Yes, those were the days!

My father's DCM-purchased M-1911 was a pretty tired specimen, having been through both world wars and many rebuilds. He gave it to one of his brothers who sadly subsequently lost it. Mine was nearly as tired but it was still a decent shooter.

I was not able to get an M-1 Garand from the DCM until several

years later when the DCM got permission to reopen M-1 sales under much more stringent requirements (proof of recent rifle competition and an FBI finger print check). At the time I was an Army Captain in Special Forces with a Top Secret security clearance, but I still had to go through all those hassles to buy my DCM M-1. John Larsen, a good friend who was one of the NCOs in my unit, and I shot in qualification matches and ordered our M-1s at the same time. John promptly got his while my order was refused because the DCM records indicated I had already purchased an M-1 in 1960. I pointed out that they had confused me with my father and that I would have been only 13 years old that year. The DCM eventually sent me my M-1, but not until I received a lot of kidding from John that the DCM obviously gave priority to NCOs because they were more important than officers.

The M-1 Garand that I received was typical of most service-grade M-1 rifles purchased from the DCM then, or the CMP today. It was used but not abused and had been totally rebuilt at least once in its history. It has an H&R receiver, but virtually all of its other parts—including its 1963-dated barrel—were made at Springfield Armory. Since it has a nice bore, it shoots quite well and

A much younger and slimmer author in Vietnam displaying some captured submachine guns. The author credits his CMP training and experiences with interesting him in military service and, once he was on active duty, helping him do well. The weapons are a French 9mm MAT 49, a Chinese copy of the Soviet 7.62x25mm PPSh41, an M-1 Thompson, and a British 9mm Sten Mk IIS with integral noise suppressor.

I have used it in a John C. Garand match and other competitions.

As you can see, between my late father's DCM purchases and my own I have quite a nice little collection of DCM guns including a Colt M-1917 revolver, a Colt M-1911, an Eddystone M-1917, a Remington M-1903A3, a Winchester and an Inland M-1 Carbine, an H&R M-1 Garand and a Springfield National Match M-1 Garand.

Thinking back, I have fired every one of them in one kind of a match or another—except for one of the M-1 Carbines, and the handguns. I have had many enjoyable hours shooting all of them at targets and, on a several occasions, hunting with some of them. The old Eddystone

M-1917 was shot one day from the bench at 100 yards with some particularly accurate match loads and repeatedly produced sub-MOA groups using its original peep sight. That's not too shabby for a WWI-vintage service rifle that cost $7.50! I hope the CMP stays alive and well for many years for many reasons, not the least of which is that I would dearly like to add to my personal DCM/CMP collection.

Everyone who can qualify should buy at least one M-1 Garand, or some other rifle through the CMP. If you are not yet qualified, get qualified. In doing so you will help finance one of the best shooter development programs in existence and you will be rescuing a great rifle from possible future government destruction. Please, write or call the CMP for more information—or visit its web site. ⊛

The author, circa 1955, trying to hold up his late father's M-1 while his younger brother Rick fiddles with his Kodak Brownie. In the background is part of Camp Perry's huge firing line.

Civilian Marksmanship Program
Camp Perry Training Site, Building 3
P. O. Box 576
Port Clinton, Ohio 43452-0576
(419) 635-2141
(888) 267-0796
FAX (419) 635-2802
web site- www.odcmp.com

PART I

THE REMINGTON
MODEL 700
LIMITED EDITION CLASSIC

by Steve Gash

Production History

Remington is America's oldest gunmaker, and has always kept abreast of the whims and wishes of shooters as they've evolved over the years. Probably no better testament to this philosophy is the

Model 700 bolt-action rifle and the Limited Edition (LE) Classic series in particular. From 1981 through 2005, Remington produced an annual series of 25 Model 700s in a variety of chamberings. With their conservative appearance, the new rifles embodied the essence of the word "classic," and

A quartet of LE Classics. Note the consistency of style and the clean, conservative lines that exude the restrained elegance usually reserved for best quality European bolt guns. From top: 35 Whelen (1988), 8x57 Mauser (2004), 300 H&H Magnum (1983) and 375 H&H Magnum (1996).

A classic hunting rifle, a 8x57 Mauser equipped with a Burris Fullfield II 3-9x40 scope.

the shooting public took to them like a sommelier to a fine wine. Some of the caliber selections themselves were true classics, such as the 300 H&H Magnum (1983) and 375 H&H Magnum (1996), as well as the 8x57 Mauser (2004). Other calibers, one may speculate, were perhaps selected to use up excess barrel inventory of a certain bore size. It is difficult to imagine that there was a shortage of 223 Remingtons (2000), 308 Winchesters (2005) or 300 Winchester Magnums (1995), for example.

Virtually all caliber niches were eventually represented over the years. Five cartridges were in the 17- to 22-caliber range, and nine were

what may be considered "medium bores" from 25- to 7mm caliber. Not surprisingly, the American standard 30-caliber came in with a total of five entries. The big bruisers were represented six times, with two 8mm rounds, as well as a 338, two 35s, and the 375. Curiously, no 24-caliber LE Classic was ever produced.

To my knowledge, no detailed history or production data for the 25-year M-700 LE Classic series have ever been assembled in one place. After over a year of research, scouring gun shows and shops, pouring over numerous references, and many phone calls to arms historians far and wide, what follows is an all-

inclusive chronology of the annual series, including contemporaneous notes on their cartridges.

A popular (but incorrect) perception within the shooting public is that Remington produced a uniform number of each LE Classic; I have often read that 5,000 were made each year. In fact, production for each year's model varied widely, from a low of 1,479 for the 308 Winchester in 2005 (the last year of the series), to 10,779 for the 300 Weatherby Magnum in 1989 (the 9th year). This is especially significant in light of the fact that each model year always sold out, usually well before production even began. Someone at Big Green certainly must have done some careful (and accurate) market research.

Total production for all 25 years was 105,981 units. A summary of shipments by year is shown in Table 1, along with barrel lengths, twist rates and action lengths for each year's rifle. I have been told, however, that occasionally a given model may have been produced with an action

꽃 ● 꽃 ● 꽃 ● 꽃 ● 꽃 ● 꽃

The Remington Model 700's trigger is fully adjustable, and contributes greatly to the rifle's well-deserved reputation for accuracy.

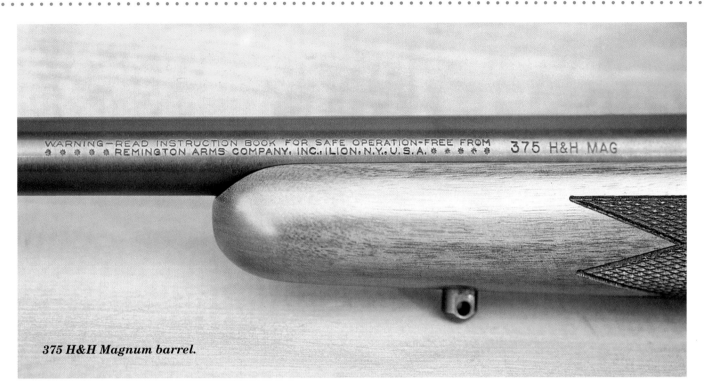

375 H&H Magnum barrel.

or barrel length other than that specified in the table. Also, confusion can ensue from the box markings. For example, the 350 Remington Magnum (1985) rifle has a 22-inch barrel. But the box end-label states that it has a 24-inch barrel. Apparently, the word "Magnum" in the caliber designation signified a 24-inch barrel to the author of the box label.

Also shown in Table 1 is the "RAMAC No." This is a unique code assigned to all Remington firearms, and is an interesting factoid in itself. The RAMAC No. has been in use at Remington for forever. Everyone there is familiar with it, but there is some disagreement as to what these letters actually stand for. The best information I could uncover is "Remington Arms Materials Authorization Code," although the "A" may stand for "Acquisition." In addition, each item had an "order no." For all of the LE Classics I have seen, this is merely the RAMAC No. preceded by a "2" (i.e., 26352 for 2004's 8x57).

The success of the LE Classics was ensured for a number of reasons, and a cult following of the series quickly developed, but it was a dichotomous assemblage. In one camp were the died-in-the-wool collectors who just had to have one of each, NIB, of course. The very thought of removing

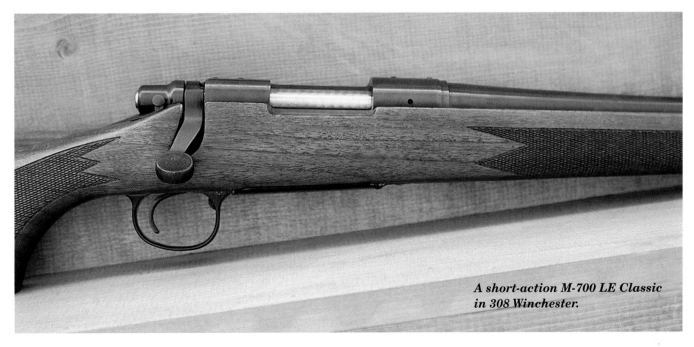

A short-action M-700 LE Classic in 308 Winchester.

an LE classic specimen from its tidy box and actually firing it was unimaginable. It just wasn't done.

Then were the "accumulators." This bunch saw the opportunity to acquire a best-quality rifle of superior design and conservative appearance in a chambering that either hadn't been offered in many years (if ever) by Remington, or after which they had lusted for decades. And what's with this "buy 'em and store 'em" policy? They figured what good is a fine piece of iron if you can't shoot it? So they bought them and had fun with them. Subsequently, if the mood so struck, accumulators had no qualms about sending an LE Classic down the road, and buying something else; probably the next year's LE Classic. Funny guys, these accumulators. (By the way, I admit to being a consumate accumulator.)

The lineage of the Model 700 goes back to the post-World War I boom and bust industrial cycle. Remington produced large numbers of 1917 Enfields for use in World War I, and

in 1921, introduced a sporterized version known as the Model 30. While a serviceable arm, the Great Depression limited sales. Around 1930, after Remington was purchased by DuPont, a fancier incarnation of the Model 30 called the Model 720 was introduced, but it was produced only until the advent of World War II.

Research and development for the 721-722 rifles began in 1942, culminating in their introduction in 1948. The new rifles had several innovative features: the stiff, round receiver, what Remington ads call the "three rings of steel" formed by the bolt, barrel, and receiver, a new type of extractor, and a new trigger mechanism. All contributed to their success, and production lasted through 1962. The 721-722s were not necessarily pretty but, as the saying goes, in function there is beauty, and the rifles certainly functioned. They also provided a solid foundation for subsequent models.

The Model 725 was a fancier bolt gun with a (then) new stock

375 H&H Magnum receiver.

concept for Remington––a Monte Carlo comb. But ever content to rest on its established laurels, the company conspicuously noted in its 1957 advertising for the M-725's introduction (in 1958) that the Model 725 had the "Same strong bolt design as famous Remington M/721-722." The M-725 was a great rifle, but production stopped in 1961.

The Model 700 was introduced in 1962, and while it incorporated many of the design features of the Models 721, 722 and 725, it was innovative and "new" in its own right. Aside from their spiffy new looks, the Model 700 rifles made their reputations on accuracy from the start. This was enhanced by the stiff, round-bottomed receiver that was easy to bed, an adjustable trigger, and a stable of neat cartridges that were themselves accurate, like the 222 Remington, which was introduced in 1950 for the short-action M-722.

The M-700 was wildly popular, due to the double wallop of the new rifle's good looks, and the simultaneous introduction of a powerful and versatile new cartridge that would become a classic in its own right – the 7mm Remington Magnum. (Interestingly, this caliber was never offered in the LE Classic.) The company carefully packaged these developments in a highly successful marketing campaign, and the new rifle was a hit. The first year alone, Remington sold more than 40,000 Model 700s – one to me, a BDL in 7mm Remington Magnum made in 1962. It was my first big-game rifle. We have shared many hunting paths. Yes, I still have it. No, it's not for sale.

The "LE" series of Classic M-700s shouldn't be confused with the regular production model called the "Classic," analogous in model hierarchy to the ADL, BDL, Mountain Rifle, etc. The regular production Classic model debuted in 1978 in seven calibers: 22-250 Remington, 243 Winchester, 6mm Remington,

270 Winchester, 280 Remington, 7mm Remington Magnum, and 30-06 Springfield. Note that of these, only the 280 was ultimately offered in the LE Classic (1997).

Aging a M-700 is a snap. Remington uses a two-letter date code on the left side of the barrel, just in front of the receiver. Reading from left to right, there are an inspector's mark, the date code, and an assembler's mark. The date code indicates the month and year that the firearm was assembled. Various components may have been made sometime before they went to production to be assembled, so the date code on an LE Classic (or any other Remington) could indicate a production date earlier or later than the release year of the gun in hand. Also, the date code is incorporated into the packer's number that appears on the box end label, which can be used to correlate the original box with its rifle. For example, "06RX" and "12/23/03" are on the box end label for a gun made in November 2002.

308 Winchester receiver.

Also, rifles were occasionally shipped before or after their official year of introduction. Here are some examples. One 7x57 rifle was shipped in 1982, as were 224 rifles in 6.5x55 Swedish Mauser in 1995. Seven 300 H&H Magnums were shipped in 1984. Three 35 Whelens were shipped from the factory in 1987, and 42 in 1989. In 1996, 346 300 Winchester Magnums were shipped. This also occurred for the 8mm Remington Magnum, of which 475 units were shipped in 1997. Five additional 375s also went out in 1997. There are probably other instances of this.

Table 2 shows the letter codes for month and year for the 25 years of the LE Classic series. Remington began this date system in 1921. The first letter is for the month, followed by the year letter. The following examples illustrate the system. My 300 H&H Magnum is coded "KD," indicating May (K) 1983 (D). My

Top: *35 Whelen barrel.*

Above: *"REP" on the right side of the barrel stands for "Remington English Proof." The mark inside the triangle to the left is the magnaflux stamp. I have no idea what the "X" to the right of the proof mark stands for.*

375 H&H Magnum is marked "WQ", for August 1996. The 35 Whelen is stamped "WI," for August 1988. The 8x57 Mauser shows "RX," which translates to November 2002 – a couple of years prior to the 2004 introduction of this unit. Other specimens I have examined include a 220 Swift with a "BM" (December 1992) code, and a 308 Winchester marked "XY" for December 2003. I even ran across an LE Classic in 221 Fireball with no inspector's mark, date code or assembler's stamp on the left side of the barrel. Lacy states that about "one in twenty rifles has a date code that is defective, missing, or otherwise illegible," but that this "is in no way indicative of a defective gun." All other barrel markings on this 221 were factory original, however.

All of the Classics (the standard and the LE series) had BDL-style hinged floor plates, and the stocks had no Monte Carlo comb, cheek piece, forend tip or grip cap. The stocks featured machine-cut checkering and a satin finish. The barrels of the Standard Classics wore BDL-style open sights, but the LE Classic barrels were usually (but not

Below: *Remington's Internal Security System (ISS) was instituted in the early 2000s, used through at least 2004, but was discontinued for the final 308 Winchester version in 2005.*

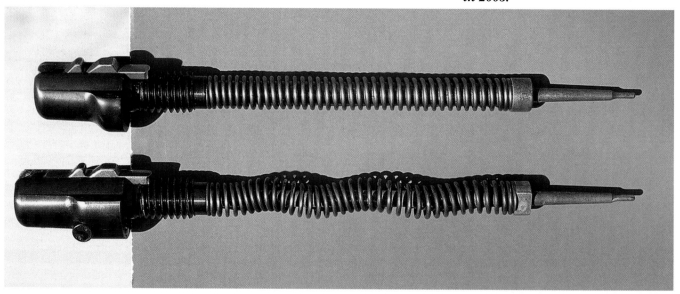

Table 1. Remington Model 700 Limited Edition Classic Production

Year Of Production	Chambering	RAMAC No.	Annual Shipments	action	Barrel Length	Twist (in.)	Cumulative Production Totals	% Of Total
1981	7mm Mauser	5758	2018	long	22	9.25	2018	1.90
1982	257 Roberts	5850	6561	long	24	10	8579	6.19
1983	300 H&H Magnum	5846	3646	long	24	10	12225	3.44
1984	250 Savage	5754	5742	short	24	10	17967	5.42
1985	350 Remington Magnum	5756	4682	short	22	16	22649	4.42
1986	264 Winchester Magnum	5898	3468	long	24	9	26117	3.27
1987	338 Winchester Magnum	5899	4792	long	24	10	30909	4.52
1988	35 Whelen	5901	8805	long	22	16	39714	8.31
1989	300 Weatherby Magnum	5903	10779	long	24	10	50493	10.17
1990	25-06 Remington	5907	6935	long	24	10	57428	6.54
1991	7mm Weatherby Magnum	5909	3092	long	24	10	60520	2.92
1992	220 Swift	5913	7594	short	24	14	68114	7.17
1993	222 Remington	5852	2021	short	24	14	70135	1.91
1994	6.5x55 Swedish Mauser	5759	3858	long	22	8	73993	3.64
1995	300 Winchester Magnum	5875	4232	long	24	10	78225	3.99
1996	375 H&H Magnum	5877	3102	long	24	12	81327	2.93
1997	280 Remington	5873	1917	long	22	9.25	83244	1.81
1998	8mm Remington Magnum	5876	2133	long	24	10	85377	2.01
1999	17 Remington	5871	3022	short	24	9	88399	2.85
2000	223 Remington	6344	3570	short	24	12	91969	3.37
2001	7mm-08 Remington	6342	2682	short	22	9.25	94651	2.53
2002	221 Remington Fireball	6348	3567	short	24	14	98218	3.37
2003	300 Savage	5869	4036	short	24	12	102254	3.81
2004	8mm Mauser	6352	2248	long	24	9.25	104502	2.12
2005	308 Winchester	6310	1479	short	24	10	105981	1.40

always) clean. The 35 Whelen and 375 H&H LEs (and perhaps others) were furnished with Remington's ramp front and brass bead, and the third generation adjustable rear sight. Nine short actions and 16 long M-700 actions were used in the LE series, depending on the caliber, and barrel lengths were either 22- or 24-inches (box markings not withstanding).

Calibers offered in the M-700 LE Classic series ran the gamut in size and application from the 17 Remington to the 375 H&H Magnum. A smart and necessary marketing adjunct for the series was ammunition availability. If Remington did not already produce a load for a year's chambering, they introduced one. An example is the 140-gr. pointed softpoint load for the 7x57, rated at 2660 fps, offered in 1981 along with the new rifle. The introduction of the entire LE

Classic line was in response to Remington's assessment of the shooting public's demand, and the calibers chosen reflect the times surrounding their introductions.

M-700 LE Classics Production History

Production data are usually difficult to come by in any industry, and this is especially true in the highly competitive gun business. A request for production figures usually results in a polite note ending with "… for competitive reasons, we cannot provide production figures …, etc." This is just business; it isn't personal.

For this project, however, that was not the case. Officials at Remington and other arms historians graciously opened their files and shared previously unpublished production data for the M-700 LE Classic series

that should gladden the hearts of collectors and shooters alike.

I wonder if, in 1981, Remington imagined what a blockbuster product the Model 700 LE Classic series would be. The annual production and especially chambering selection offer an informative look at those 25 years. Annual production varied from less than 1,500 to over 10,000 per year, and averaged about 4,239 per year, and comparing annual figures to this average offers a convenient benchmark to judge the relative popularity of each year's run.

The Early Years: 1981-1984

The LE Classic series premiered with rifles chambered to the 7x57mm Mauser, with a total of 2,018 units being shipped. As it turned out, this was one of the lowest production runs of the entire

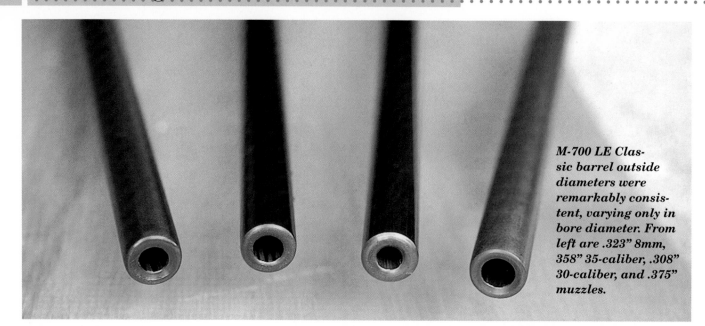

M-700 LE Classic barrel outside diameters were remarkably consistent, varying only in bore diameter. From left are .323" 8mm, 358" 35-caliber, .308" 30-caliber, and .375" muzzles.

series. Only the 280 Remington (1997), at 1,917 units, and the 308 Winchester (2005), with 1,479 rifles, had lower production.

The inaugural edition was a big hit with consumers and the Remington sales and marketing obviously took note, because the next year (1982), production of the 257 Roberts LE Classic more than tripled to 6,561 guns. It is interesting to note that all of the M-700 LE Classics were in that model year's catalog, except one – the 257 Roberts. It had to be special-ordered through the dealers. The 300 H&H Magnum followed in 1983, with 3,646 rifles, and 1984 saw the release of 5,742 neat little rifles in 250 Savage.

These early caliber selections were obviously influenced by their limited availability. Recall that the 7x57 had not been cataloged by Remington since the M-30 (1931-1940) and the 257 since the M-722 (1942-1960). The 300 H&H was only available in the M-721A Standard Grade "Magnum" in the mid-1960s. And until the 1984 LE Classic, Remington had never chambered a bolt-action rifle for the 250 Savage. Thus it is not surprising that the demand for M-700s in these heretofore popular but unavailable chamberings was substantial.

In the first four years of the program, sales of the 7x57, 257, 300 H&H, and 250 totaled 17,967 rifles. This ultimately amounted to about 17 percent of the series' production, and collectors and accumulators alike promptly gobbled them up.

The Bigger Bores: 1985-1989

After this initial flurry, production stayed up and bigger calibers were offered, some in considerable numbers. From 1985 through 1989, every cartridge selected was 30-caliber or larger. The 350 Remington Magnum, a holdover from the M-600 (1965-1968) and M-660 (1968-1971) magnum rifles, checked in 1985 with 4,682 units. I had one and not only did it shoot extremely well, but it also had a highly figured stock; I sold it in a moment of weakness.

Production dropped in 1986 to 3,468 rifles in 264 Winchester Magnum, but was right back up the following year with 4,792 guns chambered for the 338 Winchester Magnum. The big-bore trend continued in 1988 with the release of 8,805 rifles in 35 Whelen. But 1989 saw the largest production of any of the 25 years with a whopping 10,779 LE Classics in 300 Weatherby Magnum. I took a nice cow elk with mine. It, too, went down accumulator road. These four calibers amounted to 23,721 units, another 22 percent of total production.

The Medium Bores: 1990-1993

Things simmered down a little after that. In 1990, the 25-06, a popular wildcat legitimized by Remington in 1969, was released with 6,935 guns. A year later, the 7mm Weatherby Magnum appeared, but production dropped to 3,092 units. (Considering the tremendous popularity of Remington's Big 7, why the Weatherby round was chosen is a mystery.) Of course, Remington introduced 7mm Weatherby Magnum ammunition to feed the 1991 edition.

Addressing the needs of varmint hunters, the next two chamberings were 22s – the long and short of it, so to speak. In 1992, the ever-popular and much-maligned 220 Swift appeared with 7,594 sporter-weight rifles that made a lot of groundhogs very nervous.

The 222 Remington followed in 1993 with 2,021 guns. With its reputation for outstanding accuracy, and its long history in the M-722, why production was relatively low for this gem of a cartridge is anybody's guess. At any rate, it was the last of the "little" guns for a while, and these two 22s amounted to only nine percent of the total.

A Potpourri: 1994-2000

Five more "big game" calibers emerged next. A true European

classic, the 6.5x55 Swedish Mauser, was 1994's entry, and production was substantial at 3,858 rifles. Next up was everyone's favorite big-30, the 300 Winchester Magnum, with 4,232 guns. In 1996, the largest caliber of the series was produced – the perennial all-world 375 H&H Magnum, but with a production of only 3,102 guns. These 375 rifles were real gems, and mine shoots like an '06. All of the LE Classics had basically the same barrel configurations, and this makes a pretty slim barrel in a 375. But the combination of aesthetics, accuracy, power and versatility is worth a little recoil.

Production was down the next two years. In 1997, Remington's 1957 creation, the 280, checked in with a mere 1,917 units, the second lowest production of the series. The 1998 edition was one of Remington's best – but least popular – rounds, the 8mm Remington Magnum. The company must have reviewed the sales figures for the M-700 BDL from 1978 to 1985 for that caliber, because only 2,133 LE Classics so chambered hit the street. These latest five calibers amounted to another 14 percent of the total.

With a bevy of big-bores under its belt, the folks at Ilion went back to rat guns. In 1999, the 17 Remington appeared with a modest

All of the pertinent information for each year's LE Classic was provided on the box end label. In addition to the caliber, barrel length, shipping date, and serial number, the packer's code (06RX) can be used to ensure that this box is for the gun in question. Note that the "order no." is the RAMAC number with a "2" in front of it.

Table 2. Date Codes For Remington Model 700 Limited Edition Classic Rifles, 1981 to 2005.

Year Code

1981 – B	1987 – H	1993 – N	1999 – T
1982 – C	1988 – I	1994 – O	2000 – U
1983 – D	1989 – J	1995 – P	2001 – W
1984 – E	1990 – K	1996 – Q	2002 – X
1985 – F	1991 – L	1997 – R	2003 – Y
1986 – G	1992 – M	1998 – S	2004 – Z
			2005 – A

Month Code

(The acronym for months is "BLACKPOWDERX.")

Jan. – B	May – K	Sept. – D
Feb. – L	June – P	Oct. – E
Mar. – A	July – O	Nov. – R
Apr. – C	Aug. – W	Dec. - X

Note: A complete listing of Remington's date code from 1921 to 2005 can be found in the *Blue Book of Gun Values*, page 1893.

production of 3,022 units. This was followed in 2000 by 3,570 guns in 223 Remington, surely the most popular varmint round around, then and now, but these two calibers rounds amounted to only about six percent of the total production.

The Final Five: 2001-2005

The last half-decade of the series offered something for everyone. The 2001 version was chambered to the

relatively new but popular 7mm-08 Remington, with 2,682 units. Next up was a run of 3,567 rifles in 221 Fireball, a terrific rifle cartridge that was almost never chambered in rifles by any company. It is a bit baffling to note there were about as many 221s made as there were 223s, and a lot more 221s produced than 222s.

A run of 4,036 rifles in 300 Savage graced store shelves in 2002. Note that this was only slightly lower production than the super-popular 300 Winchester Magnum. The second 8mm round of the series appeared in 2004 with the 8x57mm Mauser. While it's a terrific cartridge, only 2,248 8x57s were produced.

What better cartridge to close out the series with than the 308 Winchester? Something tells me that Remington had made the decision to pull the plug sometime before 2005, since production of 308s was only 1,479 units, the lowest of the entire quarter-century period.

The End of an Era

In 2005, an era of gun-making history was over, and the demise of Remington's M-700 LE Classics marks a pivotal point in rifle history. Numerous product lines from various companies have offered this or that in the way of models and calibers, but none has embodied the continuity and diversity of the LE Classics. None has been of such a long duration or has occupied the American shooter's psyche as has this series.

The entire program was a unique and highly successful marketing concept. It provided consumers with unique, high quality rifles with similar configurations and in a wide variety of calibers to shoot,

The end of the line. Adam Gariglietti of John's Sport Center shows the author the final Model 700 LE Classic in 308 Winchester.

collect, hunt with and generally enjoy. Such an opportunity may never pass our way again.

Postscript

Both collectors and accumulators may take heart. In 2006, Remington started a new "limited" series by offering a Model 700 Limited-Edition Model CDL SF (stainless fluted) to honor "the 100-year of the 30-06 Springfield." In October 2006, the company announced the second offering of the Limited Edition Model 700 CDL SF, chambered in the new 17 Remington Fireball.

PART II

THE REMINGTON
MODEL 700
LIMITED EDITION CLASSIC

by Steve Gash

The 25 cartridges shown throughout this feature represent a comprehensive legacy of firearms history, and are a tribute to the diverse desire of the American shooter – and Remington's response to it.

Cartridge Chronology

The Remington M-700 LE Classic calibers ran the gamut in size and application from tiny (17 Remington) to tremendous (375 H&H Magnum). The introduction of the LE Classic series was in response to dynamic public demand through dealer feedback, and the chamberings chosen reflect the context of the times surrounding their introductions. Since I have owned and/or shot many of the LE Classics, I cannot resist sharing my favorite handloads for those rifles, as well.

1981 – 7mm Mauser

If you're going to do a "classic" rifle anything, what better cartridge to start with than the 7x57mm Mauser? The brainchild of Mauser in 1892, it has proven itself around the world on all sizes of game for decades. The cartridge was actually discontinued in the 1940s due to a lack of popularity! This was merely a temporary perturbation, of course. Although that year's Classic was not widely publicized, the combo was very well received by the shooting public. As a medium-game cartridge, it has few peers. Favorite handload: The 145-gr. Speer BT over 46 gr. of IMR-4350 for 2515 fps.

1982 – 257 Roberts

Another old-timer, the 257 Roberts arrived in 1934 in the Remington Model 30 bolt action. While a terrific medium-game cartridge, it now barely hangs on, although +P ammunition is available for it from a couple of companies. The ability to use 110- to 120-grain bullets helps the "Bob." Favorite handload: 38 gr. of IMR-4350 with the 115-gr. Nosler Partition bullet at 2657 fps.

1983 – 300 Holland & Holland Magnum

Like a spoiled child, the 300 H&H is, and always will be, dear to my heart. It was introduced in 1925. As a youngster, the elders of my clan regaled me with tales of their hunting exploits, not coincidentally centered on the 300 H&H which was reputed to flatten anything that walked. So when I heard that Remington's LE Classic for the year was to be this round, I ordered one immediately. I have hunted extensively with it, and have taken more mule deer and elk with this rifle than all other rifles combined. Favorite handload: The old reliable Speer 180-gr. SP over 69 gr. of IMR-4831. Velocity is 2935.

1984 – 250 Savage

Charles Newton designed the 250 in 1914 or 1915, depending on whom you read. And it was quite a stir in its day. It was originally called the "250-3000," because Savage wanted it to produce 3000 fps for marketing purposes. The bullet was lightened to 87 grains, and the goal was achieved. But eventually, the shooting public (and ammo companies) came back around to Mr. Newton's original 100-grain bullet at around 2800 fps. The 250 is a great deer and antelope round: accurate, powerful, flat-shooting, and with mild recoil. With the super bullets of today, the little 250 is more versatile than ever. Now if one could only buy a rifle chambered for it. Favorite handload: Barnes 100-gr. Triple Shock-X bullet with 35 gr. of N-150 for 2797 fps.

1985 – 350 Remington Magnum

The 350 Remington Magnum debuted in the M-600 Magnum

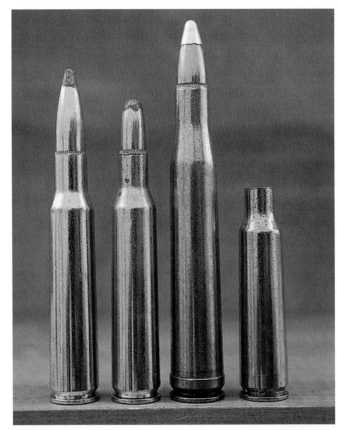

The Early Years, 1981-1983 (from left): 7x57 Mauser, 257 Roberts, 300 H&H Magnum and 250 Savage.

in 1965, and later in the M-660 Magnum, but neither was a big hit. That's too bad, because the cartridge produces ballistics all out of proportion to its short and fat "fireplug" appearance. While the 350 has been derided as a "short range" cartridge, a glance at the trajectory and energy figures indicates otherwise. It's a medium-range elk round, for sure. Favorite handload: The 225-gr. Sierra SBT launched by 58 gr. of IMR-4320. Velocity is 2491 fps.

1986 – 264 Winchester Magnum

The ill-fated 264 Winchester Magnum saw the light of day in 1958, but before it could gain a foothold, the 7mm Remington Magnum arrived in 1962, and trounced it. The 264 earned a reputation for considerable recoil (deserved) and as a barrel-burner (undeserved) in short order. But the die was cast, and Winchester's 6.5mm scream turned into a whimper as it lost favor with the shooting public. That's a shame, because it's a powerful, flat-shooting round.

1987 - 338 Winchester Magnum

Also announced in 1958 (along with the 264), the 338 Winchester Magnum quickly earned a well-deserved reputation as an elk and moose powerhouse. Many think that it takes over where the 30-caliber magnums leave off, and with good reason. Originally loaded with 200-grain Power Point and 250-gr. Silvertip bullets, a 300-grain Power Point was listed as early as 1962, and the 338 is a mainstay of American big-game hunting. Favorite handload: The 210-gr. Nosler Partition loaded over 77 gr. of Re-19 produces an honest 2949 fps and lots of bone-crunching power.

1988 - 35 Whelen

Col. Townsend Whelen was Jack O'Conner's favorite gun writer, and in 1922 the Colonel, in consort with James Howe, of the famous gun-making firm of Griffin & Howe, designed the 35-caliber cartridge that carries his name. Remington legitimized it in 1987. This fine cartridge is useful any place where deer and larger game are hunted. With proper bullet selection, the 35 Whelen can accommodate almost any species. Favorite handloads: The 225-gr. Sierra SBT and 52 gr. of 2015BR gives 2599 fps and a reasonably flat trajectory for long-range shooting. The 220-gr. Speer FP with 54 gr. of H-4895 at 2415 fps is the best deer load I have ever used.

1989 - 300 Weatherby Magnum

Roy Weatherby's most popular magnum must have made an impression on someone at Big Green, because when they decided to offer it in the LE Classic, they did it in a big way (10,779 guns). Weatherby developed the round in 1944, and for almost any game, it's tough to beat. Like most gun accumulators, I had one and sold it, but before I did, I plugged a fat cow elk with it. Needless to say, it did the job. Favorite handload: Speer's 200- SP over 75 gr. of IMR-7828 for a velocity of 2751 fps.

1990 - 25-06 Remington

Everybody's favorite 25-caliber was developed in the 1920s by A. O. Niedner, and Remington made it a factory cartridge in 1969. At its inception, the 25-06 had rough going because powders slow enough to make it work were not available. But along came Bruce

Hodgdon, World War II, surplus H-4831, and the 26-06 never looked back. While occasionally used for varmints, it is best applied to deer and antelope. Favorite handload: Try the 120-gr. Speer BT over 52.0 gr. of XMR-3100 for about 2940 fps for deer and antelope.

1991 – 7mm Weatherby Magnum

Roy Weatherby's second shortened magnum was introduced in 1944, a year after the 270 Weatherby. While never as popular as the Remington's own 7mm Magnum, its availability in the M-700 LE Classic helped, as did Remington's factory ammo introduced along with the rifle. The round offers plenty of power and a flat trajectory. Norma in Sweden loads Weatherby's factory ammo. The ability to use bullets up to 175 grains helps the versatility of the cartridge.

1992 – 220 Swift

In 1935, Winchester brought out the new Model 54 bolt action and offered it in the also new 220 Swift. The cartridge was aptly named, as it propelled a 48-grain bullet at the then-astronomical velocity of over 4000 fps. This load was simultaneously extolled and derided. Varmint hunters loved it and the nimrods that used it on deer didn't – never mind that neither Winchester nor the gun writers of the day recommended it for deer. Nowadays, most folks use 55-grain or heavier bullets at more modest velocities but with better down-range ballistics. Favorite handloads: For varmints, I use 55-gr. Sierra HPBTs over 33.5 gr. of H-4895 at 3359 fps, and the 50-gr. Sierra SP with 12.0 gr. of H-4227 at 1850 fps is a terrific turkey load.

1993 – 222 Remington

The great little 222 was introduced in 1950 along with the then-new M-722 (along with the M-721 and 700). The "deuce" was an instant hit, and dare I say, the average 222 still will outshoot the average 223. The 222 ruled the roost at benchrest matches until the advent of the PPC cartridges. Field & Stream's Warren Page was a big proponent of the 222. Essentially a 200-yard varmint cartridge, the 222 was a very popular deer cartridge in Texas until the advent of the 223. Favorite handload: Any good 50- to 53-gr. bullet works. Try the 52-gr. Nosler Ballistic Tip over 24.6 gr. of W-748 for 3049 fps.

1994 - 6.5x55mm Swedish Mauser

This fine old cartridge is a favorite in Europe because it is accurate, and fills Finnish freezers with moose meat with boring regularity. It is at least moderately popular in this country, and is a great deer and sheep round, as it can handle long, heavy bullets with its 8-inch twist. Favorite handload: The Sierra 140-gr. SBT propelled by 42.5-gr. of IMR-4350 at 2550 fps has taken many Missouri white-tails.

1995 – 300 Winchester Magnum

While fans of the 300 magnums from H&H and Weatherby hold their own court, Winchester's big 300 became popular from its introduction in 1963. Based on a lengthened "short magnum" case, the 300 WM stuffed a lot of power in a standard length action. With the tremendous selection of 30-caliber bullets, it is suitable for everything from deer to moose. Favorite handload: The 180-gr. Speer Grand Slam over 72.0 gr. of Reloder 22 at 2948 fps.

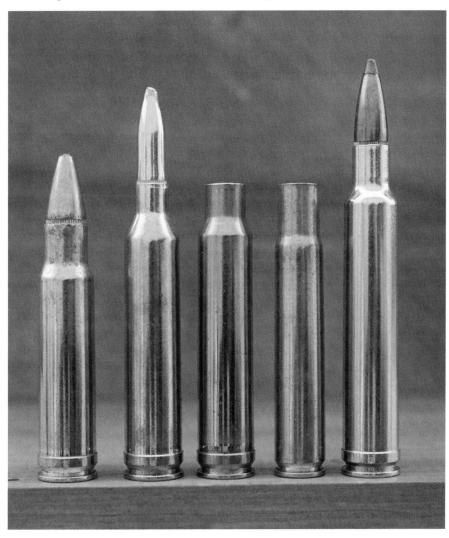

The Bigger Bores, 1984-1989 (from left): *350 Remington Magnum, 264 and 338 Winchester Magnums, 35 Whelen and 300 Weatherby Magnum.*

1996 - 375 H&H Magnum

John Taylor, in African Rifles and Cartridges (1948), states that the 375 H&H is "Undoubtedly one of the deadliest weapons in existence." What is left to be said about the most useful cartridge ever developed? Since its introduction in 1912, it has covered the world. Every serious rifleman should have (at least) one 375. My LE Classic is one of the more accurate 375s I have ever shot, and the recoil is not bad. Favorite handload: The 235-gr. Speer Semi-Spitzer over 80.0 gr. of H-205 gives 2491 fps, and is a great load for mule deer and elk.

1997 - 280 Remington

After a couple of fits and starts with its name, the 280 Remington has carved out a small but dedicated cult following. When it was introduced in 1957, to those trying to decide between the 270 Winchester or the 30-06, it seemed like the ideal compromise. Then, just five years later, the 7mm Remington Magnum was born, and potential 280 buyers were sandbagged. Why buy an '06-based 7mm when you could have a 7mm magnum? Nonetheless, the 280 is a fine round, and has a good reputation in the game fields.

1998 - 8mm Remington Magnum

Introduced in 1978 for the M-700 BDL, this is the first of only two 8mm rounds offered by the company in recent times. The M-700 BDL was never widely popular, and it was quietly dropped in 1985. Based on the full-length belted magnum case, the 8mm RM provides plenty of power – at both ends. Favorite handload: The 195-gr. Hornady InterLock SP over 84.0 gr. of Reloder 25 at 2936 fps consistently groups under 0.76-inch.

1999 - 17 Remington

The 17 Remington was introduced in 1971, and is based on the ubiquitous 223 Remington. It is the smallest bore-diameter centerfire ever offered by the company. Strictly a varmint round, it is both praised and cussed by legions – most of whom have never fired one. It is described as explosive and wind-sensitive. The 24-inch barrel of the LE Classic wrings optimum performance out of this one.

2000 - 223 Remington

Remington scored a landslide hit with their entry in the military cartridge sweepstakes in 1957, so the inclusion of the 223 in the LE Classic series was perhaps a foregone conclusion. The fact that it pretty much doomed the 222 Remington and 222 Remington Magnum pains many, but there is no denying the 223's tremendous popularity, as millions of prairie dogs will attest. It is versatile, accurate, and about as common as the 30-06 on ammo shelves across the fruited plain. Favorite handload: While 55-grain bullets are pretty much the standard for the 223, the Hornady 40-gr. V-MAX over 27.5 gr. of Benchmark gives 3496 fps, and is a varmint vaporizer.

2001 - 7mm-08 Remington

Necking military cartridges up and down has been popular sport for decades, and some real gems have been created. One is the 7mm-08 Remington. Based on the 308 Winchester case, it was introduced in 1980, and is pretty much a carbon copy of the 7mm-308 developed in the 1950s. The round pretty much embodies the ballistic attributes of the famous 7x57 Mauser, which is saying a lot.

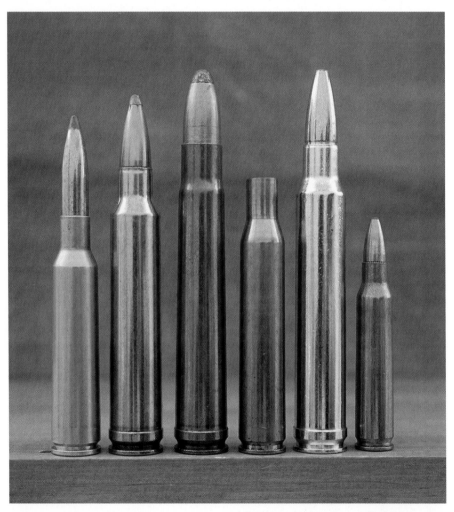

A Potpourri, 1994-2000 (from left): 6.5x55 Swedish Mauser, 300 Winchester Magnum, 375 H&H Magnum, 280 Remington, 8mm Remington Magnum and 17 Remington.

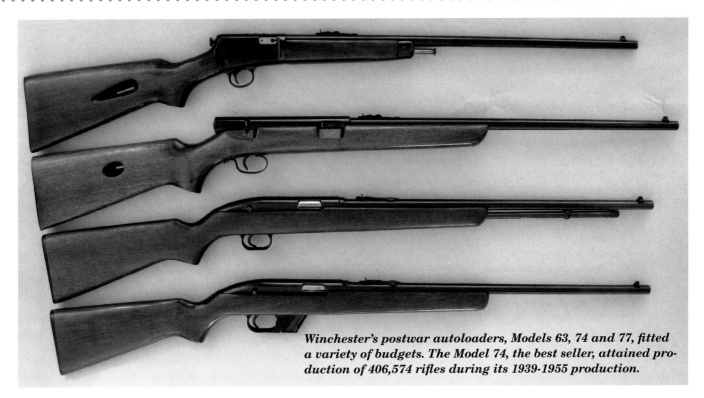

Winchester's postwar autoloaders, Models 63, 74 and 77, fitted a variety of budgets. The Model 74, the best seller, attained production of 406,574 rifles during its 1939-1955 production.

sporter rifles sold in satisfactory quantities until discontinued in 1958. A total of about 88,715 serial-numbered rifles were produced.

The Autoloading Rifles

Winchester's first 22 autoloading rifle, and first 22 autoloader ever, was the Model 1903 (1903-1932). The Model 1903 was another of Thomas C. Johnson's seminal designs for Winchester. With minor modifications, the Model 1903 became the Model 63 in 1932. The Model 63 is a fine rifle, but was relatively expensive. Winchester later recognized this and introduced the Model 74 in 1939. The Model 74 in turn became too expensive for the postwar market and was replaced by the Model 77 in 1955. Postwar production thus includes Models 63, 74 and 77. None of these survived 1963. While Winchester's 22 autoloading rifles served a range of budgets, the Model 63 was always the top of the line.

The Model 63 is a direct descendent of Winchester's first autoloading rifle, the Model 1903. Both rifles are of the balanced blowback design that utilizes a weight of metal in the forend to counterbalance the thrust of the fired cartridge. Winchester used this design in its centerfire rifles Models 1905, 1907 and 1910. The Model 63 is balanced to function reliably only with high-velocity 22 Long Rifle cartridges. The initial production rifles had the 20-inch barrel of the Model 1903 but a heavier pistol grip buttstock replaced the straight grip stock of its parent.

The new rifle was given by a scathing review in the September 1933 issue of the *American Rifleman*. F. C. Ness found the Model 63 *"...evidently designed as a handy knock-about arm for plinking and small game ..."* However, the rifle was *"...handicapped by the short forestock (only 11 inches from tip to trigger) and short barrel, which leaves the gun pronouncedly butt-heavy. It does not have the quality commonly referred to as balance."* In extensive testing of 22 Long Rifle ammunitions, the rifle proved unreliable with Winchester's own high-speed *Staynless* cartridges as well as several other ammunitions. Western *Super-X* and certain Remington and Federal loads worked well. Ness recommended a 24-inch barrel, four-inch longer forend and improvements in feeding of cartridges before it would be suitable for *"...game shooting*

beyond 40 yards...". His best groups ran about 1.6 inches at 50 yards using a Lyman tang sight. Ness concluded that *"...the Model 63 is accurate."*

The barrel length of the Model 63 was extended to 23 inches in 1934 and the 20-inch barrel was discontinued in 1936. The forend tip remained 11 inches from the trigger. The rifle is still butt-heavy and weighs about 5.5 pounds.

The Model 63 is loaded by inserting 10 cartridges through a port on the right side of the buttstock. The port is exposed by retracting the magazine tube through the butt plate. Pushing the magazine tube forward and latching it with a one-eighth turn provides spring tension on the follower and column of cartridges. The action is cycled by *"pushing quickly back"* the operating sleeve at the front of the forend. The rifle takes down into two pieces by unscrewing and pressing down the prominent screw lock at the rear of the receiver. The crossbolt safety is at the rear of the trigger guard.

The 1938 Winchester Sales Manual states: *"This is unquestionably the most popular 22 automatic rifle on the market today and fills the need of a high grade plinking or a small* game gun." The only "high grade" competition was the Remington Speedmaster Model 241 (1935-1949); both rifles are coincidentally priced at $40.15 in the 1944 GUN DIGEST.

People who have used the Model 63 mostly agree that it is the finest Winchester 22 rifle of its period. Unfortunately, collectors have pushed the prices of these rifles well beyond the reach of shooters. I am glad I got my Model 63 in 1965 for $70, a high price even then. Total production from 1933 to 1958 was about 174,000 rifles. The Model 63 is serial numbered on the lower receiver.

The Model 74 was introduced in 1939. Winchester's objective was to produce a medium-priced high quality self-loading rifle with a simple blowback design. The April issue of the *American Rifleman* announced, *"It is, wisely, made for the cheap little 22 Short cartridge, of which it holds 20 at one loading. There is also a Galley Special model which holds 15 cartridges."* It is my guess that Winchester put emphasis on sale to the popular shooting galleries with the economical Model 74. Both open and peep sights were available at $16.85 or $17.65, respectively. The retail price of the Model 63 in 1939 was $32.95, making the Model 74 much more affordable. *The American Rifleman* staff concluded, *"Sample very neat and trim, handles fine."* The barrel length was 24 inches and the rifle weighed a hefty 6.25 pounds. The 22 Long Rifle version was added in 1940 and held 14 cartridges. The barrel length was 22 inches for both chamberings after the war and the 22 Short rifles were discontinued in 1952.

The Model 74 is an interesting design built around a simple blowback action. In this case a rather heavy cylindrical bolt assembly provides the counterbalancing weight of metal. Unlike the Model 63, the Model 74 handles standard or high-velocity cartridges interchangeably. The magazine is similar to that of the Model 63, having a magazine tube inserted through the buttplate with a loading port in the right side of the buttstock. The action is cycled by a

lever on the right side of the action. The unique safety is a horizontally operating sliding bar at the top rear of the action. Removal of the bolt assembly is easily accomplished for cleaning by pressing a slotted bolt-stop cross plug from left to right at the rear of the receiver. This frees the bolt for removal from the rear. The Model 74 is a solid piece of engineering in my opinion.

The Model 74 is a relatively large and heavy 22 rifle due to its long receiver, substantial bolt and full-size stock with semi-beavertail forend. I have shot my 22 Long Rifle version, with a period Weaver B6 scope (fitted with Weaver "N" mount), enough to know it will produce one-inch 10-shot groups at 50 yards. That is as good as any of the non-target 22 rifles I have. All considered, the Model 74 is an excellent rifle. J. B. Wood agrees. He states in his book *Disassembly of Rimfire Rifles*, "The Model 74 was a simple and reliable gun." Edward Tolosky, in his *Exploded Views* in the July 1984 *American Rifleman*, states that the Model 74 continued *"...meeting the high level of quality associated with Winchester products during the early '50s."*

I have not been able to find a stated reason for discontinuing the Model 74 in 1955. By this date, both the Models 74 and 63 were priced relatively high compared to the market at $39.20 and $70.10, respectively. The probable reason for discontinuing the Model 74 was that a less expensive 22 autoloader was needed to meet the competition. The Model 74 rifles are serial numbered on the left side of the receiver. According to Watrous, *"The M/74 rifles had a very large sale, about 406,574 were made."* The Model 74 was replaced by the Model 77 series of autoloaders.

The first Model 77s with 8-shot box or 15-shot tube magazines (beneath the barrel) versions were shipped to Winchester distributors in mid-1955. The *American Rifleman* reviewed the new autoloader in the May 1955 issue: *"Intended for the low priced field, it sells for 29.95 in clip* [box] *magazine form and 34.95 with tubular magazine."* Both rifles

have 22-inch barrels and weigh about 5.5 pounds. The Model 77 functions with standard and high-velocity 22 Long Rifle cartridges. All Model 77s have grooved receivers for scope mounting. The staff reviewer found *"The appearance of this rifle is different than any other on the market. Machining and finish are much above average for an inexpensive arm..."*. The reviewer also noted the absence of sheet-metal stampings among the interior parts. Winchester obviously was not yet ready to embrace the savings of stamped parts seen in the market during the 1950s. Their one visible savings concession is the molded nylon trigger guards. The trigger guard in that version retains the box magazine. The reviewer noted that removal of the magazine was *"...not easy to the unpracticed."* Concluding, *"The Model 77 proved very easy to shoot and very accurate in its class."*

The design of the Model 77 was unconventional in many respects. The operating knob is on the left side of the action forward of the receiver. The blowback action has no bolt hold-open device and single-shot loading was *"impossible"* through the small ejection port. The *American Rifleman* reviewer felt these two shortcomings rendered the rifle unsuitable for good range practices or for junior shooters. However, properly cleaning the rifle posed the greatest problem. The barreled action is simply held to the stock by two guard screws. But further removal of the bolt can only be accomplished by removing the pinned barrel. The bolt, striker, slide and strong spring are then eased out the front of the receiver. This disassembly was *"...found by experience to be highly inadvisable."* by the reviewer. Be forewarned if you want to take your Model 77 apart.

The Model 77 rifles, regardless of magazine type, are numbered from 1001 up. The box and tube-magazine rifles were discontinued in 1962 and 1963, respectively. Total production of both rifles was about 217,180 rifles.

The Model 77 is one of the best handling Winchester 22s. The tube magazine version avoids any problems with fit of the box magazine (mine works easily) and is better balanced in my hands. My Model 77 with box magazine has a small vertical plunger on the right forward end of the receiver at the base of the barrel. Retracting the bolt and manually depressing the plunger holds the bolt open. This rifle also has no serial number. My tube-magazine rifle, serial number 69,XXX, does not have this feature. I have seen this feature on other Model 77 rifles but did not note their serial numbers. I have not found reference to this feature in any of my literature.

The Slide-Action Rifles

Winchester produced two slide-action 22 rifles during the postwar through 1963 period. Both were initiated in the 1930s Olin family resurrection of Winchester. The Model 62 was an example of updating an existing model while the Model 61 was yet another new design by staff led by Thomas C. Johnson. Both rifles were popular but their manufacture was too expensive to survive Winchester's redirection in 1963.

Ned Schwing in his book *"Winchester Slide-Action Rifles"* states: *"When the Model 61 and 62 were introduced in 1932, Winchester had already sold approximately 1,500,000 slide-action 22 caliber rifles."* Winchester already had in excellent reputation for its Models

1890 (1890-1932) and 1906 (1906-1932). Winchester advertised the Model 62 as an improved version of these two models. Watrous indicates that Winchester revised the new model *"…using essentially the same action but with several modern features."* In John Browning's basic design, rearward movement of the slide cams the breech bolt up and out of locking cuts in the receiver walls. The carrier holds the cartridge and guides it directly into the chamber on the closing stroke. This controlled round feeding works regardless of rifle orientation. Other features include the shotgun-style buttstock of the Model 1906, a round 23-inch barrel (Models 1890 and 1906 had 24 and 20-inch barrels, respectively), increased magazine capacity and retained the Model 1906's ability to use Short, Long and Long Rifle cartridges interchangeably. A prewar gallery model uses shorts only. The Model 62 was revised to the Model 62A in 1940 beginning at serial number 99,200.

The Models 62 and 62A differ primarily in their mainsprings. The Model 62 uses a leaf mainspring and has four screws in the lower tang. The Model 62 with an "A" postscript uses a coil mainspring and has one screw in the lower tang. The Model 62 of 1946 has a larger slide handle than the prewar versions. The newer handle has 17 grooves. The postwar buttstock has a more rounded comb

and length of pull increased to 13.38 inches. The diameter of the slide was reduced slightly in 1947 and given a flat bottom semi-beavertail shape in 1948. The Model 62 weighs a well-balanced 5.5 pounds. Model 62 rifles separate into two pieces by loosening the large takedown screw at the rear left side of the receiver, a design feature of all Winchester slide-action 22 rifles. The price of the Model 62 in 1946 was $37.50 compared to the hammerless Model 61 at $44.50. The Model 61 always sold at greater price than the Model 62.

The Model 62 was discontinued in 1958. These rifles are serial-numbered on the lower tang and bottom of the receiver. Approximately 409,475 Model 62 rifles were produced. Schwing provides a list of serial numbers by year for the Models 61 and 62.

As a postscript, writing in the March 1997 *American Rifleman*, Pete Dickey notes in his review of the Rossi Model 62 SAC that more than a half-million Rossi 62s were produced from 1969 to 1995. I recently bought the current Taurus version of the 62 for plinking. That 1890 Browning design just keeps going!

The Model 61 was Winchester's innovative new model slide-action 22. It was very late entering a market dominated by Remington and Savage hammerless slide-action rifles. The delay was a result of efforts to avoid infringing on John Browning's 1922

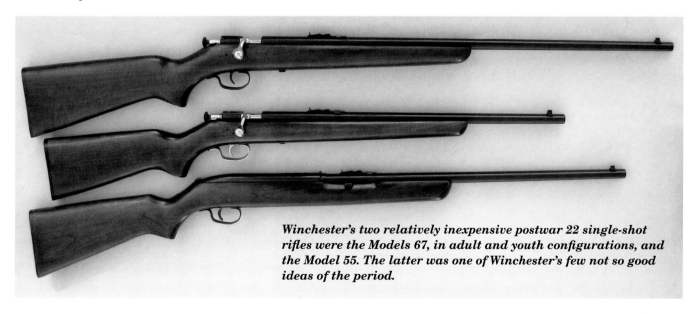

Winchester's two relatively inexpensive postwar 22 single-shot rifles were the Models 67, in adult and youth configurations, and the Model 55. The latter was one of Winchester's few not so good ideas of the period.

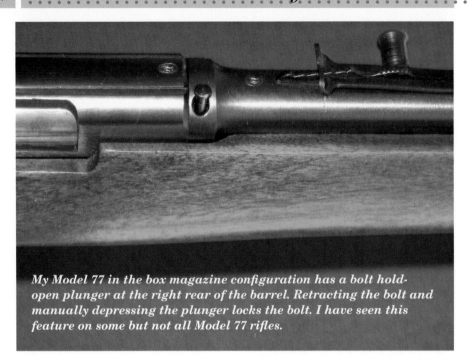

My Model 77 in the box magazine configuration has a bolt hold-open plunger at the right rear of the barrel. Retracting the bolt and manually depressing the plunger locks the bolt. I have seen this feature on some but not all Model 77 rifles.

patents for his "Trombone" 22 made by FN in Belgium. Winchester's first class design staff surmounted the turmoil of the 1920s and introduced the Model 61 in 1932 as a new hammerless repeater "...to kindle the enthusiasm of all lovers of great guns." The new rifle "...notably resembles in general design the Winchester Model 12...". The Model 61 was built to high standards using the best materials and was priced accordingly throughout its production. It was available in more variations than its stable mate, the Model 62. Prewar Model 61 rifles were available with octagon barrels, smoothbores, 22 WRF, 22 Long Rifle only and 22 Short only chamberings and drilled for tang peep sights. Prewar rifles are serial-numbered to approximately 68,775.

F. C. Ness reviewed the Model 61 in the September 1931 issue of the *American Rifleman*. The sample rifle, 22-caliber, had a 24-inch octagon barrel and weighed 6 pounds. Ness installed a Lyman tang sight on the predrilled tang. Groups from the bench ran 1.0 to 1.62 inches at 50 yards. Ness stated: *"This gun is accurate enough to justify a scope."* Ness concluded: *"Its accuracy adapts it for small-game shooting at longer ranges, and its speed of fire adapts it for work on running game at*

shorter ranges." The rifle handled all lengths and brands of 22 cartridges interchangeably without malfunction. His only complaint: *"The stock should be 0.5 inch greater in length."* That, in those days, was a good review.

The postwar Model 61 retained the 24-inch round barrel of the earlier versions. Octagon barrels were no longer available. However, postwar runs of the WRF, Short or Long Rifle only chambers occurred until 1950. Smoothbores were made in low numbers between 1952-1956. The 22 Magnum chambering was made available 1960-1963. Postwar buttstocks have more rounded combs and lengths of pull of 13.5 inches. Drop at comb and heel experienced some variation in the late 1950s. Steel buttplates were used from 1932 to 1957. Postwar forends are all 8.38 inches long with 17 grooves. Smaller and larger diameter versions are interspersed in the late 1940s to early 1950s. The larger diameter forend with blunt profile was the choice in late production. All Model 61 stocks are lacquer finished.

The Model 61 locks up just like the Model 12 shotgun. A rear shoulder on the breechbolt is cammed into a fitted recess in the top of the receiver. Feeding of cartridges was unique. J. B. Wood in his book *Firearms Assembly/Disassembly Part III:*

Rimfire Rifles states: *"The Model 61 had a virtually infallible feed system, with the cartridge firmly guided up a T-slot in the bolt face from the moment of leaving the magazine."* I note that Winchester adopted this feed system for its finest post-64 sporting 22 rifle, the Model 9422. According to Wood in *Trouble Shooting Your Rifle and Shotgun* the Model 61 is a *"...fine little rifle with few chronic ailments."* His lament: *"The main problem today is finding one."*

Conclusion

I was a teenager growing up in rural New Hampshire during much of the 1950s. I well remember Winchester's colorful ads in outdoor magazines of the period. The Model 62 "hammer pump" was my dream rifle. Most of my hunting then was in search of crows and woodchucks in farmer's fields. Plinking was a year-round activity. My father gave me a Marlin Model 81 bolt-action repeater before I was 10 years old—a big deal because we were very poor. The Marlin lasted until I had an income of my own. The only 22 rifles I collected thereafter were the Winchester 22s presented in this article. I hunted with some, plinked with all and meticulously preserved them – such was the power of Winchester's advertising in those days.

My favorite Winchester 22 rifle of the postwar pre-64 22 rifles is the Model 61. I have been a slide-action shotgun shooter for 50 years—certainly a factor in choosing the Model 61. However, the Model 61 is a beautifully designed and manufactured rifle. It is utterly reliable, accurate, and handles as nicely as any of my 22 rifles. For many years I had a scoped Model 61 (grooved receiver) in 22 WRM that shot consistent five-shot 1.5-inch groups at 100 yards. My Long Rifle version will do that at 50 yards with open sights. It is my opinion that the Model 61 is the finest of the pre-64 Winchester 22 sporting rifles for plinking and small game hunting at open sight ranges. Somebody bring out a well-made clone, please!

CHARTER ARMS
'UNDERCOVERETTE' IN 32 H&R MAGNUM

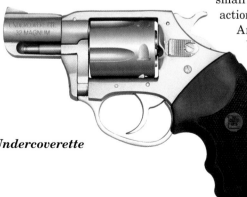

by Dave Workman

Possibly an underrated cartridge in terms of its ability to stop game and maybe a two-legged predator is the 32 H&R Magnum, a round that was developed years ago by Harrington & Richardson as an alternative to the 38 Special.

I think there were so few snubbie H&R revolvers built for this cartridge that they're kind of rare, though I doubt one could consider them collectors' items. They were inexpensive but pretty well built, and sadly they just never caught fire with consumers.

Enter the 32 H&R Magnum Undercoverette double-action revolver from Charter Arms. With its 2-inch barrel, the velocity might drop a bit from what one experiences with

a 4.5-inch tube, but you still don't want to be on the business end of this little wheelgun when it goes off.

In my experience, the 32 H&R Magnum is several rungs of the ladder above the 32 ACP as a personal defense round and, despite the small diameter of the bullet, it has been known to bring down treed mountain lions, clobber rabbits, raccoons and other small game, and it can put a real hurt on an attacker with an 85-grain JHP stroking along at 1,100 fps from the muzzle.

I have worked up handloads using 85- and 100-grain JHP bullets, and both Federal and Black Hills offer factory loads pushing an 85-grain Hornady XTP in the neighborhood of 1,100 fps, but that's out of a 4.5-inch barrel.

Black Hills also churns out a 90-grain flat-nose lead round that scoots along in the 800-900 fps realm, and in that incarnation it still has enough horsepower to make a difference in a tight spot. There are also 100-grain JHP bullets available from Speer for handloading, and they work quite well for me when pushed along by 10 grains of H110, clocking at just over 1,050 fps out of my Ruger Single-Six.

The maximum listed load in my Speer Reloading Manual is 10.5 grains of H110 behind that bullet for a muzzle velocity of 1,100 fps and, take my word for it, anything shot with that load will have its entire day ruined! So, is this cartridge destined to gather dust or just occupy a very small niche with the single-action crowd? Uh, nope! And I believe the Undercoverette is just the vehicle to give this little powerhouse load its opportunity to shine in the personal defense arena. With

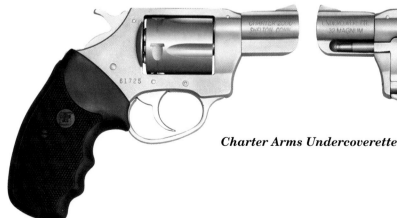

Charter Arms Undercoverette

Magnums left to right: The 32 H&R Magnum, 357 Magnum, 41 Magnum and 44 Magnum. While a little brother to the rest, the 32 H&R Magnum packs a punch.

a suggested retail price under $350, this little revolver is going to appeal to people on a budget.

According to a brief history, available on-line, Charter Arms was established more than 40 years ago by Douglas McClennahan, a veteran of the gun industry who had worked for Sturm Ruger, Colt and High Standard. The first revolver out of the gate from this fledgling company was a five-shot number chambered in 38 Special and called the Undercover, but I think it was really the 44 Special Bulldog that truly put Charter Arms on the map.

But a map is two-dimensional, and there are high points and low ones on the firearms industry's three-dimensional landscape. Let's admit it: Charter Arms had an uphill road

From left to right, the 32 ACP, 32 H&R Magnum and 38 Special.

from the outset and there have been some bumps on the way. Charter Arms went bankrupt in the 1990s, but a few years later, it was resurrected as Charter 2000 under new ownership.

The new company, according to the available history on the company's Web site and at Wikipedia, made some important improvements to the original design, primarily in the barrel. Bores are now cut with eight lands and grooves instead of six, and barrels are all one-piece, including the front sight. Also, there is a full hammer block/transfer bar to prevent accidental discharges and short hammer throw with fast lock time. In terms of safety, the Charter Arms revolver certainly qualifies as one of the safer double-action wheelguns on the market today because unless the trigger is fully depressed, that handgun cannot discharge.

Overall, today's Charter Arms revolver has going for it what the original did: A simple design with a minimum of moving parts, a solid one-piece frame with no side plate, and its inherent reliability. Frankly, Charter Arms revolvers are better guns than a lot of people might think because, quite honestly, a lot of people probably think you can't get quality for such a low price tag. Well, they're wrong.

My test revolver (Serial # 61725) came out of the box rock-solid. My dealer friend who handled the shipping for this review was equally impressed with the finish, a general feel of strength and durability, and especially that rubber grip, which fit his hand very well. It came in the box with a pretty sturdy trigger lock.

Double-action pull was pretty smooth, and the single-action pull broke crisp and clean. What I discovered at

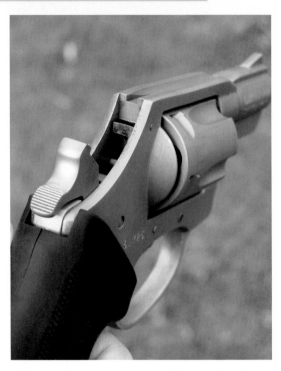

Charter Arms revolvers utilize a transfer bar as a safety feature.

the range with my test piece was that it shot low with 85-grain loads fired off a Caldwell sandbag rest at 15 yards. I found that if I held on the top of an 8-inch target, loads from Black Hills Ammo, using a Hornady XTP bullet, would drop them close to the center, clocking an average of 843 fps over a chronograph set ten feet ahead of the muzzle. Federal 85-grainers, using what appears to be the same

Revolver has a full underlug to protect the ejector rod. Notice how the crane of this revolver fits within the frame.

Basic sights are provided on this concealed-carry revolver. Workman discovered that his test gun shot low at 15 yards with 85-grain JHPs, but he still put them in the black.

bullet, ran just a little hotter and printed a bit higher. They averaged 850 fps over the chronograph screens.

In September 2005, MKS Supply, which had already made an impact on the firearms industry with Hi-Point Firearms, agreed to take on sales, marketing and distribution for Charter Arms. Looks like it was a smart move.

Most important of all in a realm that had been dominated by Smith & Wesson's 5-shot Chief's Special and the 6-round Colt Detective Special, the original Charter Arms revolvers cost considerably less while proving themselves to be well-built. The lineup now includes the Undercover Lite, with an alloy frame; Undercover Southpaw, which is built for left-handers with all the cylinder release on the right side of the frame, and a cylinder that swings out the right side; the Police Undercover, built on the same frame as the Bulldog; plus the Bulldog, Mug Pug, Off Duty, Pathfinder, Undercover and Dixie Derringer.

Today's competition still comes from Smith & Wesson, and Taurus with a series of its own J-frame clones that are very well-built and affordable. I am quite certain the Undercoverette was built with the ladies in mind, but why do they deserve all the breaks, eh?

With a swing-out cylinder, fixed sights (the rear is a notch in the top of the frame) and rubber grip, the Undercoverette is about the same size as a J-frame Smith & Wesson, and it hits the scale at a very comfortable 19 ounces. The cylinder pin tucks into an underlug shroud and, thanks to the stainless steel construction, this revolver is able to handle just about any kind of weather.

For the ladies, which could be the biggest consumer block for this caliber of handgun, it will slide readily into a purse, coat pocket or even a small

holster. It will easily ride in an ankle holster if one sticks on a set of small replacement grip panels, and just as easily tuck into an upside-down shoulder holster. Ditto if you're one of a growing number of business types who tuck a small revolver into a trouser pocket, or carry one in a deep cover, so-called "tuckable" holster (again with smaller grips installed).

And while many might figure this little revolver will not be terribly useful outside of an urban environment as a purely defensive handgun, think again. I happen to do a little hiking and backpacking out in the tall mountains of the Pacific Northwest, and have some small experience with various handguns on the trail, and these days it's kind of foolish to be without one.

Because of its all-steel construction, yet relative light weight, the Charter Arms Undercoverette would definitely be at home on the trail. Ammunition is light, and you can pack a bit more of it than if you chose, say, a 357 Magnum or 45, or even one of the lightweight trail guns chambered in 41 Magnum or 44 Magnum.

I'll admit that I pack a 45 ACP for personal defense most of the time (with a 32 ACP semi-auto as a backup) and a 357 Magnum snubbie on the trail, but from the get-go, when I first laid my hands on the Undercoverette, it just plain made sense. The 32 H&R Magnum

Hammer face is cut to fit over the firing pin so that the handgun cannot be accidentally discharged if it is dropped. The notch leaves room for the transfer bar.

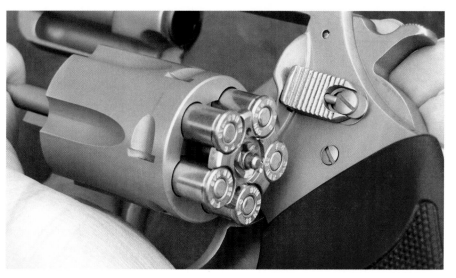

A press on the ejector rod/cylinder pin pushes cases out of the cylinder.

Black Hills loads an 85-grain JHP that clocks just under 844 fps. Notice that comfortable rubber grip with its finger groove profile.

Stainless steel construction makes the little revolver virtually impervious to rough handling and the elements.

Charter Arms, now distributed by MKS Supply, has re-established a foothold among shooters, with the 44 Bulldog and a family of 38 Special revolvers. When Charter Arms was originally a force almost a generation ago, the Undercoverette was part of the family. Now the family is reunited, to good end in my humble opinion.

This revolver has an exposed hammer, so it may be fired either double- or single-action. It has a matte stainless finish and because of the cartridge for which it is chambered, recoil is easily controllable, even for smaller shooters with smaller hands. This is particularly due to the rubber "pancake" style grips. They really soak up whatever felt recoil one might experience.

Yet, the question still may remain, why pick a 32 H&R Magnum over a 38 Special?

Well, the smaller bullet scoots along faster unless one is talking +P or +P+ cartridges in the 38 Special, and the lightweight alloy frame revolvers cannot take a steady diet of that hot ammunition. The Undercoverette can digest 32 H&R Magnums all day long. Recoil is an issue for smaller-framed shooters, and when one is introducing a woman to defensive shooting, you want to encourage them, not alienate them, and recoil is the biggest turnoff there is. This is another reason for offering a revolver in a controllable caliber that won't frighten new shooters away. Often times, they need to practice, because the reason they've purchased a defensive-type handgun has nothing to do with plinking, shooting paper targets or putting meat on the table.

cartridge, as noted earlier, does have the horsepower to clobber a rabbit for dinner, without tearing up too much meat. It also has a loud enough report to be heard some distance away in case one needs to fire the recognized three-shot emergency signal.

All Charter 2000 revolvers have a wide hammer and trigger, and for first-time shooters along with those of us wanting to make accurate shots with even small revolvers, these two features allow for sure cocking and better finger contact on the trigger.

An increasing number of women in some 40 states with shall-issue concealed carry laws are purchasing defensive handguns, and they are shopping for options, and with a discerning eye for quality at an affordable price.

The Charter Arms Undercoverette in 32 H&R Magnum is one of those "right guns at the right time."

The Undercoverette tucks into an IWB holster like this Mitch Rosen model from author Workman's original design.

SWITZERLAND'S IMPRESSIVE KARABINER 31

by Holt Bodinson

Think of it as a Swiss watch that shoots. Combining impeccable workmanship with inherent accuracy and available today at rock-bottom prices, Switzerland's K31 stands out as the military surplus bargain of the 21st Century. Viewed from any perspective, it is a remarkable weapon and mechanically intriguing.

The original design, introduced in 1889, was the product of two Swiss Army officers––Major Rudolph Schmidt of the Swiss Federal Arsenal at Bern and Lt. Col. Eduard Rubin, Director of the Swiss Federal Ammunition Factory and Research Center at Thun. Design of the rifle is attributed to Schmidt and the early semi-smokeless 7.5x53 "Gewehrpatrone" to Rubin, who is also given credit in some quarters for pioneering the development of the rimless cartridge case, the boattail bullet and the modern metal-jacketed bullet. In any case, the rifle carries both inventors' names and has become known as the Schmidt-Rubin.

By 1911, the original, semi-smokeless 7.5x53 round was replaced by the high pressure, smokeless 7.5x55mm cartridge, necessitating moving the locking lugs from the rear to the front of the bolt. The magazine capacity of the new Model 1911 Schmidt-Rubin was also reduced from 12 rounds to 6.

The 1889 and 1911 models were available in a variety of configurations including infantry rifles, short rifles, carbines, cadet rifles and even 22 rimfire trainers.

During the 1950s and 1960s, Model 1911s were fairly common in the surplus stream. I even recall seeing sporterized Model 1911s that had been commercially rechambered for the 308 Winchester. It was not a safe conversion because the long, 1911 inner bolt did not fully support the head of the case.

Speaking of Schmidt-Rubins and the 308 cartridge, recently, there were a limited number of K31 match rifles in 308 Win. imported into the United States with price tags in excess of $1,400. With service-grade K31s in fine condition currently selling for $110-$140, the Swiss carbine is an outright steal.

What is intriguing to most shooters is the K31's straight-pull action. The Swiss lavished their engineering genius on the Schmidt-Rubin bolt. The bolt actually consists of four pieces. There is an inner bolt that holds the bolt face and extractor, a striker assembly, an outer rotating bolt sleeve that carries the locking lugs and an operating handle. It is a complex assembly

At surplus prices, the K31 is an outright steal.

with tight tolerances, requiring precise machining, excellent steels and heat treatment. When buying a K31, do check to see that the serial number on the bolt sleeve matches the serial number on the receiver.

As you pull back on the operating handle, a stud on the bolt handle engages a helical groove milled into the bolt sleeve and a slot in the inner bolt. The bolt sleeve rotates, unlocking the lugs, while the striker is re-cocked, ending in the extraction and ejection of the case. You really have to hold a K31 in your hands to appreciate the operation of the massive, straight-

Stocks may be worn but the metal is generally excellent.

Disassembly of the K31 Bolt

1) Cock the action, depress the bolt release on the right side of the receiver and withdraw the bolt.
2) Pull back the finger ring and position the lug of the striker between the "Fire" and "Safe" notches.
3) Rotate locking lug sleeve clockwise until stud of the bolt handle is at the bolt head end of the helical groove.

5) Press your finger against the bolt face to keep it from turning while rotating and pulling rearward the finger loop/striker assembly until it separates from the bolt body.

4) Pull the bolt handle unit out of the helical groove and forward to remove it.

6) Separate the inner bolt from the outer locking sleeve.

7) Reassemble in reverse order. Note: When connecting the striker assembly to the bolt body, align the lugs of the inner bolt and the striker assembly so that the bolt handle slot in the striker cap aligns with the helical slot in the striker and inner bolt race. At that point, the bolt handle can be reinserted.

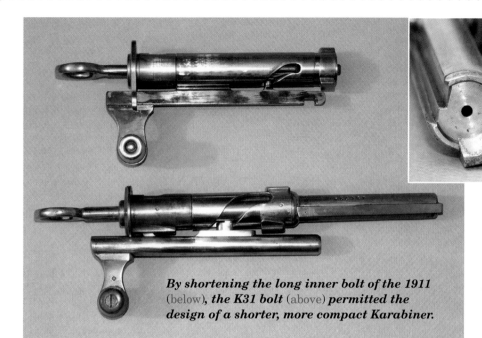

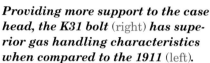

Providing more support to the case head, the K31 bolt (right) has superior gas handling characteristics when compared to the 1911 (left).

By shortening the long inner bolt of the 1911 (below), the K31 bolt (above) permitted the design of a shorter, more compact Karabiner.

pull bolt. What's interesting is that if you operate the action dry, without ammunition, the bolt will feel stiff and jerky. Ah, but fill the magazine, and the operation of the bolt is as slick as grease.

It is a fast action. The only problem one has to contend with in rapid fire is the large finger ring at the end of the striker. The characteristic Schmidt-Rubin finger ring serves three purposes. It permits the shooter to re-cock the rifle in case of a misfire, to ease the striker down on an empty chamber and to set the rifle on "Safe."

To engage the safety, pull the ring to the rear, rotate it clockwise 90 degrees and ease the cocking lug into the fixed slot. It's a very clever design, but, in rapid fire, if you don't cock the rifle a bit to the right when you are slamming the bolt back, that ring will catch you right below your right eye.

The Karabiner of 1931 is the ultimate refinement of the Schmidt-Rubin design. The 1911 action was shortened considerably by eliminating the long inner bolt that extended beyond the bolt sleeve. Note the photograph comparing the 1911 and 1931 bolts. The long inner bolt of the 1911 did not completely support the case head. In the K31, the inner bolt face is flush with the front of the bolt sleeve, providing more support to the head of the case. By reducing the length of the action, the Swiss were then able to move the magazine box back to a much handier position,

just in front of the trigger guard. The end result was that a Model 1911 infantry rifle was morphed into a Model 1931 carbine.

How does the K31 shoot?

The bores are bright, and the triggers are a delight. When it comes to the condition of milsurps, there's something to be said for neutrality. The Swiss soldiers and civilian reserves kept their firearms in superb condition. The stocks often are a little beat up, but the metal is generally excellent.

Using the military sights or, better

The Schmidt-Rubin finger rings function as a safety and as a means of re-cocking and de-cocking the action.

The rear sight of the K31 is graduated from 100-1500 meters.

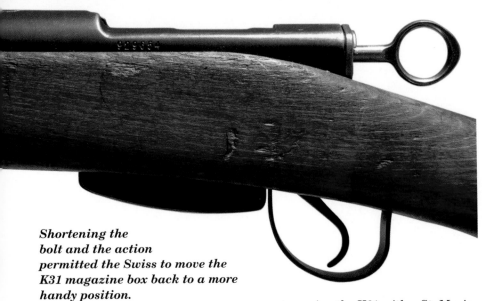

Shortening the bolt and the action permitted the Swiss to move the K31 magazine box back to a more handy position.

The K31, straight-pull bolt handle provides ample operating clearance for winter mittens.

What appears to be a cleaning rod is actually a stacking rod.

yet, scoping the K31 with a St. Marie clamp-on adapter base available from Graf & Sons (www.grafs.com) or Brownells (www.brownells.com) the K31 can generate MOA groups. Graf & Sons also offer a precision, diopter target sight, muzzlebrake and bipod adapter for the K31.

There's plenty of Swiss surplus ammunition made by RUAG still on the market. Featuring a streamlined 174-grain boattail bullet, it is match-grade material but Berdan primed. Graf & Sons carries Hornady loaded ammunition with 150-grain SST, 165-grain BTSP and 168-grain A-Max bullet options plus Norma, Prvi and Wolf brands in 7.5x55. There's plenty of Norma and Prvi brass

available, lots of reloading data in the Sierra, Hornady and Hodgdon manuals, plus a broad choice in the reloading die department. Redding dies have the reputation of being the best match for the K31 chamber. The nice thing about the 7.5 Swiss is that it takes standard .308-inch bullets so reloaders can mix up some very accurate recipes.

The Swiss K31 is the finest buy in today's milsurp market. Don't let this "Swiss watch that shoots" slip through your fingers.

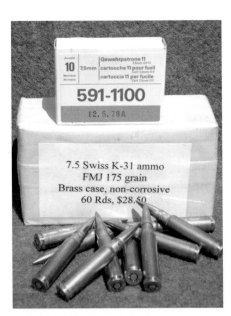

RUAG military ball is still in supply while fresh 7.5x55 ammunition is available from Hornady, Wolf, Prvi and Norma.

Unlocking, locking and cocking the K31 bolt is accomplished by the camming action of a stud on the operating handle.

CZECHOSLOVAKIA'S
REVOLUTIONARY
ROLLER-LOCKER

by Holt Bodinson

Emerging from the unraveling of the USSR and its former hammerlock on the Eastern Bloc countries has been a treasure trove of military surplus arms. Heretofore, most models were unobtainable, or so rare and obscure that they were priced like fine antiques. One of the most intriguing handguns to make a surprise appearance in great quantity and at bargain prices is Czechoslovakia's Model 52 pistol.

Designed by Frantisek Myska and produced by Presne Strojirenstvi in Uhersky Brod and by Ceska Zbrojovka in Strakonice, the Model 52, often referred to as the CZ52 or VZ52, stands apart from the typical military pistol of the early 1950s. It's a remarkably innovative and even radical design for the period. Myska took the roller-locking system invented by the engineers at Mauser for the German MG42 machinegun and scaled it down into a pistol action.

During the later post-war era, Myska's work was followed by that at Heckler & Koch and CETME which continued to refine the roller-locking design for small arms. What was once unique to the Model 52 now appears routinely in H&K models like the G3, MP5 and P9.

Apparently, the Model 52 was not the first Czech prototype to use the roller-locking action. Czech friends report that there was a Model CZ 491 double-action pistol chambered for the 9mm Parabellum that utilized the system. In fact, the CZ 491 might have been adopted by the Czech Army; however, the Soviets had other plans.

In the interests of standardizing small arms ammunition within the Warsaw Pact, the Soviets demanded "unification" in 1950, meaning that as a satellite country, you would adopt the current menu of Soviet military cartridges. What was the prevailing Soviet military pistol cartridge of the day? It was the 7.62x25 Tokarev that had proved so successful when chambered in the Tokarev TT-33 pistol as well as the PPSh 41 and PPS 43 submachine guns in WWII.

The result was Czechoslovakia shelved the Model 491 in 9mm but retained the roller-locking system. Being rather independent of mind in the design of their small arms, the Czech's were less than impressed with the Soviet Tokarev TT-33 and forged ahead to create the Model 52 chambered in 7.62x25.

The Czech, roller-locking Model 52 is still available at rock bottom prices.

Roller-shaped locking lugs are controlled by a cam that slides back and forth between them.

Officially adopted in 1952, the Model 52 is a large, nicely machined handgun, weighing 34.5 ounces unloaded. It is a single action, semiautomatic, recoil-operated, magazine-fed pistol. Its lines are pleasantly sleek except for its atrocious grip.

Flat, slab-like and wide, the grip retains a single-stack magazine, holding eight rounds of the long 7.62x25 cartridge. It's a handful. Designer Myska would have done a lot better if he had adopted the grip and grip-to-frame angle of the Tokarev.

When fired with one hand, the Tokarev points right on target. When the CZ 52 is fired one-handed, it dumps its bullets low, very low. The odd fact is that if the CZ52 is fired using a two-handed hold, it points dead on. Possibly the dimensions and profile of the CZ52 grip are intentional!

At the other end of the scale are the sights on the Model 52. The front sight blade and the notch in the standing rear sight are what might be termed "miserly." The front sight is too thin and the rear notch is too narrow. The combined sight picture they offer is slow to pick up and visually critical, even in full daylight. Inside a building or under any low-light condition, the sights of the CZ52 are marginal to useless. The remedy is to take a file and widen the rear sight notch. The rear sight is adjustable for windage by drifting it right or left, so no harm is done by opening up that pinched notch.

On the plus side is the pistol's excellent three-position safety,

giving the user three primary carry options. In the down position, the safety is "Off" – hammer down, empty chamber. In the center position, it's "ON" – hammer cocked, loaded chamber (cocked and locked), or hammer down, loaded or unloaded chamber. When the safety is flipped fully up, the hammer is decocked and the firing pin is blocked. The safety then automatically returns to the "ON" position.

The *piece-de-resistance* of the CZ52 design is its roller-locking action. It's simplicity itself, but it took a genius to create it.

The roller-locking mechanism consists of two rollers that are controlled by a cam that slides back-and-forth between them. When the slide is in the forward position, the cam spreads the rollers out, locking them into seats in the sides of the slide. At the moment of firing, the barrel and slide are locked together. As the slide begins moving rearward, the cam contacts a projection in the frame that forces the cam out of battery, permitting the rollers to withdraw from their seats and unlock the barrel from the slide. The system is simple, reliable and robust.

Does the CZ52 shoot? Yes, it does. The trigger pull is a bit long and gritty and like all 30-caliber handguns, it's a bit noisy, but does it shoot flat! The laser-like trajectory of the 7.62x25

An excellent three-position safety offers the user three primary carry options.

round has to be experienced to be appreciated. I would not want to be an exposed enemy combatant 100 meters away from a CZ52 wielding soldier. He would be duck soup.

The standard 7.62x25 loading centers around an 85-grain FMJ with a muzzle velocity of 1600 fps. Sizzling out of a pistol-length barrel at 1600 fps, the 7.62x25

is a hot number. In fact, the new Winchester "Metric Caliber" loading is manufactured in the Czech Republic and posts a velocity of 1645 fps. Just to verify the pistol velocity of the 7.62x25 ammunition, I used a PACT Professional chronograph to measure two military issue loadings – Bulgarian and Chinese ball. The Bulgarian ball plowed down range

at 1616 fps and the Chinese at 1548 fps, and those velocities were measured 10 feet from the muzzle of the CZ52. At 25 yards, typical eight-shot groups measured 2-2½ inches.

The best part of the story is that this unique pistol in excellent condition with two magazines and an issue holster is still selling for around $125. Don't pass it up.

Disassembly/Reassembly

1: With an empty, unloaded and uncocked pistol, pull down on the two grooved tabs located on either side of the trigger guard.

2: Move the slide slightly forward and lift it from the frame. The pistol is now field-stripped.

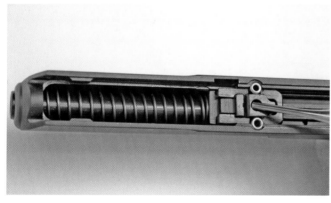

3: To remove the barrel assembly from the slide, place a punch in the hole of the roller cam, push the cam forward to unlock the rollers, and then cock and lift the assembly upward. The barrel, recoil spring and locking assembly will come out as one unit. When you remove the recoil spring, note the smaller of the two ends goes back on the barrel first.

4: Reassemble in reverse order. Note: When placing the assembled slide back on the frame, position the back end of the slide approximately 1/4" forward from the rear end of the frame. Push down firmly on the slide and pull it to the rear. It will automatically snap into place and be locked to the frame.

OLYMPIC ARMS' JOURNEYMAN

Built with selected components, this custom-grade carry gun is a gem

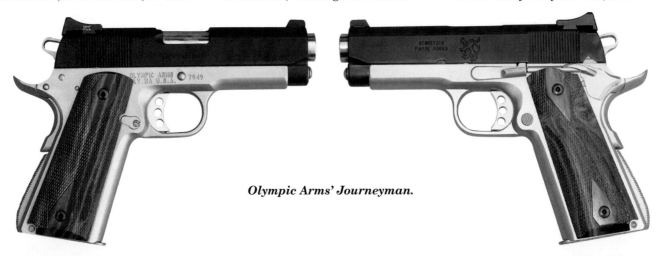

by Dave Workman

Seven years ago, for GUN DIGEST'S sister publication, the HANDGUNS annual, I delved into the process of ordering and having built a custom-level Model 1911, and the result was a pistol called the "Street Deuce" from Olympic Arms.

As readers of that article will recall, the "Deuce" is the product of Richard Niemer, who runs Olympic's Schuetzen Pistol Works (SPW) custom shop. He's a man I consider a true friend, and in some respects a genius when it comes to the Model 1911. Let me just call him *maestro*.

Now comes the good news. For shooters who are looking for a more compact carry gun than the full-frame Model 1911, SPW has been, for some

time, offering a Commander-size alternative called the Journeyman, but it seems to be a pretty well-kept secret. This rugged 45 ACP carry gun is just as snazzy as its big brother, certainly as reliable, and it can be ordered with a selection of options, such as a flat or curved Smith & Alexander stainless steel mainspring housing below a high-ride beavertail grip safety that has a "memory bump," and your choice of fixed or adjustable sights. There's more, of course, and we will detail it presently. But first a little background.

Niemer's history as a top-notch – and highly *under*-advertised – gunsmith dates back to his days at the original Detonics, then located in Bellevue, Washington. Detonics

has moved on, and so has Niemer, but with him came what he learned, and he incorporates a lifetime of experience in the production of the Street Deuce and the Journeyman.

Olympic Arms founder Bob Schuetz told me that, in his humble opinion, Niemer is "the best 45 man around." Spend an afternoon on the range with the Journeyman and you might just find yourself in complete agreement.

So, what about this carry gun? First and foremost, it is chambered in what many consider to be the finest combat pistol round on the planet, the 45 ACP. This cartridge is a proven fight-stopper (not bad for a round that is nearly 100 years old), and

Olympic Arms' Journeyman.

Journeyman is up to digesting any popular ammunition from Winchester, Black Hills and others.

in recent years, American shooters have gone through an interesting cycle that I discussed with Niemer in preparation for this article.

Back in the post-WWII days, there were really three domestic choices for a personal defense handgun: the 45 ACP, 38 Special and 357 Magnum. Lots of people couldn't handle the magnum. The 38 Special is a good round but not necessarily *that* good in a gun battle with someone

Journeyman (lower) is a compact sibling to the Street Deuce, a full-size custom-grade pistol produced by Olympic Arms' Schuetzen Pistol Works custom shop.

high on drugs, alcohol or just adrenaline. Then there was the 45, a big, slower-moving piece of lead capable of knocking somebody flat, and that was just with ball ammunition. Today's vast selection of hollowpoints that scoot along at between 950 and 1,100 fps, depending upon bullet weight and powder charge really make the 45 ACP a formidable cartridge.

But in the 1980s, something happened. America suddenly fell in love with the high-capacity 9mm. "Spray and Pray" became something of a mantra, though anyone with a grain of gray matter will affirm that the only benefit someone gets from a bullet that misses the target is a lot of confusing noise and muzzle flash. Practitioners of this high-firepower, low hit ratio seem to have forgotten that a bullet that misses its target is invariably going to hit something – or someone – else.

Thank Congress in large degree for something of a resurgence of the 45 ACP. When the misguided ban on full-capacity magazines was passed, it took a while but people eventually concluded that if they could only carry ten rounds in a pistol, they were going to make sure their pistol

carried ten of the biggest, meanest rounds available that really stop bad guys in their tracks. Say hello, again, to the 45, and at the same time, start shopping around for a quality handgun that chambers this round. Without a doubt, the Journeyman is a custom-quality pistol that arrived on the scene at the right time, and is already earning high marks from happy owners.

Incredibly, however, this pistol has not gotten the kind of attention it deserved, and one might almost consider it still a new kid on the block because of its relative anonymity.

It's a two-tone, all-steel piece of eye candy that delivers the goods inside and out. Unlike most other pistols of its size, this one utilizes a full-size Government Model frame, where frames on the Commander and other 1911 clones with shorter top ends utilize a more compact frame where the dust cover has been trimmed back a bit. Where the full size Government frame's dust cover extends two inches ahead of the trigger guard, on Commander-size guns that comes back about ¼- to ⁵/₁₆-inch.

And, yes, the Journeyman does have a full-size frame in terms of magazine capacity. It takes a full 7- or 8-round magazine, and comes with 7-round Metalforms.

Muzzle of coned bull barrel is slightly recessed. Notice dovetailed front sight.

Author Workman stacked the much fancier Journeyman up against his Commander-size pistol from Auto Ordnance. The A/O was tricked out by gunsmith Richard Niemer, who builds the Journeyman, and Renton, Washington gunsmith Tim McCullough.

SPW's Journeyman has a polished feed ramp, lowered and flared ejection port, coned 4-inch stainless steel bull barrel with a recessed target-style crown and full-length recoil spring guide rod. The result is a 6-inch sight radius. My experience with this barrel setup has been very good over the years despite the fact that I much prefer a standard diameter barrel with a match-grade bushing and "loose" recoil spring and plug/plunger up front. But that's a matter of personal preference, and I can tell readers that the way this Journeyman is set up works like a champ.

Niemer could have used any number of finishes for the top end, but the Journeyman's slide is finished with the toughest black Parkerizing I've ever seen. I've got the same finish on my Deuce, and after seven years, it is showing very little holster wear. I will, occasionally, give my pistol slide a good wipe with

Mitch Rosen's Leather Lightning, a surface treatment that does not harm a gun finish, and helps reduce friction for a life-saving fast draw.

The front sight is dovetailed and, as noted above, one has a choice of either adjustable rear or fixed rear sights. The adjustable rear is an LPA, which Niemer considers the best on the market today. The standard fixed rear offered on the Journeyman is the Heinie Slant Pro, but one can get a set of Heinie "Straight 8" tritiums as a further option, and again, Niemer believes them to be the best because they are simple.

"All you need to do is line up one dot on top of another," he observed. "You don't need to worry about lining up one dot between two others, as you have to do with a three-dot sight system."

I have guns with three-dot tritiums and I like them, but I have to admit, the Straight 8 that Niemer installed on my Street Deuce has never failed me.

For the purpose of this review, Niemer actually outfitted me with a pair of Journeyman pistols *(serial # SOF 002 and 7949)*, one with fixed Heinie night sights and the other with an adjustable rear sight. I'm delighted to report they both worked!

The bottom half is stainless steel with a handsome bead blasted matte finish that, in my experience, stands second to none in terms of durability. Consider that Niemer and the Journeyman come from the wet, sometimes-humid Pacific Northwest, and a pistol that survives in that kind of environment will survive anywhere! He adds a set of double diamond Cocobolo checkered grip panels, and the result is both beautiful and functional.

The Journeyman is fitted with an extended thumb safety, and while I sometimes prefer an ambidextrous safety so that you can use a pistol with either hand in an emergency (I had Niemer install one on the Deuce), the left-side-only setup is completely reliable.

Another option available on this handgun is a strip of Brownell's friction tape on the front strap. My humble opinion is that this

Each Journeyman comes standard with handsome double diamond cocobolo grip panels and a choice of either curved or flat Smith & Alexander mainspring housing.

For this review, Workman had two versions of the Journeyman, one with adjustable LPA sights, and the other with fixed Heinie Slant Pro Straight 8 tritium sights. Both shot very well.

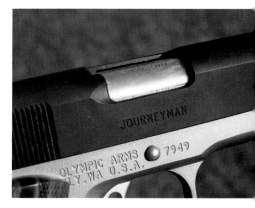

Lowered and flared ejection port contributes to Journeyman's functionality. Spent brass clears quickly and without fail.

That Heinie rear sight is one of Workman's favorites. He has the same sight installed on his Street Deuce.

Olympic/SPW made something of a niche reputation many years ago by producing a series of pistols on the 1911 frame with one distinct visible difference. This was, and remains, a finger rest/cut on the front strap that is cast into the frame in the production process. It's an odd-looking adornment that gained considerable popularity with European handgunners, and no small number of American *pistoleros*, though I personally don't care for it.

However, one of my long-time amigos owns two or three of these pistols, and he simply adores them, so there you go.

I will say this for the record: Each of these pistol models shoots very well. That 4-inch bull barrel really does wring every bit of performance out of a 45-caliber bullet, so one can see why such outfits as Kimber and Springfield also offer models with the same length tube.

One thing a carry gun of any caliber must be capable of is feeding any ammunition of the proper caliber you put into it, and the Journeyman can do that. Truncated cone target loads, 230-grain ball and, of course, jacketed hollowpoints; everything

inexpensive add-on is a preferable alternative to front strap checkering, which can be sharp and pretty tough on one's fingers, and I personally dislike on just about every 1911 I've ever fired, with the possible exception of the Taurus PT1911.

Niemer installs an adjustable trigger on the Journeyman, and my strong advice is to have him set it for a 4.5-pound letoff, which I think is plenty light for a street gun.

One thing about SPW pistols, and particularly the Journeyman, is that each part is hand-selected and fitted. Niemer does not simply wander over to a bin of frames, another with slides, a box of barrels and drawers of other components. He carefully selects each component for a total package that works, and as mentioned previously, this guy knows his 45s, and has a discerning eye for picking premium parts.

Should anyone familiar with Olympic Arms' other pistols wonder, I'll put a question to rest right now. The Journeyman setup is internally similar to that of both the Enforcer and Cohort, a couple of compact pistols that have been part of the Olympic Arms/SPW lineup for many years. Externally, there are some similarities, also, but considerable differences as well.

Stripped down for cleaning, the Journeyman essentially looks like any other 1911 platform, sort of. Bull barrel and full-length guide rod with Detonics-style recoil spring system worked flawlessly.

Now here's an innovation for anyone who lives in a damp climate, but who doesn't like checkering on the front strap: a strip of friction tape from Brownell's makes for a no-slip grip.

has to work because there may be a time when what you can find is the only stuff you can get.

I have yet to see a 4-inch 45-caliber pistol that didn't feed lots of different types of ammunition reliably. The Journeyman is certainly in that category. Let's face it, this isn't your grandfather's 45 auto.

There have been such improvements in the "little things" that, combined, they make a Model 1911 platform work like a Swiss watch.

For this evaluation, I dug into my ammunition stores and found Winchester 230-grain ball and 230-grain JHP Personal Defense loads, Federal Hydra Shok and Hi-Shok ammunition, some Black Hills JHPs using the Speer Gold Dot, Remington/UMC loads and some of my personal handloads.

I fed the following loads into the Journeyman: Federal 230-grain ball, Winchester 230-grain Personal Defense JHPs, Remington/UMC 185-grain flatpoint FMJ, Federal 185-grain Hi Shok JHPs and Black Hills 185-grain JHPs using Speer Gold Dots. Of all these loads, the Journeyman had a bit of trouble feeding the Winchester 230-grain Personal Defense round, and only because I believe there was a magazine foul-up. Once chambered, every round went downrange without a hitch.

The hottest load was the Black Hills 185-grainer clocking 981.2 fps

over a chronograph set 10 feet from the muzzle. Next up was the UMC load, stroking along at 954.3 fps. The Federal Hi-Shoks moved out at 825.9 fps, followed by he 230-grain Winchester JHPs and Federal 230-grain ball rounds right at 802 fps.

The fixed-sight model shot a bit to the right out of the box, while the pistol with an adjustable sight shot slightly to the left. Both of these problems can be fixed by simply adjusting the sights.

Before a Journeyman leaves the shop, Niemer test-fires it with both ball ammunition and hollowpoints, so he is darned certain it is going to ramp the kind of ammunition his customer is likely to use. Having seen him shoot a couple of times, I can assure readers that these pistols will hit what they are aimed at. At least, they sure hit what he aims them at!

What's the bottom line? The Journeyman is no "apprentice." It's a well-crafted, ruggedly built and carefully-assembled pistol that is certainly worth the asking price. And while we're on that subject, what's your life worth? Huh?

Federal 230-grain FMJ ball ammo performed pretty well, in model with adjustable sights. Workman fired this group off-hand. There are nine holes in that target, one covered by author's index finger.

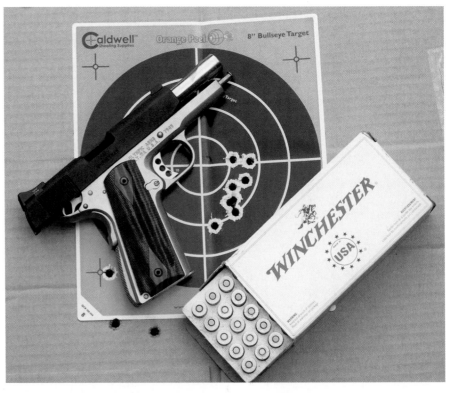

Journeyman liked 230-grain loads, whether JHPs like this Winchester stuff, GI ball ammo, or any other heavier bullet he used.

OL' NO. 7

by Steve Gash

The year was 1962, I was a college sophomore, and was immersed in the perpetual rifleman's quandry: should I buy a 30-06 or a 270? I had finally saved enough to buy my first big-game rifle, and of course, it would be my only big game rifle forever, so it had to be perfect. I had read and re-read every ballistics chart available in my corner of the world – southeast Kansas – and was torn between the heavier bullets of the '06, or the string-flat trajectory of the 270.

About this time I happened upon another contender – the 280 Remington. It looked like a perfect compromise, smack-dab in between the two front-runners in caliber, power, and trajectory. I trundled off to the B&J Army Surplus, run by a fine old gentleman named Burt Franchione. I liked Burt because he didn't run us pimple-faced, penniless gawkers out of the store as we stared, wide-eyed, at his modest inventory. He had no 270s, 280s or 30-06s, but Burt said he'd order anything I wanted.

But then Remington threw me a curve. In early 1962, the company launched a fancy new rifle called the Model 700, and a super new cartridge, the 7mm Remington Magnum. I quickly devoured every printed word on the new gun and cartridge, and was astounded to learn that it, like the 280, was in between the 27- and 30-calibers, but offered more power than either. The decision was easy. Burt placed the order and I waited. Every week I went in with the same question, "Is it in yet?" and got the same reply "No."

Eventually, the delay wore down even this star-struck kid, and I told Burt to cancel the order. I was crestfallen. Then one day, I sashayed into the B&J on a regular stop. As soon as I entered, Burt announced, "It's here." One look at the rifle and I was smitten. I would later learn that this M-700 BDL was a "type 62-210" rifle made in June 1962 from the earliest production run, but then all

I knew was that this most wonderful rifle was mine. The cost? $120.

Thus began an odyssey that continues to this day. In the intervening 45 years, Ol' No. 7 and I have trod many paths together. With it I took my first whitetail, first pronghorn, first elk, first bighorn sheep, a slew of coyotes and jackrabbits.

I shot some factory ammo, but even then I was a budding handloader. I somehow earned enough cash hauling hay and doing other odd jobs to get a press, dies and bullets. Since factory ammo came with 150- and 175-grain bullets, I bought one box each of Hornady 154-grain round nose and 175-grain Spire Point bullets. Remember, this was to be my one and only big-game rifle. Reloading life was simpler back then.

In 1966, Kansas had its first modern deer season and I worked as a biologist's aide at a deer check station at Elk City. Lots of deer were brought in, including some really nice bucks. It didn't take me long to figure

The Remington Model 700 BDL, Ol' No. 7, was made in June 1962, and has proven itself for over four decades on a variety of game, both big and small.

A Colorado mountain trail in 1974, an elk tag in hand, and Ol' No. 7 – can it get any better than this?

yesterday. As soon as I'd settled onto the campstool in my blind I had to blow my nose. Out came the red bandana, followed by a snort that should have scared every living thing within a mile. But as I replaced the handkerchief, I glanced down at the creek, and a very fat, very calm whitetail doe was standing in the shallow water, gazing away from my blind, as if without a care. It was serene. I slowly tried to lower my 7mm Magnum to a firing position, but the broom sedge was in the way. To heck with caution! I mashed the rifle down, sedge grass crunching in the process, and peered through the scope. The deer was either deaf or on drugs, as she was totally unperturbed. The range was just right for a beginner – about 20 yards.

I centered the crosshairs on the deer's shoulder, gently squeezed the trigger, and 67.1 grains of H-4831 broke the stillness, sending a 154-grain Hornady RN on its way. Instead of falling over like she was supposed to, the deer scampered up the embankment right toward me, but collapsed after a few steps. I carefully stepped from the blind

out I was on the wrong side of this table and the following year I applied for and received an "any deer" license.

I chose the state-run quail farm about four miles west of town to hunt; this was about the only thing resembling "public hunting" in those days. I built a blind out of broom sedge grass woven into chicken wire I'd fastened to a couple of 1x2s, and positioned it on a bank overlooking Cow Creek. Every morning and evening of the season I sat, Ol' No. 7 in my hands, still as the proverbial mouse, watching for deer. For the first four and a half days, I saw no deer.

Then, on the afternoon of the last day of the season, things changed. The events of those few minutes will be etched in my memory for all time. Every detail seems like it happened

and approached the deer. I distinctly remember reaching down and touching the deer to see if it was real.

After I'd calmed down, I field-dressed the deer, and dragged it the half-mile back to the county road where I was parked. Then I found the really difficult task was getting the deer into the trunk of a 1964 Plymouth.

As a kid, I had fantasized about hunting such exotic locales as Africa and Wyoming; both seemed about equally far away to me. In fact, after college, I based my job searches on where the best big-game hunting was. Eventually I worked all over the country and Ol' No. 7 was employed in most areas. In 1973 I found myself in Denver and was determined to partake of the big-game possibilities in the West.

That fall, I badgered my cousin, a Colorado resident, into a "self-guided" antelope hunt out of Casper, Wyoming. We saw lots of prairie goats, and after a careful stalk, Ol' No. 7 and I had a nice 14-inch buck. In 1974, I got a limited cow elk license in Colorado. Thus one frosty morning in a long-forgotten park, a cow poked her head over the terrace. As a midwestern varmint hunter, naive as to the tenants of shot placement, I promptly planted a 175-grain Hornady SP between her eyes, and I had my first elk.

As the years rolled by, I carried Ol' No. 7 up many a mountain and, when pointed right, it never failed to bring down game. This included several more elk, mule deer, and in 1977, a long coveted trophy – a 36-inch ¾-curl Rocky Mountain bighorn. After five weeks of hard hunting, as dusk approached one evening, I took the ram with one shot from the Big 7.

Like most rifle addicts, I have used many other rifles and other chamberings for hunting big game over the years. But, deep down, when nostalgia takes hold, and my mind drifts back to past hunts, game seen, taken or not, I cannot help but remember how Ol' No. 7 helped build my confidence and competence as a hunter. Every time I handle it, it's like meeting an old friend.

Changing jobs and moving around the country paid off. In 1974, the Big 7 and I crossed paths with this fat Colorado cow elk, the first of several.

"PA WAS A PUMP GUN MAN"

by Gerald Peterson

The year was 1967 when this new Model 760 Remington pump, chambered for the 223 Remington, showed up at our farm. For the next 29 years, this rifle and the old coyote hunter – my father – would be almost inseparable. Whether it was bouncing along on the seat beside him in his pickup truck, riding in a makeshift scabbard strapped on an early "snow cruiser" snow machine, or carried in the crook of his arm while walking the coulees for jackrabbits, fox or coyotes. From that day forward he neither had, nor wanted, another varmint rifle.

Pa was a pump-gun man. He used a Model 760 Remington in 270 Winchester that he bought back in 1957, as well as a 12-gauge model 870 Remington shotgun. Even his wedding present for his new bride was a 20-gauge Model 870 Remington. It was only a matter of time before he would have a coyote rifle in a Remington pump.

Remington introduced the Model 760 in 223 Remington in 1964, and ended the production five years later, in 1968. This was the second caliber that Remington had introduced on a small case head, the first being the 222 Remington, which was only in production for three years from 1958 to 1960.

The Model 760 pump-action rifle became available to the public in 1952; it was designed to replace the earlier pump, the Model 141 that was discontinued after the war. Among its new features was a button-rifled barrel designed by Mike Walker, an employee of Remington during WWII. Incidentally, Walker also designed the 222 Remington cartridge in 1950. A number of parts for this new pump gun were made interchangeable with Remington's semi-auto and pump-action shotguns, as well as their Model 740 semi-auto rifle.

With its front-locking, rotating bolt head and multiple locking lugs, the Model 760 is able to safely handle our high-pressure cartridges. This, plus a stiff 22-inch free-floating barrel measuring 0.650-inch at the muzzle, makes for a very accurate rifle, even by today's accuracy standards. To provide insight into the accuracy possible with this gun, during the early 1960s, the U.S. Army Marksmanship training unit at Ft. Benning, Georgia used custom 760s, with 28-inch heavy barrels chambered for the 222 Remington, in their International Running Deer matches. Also, in 1961, a U.S. shooter won the double shot aggregate at the World Championships in Oslo, Norway, and another took second place in the single shot World

Championships in Cairo, Egypt. Shortly after this, a U.S. shooter won the single shot World Championship at Ft. Benning, also with a Model 760 Remington pump-action rifle.

The new rifle arrived from the factory with impressed checkering on both the forend and the pistol grip. This was the ADL grade that was introduced in 1964, replacing the earlier 1954 ADL grade that sported cut checkering. The magazine is a detachable box holding five cartridges; the weight, with a 3-9x Leupold scope is 8¼ pounds. By no means a featherweight, this heft aids in the rifle's balance for offhand shooting. The trigger pull is a comfortable three pounds.

The buttstock was replaced in the first year. Dad was a farmer by profession, but in the early 1930s he had started making gun stocks, first for himself and his friends, and eventually fitting and stocking both rifles and shotguns for hunters across the prairies. Dad's favorite stock design was a high Monte Carlo with cheek piece. He stated this was always the preferred style for offhand shooting, and a quick look at Schuetzen and early offhand match rifles will show you why. With the high stock comb offering plenty of cheek support, the shooter can concentrate on his target without craning his neck down and forward, as on lower, straighter stocks. Also, Dad was quite adamant that cheek-to-stock contact was as crucial to hitting a running fox or coyote with a rifle, as it was to hitting clay pigeons in trap and Skeet shooting with a shotgun.

Dad was a shooter from the old school, and if one is lucky enough to watch a practiced offhand game shot these days, it is quite a sight to behold. At one time, all of the old-timers shot offhand. They shot this way while hunting birds with their shotguns in the field. When the shotguns were cleaned up, put away and the rifles were taken out, they continued to stand "on their hind legs" and shoot.

Shortly after Dad acquired the 223 pump, he started swaging his own bullets on dies made for him by Ted Smith. (Smith, from North Bend, Oregon invented the famous "Little Dripper" powder trickler, for dispensing powder to a powder scale and was also the world's largest manufacturer of bullet swage equipment at that time.) At first, jackets were made from empty 22 rimfire cases, and later, copper jackets were purchased from Corbin's. At this same time, he also ordered 200 pounds of lead wire that came in 25-pound rolls from Federated Metals in Montreal, Quebec.

Dad used 55-grain bullets almost exclusively, preferring the heavier bullet weight for its increased ability to buck the prairie winds. It would also carry up better and pack a bit more wallop over longer distances. The bullets swaged from 22 rimfire cases worked fine for shooting in settled areas. They break up upon contact with almost anything, dirt, stones, or brush. I have even seen them leave only a gray smear on a hard snow drift. Therefore, we didn't have to be too concerned with bullets ricocheting across the

countryside, especially when shooting gophers in the pastures, or hunting jackrabbits in the spring when farm machinery would be working in the fields. This is also the time of year when rabbits leave the pastures and thick brushy draws to feed, in the evenings, on the fresh green sprouts of the spring wheat and durum crops that are grown on the southern Saskatchewan prairies.

I have no idea how many of these bullets were put through his 223 over the years. Dad always believed in keeping the bore clean, especially when using the 22 rimfire jacketed bullets, because they could foul the rifling very quickly. This frequent cleaning, no doubt, prolonged the barrel life considerably.

A favorite powder through the years was IMR-4895. Although Dad had tried others, he always returned to this powder for his most accurate loads. It wasn't until the mid-80s that he switched to H-335, which produced higher velocity than other loads tried in the past, but without any difference in accuracy.

With the 55-grain Corbin jacketed bullets and 26.5 grains of H-335 powder, the old gun is still a tack-driver. Although the throat is getting a bit rough, 3-shot groups at 100 yards will still group from ⅜-inch to ½-inch for about the first 20 to 25 rounds, then the groups open to ¾ to one inch, still plenty of accuracy for hunting coyotes. Five-shot groups will average slightly over an inch from a clean barrel, which is excellent accuracy for a sporter. About this time I give the bore a good scrubbing with Shooters Choice copper remover and the accuracy is restored.

I inherited the old 223 pump, when Dad passed away back in '96. Along with his rifle, reloading dies and bullet swaging dies, was the last partial roll of lead wire. Now, all of

The Model 760 is still effective on coyotes, and goes afield several times each year.

this lead certainly didn't go through the old pump gun. My brothers and I had a hand in helping Dad use a lot of it up over the years in everything from 222s to 220 Swifts, but it is safe to say that over 6000 rounds of swaged bullets have gone down the bore of the pump-action 223 over the last 38 years. I don't shoot a lot of targets with it any more because I don't want to wear out the barrel, although I'm still fascinated with its ability to shoot small groups.

However, be that as it may, each fall I always make sure the old 223 is sighted in and ready to go along with me for a drive, while I look for a coyote or fox. Carrying his old pump is the next best thing to actually hunting, once again, with Dad. I like to think there is a bit of him in the old rifle, with his home-made stock and hand-rubbed oil finish. The small dings and character scratches accumulated over the years, the missing bluing and worn checkering from being carried many miles, on many hunts, all remind me of our many days afield.

This was always Dad's favorite rifle and someday I hope to pass it on to my son. Because it was his Grandpa's coyote rifle, it always will be "one good gun."

The family Remington Model 760. The author's father restocked it years ago.

AUTOLOADERS:
HANDGUNS TODAY

by John Malloy

Sometimes, history seems to repeat itself.

Over a century ago, in the aftermath of the Spanish-American War, U. S. forces found that their standard sidearm, the 38 Long Colt revolver, lacked stopping power. It had been considered adequate for "civilized" warfare. However, it would not reliably stop fanatical Muslim attackers in the Philippines. Such adversaries sought heavenly reward by killing infidels, even if it meant their own death.

The situation led to the Thompson/LaGarde handgun tests of 1904. The findings were that no caliber smaller than 45 should be considered. Tests were scheduled for 1906, then postponed. The tests began in 1907, and after four years of extensive testing that began in 1907, the Colt 45 ACP pistol was adopted in 1911. It served well—through World War I, World War II, Korea and Vietnam. Then, our leaders decided to use a cartridge common with our allies, and a 9mm pistol was adopted in 1985.

Recently, in the absence of "civilized" warfare, our soldiers had to once again face fanatical Muslim attackers, ones who do not mind dying as long as they can kill their targets. There has been a reevaluation of the role of the military sidearm. The 45 is being reconsidered as a military pistol. Tests were scheduled for 2006, and then postponed. At the time of this writing, military testing has been postponed indefinitely, but private development continues.

A number of companies, among them Beretta, FNH USA, Glock, Heckler & Koch, Sigarms, Smith & Wesson and Taurus, have introduced 45 ACP pistols in forms that could meet modern military specifications. Such pistols may have polymer frames, double-action trigger mechanisms, relatively large magazine capacity, grips that can fit a number of hand sizes and accessory rails. At any rate, the 45 ACP cartridge is getting a lot of attention for civilian, law enforcement and military use. Reportedly, some military combat units received small quantities of such modern new 45s. Others, again reportedly, acquired 1911s from storage, and seemed satisfied to have the nearly-century-old design available.

Here at home, the 1911 has never been more popular. More companies are making 1911s than ever before, many beginning just in the last few years. New 1911 models by established companies are essentially variations on the basic design—an effort to provide a 1911 to suit everyone's taste.

Of course, there is much more going on than just 1911s and 45s. The field of polymer-frame police service pistols in 9mm and 40 S&W—which also suit civilian self-protection—has expanded recently.

Polymer pistols continue to grow in popularity, but some new ones, such as the new Armalite and Sphinx pistols, use forged steel frames.

There are some completely new designs. Both the EAA FCP pistol and the Hogue Avenger are centerfire autoloaders that do not use a moving slide.

A compact version of the Armalite AR-24, the AR-24k, was introduced at the January 2007 SHOT Show.

New countries have recently become important in the world of autoloading handguns. Turkey, in particular, now makes pistols for companies such as Armalite, Bernardelli, Stoeger and Tristar.

The 22-caliber handgun, often just taken for granted, continues to be of interest for training, hunting and target shooting. Almost everyone can use another 22 pistol, and a number of companies are ready to provide them. New versions of proven designs are available this year.

Because pistol-caliber carbines are seldom reported along with traditional hunting rifles, we'll continue to cover them here. On the other hand, rifle-caliber semiautomatic pistols interest a lot of people. For the most part, these long-range pistols have been based on the AR-15 design. Now, new ones based on the AK-47 are being offered by Century International.

Some politicians do not like such guns, and politics continues to influence the world of autoloading handguns. Certain politicians do not like any guns, but do not like semiautomatic pistols in particular.

The future is not very clear following the November 2006 takeover of Congress by Democrats. Not all Democrats are anti-gun, of course, but a number of anti-gun members of Congress are now in positions of great power. Our first loss was John Bolton, the outspoken representative of the United States in the United Nations. He held firm against attempts to use the UN to weaken the right of Americans to keep and bear arms. The Democratic leadership made it plain he would not be confirmed, and soon, he was out. The UN now plans to produce new global gun-control proposals in September 2008, shortly before our next presidential election.

When the new Democrat-controlled Congress convened in January 2007, four anti-gun bills were proposed before the month was out. Whether or not enough anti-gun votes exist to pass any such bills is in question, but the handwriting is on the wall—we can expect more restrictive firearms bills to be introduced.

Already, many new pistols come with mechanical changes made to placate the implacable politicians who do not like autoloaders. Loaded chamber indicators and magazine disconnectors appear on many new guns.

An accessory option that many shooters prefer now consists of grip-mounted laser sighting devices. Some are available as standard equipment on autoloading pistols.

With all that as background, let's take a look at what the individual companies are doing:

Armalite

Armalite, a rifle manufacturer, is now in the pistol business. The AR-24 pistol, announced last year, is a reality. The new Armalite pistol is a 9mm, and is made in Turkey (by Sarsilmaz) of forged parts that are CNC-machined. The barrel has cut rifling. The trigger system is conventional double action, that is, first shot is double action and succeeding shots single action. The basic mechanism is similar to that of the CZ-75.

Four variants are available. First is the standard AR-24, a full-size pistol with fixed sights, 15-round magazine, and a weight of 35 ounces. Second is the AR-24K, a compact version with a 13-round magazine, weighing 33 ounces. There are also "C" variants of both, variants that have adjustable rear sights. Actually the term "fixed sights" for the standard models is not quite correct, as even the front sights are adjustable for windage—they are dovetailed and held by setscrews.

A 45 ACP prototype is in the works. Plans are to name it the AR-26, and it will use a larger frame. A 40 S&W version is also planned later, probably on the larger frame. The Armalite 45 was planned for a 2007 introduction.

Armscor

Armscor may not be a familiar name to some American shooters, but the Philippine company makes a lot of pistols. For U. S. sales, Armscor 1911-type pistols are branded with the Rock Island Armory name. Various configurations of RIA 1911 pistols are available in 45 ACP, 40 S&W, 38 Super and 9mm.

New this year is the MAP series of pistols, based on the CZ 75 pattern. The parts are made by Tanfoglio of Italy and the guns are assembled in the United States.

Automag / AMT

Recall that the AMT and AutoMag lines became associated with High Standard a few years ago, under the umbrella of the Crusader Group. By last year, the AMT BackUp pistols and the AutoMag II pistols in 22 Winchester Magnum Rimfire (22 WMR) were in production.

Now, in the AutoMag line, a new caliber—17 Hornady Magnum Rimfire (17 HMR)—is being offered, and two previous chamberings—30 Carbine and 45 Winchester Magnum—have been reintroduced in appropriately larger pistols. The AutoMag II is in 17 HMR and 22 WMR, the AutoMag III is in 30 Carbine. The 45 Winchester Magnum appears in the Auto Mag IV.

Avenger

A new semiautomatic pistol design, which has a fixed barrel and does not use a reciprocating slide, has been introduced by Hogue Grips. The pistol, of European design, will be marketed as the Avenger. (See HOGUE)

Benelli

Benelli USA is importing the Cougar pistol in 9mm and 40 S&W under the Stoeger tradename. The Stoeger Cougar is similar to the original rotating-barrel Cougar pistol introduced by Beretta a decade or so ago. (See STOEGER)

Beretta

The Beretta Storm PX4 entered into production last year as Beretta's new polymer-frame service pistol. It was designed as a modular system, with interchangeable backstraps to create an individual fit for a shooter. The PX4 was available in 9mm and 40 S&W.

Now, several new variants have been introduced. The original PX4 was shortened from muzzle and butt. The original rotating barrel locking system was not suitable for the shorter pistol, so a tilting-barrel system was used. With its 3-inch barrel, the new Storm Sub-Compact measures about 5 x 6 inches and weighs 26 ounces. Calibers remain 9mm and 40 S&W. With the short staggered-column magazines, the 9 holds 13, with 10 for the 40. A patented "Sure Grip" magazine extender flips down to form a rest for the lower finger of larger hands. There is room on the shortened frame for a tiny little rail, so lasers, lights and other accessories can still be hung on the Sub-Compact.

The new PX4 Storm in 45 ACP had been anticipated, and the new 45 shows that the Storm design can be maximized as well as minimized. The PX4 45 uses the original rotating-barrel locking system, and has a 10-round staggered-column magazine.

A variation of the Storm 45 is the PX4 Storm SD (Special Duty) pistol. Designed to meet SOCOM (Special Operations Command) military specifications, the SD version as introduced offers a corrosion-resistant finish and special sights. It comes in a Tactical Carrying Case, with one 9-round and two 10-round magazines, a cleaning kit and other items.

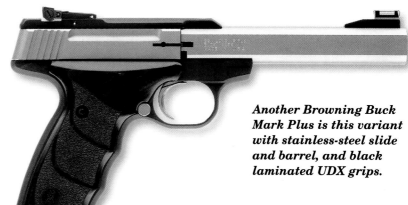

Another Browning Buck Mark Plus is this variant with stainless-steel slide and barrel, and black laminated UDX grips.

Commercial production for the new variants was scheduled for summer 2007.

Beretta also planned to make limited runs of regular-line pistols with special enhancements during 2007. The pistols included the Model 3032 Tomcat, the Model 21 Bobcat, the M9 and the Model 92FS. Embellishments were to be special laser grips, two-tone finishes, high polish and pro-shop enhancements.

Browning

Browning seems determined to tweak its popular Buck Mark 22-caliber pistol line to provide variants to please every potential shooter.

For 2007, three new Buck Mark "Plus" pistols carrying the "UDX" code were introduced, all with the recently-introduced trim grip-frame option.

The Buck Mark Plus UDX has walnut ambidextrous "Ultragrip DX" grips and has a "slabside" 5.5-inch barrel and a matte blue finish. Sights are adjustable rear and fiber-optic front.

The Buck Mark Plus Rosewood UDX is similar, but has rosewood grips.

The Buck Mark Plus Stainless Black Laminated UDX differs by having a stainless barrel and slide, and it comes with black laminated grips.

Bul

The BUL Transmark firm was begun in Israel in 1990 as a company involved with shooting ranges. It soon became a maker of polymer-frame large-capacity 1911-type pistols, which were designated as BUL M-5. Many of the pistols were supplied to other companies and sold under other names.

Now, BUL is branching out. For the first time, the company is offering a steel-frame single-column 45 of more traditional 1911 design. Made in full-size and "commander" sizes, the new Buls still retain the M-5 model number, but are designated the M-5 Classic Government and the M-5 Classic Commander. Both versions come standard with a single-column 8-round magazine.

Even a greater departure in terms of mechanism is the new BUL Cherokee pistol line.

The standard Cherokee Compact is a conventional double-action pistol with a trigger mechanism reminiscent of that of the CZ 75. With its 3.7-inch

The short rail on the Beretta Storm Subcompact's frame gives the pistol a stubby appearance, seen as Malloy gets off some aimed shots with the little pistol.

barrel, the pistol is designated a compact, but the grip still holds a 17-round staggered-column magazine.

Another variant, called the G. Cherokee Compact, is basically similar, but has a slightly larger grip backstrap. The extra dimensions allow the attachment of a special telescoping shoulder stock.

Full-size Cherokee variants are also available with 4.4-inch barrels. They are also made in standard and "G" versions.

All Cherokee variants have a forward rail that will accommodate lights, lasers and other accessories.

Bushmaster

The Bushmaster Carbon 15 9mm pistols, built on lightweight AR-15 style lower and upper receivers, have new handguards available this year. The new parts are ceramic and are ventilated for better heat control.

Chrome-lined barrels are also now offered on the Carbon 15 pistols.

Century

The line between pistols and carbines continues to waver. We have become used to long-range 223-caliber pistols built on the AR-15 action. Now, Century International Arms is offering long-range pistols built on the AK-47 action. The new AK-style pistols, cataloged as "Champion" pistols, are newly-made in Romania and are offered in three models.

The HG1844-N is in the traditional 7.62 x 39mm chambering, and comes with a 30-round magazine. The HG1845-N is chambered for the 223 round, and also is fitted with a 30-shot magazine. For those who like inexpensive plinking with a big gun feel, the HG1846-N Champion is in 22 LR and uses a modified action that utilizes a 10-round magazine.

Colt

With the spread of legal concealed carry in the 1990s, Colt had introduced the Series 90 "Defender", a short, light 45. New for 2007, Colt offered a new small 45. There seems to be no doubt as to the intended market, as the new pistol is named the Colt "Concealed Carry" model.

The Concealed Carry 45 has an aluminum-alloy frame with a beveled magazine well. With its 3-inch barrel, it weighs only 25 ounces. Length is 6.75 inches. Its shortened serrated grip frame holds a special magazine that still offers the 7-round capacity of the full-size 1911. Thus, the small new Colt is a 7 + 1 pistol.

Grips are slim "big diamond" wood grips. The long trigger and burr hammer are skeletonized, and the grip safety tang is extended. The entire pistol is finished a matte black. The sights are definitely snag-free—the sighting system is a channel along the top of the slide, in the style of pocket pistols of years past. The front slide treatment is different from that of previous Colts—instead of a scallop, the front of the slide is slightly narrowed along the entire front portion.

CZ

The subcompact CZ 2075 RAMI pistol has gained acceptance since its introduction several years ago.

Now, a new variant, the RAMI "P," has been added. The new pistol, offered in the 9mm and 40 S&W chamberings of the original, traded the aluminum alloy frame of the original for a new polymer frame.

The slide was also lightened, and internal parts have been redesigned to reduce weight. With a 3-inch barrel, the little pistol weighs about 23 ounces. Magazine capacity is 8 for the 40, and 10 for the 9mm. An extended 14-round magazine is also available for the 9mm.

Two existing CZ models, the CZ 75B and the CZ P-01, are now available factory-equipped with Crimson Trace LaserGrips.

Detonics

All Detonics USA pistol models are offered in the 45 ACP chambering. In addition, the original compact CombatMaster was planned for a number of additional calibers. Now, all these extra chamberings are available. The CombatMaster can now be had in 45 ACP, 40 S&W, 357 SIG, 38 Super and 9mm Luger.

There have been subtle changes in Detonics magazines to match the recoil characteristics of the different calibers and different models.

EAA

European American Armory has had great success with its Tanfoglio-made Witness pistol line. Now, the Witness FCP pistol promises to be one of the most unusual ever offered.

Too bad, but this is the only picture we have of EAA's new Witness FCP (Fast Cycling Pistol). EAA model Marisa Matthews holds the new pistol, which has a fixed "slide" and only four moving parts. The wire on this prototype shows the location of the "tube chamber" that holds the cartridge.

Three prototypes were displayed at the January 2007 SHOT Show.

The FCP (think "Fast Cycling Pistol") uses a Witness polymer frame and some similar firing mechanism parts. What looks like the slide, however, is immobile, fixed in place. The rear portion forms a standing breech and the forward part houses a fixed 4-inch barrel. The barrel has no chamber. A large port occupies the space between the standing breech and the rear of the barrel. A special "tube chamber," containing a loaded cartridge, can be inserted to fill this space, with additional loaded chambers in a magazine below.

The FCP pistol can only be fired double-action, as nothing reciprocates to cock the hammer. When the cartridge in the tube chamber is fired, the bullet goes through the bore. Some gas from that shot is diverted back to expel the chamber (with its contained empty cartridge case) out the port. Another loaded chamber is immediately pushed up into firing position.

The tube chambers are reusable, and can be reloaded with new cartridges. The prototypes were all in 45 ACP. Other chamberings in the offing include 38 Special, 38 Super, 380, 9mm and 40 S&W.

EAA designers apparently have a sense of humor. Because the ejection of the tube chambers can be either right or left, one of the prototypes was made with a left-side ejection port. This configuration allowed the front and rear sights to be mounted on the right side of the "slide," instead of on the top. Thus, the "shooting sideways" method employed by TV bad guys could be used. The shooter could use the sights, and the tube chambers would eject straight down.

Ed Brown

Ed Brown Products adds a new model and a new limited edition to its line of 1911-style 45 automatics.

The new Special Forces model, announced last year, is now a production gun. It is a 5-inch "government" size pistol with 7+1 capacity. Front and rear grip straps have "chainlink" pattern checkering, and the pistol is finished with GEN III severe-use coating. Novak 3-dot night sights are fitted. The long trigger and commander-style hammer are skeletonized. The grip safety and frame have been modified to provide a higher and deeper hold. Cocobolo "big diamond" grips are furnished.

The Sheriff Jim Wilson limited edition pistol was designed to honor lawman/writer Sheriff Jim Wilson. Useful as well as decorative, the pistol incorporates some of Wilson's ideas about pistols used for serious purposes. The pistol is a 5-inch Government model, with a deeply-grooved arched mainspring housing and a front grip strap with 25 lines per inch checkering. The Novak sights consist of a black rear sight teamed with a dovetailed Tritium night sight. Smooth "Tru-Ivory" grip panels and Wilson's signature in the right side of the slide make the pistol a distinctive one.

Firestorm

Last year, this report was forced to record that the Firestorm 1911-style 45 pistols were no longer available. They had been made by Llama/Gabilondo in Spain, and with the demise of that company, the manufacture of the moderately-priced pistols came to a halt.

Now, the importer, SGS, has found a new supplier. The new Firestorm 1911 45s will be made in the Philippines and promise to be of true 1911 military-specification design. Samples for BATF approval were expected early in 2007, with production guns anticipated within the first half of that year. Once the mil-spec pistols become established, deluxe models, high-capacity variants and additional calibers are anticipated.

A new Firestorm 22 LR pistol with a 6-inch barrel is also being offered now.

FNH USA

New 45 ACP pistols joined FNH USA's line of semiautomatic handguns in 2007. Similar in general design to the previous FNP-9 and FNP-40 pistols, the new FNP-45 line comprises several variants.

The FNP-45 has a conventional double-action trigger system. The high-capacity black polymer frame comes with interchangeable backstrap inserts and an integral accessory rail. The slide is stainless steel. It is available in matte stainless finish, or with a black Melonite coating. The staggered-column magazine holds 14 rounds. However, 10-shot models are available for those who live under more-restrictive government controls. With a 4.5-inch barrel, the FNP-45 weighs about 33 ounces.

The FNP-45 USG is a special variant made for submission for consideration for United States

Ed Brown Products has introduced its Sheriff Jim Wilson limited edition 45 to honor lawman/writer Wilson.

military forces. Differences include a sand-colored frame, a lanyard ring and a 15-round magazine.

The new FNP-45 pistols can be readily distinguished visually from their smaller-caliber brethren. The base of the magazine on the earlier guns is parallel to the line of the slide. The new 45 has a magazine base that is perpendicular to the grip, and at a noticeable angle to the slide line.

FNH's Five-seveN pistol, in 5.7 x 28mm, is now offered with a C-More sight system. These are snag-free 3-dot sights, available either with or without Tritium elements, and are now available as optional accessories. Plans seem to be to offer them as standard items later.

The interesting PS 90 carbine—for the same 5.7 x 28 cartridge—has a new variant. The original PS 90 had "designated" optics that were mounted as a more-or-less permanent part of the firearm. Now, the new PS 90 TR (Triple-Rail) carbine has rails to allow mounting other sights and accessories, as the user chooses. Colors are black or green.

Glock

Glock introduced a new 45 ACP pistol in 2007. The new 45, in a way, sort of breaks Glock's tradition of sequentially numbering new models. The original Glock 45, the Model 21, was introduced some years ago, and Glock numbers now go up to 39. This new 45 is introduced as the Glock Model 21 SF, with the "SF" standing for "Short Frame." The 21SF is brand new, and was not in the Glock 2007 catalog in the early part of the year.

The pistol has a full-size barrel and slide, but a smaller frame. It offers what has been described as a "subtle but noticeable" different feel. The Glock 21 has been used in limited numbers by U. S. special forces in combat zones. Reports from the troops using them were favorable, but it was felt that the grip was too large for some shooters. Glock reshaped the frame and installed a new trigger mechanism housing. Most other parts remain the same. One new innovation introduced with the SF is a true ambidextrous magazine release.

The 21 SF uses the same 13-round magazines as the original Model 21.

HK

Heckler & Koch has based most of its current line of pistols on its USP (Universal Selfloading Pistol) design, which allows a number of different mechanical and caliber variations. After getting used to HK pistols having "USP" in their model designations, it is something of a surprise that the new 45-caliber offering for 2007 was named, simply, the HK45.

The new HK45 reportedly was developed for potential U. S. military use. It can be made in a number of double-action and single-action variants. A mechanical internal recoil-reduction system was designed to improve control during rapid fire.

Two basic variants are offered. The standard HK45 has a 4.5-inch barrel and weighs about 28 ounces, and uses a 10-round magazine. A smaller version, the HK45C has a 3.9-inch barrel and tips the scales at 25 ounces. It uses an 8-round magazine. Both variants have replaceable grip panels. Both variants can be fitted with threaded barrels for use with sound suppressors.

Heckler & Koch also plans to offer the 9mm P30 pistol, based on a German customs pistol. Both rear *and side* grip panels can be changed for a very individualized grip feel. The P30 has a decocker control on the left rear of the slide.

Hi-Point

Has the long-awaited Hi-Point 45 ACP carbine become a reality yet? The 9mm and 40 S&W carbines have proved popular, and it seemed logical to bring out a 45-caliber version.

As of January 2007, a Hi-Point representative said the 45 carbine was still under development. They want it to be right before it is introduced. However, availability before the end of 2007 was anticipated.

Hogue

The prototype of a new pistol, the Hogue Avenger, was displayed at the January 2007 SHOT Show. Hogue, the grip company, plans to offer the European-designed pistol.

Dedicated readers of this publication may recall that in the 1997 edition, a new pistol called the Ultramatic was introduced by an Austrian firm. It looked a bit like a 1911, but had a fixed barrel and fixed "slide" and an internal reciprocating bolt. The bolt movement was retarded by two side-mounted locking studs. By the 1999 edition, both the company and the guns were called Wolf Sporting Pistols. However, by the following 2000 edition, the pistols had faded out of the publication.

The design had many good features, but the locking and recoil

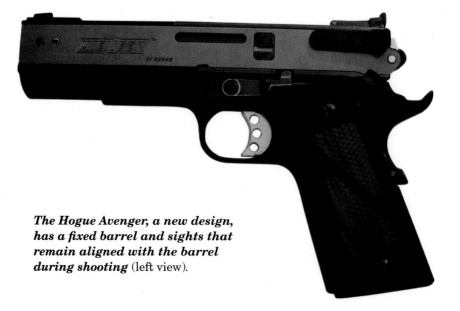

The Hogue Avenger, a new design, has a fixed barrel and sights that remain aligned with the barrel during shooting (left view).

spring systems were complex, with a lot of parts. It did some good shooting, but had some problems, and soon was gone.

During the early days, I photographed Peter Spielberger, a young man with the company, holding an Ultramatic pistol. Many years later, Spielberger rethought the design. He realized that some of the original features, such as the fixed barrel, and the non-moving sights that were always in alignment with the barrel, were good. He set about, with computer assistance, to create new spring and locking systems. The present design uses a pivoting locking wedge that locks into a recess in the top of the fixed "slide." The locking wedge controls the rearward movement of the internal bolt. The locking wedge is prevented from opening too soon by a delay block that must be cammed out of the way. The resulting mechanism is relatively simple, works well and reduces muzzle rise. The fixed, non-moving barrel and non-moving sights always stay in alignment with each other for good inherent accuracy.

Spielberger wisely refrained from reinventing the wheel for the bottom part of the pistol. The frame and trigger mechanism are straight 1911! Using the 1911 design for the lower half of the new pistol means that the Avenger can be made as a complete pistol or as a conversion unit for existing 1911 frames.

Spielberger was at the Hogue display at the January 2007 SHOT Show. So, over a decade later, I was able to take another picture of him (with his hair somewhat grayer now), holding the new pistol. Hogue will market it as the Avenger by Hogue. Limited production was scheduled for early 2007.

Iver Johnson

The new Iver Johnson 1911-style pistols, in 45 ACP and 22 LR calibers, and 22 LR conversion kits were announced year before last. Production of the 22 conversion kits began before pistol production. The production of the 45 pistol was scheduled for early 2007,

while production of the 22 version was anticipated by mid-2007. Both calibers will be available in standard (Raven Series) and deluxe (Eagle Target Series) versions. The deluxe variants will be made with adjustable sights and other niceties.

Kahr

Kahr introduced its new polymer 45 last year, and this year expands its big-bore polymer line with two more 45s. Both are double-action-only, with black polymer frames and matte stainless-steel slides.

The TP45 has a 7-shot magazine, a 4-inch barrel, and weighs about 23 ounces. The PM45 is smaller. With a 3.14-inch barrel and a 5-round magazine; it weighs about 19 ounces. Either pistol can be had with Tritium night sights.

Recall that Kahr now owns the Auto-Ordnance and Thompson firearms lines. In the Thompson line, Kahr offers two new 45 ACP Thompson long guns. The early Thompsons might be considered the first of the pistol-caliber carbines. For 2007, models with detachable buttstocks were made available, for the first time in many decades. The Thompson 1927A-1 Deluxe has a finned 16.5-inch barrel (18 inches with compensator). Thus, even with the buttstock detached, the gun measures 31.5 inches long, and the feds do not consider it a "short-barrel rifle."

However, some people are willing to jump through the necessary hoops and cough up the extra money to have an authentic semiautomatic

look-alike of the original Tommy Gun. For them, there is now the Thompson 1927A-1 SBR (Short Barrel Rifle.) Its 10.5-inch finned barrel (12 inches with compensator) gives it an overall length of 25.5 inches with the buttstock removed.

Both these new Thompson carbines will take either the 50-round drum or the 30-round box magazines.

Kimber

Kimber has evolved into one of the largest makers of 1911-type pistols. This year, three new series of 1911-style autoloaders have been introduced.

The Covert series of 45 ACP carry pistols comes from the Kimber Custom Shop. The series is composed of three models. The full-size variant, the Custom Covert II, has a 5-inch barrel and 7 + 1 capacity, and weighs 31 ounces. The 4-inch Pro Covert II has a bushingless bull barrel. Grip is full-size with 7-round magazine capacity, and the pistol weighs 28 ounces. Both the Custom Covert and Pro Covert have lanyard loops at the butt. The

Top: Kahr's new compact polymer-frame 45, the PM45, holds 5+1 rounds and weighs about 19 ounces (angled view).
Bottom: Kahr's new polymer-frame 45, the TP45, has a 4.3-inch barrel and weighs about 22 ounces (left view).

smallest Covert, the Ultra Covert II, has a 3-inch barrel and weighs 25 ounces. The frame of each Covert is Desert Tan, and the matte black slides are topped with 3-dot night sights. Each Covert pistol has camo-pattern Crimson Trace LaserGrips.

The Aegis is a series designed for 1911 lovers who somehow, for whatever reason, prefer the 9mm chambering. The Ultra Aegis II has a 3-inch barrel, the Pro Aegis II has a 4-inch barrel, and the Custom Aegis II is a full-size 5-inch version. Like the Covert series, the Aegis pistols have machined aluminum frames. Each Aegis has wide slide serrations, a spurless hammer and thin rosewood grips. Weights are about the same as for the Covert series. By the way, "Aegis" comes from the Greek, and means a shield or protection.

The SuperAmerica will be made in limited numbers. It is a full-size blued pistol, and the slide has scroll engraving inside a gold-filled border. It will come in a wooden case with a special Kimber knife. Both pistol and knife have grips made of mammoth ivory.

NAA

Grip-mounted lasers are gaining popularity on large-size pistols. Downsizing this trend, North American Arms will offer Crimson Trace LaserGrips on their little Guardian pistols. The first ones to wear the new grips will be the larger-frame 380 and 32 NAA

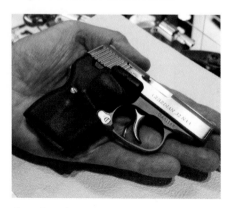

A palm-size pistol doesn't have much room for the components of a laser sight, but North American Arms is offering Crimson Trace LaserGrips on its little pistols.

versions, with the smaller 32 ACP and 25 NAA coming later. Availability was anticipated during 2007.

Para-Ordnance

Para-Ordnance has become one of the largest makers of 1911-type pistols. One can get the hint of this by looking at their 2007 catalog. On the cover, a large picture of a Para pistol overlies 51 small images of other pistols made by the company. Consider that Para makes traditional single-action and LDA (light double action) versions, offers single-column and staggered-column magazines with capacities of 6, 7, 8, 9, 10, 12, 13, 14, 15, 16 and 18 rounds, makes frames of carbon steel, stainless steel and aluminum alloy, offers barrel lengths of 3, 3.5, 4.25 and 5 inches, and can furnish pistols chambered for 9mm, 38 Super, 40 S&W, 45 GAP and 45 ACP. Small wonder that the company offers a lot of variations.

Some of Para's new offerings:

The Big Hawg can be considered the big brother of the Warthog and other compact pistols in Para's "Hawg" series. Since the small ones were well-received, why not a full-size model? The Big Hawg is a full 5-inch barrel 45 with a wide aluminum alloy frame and 14 + 1 capacity. The big pistol weighs only 28 ounces.

The Covert Black Slim Hawg is a 6 + 1 capacity 45 with a 3-inch barrel. It weighs 24 ounces.

The Carry GAP is a 6 + 1 steel-frame variant with a steel frame and 3-inch barrel, weighing 29 ounces. It is an LDA pistol chambered for the 45 G.A.P. cartridge. The grip is smaller because of the shorter cartridge.

The CCO GAP is a similar pistol with a 3.5-inch barrel and 7 + 1 capacity. Also for the 45 GAP, it weighs 31 ounces.

Because they are making the smaller grip frame, why then not make a smaller-grip 9mm? The Carry 9 is an 8 + 1 9mm pistol with a 3-inch barrel, weighing 24 ounces.

The 1911 Stainless SSP is a full-size classic single-column 8 + 1 45 ACP pistol in stainless steel.

The 1911 Limited is a similar pistol gussied up with special

Rock River Arms is now offering its Tactical Pistol, a full-size 45 with a machined frame rail.

grips and a striking black/stainless slide treatment.

Para seems determined to make a 1911 to suit just about any shooter's requirements.

Rock River

Accessory rails are becoming popular, and Rock River Arms has made a variant of their forged and machined frames which now includes a frame rail. This frame is used on the new 1911-style "Tactical Pistol" that appeared for the first time in the company's 2007 lineup. The Tactical Pistol is guaranteed to shoot 2.5-inch groups at 50 yards with specific factory ammunition.

Rohrbaugh

Rohrbaugh is the little company that came out of nowhere a few years ago with the smallest and lightest all-metal 9mm pistol. Just a little bit larger than a 3x5 index card, the Rohrbaugh R9 weighed in at 12.8 ounces. In 2005, the Rohrbaugh pistol was awarded the NRA "Golden Bullseye" award as handgun of the year. For 2007, the line expanded to include a new finish and a new chambering.

An all-black variant is now available as the "Stealth" R9. The slides are coated with "Diamond Black," which reduces friction as well as glare.

A light 9mm will kick, even as a locked-breech pistol. So, Rohrbaugh has introduced a version in 380 ACP. This variant gives a useful power level with reduced recoil.

The Ruger 22/45 MK III Hunter has a 4.5-inch fluted stainless-steel barrel (right view).

Ruger

Ruger has introduced a shorter version of its 22-caliber 22/45 Mark III Hunter pistol. The new 4.5-inch barrel Hunter pistol has a slim polymer grip with the angle and feel of the 1911. The receiver and barrel are stainless steel. Sights are an adjustable "V" rear and a "HiViz" fiber-optic front sight. If a scope is desired, the receiver is already drilled and tapped for a scope base—which is included with the pistol. Also included with each new Hunter are two 10-round magazines.

Sarsilmaz

The Turkish Sarsilmaz company, well-known as a shotgun maker, has come to the attention of American pistol shooters recently. The firm is making pistols which are sold under the names of several other companies.

Two new pistols were introduced under the Sarsilmaz name in January 2007. The 45-caliber Kilinc pistol is an enlargement of the steel-frame 9mm Kilinc pistol (a CZ 75 design) made for the Turkish military forces. Production models of the new 45 were scheduled to be offered by the end of 2007.

A new pistol, the Vatoz, is being designed for the Turkish army. It will be in the standard 9mm chambering, and will have a new light alloy frame. Early specimens were displayed at the 2007 SHOT Show.

Sigarms

45 ACP pistols are prominent in Sigarms' new offerings this year.

Sigarms is a relative newcomer to the world of 1911 pistols, but its 1911-type Revolution pistols have sixteen entries in the 2007 catalog. The latest is the Revolution Compact C3. The striking-looking pistol has a black anodized alloy frame under a stainless steel slide and controls. Rosewood grips complete the package. With its 4-inch barrel, the C3 weighs about 29 ounces.

The 45-caliber P220 was introduced back in the mid 1970s. It took a back seat to 9mm offerings when the "wondernine" era took off in the 1980s. Now, times have changed, and the P220 has moved up to the driver's seat. Most of SIG's new offerings are variants of the P220.

The P220 Super Match has had the barrel extended to 5 inches. It has a two-tone appearance, with a black beavertail frame and a stainless-steel slide. Grips are SIG custom wood panels. A factory test target comes with each pistol to prove its accuracy.

The P220 Combat is a 45 designed to meet military standards. It has an earth-tone frame, Picatinny rail and night sights. A variant, the P220 Combat TB, has a threaded barrel that can accept a sound suppressor. Unlike some of the pistols designed for military consideration, the Sigarms P220 Combat uses a single-column magazine. The standard magazine holds 8 rounds. An extended 10-shot magazine, which protrudes below the bottom of the grip, is also available.

The P220 Compact is the same general size as the compact P245 but has a new shape. The frame has a beavertail tang, and the 6-round magazine has an extended base. Several variants are made, and in 2007, it replaces the P245.

Sarsilmaz introduced a new aluminum-frame 9mm service-type pistol, the Vatos, at the 2007 SHOT Show.

The Sigarms 1911 Revolution Compact C3 pistol has a two-tone finish and rosewood grips (right view).

Top left: The new Sigarms P220 Combat 45, right view. Top right: The new Smith & Wesson M&P 45 is available in military-style configuration, with manual safety, accessory rail and earth-tone frame.
Bottom: S&W's new M&P Compact is shortened to match its 3.5-inch barrel. This one is an M&P 9c, the 9mm compact.

The P220 Carry Elite is an 8 + 1 compact pistol with a full-size frame and shorter 3.9-inch barrel of the Compact. It features the Sigarms short reset trigger (SRT).

A fundraising pistol for the group known as "Concerns of Police Survivors (C.O.P.S.)," is a special P226 designated the COPS model. For every pistol sold, Sigarms will contribute to the fund to help the families of slain police officers.

Smith & Wesson

S&W's Military & Police (M&P) polymer-frame autoloaders in 40 and 9mm were well-received. Now a 45 ACP version, the Smith & Wesson M&P45, has been added. The new 45 was offered in all-black or earth-tone variants. The earth-tone pistol, which apparently was designed with an eye to military contracts, has an additional ambidextrous

manual safety. All M&P45 pistols have a 4.5-inch barrel, with three interchangeable grips. An accessory rail is on the forward part of the frame. Weight is just under 30 ounces.

The M&P series was expanded to use the 45 cartridge, but the 9mm variant was also downsized into a compact version. The new M&P9 Compact has a 3.5-inch barrel and comes with either a 10-round or 12-round magazine. The smaller polymer-frame pistol weighs about 22 ounces. The stainless-steel barrel and slide are coated with black Melonite. Three interchangeable grip sizes allow the shooter to fit the smaller gun to a particular hand.

Sigarms has brought out a compact version of its 1911 Revolution series, the C3 Compact, in 45 ACP chambering (left view).

Robert Malloy, the writer's brother, shoots the new S&W 45-caliber M&P pistol in its earth-tone military configuration.

The S&W Model 945, available as a Performance Center gun, is a hybrid of 1911 and early S&W 45 features. Malloy shot this handsome specimen and was impressed with its accuracy.

Ken Ramage, the Editor-in-Chief of this publication, tries out the Smith & Wesson M&P 9c, the new 9mm compact version of the company's M&P line.

The Smith & Wesson Performance Center offers the 45 ACP Model 945. When S&W introduced its 45-caliber double-action autoloader, the Model 645, much pistol competition was dominated by 1911-type pistols. Long before the company gave in and brought out its own 1911, S&W made a number of attempts to create a better competition pistol. The present Model 945 is a sort of hybrid of 1911 and earlier S&W 45 features. Some think the resultant pistol is better than the 1911. Whatever the comparison, I can agree that the 945 is a very good-shooting pistol. I had a chance to shoot one recently, and it was exceptionally accurate.

Sphinx

The Sphinx, a Swiss-made pistol based on the CZ 75 with a number of modifications,

has been available as a top-end 9mm. Now, it is available in a larger version, in 45 ACP chambering.

The Sphinx design differs from the basic CZ 75 in a number of aspects. Perhaps most noticeable is that the operating frame and the grip frame are machined as two separate pieces. All parts are CNC-machined. A full slide-length frame and integral accessory rail put weight forward to reduce muzzle rise.

The new Sphinx 45 is a heavy pistol, weighing in at about 43 ounces. It should appeal to those who have admired the workmanship of the Sphinx, but wanted a 45.

Springfield

The 45 ACP chambering in Springfield's XD line was introduced last year. This year, the company

introduced the 45 ACP XD Compact. The new XD Compact seems designed to help people who can't quite decide what size pistol they want. The new XD Compact comes in a 4-inch barrel version, with a 5-incher anticipated in the near future. The Compact has had about three-quarters of an inch trimmed off the grip to match the length of a 10-shot magazine. However, two magazines are furnished with each pistol—a ten-shot "concealment" magazine that ends at the base of the grip, and a 13-round "service model" magazine that has an extension of the grip at the base. Springfield calls this the "Mag X-Tension." Each pistol comes with

The big new Sphinx 45 is made in Switzerland and handled by Sabre Defence Industries.

Springfield's Laura Lewsader displays the company's new small-grip 1911, the Springfield EMP in 9mm chambering.

special "XD Gear" items—a polymer belt holster, magazine loader and double magazine pouch.

Also new is the Springfield EMP (Enhanced Micro Pistol), a nice-looking little 9mm 1911-type pistol. The small-grip 9mm has a two-tone appearance, with dark frame and stainless-steel slide. Rosewood grips set off the colors of the metal.

STI

STI International makes 1911-type pistols and offers over 25 different models in multiple calibers. New for 2007 were five different variants.

The Escort is a compact-length pistol with a commander-size frame. Weighing about 23 ounces, this is the lightest pistol in the STI line. In 45 ACP, it has a 3-inch ramped bull barrel with a fully supported chamber. The frame is forged aluminum.

The Guardian is a commander-frame 45 with a 3.9-inch supported ramped barrel. The Guardian comes with redwood grips and weighs about 32 ounces.

The Legend is a big pistol with a modular steel/polymer frame that holds a long staggered-column magazine. The barrel is a 5-inch supported bull barrel. The hard chrome slide has a black "Legend" inlay and distinctive "Sabertooth" cocking serrations. Weight is 38 ounces. An adjustable rear sight and Dawson fiber-optic front sight

are fitted. The Legend is available in 9mm, 40 S&W and 45 ACP.

The Sentinel is a full-size 5-inch 1911 pistol available in 9mm, 40 and 45. Thick rosewood grips are fitted to the blued, matte-finish frame. Adjustable rear sight and competition front sight are fitted. The gun is suitable, out-of-the-box, for IPSC or IDPA competition.

The Spartan is a basic Parkerized 5-inch 1911-type pistol. It has a traditional barrel bushing and uncheckered frame, but comes with a number of enhancements. The Spartan has a high-ride beavertail grip safety and front and rear slide serrations. It weighs 35 ounces, and has adjustable rear and fiber-optic front sights fitted.

Stoeger

The new Stoeger Cougar may look familiar to many shooters. The design was introduced as the Beretta Cougar in the mid-1990s. As introduced, the Cougar was a fairly compact, aluminum-frame pistol of locked breech/rotating barrel design. The trigger mechanism was conventional double action.

The new Stoeger Cougar is almost identical to the original Italian-made pistol, but it is made in Turkey, imported by Benelli, and marketed under the Stoeger name. Pistols are offered in 9mm and 40 S&W. The 40-caliber magazine

holds 11 rounds and the 9mm magazine carries 15. Niceties such as 3-dot sights and ambidextrous safety/decocking levers come standard. Barrel length for either 9 or 40 is 3.6 inches, and overall length is 7 inches. Weight is about 32 ounces.

Taurus

As did a number of other manufacturers, Taurus designed a 45-caliber pistol to meet SOCOM requirements for the Joint Combat Pistol trials. With the postponement of the trials, Taurus decided to introduce the pistol to the commercial and law enforcement markets. The new 24/7 OSS pistol is now offered in 40 S&W and 9mm, as well as 45 ACP. It has an interesting single action/double action (SA/DA) trigger system. It fires normally from SA mode. However, in case of a misfire, the mechanism changes to DA mode to permit additional strikes to the primer.

The 24/7 OSS comes in two versions. The "DS" model can be carried in SA "cocked and locked" condition, with the manual safety on. The striker can be released safely by pushing up on the safety lever. Then it switches to DA mode. The "D" model is double action only, with a decocker.

Barrel length for any 24/7 OSS variant is 5.25 inches. Capacity is 17 + 1 for the 9mm, 15 + 1 for the 40 and 12 + 1 for the 45.

I cannot verify the story, but if it is true, some people at Taurus have a sense of humor. The "OSS" model designation, which calls to mind

Left: The STI Escort is a 45 with a shortened slide and 3.4-inch barrel.
Top: STI's Sentinel is a 5-inch barrel, single-column 1911, available in 9mm, 40 or 45.
Bottom: STI's new Guardian is a compact 45 with a 3.9-inch bull barrel.

Top left: This new 45-caliber Taurus PT 24/7 OSS pistol is the "DS" version, which has a unique single action/double action trigger mechanism.

Top right: The compact Millennium PRO is offered with a 3.25-inch barrel. This variant is a 12+1 9mm with a titanium slide.

Middle: The Taurus PT 1911 45 is also available with an integral frame accessory rail.

Taurus PT 24/7 PRO pistols come with a 3.3-inch barrel option. This version has a frame rail.

The 24/7 PRO from Taurus also comes in a 4-inch barrel variant, with frame rail and ribber grip.

The new Taurus PT 1911 45 is offered in blue (shown) or stainless steel.

The Taurus Millennium PRO 3.25-inch compact is available in an all-black finish. This is a 40 S&W version with 10+1 capacity.

the clandestine WWII organization that became the CIA, is said to stand for "O-Six Submission." That tongue-in-cheek designation simply meant it was made to submit for government tests in 2006.

Beside the military-type 24/7 OSS, 24/7 Pro pistols are now offered. Similar in some mechanical features to the 24/7 OSS, the 24/7 Pro pistols are made in 3.33-inch and 4-inch barrel lengths as well as 5.2 inches. They have more "civilian" features such as ribbed rubber ("ribber") grips.

Some of the same engineering has been applied to the smaller Millennium Pro series with 3.25-inch barrels. Caliber offerings should suit nearly everyone—32 ACP, 380, 9mm, 40 S&W and 45 ACP. Weights vary from 16 to 22 ounces, depending on caliber and magazine capacity.

Taurus created a stir a few years ago when the company announced they would offer a 1911-type pistol.

Now the Taurus 1911 is available. Barrel length is the traditional 5 inches. Capacity is 8 + 1. The Taurus 1911 is available in 45 ACP only and offers blued (Model 1911B) and stainless-steel (Model 1911SS) finishes. Versions with integral Picatinny rail on the frame forward extension, and versions with aluminum frames were planned for late 2007. A Novak Custom variant is also in the works. Interestingly, each Taurus 1911 pistol has the serial number not only on the frame, but on the slide and barrel. If you buy several, you don't have to worry about mixing the parts while cleaning.

Thompson

Perhaps no other firearm outline is as recognizable as that of a Thompson. The original 45 ACP Thompson submachine guns and semiautomatic carbines of the 1920s can perhaps be considered the first of the pistol-caliber carbines. They continue to have an appeal all these decades later. Kahr Arms, the current manufacturer, offers two new variants this year. (See KAHR)

Tristar

Tristar Sporting Arms imports a line of shotguns and replica Sharps rifles. New for 2007, a line of Turkish-made "Tisas" pistols will be imported.

The pistols are conventional double action, with staggered-column magazines and ambidextrous decockers. Most are expected to be offered in 9mm, but one 45 was on display at the Tristar exhibit at the January 2007 SHOT Show.

Uselton

Uselton's new pistol offering is the "Slant Six" pistol, a small 1911-type 45. It has a semi-bobtail "slant" grip treatment and a 6-round magazine.

Rick Uselton promotes exotic looks in his pistols, and displayed one with

For those who like the authentic "Tommy Gun" look and don't mind extra regulation, the 1927A1 Thompson semiautomatic carbine is available as a "short barrel rifle." It has the new detachable stock and can use either box or drum magazines.

crocodile-skin grip panels—inlaid into Cocobolo wood—at the January 2007 SHOT Show. In the works are grips with inlays of ostrich, elephant, alligator and shark skins.

Uselton race guns are planned. They will be double-column 1911s with 19 + 1 capacity. The "Desert Storm" pistol will be a full-size 5-inch 1911 with a ceramic coating finish.

U. S. Firearms

Recall that U. S. Firearms made its reputation building replicas of historic Colt revolvers. Then, a few years ago, the company started adding early Colt semiautomatic pistols, and the early 45 ACP, 38 Super and 22 Ace pistols are now in their line.

Now, USFA will reintroduce the Colt Woodsman, the historic first-ever

22-caliber autoloading pistol, which was invented by John M. Browning. The version they are planning is the "first generation" pistol initially made by Colt in 1915. The company is serious about its intention to produce the early Woodsman, but no date has been set for production.

Volquartsen

The acceptance of the little 17 Mach 2 cartridge has brought about the production of a number of rifles and also handguns, both autoloaders and revolvers, in that caliber. Owners of 22 LR pistols may have wondered if their guns could be converted to the new little 17. For Ruger owners, Volquartsen has an answer with its new Mach 2 conversion kit. The kit is suitable for Ruger Mark II and Mark III pistols. The "drop-in" kit includes a barreled receiver, with mated bolt and other necessary parts.

Postscript

More interesting autoloading handguns are available now than ever before. If you have held off, consider buying a new pistol, perhaps several. Give yourself a chance to try out new ideas—or new versions of old classics—this year. And, because autoloaders are liable to come under fire during the present Congress, take someone new with you to the range to try the guns out. The more people that understand guns, know how to handle them, and enjoy shooting them, the less the chance that anti-gun politicians can have their way. ⊛

The new Tisas 45 ACP pistol was introduced at the 2007 SHOT Show. The new 45 has unusual wood grips that extend forward on the frame.

SIX-GUNS & OTHERS :
HANDGUNS TODAY

by John Taffin

As this is written we are commemorating two very important six-gun anniversaries. The first cartridge-firing revolver, appearing 150 years ago, was the Smith & Wesson Model #1 chambered in 22 rimfire, also a new development. While this little seven-shot Tip-Up is long gone, the 22 remains our most popular cartridge. The Model #1 would evolve into the Model #2, Model #3, the Double Action Model, the Military & Police; then, 100 years ago, those evolutionary models would lead to the first N-frame, the New Century or 1st Model Hand Ejector, or as it is more affectionately known, the Triple-Lock chambered in 44 Special which a half century later would become the Smith & Wesson 44 Magnum.

I intend to shoot a lot of 22s this year to not only celebrate the cartridge's 150th anniversary, but also because they are so enjoyable. I started off the year celebrating the 44 Special by purchasing a 2nd Generation 7½-inch, ivory-stocked Colt Single Action Army 44 Special insuring more good shooting. It won't be alone as we shall see looking at the offerings for six-gunners this year.

A Dream Come True

Since this is the 100th anniversary of the 44 Special it is altogether fitting to see a museum dedicated to the person who not only did the most to popularize the 44 Special but also highly influenced the development of the 44 Magnum. From 1929 until 1955 Elmer Keith was the leading advocate of 44 Special six-guns. When he received the new 44 Magnum from Smith & Wesson in early 1956, he retired his 44 Specials and carried a 44 Magnum virtually daily from then on. In 1981 Elmer Keith suffered a stroke and died in 1984. He left a rich legacy to all shooters as well as a large collection of firearms and game trophies.

In November 2005 a friend of Ted Keith's, Al Marion, heard Cabela's planned to open a new store in Boise, Idaho and he had an idea. He contacted Jeff Montgomery of Cabela's who happens to be in charge of all the taxidermy displays at all Cabela's stores, and outlined his idea. Jeff caught the vision and, subsequently, Cabela's would do what no one else had been able to do, establish a true Elmer Keith Museum. Part of the museum is Elmer Keith sitting at his desk in front of his ancient typewriter in his office. When a button is pushed, he turns around in his chair, moves his arm with his ever-present cigar, and talks to those who are present. I used his writings to put together the seven-minute presentation.

My second job was to write the descriptions of the nearly 60 handguns, rifles and shotguns on display and then help place them in the glass cases. One side of the museum has all the six-guns while the other displays the rifles. I chose the #5 SAA 44 Special as the centerpiece of the handgun display so it would be the first thing anyone would see. On each side of it I placed two of his other most used six-guns. On one side of the #5 we have the King Custom 44 Special Colt Single Action with a 7½-inch barrel and custom sights; on the other side rests Keith's most used 44 Magnum, a 4-inch pre-29 with ivory grips carved in his favorite longhorn pattern.

I always wondered how Keith could shoot his heavy 44 Magnum load consisting of his 250-grain #429421 bullet over 22 grains of #2400. I found out the first time I handled his six-guns while serving on the Museum Board. The carving of the grip filled in the natural crease in the hand, doing much to help moderate felt recoil. All three of these famous six-guns are stocked with ivory and the #5 is fully engraved, while the other two working guns are the standard case-hardened/blue finish of a Colt Single Action and the old Smith & Wesson Bright Blue, heavily worn thus showing a lot of daily use. Other six-guns include two other 44 Special Colt Single Actions as well as several 44 Magnum Smith & Wesson and Ruger revolvers; his matched pair of 4-inch S&W 41 Magnums; a fully engraved and ivory-stocked S&W Model 1917, very rare examples of the factory 5-inch 1950 Target 44 Special and S&W 44 Magnum, and his only semi-automatic, an old 1911. Until Keith's stroke, Salmon, Idaho was the six-gunner's Mecca; now all roads lead to Cabela's in Boise, Idaho.

AWA-USA

AWA does not import complete firearms but rather parts that are finished and assembled into complete firearms in AWA's Florida facility. Originally, American Western Arms offered two basic Colt replicas, the standard model Longhorn and the top-of-the-line Peacekeeper which boasted a factory-tuned action, 11-degree forcing cone, 1st Generation-style cylinder flutes and bone/charcoal case-hardened frame. I have one of these Peacekeepers, a 45 Colt 4¾-inch single-action six-gun that has been in use for several years with nary a problem. The Longhorn and the Peacekeeper models are now gone, replaced by the Classic 1873 and the Ultimate 1873. The standard model is finished in high-polish bluing and has one-piece walnut stocks; all springs are Wolff, and the trigger pull—out of the box—is 3½ to 4 pounds. The finish of the Classic 1873 can be upgraded to blue/bone & charcoal color-case, or nickel—or even hard chrome. Polymer ivory stocks are also available.

The top-of-the-line six-gun from AWA-USA is the Ultimate, which offers many options, including a coil mainspring. Chamberings available are 32-20, 38-40, 44-40, 357 Magnum and 45 Colt, in standard barrel lengths of 4¾, 5½ and 7½ inches. The standard finish is high-polish blue, with the same finish options as the Classic to include the frame being finished in bone and charcoal color case-hardening by Doug Turnbull Restoration. Standard stocks are one-piece walnut, polymer ivory or two-piece black checkered grips as well as the full gamut of A, B, C,

Taffin shooting the AWA octagon-barreled Ultimate 1873.

or D engraving. A third offering is the Ultimate Octagon, which is the same six-gun as the Ultimate but with an octagon barrel. I have two of these from the Custom Shop, one 7½ inches and the other 10 inches; both are 44-40s with extra cylinders chambered in 44 Special, and they have consecutive serial numbers. There is no way I can pass up a good 44 Special, let alone one with an extra 44-40 cylinder. Both have proven to be excellent-shooting six-guns.

The final offering from AWA is the Lightning Bolt, based on Steve "Josh Randall" McQueen's Mare's Leg as used in the TV series "Wanted Dead Or Alive." As far as I know AWA was the first to offer a replica of the Colt Lightning and they have now pistol-ized it. The Lightning Bolt uses the basic pump action; however, it is not a rifle but ATF-classified as a handgun. Barrel length is 12 inches, magazine capacity is five rounds and it is available with round or octagon barrels, several finish options as on their six-guns, and chambered in 45 Colt, 38 Special, 38-40 and 44-40.

Charter

Charter Arms Bulldogs have been tremendously important to me and mine. Three times in my life I have really needed a firearm. Once,

when I was a teenager, it was just the sudden appearance of a 7½-inch 45 Colt that protected me from a whole lot of trouble. A Charter Arms 44 Special Bulldog was involved the other two times, and in both cases my family was present and in possible danger had that 44 Special Bulldog not been in my hand. Over the past four decades I have carried a Bulldog in my boot top, in my pocket and somewhere in a vehicle when traveling; it has been on innumerable camping and hiking trips. It is one of my most-used firearms, although

The Charter Arms Undercover offered in 38 Special is also now available in 32 Magnum.

44 SPECIAL
HORNADY
180 XTP-JHP
786 FPS

The Charter Arms 44 Special Bulldog Pug is a very accurate pocket pistol.

12 ounces with its aluminum frame and boot grip-style rubber stocks. The ejector rod is also enclosed on this little pocket pistol and the sights are the same easy-to-see square style as found on all Charter Arms revolvers. Charter now offers the Undercoverette in 32 Magnum for those unable to handle the recoil of the 38 Special, as well as the Southpaw, a left-handed version of the Undercover 38 with a cylinder that swings out to the right.

Cimarron

The Richards Conversion, the improved Richard-Mason Conversion and the 1871-72 Open-Top all served as transition revolvers from the 1860 Army to the Colt Single Action Army. For those who wish to shoot such revolvers, all three have been available as replicas for quite some time, most being chambered in 44 Colt. This cartridge, in both its original and modern version, has a smaller rim than the 44 Russian as the cylinder of the converted 1860 Army is not large enough to accept the larger rim of the Russian without overlapping. Now thanks to Cimarron Firearms we have the newest version of the Richards Conversion, the Richards II, which not only has room for the larger diameter rims, but the frame and cylinder have been made

it is very seldom fired and hardly ever brought out to show someone as an example of a great 44 Special.

One Bulldog, a stainless steel version, rests in the main bathroom medicine cabinet; another stainless steel Bulldog 44 is in the bathroom off my reloading room. One house gun can be pretty worthless if it's in one spot and I'm in the other when it is needed. Can you think of any place one can be more vulnerable in the house if trouble begins than the bathroom? My wife used to do quite a bit of fishing—both fly and otherwise—and always seemed to fall in at least once every trip. It didn't take me long to realize the gun of choice in her vest should be a stainless Bulldog.

The newest 44 Special from Charter Arms is the Bulldog Pug. The Pug is the same basic design as the two original Bulldogs, with differences. The barrel length is now 2½ inches and the ejector rod is now enclosed. This means it is no longer possible to pull forward on the ejector rod to release the cylinder so the cylinder latch release may not be removed. Another change is the grip design. The Bulldog Pug is fitted with finger-groove rubber grips that are quite narrow, very comfortable for shooting and also mate well with

the satin matte stainless steel frame. The sights are the same: easy-to-see square rear notch; the front sight is now a ramp-style rather than the post of the originals. This Bulldog Pug not only shoots closer to point of aim than the other two, it also has proven quite accurate in its own right.

A second gun from Charter Arms is the appropriately named Off Duty. This 2-inch barreled, five-shot, double-action-only 38 Special weighs only

Cimarron now offers the 1858 Remington in 45 Colt.

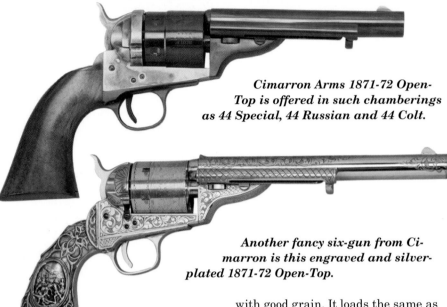

Cimarron Arms 1871-72 Open-Top is offered in such chamberings as 44 Special, 44 Russian and 44 Colt.

Another fancy six-gun from Cimarron is this engraved and silver-plated 1871-72 Open-Top.

larger to accept the 45 Colt. It is also available in 44 Colt, 44 Special and 38 Special.

The 45 Colt Cimarron Richards II is an all-steel revolver without the brass trigger guard of the original. Mainframe, hammer, breech plate and loading gate are all case-colored, with the balance of the revolver being finished in a nicely polished deep blue black. The grip frame is the comfortable 1860 Army very well fitted with one-piece walnut stocks

with good grain. It loads the same as any traditional single action—that is, the hammer is placed on half-cock to allow the cylinder to rotate and opening the loading gate accesses the chambers for loading or unloading.

A second 45 Colt new from Cimarron this year is the Remington 44 New Army percussion revolver conversion in 45 Colt. Once again it was necessary to increase the size of the cylinder to be able to place six 45 Colt chambers in the cylinder. This conversion is quite different from the Richards II. The breech plate/loading gate is somewhat of a

double saddle construction; that is, it slides into place and clips over both sides of the top strap and both sides of the mainframe. When the cylinder is removed, the breech plate can also be removed without tools and the percussion cylinder, which is supplied with this Cimarron Cartridge Conversion, placed in the frame. This conversion also follows the original in that the bullet seater is maintained and the top of the forepart is notched to hold the ejector rod in place. For loading or unloading, the bullet seater is unlatched, the ejector rod is rotated 180 degrees and is then ready for punching out empty cartridges.

The third new revolver from Cimarron is the "Man with No Name" patterned after a six-gun often used by Clint Eastwood's movie characters. Based on the 1851 Colt Navy, this conversion is not the same as the other two as the breech plate is an integral machined part of the frame and not a separate piece. The barrel and bullet seater assembly are traditional 1851 Navy with the cylinder accessed by a loading gate; however, there is no ejector rod for removing cartridges. I did not find this a problem as it is chambered in 38 Long Colt/38 Special and fired cartridges are easily removed and will often fall out of their own accord when the barrel is pointed skywards.

The finish is a cylinder and barrel nicely polished deep blue black; the mainframe, hammer, and bullet seater are case-colored; while the grip frame—both back strap and trigger guard—are brass. One-piece walnut stocks, which in this case have exceptional grain, are available in plain smooth wood, with the silver rattlesnake on the right grip.

Cimarron Firearms has come a long way since Mike Harvey first purchased a little import company known as Allen Firearms. I was the first to write up Cimarron too many years ago and I have been well pleased to see the continued upgrading of Italian replicas due in no small part to the efforts of Mike Harvey. Not only has the quality improved significantly, but it has gone hand-in-hand with a higher level of authenticity. The Cimarron

Cimarron's 1851 Navy "Man With No Name" 38 conversion.

catalog contains replicas of nearly every Colt and Remington single action offered in the last half of the 19th century. Replicas of the traditional Colt-style single action are offered as the Model P in all the standard barrel lengths and blued/ case-colored, nickel-plated, and even stainless steel. Custom engraved versions include replicas based on the fully engraved single actions of General Patton and Col. Theodore Roosevelt. One of my favorites is the "Wyatt Earp," a 10-inch Buntline Special complete with identifying medallion on the grip as seen in the movie "Tombstone." It is offered in both the antiqued traditional finish and regular blue/case-color.

Colt

I'm sitting at my desk looking through a Colt catalog. There are double-action revolvers: Python, Detective Special, Cobra, Agent, Diamondback, Trooper, Official Police and Lawman; and single-action revolvers, Single Action Army, New Frontier, Buntline Special, Peacemaker 22, and New Frontier 22. Another section has Colt Percussion Revolvers, the Third Model Dragoon and the 1851 Navy. We finally come to the section on Colt Center Fire Automatics and we find the Gold Cup National Match, Government Model, Combat Commander, Lightweight Commander, Woodsman Match Target, Woodsman, Targetsman, and Huntsman. I sigh as I put the 1975 Colt catalog back in my file.

Every single revolver save one is long gone from the production line at Colt. That is the downside. The upside is not only does the Single Action Army remain as Colt's only six-gun, the word I hear from shooters all across the country is Colt is doing an excellent job with their current 3rd Generation Single Actions. They are available in the three standard barrel lengths of 4¾-, 5½-, and 7½-inches, nickel or blued/case-colored finish and chambered for 32-20, 38-40, 44-40, 38 Special, 357 Magnum and 45 Colt. There are many grand traditional single-action six-guns out there... but only one can say it is a genuine Colt.

Freedom Arms

The first factory-produced Freedom Arms 454 left the Star Valley, Wyoming factory in 1983. When I discovered Freedom Arms in late 1985, they were building a whole lot more guns than they could sell. One of the reasons was the fear factor. Most gun writers did not want to shoot the 454. At the time I was just really getting started as a freelancer for the major publications and I called Wayne Baker and was pleasantly surprised to find he would trust me with a test gun. I subsequently purchased that 10½-inch revolver and it is as tight today as it was 25 years ago; a Freedom Arms revolver has the precision of the finest crafted machinery while at the same time having the strength of a bank vault. They are built of the finest materials obtainable and with tight as possible tolerances. They do not shoot loose.

As sales of the 454 increased, Freedom Arms branched out into other chamberings such as the 44 Magnum, 357 Magnum, 41 Magnum, 50 Action Express and even 22 Long Rifle. Both the 357 and 44 Magnum Silhouette Models became very popular among the top shooters. Next came the really big six-guns or—as far as Freedom Arms goes—five-

shooters in 475 Linebaugh. Once the 475 Linebaugh in a Freedom Arms revolver was reality, Bob Baker could take a serious look at the 500. To chamber such a cartridge in the Freedom Arms cylinder would necessitate cutting into the ratchet at the back of the cylinder as well as reducing the rim diameter significantly to fit a Freedom Arms cylinder. The result was a cartridge headspacing on a belt rather than the cartridge rim... and the 500 Wyoming Express Model 83 was born. Factory-chambered 500 WE revolvers are now available in three barrel lengths, the Perfect Packin' Pistol candidate 4¾-inch as well as 6- and 7½-inch versions, and if one has an older Model 83 chambered in 50 Action Express a new cylinder can be fitted in 500 Wyoming Express.

In 1997 Freedom Arms introduced their "90% gun," the smaller—and thus easier packin', easier-shooting Model 97. The 90% comes from the fact that they are about 9/10ths the size of the original Freedom Arms Model 83. The first Model 97 six-guns offered were just that, true six-guns with six-shot cylinders in 357 Magnum and offered with either fixed or adjustable sights. In 1998, the Model 97 arrived as a five-shot 45 Colt. This is the most compact single-

Two versions of the Freedom Arms 500 Wyoming Express.

action 45 Colt ever factory-produced. The 45 Colt Model 97 from Freedom Arms is one ounce lighter than a 5½-inch Colt SAA at 38 ounces, two ounces lighter than the same barrel length in the Colt New Frontier.

The 357 Magnum and 45 Colt were only the beginning. The Model 97 is now also available in 41 Magnum and 44 Special with five-shot cylinders, and as true six-guns in 17 HMR, 22 LR/22 Magnum, and 32 Magnum/32-20. The Model 97 is a thoroughly modern six-gun made of stainless steel, factory custom hand-fitted parts, extremely close tolerances and a modern transfer-bar action. Unlike the Model 83, which has a safety that must be engaged by placing the hammer in the safety notch, the Model 97 has an automatic safety that places a bar of steel between the hammer and the firing pin when it is lowered. With either model I prefer to carry them with the hammer down on an empty chamber.

This year Freedom Arms is offering several new custom touches such as fluted cylinders and 9mm auxiliary cylinders for the Model 97, as well as dovetail front sights for fixed-sight revolvers. These sights can be adjusted in the dovetail for windage and feature interchangeable blades of differing heights allowing fixed-sighted six-guns to be sighted in perfectly for each individual shooter.

Ruger's 44 Magnum Packin' Pistols, the 4-inch Redhawk and 2¾-inch Alaskan.

Ruger

For some reason Ruger has always seemed to have an aversion for placing short barrels on 44 Magnum revolvers. The original 44 Flat-Top came standard with the shortest length being 6½ inches. I had mine cut to 4⅝ inches in the late 1950s and Ruger made up a special 4⅝-inch Blackhawk 44 for Elmer Keith but it would never be cataloged. The 7½-inch Ruger Super Blackhawk 44 arrived in 1959 and it would be into the 1990s before it would be offered with a short barrel.

The same held true for the Redhawk until now. The Redhawk arrived in 1979 with a 7½-inch barrel, and a 5½-inch barrel was added later. Wanting an easier-to-pack 44 that would handle heavyweight bulleted loads I had my local gunsmith cut the barrel to 4 inches, install a black front sight on a ramp base, and slightly round-butt the grip frame and factory stocks. My "new" Perfect Packin' Pistol 44 Redhawk carried easily in an Idaho Leather pancake holster and handled standard 44 Magnum loads with ease; however, with heavyweight bullets at 1300-1400 fps, even the modified factory grip frame and grips left something to be desired— in my hands, at least.

Now Ruger is finally offering a 4-inch 44 Magnum Redhawk and they have fitted it with stocks which handle recoil much better than the original factory offering. It is all stainless steel as the original, with a massive six-shot cylinder, and a solid frame with no sideplate. There are two major changes in addition to the obvious shorter barrel. Instead of the interchangeable front sight

The six-shot Freedom Arms Model 97 is offered in 22/22 Magnum, 32 Magnum/32-20 and 357 Magnum.

Ruger's Anniversary Models, the 44 Magnum and 357 Magnum Blackhawks are available as a matched set with the same serial numbers.

system, the 4-inch Redhawk has a pinned-in ramp front sight with a red insert matched up with a white outline rear blade. The stocks, instead of the standard factory wood grips, are hand-filling finger-grooved Hogue rubber grips, which are much more comfortable when firing heavy 44 Magnum loads. The surface of these Hogue grips also offer a more secure feeling, thanks to their pebble-grained but non-punishing surface, than offered by the original smooth wood grips. Those grips, matched with the strength of the Redhawk and the stainless-steel construction, result

in a Perfect Packin' Pistol for hard outdoor use. For my use the holster of choice is by Rob Leahy of Simply Rugged; it is a pancake style which can be worn strong-side or crossdraw and is designed to fit tightly and cover most of the six-gun except for the grip, providing easy access and security without resorting to security straps.

When I first wrote about the Super Redhawk nearly 20 years ago I said it should be a natural for the touch of custom six-gunsmiths. By chopping the barrel of the Super Redhawk off flush with the frame, milling

off the scope recesses and fitting a front sight, the Super Redhawk would become an easily carried snub-nosed 44 Magnum. I never heard of any gunsmith doing such a project; however, this is exactly what Ruger did to come up with the Alaskan chambered in 454 Casull a few years back. Then the 480 Ruger chambering was added to the Alaskan and now the third big bore has arrived with the addition of the 44 Magnum version of the Super Redhawk Alaskan giving 44 Magnum six-gunners two choices for easy packin' while at the same time providing as much comfort as possible when firing heavy loads. To aid in this the 44 Alaskan is also fitted with Hogue soft rubber stocks. It also carries easily and securely in a pancake-style holster by Simply Rugged with six cartridge loops sewn on the holster itself making six-gun and holster a compact survival kit.

In 2005 Ruger issued the 50th Anniversary Model of the original 357 Blackhawk complete with flat-top frame and Micro rear sight, but with the New Model action. They followed up in 2006 with the same style 50th Anniversary Model of the original 44 Blackhawk. Someone at Ruger was thinking ahead and set aside 357 Blackhawks and has now mated them up with 44 Blackhawks with the same serial numbers and they are offered as a Special Anniversary pair in a glass-topped wooden box. Both of these commemorative six-guns have a steel version of the original XR3 grip frame shaped and sized just like the Colt SAA and also checkered hard rubber grips with the black Ruger eagle medallion. Good lookin' and shootin' six-guns.

Ruger produced approximately three quarters of a million Colt SAA-styled Vaqueros in just over 10 years; the original run of Colt Single Actions from 1873 to 1941 numbered about 357,000. The Vaquero was made to look much like a Colt but was slightly larger in frame size, being built on the Ruger New Model 44 Super Blackhawk frame. A few years ago Ruger dropped the Vaquero and replaced it with the New Vaquero that is basically the same size as the Colt Single Action Army. New

Ruger's 44 Magnum Alaskan packs easily in a Simply Rugged pancake holster.

Vaqueros are now offered in both blue and stainless versions in 357 Magnum and 45 Colt with the latter available in consecutively numbered, highly polished stainless steel 5½-inch Cowboy Pairs engraved in a Western scroll pattern, fitted with simulated ivory grips and in a glass-topped wooden presentation case.

Smith & Wesson

In late December 1955 Smith & Wesson called Elmer Keith to inform him his dream had come true and one of the first production 44 Magnum revolvers was on the way to the man directly responsible for it finally becoming reality. Keith had been asking for a new revolver and a new cartridge, a "44 Special Magnum" loaded with a 250-grain hard-cast bullet of his design at 1,200 fps. What he got was the Smith & Wesson 44 Magnum, for which Keith used his hard-cast 250-grain bullet over what was to become known as the Keith Load: 22.0 grains of #2400. At 1,400+ fps it is still a good load.

It was very difficult to find 44 Magnums on gun shelves in those early days. The first one I ever saw, in late 1956, was a 4-inch version at the Shell's Gun and Archery Farm. Three of us teenagers hung out there regularly and when the 4-inch 44 Magnum arrived, it was not sold but rather rented six shots at a time. All three of us paid our money, all three of us shot six rounds— and all three of us lied! The recoil was brutal in our young hands, which had never shot anything heavier than a 1911 45 ACP or a 45 Colt. We all looked at each other and said, "That's not bad!" We all lied. It would take several years,

Smith & Wesson reaches into the past for inspiration for the 44 Special Model 21 (far right) and 45 Model 22 (middle) and 45 Model 1917 (right).

custom stocks and much practice before any of us could really handle the Smith & Wesson 44 Magnum.

With its beautiful S&W Bright Blue finish, tight tolerances and superbly smooth action, the S&W 44 Magnum began a new chapter in the book of six-gunning power. In 1957 the 44 Magnum became the Model 29 when S&W decided model numbers were better than such great titles as "38/44 Heavy Duty," "Combat Magnum," "Highway Patrolman," and "Chiefs Special." In 1968 the diamond center was dropped from the S&W stocks; by 1982 both the pinned barrel and recessed case heads were gone and then the profile disappeared with the use of heavy under-lugged barrels and round-butt grip frames. In 1999 Smith & Wesson unceremoniously dumped the Model 29. How could such a thing happen? I've never really forgiven Smith and Wesson for that, I'm still smarting from 1957 and 1968. However the Model 29 is now back in its 21st century form. No, it is not the original 44 Magnum of 1956; however, it is a Model 29 complete with the original 6½-inch barrel that was dropped in 1979 in favor of the 6-inch length. I never could understand that one, either!

In 2006 S&W offered the 50th Anniversary

Model of the original Smith & Wesson 44 Magnum with a blued finish not quite as bright as the fabled Bright Blue finish of 50 years ago—almost, but not quite. The sights are the same white outline rear and red ramp front as on the original, and the barrel length is also the original 6½ inches—not the 6-inch barrel found on S&W 44s since 1979. The hammer and trigger are the original checkered and serrated style while the stocks are somewhat like the originals with the diamond around the grip screw holes and slightly thinner in overall feel and tapered quite a bit to the top of the grip frame. The grip frame itself is square-butt, not round-butt, and original 44 Magnum stocks will also fit. So we do have the original grip frame and barrel length—but missing is the pinned barrel, cylinder recessed for case heads, and the firing pin is now mounted in the frame instead of on the hammer. It also has the internal lock found on all Smith & Wesson revolvers and comes in a lockable, padded plastic case. Taking crucial measurements of this Anniversary Model 44 Magnum we find cylinder throats are a uniform 0.429-inch, and, all-in-all, it is a harmonious blending of 1956 and 2006 that results in a good-shooting, good-looking six-gun. Of even greater import is the fact it is now a standard catalog item, and

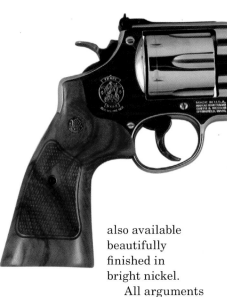

Smith & Wesson has resurrected the Model 29 in both blue and nickel finishes.

also available beautifully finished in bright nickel.

All arguments as to which is the most powerful revolver ended in 2003 with Smith & Wesson's introduction of the X-Frame Model 500 chambered in the 500 S&W Magnum with the capability of a 440-grain bullet launched from an 8⅜-inch barrel at nearly 1,700 fps. No one could argue which was the most powerful pistol now. Then, just as they did in 1964 with the 41 Magnum coming 10 years after the 44 Magnum, Smith & Wesson backed up. This time it only took two years to take a step down the ladder. Using the same basic X-Frame as on the Model 500 revolver, Smith & Wesson introduced the Model 460 XVR chambered in 460 S&W Magnum; it

was time to drop back and put a little more enjoyment in shooting while still maintaining extreme power. Even in the 4½-pound Model 500, the recoil with the full-house 440-grain bullet is brutal. With full-house loads the 460 is almost comfortable.

The original barrel lengths were 8⅜ inches, plus a compensator, and both models were soon offered in 4-inch plus compensator versions. Now Smith & Wesson is offering Emergency Survival Kits packed in a waterproof case containing a firestarter, saw, folding knife, whistle, signal mirror, compass, two space blankets and the choice of a 2¾-inch 460 with bright yellow rubber stocks, or the bright orange-stocked 500 S&W revolver. For wandering from the beaten path the other things may go in a backpack but the six-gun belongs in a good holster on the hip.

The N-frame may no longer be the largest used by Smith & Wesson but several other most interesting N-frame six-guns are offered this

year. The stainless steel, eight-shot Performance Center Model 627-5 comes in a padded, locking aluminum case with three full moon clips and two sets of grips. Shooters have a choice of wooden finger groove grips or the Hogue MonoGrip. The latter is pebble-grained and finger-grooved, and it fits my hand much better than the wooden option. With its eight-shot cylinder and slab-sided under-lugged barrel, the Model 627-5 weighs 42 ounces, making it very comfortable to shoot with all factory 357 Magnum loads—including 180s—tried. Smith & Wesson pioneered the use of scandium and titanium, super strong lightweight metals, in developing the 340Sc and 360 SC J-frame 357 Magnums. These still remain as two of the easiest-packin' and hardest-shootin' pocket pistols. Now Smith & Wesson has carried the scandium and titanium theme even further by offering the eight-shot 357 Magnum Model 327 with a black scandium alloy frame and a 2-inch Lothar-Walther button-rifled barrel.

This Perfectly Portable Packin' Pistol does not carry as easy as my 10-ounce J-frame 340Sc, but at 19½ ounces it is hardly noticeable when carried in a waist belt holster. With its short stubby barrel and eight-shot cylinder it is every bit as serious looking—maybe even more so—as the original 3½-inch 357 Magnum. The Model 327 is

Shooting the resurrected N-frame Smith & Wesson.

T/C Encore with custom barrel by SSK and Smith & Wesson X-frame —both chambered in 460 S&W Magnum.

basically built on the same platform as the Model 627. In addition to having a shorter barrel and being constructed of lighter materials than the Model 627, it also has fixed sights with a square notch rear sight and a fluorescent red front sight.

Going up in bore size, we find the 44 Magnum Mountain Gun is back with a 4-inch tapered barrel, blued finish and finger-groove wooden stocks and the 44 Magnum is also found in a 3-inch Model 29 blued with the old-style Magna stocks. Before the arrival of Magna stocks in 1935, Smith & Wesson's six-guns came with small stocks that did not extend up to the top of the frame. This year Smith & Wesson reaches back in history to resurrect this style of six-gun with the 5½-inch 45 ACP/45 Auto Rim Model 1917 complete with the old-style stocks and lanyard rings; the blued Model 21 in 44 Special and Model 22 in 45 ACP/Auto Rim are now equipped with the same style stocks and 4-inch barrels.

The Smith & Wesson Holding Co. now owns Thompson/Center so it is quite appropriate to find the single-shot Encore chambered in both the 460 and 500 S&W Magnums. These are available in factory barrels, and SSK Industries offers a large line of custom barrels for both the G2 Contender as well as the Encore, including 460 and 500 barrels for the latter. G2s are available in blued or stainless steel with wood or rubber stocks and forearms, mostly with 14-inch barrels and offered in many chamberings from 17 Mach II up to and including the 45-70, with such excellent hunting cartridges as the 30-30, 375 JDJ and 44 Magnum in-between. There is not much, if anything, as far as hunting is concerned which cannot be handled with the 375 JDJ. The stronger-actioned Encore is fitted with a 15-inch barrel and also offered in blue or stainless with wooden or rubber grips and forearms. Chamberings include the 22-250, 25-06, 270 Winchester, 30-06 and two of my favorites—308 Winchester and 7-08 Remington. The do-it-all 375 JDJ is also offered in the Encore for those who prefer a heavier single-shot pistol.

STI's latest is the Texican 45 Colt single-action revolver.

STI International

As this is written, and paraphrasing Rooster Cogburn, "The Texican is long on promise and short on production." Hopefully, by the time you read this, I will have one for testing. I can say the picture looks awfully good. STI, normally known for their 1911 semi-automatic pistols, enters the six-gunnin' scene with the blued and case-colored Texican which they describe thusly: "Proudly made in the USA, the Texican sets itself apart from the other single-action revolvers. All Texican parts are either ultra-high speed or electron discharge-machined from chrome-moly steel forgings or bar stock (no castings) to dimensions measured in ten thousands of an inch, then precisely installed, achieving an exactness of fit and smoothness of function not found in custom revolvers at twice the price of the Texican." Stay tuned.

Taurus

Taurus, long known for economically-priced, very smoothly working, good trigger double-action revolvers, introduced their first single-action revolver in 2005. Taurus is offering the Gaucho in four finishes: all blue, blue with a case-colored frame and hammer, and polished or matte stainless steel; barrel lengths of 5½ and 7½ inches in both 357 Magnum and 45 Colt. Metal-to-metal fit on the Gaucho is excellent as is grip-to-metal fit. There is no overhang or undercutting on the grips and they all fit tightly with no movement whatsoever. Taken overall, the fit and finish of the Gaucho is at least equal to—and in some cases much better than—that found on more expensive guns. Grips are very comfortable checkered black plastic, sights are the typical single-action style with a square-notch rear sight cut into the top of the frame and the traditionally styled Colt-type front sight; the cylinder base pin is held in by the spring-loaded-style catch.

Although fitted with a transfer bar safety, the action of the Gaucho is the standard four-position single-

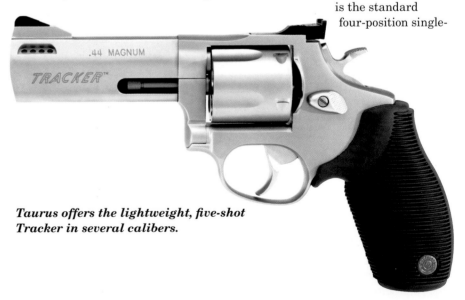

Taurus offers the lightweight, five-shot Tracker in several calibers.

action style with the hammer all the way down or the use of three notches in the hammer, the ill-named "safety" notch, a half-cock notch and the full-cock notch. The cylinder can only be rotated for loading and unloading with the hammer set at half-cock. In addition to the transfer bar safety, the Gaucho also has a key lock safety found in the back of the hammer just above the backstrap.

Taurus has a very large lineup of double-action revolvers, Trackers, Hunter Models, probably at least four dozen concealable revolvers, and the very popular Raging Bulls. I have carried a Taurus Model 85 UltraLite fitted with Crimson Trace laser grips in my jacket pocket for many years. The Raging Bull is offered in stainless steel or blue in 41 Magnum, 44 Magnum, 454 Casull and 480 Ruger. All Taurus double-action revolvers are also fitted with the safety lock Taurus security system in the back of the hammer.

Uberti

Uberti is the leading producer of replica single-action six-guns. They are owned by Beretta, from whom we get the Stampede, and the Laramie through Benelli. The three major manufacturers of single-action six-guns in the latter part of the 19th century were Colt, Remington and Smith & Wesson. Colt-style Ubertis include the traditional Single Action in blued steel or stainless steel, the Richards Conversion, Richards-Mason Conversion and the 1871-72 Open Top. Remington copies include the 1875 and 1890. In Smith & Wesson replicas we have the Model #3 Russian, the Schofield and the Laramie—which is patterned after the New Model #3 Target Model. Uberti also supplies most of the replica single actions offered by Cimarron, Navy Arms and Taylor & Co.

USFA

If ever there was a gun catalog made to fill a six-gunner's dreams it is the one from United States Firearms. This relatively new company markets all-American made single-action six-guns inspired by history and produced

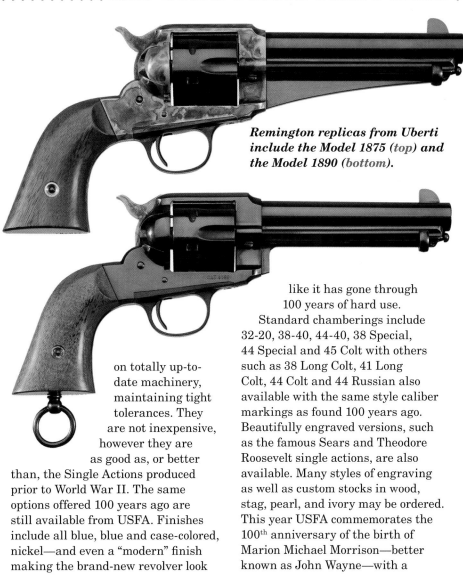

Remington replicas from Uberti include the Model 1875 (top) and the Model 1890 (bottom).

on totally up-to-date machinery, maintaining tight tolerances. They are not inexpensive, however they are as good as, or better than, the Single Actions produced prior to World War II. The same options offered 100 years ago are still available from USFA. Finishes include all blue, blue and case-colored, nickel—and even a "modern" finish making the brand-new revolver look like it has gone through 100 years of hard use.

Standard chamberings include 32-20, 38-40, 44-40, 38 Special, 44 Special and 45 Colt with others such as 38 Long Colt, 41 Long Colt, 44 Colt and 44 Russian also available with the same style caliber markings as found 100 years ago. Beautifully engraved versions, such as the famous Sears and Theodore Roosevelt single actions, are also available. Many styles of engraving as well as custom stocks in wood, stag, pearl, and ivory may be ordered. This year USFA commemorates the 100th anniversary of the birth of Marion Michael Morrison—better known as John Wayne—with a

Uberti/Beretta's Stampede has proven to be an excellent shooting revolver.

USFA's Flat-Top Target takes us back to the target-shooting days of the 1890s.

One of the special engraved six-guns offered by USFA is this replica of Theodore Roosevelt's 44-40 Frontier Six-Shooter.

They don't come much nicer-looking than this, USFA's Single Action. (left and right).

replica of the six-gun he used in so many great western movies.

USFA's Flat-Top Target Model takes us back to the target-shooting days in the 1890s and USFA has also resurrected the Bisley Model, which began as a Target Model in the 1890s and soon found favor as an everyday working gun, especially for those who had trouble reaching the hammer on the standard Single Action. Also new this year are two special military-style offerings. One is chambered in 30 Carbine and the other is the 5½-inch Lend-Lease Model chambered in 45 ACP; both versions are fitted with lanyard loops.

One of the most interesting single actions ever offered by Colt was the short-barreled, ejector-less Sheriff's Model. I even owned one once. It was chambered in 41 Long Colt and I paid $35 for it; I wish I still had it but it went in one of my teenage trades. It didn't have much finish left; however, it functioned fine and would be worth a whole lot more than $35 today. In the early 1960s Colt resurrected the Sheriff's Model (only available through Centennial Arms) as a special run of 3-inch 45 Colt Single Actions. Even though I couldn't understand why less gun cost more money, $15 more than the already too-expensive standard Single Action, I really wanted one. They were beautiful little six-guns, even looked very serious; however, for me it was not to be.

Thanks to USFA, totally American-made Sheriff's Models are now available with a choice of caliber, barrel length and finish. Mine is a 45 Colt with a 2½-inch barrel and beautifully nickel-plated. Grips are checkered hard rubber with a "US" molded into the top part and are perfectly fitted to the frame and, as with all Sheriff's Models, the USFA version has the "blackpowder" frame; that is, the base pin is held in place by a screw through the front of the frame.

Several years ago USFA introduced the Rodeo, which was nothing more than a matte-finished model allowing a significant savings in price. This year they are offering the Cowboy in full-blue chambered in 38 Special and 45 Colt and fitted with brown—not black—rubber stocks. Jim Finch, who does custom gunsmithing as Long Hunter Shooting Supply, takes the Rodeo one step further as the LHSS/USFA Rodeo. USFA ships specially LH-prefixed serial numbered Rodeos directly to Finch who gives them his custom touches. Finch's Rodeos are available in both 38 Special and 45 Colt and the choice of either a 4¾- or 5½-inch barrel. Finch makes the fixed sights of the standard Rodeo more usable by widening the rear notch from 0.108- to 0.140-inch and serrating the backside of the front sight. The forcing cone is opened to 11 degrees, the square corners of the trigger are radiused and polished, and the trigger pull is set at a crisp creep-free three pounds. To eliminate drag marks on the sides of the hammer,

USFA's Rodeo is a matte finish version of their standard Single Action.

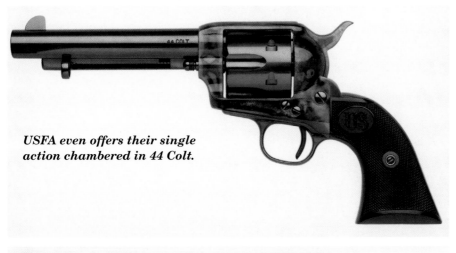

USFA even offers their single action chambered in 44 Colt.

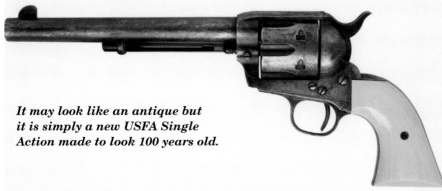

It may look like an antique but it is simply a new USFA Single Action made to look 100 years old.

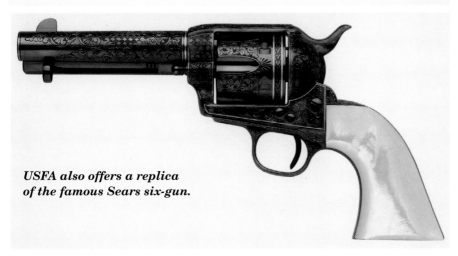

USFA also offers a replica of the famous Sears six-gun.

it is relieved .007-inch on each side where it rides in the hammer slot and, if desired, is polished and jeweled. The flat hand spring is replaced by drilling the frame for a Ruger-style coil spring, the main spring is replaced with a Lee's Gunslinger spring for smooth cocking and a fast hammer drop, while a Lee's Gunslinger wire spring replaces the trigger and bolt

spring. The Rodeo is a six-gun ready for hard duty without worrying about scratching a beautiful finish.

Wesson Firearms

Dan Wesson has a long up-and-down history since their beginning in the 1970s. Dan Wesson himself had radical ideas including interchangeable barrels, an interchangeable front sight system, and a grip stud instead of a grip frame allowing a great choice of grip styles and sizes. The Dan Wesson 357 Magnum was an early favorite among long-range silhouetters and it was followed by the large-frame 44 Magnum and then stretched-frame 357, 375, 414, and 445 SuperMags—which are the forerunners of the 460 and 500 S&W Magnums.

After Dan Wesson's death the family took over the business, lost it, got it back again, and then in the mid-1990s had to close the doors. The company was purchased by Bob Serva, moved, upgraded with all-new machinery and Wesson Firearms began producing the large-frame Dan Wesson revolvers once again. In the early part of the 21st century, Wesson Firearms began producing a large line of quality 1911s and the company was then purchased by CZ. Today revolver production is limited, with only two models currently cataloged.

Wesson was the first to offer a revolver aimed at those who wander among the large bears as the Alaskan Guide Model in 445. This rubber-stocked, short-barreled, compensated six-shot revolver remains in production as does the stainless steel standard model 445 SuperMag. Today's Dan Wesson revolvers are the finest ever built under the Wesson name. They also maintain the excellent accuracy for which Dan Wesson firearms are noted.

I ended last year's report talking of the 44s I expected to be shooting all year and also announced my working on a new book. It is appropriate that in this centennial celebration of the 44 Special *The Gun Digest Book Of The 44* is now available. It covers not only the 44 Special and 44 Magnum but all 44s—from the 44 percussion six-guns to the 44 Henry, 44 S&W American, 44 Colt, 44-40, 44 AutoMag, 444 Marlin and 445 SuperMags—and the guns and loads that go along with them. May you enjoy my labor of love. ✺

RIFLES TODAY:
RIFLE REVIEW 2008

by Layne Simpson

For no reason other than the fact that I wanted to kick off this column with something clever or thought-provoking rather than going right into the business at hand, I decided to exercise your brain with a short quiz. Answer all of them correctly and you may be qualified to become the next editor of GUN DIGEST. Answer at least one and you have the potential of becoming the star of your own television show. The answers are at the end of this report.

1. How did the Weatherby Mark V rifle come by its name?

2. What animal inspired John Nosler to develop his world-famous Partition bullet?

3. How many different bullet diameters are required to load the following cartridges?

218 Bee, 219 Zipper, 220 Swift, 221 Fireball, 222 Remington, 223 Remington, 224 Weatherby Magnum, 225 Winchester

4. What famous rifle was once offered in "African," "Alaskan" and "Westerner" versions and what were their chamberings?

5. Townsend Whelen developed the 35 Whelen cartridge, correct?

6. In what year was the Remington Model 700 introduced?

7. What rifle was called "the bolt-action with a lever" in its advertisements?

8. Which company was first to introduce a big-game rifle with a synthetic stock?

9. Are the many gunwriters who have proclaimed the 204 Ruger as our fastest commercial cartridge preaching gospel or spouting hot air?

10. What invention that converted the 1903 Springfield rifle to semiautomatic operation came too late to be used in World War I and who invented it?

Now that you have answered each question correctly, it is time to take a brief look at what's new for 2007.

Anschutz

The circa-1856 logo of company founder Julias Gottfried Anschutz can be found on the trigger guard of the special-edition Model 1710 DHB Classic and that, along with a few other details such as the circa-1901 Germania logo engraved on the 23-inch stainless steel barrel and special carving on the walnut buttstock, serves to commemorate the 150th anniversary of the Anschutz company. Other things worth noting are select-grade walnut with cut checkering, gold-plated trigger, oversized bolt handle knob and match-dimensioned 22 Long Rifle chamber.

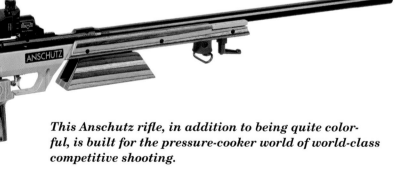

This Anschutz rifle, in addition to being quite color-ful, is built for the pressure-cooker world of world-class competitive shooting.

This Anschutz rifle is being built to commemorate the 150th anniversary of the company.

Benelli USA

Due to its gas operation, the R1 autoloading rifle was comfortable to shoot to begin with and it is even more so now that it wears the same ComforTech synthetic stock design that was first seen on Benelli shotguns. Available in black or camo, the stock has interchangeable soft comb inserts, *regular* for use with open sights or low-mounted scopes and *high* for elevating the eye to the same height as a scope with a large objective lens. Interchangeable recoil pads of various thicknesses offer three options in length of pull: 13⅝ inches, 14 inches and 14⅜ inches. A newcomer to the lineup of top-quality reproductions made by Uberti is a carbine version of the Model 1874 Sharps in 45-70 Government. Already available with 30-, 32- and 34-inch barrels, you can now buy one with a 22-inch barrel. It, and the equally new Hunter with 28-inch barrel, are quite plain and this makes them more affordable than other Sharps reproductions imported by Benelli.

Beretta USA

Beretta is not just about great shotguns, the company also imports very nice rifles made by the Italian firm of Uberti. One of the latest is called Gold Rush and it is a reproduction of the Colt Lightning pump gun in 357 Magnum or 45 Colt. Several variants are available, rifle with 24-inch barrel, carbine with 20-inch barrel and both of those in Deluxe Grade with fancy wood, jeweled hammer, case-colored receiver and gold-plated medallion in the stock. Equally interesting is the Stampede Buntline Carbine, a single-action Colt reproduction with a shoulder stock and 18-inch barrel. Said to be a copy of the guns given to Wyatt Earp and Batt Masterson during the 1870s, it is in 45 Colt and can be bought singly or in a matched pair with 1876 Philadelphia Centennial engraving.

Browning

The BLR Lightweight is now available in a takedown version in both curved-grip and straight-grip styles. Flip down a lever on the bottom of the receiver and the barrel with the forearm still attached can be removed from the receiver. An optional mount can be used to attach a long eye relief scope to the barrel rather than the receiver. Barrel lengths are 20, 22 and 25 inches depending on the caliber and your options there cover anything anyone would want to do with a lever-action rifle. To name but a few of the 14 available chamberings: 22-250, 7mm-08, 358 Winchester, 450 Marlin, 270 Winchester, 270 WSM, 323 WSM and 300 WSM. Nominal weight ranges from 6½ to 7¾ pounds depending on barrel and receiver length and caliber.

Continuing on with quick-shooting rifles, the BAR autoloader in both ShorTrac and LongTrac versions is now available with its ejection port located where left-hand shooters have long wanted it to be. Nine different chamberings are available from 243 Winchester to 300 Winchester Magnum. Right-hand versions of both rifles are also available with a Mossy Oak Break-Up camo skin.

My favorite Browning big-game rifle? That's an easy question to answer––the A-Bolt Mountain Ti. Mine is in 300 WSM and outfitted with a Zeiss 3-9X scope, a nylon carrying sling and three cartridges in its magazine it weighs only 7½ pounds. I like a lot about that rifle not the least of which are its accuracy, reliability, durability and the feel of the Dura Touch finish on its synthetic stock. Other chambering options are 243 Winchester, 7mm-08, 308, 270 WSM and 323 WSM.

Last year Browning brought back a new rifle with the old T-Bolt name and this year it is available in two versions, Standard with straight-comb stock and lightweight barrel and the new Target/Varmint with Monte Carlo-style stock and heavier barrel. Both barrels are 22 inches long and overall weights are 4¾ and 5½ pounds. Very nice and quite accurate to boot.

Chaparral Arms

Reproductions of Winchester rifles that won the West are now as abundant as fleas on a stray coon dog and Chaparral Arms adds Models 1866, 1873 and 1896 to the list. The '66 and '73 are available with 19-inch round or 24-inch octagon barrel in 38 Special, 38-40, 44-40 and 45 Colt while you can buy the '76 with a 22-, 26- or 28-inch octagon barrel in 40-60, 45-60 or 45-75 caliber.

Chiappa Firearms

This company's reproduction of the Winchester Model 92 is one of the finest I have examined lately. Barrel length options are 16, 20 and 24 inches and calibers include 38 Special, 38 Special/357 Magnum, 38-50, 44-40 and 45 Colt. Of particular interest to me are the cased takedown model with 20-inch barrel and the Trapper model with a 16-inch barrel.

CZ USA

The CZ527 American is now available with its bolt handle over on the side of left-hand shooters. For now it is available only in 223 Remington but other options will surely follow.

Ed Brown Custom Rifles

The new Gen III finish resists wear and rusting much better than bluing and is now standard on all rifles from Ed Brown Custom. Seven models of various weights are now available, Damara (6.2 lbs), Savanna (7.5 lbs), Compact Varmint (8.75 lbs), Bushveld (8.5 lbs), Express (9 lbs), Marine (10 lbs) and Tactical (11.25 lbs). All the popular chamberings are there plus a few that should be more popular than they are such as the 17 Remington, 6mm Remington, 6.5-284 Norma, 340 Weatherby Magnum and 416 Remington Magnum.

Harrington & Richardson

One of the more interesting new members of the Handi-Rifle family is the Survivor––its 20-inch barrel accepts both the .410 shotshell and the 45 Colt cartridge. The barrel is fully rifled for the 45 Colt and for .410 slug loads but it also has screw-in chokes for use with .410 shot loads. Swinging the recoil pad to the side reveals enough room inside the oversized synthetic buttstock to stow a compass, matches, fishing line, a photo of Faith Hill and other survival gear. The Survivor weighs six pounds and when taken down it carries nicely inside a backpack or when strapped to a packframe.

Henry Rifles

Henry rifles are manufactured in Brooklyn, New York of all places and they build lever-actions in 17 HMR, 22 LR, 22 WMR, 357 Magnum, 44 Magnum and 45 Colt. As rumor has it, the 30-30 Winchester is just around the corner. The guys and gals at Henry also turn out slide-action hammer guns in 22 LR and 22 WMR, as well as a mini single-shot bolt-gun that has managed to win its place in the hearts of kids, alongside the Chipmunk and the

To celebrate the 60th anniversary of the Nosler Partition bullet, I wore Filson wool clothing while using a Pre-64 Model 70 in 300 H&H Magnum and a Partition bullet made by John Nosler back in the 1940s to take this very nice woodland caribou in the Yukon.

Cricket. Last but certainly not least is a survival rifle in 22 LR that stows in its own hollow buttstock and even floats like Ivory soap when dropped overboard. Many years ago it was called the Armalite AR-7 Explorer.

Iver Johnson Arms, Inc.

The M-1 Carbine from Iver Johnson is now available in three versions––all wood, wood stock with metal handguard and synthetic stock. They say all parts will interchange with the original American-built carbine. Many years ago I bought the real McCoy through the NRA and if memory serves correctly, it cost me the princely sum of $17.50 and war-surplus ammo was only slightly more expensive than dirt. Sure wish I had kept it because the M-1 Carbine is a fun little gun.

Kimber

The action of the Kimber Model 8400 Standard Classic has been stretched just enough to allow it to accept several new chamberings including 25-06, 270 Winchester and 30-06. The magnum version is available in 300 Winchester and 338 Winchester. Latest version is a safari-style rifle in 375 H&H Magnum replete with express-style rear sight. With the exception of a couple of minor details the pre-production African rifle I examined had all the right things in all the right places.

Legacy Sports International

Howa rifles are now available wearing Hogue overmolded stocks in olive drab or black with chambering options ranging from 223 Remington to 338 Winchester Magnum. Also new is the Axiom stock with a pull-length adjustment range of 11½ to 15½ inches and a built-in Knoxx shock absorber that soaks up 70 percent of the recoil, or so its maker claims. The stock is a combination of machined aluminum and molded synthetic and the rifle is available in 204 Ruger, 223 Remington, 22-250, 243 Winchester and 308 Winchester. Just as new is a lightweight mountain rifle rated at 6¼ pounds in calibers ranging from 223

Remington to 308 Winchester. Barrel length is 20 inches. Turning from bolt guns to lever actions, the Puma is a copy of the Winchester 92 and it has been around for a very long time. It is now available with 16-, 18- or 20-inch barrel in 357 Magnum, 44 Magnum, 45 Colt, 454 Casull and 480 Ruger. In addition to stainless steel, you can get old-fashioned bluing or a case-colored receiver with a blued barrel.

Les Baer Custom

I never cease to be amazed at the accuracy of match-grade AR15 rifles and Lex Bauer continues to amaze me with the accuracy produced by those built in his shop. The barrel of the first Super Varmint I worked with several years ago had a 1:12 twist and it consistently delivered five-shot groups of less than ½-inch at 100 yards with handloads and bullets weighing up to the Berger 64-grain hollowpoint. The rifle I shot more recently was basically the same except for the quicker 1:8 inch twist rate of its barrel. With LBC precision EDM scope mounting rings holding a brilliantly clear Weaver 6-20X Grand Slam scope atop its flattop receiver, it weighed two ounces beyond 12 pounds on my postal scale and that, along with its incredible accuracy potential, made shooting tiny little groups falling-off-the-log easy. The group I am most proud of was fired with the Sierra 77-grain MatchKing seated atop 24.0 grains of RL-15. I wanted to shoot that load through the magazine so I used the Sierra-recommended cartridge overall length of 2.260 inches. Fired from a benchrest at 600 yards on a windless day, the group is a 10-shooter and it measures an incredible 2.842 inches (or roughly 0.474 minute-of-angle). Can I repeat that performance on demand? Absolutely not. Is the rifle capable of doing it all the time? I'd say it is.

One of the reasons I was able to shoot the Super Varmint so accurately is its two-stage Jewell trigger. The trigger finger first takes up the initial stage with 34 ounces of pull and then suddenly at the 42-ounce mark it breaks cleanly. AR triggers don't get any better than this. The barrel is

benchrest-grade 416R stainless and its size accounts for a good bit of the overall weight; the 24-inch barrel has a muzzle diameter of 0.925-inch. The Super Varmint is also available with 18- and 22-inch and rifling twist rate options are 1:7, 1:8, 1:9 and 1:12 inches. Upper and lower receivers are precision-machined from forgings and the former is available with or without forward assist. These and all other parts such as the chromed bolt and carrier, extractor, aluminum gas block with Picatinny top rail and the free-floating tubular handguard are manufactured in-house by LBC. Accessories included in the package are quick-detach Versa Pod, 20-round magazine, padded rifle case (with side pockets big enough to hold lots of stuff). Like several other AR15 variants offered by LBC, the Super Varmint comes with a half-minute-of-angle guarantee––believe me when I say it is no brag. Les Bauer's incredibly accurate rifles are available in 204 Ruger, 223 Remington and 6.5 Grendel.

Magnum Research

All versions of the custom Ruger 10/22 rifles from Magnum Research have barrels consisting of thin steel tubes encased in graphite/carbon fibers. The various models differ by their stocks: laminated wood on some, synthetic on others. Chambering options are 22 LR, 17 Mach 2, 17 HMR and 22 HMR. Also available is the Ruger Model 77/17 Graphite in 17 HMR only.

Marlin

The Winchester Model 71 with its curved grip, short magazine tube and 24-inch barrel has long been one of my favorite rifles and this probably explains why I like the looks of the latest Marlin Model 336 variants. For now, all have stainless steel barreled actions and laminated wood stocks and perhaps someday the decision-makers at Marlin will make me even happier by offering them in walnut and blued steel. You can choose among five different cartridges: 444 Marlin, 45-70, 30-30, 35 Remington or the new 308 Marlin.

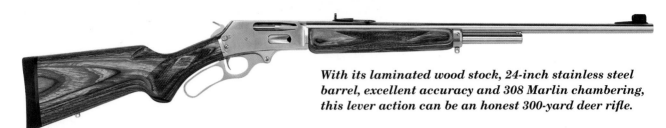

With its laminated wood stock, 24-inch stainless steel barrel, excellent accuracy and 308 Marlin chambering, this lever action can be an honest 300-yard deer rifle.

In performance, the latter cartridge treads closely on the heels of the 308 Winchester and that––along with the accuracy capability of Marlin rifles––makes the Model 308MXLR not only a mouthful but honest 300-yard deer medicine as well. The 308 Marlin chambering is also available in the Model 308MX, which is blued steel and walnut but with a 22-inch barrel. Marlin is also offering several rifles with a factory-mounted 3-9X scope: Model 336A in 30-30, Model 60SN autoloader in 22 LR and Model 917VR bolt-gun in the same caliber. And don't forget to check out the new *faux* carbon fiber pattern on the synthetic stocks of some Marlin rifles.

McMillan Tactical

The incredibly accurate, totally reliable and extremely durable McMillan tactical rifle is now available with turn-bolt actions in three lengths that will handle cartridges such as the 308 Winchester, 300 Winchester Magnum, 338 Lapua and 50 BMG. It is available with Mauser-style internal magazine with hinged floorplate or detachable box magazine. Among its many other features are match-grade stainless steel barrel, EDM-machined bolt raceway in the receiver, three-pound trigger, Fail-Safe ejector, claw extractor, detachable muzzle brake and height-adjustable comb on the synthetic stock. The stock comes in five colors and is available in a folding version.

NoslerCustom

Each production run of the limited edition bolt-action rifle from NoslerCustom is available in only one caliber and the latest is 280 Ackley Improved. To set the record straight, P.O. Ackley never got around to improving the 280 Remington cartridge but since the improving of a cartridge by decreasing its body taper and increasing its shoulder angle for an increase in powder capacity is synonymous with his name, he gets credit for it anyhow (as he should). At any rate, the NoslerCustom rifle is now chambered for the 280 Improved and match-grade unprimed cases and loaded ammunition are also available from Nosler. As can be expected, the latter is loaded with Nosler bullets in Partition, Ballistic Tip and AccuBond form. A less expensive version of the same rifle wears a black synthetic stock rather than fancy walnut and since John Nosler started the company in 1948 it is called the Model 48 Sporter. It is available in three WSM chamberings: 270, 300 and 325 WSM. On page four of the 2007 Nosler catalog is a photo of J.R. Nosler and a nice Yukon grizzly taken by him with a Model 48 in 323 WSM and the 200-grain AccuBond bullet.

During the 2006 season I spent two weeks hunting grizzly, caribou and moose in the Yukon with Bob Nosler and his son J.R. Bob and I did it the way his father John did it back in the 1940s. We wore Filson wool rather than modern synthetics and we carried Model 70 rifles in 300 H&H Magnum, which is what John Nosler hunted with. Bob's rifle even wore a Lyman Alaskan scope. To cap it all off, I used 180-grain Partition bullets that were made by John Nosler back in the 1940s. Believe it or not, my handload with that bullet and IMR-4350 powder averaged less than an inch for three shots at 100 yards when fired in the Model 70. Not bad for a rifle and a batch of bullets made before many who will read this report were born.

Remington

Biggest news from Remington for 2007 is the development for a new fire-control system for the Model 700/Seven family of rifles. Called the X-Mark Pro Trigger it blocks both the sear and the fingerpiece when engaged and it comes with a long list of improvements such as smoother component parts engagement surfaces, up to 45 percent lighter pull from the factory, greater resistance to rust and corrosion and fully adjustable for pre-travel, sear engagement and pull weight. From this point on all Model 700 and Model Seven rifles will leave the factory with the new trigger.

A new chambering for 2007 is the 17 Fireball which can be described as the 221 Fireball Case necked down or a commercial version of the 17 Mach IV. Word I get from Pat Ryan at

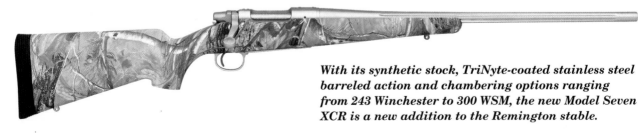

With its synthetic stock, TriNyte-coated stainless steel barreled action and chambering options ranging from 243 Winchester to 300 WSM, the new Model Seven XCR is a new addition to the Remington stable.

Redding is the body of the 17 Fireball is a few thousandths smaller at the shoulder and headspace is slightly shorter so the 17 Mach IV full-length resizing die many of us already have probably won't work. On the positive side, a 17 Mach IV bullet seating die should work fine with the Remington cartridge. The 17-221, by the way, was created by P.O. Ackley and he, along with Las Vegas gunsmith Vern O'Brien, were first to build custom rifles for it. O'Brien gave it the 17 Mach IV name but called it the 17 Mach III in custom XP-100 pistols he also built. I once owned one of his rifles in this chambering on the Sako L46 action but eventually sold it to a collector. At any rate, the 17 Fireball as Remington chooses to call it will be loaded with a 20-grain AccuTip-V bullet at 4000 fps. It is slated for availability in several rifles on the Model 700 and Model Seven actions.

And speaking of the Model Seven, the new XCR variant has a stainless steel barreled action replete with TriNyte finish, a synthetic stock with Realtree AP camo skin and fluted barrels, 20-inch in 243 Winchester, 7mm-08 and 308 and 22 inches in 270 WSM and 300 WSM. Nominal weights are seven pounds for standard cartridges and two ounces more for the magnums.

The incredibly affordable Model 710 rifle has now been replaced by an improved version called Model 770. The new synthetic stock has molded-in sling swivel posts and the rifle comes from the factory with a Bushnell 3-9X scope already mounted. Bolt travel of the 770 is smoother and it has a more durable magazine latch. With the magazine full and a cartridge in the chamber it holds four 308s and three 300 WSMs. Other available chamberings are 243 Winchester, 7mm-08, 270 Winchester, 30-06 and 300 Winchester Magnum. A youth version with shorter stock is also available, but only in 243 Winchester.

Everyone has their favorite Model 700 variation and my pick for hunting in bluebird weather is the Model 700 CDL with its trim, classical-style stock. Switch the blued steel barreled action to one made of stainless steel (and flute the barrel) and you have the Model 700 CDL SF in both short and long actions and in a variety of chamberings from 7mm-08 and 308 to 30-06 and 300 WSM. A limited-production version of that rifle sold during 2006 in 30-06 celebrated the 100th anniversary of that cartridge and for 2007 its chamber is 17 Fireball. Among other nice things it has a 24-inch barrel and special engraving on its floorplate announces the introduction of the 17 Fireball.

If the Model 700 CDL is my fair weather rifle then the Model 700 XCR with its synthetic stock and TriNyte protected stainless steel barreled action has to be my favorite for hunting during bad weather. Mine is in 7mm Remington Magnum but you can also get it in 25-06, 270 Winchester, 270 WSM, 7mm-08, 7mm Ultra Mag, 30-06, 300 Ultra Mag, 300 WSM, 300 Winchester Magnum, 338 Ultra Mag, 338 Winchester Magnum and 375 H&H Magnum. Only a few weeks before writing this I equipped my rifle with one of the first Burris LaserScopes to come off the assembly line and

From this day forward all Models 700 and Seven rifles built by Remington will have the new X-Mark Pro trigger.

used it on a successful hunt for whitetail deer in northern Wyoming.

Rossi

This company is seriously into economy-grade, break-action, single-shot rifles that come in multiple-barrel packages capable of covering lots of hunting and shooting territory. A good example is the Model S202250YM with three interchangeable barrels, 50-caliber muzzleloader, 20-gauge shotgun and 22 Long Rifle pot filler. Another model teams up a 50-caliber muzzleloader barrel with barrels in 243 Winchester and 12 gauge. Latest addition is the Trifecta with a black synthetic stock (with removable cheekpiece) and barrels in 22 LR, 243 Winchester and 20 gauge.

Ruger

The new Hawkeye version of the Model 77 rifle has one of the

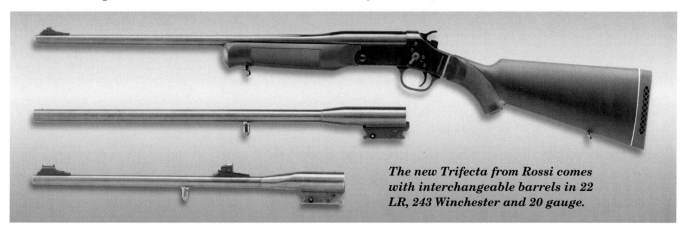

The new Trifecta from Rossi comes with interchangeable barrels in 22 LR, 243 Winchester and 20 gauge.

slimmest, trimmest, most handsome stocks ever worn by a Ruger bolt-action rifle. It is also available in a rough-weather version with synthetic stock and stainless steel barreled action. Both rifles have Ruger's new LC6 trigger and a variety of interesting chamberings including 223 Remington, 257 Roberts, 270 Winchester, 338 Federal and 358 Winchester. The African version has iron sights on its 23-inch barrel, is available only in 375 Ruger and wears a walnut stock. Switch the stock to synthetic, shorten the barrel to 20 inches and you have, in addition to plenty of muzzle blast, the Alaskan version in the same caliber. In case you are questioning the existence of the 375 Ruger, keep in mind that except for the more expensive Mark II Magnum, the company had no action long enough to handle cartridges longer than the 30-06 and 338 Winchester Magnum and other cartridges of similar lengths. The new cartridge pretty much duplicates the performance of the 375 H&H Magnum but is short enough to work in the Ruger standard-length action. Other news from Ruger includes the 10/22 Target with laminated wood stock and heavy blued steel barrel and the Mini-14 Target with its medium-weight barrel replete with boop tube and thumbhole-style stock. They say it will shoot more than one bullet inside an inch at 100 yards.

Sako

A lot of water has passed under the bridge since I traveled to Finland in October of 1996 for the unveiling of an improved version the Model 75 rifle and further refinements and improvements made since then have prompted Sako officials to give it the new name of Model 85.

Improvements made to the Model 75 action since its introduction in 1996 have prompted Sako to change its name to Model 85.

Where five action-lengths were once available there are now six ranging from X-Short for the 223 Remington to X-Long for the 416 Rigby. Bolt rotation has been reduced to 70 degrees, the receiver bridge has been slightly lengthened for a smoother bolt throw, locktime of the long action has been reduced to 1.3 milliseconds and the single-set trigger on the varmint version is the very best trigger available on a factory rifle. Latest variants of the Model 85 are the Finnlight in synthetic and stainless steel and the Laminated SS Varmint with its stock of laminated. Finnlights in 7mm-08 and 338 Federal are an especially useful pair and the varmint in 223 with its marvelous single-set trigger is one of the top three varmint rifles presently available.

Savage Arms

My old friend Gary Roberson who owns Burnham Brothers Game Calls and who I consider to be the world's greatest coyote caller came up with the idea for the new Savage Model 10 Predator Hunter. In addition to being chambered to 223 Remington which just happens to be his favorite coyote cartridge, it has other details that Gary looks for in a rifle, including 22-inch medium-heavy barrel, synthetic stock with rounded forearm for use with shooting sticks and Mossy Oak Brush camo finish. Adjustment range for its AccuTrigger is 1½ to 6 pounds.

Then we have the new Model 12 Long Range Precision Varminter, a rifle better suited for the sitting

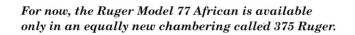

For now, the Ruger Model 77 African is available only in an equally new chambering called 375 Ruger.

varmint shooter rather than those like Gary Roberson who walk a long ways between sits. A single-shot, it has a solid-bottom receiver for rigidity and its left-side loading port combined with a right-side bolt handle allow the rifle to be loaded with one hand and shot with the other. Measuring a full inch in diameter, the barrel is heavy enough to dampen the already mild recoil generated by the 204 Ruger, 223 Remington and 22-250 cartridges and its 30-inch length shifts muzzle blast a few inches further away from the ears than most varmint rifles. The 223 barrel is available with either a 1:9 or 1:7 inches rifling twist rate.

Also new in the Model 12 lineup is the Precision Target Rifle series. The rifle built for F Class competitive shooting has a laminated wood stock with a three-inch wide ventilated forearm and a buttstock shaped specifically for resting atop a sandbag in the prone position. Its heavy, 30-inch stainless steel barrel is chambered to 6.5-284 Norma.

Taylors & Company

I have no idea why they would give it a strange name like "Spirit Overtop" but I do know it is a nice-looking, break-action, single-shot rifle in walnut and blued steel replete with case-colored receiver and in 243 Winchester.

Thompson/Center

The Icon is a totally new bolt-action centerfire rifle from T/C and while the preproduction version I handled was a bit on the heavy side it did have several interesting features. One was interchangeable bolt handles in two styles, spoon-handle and conventional with round knob. Then we have a safety that locks bolt rotation in one mode but allows the bolt to be rotated with the safety engaged in another mode. Of fat-bolt design, its three locking lugs are the same diameter as the body of the bolt and it has a Sako-style extractor along with a spring-loaded, plunger-style ejector. The shape of the bolt at the rear sort of reminds me of the Mossberg 800 of the 1970s but otherwise the Icon differs greatly from

The new stock of the TCR ProHunter makes it comfortable to shoot, even when it is chambered to 416 Rigby.

that rifle. The detachable, single-stack magazine holds three cartridges with options for 2007 being 22-250, 243 Winchester, 308 Winchester and 30 TC. The 30 TC is a shortened version of the 308 Winchester case and it is loaded by Hornady with special powders that are not available to the handloader. Those propellants enable the new cartridge to exceed the velocities of standard 308 factory loads but it runs no faster than Hornady's Light Magnum loading of that cartridge. According to the latest Hornady catalog, respective velocities for the 30 TC with 150- and 165-grain bullets are 3000 and 2850 fps versus 3000 and 2880 fps for the 308 Light Magnum.

Latest version of the Encore

I used a Remington Model 700 XCR in 7mm Magnum and wearing a Burris LaserScope to take this nice whitetail in northern Wyoming.

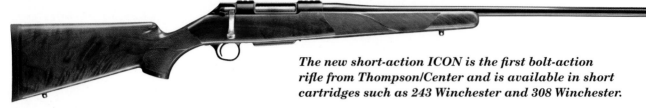

The new short-action ICON is the first bolt-action rifle from Thompson/Center and is available in short cartridges such as 243 Winchester and 308 Winchester.

rifle is the Pro Hunter with its recoil-absorbing FlexTech stock. The one I tried was in 416 Rigby and I found it quite comfortable to shoot from the offhand position, which is how most Cape buffalo are shot. Also new for 2007 are Encore barrels in 22 LR and 17 HMR.

Winchester Firearms

Imported from Russia, a bolt-action rifle called the Wildcat is chambered to 22 Long Rifle and is available in two versions, standard-weight with a thin stock combined with a lightweight barrel and varmint-weight with heavier barrel, no open sights and beavertail-style stock. Regardless of which you choose, you should also find four detachable magazines in the box, one five-rounder and three ten-rounders.

Weatherby

Back in 1961 Weatherby introduced a classy autoloading rifle in 22 Long Rifle called the Mark XXII and during its production life it was manufactured by several different companies including Beretta. The original Mark XXII (pronounced "Mark 22") was discontinued in 1988 but the name comes back to life in 2007 with the introduction of another rifle. This time around it is a bolt action, the barreled action built by Anschutz to Weatherby's specifications and stocked with American walnut in America by Americans who work for Weatherby. Built around the Anschutz Model 64 action, it is available in 22 Long

Rifle or 17 HMR and it comes with a target that certifies its sub-minute-of-angle accuracy capability. The three I shot lived up to that accuracy claim with room to spare.

The Vanguard family of centerfire rifles continues to grow and one of the latest additions is the Youth/Compact that comes with two stocks: one with a length-of-pull for short arms, the other with a standard length-of-pull for those same arms when they grow up. A Texas friend of mine bought one of these in 22-250 for his daughter and she has taken two pronghorn antelope and several whitetails with his handloads using the Nosler 60-grain Partition bullet. Other caliber options are 243 Winchester, 7mm-08 and 308 Winchester. The Vanguard Synthetic Package comes in a hard case and with a Bushnell 3-9X scope already mounted and it too has proven to be quite successful for Weatherby. I used one in 257 Magnum on several hunts and it averaged less than an inch at 100 yards with Weatherby ammo loaded with the 110-grain AccuBond and 120-grain Partition bullets. New Vanguard chamberings for 2007 are 204 Ruger and 25-06 Remington.

Answers To Questions At Beginning Of Report

1. When the fifth and final working model of his new action was completed in 1957, Roy Weatherby had not come up with a name for the rifle that would be built around

when he showed it to his friend Elgin Gates. In addition to being a world-traveled big-game hunter, Gates was the West Coast representative of Mercury outboard motors, a company that called its various models "Mark" this or "Mark" that. Gates suggested "Mark V" as a name for the new Weatherby rifle and it stuck.

2. When the bullet he was using opened up too quickly and failed to penetrate to the vitals of a Canadian moose, John Nosler went home and designed his Partition bullet.

3. All use bullets of the same .224-inch diameter.

4. Winchester Model 70: the African in 458 Magnum, the Alaskan in 338 Magnum and the Westerner in 264 Magnum.

5. Incorrect; James Howe developed the cartridge and named it in honor of Whelen.

6. The Model 700 and its new cartridge, the 7mm Remington Magnum were introduced in 1962.

7. The Winchester Model 88.

8. Weatherby.

9. Hot air. Remington's 20-grain loading of the 17 Remington and Federal's 40-grain loading of the 220 Swift are loaded to 4250 fps which is presently faster than any 204 Ruger load.

10. Invented by J.D. Pederson, the Pederson Device was officially designated "Automatic Pistol, 30 caliber, Model of 1918" as a way to preserve secrecy during its development.

Unlike the Weatherby Mark XXII autoloader of yesteryear, the new Mark XXII is a bolt action in 17 HMR and 22 LR, its barreled action built by Anschutz and stocked in walnut by Weatherby.

RIFLES TODAY ✦
SINGLE-SHOT RIFLE REVIEW

by John Campbell

The single-shot rifle is an icon. The best ones are beautiful, compact, efficient, strong, handy and romantic. Nothing else in the rifle sports embodies quite the same cachet... except, perhaps, the double rifle.

And as we press on into 2008, it's good to know that some of the greatest single-shots ever offered to sportsmen are either here already, or on their way back into production. For example, who would have ever imagined that the Wesson Long Range, Sharps-Borchardt, Sharps 1875 Long Range, and now the famed Farquharson can all be had by simply placing an order? For those of us who treasure the genre, this is truly a time of plenty. So, come on along. We have some riveting single-shot news to cover for 2008.

Axtell Rifle Co.

There are some bold moves being made by Axtell out in Sheridan, Montana. By the time you read this, Axtell will have added two new CNC tools to their shop that will improve quality even more (it will be hard to improve on "terrific") and hopefully cut production and delivery time by half.

In addition, Axtell will continue its special 1877 Sharps "Tribute" series. This year only five heavy-barrel sporting rifles will be themed for the Lakota/Sioux tribe. Each rifle will be bundled with a special gun rack that features a buffalo skull, painted by noted Western artist, Gloria D. If you want one of these five rifles, act quickly. Two of them are already gone... and the remaining three will not last long.

Axtell makes six standard versions of the 1877, sometimes known as the "English model." This was a sleek evolution of the Sharps 1874, and a very rare iteration of the Sharps "sidehammer" rifles.

Altogether, Axtell offers a Custom Express, No. 1 Creedmoor, No. 2 Long Range, Lower Sporter, Lower Business Rifle and an Overbaugh Schuetzen version of their Model 1877. Each rifle features cut rifled and hand-lapped Badger barrels plus appropriate features for its application... including a set of renowned Axell iron sights. Find all about the great stuff at Axtell at www.riflesmith.com

Ballard Arms Company

In case you hadn't noticed, Ballard Rifle is no more. Ballard Arms Company has replaced it. And Ballard Arms President Bill Northrup has taken his reinvigorated company in a bold new direction.

Along with the long-standing Ballard and Model 1885 rifles that they're so famous for, Ballard is now moving decidedly into the high-end hunting and nuevo-classic rifle market.

It all began with Ballard's Light Hunter version of the Model 1885. This single-shot is made to travel

In the finest London tradition, the Ballard Jeffery Sharps features a color case-hardened trap grip cap. The cased lever has a hand-checkered thumb pad.

the high country with a light, 24-inch rapid-taper barrel, English-style forend and quarter-rib for scope or express sights. Available in almost any reasonable caliber, this high-style rifle is essentially a "custom" that's a cataloged product.

But that wasn't enough for Bill Northrup. Now, Ballard is producing a version of the mysterious Jeffery Sharps. Actually, these were not Sharps rifles at all, but Winchester single-shots that were converted by the W. J. Jeffery Company in England around the turn of the 20th century. By calling them "Sharps," it is almost certain that Jeffery was hoping to gain some sales advantage by trading off that famous name. The problem with the Jeffery Sharps is that no complete examples are known to have survived. Bits and actions, yes. But no rifles.

Ballard will correct that deficiency their new/old Jeffery Sharps. This single-shot will look very British with a unique African Express thick-side version of the Model 1885 action, featuring a specially-shaped lever, designed by Ballard gunsmith John Mercer. Barrels will be proportional to the calibers... which will include the 400 Jeffery, 500 Nitro Express and the 577 Nitro Express. The rear express sight will feature a silvered aiming line with flip-up moonlight front bead. The stock will be shaped in the finest London tradition with trap gripcap, ebony forend tip and leather-covered Silver's butt pad.

Ballard will also produce a limited edition Model 1885 to be called the Lonesome Dove. This arm will commemorate the life and accomplishments of Texas plainsman, Charles Goodnight... the man who

Ballard's Jeffery Sharps is accented by color-case components. These included the lever, express sight rear base, front sight base, trap grip cap and more. Pure class and tradition.

inspired author/screenwriter Larry McMurtry to create the Lonesome Dove character. In fact, the very first Lonesome Dove rifle will be presented to McMurtry's son, James McMurtry, by Ballard's president, Bill Northrup. Features and details of the Lonesome Dove 1885 are in a state of development at this writing.

But the *piece de resistance* of Ballard's new direction is a recreation of the legendary Gibbs Farquharson! Yes, the most beautiful and sought-after of all Farquharsons is coming back into production at Ballard. It will not be cheap, but it will be made in the finest London tradition, superbly engraved and stocked in the sleek lines of the most admired British makers. In fact, Ballard has consulted and engaged a number of British experts and craftsmen to make this rifle a reality. Look for it to be chambered in a range of classic British sporting calibers – including 600 Nitro Express. Learn more about all these exciting rifles at www.ballardarms.com

Borchardt Rifle Co.

Al Story works a lot of overtime. That's because he's still turning

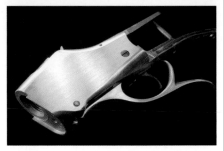

Ballard's recreation of the Jeffery Sharps is made on a Model 1885 coil mainspring action with pistol grip tang.

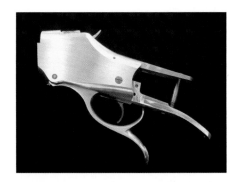

The lever of Ballard's Jeffery Sharps is a classic design by Ballard gunsmith John Mercer. It features a short lower spur with hand-checkered thumb pad.

This fine rifle could have come from a London maker a century ago. But Ballard Arms makes the Jeffery Sharps today... complete with original British Silver's pad.

REPORTS FROM THE FIELD...

out one of the best Sharps-Borchardt Model 1878 rifles in North America, plus his own action/rifle for the 50 BMG cartridge.

But it's Al's Sharps-Borchardt that keeps the light bill paid. These are fine rifles indeed, and are virtually indistinguishable from the originals. In fact, they remain a standard for the single-shot crowd, and most of the parts will interchange with the originals. For information on these rifles, call Al Story at Borchardt Rifle Co., 505-535-2923.

Cimarron

Cimarron should have been in business during the Wild West. They would have fit right in. That's because Cimarron offers no less than eight variants of the Sharps 1874. There's a Billy Dixon model as well as a Quigley model that recreates the Sharps rifle used by Tom Selleck in the movie "Quigley Down Under."

From there, you can move on to the 34-inch barreled Big 50 Sharps (in .50-90), the No. 1 Sporting, the option-laden Pride of The Plains, Texas Ranger Carbine, the Quigley II, or a more austere version of the Billy Dixon.

Cimarron also offers an Adobe Walls rolling block with double-set trigger in 45-70... this to recognize the actual rifle that buffalo hunter Billy Dixon owned and used on a daily basis (he made his famous 1583-yard shot with a Sharps).

More recently, Cimarron entered the market with a reproduction of the renowned Winchester Model 1885 Single-Shot, which can be had with either a straight grip or checkered pistol grip buttstock. There is also a Schuetzen double-set trigger available with the early Helm Schuetzen spur lever. Cimarron also offers the 1885 flat-side low-wall. Check it all out at www.cimarron-firearms.com

Classic Rifle Company

The Classic Rifle Company, of Bend, Oregon, makes Sharps 1874 rifles built to order by master machinist and gunsmith, John Mitchell. What's more, Classic can deliver *a true left hand 1874* in any configuration you'd like. Classic also makes the Sharps 1877 model.

All actions are milled from 8620 steel using original Sharps parts as patterns. Barrels are all match quality, with weight and length completely at the customer's discretion. Classic also offers tang sights machined from the same high quality steel as the rifle actions. For more information on Classic's rifles, visit www.classicrifles.net. For a quote, phone 503-789-0227 and talk to John Mitchell personally.

Cornell Publications

Sometimes I wonder about people. Really. I recently learned from the owners of Cornell that more than a few of their customers have called up and asked for one of "those Stevens you advertise for $120." That's when the caller must be gently made to understand that he's reading a catalog that's over 100 years old... and that Cornell only makes *reproductions* of old gun catalogs for enthusiast reference. They don't make guns.

But for those of us with a perspective on such things, Cornell has just added nine "new" recreations of old Stevens catalogs dating from 1877 to 1937, plus Winchester catalogs from 1891, 1893, 1907 and 1910. All of these great reference books will give single-shot fans new resources of information. So will seven new Remington catalogs from 1882 to 1906 and seven Sharps catalogs from 1859 to 1880.

They also have reproductions of the Bridgeport Gun Implement Co. catalogs from 1882 and 1912. Bridgeport made a lot of accessories for shooters... and a lot of sights for the "Big" gun companies of the day.

Cornell Publications has taken original catalogs, scanned in every page, and reprinted them just as they were originally. High-quality modern paper is used, and sometimes the catalog covers are "recreated' in color. This is done when the original cover is missing or severely damaged. Still, the inside material is all original and unaltered. It just published on new paper and saddle stitched back into a catalog format.

The great part is that prices are mostly in the $10 to $15 range, so you can feel empowered to stock up on a number of catalogs that will reveal an incredible amount of information. But it's best to visit Cornell's web site at www.cornellpubs.com and surf through the massive number of options. You can also phone Cornell at 810-225-3075.

C. Sharps Arms Co.

C. Sharps was the first company to reproduce the Sharps 1874 rifle in 1975. They also offer reproductions of the 1875 and 1877 Sharps as well as their own version of the Winchester Model 1885 high-wall.

The heart of C. Sharps' business are five models of the classic 1874 "sidehammer" Sharps. These include the 10.5-pound Hartford Sporting Model, the Bridgeport Sporting Rifle and the Boss Gun upgrade of the Hartford Sporting Rifle. It features a 34-inch barrel, engraved French grey receiver, XXX-figured wood, Hartford style forend with German Silver nose cap, globe front sight, long-range tang rear sight and a lot more.

C. Sharps also offers its interpretation of the 1875 Sharps in a Sporting Rifle and Classic Rifle configuration. Both have plain trigger and straight grip stock with an optional pistol grip available. The elegant 1877 "Presentation Grade" Sharps is also available from C. Sharps. This one is custom production only and comes with 44 or 45-caliber 32 or 34-inch tapered round barrel with Rigby flats at the breech. A custom-fitted oak-and-leather trunk case is part of the package.

C. Sharps also makes reproductions of the Winchester Model 1885: The Sporting Rifle with single trigger, shotgun butt, straight grip and the Highwall Classic with crescent butt, pistol grip stock and a silver inlay in the forend, or the custom-order Highwall Schuetzen. A Short Classic highwall is available with tapered octagon barrel at no additional cost. For the full story on C. Sharps, visit their web site at www.csharpsarms.com

Dakota Arms Inc.

To put it mildly, there's been a considerable volume of "discussion" regarding Dakota in the past year. And while I'm not about to recap it here, I will simply tell you that Dakota filed for Chapter 11 in 2006 and, as of this writing, is still in the throes of resolving the issues that led to that action.

But Dakota is still in business, according to CEO Charlie Kokesh. "We are not closing our doors, liquidating our assets or going out of business," Kokesh said.

Apparently, you can still order and obtain delivery on any Dakota single-shot, including the Model 10.

Dakota's Model 10 falling block is available in most any caliber from 22 LR to 300 Winchester Magnum. The Model 10 Magnum takes you up to the 338 Winchester, 375 H&H and 45-70. And because virtually no Model 10 is "standard," you can order any custom feature you want.

Dakota's "other single-shot" is the famous Miller. Each Miller is custom built to your specifications. The Sporter features a hand-checkered English style buttstock with XXX-wood and recoil pad. You also get the Miller action with jeweled block and 24-inch round barrel in just about any caliber up to 375 H&H. The Miller Low Boy has a case-colored receiver, half-octagon barrel and more. The Model F is Anglo-inspired with English walnut perch belly buttstock, Queen Anne grip, stainless receiver, globe front sight and Soule-type rear.

Dakota also markets a scaled-down version of the famous Model 1874 long-range rifle. In conjunction with the Little Sharps Rifle Co., of Big Sandy, Montana, Dakota reduced the size of the action by 20 percent in order to provide a rifle capable of shooting smaller rimmed handgun and hunting cartridges. So, don't let the rumors scare you off. Be bold and go to www.dakotaarms.com.

Dixie Gun Works

This year, Dixie offers a Pedersoli-made copy of the famous Remington Rolling Block Action that saw sporting and military action all over the world. This replica features a shotgun style buttstock with pistol grip, checkered wrist, and a straight forearm with silver tip. The stock is European walnut with satin oil finish. The chambering is 40/65 with a broach-rifled and blued 30-inch tapered octagon barrel. The rifle also has a color-casehardened receiver and trigger plate.

Dixie still offers its reproduction of the 1862 Confederate Sharps Carbine, made by Pedersoli. The gun is 54-caliber with a 22-inch browned, tapered round barrel with 1:48 twist and percussion ignition. Sights are browned steel base with integral blade front sight. The rear sight is blued steel, and the rifle has a single trigger. The butt and forestock are satin-finished American walnut, with the receiver, lock, lever, trigger plate and saddle bar and ring color case-hardened.

There is also a selection of Uberti high-walls at Dixie... and no less than 16 variations of the Sharps Model 1874 "sidehammer." Dixie's web site is worth checking into www.dixiegunworks.com

Steve Earle

Steve Earle is still making his incredibly precise reproduction of the famous Wesson No. 1 single-shot action.

Steve had intended to be making a recreation of the Wesson mid-range single-shot, but introduction has been delayed a bit. It's a falling block

Steve Earle has also created a set of offset scope mounts for the traditional Lyman and Unertl scopes. Much like Winchester's of a century past.

This Steve Earle Wesson was stocked and color-cased by Wisconsin single-shot gunsmith Glenn Fewless. It's beautiful.

action that has a central hammer. They only made seven originals and only four of those have survived as far as we know. Steve had one of those four to copy... but had to sell it to make his reproductions. But they will be more than worth the wait.

Steve Earle also makes scope blocks. All kinds of scope blocks. So if you want to mount an old Unertl or Lyman... or one of the new Malcolms, etc., Steve has the blocks you need. A new scope mounting system for Steve this year is an offset mount for classic Unertl and Lyman-style scopes. This is surprisingly similar to the offset mount that Winchester created in June 1910, and illustrated on page 214 of my book *The Winchester Single-Shot Vol. II, Old Secrets & New Discoveries*. It just proves that great minds think alike.

So, if you're looking for exotic Wesson actions, scope blocks and more, Steve Earle is your man. Contact him directly at 781-585-6504, e-mail him at steven.m.earle@comcast.net, or drop him a note at 24 Palmer Rd., Plympton MA 02367.

Nathan Heineke

There's a bit of London and Griffin & Howe in Nathan Heineke. And well there should be. Nathan has honed his craft in both venues, and currently plies his trade in Laramie, Wyo. There, in a well-appointed shop that would be totally at home on Bond Street, Nathan Heineke makes some of the finest single-shot rifles I've seen outside of Holland & Holland.

Nate Heineke

These rifles are built on custom or customer-supplied actions, but Nathan does all the rest of the work in the finest English tradition. The rifles that result are beautifully proportioned, meticulously stocked and magnificently finished. In every sense, they are sporting instruments of the finest caliber (actually any suitable caliber if you wish). Nathan also subscribes to an intriguing price structure. He charges a fixed price. That means he evaluates the project and its needs, quotes what he feels the job will require, then the client and Nathan agree on that price. And unless the client "ups the ante" with some new idea, Nathan delivers the rifle for his agreed price. Simple, eh?

When I last met Nathan at a Wyoming writer's seminar, he was proud to display an absolutely

This magnificent Farquharson is a product of Nathan Heineke's rifle-making skills. It's in 404 Jeffery and could pass muster in London.

marvelous Farquharson single-shot in 404 Jeffery. It was enough to tempt me into a second mortgage. For more about Nathan and his outstanding rifles, visit www.nlheineke.com. You'll swear there a little bit of London in Laramie.

Jeff's Outfitters

Jeff's Outfitters just keeps getting better... with more surprisingly cool stuff and more ways to "dress" your rifle than ever.

The classic product of this firm is classic trunk-type hard cases made along the lines of those common in the late 19th and early 20th centuries. They're leather or canvas-and-leather covered with partitioned felt-lined internal compartments for your rifle and accessories. Cases are available for Sharps, Remington rolling block, Springfield trapdoor and similarly shaped rifles. And if you want to make the kit look right, Jeff's even has the classic accessories to go along with these cases, including turnscrews, square or round nickel-plated oil cans and "Buffalo Hunter" cartridge belts.

But the single-shot stuff doesn't stop there. Jeff's also offer Pope or Winchester-style tuning fork palm rests, steel trigger guards for imported rolling blocks, plus a huge selection of sights. These range from reproductions of the standard factory sights of the era to globe and windgauge front sights, Vernier tang sights for Winchesters, Ballards, Stevens and more. Check it all out at www.jeffsoutfitters.com

Leatherwood Optics

One of the most popular scopes of the 1800s was the Malcolm. Today, thanks to Jim Leatherwood, you can still get a Malcolm scope that is, by all measures, superior to the original.

Since Leatherwood introduced these scopes, they discovered that two issues had to be addressed. First, target shooters

The Leatherwood Malcolm scope is a perfect complement to this classic 1878 Sharps Borchardt.

wanted a finer elevation adjustment. And other shooters, more interested in power than precision, needed a sturdier mount base for very heavy-recoiling rifles. Leatherwood has solved both problems. They now have a fine elevation adjustment, and a heavy recoil base and an extra ring to prevent slippage of the scope tube under heavy recoil. These accessories should be in production now, and can be easily added to existing scopes.

Leatherwood's 6x Malcolm comes in a short and long tube version with precision-adjustable mounts that affix to any 28 to 34-inch barrel. The scope has multi-coated lenses, a ¾-inch tube, crosshair reticle and is nitrogen-filled. The Leatherwood Malcolm scope is also incredibly rugged. Learn more at www.leatherwoodoptics.com

Lone Star Rifle Co., Inc.

The Lone Star Rifle Co. makes classic Remington single-shots with top quality and true-to-the-originals dimensions.

This year, Lone Star has introduced a Production Rifle to compete with the rolling block imports that have established a large presence in the marketplace. Like the original Remington production rifle, they will be plain with no checkering or engraving. But... Lone Star's Production rifle will be made one at a time and hand-fitted. That's worth a lot.

Lone Star also has a silhouette rifle (in all calibers) and a cowboy action rifle. Of course, their #5

Sporting rifle is still available, which is an exact recreation of the original Remington sporter. The Target Rifle can be ordered in Target or Silhouette configurations. The Big 50 Buffalo Rifle is chambered for the 50-90. The Custer Rifle is an authentic reproduction of the rifle actually used by Lt. Col. Custer on the Great Plains.

There's also the Gove side-lever "conversion." This is a rendition of frontier gunsmith Carlos Gove's adaptation of the classic rolling block action, and features a beautifully sculpted and lightened Pope hammer.

In addition, Lone Star offers an outstanding restoration service for rolling blocks. So whether you're interested in a factory-new roller, or the restoration of an original, you can find a great resource at www.lonestarrifle.com

Joseph Lozito and Associates

Gunsmith Joe Lozito has more up his very skilled sleeve for 2008. It's his version of the mysterious 1877 English Sharps. This is in process now… but will be ready soon.

The fascinating aspect of Joe's current 1875 Long Range action is that, by moving a kidney-shaped button at the back of the hammer axle, you can engage (or disengage) an internal mechanism that automatically re-cocks the hammer as the action's lever is closed. It is unbelievably neat.

The standard Lozito Sharps Borchardt 1878 action is cut from a block of 4130 or other chrome-moly steel to tolerances that the original Borchardts cannot match. Everything is perfect, including the finish polish. And, as with the original Sharps 1878 the Lozito-Sharps will accommodate virtually any rimmed or rimless cartridge. Want one with recessed wood panels or Zischang double set triggers? Just ask. And new for this year, Lozito will be offering an 1878 Schuetzen Model. Engraving, integral tang sight bases and more are also available.

Lozito also offers an improved 1878 with completely contained springs, improved striker arrangement, double-set triggers, integral tang

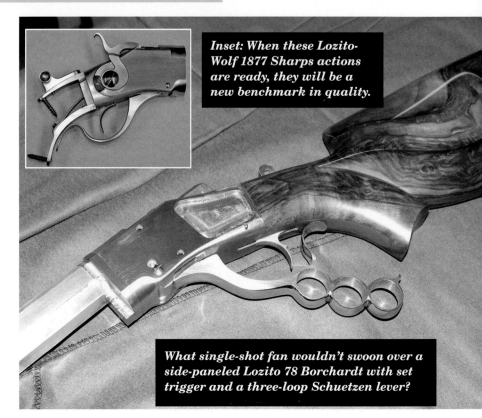

Inset: When these Lozito-Wolf 1877 Sharps actions are ready, they will be a new benchmark in quality.

What single-shot fan wouldn't swoon over a side-paneled Lozito 78 Borchardt with set trigger and a three-loop Schuetzen lever?

sight base and an ambidextrous safety located in the forward lever loop that's automatically set when you open the action. In addition, you can choose between a single hunting trigger or a double-set arrangement. Want one in take-down style? Joe Lozito has one. This would make a perfect "cased gun" with accessories.

Lozito also makes precision-machined Soule-style tang sights, globe and windgauge front sights, wood and ivory handled turnscrews, oil bottles, ball-and-needle-bearing cleaning rods, and more. Visit their web site at www.lozito-wolf.com, e-mail them at requestinfo@lozito-wolf.com or phone them at 631-242-9782. The address is Lozito-Wolf, 51 Garden City St., Bay Shore NY 11706.

Meacham Tool & Hardware

Meacham high-walls are still a benchmark for the industry. They're made in low-wall or high-wall style, and in five basic configurations: Helm Schuetzen, Special Target, Special Sporting, Benchrest and Silhouette (high-wall only).

But for 2008, the news from Meacham isn't a rifle at all. It's

a reloading tool. Meacham has created a portable reloading press called the ANYWHERE Press. It can be temporarily mounted to almost anything up to 9 inches thick, or permanently bolted to your reloading bench. The ANYWHERE Press is made of aircraft aluminum, weighs about two pounds, and its symmetrical design assures that the ammunition you load with it will be straight and accurate.

Meacham also offers a Pope-style bullet lubricator and the unbeatable Pope re-decap tool. This is a hand-operated gizmo that knocks out spent primers and seats new ones in a cartridge case. It's pretty much indispensable for the breech-seating Schuetzen enthusiast. So check Meacham's web site for one of the best Winchester Single-Shot repros available, and some very innovative accessories: www.meachamrifles.com

Montana Vintage Arms

This company's mainstay is a host of traditional tang sights based on the windage-adjustable Soule design. But they also make Winchester and Sharps style Vernier rear sights and a Marble's-type rear hunting sight.

MVA also makes a series of classic 6x scopes with ¾-inch tubes, parallax adjustment, Pope-style rib and battery stop, adjustable eyepiece and external adjustable Malcolm-type mounts. Lengths range from 23 inches on up to fit barrels as long as 34 inches.

In front sights, MVA offers Sharps, Stevens and Winchester-style globe sights, many with "wind gauge" adjustment.

Great sights aren't all that you can get from MVA. They also have a Stevens-Pope style palm rest, wooden scope cases, Winchester sight base screws (who hasn't needed these at least once?), crush-proof blackpowder cartridge blow tubes and an MVA powder measure that's the Rolls Royce of its kind for the blackpowder shooter. Peruse it all at www.montanavintagearms.com

Navy Arms

One of the greatest names in period firearms is Navy, and for 2008 they've chosen to go with what works in single-shots... the venerable 1874 Sharps.

A revitalized line of imported Sharps rifles are new at Navy this year. They include an 1874 Sharps #2 Creedmoor Rifle, a Sharps "Quigley" Rifle, Sharps sporting Rifle, and a Sharps Silhouette Rifle.

For trapdoor enthusiasts, there's an 1873 Springfield "Officer's Model" and for rolling block fans, there's a "John Bodine" rolling block, and a deluxe #2 "John Bodine" rolling block with nickel finish and select wood. For those of you who don't know, Col. John Bodine was a famous shooter of the 1800s, most closely associated with the Creedmoor range. Finally, Navy also offers a very good selection of 1885 Winchester reproductions. Check out these rifles and a lot more at Navy Arms' web site, www.navyarms.com.

Phillip Ollendorff

From a small town near Innsbruck, Austria, and from the hands of Phillip Ollendorff, comes one of the finest single-shot rifles in the world.

This lithe little arm is a perfectly made bar-in-wood sidelock "Kipplaufbuchse"... essentially a light stalking rifle. The one that Phillip had on hand at the most recent SCI convention in Reno was absolutely magnificent. It had a 25-inch barrel, weighed 5.6 kg and was chambered for the 7x57R cartridge. The scope it wore was a Swarovski 3-9x36. And to say this rifle was irresistible would be an understatement. Of course, Phillip can make a similar rifle to any specification you'd like... and in virtually any suitable caliber.

Personally, I start thinking of animals to stalk right now. Find out more at www.jagdwaffen-ollendorff.com

Ollendorff was trained in Ferlach, Austria, and his skills are perfectly suited for inletting a bar-in-wood stock.

Remington

The Remington Rolling Block is a single-shot classic that will never fade. And it's good to know you can still get one from Remington's custom shop.

The No. 1 rolling block available in two models. The first is the Mid-Range Sporter with pistol grip buttstock and blued receiver. The 30-inch round barrel has a 1:18 twist and is chambered for the 45-70 Govt. cartridge. This rifle also has a set

This neuvo-classic single-shot is a product of Austrian gunsmith Phillip Ollendorff. It's chambered for the 7x57R.

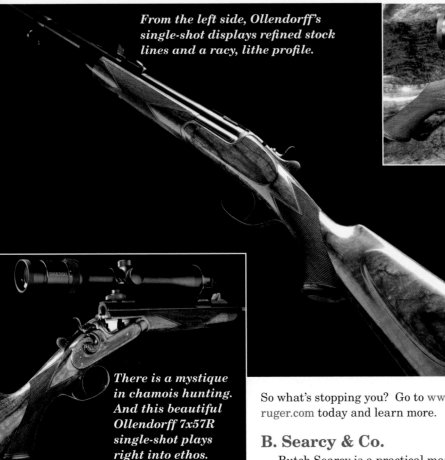

From the left side, Ollendorff's single-shot displays refined stock lines and a racy, lithe profile.

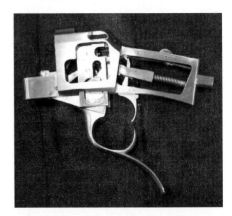

Another presentation of the Ollendorf 7x57 single-shot stalking rifle. Extra lock and polished mechanism is below.

There is a mystique in chamois hunting. And this beautiful Ollendorff 7x57R single-shot plays right into ethos.

trigger, figured wood, and color-cased receiver. Other options are available. The Mid-Range is ready to go for BPCR shooting and meets all criteria. Remember, these rifles are the real McCoy: *Remington* rolling blocks. Get the details at www.remington.com

Ruger

Once again Ruger is tempting the passions in us by offering their No. 1 Medium Sporter in a classic chambering that's too good to resist – the 9.3x74R. This 36-caliber cartridge is a very highly respected European big-game round that has been chambered in many double rifles and single-shots for over a century. For all practical purposes, it is somewhere between the 35 Whelen and 375 H&H in effectiveness. In other words, when you shoot something big with the 9.3x74R, it generally falls down and stays down. There is plenty of loaded ammunition available for the 9.3 as well as bullets and cases for reloading.

So what's stopping you? Go to www. ruger.com today and learn more.

B. Searcy & Co.

Butch Searcy is a practical man. He had the opportunity to buy the Brookings Arms Manufacturing Company's single-shot, and he did. But Butch didn't stop there. He redesigned it for better function and an improved trigger pull, added a great stock and is not offering this stout little rifle to the world. He can make one for you in just about any reasonable caliber, too. But you have to keep an eye on him. Butch handed me a 404 Jeffery at the SCI Show that weighed under 10 pounds if it weighed an ounce. And one shot from it would be just about all I'd prefer to have, thank you. But to be fair this was a prototype rifle that could easily have been a bit heftier if you wanted. Get the whole story of the Searcy single-shot at www.searcyent.com

Shiloh Sharps Rifle Co.

The spirit of Matthew Quigley lives on at Shiloh. And if the romance of a great Sharps is something you just can't resist, then a visit to the Shiloh web site will fire up your romance factor immensely.

Shiloh's 1863 rifles are a recreation the earliest Sharps design that used combustible paper cartridges. They're all offered in 50 or 54 caliber. The Sporting Rifle features a 30-inch octagon barrel with buckhorn rear sight and blade front, plus double-set triggers. The Military Rifle has a 30-inch round barrel and includes a ladder rear sight, military-style iron block front sight and single trigger. The Carbine has a 22-inch round barrel, ladder rear sight and iron block front sight.

Shiloh makes no less than a dozen variants of the 1874, including the Creedmoor Silhouette Rifle, the Carbine, Hartford Model and more. And don't worry. The Quigley model is still available. And you don't even have to go "down under" to get it. There's also a Military musket.

Shiloh also offers a 6x scope with ¾-inch tube. It has a blued steel

One of the nice features of the Searcy single-shot is that the lever throw is short, and block travel is minimal.

Searcy single-shots are classically-stocked. The top rifle is a 404 Jeffery and the bottom (unfinished) rifle a 375 H&H Flanged.

finish with Malcolm-style mounts, Pope rib, parallax adjustment, four reticle options and comes in four lengths. Get the whole story of Shiloh products, plus some music you'll recognize, at www.shilohrifle.com

Single Shot Rifles Inc.

In case you haven't heard, this is the "old" CPA Corp., under a different name. Same great people (the Shuttleworths) and the same great rifles. Just a new name. I guess it was finally discovered that someone else held prior claim to the name CPA Corp. in Pennsylvania, so CPA changed. And as the Bard once said, by any other name, SSR Inc. has been making some terrific

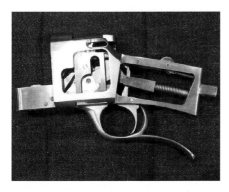

This cutaway action shows how Butch Searcy re-engineered the BAM single-shot for greater precision, smoother function and improved trigger pull.

Stevens 44½ reproductions since 1986.

Because virtually all of its rifles are built to custom order, there's not much you could call a "standard" SSR 44½. But there are three basic models: The Schuetzen, Silhouette, and the Sporting/Varmint Rifle. A host of standard features come with every one. These include a color-cased action, double-set triggers, oil-finished semi-fancy pistol grip stock, a take-down system, and your choice of most any barrel contour in most any caliber from 22 Short to 45-110.

In addition to rifles, SSR offers a large selection of "single-shot stuff" for Stevens, Sharps, Ballard, Remington, Winchester and other classic single-shots. This includes semi-inletted stocks, buttplates, levers, palm rests, scope bases and a whole bunch more.

Something new for SSR this year is their special line of Hoch nose-pour bullet moulds, made for SSR by Colorado Shooters Supply. These are specially designed by SSR to work well in their rifles as well as other single-shots of the same caliber. You can choose from .25, .32 and .38 Schuetzen designs, .38, .40 and 45 silhouette style, or .40 fast-twist and .45 long-range designs. The best part is that SSR/Hoch moulds are in stock and ready for delivery. It's worth a trip to the SSR web site just to find out, too. That's www.singleshotrifles.com

Traditions

Traditions offers a line of Pedersoli1874 Sharps rifles, all in 45-70. All models except the Standard 1874 come with double-set triggers and target sights. The Deluxe is hand-engraved with satin-finished frame. You can also obtain some very nice tang and globe front sights from Traditions. Just visit their website at www.traditionsfirearms.com

Treebone Carving

For everyone who needs a stock for whatever single-shot they're working on, there's Treebone Carving of Cimarron, New Mexico.

At Treebone, George Petersen has over 200 patterns and 4000 stock blanks to help make your project

dreams come true. Treebone pre-turned stocks are precisely made and require only a minimum of final inletting to snug up to an action. What's more, they're carefully turned "on-center" which is a big help for any amateur craftsman. Patterns are available for the Remington rolling block, Winchester Single-Shot, Ballard, Sharps, Ruger, Trapdoor, Hepburn, Marlin and Winchester lever guns and more. Treebone also offers buttplates, traditional butt plate screws, and forearm lugs.

George Petersen has also created a web site, which has valuable tutorial sections on how to fit stocks with *lots* of pictures and great information. Check it out at www.treebonecarving.com or phone George at 505-376-2145.

Uberti

This Italian manufacturer was one of the first to offer a new version of the Winchester Model 1885 Single-Shot. While the Uberti design has certain internal differences from the original Winchester "high-wall," it's still a sound and well-made rifle that offers a lot of value for the money.

The foundation of the Uberti High-Wall line is the Sporting and Special Sporting single-shots. They're offered in 45-70 Govt., 45-90, and the bison-blasting 45-120 with 30 or 32-inch tapered octagon barrels that approximate the old Winchester No. 3 contour. The steel frame and lever are color case-hardened. Walnut stocks for the Sporting rifle feature a straight grip buttstock with curved steel buttplate and traditional Schnabel forend. The Special Sporting version has a buttstock with a checkered pistol grip.

Those who prefer a slightly more compact rifle can choose Uberti's High-Wall Carbine in 45-70, but with a 28-inch tapered round barrel and a flat, shotgun style buttplate. You can also get a reproduction No. 4 rolling block from Uberti. Their forged steel frames are color case-hardened, trigger guards and buttplates are brass, and stocks are straight grip walnut. Check Uberti's web site, www.uberti.com to see these great guns for yourself. ◉

SHOTGUNS TODAY ✦
SHOTGUN REVIEW

by John Haviland

*S*hotguns are a durable product. To maintain demand, manufacturers must constantly promote innovations such as embellishments, and easier handling and shooting. Those trimmings and improvements certainly catch shooters' eyes because Americans bought approximately half a million imported shotguns and nearly 600,000 domestically produced shotguns in 2005. Let's see what shotguns manufacturers have come up with this year to tempt us.

Benelli

The ComforTech system, which consists of shock-absorbing material in recoil pad and bands in the stock, has been added to the Cordoba, Super Sport, Sport II, Super Black Eagle II, M2 Field and new M4 Tactical. The M4 Tactical uses Benelli's inertia drive operating system and has an adjustable-aperture ghost ring rear sight, fixed blade front sight and a pistol grip stock in desert camouflage or matte black. The Montefeltro Silver has nickel-plating on its aluminum receiver with scroll engraving and game birds in gold.

Beretta

The Beretta family of AL391 semi-automatics has two enhanced versions and a recoil reducer in its down-in-the-mud gun.

The Urika Premium has a high-grade finish on its wood and polished appearance on its exposed metal to match the deep black of the barrel bluing. Teknys Stonecoat, in 20- and 12-gauge standard and

This hunter is shooting a Beretta Xtrema2 with the Kick Off recoil reduction system. His quarry is sea ducks off the coast of Maine.

slug guns, feature a multi-layered finish of nickel and chrome and a final protective layer of titanium and zirconium to their receiver, bolt, bolt handle, follower and trigger.

The Xtrema2 has the option of the Kick Off recoil reduction system that features two hydraulic dampers incorporated into the stock. On a sea duck hunt on the Maine coast last season I shot Federal's 12-gauge 3- and 3½-inch shells through an Xtrema2 with the Kick Off. The recoil was almost gentle with 3-inch shells and bearable with 3½s.

The SO10 over-and-under 20-gauge is a sidelock with side plates that can be removed by hand with two hidden keys. With no pins or screws on the surface of the plates, six engraving patterns are available on the SO10. The ejectors on the gun have been increased in area to catch more of the shell rim for improved extraction and ejection. The top lever is also long and closer to the breech for more leverage to break the action. The gun has 26-, 28- or 30-inch barrels.

The Silver Pigeon and DT10 Trident L Trap and Double Trap have been dressed up. The Silver Pigeon V has color case-hardened sideplates, trigger guard, trigger plate, top lever and hinge pins. Its side plates wear game scenes of gold ducks and pheasants in the 12-gauge and quail and partridge in the 20- and 28-gauge and .410. The DT10s have English and floral engraving.

Browning

The Cynergy over and under has lots of new models. The Cynergy Feather 12-gauge weighs only six pounds, losing nearly 1½ pounds with its alloy receiver. Other lightweight Cynergys are the 20- and 28-gauge and .410-bore in the Classic Field and Classic Sporting series. The Cynergy Grade III features full receiver high-relief engraving. The 12-gauge depicts pheasants on the left side and mallards on the right, the 20-gauge teal on the left side of the receiver and partridge on the right. The Grade VI 12-gauge is embellished

This greenhead mallard was taken with a Beretta 3901 Statesman 12-gauge firing Federal's new Black Cloud steel shot. The steel pellets have a cutting band around their outside that make nasty wounds in waterfowl.

with gold-enhanced engraving of pheasants on the left side of the receiver and mallards on the right. The Cynergy Euro Sporting has a European-style rib and is available in Sporting, Sporting Adjustable with an adjustable comb, and Sporting Composite with a composite stock.

The Cynergy Field Composite 12-gauge is now available with 3½-inch chambers. Its composite buttstock and forearm are finished in Mossy Oak Duck Blind camo and have Dura-Touch rubber over moldings in the grip areas. Its comb is adjustable for drop, and features the recoil-

A Beretta Xtrema2 is posed with a common eider.

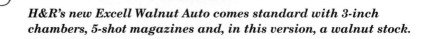

H&R's new Excell Walnut Auto comes standard with 3-inch chambers, 5-shot magazines and, in this version, a walnut stock.

H&R's Excell Waterfowl Auto is fitted with a camouflage-pattern synthetic stock.

reducing Inflex recoil pad system. The Field includes Full, Modified and Improved Cylinder choke tubes. The Cynergy Nickel Tin has a steel receiver with a matte gray nickel tin finish, gold-enhanced engraving and matte blue barrels with a ventilated rib. Its black composite stock has rubber overmolding in grip areas. The Cynergy Sporting Red, White, Blue has a blue marble gloss finish on its receiver that, to say the least, contrasts with the chopped-up American flag pattern on its composite stock. This 12-gauge has 2¾-inch chambers and ported barrels with ventilated top and side ribs. The Cynergy Classic Trap has a Monte Carlo or adjustable comb.

The Citori 525 Field Grade VI has a nitride finish with gold-enhanced engraving complimented with an oil-finished walnut stock. The 12-gauge gun has 3-inch chambers, lightweight profile barrels with a ventilated rib and Improved Cylinder, Modified and Full screw-in choke tubes. The Citori Lightning and 525 Sporting 12-gauges comes with the option of a gray laminated hardwood stock and forend with a satin finish. A gray nickel finish on the receivers and barrels match the laminate. The Lightning is also covered with Mossy Oak Duck Blind camo. A Dura-Touch coating also covers the stock and forearm. The gun is chambered for 12-gauge 3½-inch shells, just in case

someone is brave enough to fire such a big shell in the fixed-action gun. The Lightning Pheasants Forever 25th Anniversary has a blued steel receiver with silver pheasants and a glossy walnut stock. The 12-gauge has 3-inch chambers and interchangeable choke tubes at the muzzle of its 28-inch barrels and weighs 8 pounds, 2 ounces. The Citori 525 Feather has an alloy receiver with steel breech face and hinge pin, engraving and oil-finished high-grade wood. The Citori 525 Field Grade III has a steel/nitride receiver, high-relief engraving and high-grade oil-finished wood.

The BT-99 now has a more utilitarian laminate hardwood gray Monte Carlo comb stock and forearm. Its receiver and barrel match with a gray nickel finish. A matte black ventilated rib stands in contrast.

The Browning Pump Shotgun High Capacity holds seven rounds in an extended magazine tube. The 12-gauge has a 20-inch barrel with a 3-inch chamber and a fixed Cylinder choke. Its handles are composite.

After having great success shooting deer with today's 20-gauge slugs, like the Remington BuckHammer, I'm not going back to the brutal recoil of 12-gauge slugs. Browning is chambering its BPS 20-gauge with a rifled barrel and calling it the Rifled Deer Shotgun. The gun comes with a satin finished wood stock and forend and synthetic

with Mossy Oak Break-Up camo finish with Dura-Touch armor coating. A cantilever scope base is included to mount optic sights.

The Silver Hunter autoloader has been dressed up to honor Pheasants Forever's 25th anniversary. Its blued receiver has silver-enhanced engraving. The blued barrel has a ventilated rib and the Invector Plus choke tube system. The Silver Lightning has a semi-humpback receiver with a silver finish and a slim profile barrel with ventilated rib and a gloss finish and cut checkering on its wood.

Marlin

Marlin has added the 28-gauge and .410-bore to the Italian side-by-side they import and call the L.C. Smith. Both guns feature fleur-de-lis checkering patterns on their walnut stocks and forearms, single selective trigger, selective automatic ejectors and Improved Cylinder, Modified and Full screw-in choke tubes. The 26-inch chrome-lined barrels carry a solid rib and a bead front sight. The receiver is case-colored with a gold pheasant embossed on the side and bottom. The 28 has a 2¾-inch chamber and the .410 a 3-inch chamber. Both guns weigh 6½ pounds.

Marlin's H&R is importing a line of autoloading 12-gauges called the Excell Auto with 3-inch chambers and 5-shot magazines. The Excell

Marlin has added the 28-gauge and .410-bore chamberings to the Italian-made L.C. Smith line.

Synthetic has a black synthetic stock, the Waterfowl a synthetic stock with a camouflage pattern and the Walnut, a walnut stock. All three guns weigh seven pounds with a 28-inch barrel and a ventilated rib. Four screw-in choke tubes include Improved Cylinder, Modified, Improved Modified and Full. The Turkey has a camo synthetic stock with a 22-inch barrel and a ventilated rib with a fiber optic front and rear sight. It comes with Improved Cylinder, Modified, Full, Extra Full and TURKEY screw-in chokes. The Combo has a black synthetic stock with a 28-inch ventilated rib barrel and a 24-inch rifled barrel. The smoothbore barrel has a bead front sight and Improved Cylinder, Modified, Improved Modified and Full screw-in chokes. The slug barrel wears fiber optic front and rear sights.

The H&R Tamer, in 20-gauge or .410, is just right for potting grouse and rabbits. It uses the Topper break-action single-shot receiver with a nickel matte-finish and matching 20-inch barrel with a Full choke. The polymer stock has a thumbhole grip and stores four .410 or three 20-gauge shells in the right side of the stock. The receiver includes automatic spent shell ejection, transfer bar to prevent accidental firing and a locking system. The Tamer weighs six pounds.

Remington

The Premier over-under shotguns have three new models. The Premier STS Competition that was introduced in 2006 with 28- or 30-inch barrels, is now available with 32-inch barrels. The Premier Adjustable Comb has 30- or 32-inch barrels and its comb can be altered for height and cast. The Premier Field Over & Under Ruffed Grouse Society is chambered in 20-gauge. The gun has a straight grip walnut stock with a Schnabel forend and cut checkering. The 26-

The Remington Model 870 Express has three new hunting versions. The Combo includes a 12-gauge 21-inch barrel with a Turkey Extra Full choke tube for turkeys; a 23-inch fully-rifled barrel can be installed come deer season.

inch barrels have a white front bead and five ProBore choke tubes. The receiver is finished in black and offsets the gold Ruffed Grouse Society logo on both sides of the receiver and the Remington "R" on the frame bottom. The gun weighs 6½ pounds and comes in a lockable hard case.

The Model SP-10 Magnum Waterfowl is fully coated with Mossy Oak Duck Blind camo. Its 26-inch barrel accepts Briley Waterfowl Chokes that include Decoying, Intermediate and Ported Pass Shooting extended tubes. The front sight is a HiViz fiber optic bead. To tame the recoil of 10-gauge 3½-inch shells, the gun weighs 10 pounds 14 ounces and wears an R3 recoil pad.

A turkey-hunting version of the SP-10 Magnum features a thumbhole laminated wood stock that allows the palm of the hand to absorb some of the recoil from 10-gauge magnum loads. Further recoil reduction comes from an R3 recoil pad and a ported Briley choke tube. The SP-10 Thumbhole Camo has a 23-inch barrel with Williams FireSights which include a fiber-optic front bead and fully adjustable rear sight. A supplied sling will make it easier to carry the nearly 11-pound gun.

Mossy Oak Break-Up camo now completely covers the Model 11-87 Sportsman 12- and 20-gauge guns. The Camo 12-gauge has a 28-inch barrel, while the 20-gauge version has a 26-inch barrel.

The Model 11-87 SPS Super Magnum is now available in a

Waterfowl style with the Mossy Oak Duck Blind pattern. A SpeedFeed shell holder in each side of the synthetic stock holds a total of four extra shells for quick reloading. A HiViz fiber-optic sight, with interchangeable light pipes, comes on its 30-inch barrel.

The Model 870 pump Xtreme Conditions Shotgun Marine Magnum's metal is coated with Remington's TriNyte Corrosion Control System. Its trigger group parts are plated with nickel. A SpeedFeed shell holder in each side of the synthetic stock holds a total of four extra 12-gauge shells for quick reloading of its 7-round magazine. The barrel is 18 inches and has a fixed Cylinder choke.

The 870 SPS Super Magnum now has a MAX Gobbler edition. It is covered with Realtree All-Purpose Green HD camouflage and a 23-inch barrel with a super Full Turkey choke tube. Sights include Williams FireSights, which include a front and adjustable rear fiber-optic sights. The top of the receiver is also drilled and tapped to accept a Weaver-style base to mount optic sights. The synthetic stock has a pistol grip and a length of pull that is instantly adjustable from 12 to 16 inches.

The Model 870 Express has three new additions for hunting. The Super Magnum Waterfowl is offered with Mossy Oak's Duck Blind camo. The 870 Express Combo includes a 12-gauge, 3-inch chambering with a 21-inch barrel with a Turkey Extra Full choke tube for turkeys.

Remington's Model 870 pump XCS Marine Magnum's metal is coated with Remington's TriNyte Corrosion Control System.

Remington's 870 SPS Super Magnum's new MAX Gobbler edition is covered with Realtree All-Purpose Green HD camouflage.

A 23-inch barrel can be installed come deer season. It is fully rifled and has a cantilever mount for adding a scope. An 870 Express now holds 7, 20-gauge shells.

The 870 line has also been expanded to include black gun models. The Tac-2 SpecOps Stock has an 18-inch barrel with a 2-shot extension. Its synthetic stock has a Knoxx SpecOps stock with a pistol grip and a length of pull adjustable from 12 to 16 inches. The Tac-3 has a 20-inch barrel with a 3-round magazine extension and a pistol grip stock. Both models are also available with Knoxx SpecOps Folder stocks. The stocks have a wire frame over-molded with soft rubber. A push of a release unlocks the stock so it can fold over the top of the receiver.

The Model 1100 line has been expanded to include the Tac-2 and Tac-4 models, both dressed in black. The Tac-2 SpeedFeed IV version has a 2-shot magazine tube extension under its 18-inch barrel with a fixed improved cylinder choke. An extended carrier release and an oversized bolt handle make reloading quick. Accessories include a Weaver-type base for mounting a scope and front and rear swivel studs. The Tac-4 has a 4-shell magazine extension under its 22-inch barrel with three screw-in choke tubes.

Rossi

The Rossi Slug Gun is based on Rossi's break-action single shot and features a fully rifled barrel in 12- or 20-gauge. The barrel is ported at the muzzle to help reduce the kick of slug loads. Fiber optic sights are mounted on the barrel. The barrel is also drilled and tapped to mount a provided Weaver-type rail to mount a scope or other optic sights. The Slug Guns have blued steel, and wood stocks and forends.

Smith & Wesson

Smith & Wesson is importing a line of break-action and autoloading shotguns from Turkey.

The Elite Gold is a side-by-side 20 gauge with 26- or 28-inch barrels and fixed Improved Cylinder and Modified chokes. It features a trigger plate action with selective automatic ejectors and a rounded and sculpted receiver with bone charcoal case-hardening, 24 lines-per-inch hand-cut checkering on the Turkish walnut forend and straight-grip stock.

The Elite Silver is an over/under 12-gauge with many of the same cosmetic features of the Gold. The Silver, though, has 26-, 28- or 30-inch barrels with five choices of interchangeable choke tubes.

Smith & Wesson states each Elite gun comes with a lifetime warranty for the original buyer, as well as the buyer's chosen heir.

The 1000 Series of semi-automatic shotguns include the 1012, 12-gauge 3-inch, Super 12-gauge 3½-inch and 1020 20-gauge 3-inch. These gas-operated guns are made with aluminum receivers and the 12-gauge guns include two different gas rings, one for loads up to 1¼ ounces and the other for 1½ ounce and heavier loads. The barrels are chrome-lined with ventilated ribs and TRUGLO fiber optic front beads and plain beads at mid-rib. Five screw-in choke tubes of various constrictions are provided. Shim kits allow altering the cast, cant and drop of the stock. Stocks and forends are either Turkish walnut with point patterns or synthetic of black or Realtree Max-4 or APG camouflage. All in all, Smith & Wesson states there will be 29 variations of the 1000, from turkey and duck guns to youth guns.

Winchester

The Winchester Super X3 has had a makeover with flowing lines to add, as Winchester states, "a modern flair." Its stock, grip and forearm have been slimmed for a better fit in the hands. A Pachmayr Decelerator pad helps absorb recoil. Length of pull and comb drop and cast are easy to alter with provided shims. Its magazine tube and recoil spring system have also been lightened to remove half a pound of weight. A gunmetal gray Perma-Cote Ultra Tough finish on the metal is the "toughest finish ever applied to a shotgun," according to Winchester.

The Super X3 Waterfowl 3½-inch is covered with Mossy Oak Duck Blind or Brush camo. Its composite stock and forearm are covered with Dura-Touch Armor Coating finish for a sure grip. The bolt is plated with electroless nickel for corrosion resistance and the barrel incorporates

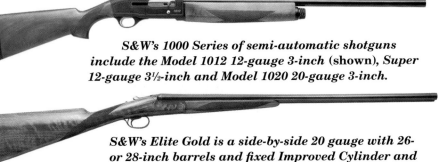

S&W's 1000 Series of semi-automatic shotguns include the Model 1012 12-gauge 3-inch (shown), Super 12-gauge 3½-inch and Model 1020 20-gauge 3-inch.

S&W's Elite Gold is a side-by-side 20 gauge with 26- or 28-inch barrels and fixed Improved Cylinder and Modified chokes.

Weatherby's Semi-Automatic Shotgun is now covered with Skyline's Fall flight pattern for waterfowl hunters.

the Invector-Plus choke tube system with three provided tubes. With a 28-inch barrel, the gun weighs 7 pounds, 4 ounces. Extra barrels are also available. The Super X3 Cantilever Deer Extra Barrels are 22 inches long. Spare barrels are also available in 26- or 28-inch lengths and 3- or 3½-inch chambers.

A few brief mentions

* Bill Hanus Birdguns continues to promote the 16-gauge. Browning made a small run of 16s in its Citori over/under and Hanus is trying to get his hands on all of them he can. Hopefully he will have a few Lightning Classics, Superlights and 525s in various grades for sale in 2007. "These guns are built on 16-gauge frames, so they usually weigh about seven ounces more than a comparable 20-gauge model and a pound less than the 12-gauge," Hanus says. "These guns appear to have about one-eighth inch of cast-off and a 14¼-inch length of pull and the field guns do not have pads."

* Mossberg's Just In Case (JIC) package includes about everything required to endure a wilderness emergency situation. Inside a plastic carrying tube, Mossberg includes one of its Model 800 pump-action shotguns in a blued Cruiser model or coated Mariner model with an 18½-inch barrel and a pistol grip. Included with the Cruiser shotgun is a survival kit complete with matches, fishing hooks and other survival items. The Mariner version includes a multi-tool and a serrated folding knife.

* Weatherby's Semi-Automatic Shotgun is now covered with Skyline Excel camouflage for turkey hunters and Fall flight pattern for waterfowl hunters.

* Birchwood Casey's Barrel Boss is a complete 12- or 20-gauge barrel cleaning kit stored in a plastic tube. The kit contains an aluminum rod for conventional cleaning and a fluffy rod to wipe the gunk out of a barrel. The hollow handle has enough room to store a provided bore brush and cleaning patches.

This young hunter has used his Benelli Nova pump 12-gauge hard for several years. The gun will no doubt last through all his shooting years. The durability of a shotgun is why manufacturers must constantly promote innovations to keep selling guns.

TODAY'S MUZZLELOADING ✦ BLACKPOWDER REVIEW

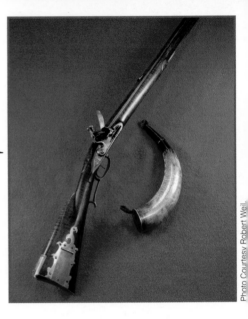

by Doc Carlson

Probably no other area of firearms offers as much diversification as the muzzleloading field. On the one hand, we have the very primitive firearm, such as the matchlock; on the other, we have today's sophisticated muzzleloaders that incorporate the very latest in modern materials and design. Both ends of the spectrum have their adherents and champions, and discussions go on and on about which is better or more "right." There are definitely more of the hunting-oriented shooters that embrace the latest in muzzleloading development, mostly due to the proliferation of special muzzleloading seasons in nearly all states. While the traditional sidehammer shooter is in the minority today, there are still large numbers of folks who want to "do it like our forefathers did."

Between custom gunsmiths and the muzzleloading industry, both groups are supplied with a wide variety of firearms and accessories that cater to whatever interest those hunters and shooters may have.

The Holy Grail for the traditional shooter is a custom hand-built gun by one of the top gunmakers. These guns are often works of art, and rank up there with fine paintings and sculpture. They quickly become heirlooms that are passed down in families from one generation to the next. While they are collectible art, they have the advantage of being completely useable and, in fact, are intended for use in the hunting field and on the target range. Guns by known makers appreciate in value, the same as paintings by known artists. Lucky is the fellow that gets a nice rifle made by a relatively unknown maker who later becomes a noted gunbuilder. His investment in the rifle will continue to grow as the reputation of the builder grows.

Mark Silver

One of the very best of the custom builders working today is Mark Silver, a Michigan gunmaker. Silver has been a full-time gunbuilder since 1976, is very well known and recognized as one of the premier builders working today. Early in his carrer, he worked as a journeyman for a couple of years

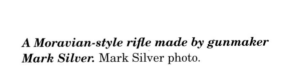

A Moravian-style rifle made by gunmaker ***Mark Silver.*** Mark Silver photo.

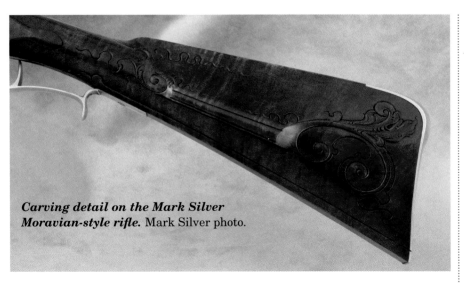

Carving detail on the Mark Silver Moravian-style rifle. Mark Silver photo.

with the late John Bivins. Bivins was considered by many to be the leading authority on early golden age rifle-building. Silver is a past president of both the Contemporary Longrifle Association and the American Custom Gunmakers Guild, which shows the regard that other custom gunmakers have for him. He regularly teaches courses related to gun-building at the gunmakers' seminars sponsored each year at Western Kentucky University by the National Muzzle Loading Rifle Association.

Silver will build most any style gun that the customer wants, but specializes in the Kentucky rifle of the Golden Age, as well as fine Continental rifles and fowlers. He builds guns using the same hand tools that the gunsmiths of the 1700s used: hand saws, planes, chisels, gouges and scrapers. The finishes he uses are the traditional nitric acid stains, spirit varnishes, oils and waxes that were available to the 18th century gunsmith.

The first rifle we'll look at is an American flintlock long rifle done in

the style of the Moravian gunmakers of Christians Spring, Pennsylvania and Bethabara (now Salem), North Carolina during the 1770-80 period. The 54-caliber rifle has a 44-inch barrel and weighs in at 9¼ pounds. The curly maple stock is stained with nitric acid stain and finished with a red-tinted varnish. The gun is brass-mounted with hand-wrought buttplate, sideplate, ramrod pipes and forend tip. The barrel is blued to duplicate the charcoal bluing that was common on these rifles. The finely tuned flintlock is custom shaped and detailed, engraved in the Moravian

style and finished with color case-hardening that is worn to enhance the relief borders and engraving. The attention to detail is fantastic, making this a serious work of art.

The second gun we'll examine is a rifle of the type that would have been made by top London gunsmiths in the 1735-55 period. This 7-pound rifle has a 28-inch 54-caliber rifled barrel and is, of course, a flintlock. The gun is steel-mounted and charcoal blued with hand-chiseled relief sideplate and hammer. There is a relief border on the lockplate with the color case-hardening selectively removed to highlight the relief work. The lock features a hand-pierced pan, 24k gold-lined, typical on finer English rifles of the period. The rifle is stocked in figured English walnut, and is carved with a shell behind the barrel tang and scrolls along the wrist. The fore-stock has a relief molding along the ramrod channel that transitions into simple relief and incised decoration behind the rear ramrod pipe. Overall, a typical high-quality rifle that

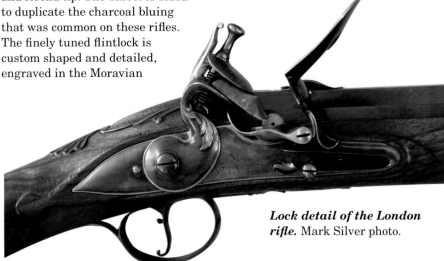

Lock detail of the London rifle. Mark Silver photo.

A mid-1700s London type rifle by Mark Silver. Clean, balanced lines mark this as a shooter's rifle. Mark Silver photo.

A very nice French Fusil by David Dodds. Robert Weil photo.

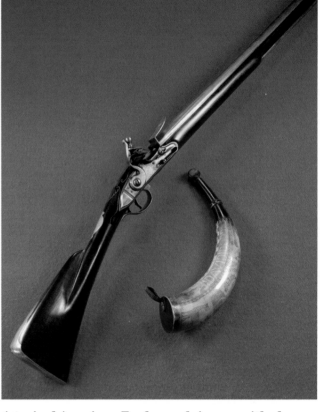

A typical American Fowler, a plain gun with clean crisp lines, by David Dodds. Robert Weil photo.

would have been made by a London gunmaker for landed aristocracy.

David L. Dodds

Another custom maker who does fine work is David L. Dodds, a full-time gunmaker who has been building since 1969. He says he got his start and early training by studying a series of articles on gunbuilding written by John Bivins for *Rifle* magazine. He was also helped with advice from close neighbor and well-known gunmaker Ron Ehlert, and another master craftsman, Jim Chambers. The above, combined with a great deal of natural talent, put him on the road to becoming a fine gunbuilder.

Dodds' major interest lies in duplicating original guns. This is a difficult task as we all tend to bring some of our own personality into whatever we are doing. Duplicating an original firearm in the style of the original gunmaker is much akin to copying someone's handwriting – some folks can do it well, but they are rare. Dodds appears to be one of those rare individuals as well as being a fine gunmaker in his own right. Presently, he is interested in the Reading school of design. These guns tend to be rather plain, with little or no carving and engraving, but they show an eye-pleasing architectural line that is very functional. Ordering a rifle from any of the better gunmakers is akin to having a tailored suit of clothes made. Measurements are taken so the finished gun will fit your physical build. You can specify style, type of wood (within limits – it has to match the gun you are ordering), barrel, caliber, lock and a myriad of other details. Be prepared for a long wait as most of these folks are several months behind on orders. You get in line and wait your turn. The wait is very much worth it, however.

Taylor's & Company

Taylor's & Company is well known for supplying high-quality

Taylor's & Co. reproduction of the rifle carried by the John C. Fremont expedition in the mid-1800s.

reproductions of early firearms, both muzzleloading and cartridge models, to traditional shooters that have interests in the various eras of blackpowder use from the pre-Revolutionary War period through the Civil War, and on into the taming of the American West. They have a new rifle that will tempt those with an interest in early exploration of the West, as well as those who just like large-caliber rifles.

The new rifle is a faithful copy of a Short Model 1842 rifle musket that was made up especially for the Fremont Expedition in 1847 at the Springfield Armory. These rifles were the same pattern as the regulation 1842 with the exception of being shortened to 48½ inches overall.

The 69-caliber rifled barrel is 33 inches long with a bayonet lug at the muzzle. An elevating rear sight is combined with a blade front, per the 1842 Model. All furniture is iron and the gun has sling swivels of standard loop size for military rifles and muskets of the time. The stock is walnut with an oil-type finish. A steel ramrod with a trumpet-shaped end is supplied and is held in place under the barrel with a spoon-type spring located in the bottom part of the ramrod channel in the stock.

The percussion lock is marked with the typical eagle head and the date 1847. The nipple takes Musket caps. The rear sling swivel is attached to the iron trigger guard.

This rifle is a very nice copy of the Fremont gun, with excellent fit and finish. The 69-caliber bore should handle either the patched roundball or the hollow-base Minie very well. I look forward to getting one of these military big bores in my hands for a shooting session.

Thompson/Center

Thompson/Center is a name well known to muzzleloaders for

The new T/C breech plug. Rotate it 90 degrees and it comes out for easy cleaning of the bore.

their line of both muzzleloading and cartridge firearms. They were one of the very first to put a mass-produced muzzleloader on the market many years ago and they continue to expand and improve their front-stuffer line to this day.

The newest addition is called the Triumph. This is a 50-caliber break-open type of modern muzzleloader. The T/C folks have added some really innovative design components that make this top-break stand out of the crowd. The gun shows a streamlined shape with a center-hung visible hammer and only 4 moving parts, including the locking system for the tip-up barrel. The hammer is a rebounding type that locks in a safety position so that an accidental blow to the hammer will not fire the rifle; the trigger must be pulled for the hammer to contact the firing mechanism. The trigger pull is crisp and factory set at 3 to 3½ pounds, just about right for hunting or target shooting. The composite stock is capped with a SIMS Limbsaver recoil pad that effectively cuts felt recoil approximaely 25 percent. A solid aluminum ramrod is supplied and the barrel is available in either the standard blue, or with the Weather Shield finish in either black or stainless. The Weather Shield finish is an advanced metal coating that protects the metal and wears very well, being much tougher than standard bluing.

The most unique design feature of the Triumph, however, is the new Speed Breech. This #209 primer

breech plug can be removed by hand for greater ease of cleaning, or for clearing a loading mistake in the field, by rotating it 90 degrees and pulling it out of the barrel; potentially a real hunt-saving feature.

There are three gas-seal rings on the front of the breech plug to stop gasses from coming back into the threads of the plug, or into the action itself. These are very similar to the piston rings in the cylinders of your car. The interrupted thread on the breech that allows easy

The gas-seal rings on the T/C Triumph keep powder gasses out of the breech threads and action of the rifle.

The very streamlined look of the new Thompson/Center Triumph rifle.

removal is very similar to that used on the breeches of large cannon for many years, so strength is certainly not a concern. The breech plug is knurled at the rear for easy grasping during removal. There's really nothing new here; several good designs were brought together to create this innovative breech plug.

This type of breech plug is also available on the Encore series of guns. This breech is partnered with a #209 extractor that rotates to the side with finger pressure to allow the Speed Breech to be easily removed. This eliminates the need to remove the extractor before breech plug removal as was necessary in the past. These T/C innovations will make the care and feeding of their muzzleloaders easier.

Knight Rifles

Another name that is associated with firsts in the muzzleloading field is Knight Rifles. The MK85 Knight rifle was the first really practical and widely distributed rifle featuring the now-familiar inline design. It seems that every year this company comes out with something new and different, often leading the pack with innovative products. Their newest offering is new thinking on a familiar style – the top-break type of muzzleloader.

Called the KPI, this rifle seems a typical center-hung, exposed hammer top-break design but it is engineered to be taken down to its component parts in less than 30 seconds – without tools. The forearm is removed by pulling down on a lever, the action is opened by the push of a button, the hinge pin is removed, which releases the barrel from the receiver, and the trigger group, with the hammer attached, is removed from the receiver by pushing a small lever in front of the trigger. It takes less time to do it than to tell about it. The ease of removing the barrel is important

for another reason besides ease of cleaning, but more on that later.

The gun is available in blue or stainless with a composite stock in either black or camo. High-visibility sights are standard and the barrel is drilled and tapped for scope mounting. What makes this rifle unique, besides the quick take-down, is that extra barrels can be interchanged in the following chamberings: (centerfire) 223, 243, 270, 30/06 and 300 Win. Mag.; (rimfire) 17 HMR and 22 LR, as well as the 50-caliber muzzle-loading barrel. This makes the KPI about as close to an all-around gun as one can get. The multicaliber range of barrels available will allow hunting a wide variety of game over various seasons. The change from centerfire to rimfire is easily accomplished with a screwdriver and Allen wrench. With an overall length of 39½ inches (centerfire/rimfire) and 43½ inches in the muzzleloader configuration and a weight of around 8 pounds, this is a trim and versatile little rifle.

Traditions Performance Firearms

Traditions has added a recoil-reducing system to their Pursuit XLT Extreme. The system, which utilizes a cam, roller and spring contained in the buttstock, is reportedly reduces felt recoil by 75 percent – a very significant amount. Given hunters' proclivity for the heavy magnum charges these days, this is good news for those of us who are recoil-sensitive.

Ballard Rifle and Cartridge Co.

Ballard, based in Cody, Wyoming, has recently undergone a change of ownership and reorganization. The company is expanding the line of fine blackpowder cartridge rifles that they are known for. They, of course, build a beautiful reproduction

of the venerable Ballard rifle. They are also doing a very nice copy of the Winchester High Wall and Low Wall rifles in various calibers. With high grade walnut and literally breathtaking authentic bone and charcoal color case-hardening, all three models are fine examples of the gunmaker's art. Dimensions are exactly the same as the original guns. In fact, part of the Ballard business is doing restorations of original guns. Their parts will interchange with originals and a "clunker" can be brought back to "as new" in the Ballard shop.

The Ballard model rifles are being seen more and more on the firing lines at various black powder cartridge silhouette competitions, including the Nationals at Raton, NM as well as Schuetzen competitions throughout the country. The Ballard action is a popular basis for fine target rifles. The record for blackpowder and lead bullets was fired in 1902 from a Ballard rifle, a 10-round group measuring 0.722-inch at 200 yards. That record still stands.

Ballard rifles can be had in most of the blackpowder-era cartridges, as well as appropriate modern smokeless calibers. Their target chamberings are done on a custom basis to extremely close tolerances; so close, in fact, that chambers are cut to match the make of brass used. No wonder the darn things shoot!

The High Wall action is well-liked by blackpowder cartridge shooters in the silhouette game and there is a high percentage of this action type seen on those firing lines. and often in the winners' circle. The very strong High Wall action lends itself not only to most any blackpowder cartridge, but it can also be chambered for some modern cartridges in the magnum family.

Ballard's attention to quality and range of models make these

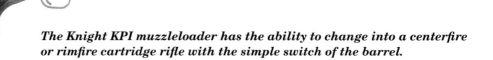

The Knight KPI muzzleloader has the ability to change into a centerfire or rimfire cartridge rifle with the simple switch of the barrel.

The Ballard Pacific rifle is very popular with hunters and target shooters alike.

Based upon the venerable Winchester High Wall action, the African Express can be ordered in a variety of blackpowder or smokeless chamberings.

guns popular with shooters of all interests, be it target shooting with blackpowder cartridges or hunting with the latest smokeless calibers. One would be hard-pressed to find better quality reproduction rifles from the late blackpowder era.

Millennium Designed Muzzleloaders

From the time of the earliest muzzleloaders, packaged loads have been used. The military, especially, used various "cartridges" to enclose powder and projectile in one package that was easy and quick for the soldier to handle when reloading. Most of these were paper-

The MDM "cartridge" combines powder and bullet in one handy package.

type cartridges that the soldier tore open with his teeth, then dumped the powder down the muzzle, followed by the bullet and, usually, the paper that wrapped the unit.

The latest upgrade of the packaged reload is one from Millennium Designed Muzzleloaders. MDM has teamed up with Magkor, the producer of Black Mag 3, a blackpowder substitute, to produce the "ThunderCharge," a consumable cartridge for muzzleloaders. Using MDM's Dyno-Core bullets of from 225 to 325 grains, the optimum charge of Black Mag 3 is compressed and attached to the bullet base. To load, the complete package is pushed down the barrel at one time, eliminating the need to handle the bullet and powder separately. As stated, the powder charge is matched to each bullet weight to deliver not only the best accuracy, but the best terminal ballistics as well.

Presently available only in 50-caliber, the consumable cartridges will come in packages of either 6 or 8. Next thing you know, someone will figure out how to wrap the whole thing in a brass case with the primer attached.

Connecticut Valley Arms

Along with self-contained cartridges, a new ignition system is coming to muzzleloading. Connecticut Valley Arms (CVA) is introducing a muzzleloading rifle with electronic ignition. Due to be on dealers' shelves by mid-year, the Electra looks like a typical inline rifle, but with a projection in front of the trigger guard that resembles the magazine of a cartridge rifle. The projection contains the electronics that fire the rifle. A thumb-operated safety disconnects the system for safe carry or loading. A pull of the trigger initiates an arc in the breech plug that ignites the powder charge. There is no primer explosion and no displacement of the powder charge from the force of a primer ignition. Trigger pull is very smooth with no release felt – the trigger is merely a switch that activates the electric arc in the breech plug. The system is supplied with a standard 9-volt battery that will fire the rifle at least 500 times and will last around 600 hours if left turned on. This is definitely something entirely new to the sport of muzzleloading. What will they think of next? ✵

TODAY'S OPTICS:
THE OPTICS FIELD IN 2007

by Wayne Van Zwoll

Better hunting optics deliver more detail, brighter images, clearer aim and less eye-strain during long glassing sessions. The best optics available now would have astonished shooters who came of age in my youth. And while prices have climbed substantially, you don't have to pay top dollar for glass that to the unpracticed eye seems as good as any on the market. Weaver's K4, the standard by which rifle-scopes were judged half a century ago, is no longer made in the U.S. It doesn't look like an original K4 or sell as cheaply. But it is still, in my view, a terrific buy. It is much better, optically, than the original. And it costs less, relative to the competition, than it did when I shot a deer with one in 1968.

Back then, hunters didn't use laser rangefinders or illuminated reticles. They were delighted by constantly centered crosswires and nitrogen-filled tubes that didn't fog. If the adjustments worked and the occasional bump didn't affect zero, if the field and eye relief allowed for quick aim, riflemen rejoiced.

Ensuing years have brought many incremental improvements, a few which qualify as pivotal. What you consider important in a sight or a binocular depends in part on what kind of hunting you do – also on your age and personal tastes. Some shooters dote on sophistication and new features; others prefer Spartan optics with traditional lines and no more complexity than necessary.

Whatever your bent, 2007 offers plenty of interesting glass to look at. And through.

Aimpoint

A sight is useless if it isn't easy to use. While rifle-scopes have become bigger, heavier and more powerful, and are now bedecked with rangefinding reticles, resettable BDC dials, parallax adjustments and scales bearing ballistic information, shooters do have an alternative.

In 1975 Swedish inventor Gunnar Sandberg came up with what he called a single-point sight. You looked into a short tube with one eye and saw a dot superimposed on the target with the other. You couldn't look *through* this sight at all! But shortly Sandberg developed more advanced devices, and now, 30 years later, his Aimpoint company has become a world leader in the broad field of "red dot" sights.

On a moose hunt not long ago, an Aimpoint Model 7000, mounted on a Blaser rifle, not only gave me fast aim in dark, thick cover; it helped me shoot 1½-inch groups at the range. The company's Kenneth Mardklint explained to me that an Aimpoint's front lens is a *compound* glass that corrects for parallax. An ordinary single lens up front still reflects the dot produced by the diode in the rear bottom of the tube. But Aimpoint's front "doublet" brings the dot to your eye *in a line parallel with the sight's optical axis.* The reflective path of a single-lens sight varies with eye position. If the dot isn't centered in the sight, you get parallax error at distances other than the one for which the sight was set. With an Aimpoint, you hit where you see the dot, even when your head position puts it off-center in the field. To ensure fine accuracy, turn the brightness dial down to the lowest practical setting. In dim light, you need very little illumination to see the dot quickly; in bright daylight, you'll need more.

Aimpoint sights with no magnification boast unlimited eye relief, so there's no time lost in finding a full field of view. You can point with both eyes open as with a shotgun. Models with magnification have generous eye relief. The 2007 Aimpoints feature ACET. Advanced Circuit Efficiency Technology reduces power demand, boosting battery life on the new Aimpoint 9000s to 50,000 hours with the brightness set on 7 (the highest setting is 10). The 9000 series comprises several models, including compact Comp

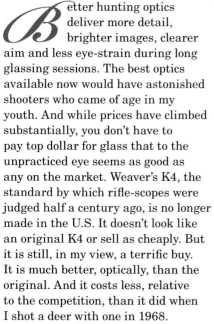

versions that weigh as little as 6.5 ounces. You get a choice of 2-minute or 4-minute dot (1- or 2-minute with the 2x converter). Adjustments are positive, each click moving point of impact 13mm at 100 meters.

Aimpoint supplies military sights to U.S. and French armies, and hunting models in 40 countries. Last May, the company signed a contract for 163,000 rifle sights for the U.S. military establishment. One of every 10 Swedish hunters using optical sights favors Aimpoint. See the complete line at aimpoint.com.

Alpen

A decade ago, Alpen Optics shouldered its way into a market already crowded with imported East Asian products. The company has steadily gained credibility with mid-priced rifle-scopes, binoculars and spotting scopes that deliver great value.

Alpen's 2007 offerings include a dozen rifle-scopes. The lightweight 4x32 and a 3-9x32 Kodiak perform better than their prices suggest. The superior Apex line has fully multi-coated lenses; it comprises a 3-9x42, a 3.5-10x50 and two sights with adjustable objectives: a 4-16x50 and a 6-24x50. Eight models in the Kodiak line, from 4x32 to 6-24x50, offer bright, sharp target images at modest cost. They complement a series of affordable spotting scopes (a 20-60x80 sells for less than $400!). Alpen's 12-36x50 Compact spotting scope, announced a few months ago, weighs just 20 ounces. There's also a 15-30x50, an 18x36x60 and a 15-45x60. Get all the details at alpenoutdoor.com.

Brunton

A 32-ounce, waterproof 8-15x35 Brunton Zoom binocular garnered a "Gear of the Year" award from *Outside* magazine in 2006. Its roof prism design, magnesium alloy frame and lockable twist-out eyecups appeared first in Brunton's top-of-the-line Epoch 10x42. The Brunton Zoom's 273-foot field of view at 8x helps you spot game

quickly. Crank it to 15x, and you have a spotting scope. Priced at $1,899, the Brunton Zoom complements a line of binoculars that includes three 43mm Epochs, in 7.5x, 8.5x and 10.5x magnification. An available doubler boosts magnification. The Eterna and Echo lines are less costly but deliver fine images. So to the Eterna spotting scopes: a 24-ounce Eterna Compact 18-38x50 and a full-size 20-60x80. Both feature fully multi-coated lenses with ED (extra-low dispersion) fluorite glass. Just 8 inches long, the Compact lists for $599 and should appeal to the hunter with long miles to hike. Even easier to pack is the new (for 2007) Echo Compact spotting scope, a 12-36x50 that weighs only 21 ounces.

Brunton's optics line includes rifle-scopes wearing the licensed NRA label. Fixed-power 4x32 and 6x42 hunting scopes sell for $109 and $119. A 6-24x50 target scope with adjustable objective lists for just $149 – a bargain, given its fully multi-coated optics, one-piece tube and mil-dot reticle. Affordability is the hallmark of NRA hunting variables too, with the 1.5-6x40 and 3.5-9x40

retailing for only $99. There's a new "fast focus" series, with eyepieces on helical threads. Four variables, from 1.5-5x to 3.5-10x, cost from $129 to $169. There's also a fast-focus 6-24x50 at $199. You'll find binoculars and spotting scopes under the NRA banner as well. Find out more at brunton.com and nrasportsoptics.com.

Burris

"There's not a lot new at Burris," said Pat Beckett at the 2007 SHOT Show. Patrick is among my favorite people, partly because he tells the story straight. "But," he added, "that's because we have to catch up with orders for all the new products from last year and before! Besides, we've extended our scope lines to the point that we're looking hard to find slots we haven't filled!"

It's all true. The company's Short Mag scopes – 1x, 4x, 2-7x, 3-9x and 4.5-14x – made headlines in 2006. Short-coupled, with 3½- to 5-inch eye relief and resettable adjustment dials, they list for $316 to $581. Burris Signature Select scopes are an upgrade from the flagship Signature

This Burris sight is among the best of many now designed for turkey hunters' shotguns.

This Bushnell 3200 Elite variable has extended eye relief for use on hand-guns like this S&W 22.

line, with more convenient turret location, index-matched lenses, rubber grips on power and AO rings. LRS versions (1.5-6x, 3-10x and 4-16x) offer resettable windage and elevation dials and lighted reticles. Both Short Mag and Signature Select scopes have 1-inch tubes, as does the fine 2-7x35 Fullfield II sight for shotguns and muzzleloading rifles. If you're a handgunner, consider the Burris 2-7x32 EER scope with illuminated reticle.

Like other manufacturers, Burris is turning out more tactical scopes, for those who need them and those who pretend they do. The XTR (Xtreme Tactical Rifle) variables come in 1.5-6x, 10x, 3-12x and now 6-24x configurations. Their 30mm tubes have side-mounted parallax dials, steel-on-steel adjustments and illuminated reticles. The Fullfield II stable also has a tactical corner now, with a 3-9x40, a 4.5-14x42 and a 6.5-20x50. All have TAC-2 adjustments and AO collars up front. Burris tactical accoutrements include the SpeedDot sight and Laser flashlight that fit on Picatinny rails.

In 2006 Burris started shipping the LaserScope, a sight with a laser-rangefinding unit built in. It's a 26-ounce 4-12x42 with ranging capabilities to 800 yards on reflective targets. I've shot with it and think it will appeal to some riflemen. More to my liking were Burris' three new 30mm Euro Diamond scopes with a 3P#4 E-Dot reticle. The 1-4x24, 2.5-10x50 and 3-12x56 feature eight light settings on a turret-mounted dial. For more information on 2007 products, key up burrisoptics.com.

Bushnell

Bushnell could make money selling its catalogs by the pound. The 2007 book is chock full of useful glass for hunters. Some of it is new. Bushnell's top-end Elite binocular series comprises four models: 10x50 and 12x50, 8x43 and 10x43. All accept Bushnell's 2.5x doubler. A new

Elite e2 binocular (8x42 and 10x42) also has the magnesium frame and XTR lenses of the Elite, but at less than $650 costs about half as much. The 8x5x45 and 10.5x45 Infinity binoculars also debut this year. Like the costlier Elites and less expensive Legend binoculars, they feature Rainguard lens coatings to shed rain.

Bushnell's long list of rifle-scopes has few new entries. A 30mm 6-24x50 in the Elite 4200 line and a 5-15x40 Tactical 3200 expand the top-end offerings. There's also a 3-10x50 in the 3200 stable, and a 3-9x50 with illuminated reticle in the affordable Sportsman group. The biggest news for shooters is still the

Bill Booth shoots while guide Pete Dube glasses. The revolver: a Bushnell-scoped S&W 500.

This Remington 223 wears a Bushnell HoloSight: fast, compact, and forgiving of eye placement.

4-12x42 rifle-scope with a built-in laser rangefinder. Announced last year, this 24-ounce sight delivers accurate range figures with the touch of a button out to over 500 yards. You get up to 8,000 ranges on its single 3-volt lithium battery, partly because the switch is programmed to shut down automatically after 30 seconds of non-use. This scope comes with a mil dot reticle and five dials to match the arc of your specific bullet and eliminate the need for holdover. The Yardage Pro laser range-finding scope has a magnesium body and lists for about $900.

For quick shooting up close, consider smaller options like the Trophy MP 1x32 red dot sight and Bushnell's latest HoloSight. The MP boasts unlimited eye relief, an integral Weaver-style mount, quarter-minute clicks. It sells for $229. The new HoloSight now uses AAA batteries. Lighter in weight and lower in profile than previous models, it costs $300 *less*!

There's little new in Bushnell's rangefinder line for 2007 – though the company still leads the industry in this field, both in numbers sold and models available. It now has an Elite 1500 with an "ARC" feature, which compensates for vertical angle. So you'll know not only actual distance, but the effective shot distance. If you shoot horizontally at a target 300 yards away, the actual and effective ranges are the same. But if the target is 300 yards away at a 45-degree vertical angle, the rifle will have to be aimed at a different place. Gravity affects only the horizontal component of the bullet's flight, which is shorter than 300 yards. Bushnell's Elite 1500 has an effective range of up to 1,600 yards on reflective targets, over 500 yards for big game animals. It features 7x magnification and a 26mm objective, lists for $499.

Bushnell's spotting scope line is essentially unchanged. The Image View 15-45x50 announced last year still qualifies as news, though. It features a digital camera with VGA resolution and 16 MB of internal memory. It comes with a shutter cable and tripod, a hard case and PhotoSuite software, and a modest $240 price tag. For a long evening's read on other Bushnell items, get a 2007 catalog or key up bushnell.com.

Elcan

Elcan is an acronym, from Ernst Leitz, Canada – the Leitz optical firm dating to 1849 in Germany. Elcan is also a subsidiary of Raytheon, one of those hulking companies with tall buildings but no human face, whose offices control the production of obscure hardware in far-flung factories with no signs on them. It's the kind of company favored by middle-age Republicans, a firm with substantial military contracts and executives in foreign countries.

But Raytheon is also a down-home company, with an office in Richardson, Texas. Rusty Maulden works there. I met him last year at the SHOT show, where he tried to explain the Elcan scope. While Elcan has been

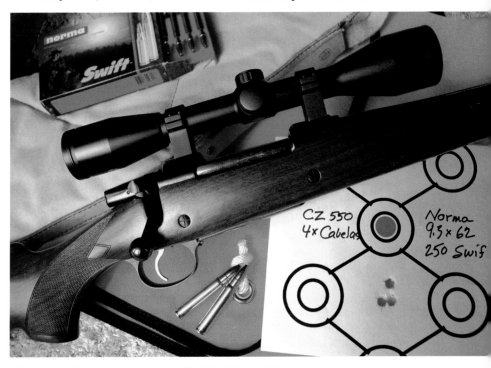

This 4x Cabela's scope, a 9.3x62 CZ 550, and Norma ammo are an accurate, deadly combination.

The Elcan DigitalHunter can be used as a variable rifle-scope and a video camera.

building infrared scopes for U.S. military units since the 1980s, it is just now tapping the civilian market with what it calls the DigitalHunter. The Elcan scope is just a year old at this writing, and already its price has been trimmed by roughly 25 percent, to less than $1,200 for 2007.

The price reflects a sophistication you won't see in ordinary optical sights. DigitalHunter shares a couple of features with most rifle-scopes: a stout alloy tube and multi-coated optics fore and aft. It mounts on a Picatinny rail or Weaver bases (you can't use rings because the body is not round). A magnification range of 2.5x to 13.5x is broader than normal, and you change power with a button, not a ring. There's no turret. A flat panel studded with buttons sits where you'd expect to find an elevation dial. That panel serves as a control center.

One of DigitalHunter's most intriguing features is its ability to record up to five seconds of video during a shooting sequence. So you can see the immediate result of your bullet strike – or why you missed! The scope operates as a still camera too. A port allows you to attach a remote screen. If you're spotting for a hunter or coaching a shooter, you see exactly what he or she sees in the sight picture. Or you can switch on the video and get up to seven five-second clips on a standard 64-mb SD card. A

small monitor atop the eyepiece shows you the images after you record them.

"Before zeroing," said Rusty, "you install software – ballistic data specific to your load. For each shot, then, you need only key in the range on the control panel and hold center. The scope self-adjusts for bullet drop." I tested the scope's compensating capability with a 30-06 to ranges beyond 400 yards. Groups were perfectly centered. No holdover. Because the target image and reticle share a common plane, there's no parallax at any range.

I didn't destroy one to test DigitalHunter's durability, but Rusty assures me it will take as much of a bruising as most scopes. In Elcan's trials, it has survived the repeated recoil of a 375 H&H.

Rusty told me that many people have asked for an integral laser range-finder – a device that would seem particularly suited to this scope. "We certainly have the means to engineer it into DigitalHunter. But a rangefinder would add weight and cost. Maybe later." I'll bet Elcan adds a rangefinder option soon.

Elcan's new sight is certainly unconventional. At 28 ounces, it's heavier than most scopes. And at dawn and dusk you'll wish for brighter images. But DigitalHunter does allow you to photograph and video during or absent a shot. It's a marvelous

instrument, parallax-free and with reticle and range-compensating options unmatched in optical sights. It's a pioneer in a field that will surely see more activity. Learn more at elcansportingoptics.com.

Leica

A few years ago, Leica announced a line of rifle-scopes manufactured to its rigid specifications by a competitor. Not surprisingly, the arrangement didn't work well, and the German firm went back to doing what it has done superbly since 1907. On May 14 of that year, a century ago, the first binocular designed by Ernst Leitz (a 6x18) went into production. Since then the company has tried hard to manufacture the best binoculars in the world. In my view, there is no better glass for hunting than those in the current Ultravid line.

After 100 years, with hunting glass that continues to set the bar for its competition, Leica certainly merits the attention of hunters and shooters who want the best optics in 2007. Visit leica-camera.com. And don't assume you've seen the last Leica rifle-scope.

Leupold & Stevens

In business now for 100 years, Leupold & Stevens has been making rifle-scopes for 50. While the latest Leupolds are nothing like the early postwar sights, some hunters, like rifle-maker Jerry Fisher, think there's nothing wrong with the 4x Pioneer. "I just recently traded up to an M8 4x. That old Pioneer helped me shoot a lot of game. Used it 40 years."

Leupold starts its second century with a new variable scope. Appropriately, the name reflects the year. VX-7 scopes feature European-style eyepieces and new "lift and lock" windage and elevation dials. The power selector ring is matched to a "Ballistic Aiming System" so you can tailor magnification and reticle to the target and distance. Like other new Leupold scopes, this series has the matched-lens system that delivers extra-sharp images. Argon/Krypton gas has replaced nitrogen in the tube, to better prevent fogging. Leupold's lifetime warranty comes with every VX-7.

Wayne prefers small, low-power hunting scopes like this Leupold 2 1/2x on a Kimber M84.

The FX-III 1x14mm Prismatic sight that debuts this year should appeal to deer hunters and tactical shooters who must get on target fast. Its long eye relief, wide field and compact profile make it ideal for shotguns, carbines and AR-15-style rifles. It's a natural pick for muzzleloading rifles. The FX-III 1x14mm Prismatic has fully multi-coated optics and a bold circle-dot reticle with illumination module. It's rugged too. This sight survived a ride on a test machine pounding it with the recoil of a 375 H&H – 28,000 times!

Binoculars are getting more and more attention from the Beaverton, Oregon firm. Leupold's top-rung Golden Ring Binocular has new HD objective lenses for 2007. Expect even brighter, sharper images from the HD (high definition, ED, extra-low dispersion, fluorite) glass. Phase-corrected prisms ensure true, crisp colors. The Golden Ring binocular comes in 8x32, 10x32, 8x42 and 10x42 configurations.

A close relationship with the Boone and Crockett Club inspired the new Pinnacles binoculars, with phase-corrected prisms and "L-coat" to reduce light loss on lenses and prism faces. These roof-prism 10x50 and 12x50 glasses come with flip-back frames and a neck strap, in a carrying case. The new Yosemite is an 8x30 that joins a 6x30 of the same model name. Its wide interpupillary adjustment range suits it to a variety of faces. Like the 6x, this glass has a slender profile and weighs less than lunch. It carries easily on a neck strap but gives you nearly 4mm of exit pupil.

For its 100th year, Leupold is marketing Cascades, Olympic and Pinnacles roof-prism binoculars in what it calls a Natural finish. It's a tan hue that should appeal to hunters wearied by green, black and camo binocular jackets. The company also offers 8x30 Yosemite and 10x42 Cascades glasses in Shadow Brown, with a laser-engraved logo of the National Wild Turkey Federation. Visit leupold.com.

Millett

Known more for its rings and bases than its scopes, Millett has been trundling along with a modest line of serviceable scopes that won't strain your budget. This year it has substantially expanded the line to include new Target and Varmint models. They wear side-mounted parallax dials and target knobs. Optional illuminated reticles include a mil dot. Like the Buck Gold and Buck Silver hunting sights, new 4-16x and 6-25x Target and Varmint scopes have 1-inch tubes. The Tactical series, augmented this year by a new 10x and a 1-4x24 variable, feature

Brian Kelly tunes out the parallax with a turret-mounted knob on a Leupold 6.5-20x scope.

Shooters are asking for more and more magnification. This Nightforce scope dials up to 22x.

30mm tubes. Lighted reticles for these and Millett's 4-16x Tactical include a Donut-Dot. There's also a Zoom Dot red-dot sight in the 2007 lineup, proofed on the S&W 500 revolver. Consistent with a trend to mounting scopes on Picatinny rails, Millett now offers its own rails for popular centerfire rifles. The company still markets a wide variety of iron sights for handguns. Go to millettsights.com.

Nightforce

NXS rifle-scopes cost a lot, and the Nightforce people make no apologies.

Their aim is to produce the best sights possible for both sportsmen and tactical applications. So the best materials come together in scopes designed to endure more abuse than any shooter could imagine imposing on a rifle-scope. Tests at the north-central Idaho firm include submersion in 100 feet of water for 24 hours, freezing in a box cooled to a minus 80 degrees F, then heating within an hour to 250 degrees F. Every scope is slammed in a recoil device delivering 1,250 Gs – both ways. Life is tough for scopes at Nightforce!

Details matter, too. The firm installs dissimilar alloys in the erector assembly to ensure repeatable movement. Lens coatings weather mil-spec abrasion tests. The 3.5-15x50 and 3.5-15x56 are typical – big 30mm scopes, and brilliant, with signature Nightforce reticles that appear only in the field's center. You'll find four-times magnification in other models as well: 5.5-22x50, 5.5-22x56 and 8-32x56. There's a super-high-power 12-43x56 – but also hunting-size compacts: a 1-4x24 and a 2.5-10x24 (that's right, a straight front end on a 2.5-10!) Nightforce sights have turret-mounted parallax knobs (except two

benchrest scopes, an 8-32x56 and a 12-42x56, which wear front-sleeve parallax adjustments). The Precision Benchrest scopes feature resettable ⅛-minute windage and elevation dials.

The company also supplies machined rings and Picatinny rails for mounting, and mil-radian knobs for NXS scopes so you can adjust in mils (.1 mil per click, 5 per revolution). There's even ballistic software so you can get the most out of your scope at long range. Visit NightforceOptics.com.

Nikon

At 26 ounces, the new Nikon IRT 4-12x42 is half a pound heavier than many scopes of its power range. But then, it incorporates a laser rangefinder that delivers 1-yard accuracy to 400 steps – and reads almost that accurately out to 800. The rangefinder, operated by the touch of a button accessible as you aim the rifle, gives you continuous readouts on moving game. A Ballistic Drop Compensating reticle helps with holdover. The IRT mounts low on most hunting rifles, is fog-proof and gives you 3 inches of eye relief.

For 2007, Nikon has overhauled its flagship Monarch rifle-scope line. Each scope has a four-times power range and 4 inches of eye relief. From the 2.5-10x42 to the 6-24x50, all scopes have one-piece main tubes and accept Nikon sunshades. Quarter-minute clicks are standard on four models, eighth-minute on the 5-20x44 and 6-24x50. Sunshades and target-style adjustments come on these two models, as does a turret-mounted parallax knob, also standard on 3-12x42 and 4-16x42 versions. The BDC reticle is available on all six. In addition, Nikon offers a new Monarch X series with 30mm tubes. The 2.5-10x and 4-16x come with either Nikoplex or mil dot reticles, both etched. The 2.5-10x is also available with an illuminated mil dot. A turret-mounted parallax knob is standard on Nikon Monarch X scopes.

To learn more about these scopes, the Nikon Buckmaster line and a new Slughunter 3-9x40 scope with a "BDC 200" reticle (rangefinders,

Wayne adjusts a Nightforce scope on a super-accurate Dakota Predator rifle in 20 Tactical.

Thompson/Center engineer Mark Laney aims a new Icon rifle wearing a Nikon Monarch variable.

spotting scopes and binoculars too), go to nikonsportoptics.com.

Pentax

Having spent a couple of seasons afield with the Pentax 8x32 DCF, I'm impressed by its sharp and bright images. The DCF roof prism series comes in 8x and 10x magnification, with objectives of 32mm to 50mm in diameter (you'll also find a 12.5x50 and 8x25 and 10x25 compacts). DCFs offer phase-corrected prisms in aluminum and polycarbonate shells. PCF Porro prism glasses in 8x40, 10x50, 12x50 and 20x60 versions remain in the line – a concession to those of us who prefer them to the more popular roof prisms. XCF Porros in 8x40, 10x50, 12x50 and 16x50 carry most PCF features at lower cost.

The Lightseeker rifle-scope series grew last year with the addition of a top-end Lightseeker 3-9x40 XL, and a compact Lightseeker 3-9x32 SL. The Gameseeker stable also appeared; for 2007 it has expanded to include eight 1-inch variable models and 4x32 and 6x42 fixed-power sights. A Whitetails Unlimited line offers mid-priced scopes from 3-9x to 6.5-20x. The big Lightseeker 30 series includes a 3-10x40, 4-16x50, 6-24x50 and 8.5-32x50. The Pioneer label covers affordable 3-9x40 and 4.5-14x42 scopes. Pentax has also developed a 2.5xSG Plus scope for slug guns and woods rifles.

Pentax's PF-65ED, which just finished its first season afield, is a top-quality spotting scope with straight and angled eyepieces. Waterproof and lightweight, it accepts 32x, 46x and 20-60x eyepieces. The 37-ounce scope is compatible with XW telescope eyepieces and the PF-CA35 camera adapter for 35mm SLRs. It joins the excellent PF-80ED and PF-100ED spotting scopes with interchangeable eyepieces, and the more compact PF-63Zoom with fixed 20-50x eyepiece. For more details, go to pentaxsportoptics.com.

Schmidt & Bender

It's been fifty years since a couple of German instrument-makers collaborated to produce hunting sights. Since then, Schmidt & Bender optics have become renowned for their high quality, the company for its innovation. No, it's not a big firm. My first visit to the plant in northern Germany conjured images of a rural veterinary clinic or college chemistry lab. The modest building lacked any industrial aspect. White-frocked technicians ghosted through spotless rooms. Scopes were tended individually, not in big batches.

Schmidt & Bender's flagship line is the Zenith, with 30mm variables in power ranges 1.1-4x24, 1.5-6x42, 2.5-6x56 and 3-12x50. Resettable windage and elevation knobs have gauges on the dial

Two superb 30mm hunting variables on Remington rifles: Schmidt & Bender (top) and Kahles.

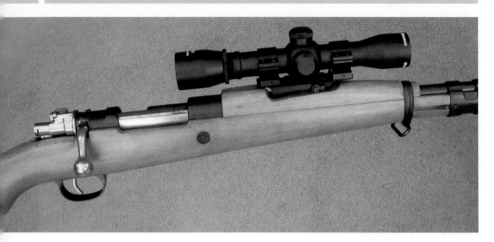

Extended-eye relief scopes suit military-style rifles like this M98 from Mitchell's Mausers.

faces to show where in the span of adjustment you are. So you can use the mount to center the optical axis in the physical axis of the scope, maximizing adjustment range. A ring under the dial face allows you to record several zeros, for quick return when shooting different loads or at various ranges. Zenith scopes come with a hollow mounting rail or, consistent with American tastes, configured for rings.

S&B's Zenith line offers illuminated reticles. My favorite is the FlashDot, which disappears from your field of view when you choose to use a black reticle. In dark conditions, switch on the Flash Dot and adjust brightness with the rheostat. A beam splitter puts the dot in the very center of the field. An automatic switch kills the dot after six hours to save battery. S&B offers traditional illuminated reticles in the Classic 30mm series 2.5-10x56, 3-12x50 and 3-12x42, and in the 8x56. The 4-16x50, 6x42 and 10x42 come with a selection of standard reticles. Depending on the model, Schmidt & Bender variables and fixed-power sights have reticles installed in the first or second focal plane. All are mechanical, save for the #9, which is etched onto the glass. Parallax is zeroed at 109 yards. S&B can retrofit illuminated reticles on some of its earlier and current-production scopes.

If you're a traditionalist, you might agree with me that Schmidt & Bender offers some of the most appealing fixed-power scopes available. Long

ago I snared a 4x36; the 6x42 and 10x42 are next on my list. If you prefer tactical sights, S&B's 34mm 3-12x50 and a new 4-16x42 merit a close look. The 3-12x was recently adopted by the U.S. Marine Corps for all its 30- and 50-caliber sniper rifles. Schmidt & Bender's entire PMII (Police Marksman) line, and its hunting scopes, can be viewed at schmidt-bender. de or on the web site of its U.S. importer: scopes@ cyberportal.net.

Shepherd

The 3-10x40 and 6-18x40 scopes from the Shepherd shop in Waterloo, Nebraska afford you long-range capabilities not shared by any other scopes. Shepherd sights have two reticles, one in the front focal plane and one in the rear. Superimposed, they appear as one. You get an aiming reticle that doesn't change

size with power changes, but a rangefinding reticle that varies in dimension as you turn the magnification ring. The rangefinding reticle comprises a series of circles spaced on a vertical stem. Top to bottom, they're of decreasing diameter to match the diminishing apparent size of a deer as distance increases. To determine the distance, just fit a deer-size target into a circle. Correct holdover has already been factored in because no matter what the scope power, the 18-inch circle (in the front plane) appears the same size in relation to the target. Choose from three rangefinding reticles calibrated to match the trajectories of popular big game cartridges. Vertical and horizontal scales are marked in minutes of angle so you can compensate for wind as well as gravity. The company also sells binoculars, but the scopes are truly remarkable. A friend whines that coyotes between 400

Sam Shaw finds that a Sightron scope helps him shoot this S&W 460 as accurately as a rifle.

Wayne mounted a 2-7x Sightron on this Tikka T3 in 308. A fast-pointing outfit!

and 500 yards are no challenge for his Remington 25-06 and a 6-18x Shepherd. Some people just like to complain. Shepherdscopes.com.

Sightron

A relative newcomer to the hunting optics industry, Sightron was incorporated in Florida in 1993. Two years later it moved to North Carolina and opened its first distribution center. Its initial products were red-dot sights; a year later it announced a line of 1-inch rifle-scopes. A year after that, binoculars appeared in the Sightron stable. Spotting scopes followed shortly. In 1999 CEO Scott Helmer hired Alan Orr as the company's product manager. I've known Alan since 30mm scopes were added in 2000. Line extensions thereafter include Premium binoculars and S1 scopes, and in 2007, SII Big Sky scopes and binoculars.

The Big Sky series comprises 15 offerings, from fixed-power 4x and 6x glass to variables 16x at the top end. They're fully multi-coated. External lenses are all treated with "Zact-7," a seven-layer coating to transmit the most light possible. They also get a hydrophobic wash to disperse

moisture when you're out in the rain. Adjustment dials are finger-friendly and resettable. Eye relief is a generous 3.8 inches. Retail prices start at $420. In addition to the 15 hunting scopes, Sightron catalogs a pair of new varmint sights in its Big Sky line. They're 6-24x42s, identical

save for the finishes (stainless and black). Both feature target knobs, adjustable objectives and plex reticles. A late addition under the Big Sky umbrella is a Dangerous Game 1.25-5x20 sight with over 6 inches of "clear tube" for mounting. Like the other sights in the line, it has a one-piece tube and comes with a lifetime replacement warranty.

There's a new target scope in Sightron's 2007 catalog, a 36x42 with ⅛-minute adjustments and ⅛-minute dot. Adjustable objective, too.

Sightron's 30mm S III-series includes a 3.5-10x44 scope, plus three 6-24x50 models. Choose a Plex, Dot or Mil Dot reticle. Fixed-power aficionados will appreciate the modestly priced SII 4x32. Deer and turkey hunters can well use the broad field and 4 inches of eye relief in the newest shotgun scope, the 2.5x32SG. Two lightweight red-dot sights feature 1x magnification and 33mm tubes.

The Big Sky moniker has been applied to Sightron's newest binoculars, all Porro-prism. The 7x, 10x and 12x have 50mm objectives. So does the new SI 18-36 spotting scope, a lightweight (20-ounce) and field-worthy glass that comes in a kit with aluminum hard case and swivel pan-lever tripod. Sightron.com.

This Remington M7 in 6.8mm Remington has a new Simmons Master Series scope from Meade.

Swarovski

"We don't want to shoot a bull near cover, or stretch the reach of that ought six." Fred obviously didn't approve of my rifle, a new Remington 700 Alaskan Ti. But I had fallen for it. On the range it drove 180-grain Swift Sciroccos from Remington loads into 1¼-inch groups with comforting consistency. Well balanced and with a sleek, open-gripped stock, it handled beautifully. I had scoped it with a new Swarovski Z6, a scope whose top magnification was fully six times its low power!

The new scope nestled tight to the Remington in Leupold rings. In shooting I'd done to ready this outfit for Texas, I'd been impressed by the scope's flat field and crisp, brilliant images. Optically, it was indeed top-drawer. The adjustments tracked true as well. Shooting "around the square," I got predictable movement grabbing 20 clicks to a shift. The last group trampled the first.

The nilgai was alone, tucked into a protected slot in the mesquite. I slipped alongside the thicket crosswind, probing for a shot alley. At just 35 yards, an opening appeared.

I knelt and pressed the trigger. As intended, the Scirocco severed the spine between the scapulae, dropping the bull instantly.

That was my introduction to Swarovski's newest rifle-scope. My Z6 is a 1.7-10x42. You can also choose a 1-6x24 or 2-12x50, and a 1-6x24 with extended (5-inch) eye relief. The scopes weigh from 15 to 18 ounces. Illuminated versions will be available shortly, I'm told; they weigh an ounce and a half more. It is no stretch to call these 30mm scopes revolutionary. Until recently, three-times magnification was all you could milk from 1-inch tubes, four-times in 30mm scopes. "A lot of hunters will appreciate the broad six-times power range," said Swarovski's Dean Capuano. "But to me the most endearing feature of this sight is its long and constant eye relief. Nearly 4 inches!" That's an increase of 19 to 50 percent. Rear-plane reticles (several are available) do not change apparent size with changes in magnification.

The last couple of years have brought significant change to the Austrian company Stateside, many of them good. The Cranston, Rhode Island-based company should fare better with the Z6 than it did with the recent SR rail mount. This toothed rail (on PH 1.25x24, PH 1-6x42 and PH 3-12x50 models) eliminates the ring/tube juncture. With rail scopes, you fear no scars or internal damage from tight rings. The scope cannot slip during heavy recoil. Tubes with rails are machined from bar stock, so a rail actually strengthens the tube. Long popular in Europe, the rail scope is making slow progress here, partly because of tradition but also because you'll find few rail bases designed for American rifles.

The PV1-2 series of Swarovski variable scopes, with rear-focal-plane reticles, are specifically built for the American market. They feature five illuminated reticles that combine lines, bars, circles and dots to provide aiming devices that are easy to see quickly but permit precise aim at distance. The 1.25-4x24, 1.5-6x42, 2.5-10x56, 3-12x50, 4-16x50 and 6-24x50 are equipped with the new BE-4 Digital Illuminator unit in the turret. High-power models have AO sleeves up front. To learn more, key up swarovskioptik.com.

Swift

Headquartered in San Jose, California, Swift Optics is 80 years old and still a family-owned firm. Its imported rifle scopes go to 3,000 dealers in 20 countries worldwide. The line includes pistol and rimfire scopes and the Premier and Standard lines for centerfire rifles. From 1.5-4.5x32 to 8-32x50, the 25 sights in Swift's stable cover all hunting and target applications and can be found at swiftoptics.com.

Trijicon

One day last fall I took a Marlin lever-action rifle, a 45-70, into a copse of still-green aspens on a sunny Colorado slope. Elk had filtered in there to bed. I moved a step at a time, glassing slivers of color as they became visible between the boles. Keeping a crosswind, I slipped past bedded cows close enough to wake with a whisper. When at last an elk nosed my scent-pool, I'd penetrated to the herd's

Wayne used this brand-new Swarovski Z6 on a Remington rifle to shoot a nilgai in Texas brush.

Many scopes, like this with a Traditions label, are built by big Japanese firms on contract.

center. Yellow rumps winked a farewell through the aspens while I searched frantically for the bull.

He rose 80 steps away, almost too far. Brush took my first bullet, and the second. I caught a bigger alley with the third and dropped him with a Hornady bullet to the shoulder.

My scope that day was a Trijicon variable, with a lighted reticle. The red tip of the post, lit not by batteries but by tritium and a fiber-optic coil, was easy to find against the mottled background, and quick to find again as I recovered from each shot. The fiber-optic coil, by the way, was exposed in a window atop the eyepiece. Adjusting reticle brightness was a simple matter of rotating the window cover open or closed.

Trijicon is a relatively new company. Even the technology is recent. Not until 1983 did the U.S. Nuclear Regulatory Commission approve a tritium-illuminated gunsight for sale. Two years later the first rifle-scope with a tritium reticle appeared. In 1987 Trijicon introduced the ACOG (Advanced Combat Optical Gunsight) to the U.S. armed forces. The next year, the FBI adopted its tritium sights for handguns.

In 1995, after many sales of tactical sights, Trijicon's 4x32 ACOG was selected by our Special Forces for the M-4 carbine. Now Trijicon optics appear on many military

and police weapons. Glock, Smith & Wesson and Springfield offer Trijicon iron sights as standard equipment on their handguns.

The company's optical sights for hunting rifles use both tritium and fiber optic strands to brighten the reticle. The 30mm TR22 2.5-10x56 AccuPoint I carried on the Colorado elk hunt is one such sight. The AccuPoint scope series comprises 1.25-4x24, 3-9x40 and 2.5-10x56 models, with red or yellow illuminated pyramid-on-post reticles. The Trijicon TriPower relies as well on a fluorescent collector. Like the ACOG, it has the profile of a red-dot sight. You can also get a compact Trijicon Reflex sight that hugs a handgun. For 2007 the Wixom, Michigan company has announced two new ACOGs and a parallax-free red-dot sight that should complement any short-range firearm. Go to trijicon.com for more information.

TruGlo

A year ago in Utah I had no luck finding a buck to match the one I'd shot the year before with an iron-sighted muzzleloader. That buck had jumped in cover that swallowed him up before I could get into action. I'd followed his tracks in the snow, through impossibly thick oak-brush. By great good fortune, he paused in an opening 100 yards ahead, and I managed to slide a sabot bullet between the limbs. He dashed off but collapsed in a flurry of snow at the top of a nearby hill.

My TruGlo sights, so effective at milking more minutes of hunting at day's end, had given me the definition I needed for a quick shot in sunshine too *bright* for ordinary sights. TruGlo's fiber-optic bars concentrate light to give you a bright red or green dot that grabs your eye. Available for most rifles, pistols and shotguns, the firm's iron sights were recently joined by four rifle-scopes – a 4x32 and three variables – with illuminated reticles. There are red-dot sights on 25-, 30-, 36-, 40- and 45mm tubes. The most recent: a 2x30mm that features an 11-position rheostat. There's more on 2007 products at truglo.com.

Trijicon's ACOG is the only sight of its type, and very popular on M16 and AR-15 rifles.

Vortex

Still new to the shooting public, Vortex optics comprise a broad selection of binoculars and two lines of rifle-scopes. The 2007 Viper series includes six variable sights, from 2-7x32 to 6.5-20x50. High-powered models include turret-mounted parallax adjustments and target knobs. All Vipers feature argon gas, fully multi-coated lenses, resettable windage and elevation dials, a fast-focus eyepiece and one-piece tube. The five offerings in the less costly Diamondback series range from a 1.75-5x32 to a 4-12x40. They too are fog-proofed with argon gas. You also get helical eyepieces, resettable dials and fully multi-coated lenses. Find out more at vortexoptics.com.

Weaver

Meade Optical, a California-based maker of telescopes, got into the rifle-scope trade a few years ago with the purchase of the Weaver, Redfield and Simmons brands. Meade chose to upgrade the Simmons line first. The Simmons overhaul went well. Engineers Mark Thomas and Forrest Babcock reconfigured the innards of the best models and renamed them. Then the design was applied to other Simmons scopes. As I understand it, these sights have sold well. Meade's next target was Redfield, a brand with a rich history and enviable reputation. A Redfield scope with five-times magnification appeared in prototype form a couple of years ago. But not everything in this new sight turned out as the Meade group (or shooters who examined the scope) desired. Since then, progress toward commercial production has been slow.

Improving Weaver scopes would entail less engineering – but even more risk. The name survives as an American institution, dating to early Depression times, when a clever young Bill Weaver fashioned a rifle-scope for the masses. His Weaver 330 seems primitive now, but it beat its competition at market. In short order Weaver built a successful company in Texas. In my youth, 30 years later, the Weaver K4 still loomed as the standard by which other scopes were judged. It retailed for $45.

You can still buy a K4, though Bill Weaver is gone and scope production was long ago moved to Japan. Weaver scopes still deliver good value. Classic K- and V-series sights, and Classic Handgun scopes, round out a selection of hunting optics anchored now by the Grand Slam series, with models from 1.5-5x32 to 6-20x40 that cover any field application. T-series target scopes rank among the most popular Weaver (or its competition) has ever produced. Two recent T-24s are identical save for reticles: a ½-minute dot and a ⅛-minute dot. Their ¼-minute windage and elevation target-style adjustments allow for fast zeroing or compensating for wind and range. Dual-spring adjustment mechanisms ensure repeatability. New T-series scopes come with extra oversized adjustment knobs, a sunshade and screw-in steel lens caps.

For 2007 Weaver has introduced a new Extreme line of top-quality rifle-scopes. Functionally and cosmetically, they offer many upgrades. The 1.5-4.5x24, 2.5-10x50 and 2.5-10x56 feature 30mm tubes, fast-focus eyepieces, an illuminated dot in plex and German #4 reticles. They have resettable windage and elevation dials, a full 4 inches of eye relief. The 2.5-10x models carry turret-mounted parallax dials. Go to weaveroptics.com for a complete product tour.

Williams

As a youngster growing up in Michigan, I knew the Williams clan – the generations of shooters and hunters who'd established a gun-sight company in Davison. Now, 81 years after its founding, I'm very pleased to see the firm still catalogs an extensive array of iron sights. You can fit your rifle or slug gun with a 5D receiver sight (though, alas, they no longer cost $5). The FP (foolproof) series comes with sleek screw adjustments or target knobs. WGRS sights fit receiver dovetails and topside factory-tapped holes. I killed my first deer with a Williams "African" open sight. Its shallow V-notch cradled a gold bead on a Williams front ramp. Very fast!

Those items are all available in 2007, with new fiber-optic sights for pistols and long guns. Williams also makes scope mounts and gunsmithing tools, and accessories like full-moon clips for revolvers, Garand clips and barrel slot blanks. Visit Williams on the range or at williamsgunsight.com.

XS goes Tritium

More than a decade ago, when I equipped woods rifles with Ashley sights, I thought them among the best I'd ever used. Simple, strong, clean-looking and compact, with clever adjustments, they seemed the perfect complement to slug guns and muzzleloaders as well. Since then, the company has changed its name a couple of times. But as XS Sights, it still makes some of the best irons out there. The line has expanded to include open sights for rifles and pistols. The shallow V rear notch with white center-line is ideal for game in thickets, where shooting is fast and close. The receiver-sight line has grown to include ghost-ring models for most popular long guns. Tritium inserts in beads and open rear sights speed shooting in dim

Wayne has taken deer and pronghorns with this Savage 99. The Ghost Ring sight is by XS Sights.

light. This "glow-in-the-dark" option appears under the "24/7" heading in the XS catalog and at xssights.com.

Zeiss

Five years ago, Zeiss courted hunters Stateside with a new line of 1-inch rifle-scopes. Conquest scopes in 3-9x, 3.5-10x, 4.5-14x and 6.5-20x came first. In 2006 4x32, 2.5-8x32 and l.8-5.5x38 appeared. The 4x and 2.5-8x weigh less than 14 ounces, and both boast 4 inches of eye relief. The 4x32 is one of my favorite big game scopes, the 2.5-8x as trim and even more versatile.

The company's Diavari scopes were recently brought under the "Victory" moniker to match that of top-ranked Zeiss binoculars. The Varipoint is optically equal but features an illuminated reticle. Recent 2.5-10x42 and 6-24x72 scopes have 30mm and 34mm tubes, respectively (there are five Varipoint and six Diavari sights). An illuminated reticle is standard on the big 6-24x72, as is a turret-mounted parallax dial. The mil dot reticle option is calibrated at 12x. The Zeiss Varipoint reticle is also available in the 2.5-10x; so is a rail-equipped tube. Incidentally, Zeiss also lists a Classic Diavari/ Diatal series (variable/fixed-power) that can cause some confusion if you're trying to track name changes. These scopes are marketed in Europe but not in the U.S.

Late in 2006 Zeiss started releasing its Diarange scope, a 30mm Victory-series 3-12x56 with laser rangefinder built in. This scope weighs 35 ounces, is optically superb and as cosmetically appealing as any sight of its type can be. The rangefinder reads reflective objects to 1,000 yards a half-second after you press a button. Now the Diarange also comes in a 2.5-10x50 version that scales 32 ounces. Both sights operate on a single 3-volt battery and feature a choice of seven reticles, including several rangefinding configurations. In 2007 Diarange and other Victory products (binoculars too) will carry hydrophobic LotuTec lens coating, a treatment that beads water for a clear view in rain.

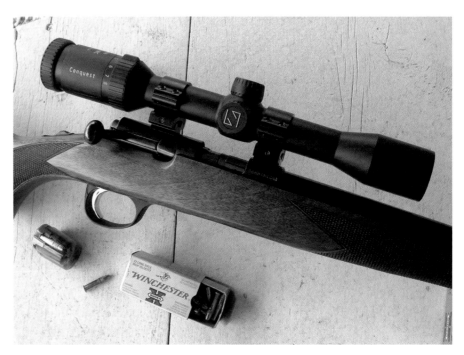

The slim, optically superb Zeiss 2.5-8x32 Conquest here complements a Browning T-Bolt 22.

As a follow-up to the compact red-dot Z-Point sight, Zeiss has just introduced a version that affixes to a bow for archers. Another one-of-a-kind item this year is the Zeiss DC4 camera-eyepiece you can attach to a Diascope spotting scope. The device allows you to photograph directly through the scope. It features a bayonet mount, operates on two 1.2-volt AA batteries and has a 2-inch display screen. You can trigger the 4-megapixel camera with a remote control. Visit Zeiss.com/sports.

A rifleman sights through the new Zeiss Diarange laser rangefinding scope, on a Weatherby rifle.

HANDLOADING UPDATE

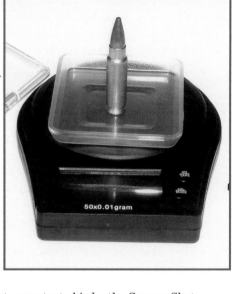

by Larry S. Sterett

The big news for handloaders in 2007 was the introduction by **Hornady Manufacturing** of so many new cartridges, or loads for previously difficult-to-obtain cartridges, ultimately resulting in more reloading die sets and components – which Hornady is also producing. Among the new loads available now are the 30 T/C (Thompson/Center), 308 Marlin Express, 9.3x74R, 375 Ruger, 450/400 Nitro Express, and the 450 Bushmaster, with the 338 Lapua Magnum on the shelves by the time you read this. That's just for a start. There's a baker's dozen new bullets, plus the 7th edition of the Hornady *Handbook of Cartridge Reloading*, and a Joyce Hornady DVD on reloading and bullet accuracy. Loading dies and components are available for some of these new cartridges already, and the others are on the way.

One of the most unusual new products this shooter has seen for handloaders is Season Shot, a non-toxic, biodegradable, seasoned, dissolving shot. Initial offerings will be garlic and herb-flavored, with lemon pepper, Cajun, Terriyaki, mesquite and Mexican (hot?) flavors to be added. Invented by Brett Holm and his partner, Dave Feig, this new shot should on the market by the time you read this. The hardened pellets are said to be comparable in range and patterning to regular steel shot, with "knock-down" power out to 45 yards on upland birds, and 25 yards on turkeys. It will take ducks and geese if they are settling in to a decoy spread, but larger size shot is being developed for use on waterfowl.

Holm stated the shot was developed after he chipped a tooth while eating a bird bagged using steel shot. "I just knew there had to be a better way." While hard enough to penetrate birds, the Season Shot pellets in the dressed birds melt from the oven heat, dissolving and providing flavor to the meat from the inside out. Bag your bird using Season Shot, clean and dress it, bake or roast, and enjoy eating garlic- and herb-flavored meat.

Lyman Products Corporation

Lyman has introduced four new loading die sets, a three-die set for the 5.7x28mm FN cartridge, plus similar

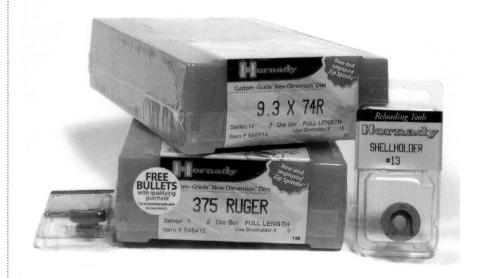

A couple of sets of Hornady's Custom Grade New Dimension loading dies for two of Hornady's new loads, along with the correct shellholder.

sets for three 'cowboy action' shooter cartridges, the 40-60, 45-60, and 45-75 Winchester rounds of yesteryear. (The new production '76 Winchester lever-action rifles are now available in these original chamberings.) Neck-sizing dies are also available for these cartridges. For those shooters wanting to take a step back further in time, the Lyman or Ideal 310 Tong Tool and dies are available for the 40-65 Winchester cartridge, in addition to some other old calibers, such as the 45-70 Government. (The 310 Tong may be slow, but having used one in his younger days, this shooter can vouch for the fact it does load shootable cartridges.)

For those handloaders who cast their own bullets, Lyman has brought back Ideal mould #403168. This mould will cast a 200-grain flat-nose bullet with two lube grooves and a plain base.

Shotshell reloaders will appreciate the new 5th edition of Lyman's *Shotshell Reloading Handbook.* This latest edition features more than 230 pages of data for reloading shotshells from the .410-bore to 10-gauge, using the most popular powders.

Discussion of non-toxic shot, including the development and history, plus case identification featuring full color drawings, tips for producing better handloads and data for loading buckshot and slug are also included.

Forster Precision Products

Forster has added several calibers to their Bench Rest die sets. Some feature full-length sizing dies, some neck-sizing and seating dies, of course. New to the Forster line are dies for the 6mm Dasher (6mm BR Improved), 6mm XC, 6.8mm Remington SPC, and the 325 WSM. Also new are the Precision Plus Bushing Bump Sizing dies. The Bump dies are matched to the caliber of a specific rifle, and a set consists of three pre-selected or 'you choose' smooth-as-silk bushings, which are available in thousandth of an inch (.001) increments. This permits the case neck to be sized for a specific chamber, and reduces the possibility of overworking the case neck.

Currently, the Bushing Bump Die, with three pre-selected bushings, is available for a baker's dozen

cartridges, from the 204 Ruger to the 30-06 Springfield. By the time you read this, dies and bushings should be available for the 6.5mm/284, 7mm Remington Magnum, and 30 BR cartridges, with others possibly later. The bushings and the Bushing Bump Die can be purchased separately.

Handloaders who don't like to change a die setting once it's established, but have to in order to return the die to its box, will like the new Forster Deluxe Die Box. With an overall length of 8½ inches, and a thickness of 2½ inches, the new double-walled boxes will handle dies for the extra-long Ultra Mag calibers, in addition to the Ultra Micrometer Bench Rest dies.

Handloaders who salvage bullets from surplus ammunition, or replace full metal jacket bullets with a soft- or hollow-point design of equal or lesser weight, should appreciate Forster's new 8mm (.323") Superfast Bullet Puller. The Puller will work in most presses taking ⅞x14-thread dies. While it will leave scratches on the pulled bullet jacket, it will pull even the tough, lacquered bullets from military rounds.

Not new – but a must for sizing cases – is a high-pressure lubricant which adheres to the case. Under the Bonanza label Forster has a lubricant that allows case resizing with a minimum of effort.

J & J Products

J&J has been in the thermoplastic injection-molding business for over three and one-half decades. Their various transparent ammunition boxes carry a lifetime guarantee against latch or hinge failure, and are designed to interlock to permit stacking of boxes for storage. Available in a variety of colors from smoke through red to camouflage, the boxes have capacities of 20, 50 or 100 rounds, depending on the model. The newest boxes in a 50-round hinge-top design will hold the 500 S&W and similar big-bore handgun cartridges – plus some of the shorter rifle cartridges of a similar size.

Some of the new cartridges being loaded by Hornady, and for which handloading dies and components will be available: L/R: 30 T/C, 308 Marlin Express, 9.3x74mmR, 375 Ruger, 450/400 Nitro Express and 450 Bushmaster.

Redding Reloading Equipment

Redding has a host of new products available for handloaders; among which are ten new die sets. These include the 17 Remington Fireball, 6x47mm Lapua, 6.5x47mm Lapua, 6.5mm Grendel, 30 T/C, 308 Marlin Express, 9.3mmx74R, 375 Ruger, 45-60 Winchester and 470 Nitro Express. New also are the Universal Decapping Dies in two sizes, Small for

The Redding Big Boss II 'O'-frame press features a one-inch diameter ram, with 3.8 inches of usable stroke. Another feature is the spent primer collection system, which funnels ejected spent primers through the ram and down a tube to a collection point below.

calibers 22 through 50 and lengths up to 2.625 inches, and the Large, which will handle cases up to three inches in length, but with a neck diameter no smaller than 25-caliber. An optional 17-caliber decapping rod is available to fit the small die, and accommodate the small (0.060-inch) flash hole PPC and BR cases.

If ten new die sets aren't news, then the introduction of the Big Boss II Reloading Press definitely is 'big news.' Featuring a one-inch diameter ram with 3.8 inches of usable stroke, this large 'O'-frame press has the largest window opening of any press in its class, making it capable of reloading most of the larger cartridges. The Boss II features the "Spent Primer Collection System" in which spent primers automatically drop through the large-diameter ram into a flexible plastic tube that can be easily routed into a collection container for later emptying. The "Smart Primer Arm" on the Boss II automatically swings into position during the ram stroke and moves out of position when not in use. Priming is done at the end of the ram stroke to ensure maximum sensitivity while at the lowest possible leverage. (An optional bushing to handle 1"x14 threaded dies is available For the Boss II, as is an extra Slide Bar Primer Assembly for the T-7 Turret Reloading Press.)

Handloaders who are also competition shooters have found the uniformity of neck wall thickness to be a contributing factor to consistently accurate

loads. Any large variation (over 0.0015-inch) in neck wall thickness can decrease accuracy. Redding has a new Case Neck Gauge that permits easy and rapid sorting of cases by neck wall thickness and uniformity. Two mandrel sizes are supplied with the Gauge to allow measurement of all cases from 17- to 338-caliber, including cases with small (0.060-inch) flash holes. The Gauge mounts directly to the reloading bench, and comes with a large dial indicator accurate to 0.001-inch. Pilot stops are required for each caliber, and two stops, 22-caliber (#06121) and 30-caliber (#06130) are provided with the Gauge. These stainless steel pilot stops, which also can be used with the flash hole deburring Tools, are currently available in fourteen sizes from 17-caliber to 338-caliber.

It may seem a small thing, but flash holes and primer pocket uniformity are more important than many handloaders realize. Redding has both primer pocket uniformers and flash hole deburring tools for small and large primer pockets and small (0.060-inch) and large (0.080-inch) flash holes. The primer pocket uniformers are designed for Large Rifle primers, but not for Large Pistol primers, while the tools for the Small Rifle primers are dimensionally correct for the Small Pistol primers. The tools come with handles and the deburrers are supplied with one pilot stop.

Redding has an easy to use SAECO Lead Hardness Tester that allows the user to check bullet

A few of the new Redding loading die sets available. Some are for old cartridges in which new interest is being shown, and many are for new, recently introduced cartridges.

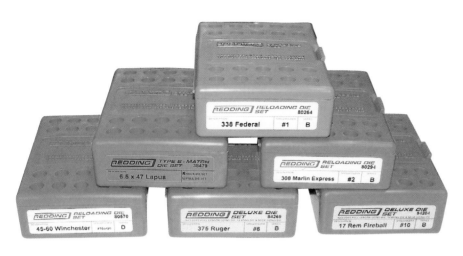

Redding loading dies are available for some cartridges, such as the 17 Remington Fireball, which weren't in the pipeline when this photo was taken.

metal up to approximately 22 Brinell. This is accomplished by the depth of penetration of a hardened steel indenter into a bullet. The relative hardness of the bullet is read off a Vernier scale calibrated in arbitrary units from 0 (pure lead) to 10 (approx. 22 Brinell). Magnum handgun and gas check rifle bullets work best if cast from an alloy with a SAECO hardness reading of 8 or over.

Cowboy Action Shooters use rather large quantities of cast lead bullets. Redding has a score of moulds to cast an assortment of classic design bullets from a 140-grain 30-caliber (#630) to a 525-grain 45-caliber (#745). All the designs feature rounded lube grooves, and a front band near bore diameter, tapering up to slightly larger than groove diameter. This type of bullet was preferred by the famed barrel-maker Harry Pope a century ago, and was frequently used by Schuetzen shooters.

RCBS/ATK

RCBS has a number of new products for handloaders, beginning with an economical new AmmoMaster Chronograph. The AmmoMaster is self-contained and has its own carrying case, operates on a 9V DC battery and features a detachable keyboard display with a 100-shot memory. Velocity range is 50 to 7,000 feet/second, and the chronograph mounts on any standard camera tripod. The detachable keypad has a twenty-foot cord to permit editing a string right at the bench. (The edit function allows the deleting of a particular shot, and will display high, low, and average velocities – plus extreme spread and standard deviation.)

Case tumblers aren't new items, but RCBS does have a new large capacity vibratory Mega Tumbler. The Mega holds up to six pounds of corncob or walnut hull media, and can clean and polish up to 1,000 38 Special cases at a time. Both 120- and 240-volt units are available, with the latter ideal for handloaders in Europe.

Ever wish trickling power onto a scale pan for weighing was easier? RCBS has a new Powder Trickler System that allows you to dispense and trickle a powder charge directly onto a scale pan without having to remove the scale pan for the initial filling. The dispensing chute adjusts to allow you to drop the powder charge directly onto the scale pan, and the unit can be adjusted for left- or right-hand use. (The Trickler system attaches to any Uniflow, Quick Change or Little Dandy powder measure, and is used in conjunction with the Advanced Powder Measure Stand.)

The Advanced Powder Measure Stand, which can be purchased separately, will accept any power measure having a ⅞-14 thread. It can be easily bolted to a reloading bench or table, and leaves plenty of space for positioning a loading block filled with cases, or a powder scale pan. RCBS has a new Black Powder Measure having a charging capacity of 120 grains. The metering cylinder is constructed of brass, with the one-pound capacity powder hopper and cap being aluminum. (The cap features a non-sparking powder level indicator to show how much powder is left in the hopper.) A 24-inch aluminum drop tube is available as an option.

New powder baffles are available for the Quick Change and Quick Change High Capacity (two pounds of powder) Powder Measures.

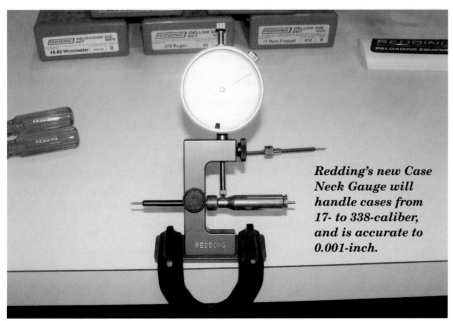

Redding's new Case Neck Gauge will handle cases from 17- to 338-caliber, and is accurate to 0.001-inch.

Extra metering assemblies can be purchased to have them preset for favorite smokeless powder charges, and Quick Change Accessories can be purchased to upgrade Uniflow Measures to the QC system.

RCBS has an extensive line of reloading dies (over 3,300, sizing and seating) available to take care of handloading almost any modern cartridge, in addition to many obsolete calibers. These range from 17-caliber, with possibly a few 10-, 12- and 14-caliber reamers still back in the stacks, to the 50 BMG round, and include the Precisioneered, Gold Medal Match Series, Competition, Legacy Series, Cowboy, X-Dies and Custom die series. The newest RCBS dies are for the 325 Winchester Short Mag (WSM), plus the Cowboy Shotshell Die.

The Shotshell Die is designed to size, decap and crimp 12-gauge brass shotshells in any single-stage RCBS press with a removable bushing. In the single stage, size the shell hull and decap it. Repriming is done using the standard priming device on this press. The sized, decapped and reprimed shell is then transferred to a regular shotshell loading press for charging with powder, seating of wads

and spacers and charging with shot. The charged but uncrimped shell is placed back on the single-stage press, the resizing ring removed from the shotshell die, an overshot wad placed on top the shot charge and the shell run up into the die to crimp the case mouth. Result: a newly-handloaded 12-gauge brass shotshell. It may sound like a lot of work, but if done in batches of fifty shells at a time in a loading block, it's not difficult. Size, decap and reprime fifty shells, move and charge fifty shells, move back to the single-stage press and crimp fifty shells. You now have fifty newly-reloaded brass shotshells.

Shellholders have a tendency to become misplaced – not lost – just misplaced. RCBS has a new Shell Holder Rack that will hold two dozen shellholders, two on each of a dozen posts, plus six Trim Pro shell holders as well. The top of the plastic rack is clear, allowing a view of the shell holder number. The rack can be used on the bench, or mounted on the wall and additional racks can be snapped together if more storage space is needed.

Handloaders of shotshells will appreciate the new RCBS *Handbook of Shotshell Reloading.* This 284-page

manual contains new information, cut-a-way and mechanical drawings, color photographs and more than 2,000 shotshell loads for various gauge shotshells. It features the use of RCBS reloading presses, contains a wealth of essential data not available elsewhere, and is destined to be a definitive handbook on the reloading of shotshells.

New cartridges require loading dies, and **Teppo Jutsu LLC**, home of the 458 SOCOM cartridge, has a couple of new ones. The big boy is the 470 Rhino, the largest of a possible line of Rhino cartridges, and the 30 HRT. The 470 is based on a shortened and necked-down 500 Jeffery case, while the 30 HRT is based on a neck-expanded 6.8x43mm SPC case. The 470 can push a 500-grain A-Frame bullet out the muzzle at about 2,150 fps and was designed to used in an compatible receiver fitted to the AR-10 lower unit, as was the 500 Phantom. The 30 HRT can do anything the rimmed 30 Herrett can do, and can be chambered and fitted to a regular AR-15 receiver. (Current Savage, Remington, etc., rifles could be rebarreled for these cartridges.)

C&H/Lee Precision

Loading dies for the Rhino and HRT cartridges are available from **C&H Tool & Die 4-D** and **Lee Precision Inc.** C&H was one of the early firms turning out top quality loading dies and H-presses for handloaders some fifty years ago. (The Swage-o-Matic was a beauty.) With the death of founder, Charles Heckman, in an automobile accident, the firm disappeared for awhile. However, like the phoenix, the firm returned. Now in Ohio, C&H has the ability to provide die sets for some 1,420 different cartridges, including at least one 12-caliber, ten 14-caliber and right on up to the 50 BMG – and larger. There are also dies for forming belts on your favorite wildcat, if needed.

The C&H loading presses include the non-progressive No. 444, 4-station H-press, and the 444-X Pistol Champ. Both presses use standard ⅞x14 dies, and are capable of loading up to 200 rounds per hour.

The spout of the RCBS Powder Trickler System trickles the powder charge from the measure directly onto the pan of the Model 750 Range Master scale.

For handloaders of the 'Big Fifty,' C&H has regular dies, a bullet puller, and a micrometer straight-line seater. All require a press capable of handling die bodies with 1½x12 threading. The regular loading dies consist of a full-length sizer and a crimp seater. The Puller die uses R-8 collets of the type used in Bridgeport milling machines, and replacement collets are available in several size increments up to one-inch, or from 4mm to 25mm. If you need to pull bullets from surplus military 50 BMG ammunition the C&H die, which has a roller thrust washer and spring ejector to ensure easy operation without marring the bullet, will do the job.

If you shoot the Big Fifty at 1,000 yards, using Barnes or Hornady bullets, you need to take a bit more care than loading with surplus 50-caliber bullets. The C&H Micrometer Die incorporates a micrometer spindle graduated in 0.001-inch with a Vernier scale to 0.0001-inch. It takes good equipment to turn out accurate loads, and if you need a precise setting when seating the 750-grain bullets, this is the die needed.

If you happen to have one of the old Herter 'C' or Lachmiller presses that used a non-standard shellholder (The shellholder on some such presses was held in position with one or two set screws.), C&H's adapter can help you. This adapter allows the use of regular snap-in shellholders used by all modern loading press manufacturers. Herter's also produced a few presses using a threaded shell holder and C&H has an adapter for this as well.

Magma Engineering Company

Magma, home of the Bullet Master and Magma Bullet Moulds, has moulds for ten new gas-check bullets, a Digital Temperature Controller for the Master Caster, Cast Master and Master Pot machines, and is now the home for the Littleton Shotmaker. The Controller, which can be located off the machines for ease and convenience of the operator, will maintain pot temperature to plus or minus 2 degrees Fahrenheit.

The Littleton Shotmaker is available with a choice of 120 or 220 VAC power unit, and is capable of producing thirty-five to forty pounds of high antimony, perfectly round shot per hour, using seven drippers. The unit measures a foot square by six inches high, and drippers are available in shot sizes 5, 6, 7, 7-½, 8, 8½ and 9.

The new Magma gas-check bullet moulds are all flat-tip designs, and include a 115-grain for the 32-20 Winchester, three 38-caliber designs, including a 260-grain for the 38-55 Winchester, a 260-grain for the 40-65 Winchester, two designs – 300 and 340 grains – for the 45-70 Government, a 265-grain for the 454 Casull and two 50-calibers: 300 and 440 grains.

Wolfe Publishing Company

Anyone in the handloading game for long should know the name of Ken Waters. Wolfe has a new book, *Ken Waters' Notebook*, available. Featuring previously unpublished personal correspondence, with many personal insights on various subjects, this new volume also contains considerable reloading information.

Corbin Mfg. & Supply

Every handloader who loads for more than one caliber has found, at one time or another, the cannelure groove on the bullet being loaded wasn't where the crimp was being made. No problem. The Oregon firm of Corbin Mfg. & Supply has a hand-operated tool, the HCT-1 Hand Cannelure Tool, which will place the cannelure where you need it, on any bullet from 17- to 72-caliber. Just set the exact depth you want the cannelure, position the bullet and turn the crank. It's handy, fast, easy to use and produces a perfect cannelure where you need it.

UniqueTek, Inc.

Users of the Fillon 550 and 650 reloading presses may have noticed a bit of looseness in the toolhead fit to the frame. UniqueTek, Inc. has a kit to tighten the fit. It eliminates looseness, reduces any overall case length variation and stabilizes the shellplate alignment. It does not require any modification to the press frame, so standard toolheads can still be used. It comes with instructions.

Ayers Arsenal

Some four or so decades back when most shotshells used paper hulls, the case mouths sometimes became frayed before the pinholes began to appear above the case head. Slipping

The new RCBS Advanced Powder Measure Stand, with measure and attached new Powder Trickler System placing the powder directly into the pan on the scale.

the cases mouth over a heated 'shell former' for a couple of seconds usually straightened the mouth, especially on Winchester-Western hulls which contained a bit of wax impregnation. The Minnesota firm of Herter's had an electrically-heated plug die which could be hand-held with an oven glove, or mounted on a single-stage press to re-form the case mouth in the step after decapping. (Leaving a plastic hull on the former for any length of time would usually ruin the case, as the plastic had a tendency to shrink.) Unfortunately, the original Herter firm is long gone.

Wisconsin's Ayers Arsenal has what they call a Thermagic Conditioner that will do the same job as the old Herter die. The Thermagic unit operates on a 110-115 VAC line and can be bench-mounted or clamped in a vise. It incorporates a thermostat for use with different plastic or paper cases. (A bit of trial and error use is necessary, as not all shotshell hulls are of the same formula plastic, plus there are paper hulls still available.) Slip the hull mouth down onto the forming mandrel with a rotating motion for a few seconds, and remove with a rotating motion in the opposite direction. Quickly slip the hot hull onto a separate cooling mandrel, rotate, remove and examine. If it's not near-perfect, try leaving the hull on the forming mandrel a second or two longer. (Roll crimps form best when using new, uncrimped hulls, but a Theermagic-treated previously crimped hull will also produced some good roll crimps.)

Caldwell Shooting Supplies

Loading ammunition is only part of the game. It has to be accurate ammunition to be worth the time and effort. Check it for accuracy is required, and the best way to accomplish that is with the aid of a mechanical rest of some type. For handgun users, Caldwell Shooting Supplies, by Battenfeld Technologies, Inc., has the H.A.M.M.R. (Handgun Accurizing Mechanical Machine Rest). If used properly, this device allows a shooter to test a handgun for accuracy free from outside interference. (It does require

In the foreground the new RCBS Black Powder Measure with non-sparking brass metering cylinder and aluminum powder hopper. To the right the new RCBS Shotshell Die in use, with a brass 12-gauge shell about to be de-primed and sized. An empty brass 12-gauge shell is shown in the far left foreground.

The new RCBS Mega Vibratory Case Tumbler can hold six pounds of cleaning media, and clean and polish up to 1,000 38 Special-size cases at a time.

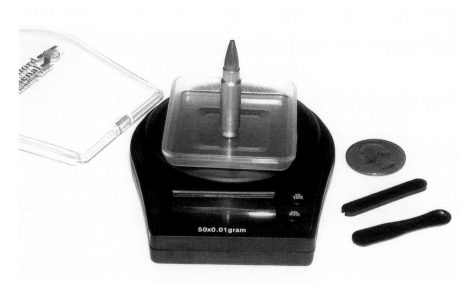

The Frankford Arsenal Micro Reloading Scale. The cartridge on the pan is a 5.7x28mm FNH, and a quarter is shown to the right, above a pair of tweezers, and a powder dipper. This scale comes with a soft case, and will fit into a shirt pocket. Accurate to 0.1 grain, it's ideal for taking to the range, along with a small press, if any reloading of handgun cartridges, etc., needs doing.

a sturdy, non-moving shooting bench to which the HAMMR can be securely clamped or mounted.) Firing is done remotely, using a cable-operated trigger actuator bar.

Currently, stock grip inserts for the HAMMR are available to fit various Smith & Wesson and Ruger revolvers, plus Beretta, SIG-Sauer, Glock, Para-Ordnance and HK pistols, as well as the M1911 Colt and clones. There is also a Universal Grip Casting Kit available, and inserts for other models are forthcoming. The original stocks on pistols and revolvers must be removed prior to installing the HAMMR inserts, and it's possible some Ransom grip inserts can be used. If handguns with polymer frames and non-removable stocks are to be used for test work, care must be taken not to over-tighten the clamping knobs during installation.

Hyskore Power Aisle, Inc.

There are a number of mechanical rests for rifle users, including the excellent Lead Sled from Caldwell Shooting Supplies. One of the best new rests for checking accuracy is the Model 30012 Dangerous Game

Machine Rest from Hyskore Power Aisle, Inc. This rest, as with the HAMMR, employs remote firing, but via a hydraulic trigger release in place of a cable. The rest should be attached to a non-moving shooting bench; a concrete bench would be ideal. The Dangerous Game Rest will handle rifles in calibers from the 223 Remington to the 416 Weatherby Magnum, using one of three compression dampers provided with the Rest. (A table listing the approximate recoil in foot-pounds of energy is provided for each of the three dampers—mild (#1), medium (#2), and heavy (#3)—when used with rifles weighing seven, eight and nine pounds. The #1 damper should be used with rifles chambered for cartridges from the 223 Remington to the 308 Winchester. Damper #2 will handle rifles chambered for cartridges from the 7mm Remington Magnum to the 375 H&H Magnum, and including 12-gauge shotguns. Damper #3 will take care of the larger cartridges, from the 338 RUM to the 416 Weatherby Magnum, including the 416 Rigby and 458 Winchester Magnum. However, the 458 is not to be used in the Rest if the

rifle weighs less than eight pounds, nor should the 416 Weatherby be used in the Rest if the rifle weighs less than nine pounds. Otherwise, damage may result to the rest and/or the rifle, according to Power Aisle.

Power Aisle stresses caution in all aspects when using the Rest, following the instructions, calculating the anticipated recoil prior to beginning so the correct damper is used, and checking everything, including the Velcro security straps, after every third shot. As the instructions state: "If you do something dumb, bad things can happen."

Ballistic Technology

Handloads intended for defensive or hunting use can be checked for expansion properties using the Bullet Test Tube by Ballistic Technology. (This shooter has used a variety of mediums over the years, from actual beef – it was cheaper then – to saturated wetpack. None provided a reliable, semi-permanent wound cavity for later analysis, although the wetpack and moist clay did well after drying for a period of time.) The bullet expansion material in the Test Tube can be melted and reused, using moulds that are available. Currently, the Bullet Test Tube can be obtained in sizes to handle handgun and/or rifle calibers. There are also moulds, material solvents, etc. available. For handloaders wanting to check the effects of their load/bullet combination, the Bullet Test Tube provides the means.

There's always something new for handloaders. It may be components, loading data, new or improved presses, dies, scale, powder measure – or even an ammunition box. What's been presented in this update represents some of what's new. There is no doubt that additional products will have been introduced by the time you read this. It's all part of what makes handloading enjoyable, that and the ability to turn out the best and most accurate handloads you can possibly produce.

THE GUNS OF EUROPE:
ONE CENTURY OF THE 25 ACP

by Raymond Caranta

William Morgan Thomas

Today obsolete in Europe and hardly surviving in America, this tiny cartridge (designed at UMC, Bridgeport, Connecticut) represented significant ballistic progress in 1906, under the "6.35mm" European nomenclature, when the first production "Petit Browning" automatic pistols were introduced by the Belgian FN (Fabrique Nationale Herstal) factory.

John Moses Browning in front of his FN office in Belgium.

William Morgan Thomas and UMC

Thanks to Jim Foral's fascinating article "UMC Thomas, a Recognition," published in the Gun Digest 1998 edition (1), we know that William Morgan Thomas, born in Wales in 1848, landed in New York in 1865 and was hired in 1869 by UMC in Bridgeport, Connecticut, a new successful company founded there in 1866. Entering the ballistics department circa 1871, the young William M. Thomas thus reached the Mecca of U.S. centerfire ammunition at the very beginning of its history.

In 1903, when John M. Browning approached UMC for the development of an original 25-caliber semi-rimmed round intended for a new vest pocket automatic pistol project, William M. Thomas was a 55-year-old highly-experienced veteran. As a matter of fact, he had been previously involved, since 1872, in the design of many famous revolver cartridges for Colt and Smith & Wesson, among others.

The following year, a batch of experimental cartridges was ready for testing and, by 1905, the first "Petit Browning" pistol could enter in production.

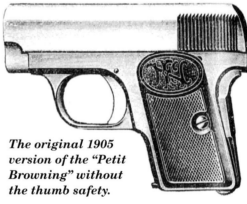

The original 1905 version of the "Petit Browning" without the thumb safety.

The 6.35mm Browning Ammunition

It features, in its original configuration, a slightly tapered centerfire case 0.62-inch long measuring 0.274-inch at the mouth,

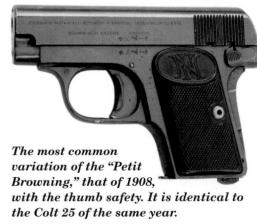

The most common variation of the "Petit Browning," that of 1908, with the thumb safety. It is identical to the Colt 25 of the same year.

0.275-inch in front of the cannelure and 0.301-inch at the rim. The round-nose 0.251-inch full-jacketed bullet is 0.46-inch long and weighs 50 grains. The overall length of the cartridge is 0.90-inch approximately, for a total weight of 78 grains.

The muzzle velocity from a 2-inch barrel was given by Major Hatcher, in 1935 (2) as 751 fps, developing a 62 foot-pounds energy (fpe) with a 10,000 psi pressure and having a 3 pine board/⅞-inch penetration (2).

The Modern Competitors

In Europe, its main competitor was the 6mm Velo Dog, marketed in France by the Paris gunsmith Galand in 1894, for small pocket revolvers (43-grain round-nose FMJ 0.222-inch bullet 0.48-inch long: muzzle velocity - 672 fps; muzzle energy – 43.4 foot-pounds). The cartridge length was 1.4 inches, for a total weight of 88 grains (3).

This modern 6mm cartridge was, at the time, highly popular everywhere on the Continent and it gallantly resisted the 25 ACP up to World War I, disappearing only in the 1920s. The Italian Fiocchi ammunition catalog listed the 6mm Velo Dog as a vintage caliber up to 1999.

In the field of the then-high tech automatic pistols, there was another competitor, the "5mm Charola Anitua calibre," better known as the 5mm

Clement, which appeared in 1898 in Spain (4). The original Charola Anitua pistol was manufactured in several versions up to 1905, when it disappeared.

However, in 1903 the Belgian designer Charles Philippe Clément, from Liège, introduced a very different automatic pistol firing this same round and produced it up to 1907, when he chambered two new versions of it for the more successful 25 and 32 ACP Browning cartridges (4). According to CARTRIDGES OF THE WORLD (5), page 298 of the tenth edition, this cartridge was still listed in the 1934 DWM catalog.

In my experience, the Charola Anitua pistols are very rare, with a total production estimated at 8400 units and the 5mm Clements chambering uncommon, as my own sample was serial-numbered 8144.

However, J. Howard Mathews (6) states that, even the 1907 32 ACP examined by him bears the serial number 7263 (page 181), while the highest-numbered 25 ACP sample mentioned is S/N 33.353, an improved model 1909. Anyway, within two years after the "Petit Browning" appearance, the unfortunate 5mm

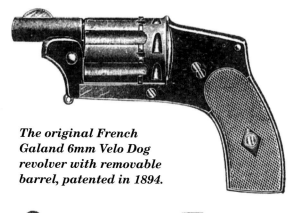

The original French Galand 6mm Velo Dog revolver with removable barrel, patented in 1894.

A more conventional Bull Dog-style 6mm Velo Dog revolver. Circa 1910, most of them were also available in 25 ACP.

chambering had been swept away.

Today, in France, an original Charola Anitua pistol in NRA Excellent condition is worth 1,500 U.S. dollars; a Clement 1903 is worth 1,000 U.S. dollars minimum, and the Model 1907, chambered for the Browning cartridges, commands about 400 U.S. dollars.

The 5mm Charola Anitua semi-rimmed bottlenecked round is 0.97-inch long, with an 0.72-inch case length. Diameters are 0.2-inch for the bullet, 0.22-inch at the case neck, 0.28-inch in front of the cannelure and 0.29-inch at the rim. It weighs about 62 grains. The FMJ bullet weight is 36 grains, with a 1030 fps nominal muzzle velocity for 61.5 fpe.

If we compare with the 25 ACP developing 62 fpe at the muzzle, the 6mm Velo Dog was 30 percent less powerful, and the 5mm Charola Anitua was equal. Concerning the bullet cross-sectional areas, the 25 ACP was the larger, with 318 cm2, against 248 cm2 for the 6mm Velo Dog and 202 cm2 for the 5mm Charola Anitua.

Accordingly, with muzzle energy of 304 foot-pounds/cm2 governing

The 25 ACP round and its competition in 1906. L-R: the 5mm and 7mm Lefaucheux pinfire cartridges, 22 Short, 5mm Charola Anitua, 6mm Velo Dog, 6.35mm Browning (.25), 8mm Gaulois, 320 Bull Dog and 32 S&W.

A French long-barrel (3.35-inch) "Policeman" version of the "Le Français" 25 ACP 8-shot pistol in its second variation (1935) designed for security agencies. This model was in service in my home-town police up to 1945.

A typical Belgian 25 ACP Bossu ("Hunchback") five-shot revolver popular circa 1910 in Europe. Five inches long, it weighed 10 oz. loaded (5 oz. less than the "Petit Browning")

its penetration potential, the 5mm Charola Anitua had the best impact ballistics, followed by the 25 ACP, at 195 foot-pounds/cm2.

However, in spite of this, the new 25 ACP cartridge had no difficulty finding commercial recognition, thanks to the huge European distribution network of the FN and the tremendous prestige of the Browning name. During the previous six years, 250,000 Brownings in 32 ACP had been sold at the same 45.00 FF ($9) unit price as the French Model 1892 service revolver!

In that time, a Smith & Wesson hammerless break-open 32-caliber revolver cost, in France, 89.00 FF or 17.80 U.S. dollars, and a good Continental 6mm Velo Dog hammerless solid-frame revolver, 34.00 FF or 6.8 U.S. dollars (7). At 2.22 FF (0.45 U.S. dollars) the box of 25, the new up-to-date 6.35mm ACP was the same price as the French 8mm service ammunition, and just above the 6mm Velo Dog, at 2.15 FF (0.43 U.S. dollars).

The Older Calibers Competition

Being admitted that a reasonable size for a true pocket pistol, as people used to carry it, is O.L. = 5.5 x H = 3.5 x TH 1.2 inches for a loaded weight not exceeding one pound, the blackpowder-era revolvers meeting this profile were the Smith & Wesson break-open 32-caliber revolvers with 2-inch barrels and their cheaper clones, or the Continental double-action solid-frame "British Bull Dogs" chambered in 320-caliber.

These 320 Bull Dog revolvers were called "vapor revolvers," because of the nice smoke wreath they produced when fired. These solid-frame hand-ejector guns were cheap and small, in the 9.00 FF to 30.00 FF (1.80 to 6.00 U.S. dollars) price bracket for the 320 Bull Dog chambering.

In 1905, many of them could also fire smokeless powder ammunition. The standard loading featured a 75-grain lead bullet with a 500 fps muzzle velocity (40 fpe muzzle energy). The bullet diameter was 0.268-inch and the 0.269-inch cylindrical case was 0.59-inch long with a 0.31-inch rim diameter. The cartridge length was 0.93-inch; the total weight was 114 grains.

The 32 Smith & Wesson was an American cartridge dating back to 1878 – like the 320 Bull Dog – but more powerful, with a .314-inch lead or jacketed round-nose bullet weighing 85 grains.

The actual muzzle velocity from a 2-inch barrel was about 655/720 fps for a resulting muzzle energy in the 80/100 fpe bracket. The actual penetration was 1.5 – 2 inches in ⅞-inch pine boards.

However, measuring L 5.9 x H 2.36 x TH 1.13 inches and weighing 16.67 oz. loaded, this revolver was heavier and bulkier than the "Petit Browning" of 1906 (L 4.45 x H 3.11 x TH 0.99-inch; 15 oz.

loaded with 6 rounds).

At the turn of the twentieth century, such nice Smith & Wesson pocket revolvers were priced at 82,00/89,00 FF, or 16.4/17.8 U.S. dollars; their American clones, with poor double-action systems, at 30,00/34,00 FF, or 6/6.8 U.S. dollars, and their Belgian or Spanish imitations, 24,00/27,00 FF, or 4.8/5.4 U.S. dollars (7).

The cost of the 32 Smith & Wesson ammunition was 3,25 FF the fifty, loaded with blackpowder, and 4,00 FF in smokeless loading, against 5,00 FF (2,25 x 2) for the new "Petit Browning" 6,35 mm rounds.

The Pioneer "Petit Browning"

When John M. Browning launched his project of a tiny vest pocket 25 auto-pistol in 1903, he had been firmly entrenched at the Belgian Fabrique Nationale for four years and, obviously, started with the basic mechanism common to the 9mm Long

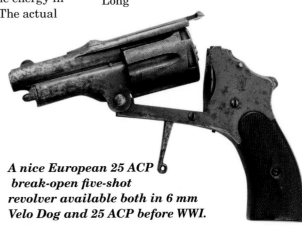

A nice European 25 ACP break-open five-shot revolver available both in 6 mm Velo Dog and 25 ACP before WWI.

"Grand Modèle" developed for them, and to the Colt "Hammerless pocket automatic" in 32 ACP simultaneously marketed in America.

The grip automatic safety was similar, like the receiver, slide, barrel mounting, magazine catch, extractor and recoil spring designs, while adapted to the desired size.

However, to keep the height above the hand as low as possible, the internal hammer mechanism was replaced by a less expensive striker, and the sights were reduced to a plain groove consisting of a minute notch and, at the muzzle, a small protrusion.

When the "Petit Browning" was released in 1905, it featured no thumb safety, which was added circa 1908 around serial number 100,000. That same year, further to its tremendous success in Europe, Colt added it to its line as the "Model 1908 Caliber .25 Hammerless Automatic Pistol." Its total production was about 410,000 units from 1909 to 1941.

Meanwhile, the European "Petit Browning" production amounted to one million units from 1906 to 1932, when it was superseded by the true "Baby Browning" of a different design. Incidentally, we have kept here its French nomenclature, which was that of the original Belgian catalogs up to the end of production.

The Contemporary Opinions

In 1911, the French importer of the "Petit Browning" stated: *"... thanks to its flat shape, it is very easy to carry; its action is both simple and sturdy.*

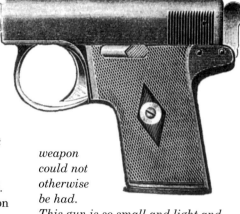

The 25 Auto Webley pistol model 1907 was one of the first competitors of the "Petit Browning." Sold at the same price, featuring an external hammer and only 4 inches long, it was shorter and lighter (11 oz.).

All components are made of the best steels and interchangeable..." (7).

In 1920 (8), the British Captain of the London Regiment, Hugh B.C. Pollard, wrote about the Colt version (identical to the Belgian one): *"... This little weapon is very accurate and very reliable... It is probably safer than any other automatic pistol, and is quite powerful enough for the purpose for which it was designed..."*

In 1935 (2), the Major Hatcher said: *"... This gun is small enough to be carried in the vest pocket, and that is its greatest recommendation. The cartridge is entirely too small to have stopping power, and while the gun is capable of inflicting a fatal injury, it does not impart enough shock to make a man feel sick as soon as he is hit. It is true that soft-point bullets are furnished for this gun, but this means nothing, as the bullet does not have enough speed to mushroom, and a soft-point bullet does no more harm than a jacketed one.*

The gun has a distinct field, however, in spite of its lack of stopping power and the fact that it can only be moderately accurate on account of its short sight radius and short barrel. This field is in its enabling one to have a weapon under circumstances where a weapon could not otherwise be had. This gun is so small and light and insignificant that it can be carried without inconvenience or without any suspicion, and no one wants to be shot even with a .25. Therefore, this gun would often be just as effective as a larger caliber, because in many cases the purpose is served if a would-be assailant simply knows that you are armed..."

The 25 Auto Handguns Available Before World War I

Since 1907, which marked the expiration of the Browning patents, the international market was opened, somewhat slowing down the sale of the "Petit Browning".

Before World War I, which started in August 1914, less than twenty 25 ACP vest pocket pistols shared the market. Most of them have been patented between 1905 and 1907 in their respective countries.

The first to be actually marketed were the Belgian Clement 1907, the Pieper "Demontant" and "Basculant,"

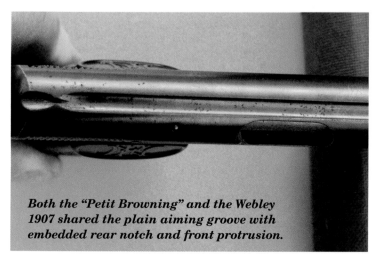

Both the "Petit Browning" and the Webley 1907 shared the plain aiming groove with embedded rear notch and front protrusion.

The Belgian 25 ACP six-shot "Baby Browning" which appeared in 1932 (O.L. = 4-inch – Empty weight = 9.8 oz./steel; 7.67 oz./light alloy). It was truly a nice gun!

The Belgian Bayard pistol, marketed in 1908, was then unique in its class as, for a size (OAL @ 4.8 inches) and weight (1 lb.) similar to those of the "Petit Browning," it was available in 32 ACP.

The German Mauser Model 1910 was beautifully made and the most accurate in its class before WWI.

whose license was sold before 1911 to Steyr, in Austria, and the external-hammer Webley, some two ounces lighter than the "Petit Browning."

The next year, in 1908, the 32 ACP Bayard appeared, as well as

the Spanish "Express," the Walther Model I, the Colt 1908 and the Spanish Star.

The year 1909 saw another Spanish model, the "Fiel" or "Diane," and appearing in 1910 the German Dreyse (marked Model 1908, but delayed two years), the Belgian Robar "Jeffeco," the Spanish Royal and Walman and – the most important – the Mauser Model 1910. This beautifully-made 10-shot pistol was slightly bigger than the others but, by far, the most accurate.

After WWI, the Mauser Model 1910 was extensively used for target shooting (11), as was the Walther Model 8. Several years ago, with such a small pistol (5.4 inches overall length – 15.35 oz. empty weight), I was able to score 244/300 using the ISU slow-fire target featuring a 2-inch ten, at 25 meters!

The 25 ACP Revolver Competitors

It goes without saying that the traditional European Bull Dog and Velo Dog revolver-makers did not accept their fate without reacting!

For the 6mm Velo Dog makers, it was easy to chamber the new cartridges,

A very special folding grip and removable barrel hammerless 25 ACP five-shot revolver sold for $8 by Alfa in 1911.

as the two bullet diameters were similar, and their 6mm cylinders longer. By 1911 more than twenty such revolvers (mostly made in France and Belgium), were available on our market at very competitive prices. However, this traditional industry was killed by the war, which unleashed the automatic pistol fad, and the revolvers soon disappeared.

After The War

With everyone wanting autoloading vest-pocket pistols, manufacturers entered the market in droves from Spain, Belgium, France, Germany, Hungary, Italy and the Czech Republic, exporting at low prices what they could not sell at home. There were so many it would be impossible to list them here.

Among the most interesting, from the technical standpoint, was the French "Le Français" double-action tip-up barrel pistol, released in 1914 just at the beginning of the war; the elegant German Walther Model 8 of 1920 and the incredibly accurate small Model 9, of 1921, which,

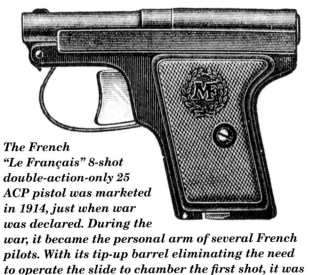

The French "Le Français" 8-shot double-action-only 25 ACP pistol was marketed in 1914, just when war was declared. During the war, it became the personal arm of several French pilots. With its tip-up barrel eliminating the need to operate the slide to chamber the first shot, it was quite revolutionary in its time (O.L. = 4.37 inch; Empty weight = 10.7-oz.).

In 1935, it was improved by changing the grip angle and magazine latch.

with the Menz "Liliput," forced the mighty FN to introduce its famous "Baby Browning" in 1932 (11).

Of course, during this golden period for the caliber, many European police departments were equipped with 25 ACP automatic pistols, some with long barrels, in the futile hope it would increase their anaemic ballistic efficiency.

World War II

Of course, during the war, the production of 25 ACP pistols was interrupted everywhere. However, in occupied Europe, such small pistols were eagerly sought by Resistance members, as it was not good to be caught by the Germans with a concealed weapon! The demand was so great that even the OSS had trouble in finding enough 25 ACP autoloaders to meet their requirements (13).

After World War II

When Colt, the only American manufacturer of 25 ACP pistols, decided after the war to abandon their production, from 1946 to 1968 the small handguns made by Beretta, Bernardelli, Belgian FN ("Browning"), Astra and Star, were massively imported from Italy, Belgium and Spain to answer the need.

However, when the U.S. government decided, by the Gun Control Act of 1968, to prohibit such imports, it ruined the most exposed of these companies which were also subject to increasingly stringent

The 2007 line of vest-pocket calibers available. L/R: the 22 Long Rifle, 22 Magnum RF, 25 ACPFMJ, 25 ACP hollowpoint, 25 NAA and 32 ACP FMJ.

Marketed after WWI, the German Ortgies 7-shot 25 ACP pistol was similar to the Walther Model 8, but featured a different barrel mounting and an original grip safety. John Dillinger, the famous bank robber, had one in his arsenal, according to the FBI archives.

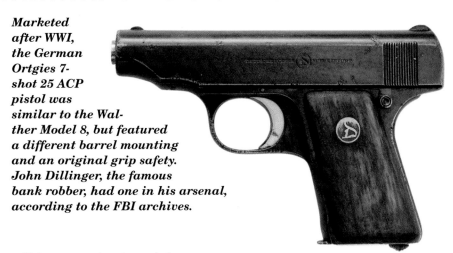

policies concerning concealed gun-carrying in their mother-countries.

Some, like Beretta and Taurus, reacted by installing factories in the United States, while others, like Walther, sold the applicable licenses to American companies. Soon, new American manufacturers started to work, and made 4,000,000 units of 25 ACP handguns from 1980 to 1999, comprising 18 percent of the total American automatic pistols production for the period.

Now, such high production figures are only a dimming memory, as the 25 ACP is waning, representing only (for 2003) 1.35 percent of America's national pistol production. In 2007, only CZ is still making a modern double-action pistol in 25 ACP with light alloy receiver, the new CZ 92, which is not imported into the United States.

Today's 25 ACP Ballistics

If the 25-caliber is dying, it is because more efficient guns of similar size are currently available. Ten years ago, one would have bet on the 22 rimfire and would have been wrong because, due to their small cross-sectional area, they need long barrels to reach the high muzzle velocity required.

When looking at special 25 ACP loadings, such as those from Hornady, Ultramax or Magsafe, we find significant improvements, but the bullet weight reductions required for meeting reasonable pressure limits, are detrimental to the penetration potential of projectiles and, therefore, to their impact efficiency for defence.

Today we see the shift to the older 32 ACP chambering, as Beretta-USA, North American and Kel-Tec have done, and now to the 9mm, as attempted by Kahr, Kel-Tec and Rohrbaugh – all contributing to dissatisfaction with the 25 ACP.

Not long ago, these caliber increases would have produce very unpleasant recoil, but thanks to new grip technologies, they are reasonably bearable. Moreover, the new North American 25 NAA and 32 NAA cartridges look highly promising but... they are no more than the 25 ACP of yesteryear!

BIBLIOGRAPHY

1 – "UMC Thomas, A Recognition" by Jim Foral, GUN DIGEST 1998. Krause Publications, 700 E. State Street, Iola WI 54990.

2 – *Textbook of Pistols and Revolvers* by Julian S. Hatcher. Small-Arms Technical Publishing Co. Plantersville, South Carolina, USA. 1935.

3 – *Le Pistolet de Epoch Moderne* by Raymond Caranta (French). Crépin-Leblond, 52902 Chaumont CEDEX 9, France. 2003.

4 – *Les Pistolets Automatiques Etrangers*, by Raymond Caranta (in French). Crépin-Leblond, 52902 Chaumont CEDEX 9, France. 2000.

5 – *Cartridges of the World*, by Frank C. Barnes/Stan Skinner. Tenth edition. Krause Publications, Iola, Wisconsin 54990-0001, USA.

6 – *Firearms Identification, Volume I*, by J. Howard Mathews. Charles C. Thomas, Springfield, Illinois, USA. 1962 and 1973.

7 – Manufrance 1911 Catalog (French). Manufrance (abbreviated nomenclature), Saint-Etienne, France.

8 – *Automatic Pistols*, by H.B. Pollard. 1921. Reprint by WE, PO Box 131, Old Greenwich, Connecticut 06870

9 – *Encyclopedia and Magazine Reference for Auto-Loading Pistols*, Triple K Mfg Co. Krasne's Inc. San Diego, California 92113. 1994

10 – *1840–1940, Cien Años de Pistolas y Revolveres Españoles*, by J.L. Calvo and E. Jimenez Sanchez-Malo (Spanish). Asociacion Española de las Coleccionistas. 1993.

11 – "The Guns of Europe – Pre-WWII Pocket Pistols" by Raymond Caranta. GUN DIGEST 1997.

12 – *Arms of the World – 1911*. Edited by Joseph J. Schroeder, Jr. Follett, Chicago IL. 1972.

13 – *U.S. Handguns of World War II*, by Charles W. Pate. Andrew Mowbray, Lincoln, RI 02865. USA. 1998.

AMMUNITION, BALLISTICS & COMPONENTS

by Holt Bodinson

The steady introduction of new calibers and high-tech loads is fueling the firearms industry. One has to look no further than Hornady to sense the pace of the ammunition market. This year Hornady is introducing four completely new cartridges – the 308 Marlin Express, 30 T/C, 375 Ruger and 460 Bushmaster. It is also bringing into production two great classics – the 450/400 N.E.-3" and the 9.3x74R. Remington, which has controlled the 17-caliber centerfire market with its swift 17 Remington for years, decided it was time to rev up the market and created the appealing 17 Remington Fireball along with five bolt-action rifles to shoot it in. The heavy end of the handgun market keeps boiling with a number of new loads for the 460 S&W and 500 S&W, including Hornady's 500-grain FP-XTP for 500 S&W shooters who like a bit of kick to their loads. Over in scattergun territory, the accent is still on the development of dense shot including Winchester's Extended Range High Density, Remington's Wingmaster HD and Federal's Black Cloud FS Steel. It's been a busy year!

A-Square Company

A-Square has aggressively tamed a number of excellent wildcats by domesticating them through the SAAMI protocols. Two of the successful cartridges, the 6.5-06 A-Square and the 338-06 A-Square, will be joined this year by the 416 Taylor A-Square. Developed by Robert Chatfield Taylor in the 1970s by necking down the 458 Win. Magnum case to .416", the compact and highly efficient 416 Taylor is capable of churning up 2400 fps with a 400-grain bullet. Move over 416 Rigby and 416 Remington, the Taylor A-Square runs on less powder and doesn't require a magnum length action to equal your classic ballistics. It's good to see that the 416 Taylor has now been standardized and is available loaded with A-Square's unique "Triad" of big game bullets. www.a-squarecompany.com

Ballistic Products

Ballistic Products new "HITS" program is changing the way shotshell reloaders optimize their choice of components around a specific game species or shooting game. Standing for "Hull Integrated Technology System," the HITS program provides the reloader with a bundle of the best components, except for powder and shot, plus reloading instructions to assemble the finest pheasant, waterfowl, sporting clays and 20-gauge shotshells. There's also a new multi-purpose 16-gauge field wad available this year. Designated the "Multi-Metal 16," it can handle lead, steel and Hevi-Shot loadings. www.ballisticproducts.com

Barnes Bullets

Celebrating their 75th anniversary, Barnes is introducing no less than 41 new bullet designs this year. Noteworthy as well is that the Barnes bullets are being factory loaded today by Black Hills, Cor-Bon, Federal, Norma and Weatherby. Brand new to the Barnes family is the "Varmint Grenade" – a 36-grain HP in .224",

Featuring a copper-tin core, Barnes' Varmint Grenade .224" bullet promises explosive performance.

Barnes' Triple-Shock X Bullet is so effective, it's being factory loaded by Federal, Black Hills and Weatherby.

featuring a highly frangible, copper-tin core. It's a "green" bullet, accurate and designed for explosive expansion of game and a minimum of ricochets. The line of Maximum-Range X-Bullets (MRX) introduced last year, featuring tungsten-alloy cores and polymer tips in the familiar Triple-Shock platform, has been expanded to cover every popular caliber from 270 through 338. Barnes' line of solids has been completely redesigned with multi-grooved shanks that reduce pressure, minimize fouling and enhance accuracy. The new "Banded Solid" line has been expanded to cover every popular caliber from 224 through 600, and this includes some classic big game calibers such as the 9.3mm, 450/400, 404 Jeffrey, 470 Nitro, 505 Gibbs and 500 Nitro. The 30/30 gets a new high performance bullet this year, a flat-nose, 150-grain Triple Shock. Finally, look for a variety of new XPB pistol bullets including new weights and designs for the 357, 357 Sig, 40 S&W, 44 Spl. and 45 GAP. www.barnesbullets.com

Berger Bullets

In an interesting turn of events, Berger is pitching its Match Grade Very Low Drag (VLD) line as perfectly suitable for hunting big game. Berger's tests, which are available on a free DVD from the company, show that the sharp nose of a VLD bullet penetrates at least 2 inches of initial tissue and then expands rapidly in the vital area. Added to the lineup this year are a 120-grain/6.5mm Match BT and a 130-grain/6.5mm Match VLD. www.bergerbullets.com

Bismuth

Working with Berger, Bismuth has developed and is loading a 175-grain/30-caliber VLD match grade bullet with a pure Bismuth, non-toxic core in the 308 Win., 30-'06, 300 Win. Mag. and 300 WSM. Test results show exceptionally fine accuracy and rapid fragmentation. Bismuth continues to offer a complete line of shotshells and Bismuth component shot for handloaders. Bismuth is the only non-toxic shot that is suitable for pre-steel shot shotgun barrels, be they breech or muzzleloaders. www.bismuth-notox.com

Black Hills

With S&W returning the Model 1917 to its line, a lot of shooters will be searching for 45 Auto Rim ammunition. It's hard to find, but not at Black Hills. Their new 45 Auto Rim loading features a hard-cast 255-grain SWC at an honest 750 fps. The hottest new varmint load this year is Black Hills' 223 "Varmint Grenade." Built around Barnes' new copper particle-cored 36-grain bullet, the Varmint Grenade is running at 3750 fps and is said to be "humanely devastating" on small critters. Long known for their custom match ammunition, Black Hills is loading a 123-grain/6.5mm Sierra MatchKing in the 6.5 Grendel cartridge for Les Baer, who is reporting .5 MOA accuracy from his custom AR-15s. Similarly, they have developed a long-range tactical match load for the 260 Rem. cartridge, featuring a 139-grain Lapua Scenar bullet at 2770 fps. The tactical match 260 Rem. load will be marketed exclusively through G.A. Precision rifles. Finally, their premium line of hunting ammunition, Black Hills Gold, is being expanded with Hornady SST bullets added to the 243

45 Auto Rim has been in short supply, but no longer. Black Hills is bringing it back.

If you don't handload, Black Hills' 223 ammunition line now includes Barnes' Varmint Grenade bullet.

Win., 270 Win. and 7mm Rem. Mag. Great people – great ammo. www.black-hills.com

Brenneke USA

The 16-gauge continues to creep up in popularity, and why not. A 16-gauge built on a 20-gauge frame is a delight to shoot and carry. Well, Brenneke has upgraded their 1 oz/16-gauge slug with a new wad system that is capable of 2.5" groups at 50 yards. Velocity is right up there at 1600 fps. Over the past year, Brenneke commissioned ballistics expert Tom Burczynski to run a series of comparative tests on all brands of shotguns slugs. Interestingly, the Brenneke 12-gauge Heavy Field Short Magnum out-penetrated the competition by a long margin and ranked second in terms of accuracy and muzzle energy. See the test results at www.brennekeusa.com

DKG Trading

DKG has emerged as a great resource if you're looking for NobelSport or Centurion shotshells. Manufactured in Italy, both lines feature some interesting variations like NobelSport's 20-gauge steel trap load and 12-gauge sporting clays spreader load. Under the Centurion banner, one will find a unique 12-gauge buckshot load featuring one 0.650" round ball and six #1 buck and a .410 shell stuffed with five #00 buck. See the whole lines at www.dkgtrading.com

Extreme Shock

Extreme Shock ammunition is designed to fragment and dump all its energy within the target. With a technology based on bullets having Tungsten powder cores, the lines now cover personal defense and aircraft safe handgun rounds, short and long range 5.56mm tactical rounds, subsonic, door-breaching and even a 675-grain 50 BMG load. See them all at www.extremeshockusa.com

Federal

Waterfowl beware! The new Black Cloud FS Steel cartridge is described as "Dropping Ducks Like Rain." Basically, a combination of Federal's proven Flitecontrol wad

Centurion packs a lethal load of one .650" ball plus six #1 buck.

and a steel shot pellet that features a cutting edge around its circumference, Black Cloud FS is a new step-up in steel shot lethality. Twelve and twenty gauge slugs also have been given a facelift by the addition of a streamlined polymer spitzer tip to Federal's Barnes Expander sabot slug. The factory standard is 2 inches at 100 yards – no exceptions. Speaking of Barnes, the 7mm/140-grain Triple Shock X-Bullet has been added to the 7mm-08, 280 Rem. and 7mm Rem. Mag. under the Premium Vital-Shok label. Also new under the same label are a 150-grain Nosler AccuBond in the 30-'06 and a 165-grain AccuBond in the 308 Win. The popularity of the 460 S&W keeps growing so Federal has once again teamed up with Barnes to load a 275-grain Expander in that big bore handgun caliber. www. federalpremium.com

Brenneke's extensive slug line-up features a new 16 ga. 1 oz. slug at 1600 fps.

Federal's 12 and 20-gauge sabot slug loads feature a spitzer-tipped Barnes Expander.

Fiocchi

Break out those Broomhandles! Fiocchi is reintroducing the 7.63 Mauser cartridge in a full-power loading sporting an 88-grain FMJ bullet at 1425 fps. www.fiocchiusa.com

Hastings

A 3½"/20-gauge slug? Famous for their slug gun barrels and sabot slug ammunition, Hastings is introducing a 3½"/20-gauge case stuffed with a 350-grain Laser Accurate Slug at 2000 fps. It's the ultimate 20-gauge magnum but suitable only for single-shot shotguns at the moment. www.hastingsammunition.com

Hodgdon

Having taken over the distribution of Winchester canister powders, Hodgdon is releasing two classic Winchester shotshell powders: WAALite – the same powder used by Winchester to create the Feather Light AA12FL shell; and Super-Handicap – useful for duplicating Winchester's clays-crushing Super-Handicap 12-gauge loading that tough competitors call the "silver bullet." There's a new short cut powder this year, IMR 4007 SSC. "SSC" stands for "Super Short Cut" and the burning rate of the new powder falls between IMR 4064 and IMR 4350. The new IMR 4007 SSC is turning in outstanding velocities and accuracy in the short magnums as well as in the 22-250, 220 Swift, 243 Win. and the classic 30-'06. Be sure to buy the new Hodgdon Reloading Manual that now includes thousands of proven recipes for IMR and Winchester, as well as the traditional Hodgdon powders. www.hodgdon.com

Hornady

After last year's introduction of the "LeverEvolution" family of cartridges, we expected Hornady to take a breather. Not so, this year Hornady is producing four completely new cartridges, the 375 Ruger, 308 Marlin Express, 30 T/C and 450 Bushmaster as well as bringing into production two great classics, the 450/400 Nitro Express 3" and the 9.3x74R. The 375 Ruger is based on a 30-'06-length case and loaded with a 270-grain SP and 300-grain SP or FMJ, it is capable of duplicating 375 H&H performance in a 20-inch barrel. The 308 Marlin Express features a 160-grain spitzer bullet with a high B.C. rating of .400 that leaves the muzzle of Marlin's new XLR lever action at 2600 fps. If you like Marlin lever actions, you'll like this new cartridge. The 30 T/C is a short-action case designed specifically for T/C's forward-looking ICON bolt-action rifle. Producing 3000 fps with a 150-grain bullet and 2850 fps with a 165-grain pill, Hornady claims the new case uses less powder than the 308 or 30-'06, exceeds the factory velocities of those classic 30s in a 20-inch barrel, and produces noticeably less recoil. Designed to take your Bushmaster AR-15 big-game hunting, the 450 Bushmaster will produce over 2000 fps with a .425-caliber/250-grain SST

Hodgdon is releasing two classic Winchester shotshell powders: AA Lite and AA Super-Handicap.

bullet. The overall length of the new cartridge matches the 223 Rem. at 2.250 inches. Just change your uppers and go hunting. www.hornady.com

Huntington

This is the handloader's emporium for bullets, cases and RCBS tooling and parts. Buzz Huntington does an exceptional job of rounding up the hardest-to-get components and will go to any length to find them. Need lead bullets for the 310 Martini, newly drawn cases for the 577 Snider, or samples of the 600 and 700 Nitro Express cases or bullets. Huntington keeps them in stock. I enjoy shooting the oddball and

Hornady's puts some muscle in the AR-15 with the new 450 Bushmaster.

obsolete cartridges, and I haven't been able to stump Buzz yet.

Huntington's catalog is as educational a reference as you will find in the trade. www.huntingtons.com

Kent Cartridge

"Speed Kills," states their catalog, and Kent has the shotshells to prove it. New this year under their "Faststeel" waterfowl label is a 12-gauge/3½" shell packing 1¼ oz of BB, 1, 2 and 3s at 1625 fps. That's fast! Then there's a new 12-gauge/2¾" upland lead load featuring 1⅜ oz of 4, 5 and 6s at 1460 fps. Look to Kent for speed. It kills. www.kentgamebore.com

Lightfield

Famous for their exceptionally accurate and lethal shotgun slugs, Lightfield has capitalized on its experience with plastic sabots and projectile design to develop a new 50-caliber muzzleloading round. Named the "Alpha Gold 300," it consists of a pure lead 300-grain boattail hollowpoint bullet wrapped in a gold-colored sabot. The hollow point is serrated to generate controlled expansion upon impact and a bullet seater is provided in each blister pack to ensure the soft spitzer point is not deformed when loading. The plastic sabot is formulated to take both blackpowder and smokeless pressures. It's a good looking round and early reports from the field indicate it's exceptionally lethal. Also new this year are several new sabot shotgun slugs and a full range of non-lethal law enforcement and wildlife control loads. Most important may be Lightfield's well-written instructional guides on benchresting and sighting in a slug gun, and analyzing recovered muzzleloading sabots to fine-tune your load. www.lightfieldslugs.com and www.lightfieldlesslethal.com

Midway

Do you have a vintage 12-gauge side-by-side that would be pleasant and safe to shoot with a low-pressure shell? Midway has the shell. Loaded by Federal to Midway's specifications, the 12-gauge/2¾" shell features ⅞ oz. of #7½ shot at 1200 fps. The chamber pressure is a mild 5,000 pounds and recoil is equally as light. The shell would be a great practice round in any 12-gauge gun and is ideal for recoil-sensitive shooters. Available by the case, see it at www.midway-usa.com.

Norma

Norma fields its "African PH" series of big game ammunition. Featuring FMJ and SP Woodleigh bullets, the new cartridge family includes the 375 H&H, 404 Jeffery, 416 Rigby and Rem. Mag., 450 Rigby, 458 Lott, 470 NE, 500 NE and 505 Gibbs. The "African PH" catalog, featuring stories on a number of past and present professional hunters, is a great read and well worth ordering. In another interesting development, Norma will be bringing out a new 6mm competition cartridge designed by David Tubb. Called the "6XC," the case is based on an improved 22-250 design with minimum case taper and a 30-degree shoulder. The 6XC will be factory loaded with a moly-coated 105-grain Berger bullet loaded to approximately 3000 fps. Norma is considering introducing the 6XC as a hunting cartridge as well, noting its superiority over the 243 Win. www.norma.cc

Nosler

Expanding its highly successful AccuBond line, Nosler is introducing four new bullets: a 130-grain/6.5mm, 130-grain/270, 225-grain/35 and a 250-grain/9.3mm. There's a new 32-grain/20 caliber Ballistic Tip varmint pill and a new 140-grain/6.5mm HPBT target bullet in the line. Nosler continues to expand its brand of custom brass and is cataloguing the 260 Rem., 280 Ackley Improved, 300 H&H and 300 SAUM this year. www.nosler.com

Polywad

Always a fertile center for shotshell innovations, Polywad is introducing the "Gram Crak-R Shell," a buffered shot load, wrapped in a high-sided craft paper shot cup. The results in the 28-gauge and .410 are amazing. With the 28-gauge shell, I was taking doves out to 50 yards this past season while the .410 Crak-R performs more like a 28-gauge. The secret is in the buffer and in the environmentally friendly shotcup that holds the shot together, producing a short shot string and a tight shot pattern with a minimum of aberrant pellets. www.polywad.com

Remington

Having opened the 17-caliber door years ago with their sensational 17 Remington, Big Green has done it again. Necking down the cute-looking 221 Fireball, they're introducing the 17 Remington Fireball with a 20-grain AccuTip-V at 4000 fps in no less than four different model rifles. Another ballistic break-through this year is Wingmaster HD waterfowl, turkey and predator loads. Utilizing their proprietary tungsten-bronze-iron alloy with a pellet density of 12 gm/cc, the new shot is perfectly spherical and offers optimum pattern densities in gauges from 10 through 20. The predator loading in the 3" and 3½"/12 gauge is based on "T" shot at 1300-1350 fps – should be deadly on coyotes at extended ranges. Working with the concept of stair-stepping loads, Remington is offering three different power level loads for the 300 Rem. Ultra Mag. Power Level 1 tames the 300 RUM to 30-'06 level performance; Level 2 to 300 Win. performance; and

Remington's traditional Core-Lokt bullet just got better with the addition of a bonded core.

SSK is the place to look for high-tech specialty bullets.

Level 3 brings out the full power level we buy the 300 RUM for in the first place. Remington states that the point-of-impact of all three power levels is within 2 inches at 200 yards, making scope adjustments unnecessary. In the shotshell slug department, there is a new Managed-Recoil addition featuring a 1 oz./12 ga. Copper Solid Sabot Slug at a mild 1200 fps. Look for Remington Core-Lokt Ultra Bonded component bullets this year in calibers 243 through 338. www.remington.com

Schroeder Bullets

For uncommon custom diameter bullets and brass, always check out Schroeder.

This year he is adding formed brass for the 204 Ruger Rimmed, 223 Rimmed, 222 Mag. Rimmed, 17-357 Maximum, 5.7x28mm Rimmed, 30 Herrett, and 7x61 S&H. New custom bullets include a 60-grain HP in .234" diameter and 225-grain and 250-grain spire points in .356" diameter. If you own a 5mm Rem.

Mag. rifle, Schroeder offers a simple and inexpensive conversion to 5mm centerfire. (619) 423-3523

Sierra Bullets

Meeting the demand for 6.5mm match bullets, Sierra has added a 123-grain HPBT MatchKing to its existing line-up of superb 6.5mm competition projectiles. www.sierrabullets.com

SSK

JD Jones and David Frickie have teamed up to produce a series of unique bullets turned from brass or copper. There are a variety of styles in 6.5mm, 6.8mm, 338, 375, 416, 458, 500, 510, 13mm, 14.5mm, 62 and 95 caliber. If you have a self-designed bullet in mind, Jones and Frickie will get it into CNC production for a modest cost of $300. Working with Michael McCourry, SSK now offers a completely new line of custom 50, 416 and 458 caliber cartridges based on WSM and Rem. Ultra Mag. brass, including a 50-caliber Alaskan cartridge that is giving outstanding performance in the Win. Model 71 and Marlin 1895. Dies, bullets, brass and custom gunsmithing are available through SSK. www.sskindustries.com

Speer

Speer's continued production of "Special Purpose Rifle Bullets" is a blessing shooters should not overlook. In spite of what must be a very limited demand, the "Special Purpose" line includes properly cannelured

bullets for the 218 Bee, 25-20, 7-30 Waters, 30 Carbine and 32-20. Stock up! www.speer-bullets.com

Swift

If you're a 25-caliber shooter, there's a great new bullet in the Scirocco line. It's a streamlined 100-grain boattail spitzer with a high BC of .429. www.swiftbullet.com

Weatherby

Weatherby was the first major company to integrate Nosler Partition bullets into their entire line. They continue to search out and load premium, high-tech component bullets. This year, Barnes Triple-Shock X-Bullet and Nosler's AccuBond bullet are being added across the Weatherby family of high-performance cartridges that already sport the Nosler Partition, Nosler Ballistic Tip and Hornady Interlock bullets. www.weatherby.com

Winchester

Winchester's top-of-the-line ammunition family, the Supreme Elite line, includes a number of firsts this year. The 243 Win and the 243 WSSM have been tipped off with Winchester's finest controlled expansion, bonded core bullet, the 95-grain/XP3. The popular 270 Win. and 270 WSM are also being upgraded with a 130-grain XP3 bullet. Respective velocities

Remington's Wingmaster HD shot is perfectly round, 10 percent denser than lead and 16 percent softer than Premium Hevi-Shot.

Weatherby's focus on premium bullets now includes the Barnes' Triple Shock.

Winchester's Supreme Elite XP3 Sabot Slug is so new its ballistics were not available at print time.

Even the old 30-30 gets a facelift this year with a slightly pointed Ballistic Silvertip ripping out at 2390 fps.

are 3050 fps and 3275 fps. Designed for rifled shotgun bores, there's a striking new XP3/12-gauge shotgun slug featuring a sharp polymer tip, controlled expansion jacket, and a refined sabot. The combination is said to be highly accurate and very flat shooting. As we go to print, the shell's velocity has not been announced. Predator hunters will like the Supreme Elite Xtended Range High Density Coyote 3"/12-gauge load featuring 1⅜ oz of Hi-Density B size pellets. Lots of knockdown power with minimum pelt damage. The 3"/20-gauge is getting some additional octane this year with the introduction of an Xtended Range turkey load packing 1⅛ oz of #5 shot at 1225 fps.

Finally, the premium line features a 3"/12-gauge Xtended Range waterfowl load, loaded with 1⅜ oz of #6 Hi-Density shot. The old 30-30 gets a facelift with a new 150-grain, slightly pointed, Ballistic Silvertip ripping out at 2390 fps. If the full-power 500 S&W seems a bit much for extended target sessions, Winchester has a new reduced recoil load consisting of a 350-grain bullet at 1400 fps. Delivering only ⅓ the recoil of the full-power cartridge, big-bore handgunners should love it. Speaking of reduced recoil, there's a new line of WinLite Low Recoil shotgun ammunition covering target, buckshot and slug applications. Finally, honoring the late John Wayne on what would be

his 100th birthday, Winchester is issuing a limited edition collector's set of ammunition in 44-40, 45 Colt and 30-30 calibers, featuring special headstamps and commemorative packaging. www.winchester.com

Woodleigh

Constructed with pure lead, bonded cores, the Woodleigh line of premium big-game bullets is being expanded this year with an ultra heavy, 240-grain protected point, Weldcore bullet for the 30-'06, 200 and 220-grain PP bullets for the 325 Win., a 400-grain FN for the 500 S&W, and a 450-grain RN in .510" diameter for the 500 Nitro. See the whole line. www.woodleighbullets.com.au

Celebrating the "Duke" legend, Winchester is offering a collector's edition of 44-40, 45 Colt and 30-30 ammunition.

Putting pizzazz in the 20-gauge, Winchester has added an Extended Range turkey load featuring 1⅛ oz of #5s at 1225 fps.

AVERAGE CENTERFIRE RIFLE CARTRIDGE BALLISTICS & PRICES

Many manufacturers do not supply suggested retail prices. Others did not get their pricing to us before press time. All pricing can vary dependent on the exact brand and style of ammo selected and/or the retail outlet from which you make your purchase. Pricing has been rounded to the nearest dollar and represents our best estimate of average pricing. An * after the cartridge means these loads are available with Nosler Partition or Swift A-Frame bullets. Listed pricing may or may not reflect this bullet type. ** = these are packed 50 to box, all others are 20 to box. Wea. Mag.= Weatherby Magnum. Spfd. = Springfield. A-Sq. = A-Square. N.E.=Nitro Express.

Cartridge	Bullet Wgt. Grs.	VELOCITY (fps)					ENERGY (ft. lbs.)					TRAJ. (in.)				Est. Price/ box
		Muzzle	100 yds.	200 yds.	300 yds.	400 yds.	Muzzle	100 yds.	200 yds.	300 yds.	400 yds.	100 yds.	200 yds.	300 yds.	400 yds.	
17, 22																
17 Remington Fireball	20	4000	3380	2840	2360	1930	710	507	358	247	165	1.6	1.5	-2.8	-13.5	NA
17 Remington	25	4040	3284	2644	2086	1606	906	599	388	242	143	+2.0	+1.7	-4.0	-17.0	$17
204 Ruger	32	4225	3632	3114	2652	2234	1268	937	689	500	355	.6	0.0	-4.2	-13.4	NA
204 Ruger	40	3900	3451	3046	2677	2336	1351	1058	824	636	485	.7	0.0	-4.5	-13.9	NA
204 Ruger	45	3625	3188	2792	2428	2093	1313	1015	778	589	438	1.00	0.0	-5.5	-16.9	NA
221 Fireball	50	2800	2137	1580	1180	988	870	507	277	155	109	+0.0	-7.0	-28.0	0.0	$14
22 Hornet	34	3050	2132	1415	1017	852	700	343	151	78	55	+0.0	-6.6	-15.5	-29.9	NA
22 Hornet	35	3100	2278	1601	1135	929	747	403	199	100	67	+2.75	0.0	-16.9	-60.4	NA
22 Hornet	45	2690	2042	1502	1128	948	723	417	225	127	90	+0.0	-7.7	-31.0	0.0	$27**
218 Bee	46	2760	2102	1550	1155	961	788	451	245	136	94	+0.0	-7.2	-29.0	0.0	$46**
222 Remington	40	3600	3117	2673	2269	1911	1151	863	634	457	324	+1.07	0.0	-6.13	-18.9	NA
222 Remington	50	3140	2602	2123	1700	1350	1094	752	500	321	202	+2.0	-0.4	-11.0	-33.0	$11
222 Remington	55	3020	2562	2147	1773	1451	1114	801	563	384	257	+2.0	-0.4	-11.0	-33.0	$12
22 PPC	52	3400	2930	2510	2130	NA	1335	990	730	525	NA	+2.0	1.4	-5.0	0.0	NA
223 Remington	40	3650	3010	2450	1950	1530	1185	805	535	340	265	+2.0	+1.0	-6.0	-22.0	$14
223 Remington	40	3800	3305	2845	2424	2044	1282	970	719	522	371	0.84	0.0	-5.34	-16.6	NA
223 Remington	50	3300	2874	2484	2130	1809	1209	917	685	504	363	1.37	0.0	-7.05	-21.8	NA
223 Remington	52/53	3330	2882	2477	2106	1770	1305	978	722	522	369	+2.0	+0.6	-6.5	-21.5	$14
223 Remington	55	3240	2748	2305	1906	1556	1282	922	649	444	296	+2.0	-0.2	-9.0	-27.0	$12
223 Remington	60	3100	2712	2355	2026	1726	1280	979	739	547	397	+2.0	+0.2	-8.0	-24.7	$16
223 Remington	64	3020	2621	2256	1920	1619	1296	977	723	524	373	+2.0	-0.2	-9.3	-23.0	$14
223 Remington	69	3000	2720	2460	2210	1980	1380	1135	925	750	600	+2.0	+0.8	-5.8	-17.5	$15
223 Remington	75	2790	2554	2330	2119	1926	1296	1086	904	747	617	2.37	0.0	-8.75	-25.1	NA
223 Remington	77	2750	2584	2354	2169	1992	1293	1110	948	804	679	1.93	0.0	-8.2	-23.8	NA
223 WSSM	55	3850	3438	3064	2721	2402	1810	1444	1147	904	704	0.7	0.0	-4.4	-13.6	NA
223 WSSM	64	3600	3144	2732	2356	2011	1841	1404	1061	789	574	1.0	0.0	-5.7	-17.7	NA
222 Rem. Mag.	55	3240	2748	2305	1906	1556	1282	922	649	444	296	+2.0	-0.2	-9.0	-27.0	$14
225 Winchester	55	3570	3066	2616	2208	1838	1556	1148	836	595	412	+2.0	+1.0	-5.0	-20.0	$19
224 Wea. Mag.	55	3650	3192	2780	2403	2057	1627	1244	943	705	516	+2.0	+1.2	-4.0	-17.0	$32
22-250 Rem.	40	4000	3320	2720	2200	1740	1420	980	660	430	265	+2.0	+1.8	-3.0	-16.0	$14
22-250 Rem.	50	3725	3264	2641	2455	2103	1540	1183	896	669	491	0.89	0.0	-5.23	-16.3	NA
22-250 Rem.	52/55	3680	3137	2656	2222	1832	1654	1201	861	603	410	+1.3	0.0	-4.0	-17.0	$13
22-250 Rem.	60	3600	3195	2826	2485	2169	1727	1360	1064	823	627	+2.0	+2.0	-2.4	-12.3	$19
220 Swift	40	4200	3678	3190	2739	2329	1566	1201	904	666	482	+0.51	0.0	-4.0	-12.9	NA
220 Swift	50	3780	3158	2617	2135	1710	1586	1107	760	506	325	+2.0	+1.4	-4.4	-17.9	$20
220 Swift	50	3850	3396	2970	2576	2215	1645	1280	979	736	545	0.74	0.0	-4.84	-15.1	NA
220 Swift	55	3800	3370	2990	2630	2310	1765	1390	1090	850	650	0.8	0.0	-4.7	-14.4	NA
220 Swift	55	3650	3194	2772	2384	2035	1627	1246	939	694	506	+2.0	+2.0	-2.6	-13.4	$19
220 Swift	60	3600	3199	2824	2475	2156	1727	1364	1063	816	619	+2.0	+1.6	-4.1	-13.1	$19
22 Savage H.P.	71	2790	2340	1930	1570	1280	1225	860	585	390	190	+2.0	-1.0	-10.4	-35.7	NA
6mm (24)																
6mm BR Rem.	100	2550	2310	2083	1870	1671	1444	1185	963	776	620	+2.5	-0.6	-11.8	0.0	$22
6mm Norma BR	107	2822	2667	2517	2372	2229	1893	1690	1506	1337	1181	+1.73	0.0	-7.24	-20.6	NA
6mm PPC	70	3140	2750	2400	2070	NA	1535	1175	895	665	NA	+2.0	+1.4	-5.0	0.0	NA
243 Winchester	55	4025	3597	3209	2853	2525	1978	1579	1257	994	779	+0.6	0.0	-4.0	-12.2	NA
243 Winchester	60	3600	3110	2660	2260	1890	1725	1285	945	680	475	+2.0	+1.8	-3.3	-15.5	$17
243 Winchester	70	3400	3040	2700	2390	2100	1795	1435	1135	890	685	1.1	0.0	-5.9	-18.0	NA
243 Winchester	75/80	3350	2955	2593	2259	1951	1993	1551	1194	906	676	+2.0	+0.9	-5.0	-19.0	$16
243 Winchester	85	3320	3070	2830	2600	2380	2080	1770	1510	1280	1070	+2.0	+1.2	-4.0	-14.0	$18
243 Winchester	90	3120	2871	2635	2411	2199	1946	1647	1388	1162	966	1.4	0.0	-6.4	-18.8	NA
243 Winchester*	100	2960	2697	2449	2215	1993	1945	1615	1332	1089	882	+2.5	+1.2	-6.0	-20.0	$16
243 Winchester	105	2920	2689	2470	2261	2062	1988	1686	1422	1192	992	+2.5	+1.6	-5.0	-18.4	$21
243 Light Mag.	100	3100	2839	2592	2358	2138	2133	1790	1491	1235	1014	+1.5	0.0	-6.8	-19.8	NA
243 WSSM	55	4060	3628	3237	2880	2550	2013	1607	1280	1013	794	0.6	0.0	-3.9	-12.0	NA
243 WSSM	95	3250	3000	2763	2538	2325	2258	1898	1610	1359	1140	1.2	0.0	-5.7	-16.9	NA
243 WSSM	100	3110	2838	2583	2341	2112	2147	1789	1481	1217	991	1.4	0.0	-6.6	-19.7	NA
6mm Remington	80	3470	3064	2694	2352	2036	2139	1667	1289	982	736	+2.0	+1.1	-5.0	-17.0	$16
6mm Remington	100	3100	2829	2573	2332	2104	2133	1777	1470	1207	983	+2.5	+1.6	-5.0	-17.0	$16
6mm Remington	105	3060	2822	2596	2381	2177	2105	1788	1512	1270	1059	+2.5	+1.1	-3.3	-15.0	$21
6mm Rem. Light Mag.	100	3250	2997	2756	2528	2311	2345	1995	1687	1418	1186	1.59	0.0	-6.33	-18.3	NA
6.17(.243) Spitfire	100	3350	3122	2905	2698	2501	2493	2164	1874	1617	1389	2.4	3.20	0.0	-8.0	NA
240 Wea. Mag.	87	3500	3202	2924	2663	2416	2366	1980	1651	1370	1127	+2.0	+2.0	-2.0	-12.0	$32
240 Wea. Mag.	100	3395	3106	2835	2581	2339	2559	2142	1785	1478	1215	+2.5	+2.8	-2.0	-11.0	$43
25																
25-20 Win.	86	1460	1194	1030	931	858	407	272	203	165	141	0.0	-23.5	0.0	0.0	$32**
25-35 Win.	117	2230	1866	1545	1282	1097	1292	904	620	427	313	+2.5	-4.2	-26.0	0.0	$24
250 Savage	100	2820	2504	2210	1936	1684	1765	1392	1084	832	630	+2.5	+0.4	-9.0	-28.0	$17
257 Roberts	100	2980	2661	2363	2085	1827	1972	1572	1240	965	741	+2.5	-0.8	-5.2	-21.6	$20
257 Roberts+P	117	2780	2411	2071	1761	1488	2009	1511	1115	806	576	+2.5	-0.2	-10.2	-32.6	$18

Many manufacturers do not supply suggested retail prices. Others did not get their pricing to us before press time. All pricing can vary dependent on the exact brand and style of ammo selected and/or the retail outlet from which you make your purchase. Pricing has been rounded to the nearest dollar and represents our best estimate of average pricing. An * after the cartridge means these loads are available with Nosler Partition or Swift A-Frame bullets. Listed pricing may or may not reflect this bullet type. ** = these are packed 50 to box, all others are 20 to box. Wea. Mag.= Weatherby Magnum. Spfd. = Springfield. A-Sq. = A-Square. N.E.=Nitro Express.

Cartridge	Bullet Wgt. Grs.	VELOCITY (fps) Muzzle	100 yds.	200 yds.	300 yds.	400 yds.	ENERGY (ft. lbs.) Muzzle	100 yds.	200 yds.	300 yds.	400 yds.	TRAJ. (in.) 100 yds.	200 yds.	300 yds.	400 yds.	Est. Price/ box
257 Roberts+P	120	2780	2560	2360	2160	1970	2060	1750	1480	1240	1030	+2.5	+1.2	-6.4	-23.6	$22
257 Roberts	122	2600	2331	2078	1842	1625	1831	1472	1169	919	715	+2.5	0.0	-10.6	-31.4	$21
257 Light Mag.	117	2940	2694	2460	2240	2031	2245	1885	1572	1303	1071	+1.7	0.0	-7.6	-21.8	NA
25-06 Rem.	87	3440	2995	2591	2222	1884	2286	1733	1297	954	686	+2.0	+1.1	-2.5	-14.4	$17
25-06 Rem.	90	3440	3043	2680	2344	2034	2364	1850	1435	1098	827	+2.0	+1.8	-3.3	-15.6	$17
25-06 Rem.	100	3230	2893	2580	2287	2014	2316	1858	1478	1161	901	+2.0	+0.8	-5.7	-18.9	$17
25-06 Rem.	117	2990	2770	2570	2370	2190	2320	2000	1715	1465	1246	+2.5	+1.0	-7.9	-26.6	$19
25-06 Rem.*	120	2990	2730	2484	2252	2032	2382	1985	1644	1351	1100	+2.5	+1.2	-5.3	-19.6	$17
25-06 Rem.	122	2930	2706	2492	2289	2095	2325	1983	1683	1419	1189	+2.5	+1.8	-4.5	-17.5	$23
25 WSSM	85	3470	3156	2863	2589	2331	2273	1880	1548	1266	1026	1.0	0.0	-5.2	-15.7	NA
25 WSSM	115	3060	284	2639	2442	2254	2392	2066	1778	1523	1398	1.4	0.0	-6.4	-18.6	NA
25 WSSM	120	2990	2717	2459	2216	1987	2383	1967	1612	1309	1053	1.6	0.0	-7.4	-21.8	NA
257 Wea. Mag.	87	3825	3456	3118	2805	2513	2826	2308	1870	1520	1220	+2.0	+2.7	-0.3	-7.6	$32
257 Wea. Mag.	100	3555	3237	2941	2665	2404	2806	2326	1920	1576	1283	+2.5	+3.2	0.0	-8.0	$32
257 Scramjet	100	3745	3450	3173	2912	2666	3114	2643	2235	1883	1578	+2.1	+2.77	0.0	-6.93	NA
6.5																
6.5x47 Lapua	123	2887	NA	2554	NA	2244	2285	NA	1788	NA	1380	NA	4.53	0.00	-10.7	NA
6.5x50mm Jap.	139	2360	2160	1970	1790	1620	1720	1440	1195	985	810	+2.5	-1.0	-13.5	0.0	NA
6.5x50mm Jap.	156	2070	1830	1610	1430	1260	1475	1155	900	695	550	+2.5	-4.0	-23.8	0.0	NA
6.5x52mm Car.	139	2580	2360	2160	1970	1790	2045	1725	1440	1195	985	+2.5	0.0	-9.9	-29.0	NA
6.5x52mm Car.	156	2430	2170	1930	1700	1500	2045	1630	1285	1005	780	+2.5	-1.0	-13.9	0.0	NA
6.5x52mm Carcano	160	2250	1963	1700	1467	1271	1798	1369	1027	764	574	+3.8	0.0	-15.9	-48.1	NA
6.5x55mm Light Mag.	129	2750	2549	2355	2171	1994	2166	1860	1589	1350	1139	+2.0	0.0	-8.2	-23.9	NA
6.5x55mm Swe.	140	2550	NA	NA	NA	NA	2020	NA	NA	NA	NA	0.0	0.0	0.0	0.0	$18
6.5x55mm Swe.*	139/140	2850	2640	2440	2250	2070	2525	2170	1855	1575	1330	+2.5	+1.6	-5.4	-18.9	$18
6.5x55mm Swe.	156	2650	2370	2110	1870	1650	2425	1950	1550	1215	945	+2.5	0.0	-10.3	-30.6	NA
260 Remington	125	2875	2669	2473	2285	2105	2294	1977	1697	1449	1230	1.71	0.0	-7.4	-21.4	NA
260 Remington	140	2750	2544	2347	2158	1979	2351	2011	1712	1448	1217	+2.2	0.0	-8.6	-24.6	NA
6.5-284 Norma	142	3025	2890	2758	2631	2507	2886	2634	2400	2183	1982	1.13	0.0	-5.7	-16.4	NA
6.71 (264) Phantom	120	3150	2929	2718	2517	2325	2645	2286	1969	1698	1440	+1.3	0.0	-6.0	-17.5	NA
6.5 Rem. Mag.	120	3210	2905	2621	2353	2102	2745	2248	1830	1475	1177	+2.5	+1.7	-4.1	-16.3	Disc.
264 Win. Mag.	140	3030	2782	2548	2326	2114	2854	2406	2018	1682	1389	+2.5	+1.4	-5.1	-18.0	$24
6.71 (264) Blackbird	140	3480	3261	3053	2855	2665	3766	3307	2899	2534	2208	+2.4	+3.1	0.0	-7.4	NA
6.8mm Rem.	115	2775	2472	2190	1926	1683	1966	1561	1224	947	723	+2.1	0.0	-3.7	-9.4	NA
27																
270 Winchester	100	3430	3021	2649	2305	1988	2612	2027	1557	1179	877	+2.0	+1.0	-4.9	-17.5	$17
270 Win. (Rem.)	115	2710	2482	2265	2059	NA	1875	1485	1161	896	NA	0.0	4.8	-17.3	0.0	NA
270 Winchester	130	3060	2776	2510	2259	2022	2702	2225	1818	1472	1180	+2.5	+1.4	-5.3	-18.2	$17
270 Win. Supreme	130	3150	2881	2628	2388	2161	2865	2396	1993	1646	1348	1.3	0.0	-6.4	-18.9	NA
270 Winchester	135	3000	2780	2570	2369	2178	2697	2315	1979	1682	1421	+2.5	+1.4	-6.0	-17.6	$23
270 Winchester*	140	2940	2700	2480	2260	2060	2685	2270	1905	1590	1315	+2.5	+1.8	-4.6	-17.9	$20
270 Win. Light Magnum	130	3215	2998	2790	2590	2400	2983	2594	2246	1936	1662	1.21	0.0	-5.83	-17.0	NA
270 Winchester*	150	2850	2585	2336	2100	1879	2705	2226	1817	1468	1175	+2.5	+1.2	-6.5	-22.0	$17
270 Win. Supreme	150	2930	2693	2468	2254	2051	2860	2416	2030	1693	1402	1.7	0.0	-7.4	-21.6	NA
270 WSM	130	3275	3041	2820	2609	2408	3096	2669	2295	1564	1673	1.1	0.0	-5.5	-16.1	NA
270 WSM	140	3125	2865	2619	2386	2165	3035	2559	2132	1769	1457	1.4	0.0	-6.5	-19.0	NA
270 WSM	150	3120	2923	2734	2554	2380	3242	2845	2490	2172	1886	1.3	0.0	-5.9	-17.2	NA
270 Wea. Mag.	100	3760	3380	3033	2712	2412	3139	2537	2042	1633	1292	+2.0	+2.4	-1.2	-10.1	$32
270 Wea. Mag.	130	3375	3119	2878	2649	2432	3287	2808	2390	2026	1707	+2.5	-2.9	-0.9	-9.9	$32
270 Wea. Mag.*	150	3245	3036	2837	2647	2465	3507	3070	2681	2334	2023	+2.5	+2.6	-1.8	-11.4	$47
7mm																
7mm BR	140	2216	2012	1821	1643	1481	1525	1259	1031	839	681	+2.0	-3.7	-20.0	0.0	$23
7mm Mauser*	139/140	2660	2435	2221	2018	1827	2199	1843	1533	1266	1037	+2.5	0.0	-9.6	-27.7	$17
7mm Mauser	145	2690	2442	2206	1985	1777	2334	1920	1568	1268	1017	+2.5	+0.1	-9.6	-28.3	$18
7mm Mauser	154	2690	2490	2300	2120	1940	2475	2120	1810	1530	1285	+2.5	+0.8	-7.5	-23.5	$17
7mm Mauser	175	2440	2137	1857	1603	1382	2313	1774	1340	998	742	+2.5	-1.7	-16.1	-1.0	$17
7x57 Light Mag.	139	2970	2730	2503	2287	2082	2722	2301	1933	1614	1337	+1.6	0.0	-7.2	-21.0	NA
7x30 Waters	120	2700	2300	1930	1600	1330	1940	1405	990	685	470	+2.5	-0.2	-12.3	0.0	$18
7mm-08 Rem.	120	3000	2725	2467	2223	1992	2398	1979	1621	1316	1058	+2.0	0.0	-7.6	-22.3	$18
7mm-08 Rem.*	140	2860	2625	2402	2189	1988	2542	2142	1793	1490	1228	+2.5	+0.8	-6.9	-21.9	$18
7mm-08 Rem.	154	2715	2510	2315	2128	1950	2520	2155	1832	1548	1300	+2.5	+1.0	-7.0	-22.7	$23
7mm-08 Light Mag.	139	3000	2790	2590	2399	2216	2777	2403	2071	1776	1515	+1.5	0.0	-6.7	-19.4	NA
7x64mm Bren.	140				Not Yet Announced											$17
7x64mm Bren.	154	2820	2610	2420	2230	2050	2720	2335	1995	1695	1430	+2.5	+1.4	-5.7	-19.9	NA
7x64mm Bren.*	160	2850	2669	2495	2327	2166	2885	2530	2211	1924	1667	+2.5	+1.6	-4.8	-17.8	$24
7x64mm Bren.	175				Not Yet Announced											$17
284 Winchester	150	2860	2595	2344	2108	1886	2724	2243	1830	1480	1185	+2.5	+0.8	-7.3	-23.2	$24
280 Remington	120	3150	2866	2599	2348	2110	2643	2188	1800	1468	1186	+2.0	+0.6	-6.0	-17.9	$17
280 Remington	140	3000	2758	2528	2309	2102	2797	2363	1986	1657	1373	+2.5	+1.4	-5.2	-18.3	$17
280 Remington*	150	2890	2624	2373	2135	1912	2781	2293	1875	1518	1217	+2.5	+0.8	-7.1	-22.6	$17

Many manufacturers do not supply suggested retail prices. Others did not get their pricing to us before press time. All pricing can vary dependent on the exact brand and style of ammo selected and/or the retail outlet from which you make your purchase. Pricing has been rounded to the nearest dollar and represents our best estimate of average pricing. An * after the cartridge means these loads are available with Nosler Partition or Swift A-Frame bullets. Listed pricing may or may not reflect this bullet type. ** = these are packed 50 to box, all others are 20 to box. Wea. Mag.= Weatherby Magnum. Spfd. = Springfield. A-Sq. = A-Square. N.E.=Nitro Express.

Cartridge	Bullet Wgt. Grs.	VELOCITY (fps)					ENERGY (ft. lbs.)					TRAJ. (in.)				Est. Price/ box
		Muzzle	100 yds.	200 yds.	300 yds.	400 yds.	Muzzle	100 yds.	200 yds.	300 yds.	400 yds.	100 yds.	200 yds.	300 yds.	400 yds.	
280 Remington	160	2840	2637	2442	2556	2078	2866	2471	2120	1809	1535	+2.5	+0.8	-6.7	-21.0	$20
280 Remington	165	2820	2510	2220	1950	1701	2913	2308	1805	1393	1060	+2.5	+0.4	-8.8	-26.5	$17
7x61mm S&H Sup.	154	3060	2720	2400	2100	1820	3200	2520	1965	1505	1135	+2.5	+1.8	-5.0	-19.8	NA
7mm Dakota	160	3200	3001	2811	2630	2455	3637	3200	2808	2456	2140	+2.1	+1.9	-2.8	-12.5	NA
7mm Rem. Mag. (Rem.)	140	2710	2482	2265	2059	NA	2283	1915	1595	1318	NA	0.0	-4.5	-1.57	0.0	NA
7mm Rem. Mag.*	139/140	3150	2930	2710	2510	2320	3085	2660	2290	1960	1670	+2.5	+2.4	-2.4	-12.7	$21
7mm Rem. Hvy Mag	139	3250	3044	2847	2657	2475	3259	2860	2501	2178	1890	1.1	0.0	-5.5	-16.2	NA
7mm Rem. Mag.	150/154	3110	2830	2568	2320	2085	3221	2667	2196	1792	1448	+2.5	+1.6	-4.6	-16.5	$21
7mm Rem. Mag.*	160/162	2950	2730	2520	2320	2120	3090	2650	2250	1910	1600	+2.5	+1.8	-4.4	-17.8	$34
7mm Rem. Mag.	165	2900	2699	2507	2324	2147	3081	2669	2303	1978	1689	+2.5	+1.2	-5.9	-19.0	$28
7mm Rem Mag.	175	2860	2645	2440	2244	2057	3178	2718	2313	1956	1644	+2.5	+1.0	-6.5	-20.7	$21
7mm Rem. SA ULTRA MAG	140	3175	2934	2707	2490	2283	3033	2676	2277	1927	1620	1.3	0.0	-6	-17.7	NA
7mm Rem. SA ULTRA MAG	150	3110	2828	2563	2313	2077	3221	2663	2188	1782	1437	2.5	2.1	-3.6	-15.8	NA
7mm Rem. SA ULTRA MAG	160	2960	2762	2572	2390	2215	3112	2709	2350	2029	1743	2.6	2.2	-3.6	-15.4	NA
7mm Rem. WSM	140	3225	3008	2801	2603	2414	3233	2812	2438	2106	1812	1.2	0.0	-5.6	-16.4	NA
7mm Rem. WSM	160	2990	2744	2512	2081	1883	3176	2675	2241	1864	1538	1.6	0.0	-7.1	-20.8	NA
7mm Wea. Mag.	140	3225	2970	2729	2501	2283	3233	2741	2315	1943	1621	+2.5	+2.0	-3.2	-14.0	$35
7mm Wea. Mag.	154	3260	3023	2799	2586	2382	3539	3044	2609	2227	1890	+2.5	+2.8	-1.5	-10.8	$32
7mm Wea. Mag.*	160	3200	3004	2816	2637	2464	3637	3205	2817	2469	2156	+2.5	+2.7	-1.5	-10.6	$47
7mm Wea. Mag.	165	2950	2747	2553	2367	2189	3188	2765	2388	2053	1756	+2.5	+1.8	-4.2	-16.4	$43
7mm Wea. Mag.	175	2910	2693	2486	2288	2098	3293	2818	2401	2033	1711	+2.5	+1.2	-5.9	-19.4	$35
7.21(.284) Tomahawk	140	3300	3118	2943	2774	2612	3386	3022	2693	2393	2122	2.3	3.20	0.0	-7.7	NA
7mm STW	140	3325	3064	2818	2585	2364	3436	2918	2468	2077	1737	+2.3	+1.8	-3.0	-13.1	NA
7mm STW Supreme	160	3150	2894	2652	2422	2204	3526	2976	2499	2085	1727	1.3	0.0	-6.3	-18.5	NA
7mm Rem. Ultra Mag.	140	3425	3184	2956	2740	2534	3646	3151	2715	2333	1995	1.7	1.60	-2.6	-11.4	NA
7mm Firehawk	140	3625	3373	3135	2909	2695	4084	3536	3054	2631	2258	+2.2	+2.9	0.0	-7.03	NA
30																
7.21 (.284) Firebird	140	3750	3522	3306	3101	2905	4372	3857	3399	2990	2625	1.6	2.4	0.0	-6.0	NA
30 Carbine	110	1990	1567	1236	1035	923	977	600	373	262	208	0.0	-13.5	0.0	0.0	$28**
303 Savage	190	1890	1612	1327	1183	1055	1507	1096	794	591	469	+2.5	-7.6	0.0	0.0	$24
30 Remington	170	2120	1822	1555	1328	1153	1696	1253	913	666	502	+2.5	-4.7	-26.3	0.0	$20
7.62x39mm Rus.	123/125	2300	2030	1780	1550	1350	1445	1125	860	655	500	+2.5	-2.0	-17.5	0.0	$13
30-30 Win.	55	3400	2693	2085	1570	1187	1412	886	521	301	172	+2.0	0.0	-10.2	-35.0	$18
30-30 Win.	125	2570	2090	1660	1320	1080	1830	1210	770	480	320	-2.0	-2.6	-19.9	0.0	$13
30-30 Win.	150	2390	2040	1723	1447	1225	1902	1386	989	697	499	0.0	-7.5	-27.0	-63.0	NA
30-30 Win. Supreme	150	2480	2095	1747	1446	1209	2049	1462	1017	697	487	0.0	-6.5	-24.5	0.0	NA
30-30 Win.	160	2300	1997	1719	1473	1268	1879	1416	1050	771	571	+2.5	-2.9	-20.2	0.0	$18
30-30 Win. Lever Evolution	160	2400	2150	1916	1699	NA	2046	1643	1304	1025	NA	3.00	0.20	-12.1	NA	NA
30-30 PMC Cowboy	170	1300	1198	1121			638	474				0.0	-27.0	0.0	0.0	NA
30-30 Win.*	170	2200	1895	1619	1381	1191	1827	1355	989	720	535	+2.5	-5.8	-23.6	0.0	$13
300 Savage	150	2630	2354	2094	1853	1631	2303	1845	1462	1143	886	+2.5	-0.4	-10.1	-30.7	$17
300 Savage	180	2350	2137	1935	1754	1570	2207	1825	1496	1217	985	+2.5	-1.6	-15.2	0.0	$17
30-40 Krag	180	2430	2213	2007	1813	1632	2360	1957	1610	1314	1064	+2.5	-1.4	-13.8	0.0	$18
7.65x53mm Arg.	180	2590	2390	2200	2010	1830	2685	2280	1925	1615	1345	+2.5	0.0	-27.6	0.0	NA
7.5x53mm Argentine	150	2785	2519	2269	2032	1814	2583	2113	1714	1376	1096	+2.0	0.0	-8.8	-25.5	NA
308 Marlin Express	160	2660	2430	2226	2026	1836	2513	2111	1761	1457	1197	3.0	1.7	-6.7	-23.5	NA
307 Winchester	150	2760	2321	1924	1575	1289	2530	1795	1233	826	554	+2.5	-1.5	-13.6	0.0	Disc.
307 Winchester	180	2510	2179	1874	1599	1362	2519	1898	1404	1022	742	+2.5	-1.6	-15.6	0.0	$20
7.5x55 Swiss	180	2650	2450	2250	2060	1880	2805	2390	2020	1700	1415	+2.5	+0.6	-8.1	-24.9	NA
7.5x55mm Swiss	165	2720	2515	2319	2132	1954	2710	2317	1970	1665	1398	+2.0	0.0	-8.5	-24.6	NA
308 Winchester	55	3770	3215	2726	2286	1888	1735	1262	907	638	435	-2.0	+1.4	-3.8	-15.8	$22
308 Winchester	150	2820	2533	2263	2009	1774	2648	2137	1705	1344	1048	+2.5	+0.4	-8.5	-26.1	$17
308 Winchester	165	2700	2440	2194	1963	1748	2670	2180	1763	1411	1199	+2.5	0.0	-9.7	-28.5	$20
308 Winchester	168	2680	2493	2314	2143	1979	2678	2318	1998	1713	1460	+2.5	0.0	-8.9	-25.3	$18
308 Win. (Fed.)	170	2000	1740	1510	NA	NA	1510	1145	860	NA	NA	0.0	0.0	0.0	0.0	NA
308 Winchester	178	2620	2415	2220	2034	1857	2713	2306	1948	1635	1363	+2.5	0.0	-9.6	-27.6	$23
308 Winchester*	180	2620	2393	2178	1974	1782	2743	2288	1896	1557	1269	+2.5	-0.2	-10.2	-28.5	$17
308 Light Mag.*	150	2980	2703	2442	2195	1964	2959	2433	1986	1606	1285	+1.6	0.0	-7.5	-22.2	NA
308 Light Mag.	165	2870	2658	2456	2263	2078	3019	2589	2211	1877	1583	+1.7	0.0	-7.5	-21.8	NA
308 High Energy	165	2870	2600	2350	2120	1890	3020	2485	2030	1640	1310	+1.8	0.0	-8.2	-24.0	NA
308 Light Mag.	168	2870	2658	2456	2263	2078	3019	2589	2211	1877	1583	+1.7	0.0	-7.5	-21.8	NA
308 High Energy	180	2740	2550	2370	2200	2030	3000	2600	2245	1925	1645	+1.9	0.0	-8.2	-23.5	NA
30-06 Spfd.	55	4080	3485	2965	2502	2083	2033	1483	1074	764	530	+2.0	+1.9	-2.1	-11.7	$22
30-06 Spfd. (Rem.)	125	2660	2335	2034	1757	NA	1964	1513	1148	856	NA	0.0	-5.2	-18.9	0.0	NA
30-06 Spfd.	125	3140	2780	2447	2138	1853	2736	2145	1662	1279	953	+2.0	+1.0	-6.2	-21.0	$17
30-06 Spfd.	150	2910	2617	2342	2083	1853	2820	2281	1827	1445	1135	+2.5	+0.8	-7.2	-23.4	$17
30-06 Spfd.	152	2910	2654	2413	2184	1968	2858	2378	1965	1610	1307	+2.5	+1.0	-6.6	-21.3	$23
30-06 Spfd.*	165	2800	2534	2283	2047	1825	2872	2352	1909	1534	1220	+2.5	+0.4	-8.4	-25.5	$17
30-06 Spfd.	168	2710	2522	2346	2169	2003	2739	2372	2045	1754	1497	+2.5	+0.4	-8.0	-23.5	$18
30-06 Spfd. (Fed.)	170	2000	1740	1510	NA	NA	1510	1145	860	NA	NA	0.0	0.0	0.0	0.0	NA

Many manufacturers do not supply suggested retail prices. Others did not get their pricing to us before press time. All pricing can vary dependent on the exact brand and style of ammo selected and/or the retail outlet from which you make your purchase. Pricing has been rounded to the nearest dollar and represents our best estimate of average pricing. An * after the cartridge means these loads are available with Nosler Partition or Swift A-Frame bullets. Listed pricing may or may not reflect this bullet type. ** = these are packed 50 to box, all others are 20 to box. Wea. Mag.= Weatherby Magnum. Spfd. = Springfield. A-Sq. = A-Square. N.E.=Nitro Express.

Cartridge	Bullet Wgt. Grs.	VELOCITY (fps)					ENERGY (ft. lbs.)					TRAJ. (in.)				Est. Price/ box
		Muzzle	100 yds.	200 yds.	300 yds.	400 yds.	Muzzle	100 yds.	200 yds.	300 yds.	400 yds.	100 yds.	200 yds.	300 yds.	400 yds.	
30 -06 Spfd.	178	2720	2511	2311	2121	1939	2924	2491	2111	1777	1486	+2.5	+0.4	-8.2	-24.6	$23
30 -06 Spfd.*	180	2700	2469	2250	2042	1846	2913	2436	2023	1666	1362	-2.5	0.0	-9.3	-27.0	$17
30 -06 Spfd.	220	2410	2130	1870	1632	1422	2837	2216	1708	1301	988	+2.5	-1.7	-18.0	0.0	$17
30 Mag.																
30-06 Light Mag.	150	3100	2815	2548	2295	2058	3200	2639	2161	1755	1410	+1.4	0.0	-6.8	-20.3	NA
30-06 Light Mag.	180	2880	2676	2480	2293	2114	3316	2862	2459	2102	1786	+1.7	0.0	-7.3	-21.3	NA
30-06 High Energy	180	2880	2690	2500	2320	2150	3315	2880	2495	2150	1845	+1.7	0.0	-7.2	-21.0	NA
30 T/C	150	3000	2772	2555	2348	2151	2997	2558	2173	1836	1540	1.5	0.0	-6.9	-20.0	NA
30 T/C	165	2850	2644	2447	2258	2078	2975	2560	2193	1868	1582	1.7	0.0	-7.6	-22.0	NA
300 REM SA ULTRA MAG	150	3200	2901	2622	2359	2112	3410	2803	2290	1854	1485	1.3	0.0	-6.4	-19.1	NA
300 REM SA ULTRA MAG	165	3075	2792	2527	2276	2040	3464	2856	2339	1898	1525	1.5	0.0	-7	-20.7	NA
300 REM SA ULTRA MAG	180	2960	2761	2571	2389	2214	3501	3047	2642	2280	1959	2.6	2.2	-3.6	-15.4	NA
7.82 (308) Patriot	150	3250	2999	2762	2537	2323	3519	2997	2542	2145	1798	+1.2	0.0	-5.8	-16.9	NA
300 WSM	150	3300	3061	2834	2619	2414	3628	3121	2676	2285	1941	1.1	0.0	-5.4	-15.9	NA
300 WSM	180	2970	2741	2524	2317	2120	3526	3005	2547	2147	1797	1.6	0.0	-7.0	-20.5	NA
300 WSM	180	3010	2923	2734	2554	2380	3242	2845	2490	2172	1886	1.3	0	-5.9	-17.2	NA
308 Norma Mag.	180	3020	2820	2630	2440	2270	3645	3175	2755	2385	2050	+2.5	+2.0	-3.5	-14.8	NA
300 Dakota	200	3000	2824	2656	2493	2336	3996	3542	3131	2760	2423	+2.2	+1.5	-4.0	-15.2	NA
300 H&H Magnum*	180	2880	2640	2412	2196	1990	3315	2785	2325	1927	1583	+2.5	+0.8	-6.8	-21.7	$24
300 H&H Magnum	220	2550	2267	2002	1757	NA	3167	2510	1958	1508	NA	-2.5	-0.4	-12.0	0.0	$24
300 Win. Mag.	150	3290	2951	2636	2342	2068	3605	2900	2314	1827	1424	+2.5	+1.9	-3.8	-15.8	$22
300 Win. Mag.	165	3100	2877	2665	2462	2269	3522	3033	2603	2221	1897	+2.5	+2.4	-3.0	-16.9	$24
300 Win. Mag.	178	2900	2760	2568	2375	2191	3509	3030	2606	2230	1897	+2.5	+1.4	-5.0	-17.6	$29
300 Win. Mag.*	180	2960	2745	2540	2344	2157	3501	3011	2578	2196	1859	+2.5	+1.2	-5.5	-18.5	$22
300 W.M. High Energy	180	3100	2830	2580	2340	2110	3840	3205	2660	2190	1790	+1.4	0.0	-6.6	-19.7	NA
300 W.M. Light Mag.	180	3100	2879	2668	2467	2275	3840	3313	2845	2431	2068	+1.39	0.0	-6.45	-18.7	NA
300 Win. Mag.	190	2885	1691	2506	2327	2156	3511	3055	2648	2285	1961	+2.5	+1.2	-5.7	-19.0	$26
300 W.M. High Energy	200	2930	2740	2550	2370	2200	3810	3325	2885	2495	2145	+1.6	0.0	-6.6	-20.1	NA
300 Win. Mag.*	200	2825	2595	2376	2167	1970	3545	2991	2508	2086	1742	-2.5	+1.6	-4.7	-17.2	$36
300 Win. Mag.	220	2680	2448	2228	2020	1823	3508	2927	2424	1993	1623	+2.5	0.0	-9.5	-27.5	$23
300 Rem. Ultra Mag.	150	3450	3208	2980	2762	2556	3964	3427	2956	2541	2175	1.7	1.5	-2.6	-11.2	NA
300 Rem. Ultra Mag.	150	2910	2686	2473	2279	2077	2820	2403	2037	1716	1436	1.7	0.0	-7.4	-21.5	NA
300 Rem. Ultra Mag.	180	3250	3037	2834	2640	2454	4221	3686	3201	2786	2407	2.4	0.0	-3.0	-12.7	NA
300 Rem. Ultra Mag.	180	2960	2774	2505	2294	2093	3501	2971	2508	2103	1751	2.7	2.2	-3.8	-16.4	NA
300 Rem. Ultra Mag.	200	3032	2791	2562	2345	2138	4083	3459	2916	2442	2030	1.5	0.0	-6.8	-19.9	NA
300 Wea. Mag.	100	3900	3441	3038	2652	2305	3714	2891	2239	1717	1297	+2.0	+2.6	-0.6	-8.7	$32
300 Wea. Mag.	150	3600	3307	3033	2776	2533	4316	3642	3064	2566	2137	+2.5	+3.2	0.0	-8.1	$32
300 Wea. Mag.	165	3450	3210	3000	2792	2593	4360	3796	3297	2855	2464	+2.5	+3.2	0.0	-7.8	NA
300 Wea. Mag.	178	3120	2902	2695	2497	2308	3847	3329	2870	2464	2104	+2.5	-1.7	-3.6	-14.7	$43
300 Wea. Mag.	180	3330	3110	2910	2710	2520	4430	3875	3375	2935	2540	+1.0	0.0	-5.2	-15.1	NA
300 Wea. Mag.	190	3030	2830	2638	2455	2279	3873	3378	2936	2542	2190	+2.5	+1.6	-4.3	-16.0	$38
300 Wea. Mag.	220	2850	2541	2283	1964	1736	3967	3155	2480	1922	1471	+2.5	+0.4	-8.5	-26.4	$35
300 Warbird	180	3400	3180	2971	2772	2582	4620	4042	3528	3071	2664	+2.59	+3.25	0.0	-7.95	NA
300 Pegasus	180	3500	3319	3145	2978	2817	4896	4401	3953	3544	3172	+2.28	+2.89	0.0	-6.79	NA
31																
32-20 Win.	100	1210	1021	913	834	769	325	231	185	154	131	0.0	-32.3	0.0	0.0	$23**
303 British	150	2685	2441	2210	1992	1787	2401	1984	1627	1321	1064	+2.5	+0.6	-8.4	-26.2	$18
303 British	180	2460	2124	1817	1542	1311	2418	1803	1319	950	687	+2.5	-1.8	-16.8	0.0	$18
303 Light Mag.	150	2830	2570	2325	2094	1884	2667	2199	1800	1461	1185	+2.0	0.0	-8.4	-24.6	NA
7.62x54mm Rus.	146	2950	2730	2520	2320	NA	2820	2415	2055	1740	NA	+2.5	+2.0	-4.4	-17.7	NA
7.62x54mm Rus.	180	2580	2370	2180	2000	1820	2650	2250	1900	1590	1100	+2.5	0.0	-9.8	-28.5	NA
7.7x58mm Jap.	150	2640	2399	2170	1954	1752	2321	1916	1568	1271	1022	+2.3	0.0	-9.7	-28.5	NA
7.7x58mm Jap.	180	2500	2300	2100	1920	1750	2490	2105	1770	1475	1225	+2.5	0.0	-10.4	-30.2	NA
8x56 R	205	2400	2188	1987	1797	1621	2621	2178	1796	1470	1196	+2.9	0.0	-11.7	-34.3	NA
8mm																
8x57mm JS Mau.	165	2850	2520	2210	1930	1670	2965	2330	1795	1360	1015	+2.5	+1.0	-7.7	0.0	NA
32 Win. Special	170	2250	1921	1626	1372	1175	1911	1393	998	710	521	+2.5	-3.5	-22.9	0.0	$14
8mm Mauser	170	2360	1969	1622	1333	1123	2102	1464	993	671	476	+2.5	-3.1	-22.2	0.0	$18
325 WSM	180	3060	2841	2632	2432	2242	3743	3226	2769	2365	2009	+1.4	0.0	-6.4	-18.7	NA
325 WSM	200	2950	2753	2565	2384	2210	3866	3367	2922	2524	2170	+1.5	0.0	-6.8	-19.8	NA
325 WSM	220	2840	2605	2382	2169	1968	3941	3316	2772	2300	1893	+1.8	0.0	-8.0	-23.3	NA
8mm Rem. Mag.	185	3080	2761	2464	2186	1927	3896	3131	2494	1963	1525	+2.5	+1.4	-5.5	-19.7	$30
8mm Rem. Mag.	220	2830	2581	2346	2123	1913	3912	3254	2688	2201	1787	+2.5	+0.6	-7.6	-23.5	Disc.
33																
338 Federal	180	2830	2590	2350	2130	1930	3200	2670	2215	1820	1480	1.80	0.00	-8.2	-23.9	NA
338 Federal	185	2750	2550	2350	2160	1980	3105	2660	2265	1920	1615	1.90	0.00	-8.3	-24.1	NA
338 Federal	210	2630	2410	2200	2010	1820	3225	2710	2265	1880	1545	2.30	0.00	-9.4	-27.3	NA
338-06	200	2750	2553	2364	2184	2011	3358	2894	2482	2118	1796	+1.9	0.0	-8.22	-23.6	NA
330 Dakota	250	2900	2719	2545	2378	2217	4668	4103	3595	3138	2727	+2.3	+1.3	-5.0	-17.5	NA

Many manufacturers do not supply suggested retail prices. Others did not get their pricing to us before press time. All pricing can vary dependent on the exact brand and style of ammo selected and/or the retail outlet from which you make your purchase. Pricing has been rounded to the nearest dollar and represents our best estimate of average pricing. An * after the cartridge means these loads are available with Nosler Partition or Swift A-Frame bullets. Listed pricing may or may not reflect this bullet type.
** = these are packed 50 to box, all others are 20 to box. Wea. Mag.= Weatherby Magnum. Spfd. = Springfield. A-Sq. = A-Square. N.E.=Nitro Express.

Cartridge	Bullet Wgt. Grs.	VELOCITY (fps)					ENERGY (ft. lbs.)					TRAJ. (in.)				Est. Price/ box
		Muzzle	100 yds.	200 yds.	300 yds.	400 yds.	Muzzle	100 yds.	200 yds.	300 yds.	400 yds.	100 yds.	200 yds.	300 yds.	400 yds.	
338 Lapua	250	2963	2795	2640	2493	NA	4842	4341	3881	3458	NA	+1.9	0.0	-7.9	0.0	NA
338 Win. Mag.	200	2960	2658	2375	2110	1862	3890	3137	2505	1977	1539	+2.5	+1.0	-6.7	-22.3	$27
338 Win. Mag.*	210	2830	2590	2370	2150	1940	3735	3130	2610	2155	1760	+2.5	+1.4	-6.0	-20.9	$33
338 Win. Mag.*	225	2785	2517	2266	2029	1808	3871	3165	2565	2057	1633	+2.5	+0.4	-8.5	-25.9	$27
338 W.M. Heavy Mag.	225	2920	2678	2449	2232	2027	4259	3583	2996	2489	2053	+1.75	0.0	-7.65	-22.0	NA
338 W.M. High Energy	225	2940	2690	2450	2230	2010	4320	3610	3000	2475	2025	+1.7	0.0	-7.5	-22.0	NA
338 Win. Mag.	230	2780	2573	2375	2186	2005	3948	3382	2881	2441	2054	+2.5	+1.2	-6.3	-21.0	$40
338 Win. Mag.*	250	2660	2456	2261	2075	1898	3927	3348	2837	2389	1999	+2.5	+0.2	-9.0	-26.2	$27
338 W.M. High Energy	250	2800	2610	2420	2250	2080	4350	3775	3260	2805	2395	+1.8	0.0	-7.8	-22.5	NA
338 Ultra Mag.	250	2860	2645	2440	2244	2057	4540	3882	3303	2794	2347	1.7	0.0	-7.6	-22.1	NA
8.59(.338) Galaxy	200	3100	2899	2707	2524	2347	4269	3734	3256	2829	2446	3	3.80	0.0	-9.3	NA
340 Wea. Mag.*	210	3250	2991	2746	2515	2295	4924	4170	3516	2948	2455	+2.5	+1.9	-1.8	-11.8	$56
340 Wea. Mag.*	250	3000	2806	2621	2443	2272	4995	4371	3812	3311	2864	+2.5	+2.0	-3.5	-14.8	$56
338 A-Square	250	3120	2799	2500	2220	1958	5403	4348	3469	2736	2128	+2.5	+2.7	-1.5	-10.5	NA
338-378 Wea. Mag.	225	3180	2974	2778	2591	2410	5052	4420	3856	3353	2902	3.1	3.80	0.0	-8.9	NA
338 Titan	225	3230	3010	2800	2600	2409	5211	4524	3916	3377	2898	+3.07	+3.80	0.0	-8.95	NA
338 Excalibur	200	3600	3361	3134	2920	2715	5755	5015	4363	3785	3274	+2.23	+2.87	0.0	-6.99	NA
338 Excalibur	250	3250	2922	2618	2333	2066	5863	4740	3804	3021	2370	+1.3	0.0	-6.35	-19.2	NA

34, 35

Cartridge	Bullet Wgt. Grs.	Muzzle	100 yds.	200 yds.	300 yds.	400 yds.	Muzzle	100 yds.	200 yds.	300 yds.	400 yds.	100 yds.	200 yds.	300 yds.	400 yds.	Est. Price/ box
348 Winchester	200	2520	2215	1931	1672	1443	2820	2178	1656	1241	925	+2.5	-1.4	-14.7	0.0	$42
357 Magnum	158	1830	1427	1138	980	883	1175	715	454	337	274	0.0	-16.2	-33.1	0.0	$25**
35 Remington	150	2300	1874	1506	1218	1039	1762	1169	755	494	359	+2.5	-4.1	-26.3	0.0	$16
35 Remington	200	2080	1698	1376	1140	1001	1921	1280	841	577	445	+2.5	-6.3	-17.1	-33.6	$16
35 Rem. Lever Evolution	200	2225	1963	1721	1503	NA	2198	1711	1315	1003	NA	3.00	-1.30	-17.5	NA	NA
356 Winchester	200	2460	2114	1797	1517	1284	2688	1985	1434	1022	732	+2.5	-1.8	-15.1	0.0	$31
356 Winchester	250	2160	1911	1682	1476	1299	2591	2028	1571	1210	937	+2.5	-3.7	-22.2	0.0	$31
358 Winchester	200	2490	2171	1876	1619	1379	2753	2093	1563	1151	844	+2.5	-1.6	-15.6	0.0	$31
358 STA	275	2850	2562	2292	2039	NA	4958	4009	3208	2539	NA	+1.9	0.0	-8.6	0.0	NA
350 Rem. Mag.	200	2710	2410	2130	1870	1631	3261	2579	2014	1553	1181	+2.5	-0.2	-10.0	-30.1	$33
35 Whelen	200	2675	2378	2100	1842	1606	3177	2510	1958	1506	1145	+2.5	-0.2	-10.3	-31.1	$20
35 Whelen	225	2500	2300	2110	1930	1770	3120	2650	2235	1870	1560	+2.6	0.0	-10.2	-29.9	NA
35 Whelen	250	2400	2197	2005	1823	1652	3197	2680	2230	1844	1515	+2.5	-1.2	-13.7	0.0	$20
358 Norma Mag.	250	2800	2510	2230	1970	1730	4350	3480	2750	2145	1655	+2.5	+1.0	-7.6	-25.2	NA
358 STA	275	2850	2562	229*2	2039	1764	4959	4009	3208	2539	1899	+1.9	0.0	-8.58	-26.1	NA

9.3mm

Cartridge	Bullet Wgt. Grs.	Muzzle	100 yds.	200 yds.	300 yds.	400 yds.	Muzzle	100 yds.	200 yds.	300 yds.	400 yds.	100 yds.	200 yds.	300 yds.	400 yds.	Est. Price/ box
9.3x57mm Mau.	286	2070	1810	1590	1390	1110	2710	2090	1600	1220	955	+2.5	-2.6	-22.5	0.0	NA
9.3x62mm Mau.	286	2360	2089	1844	1623	NA	3538	2771	2157	1670	1260	+2.5	-1.6	-21.0	0.0	NA
9.3x64mm	286	2700	2505	2318	2139	1968	4629	3984	3411	2906	2460	+2.5	+2.7	-4.5	-19.2	NA
9.3x74Rmm	286	2360	2136	1924	1727	1545	3536	2896	2351	1893	1516	0.0	-6.1	-21.7	-49.0	NA

375

Cartridge	Bullet Wgt. Grs.	Muzzle	100 yds.	200 yds.	300 yds.	400 yds.	Muzzle	100 yds.	200 yds.	300 yds.	400 yds.	100 yds.	200 yds.	300 yds.	400 yds.	Est. Price/ box
38-55 Win.	255	1320	1190	1091	1018	963	987	802	674	587	525	0.0	-23.4	0.0	0.0	$25
375 Winchester	200	2200	1841	1526	1268	1089	2150	1506	1034	714	527	+2.5	-4.0	-26.2	0.0	$27
375 Winchester	250	1900	1647	1424	1239	1103	2005	1506	1126	852	676	+2.5	-6.9	-33.3	0.0	$27
376 Steyr	225	2600	2331	2078	1842	1625	3377	2714	2157	1694	1319	2.5	0.0	-10.6	-31.4	NA
376 Steyr	270	2600	2372	2156	1951	1759	4052	3373	2787	2283	1855	2.3	0.0	-9.9	-28.9	NA
375 Dakota	300	2600	2316	2051	1804	1579	4502	3573	2800	2167	1661	+2.4	0.0	-11.0	-32.7	NA
375 N.E. 2-1/2"	270	2000	1740	1507	1310	NA	2398	1815	1362	1026	NA	+2.5	-6.0	-30.0	0.0	NA
375 Flanged	300	2450	2150	1886	1640	NA	3998	3102	2369	1790	NA	+2.5	-2.4	-17.0	0.0	NA
375 Ruger	270	2840	2600	2372	2156	1951	4835	4052	3373	2786	2283	1.8	0.0	-8.0	-23.6	NA
375 Ruger	300	2660	2344	2050	1780	1536	4713	3660	2800	2110	1572	2.4	0.0	-10.8	-32.6	NA
375 H&H Magnum	250	2670	2450	2240	2040	1850	3955	3335	2790	2315	1905	+2.5	-0.4	-10.2	-28.4	NA
375 H&H Magnum	270	2690	2420	2166	1928	1707	4337	3510	2812	2228	1747	+2.5	0.0	-10.0	-29.4	$28
375 H&H Magnum*	300	2530	2245	1979	1733	1512	4263	3357	2608	2001	1523	+2.5	-1.0	-10.5	-33.6	$28
375 H&H Hvy. Mag.	270	2870	2628	2399	2182	1976	4937	4141	3451	2150	1845	+1.7	0.0	-7.2	-21.0	NA
375 H&H Hvy. Mag.	300	2705	2386	2090	1816	1568	4873	3793	2908	2195	1637	+2.3	0.0	-10.4	-31.4	NA
375 Rem. Ultra Mag.	270	2900	2558	2241	1947	1678	5041	3922	3010	2272	1689	1.9	2.7	-8.9	-27.0	NA
375 Rem. Ultra Mag.	300	2760	2505	2263	2035	1822	5073	4178	3412	2759	2210	2.0	0.0	-8.8	-26.1	NA
375 Wea. Mag.	300	2700	2420	2157	1911	1685	4856	3901	3100	2432	1891	+2.5	-.04	-10.7	0.0	NA
378 Wea. Mag.	270	3180	2976	2781	2594	2415	6062	5308	4635	4034	3495	+2.5	+2.6	-1.8	-11.3	$71
378 Wea. Mag.	300	2929	2576	2252	1952	1680	5698	4419	3379	2538	1881	+2.5	+1.2	-7.0	-24.5	$77
375 A-Square	300	2920	2626	2351	2093	1850	5679	4594	3681	2917	2281	+2.5	+1.4	-6.0	-21.0	NA
38-40 Win.	180	1160	999	901	827	764	538	399	324	273	233	0.0	-33.9	0.0	0.0	$42**

40, 41

Cartridge	Bullet Wgt. Grs.	Muzzle	100 yds.	200 yds.	300 yds.	400 yds.	Muzzle	100 yds.	200 yds.	300 yds.	400 yds.	100 yds.	200 yds.	300 yds.	400 yds.	Est. Price/ box
400 A-Square DPM	400	2400	2146	1909	1689	NA	5116	2092	3236	2533	NA	2.98	0.00	-10.0	NA	NA
400 A-Square DPM	170	2980	2463	2001	1598	NA	3352	2289	1512	964	NA	2.16	0.00	-11.1	NA	NA
408 CheyTac	419	2850	2752	2657	2562	2470	7551	7048	6565	6108	5675	-1.02	0.00	1.9	4.2	NA
405 Win.	300	2200	1851	1545	1296		3224	2282	1589	1119		4.6	0.0	-19.5	0.0	NA
450/400-3"	400	2050	1815	1595	1402	NA	3732	2924	2259	1746	NA	0.0	NA	-33.4	NA	NA
416 Dakota	400	2450	2294	2143	1998	1859	5330	4671	4077	3544	3068	+2.5	-0.2	-10.5	-29.4	NA

Many manufacturers do not supply suggested retail prices. Others did not get their pricing to us before press time. All pricing can vary dependent on the exact brand and style of ammo selected and/or the retail outlet from which you make your purchase. Pricing has been rounded to the nearest dollar and represents our best estimate of average pricing. An * after the cartridge means these loads are available with Nosler Partition or Swift A-Frame bullets. Listed pricing may or may not reflect this bullet type. ** = these are packed 50 to box, all others are 20 to box. Wea. Mag.= Weatherby Magnum. Spfd. = Springfield. A-Sq. = A-Square. N.E.=Nitro Express.

Cartridge	Bullet Wgt. Grs.	VELOCITY (fps)					ENERGY (ft. lbs.)					TRAJ. (in.)				Est. Price/ box
		Muzzle	100 yds.	200 yds.	300 yds.	400 yds.	Muzzle	100 yds.	200 yds.	300 yds.	400 yds.	100 yds.	200 yds.	300 yds.	400 yds.	
416 Taylor	400	2350	2117	1896	1693	NA	4905	3980	3194	2547	NA	+2.5	-1.2	15.0	0.0	NA
416 Hoffman	400	2380	2145	1923	1718	1529	5031	4087	3285	2620	2077	+2.5	-1.0	-14.1	0.0	NA
416 Rigby	350	2600	2449	2303	2162	2026	5253	4661	4122	3632	3189	+2.5	-1.8	-10.2	-26.0	NA
416 Rigby	400	2370	2210	2050	1900	NA	4990	4315	3720	3185	NA	+2.5	-0.7	-12.1	0.0	NA
416 Rigby	410	2370	2110	1870	1640	NA	5115	4050	3165	2455	NA	+2.5	-2.4	-17.3	0.0	$110
416 Rem. Mag.*	350	2520	2270	2034	1814	1611	4935	4004	3216	2557	2017	+2.5	-0.8	-12.6	-35.0	$82
416 Rem. Mag.*	400	2400	2175	1962	1763	1579	5115	4201	3419	2760	2214	+2.5	-1.5	-14.6	0.0	$80
416 Wea. Mag.*	400	2700	2397	2115	1852	1613	6474	5104	3971	3047	2310	+2.5	0.0	-10.1	-30.4	$96
10.57 (416) Meteor	400	2730	2532	2342	2161	1987	6621	5695	4874	4147	3508	+1.9	0.0	-8.3	-24.0	NA
404 Jeffrey	400	2150	1924	1716	1525	NA	4105	3289	2614	2064	NA	+2.5	-4.0	-22.1	0.0	NA
425, 44																
425 Express	400	2400	2160	1934	1725	NA	5115	4145	3322	2641	NA	+2.5	-1.0	-14.0	0.0	NA
44-40 Win.	200	1190	1006	900	822	756	629	449	360	300	254	0.0	-33.3	0.0	0.0	$36**
44 Rem. Mag.	210	1920	1477	1155	982	880	1719	1017	622	450	361	0.0	-17.6	0.0	0.0	$14
44 Rem. Mag.	240	1760	1380	1114	970	878	1650	1015	661	501	411	0.0	-17.6	0.0	0.0	$13
444 Marlin	240	2350	1815	1377	1087	941	2942	1753	1001	630	472	+2.5	-15.1	-31.0	0.0	$22
444 Marlin	265	2120	1733	1405	1160	1012	2644	1768	1162	791	603	+2.5	-6.0	-32.2	0.0	Disc.
444 Marlin Light Mag	265	2335	1913	1551	1266		3208	2153	1415	943		2.0	-4.90	-26.5	0.0	NA
444 Mar. Lever Evolution	265	2325	1971	1652	1380	NA	3180	2285	1606	1120	NA	3.00	-1.40	-18.6	NA	NA
45																
45-70 Govt.	300	1810	1497	1244	1073	969	2182	1492	1031	767	625	0.0	-14.8	0.0	0.0	$21
45-70 Govt. Supreme	300	1880	1558	1292	1103	988	2355	1616	1112	811	651	0.0	-12.9	-46.0	-105.0	NA
45-70 Lever Evolution	325	2050	1729	1450	1225	NA	3032	2158	1516	1083	NA	3.00	-4.10	-27.8	NA	NA
45-70 Govt. CorBon	350	1800	1526	1296			2519	1810	1307			0.0	-14.6	0.0	0.0	NA
45-70 Govt.	405	1330	1168	1055	977	918	1590	1227	1001	858	758	0.0	-24.6	0.0	0.0	$21
45-70 Govt. PMC Cowboy	405	1550	1193				1639	1280				0.0	-23.9	0.0	0.0	NA
45-70 Govt. Garrett	415	1850					3150					3.0	-7.0	0.0	0.0	NA
45-70 Govt. Garrett	530	1550	1343	1178	1062	982	2828	2123	1633	1327	1135	0.0	-17.8	0.0	0.0	NA
450 Marlin	350	2100	1774	1488	1254	1089	3427	2446	1720	1222	922	0.0	-9.7	-35.2	0.0	NA
450 Mar. Lever Evolution	325	2225	1887	1585	1331	NA	3572	2569	1813	1278	NA	3.00	-2.20	-21.3	NA	NA
458 Win. Magnum	350	2470	1990	1570	1250	1060	4740	3065	1915	1205	870	+2.5	-2.5	-21.6	0.0	$43
458 Win. Magnum	400	2380	2170	1960	1770	NA	5030	4165	3415	2785	NA	+2.5	-0.4	-13.4	0.0	$73
458 Win. Magnum	465	2220	1999	1791	1601	NA	5088	4127	3312	2646	NA	+2.5	-2.0	-17.7	0.0	NA
458 Win. Magnum	500	2040	1823	1623	1442	1237	4620	3689	2924	2308	1839	+2.5	-3.5	-22.0	0.0	$61
458 Win. Magnum	510	2040	1770	1527	1319	1157	4712	3547	2640	1970	1516	+2.5	-4.1	-25.0	0.0	$41
450 Dakota	500	2450	2235	2030	1838	1658	6663	5544	4576	3748	3051	+2.5	-0.6	-12.0	-33.8	NA
450 N.E. 3-1/4"	465	2190	1970	1765	1577	NA	4952	4009	3216	2567	NA	+2.5	-3.0	-20.0	0.0	NA
450 N.E. 3-1/4"	500	2150	1920	1708	1514	NA	5132	4093	3238	2544	NA	+2.5	-4.0	-22.9	0.0	NA
450 No. 2	465	2190	1970	1765	1577	NA	4952	4009	3216	2567	NA	+2.5	-3.0	-20.0	0.0	NA
450 No. 2	500	2150	1920	1708	1514	NA	5132	4093	3238	2544	NA	+2.5	-4.0	-22.9	0.0	NA
458 Lott	465	2380	2150	1932	1730	NA	5848	4773	3855	3091	NA	+2.5	-1.0	-14.0	0.0	NA
458 Lott	500	2300	2062	1838	1633	NA	5873	4719	3748	2960	NA	+2.5	-1.6	-16.4	0.0	NA
450 Ackley Mag.	465	2400	2169	1950	1747	NA	5947	4857	3927	3150	NA	+2.5	-1.0	-13.7	0.0	NA
450 Ackley Mag.	500	2320	2081	1855	1649	NA	5975	4085	3820	3018	NA	+2.5	-1.2	-15.0	0.0	NA
460 Short A-Sq.	500	2420	2175	1943	1729	NA	6501	5250	4193	3319	NA	+2.5	-0.8	-12.8	0.0	NA
460 Wea. Mag.	500	2700	2404	2128	1869	1635	8092	6416	5026	3878	2969	+2.5	+0.6	-8.9	-28.0	$72
475																
500/465 N.E.	480	2150	1917	1703	1507	NA	4926	3917	3089	2419	NA	+2.5	-4.0	-22.2	0.0	NA
470 Rigby	500	2150	1940	1740	1560	NA	5130	4170	3360	2695	NA	+2.5	-2.8	-19.4	0.0	NA
470 Nitro Ex.	480	2190	1954	1735	1536	NA	5111	4070	3210	2515	NA	+2.5	-3.5	-20.8	0.0	NA
470 Nitro Ex.	500	2150	1890	1650	1440	1270	5130	3965	3040	2310	1790	+2.5	-4.3	-24.0	0.0	$177
475 No. 2	500	2200	1955	1728	1522	NA	5375	4243	3316	2573	NA	+2.5	-3.2	-20.9	0.0	NA
50, 58																
505 Gibbs	525	2300	2063	1840	1637	NA	6166	4922	3948	3122	NA	+2.5	-3.0	-18.0	0.0	NA
500 N.E.-3"	570	2150	1928	1722	1533	NA	5850	4703	3752	2975	NA	+2.5	-3.7	-22.0	0.0	NA
500 N.E.-3"	600	2150	1927	1721	1531	NA	6158	4947	3944	3124	NA	+2.5	-4.0	-22.0	0.0	NA
495 A-Square	570	2350	2117	1896	1693	NA	6925	5598	4478	3562	NA	+2.5	-1.0	-14.5	0.0	NA
495 A-Square	600	2280	2050	1833	1635	NA	6925	5598	4478	3562	NA	+2.5	-2.0	-17.0	0.0	NA
500 A-Square	600	2380	2144	1922	1766	NA	7546	6126	4920	3922	NA	+2.5	-3.0	-17.0	0.0	NA
500 A-Square	707	2250	2040	1841	1567	NA	7947	6530	5318	4311	NA	+2.5	-2.0	-17.0	0.0	NA
500 BMG PMC	660	3080	2854	2639	2444	2248	13688		500 yd. zero·			+3.1	+3.9	+4.7	+2.8	NA
577 Nitro Ex.	750	2050	1793	1562	1360	NA	6990	5356	4065	3079	NA	+2.5	-5.0	-26.0	0.0	NA
577 Tyrannosaur	750	2400	2141	1898	1675	NA	9591	7633	5996	4671	NA	+3.0	0.0	-12.9	0.0	NA
600, 700																
600 N.E.	900	1950	1680	1452	NA	NA	7596	5634	4212	NA	NA	+5.6	0.0	0.0	0.0	NA
700 N.E.	1200	1900	1676	1472	NA	NA	9618	7480	5774	NA	NA	+5.7	0.0	0.0	0.0	NA

CENTERFIRE HANDGUN CARTRIDGE—BALLISTICS & PRICES

Notes: Blanks are available in 32 S&W, 38 S&W and 38 Special. "V" after barrel length indicates test barrel was vented to produce ballistics similar to a revolver with a normal barrel-to-cylinder gap. Ammo prices are per 50 rounds except when marked with an ** which signifies a 20 round box; *** signifies a 25-round box. Not all loads are available from all ammo manufacturers. Listed loads are those made by Remington, Winchester, Federal, and others. DISC. is a discontinued load. Prices are rounded to the nearest whole dollar and will vary with brand and retail outlet. † = new bullet weight this year; "c" indicates a change in data.

Cartridge	Bullet Wgt. Grs.	VELOCITY (fps)			ENERGY (ft. lbs.)			Mid-Range Traj. (in.)		Bbl. Lgth. (in.)	Est. Price/ box
		Muzzle	50 yds.	100 yds.	Muzzle	50 yds.	100 yds.	50 yds.	100 yds.		
22, 25											
221 Rem. Fireball	50	2650	2380	2130	780	630	505	0.2	0.8	10.5"	$15
25 Automatic	35	900	813	742	63	51	43	NA	NA	2"	$18
25 Automatic	45	815	730	655	65	55	40	1.8	7.7	2"	$21
25 Automatic	50	760	705	660	65	55	50	2.0	8.7	2"	$17
30											
7.5mm Swiss	107	1010	NA	NA	240	NA	NA	NA	NA	NA	NEW
7.62mmTokarev	87	1390	NA	NA	365	NA	NA	0.6	NA	4.5"	NA
7.62 Nagant	97	790	NA	NA	134	NA	NA	NA	NA	NA	NEW
7.63 Mauser	88	1440	NA	NA	405	NA	NA	NA	NA	NA	NEW
30 Luger	93†	1220	1110	1040	305	255	225	0.9	3.5	4.5"	$34
30 Carbine	110	1790	1600	1430	785	625	500	0.4	1.7	10"	$28
30-357 AeT	123	1992	NA	NA	1084	NA	NA	NA	NA	10"	NA
32											
32 S&W	88	680	645	610	90	80	75	2.5	10.5	3"	$17
32 S&W Long	98	705	670	635	115	100	90	2.3	10.5	4"	$17
32 Short Colt	80	745	665	590	100	80	60	2.2	9.9	4"	$19
32 H&R Magnum	85	1100	1020	930	230	195	165	1.0	4.3	4.5"	$21
32 H&R Magnum	95	1030	940	900	225	190	170	1.1	4.7	4.5"	$19
32 Automatic	60	970	895	835	125	105	95	1.3	5.4	4"	$22
32 Automatic	60	1000	917	849	133	112	96			4"	NA
32 Automatic	65	950	890	830	130	115	100	1.3	5.6	NA	NA
32 Automatic	71	905	855	810	130	115	95	1.4	5.8	4"	$19
8mm Lebel Pistol	111	850	NA	NA	180	NA	NA	NA	NA	NA	NEW
8mm Steyr	112	1080	NA	NA	290	NA	NA	NA	NA	NA	NEW
8mm Gasser	126	850	NA	NA	200	NA	NA	NA	NA	NA	NEW
9mm, 38											
380 Automatic	60	1130	960	NA	170	120	NA	1.0	NA	NA	NA
380 Automatic	85/88	990	920	870	190	165	145	1.2	5.1	4"	$20
380 Automatic	90	1000	890	800	200	160	130	1.2	5.5	3.75"	$10
380 Automatic	95/100	955	865	785	190	160	130	1.4	5.9	4"	$20
38 Super Auto +P	115	1300	1145	1040	430	335	275	0.7	3.3	5"	$26
38 Super Auto +P	125/130	1215	1100	1015	425	350	300	0.8	3.6	5"	$26
38 Super Auto +P	147	1100	1050	1000	395	355	325	0.9	4.0	5"	NA
9x18mm Makarov	95	1000	NA	NA	NA	NA	NA	NA	NA	NA	NEW
9x18mm Ultra	100	1050	NA	NA	240	NA	NA	NA	NA	NA	NEW
9x23mm Largo	124	1190	1055	966	390	306	257	0.7	3.7	4"	NA
9x23mm Win.	125	1450	1249	1103	583	433	338	0.6	2.8	NA	NA
9mm Steyr	115	1180	NA	NA	350	NA	NA	NA	NA	NA	NEW
9mm Luger	88	1500	1190	1010	440	275	200	0.6	3.1	4"	$24
9mm Luger	90	1360	1112	978	370	247	191	NA	NA	4"	$26
9mm Luger	95	1300	1140	1010	350	275	215	0.8	3.4	4"	NA
9mm Luger	100	1180	1080	NA	305	255	NA	0.9	NA	4"	NA
9mm Luger	115	1155	1045	970	340	280	240	0.9	3.9	4"	$21
9mm Luger	123/125	1110	1030	970	340	290	260	1.0	4.0	4"	$23
9mm Luger	140	935	890	850	270	245	225	1.3	5.5	4"	$23
9mm Luger	147	990	940	900	320	290	265	1.1	4.9	4"	$26
9mm Luger +P	90	1475	NA	NA	437	NA	NA	NA	NA	NA	NA
9mm Luger +P	115	1250	1113	1019	399	316	265	0.8	3.5	4"	$27
9mm Federal	115	1280	1130	1040	420	330	280	0.7	3.3	4"V	$24
9mm Luger Vector	115	1155	1047	971	341	280	241	NA	NA	4"	NA
9mm Luger +P	124	1180	1089	1021	384	327	287	0.8	3.8	4"	NA
38											
38 S&W	146	685	650	620	150	135	125	2.4	10.0	4"	$19
38 Short Colt	125	730	685	645	150	130	115	2.2	9.4	6"	$19
39 Special	100	950	900	NA	200	180	NA	1.3	NA	4"V	NA
38 Special	110	945	895	850	220	195	175	1.3	5.4	4"V	$23
38 Special	110	945	895	850	220	195	175	1.3	5.4	4"V	$23
38 Special	130	775	745	710	175	160	120	1.9	7.9	4"V	$22

Notes: Blanks are available in 32 S&W, 38 S&W and 38 Special. "V" after barrel length indicates test barrel was vented to produce ballistics similar to a revolver with a normal barrel-to-cylinder gap. Ammo prices are per 50 rounds except when marked with an ** which signifies a 20 round box; *** signifies a 25-round box. Not all loads are available from all ammo manufacturers. Listed loads are those made by Remington, Winchester, Federal, and others. DISC. is a discontinued load. Prices are rounded to the nearest whole dollar and will vary with brand and retail outlet. † = new bullet weight this year; "c" indicates a change in data.

Cartridge	Bullet Wgt. Grs.	VELOCITY (fps)			ENERGY (ft. lbs.)			Mid-Range Traj. (in.)		Bbl. Lgth. (in.)	Est. Price/ box
		Muzzle	50 yds.	100 yds.	Muzzle	50 yds.	100 yds.	50 yds.	100 yds.		
38 Special Cowboy	140	800	767	735	199	183	168			7.5" V	NA
38 (Multi-Ball)	140	830	730	505	215	130	80	2.0	10.6	4"V	$10**
38 Special	148	710	635	565	165	130	105	2.4	10.6	4"V	$17
38 Special	158	755	725	690	200	185	170	2.0	8.3	4"V	$18
38 Special +P	95	1175	1045	960	290	230	195	0.9	3.9	4"V	$23
38 Special +P	110	995	925	870	240	210	185	1.2	5.1	4"V	$23
38 Special +P	125	975	929	885	264	238	218	1	5.2	4"	NA
38 Special +P	125	945	900	860	250	225	205	1.3	5.4	4"V	#23
38 Special +P	129	945	910	870	255	235	215	1.3	5.3	4"V	$11
38 Special +P	130	925	887	852	247	227	210	1.3	5.50	4"V	NA
38 Special +P	147/150(c)	884	NA	NA	264	NA	NA	NA	NA	4"V	$27
38 Special +P	158	890	855	825	280	255	240	1.4	6.0	4"V	$20
357											
357 SIG	115	1520	NA	NA	593	NA	NA	NA	NA	NA	NA
357 SIG	124	1450	NA	NA	578	NA	NA	NA	NA	NA	NA
357 SIG	125	1350	1190	1080	510	395	325	0.7	3.1	4"	NA
357 SIG	150	1130	1030	970	420	355	310	0.9	4.0	NA	NA
356 TSW	115	1520	NA	NA	593	NA	NA	NA	NA	NA	NA
356 TSW	124	1450	NA	NA	578	NA	NA	NA	NA	NA	NA
356 TSW	135	1280	1120	1010	490	375	310	0.8	3.5	NA	NA
356 TSW	147	1220	1120	1040	485	410	355	0.8	3.5	5"	NA
357 Mag., Super Clean	105	1650									NA
357 Magnum	110	1295	1095	975	410	290	230	0.8	3.5	4"V	$25
357 (Med.Vel.)	125	1220	1075	985	415	315	270	0.8	3.7	4"V	$25
357 Magnum	125	1450	1240	1090	585	425	330	0.6	2.8	4"V	$25
357 (Multi-Ball)	140	1155	830	665	420	215	135	1.2	6.4	4"V	$11**
357 Magnum	140	1360	1195	1075	575	445	360	0.7	3.0	4"V	$25
357 Magnum	145	1290	1155	1060	535	430	360	0.8	3.5	4"V	$26
357 Magnum	150/158	1235	1105	1015	535	430	360	0.8	3.5	4"V	$25
357 Mag. Cowboy	158	800	761	725	225	203	185				NA
357 Magnum	165	1290	1189	1108	610	518	450	0.7	3.1	8-3/8"	NA
357 Magnum	180	1145	1055	985	525	445	390	0.9	3.9	4"V	$25
357 Magnum	180	1180	1088	1020	557	473	416	0.8	3.6	8"V	NA
357 Mag. CorBon F.A.	180	1650	1512	1386	1088	913	767	1.66	0.0		NA
357 Mag. CorBon	200	1200	1123	1061	640	560	500	3.19	0.0		NA
357 Rem. Maximum	158	1825	1590	1380	1170	885	670	0.4	1.7	10.5"	$14**
40, 10mm											
40 S&W	135	1140	1070	NA	390	345	NA	0.9	NA	4"	NA
40 S&W	155	1140	1026	958	447	362	309	0.9	4.1	4"	$14***
40 S&W	165	1150	NA	NA	485	NA	NA	NA	NA	4"	$18***
40 S&W	180	985	936	893	388	350	319	1.4	5.0	4"	$14***
40 S&W	180	1015	960	914	412	368	334	1.3	4.5	4"	NA
400 Cor-Bon	135	1450	NA	NA	630	NA	NA	NA	NA	5"	NA
10mm Automatic	155	1125	1046	986	436	377	335	0.9	3.9	5"	$26
10mm Automatic	170	1340	1165	1145	680	510	415	0.7	3.2	5"	$31
10mm Automatic	175	1290	1140	1035	650	505	420	0.7	3.3	5.5"	$11**
10mm Auto. (FBI)	180	950	905	865	361	327	299	1.5	5.4	4"	$16**
10mm Automatic	180	1030	970	920	425	375	340	1.1	4.7	5"	$16**
10mm Auto H.V.	180†	1240	1124	1037	618	504	430	0.8	3.4	5"	$27
10mm Automatic	200	1160	1070	1010	495	510	430	0.9	3.8	5"	$14**
10.4mm Italian	177	950	NA	NA	360	NA	NA	NA	NA	NA	NEW
41 Action Exp.	180	1000	947	903	400	359	326	0.5	4.2	5"	$13**
41 Rem. Magnum	170	1420	1165	1015	760	515	390	0.7	3.2	4"V	$33
41 Rem. Magnum	175	1250	1120	1030	605	490	410	0.8	3.4	4"V	$14**
41 (Med. Vel.)	210	965	900	840	435	375	330	1.3	5.4	4"V	$30
41 Rem. Magnum	210	1300	1160	1060	790	630	535	0.7	3.2	4"V	$33
41 Rem. Magnum	240	1250	1151	1075	833	706	616	0.8	3.3	6.5V	NA
44											
44 S&W Russian	247	780	NA	NA	335	NA	NA	NA	NA	NA	NA
44 S&W Special	180	980	NA	NA	383	NA	NA	NA	NA	6.5"	NA

Notes: Blanks are available in 32 S&W, 38 S&W and 38 Special. "V" after barrel length indicates test barrel was vented to produce ballistics similar to a revolver with a normal barrel-to-cylinder gap. Ammo prices are per 50 rounds except when marked with an ** which signifies a 20 round box; *** signifies a 25-round box. Not all loads are available from all ammo manufacturers. Listed loads are those made by Remington, Winchester, Federal, and others. DISC. is a discontinued load. Prices are rounded to the nearest whole dollar and will vary with brand and retail outlet. † = new bullet weight this year; "c" indicates a change in data.

Cartridge	Bullet Wgt. Grs.	VELOCITY (fps)			ENERGY (ft. lbs.)			Mid-Range Traj. (in.)		Bbl. Lgth. (in.)	Est. Price/ box
		Muzzle	50 yds.	100 yds.	Muzzle	50 yds.	100 yds.	50 yds.	100 yds.		
44 S&W Special	180	1000	935	882	400	350	311	NA	NA	7.5"V	NA
44 S&W Special	200†	875	825	780	340	302	270	1.2	6.0	6"	$13**
44 S&W Special	200	1035	940	865	475	390	335	1.1	4.9	6.5"	$13**
44 S&W Special	240/246	755	725	695	310	285	265	2.0	8.3	6.5"	$26
44-40 Win. Cowboy	225	750	723	695	281	261	242				NA
44 Rem. Magnum	180	1610	1365	1175	1035	745	550	0.5	2.3	4"V	$18**
44 Rem. Magnum	200	1400	1192	1053	870	630	492	0.6	NA	6.5"	$20
44 Rem. Magnum	210	1495	1310	1165	1040	805	635	0.6	2.5	6.5"	$18**
44 (Med. Vel.)	240	1000	945	900	535	475	435	1.1	4.8	6.5"	$17
44 R.M. (Jacketed)	240	1180	1080	1010	740	625	545	0.9	3.7	4"V	$18**
44 R.M. (Lead)	240	1350	1185	1070	970	750	610	0.7	3.1	4"V	$29
44 Rem. Magnum	250	1180	1100	1040	775	670	600	0.8	3.6	6.5"V	$21
44 Rem. Magnum	250	1250	1148	1070	867	732	635	0.8	3.3	6.5"V	NA
44 Rem. Magnum	275	1235	1142	1070	931	797	699	0.8	3.3	6.5"	NA
44 Rem. Magnum	300	1200	1100	1026	959	806	702	NA	NA	7.5"	$17
44 Rem. Magnum	330	1385	1297	1220	1406	1234	1090	1.83	0.00	NA	NA
440 CorBon	260	1700	1544	1403	1669	1377	1136	1.58	NA	10"	NA

45, 50

Cartridge	Bullet Wgt. Grs.	Muzzle	50 yds.	100 yds.	Muzzle	50 yds.	100 yds.	50 yds.	100 yds.	Bbl. Lgth.	Est. Price/box
450 Short Colt/450 Revolver	226	830	NA	NA	350	NA	NA	NA	NA	NA	NEW
45 S&W Schofield	180	730	NA	NA	213	NA	NA	NA	NA	NA	NA
45 S&W Schofield	230	730	NA	NA	272	NA	NA	NA	NA	NA	NA
45 G.A.P.	185	1090	970	890	490	385	320	1.0	4.7	5"	NA
45 G.A.P.	230	880	842	NA	396	363	NA	NA	NA	NA	NA
45 Automatic	165	1030	930	NA	385	315	NA	1.2	NA	5"	NA
45 Automatic	185	1000	940	890	410	360	325	1.1	4.9	5"	$28
45 Auto. (Match)	185	770	705	650	245	204	175	2.0	8.7	5"	$28
45 Auto. (Match)	200	940	890	840	392	352	312	2.0	8.6	5"	$20
45 Automatic	200	975	917	860	421	372	328	1.4	5.0	5"	$18
45 Automatic	230	830	800	675	355	325	300	1.6	6.8	5"	$27
45 Automatic	230	880	846	816	396	366	340	1.5	6.1	5"	NA
45 Automatic +P	165	1250	NA	NA	573	NA	NA	NA	NA	5"	NA
45 Automatic +P	185	1140	1040	970	535	445	385	0.9	4.0	5"	$31
45 Automatic +P	200	1055	982	925	494	428	380	NA	NA	5"	NA
45 Super	185	1300	1190	1108	694	582	504	NA	NA	5"	NA
45 Win. Magnum	230	1400	1230	1105	1000	775	635	0.6	2.8	5"	$14**
45 Win. Magnum	260	1250	1137	1053	902	746	640	0.8	3.3	5"	$16**
45 Win. Mag. CorBon	320	1150	1080	1025	940	830	747	3.47			NA
455 Webley MKII	262	850	NA	NA	420	NA	NA	NA	NA	NA	NA
45 Colt	200	1000	938	889	444	391	351	1.3	4.8	5.5"	$21
45 Colt	225	960	890	830	460	395	345	1.3	5.5	5.5"	$22
45 Colt + P CorBon	265	1350	1225	1126	1073	884	746	2.65	0.0		NA
45 Colt + P CorBon	300	1300	1197	1114	1126	956	827	2.78	0.0		NA
45 Colt	250/255	860	820	780	410	375	340	1.6	6.6	5.5"	$27
454 Casull	250	1300	1151	1047	938	735	608	0.7	3.2	7.5"V	NA
454 Casull	260	1800	1577	1381	1871	1436	1101	0.4	1.8	7.5"V	NA
454 Casull	300	1625	1451	1308	1759	1413	1141	0.5	2.0	7.5"V	NA
454 Casull CorBon	360	1500	1387	1286	1800	1640	1323	2.01	0.0		NA
460 S&W	200	2300	2042	1801	2350	1851	1441	0	-1.60	NA	NA
460 S&W	260	2000	1788	1592	2309	1845	1464	NA	NA	7.5"V	NA
460 S&W	250	1900	1640	1412	2004	1494	1106	0	-2.75	NA	NA
460 S&W	395	1550	1389	1249	2108	1691	1369	0	-4.00	NA	NA
475 Linebaugh	400	1350	1217	1119	1618	1315	1112	NA	NA	NA	NA
480 Ruger	325	1350	1191	1076	1315	1023	835	2.6	0.0	7.5"	NA
50 Action Exp.	325	1400	1209	1075	1414	1055	835	0.2	2.3	6"	$24**
500 S&W	275	1665	1392	1183	1693	1184	854	1.5	NA	8.375	NA
500 S&W	350	1400	1231	1106	1523	1178	951	NA	NA	10"	NA
500 S&W	400	1675	1472	1299	2493	1926	1499	1.3	NA	8.375	NA
500 S&W	440	1625	1367	1169	2581	1825	1337	1.6	NA	8.375	NA
500 S&W	500	1425	1281	1164	2254	1823	1505	NA	NA	10"	NA

RIMFIRE AMMUNITION—BALLISTICS & PRICES

Note: The actual ballistics obtained with your firearm can vary considerably from the advertised ballistics. Also, ballistics can vary from lot to lot with the same brand and type load.

Cartridge	Bullet Wt. Grs.	Velocity (fps) 22-1/2" Bbl.		Energy (ft. lbs.) 22-1/2" Bbl.		Mid-Range Traj. (in.)	Muzzle Velocity
		Muzzle	100 yds.	Muzzle	100 yds.	100 yds.	6" Bbl.
17 Aguila	20	1850	1267	NA	NA	NA	NA
17 Hornady Mach 2	17	2100	1530	166	88	0.7	NA
17 HMR	17	2550	1902	245	136	NA	NA
17 HMR	20	2375	1776	250	140	NA	NA
22 Short Blank	—	—	—	—	—	—	—
22 Short CB	29	727	610	33	24	NA	706
22 Short Target	29	830	695	44	31	6.8	786
22 Short HP	27	1164	920	81	50	4.3	1077
22 Colibri	20	375	183	6	1	NA	NA
22 Super Colibri	20	500	441	11	9	NA	NA
22 Long CB	29	727	610	33	24	NA	706
22 Long HV	29	1180	946	90	57	4.1	1031
22 LR Pistol Match	40	1070	890	100	70	4.6	940
22 LR Sub Sonic HP	38	1050	901	93	69	4.7	NA
22 LR Standard Velocity	40	1070	890	100	70	4.6	940
22 LR AutoMatch	40	1200	990	130	85	NA	NA
22 LR HV	40	1255	1016	140	92	3.6	1060
22 LR Silhoutte	42	1220	1003	139	94	3.6	1025
22 SSS	60	950	802	120	86	NA	NA
22 LR HV HP	40	1280	1001	146	89	3.5	1085
22 Velocitor GDHP	40	1435	0	0	0	NA	NA
22 LR Hyper HP	32/33/34	1500	1075	165	85	2.8	NA
22 LR Stinger HP	32	1640	1132	191	91	2.6	1395
22 LR Hyper Vel	30	1750	1191	204	93	NA	NA
22 LR Shot #12	31	950	NA	NA	NA	NA	NA
22 WRF LFN	45	1300	1015	169	103	3	NA
22 Win. Mag.	30	2200	1373	322	127	1.4	1610
22 Win. Mag. V-Max BT	33	2000	1495	293	164	0.60	NA
22 Win. Mag. JHP	34	2120	1435	338	155	1.4	NA
22 Win. Mag. JHP	40	1910	1326	324	156	1.7	1480
22 Win. Mag. FMJ	40	1910	1326	324	156	1.7	1480
22 Win. Mag. Dyna Point	45	1550	1147	240	131	2.60	NA
22 Win. Mag. JHP	50	1650	1280	300	180	1.3	NA
22 Win. Mag. Shot #11	52	1000	—	NA	—	—	NA

SHOTSHELL LOADS & PRICES

NOTES: * = 10 rounds per box. ** = 5 rounds per box. Pricing variations and number of rounds per box can occur with type and brand of ammunition. Listed pricing is the average nominal cost for load style and box quantity shown. Not every brand is available in all shot size variations. Some manufacturers do not provide suggested list prices. All prices rounded to nearest whole dollar. The price you pay will vary dependent upon outlet of purchase. # = new load spec this year; "C" indicates a change in data.

Dram Equiv.	Shot Ozs.	Load Style	Shot Sizes	Brands	Avg. Price/ box	Velocity (fps)
10 Gauge 3-1/2" Magnum						
4-1/2	2-1/4	premium	BB, 2, 4, 5, 6	Win., Fed., Rem.	$33	1205
Max	2	premium	4, 5, 6	Fed., Win.	NA	1300
4-1/4	2	high velocity	BB, 2, 4	Rem.	$22	1210
Max	18 pellets	premium	00 buck	Fed., Win.	$7**	1100
Max	1-7/8	Bismuth	BB, 2, 4	Bis.	NA	1225
Max	1-3/4	high density	BB, 2	Rem.	NA	1300
4-1/4	1-3/4	steel	TT, T, BBB, BB, 1, 2, 3	Win., Rem.	$27	1260
Mag	1-5/8	steel	T, BBB, BB, 2	Win.	$27	1285
Max	1-5/8	Bismuth	BB, 2, 4	Bismuth	NA	1375
Max	1-1/2	steel	T, BBB, BB, 1, 2, 3	Fed.	NA	1450
Max	1-3/8	steel	T, BBB, BB, 1, 2, 3	Fed., Rem.	NA	1500
Max	1-3/8	steel	T, BBB, BB, 2	Fed., Win.	NA	1450
Max	1-3/4	slug, rifled	slug	Fed.	NA	1280
Max	24 pellets	Buckshot	1 Buck	Fed.	NA	1100
Max	54 pellets	Super-X	4 Buck	Win.	NA	1150
12 Gauge 3-1/2" Magnum						
Max	2-1/4	premium	4, 5, 6	Fed., Rem., Win.	$13*	1150
Max	2	Lead	4, 5, 6	Fed.	NA	1300
Max	2	Copper plated turkey	4, 5	Rem.	NA	1300
Max	18 pellets	premium	00 buck	Fed., Win., Rem.	$7**	1100
Max	1-7/8	Wingmaster HD	4, 6	Rem.	NA	1225
Max	1-7/8	heavyweight	5, 6	Fed.	NA	1300
Max	1-3/4	high density	BB, 2, 4, 6	Rem.		1300
Max	1-7/8	Bismuth	BB, 2, 4	Bis.	NA	1225
Max	1-5/8	Hevi-shot	T	Hevi-shot	NA	1350
Max	1-5/8	Wingmaster HD	T	Rem.	NA	1350
Max	1-5/8	high density	BB, 2	Fed.	NA	1450
Max	1-3/8	Heavyweight	2, 4, 6	Fed.	NA	1450
Max	1-3/8	steel	T, BBB, BB, 2, 4	Fed., Win., Rem.	NA	1450
Max	1-1/2	FS steel	BBB, BB, 2	Fed.	NA	1500
Max	1-1/2	Supreme H-V	BBB, BB, 2, 3	Win.	NA	1475
Max	1-3/8	H-speed steel	BB, 2	Rem.	NA	1550
Max	1-1/4	Steel	BB, 2	Win.	NA	1625
Max	24 pellets	Premium	1 Buck	Fed.	NA	1100
Max	54 pellets	Super-X	4 Buck	Win.	NA	1050
12 Gauge 3" Magnum						
4	2	premium	BB, 2, 4, 5, 6	Win., Fed., Rem.	$9*	1175
4	1-7/8	premium	BB, 2, 4, 6	Win., Fed., Rem.	$19	1210
4	1-7/8	duplex	4x6	Rem.	$9*	1210
Max	1-3/4	turkey	4, 5, 6	Fed., Fio., Win., Rem.	NA	1300
Max	1-3/4	high density	BB, 2, 4	Rem.	NA	1450
Max	1-5/8	high density	BB, 2	Fed.	NA	1450
Max	1-5/8	Wingmaster HD	4, 6	Rem.	NA	1227
Max	1-5/8	high velocity	4, 5, 6	Fed.	NA	1350
4	1-5/8	premium	2, 4, 5, 6	Win., Fed., Rem.	$18	1290
Max	1-1/2	Wingmaster HD	T	Rem.	NA	1300
Max	1-1/2	Hevi-shot	T	Hevi-shot	NA	1300
Max	1-1/2	high density	BB, 2, 4	Rem. Win.	NA	1300
Max	1-5/8	Bismuth	BB, 2, 4, 5, 6	Bis.	NA	1250
4	24 pellets	buffered	1 buck	Win., Fed., Rem.	$5**	1040
4	15 pellets	buffered	00 buck	Win., Fed., Rem.	$6**	1210
4	10 pellets	buffered	000 buck	Win., Fed., Rem.	$6**	1225
4	41 pellets	buffered	4 buck	Win., Fed., Rem.	$6**	1210
Max	1-3/8	heavyweight	5, 6	Fed.	NA	1300
Max	1-3/8	high density	B, 2, 4, 6	Rem. Win.	NA	1450
Max	1-3/8	slug	slug	Bren.	NA	1476
Max	1-1/4	slug, rifled	slug	Fed.	NA	1600
Max	1-3/16	saboted slug	copper slug	Rem.	NA	1500
Max	7/8	slug, rifled	slug	Rem.	NA	1875

Dram Equiv.	Shot Ozs.	Load Style	Shot Sizes	Brands	Avg. Price/ box	Velocity (fps)
12 Gauge 3" Magnum (cont.)						
Max	1-1/8	low recoil	BB	Fed.	NA	850
Max	1-1/8	steel	BB, 2, 3, 4	Fed., Win., Rem.	NA	1550
Max	1-1/16	high density	2, 4	Win.	NA	1400
Max	1	steel	4, 6	Fed.	NA	1330
Max	1-3/8	buckhammer	slug	Rem.	NA	1500
Max	1	slug, rifled	slug, magnum	Win., Rem.	$5**	1760
Max	1	saboted slug	slug	Rem., Win., Fed.	$10**	1550
Max	385 grs.	partition gold	slug	Win.	NA	2000
3-5/8	1-3/8	steel	BBB, BB, 1, 2, 3, 4	Win., Fed., Rem.	$19	1275
Max	1-1/8	steel	BB, 2, 4	Rem.	NA	1500
Max	1-1/8	steel	T, BBB, BB, 2, 4, 5, 6	Fed., Win.	NA	1450
Max	1-1/8	steel	BB, 2	Fed.	NA	1400
4	1-1/4	steel	T, BBB, BB, 1, 2, 3, 4, 6	Win., Fed., Rem.	$18	1400
Max	1-1/4	FS steel	BBB, BB, 2	Fed.	NA	1450
12 Gauge 2-3/4"						
Max	1-5/8	magnum	4, 5, 6	Win., Fed.	$8*	1250
Max	1-3/8	lead	4, 5, 6	Fiocchi	NA	1485
Max	1-3/8	turkey	4, 5, 6	Fio.	NA	1250
Max	1-3/8	steel	4, 5, 6	Fed.	NA	1400
Max	1-3/8	Bismuth	BB, 2, 4, 5, 6	Bis.	NA	1300
3-3/4	1-1/2	magnum	BB, 2, 4, 5, 6	Win., Fed., Rem.	$16	1260
Max	1-1/4	Supreme H-V	4, 5, 6, 7-1/2	Win. Rem.	NA	1400
3-3/4	1-1/4	high velocity	BB, 2, 4, 5, 6, 7-1/2, 8, 9	Win., Fed., Rem., Fio.	$13	1330
Max	1-1/4	high density	B, 2, 4	Win.	NA	1450
Max	1-1/4	high density	4, 6	Rem.	NA	1325
3-1/4	1-1/4	standard velocity	6, 7-1/2, 8, 9	Win., Fed., Rem., Fio.	$11	1220
Max	1-1/8	Hevi-shot	5	Hevi-shot	NA	1350
3-1/4	1-1/8	standard velocity	4, 6, 7-1/2, 8, 9	Win., Fed., Rem., Fio.	$9	1255
Max	1-1/8	steel	2, 4	Rem.	NA	1390
Max	1	steel	BB, 2	Fed.	NA	1450
3-1/4	1	standard velocity	6, 7-1/2, 8	Rem., Fed., Fio., Win.	$6	1290
3-1/4	1-1/4	target	7-1/2, 8, 9	Win., Fed., Rem.	$10	1220
3	1-1/8	spreader	7-1/2, 8, 8-1/2, 9	Fio.	NA	1200
3	1-1/8	target	7-1/2, 8, 9, 7-1/2x8	Win., Fed., Rem., Fio.	$7	1200
2-3/4	1-1/8	target	7-1/2, 8, 8-1/2, 9, 7-1/2x8	Win., Fed., Rem., Fio.	$7	1145
2-3/4	1-1/8	low recoil	7-1/2, 8	Rem.	NA	1145
2-1/2	26 grams	low recoil	8	Win.	NA	980
2-1/4	1-1/8	target	7-1/2, 8, 8-1/2, 9	Rem., Fed.	$7	1080
Max	1	spreader	7-1/2, 8, 8-1/2, 9	Fio.	NA	1300
3-1/4	28 grams (1 oz)	target	7-1/2, 8, 9	Win., Fed., Rem., Fio.	$8	1290
3	1	target	7-1/2, 8, 8-1/2, 9	Win., Fio.	NA	1235
2-3/4	1	target	7-1/2, 8, 8-1/2, 9	Fed., Rem., Fio.	NA	1180
3-1/4	24 grams	target	7-1/2, 8, 9	Fed., Win., Fio.	NA	1325
3	7/8	light	8	Fio.	NA	1200
3-3/4	8 pellets	buffered	000 buck	Win., Fed., Rem.	$4**	1325
4	12 pellets	premium	00 buck	Win., Fed., Rem.	$5**	1290
3-3/4	9 pellets	buffered	00 buck	Win., Fed., Rem., Fio.	$19	1325
3-3/4	12 pellets	buffered	0 buck	Win., Fed., Rem.	$4**	1275
4	20 pellets	buffered	1 buck	Win., Fed., Rem.	$4**	1075
3-3/4	16 pellets	buffered	1 buck	Win., Fed., Rem.	$4**	1250
4	34 pellets	premium	4 buck	Fed., Rem.	$5**	1250
3-3/4	27 pellets	buffered	4 buck	Win., Fed., Rem., Fio.	$4**	1325
Max	1	saboted slug	slug	Win., Fed., Rem.	$10**	1450

NOTES: * = 10 rounds per box. ** = 5 rounds per box. Pricing variations and number of rounds per box can occur with type and brand of ammunition. Listed pricing is the average nominal cost for load style and box quantity shown. Not every brand is available in all shot size variations. Some manufacturers do not provide suggested list prices. All prices rounded to nearest whole dollar. The price you pay will vary dependent upon outlet of purchase. # = new load spec this year; "C" indicates a change in data.

Dram Equiv.	Shot Ozs.	Load Style	Shot Sizes	Brands	Avg. Price/box	Velocity (fps)
12 Gauge 2-3/4" (cont.)						
Max	1-1/4	slug, rifled	slug	Fed.	NA	1520
Max	1-1/4	slug	slug	Lightfield		1440
Max	1-1/4	saboted slug	attached sabot	Rem.	NA	1550
Max	1	slug, rifled	slug, magnum	Rem., Fio.	$5**	1680
Max	1	slug, rifled	slug	Win., Fed., Rem.	$4**	1610
Max	1	sabot slug	slug	Sauvestre		1640
Max	7/8	slug, rifled	slug	Rem.	NA	1800
Max	400	plat. tip	sabot slug	Win.	NA	1700
Max	385 grains	Partition Gold Slug	slug	Win.	NA	1900
Max	385 grains	Core-Lokt bonded	sabot slug	Rem.	NA	1900
Max	325 grains	Barnes Sabot	slug	Fed.	NA	1900
Max	300 grains	SST Slug	sabot slug	Hornady	NA	2050
3	1-1/8	steel target	6-1/2, 7	Rem.	NA	1200
2-3/4	1-1/8	steel target	7	Rem.	NA	1145
3	1#	steel	7	Win.	$11	1235
3-1/2	1-1/4	steel	T, BBB, BB, 1, 2, 3, 4, 5, 6	Win., Fed., Rem.	$18	1275
3-3/4	1-1/8	steel	BB, 1, 2, 3, 4, 5, 6	Win., Fed., Rem., Fio.	$16	1365
3-3/4	1	steel	2, 3, 4, 5, 6, 7	Win., Fed., Rem., Fio.	$13	1390
Max	7/8	steel	7	Fio.	NA	1440
16 Gauge 2-3/4"						
3-1/4	1-1/4	magnum	2, 4, 6	Fed., Rem.	$16	1260
3-1/4	1-1/8	high velocity	4, 6, 7-1/2	Win., Fed., Rem., Fio.	$12	1295
Max	1-1/8	Bismuth	4, 5	Bis.	NA	1200
2-3/4	1-1/8	standard velocity	6, 7-1/2, 8	Fed., Rem., Fio.	$9	1185
2-1/2	1	dove	6, 7-1/2, 8, 9	Fio., Win.	NA	1165
2-3/4	1		6, 7-1/2, 8	Fio.	NA	1200
Max	15/16	steel	2, 4	Fed., Rem.	NA	1300
Max	7/8	steel	2, 4	Win.	$16	1300
3	12 pellets	buffered	1 buck	Win., Fed., Rem.	$4**	1225
Max	4/5	slug, rifled	slug	Win., Fed., Rem.	$4**	1570
Max	.92	sabot slug	slug	Sauvestre	NA	1560
20 Gauge 3" Magnum						
3	1-1/4	premium	2, 4, 5, 6, 7-1/2	Win., Fed., Rem.	$15	1185
Max	1-1/4	Wingmaster HD	4, 6	Rem.	NA	1185
3	1-1/4	turkey	4, 6	Fio.	NA	1200
Max	1-1/4	Hevi-shot	2, 4, 6	Hevi-shot	NA	1250
Max	1-1/8	high density	4, 6	Rem.	NA	1300
Max	18 pellets	buck shot	2 buck	Fed.	NA	1200
Max	24 pellets	buffered	3 buck	Win.	$5**	1150
2-3/4	20 pellets	buck	3 buck	Rem.	$4**	1200
3-1/4	1	steel	1, 2, 3, 4, 5, 6	Win., Fed., Rem.	$15	1330
Max	7/8	steel	2, 4	Win.	NA	1300
Max	1-1/16	high density	2, 4	Win.	NA	1400
Max	1-1/16	Bismuth	2, 4, 5, 6	Bismuth	NA	1250
Mag	5/8	saboted slug	275 gr.	Fed.	NA	1900

Dram Equiv.	Shot Ozs.	Load Style	Shot Sizes	Brands	Avg. Price/box	Velocity (fps)
20 Gauge 2-3/4"						
2-3/4	1-1/8	magnum	4, 6, 7-1/2	Win., Fed., Rem.	$14	1175
2-3/4	1	high velocity	4, 5, 6, 7-1/2, 8, 9	Win., Fed., Rem., Fio.	$12	1220
Max	1	Bismuth	4, 6	Bis.	NA	1200
Max	1	Hevi-shot	5	Hevi-shot	NA	1250
Max	1	Supreme H-V	4, 6, 7-1/2	Win. Rem.	NA	1300
Max	7/8	Steel	2, 3, 4	Fio.	NA	1500
2-1/2	1	standard velocity	6, 7-1/2, 8	Win., Rem., Fed., Fio.	$6	1165
2-1/2	7/8	clays	8	Rem.	NA	1200
2-1/2	7/8	promotional	6, 7-1/2, 8	Win., Rem., Fio.	$6	1210
2-1/2	1	target	8, 9	Win., Rem.	$8	1165
Max	7/8	clays	7-1/2, 8	Win.	NA	1275
2-1/2	7/8	target	8, 9	Win., Fed., Rem.	$8	1200
Max	3/4	steel	2, 4	Rem.	NA	1425
2-1/2	7/8	steel - target	7	Rem.	NA	1200
Max	1	buckhammer	slug	Rem.	NA	1500
Max	5/8	Saboted Slug	Copper Slug	Rem.	NA	1500
Max	20 pellets	buffered	3 buck	Win., Fed.	$4	1200
Max	5/8	slug, saboted	slug	Win.,	$9**	1400
2-3/4	5/8	slug, rifled	slug	Rem.	$4**	1580
Max	3/4	saboted slug	copper slug	Fed., Rem.	NA	1450
Max	3/4	slug, rifled	slug	Win., Fed., Rem., Fio.	$4**	1570
Max	.9	sabot slug	slug	Sauvestre		1480
Max	260 grains	Partition Gold Slug	slug	Win.	NA	1900
Max	260 grains	Core-Lokt Ultra	slug	Rem.	NA	1900
Max	260 grains	saboted slug	platinum tip	Win.	NA	1700
Max	3/4	steel	2, 3, 4, 6	Win., Fed., Rem.	$14	1425
Max	250 grains	SST slug	slug	Hornady	NA	1800
Max	1/2	rifled, slug	slug	Rem.	NA	1800
28 Gauge 2-3/4"						
2	1	high velocity	6, 7-1/2, 8	Win.	$12	1125
2-1/4	3/4	high velocity	6, 7-1/2, 8, 9	Win., Fed., Rem., Fio.	$11	1295
2	3/4	target	8, 9	Win., Fed., Rem.	$9	1200
Max	3/4	sporting clays	7-1/2, 8-1/2	Win.	NA	1300
Max	5/8	Bismuth	4, 6	Bis.	NA	1250
410 Bore 3"						
Max	11/16	high velocity	4, 5, 6, 7-1/2, 8, 9	Win., Fed., Rem., Fio.	$10	1135
Max	9/16	Bismuth	4	Bis.	NA	1175
410 Bore 2-1/2"						
Max	1/2	high velocity	4, 6, 7-1/2	Win., Fed., Rem.	$9	1245
Max	1/5	slug, rifled	slug	Win., Fed., Rem.	$4**	1815
1-1/2	1/2	target	8, 8-1/2, 9	Win., Fed., Rem., Fio.	$8	1200
Max	1/2	sporting clays	7-1/2, 8, 8-1/2	Win.	NA	1300
Max		Buckshot	5-000 Buck	Win.	NA	1135

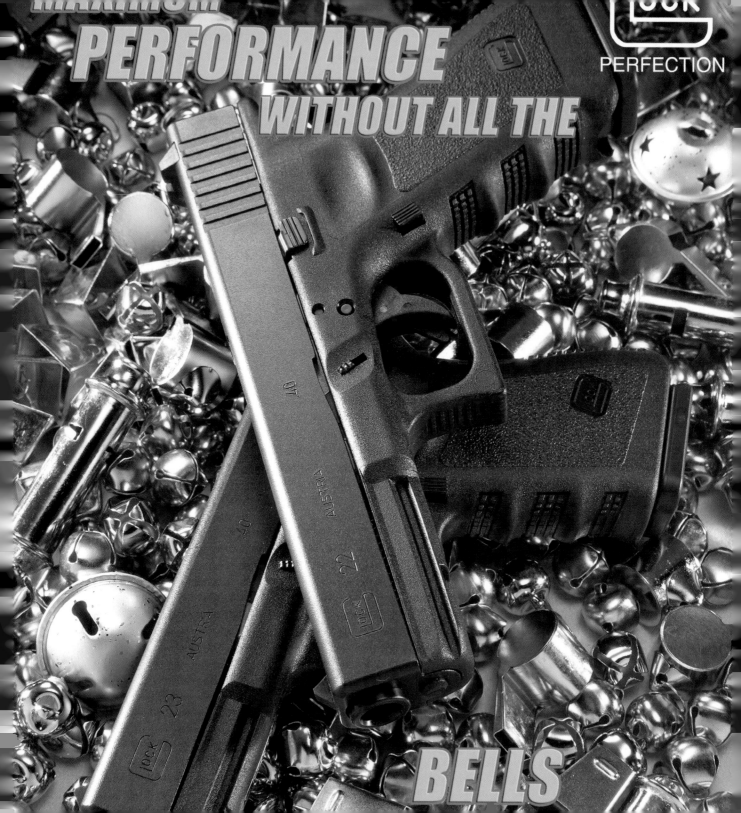

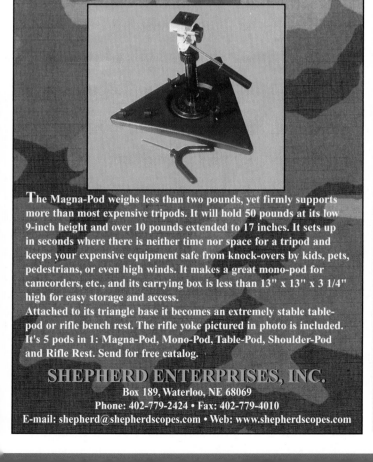
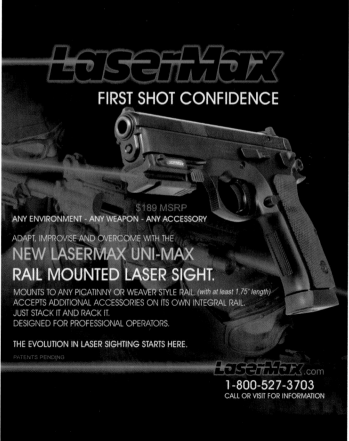

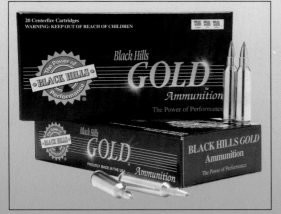
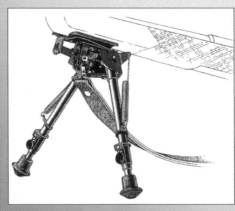

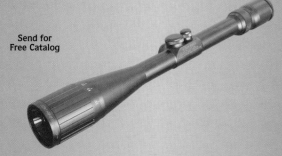

Definitive
Coverage of a Legend

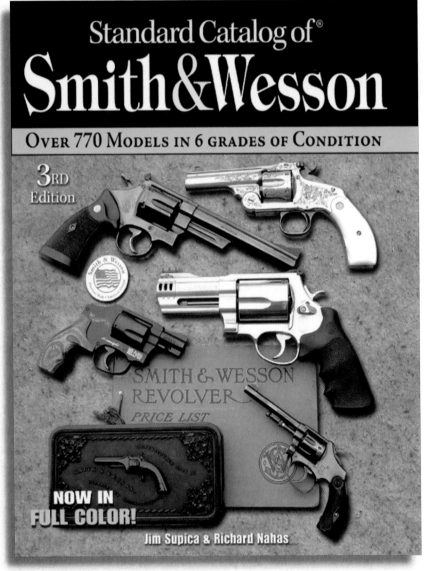

2008 GUN DIGEST *Complete Compact* CATALOG

GUNDEX

HANDGUNS

RIFLES

SHOTGUNS

BLACKPOWDER

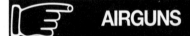

AIRGUNS

ACCESSORIES

REFERENCE

DIRECTORY OF THE ARMS TRADE

GUNDEX

GUNDEX

GUNDEX

GUNDEX

GUNDEX

GUNDEX

GUNDEX

GUNDEX

GUNDEX

Includes models suitable for several forms of competition and other sporting purposes.

Accu-Tek AT-380 II 380 ACP

Auto-Ordnance 1911A1 Standard

Auto-Ordnance Deluxe

Baer Custom Carry

Auto-Ordnance 1911PKZSEW

Baer Premium II

ACCU-TEK AT-380 II 380 ACP PISTOL

Caliber: 380 ACP, 6-shot magazine. **Barrel:** 2.8". **Weight:** 23.5 oz. **Length:** 6.125" overall. **Grips:** Textured black composition. **Sights:** Blade front, rear adjustable for windage. **Features:** Made from 17-4 stainless steel, has an exposed hammer, manual firing-pin safety block and trigger disconnect. Magazine release located on the bottom of the grip. American made, lifetime warranty. Comes with two 6-round stainless steel magazines and a California-approved cable lock. Introduced 2006. Made in U.S.A. by Accu-Tek.
Price: Satin stainless **$249.00**

AUTO-ORDNANCE 1911A1 AUTOMATIC PISTOL

Caliber: 45 ACP, 7-shot magazine. **Barrel:** 5". **Weight:** 39 oz. **Length:** 8.5" overall. **Grips:** Brown checkered plastic with medallion. **Sights:** Blade front, rear drift-adjustable for windage. **Features:** Same specs as 1911A1 military guns-parts interchangeable. Frame and slide blued; each radius has non-glare finish. Made in U.S.A. by Kahr Arms.
Price: 1911SE Standard, blued $609.00
Price: 1911WGSE Deluxe, black textured wraparound grips $615.00
Price: 1911PKZSEW Parkerized, intr. 2007 . . . . $662.00

BAER 1911 CUSTOM CARRY AUTO PISTOL

Caliber: 45 ACP, 7- or 10-shot magazine. **Barrel:** 5". **Weight:** 37 oz. **Length:** 8.5" overall. **Grips:** Checkered walnut. **Sights:** Baer improved ramp-style dovetailed front, Novak low-mount rear. **Features:** Baer forged NM frame, slide and barrel with stainless bushing. Baer speed trigger with 4-lb. pull. Partial listing shown. Made in U.S.A. by Les Baer Custom, Inc.
Price: Standard size, blued $1,640.00
Price: Standard size, stainless $1,690.00
Price: Comanche size, blued $1,640.00
Price: Comanche size, stainless $1,690.00
Price: Comanche size, aluminum frame, blued slide $1,923.00
Price: Comanche size, aluminum frame, stainless slide $1,995.00

BAER 1911 ULTIMATE RECON PISTOL

Caliber: 45 ACP, 7- or 10-shot magazine. **Barrel:** 5". **Weight:** 37 oz. **Length:** 8.5" overall. **Grips:** Checkered cocobolo. **Sights:** Baer improved ramp-style dovetailed front, Novak low-mount rear. **Features:** NM Caspian frame, slide and barrel with stainless bushing. Baer speed trigger with 4-lb. pull. Includes integral Picatinny rail and Sure-Fire X-200 light. Made in U.S.A. by Les Baer Custom, Inc. Introduced 2006.
Price: Bead blast blued **$2,988.00**
Price: Bead blast chrome **$3,230.00**

BAER 1911 PREMIER II AUTO PISTOL

Caliber: 38 Super, 400 Cor-Bon, 45 ACP, 7- or 10-shot magazine. **Barrel:** 5". **Weight:** 37 oz. **Length:** 8.5" overall. **Grips:** Checkered rosewood, double diamond pattern. **Sights:** Baer dovetailed front, low-mount Bo-Mar rear with hidden leaf. **Features:** Baer NM forged steel frame and barrel with stainless bushing, deluxe Commander hammer and sear, beavertail grip safety with pad, extended ambidextrous safety; flat mainspring housing; 30 lpi checkered front strap. Made in U.S.A. by Les Baer Custom, Inc.
Price: 5" 45 ACP $1,598.00
Price: 5" 400 Cor-Bon $1,645.00
Price: 5" 38 Super $1,789.00
Price: 6" 45 ACP (400 Cor-Bon and 38 Super available) $1,755.00
Price: Super-Tac 45 ACP (400 Cor-Bon and
38 Super available) $2,098.00

BAER 1911 S.R.P. PISTOL

Caliber: 45 ACP. **Barrel:** 5". **Weight:** 37 oz. **Length:** 8.5" overall. **Grips:** Checkered walnut. **Sights:** Trijicon night sights. **Features:** Similar to the F.B.I. contract gun except uses Baer forged steel frame. Has Baer match barrel with supported chamber, Complete tactical action. Has Baer Ultra Coat finish. Introduced 1996. Made in U.S.A. by Les Baer Custom, Inc.
Price: Government or Comanche length $2,339.00

BAER 1911 STINGER PISTOL

Caliber: 45 ACP, 7-round magazine. **Barrel:** 5". **Weight:** 34 oz. **Length:** 8.5" overall. **Grips:** Checkered cocobolo. **Sights:** Baer dovetailed front, low-mount Bo-Mar rear with hidden leaf. **Features:** Baer NM frame. Baer Commande slide, Officer's style grip frame, beveled mag well. Made in U.S.A. by Les Baer Custom, Inc.
Price: Blued $1,666.00
Price: Stainless $1,675.00

Baer 1911 Stinger

Beretta 92FS

Beretta Bobcat

Beretta Tomcat

Beretta U22 Neos

Beretta PX4 Storm

Beretta PX4 Sub-Compact with laser

Beretta Model M9

BAER 1911 PROWLER III PISTOL
Caliber: 45 ACP, 8-round magazine. **Barrel:** 5". **Weight:** 34 oz. **Length:** 8.5" overall. **Grips:** Checkered cocobolo. **Sights:** Baer dovetailed front, low-mount Bo-Mar rear with hidden leaf. **Features:** Similar to Premier II with tapered cone stub weight, rounded corners. Made in U.S.A. by Les Baer Custom, Inc.
Price: Blued **$2,215.00**

BERETTA MODEL 92FS PISTOL
Caliber: 9mm Para., 10-shot magazine. **Barrel:** 4.9". **Weight:** 34 oz. **Length:** 8.5" overall. **Grips:** Checkered black plastic. **Sights:** Blade front, rear adjustable for windage. Tritium night sights available. **Features:** Double action. Extractor acts as chamber loaded indicator, squared trigger guard, grooved front and backstraps, inertia firing pin. Matte or blued finish. Introduced 1977. Made in U.S.A.
Price: With plastic grips **$650.00**

BERETTA MODEL 80 CHEETAH SERIES DA PISTOLS
Caliber: 380 ACP, 10-shot magazine (M84); 8-shot (M85); 22 LR, 7-shot (M87). **Barrel:** 3.82". **Weight:** About 23 oz. (M84/85); 20.8 oz. (M87). **Length:** 6.8" overall. **Grips:** Glossy black plastic (wood optional at extra cost). **Sights:** Fixed front, drift-adjustable rear. **Features:** Double action, quick takedown, convenient magazine release. Introduced 1977. Made in U.S.A.
Price: Model 84 Cheetah, plastic grips **$675.00**

BERETTA MODEL 21 BOBCAT PISTOL
Caliber: 22 LR or 25 ACP. Both double action. **Barrel:** 2.4". **Weight:** 11.5 oz.; 11.8 oz. **Length:** 4.9" overall. **Grips:** Plastic. **Features:** Available in nickel, matte, engraved or blue finish. Introduced in 1985.
Price: Bobcat, 22 or 25, blue **$275.00**
Price: Bobcat, 22, stainless **$325.00**
Price: Bobcat, 22 or 25, matte **$250.00**

BERETTA MODEL 3032 TOMCAT PISTOL
Caliber: 32 ACP, 7-shot magazine. **Barrel:** 2.45". **Weight:** 14.5 oz. **Length:** 5" overall. **Grips:** Checkered black plastic. **Sights:** Blade front, drift-adjustable rear. **Features:** Double action with exposed hammer; tip-up barrel for direct loading/unloading; thumb safety; polished or matte blue finish. Made in U.S.A. Introduced 1996.
Price: Blue **$375.00**
Price: Matte **$350.00**
Price: Stainless **$450.00**
Price: With Tritium sights **$425.00**

BERETTA MODEL U22 NEOS
Caliber: 22 LR, 10-shot magazine. **Barrel:** 4.5"; 6". **Weight:** 32 oz.; 36 oz. **Length:** 8.8"; 10.3". **Sights:** Target. **Features:** Integral rail for standard scope mounts, light, perfectly weighted, 100% American made by Beretta.
Price: **$250.00**

Price: Inox **$325.00**
Price: DLX **$350.00**
Price: Inox **$375.00**

BERETTA MODEL PX4 STORM
Caliber: 9mm, 40 S&W. **Capacity:** 17 (9mm); 14 (40 S&W). **Barrel:** 4". **Weight:** 27.5 oz. **Grips:** Black checkered w/3 interchangeable backstraps. **Sights:** 3-dot ystems coated in Superluminova; removable front and rear sights. **Features:** DA/SA, manual safety/hammer decocking lever (ambi) and automatic firing pin block safety. Picatinny rail. Comes with two magazines (17/10 in 9mm and 14/10 in 40 S&W). Removable hammer unit. American made by Beretta. Introduced 2005.
Price: **$598.00**
Price: Subcompact, intr. 2007 . . . . **$575.00**

BERETTA MODEL M9
Caliber: 9mm. **Capacity:** 15. **Barrel:** 4.9". **Weight:** 32.2-35.3 oz. **Grips:** Plastic. **Sights:** Dot and post, low profile, windage adjustable rear. **Features:** DA/SA, forged aluminum alloy frame, delayed locking-bolt system, manual safety doubles as decocking lever, combat-style trigger guard, loaded chamber indicator. Comes with two magazines (15/10). American made by Beretta. Introduced 2005.
Price: **$750.00**

Beretta Model M9A1

Bersa Thunder 380

Browning Hi-Power 9mm

Browning Buckmark Stainless Plus UDX

Browning FLD Plus Rosewood UDX

Browning Buck Mark Standard

BERETTA MODEL M9A1
Caliber: 9mm. Capacity: 15. **Barrel:** 4.9". **Weight:** 32.2-35.3 oz. **Grips:** Plastic. **Sights:** Dot and post, low profile, windage adjustable rear. **Features:** Same as M9, but also includes integral Mil-Std-1913 Picatinny rail, has checkered frontstrap and backstrap. Comes with two magazines (15/10). American made by Beretta. Introduced 2005.
Price: **$750.00**

BERSA THUNDER 45 ULTRA COMPACT PISTOL
Caliber: 45 ACP. **Barrel:** 3.6". **Weight:** 27 oz. **Length:** 6.7" overall. **Grips:** Anatomicaly designed polymer. **Sights:** White outline rear. **Features:** Double action; firing pin safeties, integral locking system. Available in matte, satin nickel, gold, or duo-tone. Introduced 2003. Imported from Argentina by Eagle Imports, Inc.
Price: Thunder 45, matte blue **$441.95**
Price: Thunder 45, duo-tone **$499.95**
Price: Thunder 45, Satin nickel **$466.95**

BERSA THUNDER 380 SERIES PISTOLS
Caliber: 380 Auto, 7 rounds **Barrel:** 3.5". **Weight:** 23 oz. **Length:** 6.6" overall. **Features:** Otherwise similar to Thunder 45 Ultra Compact. 380 DLX has 9-round capacity. 380 Concealed Carry has 8 round capacity. Imported from Argentina by Eagle Imports, Inc.
Price: Thunder 380 Matte **$274.95**
Price: Thunder 380 Satin Nickle **$299.95**
Price: Thunder 380 Blue DLX **$308.95**
Price: Thunder 380 Matte CC (2006) **$291.95**

Bersa Thunder 9 Ultra Compact/40 Series Pistols
Caliber: 9mm, 40 S&W. **Barrel:** 3.5". **Weight:** 24.5 oz. **Length:** 6.6" overall. **Features:** Otherwise similar to Thunder 45 Ultra Compact. 9mm High Capacity model has 17-round capacity. 40 High Capacity model has 13-round capacity. Imported from Argentina by Eagle Imports, Inc.
Price: Thunder 9mm Matte **$441.95**
Price: Thunder 40 High Capacity Satin Nickel **$484.95**

BROWNING HI-POWER 9mm AUTOMATIC PISTOL
Caliber: 9mm Para., 13-round magazine; 40 S&W, 10-round magazine. **Barrel:** 4-5/8". **Weight:** 32 to 39 oz. Overall length: 7-3/4". Metal Finishes: Blued (Standard); black-epoxy/silver-chrome (Practical); black-epoxy (Mark III). **Grips:** Molded (Mark III); wraparound Pachmayr (Practical); or walnut grips (Standard). **Sights:** Fixed (Practical, Mark III, Standard); low-mount adjustable rear (Standard). Cable lock supplied. **Features:** External hammer with half-cock and thumb safeties. Fixed rear sight model available. Commander-style (Practical) or spur-type hammer, single action. Includes gun lock. Imported from Belgium by Browning.
Price: Mark III **$813.00**
Price: Standard, fixed sights **$836.00**
Price: Standard, adjustable sights **$896.00**

BROWNING BUCK MARK PISTOLS
Common Features: Caliber: 22 LR, 10-shot magazine. **Action:** Blowback semi-auto. Trigger: Wide grooved style. **Sights:** Ramp front, Browning Pro-Target rear adjustable for windage and elevation. **Features:** Machined aluminum frame. Includes gun lock. Introduced 1985. Hunter, Camper Stainless, STD Stainless, 5.5 Target, 5.5 Field all introduced 2005. 18 variations, as noted below. **Grips:** Cocobolo, target-style (Hunter, 5.5 Target, 5.5 Field); polymer (Camper, Camper Stainless, Micro Nickel, Standard, STD Stainless); checkered walnut (Challenge); laminated (Plus and Plus Nickel); laminated rosewood (Bullseye Target, FLD Plus); rubber (Bullseye Standard). **Metal finishes:** Matte blue (Hunter, Camper, Challenge, Plus, Bullseye Target, Bullseye Standard, 5.5 Target, 5.5 Field, FLD Plus); matte stainless (Camper Stainless, STD Stainless, Micro Standard); nickel-plated (Micro Nickel, Plus Nickel, and Nickel). Made in U.S.A. From Browning.
Price: Hunter, 7.25" heavy barrel, 38 oz., Truglo sight **$360.00**
Price: Camper, 5.5" heavy barrel, 34 oz. **$300.00**
Price: Camper Stainless, 5.5" tapered bull barrel, 34 oz. **$329.00**
Price: Standard, 5.5" flat-side bull barrel, 34 oz. **$319.00**
Price: Standard Stainless, 5.5" flat-side bull barrel, 34 oz. **$362.00**
Price: Micro Standard, 4" flat-side bull barrel, 32 oz. **$362.00**
Price: Micro Standard Stainless, 4" flat-side bull barrel, 32 oz. . . **$399.00**
Price: Challenge, 5.5" lightweight taper barrel, 25 oz. **$363.00**
Price: Bullseye URX, 7.25" fluted bull barrel, 36 oz. **$497.00**
Price: Bullseye Target, 7.25" fluted bull barrel, 36 oz. **$656.00**
Price: 5.5 Target, 5.5" round bull barrel, target sights, 35.5 oz. . . **$511.00**
Price: 5.5 Field, 5.5" round bull barrel, 35 oz. **$511.00**
Price: Plus Stainless UDX, .intr. 2007 . . . . **$461.00**
Price: Plus UDX, intr. 2007 . . . . **$425.00**
Price: FLD Plus Rosewood UDX, intr. 2007 . . . . **$425.00**

Browning Pro-9

Charles Daly Empire EFS

**Charles Daly
M-5 Government**

Cobra Patriot 380

Cobra Patriot 45

BROWNING PRO-9, PRO-40 PISTOLS
Caliber: 9mm Luger, 16-round magazine; 40 S&W, 14-round magazine. **Barrel:** 4". **Weight:** 30-33 oz. Overall length: 7.25". **Features:** Polymer frame, stainless-steel frames and barrels, double-action, ambidextrous decocker and safety. Fixed, 3-dot-style sights, 6" sight radius. Molded composite grips with interchangeable backstrap inserts. Cable lock supplied.
Price: $628.00

CHARLES DALY ENHANCED 1911 PISTOLS
Caliber: 45 ACP. **Barrel:** 5". **Weight:** 38 oz. **Length:** 8-3/4" overall. **Grips:** Checkered double diamond hardwood. **Sights:** Dovetailed front and dovetailed snag-free low profile rear sights, 3-dot system. **Features:** Extended high-rise beavertail grip safety, combat trigger, combat hammer, beveled magazine well, flared and lowered ejection port. Field Grade models are satin-finished blued steel. EMS series includes an ambidextrous safety, 4" barrel, 8-shot magazine. ECS series has a contoured left hand safety, 3.5" barrel, 6-shot magazine Two magazines, lockable carrying case. Introduced 1998. Empire series are stainless versions. Imported from the Philippines by K.B.I., Inc.
Price: EFS, blued, 39.5 oz., 5" barrel $529.00
Price: EMS, blued, 37 oz., 4" barrel $529.00
Price: ECS, blued, 34.5 oz., 3.5" barrel $529.00
Price: EFS Empire, stainless, 38.5 oz., 5" barrel $629.00
Price: EMS Empire, matte stainless, 36.5 oz., 4" barrel $619.00
Price: ECS Empire, matte stainless, 33.5 oz., 3.5" barrel $619.00

CHARLES DALY ENHANCED TARGET 1911 PISTOLS
Caliber: 45 ACP. **Barrel:** 5". **Weight:** 38.5 oz. **Length:** 8-3/4" overall. **Features:** Similar to Daly Field and Empire models but with dovetailed front and fully adjustable rear target sights. Imported from the Philippines by K.B.I., Inc.
Price: EFS Target, stainless, 38.5 oz., 5" barrel $724.00
Price: EFS Custom Match Target, high-polish stainless $799.00

CHARLES DALY HP 9MM SINGLE-ACTION PISTOL
Caliber: 9mm, 10 round magazine. **Barrel:** 4.6". **Weight:** 34.5 oz. **Length:** 7-3/8" overall. **Grips:** Uncle Mike's padded rubber grip panels. **Sights:** XS Express Sight system set into front and rear dovetails. **Features:** John Browning design. Matte-blued steel frame and slide, thumb safety. Made in the U.S. by K.B.I., Inc.
Price: Hi-Power w/XS Sights $549.00

CHARLES DALY M-5 POLYMER-FRAMED HI-CAP 1911 PISTOL
Caliber: 9mm, 12-round magazine; 40 S&W 17-round magazine; 45 ACP, 13-round magazine. **Barrel:** 5". **Weight:** 33.5 oz. **Length:** 8.5" overall. **Grips:** Checkered polymer. **Sights:** Blade front, adjustable low-profile rear. **Features:** Stainless steel beaver-tail grip safety, rounded trigger-guard, tapered bull barrel, full-length guide rod, matte blue finish on frame and slide. 40 S&W models in M-5 Govt. 1911, M-5 Commander, and M-5 IPSC introduced 2006; M-5 Ultra X Compact in 9mm and 45 ACP introduced 2006; M-5 IPSC .45 ACP introduced 2006. Made in Israel by BUL, imported by K.B.I., Inc.
Price: M-5 Govt. 1911, 40 S&W/45 ACP, matte blue $719.00
Price: M-5 Commander, 40 S&W/45 ACP, matte blue $719.00
Price: M-5 Ultra X Compact, 9mm, 3.1" barrel, 7" OAL, 28 oz. ... $719.00
Price: M-5 Ultra X Compact, 45 ACP, 3.1" barrel, 7" OAL, 28 oz. $719.00
Price: M-5 IPSC, 40 S&W/45 ACP, 5" barrel, 8.5" OAL,
 33.5 oz. $1,499.00

COBRA ENTERPRISES FS380 AUTO PISTOL
Caliber: 380 ACP, 7-shot magazine. **Barrel:** 3.5". **Weight:** 2.1 lbs. **Length:** 6-3/8" overall. **Grips:** Black composition. **Sights:** Fixed. **Features:** Choice of bright chrome, satin nickel or black finish. Introduced 2002. Made in U.S.A. by Cobra Enterprises of Utah, Inc.
Price: $130.00

COBRA ENTERPRISES FS32 AUTO PISTOL
Caliber: 32 ACP, 8-shot magazine. **Barrel:** 3.5". **Weight:** 2.1 lbs. **Length:** 6-3/8" overall. **Grips:** Black composition. **Sights:** Fixed. **Features:** Choice of black, satin nickel or bright chrome finish. Introduced 2002. Made in U.S.A. by Cobra Enterprises of Utah, Inc.
Price: $158.00

COBRA ENTERPRISES PATRIOT PISTOL
Caliber: 380 ACP, 9mm Luger, 10-shot magazine. **Barrel:** 3.3". **Weight:** 20 oz. **Length:** 6" overall. **Grips:** Checkered polymer. **Sights:** Fixed. **Features:** Stainless steel or black slide with load indicator; double-action-only trigger system. Introduced 2002. Made in U.S.A. by Cobra Enterprises of Utah, Inc.
Price: $315.00

COBRA ENTERPRISES CA32, CA380
Caliber: 32 ACP, 380 ACP. **Barrel:** 2.8" **Weight:** 22 oz. **Length:** 5.4". **Grips:** Black molded synthetic . **Sights:** Fixed. **Features:** Choice of black, satin nickle, or chorme finish. Made in U.S.A. by Cobra Enterprises of Utah, Inc.
Price: $152.00

COLT MODEL 1991 MODEL O AUTO PISTOL
Caliber: 45 ACP, 7-shot magazine. **Barrel:** 5". **Weight:** 38 oz. **Length:** 8.5" overall. **Grips:** Checkered black composition. **Sights:** Ramped blade front, fixed square notch rear, high profile. **Features:** Matte finish. Continuation of serial number range used on original G.I. 1911A1 guns. Comes with one magazine and molded carrying case. Introduced 1991.
Price: Blue $786.00
Price: Stainless $839.00

Colt XSE Government

Colt XSE Lightweight Commander

Colt Defender

Colt 38 Super Bright

Colt 38 Super

Colt Series 70

Colt 1911 WWI Replica

CZ 75B 9mm

COLT XSE SERIES MODEL O AUTO PISTOLS
Caliber: 45 ACP, 8-shot magazine. **Barrel:** 4.25", 5". **Grips:** Checkered, double diamond rosewood. **Sights:** Drift-adjustable 3-dot combat. **Features:** Brushed stainless finish; adjustable, two-cut aluminum trigger; extended ambidextrous thumb safety; upswept beavertail with palm swell; elongated slot hammer. Introduced 1999. From Colt's Mfg. Co., Inc.
Price: XSE Government (5" bbl.) **$944.00**
Price: XSE Government (4.25" bbl.) **$944.00**

COLT XSE LIGHTWEIGHT COMMANDER AUTO PISTOL
Caliber: 45 ACP, 8-shot. **Barrel:** 4-1/4". **Weight:** 26 oz. **Length:** 7-3/4" overall. **Grips:** Double diamond checkered rosewood. **Sights:** Fixed, glare-proofed blade front, square notch rear; 3-dot system. **Features:** Brushed stainless slide, nickeled aluminum frame; McCormick elongated slot enhanced hammer, McCormick two-cut adjustable aluminum hammer. Made in U.S.A. by Colt's Mfg. Co., Inc.
Price: Stainless **$944.00**

COLT DEFENDER
Caliber: 45 ACP, 7-shot magazine. **Barrel:** 3". **Weight:** 22-1/2 oz. **Length:** 6-3/4" overall. **Grips:** Pebble-finish rubber wraparound with finger grooves. **Sights:** White dot front, snag-free Colt competition rear. **Features:** Stainless finish; aluminum frame; combat-style hammer; Hi Ride grip safety, extended manual safety, disconnect safety. Introduced 1998. Made in U.S.A. by Colt's Mfg. Co., Inc.
Price: **$885.00**

COLT SERIES 70
Caliber: 45 ACP. **Barrel:** 5". **Weight:** NA. **Length:** NA. **Grips:** Rosewood with double diamond checkering pattern. **Sights:** Fixed. **Features:** Custom replica of the Original Series 70 pistol with a Series 70 firing system, original rollmarks. Introduced 2002. Made in U.S.A. by Colt's Mfg. Co., Inc.
Price: Blued **$919.00**
Price: Stainless **$950.00**

COLT 38 SUPER
Caliber: 38 Super. **Barrel:** 5". **Weight:** NA. **Length:** 8-1/2" **Grips:** Checkered rubber (stainless and blue models); wood with double diamond

checkering pattern (bright stainless model). **Sights:** 3-dot. **Features:** Beveled magazine well, standard thumb safety and service-style grip safety. Introduced 2003. Made in U.S.A. by Colt's Mfg. Co., Inc.
Price: Blued **$837.00**
Price: Stainless **$866.00**
Price: Bright Stainless **$1,090.00**

COLT 1911 WWI REPLICA
Caliber: 45 ACP, 2 7-round magazines. **Barrel:** 5". **Weight:** 38 oz. **Length:** 8.5". **Grips:** Checkered walnut with double diamond checkering pattern. **Sights:** Tapered blade front sight, U-shaped rear notch. **Features:** Reproduction based on original 1911 blueprints. Original rollmarks and inspector marks. Smooth mainspring housing with lanyard loop, WWI-style manual thumb and grip safety, Carbonia blued finish. Introduced 2005. Made in U.S.A. by Colt's Mfg. Co., Inc.
Price: Blued **$990.00**

CZ 75B AUTO PISTOL
Caliber: 9mm Para., 40 S&W, 10-shot magazine. **Barrel:** 4.7". **Weight:** 34.3 oz. **Length:** 8.1" overall. **Grips:** High impact checkered plastic. **Sights:** Square post front, rear adjustable for windage; 3-dot system. **Features:** Single action/double action design; firing pin block safety; choice of black polymer, matte or high-polish blue finishes. All-steel frame. B-SA is a single action with a drop-free magazine. Imported from the Czech Republic by CZ-USA.
Price: 75B, black polymer, 16-shot magazine **$509.00**
Price: 75B, glossy blue, dual-tone or satin nickel **$525.00**
Price: 40 S&W, black polymer, 12-shot magazine **$525.00**
Price: 75B SA, 9mm/40 S&W, single action . . . . **$518.00/$535.00**
Price: 75 Stainless 9mm (2006), 16-shot magazine **$565.00**

CZ 75B Decocker

CZ 97B

CZ 75/85 Kadet

CZ 85

CZ 100

CZ 75B Decocker
Similar to the CZ 75B except has a decocking lever in place of the safety lever. All other specifications are the same. Introduced 1999. Imported from the Czech Republic by CZ-USA.
Price: 9mm, black polymer $518.00

CZ 75B Compact Auto Pistol
Similar to the CZ 75 except has 14-shot magazine in 9mm, 3.9" barrel and weighs 32 oz. Has removable front sight, non-glare ribbed slide top. Trigger guard is squared and serrated; combat hammer. Introduced 1993. Imported from the Czech Republic by CZ-USA.
Price: 9mm, black polymer $539.00
Price: 9mm, dual tone or satin nickel $554.00
Price: 9mm D PCR Compact, alloy frame $554.00
Price: 40 S&W, black polymer, 10+1, 37.8 oz. (2006) $594.00

CZ 75 Champion Pistol
Similar to the CZ 75B except has a longer frame and slide, rubber grip to accommodate new heavy-duty magazine. Ambidextrous thumb safety, extended magazine release; three-port compensator. Blued slide and stain nickel frame finish. Introduced 2005. Imported from the Czech Republic by CZ USA.
Price: 9mm, 16-shot mag. $1,646.00

CZ 75 Tactical Sport
Similar to the CZ 75B except the CZ 75 TS is a competition ready pistol designed for IPSC standard division (USPSA limited division). Fixed target sights, tuned single-action operation, lightweight polymer match trigger with adjustments for take-up and overtravel, competition hammer, extended magazine catch, ambidextrous manual safety, checkered walnut grips, polymer magazine well, two tone finish. Introduced 2005. Imported from the Czech Republic by CZ USA.
Price: 9mm, 20-shot mag. $1,152.00
Price: 40 S&W, 16-shot mag. $1,152.00

CZ 75 SP-01 Pistol
Similar to NATO-approved CZ 75 Compact P-01 model. Features an integral 1913 accessory rail on the dust cover, rubber grip panels, black polycoat finish, extended beavertail, new grip geometry with checkering on front and back straps, and double or single action operation. Introduced 2005. The Shadow variant designed as an IPSC "production" division competition firearm. Includes competition hammer, competition rear sight and fiber-optic front sight, modified slide release, lighter recoil and main spring for use with "minor power factor" competition ammunition. Includes polycoat finish and slim walnut grips. Finished by CZ Custom Shop. Imported from the Czech Republic by CZ-USA.

Price: SP-01 9mm, black polymer, 19+1 . . . . $595.00
Price: SP-01 Shadow $615.00

CZ 85B/85 Combat Auto Pistol
Same gun as the CZ 75 except has ambidextrous slide release and safety levers; non-glare, ribbed slide top; squared, serrated trigger guard; trigger stop to prevent overtravel. Introduced 1986. The CZ 85 Combat features a fully adjustable rear sight, extended magazine release, ambidextrous slide stop and safety catch, drop free magazine and overtravel adjustment. Imported from the Czech Republic by CZ-USA.
Price: 9mm, Black polymer $536.00
Price: Combat, black polymer $599.00
Price: Combat, dual-tone, glossy blue, satin nickel $623.00

CZ 83B DOUBLE-ACTION PISTOL
Caliber: 32 ACP, 380 ACP, 12-shot magazine. **Barrel:** 3.8". **Weight:** 26.2 oz. **Length:** 6.8" overall. **Grips:** High impact checkered plastic. **Sights:** Removable square post front, rear adjustable for windage; 3-dot system. **Features:** Single action/double action; ambidextrous magazine release and safety. Blue finish; non-glare ribbed slide top. Imported from the Czech Republic by CZ-USA.
Price: Glossy blue, 32 ACP or 380 ACP $420.00
Price: Satin Nickel $420.00

CZ 97B AUTO PISTOL
Caliber: 45 ACP, 10-shot magazine. **Barrel:** 4.85". **Weight:** 40 oz. **Length:** 8.34" overall. **Grips:** Checkered walnut. **Sights:** Fixed. **Features:** Single action/double action; full-length slide rails; screw-in barrel bushing; linkless barrel; all-steel construction; chamber loaded indicator; dual transfer bars. Introduced 1999. Imported from the Czech Republic by CZ-USA.
Price: Black polymer $663.00
Price: Glossy blue $680.00

CZ 75 KADET AUTO PISTOL
Caliber: 22 LR, 10-shot magazine. **Barrel:** 4.88". **Weight:** 36 oz. **Grips:** High impact checkered plastic. **Sights:** Blade front, fully adjustable rear. **Features:** Single action/double action mechanism; all-steel construction. Introduced 1999. Kadet conversion kit consists of barrel, slide, adjustable sights, and magazine to convert the centerfire 75 to rimfire. Imported from the Czech Republic by CZ-USA.
Price: Black polymer $510.00
Price: Kadet conversion kit $299.00

CZ 100 B AUTO PISTOL
Caliber: 9mm Para., 40 S&W. **Barrel:** 3.7". **Weight:** 24 oz. **Length:** 6.9" overall. **Grips:** Grooved polymer. **Sights:** Blade front with dot, white outline rear drift adjustable for windage. **Features:** Double action only with firing pin block; polymer frame, steel slide; has laser sight mount. Introduced 1996. Imported from the Czech Republic by CZ-USA.
Price: 9mm Para, 12-shot magazine $449.00
Price: 40 S&W, 10-shot magazine $449.00

CZ 2075 RAMI AUTO PISTOL
Caliber: 9mm Para., 40 S&W. **Barrel:** 3". **Weight:** 25 oz. **Length:** 6.5" overall. **Grips:** Rubber. **Sights:** Blade front with dot, white outline rear drift adjustable for windage. **Features:** Single-action/double-action; alloy or polymer frame, steel slide; has laser sight mount. Imported from the Czech Republic by CZ-USA.
Price: 9mm Para, alloy frame, 10 and 14-shot magazines $576.00
Price: 40 S&W, alloy frame, 8-shot magazine $576.00
Price: 9mm Para, polymer frame, 10 and 14-shot magazines . . . $510.00
Price: 40 S&W, alloy frame, 8-shot magazine $510.00

Dan Wesson Pointman

Dan Wesson DW RZ-10

Desert Baby Eagle

Desert Eagle Mark XIX

EAA Witness

CZ P-01 AUTO PISTOL
Caliber: 9mm Para. **Barrel:** 3.85". **Weight:** 27 oz. **Length:** 7.2" overall. **Grips:** Checkered rubber. **Sights:** Blade front with dot, white outline rear drift adjustable for windage. **Features:** Based on the CZ 75, except with forged aircraft-grade aluminum alloy frame. Hammer forged barrel, de-cocker, firing-pin block, M3 rail, dual slide serrations, squared triggerguard, re-contoured trigger, lanyard loop on butt. Serrated front and back strap. Introduced 2006. Imported from the Czech Republic by CZ-USA.
Price: 9mm Para,14-shot magazines **$586.00**

DAN WESSON FIREARMS POINTMAN SEVEN AUTO PISTOL
Caliber: 10mm, 45 ACP. **Barrel:** 5". **Grips:** Diamond checkered cocobolo. **Sights:** Bo-Mar style adjustable target sight. **Weight:** 38 oz. **Features:** Stainless-steel frame and serrated slide. Series 70-style 1911, stainless-steel frame, forged stainless-steel slide. One-piece match-grade barrel and bushing. 20-LPI checkered mainspring housing, front and rear slide cocking serrations, beveled magwell, dehorned by hand. Lowered and flared ejection port, Ed Brown slide stop and memory groove grip safety, tactical extended thumb safety. Commander-style match hammer, match grade sear, aluminum trigger with stainless bow, Wolff springs. Introduced 2000. Made in U.S.A. by Dan Wesson Firearms, distributed by CZ-USA.
Price: 45 ACP, 7+1 . . . . **$1,079.00**
Price: 10mm, 8+1 . . . . **$1,079.00**

Dan Wesson Commander Classic Bobtail Auto Pistols
Similar to Pointman Seven, a Commander-sized frame with 4.25" barrel. Available with stainless finish, fixed night sights. Introduced 2005. Made in U.S.A. by Dan Wesson Firearms, distributed by CZ-USA.
Price: 45 ACP, 7+1, 34 oz. **$1,169.00**
Price: 10mm, 8+1, 34 oz. **$1,179.00**

DAN WESSON DW RZ-10 AUTO PISTOL
Caliber: 10mm. **Barrel:** 5". **Grips:** Diamond checkered cocobolo. **Sights:** Bo-Mar style adjustable target sight. **Weight:** 38.3 oz. **Features:** Stainless-steel frame and serrated slide. Series 70-style 1911, stainless-steel frame, forged stainless-steel slide. Commander-style match hammer. Reintroduced 2005. Made in U.S.A. by Dan Wesson Firearms, distributed by CZ-USA.
Price: 10mm, 8+1 . . . . **$1,089.00**

DESERT EAGLE MARK XIX PISTOL
Caliber: 357 Mag., 9-shot; 44 Mag., 8-shot; 50 AE, 7-shot. **Barrel:** 6", 10", interchangeable. **Weight:** 357 Mag.-62 oz.; 44 Mag.-69 oz.; 50 AE-72 oz.

Length: 10-1/4" overall (6" bbl.). **Grips:** Polymer; rubber available. **Sights:** Blade on ramp front, combat-style rear. Adjustable available. **Features:** Interchangeable barrels; rotating three-lug bolt; ambidextrous safety; adjustable trigger. Military epoxy finish. Satin, bright nickel, chrome, brushed, matte or black finishes available. 10" barrel extra. Imported from Israel by Magnum Research, Inc.
Price: 357, 6" bbl., standard pistol **$1,369.00**
Price: 44 Mag., 6", standard pistol **$1,369.00**
Price: 50 Magnum, 6" bbl., standard pistol **$1,369.00**

DESERT BABY EAGLE PISTOLS
Caliber: 9mm Para., 40 S&W, 45 ACP, 10-round magazine. **Barrel:** 3.5", 3.7", 4.72". **Weight:** 26.8-39.8 oz. **Length:** 7.25" to 8.25" overall. **Grips:** Polymer. **Sights:** Drift-adjustable rear, blade front. **Features:** Steel frame and slide; slide safety; decocker. Reintroduced in 1999. Imported from Israel by Magnum Research, Inc.
Price: Standard (9mm or 40 cal.; 4.72" barrel, 8.25" overall) **$549.00**
Price: Semi-Compact (9mm, 40 or 45 cal.; 3.7" barrel,
7.75" overall) **$549.00**
Price: Compact (9mm or 40 cal.; 3.5" barrel, 7.25" overall) **$549.00**
Price: Polymer (9mm or 40 cal; polymer frame; 3.25" barrel,
7.25" overall) **$549.00**

EAA WITNESS FULL SIZE AUTO PISTOL
Caliber: 9mm Para., 38 Super, 18-shot magazine; 40 S&W, 10mm, 15-shot magazine; 45 ACP, 10-shot magazine. **Barrel:** 4.50". **Weight:** 35.33 oz. **Length:** 8.10" overall. **Grips:** Checkered rubber. **Sights:** Undercut blade front, open rear adjustable for windage. **Features:** Double-action/single-action trigger system; round trigger guard; frame-mounted safety. Introduced 1991. Polymer frame introducted 2005. Imported from Italy by European American Armory.
Price: 9mm, 38 Super, 10mm, 40 S&W, 45 ACP, full-size steel frame,
Wonder finish **$459.00**
Price: 45/22 22 LR, full-size steel frame, blued **$429.00**
Price: 9mm, 40 S&W, 45 ACP, full-size polymer frame **$429.00**

EAA WITNESS COMPACT AUTO PISTOL
Caliber: 9mm Para., 40 S&W, 10mm, 12-shot magazine; 45 ACP, 8-shot magazine. **Barrel:** 3.6". **Weight:** 30 oz. **Length:** 7.3" overall. Otherwise similar to Full Size Witness. Polymer frame introducted 2005. Imported from Italy by European American Armory.
Price: 9mm, 10mm, 40 S&W, 45 ACP, steel frame,
Wonder finish **$459.00**
Price: 9mm, 40 S&W, 45 ACP, polymer frame **$429.00**

EAA WITNESS-P CARRY AUTO PISTOL
Caliber: 10mm, 15-shot magazine; 45 ACP, 10-shot magazine. **Barrel:** 3.6". **Weight:** 27 oz. **Length:** 7.5" overall. Otherwise similar to Full Size Witness. Polymer frame introducted 2005. Imported from Italy by European American Armory.
Price: 10mm, 45 ACP, polymer frame, from **$469.00**

Ed Brown Classic Custom

Ed Brown Kobra K-SB

Ed Brown Kobra Carry

Ed Brown Kobra

Ed Brown Executive

Ed Brown Special Forces

Excel Arms Accelerator MP-22

Firestorm 45 Gov't

Firestorm Mini

ED BROWN CLASSIC CUSTOM

Caliber: 45 ACP, 7 shot. **Barrel:** 5". **Weight:** 40 oz. Stocks: Cocobolo wood. **Sights:** Bo-Mar adjustable rear, dovetail front. **Features:** Single-action, M1911 style, custom made to order, stainless frame and slide available. Special mirror-finished slide.

Price: Model CC-BB, blued $2,895.00
Price: Model CC-SB, blued and stainless $2,995.00
Price: Model CC-SS, stainless $3,095.00

ED BROWN KOBRA AND KOBRA CARRY

Caliber: 45 ACP, 7-shot magazine. **Barrel:** 5" (Kobra); 4.25" (Kobra Carry). **Weight:** 39 oz. (Kobra); 34 oz. (Kobra Carry). **Grips:** Hogue exotic wood. **Sights:** Ramp, front; fixed Novak low-mount night sights, rear. **Features:** Has snakeskin pattern serrations on forestrap and mainspring housing, dehorned edges, beavertail grip safety.

Price: Kobra K-BB, blued $1,995.00
Price: Kobra K-SB, stainless and blued $2,095.00
Price: Kobra K-SS, stainless $2,195.00
Price: Kobra Carry KC-BB, blued $2,095.00

Ed Brown Executive Pistols

Similar to other Ed Brown products, but with 25-lpi checkered frame and mainspring housing.

Price: Elite blued, blued/stainless, or stainless, from $2,195.00
Price: Carry blued, blued/stainless, or stainless, from $2,295.00
Price: Target blued, blued/stainless, or stainless, intr. 2006,
　　　　from $2,470.00

Ed Brown Special Forces Pistol

Similar to other Ed Brown products, but with ChainLink treatment on forestrap and mainspring housing. Slide coated with Gen III finish. "Square cut" serrations on rear of slide only. Dehorned. Introduced 2006.

Price: SF-BB blued $1,995.00

EXCEL ARMS ACCELERATOR MP-17/MP-22 PISTOLS

Caliber: 17HMR, 22WMR, 9-shot magazine. **Barrel:** 8.5" bull barrel. **Weight:** 54 oz. **Length:** 12.875" overall. **Grips:** Textured black composition. **Sights:** Fully adjustable target sights. **Features:** Made from 17-4 stainless steel, comes with aluminum rib, integral Weaver base, internal hammer, firing-pin block. American made, lifetime warranty. Comes with two 9-round stainless steel magazines and a California-approved cable lock. 22 WMR Introduced 2006. Made in U.S.A. by Excel Arms.

Price: $412.00
Price: SP-17 17 Mach 2 . . . . $412.00
Price: SP-22 22LR $412.00

FIRESTORM AUTO PISTOLS

Caliber: 22LR, 32 ACP, 10-shot magazine; 380 ACP, 7-shot magazine; 9mm, 40 S&W, 10-shot magazine; 45 ACP, 7-shot magazine. **Barrel:** 3.5". **Weight:** From 23 oz. **Length:** From 6.6" overall. **Grips:** Rubber. **Sights:** 3-dot. **Features:** Double action. Distributed by SGS Importers International.

Price: 22LR, matte or duotone, from $241.95
Price: 380, matte or duotone, from $241.95
Price: Mini Firestorm 32 ACP, intr. 2006 . . . . $358.95
Price: Mini Firestorm 9mm, matte, duotone, nickel, from $358.95
Price: Mini Firestorm 40 S&W, matte, duotone, nickel, from . . . $358.95
Price: Mini Firestorm 45 ACP, matte, duotone, chrome, from . . . $308.95

Glock 17C

Glock 22

Glock 26

Glock 35

GLOCK 17/17C AUTO PISTOL
Caliber: 9mm Para., 17/19/33-shot magazines. **Barrel:** 4.49". **Weight:** 22.04 oz. (without magazine). **Length:** 7.32" overall. **Grips:** Black polymer. **Sights:** Dot on front blade, white outline rear adjustable for windage. **Features:** Polymer frame, steel slide; double-action trigger with "Safe Action" system; mechanical firing pin safety, drop safety; simple takedown without tools; locked breech, recoil operated action. ILS designation refers to Internal Locking System. Adopted by Austrian armed forces 1983. NATO approved 1984. Imported from Austria by Glock, Inc.
Price: Fixed sight $599.00
Price: Fixed sight w/ILS $624.00
Price: Adjustable sight $617.00
Price: Adjustable sight w/ILS $642.00
Price: Night sight $646.00
Price: Night sight w/ILS $671.00
Price: 17C Compensated (fixed sight) $621.00
Price: 17C Compensated (fixed sight) w/ILS $646.00

GLOCK 19/19C AUTO PISTOL
Caliber: 9mm Para., 15/17/19/33-shot magazines. **Barrel:** 4.02". **Weight:** 20.99 oz. (without magazine). **Length:** 6.85" overall. Compact version of Glock 17. Pricing the same as Model 17. Imported from Austria by Glock, Inc.
Price: Fixed sight $599.00
Price: 19C Compensated (fixed sight) $621.00

GLOCK 26 AUTO PISTOL
Caliber: 9mm Para. 10/12/15/17/19/33-shot magazines. **Barrel:** 3.46". **Weight:** 19.75 oz. **Length:** 6.29" overall. Subcompact version of Glock 17. Pricing the same as Model 17. Imported from Austria by Glock, Inc.
Price: Fixed sight $599.00

GLOCK 34 AUTO PISTOL
Caliber: 9mm Para. 17/19/33-shot magazines. **Barrel:** 5.32". **Weight:** 22.9 oz. **Length:** 8.15" overall. Competition version of Glock 17 with extended barrel, slide, and sight radius dimensions. Imported from Austria by Glock, Inc.
Price: Adjustable sight $679.00
Price: Adjustable sight w/ILS $704.00

GLOCK 22/22C AUTO PISTOL
Caliber: 40 S&W, 15/17-shot magazines. **Barrel:** 4.49". **Weight:** 22.92 oz. (without magazine). **Length:** 7.32" overall. **Features:** Otherwise similar to Model 17, including pricing. Imported from Austria by Glock, Inc. Introduced 1990.
Price: Fixed sight $599.00
Price: Fixed sight w/ILS $624.00
Price: Adjustable sight $617.00
Price: Adjustable sight w/**ILS** $642.00
Price: Night sight $646.00
Price: Night sight w/ILS $671.00
Price: 22C Compensated (fixed sight) $621.00
Price: 22C Compensated (fixed sight) w/ILS $646.00

GLOCK 23/23C AUTO PISTOL
Caliber: 40 S&W, 13/15/17-shot magazines. **Barrel:** 4.02". **Weight:** 21.16 oz. (without magazine). **Length:** 6.85" overall. **Features:** Otherwise similar to Model 22, including pricing. Compact version of Glock 22. Imported from Austria by Glock, Inc. Introduced 1990.
Price: Fixed sight $599.00
Price: 23C Compensated (fixed sight) $621.00

Glock 35

GLOCK 27 AUTO PISTOL
Caliber: 40 S&W, 9/11/13/15/17-shot magazines. **Barrel:** 3.46". **Weight:** 19.75 oz. (without magazine). **Length:** 6.29" overall. **Features:** Otherwise similar to Model 22, including pricing. Subcompact version of Glock 22. Imported from Austria by Glock, Inc. Introduced 1996.
Price: Fixed sight $599.00

GLOCK 35 AUTO PISTOL
Caliber: 40 S&W, 15/17-shot magazines. **Barrel:** 5.32". **Weight:** 24.52 oz. (without magazine). **Length:** 8.15" overall. **Features:** Otherwise similar to Model 22. Competition version of Glock 22 with extended barrel, slide, and sight radius dimensions. Imported from Austria by Glock, Inc. Introduced 1996.
Price: Fixed sight $679.00
Price: Adjustable sight w/ILS $704.00

GLOCK 20/20C 10MM AUTO PISTOL
Caliber: 10mm, 15-shot magazines. **Barrel:** 4.6". **Weight:** 27.68 oz. (without magazine). **Length:** 7.59" overall. **Features:** Otherwise similar to Model 17. Imported from Austria by Glock, Inc. Introduced 1990.
Price: Fixed sight $637.00
Price: Fixed sight w/ILS $662.00
Price: Adjustable sight $655.00
Price: Adjustable sight w/ILS $680.00
Price: Night sight . . . . , ... $684.00
Price: Night sight w/ILS $709.00
Price: 20C Compensated (fixed sight) $676.00
Price: 20C Compensated (fixed sight) w/ILS $701.00

GLOCK 29 AUTO PISTOL
Caliber: 10mm, 10/15-shot magazines. **Barrel:** 3.78". **Weight:** 24.69 oz. (without magazine). **Length:** 6.77" overall. **Features:** Otherwise similar to Model 20, including pricing. Subcompact version of Glock 20. Imported from Austria by Glock, Inc. Introduced 1997.
Price: Fixed sight $637.00

GLOCK 21/21C AUTO PISTOL
Caliber: 45 ACP, 13-shot magazines. **Barrel:** 4.6". **Weight:** 26.28 oz. (without magazine). **Length:** 7.59" overall. **Features:** Otherwise similar to Model 17. Imported from Austria by Glock, Inc. Introduced 1991.
Price: Fixed sight $637.00
Price: Fixed sight w/ILS $662.00
Price: Adjustable sight $655.00
Price: Adjustable sight w/ILS $680.00
Price: Night sight $684.00
Price: Night sight w/ILS $709.00
Price: 21C Compensated (fixed sight) $676.00
Price: 21C Compensated (fixed sight) w/ILS $701.00

Glock 30

Glock 31

Heckler & Koch USP45

Heckler & Koch
USP Compact

GLOCK 30 AUTO PISTOL
Caliber: 45 ACP, 9/10/13-shot magazines. **Barrel:** 3.78". **Weight:** 23.99 oz. (without magazine). **Length:** 6.77" overall. **Features:** Otherwise similar to Model 21, including pricing. Subcompact version of Glock 21. Imported from Austria by Glock, Inc. Introduced 1997.
Price: Fixed sight $637.00

GLOCK 36 AUTO PISTOL
Caliber: 45 ACP, 6-shot magazines. **Barrel:** 3.78". **Weight:** 20.11 oz. (without magazine). **Length:** 6.77" overall. **Features:** Single-stack magazine, slimmer grip than Glock 21/30. Subcompact. Imported from Austria by Glock, Inc. Introduced 1997.
Price: Fixed sight $637.00

GLOCK 37 AUTO PISTOL
Caliber: 45 GAP, 10-shot magazines. **Barrel:** 4.49". **Weight:** 25.95 oz. (without magazine). **Length:** 7.32" overall. **Features:** Otherwise similar to Model 17. Imported from Austria by Glock, Inc. Introduced 2005.
Price: Fixed sight $614.00
Price: Fixed sight w/ILS $639.00
Price: Adjustable sight $632.00
Price: Adjustable sight w/ILS $657.00
Price: Night sight $661.00
Price: Night sight w/ILS $686.00

GLOCK 38 AUTO PISTOL
Caliber: 45 GAP, 8/10-shot magazines. **Barrel:** 4.02". **Weight:** 24.16 oz. (without magazine). **Length:** 6.85" overall. **Features:** Otherwise similar to Model 37. Compact. Imported from Austria by Glock, Inc.
Price: Fixed sight $614.00

GLOCK 39 AUTO PISTOL
Caliber: 45 GAP, 6/8/10-shot magazines. **Barrel:** 3.46". **Weight:** 19.33 oz. (without magazine). **Length:** 6.3" overall. **Features:** Otherwise similar to Model 37. Subcompact. Imported from Austria by Glock, Inc.
Price: Fixed sight $614.00

GLOCK 25 AUTO PISTOL
Caliber: 380 ACP, 15/17/19-shot magazines. **Barrel:** 4.02". **Weight:** 20.11 oz. (without magazine). **Length:** 6.85" overall. **Features:** Otherwise similar to Model 17. Compact. Made in Austria by Glock, Inc. Not imported to U.S.
Price: . . . . NA

GLOCK 28 AUTO PISTOL
Caliber: 380 ACP, 10/12/15/17/19-shot magazines. **Barrel:** 3.46". **Weight:** 18.66 oz. (without magazine). **Length:** 6.29" overall. **Features:** Otherwise similar to Model 25. Subcompact. Made in Austria by Glock, Inc. Not imported to U.S.
Price: . . . . NA

GLOCK 31/31C AUTO PISTOL
Caliber: 357 Auto, 15/17-shot magazines. **Barrel:** 4.49". **Weight:** 23.28 oz. (without magazine). **Length:** 7.32" overall. **Features:** Otherwise similar to Model 17. Imported from Austria by Glock, Inc.
Price: Fixed sight $599.00
Price: Fixed sight w/ILS $624.00
Price: Adjustable sight $617.00

Price: Adjustable sight w/ILS $642.00
Price: Night sight $646.00
Price: Night sight w/ILS $671.00
Price: 31C Compensated (fixed sight) $621.00
Price: 31C Compensated (fixed sight) w/ILS $646.00

GLOCK 32/32C AUTO PISTOL
Caliber: 357 Auto, 13/15/17-shot magazines. **Barrel:** 4.02". **Weight:** 21.52 oz. (without magazine). **Length:** 6.85" overall. **Features:** Otherwise similar to Model 31. Compact. Imported from Austria by Glock, Inc.
Price: Fixed sight $599.00
Price: 32C Compensated (fixed sight) $621.00

GLOCK 33 AUTO PISTOL
Caliber: 357 Auto, 9/11/13/15/17-shot magazines. **Barrel:** 3.46". **Weight:** 19.75 oz. (without magazine). **Length:** 6.29" overall. **Features:** Otherwise similar to Model 31. Subcompact. Imported from Austria by Glock, Inc.
Price: Fixed sight $599.00

HAMMERLI "TRAILSIDE" TARGET PISTOL
Caliber: 22 LR. **Barrel:** 4.5", 6". **Weight:** 28 oz. **Grips:** Synthetic. **Sights:** Fixed. **Features:** 10-shot magazine. Imported from by Larry's Guns of Maine.
Price: $579.00

HECKLER & KOCH USP AUTO PISTOL
Caliber: 9mm Para., 15-shot magazine; 40 S&W, 13-shot magazine; 45 ACP, 12-shot magazine. **Barrel:** 4.25-4.41". **Weight:** 1.65 lbs. **Length:** 7.64-7.87" overall. **Grips:** Non-slip stippled black polymer. **Sights:** Blade front, rear adjustable for windage. **Features:** New HK design with polymer frame, modified Browning action with recoil reduction system, single control lever. Special "hostile environment" finish on all metal parts. Available in SA/DA, DAO, left- and right-hand versions. Introduced 1993. 45 ACP Introduced 1995. Imported from Germany by Heckler & Koch, Inc.
Price: USP 45 . . . . $839.00
Price: USP 40 and USP 9mm $769.00

Heckler & Koch USP Compact Auto Pistol
Caliber: 9mm Para., 13-shot magazine; 40 S&W and .357 SIG, 12-shot magazine; 45 ACP, 8-shot magazine. Similar to the USP except the 9mm Para., 357 SIG, and 40 S&W have 3.58" barrels, measure 6.81" overall, and weigh 1.47 lbs. (9mm). 45 ACP measures 7.09" overall. Introduced 1996. Introduced 1998. Imported from Germany by Heckler & Koch, Inc.
Price: USP Compact 45 . . . . $874.00
Price: USP Compact 9mm Para., 357 SIG, and 40 S&W $799.00

Heckler & Koch
USP45 Tactical

Heckler & Koch
Mark 23 Special Operations

Heckler & Koch
USP45 Compact

Hi-Point 9MM Comp

Hi-Point C-9

HECKLER & KOCH USP45 TACTICAL PISTOL
Caliber: 40 S&W, 13-shot magazine; 45 ACP, 12-shot magazine. **Barrel:** 4.90-5.09". **Weight:** 1.9 lbs. **Length:** 8.64" overall. **Grips:** Non-slip stippled polymer. **Sights:** Blade front, fully adjustable target rear. **Features:** Has extended threaded barrel with rubber O-ring; adjustable trigger; extended magazine floorplate; adjustable trigger stop; polymer frame. Introduced 1998. Imported from Germany by Heckler & Koch, Inc.
Price: USP Tactical 45 .... **$1,115.00**
Price: USP Tactical 40 .... **$1,019.00**

Heckler & Koch USP Compact Tactical Pistol
Caliber: 45 ACP, 8-shot magazine. Similar to the USP Tactical except measures 7.72" overall, weighs 1.72 lbs. Introduced 2006. Imported from Germany by Heckler & Koch, Inc.
Price: USP Compact Tactical **$1,115.00**

HECKLER & KOCH MARK 23 SPECIAL OPERATIONS PISTOL
Caliber: 45 ACP, 12-shot magazine. **Barrel:** 5.87". **Weight:** 2.42 lbs. **Length:** 9.65" overall. **Grips:** Integral with frame; black polymer. **Sights:** Blade front, rear drift adjustable for windage; 3-dot. **Features:** Civilian version of the SOCOM pistol. Polymer frame; double action; exposed hammer; short recoil, modified Browning action. Introduced 1996. Imported from Germany by Heckler & Koch, Inc.
Price: **$2,412.00**

HECKLER & KOCH P2000 AUTO PISTOL
Caliber: 9mm Para., 13-shot magazine; 40 S&W and .357 SIG, 12-shot magazine. **Barrel:** 3.62". **Weight:** 1.5 lbs. **Length:** 7" overall. **Grips:** Interchangeable panels. **Sights:** Fixed Patridge style, drift adjustable for windage, standard 3-dot. Incorporates features of HK USP Compact pistol, including Law Enforcement Modification (LEM) trigger, double-action hammer system, ambidextrous magazine release, dual slide-release levers, accessory mounting rails, recurved, hook trigger guard, fiber-reinforced polymer frame, modular grip with exchangeable back straps, nitro-carburized finish, lock-out safety device. Introduced 2003. Imported from Germany by Heckler & Koch, Inc.
Price: **$887.00**
Price: P2000 LEM DAO, 357 SIG, intr. 2006 .... **$887.00**
Price: P2000 SA/DA, 357 SIG, intr. 2006 .... **$887.00**

HECKLER & KOCH P2000 SK AUTO PISTOL
Caliber: 9mm Para., 10-shot magazine; 40 S&W and .357 SIG, 9-shot magazine. **Barrel:** 3.27". **Weight:** 1.3 lbs. **Length:** 6.42" overall. **Sights:** Fixed Patridge style, drift adjustable. **Features:** Standard accessory rails, ambidextrous slide release, polymer frame, polygonal bore profile. Smaller version of P2000. Introduced 2005. Imported from Germany by Heckler & Koch, Inc.
Price: **$929.00**

HI-POINT FIREARMS MODEL 9MM COMPACT PISTOL
Caliber: 9mm Para., 8-shot magazine. **Barrel:** 3.5". **Weight:** 25 oz. **Length:** 6.75" overall. **Grips:** Textured plastic. **Sights:** Combat-style adjustable 3-dot system; low profile. **Features:** Single-action design; frame-mounted magazine release; polymer frame. Scratch-resistant matte finish. Introduced 1993. Comps are similar except they have a 4" barrel with muzzle brake/compensator. Compensator is slotted for laser or flashlight mounting. Introduced 1998. Made in U.S.A. by MKS Supply, Inc.
Price: C-9 9mm **$140.00**
Price: C-9 Comp **$169.00**
Price: C-9 Comp-L w/laser sight **$219.00**

Hi-Point Firearms Model 380 Polymer Pistol
Similar to the 9mm Compact model except chambered for 380 ACP, 8-shot magazine, adjustable 3-dot sights. Weighs 25 oz. Polymer frame. Action locks open after last shot. Includes 10-shot and 8-shot magazine; trigger lock. Introduced 1998. Comps are similar except they have a 4" barrel with muzzle compensator. Introduced 2001. Made in U.S.A. by MKS Supply, Inc.
Price: CF-380 .... **$120.00**
Price: 380 Comp **$120.00**
Price: 380 Comp-L w/laser sight **$190.00**

HI-POINT FIREARMS 40SW/POLY AND 45 AUTO PISTOLS
Caliber: 40 S&W, 8-shot magazine; 45 ACP (9-shot). **Barrel:** 4.5". **Weight:** 32 oz. **Length:** 7.72" overall. **Sights:** Adjustable 3-dot. **Features:** Polymer frames, last round lock-open, grip mounted magazine release, magazine disconnect safety, integrated accessory rail, trigger lock. Introduced 2002. Made in U.S.A. by MKS Supply, Inc.
Price: 40SW Poly **$179.00**
Price: 40SW Poly w/laser **$239.00**
Price: 45 ACP **$179.00**
Price: 45 ACP w/laser **$239.00**

Kahr K9

Kahr PM45

Kahr TP45

Kel-Tec P-3AT

Kel-Tec P-32

KAHR K SERIES AUTO PISTOLS

Caliber: K9: 9mm Para., 7-shot; K40: 40 S&W, 6-shot magazine. **Barrel:** 3.5". **Weight:** 25 oz. **Length:** 6" overall. **Grips:** Wraparound textured soft polymer. **Sights:** Blade front, rear drift adjustable for windage; bar-dot combat style. **Features:** Trigger-cocking double-action mechanism with passive firing pin block. Made of 4140 ordnance steel with matte black finish. Contact maker for complete price list. Introduced 1994. Made in U.S.A. by Kahr Arms.
Price: K9093C K9, matte stainless steel **$741.00**
Price: K9093NC K9, matte stainless steel w/tritium night sights . . **$853.00**
Price: K9094C K9 matte blackened stainless stee **$772.00**
Price: K9098 K9 Elite 2003, stainless steel **$806.00**
Price: K4043 K40, matte stainless steel **$741.00**
Price: K4043N K40, matte stainless steel w/tritium night sights . . **$853.00**
Price: K4044 K40, matte blackened stainless steel **$772.00**
Price: K4048 K40 Elite 2003, stainless steel **$806.00**

Kahr MK Series Micro Pistols

Similar to the K9/K40 except is 5.35" overall, 4" high, with a 3.08" barrel. Weighs 23.1 oz. Has snag-free bar-dot sights, polished feed ramp, dual recoil spring system, DA-only trigger. Comes with 5-round flush baseplate and 6-shot grip extension magazine. Introduced 1998. Made in U.S.A. by Kahr Arms.
Price: M9093 MK9, matte stainless steel **$741.00**
Price: M9093N MK9, matte stainless steel, tritium night sights . . **$853.00**
Price: M9093-BOX MK9, matte stainless steel frame,
    matte black slide **$475.00**
Price: M9098 MK9 Elite 2003, stainless steel **$806.00**
Price: M4043 MK40, matte stainless steel **$741.00**
Price: M4043N MK40, matte stainless steel, tritium night sights . **$853.00**
Price: M4048 MK40 Elite 2003, stainless steel **$806.00**

Kahr P Series Pistols

Caliber: 9x19, 40 S&W. Similar to K9/K40 steel frame pistol except has polymer frame, matte stainless steel slide. Barrel length 3.5"; overall length 5.8"; weighs 17 oz. Includes two 7-shot magazines, hard polymer case, trigger lock. Introduced 2000. Made in U.S.A. by Kahr Arms.
Price: KP9093 P9 . . . . **$697.00**
Price: KP9093N P9, tritium night sight **$808.00**
Price: KPS9093 P9 Covert, shortened grip, 15 oz., 6+1 . . . . **$697.00**
Price: KP4043 P40 . . . . **$697.00**
Price: KPS4043N P40 Covert, shortened grip, tritium night sights **$697.00**

Kahr PM Series Pistols

Caliber: 9x19, 40 S&W. Similar to P-Series pistols except has smaller polymer frame (Polymer Micro). Barrel length 3.08"; overall length 5.35"; weighs 17 oz. Includes two 7-shot magazines, hard polymer case, trigger lock. Introduced 2000. Made in U.S.A. by Kahr Arms.
Price: PM9093 PM9 . . . . **$728.00**
Price: PM9093N PM9, tritium night sight **$839.00**
Price: PM4043 PM40 . . . . **$728.00**
Price: PM45 (2007) **$814.00**

KAHR T SERIES PISTOLS

Caliber: T9: 9mm Para., 8-shot magazine; T40: 40 S&W, 7-shot magazine. **Barrel:** 4". **Weight:** 28.1-29.1 oz. **Length:** 6.5" overall. **Grips:** Checkered Hogue Pau Ferro wood grips. **Sights:** Rear: Novak low profile 2-dot tritium night sight, front tritium night sight. **Features:** Similar to other Kahr makes, but with longer slide and barrel upper, longer butt. Trigger cocking DAO; lock breech; "Browning-type" recoil lug; passive striker block; no magazine disconnect. Comes with two magazines. Introduced 2004. Made in U.S.A. by Kahr Arms.
Price: KT9093 T9 matte stainless steel **$792.00**
Price: KT9093-NOVAK T9, "Tactical 9," Novak night sight **$921.00**

KAHR TP SERIES PISTOLS

Caliber: TP9: 9mm Para., 7-shot magazine; TP40: 40 S&W, 6-shot magazine. **Barrel:** 4". **Weight:** 19.1-20.1 oz. **Length:** 6.5-6.7" overall. **Grips:** Textured polymer. Similar to T-series guns, but with polymer frame, matte stainless slide. Comes with two magazines. TP40s introduced 2006. Made in U.S.A. by Kahr Arms.
Price: TP9093 TP9 . . . . **$697.00**
Price: TP9093-Novak TP9 . . . . **$839.00**
Price: TP4043 TP40 . . . . **$697.00**
Price: TP45 (2007) **$697.00**

KAHR CW SERIES PISTOL

Caliber: 9mm Para., 7-shot magazine; 40 S&W, 6-shot magazine. **Barrel:** 3.5-3.6". **Weight:** 17.7-18.7 oz. **Length:** 5.9-6.36" overall. **Grips:** Textured polymer. Similar to P-Series, but CW Series have conventional rifling, metal-injection-molded slide stop lever, no front dovetail cut, one magazine. CW40 introduced 2006. Made in U.S.A. by Kahr Arms.
Price: CW9093 CW9 . . . . **$533.00**
Price: CW4043 CW40 . . . . **$533.00**

KEL-TEC P-11 AUTO PISTOL

Caliber: 9mm Para., 10-shot magazine. **Barrel:** 3.1". **Weight:** 14 oz. **Length:** 5.6" overall. **Grips:** Checkered black polymer. **Sights:** Blade front, rear adjustable for windage. **Features:** Ordnance steel slide, aluminum frame. Double-action only trigger mechanism. Introduced 1995. Made in U.S.A. by Kel-Tec CNC Industries, Inc.
Price: Blue/Hard Chrome/Parkerized . . . . **$320.00/$375.00/$362.00**

KEL-TEC PF-9 PISTOL

Caliber: 9mm Luger; 7 rounds. **Weight:** 12.7 oz. **Sights:** Rear sight adjustable for windage and elevation. Barrel **Length:** 3.1". **Length:** 5.85". **Features:** Barrel, locking system, slide stop, assembly pin, front sight, recoil springs and guide rod adapted from P-11. Trigger system with integral hammer block and the extraction system adapted from P-3AT. MIL-STD-1913 Picatinny rail. Made in U.S.A. by Kel-Tec CNC Industries, Inc.
Price: Blue/Parkerized/Hard Chrome . . . . **$314.00/$355.00/$368.00**

KEL-TEC P-32 AUTO PISTOL

Caliber: 32 ACP, 7-shot magazine. **Barrel:** 2.68". **Weight:** 6.6 oz. **Length:** 5.07" overall. **Grips:** Checkered composite. **Sights:** Fixed. **Features:** Double-action-only mechanism with 6-lb. pull; internal slide stop. Textured composite grip/frame. Now available in 380 ACP. Made in U.S.A. by Kel-Tec CNC Industries, Inc.
Price: Blue/Hard Chrome/Parkerized . . . . **$300.00/$355.00/$340.00**

KEL-TEC P-3AT PISTOL

Caliber: 380 Auto; 7-rounds. **Weight:** 7.2 oz. **Length:** 5.2". **Features:** Lightest 380 auto made; aluminum frame, steel barrel.
Price: Blue/Hard Chrome/Parkerized . . . . **$300.00/$355.00/$340.00**

Kimber Pro Carry II

Kimber Ten II High Capacity Polymer

Kimber Ultra Carry II

Kimber Gold Match II

Kimber CDP II

Kimber Gold Combat II

KEL-TEC PLR-16 PISTOL

Caliber: 5.56mm NATO; 10-round magazine. **Weight:** 51 oz. **Sights:** Rear sight adjustable for windage, front sight is M-16 blade. Barrel **Length:** 9.2". **Length:** 18.5". **Features:** Muzzle is threaded 1/2"-28 to accept standard attachments such as a muzzle brake. Except for the barrel, bolt, sights, and mechanism, the PLR-16 pistol is made of high-impact glass fiber reinforced polymer. Gas-operated semi-auto. Conventional gas-piston operation with M-16 breech locking system. MIL-STD-1913 Picatinny rail. Made in U.S.A. by Kel-Tec CNC Industries, Inc.
Price: Blued **$640.00**

KIMBER CUSTOM II AUTO PISTOL

Caliber: 45 ACP, 40 S&W, 38 Super, 9mm, 10mm. **Barrel:** 5", match grade; 9mm, 10mm, 40 S&W, 38 Super barrels ramped. **Weight:** 38 oz. **Length:** 8.7" overall. **Grips:** Checkered black rubber, walnut, rosewood. **Sights:** Dovetailed front and rear, Kimber low profile adj. or fixed sights. **Features:** Slide, frame and barrel machined from steel or stainless steel. Match grade barrel, chamber and trigger group. Extended thumb safety, beveled magazine well, beveled front and rear slide serrations, high ride beavertail grip safety, checkered flat mainspring housing, kidney cut under trigger guard, high cut grip, match grade stainless steel barrel bushing, polished breech face, Commander-style hammer, lowered and flared ejection port, Wolff springs, bead blasted black oxide or matte stainless finish. Introduced in 1996. Made in U.S.A. by Kimber Mfg., Inc.
Price: Custom II **$768.00**
Price: Custom II Walnut (double-diamond walnut grips) **$775.00**
Price: Stainless II **$865.00**
Price: Stainless II 40 S&W **$884.00**
Price: Stainless II Target 45 ACP (stainless, adj. sight) **$983.00**
Price: Stainless II Target 38 Super **$1,014.00**

Kimber Compact Stainless II Auto Pistol

Similar to Pro Carry II except has stainless steel frame, 4-inch bbl., grip is .400" shorter than standard, no front serrations. Weighs 34 oz. 45 ACP only. Introduced in 1998. Made in U.S.A. by Kimber Mfg., Inc.
Price: **$907.00**

Kimber Pro Carry II Auto Pistol

Similar to Custom II, has aluminum frame, 4" bull barrel fitted directly to the slide without bushing. HD with stainless steel frame. Introduced 1998. Made in U.S.A. by Kimber Mfg., Inc.
Price: Pro Carry II **$779.00**
Price: Pro Carry II w/night sights **$902.00**
Price: Pro Carry II Stainless w/night sights **$985.00**
Price: Pro Carry HD II **$906.00**

Kimber Ultra Carry II Auto Pistol

Lightweight aluminum frame, 3" match grade bull barrel fitted to slide without bushing. Grips .4" shorter. Low effort recoil. Weighs 25 oz. Introduced in 1999. Made in U.S.A. by Kimber Mfg., Inc.
Price: **$791.00**

Price: Ultra Carry II Stainless **$875.00**
Price: Ultra Carry II Stainless 40 S&W **$921.00**

Kimber Ten II High Capacity Polymer Pistol

Similar to Custom II, Pro Carry II and Ultra Carry II depending on barrel length. Thirteen-round magazine capacity (double stack and flush fitting). Polymer grip frame molded over stainless steel or aluminum (BP Ten pistols only) frame insert. Checkered front strap and belly of trigger guard. All models have fixed sights except Gold Match Ten II, which has adjustable sight. Frame grip dimensions approximately that of the standard 1911. **Weight:** 24 to 34 oz. Improved version of the Kimber Polymer series. Made in U.S.A. by Kimber Mfg., Inc.
Price: Pro Carry Ten II **$794.00**
Price: Stainless Ten II **$786.00**

Kimber Gold Match II Auto Pistol

Similar to Custom II models. Includes stainless steel barrel with match grade chamber and barrel bushing, ambidextrous thumb safety, adjustable sight, premium aluminum trigger, hand-checkered double diamond rosewood grips. Barrel hand-fitted for target accuracy. Made in U.S.A. by Kimber Mfg., Inc.
Price: Gold Match II **$1,204.00**
Price: Gold Match Stainless II 45 ACP **$1,369.00**
Price: Gold Match Stainless II 40 S&W **$1,400.00**

Kimber Gold Match Ten II Polymer Auto Pistol

Similar to Stainless Gold Match II. High capacity polymer frame with 13-round magazine. Thumb safety. Introduced 1999. Made in U.S.A. by Kimber Mfg., Inc.
Price: **$1,072.00**

Kimber Gold Combat II Auto Pistol

Similar to Gold Match II except designed for concealed carry. Extended and beveled magazine well, Meprolight Tritium night sights; premium aluminum trigger; 30 lpi front strap checkering; extended magazine well. Introduced 1999. Made in U.S.A. by Kimber Mfg., Inc.
Price: Gold Combat II **$1,733.00**
Price: Gold Combat Stainless II **$1,674.00**

Kimber CDP II Series Auto Pistol

Similar to Custom II, but designed for concealed carry. Aluminum frame. Standard features include stainless steel slide, fixed Meprolight tritium 3-dot (green) dovetail-mounted night sights, match grade barrel and chamber, 30 LPI front strap checkering, two-tone finish, ambidextrous thumb safety, hand-checkered double diamond rosewood grips. Introduced in 2000. Made in U.S.A. by Kimber Mfg., Inc.
Price: Ultra CDP II 40 S&W **$1,215.00**
Price: Ultra CDP II (3" barrel, short grip) **$1,177.00**
Price: Compact CDP II (4" barrel, short grip) **$1,177.00**
Price: Pro CDP II (4" barrel, full length grip) **$1,177.00**
Price: Custom CDP II (5" barrel, full length grip) **$1,177.00**

Kimber Eclipse II

Kimber Eclipse Pro II

Kimber LTP II

Korth Auto Pistol

Olympic Arms
Matchmaster 5

North American
Arms Guardian

Olympic Arms
Matchmaster 6

Kimber Eclipse II Series Auto Pistol
Similar to Custom II and other stainless Kimber pistols. Stainless slide and frame, black oxide, two-tone finish. Gray/black laminated grips. 30 lpi front strap checkering. All models have night sights; Target versions have Meprolight adjustable Bar/Dot version. Made in U.S.A. by Kimber Mfg., Inc.

Price: Eclipse Ultra II (3" barrel, short grip) **$1,085.00**
Price: Eclipse Pro II (4" barrel, full length grip) **$1,085.00**
Price: Eclipse Pro Target II (4" barrel, full length grip,
   adjustable sight) **$1,189.00**
Price: Eclipse Custom II (5" barrel, full length grip) **$1,105.00**
Price: Eclipse Target II (5" barrel, full length grip,
   adjustable sight) **$1,189.00**
Price: Eclipse Custom II (10mm) **$1,220.00**

Kimber LTP II Auto Pistol
Similar to Gold Match II. Built for Limited Ten competition. First Kimber pistol with new, innovative Kimber external extractor. KimPro premium finish. Stainless steel match grade barrel. Extended and beveled magazine well. Checkered front strap and trigger guard belly. Tungsten full length guide rod. Premium aluminum trigger. Ten-round single stack magazine. Wide ambidextrous thumb safety. Made in U.S.A. by Kimber Mfg., Inc.
Price: **$2,099.00**

Kimber Super Match II Auto Pistol
Similar to Gold Match II. Built for target and action shooting competition. Tested for accuracy, target included. Stainless steel barrel and chamber. KimPro finish on stainless steel slide. Stainless steel frame. 30 lpi checkered front strap, premium aluminum trigger, Kimber adjustable sight. Introduced in 1999.
Price: **$1,986.00**

KORTH AUTO PISTOLS
Caliber: 9mm Para, 9x21 (10-shot). **Barrel:** 4", 4.5". **Weight:** 39.9 oz. **Grips:** Walnut, palisander, amboinia, ivory. **Sights:** Fully adjustable. **Features:** Recoil-operated, locking block system, forged steel, fully machine and ground to final tolerances. DA/SA, 2 models available with either rounded or combat-style trigger guard. Available finishes: high polish blue plasma, high polish or matted silver plasma, or high polish standard blue. Schalldampfer Modell has special threaded 4.5-inch barrel and thread protector, many deluxe options available. Made in Germany. Imported by Korth USA.
Price: . . . . **$7,000.00 to $12,000.00**

NORTH AMERICAN ARMS GUARDIAN DAO PISTOL
Caliber: 25 NAA, 32 ACP, 380 ACP, 32NAA, 6-shot magazine. **Barrel:** 2.49". **Weight:** 20.8 oz. **Length:** 4.75" overall. **Grips:** Black polymer. **Sights:** Low profile fixed. **Features:** Double-action only mechanism. All stainless steel construction. Introduced 1998. Made in U.S.A. by North American Arms.
Price: . . . . **$402.00 to $479.00**

OLYMPIC ARMS MATCHMASTER 5 1911 PISTOL
Caliber: 45 ACP, 7-shot magazine. **Barrel:** 5" stainless steel. **Weight:** 40 oz. **Length:** 8.75" overall. **Grips:** Smooth walnut with laser-etched scorpion icon. **Sights:** Ramped blade, LPA adjustable rear. **Features:** Matched frame and slide, fitted and head-spaced barrel, complete ramp and throat jobs, lowered and widened ejection port, beveled mag well, hand-stoned-to-match hammer and sear, lightweight long-shoe over-travel adjusted trigger, shaped and tensioned extractor, extended thumb safety, wide beavertail grip safety and full-length guide rod. Made in U.S.A. by Olympic Arms, Inc.
Price: **$714.00**

OLYMPIC ARMS MATCHMASTER 6 1911 PISTOL
Caliber: 45 ACP, 7-shot magazine. **Barrel:** 6" stainless steel. **Weight:** 44 oz. **Length:** 9.75" overall. **Grips:** Smooth walnut with laser-etched scorpion icon. **Sights:** Ramped blade, LPA adjustable rear. **Features:** Matched frame and slide, fitted and head-spaced barrel, complete ramp and throat jobs, lowered and widened ejection port, beveled mag well, hand-stoned-to-match hammer and sear, lightweight long-shoe over-travel adjusted trigger, shaped and tensioned extractor, extended thumb safety, wide beavertail grip safety and full length guide rod. Made in U.S.A. by Olympic Arms, Inc.
Price: **$774.00**

Olympic Arms Enforcer

Olympic Arms Cohort

Olympic Arms Big Deuce

Olympic Arms Westerner

Olympic Arms Constable

Olympic Arms Journeyman

Olympic Arms Trail Boss

Olympic Arms Street Deuce

OLYMPIC ARMS ENFORCER 1911 PISTOL

Caliber: 45 ACP, 6-shot magazine. **Barrel:** 4" bull stainless steel. **Weight:** 35 oz. **Length:** 7.75" overall. **Grips:** Smooth walnut with etched black widow spider icon. **Sights:** Ramped blade front, LPA adjustable rear. **Features:** Compact Enforcer frame. Busingless bull barrel with triplex counter-wound self-contained recoil system. Matched frame and slide, fitted and head-spaced barrel, complete ramp and throat jobs, lowered and widened ejection port, beveled mag well, hand-stoned-to-match hammer and sear, lightweight longshoe over-travel adjusted trigger, shaped and tensioned extractor, extended thumb safety, wide beavertail grip safety and full length guide rod. Made in U.S.A. by Olympic Arms.
Price: **$750.00**

OLYMPIC ARMS COHORT PISTOL

Caliber: 45 ACP, 7-shot magazine. **Barrel:** 4" bull stainless steel. **Weight:** 36 oz. **Length:** 7.75" overall. **Grips:** Fully checkered walnut. **Sights:** Ramped blade front, LPA adjustable rear. **Features:** Full size 1911 frame. Bushingless bull barrel with triplex counter-wound self-contained recoil system. Matched frame and slide, fitted and head-spaced barrel, complete ramp and throat jobs, lowered and widened ejection port, beveled mag well, hand-stoned-to-match hammer and sear, lightweight long-shoe over-travel adjusted trigger, shaped and tensioned extractor, extended thumb safety, wide beavertail grip safety and full length guide rod. Made in U.S.A. by Olympic Arms.
Price: **$779.00**

OLYMPIC ARMS BIG DEUCE PISTOL

Caliber: 45 ACP, 7-shot magazine. **Barrel:** 6"stainless steel. **Weight:** 44 oz. **Length:** 9.75" overall. **Grips:** Double diamond checkered exotic cocobolo wood. **Sights:** Ramped blade front, LPA adjustable rear. **Features:** Carbon steel parkerized slide with satin bead blast finish full size frame. Matched frame and slide, fitted and head-spaced barrel, complete ramp and throat jobs, lowered and widened ejection port, beveld mag well, hand-stoned-to-match hammer and sear, lightweight long-shoe over-travel adjusted trigger, shaped and tensioned extractor, extended thumb safety, wide beavertail grip safety and full length guide rod. Made in U.S.A. by Olympic Arms.
Price: **$834.00**

OLYMPIC ARMS WESTERNER SERIES 1911 PISTOLS

Caliber: 45 ACP, 7-shot magazine. **Barrel:** 4", 5", 6" stainless steel. **Weight:** 35-43 oz. **Length:** 7.75-9.75" overall. **Grips:** Smooth ivory laser-etched Westerner icon. **Sights:** Ramped blade, LPA adjustable rear. **Features:** Matched frame and slide, fitted and head-spaced barrel, complete ramp and throat jobs, lowered and widened ejection port, beveld mag well, hand-stoned-to-match hammer and sear, lightweight long-shoe over-travel adjusted trigger, shaped and tensioned extractor, extended thumb safety, wide beavertail grip safety and full length guide rod. Entire pistol is fitted and assembled, then disassembled and subjected to the color case hardening process. Made in U.S.A. by Olympic Arms, Inc.
Price: Constable, 4" barrel, 35 oz. **$935.00**
Price: Westerner, 5" barrel, 39 oz. **$834.00**
Price: Trail Boss, 6" barrel, 43 oz. **$959.00**

OLYMPIC ARMS SCHUETZEN PISTOL WORKS 1911 PISTOLS

Caliber: 45 ACP, 7-shot magazine.**Barrel:** 4", 5.2", bull stainless steel. **Weight:** 35-38 oz. **Length:** 7.75-8.75" overall. **Grips:** Double diamond checkered exotic cocobolo wood. **Sights:** Ramped blade, LPA adjustable rear. **Features:** Carbon steel parkerized slide with satin bead blast finish full size frame. Matched frame and slide, fitted and head-spaced barrel, complete ramp and throat jobs, lowered and widened ejection port, beveld mag well, hand-stoned-to-match hammer and sear, lightweight long-shoe over-travel adjusted trigger, shaped and tensioned extractor, extended thumb safety, wide beavertail grip safety and full length guide rod. Custom made by Olympic Arms Schuetzen Pistol Works. Parts are hand selected and fitted by expert pistolsmiths. Several no-cost options to choose from. Made in U.S.A. by Olympic Arms Schuetzen Pistol Works.
Price: Journeyman, 4" bull barrel, 35 oz. **$1,299.00**
Price: Street Deuce, 5.2" bull barrel, 38 oz. **$1,299.00**

Olympic Arms OA-98

Olympic Arms OA-93

Para-Ordnance SSP-SE1

Olympic Arms Whitney Wolverine

Para-Ordnance Todd Jarrett

OLYMPIC ARMS OA-93 AR PISTOL
Caliber: 5.56 NATO. **Barrel:** 6.5" button-rifled stainless steel. **Weight:** 4.46 lbs. **Length:** 17" overall. **Sights:** None. **Features:** Olympic Arms integrated recoil system on the upper receiver eliminates the buttstock, flat top upper, free floating tubular match handguard, threaded muzzle with flash suppressor. Made in U.S.A. by Olympic Arms, Inc.
Price: **$1,080.00**

Olympic Arms OA-98 AR Pistol
Caliber: 5.56 NATO. **Barrel:** 6.5" button-rifled stainless steel. **Length:** 15.25" overall. **Weight:** 49 oz. **Sights:** None. **Features:** Olympic Arms integrated recoil system on the upper receiver eliminates the buttstock, skeletonized receivers and grip for weight, flat top upper, protective barrel shroud, crowned muzzle. Conforms to AWB, legal in post-ban restricted states, except CA. Made in U.S.A. by Olympic Arms, Inc.
Price: **$1,080.00**

OLYMPIC ARMS K23PAR PISTOL
Caliber: 5.56 NATO. **Barrel:** 6.5" button-rifled chrome-moly steel. **Length:** 22.25" overall. **Weight:** 5.12 lbs. **Sights:** Adjustable A2 rear, elevation adjustable front post. **Features:** A2 upper with rear sight, free floating tubular match handguard, threaded muzzle with flash suppressor, receiver extension tube with foam cover, no bayonet lug. Made in U.S.A. by Olympic Arms, Inc. Introduced 2007.
Price: **$839.00**

OLYMPIC ARMS K23P-A3-TC AR PISTOL
Caliber: 5.56 NATO. **Barrel:** 6.5" button-rifled chrome-moly steel. **Length:** 22.25" overall. **Weight:** 5.12 lbs. **Sights:** Adjustable A2 rear, elevation adjustable front post. **Features:** Flat-top upper with detachable carry handle, free floating FIRSH rail handguard, threaded muzzle with flash suppressor, receiver extension tube with foam cover, no bayonet lug. Made in U.S.A. by Olympic Arms, Inc. Introduced 2007.
Price: **$938.00**

OLYMPIC ARMS WHITNEY WOLVERINE PISTOL
Caliber: 22 LR, 10-shot magazine. **Barrel:** 4.625" stainless steel. **Weight:** 19.2 oz. **Length:** 9" overall. **Grips:** Black checkered with fire/safe markings. **Sights:** Ramped blade front, dovetail rear. **Features:** Polymer frame with natural ergonomics and ventilated rib. Barrel with 6-groove 1x16 trwist rate. All metal magazine shell. Made in U.S.A. by Olympic Arms.
Price: **$279.50**

PARA-ORDNANCE PXT 1911 SINGLE-ACTION SINGLE-STACK AUTO PISTOLS
Caliber: 38 Super, 45 ACP. **Barrel:** 3.5", 4.25", 5". **Weight:** 28-40 oz. **Length:** 7.1-8.5" overall. **Grips:** Checkered cocobolo, textured composition, Mother of Pearl synthetic. **Sights:** Blade front, low-profile Novak Extreme Duty adjustable rear. High visibility 3-dot system. **Features:** Available with alloy, steel or stainless steel frames. Skeletonized trigger, spurred hammer. Manual thumb, grip and firing pin lock safeties. Full-length guide rod. PXT designates new Para Power Extractor throughout the line. Introduced 2004. Made in Canada by Para-Ordnance.
Price: SSP-SE1 (2006), midnight blue, 7+1, 5" barrel **$1,094.00**
Price: OPS, stainless, Griptor grooves front strap (2006) **$1,043.00**
Price: LTC, blued or stainless, 7+1, 4.25" barrel ... **$884.00 to 1,043.00**
Price: SSP, blued or stainless, 7+1, 4.25" barrel ... **$884.00 to 1,043.00**

PARA-ORDNANCE PXT 1911 SINGLE-ACTION HIGH-CAPACITY AUTO PISTOLS
Caliber: 9mm, 45 ACP, 10//14/18-shot magazines. **Barrel:** 3", 5". **Weight:** 34-40 oz. **Length:** 7.1-8.5" overall. **Grips:** Textured composition. **Sights:** Blade front, low-profile Novak Extreme Duty adjustable rear or fixed sights. High visibility 3-dot system. **Features:** Available with alloy, steel or stainless steel frames. Skeletonized match trigger, spurred hammer, flared ejection port. Manual thumb, grip and firing pin lock safeties. Full-length guide rod. Introduced 2004. Made in Canada by Para-Ordnance.
Price: P14-45MB (2006), midnight blue, 14+1, 5" barrel **$899.00**
Price: P14-45 stainless, 14+1, 5" barrel **$998.00**
Price: P18-9 stainless,18+1 9mm, 5" barrel **$1,049.00**

Para-Ordnance PXT Limited Pistols
Similar to the PXT-Series pistols except with full-length recoil guide system; fully adjustable rear sight; tuned trigger with over-travel stop; beavertail grip safety; competition hammer; front and rear slide serrations; ambidextrous safety; lowered ejection port; ramped match-grade barrel; dove-tailed front sight. Introduced 2004. Made in Canada by Para-Ordnance.
Price: S12-45 LTD, 45 ACP, 12+1, stainless, Novak sights ... **$1,163.00**
Price: Todd Jarrett 40 S&W, 16+1, stainless **$1,163.00**

HANDGUNS — Autoloaders, Service & Sport

Para-Ordnance LDA

Para-Ordnance Carry

Para-Ordnance CCO

Para-Ordnance Tac-Four

Para-Ordnance Tac-S

Para-Ordnance Limited

Para-Ordnance Slim Hawg

Para-Ordnance Nite-Trac

Para-Ordnance Colonel

Para-Ordnance Nite Hawg

Para-Ordnance Warthog

Para-Ordnance LDA Single-Stack Carry Auto Pistols

Similar to PXT-series except has double-action trigger mechanism, flush hammers, brushed stainless finish, checkered composition grips. Available in 45 ACP. Introduced 1999. Made in Canada by Para-Ordnance.

Price: Carry, 6+1, 3" barrel, stainless **$1,049.00**
Price: Carry, 6+1, 3" barrel, covert black **$1,133.00**
Price: CCO, 7+1, 3.5" barrel **$1,049.00**
Price: CCW, 7+1, 4.5" barrel **$1,049.00**

Para-Ordnance LDA High-Cap Carry Auto Pistols

Similar to LDA-series with double-action trigger mechanism. Also, bobbed beavertail, high-cap mags. Available in 9mm Para., 45 ACP. Introduced 1999. Made in Canada by Para-Ordnance.

Price: Carry 12, 12+1, 3.5" barrel, stainless **$1,133.00**
Price: Tac-Four, 13+1, 4.5" barrel, stainless **$1,028.00**
Price: C TX189B, 18+1, 5" barrel, covert black, Novak sights . **$1,163.00**

Para-Ordnance LDA Single-Stack Auto Pistols

Similar to LDA-series with double-action trigger mechanism. Cocobolo and polymer grips. Available in 45 ACP. Introduced 1999. Made in Canada by Para-Ordnance.

Price: Black Watch Companion, 7+1, 3.5" barrel **$1,133.00**
Price: Tac-S, 7+1, 4.5" barrel, Spec Ops matte finish **$944.00**
Price: Tac-S, 7+1, 4.5" barrel, stainless **$1,028.00**
Price: Limited, 7+1, 5" barrel, stainless **$1,193.00**

Para-Ordnance LDA Hi-Capacity Auto Pistols

Similar to LDA-series with double-action trigger mechanism. Polymer grips. Available in 9mm, 40 S&W, 45 ACP. Introduced 1999. Made in Canada by Para-Ordnance.

Price: Colonel, 14+1, 4.25" barrel **$944.00**
Price: Hi-Cap 45, 14+1, 5" barrel, stainless **$1,028.00**
Price: Hi-Cap 9, 18+1, 5" barrel, covert black finish **$944.00**
Price: Hi-Cap LTD 45 45 ACP, 14+1, 5" barrel, stainless **$1,193.00**
Price: Hi-Cap LTD 40 40 S&W, 15+1, 5" barrel, stainless **$1,193.00**
Price: Hi-Cap LTD 9 9mm, 18+1, 5" barrel, stainless **$1,193.00**

Para-Ordnance LDA Light Rail Pistols

Similar to PXT and LDA-series above, with built-in light rail. Polymer grips. Available in 9mm, 40 S&W, 45 ACP. Made in Canada by Para-Ordnance.

Price: Nite-Tac 45, 14+1 45 ACP, 5" barrel, covert black **$1,034.00**
Price: Nite-Tac 40, 16+1 40 S&W, 5" barrel, stainless (2006) . **$1,103.00**
Price: Nite-Tac 9, 16+1 9mm, 5" barrel, stainless (2006) **$1,103.00**

PARA-ORDNANCE WARTHOG

Caliber: 9mm, 45 ACP, 6, 10, or 12-shot magazines. **Barrel:** 3". **Weight:** 24 to 31.5 oz. **Length:** 6.5". **Grips:** Varies by model. **Features:** Single action. Made in Canada by Para-Ordnance.

Price: Slim Hawg (2006) single stack .45 ACP, stainless, 6+1 . **$1,043.00**
Price: Nite Hawg .45 ACP, black finish, 10+1 . . . . **$1,013.00**
Price: Warthog .45 ACP, Regal finish, 10+1 . . . . **$884.00**
Price: Stainless Warthog .45 ACP (2006), brushed finish, 10+1 . **$989.00**
Price: Hawg 9 9mm Regal finish, alloy frame, 12+1 . . . . **$884.00**
Price: Lite Hawg 9 9mm (2006) black finish, alloy frame, 12+1 . **$1,049.00**

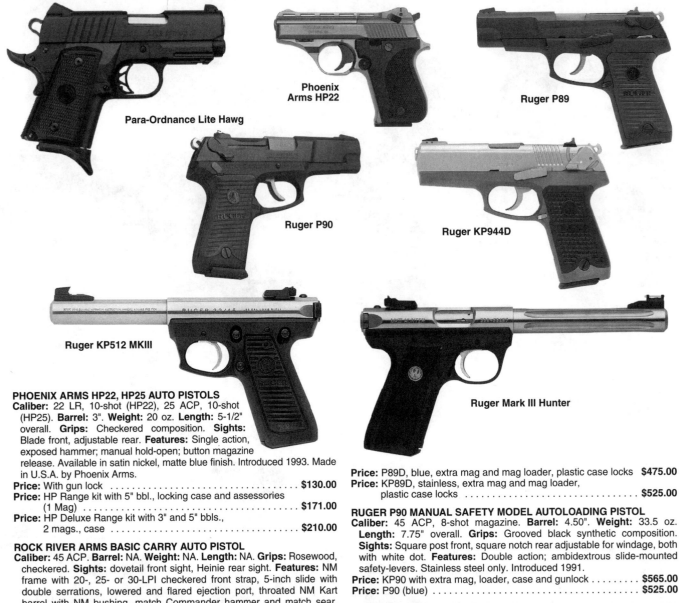

Para-Ordnance Lite Hawg

Phoenix Arms HP22

Ruger P89

Ruger P90

Ruger KP944D

Ruger KP512 MKIII

Ruger Mark III Hunter

PHOENIX ARMS HP22, HP25 AUTO PISTOLS
Caliber: 22 LR, 10-shot (HP22), 25 ACP, 10-shot (HP25). **Barrel:** 3". **Weight:** 20 oz. **Length:** 5-1/2" overall. **Grips:** Checkered composition. **Sights:** Blade front, adjustable rear. **Features:** Single action, exposed hammer; manual hold-open; button magazine release. Available in satin nickel, matte blue finish. Introduced 1993. Made in U.S.A. by Phoenix Arms.
Price: With gun lock $130.00
Price: HP Range kit with 5" bbl., locking case and assessories
(1 Mag) $171.00
Price: HP Deluxe Range kit with 3" and 5" bbls.,
2 mags., case $210.00

ROCK RIVER ARMS BASIC CARRY AUTO PISTOL
Caliber: 45 ACP. **Barrel:** NA. **Weight:** NA. **Length:** NA. **Grips:** Rosewood, checkered. **Sights:** dovetail front sight, Heinie rear sight. **Features:** NM frame with 20-, 25- or 30-LPI checkered front strap, 5-inch slide with double serrations, lowered and flared ejection port, throated NM Kart barrel with NM bushing, match Commander hammer and match sear, aluminum speed trigger, dehorned, Parkerized finish, one magazine, accuracy guarantee. 3.5 lb. Trigger pull. Introduced 2006. Made in U.S.A. From Rock River Arms.
Price: PS2700 .... $1,540.00

RUGER P89 AUTOLOADING PISTOL
Caliber: 9mm Para., 15-shot magazine. **Barrel:** 4.50". **Weight:** 32 oz. **Length:** 7.75" overall. **Grips:** Grooved black synthetic composition. **Sights:** Square post front, square notch rear adjustable for windage, both with white dot inserts. **Features:** Double action, ambidextrous slide-mounted safety-levers. Slide 4140 chrome-moly steel or 400-series stainless steel, frame lightweight aluminum alloy. Ambidextrous magazine release. Blue, stainless steel. Introduced 1986; stainless 1990.
Price: P89, blue, extra mag and mag loader, plastic case locks .. $475.00
Price: KP89, stainless, extra mag and mag loader,
plastic case locks $525.00

Ruger P89D Decocker Autoloading Pistol
Similar to standard P89 except has ambidextrous decocking levers in place of regular slide-mounted safety. Decocking levers move firing pin inside slide where hammer cannot reach. Blue, stainless steel. Introduced 1990.

Price: P89D, blue, extra mag and mag loader, plastic case locks $475.00
Price: KP89D, stainless, extra mag and mag loader,
plastic case locks $525.00

RUGER P90 MANUAL SAFETY MODEL AUTOLOADING PISTOL
Caliber: 45 ACP, 8-shot magazine. **Barrel:** 4.50". **Weight:** 33.5 oz. **Length:** 7.75" overall. **Grips:** Grooved black synthetic composition. **Sights:** Square post front, square notch rear adjustable for windage, both with white dot. **Features:** Double action; ambidextrous slide-mounted safety-levers. Stainless steel only. Introduced 1991.
Price: KP90 with extra mag, loader, case and gunlock $565.00
Price: P90 (blue) $525.00

Ruger KP94 Autoloading Pistol
Sized midway between full-size P-Series and compact KP94. 4.25" barrel, 7.5" overall length, weighs about 34 oz. KP94 manual safety model. Slide gripping grooves roll over top of slide. KP94 has ambidextrous safety-levers; Matte finish stainless slide, barrel, alloy frame. Also blue. Includes hard case and lock. Introduced 1994. Made in U.S.A. by Sturm, Ruger & Co.
Price: P944, blue (manual safety) $495.00
Price: KP944 (40-caliber) (manual safety-stainless) $575.00

RUGER P95 AUTOLOADING PISTOL
Caliber: 9mm Para., 15-shot magazine. **Barrel:** 3.9". **Weight:** 27 oz. **Length:** 7.25" overall. **Grips:** Grooved; integral with frame. **Sights:** Blade front, rear drift adjustable for windage; 3-dot system. **Features:** Molded polymer grip frame, stainless steel or chrome-moly slide. Suitable for +P+ ammunition. Safety model, decocker. Introduced 1996. Made in U.S.A. by Sturm, Ruger & Co. Comes with lockable plastic case, spare magazine, loader and lock, Picatinny rails.
Price: P95DPR15 decocker only $445.00
Price: P95PR15 stainless steel decocker only $480.00
Price: KP95PR15 safety model, stainless steel $480.00
Price: P95PR15 safety model, blued finish $445.00

Ruger KP9515

Ruger KP45HMKIII

Sabre Defence 9mm

RUGER MARK III STANDARD AUTOLOADING PISTOL

Caliber: 22 LR, 10-shot magazine. **Barrel:** 4-3/4", 5-1/2", 6", or 6-7/8". **Weight:** 35 oz. (4-3/4" bbl.). **Length:** 9" (4-3/4" bbl.). **Grips:** Checkered composition grip panels. **Sights:** Fixed, wide blade front, fixed rear. **Features:** Updated design of original Standard Auto and Mark II series. Standard models have lighter barrels. Target models have cocobolo grips; bull, target, competition, and hunter barrels; and adjustable sights. Introduced 2005.

Price: MKIII4, MKIII6 (blued) $322.00
Price: MKIII512 (blued) $382.00
Price: KMKIII512 (stainless) $483.00
Price: MKIII678 (blued) $382.00
Price: KMKIII678GC (stainless slabside barrel) . . $555.00
Price: KMKIII678GH (stainless fluted barrel) $567.00

Sabre Defence 45 ACP

Sigarms Revolution

Ruger 22/45 Mark III Pistol

Similar to other 22 Mark III autos except has Zytel grip frame that matches angle and magazine latch of Model 1911 45 ACP pistol. Available in 4" standard, 4-1/2" and 5-1/2" bull barrels. Comes with extra magazine, plastic case, lock. Introduced 1992. Hunter introduced 2006.

Price: P4MKIII, 4" bull barrel, adjustable sights $307.00
Price: P45GCMKIII, 4.5" bull barrel, fixed sights $305.00
Price: P512MKIII (5-1/2" bull blued barrel, adj. sights) $307.00
Price: KP512MKIII (5-1/2" stainless bull barrel, adj. sights $398.00
Price: Hunter KP45HMKIII 4.5" barrel (2007), KP678HMKIII,
6-7/8" stainless fluted bull barrel, adj. sights $487.00

SABRE DEFENCE SPHINX 3000 PISTOLS

Caliber: 9mm, 45 ACP., 10-shot magazine. **Barrel:** 4.43". **Weight:** 39.15 oz. **Length:** 8.27" overall. **Grips:** Textured polymer. **Sights:** Fixed Trijicon Night Sights. **Features:** CNC engineered from stainless steel billet; grip frame in stainless steel, titanium or high-strength aluminum. Integrated accessory rail, high-cut beavertail, decocking lever. Made in Switzerland. Imported by Sabre Defence Industries.

Price: 45 ACP (2007) $2,990.00
Price: 9mm Standard, titanium w/decocker $2,700.00
Price: 9mm Tactical, 3.74" barrel $2,425.00

SEECAMP LWS 32 STAINLESS DA AUTO

Caliber: 32 ACP Win. Silvertip, 6-shot magazine. **Barrel:** 2", integral with frame. **Weight:** 10.5 oz. **Length:** 4-1/8" overall. **Grips:** Glass-filled nylon. **Sights:** Smooth, no-snag, contoured slide and barrel top. **Features:** Aircraft quality 17-4 PH stainless steel. Inertia-operated firing pin. Hammer fired double-action-only. Hammer automatically follows slide down to safety rest position after each shot, no manual safety needed. Magazine safety disconnector. Polished stainless. Introduced 1985. From L.W. Seecamp.

Price: $425.00

SIGARMS REVOLUTION PISTOLS

Caliber: 45 ACP, 8-shot magazine. **Barrel:** 5". **Weight:** 40.3 oz. **Length:** 8.65" overall. **Grips:** Checkered wood grips. **Sights:** Novak night sights. Blade front, drift adjustable rear for windage. **Features:** Single-action 1911. Hand-fitted dehorned stainless-steel frame and slide; match-grade barrel, hammer/sear set and trigger; 25-lpi front strap checkering, 20-lpi mainspring housing checkering. Beavertail grip safety with speed bump, extended thumb safety, firing pin safety and hammer intercept notch. Introduced 2005. XO series has contrast sights, Ergo Grip XT textured polymer grips. Target line features adjustable target night sights, match barrel, custom wood grips, non-railed frame in stainless or Nitron finishes. TTT series is two-tone 1911 with Nitron slide and black controls on stainless frame. Includes burled maple grips, adjustable combat night sights. STX line available from SIGARMS Custom Shop; two-tone 1911, non-railed, Nitron slide, stainless frame, burled maple grips. Polished cocking serrations, flat-top slide, magwell. Carry line has Novak night sights, lanyard attachment point, gray diamondwood or rosewood grips, 8+1 capacity. Compact series has 6+1 capacity, 7.7" OAL, 4.25" barrel, slim-profile wood grips, weighs 30.3 oz. RCS line (Revolution Compact SAS) is Customs Shop version with anti-snag dehorning. Stainless or Nitron finish, Novak night sights, slim-profile gray diamondwood or rosewood grips. 6+1 capacity. Imported from Germany by SIGARMS, Inc.

Price: Revolution Nitron finish, w/ or w/o Picatinny rail $1,069.00
Price: Revolution Stainless, w/ or w/o Picatinny rail $1,050.00
Price: Revolution XO Black $890.00
Price: Revolution XO Stainless, intr. 2006 . . . . $860.00
Price: Revolution Target Nitron, intr. 2006 . . . . $1,100.00
Price: Revolution TTT, intr. 2006 . . . . $1,070.00
Price: Revolution STX, intr. 2006 . . . . $1,300.00
Price: Revolution Carry Nitron, 4.25" barrel, intr. 2006 . . . . . . $1,070.00
Price: Revolution Compact, Nitron finish $1,080.00
Price: Revolution RCS, Nitron finish $1,150.00

SIGARMS P220 AUTO PISTOLS

Caliber: 45 ACP, (7- or 8-shot magazine). **Barrel:** 4.4". **Weight:** 27.8 oz. **Length:** 7.8" overall. **Grips:** Checkered black plastic. **Sights:** Blade front, drift adjustable rear for windage. Optional Siglite night sights. **Features:** Double action. Stainless-steel slide, Nitron finish, alloy frame, M1913 Picatinny rail; safety system of decocking lever, automatic firing pin safety block, safety intercept notch, and trigger bar disconnector. Squared combat-type trigger guard. Slide stays open after last shot. Introduced 1976. P220 SAS Anti-Snag has dehorned stainless steel slide, front Siglite Night Sight, rounded trigger guard, dust cover, Custom Shop wood grips. Equinox line is Custom Shop product with Nitron stainless-steel slide with a black hard-anodized alloy frame, brush-polished flats and nickel accents. Truglo tritium fiber-optic front sight, rear Siglite night sight, gray laminated wood grips with checkering and stippling. Imported from Germany by SIGARMS, Inc.

Price: P220R $840.00
Price: P220R Two-Tone, matte-stainless slide, black alloy frame $840.00
Price: P220 Stainless $935.00
Price: P220 Crimson Trace, w/lasergrips $1,150.00
Price: P220 SAS Anti-Snag $1,000.00
Price: P220 Two-Tone SAO, single action, intr. 2006, from $929.00
Price: P220R DAK (intr. 2006) $840.00
Price: P220R Equinox (intr. 2006) $1,070.00

SIG-Sauer P220

SIG-Sauer P245 Compact

SIG-Sauer Pro 2009

SIG-Sauer P229 Sport

SIG-Sauer P232

SIG-Sauer Mosquito

SIGARMS P220 CARRY AUTO PISTOLS

Caliber: 45 ACP, 8-shot magazine. **Barrel:** 3.9". **Weight:** NA. **Length:** 7.1" overall. **Grips:** Checkered black plastic. **Sights:** Blade front, drift adjustable rear for windage. Optional Siglite night sights. **Features:** Similar to full-size P220, except is "Commander" size. Single stack, DA/SA operation, Nitron finish, Picatinny rail, and either post and dot contrast or 3-dot Siglite night sights. Introduced 2005. Imported from Germany by SIGARMS, Inc.

Price: P220 Carry, from **$840.00**
Price: P220 Carry Two-Tone, from **$915.00**
Price: P220 Carry Equinox, wood grips, two tone, from **$1,070.00**

SIG-Sauer P229 DA Auto Pistol

Similar to the P228 except chambered for 9mm Para. (10- or 15-round magazines), 40 S&W, 357 SIG (10- or 12-round magazines). Has 3.86" barrel, 7.1" overall length and 3.35" height. Weight is 32.4 oz. Introduced 1991. Frame made in Germany, stainless steel slide assembly made in U.S.; pistol assembled in U.S. From SIGARMS, Inc.

Price: P229R, from **$840.00**
Price: P229R Crimson Trace, w/lasergrips, from **$1,150.00**

SIG-SAUER SP2022 PISTOLS

Caliber: 9mm Para., 357 SIG, 40 S&W, 10-, 12-, or 15-shot magazines. **Barrel:** 3.9". **Weight:** 30.2 oz. **Length:** 7.4" overall. **Grips:** Composite and rubberized one-piece. **Sights:** Blade front, rear adjustable for windage. Optional Siglite night sights. **Features:** Polymer frame, stainless steel slide; integral frame accessory rail; replaceable steel frame rails; left- or right-handed magazine release, two interchangeable grips. From SIGARMS, Inc.

Price: SP2009, Nitron finish, from **$640.00**

SIG-Sauer P226 Pistols

Similar to the P220 pistol except has 4.4" barrel, measures 7.7" overall, weighs 34 oz. Chambered in 9mm, 357 SIG, or 40 S&W. X-Five series has factory tuned single-action trigger, 5" slide and barrel, ergonomic wood Nill grips with beavertail, ambidextrous thumb safety and stainless slide and frame with magwell, low-profile adjustable target sights, front cocking serrations and a 25-meter factory test target. Imported from Germany by SIGARMS, Inc.

Price: P226R, Nitron finish, night sights **$915.00**
Price: P226R Two Tone, Nitron/stainless finish **$969.00**
Price: P226 Stainless, from **$935.00**
Price: P226 X-Five **$2,500.00**
Price: P226 X-Five Tactical, Ilaflon finish, high cap, from **$1,500.00**

SIG-SAUER P232 PERSONAL SIZE PISTOL

Caliber: 380 ACP, 7-shot. **Barrel:** 3.6". **Weight:** 17.6-22.4 oz. **Length:** 6.6" overall. **Grips:** Checkered black composite. **Sights:** Blade front, rear adjustable for windage. **Features:** Double action/single action or DAO. Blow-

back operation, stationary barrel. Introduced 1997. Imported from Germany by SIGARMS, Inc.

Price: P232, blued **$519.00**
Price: P232 Stainless **$709.00**
Price: P232 Two-Tone **$539.00**

SIG-SAUER P239 PISTOL

Caliber: 9mm Para., 8-shot, 357 SIG 40 S&W, 7-shot magazine. **Barrel:** 3.6". **Weight:** 25.2 oz. **Length:** 6.6" overall. **Grips:** Checkered black composite. **Sights:** Blade front, rear adjustable for windage. Optional Siglite night sights. **Features:** SA/DA or DAO; blackened stainless steel slide, aluminum alloy frame. Introduced 1996. Made in U.S.A. by SIGARMS, Inc.

Price: P239 . . . . **$739.00**
Price: P239 Two-Tone, w/night sights **$895.00**
Price: P239 DAK, double action **$739.00**

SIG-SAUER MOSQUITO PISTOL

Caliber: 22LR, 10-shot magazine. **Barrel:** 3.9". **Weight:** 24.6 oz. **Length:** 7.2" overall. **Grips:** Checkered black composite. **Sights:** Blade front, rear adjustable for windage. **Features:** Blowback operated, fixed barrel, polymer frame, slide-mounted ambidextrous safety. Introduced 2005. Made in U.S.A. by SIGARMS, Inc.

Price: Mosquito, blued **$390.00**
Price: Mosquito w/threaded barrel, intr. 2006 . . . . **$500.00**
Price: Mosquito Combat Green **$460.00**

SMITH & WESSON M&P AUTO PISTOLS

Caliber: 9mm, 40 S&W, 357 SIG. **Barrel:** 4.25". **Weight:** 24.25 oz. **Length:** 7.5" overall. **Grips:** One-piece Xenoy, wraparound with straight backstrap. **Sights:** Ramp dovetail mount front; tritium sights optional; Novak Lo-mount Carry rear. **Features:** Zytel polymer frame, embedded stainless steel chassis; stainless steel slide and barrel, stainless steel structural components, black Melonite finish, reversible magazine catch, 3 interchangeable palmswell grip sizes, universal rail, sear deactivation lever, internal lock system, magazine disconnect. Ships with 2 magazines. Internal lock models available. Overall height: 5.5"; width: 1.2"; sight radius: 6.4". Introduced November 2005. 45 ACP version introduced 2007, 10+1 or 14+1 capacity. **Barrel:** 4.5". **Length:** 8.05". **Weight:** 29.6 ounces. **Features:** Picatinny-style equipment rail; black or bi-tone, dark-earth-brown frame. Bi-tone M&P45 includes ambidextrous, frame-mounted thumb safety, take down tool with lanyard attachment. Compact 9mm/357 SIG/40 S&W versions introduced 2007. Compacts have 3.5" barrel, OAL 6.7". 10+1 or 12+1 capacity. **Weight:** 21.7 ounces. **Features:** Picatinny-style equipment rail. Made in U.S.A. by Smith & Wesson.

Price: **$624.00**
Price: M&P 45 Bi-tone (2007) **$678.00**
Price: M&P Compacts (2007) **$624.00**

Smith & Wesson M&P

Smith & Wesson M&P Compact

Smith & Wesson M&P 45 Bi-Tone

Smith & Wesson 457 TDA

Smith & Wesson 908

Smith & Wesson 4013 TSW

Smith & Wesson 410 DA

Smith & Wesson 910 DA

Smith & Wesson 3913 LadySmith

SMITH & WESSON MODEL 457 TDA AUTO PISTOL

Caliber: 45 ACP, 7-shot magazine. **Barrel:** 3-3/4". **Weight:** 29 oz. **Length:** 7-1/4" overall. **Grips:** One-piece Xenoy, wraparound with straight backstrap. **Sights:** Post front, fixed rear, 3-dot system. **Features:** Aluminum alloy frame, matte blue carbon steel slide; bobbed hammer; smooth trigger. Introduced 1996. Made in U.S.A. by Smith & Wesson.
Price: Model 457, black matte finish **$711.00**
Price: Model 457S, matte finish stainless **$711.00**

SMITH & WESSON MODEL 908 AUTO PISTOL

Caliber: 9mm Para., 8-shot magazine. **Barrel:** 3-1/2". **Weight:** 24 oz. **Length:** 6-13/16". **Grips:** One-piece Xenoy, wraparound with straight backstrap. **Sights:** Post front, fixed rear, 3-dot system. **Features:** Aluminum alloy frame, matte blue carbon steel slide; bobbed hammer; smooth trigger. Introduced 1996. Made in U.S.A. by Smith & Wesson.
Price: Model 908, black matte finish **$648.00**
Price: Model 908S, stainless matte finish **$648.00**
Price: Model 908S Carry Combo, with holster **$672.00**

SMITH & WESSON MODEL 4013 TSW AUTO

Caliber: 40 S&W, 9-shot magazine. **Barrel:** 3-1/2". **Weight:** 26.8 oz. **Length:** 6 3/4" overall. **Grips:** Xenoy one-piece wraparound. **Sights:** Novak 3-dot system. **Features:** Traditional double-action system; stainless slide, alloy frame; fixed barrel bushing; ambidextrous decocker; reversible magazine catch, equipment rail. Introduced 1997. Made in U.S.A. by Smith & Wesson.
Price: Model 4013 TSW **$1,027.00**

SMITH & WESSON MODEL 410 DA AUTO PISTOL

Caliber: 40 S&W, 10-shot magazine. **Barrel:** 4". **Weight:** 28.5 oz. **Length:** 7.5". **Grips:** One-piece Xenoy, wraparound with straight backstrap.

Sights: Post front, fixed rear; 3-dot system. **Features:** Aluminum alloy frame; blued carbon steel slide; traditional double action with left-side slide-mounted decocking lever. Introduced 1996. Made in U.S.A. by Smith & Wesson.
Price: From **$687.00**

SMITH & WESSON MODEL 910 DA AUTO PISTOL

Caliber: 9mm Para., 10-shot magazine. **Barrel:** 4". **Weight:** 28 oz. **Length:** 7-3/8" overall. **Grips:** One-piece Xenoy, wraparound with straight backstrap. **Sights:** Post front with white dot, fixed 2-dot rear. **Features:** Alloy frame, blue carbon steel slide. Slide-mounted decocking lever. Introduced 1995.
Price: From **$616.00**

SMITH & WESSON MODEL 3913 TRADITIONAL DOUBLE ACTIONS

Caliber: 9mm Para., 8-shot magazine. **Barrel:** 3-1/2". **Weight:** 24.8 oz. **Length:** 6-3/4" overall. **Grips:** One-piece Delrin wraparound, textured surface. **Sights:** Post front with white dot, Novak LoMount Carry with two dots. **Features:** TSW has aluminum alloy frame, stainless slide. Bobbed hammer with no half-cock notch; smooth .304" trigger with rounded edges. Straight backstrap. Equipment rail. Extra magazine included. Introduced 1989. The 3913-LS Ladysmith has frame that is upswept at the front, rounded trigger guard. Comes in frosted stainless steel with matching gray grips. Grips are ergonomically correct for a woman's hand. Novak LoMount Carry rear sight adjustable for windage. Extra magazine included. Introduced 1990.
Price: 3913TSW **$924.00**
Price: 3913-LS **$909.00**

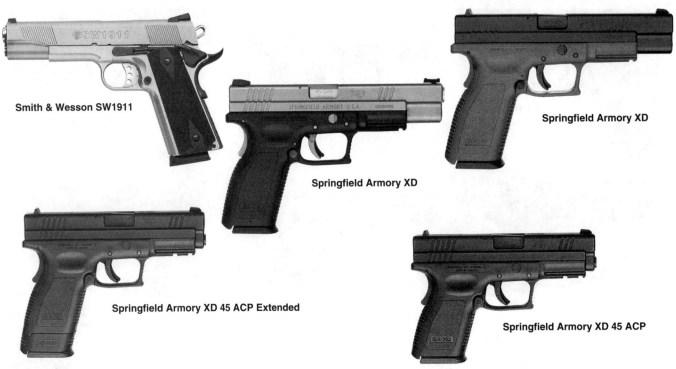

Smith & Wesson SW1911

Springfield Armory XD

Springfield Armory XD

Springfield Armory XD 45 ACP Extended

Springfield Armory XD 45 ACP

SMITH & WESSON MODEL SW1911 PISTOLS
Caliber: 45 ACP, 8 rounds. **Barrel:** 5". **Weight:** 39 oz. **Length:** 8.7". **Grips:** Wood or rubber. **Sights:** Novak Lo-Mount Carry, white dot front. **Features:** Large stainless frame and slide with matte finish, single-side external safety. No. 108284 has adjustable target rear sight, ambidextrous safety levers, 20-lpi checkered front strap, comes with two 8-round magazines. DK model (Doug Koenig) also has oversized magazine well, Doug Koenig speed hammer, flat competition speed trigger with overtravel stop, rosewood grips with Smith & Wesson silver medallions, oversized magazine well, special serial number run. No. 108295 has olive drab Crimson Trace lasergrips. No. 108299 has carbon-steel frame and slide with polished flats on slide, standard GI recoil guide, laminated double-diamond walnut grips with silver Smith & Wesson medallions, adjustable target sights. Tactical Rail No. 108293 has a Picatinny rail, black Melonite finish, Novak Lo-Mount Carry Sights, scandium alloy frame. Tactical Rail Stainless introduced 2006. SW1911PD gun is Commander size, scandium-alloy frame, 4.25" barrel, 8" OAL, 28.0 oz., non-reflective black matte finish. Gunsite edition has scandium alloy frame, beveled edges, solid match aluminum trigger, Herrett's logoed tactical oval walnut stocks, special serial number run, brass bead Novak front sight. SC model has 4.25" barrel, scandium alloy frame, stainless-steel slide, non-reflective matte finish.
Price: From **$1,011.00**

SMITH & WESSON ENHANCED SIGMA SERIES DAO PISTOLS
Caliber: 9mm Para., 40 S&W; 10-, 16-shot magazine. **Barrel:** 4". **Weight:** 24.7 oz. **Length:** 7-1/4" overall. **Grips:** Integral. **Sights:** White dot front, fixed rear; 3-dot system. Tritium night sights available. **Features:** Ergonomic polymer frame; low barrel centerline; internal striker firing system; corrosion-resistant slide; Teflon-filled, electroless-nickel coated magazine, equipment rail. Introduced 1994. Made in U.S.A. by Smith & Wesson.
Price: From **$419.00**

SMITH & WESSON MODEL CS9 CHIEF'S SPECIAL AUTO
Caliber: 9mm Para., 7-shot magazine. **Barrel:** 3". **Weight:** 20.8 oz. **Length:** 6-1/4" overall. **Grips:** Hogue wraparound rubber. **Sights:** White dot front, fixed 2-dot rear. **Features:** Traditional double-action trigger mechanism. Alloy frame, stainless slide. Ambidextrous safety. Introduced 1999. Made in U.S.A. by Smith & Wesson.
Price: Stainless **$782.00**

SMITH & WESSON MODEL CS45 CHIEF'S SPECIAL AUTO
Caliber: 45 ACP, 6-shot magazine. **Weight:** 23.9 oz. **Features:** Introduced 1999. Made in U.S.A. by Smith & Wesson.
Price: Stainless **$830.00**

SPRINGFIELD ARMORY XD POLYMER AUTO PISTOLS
Caliber: 9mm Para., 357 SIG, 40 S&W, 45 ACP, 45 GAP. **Barrel:** 3", 4", 5". **Weight:** 20.5-31 oz. **Length:** 6.26-8" overall. **Grips:** Textured polymer. **Sights:** Varies by model; Fixed sights are dovetail front and rear steel 3-dot units. **Features:** Three sizes in X-Treme Duty (XD) line: Sub-Compact (3" barrel), Service (4" barrel), Tactical (5" barrel). Three ported models available. Ergonomic polymer frame, hammer-forged barrel, no-tool disassembly, ambidextrous magazine release, visual/tactile loaded chamber indicator, visual/tactile striker status indicator, grip safety, XD gear system included. Introduced 2004. XD 45 introduced 2006. Compact line introduced 2007. Compacts ship with one extended magazine (13) and one compact magazine (10). From Springfield Armory.
Price: Sub-Compact Black 9mm, fixed sights **$536.00**
Price: Sub-Compact Black 9mm/40 S&W, Heinie night sights . . . **$633.00**
Price: Sub-Compact Bi-Tone 9mm/40 S&W, fixed sights **$566.00**
Price: Sub-Compact OD Green 9mm/40 S&W, fixed sights **$536.00**
Price: Service Black 9mm/40 S&W/357 SIG, fixed sights **$536.00**
Price: Service Black 45 ACP, fixed sights **$559.00**
Price: Service Black 45 GAP, fixed sights **$536.00**
Price: Service Black 9mm/40 S&W, Heinie night sights **$626.00**
Price: Service Bi-Tone 9mm/40 S&W/357 SIG/45 GAP,
fixed sights **$566.00**
Price: Service Bi-Tone 45 ACP, fixed sights **$595.00**
Price: Service OD Green 9mm/40 S&W/357 SIG/45 GAP,
fixed sights **$536.00**
Price: V-10 Ported Black 9mm/40 S&W/357 SIG **$566.00**
Price: Tactical Black 45 ACP, fixed sights **$595.00**
Price: Tactical Black 9mm/40 S&W/357 SIG, fixed sights **$566.00**
Price: Tactical Bi-Tone 45 ACP/45 GAP, fixed sights . . . **$626.00/$595.00**
Price: Tactical OD Green 9mm/40 S&W/357 SIG/45 GAP,
fixed sights **$566.00**
Price: Tactical OD Green 45 ACP, fixed sights **$595.00**
Price: Compact, 4" barrel (2007) **$589.00**
Price: Compact, 5" barrel (2007) **$619.00**
Price: Compact, 5" barrel, Trijicon night sights (2007) **$709.00**

Springfield Armory 1911A1 Standard

Springfield Armory Full-Size 1911A1

Springfield Armory Micro-Compact

Springfield Armory EMP

Springfield Armory TRP

SPRINGFIELD ARMORY CUSTOM LOADED FULL-SIZE 1911A1 AUTO PISTOL

Caliber: 9mm Para., 9-shot; 45 ACP, 7-shot. **Barrel:** 5". **Weight:** 30-42 oz. **Length:** 8.5" overall. **Grips:** Cocobolo, polymer. **Sights:** Fixed 3-dot system or adjustable. **Features:** Beveled magazine well; lowered and flared ejection port. All forged parts, including frame, barrel, slide. All new production. Introduced 1990. From Springfield Armory.

Price: Tactical Combat Black Stainless Steel, fixed sights $904.00
Price: Stainless Steel, fixed sights $902.00
Price: Service Model 5" Lightweight, bi-tone finish $934.00
Price: Stainless Steel, adjustable target sights $966.00
Price: Black Stainless, adjustable Bo-Mar rear, 3-dot tritium .. $1,124.00
Price: Stainless Steel 9mm, fixed combat sights $976.00

SPRINGFIELD ARMORY GI 45 1911A1 AUTO PISTOLS

Caliber: 45 ACP; 6-, 7-, 13-shot magazines. **Barrel:** 3", 4", 5". **Weight:** 28-36 oz. **Length:** 5.5-8.5" overall. **Grips:** Checkered double-diamond walnut, "U.S" logo. **Sights:** Fixed GI style. **Features:** Similar to WWII GI-issue 45s at hammer, beavertail, mainspring housing. From Springfield Armory. Enhanced Micro Pistol (EMP) introduced 2007.

Price: GI .45 4" Lightweight Champion, 7+1, 28 oz. $564.00
Price: GI .45 5" High Capacity, 13+1, 36 oz. $617.00
Price: GI .45 5" OD Green, 7+1, 36 oz. $564.00
Price: GI .45 3" Micro Compact, 6+1, 32 oz. $608.00
Price: EMP 9mm 3", (2007) $940.00

SPRINGFIELD ARMORY MIL-SPEC 1911A1 AUTO PISTOLS

Caliber: 38 Super, 9-shot magazines; 45 ACP, 7-shot magazines. **Barrel:** 5". **Weight:** 35.6-39 oz. **Length:** 8.5-8.625" overall. **Features:** Similar to GI 45s. From Springfield Armory.

Price: Mil-Spec Parkerized, 7+1, 35.6 oz. $660.00
Price: Mil-Spec Stainless Steel, 7+1, 36 oz. $724.00
Price: Mil-Spec 38 Super, Nickel finish, 9+1, 39 oz. $1,254.00

Springfield Armory Custom Loaded Champion 1911A1 Pistol

Similar to standard 1911A1, slide and barrel are 4". 7.5" OAL. Available in 45 ACP only. Novak Night Sights. Delta hammer and cocobolo grips. Parkerized or stainless. Introduced 1989.

Price: Stainless, 34 oz. $952.00
Price: Lightweight, 28 oz. $913.00

Springfield Armory Custom Loaded Ultra Compact Pistol

Similar to 1911A1 Compact, shorter slide, 3.5" barrel, 6+1, 7" OAL. Beavertail grip safety, beveled magazine well, fixed sights. Videki speed trigger, flared ejection port, stainless steel frame, blued slide, match grade barrel, rubber grips. Introduced 1996. From Springfield Armory.

Price: Stainless Steel $952.00

SPRINGFIELD ARMORY CUSTOM LOADED MICRO-COMPACT 1911A1 PISTOL

Caliber: 45 ACP, 6+1 capacity. **Barrel:** 3" 1:16 LH. **Weight:** 24-32 oz. **Length:** 4.7". **Grips:** Slimline cocobolo. **Sights:** Novak LoMount tritium. Dovetail front. **Features:** Aluminum hard-coat anodized alloy frame, forged steel slide, forged barrel, ambi-thumb safety, Extreme Carry Bevel dehorning. Lockable plastic case, 2 magazines.

Price: Bi-Tone Operator w/light rail $1,284.00
Price: Lightweight Bi-Tone $1,220.00

SPRINGFIELD ARMORY CUSTOM LOADED LONG SLIDE 1911A1 PISTOL

Caliber: 45 ACP, 7+1 capacity. **Barrel:** 6" 1:16 LH. **Weight:** 41 oz. **Length:** 9.5". **Grips:** Slimline cocobolo. **Sights:** Dovetail front; fully adjustable target rear. **Features:** Longer sight radius, 7.9".

Price: Bi-Tone Operator w/light rail $1,097.00

Springfield Armory TRP Pistols

Similar to 1911A1 except 45 ACP only, checkered front strap and main-spring housing, Novak Night Sight combat rear sight and matching dove-tailed front sight, tuned, polished extractor, oversize barrel link; lightweight speed trigger and combat action job, match barrel and bushing, extended ambidextrous thumb safety and fitted beavertail grip safety. Checkered cocobolo wood grips, comes with two Wilson 7-shot magazines. Frame is engraved "Tactical," both sides of frame with "TRP." Introduced 1998. TRP-Pro Model meets FBI specifications for SWAT Hostage Rescue Team. From Springfield Armory.

Price: Standard with Armory Kote finish $1,606.00
Price: Standard, stainless steel $1,606.00
Price: Standard with Operator Light Rail Armory Kote $1,689.00
Price: TRP-Pro, Armory Kote finish $2,395.00

Springfield Armory Loaded Operator 1911A1 Pistol

Similar to Full-Size 1911A1, except light-mounting rail is forged into frame. From Springfield Armory.

Price: Loaded Full-Size MC Operator, 42 oz., 8.5" OAL $1,254.00
Price: TRP Light Rail Armory Kote, 42 oz. $1,689.00
Price: Micro Compact LW, w/XML Mini Light, 32 oz., 6.7 OAL . $1,284.00

Springfield Armory Trophy Match 1911A1 Pistol

Similar to Full Size model, 5" match barrel and slide, fully adjustable sights. From Springfield Armory.

Price: Trophy Match 45 ACP, stainless $1,452.00

Taurus 22

Taurus 1911B-1

Stoeger Cougar 8000

Taurus 92

Taurus 24-7 OSS

Taurus 24

Taurus 99SS

STOEGER COUGAR
Caliber: 9mm, 40 S&W. Capacity: 15 (9mm); 11 (40 S&W). **Barrel:** 3.6". **Length:** 7.0". **Weight:** 32.5 oz. **Grips:** Black checkered w/3 interchangeable backstraps. **Sights:** 3-dot. **Features:** Aluminum frame, DA/SA, ambisafety. Comes with two magazines. Same design as Beretta-made version. Rotating barrel, hard-chromed bores, removable front sight, combat trigger, Made in Turkey, imported by Benelli USA. Introduced 2007.
Price: **$370.00**

TAURUS MODEL 800 Series
Caliber: 9mm, 40 S&W, 45 ACP. **Barrel:** 4". **Weight:** 32 oz. **Length:** 8.25". **Grips:** Checkered. **Sights:** Novak. **Features:** DA/SA. Blue and Stainless Steel finish. Introduced in 2007. Imported from Brazil by Taurus International.
Price: 809B, 9mm, Blue, 17+1 . . . . **NA**
Price: 809SS, 9mm, Stainless Steel, 17+1 . . . . **NA**
Price: 840B, .40 cal., Blue, 15+1 . . . . **NA**
Price: 840SS, .40 cal., Stainless Steel, 15+1 . . . . **NA**
Price: 845B, .45 ACP, Blue, 12+1 . . . . **NA**
Price: 845SS, .45ACP, Stainless Steel, 12+1 . . . . **NA**

TAURUS MODEL 1911
Caliber: 45 ACP, 8+1 capacity. **Barrel:** 5". **Weight:** 33 oz. **Length:** 8.5". **Grips:** Checkered Black. **Sights:** Heinie Straight 8. **Features:** SA. Blue, Stainless Steel, Duotone Blue, and Blue/Gray finish. Standard/Picatinny Rail, Standard Frame, Alloy Frame, and Alloy/Picatinny Rail. Introduced in 2007. Imported from Brazil by Taurus International.
Price: 1911B-1, Blue . . . . **NA**
Price: 1911SS, Stainless Steel . . . . **NA**
Price: 1911SS-1, Stainless Steel . . . . **NA**
Price: 1911 DT, Duotone Blue . . . . **NA**
Price: 1911 AL, Blue/Gray . . . . **NA**
Price: 1911 ALR, Blue/Gray . . . . **NA**

TAURUS MODEL 917
Caliber: 9mm, 19+1 capacity. **Barrel:** 4.3". **Weight:** 32.2 oz. **Length:** 8.5". **Grips:** Checkered Rubber. **Sights:** Fixed. **Features:** SA/DA. Blue and Stainless Steel finish. Medium Frame. Introduced in 2007. Imported from Brazil by Taurus International.
Price: 917B-20, Blue . . . . **NA**
Price: 917SS-20, Stainless Steel . . . . **NA**

TAURUS MODEL 22/25 AUTO PISTOLS
Caliber: 22 LR, 8-shot (PT 22); 25 ACP, 9-shot (PT 25). **Barrel:** 2.75". **Weight:** 12.3 oz. **Length:** 5.25" overall. **Grips:** Smooth rosewood or mother-of-pearl. **Sights:** Fixed. **Features:** Double action. Tip-up barrel for loading, cleaning. Blue, nickel, duo-tone or blue with gold accents. Introduced 1992. Made in U.S.A. by Taurus International.

Price: 22B or 25B, checkered wood grips,
blued finish **$236.00**
Price: 22BR or 25BR, rosewood grips,
blued finish **$236.00**
Price: 22N or 25N, nickel finish, checkered
wood grips **$236.00**
Price: 22NBR or 25NBR, two-tone,
rosewood grips **$236.00**

TAURUS MODEL 24/7
Caliber: 9mm, 40 S&W, 45 ACP. **Barrel:** 4". **Weight:** 27.2 oz. **Length:** 7-1/8". **Grips:** "Ribber" rubber-finned overlay on polymer. **Sights:** Adjustable. **Features:** SA/DA; accessory rail, four safeties, blue or stainless finish. One-piece guide rod, flush-fit magazine, flared bushingless barrel, Picatinny accessory rail, manual safety, user changeable sights, loaded chamber indicator, tuned ejector and lowered port, one piece guide rod and flat wound captive spring. Introduced 2003. Long Slide models have 5" barrels, measure 8-1/8" overall, weigh 27.2 oz. Imported from Brazil by Taurus International.
Price: 40BP, 40 S&W, blued, 10+1 or 15+1 . . . . **$503.00**
Price: 40SSP, 40 S&W, stainless slide, 10+1 or 15+1 . . . . **$520.00**
Price: 45BP, 45 ACP, blued, 10+1 or 12+1 . . . . **$503.00**
Price: Long Slide OSS-D45, 45 ACP, blued, 10+1 or 12+1, intr. 2007 . **NA**

TAURUS MODEL 92 AUTO PISTOL
Caliber: 9mm Para., 10- or 17-shot mags. **Barrel:** 5". **Weight:** 34 oz. **Length:** 8.5" overall. **Grips:** Checkered rubber, rosewood, mother-of-pearl. **Sights:** Fixed notch rear. 3-dot sight system. Also offered with micrometer-click adjustable night sights. **Features:** Double action, ambidextrous 3-way hammer drop safety, allows cocked & locked carry. Blue, stainless steel, blue with gold highlights, stainless steel with gold highlights, forged aluminum frame, integral key-lock. .22 LR conversion kit available. Imported from Brazil by Taurus International.
Price: Blued or Stainless . . . . **$602.00 to $664.00**

Taurus Model 99 Auto Pistol
Similar to 92, fully adjustable rear sight.
Price: Blue . . . . **$617.00 to $633.00**
Price: 22 Conversion kit for PT 92 and PT99
(includes barrel and slide) **$266.00**

Taurus 100

Taurus 132
Millennium Pro

Taurus 138
Millennium Pro

Taurus 140
Millennium Pro

Taurus 745
Millennium Pro

Taurus 940

Taurus 38SS

TAURUS MODEL 100/101 AUTO PISTOL
Caliber: 40 S&W, 10- or 11-shot mags. **Barrel:** 5". **Weight:** 34 oz. **Length:** 8-1/2". **Grips:** Checkered rubber, rosewood, mother-of-pearl. **Sights:** 3-dot fixed or adjustable; night sights available. **Features:** Single/double action with three-position safety/decocker. Reintroduced in 2001. Imported by Taurus International.
Price: PT100 . . . . **$602.00 to $664.00**
Price: PT101, adjustable rear sight . . . . **$617.00 to $633.00**

TAURUS MODEL 111 MILLENNIUM PRO AUTO PISTOL
Caliber: 9mm Para., 10- or 12-shot mags. **Barrel:** 3.25". **Weight:** 18.7 oz. **Length:** 6-1/8" overall. **Grips:** Checkered polymer. **Sights:** 3-dot fixed; night sights available. Low profile, 3-dot combat. **Features:** Double action only, polymer frame, matte stainless or blue steel slide, manual safety, integral key-lock. Deluxe models with wood grip inserts.
Price: . . . . **$406.00 to $422.00**
Price: Titanium Slide **$520.00**

TAURUS MODEL 132 MILLENNIUM PRO AUTO PISTOL
Caliber: 32 ACP, 10-shot mag. **Barrel:** 3.25". **Weight:** 18.7 oz. **Grips:** Polymer. **Sights:** 3-dot fixed; night sights available. **Features:** Double-action-only, polymer frame, matte stainless or blue steel slide, manual safety, integral key-lock action. Introduced 2001.
Price: . . . . **$406.00 to $422.00**

TAURUS MODEL 138 MILLENNIUM PRO SERIES
Caliber: 380 ACP, 10- or 12-shot mags. **Barrel:** 3.25". **Weight:** 18.7 oz. **Grips:** Polymer. **Sights:** Fixed 3-dot fixed. **Features:** Double-action-only, polymer frame, matte stainless or blue steel slide, manual safety, integral key-lock.
Price: . . . . **$406.00 to $422.00**

TAURUS MODEL 140 MILLENNIUM PRO AUTO PISTOL
Caliber: 40 S&W, 10-shot mag. **Barrel:** 3.25". **Weight:** 18.7 oz. **Grips:** Checkered polymer. **Sights:** 3-dot fixed; night sights available. **Features:** Double action only; matte stainless or blue steel slide, black polymer frame, manual safety, integral key-lock action. From Taurus International.
Price: . . . . **$422.00 to $439.00**

TAURUS 145 MILLENNIUM AUTO PISTOL
Caliber: 45 ACP, 10-shot mag. **Barrel:** 3.27". **Weight:** 23 oz. Stock: Checkered polymer. **Sights:** 3-dot fixed; night sights available. **Features:** Double-action only, matte stainless or blue steel slide, black polymer frame, manual safety, integral key-lock. Compact model is 6+1 with a 3.25" barrel, weighs 20.8 oz. From Taurus International.
Price: 145, blued or stainless . . . . **$422.00 to $439.00**
Price: 745 Compact, blued or stainless, intr. 2005 . . **$410.00 to $425.00**

TAURUS MODEL 911 AUTO PISTOL
Caliber: 9mm Para., 10-shot mag. **Barrel:** 4". **Weight:** 28.2 oz. **Length:** 7" overall. **Grips:** Checkered rubber, rosewood, mother-of-pearl. **Sights:** Fixed, 3-dot blue or stainless; night sights optional. **Features:** Double

action, semi-auto ambidextrous 3-way hammer drop safety, allows cocked & locked carry. Blue, stainless steel, blue with gold highlights, or stainless steel with gold highlights, forged aluminum frame, integral key-lock.
Price: **$569.00**

TAURUS MODEL 940 AUTO PISTOL
Caliber: 40 S&W, 10-shot mag. **Barrel:** 3-5/8". **Weight:** 28.2 oz. **Length:** 7" overall. **Grips:** Checkered rubber, rosewood or mother-of-pearl. **Sights:** Fixed, 3-dot blue or stainless; night sights optional. **Features:** Double action, semi-auto ambidextrous 3-way hammer drop safety, allows cocked & locked carry. Blue, stainless steel, blue with gold highlights, or stainless steel with gold hightlights, forged aluminum frame, integral key-lock.
Price: From **$569.00**

TAURUS MODEL 945/38S SERIES
Caliber: 45 ACP, 8-shot mag. **Barrel:** 4.25". **Weight:** 28.2/29.5 oz. **Length:** 7.48" overall. **Grips:** Checkered rubber, rosewood or mother-of-pearl. **Sights:** Fixed, 3-dot; night sights optional. **Features:** Double-action with ambidextrous 3-way hammer drop safety allows cocked & locked carry. Forged aluminum frame, 945C has ported barrel/slide. Blue, stainless, blue with gold highlights, stainless with gold highlights, integral key-lock. Introduced 1995. 38 Super line based on 945 frame introduced 2005. 38S series is 10+1, 30 oz., 7.5" overall. Imported by Taurus International.
Price: From **$609.00**

THOMPSON CUSTOM 1911A1 AUTOMATIC PISTOL
Caliber: 45 ACP, 7-shot magazine. **Barrel:** 4.3". **Weight:** 34 oz. **Length:** 8" overall. **Grips:** Checkered laminate grips with a Thompson bullet logo inlay. **Sights:** Front and rear sights are black with serrations and are dovetailed into the slide. **Features:** Machined from 420 stainless steel, matte finish. Thompson bullet logo on slide. Flared ejection port, angled front and rear serrations on slide, 20-lpi checkered mainspring housing and frontstrap. Adjustable trigger, combat hammer, stainless steel full-length recoil guide rod, extended beavertail grip safety; extended magazine release; checkered slide-stop lever.Made in U.S.A. by Kahr Arms.
Price: 1911CC (2006), stainless frame $775.00
Price: 1911TC, 5", 39 oz., 8.5" overall, stainless frame $775.00
Price: 1911CCF (2006), 27 oz., aluminum frame $775.00
Price: 1911CAF, 5", 31.5 oz., 8.5" overall, aluminum frame $775.00

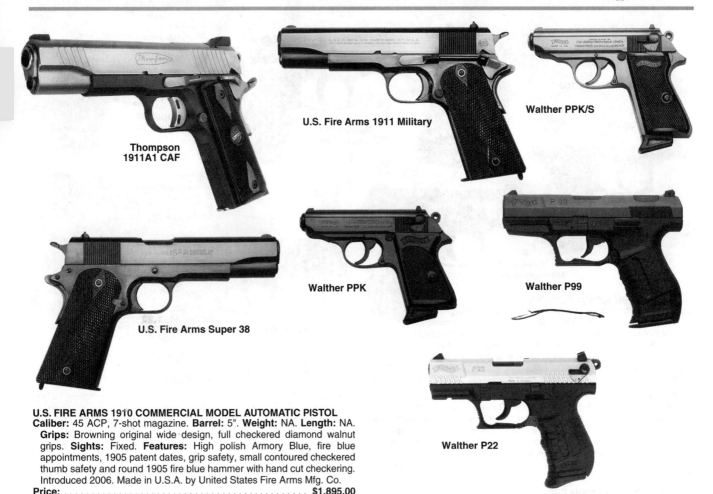

Thompson
1911A1 CAF

U.S. Fire Arms 1911 Military

Walther PPK/S

U.S. Fire Arms Super 38

Walther PPK

Walther P99

Walther P22

U.S. FIRE ARMS 1910 COMMERCIAL MODEL AUTOMATIC PISTOL
Caliber: 45 ACP, 7-shot magazine. **Barrel:** 5". **Weight:** NA. **Length:** NA. **Grips:** Browning original wide design, full checkered diamond walnut grips. **Sights:** Fixed. **Features:** High polish Armory Blue, fire blue appointments, 1905 patent dates, grip safety, small contoured checkered thumb safety and round 1905 fire blue hammer with hand cut checkering. Introduced 2006. Made in U.S.A. by United States Fire Arms Mfg. Co.
Price: **$1,895.00**

U.S. FIRE ARMS 1911 MILITARY MODEL AUTOMATIC PISTOL
Caliber: 45 ACP, 7-shot magazine. **Barrel:** 5". **Weight:** NA. **Length:** NA. **Grips:** Browning original wide design, full checkered diamond walnut grips. **Sights:** Fixed. **Features:** Military polish Armory Blue, fire blue appointments, 1905 patent dates, grip safety, small contoured checkered thumb safety and round 1905 fire blue hammer with hand cut checkering. Introduced 2006. Made in U.S.A. by United States Fire Arms Mfg. Co.
Price: **$1,895.00**

U.S. FIRE ARMS SUPER 38 AUTOMATIC PISTOL
Caliber: 38 Auto, 9-shot magazine. **Barrel:** 5". **Weight:** NA. **Length:** NA. **Grips:** Browning original wide design, full checkered diamond walnut grips. **Sights:** Fixed. **Features:** Armory blue, fire blue appointments, 1913 patent date, grip safety, small contoured checkered thumb safety and spur 1911 hammer with hand cut checkering. Supplied with two Super 38 Auto. mags. Super .38 roll mark on base. Introduced 2006. Made in U.S.A. by United States Fire Arms Mfg. Co.
Price: **$1,995.00**

U.S. FIRE ARMS ACE .22 LONG RIFLE AUTOMATIC PISTOL
Caliber: 22 LR, 10-shot magazine. **Barrel:** 5". **Weight:** NA. **Length:** NA. **Grips:** Browning original wide design, full checkered diamond walnut grips. **Sights:** Fixed. **Features:** Armory blue commercial finish, fire blue appointments, 1913 patent date, grip safety, small contoured checkered thumb safety and spur 1911 hammer with hand cut checkering. Supplied with two magazines. Ace roll mark on base. Introduced 2006. Made in U.S.A. by United States Fire Arms Mfg. Co.
Price: **$1,995.00**

WALTHER PPK/S AMERICAN AUTO PISTOL
Caliber: 380 ACP, 7-shot magazine. **Barrel:** 3.27". **Weight:** 23-1/2 oz. **Length:** 6.1" overall. **Stocks:** Checkered plastic. **Sights:** Fixed, white

markings. **Features:** Double action; manual safety blocks firing pin and drops hammer; chamber loaded indicator on 32 and 380; extra finger rest magazine provided. Made in the United States. Introduced 1980.
Price: 380 ACP only, blue **$563.00**
Price: As above, 32 ACP or 380 ACP, stainless **$543.00**

Walther PPK American Auto Pistol
Similar to Walther PPK/S except weighs 21 oz., has 6-shot capacity. Made in the U.S. Introduced 1986.
Price: Stainless, 32 ACP or 380 ACP **$543.00**
Price: Blue, 380 ACP only **$543.00**

WALTHER P99 AUTO PISTOL
Caliber: 9mm Para., 9x21, 40 S&W,10-shot magazine. **Barrel:** 4". **Weight:** 25 oz. **Length:** 7" overall. **Grips:** Textured polymer. **Sights:** Blade front (comes with three interchangeable blades for elevation adjustment), micrometer rear adjustable for windage. **Features:** Double-action mechanism with trigger safety, decock safety, internal striker safety; chamber loaded indicator; ambidextrous magazine release levers; polymer frame with interchangeable backstrap inserts. Comes with two magazines. Introduced 1997. Imported from Germany by Smith & Wesson U.S.A.
Price: **$665.00**

WALTHER P22 PISTOL
Caliber: 22 LR. **Barrel:** 3.4", 5". **Weight:** 19.6 oz. (3.4"), 20.3 oz. (5"). **Length:** 6.26", 7.83". **Grips:** NA. **Sights:** Interchangeable white dot, front, 2-dot adjustable, rear. **Features:** A rimfire version of the Walther P99 pistol, available in nickel slide with black frame, or green frame with black slide versions. Made in Germany and distributed in the U.S. by Smith & Wesson.
Price: From **$295.00**

Includes models suitable for several forms of competition and other sporting purposes.

Baer 1911 Ultimate Master

Colt Gold Cup Model O

Baer 1911 Bullseye Wadcutter

Colt Special Combat Government

Competitor Single Shot

BAER 1911 ULTIMATE MASTER COMBAT PISTOL
Caliber: 38 Super, 400 Cor-Bon 45 ACP (others available), 10-shot magazine. **Barrel:** 5", 6"; Baer NM. **Weight:** 37 oz. **Length:** 8.5" overall. **Grips:** Checkered cocobolo. **Sights:** Baer dovetail front, low-mount Bo-Mar rear with hidden leaf. **Features:** Full-house competition gun. Baer forged NM blued steel frame and double serrated slide; Baer triple port, tapered cone compensator; fitted slide to frame; lowered, flared ejection port; Baer reverse recoil plug; full-length guide rod; recoil buff; beveled magazine well; Baer Commander hammer, sear; Baer extended ambidextrous safety, extended ejector, checkered slide stop, beavertail grip safety with pad, extended magazine release button; Baer speed trigger. Made in U.S.A. by Les Baer Custom, Inc.

Price: 45 ACP Compensated $2,599.00
Price: 38 Super Compensated $2,789.00
Price: 6" 45 ACP $2,586.00
Price: 6" 38 Super $2,780.00
Price: 6" 400 Cor-Bon $2,668.00
Price: 5" 45 ACP $2,540.00
Price: 5" 38 Super $2,699.00
Price: 5" 400 Cor-Bon $2,589.00

BAER 1911 NATIONAL MATCH HARDBALL PISTOL
Caliber: 45 ACP, 7-shot magazine. **Barrel:** 5". **Weight:** 37 oz. **Length:** 8.5" overall. **Grips:** Checkered walnut. **Sights:** Baer dovetail front with under-cut post, low-mount Bo-Mar rear with hidden leaf. **Features:** Baer NM forged steel frame, double serrated slide and barrel with stainless bushing; slide fitted to frame; Baer match trigger with 4-lb. pull; polished feed ramp, throated barrel; checkered front strap, arched mainspring housing; Baer beveled magazine well; lowered, flared ejection port; tuned extractor; Baer extended ejector, checkered slide stop; recoil buff. Made in U.S.A. by Les Baer Custom, Inc.
Price: $1,689.00

Baer 1911 Bullseye Wadcutter Pistol
Similar to National Match Hardball except designed for wadcutter loads only. Polished feed ramp and barrel throat; Bo-Mar rib on slide; full length recoil rod; Baer speed trigger with 3-1/2-lb. pull; Baer deluxe hammer and sear; Baer beavertail grip safety with pad; flat mainspring housing checkered 20 lpi. Blue finish; checkered walnut grips. Made in U.S.A. by Les Baer Custom, Inc.
Price: From $1,710.00
Price: With 6" barrel, from $1,865.00

BF CLASSIC PISTOL
Caliber: Customer orders chamberings. **Barrel:** 8-15" Heavy Match Grade with 11-degree target crown. **Weight:** Approx 3.9 lbs. **Length:** From 16" overall. **Grips:** Thumbrest target style. **Sights:** Bo-Mar/Bond ScopeRib I Combo with hooded post front adjustable for height and width, rear notch available in .032", .062", .080" and .100" widths; 1/2-MOA clicks. **Features:** Hand fitted and headspaced, drilled and tapped for scope mount. Etched receiver; gold-colored trigger. Introduced 1988. Made in U.S.A. by E. Arthur Brown Co. Inc.
Price: $789.00

COLT GOLD CUP MODEL O PISTOL
Caliber: 45 ACP, 8-shot magazine. **Barrel:** 5", with new design bushing. **Weight:** 39 oz. **Length:** 8-1/2". **Grips:** Checkered rubber composite with silver-plated medallion. **Sights:** Patridge-style front, Bo-Mar-style rear adjustable for windage and elevation, sight radius 6-3/4". **Features:** Arched or flat housing; wide, grooved trigger with adjustable stop; ribbed-top slide, hand fitted, with improved ejection port.
Price: Blue $1,022.00
Price: Stainless $1,077.00

COLT SPECIAL COMBAT GOVERNMENT
Caliber: 45 ACP, 38 Super. **Barrel:** 5". **Weight:** 39 oz. **Length:** 8-1/2". **Grips:** Rosewood w/double diamond checkering pattern. **Sights:** Clark dovetail, front; Bo-Mar adjustable, rear. **Features:** A competition-ready pistol with enhancements such as skeletonized trigger, upswept grip safety, custom tuned action, polished feed ramp. Blue or satin nickel finish. Introduced 2003. Made in U.S.A. by Colt's Mfg. Co.
Price: $1,543.00

COMPETITOR SINGLE-SHOT PISTOL
Caliber: 22 LR through 50 Action Express, including belted magnums. **Barrel:** 14" standard; 10.5" silhouette; 16" optional. **Weight:** About 59 oz. (14" bbl.). **Length:** 15.12" overall. **Grips:** Ambidextrous; synthetic (standard) or laminated or natural wood. **Sights:** Ramp front, adjustable rear. **Features:** Rotary cannon-type action cocks on opening; cammed ejector; interchangeable barrels, ejectors. Adjustable single stage trigger, sliding thumb safety and trigger safety. Matte blue finish. Introduced 1988. From Competitor Corp., Inc.
Price: 14", standard calibers, synthetic grip $480.00

CZ 75 Champion

EAA Witness Gold Team

Freedom Arms 83 22 Silhouette Class

Hammerli SP 20

High Standard Trophy

CZ 75 CHAMPION COMPETITION PISTOL
Caliber: 9mm Para., 40 S&W, 16-shot mag. **Barrel:** 4.4". **Weight:** 2.5 lbs. **Length:** 9.4" overall. **Grips:** Black rubber. **Sights:** Blade front, fully adjustable rear. **Features:** Single-action trigger mechanism; three-port compensator (40 S&W, 9mm have two port) full-length guide rod; extended magazine release; ambidextrous safety; flared magazine well; fully adjustable match trigger. Introduced 1999. Imported from the Czech Republic by CZ-USA.
Price: Dual-tone finish **$1,646.00**

EAA WITNESS GOLD TEAM AUTO
Caliber: 9mm Para., 9x21, 38 Super, 40 S&W, 45 ACP. **Barrel:** 5.1". **Weight:** 44 oz. **Length:** 10.5" overall. **Grips:** Checkered walnut, competition-style. **Sights:** Square post front, fully adjustable rear. **Features:** Triple-chamber cone compensator; competition SA trigger; extended safety and magazine release; competition hammer; beveled magazine well; beavertail grip. Hand-fitted major components. Hard chrome finish. Match-grade barrel. From E.A.A. Custom Shop. Introduced 1992. From European American Armory.
Price: **$1,699.00**

FREEDOM ARMS MODEL 83 22 FIELD GRADE SILHOUETTE CLASS
Caliber: 22 LR, 5-shot cylinder. **Barrel:** 10". **Weight:** 63 oz. **Length:** 15.5" overall. **Grips:** Black Micarta. **Sights:** Removable Patridge front blade; Iron Sight Gun Works silhouette rear, click adjustable for windage and elevation (optional adj. front sight and hood). **Features:** Stainless steel, matte finish, manual sliding-bar safety system; dual firing pins, lightened hammer for fast lock time, pre-set trigger stop. Introduced 1991. Made in U.S.A. by Freedom Arms.
Price: Silhouette Class **$1,913.95**

FREEDOM ARMS MODEL 83 CENTERFIRE SILHOUETTE MODELS
Caliber: 357 Mag., 41 Mag., 44 Mag.; 5-shot cylinder. **Barrel:** 10", 9" (357 Mag. only). **Weight:** 63 oz. (41 Mag.). **Length:** 15.5", 14-1/2" (357 only). **Grips:** Pachmayr Presentation. **Sights:** Iron Sight Gun Works silhouette rear sight, replaceable adjustable front sight blade with hood. **Features:** Stainless steel, matte finish, manual sliding-bar safety system. Made in U.S.A. by Freedom Arms.
Price: Silhouette Models **$1,683.95**

HAMMERLI SP 20 TARGET PISTOL
Caliber: 22 LR, 32 S&W. **Barrel:** 4.6". **Weight:** 34.6-41.8 oz. **Length:** 11.8" overall. **Grips:** Anatomically shaped synthetic Hi-Grip available in five sizes. **Sights:** Integral front in three widths, adjustable rear with changeable notch widths. **Features:** Extremely low-level sight line; anatomically shaped trigger; adjustable JPS buffer system for different recoil characteristics. Receiver available in red, blue, gold, violet or black. Introduced 1998. Imported from Switzerland by Larry's Guns of Maine.
Price: Hammerli 22 LR **$1,450.00**
Price: Hammerli 32 S&W **$1,560.00**

HAMMERLI X-ESSE SPORT PISTOL
An all-steel .22 LR target pistol with a Hi-Grip in a new anatomical shape and an adjustable hand rest. Made in Switzerland. Introduced 2003.
Price: **$750.00**

HIGH STANDARD SUPERMATIC TROPHY TARGET PISTOL
Caliber: 22 LR, 9-shot mag. **Barrel:** 5.5" bull or 7.25" fluted. **Weight:** 44-46 oz. **Length:** 9.5-11.25" overall. **Stock:** Checkered hardwood with thumbrest. **Sights:** Undercut ramp front, frame-mounted micro-click rear adjustable for windage and elevation; drilled and tapped for scope mounting. **Features:** Gold-plated trigger, slide lock, safety-lever and magazine release; stippled front grip and backstrap; adjustable trigger and sear. Barrel weights optional. From High Standard Manufacturing Co., Inc.
Price: 5.5" barrel, adjustable sights **$795.00**
Price: 7.25", adjustable sights **$845.00**

Comprehensive Immigration
Reform is an ambiguous term.
Perhaps a spokesperson for
those here illegally can define it.
     I ask if these this "reform"
will allow those here illegally
collect benefit from no medicaid,
medicare, social security, housing
subsidized housing and food
stamps? Will these people
be able to sponsor others to
enter this country legally. If so,
who will be financially responsible
for them?

High Standard Victor

Kimber Super Match II

Ruger MKIII512

Smith & Wesson Model 41

Smith & Wesson Model 22A

Smith & Wesson Model 22S

HIGH STANDARD VICTOR TARGET PISTOL
Caliber: 22 LR, 10-shot magazine. **Barrel:** 4-1/2" or 5-1/2"; push-button takedown. **Weight:** 46 oz. **Length:** 9.5" overall. **Stock:** Checkered hardwood with thumbrest. **Sights:** Undercut ramp front, micro-click rear adjustable for windage and elevation. Also available with scope mount, rings, no sights. **Features:** Stainless steel construction. Full-length vent rib. Gold-plated trigger, slide lock, safety-lever and magazine release; stippled front grip and backstrap; polished slide; adjustable trigger and sear. Comes with barrel weight. From High Standard Manufacturing Co., Inc.
Price: 4.5" or 5.5" barrel, universal scope base **$745.00**

KIMBER SUPER MATCH II
Caliber: 45 ACP, 8-shot magazine. **Barrel:** 5". **Weight:** 38 oz. **Length:** 8.7" overall. **Grips:** Rosewood double diamond. **Sights:** Blade front, Kimber fully adjustable rear. **Features:** Guaranteed shoot 1" group at 25 yards. Stainless steel frame, black KimPro slide; two-piece magazine well; premium aluminum match-grade trigger; 30 lpi front strap checkering; stainless match-grade barrel; ambidextrous safety; special Custom Shop markings. Introduced 1999. Made in U.S.A. by Kimber Mfg., Inc.
Price: **$1,994.00**

RUGER MARK III TARGET MODEL AUTOLOADING PISTOL
Caliber: 22 LR, 10-shot magazine. **Barrel:** 5-1/2" to 6-7/8". **Weight:** 41 to 45 oz. **Length:** 9.75" to 11-1/8" overall. **Grips:** Checkered cocobolo. **Sights:** .125" blade front, micro-click rear, adjustable for windage and elevation, loaded chamber indicator; integral lock, magazine disconnect.

Plastic case with lock included. Mark II series introduced 1982, discontinued 2004. Mark III introduced 2005.
Price: MKIII512 (bull barrel, blued) **$382.00**
Price: KMKIII512 (bull barrel, stainless) **$483.00**
Price: MKIII678 (blued Target barrel, 6-7/8") **$382.00**
Price: KMKIII678GC (stainless slabside barrel) **$555.00**
Price: KMKIII678GH (stainless fluted barrel) **$567.00**

SMITH & WESSON MODEL 41 TARGET
Caliber: 22 LR, 10-shot clip. **Barrel:** 5.5", 7". **Weight:** 41 oz. (5-1/2" barrel). **Length:** 10-1/2" overall (5-1/2" barrel). **Grips:** Checkered walnut with modified thumbrest, usable with either hand. **Sights:** 1/8" Patridge on ramp base; micro-click rear adjustable for windage and elevation. **Features:** 3/8" wide, grooved trigger; adjustable trigger stop drilled and tapped.
Price: S&W Bright Blue, either barrel **$1,153.00**

SMITH & WESSON MODEL 22A PISTOLS
Caliber: 22 LR, 10-shot magazine. **Barrel:** 4", 5.5" bull. **Weight:** 28-39 oz. **Length:** 9-1/2" overall. **Grips:** Dymondwood® with ambidextrous thumbrests and flared bottom or rubber soft touch with thumbrest. **Sights:** Patridge front, fully adjustable rear. **Features:** Sight bridge with Weaver-style integral optics mount; alloy frame, stainless barrel and slide; blue/black finish. Introduced 1997. The 22S is similar to the Model 22A except has stainless steel frame. Introduced 1997. Made in U.S.A. by Smith & Wesson.
Price: From **$261.00**

Springfield Armory 1911A1 Trophy Match

STI Executive

STI Eagle 5.0

STI Trojan 6-inch

SPRINGFIELD ARMORY LEATHAM LEGEND TGO SERIES PISTOLS
Three models of 5" barrel, 45 ACP 1911 pistols built for serious competition. TGO 1 has deluxe low mount Bo-Mar rear sight, Dawson fiber optics front sight, 3.5 lb. trigger pull.
Price: TGO 1 . . . . **$2,999.00**

Springfield Armory Trophy Match Pistol
Similar to Springfield Armory's Full Size model, but designed for bullseye and action shooting competition. Available with a Service Model 5" frame with matching slide and barrel in 5" and 6" lengths. Fully adjustable sights, checkered frame front strap, match barrel and bushing. In 45 ACP only. From Springfield Inc.
Price: **$1,248.00**

STI EAGLE 5.0, 6.0 PISTOL
Caliber: 9mm, 9x21, 38 & 40 Super, 40 S&W, 10mm, 45 ACP, 10-shot magazine. **Barrel:** 5", 6" bull. **Weight:** 34.5 oz. **Length:** 8.62" overall. **Grips:** Checkered polymer. **Sights:** STI front, Novak or Heine rear. **Features:** Standard frames plus 7 others; adjustable match trigger; skeletonized hammer; extended grip safety with locator pad. Introduced 1994. Made in U.S.A. by STI International.
Price: . . . . (5.0 Eagle) $1,794.00, (6.0 Eagle) $1,894.00

STI EXECUTIVE PISTOL
Caliber: 40 S&W. **Barrel:** 5" bull. **Weight:** 39 oz. **Length:** 8-5/8". **Grips:** Gray polymer. **Sights:** Dawson fiber optic, front; STI adjustable rear. **Features:** Stainless mag. well, front and rear serrations on slide. Made in U.S.A. by STI.
Price: **$2,389.00**

STI TROJAN
Caliber: 9mm, 38 Super, 40S&W, 45 ACP. **Barrel:** 5", 6". **Weight:** 36 oz. **Length:** 8.5". **Grips:** Rosewood. **Sights:** STI front with STI adjustable rear. **Features:** Stippled front strap, flat top slide, one-piece steel guide rod.
Price: (Trojan 5") **$1,024.00**
Price: (Trojan 6", not available in 38 Super) **$1,344.00**

Includes models suitable for hunting and competitive courses of fire, both police and international.

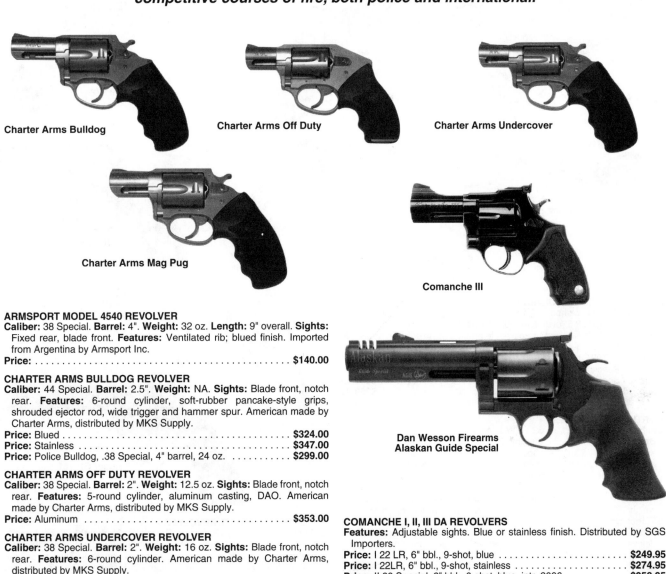

Charter Arms Bulldog

Charter Arms Off Duty

Charter Arms Undercover

Charter Arms Mag Pug

Comanche III

Dan Wesson Firearms
Alaskan Guide Special

ARMSPORT MODEL 4540 REVOLVER
Caliber: 38 Special. **Barrel:** 4". **Weight:** 32 oz. **Length:** 9" overall. **Sights:** Fixed rear, blade front. **Features:** Ventilated rib; blued finish. Imported from Argentina by Armsport Inc.
Price: **$140.00**

CHARTER ARMS BULLDOG REVOLVER
Caliber: 44 Special. **Barrel:** 2.5". **Weight:** NA. **Sights:** Blade front, notch rear. **Features:** 6-round cylinder, soft-rubber pancake-style grips, shrouded ejector rod, wide trigger and hammer spur. American made by Charter Arms, distributed by MKS Supply.
Price: Blued **$324.00**
Price: Stainless **$347.00**
Price: Police Bulldog, .38 Special, 4" barrel, 24 oz. **$299.00**

CHARTER ARMS OFF DUTY REVOLVER
Caliber: 38 Special. **Barrel:** 2". **Weight:** 12.5 oz. **Sights:** Blade front, notch rear. **Features:** 5-round cylinder, aluminum casting, DAO. American made by Charter Arms, distributed by MKS Supply.
Price: Aluminum **$353.00**

CHARTER ARMS UNDERCOVER REVOLVER
Caliber: 38 Special. **Barrel:** 2". **Weight:** 16 oz. **Sights:** Blade front, notch rear. **Features:** 6-round cylinder. American made by Charter Arms, distributed by MKS Supply.
Price: Blued **$359.00**

CHARTER ARMS UNDERCOVER SOUTHPAW REVOLVER
Caliber: 38 Special +P. **Barrel:** 2". **Weight:** 12 oz. **Sights:** NA. **Features:** Cylinder release is on the right side and the cylinder opens to the right side. Exposed hammer for both single and double-action firiing. 5-round cylinder. American made by Charter Arms, distributed by MKS Supply.
Price: Blued **$375.00**

CHARTER ARMS MAG PUG REVOLVER
Caliber: 357 Magnum. **Barrel:** 2.2". **Weight:** 23 oz. **Sights:** Blade front, notch rear. **Features:** 5-round cylinder. American made by Charter Arms, distributed by MKS Supply.
Price: Blued **$325.00**
Price: Stainless **$335.00**

COLT SINGLE-ACTION ARMY
Caliber: 32-20, 38 Special, 357 Magnum, 38-40, 44-4-, 44 Special, 45 Long Colt. **Barrel:** 4.7 5", 5.5", 7.5". **Weight:** 40-44 oz. **Sights:** Blade front, notch rear. **Features:** Available in black powder and sheriff's models; nickel, blued or case-hardened frame; 6-round cylinder.
Price: . . . . (Blued) **$1,290.00**; (Nickel) **$1,490.00**

COMANCHE I, II, III DA REVOLVERS
Features: Adjustable sights. Blue or stainless finish. Distributed by SGS Importers.
Price: I 22 LR, 6" bbl., 9-shot, blue **$249.95**
Price: I 22LR, 6" bbl., 9-shot, stainless **$274.95**
Price: II 38 Special, 2" bbl., 6-shot, blue, intr. 2006 . . . . **$258.95**
Price: II 38 Special, 4" bbl., 6-shot, stainless **$249.95**
Price: III 357 Mag, 3" bbl., 6-shot, blue **$266.95**
Price: III 357 Mag, 2" bbl., 6-shot, blue **$274.95**
Price: II 38 Special, 3" bbl., 6-shot, stainless steel **$266.95**

DAN WESSON FIREARMS ALASKAN GUIDE SPECIAL
Caliber: 445 SuperMag; also chambers and fires 44 Magnum, 44 Special, 6 shots. **Sights:** Blade front, adjustable rear. **Barrel:** Compensated 4" vent heavy barrel assembly. **Weight:** 54.4 oz. **Length:** 11.7". **Features:** Stainless steel with baked on, non-glare, matte black coating, special laser engraving. Made in U.S.A. by Dan Wesson Firearms, distributed by CZ-USA.
Price: **$1,295.00**

DAN WESSON FIREARMS VH8 445 SUPERMAG
Caliber: 445 SuperMag; also chambers and fires 44 Magnum, 44 Special, 6 shots. **Sights:** Blade front, adjustable rear. **Barrel:** 8" full-length underlug. **Weight:** 54.4 oz. **Length:** 14.6". **Features:** Stainless-steel frame and barrel. Interchangeable barrels. Made in U.S.A. by Dan Wesson Firearms, distributed by CZ-USA.
Price: **$1,070.00**

EAA Windicator

Rossi Model 971

Rossi Model 972

Rossi Model 851

Rossi Model R351

Ruger GP-100

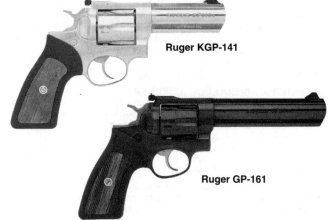

Ruger KGP-141

Ruger GP-161

EAA WINDICATOR REVOLVERS
Caliber: 38 Spec., 6-shot; 357 magnum, 6-shot. **Barrel:** 2", 4". **Weight:** 30 oz. (4"). **Length:** 8.5" overall (4" bbl.). **Grips:** Rubber with finger grooves. **Sights:** Blade front, fixed or adjustable on rimfires; fixed only on 32, 38. **Features:** Swing-out cylinder; hammer block safety; blue finish. Introduced 1991. Imported from Germany by European American Armory.
Price: 38 Special 2" barrel, alloy frame **$249.00**
Price: 38 Special 4" barrel, alloy frame **$259.00**
Price: 357 Mag, 2" barrel, steel frame **$259.00**
Price: 357 Mag, 4" barrel, steel frame **$279.00**

KORTH REVOLVERS
Caliber: 22 LR, 22 WMR, 32 S&W Long, 38 Sp., 357 Mag., 9mm Para. **Barrel:** 3", 4", 5.25", 6". **Weight:** 32-52 oz. **Grips:** Walnut, palisander, amboinia, ivory (Combat, Sport), German walnut. Matte with oil finish, adjustable ergonomic competition style (Target). **Sights:** Adjustable Patridge (Sport) or Baughman (Combat), interchangeable and adjustable rear w/Patridge front (Target) in blue and matte. **Features:** DA/SA, 3 models, over 50 configurations, externally adjustable trigger stop and weight, interchangeable cylinder, removable wide milled trigger shoe on Target model. Deluxe models are highly engraved, high polish blue finish, plasma coated in high polish or matted silver, gold, blue or charcoal. Many deluxe options available. 6-shot. Made in Germany. Imported by Korth USA.
Price: . . . . **$5000.00 to $8000.00**
Price: Deluxe . . . . **$9000.00 to $12000.00**

ROSSI R461/R462/R971/R972
Caliber: .357 Mag. **Barrel:** 2" (R46), 4" (R971), 6" (R972). **Weight:** 26-35 oz. **Grips:** Rubber. **Sights:** Fixed (R46), Fully Adjustable (R97). **Features:** DA/SA, 4 models available, +P rated frame, blue carbon or high polish stainless steel, patented Taurus Security System, 6-shot.
Price: . . . . **$343.00 to $432.00**

ROSSI MODEL R351/R352/R851REVOLVERS
Caliber: .38 Sp. **Barrel:** 2" (R35), 4" (R85). **Weight:** 24-32 oz. **Grips:** Rubber. **Sights:** Fixed (R35), Fully Adjustable (R85). **Features:** DA/SA, 3 models available, +P rated frame, blue carbon or high polish stainless steel, patented Taurus Security System, 5-shot (R35) 6-shot (R85).
Price: . . . . **$343.00 to 398.00**

ROSSI R461/R462/R971/R972
Caliber: .357Mag. **Barrel:** 2" (R46), 4" (R971), 6" (R972). **Weight:** 26-35 oz. **Grips:** Rubber. **Sights:** Fixed (R46), Fully Adjustable (R97). **Features:** DA/SA, 4 models available, +P rated frame, blue carbon or high polish stainless steel, patented Taurus Security System, 6-shot.
Price: . . . . **$343.00 to $432.00**

ROSSI MODEL 971/972 REVOLVERS
Caliber: 357 Magnum +P, 6-shot. **Barrel:** 4", 6". **Weight:** 32 oz. **Length:** 8.5" or 10.5" overall. **Grips:** Rubber. **Sights:** Blade front, adjustable rear. **Features:** Single/double action. Patented key-lock Taurus Security System; forged steel frame. Introduced 2001. Made in Brazil by Amadeo Rossi. Imported by BrazTech/Taurus.
Price: Model 971 (blued finish, 4" bbl.) **$362.00**
Price: Model 972 (stainless steel finish, 6" bbl.) **$410.00**

Rossi Model 851
Similar to Model 971/972, chambered for 38 Special +P. Blued finish, 4" barrel. Introduced 2001. Made in Brazil by Amadeo Rossi. From BrazTech/Taurus.
Price: **$313.00**

RUGER GP-100 REVOLVERS
Caliber: 38 Spec. +P, 357 Mag., 6-shot. **Barrel:** 3" full shroud, 4" full shroud, 6" full shroud. **Weight:** 3" full shroud-36 oz., 4" full shroud-38 oz. **Sights:** Fixed; adjustable on 4" full shroud, all 6" barrels. **Grips:** Ruger Santoprene Cushioned Grip with Goncalo Alves inserts. **Features:** Uses action, frame features of both the Security-Six and Redhawk revolvers. Full length, short ejector shroud. Satin blue and stainless steel.
Price: GPF-141 (357, 4" full shroud, adj. sights, blue) **$575.00**
Price: GP-161 (357, 6" full shroud, adj. sights, blue), 46 oz. **$575.00**
Price: KGP-141 (357, 4" full shroud, adj. sights, stainless) **$635.00**
Price: KGP-161 (357, 6" full shroud, adj. sights, stainless) 46 oz. **$635.00**
Price: KGPF-331 (357, 3" full shroud, stainless) **$615.00**

Ruger SP101

Ruger Redhawk

Ruger Redhawk KRH-444

Ruger Super Redhawk

Smith & Wesson Model 36LS

Smith & Wesson Model 442

Smith & Wesson Model 638

RUGER SP101 REVOLVERS

Caliber: 32 H&R Mag., 6-shot; 38 Spec. +P, 357 Mag., 5-shot. **Barrel:** 2-1/4", 3-1/16". **Weight:** (38 & 357 mag models) 2-1/4"-25 oz.; 3-1/16"-27 oz. **Sights:** Adjustable on 32, fixed on others. **Grips:** Ruger Cushioned Grip with inserts. **Features:** Compact, small frame, double-action revolver. Full-length ejector shroud. Stainless steel only. Introduced 1988.
Price: KSP-321X (2-1/4", 357 Mag.) **$550.00**
Price: KSP-3231X (3-1/16", 32 H&R), 30 oz. **$550.00**
Price: KSP-331X (3-1/16", 357 Mag.) **$550.00**
Price: KSP-821X (2-1/4", 38 Spec.) **$550.00**

Ruger SP101 Double-Action-Only Revolver

Similar to standard SP101 except double-action-only with no single-action sear notch. Spurless hammer, floating firing pin and transfer bar safety system. Available with 2-1/4" barrel in 357 Magnum. Weighs 25 oz., overall length 7.06". Natural brushed satin, high-polish stainless steel. Introduced 1993.
Price: KSP321XL (357 Mag.) **$550.00**

RUGER REDHAWK

Caliber: 44 Rem. Mag., 6-shot. **Barrel:** 5-1/2", 7-1/2". **Weight:** About 54 oz. (7-1/2" bbl.). **Length:** 13" overall (7-1/2" barrel). **Grips:** Square butt cushioned grip panels. **Sights:** Interchangeable Patridge-type front, rear adjustable for windage and elevation. **Features:** Stainless steel, brushed satin finish, blued ordnance steel. 9-1/2" sight radius. Introduced 1979.
Price: KRH-44, stainless, 7-1/2" barrel **$780.00**
Price: KRH-44R, stainless 7.5" barrel w/scope mount **$829.00**
Price: KRH-445, stainless 5.5" barrel **$780.00**
Price: RH-445, blued 5.5" barrel **$715.00**
Price: KRH-444, stainless 4" barrel (2007) **$780.00**

RUGER SUPER REDHAWK REVOLVER

Caliber: 44 Rem. Mag., 45 Colt, 454 Casull, 480 Ruger 6-shot. **Barrel:** 2.5", 5.5", 7.5", 9.5". **Weight:** About 54 oz. (7.5" bbl.). **Length:** 13" overall (7.5" barrel). **Grips:** Square butt cushioned grip panels, Hogue Tamer Monogrip. **Features:** Similar to standard Redhawk except has heavy extended frame with Ruger Integral Scope Mounting System on wide topstrap. Wide hammer spur lowered for better scope clearance. Incorporates mechanical design features and improvements of GP-100. Ramp front sight base has Redhawk-style Interchangeable Insert sight

blades, adjustable rear sight. Satin stainless steel and low-glare stainless finishes. Introduced 1987.
Price: KSRH-2454, 2.5" 454 Casull/45 Colt, Hogue Tamer
Monogrip **$899.00**
Price: KSRH-2480, 2.5" 480 Ruger, Hogue Tamer Monogrip **$899.00**
Price: KSRH-7, 7.5" 44 Mag, Ruger grip **$829.00**
Price: KSRH-7454, 7.5" 45 Colt/454 Casull, low glare stainless . . **$899.00**
Price: KSRH-7480, 7.5" 480 Ruger, low glare stainless **$899.00**
Price: KSRH-9, 9" 44 Mag, Ruger grip **$829.00**

SMITH & WESSON J-FRAME REVOLVERS

The smallest S&W wheelguns come in a variety of chamberings, barrel lengths, and materials, as noted in the individual model listings below.

SMITH & WESSON 36LS/60LS/642LS LADYSMITH REVOLVERS

Caliber: .38 Special +P, 357 Mag., 5-shot. **Barrel:** 1-7/8" (36LS, 642LS); 2-1/8" (60LS) **Weight:** 14.5 oz. (642LS); 20 oz. (36LS); 21.5 oz. (60LS); **Length:** 6.25" overall (36LS); 6.6" overall (60LS); . **Grips:** Wood. **Sights:** Black blade, serrated ramp front, fixed notch rear. **Features:** 36/60LS models have a Chiefs Special-style frame. 642LS has Centennial-style frame, frosted matte finish, smooth combat wood grips. Introduced 1996. Comes in a fitted carry/storage case. Introduced 1989. Made in U.S.A. by Smith & Wesson.
Price: From **$672.00**

SMITH & WESSON MODEL 442/637/638/642 AIRWEIGHT REVOLVERS

Caliber: 38 Special +P, 5-shot. **Barrel:** 1-7/8". **Weight:** 15 oz. (37, 442); 20 oz. (3); 21.5 oz. (); **Length:** 6-3/8" overall. **Grips:** Soft rubber. **Sights:** Fixed, serrated ramp front, square notch rear. **Features:** Aluminum-alloy frames. Models 37, 637; Chiefs Special-style frame with exposed hammer. Introduced 1996. Models 442, 642; Centennial-style frame, enclosed hammer. Model 638, Bodyguard style, shrouded hammer. Comes in a fitted carry/storage case. Introduced 1989. Made in U.S.A. by Smith & Wesson.
Price: From **$498.00**

SMITH & WESSON MODEL 60 CHIEF'S SPECIAL

Caliber: 357 Magnum, 38 Special +P, 5-shot. **Barrel:** 2-1/8", 3" or 5". **Weight:** 22.5 oz. (2-1/8" barrel). **Length:** 6-5/8 overall (2-1/8" barrel). **Grips:** Rounded butt synthetic grips. **Sights:** Fixed, serrated ramp front, square notch rear. **Features:** Stainless steel construction, satin finish, internal lock. Introduced 1965. The 5-inch-barrel model has target semi-lug barrel, rosewood grip, red ramp front sight, adjustable rear sight. Made in U.S.A. by Smith & Wesson.
Price: 2-1/8" barrel, intr. 2005 . . . . **$672.00**
Price: 3" barrel, 7.5" OAL, 24 oz. **$695.00**
Price: 5" semi-lug barrel, 9-3/8" OAL, 30.5 oz. **$735.00**

**Smith & Wesson
Model 60 Chief's Special**

**Smith & Wesson
Model 317 AirLite**

Smith & Wesson Model 340

**Smith & Wesson Model 360 PD
Airlite SC Chief's Special**

**Smith & Wesson
Model 649 Bodyguard**

**Smith & Wesson
Model 10**

Smith & Wesson Model 386

SMITH & WESSON MODEL 317 AIRLITE REVOLVERS
Caliber: 22 LR, 8-shot. **Barrel:** 1-7/8", 3". **Weight:** 10.5 oz. **Length:** 6.25" overall (1-7/8" barrel). **Grips:** Rubber. **Sights:** Serrated ramp front, fixed notch rear. **Features:** Aluminum alloy, carbon and stainless steels, Chiefs Special-style frame with exposed hammer. Smooth combat trigger. Clear Cote finish. Introduced 1997. Made in U.S.A. by Smith & Wesson.
Price: Model 317, 1-7/8" barrel **$632.00**
Price: Model 317 w/HiViz front sight, 3" barrel, 7.25 OAL **$695.00**

SMITH & WESSON MODEL 340/340PD AIRLITE SC CENTENNIAL
Caliber: 357 Magnum, 38 Spec. +P, 5-shot. **Barrel:** 1-7/8". **Weight:** 12 oz. **Length:** 6-3/8" overall (1-7/8" barrel). **Grips:** Rounded butt rubber. **Sights:** Black blade front, rear notch **Features:** Centennial-style frame, enclosed hammer. Internal lock. Matte silver finish. Scandium alloy frame, titanium cylinder, stainless steel barrel liner. Made in U.S.A. by Smith & Wesson.
Price: From **$940.00**

SMITH & WESSON MODEL 351PD REVOLVER
Caliber: 22 Mag., 7-shot. **Barrel:** 1-7/8". **Weight:** 10.6 oz. **Length:** 6.25" overall (1-7/8" barrel). **Sights:** HiViz front sight, rear notch. **Grips:** Wood. **Features:** Seven-shot, aluminum-alloy frame. Chiefs Special-style frame with exposed hammer. Nonreflective matte-black finish. Internal lock. Made in U.S.A. by Smith & Wesson.
Price: **$695.00**

SMITH & WESSON MODEL 360/360PD AIRLITE CHIEF'S SPECIAL
Caliber: 357 Magnum, 38 Spec. +P, 5-shot. **Barrel:** 1-7/8". **Weight:** 12 oz. **Length:** 6-3/8" overall (1-7/8" barrel). **Grips:** Rounded butt rubber. **Sights:** Black blade front, fixed rear notch. **Features:** Chiefs Special-style frame with exposed hammer. Internal lock. Scandium alloy frame, titanium cylinder, stainless steel barrel. Made in U.S.A. by Smith & Wesson.
Price: From **$940.00**

SMITH & WESSON MODEL 640 CENTENNIAL DA ONLY
Caliber: 357 Mag., 38 Spec. +P, 5-shot. **Barrel:** 2-1/8". **Weight:** 23 oz. **Length:** 6-3/4" overall. **Grips:** Uncle Mike's Boot grip. **Sights:** Serrated ramp front, fixed notch rear. **Features:** Stainless steel. Fully concealed hammer, snag-proof smooth edges. Internal lock. Introduced 1995 in 357 Magnum.
Price: **$672.00**

SMITH & WESSON MODEL 649 BODYGUARD REVOLVER
Caliber: 357 Mag., 38 Spec. +P, 5-shot. **Barrel:** 2-1/8". **Weight:** 23 oz. **Length:** 6-5/8" overall. **Grips:** Uncle Mike's Combat. **Sights:** Black pinned ramp front, fixed notch rear. **Features:** Stainless steel construction, satin finish. Internal lock. Bodyguard style, shrouded hammer. Made in U.S.A. by Smith & Wesson.
Price: **$672.00**

SMITH & WESSON K-FRAME/L-FRAME REVOLVERS
These mid-size S&W wheelguns come in a variety of chamberings, barrel lengths, and materials, as noted in the individual model listings below. 17 variations for 2006.

SMITH & WESSON MODEL 10 REVOLVER
Caliber: 38 Spec.+P, 6-shot. **Barrel:** 4". **Weight:** 36 oz. **Length:** 8-7/8" overall. **Grips:** Soft rubber; square butt. **Sights:** Fixed; black blade front, square notch rear. Blued carbon steel frame.
Price: Blue **$632.00**

SMITH & WESSON MODEL 64/67 REVOLVERS
Caliber: 38 Spec. +P, 6-shot. **Barrel:** 3". **Weight:** 33 oz. **Length:** 8-7/8" overall. **Grips:** Soft rubber. **Sights:** Fixed, 1/8" serrated ramp front, square notch rear. Model 67 (**Weight:** 36 oz. **Length:** 8-7/8") similar to Model 64 except for adjustable sights. **Features:** Satin finished stainless steel, square butt.
Price: From **$632.00**

SMITH & WESSON MODEL 386 SC/S
Caliber: 357 Magnum, 38 Spec. +P, 7-shot. **Barrel:** 3-1/8". **Weight:** 18.5 oz. **Length:** 8-1/8" overall. **Grips:** Rubber. **Sights:** Adjustable, HiViz front. **Features:** Scandium alloy frame, titanium cylinder, stainless steel barrel liner. Internal lock. Made in U.S.A. by Smith & Wesson.
Price: Matte silver finish **$869.00**

SMITH & WESSON MODEL 617 REVOLVERS
Caliber: 22 LR, 6- or 10-shot. **Barrel:** 4". **Weight:** 41 oz. (4" barrel). **Length:** 9-1/8" (4" barrel). **Grips:** Soft rubber. **Sights:** Patridge front, adjustable rear. Drilled and tapped for scope mount. **Features:** Stainless steel with satin finish; 4" has .312" smooth trigger, .375" semi-target hammer; 6" has either .312" combat or .400" serrated trigger, .375" semi-target or .500" target hammer; 8-3/8" with .400" serrated trigger, .500" target hammer. Introduced 1990.
Price: From **$774.00**

Smith & Wesson
Model 686 SSR

Smith & Wesson Model 21

Smith & Wesson
Model 325PD

Smith & Wesson Model 625

Smith & Wesson Model 657

SMITH & WESSON MODELS 619/620 REVOLVERS

Caliber: 38 Special +P; 357 Mag., 7 rounds. **Barrel:** 4". **Weight:** 37.5 oz. **Length:** 9-1/2". **Grips:** Rubber. **Sights:** Integral front blade, fixed rear notch on the 619; adjustable white-outline target style rear, red ramp front on 620. **Features:** Replaces Models 65 and 66. Two-piece semi-lug barrel. Satin stainless frame and cylinder. Made in U.S.A. by Smith & Wesson.
Price: $711.00

SMITH & WESSON MODEL 686/686 PLUS REVOLVERS

Caliber: 357 Mag., 38 S&W Special; 6 rounds. **Barrel:** 2.5", 4", 6". **Weight:** 35 oz. (2.5" barrel). **Length:** 7-1/2", (2.5" barrel). **Grips:** Rubber. **Sights:** White outline adjustable rear, red ramp front. **Features:** Satin stainless frame and cylinder. Plus series guns have 7-shot cylinders. Introduced 1996. Powerport (PP) has Patridge front, adjustable rear sight. Introduced early 1980s. Stock Service Revolver (SSR) intr. 2007. Capacity: 6. **Barrel:** 4". Sight: Interchangeable front, adjustable rear. Grip: Wood Finish: Satin stainless frame and cylinder. **Weight:** 38.3 oz. **Features:** Chamfered charge holes, custom barrel w/recessed crown, bossed mainspring. High-hold ergonomic grip. Made in U.S.A. by Smith & Wesson.
Price: 686 . . . . $766.00
Price: Plus, 7 rounds $790.00
Price: PP, 6" barrel, 6 rounds, 11-3/8" OAL $790.00
Price: SSR . . . . NA

SMITH & WESSON N-FRAME REVOLVERS

These large-frame S&W wheelguns come in a variety of chamberings, barrel lengths, and materials, as noted in the individual model listings below. 18 major variations for 2006.

SMITH & WESSON MODEL 21

Caliber: 44 Special, 6-round. **Barrel:** 4" tapered. **Weight:** NA. **Length:** NA. **Grips:** Smooth wood. **Sights:** Pinned half-moon service front; service rear. **Features:** Carbon steel frame, blued finish.
Price: $855.00

SMITH & WESSON MODEL 29 50TH ANNIVERSARY REVOLVER

Caliber: 44 Mag, 6-round. **Barrel:** 6.5". **Weight:** 48.5 oz. **Length:** 12". **Grips:** Cocobolo. **Sights:** Adjustable white-outline rear, red ramp front. **Features:** Carbon steel frame, polished-blued finish. Introduced 2005. Includes 24 carat gold-plated anniversary logo on frame, cleaning kit with screwdriver, mahogany presentation case, square-butt frame, serrated trigger. Original Model 29 made famous by "Dirty Harry" character created in 1971 by Clint Eastwood.
Price: Dealer pricing, no MSRP . . . . NA

SMITH & WESSON MODEL 325PD/329PD/357PD AIRLITE REVOLVERS

Caliber: 41 Mag. (357PD); 44 Spec., 44 Mag. (329PD); 45 ACP (325PD); 6-round. **Barrel:** 2-3/4" (325PD). **Weight:** 21.5 oz. (325PD, 2-3/4" barrel).

Length: 7-1/4" (325PD, 2-3/4" barrel). **Grips:** Wood. **Sights:** Adj. rear, HiViz orange-dot front. **Features:** Scandium alloy frame, titanium cylinder. 4" model has HiViz green front sight and Ahrends finger-groove wood grips. Weighs 26.5 oz.
Price: From $1,067.00

SMITH & WESSON MODEL 625 REVOLVERS

Caliber: 45 ACP, 6-shot. **Barrel:** 4", 5". **Weight:** 43 oz. (4" barrel). **Length:** 9-3/8" overall (4" barrel). **Grips:** Soft rubber; wood optional. **Sights:** Patridge front on ramp, S&W micrometer click rear adjustable for windage and elevation. **Features:** Stainless steel construction with .400" semi-target hammer, .312" smooth combat trigger; full lug barrel. Glass beaded finish. Introduced 1989. "Jerry Miculek" Professional (JMP) Series has .265"-wide grooved trigger, special wooden Miculek Grip, five full moon clips, gold bead Patridge front sight on interchangeable front sight base, bead blast finish. Unique serial number run. Mountain Gun has 4" tapered barrel, drilled and tapped, Hogue Rubber Monogrip, pinned black ramp front sight, micrometer click-adjustable rear sight, satin stainless frame and barrel, weighs 39.5 oz.
Price: From $869.00

SMITH & WESSON MODEL 629 REVOLVERS

Caliber: 44 Magnum, 44 S&W Special, 6-shot. **Barrel:** 4", 5", 6-1/2". **Weight:** 41.5 oz. (4" bbl.). **Length:** 9-5/8" overall (4" bbl.). **Grips:** Soft rubber; wood optional. **Sights:** 1/8" red ramp front, white outline rear, internal lock, adjustable for windage and elevation. Classic similar to standard Model 629, except Classic has full-lug 5" barrel, chamfered front of cylinder, interchangeable red ramp front sight with adjustable white outline rear, Hogue grips with S&W monogram, drilled and tapped for scope mounting. Factory accurizing and endurance packages. Introduced 1990. Classic Power Port has Patridge front sight and adjustable rear sight. Model 629CT has 5" barrel, Crimson Trace Hoghunter Lasergrips, 10.5" OAL, 45.5 oz. weight. Introduced 2006.
Price: From $869.00

SMITH & WESSON MODEL 657 REVOLVER

Caliber: 41 Mag., 6-shot. **Barrel:** 7-1/2" full lug. **Weight:** 52 oz. **Grips:** Soft rubber. **Sights:** Pinned 1/8" red ramp front, micro-click rear adjustable for windage and elevation. Target hammer, drilled and tapped, unfluted cylinder. **Features:** Stainless steel construction.
Price: $869.00

SMITH & WESSON X-FRAME REVOLVERS

These extra-large X-frame S&W wheelguns come in a variety of chamberings, barrel lengths, and materials, as noted in the individual model listings below. 7 variations for 2006.

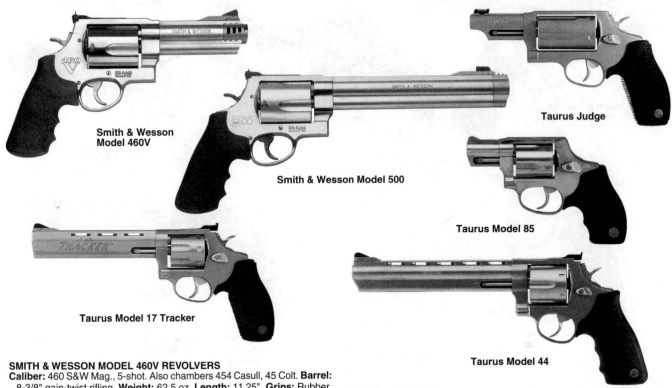

Smith & Wesson Model 460V

Smith & Wesson Model 500

Taurus Judge

Taurus Model 85

Taurus Model 17 Tracker

Taurus Model 44

SMITH & WESSON MODEL 460V REVOLVERS
Caliber: 460 S&W Mag., 5-shot. Also chambers 454 Casull, 45 Colt. **Barrel:** 8-3/8" gain-twist rifling. **Weight:** 62.5 oz. **Length:** 11.25". **Grips:** Rubber. **Sights:** Adj. rear, red ramp front. **Features:** Satin stainless steel frame and cylinder, interchangeable compensator. 460XVR (X-treme Velocity Revolver) has black blade front sight with interchangeable green Hi-Viz tubes, adjustable rear sight. 7.5"-barrel version has Lothar-Walther barrel, 360-degree recoil compensator, tuned Performance Center action, pinned sear, integral Weaver base, non-glare surfaces, scope mount accessory kit for mounting full-size scopes, flashed-chromed hammer and trigger, Performance Center gun rug and shoulder sling. Interchangeable Hi-Viz green dot front sight, adjustable black rear sight, Hogue Dual Density Monogrip, matte-black frame and shroud finish with glass-bead cylinder finish, 72 oz. Compensated Hunter has tear drop chrome hammer, .312 chrome trigger, Hogue Dual Density Monogrip, satin/matte stainless finish, HiViz interchangeable front sight, adjustable black rear sight. XVR introduced 2006.
Price: 460V **$1,256.00**
Price: 460XVR, from **$1,401.00**

SMITH & WESSON MODEL 500 REVOLVERS
Caliber: 500 S&W Mag., 5 rounds. **Barrel:** 4", 8-3/8". **Weight:** 72.5 oz. **Length:** 15" (8-3/8" barrel). **Grips:** Hogue Sorbothane Rubber. **Sights:** Interchangeable blade, front, adjustable rear. **Features:** Recoil compensator, ball detent cylinder latch, internal lock. 6-1/2"-barrel model has orange-ramp dovetail Millett front sight, adjustable black rear sight, Hogue Dual Density Monogrip, .312" chrome trigger with over-travel stop, chrome tear-drop hammer, glassbead finish. 10-1/2"-barrel model has red ramp front front sight, adjustable rear sight, .312 chrome trigger with overtravel stop, chrome tear drop hammer with pinned sear, hunting sling. Compensated Hunter has .400 orange ramp dovetail front sight, adjustable black blade rear sight, Hogue Dual Density Monogrip, glassbead finish w/black passivate clear coat. Made in U.S.A. by Smith & Wesson.
Price: From **$1,256.00**

TAURUS MODEL JUDGE
Caliber: 3" mag 410ga./.45LC, 2-1/2" 410ga./.45LC. **Barrel:** 3". **Weight:** 35.2 oz., 22.4 oz. **Length:** 7.5". **Grips:** Ribber. **Sights:** Fiber Optic. **Features:** DA/SA. Matte Stainless and Ultra-Lite Stainless finish. Introduced in 2007. Imported from Brazil by Taurus International.
Price: 4510TKR-3MAG, Matte Stainless . . . . **NA**
Price: 4510TKR-3UL, Ultra-Lite Stainless . . . . **NA**

TAURUS MODEL 85
Caliber: .38 Special +P. **Barrel:** 2". **Weight:** 12.4 oz. **Length:** 6.5". **Grips:** Rubber. **Sights:** Fixed, Fiber Optic. **Features:** DA/SA. Hy-Lite Magnesium and Ultra-Lite Gray finish. Introduced in 2007. Imported from Brazil by Taurus International.
Price: 85HL2MG, Hy-Lite Magnesium . . . . **NA**
Price: 85ULGRYFO, Ultra-Lite Gray . . . . **NA**
Price: 85ULGRY, Ultra-Lite Gray . . . . **NA**
Price: 85SS2CHUL **$398.00**

TAURUS MODEL 850
Caliber: .38 Special +P. **Barrel:** 2". **Weight:** 15.6 oz. **Length:** 6.5". **Grips:** Rubber. **Sights:** Fixed. **Features:** DAO. Small Frame. Ultra-Lite Blue and Ultra-Lite Stainless. Incredibly Strong, Lightweight Forged Alloy Frame. Introduced in 2007. Imported from Brazil by Taurus International.
Price: 850B2UL, Ultra-Lite Blue . . . . **NA**
Price: 850SS2UL, Ultra-Lite Stainless . . . . **NA**

TAURUS MODEL 17 "TRACKER"
Caliber: 17 HMR, 7-shot. **Barrel:** 6-1/2". **Weight:** 45.8 oz. **Grips:** Rubber. **Sights:** Adjustable. **Features:** Double action, matte stainless, integral key-lock.
Price: From **$390.00**

TAURUS MODEL 44 REVOLVER
Caliber: 44 Mag., 6-shot. **Barrel:** 4", 6-1/2", 8-3/8". **Weight:** 44-3/4 oz. **Grips:** Rubber. **Sights:** Adjustable. **Features:** Double-action. Integral key-lock. Introduced 1994. New Model 44S12 has 12" vent rib barrel. Imported from Brazil by Taurus International Manufacturing, Inc.
Price: Blue or stainless steel . . . . **$445.00 to $602.00**

Taurus Model 44 Series Revolver
Similar to Taurus Model 60 series, but in .44 Rem. Mag. With six-shot cylinder, blue and matte stainless finishes.
Price: From **$602.00**

TAURUS MODEL 65 REVOLVER
Caliber: 357 Mag., 6-shot. **Barrel:** 4". **Weight:** 38 oz. **Length:** 10-1/2" overall. **Grips:** Soft rubber. **Sights:** Fixed. **Features:** Double action, integral key-lock. Seven models for 2006 Imported by Taurus International.
Price: From **$406.00**

Taurus Model 65

Taurus Model 66

Taurus Model 82

Taurus Model 85

Taurus Model 94

Taurus Model 444
Raging Bull

Taurus Model 605

Taurus Model 731

Taurus Model 608

Taurus Model 66 Revolver
Similar to Model 65, 4" or 6" barrel, 7-shot cylinder, adjustable rear sight. Integral key-lock action. Imported by Taurus International.
Price: From $455.00

TAURUS MODEL 82 HEAVY BARREL REVOLVER
Caliber: 38 Spec., 6-shot. **Barrel:** 4", heavy. **Weight:** 36.5 oz. **Length:** 9-1/4" overall (4" bbl.). **Grips:** Soft black rubber. **Sights:** Serrated ramp front, square notch rear. **Features:** Double action, solid rib, integral key-lock. Imported by Taurus International.
Price: From $391.00

TAURUS MODEL 85 REVOLVER
Caliber: 38 Spec., 5-shot. **Barrel:** 2". **Weight:** 17-24.5 oz., titanium 13.5-15.4 oz. **Grips:** Rubber, rosewood or mother-of-pearl. **Sights:** Ramp front, square notch rear. **Features:** Blue, matte stainless, blue with gold accents, stainless with gold accents; rated for +P ammo. Integral keylock. Some models have titantium frame. Introduced 1980. Imported by Taurus International.
Price: From $391.00

TAURUS MODEL 94 REVOLVER
Caliber: 22 LR, 9-shot cylinder; 22 Mag, 8-shot cylinder **Barrel:** 2", 4", 5". **Weight:** 18.5-27.5 oz. **Grips:** Soft black rubber. **Sights:** Serrated ramp front, click-adjustable rear. **Features:** Double action, integral key-lock. Introduced 1989. Imported by Taurus International.
Price: From $358.00

TAURUS RAGING BULL MODEL 416
Caliber: 41 Magnum, 6-shot. **Barrel:** 6-1/2". **Weight:** 61.9 oz. **Grips:** Rubber. **Sights:** Adjustable. **Features:** Double-action, ported, ventilated rib, matte stainless, integral key-lock.
Price: $691.00

TAURUS MODEL 425/627 TRACKER REVOLVERS
Caliber: 357 Mag., 7-shot; 41 Mag., 5-shot. **Barrel:** 4" and 6". **Weight:** 28.8-40 oz. (titanium) 24.3-28. (6"). **Grips:** Rubber. **Sights:** Fixed front, adjustable rear. **Features:** Double-action stainless steel, Shadow Gray or Total Titanium; vent rib (steel models only); integral key-lock action. Imported by Taurus International.

Price: . . . . $531.00 to $766.00
Price: Total Titanium $766.00

TAURUS MODEL 444 ULTRALIGHT
Caliber: 44 Mag, 5-shot. **Barrel:** 4". **Weight:** 28.3 oz. **Length:** 9.8" overall. **Grips:** Cushioned inset rubber. **Sights:** Fixed red-fiber optic front, adjustable rear. **Features:** UltraLite titanium blue finish, titanium/alloy frame built on Raging Bull design. Smooth trigger shoe, 1.760" wide, 6.280" tall. Barrel rate of twist 1:16", 6 grooves. Introduced 2005. Imported by Taurus International.
Price: $650.00

TAURUS MODEL 444/454/480 RAGING BULL REVOLVERS
Caliber: 44 Mag., 45 LC, 454 Casull, 480 Ruger, 5-shot. **Barrel:** 5", 6-1/2", 8-3/8". **Weight:** 53-63 oz. **Length:** 12" overall (6-1/2" barrel). **Grips:** Soft black rubber. **Sights:** Patridge front, adjustable rear. **Features:** Double-action, ventilated rib, ported, integral key-lock. Introduced 1997. Imported by Taurus International.
Price: From $619.00

TAURUS MODEL 605 REVOLVER
Caliber: 357 Mag., 5-shot. **Barrel:** 2". **Weight:** 24 oz. **Grips:** Rubber. **Sights:** Fixed. **Features:** Double-action, blue or stainless or titanium, concealed hammer models DAO, porting optional, integral key-lock. Introduced 1995. Imported by Taurus International.
Price: From $391.00

Taurus Model 731 Revolver
Similar to the Taurus Model 605, except in .32 Magnum.
Price: $455.00

TAURUS MODEL 608 REVOLVER
Caliber: 357 Mag. 38 Spec., 8-shot. **Barrel:** 4", 6-1/2", 8-3/8". **Weight:** 44-57 oz. **Length:** 9-3/8" overall. **Grips:** Soft black rubber. **Sights:** Adjustable. **Features:** Double-action, integral key-lock action. Available in blue or stainless. Introduced 1995. Imported by Taurus International.
Price: $569.00

Taurus Model 617

Taurus Model 650

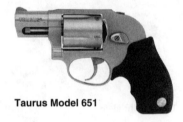

Taurus Model 651

Taurus Model 817

Taurus Model 850

Taurus Model 941

TAURUS MODEL 617 REVOLVER
Caliber: 357 Magnum, 7-shot. **Barrel:** 2". **Weight:** 28.3 oz. **Length:** 6-3/4" overall. **Grips:** Soft black rubber. **Sights:** Fixed. **Features:** Double-action, blue, Shadow Gray, bright spectrum blue or matte stainless steel, integral key-lock. Available with porting, concealed hammer. Introduced 1998. Imported by Taurus International.
Price: . . . . **$391.00 to $453.00**
Price: Total Titanium, 19.9 oz. **$602.00**

TAURUS MODEL 650CIA REVOLVER
Caliber: 357 Magnum, 5-shot. **Barrel:** 2". **Weight:** 24.5 oz. **Grips:** Rubber. **Sights:** Ramp front, square notch rear. **Features:** Double-action only, blue or matte stainless steel, integral key-lock, internal hammer. Introduced 2001. From Taurus International.
Price: From **$398.00**

TAURUS MODEL 651 PROTECTOR REVOLVER
Caliber: 357 Magnum, 5-shot. **Barrel:** 2". **Weight:** 17-24.5 oz. **Grips:** Rubber. **Sights:** Fixed. **Features:** Concealed single-action/double-action design. Shrouded cockable hammer, blue, matte stainless, Shadow Gray, Total Titanium, integral key-lock. Made in Brazil. Imported by Taurus International Manufacturing, Inc.
Price: From **$398.00**

TAURUS MODEL 817 ULTRA-LITE REVOLVER
Caliber: 38 Spec., 7-shot. **Barrel:** 2". **Weight:** 21 oz. **Length:** 6-1/2" overall. **Grips:** Soft rubber. **Sights:** Fixed. **Features:** Double-action, integral key-lock. Rated for +P ammo. Introduced 1999. Imported from Brazil by Taurus International.
Price: From **$422.00**

TAURUS MODEL 850CIA REVOLVER
Caliber: 38 Special, 5-shot. **Barrel:** 2". **Weight:** 17-24.5 oz. **Grips:** Rubber, mother-of-pearl. **Sights:** Ramp front, square notch rear. **Features:**

Taurus Model 970 Tracker

Double-action only, blue or matte stainless steel, rated for +P ammo, integral key-lock, internal hammer. Introduced 2001. From Taurus International.
Price: From **$398.00**

TAURUS MODEL 941 REVOLVER
Caliber: 22 LR (Mod. 94), 22 WMR (Mod. 941), 8-shot. **Barrel:** 2", 4", 5". **Weight:** 27.5 oz. (4" barrel). **Grips:** Soft black rubber. **Sights:** Serrated ramp front, rear adjustable. **Features:** Double-action, integral key-lock. Introduced 1992. Imported by Taurus International.
Price: From **$373.00**

TAURUS MODEL 970/971 TRACKER REVOLVERS
Caliber: 22 LR (Model 970), 22 Magnum (Model 971); 7-shot. **Barrel:** 6". **Weight:** 53.6 oz. **Grips:** Rubber. **Sights:** Adjustable. **Features:** Double barrel, heavy barrel with ventilated rib; matte stainless finish, integral key-lock. Introduced 2001. From Taurus International.
Price: From **$439.00**

Both classic six-shooters and modern adaptations for hunting and sport.

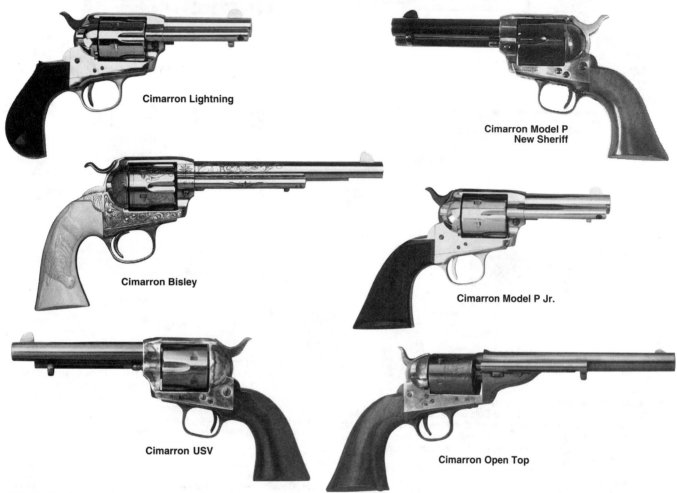

Cimarron Lightning

Cimarron Model P
New Sheriff

Cimarron Bisley

Cimarron Model P Jr.

Cimarron USV

Cimarron Open Top

CHARLES DALY 1873 SINGLE-ACTION REVOLVER
Caliber: 357 Mag., 45 Colt, 6-shot. **Barrel:** 4.75", 5.5", 7.5". **Weight:** 36 oz. (4.75" barrel). **Length:** 10" overall (4.75" barrel). **Grips:** Hardwood with company logo near tang. **Sights:** Blade front, notch rear. **Features:** Stainless steel and color case hardened finishes. From K.B.I., Inc.
Price: 1873 Steel, 45 Colt, 4.75", 5.5", 7.5" barrel, brass frame . . **$449.00**
Price: 1873 Steel, 357 Mag, 4.75", 5.5", 7.5" barrel, brass frame . **$479.00**
Price: 1873 Steel, 45 Colt, 4.75", 5.5", 7.5" barrel, steel frame . . **$449.00**
Price: 1873 Stainless Steel, 357 Mag, 4.75", 5.5", 7.5" barrel . . **$659.00**
Price: 1873 Stainless Steel, 45 Colt, 4.75", 5.5", 7.5" barrel **$659.00**

CIMARRON LIGHTNING SA
Caliber: 32-20, 32 H&R, 38 Colt, 38 Special. **Barrel:** 3-1/2", 4-3/4", 5-1/2". **Grips:** Smooth or checkered walnut. **Sights:** Blade front. **Features:** Replica of the Colt 1877 Lightning DA. Similar to Cimarron Thunderer™, except smaller grip frame to fit smaller hands. Standard blue, charcoal blue or nickel finish with forged, old model, or color case hardened frame. Introduced 2001. From Cimarron F.A. Co.
Price: . . . . **$499.00 to $559.00**

CIMARRON MODEL P
Caliber: 32 WCF, 38 WCF, 357 Mag., 44 WCF, 44 Spec., 45 Colt, 45 LC and 45 ACP. **Barrel:** 4-3/4", 5-1/2", 7-1/2". **Weight:** 39 oz. **Length:** 10" overall (4" barrel). **Grips:** Walnut. **Sights:** Blade front, fixed or adjustable rear. **Features:** Uses "old model" black powder frame with "Bullseye" ejector or New Model frame. Imported by Cimarron F.A. Co.
Price: . . . . **$499.00 to $559.00**
Price: Laser Engraved **$843.70**
Price: New Sheriff . . . . **$499.00 to $559.00**

Cimarron Bisley Model Single-Action Revolvers
Similar to 1873 Model P, special grip frame and trigger guard, knurled wide-spur hammer, curved trigger. Available in 357 Mag., 44 WCF, 44 Spl., 45 Colt. Introduced 1999. Imported by Cimarron F.A. Co.
Price: **$525.00**

CIMARRON MODEL "P" JR.
Caliber: 32-20, 32 H&R, 38 Special. **Barrel:** 3-1/2", 4-3/4", 5-1/2". **Grips:** Checkered walnut. **Sights:** Blade front. **Features:** Styled after 1873 Colt Peacemaker, except 20 percent smaller. Blue finish with color case-hardened frame; Cowboy Comp® action. Introduced 2001. From Cimarron F.A. Co.
Price: . . . . **$489.00 to $529.00**

CIMARRON U. S. VOLUNTEER ARTILLERY MODEL SINGLE-ACTION
Caliber: 45 Colt. **Barrel:** 5-1/2". **Weight:** 39 oz. **Length:** 11-1/2" overall. **Grips:** Walnut. **Sights:** Fixed. **Features:** U.S. markings and cartouche, case-hardened frame and hammer; 45 Colt only. Imported by Cimarron F.A. Co.
Price: . . . . **$549.00 to $599.00**

CIMARRON 1872 OPEN TOP REVOLVER
Caliber: 38, 44 Special, 44 Colt, 44 Russian, 45LC, 45 S&W Schofield. **Barrel:** 5-1/2" and 7-1/2". **Grips:** Walnut. **Sights:** Blade front, fixed rear. **Features:** Replica of first cartridge-firing revolver. Blue, charcoal blue, nickel or Original® finish; Navy-style brass or steel Army-style frame. Introduced 2001 by Cimarron F.A. Co.
Price: . . . . **$529.00 to $599.00**

Cimarron Thunderer

Colt Single-Action Army

EAA Bounty Hunter

EMF Hartford

EMF 1875 Outlaw

EMF 1894 Bisley

CIMARRON THUNDERER REVOLVER

Caliber: 357 Mag., 44 WCF, 44 Spl, 45 Colt, 6-shot. **Barrel:** 3-1/2", 4-3/4", 5-1/2", 7-1/2", with ejector. **Weight:** 38 oz. (3-1/2" barrel). **Grips:** Smooth or checkered walnut. **Sights:** Blade front, notch rear. **Features:** Thunderer grip; color case-hardened frame with balance blued. Introduced 1993. Imported by Cimarron F.A. Co.

Price: 3-1/2", 4-3/4", smooth grips	$519.00 to $549.00
Price: As above, checkered grips	$564.00 to $584.00
Price: 5-1/2", 7-1/2", smooth grips	$519.00 to $549.00
Price: As above, checkered grips	$564.00 to $584.00

COLT SINGLE-ACTION ARMY REVOLVER

Caliber: 357 Mag., 38 Special, .32/20, 44-40, 45 Colt, 6-shot. **Barrel:** 4-3/4", 5-1/2", 7-1/2". **Weight:** 40 oz. (4-3/4" barrel). **Length:** 10-1/4" overall (4-3/4" barrel). **Grips:** Black Eagle composite. **Sights:** Blade front, notch rear. **Features:** Available in full nickel finish with nickel grip medallions, or Royal Blue with color case-hardened frame. Reintroduced 1992.

Price: .... $1,290.00 to $1,490.00

EAA BOUNTY HUNTER SA REVOLVERS

Caliber: 22 LR/22 WMR, 357 Mag., 44 Mag., 45 Colt, 6-shot. **Barrel:** 4-1/2", 7-1/2". **Weight:** 2.5 lbs. **Length:** 11" overall (4-5/8" barrel). **Grips:** Smooth walnut. **Sights:** Blade front, grooved topstrap rear. **Features:** Transfer bar safety; 3-position hammer; hammer forged barrel. Introduced 1992. Imported by European American Armory.

Price: Blue or case-hardened	$369.00
Price: Nickel	$399.00
Price: 22LR/22WMR, blue	$269.00
Price: As above, nickel	$299.00

EMF MODEL 1873 FRONTIER MARSHAL

Caliber: 357 Mag., 45 Colt. **Barrel:** 4-3/4", 5-1/2, 7-1/2". **Weight:** 39 oz. **Length:** 10-1/2" overall. **Grips:** One-piece walnut. **Sights:** Blade front, notch rear. **Features:** Bright brass trigger guard and backstrap, color case-hardened frame, blued barrel and cylinder. Introduced 1998. Imported from Italy.

Price: $390.00

EMF HARTFORD SINGLE-ACTION REVOLVERS

Caliber: 357 Mag., 32-20, 38-40, 44-40, 44 Spec., 45 Colt. **Barrel:** 4-3/4", 5-1/2", 7-1/2". **Weight:** 45 oz. **Length:** 13" overall (7-1/2" barrel). **Grips:** Smooth walnut. **Sights:** Blade front, fixed rear. **Features:** Identical to the original Colts. All major parts serial numbered using original Colt-style lettering, numbering. Bullseye ejector head and color case-hardening on old model frame and hammer. Introduced 1990. Imported by E.M.F.

Price: Old Model	$450.00
Price: Cavalry or Artillery	$475.00
Price: Nickel plated, add	$200.00
Price: Case-hardened New Model frame	$450.00

EMF 1894 Bisley Revolver

Similar to the Hartford single-action revolver except has special grip frame and trigger guard, wide spur hammer; available in 45 Colt, 4-3/4", 5-1/2" or 7-1/2" barrel. Introduced 1995. Imported by E.M.F.

Price: Case-hardened/blue	$490.00
Price: Nickel, add	$200.00

EMF Hartford Pinkerton Single-Action Revolver

Same as the regular Hartford except has 4" barrel with ejector tube and bird's-head grip. Calibers: 357 Mag., 45 Colt. Introduced 1997. Imported by E.M.F.

Price: $450.00

EMF GWII Express Single-Action Revolver

Same as the regular model except uses grip of the Colt Lightning revolver. Barrel lengths of 4-3/4". Introduced 2006. Imported by E.M.F.

Price: Standard	$490.00
Price: Custom	$665.00

EMF 1875 OUTLAW REVOLVER

Caliber: 357 Mag., 44-40, 45 Colt. **Barrel:** 7-1/2", 9-1/2". **Weight:** 46 oz. **Length:** 13-1/2" overall. **Grips:** Smooth walnut. **Sights:** Blade front, fixed groove rear. **Features:** Authentic copy of 1875 Remington with firing pin in hammer; color case-hardened frame, blue cylinder, barrel, steel backstrap and trigger guard. Also available in nickel, factory engraved. Imported by E.M.F.

Price: All calibers	$450.00
Price: Nickel	$650.00
Price: Laser Engraved	$660.00

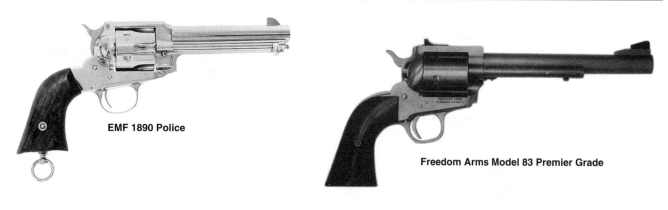

EMF 1890 Police

Freedom Arms Model 83 Premier Grade

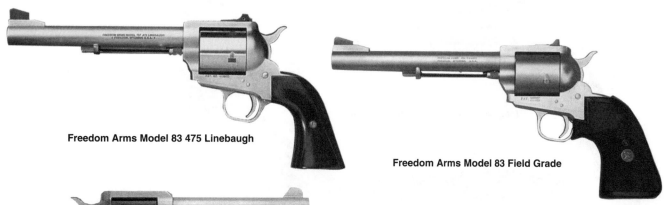

Freedom Arms Model 83 475 Linebaugh

Freedom Arms Model 83 Field Grade

Freedom Arms Model 97 Premier Grade

EMF 1890 Police Revolver
Similar to the 1875 Outlaw except has 5-1/2" barrel, weighs 40 oz., with 12-1/2" overall length. Has lanyard ring in butt. No web under barrel. Calibers: 45 Colt. Imported by E.M.F.
Price: **$450.00**
Price: Nickel **$650.00**

EMF 1873 GREAT WESTERN II
Caliber: .357, 45LC, 44/40. **Barrel:** 4 3/4", 5-1/2", 7-1/2". **Weight:** 36 oz. **Length:** 11" (5-1/2"). **Grips:** Walnut. **Sights:** Blade front, notch rear.
Features: Authentic reproduction of the original 2nd generation Colt single-action revolver. Standard and bone case hardening. Coil hammer spring. Hammer-forged barrel.
Price: 1873 Californian **$460.00**
Price: 1873 Custom series, bone or nickel, ivory-like grips **$650.00**
Price: 1873 Stainless steel, ivory-like grips **$640.00**

FREEDOM ARMS MODEL 83 PREMIER GRADE REVOLVER
Caliber: 357 Mag., 41 Mag., 44 Mag., 454 Casull, 475 Linebaugh, 500 Wyo. Exp., 5-shot. **Barrel:** 4-3/4", 6", 7-1/2", 9" (357 Mag. only), 10" (except 357 Mag. and 500 Wyo. Exp. **Weight:** 53 oz. (7-1/2" bbl. In 454 Casull). **Length:** 13" (7-1/2" bbl.). **Grips:** Impregnated hardwood. **Sights:** Adjustable rear with replaceable front sight. Fixed rear notch and front blade. **Features:** Stainless steel construction with brushed finish; manual sliding safety bar. Micarta grips optional. 500 Wyo. Exp. Introduced 2006. Lifetime warranty. Made in U.S.A. by Freedom Arms, Inc.

Price: 500 WE, 454 Casull, 475 Linebaugh, 454 Casull **$2,120.00**
Price: 454 Casull, fixed sight **$2,038.00**
Price: 357 Mag., 41 Mag., 44 Mag. **$2,035.00**

FREEDOM ARMS MODEL 83 FIELD GRADE REVOLVER
Caliber: 22 LR, 357 Mag., 41 Mag., 44 Mag., 454 Casull, 475 Linebaugh, 500 Wyo. Exp., 5-shot. **Barrel:** 4-3/4", 6", 7-1/2", 9" (357 Mag. only), 10" (except 357 Mag. and 500 Wyo. Exp.) **Weight:** 56 oz. (7-1/2" bbl. In 454 Casull). **Length:** 13.1" (7-1/2" bbl.). **Grips:** Pachmayr standard, impregnated hardwood or Micarta optional. **Sights:** Adjustable rear with replaceable front sight. Model 83 frame. All stainless steel. Introduced 1988. Made in U.S.A. by Freedom Arms Inc.
Price: 454 Casull, 475 Linebaugh, 500 WE adj. sights **$1,639.00**
Price: 357 Mag., 41 Mag., 44 Mag. **$1,573.00**
Price: 22 LR with match chambers and 10" barrel **$1,803.00**

FREEDOM ARMS MODEL 97 PREMIER GRADE REVOLVER
Caliber: 17HMR, 22 LR, 32 H&R, 357 Mag., 6-shot; 41 Mag., 44 Special, 45 Colt, 5-shot. **Barrel:** 4-1/4", 5-1/2", 7-1/2", 10" (17 HMR, 22LR & 32 H&R). **Weight:** 40 oz. (5-1/2" 357 Mag.). **Length:** 10-3/4" (5-1/2" bbl.). **Grips:** Impregnated hardwood; Micarta optional. **Sights:** Adjustable rear, replaceable blade front. Fixed rear notch and front blade. **Features:** Stainless steel construction, brushed finish, automatic transfer bar safety system. Introduced in 1997. Lifetime warranty. Made in U.S.A. by Freedom Arms.
Price: Centerfire cartridges, adjustable sights **$1,718.00**
Price: Rimfire cartridges **$1,784.00**
Price: 32 H&R, 357 Mag., 6-shot; 45 Colt, fixed sights **$1,624.00**
Price: Extra fitted cylinders, centerfire, 22 WMR, 17 Mach II **$272.00**
Price: Extra fitted 22 LR match grade cylinder **$404.00**
Price: 22 LR match cylinder in place of 22 LR sporting cylinde . . **$132.00**
Price: 357 Mag., 45 Colt, fixed sight **$1,576.00**
Price: Extra fitted cylinders 38 Special, 45 ACP **$264.00**
Price: 22 LR with sporting chambers **$1,732.00**
Price: Extra fitted 22 WMR cylinder **$264.00**
Price: Extra fitted 22 LR match grade cylinder **$476.00**
Price: 22 match grade chamber instead of 22 LR sport chamber . **$214.00**

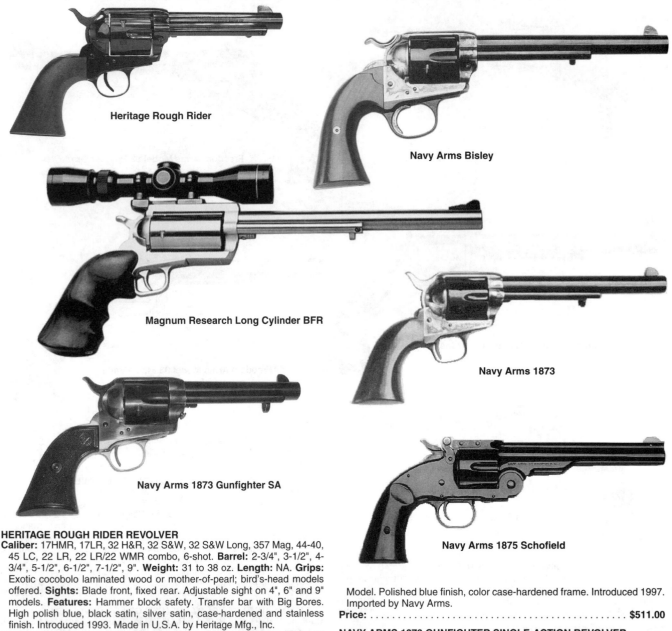

Heritage Rough Rider

Navy Arms Bisley

Magnum Research Long Cylinder BFR

Navy Arms 1873

Navy Arms 1873 Gunfighter SA

Navy Arms 1875 Schofield

HERITAGE ROUGH RIDER REVOLVER
Caliber: 17HMR, 17LR, 32 H&R, 32 S&W, 32 S&W Long, 357 Mag, 44-40, 45 LC, 22 LR, 22 LR/22 WMR combo, 6-shot. **Barrel:** 2-3/4", 3-1/2", 4-3/4", 5-1/2", 6-1/2", 7-1/2", 9". **Weight:** 31 to 38 oz. **Length:** NA. **Grips:** Exotic cocobolo laminated wood or mother-of-pearl; bird's-head models offered. **Sights:** Blade front, fixed rear. Adjustable sight on 4", 6" and 9" models. **Features:** Hammer block safety. Transfer bar with Big Bores. High polish blue, black satin, silver satin, case-hardened and stainless finish. Introduced 1993. Made in U.S.A. by Heritage Mfg., Inc.
Price: . . . . **$159.95 to $499.95**

MAGNUM RESEARCH BFR SINGLE-ACTION REVOLVER
(Long cylinder) **Caliber:** 30/30, 45/70 Government, 444 Marlin, 460 S&W, 45 LC/410, 450 Marlin, .500 S&W. **Barrel:** 7.5", 10". **Weight:** 4 lbs., 4.36 lbs. **Length:** 15", 17.5".
(Short cylinder) Caliber: 50AE, 454 Casull, 22 Hornet, BFR 480/475. **Barrel:** 6.5", 7.5", 10". **Weight:** 3.2 lbs, 3.5 lbs., 4.36 lbs. (10"). **Length:** 12.75 (6"), 13.75", 16.25".
Sights: All have fully adjustable rear, black blade ramp front. **Features:** Stainless steel construction, rubber grips, all 5-shot capacity. Barrels are stress-relieved and cut rifled. Made in U.S.A. From Magnum Research, Inc.
Price: **$899.00**

NAVY ARMS BISLEY MODEL SINGLE-ACTION REVOLVER
Caliber: 44-40 or 45 Colt, 6-shot cylinder. **Barrel:** 4-3/4", 5-1/2", 7-1/2". **Weight:** 40 oz. **Length:** 12-1/2" overall (7-1/2" barrel). **Grips:** Smooth walnut. **Sights:** Blade front, notch rear. **Features:** Replica of Colt's Bisley

Model. Polished blue finish, color case-hardened frame. Introduced 1997. Imported by Navy Arms.
Price: **$511.00**

NAVY ARMS 1873 GUNFIGHTER SINGLE-ACTION REVOLVER
Caliber: 357 Mag., 44-40, 45 Colt, 6-shot cylinder. **Barrel:** 4-3/4", 5-1/2", 7-1/2". **Weight:** 37 oz. **Length:** 10-1/4" overall (4-3/4" barrel). **Grips:** Checkered black polymer. **Sights:** Blade front, notch rear. **Features:** Blued with color case-hardened receiver, trigger and hammer; German Silver backstrap and triggerguard. American made Wolff trigger and mainsprings installed. Introduced 2005. Imported by Navy Arms.
Price: **$511.00**
Price: Stainless steel **$608.00**

NAVY ARMS 1875 SCHOFIELD REVOLVER
Caliber: 44-40, 45 Colt, 6-shot cylinder. **Barrel:** 3-1/2", 5", 7". **Weight:** 39 oz. **Length:** 10-3/4" overall (5" barrel). **Grips:** Smooth walnut. **Sights:** Blade front, notch rear. **Features:** Replica of Smith & Wesson Model 3 Schofield. Single-action, top-break with automatic ejection. Polished blue finish. Introduced 1994. Imported by Navy Arms.
Price: Hideout Model, 3-1/2" barrel **$849.00**
Price: Wells Fargo, 5" barrel **$849.00**
Price: U.S. Cavalry model, 7" barrel, military markings **$849.00**

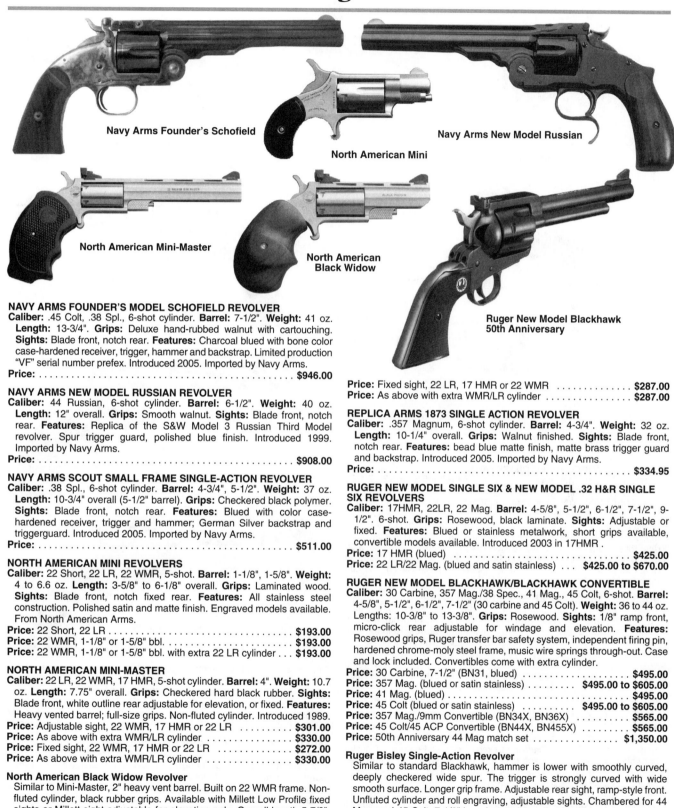

Navy Arms Founder's Schofield

North American Mini

Navy Arms New Model Russian

North American Mini-Master

North American Black Widow

Ruger New Model Blackhawk 50th Anniversary

NAVY ARMS FOUNDER'S MODEL SCHOFIELD REVOLVER
Caliber: .45 Colt, .38 Spl., 6-shot cylinder. **Barrel:** 7-1/2". **Weight:** 41 oz. **Length:** 13-3/4". **Grips:** Deluxe hand-rubbed walnut with cartouching. **Sights:** Blade front, notch rear. **Features:** Charcoal blued with bone color case-hardened receiver, trigger, hammer and backstrap. Limited production "VF" serial number prefex. Introduced 2005. Imported by Navy Arms.
Price: **$946.00**

NAVY ARMS NEW MODEL RUSSIAN REVOLVER
Caliber: 44 Russian, 6-shot cylinder. **Barrel:** 6-1/2". **Weight:** 40 oz. **Length:** 12" overall. **Grips:** Smooth walnut. **Sights:** Blade front, notch rear. **Features:** Replica of the S&W Model 3 Russian Third Model revolver. Spur trigger guard, polished blue finish. Introduced 1999. Imported by Navy Arms.
Price: **$908.00**

NAVY ARMS SCOUT SMALL FRAME SINGLE-ACTION REVOLVER
Caliber: .38 Spl., 6-shot cylinder. **Barrel:** 4-3/4", 5-1/2". **Weight:** 37 oz. **Length:** 10-3/4" overall (5-1/2" barrel). **Grips:** Checkered black polymer. **Sights:** Blade front, notch rear. **Features:** Blued with color case-hardened receiver, trigger and hammer; German Silver backstrap and triggerguard. Introduced 2005. Imported by Navy Arms.
Price: **$511.00**

NORTH AMERICAN MINI REVOLVERS
Caliber: 22 Short, 22 LR, 22 WMR, 5-shot. **Barrel:** 1-1/8", 1-5/8". **Weight:** 4 to 6.6 oz. **Length:** 3-5/8" to 6-1/8" overall. **Grips:** Laminated wood. **Sights:** Blade front, notch fixed rear. **Features:** All stainless steel construction. Polished satin and matte finish. Engraved models available. From North American Arms.
Price: 22 Short, 22 LR **$193.00**
Price: 22 WMR, 1-1/8" or 1-5/8" bbl. **$193.00**
Price: 22 WMR, 1-1/8" or 1-5/8" bbl. with extra 22 LR cylinder ... **$193.00**

NORTH AMERICAN MINI-MASTER
Caliber: 22 LR, 22 WMR, 17 HMR, 5-shot cylinder. **Barrel:** 4". **Weight:** 10.7 oz. **Length:** 7.75" overall. **Grips:** Checkered hard black rubber. **Sights:** Blade front, white outline rear adjustable for elevation, or fixed. **Features:** Heavy vented barrel; full-size grips. Non-fluted cylinder. Introduced 1989.
Price: Adjustable sight, 22 WMR, 17 HMR or 22 LR **$301.00**
Price: As above with extra WMR/LR cylinder **$330.00**
Price: Fixed sight, 22 WMR, 17 HMR or 22 LR **$272.00**
Price: As above with extra WMR/LR cylinder **$330.00**

North American Black Widow Revolver
Similar to Mini-Master, 2" heavy vent barrel. Built on 22 WMR frame. Non-fluted cylinder, black rubber grips. Available with Millett Low Profile fixed sights or Millett sight adjustable for elevation only. Overall length 5-7/8", weighs 8.8 oz. From North American Arms.
Price: Adjustable sight, 22 LR, 17 HMR or 22 WMR **$287.00**
Price: As above with extra WMR/LR cylinder **$316.00**

Price: Fixed sight, 22 LR, 17 HMR or 22 WMR **$287.00**
Price: As above with extra WMR/LR cylinder **$287.00**

REPLICA ARMS 1873 SINGLE ACTION REVOLVER
Caliber: .357 Magnum, 6-shot cylinder. **Barrel:** 4-3/4". **Weight:** 32 oz. **Length:** 10-1/4" overall. **Grips:** Walnut finished. **Sights:** Blade front, notch rear. **Features:** bead blue matte finish, matte brass trigger guard and backstrap. Introduced 2005. Imported by Navy Arms.
Price: **$334.95**

RUGER NEW MODEL SINGLE SIX & NEW MODEL .32 H&R SINGLE SIX REVOLVERS
Caliber: 17HMR, 22LR, 22 Mag. **Barrel:** 4-5/8", 5-1/2", 6-1/2", 7-1/2", 9-1/2". 6-shot. **Grips:** Rosewood, black laminate. **Sights:** Adjustable or fixed. **Features:** Blued or stainless metalwork, short grips available, convertible models available. Introduced 2003 in 17HMR .
Price: 17 HMR (blued) **$425.00**
Price: 22 LR/22 Mag. (blued and satin stainless) ... **$425.00 to $670.00**

RUGER NEW MODEL BLACKHAWK/BLACKHAWK CONVERTIBLE
Caliber: 30 Carbine, 357 Mag./38 Spec., 41 Mag., 45 Colt, 6-shot. **Barrel:** 4-5/8", 5-1/2", 6-1/2", 7-1/2" (30 carbine and 45 Colt). **Weight:** 36 to 44 oz. **Lengths:** 10-3/8" to 13-3/8". **Grips:** Rosewood. **Sights:** 1/8" ramp front, micro-click rear adjustable for windage and elevation. **Features:** Rosewood grips, Ruger transfer bar safety system, independent firing pin, hardened chrome-moly steel frame, music wire springs through-out. Case and lock included. Convertibles come with extra cylinder.
Price: 30 Carbine, 7-1/2" (BN31, blued) **$495.00**
Price: 357 Mag. (blued or satin stainless) .... **$495.00 to $605.00**
Price: 41 Mag. (blued) **$495.00**
Price: 45 Colt (blued or satin stainless) .... **$495.00 to $605.00**
Price: 357 Mag./9mm Convertible (BN34X, BN36X) **$565.00**
Price: 45 Colt/45 ACP Convertible (BN44X, BN455X) ... **$565.00**
Price: 50th Anniversary 44 Mag match set **$1,350.00**

Ruger Bisley Single-Action Revolver
Similar to standard Blackhawk, hammer is lower with smoothly curved, deeply checkered wide spur. The trigger is strongly curved with wide smooth surface. Longer grip frame. Adjustable rear sight, ramp-style front. Unfluted cylinder and roll engraving, adjustable sights. Chambered for 44 Mag. and 45 Colt; 7-1/2" barrel; overall length 13-1/2"; weighs 48-51 oz. Plastic lockable case. Orig. fluted cylinder introduced 1985; discontinued 1991. Unfluted cylinder introduced 1986.
Price: RB-44W (44 Mag), RB45W (45 Colt) **$625.00**

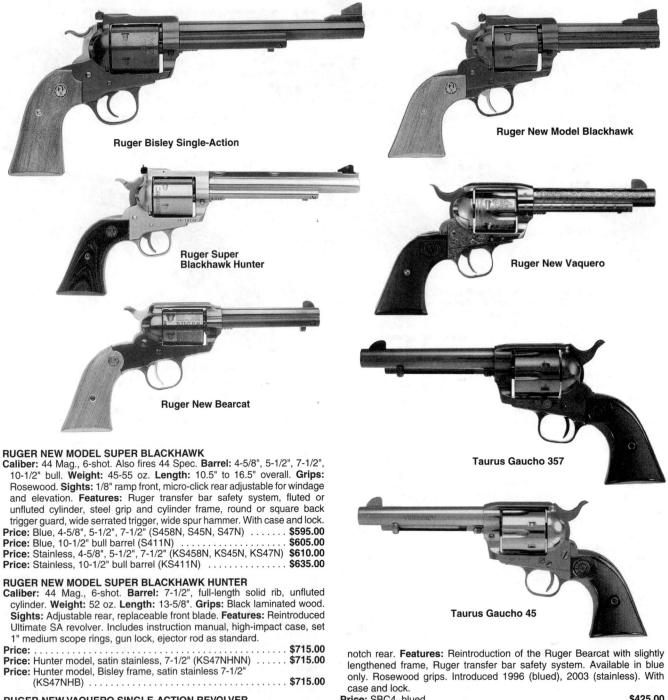

Ruger Bisley Single-Action

Ruger New Model Blackhawk

Ruger Super Blackhawk Hunter

Ruger New Vaquero

Ruger New Bearcat

Taurus Gaucho 357

Taurus Gaucho 45

RUGER NEW MODEL SUPER BLACKHAWK

Caliber: 44 Mag., 6-shot. Also fires 44 Spec. **Barrel:** 4-5/8", 5-1/2", 7-1/2", 10-1/2" bull. **Weight:** 45-55 oz. **Length:** 10.5" to 16.5" overall. **Grips:** Rosewood. **Sights:** 1/8" ramp front, micro-click rear adjustable for windage and elevation. **Features:** Ruger transfer bar safety system, fluted or unfluted cylinder, steel grip and cylinder frame, round or square back trigger guard, wide serrated trigger, wide spur hammer. With case and lock.
Price: Blue, 4-5/8", 5-1/2", 7-1/2" (S458N, S45N, S47N) **$595.00**
Price: Blue, 10-1/2" bull barrel (S411N) **$605.00**
Price: Stainless, 4-5/8", 5-1/2", 7-1/2" (KS458N, KS45N, KS47N) **$610.00**
Price: Stainless, 10-1/2" bull barrel (KS411N) **$635.00**

RUGER NEW MODEL SUPER BLACKHAWK HUNTER

Caliber: 44 Mag., 6-shot. **Barrel:** 7-1/2", full-length solid rib, unfluted cylinder. **Weight:** 52 oz. **Length:** 13-5/8". **Grips:** Black laminated wood. **Sights:** Adjustable rear, replaceable front blade. **Features:** Reintroduced Ultimate SA revolver. Includes instruction manual, high-impact case, set 1" medium scope rings, gun lock, ejector rod as standard.
Price: **$715.00**
Price: Hunter model, satin stainless, 7-1/2" (KS47NHNN) **$715.00**
Price: Hunter model, Bisley frame, satin stainless 7-1/2"
(KS47NHB) **$715.00**

RUGER NEW VAQUERO SINGLE-ACTION REVOLVER

Caliber: 357 Mag., 45 Colt, 6-shot. **Barrel:** 4-5/8", 5-1/2", 7-1/2". **Weight:** 39-45 oz. **Length:** 10-1/2" overall (4-5/8" barrel). **Grips:** Rubber with Ruger medallion. **Sights:** Blade front, fixed notch rear. **Features:** Transfer bar safety system and loading gate interlock. Blued model color case-hardened finish on frame, rest polished and blued. Engraved model available. Gloss stainless. Introduced 2005.
Price: 357 Mag., blued or stainless **$609.00**
Price: 45 Colt, blued or stainless **$609.00**

RUGER NEW BEARCAT SINGLE-ACTION

Caliber: 22 LR, 6-shot. **Barrel:** 4". **Weight:** 24 oz. **Length:** 9" overall. **Grips:** Smooth rosewood with Ruger medallion. **Sights:** Blade front, fixed notch rear. **Features:** Reintroduction of the Ruger Bearcat with slightly lengthened frame, Ruger transfer bar safety system. Available in blue only. Rosewood grips. Introduced 1996 (blued), 2003 (stainless). With case and lock.
Price: SBC4, blued **$425.00**
Price: KSBC-4, satin stainless **$480.00**

TAURUS SINGLE-ACTION GAUCHO REVOLVERS

Caliber: 38 Spl, 357 Mag, 44-40, 45 Colt, 6-shot. **Barrel:** 4.75", 5.5", 7.5", 12". **Weight:** 36.7-37.7 oz. **Length:** 13". **Grips:** Checkered black polymer. **Sights:** Blade front, fixed notch rear. Integral transfer bar; blue, blue with case hardened frame, matte stainless and the hand polished "Sundance" stainless finish. Removable cylinder, half-cock notch. Introduced 2005. Imported from Brazil by Taurus International.
Price: S/A-357-B, 357 Mag., Sundance blue finish, 5.5" barrel . . **$520.00**
Price: S/A-357-S/S7, 357 Mag., polished stainless, 7.5" barrel . . **$536.00**
Price: S/A-45-B **$52.00**

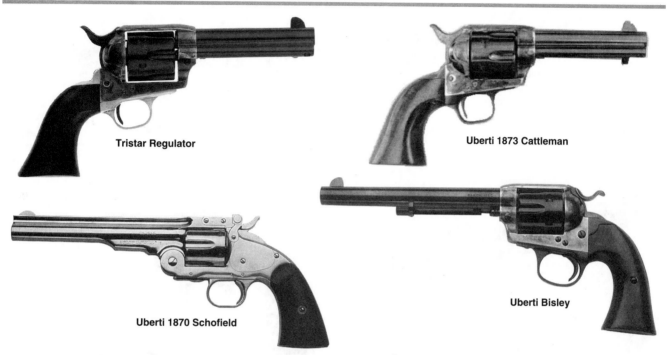

Tristar Regulator

Uberti 1873 Cattleman

Uberti 1870 Schofield

Uberti Bisley

Uberti 1875 Outlaw

TRISTAR/UBERTI REGULATOR REVOLVER
Caliber: 45 Colt. **Barrel:** 4-3/4", 5.5". **Weight:** 32-38 oz. **Length:** 8-1/4" overall (4-3/4" bbl.) **Grips:** One-piece walnut. **Sights:** Blade front, notch rear. **Features:** Uberti replica of 1873 Colt Model "P" revolver. Color-case hardened steel frame, brass backstrap and trigger guard, hammer-block safety. Imported from Italy by Tristar Sporting Arms.
Price: Regulator **$455.00**
Price: Regulator Deluxe (blued backstrap, trigger guard) **$489.00**
Price: Stallion (.17 HMR and .17 M2 Cylinders) **$459.00**

UBERTI 1858 NEW ARMY CONVERSION REVOLVER
Caliber: 45 Colt, 6-shot engraved cylinlder. **Barrel:** 8" **Weight:** 2.6 lbs. **Length:** 13.8". **Grips:** One-piece walnut. **Sights:** Blade front, groove rear. **Features:** Brass backstrap, trigger guard; color case-hardened frame, blued barrel, cylinder. Introduced 2007. Imported from Italy by Uberti U.S.A.
Price: **$450.00**

UBERTI 1851-1860 CONVERSION REVOLVERS
Caliber: 38 Sp., 45 Colt, 6-shot engraved cylinlder. **Barrel:** 4-3/4", 5-1/2", 7-1/2", 8" **Weight:** 2.6 lbs. (5-1/2" bbl.). **Length:** 13" overall (5-1/2" bbl.). **Grips:** Walnut. **Features:** Brass backstrap, trigger guard; color case-hardened frame, blued barrel, cylinder. Introduced 2007. Imported from Italy by Uberti U.S.A.
Price: 1851 Navy, 38 Special **$435.00**
Price: 1860 Army, 45 Colt **$485.00**

UBERTI 1871-1872 OPEN TOP REVOLVERS
Caliber: 38 Sp., 45 Colt, 6-shot engraved cylinlder. **Barrel:** 4-3/4", 5-1/2", 7-1/2". **Weight:** 2.6 lbs. (5-1/2" bbl.). **Length:** 13" overall (5-1/2" bbl.). **Grips:** Walnut. **Features:** Blued backstrap, trigger guard; color case-hardened frame, blued barrel, cylinder. Introduced 2007. Imported from Italy by Uberti U.S.A.
Price: 1872 Open Top **$445.00**
Price: 1871 Open Top **$415.00**

UBERTI 1873 CATTLEMAN SINGLE-ACTION
Caliber: 45 Colt; 6-shot fluted cylinder **Barrel:** 4-3/4", 5-1/2", 7-1/2". **Weight:** 2.3 lbs. (5-1/2" bbl.). **Length:** 11" overall (5-1/2" bbl.). **Grips:** Styles: Frisco (pearl styled); Desperado (buffalo horn styled); Chisholm (checkered walnut); Gunfighter (black checkered), Cody (ivory styled), one-piece walnut. **Sights:** Blade front, groove rear. **Features:** Steel or brass backstrap, trigger guard; color case-hardened frame, blued barrel, cylinder. NM designates New Model plunger style frame; OM designates Old Model screw cylinder pin retainer. Imported from Italy by Uberti U.S.A.
Price: 1873 Cattleman Frisco **$650.00**

Price: 1873 Cattleman Desperado (2006) **$650.00**
Price: 1873 Cattleman Chisholm (2006) **$390.00**
Price: 1873 Cattleman NM, blued 4-3/4" barrel **$400.00**
Price: 1873 Cattleman NM, stainless steel 7-1/2" barrel **$535.00**
Price: 1873 Cattleman OM, Old West finish, 5-1/2" barrel **$535.00**
Price: 1873 Cattleman NM, Nickel finish, 7-1/2" barrel **$555.00**

UBERTI 1873 CATTLEMAN BIRD'S HEAD SINGLE ACTION
Caliber: 357 Mag., 45 Colt; 6-shot fluted cylinder **Barrel:** 3-1/2", 4", 4-3/4", 5-1/2". **Weight:** 2.3 lbs. (5-1/2" bbl.). **Length:** 10.9" overall (5-1/2" bbl.). **Grips:** One-piece walnut. **Sights:** Blade front, groove rear. **Features:** Steel or brass backstrap, trigger guard; color case-hardened frame, blued barrel, cylinder. Imported from Italy by Uberti U.S.A.
Price: 1873 Cattleman Bird's Head OM 3-1/2" barrel **$500.00**

UBERTI 1873 BUNTLINE AND REVOLVER CARBINE SINGLE ACTION
Caliber: 357 Mag., 44-40, 45 Colt; 6-shot fluted cylinder **Barrel:** 18". **Length:** 22.9" to 34". **Grips:** Walnut pistol grip or rifle stock. **Sights:** Fixed or adjustable. **Features:** Imported from Italy by Uberti U.S.A.
Price: 1873 Revolver Carbine, 18" barrel, 34" OAL **$585.00**
Price: 1873 Catttleman Buntline Target, 18" barrel, 22.9" OAL . . **$520.00**

UBERTI OUTLAW, FRONTIER, AND POLICE REVOLVERS
Caliber: 45 Colt, 6-shot fluted cylinder. **Barrel:** 5-1/2", 7-1/2". **Weight:** 2.5 to 2.8 lbs. **Length:** 10.8" to 13.6" overall. **Grips:** Two-piece smooth walnut. **Sights:** Blade front, notch rear. **Features:** Cartridge version of 1858 Remington percussion revolver. Nickel and blued finishes. Imported by Uberti U.S.A.
Price: 1875 Outlaw nickel finish **$515.00**
Price: 1875 Frontier, blued finish **$435.00**
Price: 1890 Police, blued finish **$440.00**

U.S. Fire Arms Single Action Army Revolver

U.S. Fire Arms Single Action Flattop Target

U.S. Fire Arms Single Action Omni-Potent

U.S. Fire Arms Single Action Bisley

U.S. Fire Arms Rodeo Cowboy Action

U.S. Firearms United States Pre-War

UBERTI 1870 SCHOFIELD-STYLE BREAK-TOP REVOLVER

Caliber: 38, 44 Russian, 44-40, 45 Colt, 6-shot cylinder. **Barrel:** 3-1/2", 5", 7". **Weight:** 2.4 lbs. (5" barrel) **Length:** 10.8" overall (5" barrel). **Grips:** Two-piece smooth walnut or pearl. **Sights:** Blade front, notch rear. **Features:** Replica of Smith & Wesson Model 3 Schofield. Single-action, top-break with automatic ejection. Polished blue finish (first model). Introduced 1994. Imported by Uberti U.S.A.
Price: No. 3-2nd Model, nickel finish **$975.00**

UBERTI BISLEY AND STALLION MODELS SINGLE-ACTION REVOLVERS

Caliber: 357 Mag., 45 Colt (Bisley); 22LR and 38 Special (Stallion), both with 6-shot fluted cylinder. **Barrel:** 4-3/4", 5-1/2", 7-1/2". **Weight:** 2 to 2.5 lbs. **Length:** 12.7" overall (7-1/2" barrel). **Grips:** Two-piece walnut. **Sights:** Blade front, notch rear. **Features:** Replica of Colt's Bisley Model. Polished blue finish, color case-hardened frame. Introduced 1997. Imported by Uberti U.S.A.
Price: 1873 Stallion, 5-1/2" barrel **$425.00**
Price: 1873 Bisley, 7-1/2" barrel **$500.00**

U.S. FIRE ARMS SINGLE-ACTION REVOLVER

Caliber: 45 Colt (standard); 32 WCF, 38 WCF, 38 Special, 44 WCF, 44 Special, 6-shot cylinder. **Barrel:** 4-3/4", 5-1/2", 7-1/2". **Weight:** 37 oz. **Length:** NA. **Grips:** Hard rubber. **Sights:** Blade front, notch rear. **Features:** Recreation of original guns; 3" and 4" have no ejector. Available with all-blue, blue with color case-hardening, or full nickel-plate finish. Other models include Government Inspector Series ($1,485, walnut grips), Custer Battlefield Gun ($1,485, 7-1/2" barrel), Patriot Series ($1,280, lanyard loop in 30 Carbine), Flattop Target ($1,495), Sheriff's Model ($1,085, with barrel lengths starting at 2"), Snubnose ($1,295, barrel lengths 2", 3", 4"), Omni-Potent Six-Shooter and Omni-Target Six-Shooter (from $1,485), Bisley and Bisley Target (from $1,485, introduced 2006). Made in U.S.A. by United States Fire Arms Mfg. Co.
Price: Blue/cased-colors **$1,085.00**
Price: Nickel **$1,485.00**

U.S. FIRE ARMS RODEO COWBOY ACTION REVOLVER

Caliber: 45 Colt, 38 Special. **Barrel:** 4-3/4", 5-1/2". **Grips:** Rubber. **Features:** Historically correct Armory bone case hammer, blue satin finish, transfer bar safety system, correct solid firing pin. Entry level basic cowboy SASS gun. Other models include Cowboy ($945) and Gunslinger ($1,045). 2006 version includes brown-rubber stocks.
Price: **$649.00**

U.S. FIRE ARMS U.S. PRE-WAR

Caliber: 45 Colt (standard); 32 WCF, 38 WCF, 38 Special, 44 WCF, 44 Special. **Barrel:** 4-3/4", 5-1/2", 7-1/2". **Grips:** Hard rubber. **Features:** Armory bone case/Armory blue finish standard, cross-pin or black powder frame. Introduced 2002. Made in U.S.A. by United States Firearms Mfg. Co.
Price: **$1,345.00**

HANDGUNS — Miscellaneous

Specially adapted single-shot and multi-barrel arms.

Bond Arms Texas Defender

Bond Arms Century 2000 Defender

Cobra Big Bore

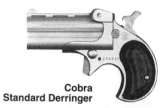

Cobra Standard Derringer

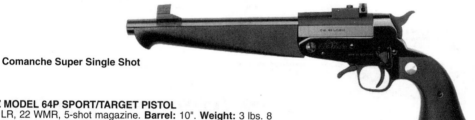

Comanche Super Single Shot

Downsizer WSP Single Shot

ANSCHUTZ MODEL 64P SPORT/TARGET PISTOL
Caliber: 22 LR, 22 WMR, 5-shot magazine. **Barrel:** 10". **Weight:** 3 lbs. 8 oz. **Length:** 18-1/2" overall. Stock: Choate Rynite. **Sights:** None furnished; grooved for scope mounting. **Features:** Right-hand bolt; polished blue finish. Introduced 1998. Imported from Germany by AcuSport.
Price: 22 LR **$455.95**
Price: 22 WMR **$479.95**

BOND ARMS TEXAS DEFENDER DERRINGER
Caliber: From 22 LR to 45 LC/410 shotshells. **Barrel:** 3". **Weight:** 20 oz. **Length:** 5". **Grips:** Rosewood. **Sights:** Blade front, fixed rear. **Features:** Interchangeable barrels, stainless steel firing pins, cross-bolt safety, automatic extractor for rimmed calibers. Stainless steel construction, brushed finish. Right or left hand.
Price: **$389.00**
Price: Interchangeable barrels, 22 LR thru 45 LC, 3" **$139.00**
Price: Interchangeable barrels, 45 LC, 3.5" **$159.00**

BOND ARMS CENTURY 2000 DEFENDER
Caliber: 45LC/410 shotshells. **Barrel:** 3.5". **Weight:** 21 oz. **Length:** 5.5". **Features:** Similar to Defender series.
Price: **$404.00**

BOND ARMS COWBOY DEFENDER
Caliber: From 22 LR to 45 LC/410 shotshells. **Barrel:** 3". **Weight:** 19 oz. **Length:** 5.5". **Features:** Similar to Defender series. No trigger guard.
Price: **$389.00**

BOND ARMS SNAKE SLAYER
Caliber: 45 LC/410 shotshell (2-1/2" or 3"). **Barrel:** 3.5". **Weight:** 21 oz. **Length:** 5.5". **Grips:** Extended rosewood. **Sights:** Blade front, fixed rear. **Features:** Single-action; interchangeable barrels; stainless steel firing pin. Introduced 2005.
Price: **$455.00**

BOND ARMS SNAKE SLAYER IV
Caliber: 45 LC/410 shotshell (2-1/2" or 3"). **Barrel:** 4.25". **Weight:** 22 oz. **Length:** 6.25". **Grips:** Extended rosewood. **Sights:** Blade front, fixed rear. **Features:** Single-action; interchangeable barrels; stainless steel firing pin. Introduced 2006.
Price: **$485.00**

BROWN CLASSIC SINGLE-SHOT PISTOL
Caliber: 17 Ackley Hornet through 375x444. **Barrel:** 15" air-gauged match grade. **Weight:** About 3 lbs. 7 oz. **Grips:** Walnut; thumb rest target-style. **Sights:** None furnished; drilled and tapped for scope mounting. **Features:** Falling block action gives rigid barrel-receiver mating; hand fitted and headspaced. Introduced 1998. Made in U.S.A. by E.A. Brown Mfg.
Price: **$589.00**

CHARTER ARMS DIXIE DERRINGERS
Caliber: 22 LR, 22 WMR. **Barrel:** 1.125". **Weight:** 5-6 oz. **Length:** 4" overall. **Grips:** Black polymer **Sights:** Blade front, fixed notch rear.

Features: Stainless finish. Introduced 2006. Made in U.S.A. by Charter Arms, distributed by MKS Supply.
Price: **$112.00**

COBRA BIG BORE DERRINGERS
Caliber: 22 WMR, 32 H&R Mag., 38 Spec., 9mm, 380 ACP. **Barrel:** 2.75". **Weight:** 14 oz. **Length:** 4.65" overall. **Grips:** Textured black synthetic or laminated rosewood. **Sights:** Blade front, fixed notch rear. **Features:** Alloy frame, steel-lined barrels, steel breech block. Plunger-type safety with integral hammer block. Black, chrome or satin finish. Introduced 2002. Made in U.S.A. by Cobra Enterprises of Utah, Inc.
Price: **$160.00**

COBRA LONG-BORE DERRINGERS
Caliber: 22 WMR, 38 Spec., 9mm. **Barrel:** 3.5". **Weight:** 16 oz. **Length:** 5.4" overall. **Grips:** Black synthetic or rosewood. **Sights:** Fixed. **Features:** Chrome, satin nickel, or black Teflon finish. Introduced 2002. Made in U.S.A. by Cobra Enterprises of Utah, Inc.
Price: **$160.00**

COBRA STANDARD SERIES DERRINGERS
Caliber: 22 LR, 22 WMR, 25 ACP, 32 ACP. **Barrel:** 2.4". **Weight:** 9.5 oz. **Length:** 4" overall. **Grips:** Laminated wood or pearl. **Sights:** Blade front, fixed notch rear. **Features:** Choice of black powder coat, satin nickel or chrome finish. Introduced 2002. Made in U.S.A. by Cobra Enterprises of Utah, Inc.
Price: **$140.00**

COMANCHE SUPER SINGLE-SHOT PISTOL
Caliber: 45 LC, 410 ga. **Barrel:** 10". **Sights:** Adjustable. **Features:** Blue finish, not available for sale in CA, MA. Distributed by SGS Importers International, Inc.
Price: **$183.95**
Price: Satin nickel **$199.95**
Price: Camo, intr. 2006 .... **$216.95**

DOWNSIZER WSP SINGLE-SHOT PISTOL
Caliber: 357 Magnum, 45 ACP, 38 Special. **Barrel:** 2.10". **Weight:** 11 oz. **Length:** 3.25" overall. **Grips:** Black polymer. **Sights:** None. **Features:** Single shot, tip-up barrel. Double action only. Stainless steel construction. Measures .900" thick. Introduced 1997. From Downsizer Corp.
Price: **$499.00**

GAUCHER GN1 SILHOUETTE PISTOL
Caliber: 22 LR, single shot. **Barrel:** 10". **Weight:** 2.4 lbs. **Length:** 15.5" overall. **Grips:** European hardwood. **Sights:** Blade front, open adjustable rear. **Features:** Bolt action, adjustable trigger. Introduced 1990. Imported from France by Mandall Shooting Supplies.
Price: About **$525.00**
Price: Model GP Silhouette **$425.00**

"62ND EDITION, 2008 305"

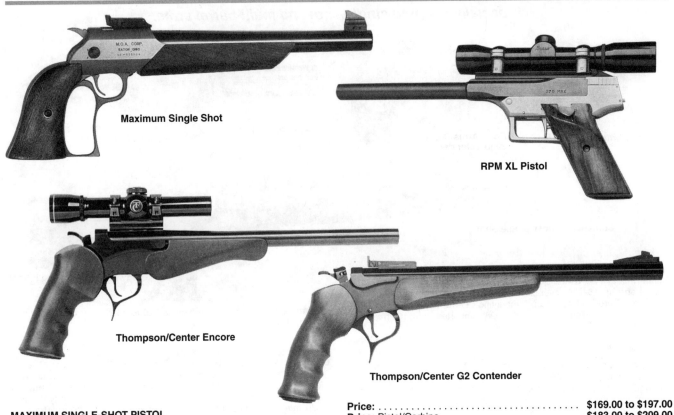

Maximum Single Shot

RPM XL Pistol

Thompson/Center Encore

Thompson/Center G2 Contender

MAXIMUM SINGLE-SHOT PISTOL

Caliber: 22 LR, 22 Hornet, 22 BR, 22 PPC, 223 Rem., 22-250, 6mm BR, 6mm PPC, 243, 250 Savage, 6.5mm-35M, 270 MAX, 270 Win., 7mm TCU, 7mm BR, 7mm-35, 7mm INT-R, 7mm-08, 7mm Rocket, 7mm Super-Mag., 30 Herrett, 30 Carbine, 30-30, 308 Win., 30x39, 32-20, 350 Rem. Mag., 357 Mag., 357 Maximum, 358 Win., 375 H&H, 44 Mag., 454 Casull. **Barrel:** 8-3/4", 10-1/2", 14". **Weight:** 61 oz. (10-1/2" bbl.); 78 oz. (14" bbl.). **Length:** 15", 18-1/2" overall (with 10-1/2" and 14" bbl., respectively). **Grips:** Smooth walnut stocks and forend. Also available with 17" finger groove grip. **Sights:** Ramp front, fully adjustable open rear. **Features:** Falling block action; drilled and tapped for M.O.A. scope mounts; integral grip frame/receiver; adjustable trigger; Douglas barrel (interchangeable). Introduced 1983. Made in U.S.A. by M.O.A. Corp.

Price: Stainless receiver, blue barrel $799.00
Price: Stainless receiver, stainless barrel $883.00
Price: Extra blued barrel $254.00
Price: Extra stainless barrel $317.00
Price: Scope mount $60.00

RPM XL SINGLE SHOT PISTOL

Caliber: 22 LR through 45-70. **Barrel:** 8", 10-3/4", 12", 14". **Weight:** About 60 oz. **Grips:** Smooth Goncalo Alves with thumb and heel rests. **Features:** Barrel drilled and tapped for scope mount. Visible cocking indicator. Spring-loaded barrel lock, positive hammer-block safety. Trigger adjustable for weight of pull and over-travel. Contact maker for complete price list. Made in U.S.A. by RPM.

Price: XL Hunter model (action only) $1,045.00
Price: Extra barrel . . . . $250.00 to $300.00

SPRINGFIELD M6 SCOUT PISTOL

Caliber: 22 LR/45 LC/410, 22 Hornet, 45 LC/410. **Barrel:** 10". **Weight:** NA. **Length:** NA. **Grips:** NA. **Sights:** NA. **Features:** Adapted from the U.S. Air Force M6 Survival Rifle, also available as a carbine with 16" barrel.

Price: . . . . $169.00 to $197.00
Price: Pistol/Carbine . . . . $183.00 to $209.00

THOMPSON/CENTER ENCORE PISTOL

Caliber: 22-250, 223, 204 Ruger, 6.8 Rem., 260 Rem., 7mm-08, 243, 308, 270, 30-06, 375 JDJ, 204 Ruger, 44 Mag., 454 Casull, 480 Ruger, 444 Marlin single shot, 450 Marlin with muzzle tamer, no sights. **Barrel:** 12", 15", tapered round. **Weight:** NA. **Length:** 21" overall with 12" barrel. **Grips:** American walnut with finger grooves, walnut forend. **Sights:** Blade on ramp front, adjustable rear, or none. **Features:** Interchangeable barrels; action opens by squeezing the trigger guard; drilled and tapped for scope mounting; blue finish. Announced 1996. Made in U.S.A. by Thompson/Center Arms.

Price: . . . . $589.00 to $592.00
Price: Extra 12" barrels $262.00
Price: Extra 15" barrels $270.00
Price: 45 Colt/410 barrel, 12" $292.00
Price: 45 Colt/410 barrel, 15" $299.00

Thompson/Center Stainless Encore Pistol

Similar to blued Encore, made of stainless steel, available with 15" barrel in 223, 22-250, 243 Win., 7mm-08, 308, 30/06 Sprgfld., 45/70 Gov't., 45/410 VR. With black rubber grip and forend. Made in U.S.A. by Thompson/Center Arms.

Price: . . . . $636.00 to $644.00

Thompson/Center G2 Contender Pistol

A second generation Contender pistol maintaining the same barrel interchangeability with older Contender barrels and their corresponding forends (except Herrett forend). The G2 frame will not accept old-style grips due to the change in grip angle. Incorporates an automatic hammer block safety with built-in interlock. Features include trigger adjustable for overtravel, adjustable rear sight; ramp front sight blade, blued steel finish.

Price: $570.00

Both classic arms and recent designs in American-style repeaters for sport and field shooting.

Armalite M15A2

Armalite AR-10A4

Armalite AR-180B

ARMALITE M15A2 CARBINE
Caliber: 223, 30-round magazine. **Barrel:** 16" heavy chrome lined; 1:9" twist. **Weight:** 7 lbs. **Length:** 35-11/16" overall. **Stock:** Green or black composition. **Sights:** Standard A2. **Features:** Upper and lower receivers have push-type pivot pin; hard coat anodized; A2-style forward assist; M16A2-type raised fence around magazine release button. Made in U.S.A. by ArmaLite, Inc.
Price: Green **$1,100.00**
Price: Black **$1,100.00**

ARMALITE AR-10A4 SPECIAL PURPOSE RIFLE
Caliber: 308 Win., 10- and 20-round magazine. **Barrel:** 20" chrome-lined, 1:11.25" twist. **Weight:** 9.6 lbs. **Length:** 41" overall. **Stock:** Green or black composition. **Sights:** Detachable handle, front sight, or scope mount available; comes with international style flattop receiver with Picatinny rail. **Features:** Forged upper receiver with case deflector. Receivers are hard-coat anodized. Introduced 1995. Made in U.S.A. by ArmaLite, Inc.
Price: Green **$1,506.00**
Price: Black **$1,506.00**

ArmaLite AR-10(T)
Similar to the ArmaLite AR-10A4 but with stainless steel, barrel, machined tool steel, two-stage National Match trigger group and other features.
Price: AR-10(T) rifle **$2,126.00**

ArmaLite AR-10A2
Utilizing the same 20" double-lapped, heavy barrel as the ArmaLite AR-10A4 Special Purpose Rifle. Offered in 308 caliber only. Made in U.S.A. by ArmaLite, Inc.
Price: AR-10A2 rifle or carbine **$1,506.00**

ARMALITE AR-180B RIFLE
Caliber: 223, 10-shot magazine. **Barrel:** 19.8". **Weight:** 6 lbs. **Length:** 38". **Stock:** Synthetic. **Sights:** Rear sight adjustable for windage, small and large apertures. **Features:** Lower receiver made of polymer, upper formed of sheet metal. Uses standard AR-15 magazines. Made in U.S.A. by Armalite.
Price: **$750.00**

ARSENAL USA SSR-56
Caliber: 7.62x39mm. **Barrel:** 16.25". **Weight:** 7.4 lbs. **Length:** 35.5". **Stock:** Black polymer. **Sights:** Adjustable rear. **Features:** An AK-47-style rifle built on a hardened Hungarian FEG receiver with the required six U.S.-made parts to make it legal for use with all extra-capacity magazines. From Arsenal I, LLC.
Price: **$565.00**

ARSENAL USA SSR-74-2
Caliber: 5.45x39mm **Barrel:** 16.25" **Weight:** 7 lbs. **Length:** 36.75" **Stock:** Polymer or wood. **Sights:** Adjustable. **Features:** Built with parts from an unissued Bulgarian AK-47 rifle, it has a Buffer Technologies recoil buffer, enough U.S.-made parts to allow pistol grip stock and use with all extra-capacity magazines. Assembled in U.S.A. From Arsenal I, LLC.
Price: **$499.00**

ARSENAL USA SSR-85C-2
Caliber: 7.62x39mm. **Barrel:** 16.25". **Weight:** 7.1 lbs. **Length:** 35.5". **Stock:** Polymer or wood. **Sights:** Adjustable rear calibrated to 800 meters. **Features:** Built from parts obtained from unissued Polish AK-47 rifles, the gas tube is vented and the receiver cover is plain. Rifle contains enough U.S.-sourced parts to allow pistol grip stock and use with all extra-capacity magazines. Assembled in U.S.A. by Arsenal I, LLC.
Price: **$499.00**

Auto-Ordnance 1927 A-1 Thompson

Benelli R1

Benelli R1 APG Camo

Barrett Model 82A-1

AUTO-ORDNANCE 1927 A-1 THOMPSON
Caliber: 45 ACP. **Barrel:** 16-1/2". **Weight:** 13 lbs. **Length:** About 41"
overall (Deluxe). **Stock:** Walnut stock and vertical forend. **Sights:** Blade
front, open rear adjustable for windage. **Features:** Recreation of
Thompson Model 1927. Semi-auto only. Deluxe model has finned barrel,
adjustable rear sight and compensator; Standard model has plain barrel
and military sight. From Auto-Ordnance Corp.
Price: Deluxe $950.00
Price: 1927A1C lightweight model (9-1/2 lbs.) $950.00

Auto-Ordnance Thompson M1/M1-C
Similar to the 1927 A-1 except is in the M-1 configuration with side cocking
knob, horizontal forend, smooth unfinned barrel, sling swivels on butt and
forend. Matte black finish. Introduced 1985.
Price: M1 semi-auto carbine $950.00
Price: M1-C lightweight semi-auto $925.00

Auto-Ordnance 1927 A-1 Commando
Similar to the 1927 A-1 except has Parkerized finish, black-finish wood
butt, pistol grip, horizontal forend. Comes with black nylon sling.
Introduced 1998. Made in U.S.A. by Auto-Ordnance Corp.
Price: $950.00

BARRETT MODEL 82A-1 SEMI-AUTOMATIC RIFLE
Caliber: 50 BMG, 10-shot detachable box magazine. **Barrel:** 29". **Weight:**
28.5 lbs. **Length:** 57" overall. **Stock:** Composition with energy-absorbing
recoil pad. **Sights:** Scope optional. **Features:** Semi-automatic, recoil
operated with recoiling barrel. Three-lug locking bolt; muzzle brake.
Adjustable bipod. Introduced 1985. Made in U.S.A. by Barrett Firearms.
Price: From $7,200.00

BENELLI R1 RIFLE
Caliber: 300 Win. Mag., 300 WSM, 270 WSM (24" barrel); 30-06, 308 (22"
barrel); 300 Win. Mag., 30-06, (20" barrel). **Weight:** 7.1 lbs. **Length:**
43.75" to 45.75" **Stock:** Select satin walnut or synthetic. **Sights:** None.
Features: Auto-regulating gas-operated system, three-lug rotary bolt,
interchangeable barrels, optional recoil pads. Introduced 2003. Imported
from Italy by Benelli USA.
Price: Synthetic with ComforTech gel recoil pad $1,435.00
Price: Satin walnut $1,265.00
Price: Black synthetic , Grip Tight, ComforTech , .270 WSM or
.300 WSM (2007) $1,435.00

Beretta CX4 Carbine

Browning Mark II Safari

Browning Lightweight Stalker

Browning Lightweight Stalker

Bushmaster M17S Bullpup

BERETTA CX4/PX4 STORM CARBINE
Caliber: 9mm Para, 40 S&W, 45 ACP. **Weight:** 5.75 lbs. **Barrel Length:** 16.6", chrome lined, rate of twist 1:16 (40 S&W) or 1:10 (9mm). **Length:** NA. **Stock:** Black synthetic. **Sights:** NA. **Features:** Introduced 2005. Imported from Italy by Beretta USA.
Price: Cx4 Carbine, 40 S&W, 10+1 . . . . $800.00
Price: Cx4 Carbine, 8000 Series, 9mm, 10+1 . . . . $775.00
Price: Cx4 Carbine, 8045 Series,45 ACP, 8+1 . . . . $800.00
Price: Cx4 Px4 Carbine, 40 S&W, 14+1 . . . . $850.00
Price: Cx4 Px4 Carbine, 9mm, 17+1 . . . . $850.00

BROWNING BAR SAFARI AND SAFARI W/BOSS SEMI-AUTO RIFLES
Caliber: Safari: 243, 25-06, 270, 7mm Rem Mag., 30-06, 308, 300 Win. Mag., 338 Win Mag. Safari w/BOSS: 270, 7mm Rem Mag., 30-06, 300 Win. Mag., 338 Win Mag., plus 270 WSM, 7mm WSM, 300 WSM. **Barrel:** 22-24" round tapered. **Weight:** 7.4-8.2 lbs. **Length:** 43-45" overall. **Stock:** French walnut pistol grip stock and forend, hand checkered. **Sights:** No sights. **Features:** Has new bolt release lever; removable trigger assembly with larger trigger guard; redesigned gas and buffer systems. Detachable 4-round box magazine. Scroll-engraved receiver is tapped for scope mounting. BOSS barrel vibration modulator and muzzle brake system available. Mark II Safari introduced 1993. Imported from Belgium by Browning.
Price: BAR MK IISafari, from. $934.00
Price: BAR Safari w/BOSS, from $1,038.00

BROWNING BAR SHORTTRAC/LONGTRAC AUTO RIFLES
Caliber: (ShortTrac models) 270 WSM, 7mm WSM, 300 WSM, 243 Win., 308 Win.; (Long Trac models) 270 Win., 30-06 Sprfld., 7mm Rem. Mag., 300 Win. Mag. **Barrel:** 23". **Weight:** 6 lbs. 10 oz. to 7 lbs. 4 oz. **Length:** 41-1/2" to 44". **Stock:** Satin-finish walnut, pistol-grip, fluted forend. **Sights:** Adj. rear, bead front standard, no sights on BOSS models

(optional). **Features:** Designed to handle new WSM chamberings. Gas-operated, blued finish, rotary bolt design (Long Trac models).
Price: BAR ShortTrac, 243 Win., 308 Win. from $930.00
Price: BAR ShortTrac Left-Hand, intr. 2007, from $967.00
Price: BAR ShortTrac WSM, 270 WSM, 7mm WSM, 300 WSM . . . $965.00
Price: BAR LongTrac, 270 Win., 30-06 Sprfld. $885.00
Price: BAR LongTrac, 7mm Rem. Mag., 300 Win. Mag. $965.00
Price: BAR LongTrac Mossy Oak Break Up, intr. 2007, from $1,055.00

BROWNING BAR LIGHTWEIGHT STALKER AUTO RIFLE
Caliber: 243, 308, 270, 30-06, 270 WSM, 7mm WSM, 300 WSM, 300 Win. Mag., 338 Win. Mag. **Barrel:** 20-24". **Weight:** 7.1-7.75 LBS. **Length:** 41-45" overall. **Stock:** Black composite stock and forearm. **Sights:** Hooded front and adjustable rear. **Features:** Gas-operated action with seven-lug rotary bolt; dual action bars; 2-, 3- or 4-shot magazine (depending on cartridge). Introduced 2001. Imported by Browning.
Price: BAR Lightweight Stalker, from $927.00
Price: BAR Lightweight Stalker, WSM and magnums $964.00

BUSHMASTER M17S BULLPUP RIFLE
Caliber: 223, 10-shot magazine. **Barrel:** 21.5", chrome lined; 1:9" twist. **Weight:** 8.2 lbs. **Length:** 30" overall. **Stock:** Fiberglass-filled nylon. **Sights:** Designed for optics-carrying handle incorporates scope mount rail for Weaver-type rings; also includes 25-meter open iron sights. **Features:** Gas-operated, short-stroke piston system; ambidextrous magazine release. Introduced 1993. Made in U.S.A. by Bushmaster Firearms, Inc./Quality Parts Co.
Price: $765.00

Bushmaster XM15 E2S Carbine

Bushmaster Varminter

Century International AES-10 Hi-Cap with bipod

Century International WASR-10 Hi-Cap

BUSHMASTER SHORTY XM15 E2S CARBINE
Caliber: 223,10-shot magazine. **Barrel:** 16", heavy; 1:9" twist. **Weight:** 7.2 lbs. **Length:** 34.75" overall. **Stock:** A2 type; fixed black composition. **Sights:** Fully adjustable M16A2 sight system. **Features:** Patterned after Colt M-16A2. Chrome-lined barrel with manganese phosphate finish. "Shorty" handguards. Has forged aluminum receivers with pushpin. Made in U.S.A. by Bushmaster Firearms, Inc.
Price: (A2) **$985.00**
Price: (A3) **$1,085.00**

Bushmaster XM15 E2S Dissipator Carbine
Similar to the XM15 E2S Shorty carbine except has full-length "Dissipator" handguards. Weighs 7.6 lbs.; 34.75" overall; forged aluminum receivers with push-pin style takedown. Made in U.S.A. by Bushmaster Firearms, Inc.
Price: (A2 type) **$995.00**
Price: (A3 type) **$1,095.00**

Bushmaster XM15 E25 AK Shorty Carbine
Similar to the XM15 E2S Shorty except has 14.5" barrel with an AK muzzle brake permanently attached giving 16" barrel length. Weighs 7.3 lbs. Introduced 1999. Made in U.S.A. by Bushmaster Firearms, Inc.
Price: (A2 type) **$1,005.00**
Price: (A3 type) **$1,105.00**

Bushmaster M4/M4A3 Post-Ban Carbine
Similar to the XM15 E2S except has 14.5" barrel with Mini Y compensator, and fixed telestock. MR configuration has fixed carry handle; M4A3 has removeable carry handle.

Price: (M4) **$1,065.00**
Price: (M4A3) **$1,165.00**

BUSHMASTER VARMINTER RIFLE
Caliber: 223 Rem., 5-shot. **Barrel:** 24", 1:9" twist, fluted, heavy, stainless. **Weight:** 8-3/4 lbs. **Length:** 42-1/4". **Stock:** Rubberized pistol grip. **Sights:** 1/2" scope risers. **Features:** Gas-operated, semi-auto, two-stage trigger, slotted free floater forend, lockable hard case.
Price: **$1,245.00**

CENTURY INTERNATIONAL AES-10 HI-CAP RIFLE
Caliber: 7.62x39mm. 30-shot magazine. **Barrel:** 23.2". **Weight:** NA. **Length:** 41.5" overall. **Stock:** Wood grip, forend. **Sights:** Fixed-notch rear, windage-adjustable post front. **Features:** RPK-style, accepts standard double-stack AK-type mags. Side-mounted scope mount, integral carry handle, bipod. Imported by Century Arms Int'l.
Price: AES-10, from **$450.00**

CENTURY INTERNATIONAL GP WASR-10 HI-CAP RIFLE
Caliber: 7.62x39mm. 30-shot magazine. **Barrel:** 16.25", 1:10 rh twist. **Weight:** 7.2 lbs. **Length:** 34.25" overall. **Stock:** Wood laminate or composite, grip, forend. **Sights:** Fixed-notch rear, windage-adjustable post front. **Features:** Two 30-rd. detachable box magazines, cleaning kit, bayonet. Version of AKM rifle; U.S.-parts added for BATFE compliance. Threaded muzzle, folding stock, bayonet lug, compensator, Dragunov stock available. Made in Romania by Cugir Arsenal. Imported by Century Arms Int'l.
Price: GP WASR-10, from **$350.00**

Century Arms M70AB2 Sporter

Century Arms WASR-2 Hi-Cap

Colt Match Target Lightweight

CENTURY INTERNATIONAL WASR-2 HI-CAP RIFLE
Caliber: 5.45x39mm. 30-shot magazine. **Barrel:** 16.25". **Weight:** 7.5 lbs. **Length:** 34.25" overall. **Stocks:** Wood laminate. **Sights:** Fixed-notch rear, windage-adjustable post front. **Features:** 1 30-rd. detachable box magazine, cleaning kit, sling. WASR-3 HI-CAP chambered in 223 Rem. Imported by Century Arms Int'l.
Price: GP WASR-2/3, from **$250.00**

CENTURY INTERNATIONAL M70AB2 SPORTER RIFLE
Caliber: 7.62x39mm. 30-shot magazine. **Barrel:** 16.25". **Weight:** 7.5 lbs. **Length:** 34.25" overall. **Stocks:** Metal grip, wood forend. **Sights:** Fixed-notch rear, windage-adjustable post front. **Features:** 2 30-rd. double-stack magazine, cleaning kit, compensator, bayonet lug and bayonet. Paratrooper-style Kalashnikov with under-folding stock. Imported by Century Arms Int'l.
Price: M70AB2, from.................................. **$480.00**

COLT MATCH TARGET MODEL RIFLE
Caliber: 223 Rem., 5-shot magazine. **Barrel:** 16.1" or 20". **Weight:** 7.1 to 8-1/2 lbs. **Length:** 34-1/2" to 39" overall. **Stock:** Composition stock, grip, forend. **Sights:** Post front, rear adjustable for windage and elevation. **Features:** 5-round detachable box magazine, flash suppressor, sling swivels. Forward bolt assist included. Introduced 1991. Made in U.S.A. by Colt's Mfg. Co., Inc.
Price: Match Target HBAR, from......................... **$1,172.00**

DPMS PANTHER ARMS AR-15 RIFLES
Caliber: 223 Rem., 7.62x39. **Barrel:** 16" to 24". **Weight:** 7-3/4 to 11-3/4 lbs. **Length:** 34-1/2" to 42-1/4" overall. **Stock:** Black Zytel® composite. **Sights:** Square front post, adjustable A2 rear. **Features:** Steel or stainless steel heavy or bull barrel; hardcoat anodized receiver; aluminum free-float tube handguard; many options. From DPMS Panther Arms.
Price: Panther Bull A-15 (20" stainless bull bbl.)............... **$915.00**
Price: Panther Bull Twenty-Four (24" stainless bull bbl.) **$945.00**
Price: Bulldog (20" stainless fluted bbl., flattop receiver) **$1,219.00**

Price: Panther Bull Sweet Sixteen (16" stainless bull bbl.) **$885.00**
Price: DCM Panther (20" stainless heavy bbl., n.m. sights) **$1,099.00**
Price: Panther 7.62x39 (20" steel heavy bbl.) **$849.00**

DSA Z4 GTC CARBINE WITH C.R.O.S.
Caliber: 5.56 NATO **Barrel:** 16" 1:9 twist M4 profile fluted chrome lined heavy barrel with threaded Vortec flash hider. **Weight:** 7.6 lbs. **Stock:** 6 position collapsible M4 stock, Predator P4X free float tactical rail. **Sights:** Chrome lined Picatinny gas block w/removable front sight. **Features:** The Corrosion Resistant Operating System incorporates the new P.O.F. Gas Trap System with removable gas plug eliminates problematic features of standard AR gas system, Forged 7075T6 DSA lower receiver. Introduced 2006. Made in U.S.A. by DSA, Inc.
Price: **$1,700.00**

DSA CQB MRP, STANDARD MRP
Caliber: 5.56 NATO **Barrel:** 16" or 18" 1:7 twist chrome-lined or stainless steel barrel with A2 flash hider **Stock:** 6 position collapsible M4 stock. **Features:** LMT_1/2" MRP upper receiver with 20-1/2" Standard quad rail or 16-1/2" CQB quad rail, LMT_enhanced bolt with dual extractor springs, free float barrel, quick change barrel system, forged 7075T6 DSA lower receiver. EOTech and vertical grip additional. Introduced 2006. Made in U.S.A. by DSA, Inc.
Price: CQB MRP w/16" chrome lined barrel **$2,420.00**
Price: CQB MRP w/16" stainless steel barrel **$2,540.00**
Price: Standard MRP w/16" chrome lined barrel **$2,620.00**
Price: Standard MRP w/16" or 18" stainless steel barrel....... **$2,720.00**

DSA STD CARBINE
Caliber: 5.56 NATO. **Barrel:** 16" 1:9 twist D4 w/A2 flash hider. **Weight:** 6.25 lbs. **Length:** 31". **Stock:** A2 buttstock, D4 handguard w/heatshield. **Sights:** Forged A2 front sight with lug. **Features:** Forged 7075T6 DSA lower receiver, forged A2 or flattop upper receiver. Introduced 2006. Made in U.S.A. by DSA, Inc.
Price: A2 or Flattop STD Carbine........................ **$1,025.00**
Price: With LMT SOPMOD stock **$1,267.00**

DSA SA58 Congo

DSA SA58 Para Congo

DSA SA58 Gray Wolf

DSA 1R CARBINE
Caliber: 5.56 NATO. **Barrel:** 16" 1:9 twist D4 w/A2 flash hider. **Weight:** 6.25 lbs. **Length:** Variable. **Stock:** 6 position collapsible M4 stock, D4 handguard w/heatshield. **Sights:** Forged A2 front sight with lug. **Features:** Forged 7075T6 DSA lower receiver, forged A2 or flattop upper receiver. Introduced 2006. Made in U.S.A. by DSA, Inc.
Price: A2 or Flattop 1R Carbine **$1,055.00**
Price: With VLTOR ModStock **$1,175.00**

DSA XM CARBINE
Caliber: 5.56 NATO. **Barrel:** 11-1/2" 1:9 twist D4 with 5-1/2" permanently attached flash hider. **Weight:** 6.25 lbs. **Length:** Variable. **Stock:** Collapsible, Handguard w/heatshield. **Sights:** Forged A2 front sight with lug. **Features:** Forged 7075T6 DSA lower receiver, forged A2 upper receiver. Introduced 2006. Made in U.S.A. by DSA, Inc.
Price: **$1,055.00**

DSA STANDARD
Caliber: 5.56 NATO. **Barrel:** 20" 1:9 twist heavy barrel w/A2 flash hider. **Weight:** 6.25 lbs. **Length:** 38-7/16". **Stock:** A2 buttstock, A2 handguard w/heatshield. **Sights:** Forged A2 front sight with lug. **Features:** Forged 7075T6 DSA lower receiver, forged A2 or flattop upper receiver. Introduced 2006. Made in U.S.A. by DSA, Inc.
Price: A2 or Flattop Standard **$1,025.00**

DSA DCM Rifle
Caliber: .223 Wylde Chamber. **Barrel:** 20" 1:8 twist chrome moly match grade Badger Barrel. **Weight:** 10 lbs. **Length:** 39.5". **Stock:** DCM freefloat handguard system, A2 buttstock. **Sights:** Forged A2 front sight with lug. **Features:** NM two stage trigger, NM rear sight, forged 7075T6 DSA lower receiver, forged A2 upper receiver. Introduced 2006. Made in U.S.A. by DSA, Inc.
Price: **$1,520.00**

DSA S1
Caliber: .223 Match Chamber. **Barrel:** 16", 20" or 24" 1:8 twist stainless steel bull barrel. **Weight:** 8.0, 9.5 and 10 lbs. **Length:** 34.25", 38.25" and 42.25". **Stock:** A2 buttstock with free float aluminum handguard. **Sights:**

Picatinny gas block sight base. **Features:** Forged 7075T6 DSA lower receiver, Match two stage trigger, forged flattop upper receiver, fluted barrel optional. Introduced 2006. Made in U.S.A. by DSA, Inc.
Price: **$1,155.00**

DSA SA58 CONGO, PARA CONGO
Caliber: 308 Win. **Barrel:** 18" w/short Belgian short flash hider. **Weight:** 8.6 lbs. (Congo); 9.85 lbs. (Para Congo). **Length:** 39.75" **Stock:** Synthetic w/military grade furniture (Congo); Synthetic with non-folding steel para stock (Para Congo). **Sights:** Elevation adjustable protected post front sight, windage adjustable rear peep (Congo); Belgian type Para Flip Rear (Para Congo). **Features:** Fully-adjustable gas system, high-grade steel upper receiver with carry handle. Made in U.S.A. by DSA, Inc.
Price: Congo. **$1,695.00**
Price: Para Congo **$1,995.00**

DSA SA58 GRAY WOLF
Caliber: 308 Win. **Barrel:** 21" match-grade bull w/target crown. **Weight:** 13 lbs. **Length:** 41.75". **Stock:** Synthetic. **Sights:** Elevation-adjustable post front sight, windage-adjustable match rear peep. **Features:** Fully-adjustable gas system, high-grade steel upper receiver, Picatinny scope mount, DuraCoat finish. Made in U.S.A. by DSA, Inc.
Price: **$2,120.00**

DSA SA58 PREDATOR
Caliber: 243 Win., 260 Rem., 308 Win. **Barrel:** 16" and 19" w/target crown. **Weight:** 9 to 9.3 lbs. **Length:** 36.25" to 39.25". **Stock:** Green synthetic. **Sights:** Elevation-adjustable post front; windage-adjustable match rear peep. **Features:** Fully-adjustable gas system, high-grade steel upper receiver, Picatinny scope mount, DuraCoat solid and camo finishes. Made in U.S.A. by DSA, Inc.
Price: 243 Win., 260 Rem. **$1,695.00**
Price: 308 Win. **$1,640.00**

DSA SA58 Predator

DSA SA58 T48

DSA SA58 G1

DSA SA58 Standard

DSA SA58 Carbine

DSA SA58 T48
Caliber: 308 Win. **Barrel:** 21" with Browning long flash hider. **Weight:** 9.3 lbs. **Length:** 44.5". **Stock:** European walnut. **Sights:** Elevation-adjustable post front, windage adjustable rear peep. **Features:** Gas-operated semi-auto with fully adjustable gas system, high grade steel upper receiver with carry handle. DuraCoat finishes. Made in U.S.A. by DSA, Inc.
Price: **$1,995.00**

DSA SA58 G1
Caliber: 308 Win. **Barrel:** 21" with quick-detach flash hider. **Weight:** 10.65 lbs. **Length:** 44". **Stock:** Steel bipod cut handguard with hardwood stock and synthetic pistol grip. **Sights:** Elevation-adjustable post front, windage adjustable rear peep. **Features:** Gas-operated semi-auto with fully adjustable gas system, high grade steel upper receiver with carry handle, original GI steel lower receiver with GI bipod. DuraCoat finishes. Made in U.S.A. by DSA, Inc.
Price: **$1,850.00**

DSA SA58 STANDARD
Caliber: 308 Win. **Barrel:** 21" bipod cut w/threaded flash hider. **Weight:** 8.75 lbs. **Length:** 43". **Stock:** Synthetic, X-Series or optional folding para stock. **Sights:** Elevation-adjustable post front, windage-adjustable rear peep. **Features:** Fully adjustable short gas system, high grade steel or 416 stainless upper receiver. Made in U.S.A. by DSA, Inc.
Price: High-grade steel **$1,595.00**
Price: Folding para stock **$1,845.00**

DSA SA58 CARBINE
Caliber: 308 Win. **Barrel:** 16.25" bipod cut w/threaded flash hider. **Weight:** 8.35 lbs. **Length:** 37.5". **Stock:** Synthetic, X-Series or optional folding para stock. **Sights:** Elevation-adjustable post front, windage-adjustable rear peep. **Features:** Fully adjustable short gas system, high grade steel or 416 stainless upper receiver. Made in U.S.A. by DSA, Inc.
Price: High-grade steel................................. **$1,595.00**
Price: Stainless steel **$1,850.00**

DSA SA58 TACTICAL CARBINE
Caliber: 308 Win. **Barrel:** 16.25" fluted with A2 flash hider. **Weight:** 8.25 lbs. **Length:** 36.5". **Stock:** Synthetic, X-Series or optional folding para stock. **Sights:** Elevation-adjustable post front, windage-adjustable match rear peep. **Features:** Shortened fully adjustable short gas system, high grade steel or 416 stainless upper receiver. Made in U.S.A. by DSA, Inc.
Price: High-grade steel................................. **$1,595.00**
Price: Stainless steel **$1,850.00**

DSA SA58 Medium Contour Tactical

DSA SA58 Medium Contour

DSA SA58 Bull

DSA SA58 OSW

EAA/Saiga 308

DSA SA58 MEDIUM CONTOUR
Caliber: 308 Win. **Barrel:** 21" w/threaded flash hider. **Weight:** 9.75 lbs. **Length:** 43". **Stock:** Synthetic military grade. **Sights:** Elevation-adjustable post front, windage-adjustable match rear peep. **Features:** Gas-operated semi-auto with fully adjustable gas system, high grade steel receiver. Made in U.S.A. by DSA, Inc.
Price: **$1,595.00**

DSA SA58 BULL BARREL RIFLE
Caliber: 308 Win. **Barrel:** 21". **Weight:** 11.1 lbs. **Length:** 41.5". **Stock:** Synthetic, free floating handguard. **Sights:** Elevation-adjustable windage-adjustable post front, match rear peep. **Features:** Gas-operated semi-auto with fully adjustable gas system, high grade steel or stainless upper receiver. Made in U.S.A. by DSA, Inc.
Price: **$1,745.00**
Price: Stainless steel **$1,995.00**

DSA SA58 MINI OSW
Caliber: 308 Win. **Barrel:** 11" or 13" w/A2 flash hider. **Weight:** 9 to 9.35 lbs. **Length:** 32.75" to 35". **Stock:** Fiberglass reinforced short synthetic handguard, para folding stock and synthetic pistol grip. **Sights:** Adjustable post front, para rear sight. **Features:** Semi-auto or select fire with fully adjustable short gas system, optional FAL rail handguard, SureFire Vertical Foregrip System, EOTech HOLOgraphic Sight and ITC cheekrest. Made in U.S.A. by DSA, Inc.
Price: **$1,845.00**

EAA/SAIGA SEMI-AUTO RIFLE
Caliber: 7.62x39, 308, 223. **Barrel:** 20.5", 22", 16.3". **Weight:** 7 to 8-1/2 lbs. **Length:** 43". **Stock:** Synthetic or wood. **Sights:** Adjustable, sight base. **Features:** Based on AK Combat rifle by Kalashnikov. Imported from Russia by EAA Corp.
Price: 7.62x39 (syn.). **$239.00**
Price: 308 (syn. or wood) **$429.00**
Price: 223 (syn.) **$389.00**

Excel Arms Accelerator

Heckler & Koch USC

Hi-Point Carbine

Les Baer Flattop

chrome finish. Sling swivels. Available with laser or red dot sights. Introduced 1996. Made in U.S.A. by MKS Supply, Inc.
Price: Black or chrome, 9mm **$199.00**
Price: 40 S&W **$225.00**
Price: Camo stock **$210.00**

IAI M-333 M1 GARAND
Caliber: 30-06, 8-shot clip. **Barrel:** 24". **Weight:** 9-1/2 lbs. **Length:** 43.6" overall. **Stock:** Hardwood. **Sights:** Blade front, aperture adjustable rear. **Features:** Parkerized finish; gas-operated semi-automatic; remanufactured to military specifications. From Intrac Arms International, Inc.
Price: **$971.75**

IAI M-888 M1 CARBINE SEMI-AUTOMATIC RIFLE
Caliber: 22, 30 carbine. **Barrel:** 18"-20". **Weight:** 5-1/2 lbs. **Length:** 35"-37" overall. **Stock:** Laminate, walnut or birch. **Sights:** Blade front, adjustable rear. **Features:** Gas-operated, air cooled, manufactured to military specifications. 10/15/30 rnd. mag. scope available. From Intrac Arms International, Inc.
Price: 30 cal. . . . . **$556.00 to $604.00**
Price: 22 cal. . . . . **$567.00 to $654.00**

IAI-65 Rifle
A civilian-legal version of the original HKM rifle manufactured in Hungary. Manufactured by Gordon Technologies using an original AMD-65 matching parts kit built on an AKM receiver. The original wire stock is present, but it is welded in the open position as per BATF regulations. Furnished with a 12.6" barrel with large weld-in-place muzzle brake to bring its length over the 16" federal minimum. This rifle accepts all 7.62x39mm magazines and drums. Introduced 2002. From Intrac Arms International, Inc.
Price: **$799.00**

LES BAER CUSTOM ULTIMATE AR 223 RIFLES
Caliber: 223. **Barrel:** 18", 20", 22", 24". **Weight:** 7-3/4 to 9-3/4 lb. **Length:** NA. **Stock:** Black synthetic. **Sights:** None furnished; Picatinny-style flattop rail for scope mounting. **Features:** Forged receiver; Ultra single-stage trigger (Jewell two-stage trigger optional); titanium firing pin; Versa-Pod bipod; chromed National Match carrier; stainless steel, hand-lapped and cryo-treated barrel; guaranteed to shoot 1/2 or 3/4 MOA, depending on model. Made in U.S.A. by Les Baer Custom Inc.
Price: Super Varmint Model **$1,989.00**
Price: Super Match Model (introduced 2006) **$2,144.00**
Price: M4 flattop model **$2,195.00**
Price: IPSC action model **$2,310.00**

EXCEL ARMS ACCELERATOR RIFLES
Caliber: 17HMR, 22WMR, 17M2, 22LR, 9-shot magazine. **Barrel:** 18" fluted stainless steel bull barrel. **Weight:** 8 lbs. **Length:** 32.5" overall. **Grips:** Textured black polymer. **Sights:** Fully adjustable target sights. **Features:** Made from 17-4 stainless steel, aluminum shroud w/Weaver rail, manual safety, firing-pin block, last-round bolt-hold-open feature. Four packages with various equipment available. American made, lifetime warranty. Comes with one 9-round stainless steel magazine and a California-approved cable lock. Introduced 2006. Made in U.S.A. by Excel Arms.
Price: MR-17 17HMR **$498.00**
Price: MR-22 22WMR **$498.00**
Price: SR-17 17 Mach 2 . . . . **$498.00**
Price: SR-22 22LR **$498.00**

HECKLER & KOCH USC CARBINE
Caliber: 45 ACP, 10-shot magazine. **Barrel:** 16". **Weight:** 8.6 lb. **Length:** 35.4" overall. **Stock:** Skeletonized polymer thumbhole. **Sights:** Blade front with integral hood, fully adjustable diopter. **Features:** Based on German UMP submachine gun. Blowback operation; almost entirely constructed of carbon fiber-reinforced polymer. Free-floating heavy target barrel. Introduced 2000. From H&K.
Price: **$1,249.00**

HI-POINT 9MM CARBINE
Caliber: 9mm Para., 40 S&W, 10-shot magazine. **Barrel:** 16-1/2" (17-1/2" for 40 S&W). **Weight:** 4-1/2 lbs. **Length:** 31-1/2" overall. **Stock:** Black polymer, camouflage. **Sights:** Protected post front, aperture rear. Integral scope mount. **Features:** Grip-mounted magazine release. Black or

Les Baer IPSC

Olympic Arms K9 Carbine

Olympic Arms K3B

Olympic Arms Plinker Plus AR15

LR 300 SR LIGHT SPORT RIFLE
Caliber: 223. **Barrel:** 16-1/4"; 1:9" twist. **Weight:** 7.2 lbs. **Length:** 36" overall (extended stock), 26-1/4" (stock folded). **Stock:** Folding, tubular steel, with thumbhole-type grip. **Sights:** Trijicon post front, Trijicon rear. **Features:** Uses AR-15 type upper and lower receivers; flattop receiver with weaver base. Accepts all AR-15/M-16 magazines. Introduced 1996. Made in U.S.A. from Z-M Weapons.
Price: **$2,550.00**

OLYMPIC ARMS K9, K10, K40, K45 PISTOL-CALIBER AR15 CARBINES
Caliber: 9mm, 10mm, 40 S&W, 45 ACP; 32/10-shot modified magazines. **Barrel:** 16" button rifled stainless steel, 1x16 twist rate. **Weight:** 6.73 lbs. **Length:** 31.625" overall. **Stock:** A2 grip, M4 6-point collapsible stock. **Features:** A2 upper with adjustable rear sight, elevation adjustable front post, bayonet lug, sling swivel, threaded muzzle, flash suppressor, carbine length handguards. Made in U.S.A. by Olympic Arms, Inc.
Price: K9, 9mm, modified 32-round Sten magazine............. **$834.00**
Price: K10, 10mm, modified 10-round Uzi magazine............ **$834.00**
Price: K40, 40 S&W, modified 10-round Uzi magazine........... **$834.00**
Price: K45, 45 ACP, modified 10-round Uzi magazine **$834.00**

OLYMPIC ARMS K3B SERIES AR15 CARBINES
Caliber: 5.56 NATO, 30-shot magazines. **Barrel:** 16" button rifled chromemoly steel, 1x9 twist rate. **Weight:** 5-7 lbs. **Length:** 31.75" overall. **Stock:** A2 grip, M4 6-point collapsible buttstock. **Features:** A2 upper with adjustable rear sight, elevation adjustable front post, bayonet lug, sling swivel, threaded muzzle, flash suppressor, carbine length handguards. Made in U.S.A. by Olympic Arms, Inc.
Price: K3B base model, A2 upper **$780.00**
Price: K3B-A3 flat-top upper, detachable carry handle **$875.00**
Price: K3B-M4 M4 contoured barrel & handguards............ **$839.00**
Price: K3B-M4-A3-TC A3 upper, M4 barrel, FIRSH rail
   handguard **$1,012.00**
Price: K3B-CAR 11.5" barrel with 5.5" permanent flash suppressor **$810.00**
Price: K3B-FAR 16" featherweight contoured barrel **$822.00**

OLYMPIC ARMS PLINKER PLUS AR15 MODELS
Caliber: 5.56 NATO, 30-shot magazine. Barrel 16" or 20" button-rifled chrome-moly steel, 1x9 twist. **Weight:** 7.5-8.5 lbs. **Length:** 35.5"-39.5" overall. **Stock:** A2 grip, A2 buttstock with trapdoor. **Sights:** A1 windage rear, elevation-adjustable front post. **Features:** A1 upper, fiberite handguards, bayonet lug, threaded muzzle and flash suppressor. Made in U.S.A. by Olympic Arms, Inc.
Price: Plinker Plus................................... **$595.00**
Price: Plinker Plus 20 .... **$749.00**

Olympic Arms Plinker Plus 20

Ruger Ranch Mini 14/5R

Sabre Defence
Ayoob Professional

PANTHER ARMS CLASSIC AUTO RIFLE
Caliber: 5.56x45mm. **Barrel:** Heavy 16" to 20" w/flash hider. **Weight:** 7 to 9 lbs. **Length:** 34-11/16" to 38-7/16". **Sights:** Adj. rear and front. **Stock:** Black Zytel w/trap door assembly. **Features:** Gas operated rotating bolt, mil spec or Teflon black finish.

Price: **$809.00**
Price: Stainless, match sights **$1,099.00**
Price: Southpaw **$875.00**
Price: 16" bbl. **$799.00**
Price: Panther Lite, 16" bbl. **$720.00**
Price: Panther carbine . . . . **$799.00 to $989.00**
Price: Panther bull bbl . . . . **$885.00 to $1,199.00**

REMINGTON MODEL 750 WOODSMASTER
Caliber: 243 Win., 270 Win., 308 Win., 30-06, 35 Whelen. 4-shot magazine. **Barrel:** 22" round tapered. **Weight:** 7.5 lbs. **Length:** 42.6" overall. **Stock:** Restyled American walnut forend and stock with machine-cut checkering. Satin finish. **Sights:** Gold bead front sight on ramp; step rear sight with windage adjustable. **Features:** Replaces wood-stocked Model 7400 line introduced 1981. Gas action, R3 recoil pad. Positive cross-bolt safety. Carbine chambered in 308, 30-06, 35 Whelen. Receiver tapped for scope mount. Introduced 2006. Made in U.S.A. by Remington Arms Co.
Price: 750 Woodsmaster **$831.00**
Price: 750 Woodsmaster Carbine (18.5" bbl.) **$831.00**
Price: 750 Synthetic stock (2007) **$732.00**

ROCK RIVER ARMS STANDARD A2 RIFLE
Caliber: 45 ACP. **Barrel:** NA. **Weight:** 8.2 lbs. **Length:** NA. **Stock:** Thermoplastic. **Sights:** Standard AR-15 style sights. **Features:** Two-stage, national match trigger; optional muzzle brake. Made in U.S.A. From Rock River Arms.
Price: **$925.00**

RUGER RANCH RIFLE AUTOLOADING RIFLE
Caliber: 223 Rem., 5-shot detachable box magazine. **Barrel:** 18-1/2". Rifling twist 1:9". **Weight:** 6.4 lbs. **Length:** 37-1/4" overall. **Stock:** American hardwood, steel reinforced. **Sights:** Protected blade front, fully adjustable Ghost Ring rear. **Features:** Fixed piston gas-operated, positive primary extraction. New buffer system, redesigned ejector system. Ruger S100RM scope rings included on Ranch Rifle.
Price: Mini-14/5, Ranch Rifle, blued, scope rings **$775.00**
Price: K-Mini-14/5, Ranch Rifle, stainless, scope rings **$835.00**
Price: K-Mini-14/5P, Ranch Rifle, stainless, synthetic stock **$835.00**
Price: K-Mini-14/5T, laminate stock, adjustable harmonic barrel weight
(2007) **$995.00**

Ruger Mini Thirty Rifle
Similar to the Mini-14 Ranch Rifle except modified to chamber the 7.62x39 Russian service round. Weight is about 6-7/8 lbs. Has 6-groove barrel with 1:10" twist, Ruger Integral Scope Mount bases and protected blade front, fully adjustable Ghost Ring rear. Detachable 5-shot staggered box magazine. Stainless w/synthetic stock. Introduced 1987.
Price: Stainless, scope rings **$809.00**

SABRE DEFENCE XR15A3 SPR
Caliber: 5.56 NATO, 6.5 Grendel, 30-shot magazines. **Barrel:** 20" 410 stainless steel, 1x8 twist rate; or 18" vanadium alloy, chrome lined barrel with Sabre Gill-Brake. **Weight:** 6.77 lbs. **Length:** 31.75" overall. **Stock:** SOCOM 3-position stock with Samson M-EX handguards. **Sights:** Flip-up front and rear sights. **Features:** Fluted barrel, Harris bipod, and two-stage match trigger, Ergo Grips; upper and matched lower CNC machined from 7075-T6 forgings. SOCOM adjustable stock, Samson tactical handguards, M4 contour barrels available in 14.5" and 16" are made of MIL-B-11595 vanadium alloy and chrome lined. Introduced 2002. From Sabre Defence Industries.
Price: 6.5 Grendel (2007) **$2,699.00**
Price: XR15A3 Competition Deluxe, 6.5 Grendel, 20" barrel **$2,499.00**
Price: XR15A3 Competition Standard, 5.56mm, 18" barrel **$1,899.00**
Price: Massad Ayoob Professional **$1,999.00**
Price: SPR Carbine **$2,499.00**
Price: M4 Carbine, 14.5" barrel **$1,429.00**
Price: M4 Flat-top Carbine, 16" barrel **$1,349.00**

Springfield M1A

Stoner SR-25

Winchester Super X

SIG 556 AUTOLOADING RIFLE
Caliber: 223 Rem., 30-shot detachable box magazine. **Barrel:** 16". Rifling twist 1:9". **Weight:** 6.8 lbs. **Length:** 36.5" overall. **Stock:** Polymer, folding style. **Sights:** Flip-up front combat sight, adjustable for windage and elevation. **Features:** Based on SG 550 series rifle. Two-position adjustable gas piston operating rod system, accepts standard AR magazines. Polymer forearm, three integrated Picatinny rails, forward mount for right- or left-side sling attachment. Aircraft-grade aluminum alloy trigger housing, hard-coat anodized finish; two-stage trigger, ambidextrous safety, 30-round polymer magazine, battery compartments, pistol-grip rubber-padded watertight adjustable butt stock with sling-attachment points. SIG 556 SWAT model has flat-top Picatinny railed receiver, tactical quad rail. Imported by SIGARMS, Inc.
Price: SIG 556 . . . . **$1,300.00**

SPRINGFIELD ARMORY M1A RIFLE
Caliber: 7.62mm NATO (308), 5- or 10-shot box magazine. **Barrel:** 25-1/16" with flash suppressor, 22" without suppressor. **Weight:** 9-3/4 lbs. **Length:** 44-1/4" overall. **Stock:** American walnut with walnut-colored heat-resistant fiberglass handguard. Matching walnut handguard available. Also available with fiberglass stock. **Sights:** Military, square blade front, full click-adjustable aperture rear. **Features:** Commercial equivalent of the U.S. M-14 service rifle with no provision for automatic firing. From Springfield Armory
Price: Standard M1A, black fiberglass stock. **$1,498.00**
Price: Standard M1A, black fiberglass stock, stainless **$1,727.00**
Price: Standard M1A, black stock, carbon barrel **$1,379.00**
Price: Standard M1A, Mossy Oak stock, carbon barrel **$1,507.00**
Price: Scout Squad M1A . . . . **$1,653.00 to $1,727.00**
Price: National Match . . . . **$2,049.00 to $2,098.00**
Price: Super Match (heavy premium barrel) about **$3,149.00**
Price: M1A SOCOM II rifle **$1,948.00**
Price: M25 White Feather Tactical rifle **$4,648.00**

SPRINGFIELD M1 GARAND RIFLE
Caliber: 308, 30-06. **Barrel:** 24". **Weight:** 9.5 lbs. **Length:** 43-3/5". **Stock:** Walnut. **Sights:** Military aperture with MOA adjustments for both windage

and elevation, rear; military square post, front. **Features:** Original U.S. government-issue parts on a new walnut stock.
Price: . . . . **$1,348.00 to $1,378.00**

STONER SR-15 M-5 RIFLE
Caliber: 223. **Barrel:** 20". **Weight:** 7.6 lbs. **Length:** 38" overall. **Stock:** Black synthetic. **Sights:** Post front, fully adjustable rear (300-meter sight). **Features:** Modular weapon system; two-stage trigger. Black finish. Introduced 1998. Made in U.S.A. by Knight's Mfg.
Price: **$1,650.00**
Price: M-4 Carbine (16" barrel, 6.8 lbs) **$1,555.00**

STONER SR-25 CARBINE
Caliber: 7.62 NATO, 10-shot steel magazine. **Barrel:** 16" free-floating **Weight:** 7-3/4 lbs. **Length:** 35.75" overall. **Stock:** Black synthetic. **Sights:** Integral Weaver-style rail. Scope rings, iron sights optional. **Features:** Shortened, non-slip handguard; removable carrying handle. Matte black finish. Introduced 1995. Made in U.S.A. by Knight's Mfg. Co.
Price: **$3,345.00**

SMITH & WESSON M&P15 RIFLES
Caliber: 5.56mm NATO/223, 30-shot steel magazine. **Barrel:** 16", 1:9 **Weight:** 6.74 lbs., w/o magazine. **Length:** 32-35" overall. **Stock:** Black synthetic. **Sights:** Adjustable post front sight, adjustable dual aperture rear sight. **Features:** 6-position telescopic stock, thermo-set M4 handguard. 14.75" sight radius. 7-lbs. (approx.) trigger pull. 7075 T6 aluminum upper, 4140 steel barrel. Chromed barrel bore, gas key, bolt carrier. Hard-coat black-anodized receiver and barrel finish. Introduced 2006. Made in U.S.A. by Smith & Wesson.
Price: M&P15 No. 811000 . . . . **$1,200.00**
Price: M&P15T No. 811001, free float modular rail forend **$1,700.00**
Price: M&P15A No. 811002, folding battle rear sight **$1,300.00**

WINCHESTER SUPER X RIFLE
Caliber: 270 WSM, 30-06, 300 Win. Mag., 300 WSM, 4-shot steel magazine. **Barrel:** 22", 1:10", blued. **Weight:** 7.25 lbs. **Length:** 41-3/8". **Stock:** Walnut, 14-1/8"x 7/8"x 1-1/4". **Sights:** None. **Features:** Gas operated, removable trigger assembly, detachable box magazine, drilled and tapped, alloy receiver, enlarged trigger guard, crossbolt safety.Introduced 2007. Made in U.S.A. by Winchester Repeating Arms.
Price: Super X Rifle, from **$811.00**

Both classic arms and recent designs in American-style repeaters for sport and field shooting.

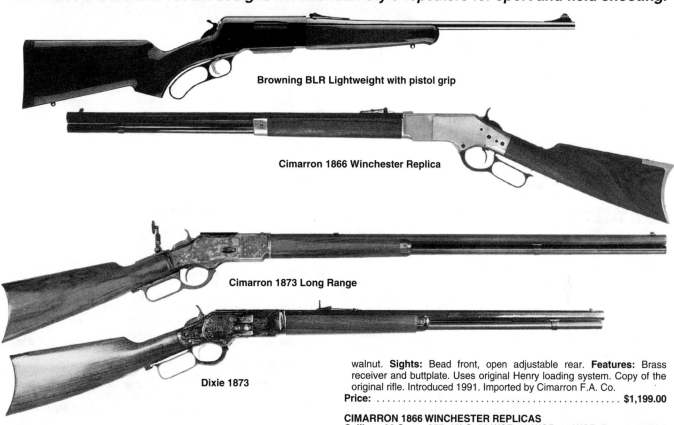

Browning BLR Lightweight with pistol grip

Cimarron 1866 Winchester Replica

Cimarron 1873 Long Range

Dixie 1873

BROWNING BLR RIFLES

Action: Lever action with rotating bolt head, multiple-lug breech bolt with recessed bolt face, side ejection. Rack-and-pinion lever. Flush-mounted detachable magazines, with 4+1 capacity for magnum cartridges, 5+1 for standard rounds. **Barrel:** Button-rifled chrome-moly steel with crowned muzzle. **Stock:** Buttstocks and forends are American walnut with grip and forend checkering. Recoil pad installed. **Trigger:** Wide-groove design, trigger travels with lever. Half-cock hammer safety; fold-down hammer. **Sights:** Gold bead on ramp front; low-profile square-notch adjustable rear. **Features:** Blued barrel and receiver, high-gloss wood finish. Receivers are drilled and tapped for scope mounts, swivel studs included. Action lock provided. Introduced 1996. Four model name variations for 2006, as noted below. Imported from Japan by Browning.

BROWNING BLR LIGHTWEIGHT W/PISTOL GRIP, SHORT AND LONG ACTION; LIGHTWEIGHT '81, SHORT AND LONG ACTION

Calibers, Short Action, 20" barrel: 22-250, 243, 7mm-08, 308, 358, 450 Marlin. **Calibers, Short Action, 22" barrel:** 270 WSM, 7mm WSM, 300 WSM, 325 WSM. **Calibers, Long Action 22" barrel:** 270, 30-06. **Calibers, Long Action 24" barrel:** 7mm Rem. Mag., 300 Win. Mag. **Weight:** 6.5-7.75 lbs. **Length:** 40-45" overall. **Stock:** New checkered pistol grip and Schnabel forearm. Lightweight '81 differs from Pistol Grip models with a Western-style straight grip stock and banded forearm. Lightweight w/Pistol Grip Short Action and Long Action introduced 2005. Model '81 Lightning Long Action introduced 1996.

Price: Lightweight w/Pistol Grip Short Action, from **$796.00**
Price: Lightweight w/Pistol Grip Long Action **$842.00**
Price: Lightweight '81 Short Action **$878.00**
Price: Lightweight '81 Long Action **$807.00**
Price: Lightweight Takedown, intr. 2007, from **$867.00**
Price: Lightweight '81 Takedown, intr. 2007, from **$832.00**

CIMARRON 1860 HENRY REPLICA

Caliber: 44 WCF, 45LC; 13-shot magazine. **Barrel:** 24-1/4" (rifle), 22" (carbine). **Weight:** 9-1/2 lbs. **Length:** 43" overall (rifle). **Stock:** European walnut. **Sights:** Bead front, open adjustable rear. **Features:** Brass receiver and buttplate. Uses original Henry loading system. Copy of the original rifle. Introduced 1991. Imported by Cimarron F.A. Co.
Price: **$1,199.00**

CIMARRON 1866 WINCHESTER REPLICAS

Caliber: 38 Spec., 357, 45LC, 32 WCF, 38 WCF, 44 WCF. **Barrel:** 24-1/4" (rifle), 19" (carbine). **Weight:** 9 lbs. **Length:** 43" overall (rifle). **Stock:** European walnut. **Sights:** Bead front, open adjustable rear. **Features:** Solid brass receiver, buttplate, forend cap. Octagonal barrel. Copy of the original Winchester '66 rifle. Introduced 1991. Imported by Cimarron F.A. Co.
Price: Rifle **$965.00**
Price: Carbine **$950.00**

CIMARRON 1873 SHORT RIFLE

Caliber: 357 Mag., 38 Spec., 32 WCF, 38 WCF, 44 Spec., 44 WCF, 45 Colt. **Barrel:** 20" tapered octagon. **Weight:** 7.5 lbs. **Length:** 39" overall. **Stock:** Walnut. **Sights:** Bead front, adjustable semi-buckhorn rear. **Features:** Has half "button" magazine. Original-type markings, including caliber, on barrel and elevator and "Kings" patent. From Cimarron F.A. Co.
Price: **$1,149.00**

Cimarron 1873 Sporting Rifle

Similar to the 1873 Short Rifle except has 24" barrel with half-magazine.
Price: **$1,149.00**

CIMARRON 1873 LONG RANGE RIFLE

Caliber: 44 WCF, 45 Colt. **Barrel:** 30", octagonal. **Weight:** 8-1/2 lbs. **Length:** 48" overall. **Stock:** Walnut. **Sights:** Blade front, semi-buckhorn ramp rear. Tang sight optional. **Features:** Color case-hardened frame; choice of modern blue-black or charcoal blue for other parts. Barrel marked "Kings Improvement." From Cimarron F.A. Co.
Price: **$1,199.00**

DIXIE ENGRAVED 1873 RIFLE

Caliber: 44-40, 11-shot magazine. **Barrel:** 20", round. **Weight:** 7-3/4 lbs. **Length:** 39" overall. **Stock:** Walnut. **Sights:** Blade front, adjustable rear. **Features:** Engraved and case-hardened frame. Replica of Winchester 1873. Made in Italy. From 21 Gun Works.
Price: CR204A **$1,425.00**
Price: Plain, blued carbine, CR201 . . . . **$1,015.00**

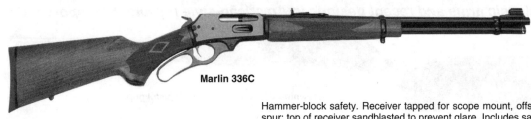

Marlin 336C

E.M.F. 1876 SPORTING RIFLE
Caliber: 40/60, 45/75. **Barrel:** 28". **Weight:** 10 lbs. **Length:** NA. **Stock:** Walnut. **Sight:** Bead front. **Features:** Case-hardened frame, blue barrel, first repeater in heavier loads. Imported by E.M.F.
Price: (2007) $1,265.00

E.M.F. 1860 HENRY RIFLE
Caliber: 44-40 or 45 Colt. **Barrel:** 24.25". **Weight:** About 9 lbs. **Length:** About 43.75" overall. **Stock:** Oil-stained American walnut. **Sights:** Blade front, rear adjustable for elevation. **Features:** Reproduction of the original Henry rifle with brass frame and buttplate, rest blued. Imported by E.M.F.
Price: Brass frame. $1,050.00
Price: Steel frame. $1,140.00

E.M.F. 1866 YELLOWBOY LEVER ACTIONS
Caliber: 38 Spec., 44-40, 45 LC. **Barrel:** 19" (carbine), 24" (rifle). **Weight:** 9 lbs. **Length:** 43" overall (rifle). **Stock:** European walnut. **Sights:** Bead front, open adjustable rear. **Features:** Solid brass frame, blued barrel, lever, hammer, buttplate. Imported from Italy by E.M.F.
Price: Rifle $920.00
Price: Carbine $870.00
Price: Border Rifle. $970.00

E.M.F. HARTFORD MODEL 1892 LEVER-ACTION RIFLE
Caliber: .357, .44Mag., 44/40, 45LC. **Barrel:** 20", 24" **Weight:** 7 lbs. **Length:** 42" overall. **Stock:** Smooth hardwood. **Sights:** Bead front, rear adjustable for windage and evaluation. **Features:** Color case-hardened frame, blue frame, brass frame or stainless steel frame. Crescent shaped butt plate. Imported by E.M.F.
Price: Blued carbine, round 20" barrel, saddle ring $430.00
Price: Brass or stainless frame, carbine $475.00
Price: Case-hardened rifle, octagonal 20" or 24" barrel $510.00
Price: Stainless-steel rifle, octagonal 20" or 24" barrel. $550.00

E.M.F. MODEL 1873 LEVER-ACTION RIFLE
Caliber: 32/20, 357 Mag., 38/40, 44-40, 45 Colt. **Barrel:** 18", 20", 24", 30". **Weight:** 8 lbs. **Length:** 43-1/4" overall. **Stock:** European walnut. **Sights:** Bead front, rear adjustable for windage and elevation. **Features:** Color case-hardened frame (blue on carbine). Imported by E.M.F.
Price: Rifle $1,050.00
Price: Carbine, 19" barrel $1,040.00
Price: Deluxe Cowboy $1,100.00

E.M.F. MODEL 1873 REVOLVER CARBINE
Caliber: 357 Mag., 45 Colt. **Barrel:** 18". **Weight:** 4 lbs., 8 oz. **Length:** 34" overall. **Stock:** One-piece walnut. **Sights:** Blade front, notch rear. **Features:** Color case-hardened frame, blue barrel, backstrap and trigger guard. Introduced 1998. Imported from Italy by EMF, Inc.
Price: Standard $580.00

E.M.F. LIGHTNING PUMP-ACTION RIFLES
Caliber: 44/40, 45LC. **Barrel:** 20", 24", 26". **Weight:** NA. **Length:** NA. **Stock:** Walnut. **Sight:** Bead front. **Features:** Blued or deluxe case-hardened frames. Imported from Pedersoli by E.M.F.
Price: Carbine $1,300.00
Price: Regular $1,425.00
Price: Deluxe case-hardened fram $1,600.00

MARLIN MODEL 336C LEVER-ACTION CARBINE
Caliber: 30-30 or 35 Rem., 6-shot tubular magazine. **Barrel:** 20" Micro-Groove®. **Weight:** 7 lbs. **Length:** 38-1/2". **Stock:** Checkered American black walnut, capped pistol grip. Mar-Shield® finish; rubber buttpad; swivel studs. **Sights:** Ramp front with Wide-Scan hood, semi-buckhorn folding rear adjustable for windage and elevation. **Features:** Hammer-block safety. Receiver tapped for scope mount, offset hammer spur; top of receiver sandblasted to prevent glare. Includes safety lock.
Price: $570.00

Marlin Model 336A Lever-Action Carbine
Same as the Marlin 336C except has cut-checkered, walnut-finished hardwood pistol grip stock with swivel studs, 30-30 only, 6-shot. Hammer-block safety. Adjustable rear sight, brass bead front. Includes safety lock.
Price: $477.00
Price: With 4x scope and mount $527.00

Marlin Model 336SS Lever-Action Carbine
Same as the 336C except receiver, barrel and other major parts are machined from stainless steel. 30-30 only, 6-shot; receiver tapped for scope. Includes safety lock.
Price: $692.00

Marlin Model 336W Lever-Action Rifle
Similar to the Model 336C except has walnut-finished, cut-checkered Maine birch stock; blued steel barrel band has integral sling swivel; no front sight hood; comes with padded nylon sling; hard rubber buttplate. Introduced 1998. Includes safety lock. Made in U.S.A. by Marlin.
Price: $482.00
Price: With 4x scope and mount $535.00

Marlin Model 336XLR Lever-Action Rifle
Similar to Model 336C except has an 24" stainless barrel with Ballard-type cut rifling, stainless steel receiver and other parts, laminated hardwood stock with pistol grip, nickel-plated swivel studs. Chambered for 30-30 Win. with Hornady Evolution spire-pointed Flex-Tip cartridges. Includes safety lock. Introduced 2006.
Price: (Model 336XLR) $874.00

MARLIN MODEL 444 LEVER-ACTION SPORTER
Caliber: 444 Marlin, 5-shot tubular magazine. **Barrel:** 22" deep cut Ballard rifling. **Weight:** 7-1/2 lbs. **Length:** 40-1/2" overall. **Stock:** Checkered American black walnut, capped pistol grip, rubber rifle buttpad. Mar-Shield® finish; swivel studs. **Sights:** Hooded ramp front, folding semi-buckhorn rear adjustable for windage and elevation. **Features:** Hammer-block safety. Receiver tapped for scope mount; offset hammer spur. Includes safety lock.
Price: $665.00

Marlin Model 444XLR Lever-Action Rifle
Similar to Model 444 except has an 24" stainless barrel with Ballard-type cut rifling, stainless steel receiver and other parts, laminated hardwood stock with pistol grip, nickel-plated swivel studs. Chambered for 444 Marlin with Hornady Evolution spire-pointed Flex-Tip cartridges. Includes safety lock. Introduced 2006.
Price: (Model 444XLR) $874.00

MARLIN MODEL 1894 LEVER-ACTION CARBINE
Caliber: 44 Spec./44 Mag., 10-shot tubular magazine. **Barrel:** 20" Ballard-type rifling. **Weight:** 6 lbs. **Length:** 37-1/2" overall. **Stock:** Checkered American black walnut, straight grip and forend. Mar-Shield® finish. Rubber rifle buttpad; swivel studs. **Sights:** Wide-Scan hooded ramp front, semi-buckhorn folding rear adjustable for windage and elevation. **Features:** Hammer-block safety. Receiver tapped for scope mount, offset hammer spur, solid top receiver sand blasted to prevent glare. Includes safety lock.
Price: $614.00

Marlin Model 1894C Carbine
Similar to the standard Model 1894 except chambered for 38 Spec./357 Mag. with full-length 9-shot magazine, 18-1/2" barrel, hammer-block safety, hooded front sight. Introduced 1983. Includes safety lock.
Price: $614.00

Marlin 1894 Cowboy

Marlin 1895

Marlin 1895M

Navy Arms Iron Frame Henry

MARLIN MODEL 1894 COWBOY
Caliber: 357 Mag., 44 Mag., 45 Colt, 10-shot magazine. **Barrel:** 20" tapered octagon, deep cut rifling. **Weight:** 7-1/2 lbs. **Length:** 41-1/2" overall. **Stock:** Straight grip American black walnut, hard rubber buttplate, Mar-Shield® finish. **Sights:** Marble carbine front, adjustable Marble semi-buckhorn rear. **Features:** Squared finger lever; straight grip stock; blued steel forend tip. Designed for Cowboy Shooting events. Introduced 1996. Includes safety lock. Made in U.S.A. by Marlin.
Price: **$889.00**

Marlin Model 1894SS
Similar to Model 1894 except has stainless steel barrel, receiver, lever, guard plate, magazine tube and loading plate. Nickel-plated swivel studs.
Price: **$752.00**

MARLIN MODEL 1895 LEVER-ACTION RIFLE
Caliber: 45-70, 4-shot tubular magazine. **Barrel:** 22" round. **Weight:** 7-1/2 lbs. **Length:** 40-1/2" overall. **Stock:** Checkered American black walnut, full pistol grip. Mar-Shield® finish; rubber buttpad; quick detachable swivel studs. **Sights:** Bead front with Wide-Scan hood, semi-buckhorn folding rear adjustable for windage and elevation. **Features:** Hammer-block safety. Solid receiver tapped for scope mounts or receiver sights; offset hammer spur. Includes safety lock.
Price: **$665.00**

Marlin Model 1895G Guide Gun Lever-Action Rifle
Similar to Model 1895 with deep-cut Ballard-type rifling; straight-grip walnut stock. Overall length is 37", weighs 7 lbs. Introduced 1998. Includes safety lock. Made in U.S.A. by Marlin.
Price: **$681.00**

Marlin Model 1895GS Guide Gun
Similar to Model 1895G except receiver, barrel and most metal parts are machined from stainless steel. Chambered for 45-70, 4-shot, 18-1/2" barrel. Overall length is 37", weighs 7 lbs. Introduced 2001. Includes safety lock. Made in U.S.A. by Marlin.
Price: **$805.00**

Marlin Model 1895 Cowboy Lever-Action Rifle
Similar to Model 1895 except has 26" tapered octagon barrel with Ballard-type rifling, Marble carbine front sight and Marble adjustable semi-buckhorn rear sight. Receiver tapped for scope or receiver sight. Overall length is 44-1/2", weighs about 8 lbs. Introduced 2001. Includes safety lock. Made in U.S.A. by Marlin.
Price: **$849.00**

Marlin Model 1895XLR Lever-Action Rifle
Similar to Model 1895 except has an 24" stainless barrel with Ballard-type cut rifling, stainless steel receiver and other parts, laminated hardwood stock with pistol grip, nickel-plated swivel studs. Chambered for 45-70 Government with Hornady Evolution spire-pointed Flex-Tip cartridges. Includes safety lock. Introduced 2006.
Price: (Model 1895MXLR) **$874.00**

Marlin Model 1895M Lever-Action Rifle
Similar to Model 1895G except has an 18-1/2" barrel with Ballard-type cut rifling. Chambered for 450 Marlin. Includes safety lock.
Price: (Model 1895M) **$733.00**

Marlin Model 1895MXLR Lever-Action Rifle
Similar to Model 1895M except has an 24" stainless barrel with Ballard-type cut rifling, stainless steel receiver and other parts, laminated hardwood stock with pistol grip, nickel-plated swivel studs. Chambered for 450 Marlin with Hornady Evolution spire-pointed Flex-Tip cartridges. Includes safety lock. Introduced 2006.
Price: (Model 1895MXLR) **$874.00**

NAVY ARMS MILITARY HENRY RIFLE
Caliber: 44-40 or 45 Colt, 12-shot magazine. **Barrel:** 24-1/4". **Weight:** 9 lbs., 4 oz. **Stock:** European walnut. **Sights:** Blade front, adjustable ladder-type rear. **Features:** Brass frame, buttplate, rest blued. Replica of the model used by cavalry units in the Civil War. Has full-length magazine tube, sling swivels; no forend. Imported from Italy by Navy Arms.
Price: **$1,199.00**

Navy Arms Iron Frame Henry
Similar to the Military Henry Rifle except receiver is blued or color case-hardened steel. Imported by Navy Arms.
Price: . . . . **$1,258.00 to $1,275.00**

Navy Arms 1866 Yellow Boy

Navy Arms 1892 Rifle

Puma Model 92

Remington 7600 Rifle

NAVY ARMS 1866 YELLOW BOY RIFLE
Caliber: 38 Spec., 44-40, 45 Colt, 12-shot magazine. **Barrel:** 20" or 24", full octagon. **Weight:** 8-1/2 lbs. **Length:** 42-1/2" overall. **Stock:** Walnut. **Sights:** Blade front, adjustable ladder-type rear. **Features:** Brass frame, forend tip, buttplate, blued barrel, lever, hammer. Introduced 1991. Imported from Italy by Navy Arms.
Price: **$942.00**
Price: Carbine, 19" barrel **$908.00**

NAVY ARMS 1866 SPORTING YELLOW BOY RIFLES
Caliber: 45 Colt. **Barrel:** 24-1/4" octagonal; 1:16" twist. **Weight:** 8.16 lbs. **Length:** 43-3/4" overall. **Stock:** Walnut. **Sights:** Blade front, adjustable folding rear. **Features:** Brass receiver; blued or white barrel; 13-shot magazine. Introduced 2001. Imported from Uberti by Navy Arms.
Price: (blued barrel)................................ **$942.00**

NAVY ARMS 1873 WINCHESTER-STYLE RIFLE
Caliber: 357 Mag., 44-40, 45 Colt, 12-shot magazine. **Barrel:** 24-1/4". **Weight:** 8-1/4 lbs. **Length:** 43" overall. **Stock:** European walnut. **Sights:** Blade front, buckhorn rear. **Features:** Color case-hardened frame, rest blued. Full-octagon barrel. Imported by Navy Arms.
Price: **$1,079.00**
Price: 1873 Carbine, 19" barrel **$1,054.00**
Price: 1873 Sporting Rifle (full oct. bbl., checkered walnut stock
 and forend) **$1,218.00**
Price: 1873 Border Model, 20" octagon barrel **$1,079.00**
Price: 1873 Deluxe Border Model **$1,218.00**

NAVY ARMS 1892 RIFLE
Caliber: 357 Mag., 44-40, 45 Colt. **Barrel:** 24-1/4" octagonal. **Weight:** 7 lbs. **Length:** 42" overall. **Stock:** American walnut. **Sights:** Blade front, semi-buckhorn rear. **Features:** Replica of Winchester's early Model 1892 with octagonal barrel, forend cap and crescent buttplate. Blued or color case-hardened receiver. Introduced 1998. Imported by Navy Arms.
Price: **$355.00**

Navy Arms 1892 Stainless Carbine
 Similar to the 1892 Rifle except stainless steel, has 20" round barrel, weighs 5-3/4 lbs., and is 37-1/2" overall. Introduced 1998. Imported by Navy Arms.
Price: **$345.00**

Navy Arms 1892 Short Rifle
 Similar to the 1892 Rifle except has 20" octagonal barrel, weighs 6-1/4 lbs., and is 37-3/4" overall. Replica of the rare, special order 1892 Winchester nicknamed the "Texas Special." Blued or color case-hardened receiver and furniture. Introduced 1998. Imported by Navy Arms.
Price: **$355.00**

PUMA MODEL 92 RIFLES & CARBINES
Caliber: 38 Spec./357 Mag., 44 Mag., 45 Colt, 454 Casull, 480 Ruger. **Barrel:** 16". 18", 20" round, 24" octagonal; porting and large lever loop available. **Weight:** 6.1 to 7.7 lbs. **Stock:** Walnut-stained hardwood. **Sights:** Open, buckhorn front & rear; HiViz also available. **Features:** Blue, case-hardened, stainless steel and brass receivers, matching buttplates. Blued, stainless steel barrels, full-length magazines. Thumb safety. 45 Colt and 454 Casull carbine introduced in 2002. The 480 Ruger version introduced in 2003. Imported from Brazil by Legacy Sports International.
Price: .... **$450.00 to $617.00**

REMINGTON MODEL 7600/7615 PUMP ACTION
Caliber: 243, 270, 30-06, 308. **Barrel:** 22" round tapered. **Weight:** 7.5 lbs. **Length:** 42.6" overall. **Stock:** Cut-checkered walnut pistol grip and forend, Monte Carlo with full cheekpiece. Satin or high-gloss finish. Also, black synthetic. **Sights:** Gold bead front sight on matted ramp, open step adjustable sporting rear. **Features:** Redesigned and improved version of the Model 760. Detachable 4-shot clip. Cross-bolt safety. Receiver tapped for scope mount. Introduced 1981. Model 7615 Tactical chambered in 223 Rem. **Features:** Knoxx SpecOps NRS (Non Recoil Suppressing) adjustable stock, parkerized finish, 10-round detachable magazine box, sling swivel studs. Introduced 2007.
Price: **$749.00**
Price: Carbine (18-1/2" bbl., 30-06 only) **$749.00**
Price: Model 7615 (2007) **$932.00**

CENTERFIRE RIFLES — Lever & Slide

Ruger Model 96/44

Tristar 1873 Sporting Rifle

Tristar 1866 Yellowboy Carbine

Tristar 1860 Henry

Uberti 1873 Sport

RUGER MODEL 96/44 LEVER-ACTION RIFLE
Caliber: 44 Mag., 4-shot rotary magazine. **Barrel:** 18-1/2". **Weight:** 6 lbs. **Length:** 37.75" overall. **Stock:** American hardwood. **Sights:** Gold bead front, folding leaf rear. **Features:** Solid chrome-moly steel receiver. Manual cross-bolt safety, visible cocking indicator; short-throw lever action; integral scope mount; blued finish; color case-hardened lever. Introduced 1996. Made In U.S. by Sturm, Ruger & Co.
Price: 96/44M, 44 Mag $599.00

TRISTAR/SHARPS 1874 SPORTING RIFLE
Caliber: 45-70. **Barrel:** 28", 32", 34" octagonal. **Weight:** 9.75 lbs. **Length:** 44.5" overall. **Stock:** Walnut. **Sights:** Dovetail front, adjustable rear. **Features:** Cut checkering, case colored frame finish.
Price: $839.00
Price: Bridgeport Sharps $899.00

TRISTAR/UBERTI 1866 SPORTING RIFLE, CARBINE
Caliber: 45 Colt. **Barrel:** 24-1/4", octagonal. **Weight:** 8.1 lbs. **Length:** 43-1/4" overall. **Stock:** Walnut. **Sights:** Blade front adjustable for windage, rear adjustable for elevation. **Features:** Frame, buttplate, forend cap of polished brass, balance charcoal blued. Imported by Tristar Sporting Arms Ltd.

Price: $1,109.00
Price: Yellowboy carbine (19" round bbl.) $999.00

TRISTAR/UBERTI 1860 HENRY RIFLE
Caliber: 45 Colt. **Barrel:** 24-1/4", half-octagon. **Weight:** 9.2 lbs. **Length:** 43-3/4" overall. **Stock:** American walnut. **Sights:** Blade front, rear adjustable for elevation. **Features:** Frame, elevator, magazine follower, buttplate are brass, balance blue. Imported by Tristar Sporting Arms Ltd. Arms, Inc.
Price: $1,359.00

TRISTAR/UBERTI 1873 SPORTING RIFLE
Caliber: 45 Colt. **Barrel:** 24-1/4", 30", octagonal. **Weight:** 8.1 lbs. **Length:** 43-1/4" overall. **Stock:** Walnut. **Sights:** Blade front adjustable for windage, open rear adjustable for elevation. **Features:** Color case-hardened frame, blued barrel, hammer, lever, buttplate, brass elevator. Imported from Italy by Tristar Sporting Arms Ltd.
Price: 24-1/4" barrel $1,259.00

UBERTI 1873 SPORTING RIFLE
Caliber: 357 Mag., 44-40, 45 Colt. **Barrel:** 19", to 24-1/4". **Weight:** Up to 8.2 lbs. **Length:** Up to 43.3" overall. **Stock:** Walnut, straight grip and pistol grip. **Sights:** Blade front adjustable for windage, open rear adjustable for elevation. **Features:** Color case-hardened frame, blued barrel, hammer, lever, buttplate, brass elevator. Imported by Benelli USA.
Price: 1873 Carbine, 19" round barrel $945.00
Price: 1873 Short Rifle, 20" octagonal barrel $985.00
Price: 1873 Special Sporting Rifle, 24.25" octagonal barrel $1,100.00

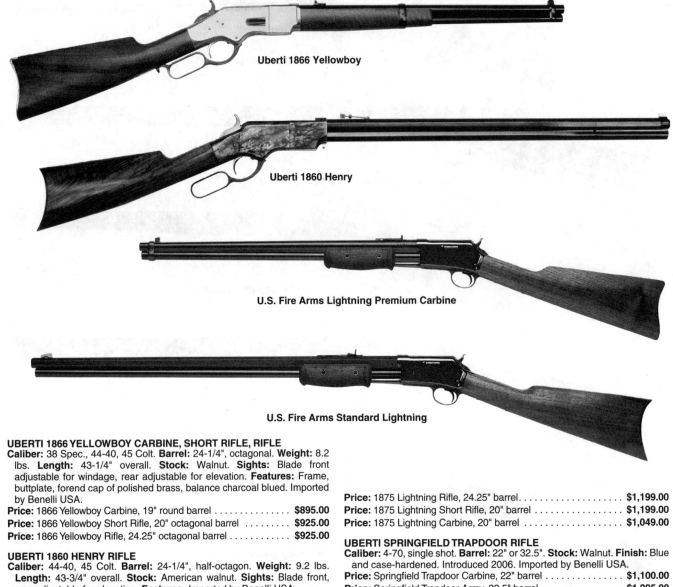

Uberti 1866 Yellowboy

Uberti 1860 Henry

U.S. Fire Arms Lightning Premium Carbine

U.S. Fire Arms Standard Lightning

UBERTI 1866 YELLOWBOY CARBINE, SHORT RIFLE, RIFLE
Caliber: 38 Spec., 44-40, 45 Colt. **Barrel:** 24-1/4", octagonal. **Weight:** 8.2 lbs. **Length:** 43-1/4" overall. **Stock:** Walnut. **Sights:** Blade front adjustable for windage, rear adjustable for elevation. **Features:** Frame, buttplate, forend cap of polished brass, balance charcoal blued. Imported by Benelli USA.
Price: 1866 Yellowboy Carbine, 19" round barrel **$895.00**
Price: 1866 Yellowboy Short Rifle, 20" octagonal barrel **$925.00**
Price: 1866 Yellowboy Rifle, 24.25" octagonal barrel **$925.00**

UBERTI 1860 HENRY RIFLE
Caliber: 44-40, 45 Colt. **Barrel:** 24-1/4", half-octagon. **Weight:** 9.2 lbs. **Length:** 43-3/4" overall. **Stock:** American walnut. **Sights:** Blade front, rear adjustable for elevation. **Features:** Imported by Benelli USA.
Price: 1860 Henry Trapper, 18.5" barrel, brass frame **$1,050.00**
Price: 1860 Henry Rifle, 24.25" barrel, brass frame **$1,050.00**
Price: 1860 Henry Rifle steel, 24.25" barrel, case-hardened
 frame **$1,150.00**
Price: 1860 Henry Rifle Iron Frame, 24.25" barrel **$1,050.00**

Uberti 1860 Henry Trapper Carbine
 Similar to the 1860 Henry Rifle except has 18-1/2" barrel, measures 37-3/4" overall, and weighs 8 lbs. Introduced 1999. Imported by Benelli USA.
Price: Brass frame, blued barrel **$1,050.00**

UBERTI LIGHTNING RIFLE
Caliber: 357 Mag., 45 Colt, 10+1. **Barrel:** 20" to 24.25". **Stock:** Walnut. **Finish:** Blue or case-hardened. Introduced 2006. Imported by Benelli USA.

Price: 1875 Lightning Rifle, 24.25" barrel **$1,199.00**
Price: 1875 Lightning Short Rifle, 20" barrel **$1,199.00**
Price: 1875 Lightning Carbine, 20" barrel **$1,049.00**

UBERTI SPRINGFIELD TRAPDOOR RIFLE
Caliber: 4-70, single shot. **Barrel:** 22" or 32.5". **Stock:** Walnut. **Finish:** Blue and case-hardened. Introduced 2006. Imported by Benelli USA.
Price: Springfield Trapdoor Carbine, 22" barrel **$1,100.00**
Price: Springfield Trapdoor Army, 32.5" barrel **$1,295.00**

U.S. FIRE ARMS STANDARD LIGHTNING MAGAZINE RIFLE
Caliber: 45 Colt, 44 WCF, 44 Spl., 38 WCF, 15-shot. **Barrel:** 26". **Stock:** Oiled walnut. **Finish:** High polish blue. Nickel finish also available. Introduced 2002. Made in U.S.A. by United States Fire-Arms Manufacturing Co.
Price: Round barrel. **$1,480.00**
Price: Octagonal barrel, checkered forend **$1,750.00**
Price: Half-round barrel, checkered forend **$1,999.00**
Price: Premium Carbine, 20" round barrel **$1,480.00**
Price: Baby Carbine, 20" special taper barrel **$1,999.00**
Price: Trapper, 16" special taper barrel **$2,155.00**
Price: Cowboy Action Lightning **$1,345.00**
Price: Cowboy Action Lightning Carbine, 20" round barrel **$1,345.00**

Includes models for a wide variety of sporting and competitive purposes and uses.

Anschutz 1733D

Barrett Model 95

Blaser R93 Classic

ANSCHUTZ 1743D BOLT-ACTION RIFLE
Caliber: 222 Rem., 3-shot magazine. **Barrel:** 19.7". **Weight:** 6.4 lbs. **Length:** 39" overall. **Stock:** European walnut. **Sights:** Hooded blade front, folding leaf rear. **Features:** Receiver grooved for scope mounting; single stage trigger; claw extractor; sling safety; sling swivels. Imported from Germany by AcuSport Corp.
Price: **$1,588.95**

ANSCHUTZ 1740 MONTE CARLO RIFLE
Caliber: 22 Hornet, 5-shot clip; 222 Rem., 3-shot clip. **Barrel:** 24". **Weight:** 6-1/2 lbs. **Length:** 43.25" overall. **Stock:** Select European walnut. **Sights:** Hooded ramp front, folding leaf rear; drilled and tapped for scope mounting. **Features:** Uses Match 54 action. Adjustable single stage trigger. Stock has roll-over Monte Carlo cheekpiece, slim forend with Schnabel tip, Wundhammer palm swell on grip, rosewood gripcap with white diamond insert. Skip-line checkering on grip and forend. Introduced 1997. Imported from Germany by AcuSport Corp.
Price: From **$1,439.00**
Price: Model 1730 Monte Carlo, as above except in
    22 Hornet **$1,439.00**

Anschutz 1733D Rifle
Similar to the 1740 Monte Carlo except has full-length, walnut, Mannlicher-style stock with skip-line checkering, rosewood Schnabel tip, and is chambered for 22 Hornet. Weighs 6.4 lbs., overall length 39", barrel length 19.7". Imported from Germany by AcuSport Corp.
Price: **$1,588.95**

BARRETT MODEL 95 BOLT-ACTION RIFLE
Caliber: 50 BMG, 5-shot magazine. **Barrel:** 29". **Weight:** 22 lbs. **Length:** 45" overall. **Stock:** Energy-absorbing recoil pad. **Sights:** Scope optional. **Features:** Bolt-action, bullpup design. Disassembles without tools; extendable bipod legs; match-grade barrel; muzzle brake. Introduced 1995. Made in U.S.A. by Barrett Firearms Mfg., Inc.
Price: From **$4,950.00**

BLASER R93 BOLT-ACTION RIFLE
Caliber: 22-250, 243, 6.5x55, 270, 7x57, 7mm-08, 308, 30-06, 257 Wby. Mag., 7mm Rem. Mag., 300 Win. Mag., 300 Wby. Mag., 338 Win Mag., 375 H&H, 416 Rem. Mag. **Barrel:** 22" (standard calibers), 26" (magnum). **Weight:** 7 lbs. **Length:** 40" overall (22" barrel). **Stock:** Two-piece European walnut. **Sights:** None furnished; drilled and tapped for scope mounting. **Features:** Straight pull-back bolt action with thumb-activated safety slide/cocking mechanism; interchangeable barrels and bolt heads. Introduced 1994. Imported from Germany by SIGARMS.
Price: R93 Classic **$3,680.00**
Price: R93 LX **$1,895.00**
Price: R93 Synthetic (black synthetic stock) **$1,595.00**
Price: R93 Safari Synthetic (416 Rem. Mag. only) **$1,855.00**
Price: R93 Grand Lux **$4,915.00**
Price: R93 Attaché **$5,390.00**

BROWNING A-BOLT RIFLES
Common Features: Short-throw (60°) fluted bolt, three locking lugs, plunger-type ejector; adjustable trigger is grooved. Chrome-plated trigger sear. Hinged floorplate, detachable box magazine. Slide tang safety. Receivers are drilled and tapped for scope mounts, swivel studs included. Barrel is free-floating and glass-bedded, recessed muzzle. Safety is top-tang sliding button. Engraving available for bolt sleeve or rifle body. Introduced 1985. 30 model name variations, as noted below. Imported from Japan by Browning.

BROWNING A-BOLT HUNTER
Calibers, 22" barrel: 223, 22-250, 243, 270 Win., 30-06, 7mm-08, 308. **Calibers, 23" barrel:** 270 WSM, 7mm WSM, 300 WSM, 325 WSM (intr. 2005). **Calibers, 24" barrel:** 25-06. **Calibers, 26" barrel:** 7mm Rem. Mag., 300 Win. Mag., 338 Win. Mag. **Weight:** 6.25-7.2 lbs. **Length:** 41.25-46.5" overall. **Stock:** Sporter-style walnut; checkered grip and forend. **Metal Finish:** Low-luster blueing.
Price: Hunter, from **$719.00**
Price: Hunter, Left-hand, from **$750.00**

Browning A-Bolt Hunter

Browning A-Bolt Medallion

Browning A-Bolt White Gold Medallion

Browning A-Bolt Stainless Stalker

BROWNING A-BOLT HUNTER FLD
Caliber, 23" barrel: 270 WSM, 7mm WSM, 300 WSM, 325 WSM (intr. 2005). **Weight:** 6.6 lbs. **Length:** 42.75" overall. **Features:** FLD has low-luster blueing and select Monte Carlo stock with right-hand palm swell, double-border checkering. Otherwise similar to A-Bolt Hunter.
Price: FLD **$808.00**

BROWNING A-BOLT HUNTER WSSM, FLD WSSM
Calibers, 22" barrel: 223 WSSM, 243 WSSM, 25 WSSM. **Weight:** 6.3 lbs. **Length:** 41.25" overall. **Features:** WSSM has classic walnut stock. FLD has low-luster blueing and select Monte Carlo stock with right-hand palm swell, double-border checkering. Otherwise similar to A-Bolt Hunter.
Price: WSSM **$755.00**
Price: FLD WSSM **$829.00**

BROWNING A-BOLT MOUNTAIN TI
Caliber: 223 WSSM, 243 WSSM, 25 WSSM (all added 2005); 270 WSM, 7mm WSM, 300 WSM. **Barrel:** 22" or 23". **Weight:** 5.25-5.5 lbs. **Length:** 41.25-42.75" overall. **Stock:** Lightweight fiberglass Bell & Carlson model in Mossy-Oak New Break Up camo. **Metal Finish:** Stainless barrel, titanium receiver. **Features:** Pachmayr Decelerator recoil pad. Introduced 1999.
Price: From **$1,673.00**

Browning A-Bolt Micro Hunter and Micro Hunter Left-Hand
Calibers, 20" barrel: 22-250, 243, 308, 7mm-08. **Calibers, 22" barrel:** 22 Hornet, 270 WSM, 7mm WSM, 300 WSM, 325 WSM (2005). **Weight:** 6.25-6.4 lbs. **Length:** 39.5-41.5" overall. **Features:** Classic walnut stock with 13.3" LOP. Otherwise similar to A-Bolt Hunter.
Price: Micro Hunter, from **$698.00**
Price: Micro Hunter Left-hand, from **$728.00**

BROWNING A-BOLT MEDALLION
Calibers, 22" barrel: 223, 22-250, 243, 308, 270 Win., 280, 30-06. **Calibers, 23" barrel:** 270 WSM, 7mm WSM, 300 WSM, 325 WSM (intr. 2005). **Calibers, 24" barrel:** 25-06. **Calibers, 26" barrel:** 7mm Rem. Mag., 300 Win. Mag., 338 Win. Mag., 375 H&H. **Weight:** 6.25-7.1 lbs. **Length:** 41.25-46.5" overall. **Stock:** Select walnut stock, glossy finish, rosewood grip and forend caps, checkered grip and forend. **Metal Finish:** Engraved high-polish blued receiver.
Price: Medallion, from. **$821.00**
Price: Medallion WSSM in 223/243/25 WSSM **$872.00**
Price: Medallion w/BOSS, intr. 1987, from **$901.00**
Price: Medallion w/Boss, left-hand, from **$854.00**

BROWNING A-BOLT WHITE GOLD MEDALLION, RMEF WHITE GOLD, WHITE GOLD MEDALLION W/BOSS
Calibers, 22" barrel: 270 Win., 30-06. **Calibers, 23" barrel:** 270 WSM, 7mm WSM, 300 WSM, 325 WSM (intr. 2005). **Calibers, 26" barrel:** 7mm Rem. Mag., 300 Win. Mag. **Weight:** 6.4-7.7 lbs. **Length:** 42.75-46.5" overall. **Stock:** select walnut stock with brass spacers between rubber recoil pad and between the rosewood gripcap and forend tip; gold-filled barrel inscription; palm-swell pistol grip, Monte Carlo comb, 22 lpi checkering with double borders. **Metal Finish:** Engraved high-polish stainless receiver and barrel. BOSS version chambered in 270 Win. and 30-06 (22" barrel) and 7mm Rem. Mag. and 300 Win. Mag. (26" barrel) Introduced 1988. RMEF version has engraved gripcap, continental cheekpiece; gold engraved, stainless receiver and bbl. Introduced 2004.
Price: White Gold Medallion, from **$1,178.00**
Price: Rocky Mt. Elk Foundation White Gold, 325 WSM, intr. 2007 . **$1,286.00**
Price: White Gold Medallion w/BOSS . . . . **$1,235.00 to $1,263.00**

BROWNING A-BOLT STAINLESS STALKER, STAINLESS STALKER LEFT-HAND
Calibers, 22" barrel: 223, 243, 270, 280, 7mm-08, 30-06, 308. **Calibers, 23" barrel:** 270 WSM, 7mm WSM, 300 WSM, 325 WSM (intr. 2005). **Calibers, 24" barrel:** 25-06. **Calibers, 26" barrel:** 7mm Rem. Mag., 300 Win. Mag., 338 Win. Mag., 375 H&H. **Weight:** 6.1-7.2 lbs. **Length:** 40.9-46.5" overall. **Features:** Similar to the A-Bolt Hunter model except receiver and barrel are made of stainless steel; other exposed metal surfaces are finished silver-gray matte. Graphite-fiberglass composite textured stock. No sights are furnished, except on 375 H&H, which comes with open sights. Introduced 1987.
Price: Stainless Stalker, from **$915.00**
Price: Stainless Stalker left-hand, from **$944.00**
Price: Stainless Stalker WSSM, 223/243/25 WSSM **$808.00**

Browning A-Bolt Varmint Stalker

Browning A-Bolt Composite Stalker

Browning A-Bolt Eclipse Hunter

Browning A-Bolt Eclipse M-1000

Browning A-Bolt Stainless Stalker, Stainless Stalker Left-Hand, w/BOSS

Calibers, 22" barrel: 223 WSSM, 243 WSSM, 25 WSSM, 270, 30-06. **Calibers, 23" barrel:** 270 WSM, 7mm WSM, 300 WSM, 325 WSM (intr. 2005). **Calibers, 24" barrel:** 375 H&H. **Calibers, 26" barrel:** 7mm Rem. Mag., 300 Win. Mag., 338 Win. Mag. **Features:** Similar to the A-Bolt Stainless Stalker, except includes BOSS.

Price: Stainless Stalker w/BOSS, from **$995.00**
Price: Stainless Stalker left-hand w/BOSS, from **$1,024.00**

BROWNING A-BOLT VARMINT STALKER, VARMINT STALKER WSSM

Calibers, 24" barrel: 223 Rem., 223 WSSM, 243 WSSM, 25 WSSM. **Calibers, 26" barrel:** 22-250. **Weight:** 7.8-8.2 lbs. **Length:** 42.75-45.75" overall. **Features:** Similar to the A-Bolt Stainless Stalker except has black graphite-fiberglass stock with textured finish and matte blue-finish on all exposed metal surfaces. Medium-heavy varmint barrel. No sights are furnished. Introduced 1987.

Price: Varmint Stalker **$877.00**
Price: Varmint Stalker WSSM **$928.00**

BROWNING A-BOLT COMPOSITE STALKER

Calibers, 22" barrel: 223, 22-250, 243, 270, 280, 7mm-08, 30-06, 308. **Calibers, 23" barrel:** 270 WSM, 7mm WSM, 300 WSM, 325 WSM (intr. 2005). **Calibers, 24" barrel:** 25-06. **Calibers, 26" barrel:** 7mm Rem. Mag., 300 Win. Mag., 338 Win. Mag. **Weight:** 6.1-7.2 lbs. **Length:** 40.75-46.5" overall. **Features:** Similar to the A-Bolt Stainless Stalker except has black composite stock with textured finish and matte-blued finish on all exposed metal surfaces except bolt sleeve. No sights are furnished.

Price: Composite Stalker, from **$719.00**
Price: Composite Stalker, w/BOSS, from **$799.00**

BROWNING A-BOLT ECLIPSE HUNTER W/BOSS, M-1000 ECLIPSE W/BOSS, M-1000 ECLIPSE WSM, STAINLESS M-1000 ECLIPSE WSM

Calibers, 22" barrel: 270, 30-06. **Calibers, 26" barrel:** 7mm Rem. Mag., 300 Win. Mag., 270 WSM, 7mm WSM, 300 WSM. **Weight:** 7.5-9.9 lbs.

Length: 42.75-46.5" overall. **Features:** All models have gray/black laminated thumbhole stock. Introduced 1996. Two versions have BOSS barrel vibration modulator and muzzle brake. Hunter has sporter-weight barrel. M-1000 Eclipses have long actions and heavy target barrels, adjustable triggers, bench-style forends, 3-shot magazines. Introduced 1997.

Price: Eclipse Hunter w/BOSS, from **$1,157.00**
Price: M-1000 Eclipse, from **$1,078.00**
Price: M-1000 Eclipse w/BOSS, from **$1,188.00**
Price: Stainless M-1000 Eclipse WSM, from **$1,288.00**

CARBON ONE BOLT-ACTION RIFLE

Caliber: 22-250 to 375 H&H. **Barrel:** Up to 28". **Weight:** 5-1/2 to 7-1/4 lbs. **Length:** Varies. **Stock:** Synthetic or wood. **Sights:** None furnished. **Features:** Choice of Remington, Browning or Winchester action with free-floated Christensen graphite/epoxy/steel barrel, trigger pull tuned to 3 to 3-1/2 lbs. Made in U.S.A. by Christensen Arms.

Price: Carbon One Hunter Rifle, 6-1/2 to 7 lbs. **$1,499.00**
Price: Carbon One Custom, 5-1/2 to 6-1/2 lbs., Shilen trigger . . . **$2,750.00**
Price: Carbon Ranger, 50 BMG, 5-shot repeater **$4,750.00**
Price: Carbon Ranger, 50 BMG, single shot **$3,950.00**

CENTURY INTERNATIONAL M70 SPORTER DOUBLE-TRIGGER BOLT-ACTION RIFLE

Caliber: 22-250, 270, 300 Win. Mag., 308 Win., 24" barrel. **Weight:** 7.95 lbs. **Length:** 44.5" **Sights:** Flip-up U-notch rear sight, hooded blade front sight. **Features:** Mauser M98-type action; 5-rd fixed box magazine. 22-250 has hinged floorplate. Monte Carlo stock, oil finish. Adjustable trigger on double-trigger models. 300 Win. Mag. Has 3-rd. fixed box magazine. 308 holds 5 rds. 300 and 308 have buttpads. Manufactured by Zastava in Yugoslavia, imported by Century International.

Price: M70 Sporter Double-Trigger. **$500.00**
Price: M70 Sporter Double-Trigger 22-250 . . . . **$475.00**
Price: M70 Sporter Single-Trigger .300 Win. Mag. **$475.00**
Price: M70 Sporter Single/Double Trigger .308 Win. **$500.00**

Charles Daly Field Mauser

Cooper Model 21 Bolt

CZ 527 Lux

CHARLES DALY FIELD MAUSER RIFLE
Caliber: 22-250, 243, 25-06, 270, 308, 30-06 (in 22" barrels); 7mm Rem. Mag. and 300 Win. Mag. in 24" barrels. **Weight:** NA. **Sights:** None; drilled and tapped for scope mounts. **Features:** Mauser Model 98-type action; carbon or stainless steel barrels; slide safety; polymer stock; fully adjustable trigger.
Price: Field Grade Mauser **$459.00**
Price: Mauser SS **$549.00**
Price: Magnum calibers **$579.00**

CHEYTAC M-200
Caliber: 408 CheyTac, 7-round mag. **Barrel:** 30". **Length:** 55", stock extended. **Weight:** 27 lbs. (steel barrel); 24 lbs. (carbon fiber barrel). **Stock:** Retractable. **Sights:** None, scope rail provided. **Features:** CNC-machined receiver, attachable Picatinny rail M-1913, detachable barrel, integral bipod, 3.5-lb. trigger pull, muzzle brake. Made in U.S. by CheyTac, LLC.
Price: **$13,795.00**

COOPER MODEL 16 BOLT-ACTION RIFLE
Caliber: .223 WSSM, .243 WSSM, .25 WSSM, .22BR, 6mmBR, .22 PPC, 6mm PPC. **Barrel:** 26" stainless steel match barrel. **Weight:** 6.5-7.5 lbs. **Stock:** AA-AAA select claro walnut, 20 lpi checkering. **Sights:** None furnished. **Features:** Three front locking-lug bolt-action.
Price: Varminter. **$1.550.00**
Price: Montana Varminter **$1,520.00**
Price: Varmint Extreme **$1,995.00**

COOPER MODEL 21 BOLT-ACTION RIFLE
Caliber: .17 Rem., 19-.223, Tactical 20, .204 Ruger, .20 VarTarg, .222 Rem, .222 Rem Mag, .223 Rem, .223 Rem A.I., .22 PPC, 6mm PPC, 6x45, 6x47. **Barrel:** 22" or 24" in Classic configurations, 24"-26" in Varminter configurations. **Weight:** 6.5-8.0 lbs., depending on type. **Stock:** AA-AAA select claro walnut, 20 lpi checkering. **Sights:** None furnished. **Features:** Three front locking-lug bolt-action single shot. **Action:** 7.75" long, Sako extractor. Button ejector. Fully adjustable single-stage trigger. Options include wood upgrades, case-color metalwork, barrel fluting, custom LOP, and many others.
Price: Phoenix. **$1,298.00**
Price: Varminter **$1,298.00**
Price: Montana Varminter **$1,520.00**
Price: Varmint Extreme **$1,995.00**
Price: Classic (blued barrel) **$1,450.00**

Price: Custom Classic (blued barrel) **$2,100.00**
Price: Western Classic (blued barrel) **$2,800.00**

COOPER MODEL 22 BOLT-ACTION RIFLE
Caliber: 22-250 Rem., 22-250 Rem. AI, 25-06 Rem., 25-06 Rem. AI, 243 Win., 243 Win. AI, 220 Swift, 250/3000 AI, 257 Roberts, 257 Roberts AI, 7mm-08, 6mm Rem., 260 Rem., 6 x 284, 6.5 x 284, 22 BR, 6mm BR, 308 Win. **Barrel:** 24" or 26" stainless match in Classic configurations. 24" or 26" in Varminter configurations. **Weight:** 7.5 to 8.0 lbs. depending on type. **Stock:** AA-AAA select claro walnut, 20 lpi checkering. **Sights:** None furnished. **Features:** Three front locking-lug bolt-action single shot. **Action:** 8.25" long, Sako style extractor. Button ejector. Fully adjustable single-stage trigger. Options include wood upgrades, case-color metalwork, barrel fluting, custom LOP, and many others.
Price: Phoenix. **$1,398.00**
Price: Varminter **$1,398.00**
Price: Montana Varminter **$1,600.00**
Price: Varmint Extreme **$2,100.00**
Price: Classic (blued barrel) **$1,498.00**
Price: Custom Classic (blued barrel) **$2,195.00**
Price: Western Classic (blued barrel) **$2,895.00**

COOPER MODEL 38 BOLT-ACTION RIFLE
Caliber: 17 Squirrel, 17 He Bee, 17 Ackley Hornet, 17 Mach IV, 19 Calhoon, 20 VarTarg, 221 Fireball, 22 Hornet, 22 K-Hornet, 22 Squirrel, 218 Bee, 218 Mashburn Bee. **Barrel:** 22" or 24" in Classic configurations, 24" or 26" in Varminter configurations. **Weight:** 6.5-8.0 lbs. depending on type. **Stock:** AA-AAA select claro walnut, 20 lpi checkering. **Sights:** None furnished. **Features:** Three front locking-lug bolt-action single shot. **Action:** 7" long, Sako style extractor. Button ejector. Fully adjustable single-stage trigger. Options include wood upgrades, case-color metalwork, barrel fluting, custom LOP, and many others.
Price: **$1,298.00**
Price: Montana Varminter **$1,520.00**
Price: Varmint Extreme **$1,995.00**
Price: Classic (blued barrel) **$1,450.00**
Price: Custom Classic (blued barrel) **$2,100.00**
Price: Western Classic (blued barrel) **$2,800.00**

CZ 527 LUX BOLT-ACTION RIFLE
Caliber: 22 Hornet, 222 Rem., 223 Rem., detachable 5-shot magazine. **Barrel:** 23-1/2"; standard or heavy barrel. **Weight:** 6 lbs., 1 oz. **Length:** 42-1/2" overall. **Stock:** European walnut with Monte Carlo. **Sights:** Hooded front, open adjustable rear. **Features:** Improved mini-Mauser action with non-rotating claw extractor; single set trigger; grooved receiver. Imported from the Czech Republic by CZ-USA.
Price: **$566.00**
Price: Model FS, full-length stock, cheekpiece **$658.00**

CZ 527 FS

CZ 527 American

CZ 550 Lux

CZ 550 Medium Magnum

CZ 550 Magnum

CZ 527 American Classic Bolt-Action Rifle
Similar to the CZ 527 Lux except has classic-style stock with 18 lpi checkering; free-floating barrel; recessed target crown on barrel. No sights furnished. Introduced 1999. Imported from the Czech Republic by CZ-USA.
Price: 22 Hornet, 222 Rem., 223 Rem. . . . . **$586.00 to $609.00**

CZ 550 LUX BOLT-ACTION RIFLE
Caliber: 22-250, 243, 6.5x55, 7x57, 7x64, 308 Win., 9.3x62, 270 Win., 30-06. **Barrel:** 20.47". **Weight:** 7.5 lbs. **Length:** 44.68" overall. **Stock:** Turkish walnut in Bavarian style or FS (Mannlicher). **Sights:** Hooded front, adjustable rear. **Features:** Improved Mauser-style action with claw extractor, fixed ejector, square bridge dovetailed receiver; single set trigger. Imported from the Czech Republic by CZ-USA.
Price: Lux. . . . . **$566.00 to $609.00**
Price: FS (full stock) **$706.00**

CZ 550 American Classic Bolt-Action Rifle
Similar to CZ 550 Lux except has American classic-style stock with 18 lpi checkering; free-floating barrel; recessed target crown. Has 25.6" barrel; weighs 7.48 lbs. No sights furnished. Introduced 1999. Imported from the Czech Republic by CZ-USA.
Price: . . . . **$586.00 to $609.00**

CZ 550 Medium Magnum Bolt-Action Rifle
Similar to the CZ 550 Lux except chambered for the 300 Win. Mag. and 7mm Rem. Mag.; 5-shot magazine. Adjustable iron sights, hammer-forged barrel, single-set trigger, Turkish walnut stock. Weighs 7.5 lbs. Introduced 2001. Imported from the Czech Republic by CZ-USA.
Price: **$621.00**

CZ 550 Magnum Bolt-Action Rifle
Similar to CZ 550 Lux except has long action for 300 Win. Mag., 375 H&H, 416 Rigby, 458 Win. Mag. Overall length is 46.45"; barrel length 25"; weighs 9.24 lbs. Hooded front sight, express rear with one standing, two folding leaves. Imported from the Czech Republic by CZ-USA.
Price: 300 Win. Mag. **$717.00**
Price: 375 H&H **$756.00**
Price: 416 Rigby **$809.00**
Price: 458 Win. Mag. **$744.00**

Dakota 76 Traveler

Dakota 76 Classic

Dakota 76 Safari

Dakota Longbow

CZ 700 M1 SNIPER RIFLE

Caliber: 308 Winchester, 10-shot magazine. **Barrel:** 25.6". **Weight:** 11.9 lbs. **Length:** 45" overall. **Stock:** Laminated wood thumbhole with adjustable buttplate and cheekpiece. **Sights:** None furnished; permanently attached Weaver rail for scope mounting. **Features:** 60-degree bolt throw; oversized trigger guard and bolt handle for use with gloves; full-length equipment rail on forend; fully adjustable trigger. Introduced 2001. Imported from the Czech Republic by CZ-USA.
Price: **$2,097.00**

DAKOTA 76 TRAVELER TAKEDOWN RIFLE

Caliber: 257 Roberts, 25-06, 7x57, 270, 280, 30-06, 338-06, 35 Whelen (standard length); 7mm Rem. Mag., 300 Win. Mag., 338 Win. Mag., 416 Taylor, 458 Win. Mag. (short magnums); 7mm, 300, 330, 375 Dakota Magnums. **Barrel:** 23". **Weight:** 7-1/2 lbs. **Length:** 43-1/2" overall. **Stock:** Medium fancy-grade walnut in classic style. Checkered grip and forend; solid buttpad. **Sights:** None furnished; drilled and tapped for scope mounts. **Features:** Threadless disassembly. Uses modified Model 76 design with many features of the Model 70 Winchester. Left-hand model also available. Introduced 1989. African chambered for 338 Lapua Mag., 404 Jeffery, 416 Rigby, 416 Dakota, 450 Dakota, 4-round magazine, select wood, two stock cross-bolts. 24" barrel, weighs 9-10 lbs. Ramp front sight, standing leaf rear. Introduced 1989. Made in U.S.A. by Dakota Arms, Inc.
Price: Classic. **$6,095.00**
Price: Safari **$6,995.00**
Price: African **$7,995.00**

DAKOTA 76 CLASSIC BOLT-ACTION RIFLE

Caliber: 257 Roberts, 270, 280, 30-06, 7mm Rem. Mag., 338 Win. Mag., 300 Win. Mag., 375 H&H, 458 Win. Mag. **Barrel:** 23". **Weight:** 7-1/2 lbs. **Length:** 43-1/2" overall. **Stock:** Medium fancy grade walnut in classic style. Checkered pistol grip and forend; solid buttpad. **Sights:** None furnished; drilled and tapped for scope mounts. **Features:** Has many features of the original Winchester Model 70. One-piece rail trigger guard assembly; steel gripcap. Model 70-style trigger. Many options available. Left-hand rifle available at same price. Introduced 1988. From Dakota Arms, Inc.
Price: From **$4,595.00**

DAKOTA 76 SAFARI BOLT-ACTION RIFLE

Caliber: 270 Win., 7x57, 280, 30-06, 7mm Dakota, 7mm Rem. Mag., 300 Dakota, 300 Win. Mag., 330 Dakota, 338 Win. Mag., 375 Dakota, 458 Win. Mag., 300 H&H, 375 H&H, 416 Rem. **Barrel:** 23". **Weight:** 8-1/2 lbs. **Length:** 43-1/2" overall. **Stock:** XXX fancy walnut with ebony forend tip; point-pattern with wraparound forend checkering. **Sights:** Ramp front, standing leaf rear. **Features:** Has many features of the original Winchester Model 70. Barrel band front swivel, inletted rear. Cheekpiece with shadow line. Steel gripcap. Introduced 1988. From Dakota Arms, Inc.
Price: Wood stock **$5,595.00**

DAKOTA LONGBOW TACTICAL E.R. RIFLE

Caliber: 300 Dakota Magnum, 330 Dakota Magnum, 338 Lapua Magnum. **Barrel:** 28", .950" at muzzle **Weight:** 13.7 lbs. **Length:** 50" to 52" overall. **Stock:** Ambidextrous McMillan A-2 fiberglass, black or olive green color; adjustable cheekpiece and buttplate. **Sights:** None furnished. Comes with Picatinny one-piece optical rail. **Features:** Uses the Dakota 76 action with controlled-round feed; three-position firing pin block safety; claw extractor; Model 70-style trigger. Comes with bipod, case tool kit. Introduced 1997. Made in U.S.A. by Dakota Arms, Inc.
Price: **$4,250.00**

Dakota 97 Lightweight Hunter

Dakota Hunter

DSA DS-MP1

Ed Brown 702 Savanna

DAKOTA 97 LIGHTWEIGHT HUNTER

Caliber: 22-250 to 330. **Barrel:** 22" to 24". **Weight:** 6.1 to 6.5 lbs. **Length:** 43" overall. **Stock:** Fiberglass. **Sights:** Optional. **Features:** Matte blue finish, black stock. Right-hand action only. Introduced 1998. Made in U.S.A. by Dakota Arms, Inc.
Price: **$1,995.00**

DAKOTA LONG-RANGE HUNTER RIFLE

Caliber: 25-06, 257 Roberts, 270 Win., 280 Rem., 7mm Rem. Mag., 7mm Dakota Mag., 30-06, 300 Win. Mag., 300 Dakota Mag., 338 Win. Mag., 330 Dakota Mag., 375 H&H Mag., 375 Dakota Mag. **Barrel:** 24", 26", match-quality; free-floating. **Weight:** 7.7 lbs. **Length:** 45" to 47" overall. **Stock:** H-S Precision black synthetic, with one-piece bedding block system. **Sights:** None furnished. Drilled and tapped for scope mounting. **Features:** Cylindrical machined receiver controlled round feed; Mauser-style extractor; three-position striker blocking safety; fully adjustable match trigger. Right-hand action only. Introduced 1997. Made in U.S.A. by Dakota Arms, Inc.
Price: From **$2,995.00**

DAKOTA PREDATOR RIFLE

Caliber: 17 VarTarg, 17 Rem., 17 Tactical , 20 VarTarg , 20 Tactical , .20 PPC, 204 Ruger, 221 Rem Fireball, 222 Remington, 22 PPC, 223 Rem., 6mm PPC, 6.5 Grendel. **Barrel:** 22" match grade stainless;. **Weight:** NA. **Length:** NA. **Stock:** Special select walnut, sporter-style stock, 23 lpi checkering on forend and grip. **Sights:** None furnished. Drilled and tapped for scope mounting. **Features:** 13-5/8" LOP, 1/2" black presentation pad,

11˚ recessed target crown. Serious Predator includes XXX walnut varmint style stock w/semi-beavertail forend, stainless receiver. All-Weather Predator includes varmint style composite stock w/semi-beavertail forend, stainless receiver. Introduced 2007. Made in U.S.A. by Dakota Arms, Inc.
Price: Classic **$4,295.00**
Price: Serious **$3,295.00**
Price: All-Weather **$2,595.00**

DSA DS-MP1

Caliber: 308 Win. match chamber. **Barrel:** 22", 1:10 twist, hand-lapped stainless-steel match-grade Badger Barrel with recessed target crown. **Weight:** 11.5 lbs. **Length:** 41.75". **Stock:** Black McMillan A5 pillar bedded in Marine-Tex with 13.5" length of pull. **Sights:** Tactical Picatinny rail. **Features:** Action, action threads and action bolt locking shoulder completely trued, Badger Ordnance precision ground heavy recoil lug, machined steel Picatinny rail sight mount, trued action threads, action bolt locking shoulder, bolt face and lugs, 2.5-lb. trigger pull, barrel and action finished in Black DuraCoat, guaranteed to shoot 1/2 MOA at 100 yards with match-grade ammo. Introduced 2006. Made in U.S.A. by DSA, Inc.
Price: **$2,800.00**

ED BROWN SAVANNA RIFLE

Caliber: 30-06, 300 Win. Mag., 300 Weatherby, 338 Win. Mag. **Barrel:** 22", 23", 24". **Weight:** 8 to 8-1/2 lbs. **Stock:** Fully glass-bedded McMillan fiberglass sporter. **Sights:** None furnished. Talley scope mounts utilizing heavy duty 8-40 screws. **Features:** Custom action with machined steel trigger guard and hinged floor plate.
Price: **$3,195.00**

Howa Lightning

Howa M-1500 Hunter

Howa M-1500 Ultralight

Howa M-1500 Varmint Supreme

ED BROWN MODEL 704 BUSHVELD

Caliber: 338 Win. Mag., 375 H&H, 416 Rem. Mag., 458 Win. Mag., 458 Lott and all Ed Brown Savanna long action calibers. **Barrel:** 24" medium or heavy weight. **Weight:** 8.25 lbs. **Stock:** Fully bedded McMillan fiberglass with Monte Carlo style cheekpiece, Pachmayr Decelerator recoil pad. **Sights:** None furnished. Talley scope mounts utilizing heavy duty 8-40 screws. **Features:** Stainless steel barrel, additional calibers, iron sights.
Price: From .... **$2,895.00 to $3,195.00**

ED BROWN Model 704 EXPRESS

Caliber: 375 H&H, 416 Rem, 458 Lott, other calibers available. **Barrel:** 24" #4 Stainless barrel with black Gen III coating for superior rust protection. **Weight:** 9 lbs. **Stocks:** Hand-bedded McMillan fiberglass stock. Monte Carlo style with cheek piece and full 1" thick Pachmayr Decel recoil pad. **Sights:** Adjustable iron sights. **Features:** Ed Brown controlled feed action. A special dropped box magazine ensures feeding and allows a full four-round capacity in the magazine, plus one in the chamber. Barrel band is standard for lower profile when carrying the rifle through heavy brush.
Price: From **$3,695.00**

HOWA LIGHTNING BOLT-ACTION RIFLE

Caliber: 223, 22-250, 243, 204 Ruger, 270, 308, 30-06, 7mm Rem. Mag., 300 Win. Mag., 338 Win. Mag, 300 WSM, 7mm WSM, 270 WSM. **Barrel:** 22", 24" magnum calibers. **Weight:** 7-1/2 lbs. **Length:** 42-44" overall (22" barrel). **Stock:** Black Bell & Carlson Carbelite composite with Monte Carlo comb; checkered grip and forend; also Realtree camo available. **Sights:** None furnished. Drilled and tapped for scope mounting. **Features:** Three-position thumb safety; hinged floorplate; polished blue/black finish. Introduced 1993. From Legacy Sports International.
Price: Blue, standard calibers $439.00
Price: Blue, magnum calibers $470.00
Price: Stainless, standard calibers $661.00
Price: Stainless, magnum calibers $690.00

Howa M-1500 Hunter Bolt-Action Rifle

Similar to Lightning Model except has walnut-finished hardwood stock, three-position safety. Polished blue finish or stainless steel. Introduced 1999. From Legacy Sports International.
Price: Blue, standard calibers **$574.00**
Price: Stainless, standard calibers **$682.00**
Price: Blue, magnum calibers **$595.00**
Price: Stainless, magnum calibers **$704.00**
Price: Blued, camo stock **$545.00**

Howa M-1500 Supreme Rifles

Similar to Howa M-1500 Lightning except stocked with JRS Classic or Thumbhole Sporter laminated wood stocks in Nutmeg (brown/black) or Pepper (gray/black) colors. **Barrel:** 22"; 24" magnum calibers. Weights are JRS stock 8 lbs., THS stock 8.3 lbs. Three-position safety. Introduced 2001. Imported from Japan by Legacy Sports International.
Price: Blue, standard calibers, JRS stock **$646.00**
Price: Blue, standard calibers, THS stock **$704.00**
Price: Blue, magnum calibers, JRS stock **$675.00**
Price: Blue, magnum calibers, THS stock **$733.00**
Price: Stainless, standard calibers, JRS stock **$755.00**
Price: Stainless, standard calibers, THS stock **$813.00**
Price: Stainless, magnum calibers, JRS stock **$784.00**
Price: Stainless, magnum calibers, THS stock **$842.00**

Howa M-1500 Ultralight

Similar to Howa M-1500 Lightning except receiver milled to reduce weight; three-position safety; tapered 22" barrel; 1-10" twist. Chambered for 243 Win. Stocks are black texture-finished hardwood. Weighs 6.4 lbs. Length 40" overall.
Price: Blued **$539.00**
Price: Stainless model **$658.00**

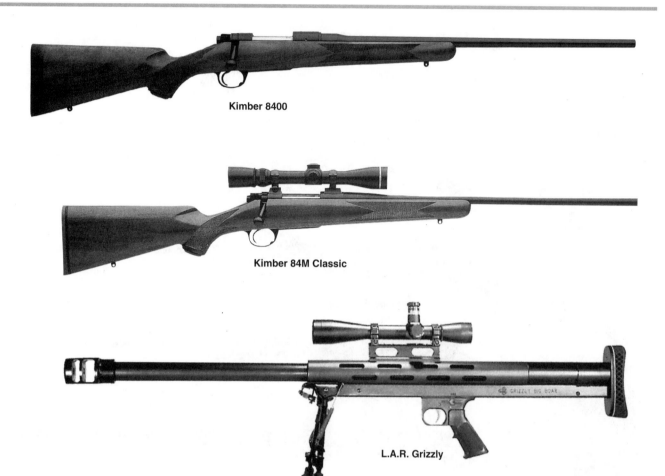

Kimber 8400

Kimber 84M Classic

L.A.R. Grizzly

Howa M-1500 Varmint and Varmint Supreme Rifles
Similar to M-1500 Lightning except has heavy 24" hammer-forged barrel. Chambered for 223, 22-250, 308. Weighs 9.3 lbs.; overall length 44.5". Introduced 1999. Imported from Japan by Interarms/Howa. Varminter Supreme has heavy barrel, target crown muzzle; three-position safety. Heavy 24" barrel, laminated wood with raised comb stocks, rollover cheekpiece, vented beavertail forearm; available in 223 Rem., 22-250 Rem., 204 Ruger, 308 Win. Weighs 9.9 lbs. Carbon fiber thumbhole stock option available. Introduced 2001. Imported from Japan by Legacy Sports International.
Price: Varminter, blue, polymer stock **$546.00**
Price: Varminter, stainless, polymer stock **$664.00**
Price: Varminter, blue, wood stock **$610.00**
Price: Varminter, stainless, wood stock **$719.00**
Price: Varminter Supreme, blued . . . . **$711.00 to $733.00**
Price: Varminter Supreme, stainless . . . . **$820.00 to $842.00**
Price: Varminter, blued, camo stock **$582.00**
Price: Varminter, stainless, camo stock **$704.00**

KENNY JARRETT BOLT-ACTION RIFLE
Caliber: 223 Rem., 243 Improved, 243 Catbird, 7mm-08 Improved, 280 Remington, .280 Ackley Improved, 7mm Rem. Mag., 284 Jarrett, 30-06 Springfield, 300 Win. Mag., .300 Jarrett, 323 Jarrett, 338 Jarrett, 375 H&H, 416 Rem., 450 Rigby., other modern cartridges. **Barrel:** NA. **Weight:** NA. **Length:** NA. **Stock:** NA. **Features:** Tri-Lock receiver. Talley rings and bases. Accuracy guarantees and custom loaded ammunition.
Price: Signature Series **$6,880.00**
Price: Wind Walker **$6,650.00**
Price: Original Beanfield (customer's receiver) **$4,850.00**
Price: Professional Hunter **$9,390.00**

KIMBER MODEL 8400 BOLT-ACTION RIFLE
Caliber: 270, 7mm, 300 or 325 WSM, 4 shot. **Barrel:** 24". **Weight:** 6 lbs. 3 oz. to 6 lbs 10 oz. **Length:** 43.25". **Stock:** Claro walnut or Kevlar-reinforced fiberglass. **Sights:** None; drilled and tapped for bases. **Features:** Mauser claw extractor, two-position wing safety, action bedded on aluminum pillars and fiberglass, free-floated barrel, match grade adjustable trigger set at 4 lbs., matte or polished blue or matte stainless finish. Introduced 2003. Made in U.S.A. by Kimber Mfg. Inc.
Price: Classic . . . . **$1,080.00 to $2,030.00**

KIMBER MODEL 84M BOLT-ACTION RIFLE
Caliber: 22-250, 204 Ruger, 223, 243, 260 Rem., 7mm-08, 308, 5-shot. **Barrel:** 22", 24", 26". **Weight:** 5 lbs., 10 oz. to 10 lbs. **Length:** 41" to 45". **Stock:** Claro walnut, checkered with steel gripcap; synthetic or gray laminate. **Sights:** None; drilled and tapped for bases. **Features:** Mauser claw extractor, three-position wing safety, action bedded on aluminum pillars, free-floated barrel, match-grade trigger set at 4 lbs., matte blue finish. Includes cable lock. Introduced 2001. Made in U.S.A. by Kimber Mfg. Inc.
Price: Classic (243, 260, 7mm-08, 308) . . . . **$945.00 to $1,828.00**
Price: Varmint (22-250) **$1,038.00**

L.A.R. GRIZZLY 50 BIG BOAR RIFLE
Caliber: 50 BMG, single shot. **Barrel:** 36". **Weight:** 30.4 lbs. **Length:** 45.5" overall. **Stock:** Integral. Ventilated rubber recoil pad. **Sights:** None furnished; scope mount. **Features:** Bolt-action bullpup design, thumb and bolt stop safety. All-steel construction. Introduced 1994. Made in U.S.A. by L.A.R. Mfg., Inc.
Price: **$2,350.00**

Magnum Research Tactical

Remington 700 Classic

Remington 700 BDL

Remington 700 SPS Buckmaster

Remington 700 SPS Varmint

MAGNUM RESEARCH MAGNUM LITE RIFLES

Caliber: 22-250, 223, 280, 7mm WSM, 30-06, 308, 300 WSM, 300 Win. Mag., 3-shot magazine. **Barrel:** 24" sport taper graphite; 26" bull barrel graphite. **Weight:** 7.1-9.2 lbs. **Length:** 44.5-48.25" overall (adjustable on Tactical model). **Stock:** Hogue OverMolded synthetic, H-S Precision Tactical synthetic, H-S Precision Varmint synthetic. **Sights:** None. **Features:** Remington Model 700 receiver. Introduced: 2001. From Magnum Research, Inc.

Price: MLR3006B26 H-S Tactical stock	**$2,295.00**
Price: MLR7MMBST24 Hogue stock	**$2,295.00**
Price: MLRT22250 H-S Tactical stock, 26" bull barrel	**$2,400.00**

REMINGTON MODEL 700 CDL CLASSIC DELUXE RIFLE

Caliber: 223, 243, 25-06, 270, 7mm-08, 7mm Rem. Ultra Mag., 30-06, 300 Rem. Mag., 35 Whelen. **Barrel:** 24" or 26" round tapered. **Weight:** 7.4 to 7.6 lbs. **Length:** 43.6" to 46.5" overall. **Stock:** Straight-comb American walnut stock, satin finish, checkering, right-handed cheek piece, black fore-end tip and grip cap, sling swivel studs. **Sights:** None. **Features:** Satin blued finish, jeweled bolt body, drilled and tapped for scope mounts. Hinged-floorplate magazine capacity: 4, standard calibers; 3, magnum calibers. R3 gel recoil pad, cylindrical receiver, integral extractor. Introduced 2004. CDL SF (stainless fluted) introduced 2007. SF chambered for 17 Rem Fireball, 270, 270 WSM, 7mm-08, 7mm Rem. Mag., 30-06, 300 WSM. Made in U.S. by Remington Arms Co., Inc.

Price: Standard calibers, 24" barrel	**$907.00**
Price: Magnum calibers, 26" barrel	**$933.00**
Price: SF (2007), from	**$1,039.00**

REMINGTON MODEL 700 BDL RIFLE

Caliber: 243, 270, 7mm Rem. Mag. 30-06, 300 Rem Ultra Mag. **Barrel:** 22, 24, 26" round tapered. **Weight:** 7.25-7.4 lbs. **Length:** 41.6-46.5" overall. **Stock:** Walnut. Gloss-finish pistol grip stock with skip-line checkering, black forend tip and gripcap with white line spacers. Quick-release floorplate. **Sights:** Gold bead ramp front; hooded ramp, removable step-adjustable rear with windage screw. **Features:** Side safety, receiver tapped for scope mounts, matte receiver top, quick detachable swivels.

Price: 243, 270, 30-06	**$877.00**
Price: 7mm Rem. Mag. 300 Rem Ultra Mag	**$904.00**

REMINGTON MODEL 700 SPS RIFLES

Caliber: 6.8 Rem SPC, 223 Rem., 243 Win., 270 Win. 270 WSM, 7mm-08 Rem., 7mm Rem. Mag., 30-06, 308 Win., 300 WSM, 300 Win. Mag., 300 Rem. Ultra Mag. **Barrel:** 20", 24" or 26" carbon steel. **Weight:** 7 to 7.6 lbs. **Length:** 39.6" to 46.5" overall. **Stock:** Black synthetic, sling swivel studs, R3 recoil pad. **Sights:** None. Introduced 2005. SPS Stainless replaces Model 700 BDL Stainless Synthetic. **Barrel:** Bead-blasted 416 stainless steel. **Features:** Plated internal fire control components; additional calibers: 204 Ruger, 22-250 Rem., 25-06 Rem. SPS DM features detachable box magazine. Buckmaster Edition versions feature Realtree Hardwoods HD camouflage and Buckmasters logo engraved on floorplate. SPS Varmint includes X-Mark Pro trigger, 26" heavy contour barrel, vented beavertail forend, dual front sling swivel studs. Made in U.S. by Remington Arms Co., Inc.

Price: SPS 17 Rem. Fireball (2007)	**$604.00**
Price: SPS Youth, 20" barrel (2007)	**$604.00**
Price: SPS Buckmasters (2007)	**$665.00**
Price: SPS Varmint (2007)	**$647.00**
Price: SPS Stainless, (2005)	**$604.00**
Price: SPS DM (2005)	**$633.00**

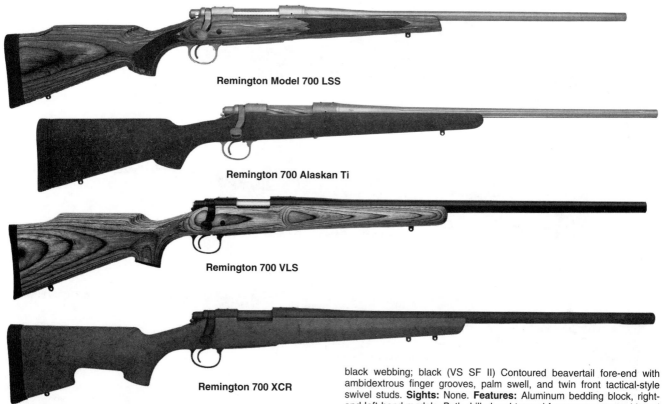

Remington Model 700 LSS

Remington 700 Alaskan Ti

Remington 700 VLS

Remington 700 XCR

REMINGTON MODEL 700 MOUNTAIN LSS RIFLES
Caliber: 270 Win., 280 Rem., 7mm-08 Rem., 30-06. **Barrel:** 22" satin stainless steel. **Weight:** 6.6 lbs. **Length:** 41.6" to 42.5" overall. **Stock:** Brown laminated, sling swivel studs, R3 recoil pad, black forend tip. **Sights:** None. **Barrel:** Bead-blasted 416 stainless steel, lightweight contour. Made in U.S. by Remington Arms Co., Inc.
Price: 280 Rem. (2007) **$1,015.00**

REMINGTON MODEL 700 ALASKAN TI
Caliber: 25-06, 270 Win., 270 WSM, 280 Rem., 7mm-08 Rem., 7mm Rem. Mag., 30-06, 300 WSM, 300 Win. Mag. **Barrel:** 24" round tapered. **Weight:** 6 lbs. **Length:** 43.6" to 44.5" overall. **Stock:** Bell & Carlson carbon-fiber synthetic, sling swivel studs, R3 gel recoil pad. **Sights:** None. **Features:** Formerly Model 700 Titanium, introduced 2001. Titanium receiver, spiral-cut fluted bolt, skeletonized bolt handle, X-Mark Pro trigger, satin stainless finish. Drilled and tapped for scope mounts. Hinged-floorplate magazine capacity: 4, standard calibers; 3, magnum calibers. Introduced 2007. Made in U.S. by Remington Arms Co., Inc.
Price: From **$2,105.00**

REMINGTON MODEL 700 VLS/VLSS RIFLES
Caliber: 204 Ruger, 223 Rem., 22-250, 6mm, 243, 308. **Barrel:** 26" heavy contour barrel (0.820" muzzle O.D.), concave target-style barrel crown **Weight:** 9.4 lbs. **Length:** 45.75" overall. **Stock:** Brown laminated stock, satin finish, with beavertail forend, gripcap, rubber buttpad. **Sights:** None. **Features:** Introduced 1995. VLSS (varmint laminate stock stainless) thumbhole model introduced 2007. Made in U.S. by Remington Arms Co., Inc.
Price: VLS **$928.00**
Price: VLSS TH **$1,028.00**

REMINGTON MODEL 700 VSF/VS SF II/SENDERO SF II RIFLES
Caliber: 17 Rem. Mag., 223 Rem., 22-250 Rem., 308 Win. **Barrel:** satin blued 26" heavy contour (0.820" muzzle O.D.), concave target-style barrel crown on VSF. VS SF has satin-finish stainless barreled action with 26" fluted barrel. **Weight:** 8.5 lbs. **Length:** 45.75" overall. **Stock:** H.S. Precision composite reinforced with aramid fibers, desert tan (VSF) with black webbing; black (VS SF II) Contoured beavertail fore-end with ambidextrous finger grooves, palm swell, and twin front tactical-style swivel studs. **Sights:** None. **Features:** Aluminum bedding block, right- and left-hand models. Both drilled and tapped for scope mounts, hinged floorplate magazines. VSF Introduced 1992. VS SF additionally chambered for 204 Ruger, 220 Swift. Introduced 1994. Sendero model is similar to VS SF II except chambered for 264 Win. Mag., 7mm Rem. Mag., 7mm Rem. Ultra Mag., 300 Win. Mag., 300 Rem. Ultra Mag. Polished stainless barrel. Introduced 1996. Made in U.S. by Remington Arms Co., Inc.
Price: VSF, 17 Rem. Fireball (2007) **$1,159.00**
Price: VS SF II **$1,252.00**
Price: Sendero SF II **$1,279.00**

REMINGTON MODEL 700 LV SF
Caliber: 17 Rem., 204 Ruger, 221 Rem. Fireball, 223 Rem., 22-250 Rem. **Barrel:** 22" satin stainless steel medium contour (0.657" muzzle O.D.), fluted. **Weight:** 6.75 lbs. **Length:** 41.6" overall. **Stock:** Black Bell & Carlson composite, semi-beavertail forend, swivel studs, R3 recoil pad. **Features:** Short action, pillar-bedded receiver, blind box magazine, jeweled bolt.
Price: **$1,040.00**

REMINGTON MODEL 700 XCR RIFLE
Caliber: 25-06 Rem., 270 Win., 270 WSM, 7mm-08 Rem., 7mm Rem. Mag., 7mm Rem Ultra Mag, 30-06, 300 WSM, 300 Win. Mag., 300 Rem. Ultra Mag., 338 Rem. Ultra Mag., 338 Win. Mag., 375 H&H Mag., 375 Rem. Ultra Mag. **Barrel:** 24" standard caliber; 26" magnum. **Weight:** 7.4 to 7.6 lbs. **Length:** 43.6" to 46.5" overall. **Stock:** Black synthetic, R3 recoil pad, rubber overmolded grip and forend. **Sights:** None. **Features:** XCR (Xtreme Conditions Rifle) includes TriNyte Corrosion Control System; drilled and tapped for scope mounts. 375 H&H Mag., 375 Rem. Ultra Mag. chamberings come with iron sights. Introduced 2005. XCR Tactical model introduced 2007. **Features:** Bell & Carlson OD green tactical stock, beavertail forend, recessed thumbhook behind pistol grip, TriNyte coating over stainless steel barrel, LTR fluting. Chambered in 223 Rem., 300 Win. Mag., 308 Win. Made in U.S. by Remington Arms Co., Inc.
Price: 25-06 Rem., 24" barrel (2007) **$1,029.00**
Price: 270 WSM, 24" barrel **$1,103.00**
Price: 7mm Rem. Mag., 26" barrel **$1,056.00**
Price: XCR Tactical (2007) **$1,332.00**

Remington 770

Remington Seven XCR Camo

Remington 798 SS Laminate

Ruger Magnum

REMINGTON MODEL 770 BOLT-ACTION RIFLE

Caliber: 243 Win., 270 Win., 7mm Rem. Mag., 30-06, 300 Win. Mag. **Barrel:** 22" or 24". **Weight:** 8.5 lbs. **Length:** 42.5" to 44.5" overall. **Stock:** Black synthetic. **Sights:** Bushnell Sharpshooter 3-9x scope mounted and bore-sighted. **Features:** Upgrade of Model 710 introduced 2001. Unique action locks bolt directly into barrel; 60-degree bolt throw; 4-shot dual-stack magazine; key-operated Integrated Security System locks bolt open. Introduced 2007. Made in U.S.A. by Remington Arms Co.

Price: $452.00
Price: Youth $452.00

REMINGTON MODEL SEVEN CDL/CDL MAGNUM

Caliber: 17 Rem. Mag., 204 Ruger, 22-250, 223 Rem., 243 Win., 260 Rem., 6.8 Rem. PC, 270 WSM, 7mm-08 Rem., 308 Win. 7mm Rem SA Ultra Mag., 300 WSM, 300 Rem. SA Ultra Mag., 350 Rem. Mag. **Barrel:** 20"; 22" magnum. **Weight:** 6.5 to 7.4 lbs. **Length:** 39.25" to 41.25" overall. **Stock:** American walnut, R3 recoil pad, satin finished. **Sights:** None. **Features:** Satin finished carbon steel barrel and action, 3- or 4-round magazine, hinged magazine floorplate. Furnished with iron sights and sling swivel studs, drilled and tapped for scope mounts. CDL versions introduced 2007. XCR Camo line chambered in 243 Win., 270 WSM, 7mm-08 Rem., 300 WSM, 308 Win.

Price: CDL $907.00
Price: CDL Magnum $973.00
Price: CDL XCR Camo from $1,080.00
Price: Youth, 6.8 Rem. PC (2007) $684.00

REMINGTON MODEL 798/799 BOLT-ACTION RIFLES

Caliber: 243 Win., 25-06 Rem., .270 Win., 7mm Rem. Mag., .308 Win., .30-06 Sprg., .300 Win. Mag., .375 H&H Mag., .458 Win. Mag. **Barrel:** 20" short actions, 22" standard actions; 24" long actions. **Weight:** 7.75 lbs. **Length:** 39.5" to 42.5" overall. **Stock:** Brown or green laminated, 1-inch rubber butt pad. **Sights:** None. Receiver drilled and tapped for standard Mauser 98 (long- and short-action) scope mounts. **Features:** Model 98 Mauser action (square-bridge Mauser 98). Claw extractor, sporter style 2-position safety, solid steel hinged floorplate magazine. Introduced 2006. Made in U.S.A. by Remington Arms Co.

Price: Model 798, 22" barrel, 42.5" OAL, 7 lbs., green laminate stock (2007) 243 Win., 25-06 Rem., 270 Win., .308 Win., .30-06 Sprg. $710.00
Price: Model 798, 24" barrel, 44.5" OAL, 7 lbs., 7mm Rem. Mag, .300 Win. Mag. $690.00
Price: Model 798, 26" barrel, 46.5" OAL, 7 lbs., .375 H&H Mag., .458 Win. Mag. $1,032.00
Price: Model 799, 20" barrel, 39.5" OAL, 6.75 lbs., .22 Hornet, .222 Rem., .22-250 Rem., .223 Rem., 7.62x39mm $648.00

RUGER MAGNUM RIFLE

Caliber: 375 H&H, 416 Rigby, 458 Lott. **Barrel:** 23". **Weight:** 9-1/2 to 10-1/4 lbs. **Length:** 44". **Stock:** AAA Premium Grade Circassian walnut with live-rubber recoil pad, metal gripcap, and studs for mounting sling swivels. **Sights:** Blade, front; V-notch rear express sights (one stationary, two folding) drift-adjustable for windage. **Features:** Floorplate latch secures the hinged floorplate against accidental dumping of cartridges; one-piece bolt has a non-rotating Mauser-type controlled-feed extractor; fixed-blade ejector.

Price: M77RSMMKII $2,200.00

Ruger 77/22 Hornet Varmint

Ruger M77 Mark II

Ruger M77 Hawkeye

Ruger M77 Hawkeye Alaskan

Ruger KM77RLFP MKII

RUGER 77/22 HORNET BOLT-ACTION RIFLE

Caliber: 22 Hornet, 6-shot rotary magazine. **Barrel:** 20". **Weight:** About 6 lbs. **Length:** 39-3/4" overall. **Stock:** Checkered American walnut, black rubber buttpad. **Sights:** None. **Features:** Same basic features as rimfire model except slightly lengthened receiver. Uses Ruger rotary magazine. Three-position safety. Comes with 1" Ruger scope rings. Introduced 1994.
Price: 77/22RH (rings only, no sights). **$690.00**
Price: K77/22VHZ Varmint, laminated stock, no sights **$765.00**

RUGER M77 MARK II RIFLE

Caliber: 223, 22-250, 204 Ruger, 243, 257 Roberts, 25-06, 270, 308, 30-06, 7mm Rem. Mag., 7mm/08, 300 Win. Mag., 338 Win. Mag., 3-shot magazine. **Barrel:** 20", 22"; 24" (magnums). **Weight:** About 7 lbs. **Length:** 39-3/4" overall. **Stock:** Synthetic American walnut; swivel studs, rubber buttpad. **Sights:** None furnished. Receiver has Ruger integral scope mount base, Ruger 1" rings. **Features:** All with new triggers, 3-position safety. Steel trigger guard. Left-hand available. Introduced 1989.
Price: M77LRMKII (left-hand, 25/06, 270, 30-06, 7mm Rem.
Mag.,300 Win. Mag.) **$749.00**

RUGER M77 HAWKEYE RIFLES

Caliber: 204 Ruger, 223, 22-250, 243, 257 Roberts, 25-06, 270, 280 Rem., 7mm/08, 7mm Rem. Mag., 308, 30-06, 300 Win. Mag., 338 Win. Mag., 338 Federal, 358 Win. Mag.,4-shot magazine, except 3-shot magazine for magnums; 5-shot magazine for 204 Ruger and 223 Rem. **Barrel:** 22", 24". **Weight:** 7-8.25 lbs. **Length:** 42-44.4" overall. **Stock:** American walnut. **Sights:** None furnished. Receiver has Ruger integral scope mount base, Ruger 1" rings. **Features:** Includes Ruger LC6™trigger, new red rubber recoil pad, Mauser-type controlled feeding, claw extractor, 3-position safety, hammer-forged steel barrels, Ruger scope rings. Walnut stock includes wrap-around cut checkering on the forearm and, more rounded contours on stock and top of pistol grips. Matte stainless version features synthetic stock. Hawkeye Alaskan and African chambered in 375 Ruger. Alaskan features matte-black finish, 20" barrel, Hogue OverMolded synthetic stock. African has 23" blued barrel, checkered walnut stock, left-handed model. 375s have windage adjustable shallow "V" notch rear sight, white bead front sights. Introduced 2007.
Price: HM77R walnut/blued **$749.00**
Price: HKM77RFP synthetic/stainless **$749.00**
Price: Alaska synthetic/Diamondblack **$1,095.00**
Price: African walnut/blued. **$1,095.00**

Ruger M77RSI International Carbine

Same as standard Model 77 except 18" barrel, full-length International-style stock, steel forend cap, loop-type steel sling swivels. Integral base receiver, open sights, Ruger 1" steel rings. Improved front sight. Available in 243, 270, 308, 30-06. Weighs 7 lbs. Length overall is 38-3/8".
Price: M77RSIMKII. **$876.00**

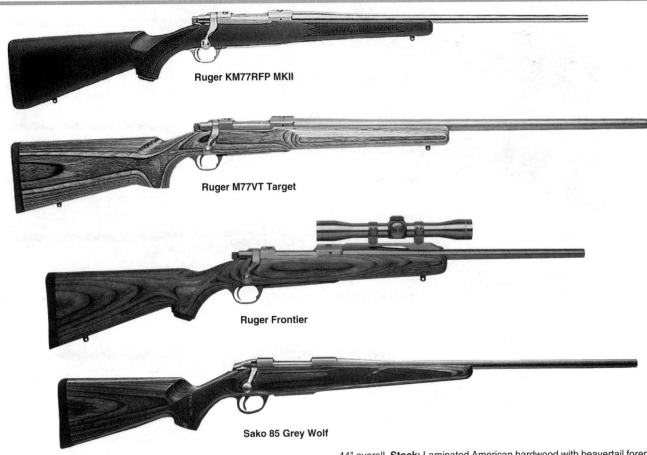

Ruger KM77RFP MKII

Ruger M77VT Target

Ruger Frontier

Sako 85 Grey Wolf

Ruger M77 Mark II All-Weather and Sporter Model Stainless Rifle

Similar to wood-stock M77 Mark II except all metal parts are stainless steel, has an injection-molded, glass-fiber-reinforced polymer stock. Laminated wood stock. Chambered for 223, 22/250, 25/06, 260 Rem., 7mm WSM, 7mm/08, 7mm SWM, 280 Rem., 300 WSM, 204 Ruger, 243, 270, 308, 30-06, 7mm Rem. Mag., 300 Win. Mag., 325 WSM, 338 Win. Mag. Fixed-blade-type ejector, three-position safety, new trigger guard with patented floorplate latch. Integral Scope Base Receiver, 1" Ruger scope rings, built-in sling swivel loops. Introduced 1990.

Price: K77RLFPMKII Ultra-Light, synthetic stock, rings, no sights . **$759.00**
Price: K77LRBBZMKII, left-hand bolt, rings, no sights,
laminated
stock **$805.00**
Price: K77RBZMKII, no sights, laminated wood stock, 223,
22/250, 243, 270, 280 Rem., 7mm Rem. Mag., 30-06,
308, 300 Win. Mag., 338 Win. Mag. **$805.00**
Price: KM77RFPMKII, synthetic stock, no sights **$695.00**

Ruger M77RL Ultra Light

Similar to standard M77 except weighs 6 lbs., chambered for 223, 243, 257 Roberts, 25-06, 270, 308, 30-06, barrel tapped for target scope blocks, 20" Ultra Light barrel. Overall length 40". Ruger's steel 1" scope rings supplied. Introduced 1983.
Price: M77RLMKII **$805.00**

Ruger M77 Mark II Compact Rifles

Similar to standard M77 except reduced 16-1/2" barrel, weighs 5-3/4 lbs. Chambered for 223, 243, 260 Rem., 308, and 7mm-08.
Price: M77CR MKII (blued finish, walnut stock) **$749.00**
Price: KM77CRBBZ MKII (stainless finish, black laminated stock) . **$805.00**

RUGER M77VT TARGET RIFLE

Caliber: 22-250, 223, 204 Ruger, 243, 25-06, 308. **Barrel:** 26" heavy stainless steel with target gray finish. **Weight:** 9-3/4 lbs. **Length:** Approx.

44" overall. **Stock:** Laminated American hardwood with beavertail forend, steel swivel studs; no checkering or gripcap. **Sights:** Integral scope mount bases in receiver. **Features:** Ruger diagonal bedding system. Ruger steel 1" scope rings supplied. Fully adjustable trigger. Steel floorplate and trigger guard. New version introduced 1992.
Price: K77VTMKII **$899.00**

RUGER FRONTIER RIFLE

Caliber: 243, 7mm/08, 308, 338 Fed., 358 Win. **Barrel:** 16-1/2". **Weight:** 6-1/4 lbs. **Stock:** Black laminate. **Features:** Front scope mounting rib, blued finish; overall length 35-1/2". Introduced 2005, stainless in 2006.
Price: Blued, walnut **$799.00**
Price: Stainless, laminate **$900.00**

SAKO TRG-42 BOLT-ACTION RIFLE

Caliber: 338 Lapua Mag. and 300 Win. Mag. **Barrel:** 27-1/8". **Weight:** 11-1/4 lbs. **Length:** NA. **Stock:** NA. **Sights:** NA. **Features:** 5-shot magazine, fully adjustable stock and competition trigger. Imported from Finland by Beretta USA.
Price: **$3,525.00**

SAKO MODEL 85 BOLT-ACTION RIFLES

Caliber: 22-250, 243, 25-06, 260, 6.5x55mm, 270, 270 WSM, 7mm-08, 308, 30-06; 7mm WSM, 300 WSM, 338 Federal. **Barrel:** 22.4", 22.9", 24.4". **Weight:** 7.75 lbs. **Length:** NA. **Stock:** Polymer, laminated or high-grade walnut, straight comb, shadow-line cheekpiece. **Sights:** None furnished. **Features:** Controlled-round feeding, adjustable trigger, matte stainless or nonreflective satin blue. Quad model is polymer/stainless with four interchangeable barrels in 22LR, 22 WMR 17 HMR and 17 Mach 2; 50-degree bolt-lift, ambidextrous palm-swell, adjustable butt-pad. Introduced 2006. Imported from Finland by Beretta USA.
Price: Sako 85 Hunter, walnut/blued **$1,595.00**
Price: Sako 85 Grey Wolf, laminated/stainless **$1,495.00**
Price: Sako 85 Quad, polymer/stainless **$925.00**
Price: Sako 85 Quad Combo, four barrels **$1,800.00**

Sako 75 Hunter

Sako 75 Stainless Hunter

Sako 75 Deluxe

Sako 75 Varmint

Savage 110GXP3

SAKO 75 HUNTER BOLT-ACTION RIFLE

Caliber: 223, 22-250, 243, 25-06, 260, 270, 270 WSM, 280, 300 Win. Mag., 30-06; 7mm-08, 308 Win., 270 Wby. Mag., 7mm Rem. Mag., 7mm STW, 7mm Wby. Mag., 300 Wby. Mag., 338 Win. Mag., 340 Wby. Mag., 375 H&H. **Barrel:** 22", standard calibers; 24", 26" magnum calibers. **Weight:** About 6 lbs. **Length:** NA. **Stock:** European walnut with matte lacquer finish. **Sights:** None furnished; dovetail scope mount rails. **Features:** New design with three locking lugs and a mechanical ejector, key locks firing pin and bolt, cold hammer-forged barrel is free-floating, two-position safety, hinged floorplate or detachable magazine that can be loaded from the top, short 70-degree bolt lift. Five action lengths. Introduced 1997. Imported from Finland by Beretta USA.
Price: From **$1,375.00**

Sako 75 Stainless Synthetic Rifle

Similar to 75 Hunter except all metal is stainless steel, synthetic stock has soft composite panels molded into forend and pistol grip. Available in 22-250, 243, 308 Win., 25-06, 270, 30-06 with 22" barrel, 7mm Rem. Mag., 7mm STW, 300 Win. Mag., 338 Win. Mag. and 375 H&H Mag. with 24" barrel and 300 Wby. Mag., 300 Rem. Ultra Mag. with 26" barrel. Introduced 1997. Imported from Finland by Beretta USA.
Price: from. **$1,495.00**

Sako 75 Deluxe Rifle

Similar to 75 Hunter except select wood rosewood gripcap and forend tip. Available in 17 Rem., 222, 223, 25-06, 243, 7mm-08, 308, 25-06, 270, 280, 30-06; 270 Wby. Mag., 7mm Rem. Mag., 7mm STW, 7mm Wby. Mag., 300 Win. Mag., 300 Wby. Mag., 338 Win. Mag., 340 Wby. Mag., 375 H&H Mag., 416 Rem. Mag. Introduced 1997. Imported from Finland by Beretta USA.
Price: from. **$2,050.00**

Sako 75 Varmint Stainless Laminated Rifle

Similar to Sako 75 Hunter except chambered only for 222, 223, 22-250, 22 PPC USA, 6mm PPC, heavy 24" barrel with recessed crown; set trigger; all metal is stainless steel, laminated wood stock with beavertail forend. Introduced 1999. Imported from Finland by Beretta USA.
Price: **$1,959.00**

Sako 75 Varmint Rifle

Similar to Model 75 Hunter except chambered only for 17 Rem., 222 Rem., 223 Rem., 22-250 Rem., 22 PPC and 6mm PPC, 24" heavy barrel with recessed crown; set trigger; beavertail forend. Introduced 1998. Imported from Finland by Beretta USA.
Price: **$1,850.00**

SAUER 202 BOLT-ACTION RIFLE

Caliber: Standard 243, 6.5x55, 270 Win., 308 Win., 30-06; magnum 7mm Rem. Mag., 300 Win. Mag., 300 Wby. Mag., 375 H&H. **Barrel:** 23.6" (standard), 26" (magnum). **Weight:** 7.7 lbs. (standard). **Length:** 44.3" overall (23.6" barrel). **Stock:** Select American Claro walnut with high-gloss epoxy finish, rosewood grip and forend caps; 22 lpi checkering. Synthetic also available. **Sights:** None furnished; drilled and tapped for scope mounting. **Features:** Short 60" bolt throw; detachable box magazine; six-lug bolt; quick-change barrel; tapered bore; adjustable two-stage trigger; firing pin cocking indicator. Introduced 1994. Imported from Germany by SIGARMS, Inc.
Price: Standard calibers, right-hand. **$1,035.00**
Price: Magnum calibers, right-hand **$1,106.00**
Price: Standard calibers, synthetic stock **$985.00**
Price: Magnum calibers, synthetic stock **$1,056.00**

SAVAGE MODEL 10GXP3, 110GXP3 PACKAGE GUNS

Caliber: 223 Rem., 22-250 Rem., 243 Win., 7mm-08 Rem., 308 Win., 300 WSM (10GXP3). 25-06 Rem., 270 Win., 30-06 Spfld., 7mm Rem. Mag., 300 Win. Mag., 300 Rem. Ultra Mag. (110GXP3). **Barrel:** 22" 24", 26". **Weight:** 7.5 lbs. average. **Length:** 43" to 47". **Stock:** Walnut Monte Carlo with checkering. **Sights:** 3-9x40mm scope, mounted & bore sighted. **Features:** Blued, free floating and button rifled, internal box magazines, swivel studs, leather sling. Left-hand available.
Price: Accu-trigger **$539.00**

Savage Model 10FP

Savage Model 10FPLE1

Savage Model 10FPXP-LE

SAVAGE MODEL 11FXP3, 111FXP3, 111FCXP3, 11FYXP3 (Youth) PACKAGE GUNS

Caliber: 223 Rem., 22-250 Rem., 243 Win., 308 Win., 300 WSM (11FXP3). 270 Win., 30-06 Spfld., 25-06 Rem., 7mm Rem. Mag., 300 Win. Mag., 338 Win. Mag., 300 Rem. Ultra Mag. (11FCXPE & 111FXP3). **Barrel:** 22" to 26". **Weight:** 6.5 lbs. **Length:** 41" to 47". **Stock:** Synthetic checkering, dual pillar bed. **Sights:** 3-9X40mm scope, mounted & bore sighted. **Features:** Blued, free floating and button rifled, Top loading internal box mag (except 111FXCP3 has detachable box mag.). Nylon sling and swivel studs. Some left-hand available.
Price: Model 11FXP3 . . . . **$516.00**
Price: Model 111FCXP3 . . . . **$411.00**
Price: Model 11FYXP3, 243 Win., 12.5" pull (youth) **$501.00**

SAVAGE MODEL 16FXP3, 116FXP3 SS ACTION PACKAGE GUNS

Caliber: 223 Rem., 243 Win., 308 Win., 300 WSM, 270 Win., 30-06 Spfld., 7mm Rem. Mag., 300 Win. Mag., 338 Win. Mag., 375 H&H, 7mm S&W, 7mm Rem. Ultra Mag., 300 Rem. Ultra Mag. **Barrel:** 22", 24", 26". **Weight:** 6.75 lbs. average. **Length:** 41" to 46". **Stock:** Synthetic checkering, dual pillar bed. **Sights:** 3-9X40mm scope, mounted & bore sighted. **Features:** Free floating and button rifled. Internal box mag., nylon sling and swivel studs.
Price: **$601.00**

SAVAGE MODEL 10FM SIERRA ULTRA LIGHT RIFLE

Caliber: 223, 243, 308. **Barrel:** 20". **Weight:** 6 lbs. **Length:** 41-1/2". **Stock:** "Dual Pillar" bedding in black synthetic stock with silver medallion in gripcap. **Sights:** None furnished; drilled and tapped for scope mounting. **Features:** True short action. Model 10FCM has detachable box magazine. Comes with sling and quick-detachable swivels. Introduced 1998. Made in U.S.A. by Savage Arms, Inc.
Price: **$552.00**

SAVAGE MODEL 10/110FP LONG RANGE RIFLE

Caliber: 223, 25-06, 308, 30-06, 300 Win. Mag., 7mm Rem. Mag., 4-shot magazine. **Barrel:** 24", heavy; recessed target muzzle. **Weight:** 8-1/2 lbs. **Length:** 45.5" overall. **Stock:** Black graphite/fiberglass composition; positive checkering. **Sights:** None furnished. Receiver drilled and tapped for scope mounting. **Features:** Pillar-bedded stock. Black matte finish on all metal parts. Double swivel studs on the forend for sling and/or bipod mount. Right- or left-hand. Introduced 1990. From Savage Arms, Inc.
Price: Right- or left-hand. **$601.00**

Savage Model 10FP Tactical Rifle

Similar to the Model 110FP except has true short action, chambered for 223, 308; black synthetic stock with "Dual Pillar" bedding. Introduced 1998. Made in U.S.A. by Savage Arms, Inc.
Price: **$601.00**
Price: Model 10FLP (left-hand) **$601.00**
Price: Model 10FP-LE1 (20"), 10FPLE2 (26") **$601.00**
Price: Model 10FPXP-LE w/Burris 3.5-10x50 scope,
Harris bipod package **$1,805.00**

Savage Model 10FP-LE1A Tactical Rifle

Similar to the Model 110FP except weighs 10.75 lbs. and has overall length of 39.75". Chambered for 223 Rem., 308 Win. Black synthetic Choate™ adjustable stock with accessory rail and swivel studs.
Price: **$729.00**

SAVAGE MODEL 111 CLASSIC HUNTER RIFLES

Caliber: 25-06 Rem., 270 Win., 30-06 Spfld., 7mm Rem. Mag, 300 Win. Mag., 7mm RUM, 300 RUM. **Barrel:** 22", 24", 26" (magnum calibers). **Weight:** 6.5 to 7.5 lbs. **Length:** 42.75" to 47.25". **Stock:** Walnut-finished hardwood (M111G, GC); graphite/fiberglass filled composite. **Sights:** Ramp front, open fully adjustable rear; drilled and tapped for scope mounting. **Features:** Three-position top tang safety, double front locking lugs, free-floated button-rifled barrel. Comes with trigger lock, target, ear puffs. Introduced 1994. Made in U.S.A. by Savage Arms, Inc.
Price: Model 111F (270 Win., 30-06 Spfld., 7mm Rem. Mag., 300 Win. Mag.) **$486.00**
Price: Model 111F (25-06 Rem., 338 Win. Mag., 7mm Rem. Ultra Mag, 300 Rem. Ultra Mag.) **$486.00**
Price: Model 111G
(wood stock, top-loading magazine, right- or left-hand) **$436.00**
Price: Model 111GNS (wood stock, detachable box magazine, no sights, right-hand only) **$518.00**

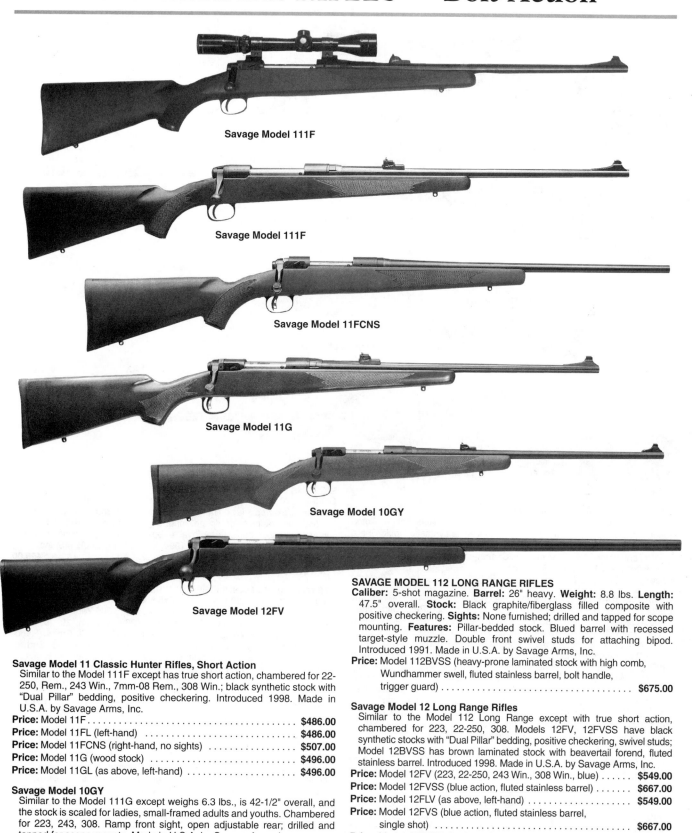

Savage Model 111F

Savage Model 111F

Savage Model 11FCNS

Savage Model 11G

Savage Model 10GY

Savage Model 12FV

Savage Model 11 Classic Hunter Rifles, Short Action
Similar to the Model 111F except has true short action, chambered for 22-250, Rem., 243 Win., 7mm-08 Rem., 308 Win.; black synthetic stock with "Dual Pillar" bedding, positive checkering. Introduced 1998. Made in U.S.A. by Savage Arms, Inc.

Price: Model 11F **$486.00**
Price: Model 11FL (left-hand) **$486.00**
Price: Model 11FCNS (right-hand, no sights) **$507.00**
Price: Model 11G (wood stock) **$496.00**
Price: Model 11GL (as above, left-hand) **$496.00**

Savage Model 10GY
Similar to the Model 111G except weighs 6.3 lbs., is 42-1/2" overall, and the stock is scaled for ladies, small-framed adults and youths. Chambered for 223, 243, 308. Ramp front sight, open adjustable rear; drilled and tapped for scope mounts. Made in U.S.A. by Savage Arms, Inc.
Price: Model 10GY (short action, calibers 223, 243, 308) **$496.00**

SAVAGE MODEL 112 LONG RANGE RIFLES
Caliber: 5-shot magazine. **Barrel:** 26" heavy. **Weight:** 8.8 lbs. **Length:** 47.5" overall. **Stock:** Black graphite/fiberglass filled composite with positive checkering. **Sights:** None furnished; drilled and tapped for scope mounting. **Features:** Pillar-bedded stock. Blued barrel with recessed target-style muzzle. Double front swivel studs for attaching bipod. Introduced 1991. Made in U.S.A. by Savage Arms, Inc.
Price: Model 112BVSS (heavy-prone laminated stock with high comb, Wundhammer swell, fluted stainless barrel, bolt handle, trigger guard) **$675.00**

Savage Model 12 Long Range Rifles
Similar to the Model 112 Long Range except with true short action, chambered for 223, 22-250, 308. Models 12FV, 12FVSS have black synthetic stocks with "Dual Pillar" bedding, positive checkering, swivel studs; Model 12BVSS has brown laminated stock with beavertail forend, fluted stainless barrel. Introduced 1998. Made in U.S.A. by Savage Arms, Inc.
Price: Model 12FV (223, 22-250, 243 Win., 308 Win., blue) **$549.00**
Price: Model 12FVSS (blue action, fluted stainless barrel) **$667.00**
Price: Model 12FLV (as above, left-hand) **$549.00**
Price: Model 12FVS (blue action, fluted stainless barrel, single shot) **$667.00**
Price: Model 12BVSS (laminated stock) **$721.00**
Price: Model 12BVSS-S (as above, single shot) **$721.00**

Savage Model 12VSS

Savage Model 116FSAK

Steyr Mannlicher SBS

Steyr SBS Forester

Savage Model 12VSS Varminter Rifle
Similar to other Model 12s except blue/stainless steel action, fluted stainless barrel, Choate full pistol grip, adjustable synthetic stock, Sharp Shooter trigger. Overall length 47-1/2", weighs appx. 15 lbs. No sights; drilled and tapped for scope mounts. Chambered in 223, 22-250, 308 Win. Made in U.S.A. by Savage Arms, Inc.
Price: **$934.00**

SAVAGE MODEL 116 WEATHER WARRIORS
Caliber: 375 H&H, 300 Rem. Ultra Mag., 308 Win., 300 Rem. Ultra Mag., 300 WSM, 7mm Rem. Ultra Mag., 7mm Rem. Short Ultra Mag., 7mm S&W, 7mm-08 Rem. **Barrel:** 22", 24" for 7mm Rem. Mag., 300 Win. Mag., 338 Win. Mag. (M116FSS only). **Weight:** 6.25 to 6.5 lbs. **Length:** 41" to 47". **Stock:** Graphite/fiberglass filled composite. **Sights:** None furnished; drilled and tapped for scope mounting. **Features:** Stainless steel with matte finish; free-floated barrel; quick-detachable swivel studs; laser-etched bolt; scope bases and rings. Left-hand models available in all models, calibers at same price. Model 116FSS introduced 1991; 116FSAK introduced 1994. Made in U.S.A. by Savage Arms, Inc.
Price: Model 116FSS (top-loading magazine) **$520.00**
Price: Model 116FSAK (top-loading magazine,
    Savage adjustable muzzle brake system) **$601.00**
Price: Model 116BSS (brown laminate, 24") **$668.00**
Price: Model 116BSS (brown laminate, 26") **$668.00**

Savage Model 16FCSS Rifle
Similar to Model 116FSS except true short action, chambered for 223, 243, 22" free-floated barrel; black graphite/fiberglass stock, "Dual Pillar" bedding. Also left-hand version available. Introduced 1998. Made in U.S.A. by Savage Arms, Inc.
Price: **$552.00**

SIGARMS SHR 970 SYNTHETIC RIFLE
Caliber: 270, 30-06. **Barrel:** 22". **Weight:** 7.2 lbs. **Length:** 41.9" overall. **Stock:** Textured black fiberglass or walnut. **Sights:** None furnished; drilled and tapped for scope mounting. **Features:** Quick takedown; interchangeable barrels; removable box magazine; cocking indicator; three-position safety. Introduced 1998. Imported by SIGARMS, Inc.
Price: Synthetic stock **$499.00**
Price: Walnut stock **$550.00**

STEYR CLASSIC MANNLICHER SBS RIFLE
Caliber: 243, 25-06, 308, 6.5x55, 6.5x57, 270, 7x64 Brenneke, 7mm-08, 7.5x55, 30-06, 9.3x62, 6.5x68, 7mm Rem. Mag., 300 Win. Mag., 8x68S, 4-shot magazine. **Barrel:** 23.6" standard; 26" magnum; 20" full stock standard calibers. **Weight:** 7 lbs. **Length:** 40.1" overall. **Stock:** Hand-checkered fancy European oiled walnut with standard forend. **Sights:** Ramp front adjustable for elevation, V-notch rear adjustable for windage. **Features:** Single adjustable trigger; 3-position roller safety with "safe-bolt" setting; drilled and tapped for Steyr factory scope mounts. Introduced 1997. Imported from Austria by GSI, Inc.
Price: Full-stock, standard calibers **$1,749.00**

STEYR SBS FORESTER RIFLE
Caliber: 243, 25-06, 270, 7mm-08, 308 Win., 30-06, 7mm Rem. Mag., 300 Win. Mag. Detachable 4-shot magazine. **Barrel:** 23.6", standard calibers; 25.6", magnum calibers. **Weight:** 7.5 lbs. **Length:** 44.5" overall (23.6" barrel). **Stock:** Oil-finished American walnut with Monte Carlo cheekpiece. Pachmayr 1" swivels. **Sights:** None furnished. Drilled and tapped for Browning A-Bolt mounts. **Features:** Three-position ambidextrous roller tang safety. Matte finish on barrel and receiver; adjustable trigger. Rotary cold-hammer forged barrel. Introduced 1997. Imported by GSI, Inc.
Price: Standard calibers **$799.00**
Price: Magnum calibers **$829.00**

Steyr SBS Prohunter

Steyr Scout Rifle

Thompson/Center Icon

Tikka T-3 Hunter

Steyr SBS Prohunter Rifle

Similar to the SBS Forester except has ABS synthetic stock with adjustable butt spacers, straight comb without cheekpiece, palm swell, Pachmayr 1" swivels. Special 10-round magazine conversion kit available. Introduced 1997. Imported by GSI.

Price: Standard calibers **$769.00**
Price: Magnum calibers **$799.00**

STEYR SCOUT BOLT-ACTION RIFLE

Caliber: 308 Win., 5-shot magazine. **Barrel:** 19", fluted. **Weight:** NA. **Length:** NA. **Stock:** Gray Zytel. **Sights:** Pop-up front & rear, Leupold M8 2.5x28 IER scope on Picatinny optic rail with Steyr mounts. **Features:** luggage case, scout sling, two stock spacers, two magazines. Introduced 1998. From GSI.

Price: From **$1,969.00**

STEYR SSG BOLT-ACTION RIFLE

Caliber: 308 Win., detachable 5-shot rotary magazine. **Barrel:** 26". **Weight:** 8.5 lbs. **Length:** 44.5" overall. **Stock:** Black ABS Cycolac with spacers for length of pull adjustment. **Sights:** Hooded ramp front adjustable for elevation, V-notch rear adjustable for windage. **Features:** Sliding safety; NATO rail for bipod; 1" swivels; Parkerized finish; single or double-set triggers. Imported from Austria by GSI, Inc.

Price: SSG-PI, iron sights **$1,699.00**
Price: SSG-PII, heavy barrel, no sights **$1,699.00**
Price: SSG-PIIK, 20" heavy barrel, no sights **$1,699.00**
Price: SSG-PIV, 16.75" threaded heavy barrel with flash hider . . **$2,659.00**

THOMPSON/CENTER ICON BOLT-ACTION RIFLE

Caliber: 22-250, 243, 308, 30TC, 3-round box magazine. **Barrel:** 24", button rifled. **Weight:** 7.5 lbs. **Length:** 44.5" overall. **Stock:** Walnut, 20-lpi grip and forend cut checkering with ribbon detail. **Sights:** None; integral Weaver style scope mounts. **Features:** Interchangeable bolt handle, 60-degree bolt lift, Interlok Bedding System, 3-lug bolt with T-Slot extractor, cocking indicator, adjustable trigger, preset to 3 to 3.5 lbs of pull. Introduced 2007. From Thompson/Center Arms.

Price: . . . . **NA**

TIKKA T-3 BIG BOAR SYNTHETIC BOLT-ACTION RIFLE

Caliber: 308, 30-06, 300 WSM. **Barrel:** 19". **Weight:** 6 lbs. **Length:** 39.5" overall. **Stock:** Laminated. **Sights:** None furnished. **Features:** Detachable, 3-round. Receiver dove-tailed for scope mounting. Reintroduced 1996. Imported from Finland by Beretta USA.

Price: Left-hand **$695.00**

Tikka T-3 Super Varmint Rifle

Similar to the standard T-3 rifle except has 23-3/8" heavy stainless barrel. Chambered for 22-250, 223, 308. Reintroduced 2005. Made in Finland by Sako. Imported by Beretta USA.

Price: **$1,425.00**

TIKKA T-3 HUNTER

Caliber: 223, 22-250, 243, 308, 25-06, 270, 30-06, 300 Win. Mag., 338 Win. Mag., 270 WSM, 300 WSM, 6.5x55 Swedish Mauser, 7mm Rem. Mag. **Stock:** Walnut. **Sight:** None furnished. **Barrel:** 22-7/16", 24-3/8". **Features:** Detachable magazine, aluminum scope rings. Introduced 2005. Imported from Finland by Beretta USA.

Price: **$695.00**

Tikka T-3 Stainless Synthetic

Similar to the T-3 Hunter except stainless steel, synthetic stock. Available in 243, 25-06, 270, 308, 30-06, 270 WSM, 300 WSM, 7mm Rem. Mag., 300 Win. Mag., 338 Win. Mag. Introduced 2005. Imported from Finland by Beretta USA.

Price: **$895.00**

ULTRA LIGHT ARMS BOLT-ACTION RIFLES

Caliber: 17 Rem. to 416 Rigby. **Barrel:** Douglas, length to order. **Weight:** 4-3/4 to 7-1/2 lbs. **Length:** Varies. **Stock:** Kevlar® graphite composite, variety of finishes. **Sights:** None furnished; drilled and tapped for scope mounts. **Features:** Timney trigger, hand-lapped action, button-rifled barrel, hand-bedded action, recoil pad, sling-swivel studs, optional Jewell trigger. Made in U.S.A. by New Ultra Light Arms.

Price: Model 20 (short action) **$2,800.00**
Price: Model 24 (long action) **$2,900.00**
Price: Model 28 (magnum action) **$3,200.00**
Price: Model 40 (300 Wby. Mag., 416 Rigby) **$3,200.00**
Price: Left-hand models, add **$100.00**

Weatherby Mark V Lazermark

Weatherby Mark V Sporter

Weatherby Mark V Stainless

Weatherby Mark V Synthetic

WEATHERBY MARK V DELUXE BOLT-ACTION RIFLE
Caliber: All Weatherby calibers plus 22-250, 243, 25-06, 270 Win., 280 Rem., 7mm-08, 30-06, 308 Win. **Barrel:** 24" barrel on standard calibers. **Weight:** 8-1/2 to 10-1/2 lbs. **Length:** 46-5/8" to 46-3/4" overall. **Stock:** Walnut, Monte Carlo with cheekpiece; high luster finish; checkered pistol grip and forend; recoil pad. **Sights:** None furnished. **Features:** Cocking indicator; adjustable trigger; hinged floorplate, thumb safety; quick detachable sling swivels. Made in U.S.A. From Weatherby.

Price: 257, 270, 7mm. 300, 340 Wby. Mags., 26" barrel **$1,767.00**
Price: 416 Wby. Mag. with Accubrake, 28" barrel **$2,079.00**
Price: 460 Wby. Mag. with Accubrake, 28" barrel **$2,443.00**
Price: 24" barrel **$1,715.00**

Weatherby Mark V Lazermark Rifle
Same as Mark V Deluxe except stock has extensive oak leaf pattern laser carving on pistol grip and forend. Introduced 1981.

Price: 257, 270, 7mm Wby. Mag., 300, 340, 26". **$1,923.00**
Price: 378 Wby. Mag., 28" **$2,266.00**
Price: 416 Wby. Mag., 28", Accubrake **$2,266.00**
Price: 460 Wby. Mag., 28", Accubrake **$2,661.00**

Weatherby Mark V Sporter Rifle
Same as the Mark V Deluxe without the embellishments. Metal has low-luster blue, stock is Claro walnut with matte finish, Monte Carlo comb, recoil pad. Introduced 1993. From Weatherby.

Price: 22-250, 243, 240 Wby. Mag., 25-06, 7mm-08,
270 WCF, 280, 30-06, 308; 24". **$1,091.00**

Price: 257 Wby., 270, 7 mm Wby., 7mm Rem., 300 Wby.,
300 Win., 340 Wby., 338 Win. Mag., 26" barrel for Wby. calibers;
24" for non-Wby. calibers **$1,143.00**

Weatherby Mark V Stainless Rifle
Similar to the Mark V Deluxe except made of 410-series stainless steel. Also available in 30-378 Wby. Mag. Has lightweight injection-molded synthetic stock with raised Monte Carlo comb, checkered grip and forend, custom floorplate release. Right-hand only. Introduced 1995. Made in U.S.A. From Weatherby.

Price: 22-250 Rem., 243 Win., 240 Wby. Mag., 25-06 Rem.,
270 Win., 280 Rem., 7mm-08 Rem., 30-06 Spfld., 308 Win.,
24" barrel **$1,018.00**
Price: 257, 270, 7mm, 300, 340 Wby. Mag., 26" barrel **$1,070.00**
Price: 7mm Rem. Mag., 300 Win. Mag., 338 Win. Mag.,
375 H&H Mag., 24" barrel **$1,070.00**

Weatherby Mark V Synthetic
Similar to the Mark V Stainless except made of matte finished blued steel. Injection molded synthetic stock. Weighs 6-1/2 lbs., 24" barrel. Available in 22-250, 240 Wby. Mag., 243, 25-06, 270, 7mm-08, 280, 30-06, 308. Introduced 1997. Made in U.S.A. From Weatherby.

Price: **$923.00**
Price: 257, 270, 7mm, 300, 340 Wby. Mags., 26" barrel **$975.00**
Price: 7mm STW, 7mm Rem. Mag., 300, 338 Win. Mags **$975.00**
Price: 375 H&H, 24" barrel **$975.00**
Price: 30-378 Wby. Mag., 338-378 Wby. 28" barrel **$1,151.00**

Weatherby Mark V Accumark

Weatherby Mark V SVR

Weatherby Mark V
Dangerous Game Rifle

WEATHERBY MARK V ACCUMARK RIFLE

Caliber: 257, 270, 7mm, 300, 340 Wby. Mags., 338-378 Wby. Mag., 30-378 Wby. Mag., 7mm STW, 7mm Rem. Mag., 300 Win. Mag. **Barrel:** 26", 28". **Weight:** 8-1/2 lbs. **Length:** 46-5/8" overall. **Stock:** Bell & Carlson with full length aluminum bedding block. **Sights:** None furnished. Drilled and tapped for scope mounting. **Features:** Uses Mark V action with heavy-contour stainless barrel with black oxidized flutes, muzzle diameter of .705". Introduced 1996. Made in U.S.A. From Weatherby.

Price: 26" **$1,507.00**
Price: 30-378 Wby. Mag., 338-378 Wby. Mag., 28",
Accubrake **$1,724.00**
Price: 223, 22-250, 243, 240 Wby. Mag., 25-06, 270,
280 Rem., 7mm-08, 30-06, 308; 24" **$1,455.00**
Price: Accumark left-hand 257, 270, 7mm, 300, 340 Wby.
Mag., 7mm Rem. Mag., 7mm STW, 300 Win. Mag. **$1,559.00**
Price: Accumark left-hand 30-378, 333-378 Wby. Mags. **$1,788.00**

Weatherby Mark V Accumark Ultra Lightweight Rifles

Similar to the Mark V Accumark except weighs 5-3/4 lbs., 6-3/4 lbs. in Mag. calibers.; 24", 26" fluted barrel with recessed target crown; hand-laminated stock with CNC-machined aluminum bedding plate and faint gray "spider web" finish. Available in 257, 270, 7mm, 300 Wby. Mags., (26"); 243, 240 Wby. Mag., 25-06, 270 Win., 280 Rem., 7mm-08, 7mm Rem. Mag., 30-06, 338-06 A-Square, 308, 300 Win. Mag. (24"). Introduced 1998. Made in U.S.A. by Weatherby.

Price: . . . . **$1,459.00 to $1,517.00**
Price: Left-hand models **$1,559.00**

Weatherby Mark V SVM/SPM Rifles

Similar to the Mark V Accumark except has 26" fluted (SVM) or 24" fluted Krieger barrel, spiderweb-pattern tan laminated synthetic stock. SVM has a fully adjustable trigger. Chambered for 223, 22-250, 220 Swift (SVM only), 243, 7mm-08 and 308. Made in U.S.A. by Weatherby.

Price: SVM (Super VarmintMaster), repeater or single-shot **$1,517.00**
Price: SPM (Super Predator Master) **$1,459.00**

Weatherby Mark V Special Varmint Rifle (SVR)

Similar to the Super VarmintMaster and Accumark with 22", #3 contour chrome-moly 4140 steel Krieger Criterion button-rifled barrel with one-degree target crown and hand-laminated composite stock. Available in .223 Rem. (5+1 magazine capacity) and .22-250 Rem. (4+1 magazine capacity) in right-hand models only.

Price: **$999.00**

Weatherby Mark V Fibermark Rifles

Similar to other Mark V models except has black Kevlar® and fiberglass composite stock and bead-blast blue or stainless finish. Chambered for 19 standard and magnum calibers. Introduced 1983; reintroduced 2001. Made in U.S.A. by Weatherby.

Price: Fibermark . . . . **$1,070.00 to $1,347.00**
Price: Fibermark stainless . . . . **$1,165.00 to $1,390.00**

WEATHERBY MARK V DANGEROUS GAME RIFLE

Caliber: 375 H&H, 375 Wby. Mag., 378 Wby. Mag., 416 Rem. Mag., 416 Wby. Mag., 458 Win. Mag., .458 Lott, 460 Wby. Mag. 300 Win. Mag., 300 Wby., Mag., 338 Win. Mag., 340 Wby. Mag., 24" only **Barrel:** 24" or 26". **Weight:** 8-3/4 to 9-1/2 lbs. **Length:** 44-5/8" to 46-5/8" overall. **Stock:** Kevlar® and fiberglass composite. **Sights:** Barrel-band hooded front with large gold bead, adjustable ramp/shallow "V" rear. **Features:** Designed for dangerous game hunting. Black oxide matte finish on all metalwork; Pachmayr Decelerator™ recoil pad, short-throw Mark V action. Introduced 2001. Made in U.S.A. by Weatherby.

Price: . . . . **$2,703.00 to $2,935.00**

WEATHERBY MARK V SUPER BIG GAMEMASTER DEER RIFLE

Caliber: 240 Wby. Mag., 25-06 Rem., 270 Win., 280 Rem., 30-06 Spfld., 257 Wby. Mag., 270 Wby. Mag., 7mm Rem. Mag., 7mm Wby. Mag., 338-06 A-Square, 300 Win. Mag., 300 Wby. Mag. **Barrel:** 26", target crown. **Weight:** 5-3/4 lbs., (6-3/4 lbs. Magnum). **Stock:** Raised comb Monte Carlo composite. **Features:** Fluted barrel, aluminum bedding block, Pachmayr decelerator, 54-degree bolt lift, adj. trigger.

Price: **$1,459.00**
Price: Magnum **$1,517.00**

WEATHERBY MARK V ROYAL CUSTOM RIFLE

Caliber: 257, 270, 7mm, 300, 340 all Wby. Mags. Other calibers available upon request. **Barrel:** 26". **Stock:** Monte Carlo hand-checkered Claro walnut with high gloss finish. **Features:** Bolt and follower are damascened with checkered knob. Engraved receiver, bolt sleeve and floorplate sport scroll pattern. Animal images on floorplate optional. High gloss blue, 24-karat gold and nickel-plating. Made in U.S.A. From Weatherby.

Price: **$5,831.00**

WEATHERBY THREAT RESPONSE RIFLES (TRR) SERIES

Caliber: TRR 223 Rem., 300 Win. TRR Magnum and Magnum Custom 300 Win. Mag., 300 Wby. Mag., 30-378 Wby. Mag., 328-378 Wby. Mag. **Barrel:** 22", 26", target crown. **Stock:** Hand-laminated composite. TTR & TRR Magnum have raised comb Monte Carlo style. TRR Magnum Custom adjustable ergonomic stock. **Features:** Adjustable trigger, aluminum bedding block, beavertail forearms dual tapered, flat-bottomed. "Rocker Arm" lockdown scope mounting. 54 degree bolt. Pachmayr decelerator pad. Made in U.S.A.

Price: TRR Magnum Custom 300 . . . . **$2,699.00**
Price: 30-378, 338-378 with accubrake **$2,861.00**

WILDERNESS EXPLORER MULTI-CALIBER CARBINE

Caliber: 22 Hornet, 218 Bee, 44 Magnum, 50 A.E. (interchangeable). **Barrel:** 18", match grade. **Weight:** 5.5 lbs **Length:** 38-1/2" overall. **Stock:** Synthetic or wood. **Sights:** None furnished; comes with Weaver-style mount on barrel. **Features:** Quick-change barrel and bolt face for caliber switch. Removable box magazine; adjustable trigger with side safety; detachable swivel studs. Introduced 1997. Made in U.S.A. by Phillips & Rogers, Inc.

Price: **$995.00**

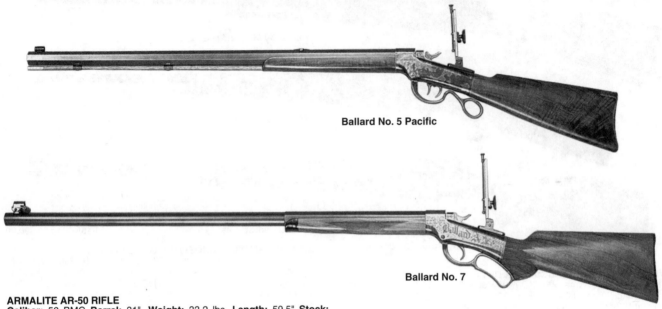

Ballard No. 5 Pacific

Ballard No. 7

ARMALITE AR-50 RIFLE
Caliber: 50 BMG **Barrel:** 31". **Weight:** 33.2 lbs. **Length:** 59.5" **Stock:** Synthetic. **Sights:** None furnished. **Features:** A single-shot bolt action rifle designed for long range shooting. Available in left-hand model. Made in U.S.A. by Armalite.
Price: **$2,999.00**

ARMSPORT 1866 SHARPS RIFLE, CARBINE
Caliber: 45-70. **Barrel:** 28", round or octagonal. **Weight:** 8.10 lbs. **Length:** 46" overall. **Stock:** Walnut. **Sights:** Blade front, folding adjustable rear. Tang sight set optionally available. **Features:** Replica of the 1866 Sharps. Color case-hardened frame, rest blued. Imported by Armsport.
Price: **$865.00**
Price: With octagonal barrel **$900.00**
Price: Carbine, 22" round barrel **$850.00**

BALLARD NO. 1 3/4 FAR WEST RIFLE
Caliber: 22 LR, 32-40, 38-55, 40-65, 40-70, 45-70, 45-110, 50-70, 50-90. **Barrel:** 30" std. or heavyweight. **Weight:** 10-1/2 lbs. (std.) or 11-3/4 lbs. (heavyweight bbl.) **Length:** NA. **Stock:** Walnut. **Sights:** Blade front, Rocky Mountain rear. **Features:** Single- or double-set triggers, S-lever or ring-style lever; color case-hardened finish; hand polished and lapped Badger barrel. Made in U.S.A. by Ballard Rifle & Cartridge Co.
Price: **$2,250.00**

BALLARD NO. 4 PERFECTION RIFLE
Caliber: 22 LR, 32-40, 38-55, 40-65, 40-70, 45-70, 45-90, 45-110, 50-70, 50-90. **Barrel:** 30" or 32" octagon, standard or heavyweight. **Weight:** 10-1/2 lbs. (standard) or 11-3/4 lbs. (heavyweight bbl.). **Length:** NA. **Stock:** Smooth walnut. **Sights:** Blade front, Rocky Mountain rear. **Features:** Rifle or shotgun-style buttstock, straight grip action, single or double-set trigger, "S" or right lever, hand polished and lapped Badger barrel. Made in U.S.A. by Ballard Rifle & Cartridge Co.
Price: **$2,250.00**

BALLARD NO. 5 PACIFIC SINGLE-SHOT RIFLE
Caliber: 32-40, 38-55, 40-65, 40-90, 40-70 SS, 45-70 Gov't., 45-110 SS, 50-70 Gov't., 50-90 SS. **Barrel:** 30", or 32" octagonal. **Weight:** 10-1/2 lbs. **Length:** NA. **Stock:** High-grade walnut; rifle or shotgun style. **Sights:** Blade front, Rocky Mountain rear. **Features:** Standard or heavy barrel; double-set triggers; under-barrel wiping rod; ring lever. Introduced 1999. Made in U.S.A. by Ballard Rifle & Cartridge Co.
Price: **$2,575.00**

BALLARD NO. 7 LONG RANGE RIFLE
Caliber: 32-40, 38-55, 40-65, 40-70 SS, 45-70 Gov't., 45-90, 45-110. **Barrel:** 32", 34" half-octagon. **Weight:** 11-3/4 lbs. **Length:** NA. **Stock:** Walnut; checkered pistol grip shotgun butt, ebony forend cap. **Sights:** Globe front. **Features:** Designed for shooting up to 1000 yards. Standard or heavy barrel; single or double-set trigger; hard rubber or steel buttplate. Introduced 1999. Made in U.S.A. by Ballard Rifle & Cartridge Co.
Price: From **$2,475.00**

BALLARD NO. 8 UNION HILL RIFLE
Caliber: 22 LR, 32-40, 38-55, 40-65, 40-70 SS. **Barrel:** 30" half-octagon. **Weight:** About 10-1/2 lbs. **Length:** NA. **Stock:** Walnut; pistol grip butt with cheekpiece. **Sights:** Globe front. **Features:** Designed for 200-yard offhand shooting. Standard or heavy barrel; double-set triggers; full loop lever; hook Schuetzen buttplate. Introduced 1999. Made in U.S.A. by Ballard Rifle & Cartridge Co.
Price: From **$2,500.00**

BALLARD MODEL 1885 HIGH WALL SINGLE SHOT RIFLE
Caliber: 17 Bee, 22 Hornet, 218 Bee, 219 Don Wasp, 219 Zipper, 22 Hi-Power, 225 Win., 25-20 WCF, 25-35 WCF, 25 Krag, 7mmx57R, 30-30, 30-40 Krag, 303 British, 33 WCF, 348 WCF, 35 WCF, 35-30/30, 9.3x74R, 405 WCF, 50-110 WCF, 500 Express, 577 Express. **Barrel:** Lengths to 34". **Weight:** NA. **Length:** NA. **Stock:** Straight-grain American walnut. **Sights:** buckhorn or flattop rear, blade front. **Features:** Faithful copy of original Model 1885 High Wall; parts interchange with original rifles; variety of options available. Introduced 2000. Made in U.S.A. by Ballard Rifle & Cartridge LLC.
Price: From **$2,313.00**
Price: With single set trigger from **$2,355.00**

BARRETT MODEL 99 SINGLE SHOT RIFLE
Caliber: 50 BMG. **Barrel:** 33". **Weight:** 25 lbs. **Length:** 50.4" overall. **Stock:** Anodized aluminum with energy-absorbing recoil pad. **Sights:** None furnished; integral M1913 scope rail. **Features:** Bolt action; detachable bipod; match-grade barrel with high-efficiency muzzle brake. Introduced 1999. Made in U.S.A. by Barrett Firearms.
Price: From **$3,000.00**

BROWN MODEL 97D SINGLE SHOT RIFLE
Caliber: 17 Ackley Hornet through 45-70 Gov't. **Barrel:** Up to 26", air gauged match grade. **Weight:** About 5 lbs., 11 oz. **Stock:** Sporter style with pistol grip, cheekpiece and Schnabel forend. **Sights:** None furnished; drilled and tapped for scope mounting. **Features:** Falling block action gives rigid barrel-receiver matting; polished blue/black finish. Hand-fitted action. Many options. Made in U.S.A. by E. Arthur Brown Co., Inc.
Price: From **$699.00**

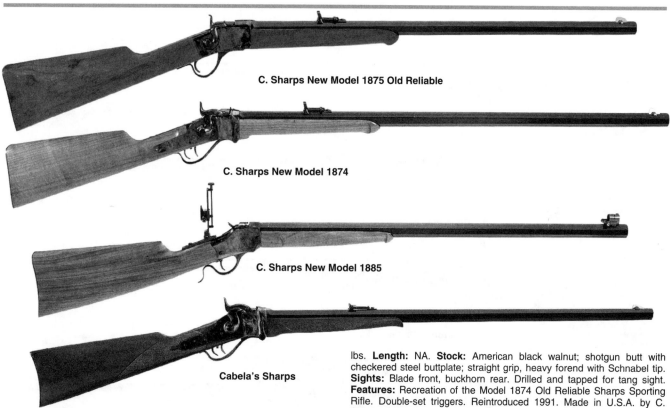

C. Sharps New Model 1875 Old Reliable

C. Sharps New Model 1874

C. Sharps New Model 1885

Cabela's Sharps

BROWNING MODEL 1885 HIGH WALL SINGLE SHOT RIFLE
Caliber: 22-250, 30-06, 270, 7mm Rem. Mag., 454 Casull, 45-70. **Barrel:** 28". **Weight:** 8 lbs., 12 oz. **Length:** 43-1/2" overall. **Stock:** Walnut with straight grip, Schnabel forend. **Sights:** None furnished; drilled and tapped for scope mounting. **Features:** Replica of J.M. Browning's high-wall falling block rifle. Octagon barrel with recessed muzzle. Imported from Japan by Browning. Introduced 1985.
Price: **$1,027.00**

C. SHARPS ARMS NEW MODEL 1875 OLD RELIABLE RIFLE
Caliber: 22LR, 32-40 & 38-55 Ballard, 38-56 WCF, 40-65 WCF, 40-90 3-1/4", 40-90 2-5/8", 40-70 2-1/10", 40-70 2-1/4", 40-70 2-1/2", 40-50 1-11/16", 40-50 1-7/8", 45-90, 45-70, 45-100, 45-110, 45-120. Also available on special order only in 50-70, 50-90, 50-140. **Barrel:** 24", 26", 30" (standard), 32", 34" optional. **Weight:** 8-12 lbs. **Stock:** Walnut, straight grip, shotgun butt with checkered steel buttplate. **Sights:** Silver blade front, Rocky Mountain buckhorn rear. **Features:** Recreation of the 1875 Sharps rifle. Production guns will have case-colored receiver. Available in Custom Sporting and Target versions upon request. Announced 1986. From C. Sharps Arms Co.
Price: 1875 Sporting Rifle (30" tapered oct. bbl.) **$1,185.00**

C. Sharps Arms 1875 Classic Sharps
Similar to New Model 1875 Sporting Rifle except 26", 28" or 30" full octagon barrel, crescent buttplate with toe plate, Hartford-style forend with cast German silver nose cap. Blade front sight, Rocky Mountain buckhorn rear. Weighs 10 lbs. Introduced 1987. From C. Sharps Arms Co.
Price: **$1,470.00**

C. Sharps Arms New Model 1875 Target & Long Range
Similar to New Model 1875 in all listed calibers except 22 LR; 34" tapered octagon barrel; globe with post front sight, Long Range Vernier tang sight with windage adjustments. Pistol grip stock with cheek rest; checkered steel buttplate. Introduced 1991. From C. Sharps Arms Co.
Price: **$1,549.50**

C. SHARPS ARMS NEW MODEL 1874 OLD RELIABLE
Caliber: 40-50, 40-70, 40-90, 45-70, 45-90, 45-100, 45-110, 45-120, 50-70, 50-90, 50-140. **Barrel:** 26", 28", 30" tapered octagon. **Weight:** About 10 lbs. **Length:** NA. **Stock:** American black walnut; shotgun butt with checkered steel buttplate; straight grip, heavy forend with Schnabel tip. **Sights:** Blade front, buckhorn rear. Drilled and tapped for tang sight. **Features:** Recreation of the Model 1874 Old Reliable Sharps Sporting Rifle. Double-set triggers. Reintroduced 1991. Made in U.S.A. by C. Sharps Arms.
Price: **$1,584.00**

C. SHARPS ARMS NEW MODEL 1885 HIGHWALL RIFLE
Caliber: 22 LR, 22 Hornet, 219 Zipper, 25-35 WCF, 32-40 WCF, 38-55 WCF, 40-65, 30-40 Krag, 40-50 ST or BN, 40-70 ST or BN, 40-90 ST or BN, 45-70 2-1/10" ST, 45-90 2-4/10" ST, 45-100 2-6/10" ST, 45-110 2-7/8" ST, 45-120 3-1/4" ST. **Barrel:** 26", 28", 30", tapered full octagon. **Weight:** About 9 lbs., 4 oz. **Length:** 47" overall. **Stock:** Oil-finished American walnut; Schnabel-style forend. **Sights:** Blade front, buckhorn rear. Drilled and tapped for optional tang sight. **Features:** Single trigger; octagonal receiver top; checkered steel buttplate; color case-hardened receiver and buttplate, blued barrel. Many options available. Made in U.S.A. by C. Sharps Arms Co.
Price: From **$1,439.00**

C. SHARPS ARMS CUSTOM NEW MODEL 1877 LONG RANGE TARGET RIFLE
Caliber: 44-90 Sharps/Rem., 45-70, 45-90, 45-100 Sharps. **Barrel:** 32", 34" tapered round with Rigby flat. **Weight:** Appx. 10 lbs. **Stock:** Walnut checkered. Pistol grip/forend. **Sights:** Classic long range with windage. **Features:** Custom production only.
Price: . . . . **$5,550.00 and up**

CABELA'S SHARPS SPORTING RIFLE
Caliber: 45-70, 45-120, 45-110. **Barrel:** 32", tapered octagon. **Weight:** 9 lbs. **Length:** 47-1/4" overall. **Stock:** Checkered walnut. **Sights:** Blade front, open adjustable rear. **Features:** Color case-hardened receiver and hammer, rest blued. Introduced 1995. Imported by Cabela's.
Price: 45-70, 45-90 . . . . **$1399.99**
Price: (Heavy Target Sharps, 45-70, 45-120) **$1,599.99**
Price: (Quigley Sharps, 45-70, 45-120, 45-110) **$1,899.99**

CIMARRON BILLY DIXON 1874 SHARPS SPORTING RIFLE
Caliber: 40-40, 50-90, 50-70, 45-70. **Barrel:** 32" tapered octagonal. **Weight:** NA. **Length:** NA. **Stock:** European walnut. **Sights:** Blade front, Creedmoor rear. **Features:** Color case-hardened frame, blued barrel. Hand-checkered grip and forend; hand-rubbed oil finish. Introduced 1999. Imported by Cimarron F.A. Co.
Price: **$1,670.00**

Cimarron Billy Dixon

Cimarron Quigley

Cimarron 1885 High Wall

Dakota Single Shot

Dixie 1874 Sharps Silhouette

CIMARRON QUIGLEY MODEL 1874 SHARPS SPORTING RIFLE
Caliber: 45-110, 50-70, 50-40, 45-70, 45-90, 45-120. **Barrel:** 34" octagonal. **Weight:** NA. **Length:** NA. **Stock:** Checkered walnut. **Sights:** Blade front, adjustable rear. **Features:** Blued finish; double-set triggers. From Cimarron F.A. Co.
Price: **$1,805.00**

CIMARRON SILHOUETTE MODEL 1874 SHARPS SPORTING RIFLE
Caliber: 45-70, 50-70. **Barrel:** 32" octagonal. **Weight:** NA. **Length:** NA. **Stock:** Walnut. **Sights:** Blade front, adjustable rear. **Features:** Pistol-grip stock with shotgun-style buttplate; cut-rifled barrel. From Cimarron F.A. Co.
Price: **$1,620.00**

CIMARRON MODEL 1885 HIGH WALL RIFLE
Caliber: 38-55, 40-65, 45-70, 45-90, 45-120, 30-40 Krag, 348 Winchester. **Barrel:** 30" octagonal. **Weight:** NA. **Length:** NA. **Stock:** European walnut. **Sights:** Bead front, semi-buckhorn rear. **Features:** Replica of the Winchester 1885 High Wall rifle. Color case-hardened receiver and lever, blued barrel. Curved buttplate. Optional double-set triggers. Introduced 1999. Imported by Cimarron F.A. Co.

Price: **$995.00**
Price: With pistol grip **$1,175.00**

DAKOTA MODEL 10 SINGLE SHOT RIFLE
Caliber: Most rimmed and rimless commercial calibers. **Barrel:** 23". **Weight:** 6 lbs. **Length:** 39-1/2" overall. **Stock:** Medium fancy grade walnut in classic style. Checkered grip and forend. **Sights:** None furnished. Drilled and tapped for scope mounting. **Features:** Falling block action with underlever. Top tang safety. Removable trigger plate for conversion to single set trigger. Introduced 1990. Made in U.S.A. by Dakota Arms.
Price: **$3,595.00**
Price: Barreled action **$2,095.00**
Price: Action only **$1,850.00**
Price: Magnum calibers **$3,595.00**
Price: Magnum barreled action **$2,050.00**
Price: Magnum action only **$1,675.00**

DIXIE 1874 SHARPS BLACK POWDER SILHOUETTE RIFLE
Caliber: 45-70. **Barrel:** 30"; tapered octagon; blued; 1:18" twist. **Weight:** 10 lbs., 3 oz. **Length:** 47-1/2" overall. **Stock:** Oiled walnut. **Sights:** Blade front, ladder-type hunting rear. **Features:** Replica of the Sharps #1 Sporter. Shotgun-style butt with checkered metal buttplate; color case-hardened receiver, hammer, lever and buttplate. Tang is drilled and tapped for tang sight. Double-set triggers. Meets standards for NRA blackpowder cartridge matches. Introduced 1995. Imported from Italy by Dixie Gun Works.
Price: CR0145 .... **$1,100.00**

H&R Ultra Varmint

H&R Ultra Hunter

H&R Buffalo

Dixie 1874 Sharps Lightweight Hunter/Target Rifle
Same as the Dixie 1874 Sharps Black Powder Silhouette model except has a straight-grip buttstock with military-style buttplate. Based on the 1874 military model. Introduced 1995. Imported from Italy by Dixie Gun Works.
Price: CR0212. . . . . **$1,050.00**

E.M.F. PREMIER 1874 SHARPS RIFLE
Caliber: 45/70, 45/110, 45/120. **Barrel:** 32", 34". **Weight:** 11-13 lbs. **Length:** 49", 51" overall. **Stock:** Pistol grip, European walnut. **Sights:** Blade front, adjustable rear. **Features:** Superb quality reproductions of the 1874 Shaprs Sporting Rifles; casehardened locks; double-set triggers; blue barrels. Imported from Pedersoli by E.M.F.
Price: Business Rifle. **$1,130.00**
Price: "Quigley", Patchbox, heavy barrel **$1,800.00**
Price: Silhouette, pistol-grip **$1,500.00**
Price: Super Deluxe Hand Engraved **$3,150.00**

E.M.F. 1885 HIGHWALL RIFLES
Caliber: 38/55, 45/70. **Barrel:** 30". **Weight:** 10 lbs. **Length:** 47". **Stock:** Walnut, straight or pistol grip.. **Sights:** Bead front, semi-buckhorn rear. **Features:** Reproduction of the Winchester 1885 Highwall Rifle, curved butt plate. Case-hardened receiver and lever, blue barrel. Imported by E.M.F.
Price: Standard **$900.00**
Price: Deluxe pistol grip **$1,020.00**

HARRINGTON & RICHARDSON ULTRA VARMINT/ULTRA HUNTER RIFLES
Caliber: 204 Ruger, 22 WMR, 22-250, 223, 243, 25-06, 30-06. **Barrel:** 22" to 26" heavy taper. **Weight:** About 7.5 lbs. **Stock:** Laminated birch with Monte Carlo comb or skeletonized polymer. **Sights:** None furnished. Drilled and tapped for scope mounting. **Features:** Break-open action with side-lever release, positive ejection. Scope mount. Blued receiver and barrel. Swivel studs. Introduced 1993. Ultra Hunter introduced 1995. From H&R 1871, Inc.

Price: Ultra Varmint Fluted, 24" bull barrel, polymer stock. **$406.00**
Price: Ultra Hunter Rifle, 26" bull barrel in 25-06, laminated stock . **$357.00**
Price: Ultra Varmint Rifle, 22" bull barrel in 223, laminated stock . . **$357.00**

HARRINGTON & RICHARDSON BUFFALO CLASSIC & TARGET RIFLES
Caliber: 45-70. **Barrel:** 32" heavy. **Weight:** 8 lbs. **Length:** 46" overall. **Stock:** Cut-checkered American black walnut. **Sights:** Williams receiver sight; Lyman target front sight with 8 aperture inserts. **Features:** Color case-hardened Handi-Rifle action with exposed hammer; color case-hardened crescent buttplate; 19th century checkering pattern. Introduced 1995. Target model (introduced 1998) is similar to the Buffalo Classic rifle except chambered for 38-55 Win., has 28" barrel. The barrel, steel trigger guard and forend spacer, are highly polished and blued. Color case-hardened receiver and buttplate. Made in U.S.A. by H&R 1871, LLC.
Price: Buffalo Classic Rifle **$449.00**
Price: Target Model Rifle **$449.00**

HARRIS GUNWORKS ANTIETAM SHARPS RIFLE
Caliber: 40-65, 45-75. **Barrel:** 30", 32", octagon or round, hand-lapped stainless or chrome-moly. **Weight:** 11.25 lbs. **Length:** 47" overall. **Stock:** Choice of straight grip, pistol grip or Creedmoor with Schnabel forend; pewter tip optional. Standard wood is A Fancy; higher grades available. **Sights:** Montana Vintage Arms #111 Low Profile Spirit Level front, #108 mid-range tang rear with windage adjustments. **Features:** Recreation of the 1874 Sharps sidehammer. Action is color case-hardened, barrel satin black. Chrome-moly barrel optionally blued. Optional sights include #112 Spirit Level Globe front with windage, #107 Long Range rear with windage. Introduced 1994. Made in U.S.A. by Harris Gunworks.
Price: **$2,400.00**

KRIEGHOFF HUBERTUS SINGLE-SHOT RIFLE
Caliber: 222, 243, 270, 308, 30-06, 5.6x50R Mag., 5.6x52R, 6x62R Freres, 6.5x57R, 6.5x65R, 7x57R, 7x65R, 8x57JRS, 8x75RS, 9.3x74R, 7mm Rem. Mag., 300 Win. Mag. **Barrel:** 23-1/2". **Weight:** 6-1/2 lbs. **Length:** 40.5. **Stock:** High-grade walnut. **Sights:** Blade front, open rear. **Features:** Break-open loading with manual cocking lever on top tang; takedown; extractor; Schnabel forearm; many options. Imported from Germany by Krieghoff International Inc.
Price: Hubertus single shot, from. **$5,995.00**
Price: Hubertus, magnum calibers **$6,995.00**

Model 1885 High Wall

Mossberg SSi-One Sporter

Mossberg SSi-One Varminter

Navy Arms #2 Creedmoor

MEACHAM HIGHWALL SILHOUETTE or SCHUETZEN RIFLE
Caliber: any rimmed cartridge. **Barrel:** 26-34". **Weight:** 8-15 lbs. **Sights:** none. Tang drilled for Win. base, 3/8 dovetail slot front. **Stock:** Fancy eastern walnut with cheekpiece; ebony insert in forearm tip. **Features:** Exact copy of 1885 Winchester. With most Winchester factory options available, including double set triggers. Introduced 1994. Made in U.S.A. by Meacham T&H Inc.
Price: From **$3,899.00**

MERKEL K-1 MODEL LIGHTWEIGHT STALKING RIFLE
Caliber: 243 Win., 270 Win., 7x57R, 308 Win., 30-06, 7mm Rem. Mag., 300 Win. Mag., 9.3x74R. **Barrel:** 23.6". **Weight:** 5.6 lbs. unscoped. **Stock:** Satin-finished walnut, fluted and checkered; sling-swivel studs. **Sights:** None (scope base furnished). **Features:** Franz Jager single-shot break-open action, cocking/uncocking slide-type safety, matte silver receiver, selectable trigger pull weights, integrated, quick detach 1" or 30mm optic mounts (optic not included). Imported from Germany by GSI.
Price: Standard, simple border engraving. **$3,795.00**
Price: Premium, light arabesque scroll **$3,795.00**
Price: Jagd, fine engraved hunting scenes **$4,395.00**

MODEL 1885 HIGH WALL RIFLE
Caliber: 30-40 Krag, 32-40, 38-55, 40-65 WCF, 45-70. **Barrel:** 26" (30-40), 28" to 30" all others. Douglas Premium #3 tapered octagon. **Weight:** 9 lbs, 4 oz. **Length:** 47" overall. **Stock:** Premium American black walnut. **Sights:** Marble's standard ivory bead front, #66 long blade top rear with reversible notch and elevator. **Features:** Receiver with octagon top, thick-

wall High Wall with coil spring action. Tang drilled, tapped for High Wall tang sight. Receiver, lever, hammer and breechblock color case-hardened. Available from Montana Armory, Inc.
Price: **$1,350.00**

MOSSBERG SSi-ONE SINGLE SHOT RIFLE
Caliber: 223 Rem., 22-250 Rem., 243 Win., 270 Win., 308 Rem., 30-06. **Barrel:** 24". **Weight:** 8 lbs. **Length:** 40". **Stock:** Satin-finished walnut, fluted and checkered; sling-swivel studs. **Sights:** None (scope base furnished). **Features:** Frame accepts interchangeable barrels including 12 gauge, fully rifled slug barrel and 12 ga., 3-1/2" chambered barrel with Ulti-Full Turkey choke tube. Lever-opening, break-action design; single-stage trigger; ambidextrous, top-tang safety; internal eject/extract selector. Introduced 2000. From Mossberg.
Price: SSi-One Sporter (standard barrel) or 12 ga., 3-1/2" chamber **$459.00**
Price: SSi-One Varmint (bull barrel, 22-250 Rem. only;
    weighs 10 lbs.) **$480.00**
Price: SSi-One 12 gauge Slug (fully rifled barrel, no sights,
    scope base) **$480.00**

NAVY ARMS 1873 SHARPS "QUIGLEY" RIFLE
Caliber: 45/70. **Barrel:** 34" heavy octagonal. **Stock:** Walnut. **Features:** Case-hardened receiver and military patchbox. Exact reproduction from "Quigley Down Under."
Price: **$1,826.00**

NAVY ARMS 1873 SHARPS NO. 2 CREEDMOOR RIFLE
Caliber: 45/70. **Barrel:** 30" tapered round. **Stock:** Walnut. **Sights:** Front globe, "soule" tang rear. **Features:** Nickel receiver and action. Lightweight sporting rifle.
Price: **$1,739.00**

Navy Arms 1874 Sharps Cavalry Carbine

Navy Arms Sharps #2 Sporting

Navy Arms Sharps #2 Silhouette

Navy Arms 1873 Springfield

Navy Arms John Bodine

NAVY ARMS 1874 SHARPS CAVALRY CARBINE
Caliber: 45-70. **Barrel:** 22". **Weight:** 7 lbs., 12 oz. **Length:** 39" overall. **Stock:** Walnut. **Sights:** Blade front, military ladder-type rear. **Features:** Replica of the 1874 Sharps military carbine. Color case-hardened receiver and furniture. Imported by Navy Arms.
Price: **$1,245.00**

Navy Arms Sharps Sporting Rifle
Same as the Navy Arms Sharps Plains Rifle except has pistol grip stock. Introduced 1997. Imported by Navy Arms.
Price: 45-70 only **$1,739.00**
Price: #2 Sporting with case-hardened receiver **$1,739.00**
Price: #2 Silhouette with full octagonal barrel **$1,739.00**

NAVY ARMS 1885 HIGH WALL RIFLE
Caliber: 45-70; others available on special order. **Barrel:** 28" round, 30" octagonal. **Weight:** 9.5 lbs. **Length:** 45-1/2" overall (30" barrel). **Stock:** Walnut. **Sights:** Blade front, vernier tang-mounted peep rear. **Features:** Replica of Winchester's High Wall designed by Browning. Color case-hardened receiver, blued barrel. Introduced 1998. Imported by Navy Arms.
Price: 28", round barrel, target sights **$1,169.00**
Price: 30" octagonal barrel, target sights **$1,169.00**

NAVY ARMS 1873 SPRINGFIELD CAVALRY CARBINE
Caliber: 45-70. **Barrel:** 22". **Weight:** 7 lbs. **Length:** 40-1/2" overall. **Stock:** Walnut. **Sights:** Blade front, military ladder rear. **Features:** Blued lockplate and barrel; color case-hardened breechblock; saddle ring with bar. Replica of 7th Cavalry gun. Imported by Navy Arms.
Price: **$1,195.00**

NAVY ARMS "JOHN BODINE" ROLLING BLOCK RIFLE
Caliber: 45-70. **Barrel:** 30" heavy octagonal. **Stock:** Walnut. **Sights:** Globe front, "soule" tang rear. **Features:** Double-set triggers.
Price: **$1,856.00**
Price: (#2 with deluxe nickel finished receiver) **$1,856.00**

Navy Arms Rolling Block Buffalo

New England
Firearms Handi-Rifle

New England Firearms Superlight

New England Firearms Survivor

NAVY ARMS ROLLING BLOCK BUFFALO RIFLE
Caliber: 45-70. **Barrel:** 26" heavy full octagon. **Weight:** 10 lbs., 12 oz.
Length: 43". **Stock:** European walnut. **Sights:** Rocky Mountain style front
blade and open notch rear. **Features:** Color case hardened receiver,
trigger guard, barrel band and buttplate.
Price: **$910.00**

NAVY ARMS SHARPS NO. 3 LONG RANGE RIFLE
Caliber: 45-70, 45-90. **Barrel:** 34" octagon. **Weight:** 10 lbs., 12 oz. **Length:**
51-1/2". **Stock:** Deluxe walnut. **Sights:** Globe target front and match
grade rear tang. **Features:** Shotgun buttplate, German silver forend cap,
color case hardenend receiver. Imported by Navy Arms.
Price: **$2,194.00**

NEW ENGLAND FIREARMS HANDI-RIFLE
Caliber: 204 Ruger, 22 Hornet, 223, 243, 30-30, 270, 280 Rem., 7mm-08,
308, 7.62x39 Russian, 30-06, 357 Mag., 35 Whelen, 44 Mag., 45-70, 500
S&W. **Barrel:** from 20" to 26", blued or stainless. **Weight:** 5.5 to 7 lbs.
Stock: Walnut-finished hardwood or synthetic. **Sights:** Vary by model, but

most have ramp front, folding rear, or are drilled and tapped for scope
mount. **Features:** Break-open action with side-lever release. Swivel studs
on all models. Blue finish. Introduced 1989. From New England Firearms.
Price: Various cartridges. **$292.00**
Price: 7.62x39 Russian, 35 Whelen, intr. 2006 . . . . **$292.00**
Price: Youth, 37" OAL, 11.75" LOP, 6.75 lbs. **$292.00**
Price: Handi-Rifle/Pardner combo, 20 ga. synthetic, intr. 2006 . . . . **$325.00**
Price: Handi-Rifle/Pardner Superlight, 20 ga., 5.5 lbs., intr. 2006 . . **$325.00**
Price: Synthetic **$302.00**
Price: Stainless **$364.00**
Price: Superlight, 20" barrel, 35.25" OAL, 5.5 lbs. **$302.00**

NEW ENGLAND FIREARMS SURVIVOR RIFLE
Caliber: 223, 308 Win., .410 shotgun, 45 Colt, single shot. **Barrel:** 20" to
22". **Weight:** 6 lbs. **Length:** 34.5" to 36" overall. **Stock:** Black polymer,
thumbhole design. **Sights:** None furnished; scope mount provided.
Features: Receiver drilled and tapped for scope mounting. Stock and
forend have storage compartments for ammo, etc.; comes with integral
swivels and black nylon sling. Introduced 1996. Made in U.S.A. by New
England Firearms.
Price: Blue or nickel finish **$304.00**

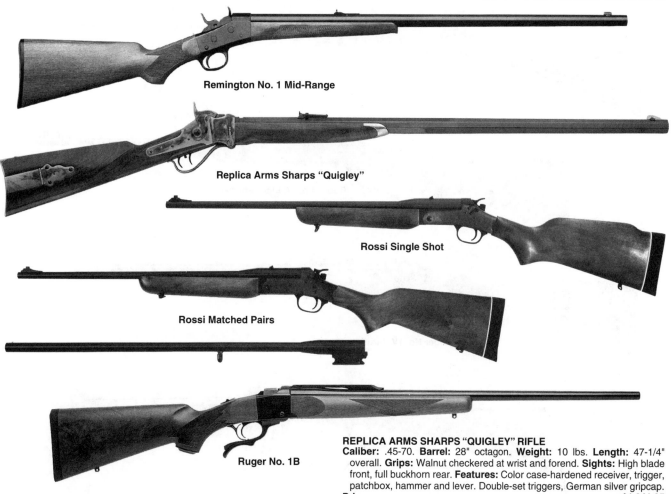

Remington No. 1 Mid-Range

Replica Arms Sharps "Quigley"

Rossi Single Shot

Rossi Matched Pairs

Ruger No. 1B

NEW ENGLAND FIREARMS SPORTSTER/VERSA PACK RIFLE
Caliber: 17M2, 17HMR, 22LR, 22 WMR, .410 bore single shot. **Barrel:** 20" to 22". **Weight:** 5.4 to 7 lbs. **Length:** 33" to 38.25" overall. **Stock:** Black polymer. **Sights:** Adjustable rear, ramp front. **Features:** Receiver drilled and tapped for scope mounting. Made in U.S.A. by New England Firearms.
Price: Sportster 17M2, 17HMR $193.00
Price: Sportster $161.00
Price: Sportster Youth $161.00
Price: Sportster 22/410 Versa Pack $176.00

REMINGTON MODEL XR-100 RANGEMASTER
Caliber: 204 Ruger, 223 Rem., 22-250 Rem. **Barrel:** 26" varmint-contour barrel with concave target crown, satin blued. **Weight:** 9.1 lbs. **Length:** 45.4" overall. **Stock:** Black-and-gray laminated thumbhole, rollover cheekpiece, beavertail forend with lightening-vent cuts under barrel channel, swivel studs. **Sights:** None. **Features:** Single-shot target rifle, based on Remington XP-100 pistol action. Externally adjustable Model 40-X target trigger adjustable from 1.5 to 3.5 pounds. Introduced 2005. Made in U.S. by Remington Arms Co., Inc.
Price: (2007) $1,057.00

REMINGTON NO. 1 ROLLING BLOCK MID-RANGE SPORTER
Caliber: 45-70. **Barrel:** 30" round. **Weight:** 8-3/4 lbs. **Length:** 46-1/2" overall. **Stock:** American walnut with checkered pistol grip and forend. **Sights:** Beaded blade front, adjustable center-notch buckhorn rear. **Features:** Recreation of the original. Polished blue metal finish. Many options available. Introduced 1998. Made in U.S.A. by Remington.
Price: $1,450.00
Price: Silhouette model with single-set trigger, heavy barrel $1,560.00

REPLICA ARMS SHARPS "QUIGLEY" RIFLE
Caliber: .45-70. **Barrel:** 28" octagon. **Weight:** 10 lbs. **Length:** 47-1/4" overall. **Grips:** Walnut checkered at wrist and forend. **Sights:** High blade front, full buckhorn rear. **Features:** Color case-hardened receiver, trigger, patchbox, hammer and lever. Double-set triggers, German silver gripcap.
Price: $1,241.95

REPLICA ARMS SHARPS "BIG GAME" RIFLE
Caliber: .45-70. **Barrel:** 28" Deluxe Heavy Round. **Weight:** 8.8 lbs. **Length:** 44.8" overall. **Grips:** Walnut. **Sights:** Gold bead front, full buckhorn rear. **Features:** Color case-hardened receiver, trigger, hammer and lever. Double-set triggers.
Price: $1,014.00

ROSSI SINGLE-SHOT RIFLES
Caliber: .17, .223, .243Win, .270Win, .30-06, .308, 7.62x39, .22-250. **Barrel:** 22" (Youth), 23". **Weight:** 6.25-7 lbs. **Stocks:** Wood, Black Synthetic (Youth). **Sights:** Adjustable sights, drilled and tapped for scope. **Features:** Single-shot break open, 13 models available, positive ejection, internal transfer bar mechanism, manual external safety, trigger block system, Taurus Security System, Matte blue finish, youth models available.
Price: . . . . $175.00 to $258.00

ROSSI MATCHED PAIRS
Gauge/Caliber: 12, 20, .410, .22Mag, .22LR, .17HMR, .223Rem, .243Win, .270Win, .30-06, .308Win, .50 (black powder). **Barrel:** 23", 28". **Weight:** 5-6.3 lbs. **Stocks:** Wood or black synthetic. **Sights:** Bead front on shotgun barrel, fully adjustable front and rear on rifle barrel, drilled and tapped for scope, fully adjustable fiber optic sights (black powder). **Features:** Single-shot break open, 27 models available, internal transfer bar mechanism, manual external safety, blue finish, trigger block system, Taurus Security System, youth models available.
Price: Rimfire/Shotgun . . . . $169.00 to $253.00
Price: Centerfire/Shotgun $297.00
Price: Black Powder Matched Pair . . . . $249.00 to $313.00

Ruger K1-B-BBZ

Ruger No. 1A Light Sporter

Ruger No. 1V Varminter

Ruger No. 1 RSI

Ruger No. 1H Tropical

RUGER NO. 1B SINGLE SHOT
Caliber: 23, 204 Ruger, 25-06, 270, 30-06, 7mm Rem. Mag., 300 Win. Mag., 308 Win. **Barrel:** 26" round tapered with quarter-rib; with Ruger 1" rings. **Weight:** 8.25 lbs. **Length:** 42.25" overall. **Stock:** Walnut, two-piece, checkered pistol grip and semi-beavertail forend. **Sights:** None, 1" scope rings supplied for integral mounts. **Features:** Under-lever, hammerless falling block design has auto ejector, top tang safety.
Price: 1B **$1,030.00**
Price: K1-B-BBZ stainless steel, laminated stock 25-06, 7mm mag,
270, 300 Win Mag., 243 Win., 30-06 . . . . **$1,032.00**

Ruger No. 1A Light Sporter
Caliber: 243, 270, 7x57, 30-06. **Weight:** 7.25 lbs. Similar to the No. 1B Standard Rifle except has lightweight 22" barrel, Alexander Henry-style forend, adjustable folding leaf rear sight on quarter-rib, dovetailed ramp front with gold bead.
Price: No. 1A **$1,030.00**

Ruger No. 1A Light Standard
Caliber: 204 Ruger. **Weight:** About 7.25 lbs. **Length:** 38.25" overall. Similar to the No. 1A Light Sporter but doesn't come with sights.
Price: No. 1-AB **$1,030.00**

Ruger No. 1V Varminter
Similar to the No. 1B Standard Rifle except has 24" heavy barrel. Semi-beavertail forend, barrel ribbed for target scope block, with 1" Ruger scope rings. Calibers 204 Ruger, 22-250, 223, 25-06. Weight about 9 lbs.
Price: No. 1V **$1,030.00**
Price: K1-V-BBZ stainless steel, laminated stock 204 Ruger **$1,065.00**

Ruger No. 1 RSI International
Similar to the No. 1B Standard Rifle except has lightweight 20" barrel, full-length International-style forend with loop sling swivel, adjustable folding leaf rear sight on quarter-rib, ramp front with gold bead. Calibers 243, 30-06, 270 and 7x57. Weight is about 7-1/4 lbs.
Price: No. 1 RSI **$1,065.00**

Ruger No. 1H Tropical Rifle
Similar to the No. 1B Standard Rifle except has Alexander Henry forend, adjustable folding leaf rear sight on quarter-rib, ramp front with dovetail gold bead. 24" heavy barrel. Calibers 375 H&H, 416 Rigby, 458 Lott, 405 Win. (weighs about 9 lbs.).
Price: No. 1H. **$1,030.00**
Price: K1-H-BBZ, S/S, 375 H&H, 458 Lott, 416 Rigby **$1,065.00**

Ruger No. 1S Medium Sporter

Shiloh 1874 Long Range Express

Shiloh 1874 Quigley

Shiloh 1874 Saddle

Shiloh 1874 Montana Roughrider

Ruger No. 1S Medium Sporter
Similar to the No. 1B Standard Rifle except has Alexander Henry-style forend, adjustable folding leaf rear sight on quarter-rib, ramp front sight base and dovetail-type gold bead front sight. Calibers: 9.3x74R, 45-70 with 22" barrel. Weighs about 7-1/2 lbs.
Price: No. 1S **$1,030.00**
Price: K1-S-BBZ, S/S, 45-70 . . . . **$1,065.00**

SHILOH RIFLE CO. SHARPS 1874 LONG RANGE EXPRESS
Caliber: 40-50 BN, 40-70 BN, 40-90 BN, 45-70 ST, 45-90 ST, 45-110 ST, 50-70 ST, 50-90 ST, 38-55, 40-70 ST, 40-90 ST. **Barrel:** 34" tapered octagon. **Weight:** 10-1/2 lbs. **Length:** 51" overall. **Stock:** Oil-finished walnut (upgrades available) with pistol grip, shotgun-style butt, traditional cheek rest, Schnabel forend. **Sights:** Customer's choice. **Features:** Re-creation of the Model 1874 Sharps rifle. Double-set triggers. Made in U.S.A. by Shiloh Rifle Mfg. Co.
Price: **$1,638.00**
Price: Sporting Rifle No. 1 (similar to above except with 30" bbl., blade front, buckhorn rear sight) **$1,638.00**
Price: Sporting Rifle No. 3 (similar to No. 1 except straight-grip stock, standard wood) **$1,547.00**

SHILOH RIFLE CO. SHARPS 1874 QUIGLEY
Caliber: 45-70, 45-110. **Barrel:** 34" heavy octagon. **Stock:** Military-style with patch box, standard grade American walnut. **Sights:** Semi buckhorn, interchangeable front and midrange vernier tang sight with windage. **Features:** Gold inlay initials, pewter tip, Hartford collar, case color or antique finish. Double-set triggers.
Price: **$2,903.00**

SHILOH RIFLE CO. SHARPS 1874 SADDLE RIFLE
Caliber: 38-55, 40-50 BN, 40-65 Win., 40-70 BN, 40-70 ST, 40-90 BN, 40-90 ST, 44-77 BN, 44-90 BN, 45-70 ST, 45-90 ST, 45-100 ST, 45-110 ST, 45-120 ST, 50-70 ST, 50-90 ST. **Barrel:** 26" full or half octagon. **Stock:** Semi fancy American walnut. Shotgun style with cheekrest. **Sights:** Buckhorn and blade. **Features:** Double-set trigger, numerous custom features can be added.
Price: **$1,594.00**

SHILOH RIFLE CO. SHARPS 1874 MONTANA ROUGHRIDER
Caliber: 38-55, 40-50 BN, 40-65 Win., 40-70 BN, 40-70 ST, 40-90 BN, 40-90 ST, 44-77 BN, 44-90 BN, 45-70 ST, 45-90 ST, 45-100 ST, 45-110 ST, 45-120 ST, 50-70 ST, 50-90 ST. **Barrel:** 30" full or half octagon. **Stock:** American walnut in shotgun or military style. **Sights:** Buckhorn and blade. **Features:** Double-set triggers, numerous custom features can be added.
Price: **$1,638.00**

Shiloh 1874 Creedmoor

Thompson/Center Encore

Thompson/Center Encore "Katahdin"

Thompson/Center Contender

Traditions 1874 Sharps Deluxe

SHILOH RIFLE CO. SHARPS CREEDMOOR TARGET
Caliber: 38-55, 40-50 BN, 40-65 Win., 40-70 BN, 40-70 ST, 40-90 BN, 40-90 ST, 44-77 BN, 44-90 BN, 45-70 ST, 45-90 ST, 45-100 ST, 45-110 ST, 45-120 ST, 50-70 ST, 50-90 ST. **Barrel:** 32", half round-half octagon. **Stock:** Extra fancy American walnut. Shotgun style with pistol grip. **Sights:** Customer's choice. **Features:** Single trigger, AA finish on stock, polished barrel and screws, pewter tip.
Price: **$2,485.00**

THOMPSON/CENTER ENCORE RIFLE
Caliber: 22-250, 223, 243, 204 Ruger, 6.8 Rem. Spec., 25-06, 270, 7mm-08, 308, 30-06, 7mm Rem. Mag., 300 Win. Mag. **Barrel:** 24", 26". **Weight:** 6 lbs., 12 oz. (24" barrel). **Length:** 38-1/2" (24" barrel). **Stock:** American walnut. Monte Carlo style; Schnabel forend or black composite. **Sights:** Ramp-style white bead front, fully adjustable leaf-type rear. **Features:** Interchangeable barrels; action opens by squeezing trigger guard; drilled and tapped for T/C scope mounts; polished blue finish. Introduced 1996. Made in U.S.A. by Thompson/Center Arms.
Price: . . . . $604.00 to $663.00
Price: Extra barrels **$277.00**

Thompson/Center Stainless Encore Rifle
Similar to blued Encore except stainless steel with blued sights, black composite stock and forend. Available in 22-250, 223, 7mm-08, 30-06, 308. Introduced 1999. Made in U.S.A. by Thompson/Center Arms.
Price: . . . . $680.00 to $738.00

THOMPSON/CENTER ENCORE "KATAHDIN" CARBINE
Caliber: 45-70 Gov't., 450 Marlin. **Barrel:** 18" with muzzle tamer. **Stock:** Composite.
Price: **$619.00**

Thompson/Center G2 Contender Rifle
Similar to the G2 Contender pistol, but in a compact rifle format. Weighs 5-1/2 lbs. Features interchangeable 23" barrels, chambered for 17 HMR, 22LR, 223 Rem., 30/30 Win. and 45/70 Gov't; plus a 45 Cal. Muzzleloading barrel. All of the 16-1/4" and 21" barrels made for the old-style Contender will fit. Introduced 2003. Made in U.S.A. by Thompson/Center Arms.
Price: . . . . $622.00 to $637.00

TRADITIONS 1874 SHARPS DELUXE RIFLE
Caliber: 45-70. **Barrel:** 32" octagonal; 1:18" twist. **Weight:** 11.67 lbs. **Length:** 48.8" overall. **Stock:** Checkered walnut with German silver nose cap and steel buttplate. **Sights:** Globe front, adjustable Creedmore rear with 12 inserts. **Features:** Color case-hardened receiver; double-set triggers. Introduced 2001. Imported from Pedersoli by Traditions.
Price: **$999.00**

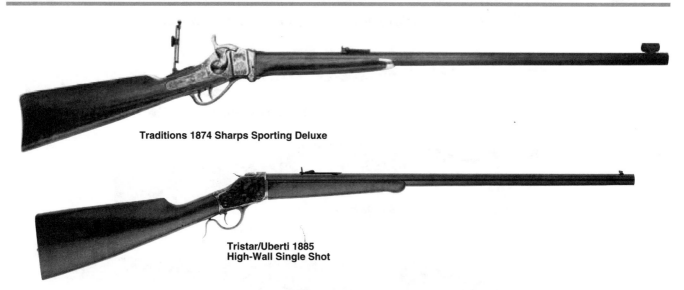

Traditions 1874 Sharps Sporting Deluxe

**Tristar/Uberti 1885
High-Wall Single Shot**

Traditions 1874 Sharps Sporting Deluxe Rifle
Similar to Sharps Deluxe but custom silver engraved receiver, European walnut stock and forend, satin finish, set trigger, fully adjustable.
Price: **$1,999.00**

Traditions 1874 Sharps Standard Rifle
Similar to 1874 Sharps Deluxe except has blade front and adjustable buckhorn-style rear sight. Weighs 10.67 pounds. Introduced 2001. Imported from Pedersoli by Traditions.
Price: **$769.00**

TRADITIONS ROLLING BLOCK SPORTING RIFLE
Caliber: 45-70. **Barrel:** 30" octagonal; 1:18" twist. **Weight:** 11.67 lbs. **Length:** 46.7" overall. **Stock:** Walnut. **Sights:** Blade front, adjustable rear. **Features:** Antique silver, color case-hardened receiver, drilled and tapped for tang/globe sights; brass buttplate and trigger guard. Introduced 2001. Imported from Pedersoli by Traditions.
Price: **$769.00**

TRADITIONS ROLLING BLOCK SPORTING RIFLE IN 30-30 WINCHESTER
Caliber: 30-30. **Barrel:** 28" round, blued. **Weight:** 8.25 lbs. **Stock:** Walnut. **Sights:** Fixed front, adjustable rear. **Features:** Steel buttplate, trigger guard, barrel band.
Price: **$769.00**

UBERTI 1874 SHARPS SPORTING RIFLE
Caliber: 45-70. **Barrel:** 30", 32", 34" octagonal. **Weight:** 10.57 lbs. with 32" barrel. **Length:** 48.9" with 32" barrel. **Stock:** Walnut. **Sights:** Dovetail front, Vernier tang rear. **Features:** Cut checkering, case-colored finish on frame, buttplate, and lever.
Price: Standard Sharps (2006), 30" barrel................... **$1,195.00**
Price: Special Sharps (2006) 32" barrel **$1,450.00**
Price: Deluxe Sharps (2006) 34" barrel.................... **$2,200.00**
Price: Down Under Sharps (2006) 34" barrel **$1,799.00**
Price: Adobe Walls Sharps (2006) 32" barrel **$1,750.00**
Price: Longe Range Sharps (2006) 34" barrel **$1,799.00**

UBERTI ROLLING BLOCK CARBINE AND RIFLE
Caliber: 22 LR, 22 WMR, 22 Hornet, 357 Mag., single shot. **Barrel:** 22" to 26". **Weight:** 4.9 lbs. (Carbine) **Length:** 35.5" overall. **Stock:** Walnut stock and forend. **Sights:** Blade front, fully adjustable open rear. **Features:** Resembles Remington New Model No. 4 carbine. Brass trigger guard and buttplate; color case-hardened frame, blued barrel. Imported by Uberti USA Inc.
Price: Carbine, 22" barrel................................ **$535.00**
Price: Rifle, 26" barrel **$600.00**

UBERTI HIGH-WALL RIFLE
Caliber: 45-70, 45-90, 45-120 single shot. **Barrel:** 28" to 23". **Weight:** 9.3 to 9.9 lbs. **Length:** 44.5" to 47" overall. **Stock:** Walnut stock and forend. **Sights:** Blade front, fully adjustable open rear. **Features:** Based on Winchester High-Wall design by John Browning. Color case-hardened frame and lever, blued barrel and buttplate. Imported by Uberti USA Inc.
Price: 1885 High-Wall, 28" round barrel..................... **$850.00**
Price: 1885 High-Wall Sporting, 30" octagonal barrel **$850.00**
Price: 1885 High-Wall Special Sporting, 32" octagonal barrel ... **$1,015.00**

Designs for sporting and utility purposes worldwide.

Beretta Express SSO

Beretta Model 455 SxS

Charles Daly Superior

Charles Daly Empire Combo

CZ 584 Solo

BERETTA EXPRESS SSO O/U DOUBLE RIFLES
Caliber: 375 H&H, 458 Win. Mag., 9.3x74R. **Barrel:** 25.5". **Weight:** 11 lbs. **Stock:** European walnut with hand-checkered grip and forend. **Sights:** Blade front on ramp, open V-notch rear. **Features:** Sidelock action with color case-hardened receiver (gold inlays on SSO6 Gold). Ejectors, double triggers, recoil pad. Introduced 1990. Imported from Italy by Beretta U.S.A.
Price: SSO6. . . . . **$21,000.00**
Price: SSO6 Gold **$23,500.00**

BERETTA MODEL 455 SxS EXPRESS RIFLE
Caliber: 375 H&H, 458 Win. Mag., 470 NE, 500 NE 3", 416 Rigby. **Barrel:** 23-1/2" or 25-1/2". **Weight:** 11 lbs. **Stock:** European walnut with hand-checkered grip and forend. **Sights:** Blade front, folding leaf V-notch rear. **Features:** Sidelock action with easily removable sideplates; color case-hardened finish (455), custom big game or floral motif engraving (455EELL). Double triggers, recoil pad. Introduced 1990. Imported from Italy by Beretta U.S.A.
Price: Model 455 . . . . **$36,000.00**
Price: Model 455EELL **$47,000.00**

CHARLES DALY SUPERIOR COMBINATION GUN
Caliber/Gauge: 12 ga. over 22 Hornet, 223 Rem., 22-250, 243 Win., 270 Win., 308 Win., 30-06. **Barrel:** 23.5", shotgun choked Imp. Cyl. **Weight:** About 7.5 lbs. **Stock:** Checkered walnut pistol grip buttstock and semi-beavertail forend. **Features:** Silvered, engraved receiver; chrome-moly steel barrels; double triggers; extractors; sling swivels; gold bead front sight. Introduced 1997. Imported from Italy by K.B.I. Inc.
Price: **$1,479.00**

Charles Daly Empire Combination Gun
Same as the Superior grade except has deluxe wood with European-style comb and cheekpiece; slim forend. Introduced 1997. Imported from Italy by K.B.I., Inc.
Price: **$2,189.00**

CZ 584 SOLO COMBINATION GUN
Caliber/Gauge: 7x57R; 12, 2-3/4" chamber. **Barrel:** 24.4". **Weight:** 7.37 lbs. **Length:** 45.25" overall. **Stock:** Circassian walnut. **Sights:** Blade front, open rear adjustable for windage. **Features:** Kersten-style double lump locking system; double-trigger Blitz-type mechanism with drop safety and adjustable set trigger for the rifle barrel; auto safety, dual extractors; receiver dovetailed for scope mounting. Imported from the Czech Republic by CZ-USA.
Price: **$851.00**

CZ 589 STOPPER OVER/UNDER GUN
Caliber: 458 Win. Magnum. **Barrels:** 21.7". **Weight:** 9.3 lbs. **Length:** 37.7" overall. **Stock:** Turkish walnut with sling swivels. **Sights:** Blade front, fixed rear. **Features:** Kersten-style action; Blitz-type double trigger; hammer-forged, blued barrels; satin-nickel, engraved receiver. Introduced 2001. Imported from the Czech Republic by CZ USA.
Price: **$2,999.00**
Price: Fully engraved model **$3,999.00**

Hoenig Rotary Round Action Double Rifle

Hoenig Rotary Round Action Combination

Krieghoff Classic Double Rifle

DAKOTA DOUBLE RIFLE
Caliber: 470 Nitro Express, 500 Nitro Express. **Barrel:** 25". **Stock:** Exhibition-grade walnut. **Sights:** Express-style. **Features:** Round action; selective ejectors; recoil pad; Americase. From Dakota Arms Inc.
Price: **$25,000.00**

EAA/BAIKAL IZH-94 COMBINATION GUN
Caliber/Gauge: 12, 3" chamber; 222 Rem., 223, 5.6x50R, 5.6x55E, 7x57R, 7x65R, 7.62x39, 7.62x51, 308, 7.62x53R, 7.62x54R, 30-06. **Barrel:** 24", 26"; imp., mod. and full choke tubes. **Weight:** 7.28 lbs. **Stock:** Walnut; rubber buttpad. **Sights:** Express-style. **Features:** Hammer-forged barrels with chrome-lined bores; machined receiver; single-selective or double triggers. Imported by European American Armory.
Price: Blued finish **$549.00**
Price: 20 ga./22 LR, 20/22 Mag, 3" **$629.00**

GARBI EXPRESS DOUBLE RIFLE
Caliber: 7x65R, 9.3x74R, 375 H&H. **Barrel:** 24-3/4". **Weight:** 7-3/4 to 8-1/2 lbs. **Length:** 41-1/2" overall. **Stock:** Turkish walnut. **Sights:** Quarter-rib with express sight. **Features:** Side-by-side double; H&H-pattern sidelock ejector with reinforced action, chopper lump barrels of Boehler steel; double triggers; fine scroll and rosette engraving, or full coverage ornamental; coin-finished action. Introduced 1997. Imported from Spain by Wm. Larkin Moore.
Price: **$19,900.00**

HOENIG ROTARY ROUND ACTION DOUBLE RIFLE
Caliber: Most popular calibers from 225 Win. to 9.3x74R. **Barrel:** 22" to 26". **Stock:** English Walnut; to customer specs. **Sights:** Swivel hood front with button release (extra bead stored in trap door gripcap), express-style rear on quarter-rib adjustable for windage and elevation; scope mount. **Features:** Round action opens by rotating barrels, pulling forward. Inertia extractor system, rotary safety blocks strikers. Single lever quick-detachable scope mount. Simple takedown without removing forend. Introduced 1997. Made in U.S.A. by George Hoenig.
Price: **$25,000.00**

HOENIG ROTARY ROUND ACTION COMBINATION
Caliber: 28 ga. **Barrel:** 26". **Weight:** 7 lbs. **Stock:** English Walnut to customer specs. **Sights:** Front ramp with button release blades. Foldable aperture tang sight windage and elevation adjustable. Quarter-rib with scope mount. **Features:** Round action opens by rotating barrels, pulling forward. Inertia extractor; rotary safety blocks strikers. Simple takedown without removing forend. Made in U.S.A. by George Hoenig.
Price: **$25,000.00**

KRIEGHOFF CLASSIC DOUBLE RIFLE
Caliber: 7x57R, 7x65R, 308 Win., 30-06, 8x57 JRS, 8x75RS, 9.3x74R, 375NE, 500/416NE, 470NE, 500NE. **Barrel:** 23.5". **Weight:** 7.3 to 8 lbs; 10-11 lbs. Big 5. **Stock:** High grade European walnut. Standard model

has conventional rounded cheekpiece, Bavaria model has Bavarian-style cheekpiece. **Sights:** Bead front with removable, adjustable wedge (375 H&H and below), standing leaf rear on quarter-rib. **Features:** Boxlock action; double triggers; short opening angle for fast loading; quiet extractors; sliding, self-adjusting wedge for secure bolting; Purdey-style barrel extension; horizontal firing pin placement. Many options available. Introduced 1997. Imported from Germany by Krieghoff International.
Price: With small Arabesque engraving **$8,950.00**
Price: With engraved sideplates **$12,300.00**
Price: For extra barrels **$5,450.00**
Price: Extra 20-ga., 28" shotshell barrels **$3,950.00**

Krieghoff Classic Big Five Double Rifle
Similar to the standard Classic except available in 375 Flanged Mag. N.E., 500/416 NE, 470 NE, 500 NE. Has hinged front trigger, non-removable muzzle wedge (models larger than 375 caliber), Universal Trigger System, Combi Cocking Device, steel trigger guard, specially weighted stock bolt for weight and balance. Many options available. Introduced 1997. Imported from Germany by Krieghoff International. Imperial Model introduced 2006.
Price: **$11,450.00**
Price: With engraved sideplates **$14,800.00**

LEBEAU-COURALLY EXPRESS RIFLE SxS
Caliber: 7x65R, 8x57JRS, 9.3x74R, 375 H&H, 470 N.E. **Barrel:** 24" to 26". **Weight:** 7-3/4 to 10-1/2 lbs. **Stock:** Fancy French walnut with cheekpiece. **Sights:** Bead on ramp front, standing left express rear on quarter-rib. **Features:** Holland & Holland-type sidelock with automatic ejectors; double triggers. Built to order only. Imported from Belgium by Wm. Larkin Moore.
Price: **$41,000.00**

MERKEL DRILLINGS
Caliber/Gauge: 12, 20, 3" chambers, 16, 2-3/4" chambers; 22 Hornet, 5.6x50R Mag., 5.6x52R, 222 Rem., 243 Win., 6.5x55, 6.5x57R, 7x57R, 7x65R, 308, 30-06, 8x57JRS, 9.3x74R, 375 H&H. **Barrel:** 25.6". **Weight:** 7.9 to 8.4 lbs. depending upon caliber. **Stock:** Oil-finished walnut with pistol grip; cheekpiece on 12-, 16-gauge. **Sights:** Blade front, fixed rear. **Features:** Double barrel locking lug with Greener cross bolt; scroll-engraved, case-hardened receiver; automatic trigger safety; Blitz action; double triggers. Imported from Germany by GSI.
Price: Model 96K (manually cocked rifle system), from **$7,495.00**
Price: Model 96K Engraved (hunting series on receiver) **$8,595.00**

Merkel 96K Engraved

Merkel 140-1

Rizzini Express

Savage 24F Combination

Springfield M6 Scout

MERKEL BOXLOCK DOUBLE RIFLES
Caliber: 5.6x52R, 243 Winchester, 6.5x55, 6.5x57R, 7x57R, 7x65R, 308 Winchester, 30-06 Springfield, 8x57 IRS, 9.3x74R. **Barrel:** 23.6". **Weight:** 7.7 oz. **Length:** NA. **Stock:** Walnut, oil finished, pistol grip. **Sights:** Fixed 100 meter. **Features:** Anson & Deely boxlock action with cocking indicators, double triggers, engraved color case-hardened receiver. Introduced 1995. Imported from Germany by GSI.
Price: Model 140-1, from. **$6,695.00**
Price: Model 140-1.1 (engraved silver-gray receiver), from **$7,795.00**

RIZZINI EXPRESS 90L DOUBLE RIFLE
Caliber: 30-06, 7x65R, 9.3x74R. **Barrel:** 24". **Weight:** 7-1/2 lbs. **Length:** 40" overall. **Stock:** Select European walnut with satin oil finish; English-style cheekpiece. **Sights:** Ramp front, quarter-rib with express sight. **Features:** Color case-hardened boxlock action; automatic ejectors; single selective trigger; polished blue barrels. Extra 20 gauge shotgun barrels available. Imported for Italy by Wm. Larkin Moore.
Price: With case. **$3,850.00**

SAVAGE 24F PREDATOR O/U COMBINATION GUN
Caliber/Gauge: 22 Hornet, 223, 30-30 over 12 (24F-12) or 22 LR, 22 Hornet, 223, 30-30 over 20 ga. (24F-20); 3" chambers. **Action:** Takedown, low rebounding visible hammer. Single trigger, barrel selector spur on hammer. **Barrel:** 24" separated barrels; 12 ga. has mod. choke tubes, 20 ga. has fixed Mod. choke. **Weight:** 8 lbs. **Length:** 40-1/2" overall. **Stock:** Black Rynite composition. **Sights:** Blade front, rear open adjustable for elevation. **Features:** Introduced 1989.
Price: 24F-12 . . . . **$661.00**
Price: 24F-20 . . . . **$628.00**

SPRINGFIELD ARMORY M6 SCOUT RIFLE/SHOTGUN
Caliber/Gauge: 22 LR or 22 Hornet over 410 bore. **Barrel:** 18.25". **Weight:** 4 lbs. **Length:** 32" overall. **Stock:** Folding detachable with storage for 15 22 LR, four 410 shells. **Sights:** Blade front, military aperture for 22; V-notch for 410. **Features:** All metal construction. Designed for quick disassembly and minimum maintenance. Folds for compact storage. Introduced 1982; reintroduced 1996. Imported from the Czech Republic by Springfield Armory.
Price: Parkerized **$185.00**
Price: Stainless steel **$219.00**

Designs for hunting, utility and sporting purposes, including training for competition.

Browning Buck Mark Target

Browning Semi-Auto 22

CZ 511 Auto

Henry U.S. Survival

AR-7 EXPLORER CARBINE

Caliber: 22 LR, 8-shot magazine. **Barrel:** 16". **Weight:** 2-1/2 lbs. **Length:** 34-1/2", 16-1/2" stowed. **Stock:** Molded Cycolac; snap-on rubber buttpad. **Sights:** Square blade front, aperture rear. **Features:** Takedown design stores barrel and action in hollow stock. Light enough to float. Reintroduced 1999. From AR-7 Industries, LLC.

Price: Black matte finish **$150.00**
Price: AR-20 Sporter (tubular stock, barrel shroud) **$200.00**
Price: AR-7 camo- or walnut-finish stock **$164.95**

BROWNING BUCK MARK SEMI-AUTO RIFLES

Caliber: 22 LR, 10+1. **Action:** A rifle version of the Buck Mark Pistol; straight blowback action; machined aluminum receiver with integral rail scope mount; manual thumb safety. **Barrel:** Recessed crowns. **Stock:** Stock and forearm with full pistol grip. **Features:** Action lock provided. Introduced 2001. Four model name variations for 2006, as noted below. **Sights:** FLD Target, FLD Carbon, and Target models have integrated scope rails. Sporter has Truglo/Marble fiber optic sights. Imported from Japan by Browning.

Price: FLD Target, 5.5 lbs., bull barrel, laminated stock **$601.00**
Price: Target, 5.4 lbs., blued bull barrel, wood stock **$583.00**
Price: Sporter, 4.4 lbs., blued sporter barrel w/sights **$583.00**

BROWNING SEMI-AUTO 22 RIFLE

Caliber: 22 LR, 11+1. **Barrel:** 16.25". **Weight:** 5.2 lbs. **Length:** 37" overall. **Stock:** Checkered select walnut with pistol grip and semi-beavertail forend. **Sights:** Gold bead front, folding leaf rear. **Features:** Engraved receiver with polished blue finish; cross-bolt safety; tubular magazine in buttstock; easy takedown for carrying or storage. The Grade VI is available with either grayed or blued receiver with extensive engraving with gold-plated animals: right side pictures a fox and squirrel in a woodland scene; left side shows a beagle chasing a rabbit. On top is a portrait of the beagle. Stock and forend are of high-grade walnut with a double-bordered cut checkering design. Introduced 1987. Imported from Japan by Browning.

Price: Grade I, scroll-engraved blued receiver **$557.00**
Price: Grade VI BL, gold-plated engraved blued receiver **$1,191.00**
Price: Grade VI GR, gold-plated engraved grayed receiver **$1,191.00**

CZ 511 AUTO RIFLE

Caliber: 22 LR, 8-shot magazine. **Barrel:** 22.2". **Weight:** 5.39 lbs. **Length:** 38.6" overall. **Stock:** Walnut with checkered pistol grip. **Sights:** Hooded front, adjustable rear. **Features:** Polished blue finish; detachable magazine; sling swivel studs. Imported from the Czech Republic by CZ-USA.

Price: **$351.00**

HENRY U.S. SURVIVAL RIFLE .22

Caliber: 22 LR, 8-shot magazine. **Barrel:** 16" steel lined. **Weight:** 2.5 lbs. **Stock:** ABS plastic. **Sights:** Blade front on ramp, aperture rear. **Features:** Takedown design stores barrel and action in hollow stock. Light enough to float. Silver, black or camo finish. Comes with two magazines. Introduced 1998. From Henry Repeating Arms Co.

Price: **$205.00**

MAGNUM RESEARCH MAGNUMLITE RIFLES

Caliber: 22 WMR, 17 HMR, 22 LR 17M2, 10-shot magazine. **Barrel:** 17" graphite. **Weight:** 4.45 lbs. **Length:** 35.5" overall. **Stock:** Hogue OverMolded synthetic or walnut. **Sights:** Integral scope base. **Features:** Magnum Lite graphite barrel, French grey anodizing, match bolt, target trigger. 22LR/17M2 rifles use factory Ruger 10/22 magazines. 4-5 lbs. average trigger pull. Graphite carbon-fiber barrel weighs approx. 13.04 ounces in .22 LR, 1:16 twist. Introduced: 2007. From Magnum Research, Inc.

Price: MLR22H 22 LR **$629.00**
Price: MLR22WMH 22 WMR **$719.00**
Price: MLR22WC, walnut stock **$799.00**

MARLIN MODEL 60 AUTO RIFLE

Caliber: 22 LR, 14-shot tubular magazine. **Barrel:** 19" round tapered. **Weight:** About 5-1/2 lbs. **Length:** 37-1/2" overall. **Stock:** Press-checkered, walnut-finished Maine birch with Monte Carlo, full pistol grip; Mar-Shield® finish. **Sights:** Ramp front, open adjustable rear. **Features:** Matted receiver is grooved for scope mount. Manual bolt hold-open; automatic last-shot bolt hold-open. Model 60C is similar except has hardwood Monte Carlo stock with Mossy Oak Break-Up camouflage pattern. From Marlin.

Price: **$200.00**
Price: With 4x scope **$208.00**
Price: (Model 60C camo) **$236.00**
Price: (Model 60DL walnut tone finish) **$236.00**

Marlin Model 60

Marlin Model 70PSS Papoose

Marlin 795

Remington 552 BDL Speedmaster

Marlin Model 60SS Self-Loading Rifle
Same as the Model 60 except breech bolt, barrel and outer magazine tube are made of stainless steel; most other parts are either nickel-plated or coated to match the stainless finish. Monte Carlo stock is of black/gray Maine birch laminate, and has nickel-plated swivel studs, rubber buttpad. Introduced 1993. From Marlin.
Price:	**$318.00**
Price: Model 60SSK (black fiberglass-filled stock)	**$269.00**
Price: Model 60SB (walnut-finished birch stock)	**$235.00**
Price: Model 60SB with 4x scope	**$270.00**

MARLIN 70PSS PAPOOSE STAINLESS RIFLE
Caliber: 22 LR, 7-shot magazine. **Barrel:** 16-1/4" stainless steel, Micro-Groove® rifling. **Weight:** 3-1/4 lbs. **Length:** 35-1/4" overall. **Stock:** Black fiberglass-filled synthetic with abbreviated forend, nickel-plated swivel studs, molded-in checkering. **Sights:** Ramp front with orange post, cut-away Wide Scan™ hood; adjustable open rear. Receiver grooved for scope mounting. **Features:** Takedown barrel; cross-bolt safety; manual bolt hold-open; last shot bolt hold-open; comes with padded carrying case. Introduced 1986. Made in U.S.A. by Marlin.
Price: **$318.00**

MARLIN MODEL 717M2 17 MACH 2 RIFLE
Caliber: 17 Mach 2, 7-shot. **Barrel:** 22" sporter. **Weight:** 5.5 lbs. **Length:** 37". **Stock:** Walnut-finished hardwood stock. **Sights:** Adjustable open rear, ramp front, grooved for scope mount. **Features:** Swivel studs, cross-bolt safety. Similar in design to 917 series bolt guns.
Price: 717M2 .... **$264.00**

MARLIN MODEL 7000 AUTO RIFLE
Caliber: 22 LR, 10-shot magazine. **Barrel:** 18" heavy target with 12-groove Micro-Groove® rifling, recessed muzzle. **Weight:** 5-1/2 lbs. **Length:** 37" overall. **Stock:** Black fiberglass-filled synthetic with Monte Carlo combo, swivel studs, molded-in checkering. **Sights:** None furnished; comes with

ring mounts. **Features:** Automatic last-shot bolt hold-open, manual bolt hold-open; cross-bolt safety; steel charging handle; blue finish, nickel-plated magazine. Introduced 1997. Made in U.S.A. by Marlin Firearms Co.
Price: **$263.00**

MARLIN MODEL 795 AUTO RIFLE
Caliber: 22. **Barrel:** 18" with 16-groove Micro-Groove® rifling. Ramp front sight, adjustable rear. Receiver grooved for scope mount. **Stock:** Black synthetic. **Features:** 10-round magazine, last shot hold-open feature. Introduced 1997. SS is similar to Model 795 excapt stainless steel barrel. Most other parts nickel-plated. Adjustable folding semi-buckhorn rear sights, ramp front high-visibility post and removeable cutaway wide scan hood. Made in U.S.A. by Marlin Firearms Co.
Price: 795	**$172.00**
Price: 795SS	**$255.00**

REMINGTON MODEL 552 BDL DELUXE SPEEDMASTER RIFLE
Caliber: 22 S (20), L (17) or LR (15) tubular mag. **Barrel:** 21" round tapered. **Weight:** 5-3/4 lbs. **Length:** 40" overall. **Stock:** Walnut. Checkered grip and forend. **Sights:** Big game. **Features:** Positive cross-bolt safety, receiver grooved for tip-off mount.
Price:	**$536.00**
Price: Smoothbore model (2007)	**$575.00**

REMINGTON 597 AUTO RIFLE
Caliber: 22 LR, 10-shot clip. **Barrel:** 20". **Weight:** 5-1/2 lbs. **Length:** 40" overall. **Stock:** Black synthetic. **Sights:** Big game. **Features:** Matte black finish, nickel-plated bolt. Receiver is grooved and drilled and tapped for scope mounts. Introduced 1997. Made in U.S.A. by Remington.
Price: Synthetic Scope Combo (2007)	**$229.00**
Price: Model 597 Magnum, 17 HMR, 8-shot clip	**$505.00**
Price: Model 597 LSS (laminated stock, stainless)	**$348.00**
Price: Model 597 SS (22 LR, stainless steel, black synthetic stock)	**$283.00**
Price: Model 597 LS heavy barrel (22 LR, laminated stock)	**$265.00**
Price: Model 597 Magnum LS heavy barrel (22 WMR, lam. stock)	**$569.00**
Price: Model 597 LS HB, 10-shot clip	**$337.00**

Remington 597

Ruger 10/22 Deluxe Sporter

Ruger 10/22 Target

Savage Model 64FV

RUGER 10/22 AUTOLOADING CARBINE
Caliber: 22 LR, 10-shot rotary magazine. **Barrel:** 18-1/2" round tapered. **Weight:** 5 lbs. **Length:** 37-1/4" overall. **Stock:** American hardwood with pistol grip and barrel band or synthetic. **Sights:** Brass bead front, folding leaf rear adjustable for elevation. **Features:** Detachable rotary magazine fits flush into stock, cross-bolt safety, receiver tapped and grooved for scope blocks or tip-off mount. Scope base adaptor furnished with each rifle.
Price: Model 10/22 RB (blue) **$250.00**
Price: Model 10/22CRR Compact RB (blued), intr. 2006 . . . . **$285.00**

Ruger 10/22 Deluxe Sporter
Same as 10/22 Carbine except walnut stock with hand checkered pistol grip and forend; straight buttplate, no barrel band, has sling swivels.
Price: Model 10/22 DSP **$330.00**

Ruger 10/22T Target Rifle
Similar to the 10/22 except has 20" heavy, hammer-forged barrel with tight chamber dimensions, improved trigger pull, laminated hardwood stock dimensioned for optical sights. No iron sights supplied. Introduced 1996. Made in U.S.A. by Sturm, Ruger & Co.
Price: 10/22T **$450.00**
Price: K10/22T, stainless steel **$485.00**

Ruger K10/22RPF All-Weather Rifle
Similar to the stainless K10/22/RB except has black composite stock of thermoplastic polyester resin reinforced with fiberglass; checkered grip and forend. Brushed satin, natural metal finish with clear hardcoat finish. Weighs 5 lbs., measures 36-3/4" overall. Introduced 1997. From Sturm, Ruger & Co.
Price: **$295.00**

SAVAGE MODEL 64G AUTO RIFLE
Caliber: 22 LR, 10-shot magazine. **Barrel:** 20", 21". **Weight:** 5-1/2 lbs. **Length:** 40", 41". **Stock:** Walnut-finished hardwood with Monte Carlo-type comb, checkered grip and forend. **Sights:** Bead front, open adjustable rear. Receiver grooved for scope mounting. **Features:** Thumb-operated rotating safety. Blue finish. Side ejection, bolt hold-open device. Introduced 1990. Made in Canada, from Savage Arms.
Price: **$162.00**
Price: Model 64FSS, stainless **$202.00**
Price: Model 64F, black synthetic stock **$135.00**
Price: Model 64GXP package gun includes
    4x15 scope and mounts **$171.00**
Price: Model 64FXP (black stock, 4x15 scope) **$142.00**
Price: Model 64F Camo **$135.00**

Savage Model 64FV Auto Rifle
Similar to the Model 64F except has heavy 21" barrel with recessed crown; no sights provided, comes with Weaver-style bases. Introduced 1998. Imported from Canada by Savage Arms, Inc.
Price: **$135.00**
Price: Model 64FSS, stainless **$202.00**

62 63 RIFLE
Caliber: 22 LR, 10-shot tube-fed magazine. **Barrel:** 23". **Weight:** 72 oz. **Length:** 32-1/2". **Stock:** Hand-fitted walnut-finished hardwood. **Sights:** Adjustable rear, fixed front. **Features:** Manual safety, metal buttplate, can accept Taurus tang sight. Charged and cocked with operating plunger at front of forend. Available in blue or polished stainless steel.
Price: 63 . . . . **$329.00**
Price: 63SS **$349.00**

THOMPSON/CENTER 22 LR CLASSIC RIFLE
Caliber: 22 LR, 8-shot magazine. **Barrel:** 22" match-grade. **Weight:** 5-1/2 pounds. **Length:** 39-1/2" overall. **Stock:** Satin-finished American walnut with Monte Carlo-type comb and pistol gripcap, swivel studs. **Sights:** Ramp-style front and fully adjustable rear, both with fiber optics. **Features:** All-steel receiver drilled and tapped for scope mounting; barrel threaded to receiver; thumb-operated safety; trigger guard safety lock included. New .22 Classic Benchmark TGT target rifle variant has 18" heavy barrel, brown laminated target stock, blued with matte finish, 10-shot magazine and no sights; drilled and tapped.
Price: T/C 22 LR Classic (blue) **$396.00**
Price: T/C 22 LR Classic Benchmark **$505.00**

Classic and modern models for sport and utility, including training.

Browning BL-22

Henry Lever-Action 22

Henry Golden Boy 22

Henry Pump-Action 22

Marlin Model 39A

BROWNING BL-22 RIFLES

Action: Short-throw lever action, side ejection. Rack-and-pinion lever. Tubular magazines, with 15+1 capacity for 22LR. **Barrel:** Recessed muzzle. **Stock:** Walnut, two-piece straight grip Western style. **Trigger:** Half-cock hammer safety; fold-down hammer. **Sights:** Bead post front, folding-leaf rear. Steel receiver grooved for scope mount. **Weight:** 5-5.4 lbs. **Length:** 36.75-40.75" overall. **Features:** Action lock provided. Introduced 1996. FLD Grade II Octagon has octagonal 24" barrel, silver nitride receiver with scroll engraving, gold-colored trigger. FLD Grade I has satin-nickel receiver, blued trigger, no stock checkering. FLD Grade II has satin-nickel receivers with scroll engraving; gold-colored trigger, cut checkering. Both introduced 2005. Grade I has blued receiver and trigger, no stock checkering. Grade II has gold-colored trigger, cut checkering, blued receiver with scroll engraving. Imported from Japan by Browning.

Price: BL-22 Grade I/II, from **$480.00**
Price: BL-22 FLD Grade I/II, from **$514.00**
Price: BL-22 FLD, Grade II Octagon **$756.00**

HENRY LEVER-ACTION 22

Caliber: 22 Long Rifle (15-shot). **Barrel:** 18-1/4" round. **Weight:** 5-1/2 lbs. **Length:** 34" overall. **Stock:** Walnut. **Sights:** Hooded blade front, open adjustable rear. **Features:** Polished blue finish; full-length tubular magazine; side ejection; receiver grooved for scope mounting. Introduced 1997. Made in U.S.A. by Henry Repeating Arms Co.

Price: **$279.95**
Price: Youth model (33" overall, 11-round 22 LR) **$279.95**

HENRY GOLDEN BOY 22 LEVER-ACTION RIFLE

Caliber: 22 LR, 22 Magnum, 16-shot. **Barrel:** 20" octagonal. **Weight:** 6.25 lbs. **Length:** 38" overall. **Stock:** American walnut. **Sights:** Blade front, open rear. **Features:** Brasslite receiver, brass buttplate, blued barrel and lever. Introduced 1998. Made in U.S.A. from Henry Repeating Arms Co.

Price: **$409.95**
Price: Magnum **$485.00**

HENRY PUMP-ACTION 22 PUMP RIFLE

Caliber: 22 LR, 15-shot. **Barrel:** 18.25". **Weight:** 5.5 lbs. **Length:** NA. **Stock:** American walnut. **Sights:** Bead on ramp front, open adjustable rear. **Features:** Polished blue finish; receiver groved for scope mount; grooved slide handle; two barrel bands. Introduced 1998. Made in U.S.A. from Henry Repeating Arms Co.

Price: **$309.95**

MARLIN MODEL 39A GOLDEN LEVER-ACTION RIFLE

Caliber: 22, S (26), L (21), LR (19), tubular mag. **Barrel:** 24" Micro-Groove®. **Weight:** 6-1/2 lbs. **Length:** 40" overall. **Stock:** Checkered American black walnut; Mar-Shield® finish. Swivel studs; rubber buttpad. **Sights:** Bead ramp front with detachable Wide-Scan™ hood, folding rear semi-buckhorn adjustable for windage and elevation. **Features:** Hammer block safety; rebounding hammer. Takedown action, receiver tapped for scope mount (supplied), offset hammer spur, gold-colored steel trigger. From Marlin Firearms.

Price: **$552.00**

Remington Model 572 BDL Deluxe Fieldmaster

Ruger Model 96/22

Ruger Model 96/17

Taurus 62R

Taurus 72C-SS

REMINGTON 572 BDL DELUXE FIELDMASTER PUMP RIFLE
Caliber: 22 S (20), L (17) or LR (15), tubular mag. **Barrel:** 21" round tapered. **Weight:** 5-1/2 lbs. **Length:** 40" overall. **Stock:** Walnut with checkered pistol grip and slide handle. **Sights:** Big game. **Features:** Cross-bolt safety; removing inner magazine tube converts rifle to single shot; receiver grooved for tip-off scope mount.
Price: **$407.00**

RUGER MODEL 96 LEVER-ACTION RIFLE
Caliber: 22 WMR, 9 rounds; 44 Magnum, 4 rounds; 17 HMR 9 rounds. **Barrel:** 18-1/2". **Weight:** 5-1/4 lbs. **Length:** 37-1/4" overall. **Stock:** Hardwood. **Sights:** Gold bead front, folding leaf rear. **Features:** Sliding cross button safety, visible cocking indicator; short-throw lever action. Introduced 1996. Made in U.S.A. by Sturm, Ruger & Co.
Price: 96/22M (22 WMR). **$435.00**
Price: 96/22M (44 Mag.) **$599.00**
Price: 96/17M (17 HMR) **$425.00**

TAURUS MODEL 62 PUMP RIFLE
Caliber: 22 LR, 12- or 13-shot. **Barrel:** 16-1/2" or 23" round. **Weight:** 72 oz. to 80 oz. **Length:** 39" overall. **Stock:** Premium hardwood. **Sights:** Adjustable rear, bead blade front, optional tang. **Features:** Blue, case

hardened or stainless, bolt-mounted safety, pump action, manual firing pin block, integral security lock system. Imported from Brazil by Taurus International.
Price: From **$299.00**

Taurus Model 72 Pump Rifle
Same as Model 62 except chambered in 22 Magnum or .17 HMR; 16-1/2" bbl. holds 10-12 shots, 23" bbl. holds 11-13 shots. Weighs 72 oz. to 80 oz. Introduced 2001. Imported from Brazil by Taurus International.
Price: From **$329.00**

TAURUS THUNDERBOLT PUMP ACTION
Caliber: 38/.357, 45 Long Colt, 12 or 14 rounds. **Barrel:** 26" blue or polished stainless. **Weight:** 8.1 lbs. **Length:** 43" overall. **Stock:** Hardwood stock and forend. Gloss finish. **Sights:** Longhorn adjustable rear. Introduced 2004. Imported from Brazil by Taurus International.
Price: C357BC **$515.00**
Price: C45BR **$639.00**

Includes models for a variety of sports, utility and competitive shooting.

Anchutz 1710D

Browning T-Bolt

Chipmunk Standard

Chipmunk Deluxe

ANSCHUTZ 1416D/1516D CLASSIC RIFLES
Caliber: 22 LR (1416D), 5-shot clip; 22 WMR (1516D), 4-shot clip. **Barrel:** 22-1/2". **Weight:** 6 lbs. **Length:** 41" overall. **Stock:** European hardwood with walnut finish; classic style with straight comb, checkered pistol grip and forend. **Sights:** Hooded ramp front, folding leaf rear. **Features:** Uses Match 64 action. Adjustable single stage trigger. Receiver grooved for scope mounting. Imported from Germany by AcuSport Corp.
Price: 1416D, 22 LR **$755.95**
Price: 1516D, 22 WMR **$779.95**
Price: 1416D Classic left-hand **$679.95**

Anschutz 1416D/1516D Walnut Luxus Rifles
Similar to the Classic models except have European walnut stocks with Monte Carlo cheekpiece, slim forend with Schnabel tip, cut checkering on grip and forend. Introduced 1997. Imported from Germany by AcuSport Corp.
Price: 1416D (22 LR) **$755.95**
Price: 1516D (22 WMR) **$779.95**

ANSCHUTZ 1518D LUXUS BOLT-ACTION RIFLE
Caliber: 22 WMR, 4-shot magazine. **Barrel:** 19-3/4". **Weight:** 5-1/2 lbs. **Length:** 37-1/2" overall. **Stock:** European walnut. **Sights:** Blade on ramp front, folding leaf rear. **Features:** Receiver grooved for scope mounting; single stage trigger; skip-line checkering; rosewood forend tip; sling swivels. Imported from Germany by AcuSport Corp.
Price: **$1,186.95**

ANSCHUTZ 1710D CUSTOM RIFLE
Caliber: 22 LR, 5-shot clip. **Barrel:** 24-1/4". **Weight:** 7-3/8 lbs. **Length:** 42-1/2" overall. **Stock:** Select European walnut. **Sights:** Hooded ramp front, folding leaf rear; drilled and tapped for scope mounting. **Features:** Match 54 action with adjustable single-stage trigger; roll-over Monte Carlo cheekpiece, slim forend with Schnabel tip, Wundhammer palm swell on pistol grip, rosewood gripcap with white diamond insert; skip-line checkering on grip and forend. Introduced 1988. Imported from Germany by AcuSport Corp.
Price: **$1,289.95**

BROWNING T-BOLT RIMFIRE RIFLE
Caliber: 22 LR, 10-round rotary box Double Helix magazine. **Barrel:** 22", free-floating, semi-match chamber, target muzzle crown. **Weight:** 4.8 lbs. **Length:** 40.1" overall. **Stock:** Walnut, satin finish, synthetic buttplate. **Sights:** None. **Features:** Straight-pull bolt-action, three-lever trigger adjustable for pull weight, dual action screws, sling swivel studs. Crossbolt lockup, enlarged bolt handle, one-piece dual extractor with integral spring and red cocking indicator band, gold-tone trigger. Top-tang, thumb-operated two-position safety, drilled and tapped for scope mounts. Varmint model has raised Monte Carlo comb, heavy barrel, wide forearm. Introduced 2006. Imported from Japan by Browning.
Price: Sporter **$623.00**
Price: Target/Varmint, intr. 2007 . . . . **$647.95**

CHARLES DALY SUPERIOR II RIMFIRE RIFLE
Caliber: 22LR, 22MRF, 17HRM. **Barrel:** 22". **Weight:** 6 pounds. **Sights:** None. Drilled and tapped for scope mounts. **Features:** Manufactured by Zastava. Walnut stock, two-position safety; 5-round magazine capacity. Introduced 2005.
Price: 22LR **$259.00**
Price: 22WMR **$299.00**
Price: 17HMR **$334.00**

CHIPMUNK SINGLE SHOT RIFLE
Caliber: 22 LR, 22 WMR, single shot. **Barrel:** 16-1/8". **Weight:** About 2-1/2 lbs. **Length:** 30" overall. **Stocks:** American walnut. **Sights:** Post on ramp front, peep rear adjustable for windage and elevation. **Features:** Drilled and tapped for scope mounting using special Chipmunk base ($13.95). Engraved model also available. Made in U.S.A. Introduced 1982. From Rogue Rifle Co., Inc.
Price: Standard **$194.25**
Price: Standard 22 WMR **$209.95**
Price: Deluxe (better wood, checkering) **$246.95**
Price: Deluxe 22 WMR **$262.95**
Price: Laminated stock **$209.95**
Price: Laminated stock, 22 WMR **$225.95**
Price: Bull barrel models of above, add **$16.00**

Cooper Model 57 Classic

Cooper Custom Classic

CZ 452 Lux

CZ 452 Varmint

CZ 452 American Classic

CHIPMUNK TM (TARGET MODEL)
Caliber: 22 S, L, or LR. **Barrel:** 18" blue. **Weight:** 5 lbs. **Length:** 33". Stocks: Walnut with accessory rail. **Sights:** 1/4 minute micrometer adjustable. **Features:** Manually cocking single shot bolt action, blue receiver, adjustable buttplate and buttpad.
Price: $329.95

COOPER MODEL 57-M BOLT-ACTION RIFLE
Caliber: 22 LR, 22 WMR, 17 HMR, 17 Mach 2. **Barrel:** 22" or 24" stainless steel or 4140 match grade. **Weight:** 6.5-7.5 lbs. **Stock:** AA-AAA select Claro walnut, 22 lpi hand checkering. **Sights:** None furnished. **Features:** Three rear locking lug, repeating bolt-action with 5-shot mag. for 22 LR and 17M2; 4-shot mag for 22 WMR and 17 HMR. Fully adjustable trigger. Left-hand models add $150 to base rifle price. 1/4"-group rimfire accuracy guarantee at 50 yds.; 1/2"-group centerfire accuracy guarantee at 100 yds. Options include wood upgrades, case-color metalwork, barrel fluting, custom LOP, and many others.
Price: Classic.. $1,349.00
Price: LVT $1,459.00
Price: Custom Classic $1,995.00
Price: Western Classic $2,698.00
Price: TRP-3 (22 LR only, benchrest style) $1,295.00
Price: Jackson Squirrel Rifle $1,498.00
Price: Jackson Hunter (synthetic) $1,298.00

CZ 452 LUX BOLT-ACTION RIFLE
Caliber: 22 LR, 22 WMR, 5-shot detachable magazine. **Barrel:** 24.8". **Weight:** 6.6 lbs. **Length:** 42.63" overall. **Stock:** Walnut with checkered pistol grip. **Sights:** Hooded front, fully adjustable tangent rear. **Features:** All-steel construction, adjustable trigger, polished blue finish. Imported from the Czech Republic by CZ-USA.
Price: 22 LR, 22 WMR $378.00

CZ 452 Varmint Rifle
Similar to the Lux model except has heavy 20.8" barrel; stock has beavertail forend; weighs 7 lbs.; no sights furnished. Available only in 22 LR. Imported from the Czech Republic by CZ-USA.
Price: $407.00

CZ 452 American Classic Bolt-Action Rifle
Similar to the CZ 452 M 2E Lux except has classic-style stock of Circassian walnut; 22.5" free-floating barrel with recessed target crown; receiver dovetail for scope mounting. Introduced 1999. Imported from the Czech Republic by CZ-USA.
Price: 22 LR, 22 WMR $420.00

HARRINGTON & RICHARDSON
ULTRA HEAVY BARREL 22 MAG RIFLE
Caliber: 22 WMR, single shot. **Barrel:** 22" bull. **Stock:** Cinnamon laminated wood with Monte Carlo cheekpiece. **Sights:** None furnished; scope mount rail included. **Features:** Hand-checkered stock and forend; deep-crown rifling; tuned trigger; trigger locking system; hammer extension. Introduced 2001. From H&R 1871 LLC.
Price: $193.00

Henry "Mini" Bolt 22

Kimber 22 Classic

Kimber 22 SuperAmerica

Kimber 22 SVT

Kimber 22 HS

HENRY ACU-BOLT RIFLE
Caliber: 22, 22 Mag., 17HMR; single shot. **Barrel:** 20". **Weight:** 4.15 lbs. **Length:** 36". **Stock:** One-piece fiberglass synthetic. **Sights:** Scope mount and 4x scope included. **Features:** Stainless barrel and receiver, bolt-action.
Price: **$325.00**

HENRY "MINI" BOLT ACTION 22 RIFLE
Caliber: 22 LR, single shot youth gun. **Barrel:** 16" stainless, 8-groove rifling. **Weight:** 3.25 lbs. **Length:** 30", LOP 11-1/2". **Stock:** Synthetic, pistol grip, wraparound checkering and beavertail forearm. **Sights:** William Fire sights. **Features:** One-piece bolt configuration manually operated safety.
Price: **$169.95**

KIMBER 22 CLASSIC BOLT-ACTION RIFLE
Caliber: 22 LR and 17 Mach 2, 5-shot magazine. **Barrel:** 18", 22", 24" match grade; 11-degree target crown. **Weight:** 5 to 8 lbs. **Length:** 35" to 43". **Stock:** Classic Claro walnut, hand-cut checkering, steel gripcap, swivel studs. **Sights:** None, drilled and tapped. **Features:** All-new action with Mauser-style full-length claw extractor, two-position wing safety, match trigger, pillar-bedded action with recoil lug. Introduced 1999. Made in U.S.A. by Kimber Mfg., Inc.

Price: Classic 22. .... **$1,147.00**
Price: Classic Varmint (22 or17M2) **$1,055.00**
Price: Hunter (22) **$809.00**
Price: Hunter (17M2) **$846.00**

Kimber 22 SuperAmerica Bolt-Action Rifle
Similar to 22 Classic except has AAA Claro walnut stock with wraparound 22 lpi hand-cut checkering, ebony forend tip, beaded cheekpiece. Introduced 1999. Made in U.S.A. by Kimber Mfg., Inc.
Price: **$1,865.00**

Kimber 22 SVT Bolt-Action Rifle
Similar to 22 Classic except has 18" stainless steel, fluted bull barrel, gray laminated, high-comb target-style stock with deep pistol grip, high comb, beavertail forend with bipod stud. Weighs 7.5 lbs., overall length 36.5". Matte finish on action. Introduced 1999. Made in U.S.A. by Kimber Mfg., Inc.
Price: 22 model. **$1,007.00**
Price: 17M2 model **$1,055.00**

Kimber 22 HS (Hunter Silhouette) Bolt-Action Rifle
Similar to 22 Classic except 24" medium sporter match-grade barrel with half-fluting; high comb, walnut, Monte Carlo target stock with 18 lpi checkering; matte blue metal finish. Introduced 1999. Made in U.S.A. by Kimber Mfg., Inc.
Price: **$915.00**

Marlin 917V

Marlin Model 915YN "Little Buckaroo"

Marlin Model 980S

Marlin 980V

Marlin 925

Marlin 925C

MARLIN MODEL 917/717 17 HMR/17 MACH 2 BOLT-ACTION RIFLES
Caliber: 17 HMR, 17 Mach 2, 7-shot. **Barrel:** 22". **Weight:** 6 lbs., stainless 7 lbs. **Length:** 41". **Stock:** Checkered walnut Monte Carlo SS, laminated black/grey. **Sights:** No sights but receiver grooved. **Features:** Swivel studs, positive thumb safety, red cocking indicator, safety lock, SS 1" brushed aluminum scope rings.
Price: 917 (new version 17 HMR intr. 2006, black synthetic stock) . **$269.00**
Price: 917V (17 HMR, walnut-finished hardwood stock) **$292.00**
Price: 917VS (17 HMR, heavy stainless barrel) **$433.00**
Price: 917VR (17 HMR, intr. 2006, heavy barrel) **$282.00**
Price: 917VR (17 HMR, heavy stainless fluted barrel) **$459.00**
Price: 917M2 (17 Mach 2, walnut-finished hardwood stock) **$274.00**
Price: 917M2S (17 Mach 2, 22" heavy stainless barrel) **$410.00**

MARLIN MODEL 915YN "LITTLE BUCKAROO"
Caliber: 22 S, L, LR, single shot. **Barrel:** 16-1/4" Micro-Groove®. **Weight:** 4-1/4 lbs. **Length:** 33-1/4" overall. **Stock:** One-piece walnut-finished, press-checkered Maine birch with Monte Carlo; Mar-Shield® finish. **Sights:** Ramp front, adjustable open rear. **Features:** Beginner's rifle with thumb safety, easy-load feed throat, red cocking indicator. Receiver grooved for scope mounting. Introduced 1989.
Price: **$225.00**
Price: 915YS (stainless steel with fire sights) **$255.00**

MARLIN MODEL 980S BOLT-ACTION RIFLE
Caliber: 22 LR, 7-shot clip magazine. **Barrel:** 22" Micro-Groove®. **Weight:** 6 lbs. **Length:** 41" overall. **Stock:** Black fiberglass-filled synthetic with

nickel-plated swivel studs and molded-in checkering. **Sights:** Ramp front with orange post and cutaway Wide-Scan™ hood, adjustable semi-buckhorn folding rear. **Features:** Stainless steel barrel, receiver, front breech bolt and striker; receiver grooved for scope mounting. Introduced 1994. Model 880SQ (Squirrel Rifle) is similar but has heavy 22" barrel. Made in U.S.A. by Marlin.
Price: 980S **$349.00**
Price: 980V, heavy target barrel, 7 lbs., no sights **$349.00**

Marlin Model 981T Bolt-Action Rifle
Same as Marlin 980S except blued steel, tubular magazine, holds 17 Long Rifle cartridges. Weighs 6 lbs.
Price: **$229.00**

Marlin Model 925 Bolt-Action Repeater
Similar to Marlin 980S, except walnut-finished hardwood stock, adjustable open rear sight, ramp front. Weighs 5.5 lbs.
Price: **$229.00**
Price: With 4x scope and mount **$239.00**

Marlin Model 925R Bolt-Action Repeater
Similar to Marlin 925, except Monte Carlo black-fiberglass synthetic stock. Weighs 5.5 lbs. OAL: 41". Introduced 2006.
Price: **$229.00**
Price: With 4x scope and mount **$239.00**

Marlin Model 925C Bolt-Action Repeater
Same as Model 980S except Mossy Oak® Break-Up camouflage stock. Made in U.S.A. by Marlin. Weighs 5.5 lbs.
Price: **$268.00**

Marlin 983T

Rossi Matched Pair

Ruger K77/22 Varmint

MARLIN MODEL 982 BOLT-ACTION RIFLE
Caliber: 22 WMR. **Barrel:** 22" Micro-Groove®. **Weight:** 6 lbs. **Length:** 41" overall. **Stock:** Walnut Monte Carlo genuine American black walnut with swivel studs; full pistol grip; classic cut checkering; rubber rifle butt pad; tough Mar-Shield® finish. **Sights:** Adjustable semi-buckhorn folding rear, ramp front sight with brass bead and Wide-Scan™ front sight hood. **Features:** 7-shot clip, thumb safety, red cocking indicator, receiver grooved for scope mount. 982S has stainless steel front breech bolt, barrel, receiver and bolt knob. All other parts are either stainless steel or nickel-plated. Has black Monte Carlo stock of fiberglass-filled polycarbonate with molded-in checkering, nickel-plated swivel studs. Introduced 2005. Model 982S has selected heavy 22" stainless steel barrel with recessed muzzle, and comes without sights; receiver is grooved for scope mount and 1" ring mounts are included. Weighs 7 lbs. Introduced 1997. Made in U.S.A. by Marlin Firearms Co.
Price: 982 . . . . **$341.00**
Price: 982L (laminated hardwood stock, 6.25 lbs). **$361.00**
Price: 982S (stainless parts, 6.25 lbs). **$377.00**
Price: 982VS (heavy stainless barrel, 7 lbs). **$357.00**

Marlin Model 925M/925MC Bolt-Action Rifles
Similar to the Model 982 except chambered for 22 WMR. Has 7-shot clip magazine, 22" Micro-Groove® barrel, checkered walnut-finished Maine birch stock. Introduced 1989.
Price: 925M **$260.00**
Price: 925MC (Mossy Oak Break-Up camouflage stock) **$300.00**

MARLIN MODEL 983 BOLT-ACTION RIFLE
Caliber: 22 WMR. **Barrel:** 22"; 1:16" twist. **Weight:** 6 lbs. **Length:** 41" overall. **Stock:** Walnut Monte Carlo with sling swivel studs, rubber buttpad. **Sights:** Ramp front with brass bead, removable hood; adjustable semi-buckhorn folding rear. **Features:** Thumb safety, red cocking indicator, receiver grooved for scope mount. 983S is same as the Model 983 except front breech bolt, striker knob, trigger stud, cartridge lifter stud and outer magazine tube are of stainless steel; other parts are nickel-plated. Introduced 1993. 983T has a black Monte Carlo fiberglass-filled synthetic stock with sling swivel studs. Introduced 2001. Made in U.S.A. by Marlin Firearms Co.
Price: 983 . . . . **$356.00**
Price: 983S (stainless barrel) **$377.00**
Price: 983T (fiberglass stock) **$273.00**

MEACHAM LOW-WALL RIFLE
Caliber: Any rimfire cartridge. **Barrel:** 26-34". **Weight:** 7-15 lbs. **Sights:** none. Tang drilled for Win. base, 3/8 dovetail slot front. **Stock:** Fancy eastern walnut with cheekpiece; ebony insert in forearm tip. **Features;** Exact copy of 1885 Winchester. With most Winchester factory options available including double set triggers. Introduced 1994. Made in U.S.A. by Meacham T&H Inc.
Price: From **$3,899.00**

NEW ENGLAND FIREARMS SPORTSTER™ SINGLE-SHOT RIFLES
Caliber: 22 LR, 22 WMR, 17 HMR, single-shot. **Barrel:** 20". **Weight:** 5-1/2 lbs. **Length:** 36-1/4" overall. **Stock:** Black polymer. **Sights:** None furnished; scope mount included. **Features:** Break open, side-lever release; automatic ejection; recoil pad; sling swivel studs; trigger locking system. Introduced 2001. Made in U.S.A. by New England Firearms.
Price: **$149.00**
Price: Youth model (20" bbl., 33" overall, weighs 5-1/3 lbs.) **$149.00**
Price: Sportster 17 HMR **$180.00**

NEW ULTRA LIGHT ARMS 20RF BOLT-ACTION RIFLE
Caliber: 22 LR, single shot or repeater. **Barrel:** Douglas, length to order. **Weight:** 5-1/4 lbs. **Length:** Varies. **Stock:** Kevlar®/graphite composite, variety of finishes. **Sights:** None furnished; drilled and tapped for scope mount. **Features:** Timney trigger, hand-lapped action, button-rifled barrel, hand-bedded action, recoil pad, sling-swivel studs, optional Jewell trigger. Made in U.S.A. by New Ultra Light Arms.
Price: 20 RF single shot **$800.00**
Price: 20 RF repeater **$850.00**

ROSSI MATCHED PAIR SINGLE-SHOT RIFLE/SHOTGUN
Caliber: 22 LR or 22 Mag. **Barrel:** 18-1/2" or 23". **Weight:** 6 lbs. **Stock:** Hardwood (brown or black finish). **Sights:** Fully adjustable front and rear. **Features:** Break-open breech, transfer-bar manual safety, includes matched 410-, 20 or 12 gauge shotgun barrel with bead front sight. Introduced 2001. Imported by BrazTech/Taurus.
Price: Blue **$139.95**
Price: Stainless steel **$169.95**

RUGER K77/22 VARMINT RIFLE
Caliber: 22 LR, 10-shot, 22 WMR, 9-shot detachable rotary magazine. **Barrel:** 24", heavy. **Weight:** 6-7/8 lbs. **Length:** 43.25" overall. **Stock:** Laminated hardwood with rubber buttpad, quick-detachable swivel studs. **Sights:** None furnished. Comes with Ruger 1" scope rings. **Features:** Stainless steel or blued finish. Three-position safety, dual extractors. Stock has wide, flat forend. Introduced 1993.
Price: K77/22VBZ, 22 LR **$765.00**
Price: K77/22VMBZ, 22 WMR **$765.00**

Ruger 77/22R

Ruger 77/17

Savage Mark I-G

Savage Mark II-BV

Savage Mark II-FXP

RUGER 77/22 RIMFIRE BOLT-ACTION RIFLE

Caliber: 22 LR, 10-shot rotary magazine; 22 WMR, 9-shot rotary magazine. **Barrel:** 20". **Weight:** About 6 lbs. **Length:** 39-3/4" overall. **Stock:** Checkered American walnut, laminated hardwood, or synthetic stocks, stainless sling swivels. **Sights:** Plain barrel with 1" Ruger rings. **Features:** Mauser-type action uses Ruger's rotary magazine. Three-position safety, simplified bolt stop, patented bolt locking system. Uses the dual-screw barrel attachment system of the 10/22 rifle. Integral scope mounting system with 1" Ruger rings. Blued model introduced 1983. Stainless steel and blued with synthetic stock introduced 1989.

Price: 77/22R (no sights, rings, walnut stock) **$690.00**
Price: K77/22RP (stainless, no sights, rings, synthetic stock) **$690.00**
Price: 77/22RM (22 WMR, blue, walnut stock) **$690.00**
Price: K77/22RMP (22 WMR, stainless, synthetic stock) **$690.00**

RUGER 77/17 RIMFIRE BOLT-ACTION RIFLE

Caliber: 17HMR (9-shot rotary magazine. **Barrel:** 22" to 24". **Weight:** 6.5-7.5 lbs. **Length:** 41.25-43.25" overall. **Stock:** Checkered American walnut, laminated hardwood; stainless sling swivels. **Sights:** Plain barrel with 1" Ruger rings. **Features:** Mauser-type action uses Ruger's rotary magazine. Three-position safety, simplified bolt stop, patented bolt locking system. Uses the dual-screw barrel attachment system of the 10/22 rifle. Integral scope mounting system with 1" Ruger rings. Introduced 2002.

Price: 77/17RM (no sights, rings, walnut stock) **$690.00**
Price: K77/17VMBBZ (Target grey bbl, black laminate stock) **$746.00**

SAVAGE MARK I-G BOLT-ACTION RIFLE

Caliber: 22 LR, single shot. **Barrel:** 20-3/4". **Weight:** 5-1/2 lbs. **Length:** 39-1/2" overall. **Stock:** Walnut-finished hardwood with Monte Carlo-type comb, checkered grip and forend. **Sights:** Bead front, open adjustable rear. Receiver grooved for scope mounting. **Features:** Thumb-operated rotating safety. Blue finish. Rifled or smooth bore. Introduced 1990. Made in Canada, from Savage Arms Inc.

Price: Mark IG, rifled or smooth bore, right- or left-handed **$152.00**
Price: Mark I-GY (Youth), 19" bbl., 37" overall, 5 lbs. **$152.00**
Price: Mark I-LY (Youth), 19" bbl., color laminate **$187.00**
Price: Mark I-GSB (22 LR shot cartridge) **$152.00**

SAVAGE MARK II BOLT-ACTION RIFLE

Caliber: 22 LR, 10-shot magazine. **Barrel:** 20-1/2". **Weight:** 5-1/2 lbs. **Length:** 39-1/2" overall. **Stock:** Walnut-finished hardwood with Monte Carlo-type comb, checkered grip and forend. **Sights:** Bead front, open adjustable rear. Receiver grooved for scope mounting. **Features:** Thumb-operated rotating safety. Blue finish. Introduced 1990. Made in Canada, from Savage Arms, Inc.

Price: Mark II-BV **$264.00**
Price: Mark II Camo **$184.00**
Price: Mark II-GY (youth), 19" barrel, 37" overall, 5 lbs. **$169.00**
Price: Mark II-GL, left-hand **$169.00**
Price: Mark II-GLY (youth) left-hand **$169.00**
Price: Mark II-FXP (as above with black synthetic stock) **$158.00**
Price: Mark II-F (as above, no scope) **$151.00**

Savage Mark II-FSS Stainless Rifle

Similar to the Mark II except has stainless steel barreled action and black synthetic stock with positive checkering, swivel studs, and 20.75" free-floating and button-rifled barrel with detacheable magazine. Weighs 5.5 lbs. Introduced 1997. Imported from Canada by Savage Arms, Inc.

Price: **$213.00**

Savage Model 93G

Savage Model 93FSS

Savage Model 93FVSS

Savage Model 30G Stevens "Favorite"

Savage Cub G Youth

Winchester Wildcat

SAVAGE MODEL 93G MAGNUM BOLT-ACTION RIFLE
Caliber: 22 WMR, 5-shot magazine. **Barrel:** 20-3/4". **Weight:** 5-3/4 lbs. **Length:** 39-1/2" overall. **Stock:** Walnut-finished hardwood with Monte Carlo-type comb, checkered grip and forend. **Sights:** Bead front, adjustable open rear. Receiver grooved for scope mount. **Features:** Thumb-operated rotary safety. Blue finish. Introduced 1994. Made in Canada, from Savage Arms.

Price: **$195.00**
Price: Model 93F (as above with black graphite/fiberglass stock) . . **$187.00**

Savage Model 93FSS Magnum Rifle
Similar to Model 93G except stainless steel barreled action and black synthetic stock with positive checkering. Weighs 5-1/2 lbs. Introduced 1997. Imported from Canada by Savage Arms, Inc.

Price: **$236.00**

Savage Model 93FVSS Magnum Rifle
Similar to Model 93FSS Magnum except 21" heavy barrel with recessed target-style crown, satin-finished stainless barreled action, black graphite/fiberglass stock. Drilled and tapped for scope mounting; comes with Weaver-style bases. Introduced 1998. Imported from Canada by Savage Arms, Inc.

Price: **$267.00**
Price: With scope **$305.00**

SAVAGE MODEL 30G STEVENS "FAVORITE"
Caliber: 22 LR, 22WMR Model 30GM, 17 HMR Model 30R17. **Barrel:** 21". **Weight:** 4.25 lbs. **Length:** 36.75". **Stock:** Walnut, straight grip, Schnabel forend. **Sights:** Adjustable rear, bead post front. **Features:** Lever action falling block, inertia firing pin system, Model 30G half octagonal bbl. Model 30GM full octagonal bbl.

Price: Model 30G **$228.00**
Price: Model 30GM **$266.00**
Price: Model 30R17 . . . . **$292.00**

SAVAGE CUB G YOUTH
Caliber: 22 S, L, LR; 17 Mach 2. **Barrel:** 16.125" **Weight:** 3.3 lbs. **Length:** 33" **Stock:** Walnut finished hardwood. **Sights:** Bead post, front; peep, rear. **Features:** Mini single shot bolt action, free-floating button-rifled barrel, blued finish. From Savage Arms.

Price: 22 S, L, LR **$156.00**
Price: 17 Mach 2 . . . . **$165.00**

WINCHESTER WILDCAT BOLT ACTION 22
Caliber: 22 S, L, LR; one 5-round and three 10-round magazines. **Barrel:** 21" **Weight:** NA. **Length:** NA. **Stock:** Checkered hardwood stock, checkered black synthetic Winchester buttplate, Schnabel fore-end, identical grip. cap **Sights:** Bead post, front; buckhorn rear. **Features:** Steel sling swivel studs, blued finish. Wildcat Target/Varmint rifle has .866" diameter bull barrel. Receiver drilled, tapped, and grooved for bases. Adjustable trigger, dual front steel swivel studs. Introduced 2007. From Winchester Rifles.

Price:. **$230.00**
Price: Wildcat/Varmint **$265.00**

Includes models for classic American and ISU target competition and other sporting and competitive shooting.

Anschutz 1451 Target

Anschutz 2013

ANSCHUTZ 1451R SPORTER TARGET RIFLE
Caliber: 22 LR, 5-shot magazine. **Barrel:** 22" heavy match. **Weight:** 6.4 lbs. **Length:** 39.75" overall. **Stock:** European hardwood with walnut finish. **Sights:** None furnished. Grooved receiver for scope mounting or Anschutz micrometer rear sight. **Features:** Sliding safety, two-stage trigger. Adjustable buttplate; forend slide rail to accept Anschutz accessories. Imported from Germany by GSI.
Price: **$549.00**

ANSCHUTZ 1451 TARGET RIFLE
Caliber: 22 LR. **Barrel:** 22". **Weight:** About 6.5 lbs. **Length:** 40". **Sights:** Optional. Receiver grooved for scope mounting. **Features:** Designed for the beginning junior shooter with adjustable length of pull from 13.25" to 14.25" via removable butt spacers. Two-stage trigger factory set at 2.6 lbs. Introduced 1999. Imported from Germany by Gunsmithing, Inc.
Price: **$347.00**
Price: #6834 Match Sight Set **$227.10**

ANSCHUTZ 1808D-RT SUPER RUNNING TARGET RIFLE
Caliber: 22 LR, single shot. **Barrel:** 32-1/2". **Weight:** 9 lbs. **Length:** 50" overall. **Stock:** European walnut. Heavy beavertail forend; adjustable cheekpiece and buttplate. Stippled grip and forend. **Sights:** None furnished. Grooved for scope mounting. **Features:** Designed for Running Target competition. Nine-way adjustable single-stage trigger, slide safety. Introduced 1991. Imported from Germany by Gunsmithing, Inc.
Price: Right-hand. **$1,364.10**

ANSCHUTZ 1903 MATCH RIFLE
Caliber: 22 LR, single shot. **Barrel:** 25.5", .75" diameter. **Weight:** 10.1 lbs. **Length:** 43.75" overall. **Stock:** Walnut-finished hardwood with adjustable cheekpiece; stippled grip and forend. **Sights:** None furnished. **Features:** Uses Anschutz Match 64 action and #5098 two-stage trigger. A medium weight rifle for intermediate and advanced Junior Match competition. Introduced 1987. Imported from Germany by Gunsmithing, Inc.
Price: Right-hand. **$720.40**
Price: Left-hand **$757.90**

ANSCHUTZ 64-MS R SILHOUETTE RIFLE
Caliber: 22 LR, 5-shot magazine. **Barrel:** 21-1/2", medium heavy; 7/8" diameter. **Weight:** 8 lbs. **Length:** 39.5" overall. **Stock:** Walnut-finished hardwood, silhouette-type. **Sights:** None furnished. **Features:** Uses Match 64 action. Designed for metallic silhouette competition. Stock has stippled checkering, contoured thumb groove with Wundhammer swell. Two-stage #5098 trigger. Slide safety locks sear and bolt. Introduced 1980. Imported from Germany by AcuSport Corp., Gunsmithing, Inc.
Price: 64-MS R **$704.30**

ANSCHUTZ 2013 BENCHREST RIFLE
Caliber: 22 LR, single shot. **Barrel:** 19.6". **Weight:** About 10.3 lbs. **Length:** 37.75" to 42.5" overall. **Stock:** Benchrest style of European hardwood. Stock length adjustable via spacers and buttplate. **Sights:** None furnished. Receiver grooved for mounts. **Features:** Uses the Anschutz 2013 target action; two-stage adjustable target trigger factory set at 3.9 oz. Introduced 1994. Imported from Germany by Gunsmithing, Inc.
Price: **$1,757.20**

Anschutz 2007 Match Rifle
Uses same action as the Model 2013, but has a lighter barrel. European walnut stock in right-hand, true left-hand or extra-short models. Sights optional. Available with 19.6" barrel with extension tube, or 26", both in stainless or blue. Introduced 1998. Imported from Germany by Gunsmithing, Inc.
Price: Right-hand, blue, no sights **$1,766.60**
Price: Right-hand, blue, no sights, extra-short stock **$1,756.60**
Price: Left-hand, blue, no sights **$1,856.80**

ANSCHUTZ 1827 BIATHLON RIFLE
Caliber: 22 LR, 5-shot magazine. **Barrel:** 21-1/2". **Weight:** 8-1/2 lbs. with sights. **Length:** 42-1/2" overall. **Stock:** European walnut with cheekpiece, stippled pistol grip and forend. **Sights:** Optional globe front specially designed for Biathlon shooting, micrometer rear with hinged snow cap. **Features:** Uses Super Match 54 action and nine-way adjustable trigger; adjustable wooden buttplate, biathlon butthook, adjustable hand-stop rail. Introduced 1982. Imported from Germany by Gunsmithing, Inc.
Price: Right-hand, with sights, about .... **$1,500.50 to $1,555.00**

Anschutz 1827BT Fortner Biathlon Rifle
Similar to the Anschutz 1827 Biathlon rifle except uses Anschutz/Fortner system straight-pull bolt action, blued or stainless steel barrel. Introduced 1982. Imported from Germany by Gunsmithing, Inc.
Price: Right-hand, with sights................... **$1,908.00 to $2,210.00**
Price: Left-hand, with sights .... **$2,099.20 to $2,395.00**
Price: Right-hand, sights, stainless barrel **$2,045.20**

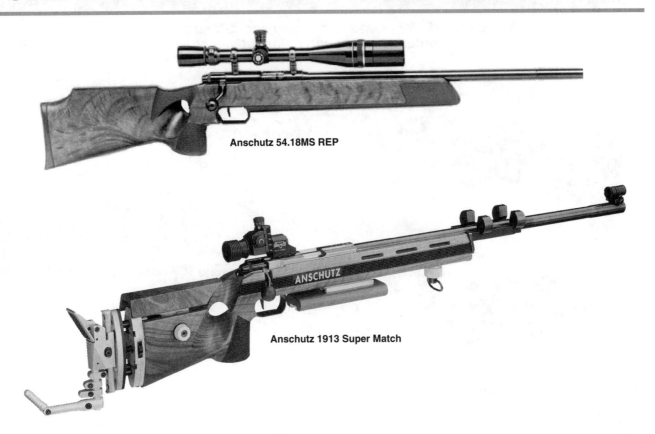

Anschutz 54.18MS REP

Anschutz 1913 Super Match

ANSCHUTZ SUPER MATCH SPECIAL MODEL 2013 RIFLE
Caliber: 22 LR, single shot. **Barrel:** 25.9". **Weight:** 13 lbs. **Length:** 41.7" to 42.9". **Stock:** A thumbhole version made of European walnut, both the cheekpiece and buttplate are highly adjustable. **Sights:** None furnished. **Features:** Developed by Anschütz for women to shoot in the sport rifle category. Stainless or blue. Introduced in 1997.
Price: Right-hand, blue, no sights, walnut.................. **$2,219.30**
Price: Right-hand, stainless, no sights, walnut **$2,345.30**
Price: Left-hand, blue, no sights, walnut **$2,319.50**

ANSCHUTZ 2012 SPORT RIFLE
Caliber: 22 LR, 5-shot magazine. **Barrel:** 22.4" match; detachable muzzle tube. **Weight:** 7.9 lbs. **Length:** 40.9" overall. **Stock:** European walnut, thumbhole design. **Sights:** None furnished. **Features:** Uses Anschutz 54.18 barreled action with two-stage match trigger. Introduced 1997. Imported from Germany by AcuSport Corp.
Price: .... **$1,425.00 to $2,219.95**

ANSCHUTZ 1911 PRONE MATCH RIFLE
Caliber: 22 LR, single shot. **Barrel:** 27-1/4". **Weight:** 11 lbs. **Length:** 46" overall. **Stock:** Walnut-finished European hardwood; American prone-style with adjustable cheekpiece, textured pistol grip, forend with swivel rail and adjustable rubber buttplate. **Sights:** None furnished. Receiver grooved for Anschutz sights (extra). **Features:** Two-stage trigger adjustable from 2.1 to 8.6 oz. Extremely fast lock time. Stainless or blue barrel. Imported from Germany by Gunsmithing, Inc.
Price: Right-hand, no sights **$1,714.20**

ANSCHUTZ 1912 SPORT RIFLE
Caliber: 22 LR, single shot. **Barrel:** 25.9". **Weight:** About 11.4 lbs. **Length:** 41.7 to 42.9". **Stock:** European walnut or aluminum. **Sights:** None furnished. **Features:** Lightweight sport rifle version of the 1913 but weighs 1.5 pounds less. Stainless or blue barrel. Introduced 1997.
Price: Right-hand, blue, no sights, walnut................. **$1,789.50**
Price: Right-hand, blue, no sights, aluminum **$2,129.80**
Price: Right-hand, stainless, no sights, walnut **$1,910.30**
Price: Left-hand, blue, no sights, walnut **$1,879.00**

Anschutz 1913 Super Match Rifle
Same as the Model 1911 except European walnut International-type stock with adjustable cheekpiece, or color laminate, both available with straight or lowered forend, adjustable aluminum hook buttplate, adjustable hand stop, weighs 15.5 lbs., 46" overall. Stainless or blue barrel. Imported from Germany by Gunsmithing, Inc.
Price: Right-hand, blue, no sights, walnut stock.... **$2,139.00 to $2,175.00**
Price: Right-hand, blue, no sights, color laminate stock **$2,199.40**
Price: Right-hand, blue, no sights, walnut, lowered forend **$2,181.80**
Price: Right-hand, blue, no sights, color laminate,
  lowered forend **$2,242.20**
Price: Left-hand, blue, no sights, walnut stock .... **$2,233.10 to $2,275.00**

Anschutz 54.18MS REP Deluxe Silhouette Rifle
Same basic action and trigger specifications as the Anschutz 1913 Super Match but with removable 5-shot clip magazine, 22.4" barrel extendable to 30" using optional extension and weight set. Weight is 8.1 lbs. Receiver drilled and tapped for scope mounting. Stock is thumbhole silhouette version or standard silhouette version, both are European walnut. Introduced 1990. Imported from Germany by Gunsmithing, Inc.
Price: Thumbhole stock **$1,461.40**
Price: Standard stock **$1,212.10**

Anschutz 1907 Standard Match Rifle
Same action as Model 1913 but with 7/8" diameter 26" barrel (stainless or blue). Length is 44.5" overall, weighs 10.5 lbs. Choice of stock configurations. Vented forend. Designed for prone and position shooting ISU requirements; suitable for NRA matches. Also available with walnut flat-forend stock for benchrest shooting. Imported from Germany by Gunsmithing, Inc.
Price: Right-hand, blue, no sights,
  hardwood stock .... **$1,253.40 to $1,299.00**
Price: Right-hand, blue, no sights, colored laminated
  stock .... **$1,316.10 to $1,375.00**
Price: Right-hand, blue, no sights, walnut stock **$1,521.10**
Price: Left-hand, blue barrel, no sights, walnut stock **$1,584.60**

Anschutz 1907

Armalite
AR-10(T)

Bushmaster A2

Bushmaster DCM

ARMALITE AR-10(T) RIFLE
Caliber: 308, 10-shot magazine. **Barrel:** 24" target-weight Rock 5R custom. **Weight:** 10.4 lbs. **Length:** 43.5" overall. **Stock:** Green or black compostion; N.M. fiberglass handguard tube. **Sights:** Detachable handle, front sight, or scope mount available. Comes with international-style flattop receiver with Picatinny rail. **Features:** National Match two-stage trigger. Forged upper receiver. Receivers hard-coat anodized. Introduced 1995. Made in U.S.A. by ArmaLite, Inc.
Price: Green $2,126.00
Price: Black $2,126.00

ARMALITE M15A4(T) EAGLE EYE RIFLE
Caliber: 223, 10-round magazine. **Barrel:** 24" heavy stainless; 1:8" twist. **Weight:** 9.2 lbs. **Length:** 42-3/8" overall. **Stock:** Green or black butt, N.M. fiberglass handguard tube. **Sights:** One-piece international-style flattop receiver with Weaver-type rail, including case deflector. **Features:** Detachable carry handle, front sight and scope mount (30mm or 1") available. Upper and lower receivers have push-type pivot pin, hard coat anodized. Made in U.S.A. by ArmaLite, Inc.
Price: Green $1,378.00
Price: Black $1,504.00

BLASER R93 LONG RANGE RIFLE
Caliber: 308 Win., 10-shot detachable box magazine. **Barrel:** 24". **Weight:** 10.4 lbs. **Length:** 44" overall. **Stock:** Aluminum with synthetic lining. **Sights:** None furnished; accepts detachable scope mount. **Features:** Straight-pull bolt action with adjustable trigger; fully adjustable stock; quick takedown; corrosion resistant finish. Introduced 1998. Imported from Germany by SIGARMS.
Price: $2,360.00

BUSHMASTER A2 RIFLE
Caliber: 308, 5.56mm. **Barrel:** 16", 20". **Weight:** 8.3 lbs. **Length:** 38.25" overall (20" barrel). **Stock:** Black composition; A2 type. **Sights:** Adjustable post front, adjustable aperture rear. **Features:** Patterned after Colt M-16A2. Chrome-lined barrel with manganese phosphate exterior. Forged aluminum receivers with push-pin takedown. Available in stainless barrel and camo stock versions. Made in U.S.A. by Bushmaster Firearms Co.
Price: 20" match heavy barrel (A2 type). . . . . **$1,025.00 to $1,185.00**
Price: (A3 type) $1,135.00

BUSHMASTER DCM COMPETITION RIFLE
Caliber: 223. **Barrel:** 20" extra-heavy (1" diameter) barrel with 1.8" twist for heavier competition bullets. **Weight:** Appx. 12 lbs. with balance weights. **Length:** NA. **Stock:** NA. **Sights:** A2 rear sight. **Features:** Has special competition rear sight with interchangeable apertures, extra-fine 1/2- or 1/4-MOA windage and elevation adjustments; specially ground front sight post in choice of three widths. Full-length handguards over free-floater barrel tube. Introduced 1998. Made in U.S.A. by Bushmaster Firearms, Inc.
Price: $1,395.00

Colt Accurized

Colt Match Target HBAR

Colt Match Target HBAR II

EAA/Izhmash URAL 5.1

BUSHMASTER VARMINTER RIFLE
Caliber: 5.56mm. **Barrel:** 24", fluted. **Weight:** 8.4 lbs. **Length:** 42.25" overall. **Stock:** Black composition, A2 type. **Sights:** None furnished; upper receiver has integral scope mount base. **Features:** Chrome-lined .950" extra heavy barrel with counter-bored crown, manganese phosphate finish, free-floating aluminum handguard, forged aluminum receivers with push-pin takedown, hard anodized mil-spec finish. Competition trigger optional. Made in U.S.A. by Bushmaster Firearms, Inc.
Price: 20" Match heavy barrel **$1,265.00**
Price: Stainless barrel **$1,265.00**

COLT MATCH TARGET HBAR RIFLE
Caliber: 223 Rem. **Barrel:** 20". **Weight:** 8 lbs. **Length:** 39" overall. **Stock:** Synthetic. **Sights:** Front: elevation adj. post; rear: 800-meter, aperture adj. for windage and elevation. **Features:** Heavy barrel, rate of rifling twist 1:7. Introduced 1991. Made in U.S.A. by Colt.
Price: Model MT6601, MT6601C **$1,183.00**

Colt Match Target Competition HBAR Rifle
Similar to the Match Target except has removeable carry handle for scope mounting, 1:9" rifling twist, 9-round magazine. Weighs 8.5 lbs. Introduced 1991.
Price: Model MT6700, MT6700C **$1,250.00**

Colt Match Target Competition HBAR II Rifle
Similar to the Match Target Competition HBAR except has 16:1" barrel, overall length 34.5", and weighs 7.1 lbs. Introduced 1995.
Price: Model MT6731 . . . . **$1,172.00**

Colt Accurized Rifle
Similar to the Match Target Model except has 24" barrel. Features flat-top receiver for scope mounting, stainless steel heavy barrel, tubular handguard, and free-floating barrel. Matte black finish. Weighs 9.25 lbs. Made in U.S.A. by Colt's Mfg. Co., Inc.
Price: Model CR6724 . . . . **$1,334.00**

EAA/HW 660 MATCH RIFLE
Caliber: 22 LR. **Barrel:** 26". **Weight:** 10.7 lbs. **Length:** 45.3" overall. **Stock:** Match-type walnut with adjustable cheekpiece and buttplate. **Sights:** Globe front, match aperture rear. **Features:** Adjustable match trigger; stippled pistol grip and forend; forend accessory rail. Introduced 1991. Imported from Germany by European American Armory.
Price: About **$999.00**
Price: With laminate stock **$1,159.00**

EAA/IZHMASH URAL 5.1 TARGET RIFLE
Caliber: 22 LR. **Barrel:** 26.5". **Weight:** 11.3 lbs. **Length:** 44.5". **Stock:** Wood, international style. **Sights:** Adjustable click rear, hooded front with inserts. **Features:** Forged barrel with rifling, adjustable trigger, aluminum rail for accessories, hooked adjustable buttplate. Adjustable comb, adjustable large palm rest. Hand stippling on grip area.
Price: . . . . **NA**

EAA/Izhmash Biathlon Target Rifle
Similar to URAL with addition of snow covers for barrel and sights, stock holding extra mags, round trigger block. Unique bolt utilizes toggle action. Designed to compete in 40 meter biathlon event. 22 LR, 19.5" bbl.
Price: **$979.00**

EAA/IZHMASH Biathlon Target

Ed Brown Marine Sniper

Olympic Arms SM-1

Olympic Arms SM-1P

Olympic Arms UM-1

ED BROWN MODEL 704 TACTICAL
Caliber: 308, 300 Win. Mag. **Barrel:** 26". SS with GEN III Coating. **Weight:** 11.25 lbs. **Stock:** Hand bedded McMillan A-3 fiberglass tactical stock with recoil pad. **Sights:** None furnished. Leupold Mark 4 30mm scope mounts utilizing heavy-duty screws. **Features:** Custom short or long action, steel trigger guard, hinged floor plate, additional calibers available.
Price: From **$2,995.00**

ED BROWN MODEL 704, M40A2 MARINE SNIPER
Caliber: 308 Win., 30-06 Springfield. **Barrel:** Match-grade 24". **Weight:** 9.25 lbs. **Stock:** Hand bedded McMillan GP fiberglass tactical stock with recoil pad in special Woodland Camo molded-in colors. **Sights:** None furnished. Leupold Mark 4 30mm scope mounts with heavy-duty screws. **Features:** Steel trigger guard, hinged floor plate, three position safety. Left-hand model available.
Price: From **$2,995.00**

OLYMPIC ARMS SM SERVICEMATCH AR15 RIFLES
Caliber: 223 Rem. minimum SAAMI spec, 30-shot magazine. **Barrel:** 20" broach-cut Ultramatch stainless steel 1x8 twist rate. **Weight:** 10 lbs. **Length:** 39.5" overall. **Stock:** A2 grip, A2 buttstock with trapdoor. **Sights:** A2 NM rear, elevation adjustable front post. **Features:** DCM-ready AR15, free-floating handguard looks standard, A2 upper, threaded muzzle, flash suppressor. Premium model adds pneumatic recoil buffer, Bob Jones interchangeable sights, two-stage trigger and Turner Saddlery sling. Made in U.S.A. by Olympic Arms, Inc.
Price: SM-1, 20" DCM ready **$1,099.00**
Price: SM-1P, Premium 20" DCM ready. **$1,493.00**

OLYMPIC ARMS UM ULTRAMATCH AR15 RIFLES
Caliber: 223 Rem. minimum SAAMI spec, 30-shot magazine. **Barrel:** 20"or 24" bull broach-cut Ultramatch stainless steel 1x10 twist rate. **Weight:** 8-10 lbs. **Length:** 38.25" overall. **Stock:** A2 grip, A2 buttstock with trapdoor. **Sights:** None, flat-top upper and gas block with rails. **Features:** Flat top upper, free floating tubular match handguard, picatinny gas block, crowned muzzle, factory trigger job and "Ultramatch" pantograph. Premium model adds pneumatic recoil buffer, Harris S-series bipod, hand selected premium receivers and William Set Trigger. Made in U.S.A. by Olympic Arms, Inc.
Price: UM-1, 20" Ultramatch. **$1,074.00**
Price: UM-1P, Premium 24" Ultramatch **$1,559.00**

Olympic Arms ML-1

Remington 40-XB Rangemaster

Remington 40-XC KS

Sako TRG-22

OLYMPIC ARMS ML-1/ML-2 MULTIMATCH AR15 CARBINES

Caliber: 223 Rem. minimum SAAMI spec, 30-shot magazine. **Barrel:** 16" broach-cut Ultramatch stainless steel 1x10 twist rate. **Weight:** 7-8 lbs. **Length:** 34-36" overall. **Stock:** A2 grip and varying buttstock. **Sights:** None. **Features:** The ML-1 includes A2 upper with adjustable rear sight, elevation adjustable front post, free floating tubular match handguard, bayonet lug, threaded muzzle, flash suppressor and M4 6-point collapsible buttstock. The ML-2 includes bull diameter barrel, flat top upper, free floating tubular match handguard, picatinny gas block, crowned muzzle and A2 buttstock with trapdoor. Made in U.S.A. by Olympic Arms, Inc.
Price: ML-1 or ML-2 . . . . **$957.00**

OLYMPIC ARMS K8 TARGETMATCH AR15 RIFLES

Caliber: 5.56 NATO, .223 WSSM, .243 WSSM, .25 WSSM 30/7-shot magazine. **Barrel:** 20", 24" bull button-rifled stainless/chrome-moly steel 1x9/1x10 twist rate. **Weight:** 8-10 lbs. **Length:** 38"-42" overall. **Stock:** A2 grip, A2 buttstock with trapdoor. **Sights:** None. **Features:** Barrel has satin bead-blast finish; flat-top upper, free-floating tubular match handguard, Picatinny gas block, crowned muzzle and "Targetmatch" pantograph on lower receiver. K8-MAG model uses Winchester Super Short Magnum cartridges. Includes 24" bull chrome-moly barrel, flat-top upper, free-floating tubular match handguard, Picatinny gas block, crowned muzzle and 7-shot magazine. Made in U.S.A. by Olympic Arms, Inc.
Price: K8 . . . . **$803.00**
Price: K8-MAG **$1,074.00**

REMINGTON 40-XB RANGEMASTER TARGET CENTERFIRE

Caliber: 15 calibers from 220 Swift to 300 Win. Mag. **Barrel:** 27-1/4". **Weight:** 11-1/4 lbs. **Length:** 47" overall. **Stock:** American walnut, laminated thumbhole or Kevlar with high comb and beavertail forend stop. Rubber non-slip buttplate. **Sights:** None. Scope blocks installed. **Features:** Adjustable trigger. Stainless barrel and action. Receiver drilled and tapped for sights.

Price: Standard single shot (right-hand)
   $1,636.00; (left-hand) **$1,761.00**
Price: Repeater **$1,734.00**

REMINGTON 40-XBBR KS

Caliber: Five calibers from 22 BR to 308 Win. **Barrel:** 20" (light varmint class), 24" (heavy varmint class). **Weight:** 7-1/4 lbs. (light varmint class); 12 lbs. (heavy varmint class). **Length:** 38" (20" bbl.), 42" (24" bbl.). **Stock:** Aramid fiber. **Sights:** None. Supplied with scope blocks. **Features:** Unblued benchrest with stainless steel barrel, trigger adjustable from 1-1/2 lbs. to 3-1/2 lbs. Special two-oz. trigger extra cost. Scope and mounts extra.
Price: Single shot **$1,876.00**

REMINGTON 40-XC KS TARGET RIFLE

Caliber: 7.62 NATO, 5-shot. **Barrel:** 24", stainless steel. **Weight:** 11 lbs. without sights. **Length:** 43-1/2" overall. **Stock:** Aramid fiber. **Sights:** None furnished. **Features:** Designed to meet the needs of competitive shooters. Stainless steel barrel and action.
Price: **$1,821.00**

REMINGTON 40-XR CUSTOM SPORTER

Caliber: 22 LR, 22 WM. **Features:** Model XR-40 Target rifle action. Many options available.
Price: Single shot **$3,383.00**

SAKO TRG-22/TRG-42 BOLT-ACTION RIFLE

Caliber: 308 Win., 10-shot magazine. **Barrel:** 26". **Weight:** 10-1/4 lbs. **Length:** 45-1/4" overall. **Stock:** Reinforced polyurethane with fully adjustable cheekpiece and buttplate. **Sights:** None furnished. Optional quick-detachable, one-piece scope mount base, 1" or 30mm rings. **Features:** Resistance-free bolt, free-floating heavy stainless barrel, 60-degree bolt lift. Two-stage trigger is adjustable for length, pull, horizontal or vertical pitch. Introduced 2000. Imported from Finland by Beretta USA.
Price: TRG-22 Green Folding Stock. **$4,525.00**
Price: TRG-22 Green or black stock **$2,825.00**
Price: TRG-42 300 Win Mag., green stock . . . . . . **$2,825.00 to $3,525.00**
Price: TRG-42 338 Lapua Mag., green stock . . . . . **$2,825.00 to $3,525.00**

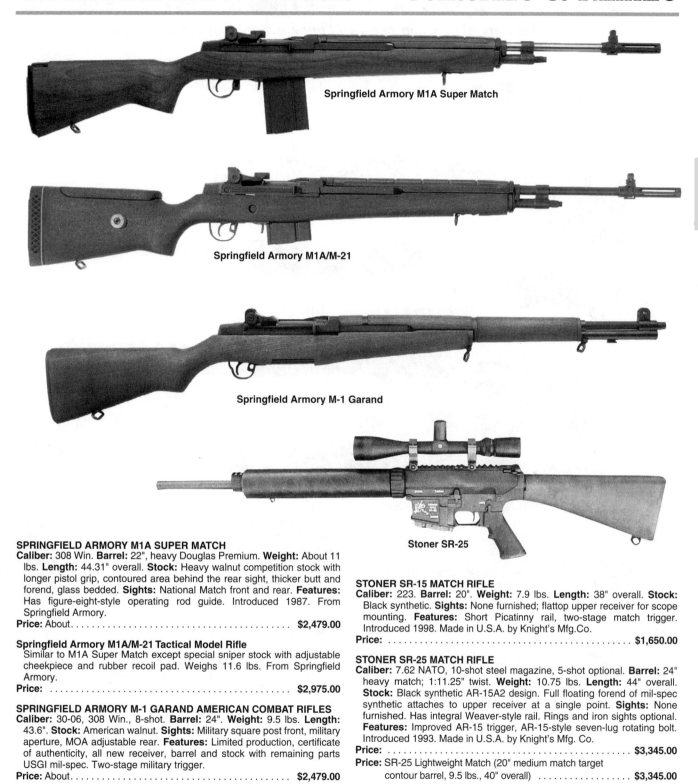

Springfield Armory M1A Super Match

Springfield Armory M1A/M-21

Springfield Armory M-1 Garand

Stoner SR-25

SPRINGFIELD ARMORY M1A SUPER MATCH
Caliber: 308 Win. **Barrel:** 22", heavy Douglas Premium. **Weight:** About 11 lbs. **Length:** 44.31" overall. **Stock:** Heavy walnut competition stock with longer pistol grip, contoured area behind the rear sight, thicker butt and forend, glass bedded. **Sights:** National Match front and rear. **Features:** Has figure-eight-style operating rod guide. Introduced 1987. From Springfield Armory.
Price: About. $2,479.00

Springfield Armory M1A/M-21 Tactical Model Rifle
Similar to M1A Super Match except special sniper stock with adjustable cheekpiece and rubber recoil pad. Weighs 11.6 lbs. From Springfield Armory.
Price: $2,975.00

SPRINGFIELD ARMORY M-1 GARAND AMERICAN COMBAT RIFLES
Caliber: 30-06, 308 Win., 8-shot. **Barrel:** 24". **Weight:** 9.5 lbs. **Length:** 43.6". **Stock:** American walnut. **Sights:** Military square post front, military aperture, MOA adjustable rear. **Features:** Limited production, certificate of authenticity, all new receiver, barrel and stock with remaining parts USGI mil-spec. Two-stage military trigger.
Price: About. $2,479.00

STONER SR-15 MATCH RIFLE
Caliber: 223. **Barrel:** 20". **Weight:** 7.9 lbs. **Length:** 38" overall. **Stock:** Black synthetic. **Sights:** None furnished; flattop upper receiver for scope mounting. **Features:** Short Picatinny rail, two-stage match trigger. Introduced 1998. Made in U.S.A. by Knight's Mfg.Co.
Price: $1,650.00

STONER SR-25 MATCH RIFLE
Caliber: 7.62 NATO, 10-shot steel magazine, 5-shot optional. **Barrel:** 24" heavy match; 1:11.25" twist. **Weight:** 10.75 lbs. **Length:** 44" overall. **Stock:** Black synthetic AR-15A2 design. Full floating forend of mil-spec synthetic attaches to upper receiver at a single point. **Sights:** None furnished. Has integral Weaver-style rail. Rings and iron sights optional. **Features:** Improved AR-15 trigger, AR-15-style seven-lug rotating bolt. Introduced 1993. Made in U.S.A. by Knight's Mfg. Co.
Price: $3,345.00
Price: SR-25 Lightweight Match (20" medium match target
     contour barrel, 9.5 lbs., 40" overall) $3,345.00

Includes a wide variety of sporting guns and guns suitable for various competitions.

Benelli Legacy

Benelli M2 20 gauge Realtree APG HD

Benelli M2 20 gauge Realtree APG HD

Benelli M4

Benelli Montefeltro

BENELLI LEGACY SHOTGUN

Gauge: 12, 20, 2-3/4" and 3" chamber. **Barrel:** 24", 26", 28" (Full, Mod., Imp. Cyl., Imp. Mod., cylinder choke tubes). Mid-bead sight. **Weight:** 5.8 to 7.4 lbs. **Length:** 49-5/8" overall (28" barrel). **Stock:** Select AA European walnut with satin finish. **Features:** Uses the rotating bolt inertia recoil operating system with a two-piece steel/aluminum etched receiver (bright on lower, blue upper). Drop adjustment kit allows the stock to be custom fitted without modifying the stock. Introduced 1998. Ultralight model has gloss-blued finish receiver. Weight is 6.0 lbs., 24" barrel, 45.5 overall length. WeatherCoat walnut stock. Introduced 2006. Imported from Italy by Benelli USA, Corp.

Price: **$1,565.00**
Price: Ultralight model, Weathercoat finish, 2+1 (2007) **$1,385.00**

BENELLI M2 FIELD SHOTGUNS

Gauge: 20 ga., 12 ga., 3" chamber. **Barrel:** 21", 24", 26", 28". **Weight:** 5.4 to 7.2 lbs. **Length:** 42.5 to 49.5" overall. **Stock:** Synthetic, Advantage® Max-4 HD, Advantage® Timber HD, APG HD. **Sights:** Red bar. **Features:** Uses the Inertia Driven™ bolt mechanism. Vent rib. Comes with set of five choke tubes. Imported from Italy by Benelli USA.

Price: Synthetic ComforTech gel recoil pad **$1,215.00**
Price: Camo ComforTech gel recoil pad **$1,335.00**
Price: Satin walnut **$1,145.00**
Price: Rifled slug synthetic **$1,280.00**
Price: Camo turkey model w/SteadyGrip stock **$1,375.00**
Price: Realtree APG HD ComforTech stock (2007) **$1,335.00**

Price: Realtree APG HD ComforTech 20 ga. (2007) **$1,335.00**
Price: Realtree APG HD LH ComforTech (2007) **$1,365.00**
Price: Realtree APG HD ComforTech Slug (2007) **$1,400.00**
Price: Realtree APG HD w/SteadyGrip stock (2007) **$1,375.00**
Price: Black Synthetic Grip Tight 20 ga. (2007) **$1,215.00**
Price: Timber HD ComforTech 20 ga. (2007) **$1,335.00**
Price: Realtree APG HD ComforTech 20 ga. (2007) **$1,335.00**

BENELLI M4 TACTICAL SHOTGUN

Gauge: 12 ga., 3" chamber. **Barrel:** 18.5". **Weight:** 7.8 lbs. **Length:** 40" overall. **Stock:** Synthetic. **Sights:** Ghost Ring rear, fixed blade front. **Features:** Auto-regulating gas-operated (ARGO) action, choke tube, Picatinny rail, standard and collapsible stocks available, optional LE tactical gun case. Introduced 2006. Imported from Italy by Benelli USA.

Price: Pistol grip stock, black synthetic. **$1,600.00**
Price: Desert camo pistol grip (2007). **$1,735.00**

BENELLI MONTEFELTRO SHOTGUNS

Gauge: 12 and 20 ga. Full, Imp. Mod., Mod., Imp. Cyl., Cyl. choke tubes. **Barrel:** 24", 26", 28". **Weight:** 5.3 to 7.1 lbs. **Stock:** Checkered walnut with satin finish. **Length of Pull:** 12-1/2 to 14-3/8" overall. **Length:** 43.6 to 49.5" overall. **Features:** Uses the Inertia Driven rotating bolt system with a simple inertia recoil design. Finish is blue. Introduced 1987.

Price: 24", 26", 28" **$1,110.00**
Price: Left hand. **$1,120.00**
Price: 20 ga. **$1,110.00**
Price: 20 ga. short stock (LOP: 12.5") **$1,120.00**
Price: Silver (AA walnut; nickle-blue receiver) **$1,535.00**
Price: Silver 20 ga. **$1,535.00**

Benelli Super Black Eagle II Realtree APG HD

Benelli Super Black Eagle II Slug

Beretta 3901 Ambassador

Beretta 3901 Citizen

BENELLI SUPER BLACK EAGLE II SHOTGUNS
Gauge: 12, 3-1/2" chamber. **Barrel:** 24", 26", 28" (Cyl. Imp. Cyl., Mod., Imp. Mod., Full choke tubes). **Weight:** 7.1 to 7.3 lbs. **Length:** 45.6 to 49.6" overall. **Stock:** European walnut with satin finish, polymer, or camo. Adjustable for drop. **Sights:** Red bar front. **Features:** Uses Benelli inertia recoil bolt system. Vent rib. Advantage® Max-4 HD™, Advantage® Timber HD™ camo patterns. Features ComforTech stock. Introduced 1991. Left-hand models available. Imported from Italy by Benelli USA.

Price: Satin walnut, non-ComforTech **$1,480.00**
Price: Camo stock, ComforTech gel recoil pad **$1,635.00**
Price: Black Synthetic stock **$1,415.00**
Price: Max-4 or Timber HD Camo stock **$1,535.00**
Price: Satin walnut Rifled slug **$1,560.00**
Price: Timber HD turkey model w/SteadyGrip stock **$1,615.00**
Price: Realtree APG HD SteadyGrip stock (2007) **$1,615.00**
Price: Realtree APG HD w/ComforTech stock (2007) **$1,665.00**
Price: Realtree APG HD LH ComforTech stock (2007) **$1,700.00**
Price: Realtree APG HD Slug Gun (2007) **$1,735.00**

BENELLI CORDOBA SHOTGUN
Gauge: 20; 12; 3" chamber. **Barrel:** 28" and 30", ported, 10mm sporting rib. **Weight:** 7.2 to 7.3 lbs. **Length:** 49.6 to 51.6". **Features:** Designed for high-volume sporting clays and Argentina dove shooting. Inertia-driven action, Extended Sport CrioChokes, 4+1 capacity. Ported. Imported from Italy by Benelli USA.

Price: Black synthetic GripTight ComforTech stock **$1,735.00**
Price: Black synthetic GripTight ComforTech stock, 20 ga.,
    (2007) **$1,735.00**
Price: Max-4 HD ComforTech stock (2007) **$1,870.00**

BENELLI SUPERSPORT & SPORT II SHOTGUNS
Gauge: 20; 12; 3" chamber. **Barrel:** 28" and 30", ported, 10mm sporting rib. **Weight:** 7.2 to 7.3 lbs. **Length:** 49.6 to 51.6". **Stock:** Carbon fiber, ComforTech (Supersport) or walnut (Sport II). **Sights:** Red bar front, metal midbead. Sport II is similar to the Legacy model except has nonengraved dual tone blue/silver receiver, ported wide-rib barrel, adjustable buttstock, and functions with all loads. Walnut stock with satin finish. Introduced 1997. **Features:** Designed for high-volume sporting clays. Inertia-driven action, Extended CrioChokes, 4+1 capacity. Ported. Imported from Italy by Benelli USA.

Price: Carbon fiber ComforTech stock **$1,800.00**
Price: Carbon fiber ComforTech stock, 20 ga. (2007) **$1,800.00**
Price: Sport II 20 ga. (2007) **$1,580.00**

BERETTA 3901 SHOTGUNS
Gauge: 12, 20 gauge; 3" chamber, semi-auto. **Barrel:** 26", 28". **Weight:** 6.55 lbs. (20 ga.), 7.2 lbs. (12 ga.). **Length:** NA. **Stock:** Wood, X-tra wood (special process wood enhancement), and polymer. **Features:** Based on A390 shotgun introduced in 1996. Mobilchokes, removable trigger group. 3901 Target RL uses gas operating system; Sporting style flat rib with steel front bead and mid-bead, walnut stock and forearm, satin matte finish, adjustable LOP from 12–13", adjustable for cast on/off, Beretta's Memory System II to adjust the parallel comb. Weighs 7.2 lbs. 3901 Citizen has polymer stock. 3901 Statesman has basic wood and checkering treatment. 3901 Ambassador has X-tra wood stock and fore end; high-polished receiver with engraving, Gel-Tek recoil pad, optional TruGlo fiber-optic front sight. 3901 Rifled Slug Shotgun has black high-impact synthetic stock and fore end, 24" barrel,1:28 twist, Picatinny cantilever rail. Introduced 2006. Made in U.S. by Beretta USA.

Price: **$1,295.00**
Price: 3901 Target RL **$898.00**
Price: 3901 Citizen **$750.00**
Price: 3901 Citizen **$898.00**
Price: 3901 Ambassador **$998.00**
Price: 3901 Rifled Slug Shotgun **$799.00**

Beretta UGB

Beretta AL391 Urika Sporting

Beretta AL391 Urika Gold Sporting

Beretta A391 Xtrema2 3.5

BERETTA UGB25 XCEL
Gauge: 12, 2-3/4" chambers. **Barrel:** 28", 30", 32"; competition-style interchangeable vent rib; Optima choke tubes. **Weight:** 7.7-9 lbs. **Stock:** High-grade walnut with oil finish; hand-checkered grip and forend, adjustable. **Features:** Break-open semiautomatic. High-resistance fiberglass-reinforced technopolymer trigger plate, self-lubricating firing mechanism. Rounded alloy receiver, polished sides, external cartridge carrier and feeding port, bottom eject. two technopolymer recoil dampers on breech bolt, double recoil dampers located in the receiver, Beretta Recoil Reduction System, recoil-absorbing Beretta Gel Tek recoil pad. Optima-Bore barrel with a lengthened forcing cone, Optimachoke and Extended Optimachoke tubes. Steel-shot capable, interchangeable aluminum alloy top rib. Introduced 2006. Imported from Italy by Beretta USA.
Price: .... **$,3,275.00**

BERETTA AL391 TEKNYS SHOTGUNS
Gauge: 12, 20 gauge; 3" chamber, semi-auto. **Barrel:** 26", 28". **Weight:** 5.9 lbs. (20 ga.), 7.3 lbs. (12 ga.). **Length:** NA. **Stock:** X-tra wood (special process wood enhancement). **Features:** Flat 1/4 rib, TruGlo Tru-Bead sight, recoil reducer, stock spacers, overbored bbls., flush choke tubes. Comes with fitted, lined case.
Price: From **$1,425.00**

BERETTA AL391 URIKA AND URIKA OPTIMA AUTO SHOTGUNS
Gauge: 12, 20 gauge; 3" chamber. **Barrel:** 22", 24", 26", 28", 30"; five Mobilchoke choke tubes. **Weight:** 5.95 to 7.28 lbs. **Length:** Varies by model. **Stock:** Walnut, black or camo synthetic; shims, spacers and interchangeable recoil pads allow custom fit. **Features:** Self-compensating gas operation handles full range of loads; recoil reducer in receiver; enlarged trigger guard; reduced-weight receiver, barrel and forend; hard-chromed bore. Introduced 2000. Urika Gold and Gold Sporting models are similar to AL391 Urika except features deluxe wood, jewelled bolt and carrier, gold-inlaid receiver with black or silver finish. Introduced 2000. Urika Sporting models are similar to AL391 Urika except has competition sporting stock with rounded rubber recoil pad, wide vent rib with white front and mid-rib beads, satin-black receiver with silver markings. Available in 12 and 20 gauge. Introduced 2000. Urika Trap has wide vent rib with white front and mid-rib beads, Monte Carlo stock and special trap recoil pad. Gold Trap features highly figured walnut stock and forend, gold-filled Beretta logo and signature on receiver. Optima bore and Optima choke tubes. Introduced 2000. Urika Parallel Target RL and SL models have parallel comb, Monte Carlo stock with tighter grip radius and stepped vent rib. SL model has same features but with 13.5" length of pull stock. Introduced 2000. Urika Youth has a 24" or 26" barrel with 13.5" stock for youths and smaller shooters. Introduced 2000. Imported from Italy by Beretta USA.
Price: .... **$998.00 to $1,500.00**

BERETTA A391 XTREMA2 3.5 AUTO SHOTGUNS
Gauge: 12 ga. 3.5" chamber. **Barrel:** 24", 26", 28". **Weight:** 7.8 lbs. **Stock:** Synthetic. **Features:** Semi-auto goes with two-lug rotating bolt and self-compensating gas valve, extended tang, cross bolt safety, self-cleaning, with case.
Price: From **$1,098.00**

BROWNING GOLD AUTO SHOTGUNS
Gauge: 12, 3" or 3-1/2" chamber; 20, 3" chamber. **Barrel:** 12 ga.-26", 28", 30", Invector Plus choke tubes; 20 ga.-26", 30", Invector choke tubes. **Weight:** 7 lbs., 9 oz. (12 ga.), 6 lbs., 12 oz. (20 ga.). **Length:** 46-1/4" overall (20 ga., 26" barrel). **Stock:** 14"x1-1/2"x2-1/3"; select walnut with gloss finish; palm swell grip. **Features:** Self-regulating, self-cleaning gas system shoots all loads; lightweight receiver with special non-glare deep black finish; large reversible safety button; large rounded trigger guard, gold trigger. The 20 gauge has slightly smaller dimensions; 12 gauge have back-bored barrels, Invector Plus tube system. Introduced 1994. Gold Evolve shotguns have new rib design, HiViz sights. Gold Micro has a 26" barrel, 13-7/8" pull length and smaller pistol grip for youths and other small shooters. Introduced 2001. Gold Fusion has front HiViz Pro-Comp and center bead on tapered vent rib; ported and back-bored Invector Plus barrel; 2-3/4" chamber; satin-finished stock with solid, radiused recoil pad with hard heel insert; non-glare black alloy receiver, shim-adj. stock. Imported by Browning.
Price: Gold Evolve, 12 or 20 ga., 3" chamber **$1,220.00**
Price: Gold Hunter, 12 or 20 ga., 3" or 3-1/2" chamber, from **$1,025.00**
Price: Gold FLD, 12 or 20 ga., semi-humpback receiver **$1,025.00**
Price: Gold Rifled Deer Hunter, 12 or 20 ga., scope mount **$1,131.00**
Price: Gold Upland Special, 12 or 20 ga., 24" or 26" barrel **$1,025.00**
Price: Gold Superlite Micro, 20 ga., 24" or 26" barrel, 6.6 lbs. ... **$1,105.00**
Price: Gold Fusion, 12 or 20 ga., 6.4 to 7 lbs., ... **$1,152.00**
Price: Gold Fusion High Grade, 12 or 20 ga., intr. 2005 .... **$2,137.00**

Browning Gold Deer Hunter

Browning Gold Fusion

Browning Gold Superlite Micro

Browning NWTF Mossy Oak® Break-Up™

Browning Gold Light 10 Gauge

Browning Gold Stalker Auto Shotgun
Similar to the Gold Hunter except has black composite stock and forend. Chambered in 12 gauge, 3" or 3-1/2" chamber. Gold Deer Stalker has fully rifled barrel, cantilever scope mount. Introduced 1999. Imported by Browning.
Price: Gold Stalker, 3" or 3-1/2" chamber, 26" or 28" barrel,
from . . . . **$ 1,171.00**
Price: Gold FLD Stalker, 3" chamber, semi-humpback receiver . . . **$981.00**
Price: Gold Rifled Deer Stalker, 12 ga. 3" chamber, 22" barrel . . **$1,241.00**

Browning Gold NWTF Turkey Series and Mossy Oak Shotguns
Similar to the Gold Hunter except has specialized camouflage patterns, including National Wild Turkey Federation design. Includes extra-full choke tube and HiViz fiber-optic sights on some models and Dura-Touch coating. Camouflage patterns include Mossy Oak New Break-Up (NBU) or Mossy Oak New Shadow Grass (NSG). NWTF models include NWTF logo on stock. Introduced 2001. From Browning.
Price: NWFT Gold Ultimate Turkey, 24" barrel, 3-1/2" chamber . **$1,469.00**
Price: NWFT Gold Turkey, 24" barrel, 3" chamber **$1,202.00**
Price: Gold NSG, 26" or 28" barrel, 3" or 3-1/2" chamber, from . . **$1,127.00**
Price: Gold NBU, 26" barrel, 3" or 3-1/2" chamber, from **$1,127.00**
Price: Gold Rifle Deer NBU, 22" barrel, 3" chamber, from **$1,218.00**

BROWNING GOLD "CLAYS" AUTO SHOTGUNS
Gauge: 12, 2-3/4" chamber. **Barrel:** 28", 30", Invector Plus choke tubes. **Weight:** about 7.75 lbs. **Length:** From 47.75 to 50.5". **Stock:** Select walnut with gloss finish; palm swell grip, shim adjustable. **Features:** Ported barrels, "Golden Clays" models feature gold inlays and engraving. Otherwise similar to Gold series guns. Imported by Browning.
Price: Gold "Golden Clays" Sporting Clays, intr. 2005 . . . . **$1,848.00**
Price: Gold Sporting Clays **$1,127.00**
Price: Gold "Golden Clays" Ladies Sporting Clays, intr. 2005 . . . . **$1,848.00**
Price: Gold Ladies Sporting Clays **$1,127.00**

Browning Gold Light 10 Gauge Auto Shotgun
Similar to the Gold Hunter except has an alloy receiver that is 1 lb. lighter than standard model. Offered in 26" or 28" bbls. With Mossy Oak® Break-Up™ or Shadow Grass coverage; 5-shot magazine. Weighs 9 lbs., 10 oz. (28" bbl.). Introduced 2001. Imported by Browning.
Price: Camo model only **$1,390.00**

CHARLES DALY FIELD SEMI-AUTO SHOTGUNS
Gauge: 12, 20, 28. **Barrel:** 22", 24", 26", 28" or 30". **Stock:** Synthetic black, Realtree Hardwoods or Advantage Timber. **Features:** Interchangeable barrels handle all loads including steel shot. Slug model has adjustable sights. Maxi-Mag is 3.5" chamber.
Price: Field Hunter **$389.00**

Charles Daly Field Pump

Charles Daly Maxi-Mag Field Hunter VR-MC

Charles Daly Superior II

Escort Model AS

Franchi 48AL Deluxe

CHARLES DALY SUPERIOR II SEMI-AUTO SHOTGUNS
Gauge: 12, 20, 28. **Barrel:** 26", 28" or 30". **Stock:** Select Turkish walnut. **Features:** Factory ported interchangeable barrels; wide vent rib on Trap and Sport models; fluorescent red sights.
Price: Superior Hunter VR-MC $539.00
Price: Superior Sport $569.00

ESCORT SEMI-AUTO SHOTGUNS
Gauge: 12, 20. **Barrel:** 22", 24", 26", 18" (AimGuard model); 3" chambers. **Weight:** 6 lbs, 4 0. to 7 lbs., 6 oz. **Stock:** Polymer, black, or camo finish; also Turkish walnut. **Features:** Black chrome finish; top of receiver dovetailed for sight mounting. Gold-plated trigger, trigger guard safety, magazine cut-off. Three choke tubes (IC, M, F — except AimGuard); 24" bbl. model comes with turkey choke tube. **Sights:** Optional HiViz Spark and TriViz fiber-optic sights. Introduced 2002. Camo model introduced 2003. Youth, Slug, Obsession Camo models introduced 2005. Three-barrel pumpset introduced 2006. Imported from Turkey by Legacy Sports International.
Price: From $392.00

FRANCHI INERTIA I-12 SHOTGUN
Gauge: 12, 3" chamber. **Barrel:** 24", 26", 28" (Cyl., IC, Mod., IM, F choke tubes). **Weight:** 7.5 to 7.7. lbs. **Length:** 45" to 49". **Stock:** 14-3.8" LOP, satin walnut with checkered grip and forend, synthetic, Advantage Timber

HD or Max-4 camo patterns. **Features:** Inertia-Driven action. AA walnut stock. Red bar front sight, metal mid sight. Imported from Italy by Benelli USA.
Price: Synthetic $759.00
Price: Camo $839.00
Price: Satin walnut $839.00
Price: Limited engraved receiver, hard case $1,399.00

FRANCHI MODEL 720 SHOTGUNS
Gauge: 20, 3" chamber. **Barrel:** 24", 26", 28" w/(IC, Mod., F choke tubes). **Weight:** 5.9 to 6.1 lbs. **Length:** 43.25" to 49". **Stock:** WeatherCoat finish walnut, Max-4 and Timber HD camo. **Sights:** Front bead. **Features:** Made in Italy and imported by Benelli USA.
Price: Walnut w/Weathercoat $889.00
Price: Camo $919.00
Price: Walnut, 12.5" LOP, 43.25" OAL $789.00
Price: Competition Weathercoat 20 ga. $999.00

FRANCHI 48AL FIELD AND DELUXE SHOTGUNS
Gauge: 20 or 28, 2-3/4" chamber. **Barrel:** 24", 26", 28" (Full, Cyl., Mod., choke tubes). **Weight:** 5.4 to 5.7 lbs. **Length:** 42.25" to 48". **Stock:** Walnut with checkered grip and forend. **Features:** Long recoil-operated action. Chrome-lined bore; cross-bolt safety. Imported from Italy by Benelli USA.
Price: 20 ga. $779.00
Price: 20 ga. Deluxe A grade walnut $979.00
Price: 28 ga. $1089.00

Remington Model 105 CTI

Remington Model 11-87 Special Purpose Magnum

Remington Model 11-87 SPS Cantilever

Remington Model 11-87 SPS Camo

FRANCHI 712 COMPETITION SHOTGUN
Gauge: 12 ; 4+1. **Barrel:** 30" ported; tapered target rib and bead front sight. **Weight:** 7.1 lbs. **Stock:** Walnut with WeatherCoat (impervious to weather). **Features:** Gas-operated, satin nickel receiver.
Price: **$999.00**

HARRINGTON & RICHARDSON EXCELL AUTO 5 SHOTGUNS
Gauge: 12, 3" chamber. **Barrel:** 22", 24", 28", four screw-in choke tubes (IC, M, IM, F). **Weight:** About 7 lbs. **Length:** 42.5" to 48.5" overall, depending on barrel length. **Stock:** American walnut with satin finish; cut checkering; ventilated buttpad. Synthetic stock or camo-finish. **Sights:** Metal bead front or fiber-optic front and rear. **Features:** Ventilated rib on all models except slug gun. Imported by H&R 1871, Inc.
Price: Synthetic, black, 28" barrel, 48.5" OAL................. **$415.00**
Price: Walnut, checkered grip/forend, 28" barrel, 48.5" OAL **$461.00**
Price: Waterfowl, camo finish **$521.00**
Price: Turkey, camo finish, 22" barrel, fiber optic sights **$521.00**
Price: Combo, synthetic black stock, with slug barrel **$583.00**

REMINGTON MODEL 105 CTI SHOTGUN
Gauge: 12, 3" chamber, 2-shot magazine. **Barrel:** 26", 28" (IC, Mod., Full ProBore chokes). **Weight:** 7 lbs. **Length:** 46.25" overall (26" barrel). **Stock:** Walnut with satin finish. Checkered grip and forend. **Sights:** Front bead. **Features:** Aircraft-grade titanium receiver body, skeletonized receiver with carbon fiber shell. Bottom feed and eject, target grade trigger, R3 recoil pad, FAA-approved lockable hard case, .735" overbored barrel with lengthened forcing cones. TriNyte coating; carbon/aramid barrel rib. Introduced 2006.
Price: **$1,511.00**

REMINGTON MODEL SPR453 SHOTGUN
Gauge: 12; 3.5" chamber, 4+1 capacity. **Barrel:** 24", 26", 28" vent rib. **Weight:** 8 to 8.25 lbs. **Stock:** Black synthetic and Mossy Oak Break-Up stock and forend. **Features:** Matte finish, dual extractors, four extended screw-in SPR choke tubes (improved cylinder, modified, full and super-full turkey. Introduced 2006. From Remington Arms Co.
Price: Black synthetic **$461.00**

REMINGTON MODEL 11-87 SPORTSMAN SHOTGUNS
Gauge: 12, 20, 3" chamber. **Barrel:** 26", 28", RemChoke tubes. Standard contour, vent rib. **Weight:** About 7.75 to 8.25 lbs. **Length:** 46" to 48" overall. **Stock:** Black synthetic or Mossy Oak Break Up. **Sights:** Single bead front. **Features:** Matte-black metal finish, magazine cap swivel studs. Sportsman Deer gun has 21-inch fully rifled barrel, cantilever scope mount.
Price: Sportsman Camo (2007) **$845.00**
Price: Sportsman black synthetic.......................... **$739.00**
Price: Sportsman Deer................................... **$845.00**

Remington Model 11-87 Special Purpose Magnum
Similar to the 11-87 Sportsman except has dull stock finish, Parkerized exposed metal surfaces. Bolt and carrier have dull blackened coloring. Comes with 26" or 28" barrel with RemChokes, padded Cordura nylon sling and quick detachable swivels. Introduced 1987. Thumbhole model available. Cantilever model has fully rifled barrel; synthetic stock with Monte Carlo comb; cantilever scope mount deer barrel. Comes with sling and swivels. Introduced 1994. Turkey Camo model has 21" vent rib barrel with RemChoke tube. Super Magnum Synthetic Camo has 23" vent rib barrel with Turkey Super full choke tube, chambered for 12 ga., 3-1/2", TruGlo rifle sights. Version available without TruGlo sights. Introduced 2001. Special Purpose-Deer Shotgun has fully-rifled 21" barrel with rifle sights, black non-reflective, synthetic stock and forend, black carrying sling. Introduced 1993. SPS Super Magnums have 3.5" chamber. Introduced 2000. From Remington Arms Co.
Price: SP Thumbhole rifled barrel **$1,135.00**
Price: SP-T Thumbhole, Mossy Oak Obsession camo **$1,241.00**
Price: SPS-T, Mossy Oak Obsession camo.................. **$1,175.00**
Price: SPS Super Magnum **$1,076.00**
Price: SPS Super Magnum Camo **$1,175.00**

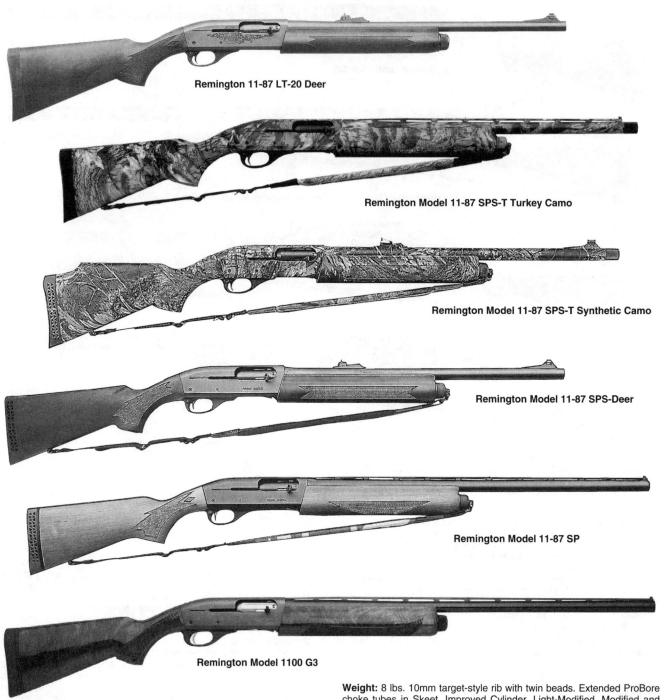

Remington 11-87 LT-20 Deer

Remington Model 11-87 SPS-T Turkey Camo

Remington Model 11-87 SPS-T Synthetic Camo

Remington Model 11-87 SPS-Deer

Remington Model 11-87 SP

Remington Model 1100 G3

REMINGTON MODEL 1100 G3 SHOTGUN

Gauge: 20, 12; 3" chamber. **Barrel:** 26", 28". **Weight:** 6.75-7.6 lbs. **Stock:** Realwood semi-Fancy carbon fiber laminate stock, high gloss finish, machine cut checkering. **Features:** Gas operating system, pressure compensated barrel, solid carbon-steel engraved receiver, titanium coating. Action bars, trigger and extended carrier release, action bar sleeve, action spring, locking block, hammer, sear and magazine tube have nickel-plated, Teflon coating. R3 recoil pad, overbored (.735" dia.) vent rib barrels, ProBore choke tubes. 20-gauges have Rem Chokes. Comes with lockable hard case. Introduced 2006. Competition model (12 gauge 2.75" chamber) has overbored (0.735" bore diameter) 30" barrel.

Weight: 8 lbs. 10mm target-style rib with twin beads. Extended ProBore choke tubes in Skeet, Improved Cylinder, Light-Modified, Modified and Full. Semi-fancy American walnut stock and forend. Classic Trap model has polished blue receiver with scroll engraving, gold accents, 30" low-profile, light-target contoured vent rib barrel with standard .727" dimensions. Comes with specialized Rem Choke trap tubes: Singles (.027"), Mid Handicap (.034"), and Long Handicap (.041"). Monte Carlo stock of semi-fancy American walnut, deep-cut checkering, high-gloss finish.

Price: G3, 12 or 20 gauge **$1,208.00**
Price: Competition, standard stock. **$1,492.00**
Price: Competition, adjustable comb **$1,651.00**
Price: Classic Trap **$1,101.00**

Remington Model 1100 Sporting 28

Remington Model 1100 Classic Trap

Remington Model 1100 Sporting 12

Remington Model SP-10

Remington Model SP-10 Thumbhole

Remington Model 1100 Sporting Shotguns

Similar to 1100 G3 but in .410 bore, 28, 20, 12 gauge. **Barrel:** 27" or 28" light target contoured vent rib barrel with twin bead target sights. **Stock:** Semi-fancy American walnut stock and forend, cut checkering, high gloss finish. **Features:** Gold-plated trigger. Four extended choke tubes: Skeet, Improved Cylinder, Light Modified and Modified. 1100 Tournament Skeet (20 and 12 gauge) receiver is roll-marked with "Tournament Skeet." 26-inch light contour, vent rib barrel has twin bead sights, Extended Target Choke Tubes (Skeet and Improved Cylinder).

Price: Sporting 12, 49" OAL, 8 lbs. **$1,057.00**
Price: Sporting 20, 48.75" OAL, 7 lbs. **$1,057.00**
Price: Sporting 28, 47.75" OAL, 6.75 lbs. **$1,101.00**
Price: Sporting 410, 47.75" OAL, 6.75 lbs. **$1,101.00**
Price: Tournament Skeet 12 gauge, 47" OAL, 7.75 lbs. **$1,057.00**

REMINGTON MODEL SP-10 MAGNUM SHOTGUN

Gauge: 10, 3-1/2" chamber, 2-shot magazine. **Barrel:** 26", 30" (full and mod. RemChokes). **Weight:** 10-3/4 to 11 lbs. **Length:** 47-1/2" overall (26" barrel). **Stock:** Walnut with satin finish or black synthetic with 26" barrel. Checkered grip and forend. **Sights:** Twin bead. **Features:** Stainless steel gas system with moving cylinder; 3/8" vent rib. Receiver and barrel have matte finish. Brown recoil pad. Comes with padded Cordura nylon sling. Introduced 1989. SP-10 Magnum Camo has buttstock, forend, receiver, barrel and magazine cap covered with Mossy Oak® Break-Up™ camo finish; bolt body and trigger guard have matte black finish. RemChoke tube, 26" vent rib barrel with mid-rib bead and Bradley-style front sight, swivel studs and quick-detachable swivels, non-slip Cordura carrying sling in same camo pattern. Introduced 1993.

Price: . . . . **$1,684.00 to $1,844.00**
Price: Thumbhole Camo, Mossy Oak Obsession (2007) **$1,952.00**

SARSILMAZ SEMI-AUTOMATIC SHOTGUN

Gauge: 12, 3" chamber. **Barrel:** 26" or 28"; fixed chokes. **Stock:** Walnut or synthetic. **Features:** Handles 2-3/4" or 3" magnum loads. Introduced 2000. Imported from Turkey by Armsport Inc.

Price: With walnut stock **$969.95**
Price: With synthetic stock **$919.95**

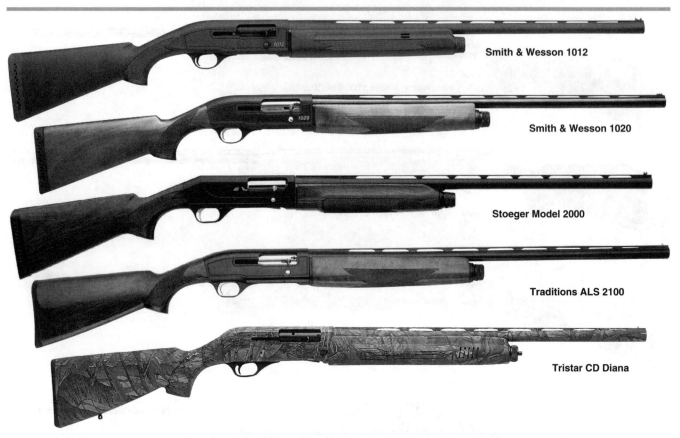

Smith & Wesson 1012

Smith & Wesson 1020

Stoeger Model 2000

Traditions ALS 2100

Tristar CD Diana

SMITH & WESSON 1000/1020/1012 SUPER SEMI-AUTO SHOTGUNS
Gauge: 12, 20; 3" in 1000; 3.5" chamber in Super. **Barrel:** 24", 26", 28", 30". **Stock:** Walnut. Synthetic finishes are satin, black, Realtree MAX-4, Realtree APG. **Sights:** TruGlo fiber-optic. **Features:** 29 configurations. Gas operated, dual-piston action; chrome-lined barrels, five choke tubes, shim kit for adjusting stock. 20-ga. models are Model 1020 or Model 1020SS (short stock). Lifetime warranty. Introduced 2007. Imported from Turkey by Smith & Wesson.
Price: Black synthetic stock. . . . . **NA**

STOEGER MODEL 2000 SHOTGUNS
Gauge: 12, 3" chamber, set of five choke tubes (C, IC, M, F, XFT). **Barrel:** 24", 26", 28", 30". **Stock:** Walnut, synthetic, Timber HD, Max-4. **Sights:** Red bar front. **Features:** Inertia-recoil. Minimum recommended load: 3 dram, 1-1/8 oz. Imported by Benelli USA.
Price: Walnut $445.00
Price: Synthetic $435.00
Price: Max-4, Timber HD $495.00
Price: Field and slug barrel combo $725.00
Price: Black synthetic pistol grip (2007) $475.00
Price: APG HD camo pistol grip (2007) $535.00

TRADITIONS ALS 2100 SERIES SEMI-AUTOMATIC SHOTGUNS
Gauge: 12, 3" chamber; 20, 3" chamber. **Barrel:** 24", 26", 28" (Imp. Cyl., Mod. and Full choke tubes). **Weight:** 5 lbs., 10 oz. to 6 lbs., 5 oz. **Length:** 44" to 48" overall. **Stock:** Walnut or black composite. **Features:** Gas-operated; vent rib barrel with Beretta-style threaded muzzle. Introduced 2001 by Traditions.
Price: Field Model (12 or 20 ga., 26" or 28" bbl., walnut stock) $479.00
Price: Youth Model (12 or 20 ga., 24" bbl., walnut stock) $479.00
Price: (12 or 20 ga., 26" or 28" barrel, composite stock) $459.00

Traditions ALS 2100 Turkey Semi-Automatic Shotgun
Similar to ALS 2100 Field Model except chambered in 12 gauge, 3" only with 26" barrel and Mossy Oak® Break Up™ camo finish. Weighs 6 lbs.; 46" overall.
Price: $519.00

Traditions ALS 2100 Waterfowl Semi-Automatic Shotgun
Similar to ALS 2100 Field Model except chambered in 12 gauge, 3" only with 28" barrel and Advantage® Wetlands™ camo finish. Weighs 6.25 lbs.; 48" overall. Multi chokes.
Price: $529.00

Traditions ALS 2100 Hunter Combo
Similar to ALS 2100 Field Model except 2 barrels, 28" vent rib and 24" fully rifled deer. Weighs 6 to 6.5 lbs.; 48" overall. Choice TruGlo adj. sights or fixed cantilever mount on rifled barrel. Multi chokes.
Price: Walnut, rifle barrel $609.00
Price: Walnut, cantilever $629.00
Price: Synthetic $579.00

Traditions ALS 2100 Slug Hunter Shotgun
Similar to ALS 2100 Field Model, 12 ga., 24" barrel, overall length 44"; weighs 6.25 lbs. Designed specifically for the deer hunter. Rifled barrel has 1 in 36" twist. Fully adjustable fiber-optic sights.
Price: Walnut, rifle barrel $529.00
Price: Synthetic, rifle barrel $499.00
Price: Walnut, cantilever $549.00
Price: Synthetic, cantilever $529.00

Traditions ALS 2100 Home Security Shotgun
Similar to ALS 2100 Field Model, 12 ga., 20" barrel, overall length 40", weighs 6 lbs. Can be reloaded with one hand while shouldered and on-target. Swivel studs installed in stock.
Price: $399.00

TRISTAR CD DIANA AUTO SHOTGUNS
Gauge: 12, shoots 2-3/4" or 3" interchangeably. **Barrel:** 24", 26", 28" (Imp. Cyl., Mod., Full choke tubes). **Stock:** European walnut or black synthetic. **Features:** Gas-operated action; blued barrel; checkered pistol grip and forend; vent rib barrel. Available with synthetic and camo stock and in slug model. First introduced 1999 under the name "Tristar Phantom." Imported by Tristar Sporting Arms Ltd.
Price: . . . . $399.00 to $535.00

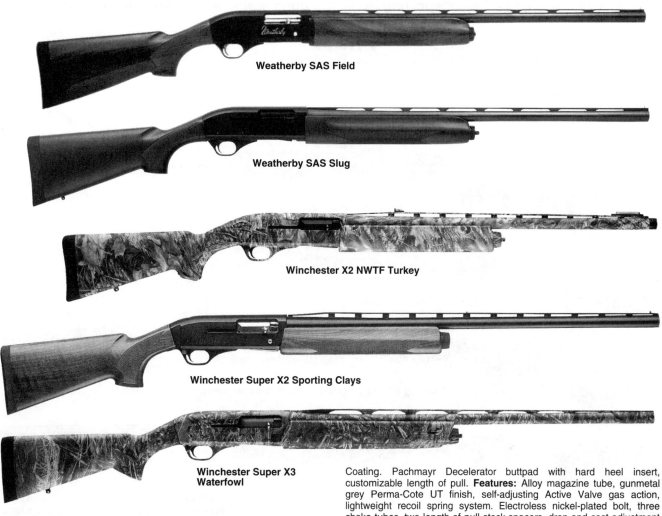

Weatherby SAS Field

Weatherby SAS Slug

Winchester X2 NWTF Turkey

Winchester Super X2 Sporting Clays

Winchester Super X3 Waterfowl

VERONA MODEL SX400 SEMI AUTO SHOTGUNS
Gauge: 12. **Barrel:** 26", 30". **Weight:** 6-1/2 lbs. **Stock:** Walnut, black composite. **Sights:** Red dot. **Features:** Aluminum receivers, gas-operated, 2-3/4" or 3" Magnum shells without adj. or Mod., 4 screw-in chokes and wrench included. Sling swivels, gold trigger. Blued barrel. Imported from Italy by B.C. Outdoors.

Price: 401S, 12 ga. **$398.40**
Price: 405SDS, 12 ga. **$610.00**
Price: 405L, 12 ga. **$331.20**

WEATHERBY SAS (SEMI-AUTOMATIC SHOTGUNS)
Gauge: 12 ga. **Barrel:** Vent ribbed, 24" to 30". **Weight:** 7 lbs. to 7-3/4 lbs. **Stock:** SAS field and sporting clays, walnut. SAS Shadow Grass, Break-Up™, Synthetic, composite. **Sights:** SAS sporting clays, brass front and mid-point rear. SAS Shadow Grass and Break-Up™, HiViz front and brass mid. Synthetic has brass front. **Features:** Easy to shoot, load, clean; lightweight, reduced recoil, IMC system includes 3 chrome-moly screw-in choke tubes. Slug gun has 22" rifled barrel with matte blue finish and cantilever base for scope mounting.

Price: Field, Sporting Clays, Shadow Grass, Break-Up™,
Synthetic, Slug Gun .... **$879.00 to $969.00**

WINCHESTER SUPER X3 SHOTGUNS
Gauge: 12, 3" and 3.5" chambers. **Barrel:** 26", 28", .742" back-bored; Invector Plus choke tubes. **Weight:** 7 to 7.25 lbs. **Stock:** Composite, 14.25"x1.75"x2". Mossy Oak New Break-Up camo with Dura-Touch Armor Coating. Pachmayr Decelerator buttpad with hard heel insert, customizable length of pull. **Features:** Alloy magazine tube, gunmetal grey Perma-Cote UT finish, self-adjusting Active Valve gas action, lightweight recoil spring system. Electroless nickel-plated bolt, three choke tubes, two length-of-pull stock spacers, drop and cast adjustment spacers, sling swivel studs. Introduced 2006. Made in Belgium, assembled in Portugal by U.S. Repeating Arms Co.

Price: from **$945.00**
Price: Cantilever Deer. **$995.00**
Price: Waterfowl w/Mossy Oak Brush camo, intr. 2007 .... **$1,216.00**
Price: Field model, walnut stock, intr. 2007 .... **$979.00**

WINCHESTER SUPER X2 AUTO SHOTGUNS
Gauge: 12, 3", 3-1/2" chamber. **Barrel:** Belgian, 24", 26", 28"; Invector Plus choke tubes. **Weight:** 7-1/4 to 7-1/2 lbs. **Stock:** 14-1/4"x1-3/4"x2". Walnut or black synthetic. **Features:** Gas-operated action shoots all loads without adjustment; vent rib barrels; 4-shot magazine. Introduced 1999. Assembled in Portugal by U.S. Repeating Arms Co.

Price: Universal Hunter T **$1,252.00**
Price: NWTF Turkey, 3-1/2", Mossy Oak Break-Up camo **$1,236.00**
Price: Universal Hunter Model **$1,252.00**

Winchester Super X2 Sporting Clays Auto Shotguns
Similar to the Super X2 except has two gas pistons (one for target loads, one for heavy 3" loads), adjustable comb system and high-post rib. Back-bored barrel with Invector Plus choke tubes. Offered in 28" and 30" barrels. Introduced 2001. From U.S. Repeating Arms Co.

Price: Super X2 sporting clays **$999.00**
Price: Signature red stock **$1,015.00**
Price: Practical MK I, composite stock, TruGlo sights **$1,116.00**

Includes a wide variety of sporting guns and guns suitable for competitive shooting.

Benelli Nova Pump

Benelli Nova Pump Slug

Browning BPS 10 gauge

Browning BPS 10 gauge Mossy Oak® Shadow Grass

Browning BPS Trap

BENELLI SUPERNOVA PUMP SHOTGUNS
Gauge: 12; 3.5" chamber. **Barrel:** 24", 26", 28". **Length:** 45.5-49.5". **Stock:** Synthetic; Max-4 , Timber, APG HD (2007). **Sights:** Red bar front, metal midbead. **Features:** 2-3/ 4", 3" chamber (3-1/2" 12 ga. only). Montefeltro rotating bolt design with dual action bars, magazine cut-off, synthetic trigger assembly, adjustable combs, shim kit, choice of buttstocks. 4-shot magazine. Introduced 2006. Imported from Italy by Benelli USA.
Price: Synthetic ComforTech **$455.00**
Price: Camo ComforTech **$545.00**
Price: SteadyGrip . . . . **$465.00 to $560.00**
Price: Tactical, Ghost Ring sight . . . . **$400.00 to $545.00**
Price: Field & Slug combo (2007) **$655.00**
Price: Rifled Slug ComforTech (2007) **$645.00**
Price: Tactical desert camo pistol grip, 18" barrel (2007) **$545.00**

BENELLI NOVA PUMP SHOTGUNS
Gauge: 12, 20. **Barrel:** 24", 26", 28". **Stock:** Black synthetic, Max-4, Timber and APG HD. **Sights:** Red bar. **Features:** 2-3/ 4", 3" chamber (3-1/2" 12 ga. only). Montefeltro rotating bolt design with dual action bars, magazine cut-off, synthetic trigger assembly, 4-shot magazine. Introduced 1999. Field & Slug Combo has 24" barrel and rifled bore; open rifle sights; synthetic stock; weighs 8.1 lbs. Imported from Italy by Benelli USA.
Price: Black synthetic stock **$360.00**
Price: Timber HD or Max-4 camo stock **$455.00**
Price: H20 model, black synthetic, matte nickel finish **$535.00**
Price: APG HD stock (2007) **$455.00**

Price: Tactical, 18.5" barrel, Ghost Ring sight **$375.00**
Price: Black synthetic stock, 20 ga. **$360.00**
Price: Black synthetic youth stock, 20 ga. **$375.00**
Price: Timber HD stock or APG HD stock (2007), 20 ga. **$455.00**
Price: Field & Slug Combo, black synthetic, cantilever mount **$560.00**

BROWNING BPS PUMP SHOTGUNS
Gauge: 10, 12, 3-1/2" chamber; 12 or 20, 3" chamber (2-3/4" in target guns), 28, 2-3/4" chamber, 5-shot magazine, .410, 3" chamber. **Barrel:** 10 ga.-24" Buck Special, 28", 30", 32" Invector; 12, 20 ga.-22", 24", 26", 28", 30", 32" (Imp. Cyl., Mod. or Full), .410-26" barrel. (Imp. Cyl., Mod. and Full choke tubes.) Also available with Invector choke tubes, 12 or 20 ga.; Upland Special has 22" barrel with Invector tubes. BPS 3" and 3-1/2" have back-bored barrel. **Weight:** 7 lbs., 8 oz. (28" barrel). **Length:** 48-3/4" overall (28" barrel). **Stock:** 14-1/4"x1-1/2"x2-1/2". Select walnut, semi-beavertail forend, full pistol grip stock. **Features:** All 12 gauge 3" guns except Buck Special and game guns have back-bored barrels with Invector Plus choke tubes. Bottom feeding and ejection, receiver top safety, high post vent rib. Double action bars eliminate binding. Vent rib barrels only. All 12 and 20 gauge guns with 3" chamber available with fully engraved receiver flats at no extra cost. Each gauge has its own unique game scene. Introduced 1977. Imported from Japan by Browning.
Price: 12 ga., 3-1/2" Stalker (black syn. stock) **$608.00**
Price: 12, 20 ga., Hunter, Invector Plus **$519.00**
Price: 20 ga. Deer Hunter (22" rifled bbl., cantilever mount),
    intr. 2007 . . . . **$651.00**
Price: 28 ga., Hunter, Invector **$555.00**
Price: .410, Hunter, Invector **$555.00**
Price: Trap, intr. 2007 . . . . **$663.00**

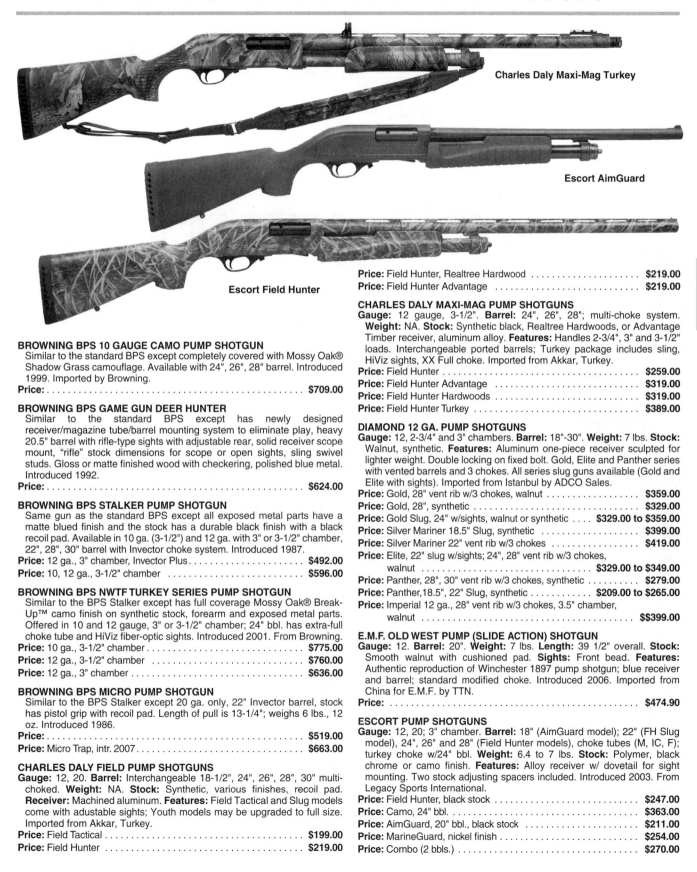

Charles Daly Maxi-Mag Turkey

Escort AimGuard

Escort Field Hunter

BROWNING BPS 10 GAUGE CAMO PUMP SHOTGUN
Similar to the standard BPS except completely covered with Mossy Oak® Shadow Grass camouflage. Available with 24", 26", 28" barrel. Introduced 1999. Imported by Browning.
Price: **$709.00**

BROWNING BPS GAME GUN DEER HUNTER
Similar to the standard BPS except has newly designed receiver/magazine tube/barrel mounting system to eliminate play, heavy 20.5" barrel with rifle-type sights with adjustable rear, solid receiver scope mount, "rifle" stock dimensions for scope or open sights, sling swivel studs. Gloss or matte finished wood with checkering, polished blue metal. Introduced 1992.
Price: **$624.00**

BROWNING BPS STALKER PUMP SHOTGUN
Same gun as the standard BPS except all exposed metal parts have a matte blued finish and the stock has a durable black finish with a black recoil pad. Available in 10 ga. (3-1/2") and 12 ga. with 3" or 3-1/2" chamber, 22", 28", 30" barrel with Invector choke system. Introduced 1987.
Price: 12 ga., 3" chamber, Invector Plus..................... **$492.00**
Price: 10, 12 ga., 3-1/2" chamber **$596.00**

BROWNING BPS NWTF TURKEY SERIES PUMP SHOTGUN
Similar to the BPS Stalker except has full coverage Mossy Oak® Break-Up™ camo finish on synthetic stock, forearm and exposed metal parts. Offered in 10 and 12 gauge, 3" or 3-1/2" chamber; 24" bbl. has extra-full choke tube and HiViz fiber-optic sights. Introduced 2001. From Browning.
Price: 10 ga., 3-1/2" chamber **$775.00**
Price: 12 ga., 3-1/2" chamber **$760.00**
Price: 12 ga., 3" chamber **$636.00**

BROWNING BPS MICRO PUMP SHOTGUN
Similar to the BPS Stalker except 20 ga. only, 22" Invector barrel, stock has pistol grip with recoil pad. Length of pull is 13-1/4"; weighs 6 lbs., 12 oz. Introduced 1986.
Price: **$519.00**
Price: Micro Trap, intr. 2007.............................. **$663.00**

CHARLES DALY FIELD PUMP SHOTGUNS
Gauge: 12, 20. **Barrel:** Interchangeable 18-1/2", 24", 26", 28", 30" multi-choked. **Weight:** NA. **Stock:** Synthetic, various finishes, recoil pad. **Receiver:** Machined aluminum. **Features:** Field Tactical and Slug models come with adustable sights; Youth models may be upgraded to full size. Imported from Akkar, Turkey.
Price: Field Tactical **$199.00**
Price: Field Hunter **$219.00**

Price: Field Hunter, Realtree Hardwood **$219.00**
Price: Field Hunter Advantage **$219.00**

CHARLES DALY MAXI-MAG PUMP SHOTGUNS
Gauge: 12 gauge, 3-1/2". **Barrel:** 24", 26", 28"; multi-choke system. **Weight:** NA. **Stock:** Synthetic black, Realtree Hardwoods, or Advantage Timber receiver, aluminum alloy. **Features:** Handles 2-3/4", 3" and 3-1/2" loads. Interchangeable ported barrels; Turkey package includes sling, HiViz sights, XX Full choke. Imported from Akkar, Turkey.
Price: Field Hunter **$259.00**
Price: Field Hunter Advantage **$319.00**
Price: Field Hunter Hardwoods **$319.00**
Price: Field Hunter Turkey **$389.00**

DIAMOND 12 GA. PUMP SHOTGUNS
Gauge: 12, 2-3/4" and 3" chambers. **Barrel:** 18"-30". **Weight:** 7 lbs. **Stock:** Walnut, synthetic. **Features:** Aluminum one-piece receiver sculpted for lighter weight. Double locking on fixed bolt. Gold, Elite and Panther series with vented barrels and 3 chokes. All series slug guns available (Gold and Elite with sights). Imported from Istanbul by ADCO Sales.
Price: Gold, 28" vent rib w/3 chokes, walnut **$359.00**
Price: Gold, 28", synthetic **$329.00**
Price: Gold Slug, 24" w/sights, walnut or synthetic .... **$329.00 to $359.00**
Price: Silver Mariner 18.5" Slug, synthetic **$399.00**
Price: Silver Mariner 22" vent rib w/3 chokes **$419.00**
Price: Elite, 22" slug w/sights; 24", 28" vent rib w/3 chokes,
walnut .... **$329.00 to $349.00**
Price: Panther, 28", 30" vent rib w/3 chokes, synthetic **$279.00**
Price: Panther,18.5", 22" Slug, synthetic .... **$209.00 to $265.00**
Price: Imperial 12 ga., 28" vent rib w/3 chokes, 3.5" chamber,
walnut .... **$$399.00**

E.M.F. OLD WEST PUMP (SLIDE ACTION) SHOTGUN
Gauge: 12. **Barrel:** 20". **Weight:** 7 lbs. **Length:** 39 1/2" overall. **Stock:** Smooth walnut with cushioned pad. **Sights:** Front bead. **Features:** Authentic reproduction of Winchester 1897 pump shotgun; blue receiver and barrel; standard modified choke. Introduced 2006. Imported from China for E.M.F. by TTN.
Price: **$474.90**

ESCORT PUMP SHOTGUNS
Gauge: 12, 20; 3" chamber. **Barrel:** 18" (AimGuard model); 22" (FH Slug model), 24", 26" and 28" (Field Hunter models), choke tubes (M, IC, F); turkey choke w/24" bbl. **Weight:** 6.4 to 7 lbs. **Stock:** Polymer, black chrome or camo finish. **Features:** Alloy receiver w/ dovetail for sight mounting. Two stock adjusting spacers included. Introduced 2003. From Legacy Sports International.
Price: Field Hunter, black stock **$247.00**
Price: Camo, 24" bbl. **$363.00**
Price: AimGuard, 20" bbl., black stock **$211.00**
Price: MarineGuard, nickel finish **$254.00**
Price: Combo (2 bbls.) **$270.00**

**Mossberg Model 835
Mossy Oak Camo**

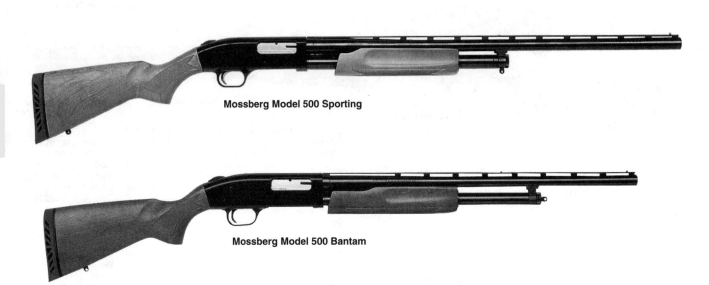

Mossberg Model 500 Sporting

Mossberg Model 500 Bantam

MOSSBERG MODEL 835 ULTI-MAG PUMP SHOTGUNS
Gauge: 12, 3-1/2" chamber. **Barrel:** Ported 24" rifled bore, 24", 28", Accu-Mag choke tubes for steel or lead shot. **Weight:** 7-3/4 lbs. **Length:** 48-1/2" overall. **Stock:** 14"x1-1/2"x2-1/2". Dual Comb. Cut-checkered hardwood or camo synthetic; both have recoil pad. **Sights:** White bead front, brass mid-bead; fiber-optic rear. **Features:** Shoots 2-3/4", 3" or 3-1/2" shells. Back-bored and ported barrel to reduce recoil, improve patterns. Ambidextrous thumb safety, twin extractors, dual slide bars. Mossberg Cablelock included. Introduced 1988.
Price: 28" vent rib, hardwood stock. $394.00
Price: Combos, 24" rifled or smooth bore, rifle sights, 24" vent rib
    Accu-Mag Ulti-Full choke tube, Mossy Oak® camo finish . . $556.00
Price: RealTree Camo Turkey, 24" vent rib, Accu-Mag extra-full
    tube, synthetic stock $574.00
Price: Mossy Oak® Camo, 28" vent rib, Accu-Mag tubes,
    synthetic stock $574.00
Price: OFM Camo, 28" vent rib, Accu-Mag Mod. tube,
    synthetic stock $438.00

Mossberg Model 835 Synthetic Stock Shotgun
Similar to the Model 835, except with 28" ported barrel with Accu-Mag Mod. choke tube, Parkerized finish, black synthetic stock and forend. Introduced 1998. Made in U.S. by Mossberg.
Price: $394.00

MOSSBERG MODEL 500 SPORTING PUMP SHOTGUNS
Gauge: 12, 20, .410, 3" chamber. **Barrel:** 18-1/2" to 28" with fixed or Accu-Choke, plain or vent rib. **Weight:** 6-1/4 lbs. (.410), 7-1/4 lbs. (12). **Length:** 48" overall (28" barrel). **Stock:** 14"x1-1/2"x2-1/2". Walnut-stained hardwood. Cut-checkered grip and forend. **Sights:** White bead front, brass mid-bead; fiber-optic. **Features:** Ambidextrous thumb safety, twin

extractors, disconnecting safety, dual action bars. Quiet Carry forend. Many barrels are ported. From Mossberg.
Price: From about $316.00
Price: Sporting Combos (field barrel and Slugster barrel). From . . $381.00

Mossberg Model 500 Bantam Pump Shotgun
Same as the Model 500 Sporting Pump except 12 or 20 gauge, 22" vent rib Accu-Choke barrel with choke tube set; has 1" shorter stock, reduced length from pistol grip to trigger, reduced forend reach. Introduced 1992.
Price: $316.00
Price: With Realtree Hardwoods camouflage finish (20 ga. only) . . $364.00

Mossberg Model 500 Camo Pump Shotgun
Same as the Model 500 Sporting Pump except 12 gauge only and entire gun is covered with Mossy Oak® Advantage camouflage finish. Receiver drilled and tapped for scope mounting. Comes with quick detachable swivel studs, swivels, camouflage sling, Mossberg Cablelock.
Price: From about $364.00

Mossberg Model 500 Persuader/Cruiser Shotguns
Similar to Mossberg Model 500 except has 18-1/2" or 20" barrel with cylinder bore choke, synthetic stock and blue or Parkerized finish. Available in 12, 20 and .410 with bead or ghost ring sights, 6- or 8-shot magazines. From Mossberg.
Price: 12 gauge, 20" barrel, 8-shot, bead sight. $357.00
Price: 20 gauge or .410, 18-1/2" barrel, 6-shot, bead sight $357.00
Price: Home Security 410 (.410, 18-1/2" barrel with
    spreader choke) $360.00

Mossberg Model 590 Special Purpose Shotgun
Similar to Model 500 except has Parkerized or Marinecote finish, 9-shot magazine and black synthetic stock (some models feature Speed Feed). Available in 12 gauge only with 20", cylinder bore barrel. Weighs 7-1/4 lbs. From Mossberg.
Price: Bead sight, heat shield over barrel $525.00

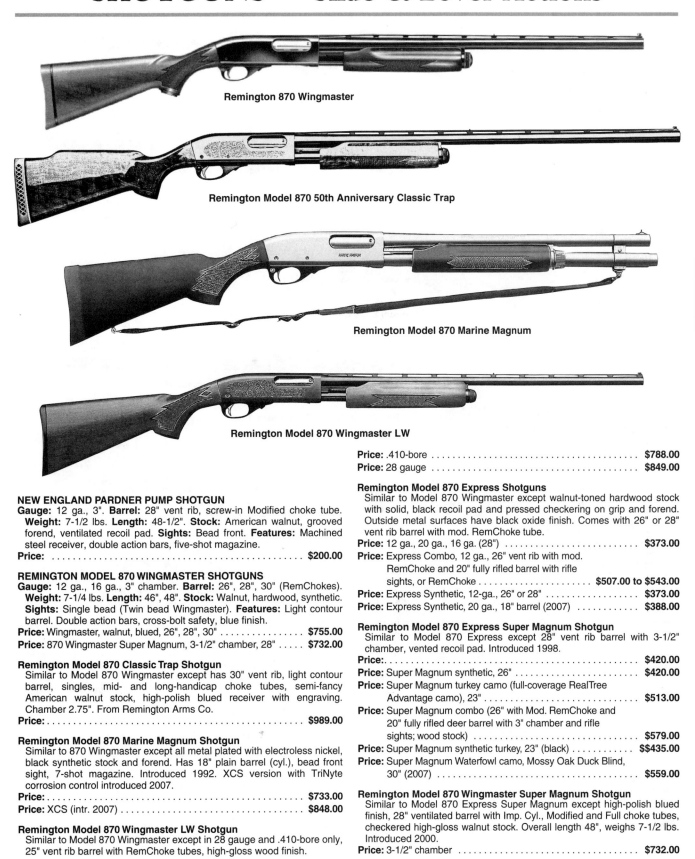

Remington 870 Wingmaster

Remington Model 870 50th Anniversary Classic Trap

Remington Model 870 Marine Magnum

Remington Model 870 Wingmaster LW

NEW ENGLAND PARDNER PUMP SHOTGUN
Gauge: 12 ga., 3". **Barrel:** 28" vent rib, screw-in Modified choke tube. **Weight:** 7-1/2 lbs. **Length:** 48-1/2". **Stock:** American walnut, grooved forend, ventilated recoil pad. **Sights:** Bead front. **Features:** Machined steel receiver, double action bars, five-shot magazine.
Price: **$200.00**

REMINGTON MODEL 870 WINGMASTER SHOTGUNS
Gauge: 12 ga., 16 ga., 3" chamber. **Barrel:** 26", 28", 30" (RemChokes). **Weight:** 7-1/4 lbs. **Length:** 46", 48". **Stock:** Walnut, hardwood, synthetic. **Sights:** Single bead (Twin bead Wingmaster). **Features:** Light contour barrel. Double action bars, cross-bolt safety, blue finish.
Price: Wingmaster, walnut, blued, 26", 28", 30" **$755.00**
Price: 870 Wingmaster Super Magnum, 3-1/2" chamber, 28" **$732.00**

Remington Model 870 Classic Trap Shotgun
Similar to Model 870 Wingmaster except has 30" vent rib, light contour barrel, singles, mid- and long-handicap choke tubes, semi-fancy American walnut stock, high-polish blued receiver with engraving. Chamber 2.75". From Remington Arms Co.
Price: **$989.00**

Remington Model 870 Marine Magnum Shotgun
Similar to 870 Wingmaster except all metal plated with electroless nickel, black synthetic stock and forend. Has 18" plain barrel (cyl.), bead front sight, 7-shot magazine. Introduced 1992. XCS version with TriNyte corrosion control introduced 2007.
Price: **$733.00**
Price: XCS (intr. 2007) **$848.00**

Remington Model 870 Wingmaster LW Shotgun
Similar to Model 870 Wingmaster except in 28 gauge and .410-bore only, 25" vent rib barrel with RemChoke tubes, high-gloss wood finish.

Price: .410-bore **$788.00**
Price: 28 gauge **$849.00**

Remington Model 870 Express Shotguns
Similar to Model 870 Wingmaster except walnut-toned hardwood stock with solid, black recoil pad and pressed checkering on grip and forend. Outside metal surfaces have black oxide finish. Comes with 26" or 28" vent rib barrel with mod. RemChoke tube.
Price: 12 ga., 20 ga., 16 ga. (28") **$373.00**
Price: Express Combo, 12 ga., 26" vent rib with mod.
RemChoke and 20" fully rifled barrel with rifle
sights, or RemChoke .... **$507.00 to $543.00**
Price: Express Synthetic, 12-ga., 26" or 28" **$373.00**
Price: Express Synthetic, 20 ga., 18" barrel (2007) **$388.00**

Remington Model 870 Express Super Magnum Shotgun
Similar to Model 870 Express except 28" vent rib barrel with 3-1/2" chamber, vented recoil pad. Introduced 1998.
Price:. **$420.00**
Price: Super Magnum synthetic, 26" **$420.00**
Price: Super Magnum turkey camo (full-coverage RealTree
Advantage camo), 23" **$513.00**
Price: Super Magnum combo (26" with Mod. RemChoke and
20" fully rifled deer barrel with 3" chamber and rifle
sights; wood stock) **$579.00**
Price: Super Magnum synthetic turkey, 23" (black) .... **$$435.00**
Price: Super Magnum Waterfowl camo, Mossy Oak Duck Blind,
30" (2007) **$559.00**

Remington Model 870 Wingmaster Super Magnum Shotgun
Similar to Model 870 Express Super Magnum except high-polish blued finish, 28" ventilated barrel with Imp. Cyl., Modified and Full choke tubes, checkered high-gloss walnut stock. Overall length 48", weighs 7-1/2 lbs. Introduced 2000.
Price: 3-1/2" chamber **$732.00**

Remington Model 870 Express Super Magnum

Remington Model 870 Express Deer Gun

Remington Model 870 Express Turkey

Remington Model 870 Express Youth Turkey Camo

Remington Model 870 SPS-T Camo

Remington Model 870 SPS-T Super Magnum Camo Shotguns
   Similar to the Model 870 Express synthetic, chambered for 12 ga., 3"
shells, has Mossy Oak® Break-Up™ synthetic stock and metal treatment,
TruGlo fiber-optic sights. Introduced 2001. SPS Max Gobbler introduced
2007. Knoxx SpecOps adjustable stock, Williams Fire Sights fiber-optic
sights, R3 recoil pad, Realtree APG HD camo. Drilled and tapped for
Weaver-style rail
Price: 20" RS, Rem. choke **$653.00**
Price: SPS Super Mag Max Gobbler (2007). **$799.00**

Remington Model 870 Express Deer Shotguns
   Same as Model 870 Express except 20" barrel with fixed imp. cyl. choke,
open iron sights, Monte Carlo stock. Introduced 1991.
Price: **$416.00**
Price: With fully rifled barrel **$385.00**

Remington Model 870 Express Turkey Shotguns
   Same as Model 870 Express except 3" chamber, 21" vent rib turkey barrel
and extra-full Rem. choke turkey tube; 12 ga. only. Introduced 1991.
Price: **$359.00**
Price: Express Turkey Camo stock has Skyline Excel camo, matte black
        metal **$412.00**
Price: Express Turkey Youth Camo **$445.00**

Remington Model 870 Express Synthetic 18" Shotgun
   Similar to Model 870 Express with 18" barrel except synthetic stock and
forend; 7-shot. Introduced 1994.
Price: **$332.00**

REMINGTON MODEL 870 SPS SUPER MAGNUM CAMO SHOTGUN
Gauge: 12, 3-1/2" chamber. **Barrel:** 26", 28", vent rib, with Full, Mod., Imp.
   Cyl. RemChoke. **Weight:** 7-1/4 lbs. to 7-1/2 lbs. **Length:** 46" to 481/2"
   overall. **Stock:** Mossy Oak® Break-Up™ camo finish. **Sights:** Metal bead
   front. **Features:** Synthetic stock and all metal (except bolt and trigger
   guard) and stock covered with Mossy Oak® Break-Up™ camo finish.
   Comes with camo sling, swivels.
Price: **$741.00**
Price: Max Gobbler, Realtree All-Purpose Green HD (2007) **$799.00**

STOEGER MODEL P350 SHOTGUNS
Gauge: 12, 3.5" chamber, set of five choke tubes (C, IC, M, IM, XF). **Barrel:**
   18.5",24", 26", 28". **Stock:** Black synthetic, Timber HD, Max-4 HD, APG
   HD camos. **Sights:** Red bar front. **Features:** Inertia-recoil, mercury recoil
   reducer, pistol grip stocks. Imported by Benelli USA.
Price: Synthetic **$290.00**
Price: Max-4, Timber HD **$350.00**
Price: Black synthetic pistol grip (2007) **$325.00**
Price: APG HD camo pistol grip (2007) **$350.00**

Includes a variety of game guns and guns for competitive shooting.

Beretta DT Trident Skeet

Beretta Series 682 Gold E Sporting

Beretta Series 682 Gold E Trap Combo

Beretta S687 EELL Combo

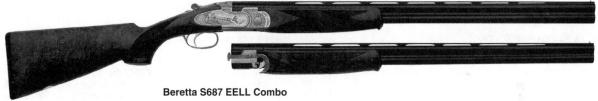

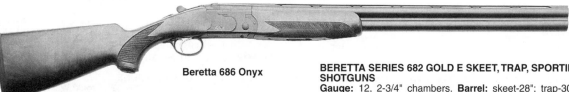

Beretta 686 Onyx

BERETTA DT10 TRIDENT SHOTGUNS

Gauge: 12, 2-3/4", 3" chambers. **Barrel:** 28", 30", 32", 34"; competition-style vent rib; fixed or Optima choke tubes. **Weight:** 7.9 to 9 lbs. **Stock:** High-grade walnut stock with oil finish; hand-checkered grip and forend, adjustable stocks available. **Features:** Detachable, adjustable trigger group, raised and thickened receiver, forend iron has adjustment nut to guarantee wood-to-metal fit. Introduced 2000. Imported from Italy by Beretta USA.

Price: DT10 Trident Trap (selective, lockable single trigger,
   adjustable stock. **$8,500.00**
Price: DT10 Trident Top Single **$10,790.00**
Price: DT10 Trident X Trap Combo
   (single and o/u barrels) **$11,040.00**
Price: DT10 Trident Skeet (skeet stock with rounded recoil
   pad, tapered rib) **$8,030.00**
Price: DT10 Trident Sporting (sporting clays stock with
   rounded recoil pad) **$7,850.00**
Price: DT10L Sporting **$8,475.00**

BERETTA SERIES 682 GOLD E SKEET, TRAP, SPORTING O/U SHOTGUNS

Gauge: 12, 2-3/4" chambers. **Barrel:** skeet-28"; trap-30" and 32", Imp. Mod. & Full and Mobilchoke; trap mono shotguns-32" and 34" Mobilchoke; trap top single guns-32" and 34" Full and Mobilchoke; trap combo sets-from 30" O/U, to 32" O/U, 34" top single. **Stock:** Close-grained walnut, hand checkered. **Sights:** White Bradley bead front sight and center bead. **Features:** Receiver has Greystone gunmetal gray finish with gold accents. Trap Monte Carlo stock has deluxe trap recoil pad. Various grades available. Imported from Italy by Beretta USA.

Price: 682 Gold E Trap with adjustable stock. **$4,325.00**
Price: 682 Gold E Trap Top Combo **$5,475.00**
Price: 682 Gold E Sporting **$3,550.00**
Price: 682 Gold E skeet, adjustable stock **$4,325.00**

BERETTA 686 ONYX O/U SHOTGUNS

Gauge: 12, 20, 28; 3", 3.5" chambers. **Barrel:** 26", 28" (Mobilchoke tubes). **Weight:** 6.8-6.9 lbs. **Stock:** Checkered American walnut. **Features:** Intended for the beginning sporting clays shooter. Has wide, vented target rib, radiused recoil pad. Polished black finish on receiver and barrels. Introduced 1993. Imported from Italy by Beretta U.S.A.

Price: White Onyx. **$1,875.00**
Price: Onyx Pro **$1,875.00**
Price: Onyx Pro 3.5 . . . . **$1,975.00**

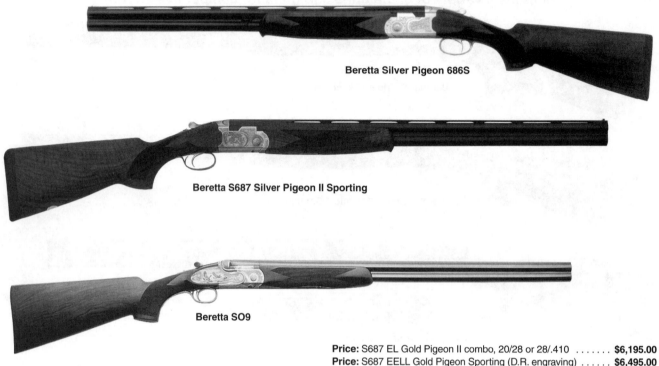

Beretta Silver Pigeon 686S

Beretta S687 Silver Pigeon II Sporting

Beretta SO9

BERETTA SILVER PIGEON O/U SHOTGUNS
Gauge: 12, 20, 28, 3" chambers (2-3/4" 28 ga.). .410 bore, 3" chamber. **Barrel:** 26", 28". **Weight:** 6.8 lbs. **Stock:** Checkered walnut. **Features:** Interchangeable barrels (20 and 28 ga.), single selective gold-plated trigger, boxlock action, auto safety, Schnabel forend.
Price: Silver Pigeon S **$2,150.00**
Price: Silver Pigeon S Combo **$2,975.00**
Price: Silver Pigeon II **$2,525.00**
Price: Silver Pigeon II, 28 ga. **$3,475.00**
Price: Silver Pigeon III **$2,650.00**
Price: Silver Pigeon IV **$2,955.00**
Price: Silver Pigeon V **$3,495.00**

BERETTA ULTRALIGHT O/U SHOTGUNS
Gauge: 12, 2-3/4" chambers. **Barrel:** 26", 28", Mobilchoke tubes. **Weight:** About 5 lbs., 13 oz. **Stock:** Select American walnut with checkered grip and forend. **Features:** Low-profile aluminum alloy receiver with titanium breech face insert. Electroless nickel receiver with game scene engraving. Single selective trigger; automatic safety. Introduced 1992. Ultralight Deluxe except has matte electroless nickel finish receiver with gold game scene engraving; matte oil-finished, select walnut stock and forend. Imported from Italy by Beretta U.S.A.
Price: **$1,975.00**
Price: Ultralight Deluxe **$2,350.00**

BERETTA COMPETITION SHOTGUNS
Gauge: 12, 20, 28, and .410 bore, 2-3/4", 3" and 3-1/2" chambers. **Barrel:** 26" and 28" (Mobilchoke tubes). **Stock:** Close-grained walnut. **Features:** Highly-figured, American walnut stocks and forends, and a unique, weather-resistant finish on barrels. Silver designates standard 686, 687 models with silver receivers; 686 Silver Pigeon has enhanced engraving pattern, Schnabel forend; Gold indicates higher grade 686EL, 687EL models with full sideplates; Diamond is for 687EELL models with highest grade wood, engraving. Case provided with Gold and Diamond grades. Imported from Italy by Beretta U.S.A.
Price: S687 Silver Pigeon II Sporting **$2,850.00**
Price: S687 EL Gold Pigeon II (deep relief engraving) **$5,095.00**

Price: S687 EL Gold Pigeon II combo, 20/28 or 28/.410 . . . . . . **$6,195.00**
Price: S687 EELL Gold Pigeon Sporting (D.R. engraving) **$6,495.00**
Price: Gold Sporting Pigeon **$4,971.00**
Price: 28 and 410 combo . . . . **NA**

BERETTA MODEL SO5, SO6, SO9 SHOTGUNS
Gauge: 12, 2-3/4" chambers. **Barrel:** To customer specs. **Stock:** To customer specs. **Features:** SO5-trap, skeet and sporting clays models SO5; SO6-SO6 and SO6 EELL are field models. SO6 has a case-hardened or silver receiver with contour hand engraving. SO6 EELL has hand-engraved receiver in a fine floral or "fine English" pattern or game scene, with bas-relief chisel work and gold inlays. SO6 and SO6 EELL are available with sidelocks removable by hand. Imported from Italy by Beretta U.S.A.
Price: SO5 Trap, skeet, Sporting **$13,000.00**
Price: SO6 Trap, skeet, Sporting **$17,500.00**
Price: SO6 EELL Field, custom specs **$28,000.00**
Price: SO9 (12, 20, 28, .410, 26", 28", 30", any choke) **$31,000.00**

BROWNING CYNERGY O/U SHOTGUNS
Gauge: 12, 20, 28. **Barrel:** 26", 28", 30", 32". **Stock:** Walnut or composite. **Sights:** White bead front most models; HiViz Pro-Comp sight on some models; mid bead. **Features:** Mono-Lock hinge, recoil-reducing interchangeable Inflex recoil pad, silver nitride receiver; striker-based trigger, ported barrel option. 12 models cataloged for 2006. Nine new models introduced 2006: Cynergy Sporting, Adjustable Comb; Cynergy Sporting Composite with TopCote; Cynergy Sporting Composite CF; Cynergy Field, Composite; Cynergy Classic Sporting; Cynergy Classic Field; Cynergy Camo Mossy Oak New Shadow Grass; Cynergy Camo Mossy Oak New Break-Up; and Cynergy Camo Mossy Oak Brush. Imported from Japan by Browning.
Price: Cynergy Field, 12 ga., Grade 1 walnut, ... **$2,048.00**
Price: Cynergy Field Small Gauge, 20 /28 ga., intr. 2005 . . . . . . **$2,062.00**
Price: Cynergy Sporting Small Gauge, 20 /28 ga., intr. 2005 . . . . **$3,080.00**
Price: Cynergy Field Composite, 12 ga., ... **$1,890.00**
Price: Cynergy Sporting, 12 ga.; 28", 30", or 32" barrels **$3,046.00**
Price: Cynergy Sporting Composite 12 ga. **$2,846.00**
Price: Cynergy Sporting, adjustable comb, intr. 2006 . . . . **$3,351.00**
Price: Cynergy Sporting Composite w/TopCote, intr. 2006 . . . . . . **$2,979.00**
Price: Cynergy Feather, intr. 2007 . . . . **$2,359.00**
Price: Cynergy Euro Sporting Composite, intr. 2007 . . . . **$3,199.00**

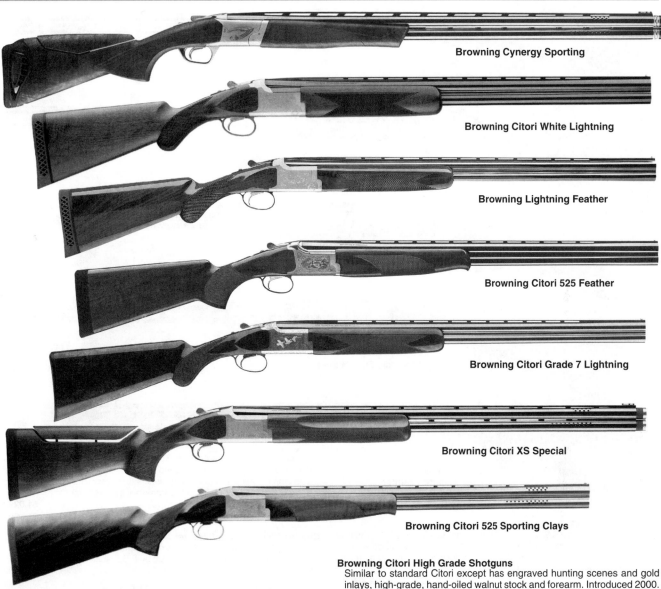

Browning Cynergy Sporting

Browning Citori White Lightning

Browning Lightning Feather

Browning Citori 525 Feather

Browning Citori Grade 7 Lightning

Browning Citori XS Special

Browning Citori 525 Sporting Clays

BROWNING CITORI O/U SHOTGUNS

Gauge: 12, 20, 28 and .410. **Barrel:** 26", 28" in 28 and .410. Offered with Invector choke tubes. All 12 and 20 gauge models have back-bored barrels and Invector Plus choke system. **Weight:** 6 lbs., 8 oz. (26" .410) to 7 lbs., 13 oz. (30" 12 ga.). **Length:** 43" overall (26" bbl.). **Stock:** Dense walnut, hand checkered, full pistol grip, beavertail forend. Field-type recoil pad on 12 ga. field guns and trap and skeet models. **Sights:** Medium raised beads, German nickel silver. **Features:** Barrel selector integral with safety, automatic ejectors, three-piece takedown. 25 models cataloged for 2006. Two limited-run models reintroduced 2006: Citori 4-Barrel Skeet Set, Grade I; Citori 4-Barrel Skeet Set, Grade VII. Imported from Japan by Browning.

Price: Lightning, 12 and 20 ga. $1,645.00
Price: Lightning, 28 ga. and .410 bore $1,709.00
Price: White Lightning, 12 and 20 ga. $1,714.00
Price: White Lightning, 28 ga. and .410 bore $1,790.00
Price: 525 Field, 12 and 20 ga.. . . . . $1,981.00
Price: 525 Field, 28 ga. and .410 bore. $2,010.00
Price: Superlight Feather, 12 and 20 ga. (2-3/4"), 6.25/5.7 lbs. . . $1,938.00
Price: Lightning Feather, 12 and 20 ga., ... $1,869.00
Price: Citori 4-Barrel Skeet Set, Grade I, intr. 2006 . . . . $8,412.00
Price: 525 Feather, 12 ga. intr. 2007 . . . . $2,212.00

Browning Citori High Grade Shotguns

Similar to standard Citori except has engraved hunting scenes and gold inlays, high-grade, hand-oiled walnut stock and forearm. Introduced 2000. From Browning.

Price: Gran Lightning, engraved receiver, from $2,429.00
Price: Grade IV Lightning, engraved gray receiver,
    introduced 2005, from $2,608.00
Price: Grade VII Lightning, engraved gray or blue receiver,
    introduced 2005, from $4,146.00
Price: GTS High Grade, intr. 2007 . . . . $3,900.00

Browning Citori XS Sporting O/U Shotguns

Similar to the standard Citori except available in 12, 20, 28 or .410 with 28", 30", 32" ported barrels with various screw-in choke combinations: S (Skeet), C (Cylinder), IC (Improved Cylinder), M (Modified), and IM (Improved Modified). Has pistol grip stock, rounded or Schnabel forend. Weighs 7.1 lbs. to 8.75 lbs. Introduced 2004.

Price: XS Special, 12 ga.; 30", 32" barrels $2,727.00
Price: XS Sporting, 12 or 20 ga. $2,472.00
Price: XS Skeet, 12 or 20 ga. $2,434.00
Price: 525 Sporting Grade I, 12 ga. intr. 2005 . . . . $2,319.00
Price: 525 Golden Clays, 12 or 20 gauge $3,058.00
Price: 525 Golden Clays, 28 or .410 . . . . $4,653.00
Price: High Post Rib, intr. 2007 . . . . $2,865.00

SHOTGUNS — Over/Unders

Browning Citori High Post Rib

Browning Citori XT Trap

Charles Daly Superior II Trap AE-MC

Charles Daly Field Hunter

Charles Daly Superior Hunter

Browning Citori XT Trap O/U Shotgun
Similar to the Citori XS Special except has engraved silver nitride receiver with gold highlights, vented side barrel rib. Available in 12 gauge with 30" or 32" barrels, Invector-Plus choke tubes, adjustable comb and buttplate. Introduced 1999. Imported by Browning.
Price: XT Trap **$2,390.00**
Price: XT Trap w/adjustable comb **$2,678.00**
Price: XT Trap Gold w/adjustable comb, introduced 2005 . . . . . . **$4,435.00**

CENTURION O/U SHOTGUN
Gauge: 12, 2-3/4" & 3" chambers, 20, 28, 410. **Barrel:** 28", 5 choke tubes. **Weight:** 7.35 lbs. (12); 6.14 lbs. (20); 5.8 lbs. (28); 5.3 lbs. (410). **Length:** 45". **Stock:** Glossy Turkish walnut. **Features:** Single selective trigger, automatic safety, extractors, ventilated recoil pad, front bead sight. Manufactured by CFS in Turkey. Imported by Century International.
Price: **$470.00**

CHARLES DALY SUPERIOR II TRAP AE-MC O/U SHOTGUN
Gauge: 12, 2-3/4" chambers. **Barrel:** 30" choke tubes. **Weight:** About 7 lbs. **Length:** 47-3/8". **Stock:** Checkered walnut; pistol grip, semi-beavertail forend. **Features:** Silver engraved receiver, chrome-moly steel barrels; gold single selective trigger; automatic safety, automatic ejectors; red bead front sight, metal bead center; recoil pad. Introduced 1997. Imported from Italy by K.B.I., Inc.
Price: **$1,699.00**

CHARLES DALY FIELD II HUNTER O/U SHOTGUN
Gauge: 12, 20, 28 and .410 bore (3" chambers, 28 ga. has 2-3/4"). **Barrel:** 28" Mod & Full, 26" Imp. Cyl. & Mod (.410 is Full & Full). **Weight:** About 7

lbs. **Length:** 42-3/4" to 44-3/4". **Stock:** Checkered walnut pistol grip and forend. **Features:** Blued engraved receiver, chrome-moly steel barrels; gold single selective trigger; automatic safety; extractors; gold bead front sight. Introduced 1997. Imported from Italy by K.B.I., Inc.
Price: 12 or 20 ga. **$1,029.00**
Price: 28 ga., .410 bore **$1,129.00**

Charles Daly Superior II Hunter AE O/U Shotgun
Similar to the Field Hunter AE except has silvered, engraved receiver. Introduced 1997. Imported from Italy by F.B.I., Inc.
Price: 28 ga., .410 bore **$1,519.00**

Charles Daly Field Hunter AE-MC O/U Shotgun
Similar to the Field Hunter except in 12 or 20 only, 26" or 28" barrels with five multi-choke tubes; automatic ejectors. Introduced 1997. Imported from Italy by K.B.I., Inc.
Price: 12 or 20 ga. **$1,279.00**

Charles Daly Superior II Sporting O/U Shotgun
Similar to the Field Hunter AE-MC except 28" or 30" barrels; silvered, engraved receiver; five choke tubes; ported barrels; red bead front sight. Introduced 1997. Imported from Italy by K.B.I., Inc.
Price: **$1,659.00**

CHARLES DALY EMPIRE II EDL HUNTER AE, AE-MC O/U SHOTGUNS
Gauge: 12, 20, .410, 3" chambers, 28 ga., 2-3/4". **Barrel:** 26", 28" (12, 20, choke tubes), 26" (Imp. Cyl. & Mod., 28 ga.), 26" (Full & Full, .410). **Weight:** About 7 lbs. **Stocks:** Checkered walnut pistol grip buttstock, semi-beavertail forend; recoil pad. **Features:** Silvered, engraved receiver; chrome-moly barrels; gold single selective trigger; automatic safety; automatic ejectors; red bead front sight, metal bead middle sight. Introduced 1997. Imported from Italy by K.B.I., Inc.
Price: Empire II EDL AE-MC (dummy sideplates) 12 or 20 . . . . . . **$2,029.00**
Price: Empire II EDL AE, 28 . . . . **$2,019.00**
Price: Empire II EDL AE, .410 . . . . **$2,019.00**

Charles Daly Empire II Mono Trap

Charles Daly Empire II EDL Hunter

Charles Daly Empire Sporting O/U

Charles Daly Diamond Regent GTX DL

Charles Daly Empire II Sporting AE-MC O/U Shotgun
Similar to the Empire II EDL Hunter except 12 or 20 gauge only, 28", 30" barrels with choke tubes; ported barrels; special stock dimensions. Introduced 1997. Imported from Italy by K.B.I., Inc.
Price: **$2,049.00**

CHARLES DALY EMPIRE II TRAP AE-MC O/U SHOTGUNS
Gauge: 12, 2-3/4" chambers. **Barrel:** 30" choke tubes. **Weight:** About 7 lbs. **Stock:** Checkered walnut; pistol grip, semi-beavertail forend. **Features:** Silvered, engraved, reinforced receiver; chrome-moly steel barrels; gold single selective trigger; automatic safety, automatic ejector; red bead front sight, metal bead center; recoil pad. Imported from Italy by K.B.I., Inc.
Price: **$2,099.00**
Price: Mono AE-MC, adj. comb **$2,999.00**
Price: AE-MC combo set, adj. comb **$3,919.00**

CHARLES DALY DIAMOND REGENT GTX DL HUNTER O/U SHOTGUNS
Gauge: 12, 20, .410, 3" chambers, 28, 2-3/4" chambers. **Barrel:** 26", 28", 30" (choke tubes), 26" (Imp. Cyl. & Mod. in 28, 26" (Full & Full) in .410. **Weight:** About 7 lbs. **Stock:** Extra select fancy European walnut with 24" hand checkering, hand rubbed oil finish. **Features:** Boss-type action with internal side lumps. Deep cut hand-engraved scrollwork and game scene set in full sideplates. GTX detachable single selective trigger system with coil springs; chrome-moly steel barrels; automatic safety; automatic ejectors, white bead front sight, metal bead center sight. Introduced 1997. Imported from Italy by K.B.I., Inc.
Price: 12 or 20 . . . . **Special order only**
Price: 28 . . . . **Special order only**
Price: .410 bore . . . . **Special order only**
Price: Diamond Regent GTX EDL Hunter (as above with engraved
scroll and birds, 10 gold inlays), 12 or 20 . . . . . . **Special order only**
Price: As above, 28 . . . . **Special order only**
Price: As above, .410 . . . . **Special order only**

CHARLES DALY DIAMOND GTX SPORTING O/U SHOTGUN
Gauge: 12, 20, 3" chambers. **Barrel:** 28", 30" with choke tubes. **Weight:** About 8.5 lbs. **Stock:** Checkered deluxe walnut; sporting clays dimensions. Pistol grip; semi-beavertail forend; hand rubbed oil finish. **Features:** Chromed, hand-engraved receiver; chrome-moly steel barrels; GTX detachable single selective trigger system with coil springs, automatic safety; automatic ejectors; red bead front sight; ported barrels. Introduced 1997. Imported from Italy by K.B.I., Inc.
Price: . . . . **Price on request**

CHARLES DALY DIAMOND GTX TRAP AE-MC O/U SHOTGUN
Gauge: 12, 2-3/4" chambers. **Barrel:** 30" (Full & Full). **Weight:** About 8.5 lbs. **Stock:** Checkered deluxe walnut; pistol grip; trap dimensions; semi-beavertail forend; hand-rubbed oil finish. **Features:** Silvered, hand-engraved receiver; chrome-moly steel barrels; GTX detachable single selective trigger system with coil springs, automatic safety, automatic ejectors, red bead front sight, metal bead middle; recoil pad. Imported from Italy by K.B.I., Inc.
Price: . . . . **Price on request**

CHARLES DALY DIAMOND GTX DL HUNTER O/U SHOTGUN
Gauge: 12, 20, .410, 3" chambers, 28, 2-3/4" chambers. **Barrel:** 26", 28", choke tubes in 12 and 20 ga., 26" (Imp. Cyl. & Mod.), 26" (Full & Full) in .410-bore. **Weight:** About 8.5 lbs. **Stock:** Select fancy European walnut stock, with 24 lpi hand checkering; hand-rubbed oil finish. **Features:** Boss-type action with internal side lugs, hand-engraved scrollwork and game scene. GTX detachable single selective trigger system with coil springs; chrome-moly steel barrels, automatic safety, automatic ejectors, red bead front sight, recoil pad. Introduced 1997. Imported from Italy by K.B.I., Inc.
Price: . . . . **Special order only**

CZ CANVASBACK
Gauge: 12, 20, 3" chambers. **Barrel:** 26", 28". **Weight:** 7.3 lbs. **Length:** NA. **Stock:** NA. **Features:** Single selective trigger, set of 5 screw-in chokes, black chrome finished receiver, Schnable forend. From CZ-USA.
Price: **$708.00**

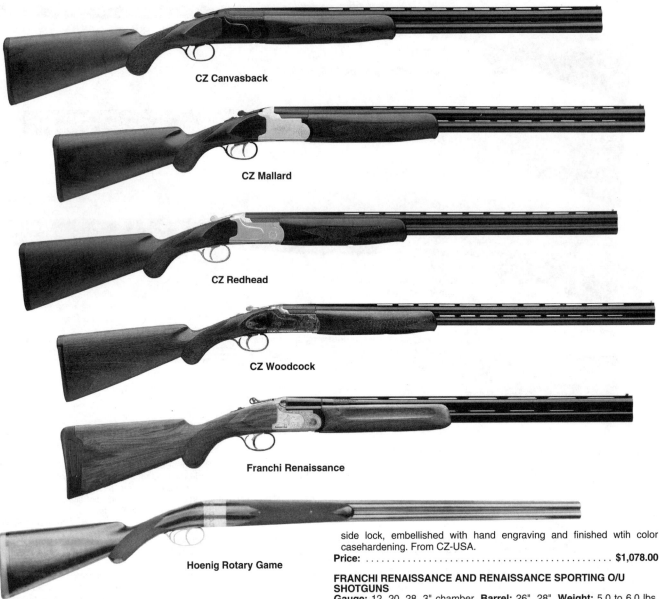

CZ Canvasback

CZ Mallard

CZ Redhead

CZ Woodcock

Franchi Renaissance

Hoenig Rotary Game

CZ MALLARD
Gauge: 12, 20, 28, .410, 3" chambers. **Barrel:** 26". **Weight:** 7.7 lbs. **Length:** NA. **Stock:** NA. **Features:** Double triggers and extractors, coin finished receiver, Schnable forend, multi chokes. From CZ-USA.
Price: **$487.00**

CZ REDHEAD
Gauge: 12, 20, 3" chambers. **Barrel:** 28". **Weight:** 7.4 lbs. **Length:** NA. **Stock:** NA. **Features:** Single selective triggers and extractors (12 & 20 ga.), screw-in chokes (12, 20, 28 ga.) choked IC and Mod (.410), coin finished receiver, Schnable forend, multi chokes. From CZ-USA.
Price: **$836.00**

CZ WOODCOCK
Gauge: 12, 20, 28, .410, 3" chambers. **Barrel:** 26". **Weight:** 7.7 lbs. **Length:** NA. **Stock:** NA. **Features:** Single selective triggers and extractors (auto ejectors on 12 & 20 ga.), screw-in chokes (12, 20, 28 ga.) choked IC and Mod (.410), coin finished receiver, Schnable forend, multi chokes. The sculptured frame incorporates a side plate, resembling a true side lock, embellished with hand engraving and finished wtih color casehardening. From CZ-USA.
Price: **$1,078.00**

FRANCHI RENAISSANCE AND RENAISSANCE SPORTING O/U SHOTGUNS
Gauge: 12, 20, 28, 3" chamber. **Barrel:** 26", 28". **Weight:** 5.0 to 6.0 lbs. **Length:** 42 5/8" to 44 5/8". **Stock:** 14.5" LOP, European oil-finished walnut with standard grade A grade, and AA grade choices. Prince of Wales grip. **Features:** TSA recoil pad, interchangeable chokes, hard case. Introduced 2006. Sporting model : **Gauge:** 12 , 3". **Barrel:** 30" ported. **Weight:** 7.9 lbs. **Length:** 46 5/8". **Stock:** 14.5" LOP, A-grade European oil-finished walnut. **Features:** TSA recoil pad, adjustable comb, lengthened forcing cones, extended choke tubes (C, IC, M and wrench), hard case. Introduced 2007. Imported from Italy by Benelli USA.
Price: Field **$1,320.00**
Price: Classic **$1,545.00**
Price: Elite **$2,110.00**
Price: Sporting **$2,039.00**

HOENIG ROTARY ROUND ACTION GAME GUN O/U SHOTGUN
Gauge: 20, 28. **Barrel:** 26", 28", solid tapered rib. **Weight:** 6 lbs. and 6-1/4 lbs. **Stock:** English walnut to customer specifications. **Features:** Round action opens by rotating barrels, pulling forward. Inertia extraction system, rotary wing safety blocks strikers. Simple takedown without removing forend. Introduced 1997. Made in U.S.A. by George Hoenig.
Price: **$20,000.00**

Kolar Sporting Clays

Krieghoff K-80 Sporting Clays

Ljutic LM-6 Super Deluxe

KIMBER MARIAS O/U SHOTGUNS
Gauge: 12, 20; 3". **Barrel:** 26", 28", 30". **Weight:** 7.4 lbs. **Length:** NA. **Stock:** Turkish walnut stocks, 24-lpi checkering, oil finish. LOP: 14.75 inches. **Features:** Hand-detachable back-action sidelock, bone-charcoal case coloring. Hand-engraving on receiver and locks, Belgian rust blue barrels, chrome lined. Five thinwall choke tubes, automatic ejectors, ventilated rib. Gold line cocking indicators on locks. Grade I has 28-inch barrels, Prince of Wales stock in grade three Turkish walnut in either 12 or 20 gauge. Grade II shas grade four Turkish walnut stocks, 12 gauge in Prince of Wales and 20 with either Prince of Wales or English profiles. Imported from Italy by Kimber Mfg., Inc.
Price: Grade I . . . . **NA**
Price: Grade II . . . . **NA**

KOLAR SPORTING CLAYS O/U SHOTGUNS
Gauge: 12, 2-3/4" chambers. **Barrel:** 30", 32", 34"; extended choke tubes. **Stock:** 14-5/8"x2-1/2"x1-7/8"x1-3/8". French walnut. Four stock versions available. **Features:** Single selective trigger, detachable, adjustable for length; overbored barrels with long forcing cones; flat tramline rib; matte blue finish. Made in U.S. by Kolar.
Price: Standard **$8,995.00**
Price: Elite **$12,495.00**
Price: Elite Gold **$15,295.00**
Price: Legend **$15,995.00**
Price: Select **$18,995.00**
Price: Custom . . . . **Price on request**

Kolar AAA Competition Trap O/U Shotgun
Similar to the Sporting Clays gun except has 32" O/U /34" Unsingle or 30" O/U /34" Unsingle barrels as an over/under, unsingle, or combination set. Stock dimensions are 14-1/2"x2-1/2"x1-1/2"; American or French walnut; step parallel rib standard. Contact maker for full listings. Made in U.S.A. by Kolar.
Price: Over/under, choke tubes, standard. **$9,595.00**
Price: Unsingle, choke tubes, standard **$10,195.00**
Price: Combo (30"/34", 32"/34"), standard **$12,595.00**

Kolar AAA Competition Skeet O/U Shotgun
Similar to the Sporting Clays gun except has 28" or 30" barrels with Kolarite AAA sub gauge tubes; stock of American or French walnut with matte finish; flat tramline rib; under barrel adjustable for point of impact. Many options available. Contact maker for complete listing. Made in U.S.A. by Kolar.
Price: Standard, choke tubes **$10,495.00**
Price: Standard, choke tubes, two-barrel set **$12,995.00**

KRIEGHOFF K-80 SPORTING CLAYS O/U SHOTGUNS
Gauge: 12. **Barrel:** 28", 30", 32", 34" with choke tubes. **Weight:** About 8 lbs. **Stock:** #3 Sporting stock designed for gun-down shooting. **Features:** Standard receiver with satin nickel finish and classic scroll engraving.

Selective mechanical trigger adjustable for position. Choice of tapered flat or 8mm parallel flat barrel rib. Free-floating barrels. Aluminum case. Imported from Germany by Krieghoff International, Inc.
Price: Standard grade with five choke tubes, from **$9,395.00**

KRIEGHOFF K-80 SKEET O/U SHOTGUNS
Gauge: 12, 2-3/4" chambers. **Barrel:** 28", 30", 32", (skeet & skeet), optional choke tubes). **Weight:** About 7-3/4 lbs. **Stock:** American skeet or straight skeet stocks, with palm-swell grips. Walnut. **Features:** Satin gray receiver finish. Selective mechanical trigger adjustable for position. Choice of ventilated 8mm parallel flat rib or ventilated 8-12mm tapered flat rib. Introduced 1980. Imported from Germany by Krieghoff International, Inc.
Price: Standard, skeet chokes **$8,375.00**
Price: Skeet Special (28", 30", 32" tapered flat rib,
          skeet & skeet choke tubes) **$9,100.00**

KRIEGHOFF K-80 TRAP O/U SHOTGUNS
Gauge: 12, 2-3/4" chambers. **Barrel:** 30", 32" (Imp. Mod. & Full or choke tubes). **Weight:** About 8-1/2 lbs. **Stock:** Four stock dimensions or adjustable stock available; all have palm-swell grips. Checkered European walnut. **Features:** Satin nickel receiver. Selective mechanical trigger, adjustable for position. Ventilated step rib. Introduced 1980. Imported from Germany by Krieghoff International, Inc.
Price: K-80 O/U (30", 32", Imp. Mod. & Full), from **$8,850.00**
Price: K-80 Unsingle (32", 34", Full), standard, from **$10,080.00**
Price: K-80 Combo (two-barrel set), standard, from **$13,275.00**

Krieghoff K-20 O/U Shotgun
Similar to the K-80 except built on a 20-gauge frame. Designed for skeet, sporting clays and field use. Offered in 20, 28 and .410; 28", 30" and 32" barrels. Imported from Germany by Krieghoff International Inc.
Price: K-20, 20 gauge, from **$9,575.00**
Price: K-20, 28 gauge, from **$9,725.00**
Price: K-20, .410, from **$9,725.00**

LEBEAU-COURALLY BOSS-VEREES O/U SHOTGUN
Gauge: 12, 20, 2-3/4" chambers. **Barrel:** 25" to 32". **Weight:** To customer specifications. **Stock:** Exhibition-quality French walnut. **Features:** Boss-type sidelock with automatic ejectors; single or double triggers; chopper lump barrels. A custom gun built to customer specifications. Imported from Belgium by Wm. Larkin Moore.
Price: From **$96,000.00**

LJUTIC LM-6 SUPER DELUXE O/U SHOTGUNS
Gauge: 12. **Barrel:** 28" to 34", choked to customer specs for live birds, trap, international trap. **Weight:** To customer specs. **Stock:** To customer specs. Oil finish, hand checkered. **Features:** Custom-made gun. Hollow-milled rib, pull or release trigger, push-button opener in front of trigger guard. From Ljutic Industries.
Price: Super Deluxe LM-6 O/U. **$19,995.00**
Price: Over/Under combo (interchangeable single barrel, two
          trigger guards, one for single trigger, one for doubles) . . . **$27,995.00**
Price: Extra over/under barrel sets, 29"-32" **$6,995.00**

Marlin L. C. Smith 12 gauge

Marocchi Conquista Sporting Clay

Merkel Model 2001EL

LUGER CLASSIC O/U SHOTGUNS
Gauge: 12, 3" and 3-1/2" chambers. **Barrel:** 26", 28", 30"; Imp. Cyl. Mod. and Full choke tubes. **Weight:** 7-1/2 lbs. **Length:** 45" overall (28" barrel) **Stock:** Select-grade European walnut, hand-checkered grip and forend. **Features:** Gold, single selective trigger; automatic ejectors. Introduced 2000.
Price: Classic (26", 28" or 30" barrel; 3-1/2" chambers) **$919.00**
Price: Classic Sporting (30" barrel; 3" chambers) **$964.00**

MARLIN L. C. SMITH O/U SHOTGUNS
Gauge: 12, 20. **Barrel:** 26", 28". **Stock:** Checkered walnut w/recoil pad. **Length:** 45". **Weight:** 7.25 lbs. **Features:** 3" chambers; 3 choke tubes (IC, Mod., Full), single selective trigger, selective automatic ejectors; vent rib; bead front sight. Imported from Italy by Marlin. Introduced 2005.
Price: LC12-OU (12 ga., 28" barrel) **$1,416.00**
Price: LC20-OU (20 ga., 26" barrel, 6.25 lbs., OAL 43") **$1,416.00**

MAROCCHI CONQUISTA SPORTING CLAYS O/U SHOTGUNS
Gauge: 12, 2-3/4" chambers. **Barrel:** 28", 30", 32" (ContreChoke tubes); 10mm concave vent rib. **Weight:** About 8 lbs. **Stock:** 14-1/2"-14-7/8"x2-3/16"x1-7/16"; American walnut with checkered grip and forend; sporting clays butt pad. **Sights:** 16mm luminescent front. **Features:** Lower mono-block and frame profile. Fast lock time. Ergonomically-shaped trigger adjustable for pull length. Automatic selective ejectors. Coin-finished receiver, blued barrels. Five choke tubes, hard case. Available as true left-hand model, opening lever operates from left to right; stock has left-hand cast. Introduced 1994. Imported from Italy by Precision Sales International.
Price: Grade I, right-hand **$1,490.00**
Price: Grade I, left-hand **$1,615.00**
Price: Grade II, right-hand **$1,828.00**
Price: Grade II, left-hand **$2,180.00**
Price: Grade III, right-hand, from **$3,093.00**
Price: Grade III, left-hand, from **$3,093.00**

Marocchi Conquista Trap O/U Shotguns
Similar to Conquista Sporting Clays model except 30" or 32" barrels choked Full & Full, stock dimensions of 14-1/2"-14-7/8"x1-11/16"x1-9/32"; weighs about 8-1/4 lbs. Introduced 1994. Imported from Italy by Precision Sales International.
Price: Grade I, right-hand **$1,490.00**
Price: Grade II, right-hand **$1,828.00**
Price: Grade III, right-hand, from **$3,093.00**

Marocchi Conquista Skeet O/U Shotguns
Similar to Conquista Sporting Clays model except 28" (skeet & skeet) barrels, stock dimensions of 14-3/8"-14-3/4"x2-3/16"x1-1/2". Weighs about 7-3/4 lbs. Introduced 1994. Imported from Italy by Precision Sales International.
Price: Grade I, right-hand. **$1,490.00**
Price: Grade II, right-hand **$1,828.00**
Price: Grade III, right-hand, from **$3,093.00**

MAROCCHI MODEL 99 SPORTING TRAP AND SKEET O/U SHOTGUNS
Gauge: 12, 2-3/4", 3" chambers. **Barrel:** 28", 30", 32". **Stock:** French walnut. **Features:** Boss Locking system, screw-in chokes, low recoil, lightweight Monoblock barrels and ribs. Imported from Italy by Precision Sales International.
Price: Grade I **$2,350.00**
Price: Grade II **$2,870.00**
Price: Grade II Gold **$3,025.00**
Price: Grade III **$3,275.00**
Price: Grade III Gold **$3,450.00**
Price: Blackgold **$4,150.00**
Price: Lodestar **$5,125.00**
Price: Brittania **$5,125.00**
Price: Diana **$6,350.00**

MAROCCHI CONQUISTA USA MODEL 92 SPORTING CLAYS O/U SHOTGUN
Gauge: 12, 3" chambers. **Barrel:** 30"; back-bored, ported (ContreChoke Plus tubes); 10 mm concave ventilated top rib, ventilated middle rib. **Weight:** 8 lbs. 2 oz. **Stock:** 14-1/4"-14-5/8"x 2-1/8"x1-3/8"; American walnut with checkered grip and forend; sporting clays butt pad. **Features:** Low profile frame; fast lock time; automatic selective ejectors; blued receiver and barrels. Comes with three choke tubes. Ergonomically shaped trigger adjustable for pull length without tools. Barrels are back-bored and ported. Introduced 1996. Imported from Italy by Precision Sales International.
Price: **$1,490.00**

MERKEL MODEL 2001EL O/U SHOTGUN
Gauge: 12, 20, 3" chambers, 28, 2-3/4" chambers. **Barrel:** 12-28"; 20, 28 ga.-26-3/4". **Weight:** About 7 lbs. (12 ga.). **Stock:** Oil-finished walnut; English or pistol grip. **Features:** Self-cocking Blitz boxlock action with cocking indicators; Kersten double cross-bolt lock; silver-grayed receiver with engraved hunting scenes; coil spring ejectors; single selective or double triggers. Imported from Germany by GSI, Inc.
Price: 12, 20 . . . . **$7,295.00**
Price: 28 ga. **$7,295.00**
Price: Model 2000EL (scroll engraving, 12, 20 or 28) **$5,795.00**

Merkel Model 303EL

Merkel Model 2002EL

Perazzi MX8

Perazzi MX28

Merkel Model 303EL O/U Shotgun
Similar to Model 2001EL except Holland & Holland-style sidelock action with cocking indicators; English-style arabesque engraving. Available in 12, 20, 28 gauge. Imported from Germany by GSI, Inc.
Price: **$19,995.00**

Merkel Model 2002EL O/U Shotgun
Similar to Model 2001EL except dummy sideplates, arabesque engraving with hunting scenes; 12, 20, 28 gauge. Imported from Germany by GSI, Inc.
Price: **$10,995.00**

PERAZZI MX8/MX8 SPECIAL TRAP, SKEET O/U SHOTGUNS
Gauge: 12, 2-3/4" chambers. **Barrel:** Trap: 29-1/2" (Imp. Mod. & Extra Full), 31-1/2" (Full & Extra Full). Choke tubes optional. Skeet: 27-5/8" (skeet & skeet). **Weight:** About 8-1/2 lbs. (trap); 7 lbs., 15 oz. (skeet). **Stock:** Interchangeable and custom made to customer specs. **Features:** Has detachable and interchangeable trigger group with flat V springs. Flat 7/16" vent rib. Many options available. Imported from Italy by Perazzi U.S.A., Inc.
Price: MX Trap Single **$10,934.00**

Perazzi MX8 Special Skeet O/U Shotgun
Similar to the MX8 Skeet except has adjustable four-position trigger, skeet stock dimensions. Imported from Italy by Perazzi U.S.A., Inc.
Price: From **$11,166.00**

PERAZZI MX8 O/U SHOTGUNS
Gauge: 12, 2-3/4" chambers. **Barrel:** 28-3/8" (Imp. Mod. & Extra Full), 29-1/2" (choke tubes). **Weight:** 7 lbs., 12 oz. **Stock:** Special specifications. **Features:** Has single selective trigger; flat 7/16" x 5/16" vent rib. Many options available. Imported from Italy by Perazzi U.S.A., Inc.
Price: Standard **$12,532.00**
Price: Sporting **$11,166.00**
Price: Trap Double Trap (removable trigger group) **$15,581.00**
Price: Skeet **$12,756.00**
Price: SC3 grade (variety of engraving patterns) .... **$23,000.00+**
Price: SCO grade (more intricate engraving, gold inlays) .... **$39,199.00+**

Perazzi MX8/20 O/U Shotgun
Similar to the MX8 except has smaller frame and has a removable trigger mechanism. Available in trap, skeet, sporting or game models with fixed chokes or choke tubes. Stock is made to customer specifications. Introduced 1993. Imported from Italy by Perazzi U.S.A., Inc.
Price: From **$11,731.00**

PERAZZI MX12 HUNTING O/U SHOTGUNS
Gauge: 12, 2-3/4" chambers. **Barrel:** 26-3/4", 27-1/2", 28-3/8", 29-1/2" (Mod. & Full); choke tubes available in 27-5/8", 29-1/2" only (MX12C). **Weight:** 7 lbs., 4 oz. **Stock:** To customer specs; interchangeable. **Features:** Single selective trigger; coil springs used in action; Schnabel forend tip. Imported from Italy by Perazzi U.S.A., Inc.
Price: From **$11,166.00**
Price: MX12C (with choke tubes). From **$11,960.00**

Perazzi MX20 Hunting O/U Shotguns
Similar to the MX12 except 20 ga. frame size. Non-removable trigger group. Available in 20, 28, .410 with 2-3/4" or 3" chambers. 26" standard, and choked Mod. & Full. Weight is 6 lbs., 6 oz. Imported from Italy by Perazzi U.S.A., Inc.
Price: From **$11,166.00**
Price: MX20C (as above, 20 ga. only, choke tubes). From **$11,960.00**

PERAZZI MX10 O/U SHOTGUN
Gauge: 12, 2-3/4" chambers. **Barrel:** 29.5", 31.5" (fixed chokes). **Weight:** NA. **Stock:** Walnut; cheekpiece adjustable for elevation and cast. **Features:** Adjustable rib; vent side rib. Externally selective trigger. Available in single barrel, combo, over/under trap, skeet, pigeon and sporting models. Introduced 1993. Imported from Italy by Perazzi U.S.A., Inc.
Price: MX200410 .... **$18,007.00**

PERAZZI MX28, MX410 GAME O/U SHOTGUN
Gauge: 28, 2-3/4" chambers, .410, 3" chambers. **Barrel:** 26" (Imp. Cyl. & Full). **Weight:** NA. **Stock:** To customer specifications. **Features:** Made on scaled-down frames proportioned to the gauge. Introduced 1993. Imported from Italy by Perazzi U.S.A., Inc.
Price: From **$22,332.00**

Piotti Boss

Remington Premier Field Grade

Remington Premier Upland Grade

Rizzini S790 Emel

PIOTTI BOSS O/U SHOTGUN
Gauge: 12, 20. **Barrel:** 26" to 32", chokes as specified. **Weight:** 6.5 to 8 lbs. **Stock:** Dimensions to customer specs. Best quality figured walnut. **Features:** Essentially a custom-made gun with many options. Introduced 1993. Imported from Italy by Wm. Larkin Moore.
Price: From **$48,000.00**

POINTER O/U SHOTGUN
Gauge: 12. **Barrel:** 28". **Stock:** Walnut. **Features:** Kickeez buttpad, Tru-Glo sight, extractors, barrel selector, engraved receiver, gold trigger and 5 choke tubes. Introduced 2006. Imported by Legacy Sports Int.
Price: **$599.00**

REMINGTON PREMIER FIELD GRADE OVER/UNDER SHOTGUNS
Gauge: 12, 20, 28, 3" chambers; 28 2-3/4" chambers. **Barrel:** 26", 28", 30" in 12 gauge; overbored (.735), polished blue; 7mm vent rib. **Sights:** Ivory front bead, steel mid bead. **Weight:** 6.5 to 7.5 lbs. **Length:** 43.125" to 45.125" overall. **Stock:** 14.25" LOP; 1.5" drop at comb; 2.4" drop at heel. Walnut, cut checkering, Schnabeled forends. Checkered pistol grip, checkered forend, satin finish, rubber butt pad. Right-hand palm swell. **Features:** Nickel finish receiver, game-scene engraving. Single selective mechanical trigger, selective automatic ejectors; serrated free-floating vent rib. Five flush mount ProBore choke tubes for 12s and 20s; 28-gauge equipped with 3 flush mount ProBore choke tubes. Hard case included. Introduced 2006. Premier Upland Grade includes engraved game scenes on receiver; 12-, 20- and 28-gauge, 26" or 28" barrels. Oil-finished woodwork, case-colored receiver. Introduced 2006. Ruffed Grouse Edition has Ruffed Grouse Society logo in 14k gold on both sides of the black onyx frame. Gold-script Remington insignia "R" appears on underbelly. 20 gauge, 26" barrel, straight-grip, English-style stock, oil finish. Introduced 2007. STS Series Competition line offers adjustable-comb model with 30" or 32" barrels, and a 32" barrel in non-adjustable stocks. 10mm target-style rib with ivory front bead and steel midpost, gold trigger, engraved receiver. Introduced 2007. Made in Italy, imported by Remington Arms Co.
Price: Premier Field 12 gauge, 26" barrel, 7 lbs. **$2,086.00**
Price: Premier Field 20 gauge, 28" barrel, 6.75 lbs. **$2,086.00**

Price: Premier Field 28 gauge, 27" barrel, 6.75 lbs. **$2,086.00**
Price: Premier Upland **$2,268.00**
Price: Premier Ruffed Grouse **$2,380.00**
Price: Premier STS Series Competition (2007) **$2,540.00**
Price: Premier STS Series Competition Adj. Comb (2007) **$2,890.00**

RIZZINI S790 EMEL O/U SHOTGUN
Gauge: 20, 28, .410. **Barrel:** 26", 27.5" (Imp. Cyl. & Imp. Mod.). **Weight:** About 6 lbs. **Stock:** 14"x1-1/2"x2-1/8". Extra fancy select walnut. **Features:** Boxlock action with profuse engraving; automatic ejectors; single selective trigger; silvered receiver. Comes with Nizzoli leather case. Introduced 1996. Imported from Italy by Wm. Larkin Moore & Co.
Price: From **$9,725.00**

Rizzini S792 EMEL O/U Shotgun
Similar to S790 EMEL except dummy sideplates with extensive engraving coverage. Nizzoli leather case. Introduced 1996. Imported from Italy by Wm. Larkin Moore & Co.
Price: From **$9,075.00**

RIZZINI UPLAND EL O/U SHOTGUN
Gauge: 12, 16, 20, 28, .410. **Barrel:** 26", 27-1/2", Mod. & Full, Imp. Cyl. & Imp. Mod. choke tubes. **Weight:** About 6.6 lbs. **Stock:** 14-1/2"x1-1/2"x2-1/4". **Features:** Boxlock action; single selective trigger; ejectors; profuse engraving on silvered receiver. Comes with fitted case. Introduced 1996. Imported from Italy by Wm. Larkin Moore & Co.
Price: From **$3,350.00**

Rizzini Artemis O/U Shotgun
Same as Upland EL model except dummy sideplates with extensive game scene engraving. Fancy European walnut stock. Fitted case. Introduced 1996. Imported from Italy by Wm. Larkin Moore & Co.
Price: From **$2,100.00**

RIZZINI S782 EMEL O/U SHOTGUN
Gauge: 12, 2-3/4" chambers. **Barrel:** 26", 27.5" (Imp. Cyl. & Imp. Mod.). **Weight:** About 6.75 lbs. **Stock:** 14-1/2"x1-1/2"x2-1/4". Extra fancy select walnut. **Features:** Boxlock action with dummy sideplates, extensive engraving with gold inlaid game birds, silvered receiver, automatic ejectors, single selective trigger. Nizzoli leather case. Introduced 1996. Imported from Italy by Wm. Larkin Moore & Co.
Price: From **$11,450.00**

Ruger Red Label

Ruger Red Label Low-Glare Stainless

Ruger Red Label All-Weather Camo

SIGARMS SA5 Field

SKB 85TSS

RUGER RED LABEL O/U SHOTGUNS
Gauge: 12, 20, 3" chambers; 28 2-3/4" chambers. **Barrel:** 26", 28", 30" in 12 gauge. **Weight:** About 7 lbs. (20 ga.); 7-1/2 lbs. (12 ga.). **Length:** 43" overall (26" barrels). **Stock:** 14"x1-1/2"x2-1/2". Straight grain American walnut. Checkered pistol grip or straight grip, checkered forend, rubber butt pad. **Features:** Stainless steel receiver. Single selective mechanical trigger, selective automatic ejectors; serrated free-floating vent rib. Comes with two skeet, one Imp. Cyl., one Mod., one Full choke tube and wrench. Made in U.S. by Sturm, Ruger & Co.
Price: Red Label with pistol grip stock **$1,790.00**
Price: English Field with straight-grip stock **$1,790.00**
Price: Sporting clays (30" bbl.) **$1,790.00**

Ruger Engraved Red Label O/U Shotgun
Similar to Red Label except scroll engraved receiver with 24-carat gold game bird (pheasant in 12 gauge, grouse in 20 gauge, woodcock in 28 gauge). Introduced 2000.
Price: Engraved Red Label, pistol grip only **$1,995.00**

SARSILMAZ O/U SHOTGUNS
Gauge: 12, 3" chambers. **Barrel:** 26", 28"; fixed chokes or choke tubes. **Weight:** NA. **Length:** NA. **Stock:** Oil-finished hardwood. **Features:** Double or single selective trigger, wide vent rib, chrome-plated parts, blued finish. Introduced 2000. Imported from Turkey by Armsport Inc.
Price: Double triggers; mod. and full or imp. cyl.
and mod. fixed chokes **$499.95**
Price: Single selective trigger; imp. cyl. and mod. or mod.
and full fixed chokes **$575.00**
Price: Single selective trigger; five choke tubes and wrench **$695.00**

SIGARMS SA5 O/U SHOTGUNS
Gauge: 12, 20, 3" chamber. **Barrel:** 26-1/2", 27" (Full, Imp. Mod., Mod., Imp. Cyl., Cyl. choke tubes). **Weight:** 6.9 lbs. (12 gauge), 5.9 lbs. (20 gauge). **Stock:** 14-1/2" x 1-1/2" x 2-1/2". Select grade walnut; checkered 20 lpi at grip and forend. **Features:** Single selective trigger, automatic ejectors; hand engraved detachable side plate; matte nickel receiver, rest blued; tapered bolt lock-up. Introduced 1997. Imported by SIGARMS, Inc.
Price: Field, 12 gauge **$2,670.00**
Price: Sporting clays **$2,800.00**
Price: Field 20 gauge **$2,670.00**

SKB MODEL 85TSS O/U SHOTGUNS
Gauge: 12, 20, .410: 3"; 28, 2-3/4". **Barrel:** Chrome lined 26", 28", 30", 32" (w/choke tubes). **Weight:** 7 lbs., 7 oz. to 8 lbs., 14 oz. **Stock:** Hand-checkered American walnut with matte finish, Schnabel or grooved forend. Target stocks available in various styles. **Sights:** HiViz competition sights. **Features:** Low profile boxlock action with Greener-style cross bolt; single selective trigger; manual safety. Back-bored barrels with lengthened forcing cones. Introduced 2004. Imported from Japan by G.U. Inc.
Price: Sporting clays, 12 , 20, 28 . . . . **$2,199.00**
Price: Sporting clays, 410 . . . . **$2,899.00**
Price: Sporting clays set, 12 and 20 . . . . **$3,549.00**
Price: Skeet, 12, 20, 28 . . . . **$2,199.00**
Price: Skeet, .410 . . . . **$2,229.00**
Price: Skeet, three-barrel set, 20, 28, .410 . . . . **$5,349.00**
Price: Trap, standard or Monte Carlo **$2,199.00**
Price: Trap adjustable comb **$2,429.00**
Price: Trap Unsingle (2007) **$2,499.00**
Price: Trap Combo (2007) **$3,489.00**

SKB Model 585 Gold

SKB Model 505 Field

Smith & Wesson Elite Silver

Stoeger Condor Combo

SKB MODEL 585 O/U SHOTGUNS
Gauge: 12 or 20, 3"; 28, 2-3/4"; .410, 3". **Barrel:** 12 ga.-26", 28", (InterChoke tubes); 20 ga.-26", 28" (InterChoke tubes); 28-26", 28" (InterChoke tubes); .410-26", 28" (InterChoke tubes). **Weight:** 6.6 to 8.5 lbs. **Length:** 43" to 51-3/8" overall. **Stock:** 14-1/8"x1-1/2"x2-3/16". Hand checkered walnut with matte finish. **Sights:** Metal bead front (field). **Features:** Boxlock action; silver nitride finish; manual safety, automatic ejectors, single selective trigger. All 12 gauge barrels are back-bored, have lengthened forcing cones and longer choke tube system. Introduced 1992. Imported from Japan by G.U., Inc.

Price: Field. **$1,699.00**
Price: Two-barrel field set, 12 & 20 . . . . **$2,749.00**
Price: Two-barrel field set, 20 & 28 or 28 & .410 . . . . **$2,829.00**

SKB Model 585 Gold Package
Similar to Model 585 Field except gold-plated trigger, two gold-plated game inlays, Schnabel forend. Silver or blue receiver. Introduced 1998. Imported from Japan by G.U. Inc.

Price: 12, 20 ga. **$1,899.00**
Price: 28, .410 . . . . **$1,989.00**

SKB Model 505 O/U Shotgun
Similar to Model 585 except blued receiver, standard bore diameter, standard InterChoke system on 12, 20, 28, different receiver engraving. Imported from Japan by G.U. Inc.

Price: Field, 12 (26", 28"), 20 (26", 28") **$1,429.00**

SMITH & WESSON ELITE SILVER SHOTGUNS
Gauge: 12, 3" chambers. **Barrel:** 26", 28", 30", rust-blued chopper-lump. **Weight:** 7.8 lbs. Length: 46-48". **Sights:** Ivory front bead, metal mid-bead. **Stock:** AAA (grade III) Turkish walnut stocks, hand-cut checkering, satin finish. **Features:** Smith & Wesson–designed trigger-plate action, hand-engraved receivers, bone-charcoal case hardening, lifetime warranty. Five choke tubes. Introduced 2007. Made in Turkey, imported by Smith & Wesson.

Price:. . . . . **NA**

STOEGER CONDOR O/U SHOTGUNS
Gauge: 12, 20, 2-3/4" 3" chambers; 16, .410. **Barrel:** 22", 24", 26", 28", 30". **Weight:** 5.5 to 7.8 lbs. **Sights:** Brass bead. **Features:** IC, M, or F screw-in choke tubes with each gun. Oil finished hardwood with pistol grip and forend. Auto safety, single trigger, automatic extractors.

Price: Condor, 12, 20, 16 ga. or .410 . . . . **$350.00**
Price: Condor Supreme (w/mid bead), 12 or 20 ga. **$599.00**
Price: Condor Combo, 12 and 20 ga. barrels . . . . **$550.00 to $700.00**
Price: Condor Youth, 20 ga. or .410 . . . . **$350.00**
Price: Condor Competition, 12 or 20 ga. **$629.00**
Price: Condor Combo, 12/20 ga., RH or LH (2007) **$749.00**
Price: Condor Outback, 12 or 20 ga., 20" barrel **$410.00**

TRADITIONS CLASSIC SERIES O/U SHOTGUNS
Gauge: 12, 3"; 20, 3"; 16, 2-3/4"; 28, 2-3/4"; .410, 3". **Barrel:** 26" and 28". **Weight:** 6 lbs. 5 oz. to 7 lbs. 6 oz. **Length:** 43" to 45" overall. **Stock:** Walnut. **Features:** Single-selective trigger; chrome-lined barrels with screw-in choke tubes; extractors (Field Hunter and Field I models) or automatic ejectors (Field II and Field III models); rubber butt pad; top tang safety. Imported from Fausti of Italy by Traditions.

Price: Field Hunter: Blued receiver; 12 or 20 ga.; 26" bbl. has IC and Mod. tubes, 28" has mod. and full tubes **$669.00**
Price: Field I: Blued receiver; 12, 20, 28 ga. or .410; fixed chokes (26" has I.C. and mod., 28" has mod. and full) **$619.00**
Price: Field II: Coin-finish receiver; 12, 16, 20, 28 ga. or .410; gold trigger; choke tubes **$789.00**
Price: Field III: Coin-finish receiver; gold engraving and trigger; 12 ga.; 26" or 28" bbl.; choke tubes **$999.00**
Price: Upland II: Blued receiver; 12 or 20 ga.; English-style straight walnut stock; choke tubes **$839.00**
Price: Upland III: Blued receiver, gold engraving; 20 ga.; high-grade pistol grip walnut stock; choke tubes **$1,059.00**
Price: Upland III: Blued, gold engraved receiver, 12 ga. Round pistol grip stock, choke tubes **$1,059.00**
Price: Sporting Clay II: Silver receiver; 12 ga.; ported barrels with skeet, i.c., mod. and full extended tubes **$959.00**
Price: Sporting Clay III: Engraved receivers, 12 and 20 ga., walnut stock, vent rib, extended choke tubes **$1,189.00**

SHOTGUNS — Over/Unders

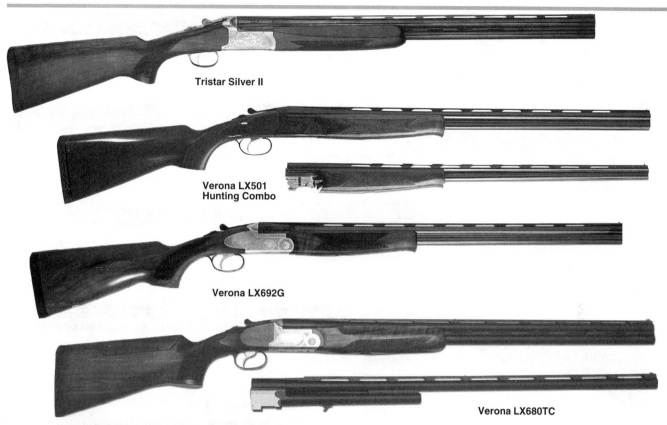

Tristar Silver II

Verona LX501 Hunting Combo

Verona LX692G

Verona LX680TC

TRADITIONS MAG 350 SERIES O/U SHOTGUNS
Gauge: 12, 3-1/2". **Barrel:** 24", 26" and 28". **Weight:** 7 lbs. to 7 lbs., 4 oz. **Length:** 41" to 45" overall. **Stock:** Walnut or composite with Mossy Oak® Break-Up™ or Advantage® Wetlands ™ camouflage. **Features:** Black matte, engraved receiver; vent rib; automatic ejectors; single-selective trigger; three screw-in choke tubes; rubber recoil pad; top tang safety. Imported from Fausti of Italy by Traditions.
Price: (Mag Hunter II: 28" black matte barrels, walnut stock, includes I.C., Mod. and Full tubes) **$799.00**
Price: (Turkey II: 24" or 26" camo barrels, Break-Up™ camo stock, includes Mod., Full and X-Full tubes) **$889.00**
Price: (Waterfowl II: 28" camo barrels, Advantage Wetlands camo stock, includes IC, Mod. and Full tubes) **$899.00**

TRISTAR SILVER II O/U SHOTGUN
Gauge: 12, 20, .410. **Barrel:** 26" barrel (Imp. Cyl., Mod., Full choke tubes, 12 and 20 ga.), 28" (Imp. Cyl., Mod., Full choke tubes, 12 ga. only), 26" (Imp. Cyl. & Mod. fixed chokes, 28 and .410) automatic selective ejectors. **Weight:** 6 lbs., 15 oz. (12 ga., 26"). **Length:** 45-1/2" overall. **Stock:** 14-3/8"x1-1/2"x2-3/8". Figured walnut, cut checkering; sporting clays quick-mount buttpad. **Sights:** Target bead front. **Features:** Boxlock action with single selective trigger, automatic selective ejectors; special broadway channeled rib; vented barrel rib; chrome bores. Chrome-nickel finish on frame, with engraving. Imported from Italy by Tristar Sporting Arms Ltd.
Price: **$669.00**

VERONA LX501 HUNTING O/U SHOTGUNS
Gauge: 12, 20, 28, .410 (2-3/4", 3" chambers). **Barrel:** 28"; 12, 20 ga. have Interchoke tubes, 28 ga. and .410 have fixed Full & Mod. **Weight:** 6-7 lbs. **Stock:** Matte-finished walnut with machine-cut checkering. **Features:** Gold-plated single-selective trigger; ejectors; engraved, blued receiver; non-automatic safety; coil spring-operated firing pins. Introduced 1999. Imported from Italy by B.C. Outdoors.
Price: 12 and 20 ga. **$878.08**
Price: 28 ga. and .410 . . . . **$926.72**
Price: .410 . . . . **$907.01**
Price: Combos 20/28, 28/.410 . . . . **$1,459.20**

Verona LX692 Gold Hunting O/U Shotguns
Similar to Verona LX501 except engraved, silvered receiver with false sideplates showing gold inlaid bird hunting scenes on three sides; Schnabel forend tip; hand-cut checkering; black rubber butt pad. Available in 12 and 20 gauge only, five Interchoke tubes. Introduced 1999. Imported from Italy by B.C. Outdoors.
Price: **$1,295.00**
Price: LX692G Combo 28/.410 . . . . **$2,192.40**

Verona LX680 Sporting O/U Shotgun
Similar to Verona LX501 except engraved, silvered receiver; ventilated middle rib; beavertail forend; hand-cut checkering; available in 12 or 20 gauge only with 2-3/4" chambers. Introduced 1999. Imported from Italy by B.C. Outdoors.
Price: **$1,159.68**

Verona LX680 Skeet/Sporting/Trap O/U Shotgun
Similar to Verona LX501 except skeet or trap stock dimensions; beavertail forend, palm swell on pistol grip; ventilated center barrel rib. Introduced 1999. Imported from Italy by B.C. Outdoors.
Price: **$1,736.96**

Verona LX692 Gold Sporting O/U Shotgun
Similar to Verona LX680 except false sideplates have gold-inlaid bird hunting scenes on three sides; red high-visibility front sight. Introduced 1999. Imported from Italy by B.C. Outdoors.
Price: Skeet/sporting **$1,765.12**
Price: Trap (32" barrel, 7-7/8 lbs.) **$1,594.80**

VERONA LX680 COMPETITION TRAP O/U SHOTGUNS
Gauge: 12. **Barrel:** 30" O/U, 32" single bbl. **Weight:** 8-3/8 lbs. combo, 7 lbs. single. **Stock:** Walnut. **Sights:** White front, mid-rib bead. **Features:** Interchangeable barrels switch from o/u to single configurations. 5 Briley chokes in combo, 4 in single bbl. extended forcing cones, ported barrels 32" with raised rib. By B.C. Outdoors.
Price: Trap Single (LX680TGTSB) **$1,736.96**
Price: Trap Combo (LX680TC) **$2,553.60**

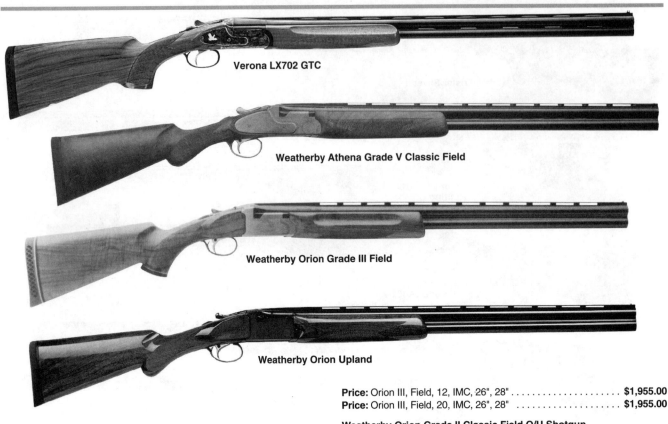

Verona LX702 GTC

Weatherby Athena Grade V Classic Field

Weatherby Orion Grade III Field

Weatherby Orion Upland

VERONA LX702 GOLD TRAP COMBO O/U SHOTGUNS
Gauge: 20/28, 2-3/4" chamber. **Barrel:** 30". **Weight:** 7 lbs. **Stock:** Turkish walnut with beavertail forearm. **Sights:** White front bead. **Features:** 2-barrel competition gun. Color case-hardened side plates and receiver with gold inlaid pheasant. Vent rib between barrels. 5 Interchokes. Imported from Italy by B.C. Outdoors.
Price: Combo $2,467.84
Price: 20 ga. $1,829.12

Verona LX702 Skeet/Trap O/U Shotguns
Similar to Verona LX702. Both are 12 gauge and 2-3/4" chamber. Skeet has 28" barrel and weighs 7-3/4 lbs. Trap has 32" barrel and weighs 7-7/8 lbs. By B.C. Outdoors.
Price: Skeet $1,829.12
Price: Trap $1,829.12

WEATHERBY ATHENA GRADE V CLASSIC FIELD O/U SHOTGUN
Gauge: 12, 20, 3" chambers. **Barrel:** 26", 28", IMC multi-choke tubes. **Weight:** 12 ga., 7-1/4 to 8 lbs.; 20 ga. 6-1/2 to 7-1/4 lbs. **Stock:** Oil-finished American Claro walnut with fine-line checkering, rounded pistol grip and slender forend. **Features:** Old English recoil pad. Sideplate receiver has rose and scroll engraving.
Price: $3,037.00

Weatherby Athena Grade III Classic Field O/U Shotgun
Similar to Athena Grade V, has Grade III Claro walnut with oil finish, rounded pistol grip, slender forend; silver nitride/gray receiver has rose and scroll engraving with gold-overlay upland game scenes. Introduced 1999. Imported from Japan by Weatherby.
Price: 12, 20, 28 ga. $2,173.00

WEATHERBY ORION GRADE III FIELD O/U SHOTGUNS
Gauge: 12, 20, 3" chambers. **Barrel:** 26", 28", IMC multi-choke tubes. **Weight:** 6-1/2 to 8 lbs. **Stock:** 14-1/4"x1-1/2"x2-1/2". American walnut, checkered grip and forend. Rubber recoil pad. **Features:** Selective automatic ejectors, single selective inertia trigger. Top tang safety, Greener cross bolt. Has silver-gray receiver with engraving and gold duck/pheasant. Imported from Japan by Weatherby.

Price: Orion III, Field, 12, IMC, 26", 28" $1,955.00
Price: Orion III, Field, 20, IMC, 26", 28" $1,955.00

Weatherby Orion Grade II Classic Field O/U Shotgun
Similar to Orion Grade III Field except stock has high-gloss finish, and bird on receiver is not gold. Available in 12 gauge, 26", 28", 30" barrels, 20 gauge, 26" 28", both with 3" chambers, 28 gauge, 26", 2-3/4" chambers. All have IMC choke tubes. Imported from Japan by Weatherby.
Price: $1,622.00

Weatherby Orion Upland O/U Shotgun
Similar to Orion Grade III Field. Plain blued receiver, gold W on trigger guard; rounded pistol grip, slender forend of Claro walnut with high-gloss finish; black butt pad. Available in 12 and 20 gauge with 26" and 28" barrels. Introduced 1999. Imported from Japan by Weatherby.
Price: $1,299.00

WEATHERBY ORION SSC O/U SHOTGUN
Gauge: 12, 3" chambers. **Barrel:** 28", 30", 32" (skeet, SC1, Imp. Cyl., SC2, Mod. IMC choke tubes). **Weight:** About 8 lbs. **Stock:** 14-3/4"x2-1/4"x1-1/2". Claro walnut with satin oil finish; Schnabel forend tip; sporter-style pistol grip; Pachmayr Decelerator recoil pad. **Features:** Designed for sporting clays competition. Has lengthened forcing cones and back-boring; ported barrels with 12mm grooved rib with mid-bead sight; mechanical trigger is adjustable for length of pull. Introduced 1998. Imported from Japan by Weatherby.
Price: SSC (Super Sporting Clays) $2,059.00

WINCHESTER SELECT O/U SHOTGUNS
Gauge: 12, 2-3/4", 3" chambers. **Barrel:** 28", 30", Invector Plus choke tubes. **Weight:** 7 lbs. 6 oz. to 7 lbs. 12. oz. **Length:** 45" overall (28" barrel). **Stock:** Checkered walnut stock. **Features:** Chrome-plated chambers; back-bored barrels; tang barrel selector/safety; deep-blued finish. Introduced 2000. From U.S. Repeating Arms. Co.
Price: Select Model 101 Field, intr. 2007 . . . . $2,061.00
Price: Select Model 101 Sporting, intr. 2007, from $2,328.00
Price: Select Platinum Sporting, intr. 2007, from $2,625.00
Price: Select Platinum Field, intr. 2007, from $2,359.00
Price: Select Deluxe Field, intr. 2007, from $1,607.00
Price: Select Energy Trap $1,948.00
Price: Select Energy Trap adjustable $2,112.00

Variety of models for utility and sporting use, including some competitive shooting.

Bill Hanus Birdgun

Charles Daly Superior Hunter

Charles Daly Empire Hunter AE-MC

Charles Daly Diamond DL

ARRIETA SIDELOCK DOUBLE SHOTGUNS
Gauge: 12, 16, 20, 28, .410. **Barrel:** Length and chokes to customer specs. **Weight:** To customer specs. **Stock:** To customer specs. Straight English with checkered butt (standard), or pistol grip. Select European walnut with oil finish. **Features:** Essentially custom gun with myriad options. H&H pattern hand-detachable sidelocks, selective automatic ejectors, double triggers (hinged front) standard. Some have self-opening action. Finish and engraving to customer specs. Imported from Spain by Wingshooting Adventures.

Price: Model 557, auto ejectors. From	$3,250.00
Price: Model 570, auto ejectors. From	$3,950.00
Price: Model 578, auto ejectors. From	$4,350.00
Price: Model 600 Imperial, self-opening. From	$6,050.00
Price: Model 601 Imperial Tiro, self-opening. From	$6,950.00
Price: Model 801. From	$9,135.00
Price: Model 802. From	$9,135.00
Price: Model 803. From	$6,930.00
Price: Model 871, auto ejectors. From	$5,060.00
Price: Model 872, self-opening. From	$12,375.00
Price: Model 873, self-opening. From	$8,200.00
Price: Model 874, self-opening. From	$9,250.00
Price: Model 875, self-opening. From	$14,900.00

AYA MODEL 4/53 SHOTGUNS
Gauge: 12, 16, 20, 28, 410. **Barrel:** 26", 27", 28", 30". **Weight:** To customer specifications. **Length:** To customer specifications. **Features:** Hammerless boxlock action; double triggers; light scroll engraving; automatic safety; straight grip oil finish walnut stock; checkered butt. Made in Spain. Imported by New England Custom Gun Service, Lt.

Price:	$2,799.00
Price: No. 2	$4,499.00
Price: No. 2 Rounded Action	$4,899.00

BILL HANUS BIRDGUNS BY AYA
Gauge: 16, 20, 28. **Barrel:** 27", 20 and 28 ga.; 28", 16 ga. (skeet 1 & skeet 2). **Weight:** 5 lbs., 4 oz. to 6 lbs., 4 oz. **Stock:** 14-3/8"x1-1/2"x2-3/8", with 1/4" cast-off. Select walnut. **Features:** Boxlock action with ejectors; splinter forend, straight English grip; checkered butt; English leather-covered handguard and AyA snap caps included. Made by AyA. Introduced 1998. Imported from Spain by Bill Hanus Birdguns.

Price:	$2,995.00

CHARLES DALY SUPERIOR HUNTER AND SUPERIOR MC DOUBLE SHOTGUNS
Gauge: 12, 20, 3" chambers, 28, 2-3/4" chambers. **Barrel:** 28" (Mod. & Full) 26" (Imp. Cyl. & Mod.). **Weight:** About 7 lbs. **Stock:** Checkered walnut pistol grip buttstock, splinter forend. **Features:** Silvered, engraved receiver; chrome-lined barrels; gold single trigger; automatic safety; extractors; gold bead front sight. Introduced 1997. Imported from Italy by K.B.I., Inc.

Price: Superior Hunter, 28 gauge and .410	$1,659.00
Price: Superior Hunter MC 26"-28"	$1,629.00

Charles Daly Empire Hunter AE-MC Double Shotgun
Similar to Superior Hunter except deluxe wood English-style stock, game scene engraving, automatic ejectors. Introduced 1997. Imported from Italy by K.B.I., Inc.

Price: 12 or 20	$2,119.00

CHARLES DALY DIAMOND DL DOUBLE SHOTGUN
Gauge: 12, 20, .410, 3" chambers, 28, 2-3/4" chambers. **Barrel:** 28" (Mod. & Full), 26" (Imp. Cyl. & Mod.), 26" (Full & Full, .410). **Weight:** From 5 lbs. to 7 lbs. **Stock:** Select fancy European walnut, English-style butt, beavertail forend; hand-checkered, hand-rubbed oil finish. **Features:** Drop-forged action with gas escape valves; demi-block barrels with concave rib; selective automatic ejectors; hand-detachable double safety sidelocks with hand-engraved rose and scrollwork. Hinged front trigger. Color case-hardened receiver. Introduced 1997. Imported from Spain by K.B.I., Inc.

Price:	Special order only

Charles Daly Diamond Regent DL

Charles Daly Field II Hunter

CZ Bobwhite

CZ Ringneck

CZ Durango

CZ Hammer Coach

CHARLES DALY DIAMOND REGENT DL DOUBLE SHOTGUN
Gauge: 12, 20, .410, 3" chambers, 28, 2-3/4" chambers. **Barrel:** 28" (Mod. & Full), 26" (Imp. Cyl. & Mod.), 26" (Full & Full, .410). **Weight:** About 5-7 lbs. **Stock:** Special select fancy European walnut, English-style butt, splinter forend; hand-checkered; hand-rubbed oil finish. **Features:** Drop-forged action with gas escape valves; demi-block barrels of chrome-nickel steel with concave rib; selective automatic-ejectors; hand-detachable, double-safety H&H sidelocks with demi-relief hand engraving; H&H pattern easy-opening feature; hinged trigger; coin finished action. Introduced 1997. Imported from Spain by K.B.I., Inc.
Price: Special Custom Order .... **NA**

CHARLES DALY FIELD II, AE-MC HUNTER DOUBLE SHOTGUN
Gauge: 12, 20, 28, .410 (3" chambers; 28 has 2-3/4"). **Barrel:** 32" (Mod. & Mod.), 28, 30" (Mod. & Full), 26" (Imp. Cyl. & Mod.) .410 (Full & Full). **Weight:** 6 lbs. to 11.4 lbs. **Stock:** Checkered walnut pistol grip and forend. **Features:** Silvered, engraved receiver; gold single selective trigger in 10, 12, and 20 ga.; double triggers in 28 and .410; automatic safety; extractors; gold bead front sight. Introduced 1997. Imported from Spain by K.B.I., Inc.
Price: 28 ga., .410-bore............................. **$1,189.00**
Price: 12 or 20 AE-MC **$1,099.00**

CZ BOBWHITE AND RINGNECK SHOTGUNS
Gauge: 12, 20, 28, .410. (5 screw-in chokes in 12 and 20 ga. and fixed chokes in IC and Mod in .410). **Barrel:** 20". **Weight:** 6.5 lbs. **Length:** NA. **Stock:** Sculptured Turkish walnut with straight English-style grip and double triggers (Bobwhite) or conventional American pistol grip with a single trigger (Ringneck). Both are hand checkered 20 lpi. **Features:** Both color case-hardened shotguns are hand engraved.
Price: Bobwhite **$695.00**
Price: Ringneck **$912.00**

CZ DURANGO AND AMARILLO SHOTGUNS
Gauge: 12, 3" chambers. **Barrel:** 20". **Weight:** 6.7 lbs. **Length:** NA. **Stock:** Hand checkered walnut with old style round knob pistol grip. **Features:** The Durango comes with a single trigger, while the Amarillo is a double trigger shotgun The receiver, trigger guard, and forend metal are finished in 19th century color case-hardening.
Price: **$795.00**

CZ HAMMER COACH SHOTGUNS
Gauge: 12, 3" chambers. **Barrel:** 20". **Weight:** 6.7 lbs. **Length:** NA. **Stock:** NA. **Features:** Following in the tradition of the guns used by the stagecoach guards of the 1880's, this cowboy gun features double triggers, 19th century color case-hardening and fully functional external hammers.
Price: **$795.00**

A.H. Fox DE Grade

Garbi Model 100

Marlin L. C. Smith 12 gauge

DAKOTA PREMIER GRADE SHOTGUN
Gauge: 12, 16, 20, 28, .410. **Barrel:** 27". **Weight:** NA. **Length:** NA. **Stock:** Exhibition-grade English walnut, hand-rubbed oil finish with straight grip and splinter forend. **Features:** French grey finish; 50 percent coverage engraving; double triggers; selective ejectors. Finished to customer specifications. Made in U.S. by Dakota Arms.
Price: From **$14,950.00**

Dakota Legend Shotgun
Similar to Premier Grade except has special selection English walnut, full-coverage scroll engraving, oak and leather case. Made in U.S. by Dakota Arms.
Price: From **$19,000.00**

E.M.F. OLD WEST HAMMER SHOTGUN
Gauge: 12. **Barrel:** 20". **Weight:** 8 lbs. **Length:** 37" overall. **Stock:** Smooth walnut with steel butt place. **Sights:** Large brass bead. **Features:** Colt-style exposed hammers rebounding type; blued receiver and barrels; cylinder bore. Introduced 2006. Imported from China for E.M.F. by TTN.
Price: **$449.90**

FOX, A.H., SIDE-BY-SIDE SHOTGUNS
Gauge: 16, 20, 28, .410. **Barrel:** Length and chokes to customer specifications. Rust-blued Chromox or Krupp steel. **Weight:** 5-1/2 to 6-3/4 lbs. **Stock:** Dimensions to customer specifications. Hand-checkered Turkish Circassian walnut with hand-rubbed oil finish. Straight, semi or full pistol grip; splinter, Schnabel or beavertail forend; traditional pad, hard rubber buttplate or skeleton butt. **Features:** Boxlock action with automatic ejectors; double or Fox single selective trigger. Scalloped, rebated and color case-hardened receiver; hand finished and hand-engraved. Grades differ in engraving, inlays, grade of wood, amount of hand finishing. Introduced 1993. Made in U.S. by Connecticut Shotgun Mfg.
Price: CE Grade **$13,500.00**
Price: XE Grade **$15,500.00**
Price: DE Grade **$18,000.00**
Price: FE Grade **$23,000.00**
Price: Exhibition Grade **$36,500.00**
Price: 28/.410 CE Grade **$15,500.00**
Price: 28/.410 XE Grade **$17,500.00**
Price: 28/.410 DE Grade **$20,000.00**
Price: 28/.410 FE Grade **$25,000.00**

GARBI MODEL 100 DOUBLE SHOTGUN
Gauge: 12, 16, 20, 28. **Barrel:** 26", 28", choked to customer specs. **Weight:** 5-1/2 to 7-1/2 lbs. **Stock:** 14-1/2"x2-1/4"x1-1/2". European walnut. Straight grip, checkered butt, classic forend. **Features:** Sidelock action, automatic ejectors, double triggers standard. Color case-hardened action, coin finish optional. Single trigger; beavertail forend, etc. optional. Five additional models available. Imported from Spain by Wm. Larkin Moore.
Price: From **$4,850.00**

Garbi Model 101 Side-by-Side Shotgun
Similar to the Garbi Model 100 except hand engraved with scroll engraving; select walnut stock; better overall quality than the Model 100. Imported from Spain by Wm. Larkin Moore.
Price: From **$6,250.00**

Garbi Model 103 A & B Side-by-Side Shotguns
Similar to the Garbi Model 100 except has Purdey-type fine scroll and rosette engraving. Better overall quality than the Model 101. Model 103B has nickel-chrome steel barrels, H&H-type easy opening mechanism; other mechanical details remain the same. Imported from Spain by Wm. Larkin Moore.
Price: Model 103A. From **$8,000.00**
Price: Model 103B. From **$11,800.00**

Garbi Model 200 Side-by-Side Shotgun
Similar to the Garbi Model 100 except has heavy-duty locks, magnum proofed. Very fine Continental-style floral and scroll engraving, well figured walnut stock. Other mechanical features remain the same. Imported from Spain by Wm. Larkin Moore.
Price: **$11,200.00**

KIMBER VALIER GRADE I and II SHOTGUN
Gauge: 20, 3" chambers. **Barrels:** 26" or 28", IC and M. **Weight:** 6 lbs. 8 oz. **Stock:** Turkish walnut, English style. **Features:** Sidelock design, double triggers, 50-percent engraving; 24 lpi checkering; auto-ejectors (extractors only on Grade I). Color case-hardened sidelocks, rust blue barrels. Imported from Turkey by Kimber Mfg., Inc.
Price: Grade I **$3,879.00**
Price: Grade II **$4,480.00**

LEBEAU-COURALLY BOXLOCK SIDE-BY-SIDE SHOTGUN
Gauge: 12, 16, 20, 28, .410-bore. **Barrel:** 25" to 32". **Weight:** To customer specifications. **Stock:** French walnut. **Features:** Anson & Deely-type action with automatic ejectors; single or double triggers. Custom gun built to customer specifications. Imported from Belgium by Wm. Larkin Moore.
Price: From **$25,500.00**

LEBEAU-COURALLY SIDELOCK SIDE-BY-SIDE SHOTGUN
Gauge: 12, 16, 20, 28, .410-bore. **Barrel:** 25" to 32". **Weight:** To customer specifications. **Stock:** Fancy French walnut. **Features:** Holland & Holland-type action with automatic ejectors; single or double triggers. Custom gun built to customer specifications. Imported from Belgium by Wm. Larkin Moore.
Price: From **$56,000.00**

MARLIN L. C. SMITH SIDE-BY-SIDE SHOTGUN
Gauge: 12, 20. **Stock:** Checkered walnut w/recoil pad. **Features:** 3" chambers, single trigger, selective automatic ejectors; 3 choke tubes (IC, Mod., Full); solid rib, bead front sight. Imported from Italy by Marlin. Introduced 2005.
Price: LC12-DB (28" barrel, 43" OAL, 6.25 lbs) **$2,109.00**
Price: LC20-DB (26" barrel, 41" OAL, 6 lbs) **$2,109.00**

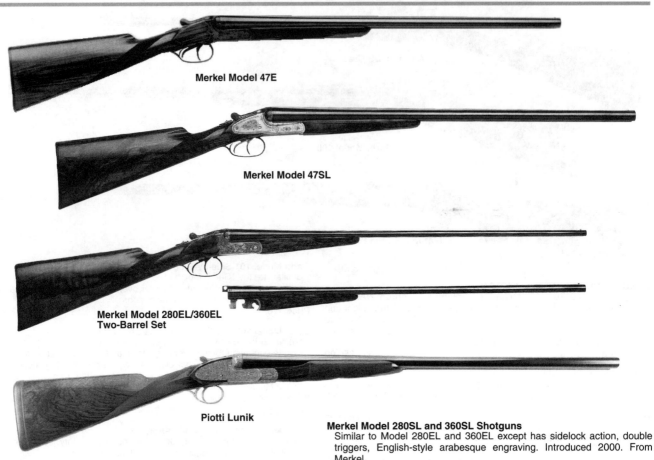

Merkel Model 47E

Merkel Model 47SL

Merkel Model 280EL/360EL Two-Barrel Set

Piotti Lunik

MERKEL MODEL 47E, 147E SIDE-BY-SIDE SHOTGUNS

Gauge: 12, 3" chambers, 16, 2-3/4" chambers, 20, 3" chambers. **Barrel:** 12, 16 ga.-28"; 20 ga.-26-3/4" (Imp. Cyl. & Mod., Mod. & Full). **Weight:** About 6-3/4 lbs. (12 ga.). **Stock:** Oil-finished walnut; straight English or pistol grip. **Features:** Anson & Deeley-type boxlock action with single selective or double triggers, automatic safety, cocking indicators. Color case-hardened receiver with standard arabesque engraving. Imported from Germany by GSI.

Price: Model 47E (H&H ejectors) **$3,295.00**
Price: Model 147E (as above with ejectors) **$3,995.00**

Merkel Model 47SL, 147SL Side-by-Side Shotguns

Similar to Model 47E except H&H style sidelock action with cocking indicators, ejectors. Silver-grayed receiver and sideplates have arabesque engraving, engraved border and screws (Model 47S), or fine hunting scene engraving (Model 147S). Imported from Germany by GSI.

Price: Model 47SL **$5,995.00**
Price: Model 147SL **$7,995.00**
Price: Model 247SL (English-style engraving, large scrolls) **$7,995.00**
Price: Model 447SL (English-style engraving, small scrolls) **$9,995.00**

Merkel Model 280EL, 360EL Shotguns

Similar to Model 47E except smaller frame. Greener cross bolt with double under-barrel locking lugs, fine engraved hunting scenes on silver-grayed receiver, luxury-grade wood, Anson and Deely box-lock action. H&H ejectors, single-selective or double triggers. Introduced 2000. From Merkel.

Price: Model 280EL (28 gauge, 28" barrel, Imp. Cyl. and
  Mod. chokes) **$5,795.00**
Price: Model 360EL (.410, 28" barrel, Mod. and
  Full chokes) **$5,795.00**
Price: Model 280/360EL two-barrel set (28 and .410 gauge
  as above) **$8,295.00**

Merkel Model 280SL and 360SL Shotguns

Similar to Model 280EL and 360EL except has sidelock action, double triggers, English-style arabesque engraving. Introduced 2000. From Merkel.

Price: Model 280SL (28 gauge, 28" barrel, Imp. Cyl. and
  Mod. chokes) **$8,495.00**
Price: Model 360SL (.410, 28" barrel, Mod. and
  Full chokes) **$8,495.00**
Price: Model 280/360SL two-barrel set **$11,995.00**

PIOTTI KING NO. 1 SIDE-BY-SIDE SHOTGUN

Gauge: 12, 16, 20, 28, .410. **Barrel:** 25" to 30" (12 ga.), 25" to 28" (16, 20, 28, .410). To customer specs. Chokes as specified. **Weight:** 6-1/2 lbs. to 8 lbs. (12 ga. to customer specs.). **Stock:** Dimensions to customer specs. Finely figured walnut; straight grip with checkered butt with classic splinter forend and hand-rubbed oil finish standard. Pistol grip, beavertail forend. **Features:** Holland & Holland pattern sidelock action, automatic ejectors. Double trigger; non-selective single trigger optional. Coin finish standard; color case-hardened optional. Top rib; level, file-cut; concave, ventilated optional. Very fine, full coverage scroll engraving with small floral bouquets. Imported from Italy by Wm. Larkin Moore.

Price: From **$29,600.00**

Piotti King Extra Side-by-Side Shotgun

Similar to the Piotti King No. 1 except with upgraded engraving. Choice of any type of engraving, including bulino game scene engraving and game scene engraving with gold inlays. Engraved and signed by a master engraver. Other mechanical specifications remain the same. Imported from Italy by Wm. Larkin Moore.

Price: From **$35,000.00**

Piotti Lunik Side-by-Side Shotgun

Similar to the Piotti King No. 1 in overall quality. Has Renaissance-style large scroll engraving in relief. Best quality Holland & Holland-pattern sidelock ejector double with chopper lump (demi-bloc) barrels. Other mechanical specifications remain the same. Imported from Italy by Wm. Larkin Moore.

Price: From **$30,900.00**

Rizzini Sidelock

Ruger Gold Label

Smith & Wesson Elite Gold

Stoeger Uplander

Stoeger Silverado Coach

PIOTTI PIUMA SIDE-BY-SIDE SHOTGUN
Gauge: 12, 16, 20, 28, .410. **Barrel:** 25" to 30" (12 ga.), 25" to 28" (16, 20, 28, .410). **Weight:** 5-1/2 to 6-1/4 lbs. (20 ga.). **Stock:** Dimensions to customer specs. Straight grip stock with walnut checkered butt, classic splinter forend, hand-rubbed oil finish are standard; pistol grip, beavertail forend, satin luster finish optional. **Features:** Anson & Deeley boxlock ejector double with chopper lump barrels. Level, file-cut rib, light scroll and rosette engraving, scalloped frame. Double triggers; single non-selective optional. Coin finish standard, color case-hardened optional. Imported from Italy by Wm. Larkin Moore.
Price: From **$14,800.00**

REMINGTON PREMIER UPLAND & UPLAND SPECIAL SIDE-BY-SIDE SHOTGUNS
Gauge: 12, 20, 28, .410 bore, 3" chamber; **Barrel:** 28" in 12, 20 gauge; polished blue; vent rib. **Sights:** front bead. **Weight:** 6.5 to 7.5 lbs. **Length:** 44.125" to 45.125" overall. **Stock:** 14.25" LOP; 1.5" drop at comb; 2.4" drop at heel. Checkered pistol grip, checkered fore-end, oil finish, rubber butt pad. Semi-beavertail fore-end. Upland Special has straight grip English-style stock. **Features:** Case-colored receiver, game-scene engraving. Single-selective mechanical trigger, selective automatic ejectors; serrated free-floating vent rib. Five flush-mount ProBore choke tubes for 12s and 20s; 28-gauge equipped with 3 flush mount ProBore choke tubes. Hard case included. Introduced 2007. Made in Italy, imported by Remington Arms Co.

Price: Premier Upland 12 gauge, 28" barrel, 7.5 lbs.	**$2,030.00**
Price: Premier Upland 20 gauge, 28" barrel, 6.75 lbs.	**$2,030.00**
Price: Premier Upland 28 gauge, 27" barrel, 6.5 lbs.	**$2,086.00**
Price: Premier Upland .410, 27" barrel, 6.5 lbs.	**$2,086.00**
Price: Premier Upland Special 28 ga. or .410 bore, 27" barrel, 6.5 lbs.	**$2,086.00**

RIZZINI SIDELOCK SIDE-BY-SIDE SHOTGUN
Gauge: 12, 16, 20, 28, .410. **Barrel:** 25" to 30" (12, 16, 20 ga.), 25" to 28" (28, .410). To customer specs. Chokes as specified. **Weight:** 6-1/2 lbs. to 8 lbs. (12 ga. to customer specs). **Stock:** Dimensions to customer specs. Finely figured walnut; straight grip with checkered butt with classic splinter forend and hand-rubbed oil finish standard. Pistol grip, beavertail forend. **Features:** Sidelock action, auto ejectors. Double triggers or non-selective single trigger standard. Coin finish standard. Imported from Italy by Wm. Larkin Moore.

Price: 12, 20 ga. From	**$66,900.00**
Price: 28, .410 bore. From	**$75,500.00**

RUGER GOLD LABEL SIDE-BY-SIDE SHOTGUN
Gauge: 12, 3" chambers. **Barrel:** 28" with skeet tubes. **Weight:** 6-1/2 lbs. **Length:** 45". **Stock:** American walnut straight or pistol grip. **Sights:** Gold bead front, full length rib, serrated top. **Features:** Spring-assisted break-open, SS trigger, auto eject. Five interchangeable screw-in choke tubes, combination safety/barrel selector with auto safety reset.
Price: **$2,650.00**

SMITH & WESSON ELITE GOLD SHOTGUNS
Gauge: 20, 3" chambers. **Barrel:** 26", 28", 30", rust-blued chopper-lump. **Weight:** 6.5 lbs. **Length:** 43.5-45.5". **Sights:** Ivory front bead, metal mid-bead. **Stock:** AAA (grade III) Turkish walnut stocks, hand-cut checkering, satin finish. English grip or pistol grip. **Features:** Smith & Wesson-designed trigger-plate action, hand-engraved receivers, bone-charcoal case hardening, lifetime warranty. Five choke tubes. Introduced 2007. Made in Turkey, imported by Smith & Wesson.
Price: . . . . **NA**

STOEGER UPLANDER SIDE-BY-SIDE SHOTGUNS
Gauge: 16, 28, 2-3/4 chambers. 12, 20, .410, 3" chambers. **Barrel:** 22", 24", 26", 28". **Weight:** 7.3 lbs. **Sights:** Brass bead. **Features:** Double trigger, IC & M fixed choke tubes with gun.

Price: With fixed or screw-in chokes	**$350.00**
Price: Supreme, screw-in chokes, 12 or 20 ga.	**$485.00**
Price: Youth, 20 ga. or .410, 22" barrel, double trigger	**$350.00**
Price: Combo, 20/28 ga. or 12/20 ga.	**$649.00**

Traditions Elite Hunter

Traditions Uplander V

Tristar Brittany

Tristar-Gentry

STOEGER COACH GUN SIDE-BY-SIDE SHOTGUNS
Gauge: 12, 20, 2-3/4", 3" chambers. **Barrel:** 20". **Weight:** 6-1/2 lbs. **Stock:** Brown hardwood, classic beavertail forend. **Sights:** Brass bead. **Features:** IC & M fixed chokes, tang auto safety, auto extractors, black plastic buttplate. Imported by Benelli USA.

Price: Supreme blued finish **$410.00**
Price: Supreme blued barrel, stainless receiver **$430.00**
Price: Supreme polished nickel receiver **$460.00**
Price: Coach Gun black walnut stock, polished nickel receiver **$410.00**
Price: Nickel Coach Gun synthetic stock, stainless **$400.00**
Price: Silverado Coach Gun with English synthetic stock **$400.00**

TRADITIONS ELITE SERIES SIDE-BY-SIDE SHOTGUNS
Gauge: 12, 3"; 20, 3"; 28, 2-3/4"; .410, 3". **Barrel:** 26". **Weight:** 5 lbs., 12 oz. to 6-1/2 lbs. **Length:** 43" overall. **Stock:** Walnut. **Features:** Chrome-lined barrels; fixed chokes (Elite Field III ST, Field I DT and Field I ST) or choke tubes (Elite Hunter ST); extractors (Hunter ST and Field I models) or automatic ejectors (Field III ST); top tang safety. Imported from Fausti of Italy by Traditions.

Price: Elite Field I DT — 12, 20, 28 ga. or .410; IC and Mod. fixed chokes
(F and F on .410); double triggers . . . . **$789.00 to $969.00**
Price: Elite Field I ST — 12, 20, 28 ga. or .410; same as DT
but with single trigger . . . . **$969.00 to $1,169.00**

Price: Elite Field III ST — 28 ga. or .410; gold-engraved receiver;
high-grade walnut stock **$2,099.00**
Price: Elite Hunter ST — 12 or 20 ga.; blued receiver; IC and
Mod. choke tubes **$999.00**

TRADITIONS UPLANDER SERIES SIDE-BY-SIDE SHOTGUNS
Gauge: 12, 3"; 20, 3". **Barrel:** 26", 28". **Weight:** 6-1/4 lbs. to 6-1/2 lbs. **Length:** 43" to 45" overall. **Stock:** Walnut. **Features:** Barrels threaded for choke tubes (Improved Cylinder, Modified and Full); top tang safety, extended trigger guard. Engraved silver receiver with side plates and lavish gold inlays. Imported from Fausti of Italy by Traditions.

Price: Uplander III Silver 12, 20 ga. **$2,699.00**
Price: Uplander V Silver 12, 20 ga. **$3,199.00**

TRISTAR BRITTANY SIDE-BY-SIDE SHOTGUN
Gauge: 12, 16, 20, 28, .410, 3" chambers. **Barrel:** 12 ga., 20 ga., 26", 28"; 16 ga., 27", 28 ga., 27", 410 ga., 27". All have CT-3 Chokes. **Weight:** 6.2 to 7.2 lbs. **Stock:** Walnut English-style, semi-beavertail forearm with cut checkering, standard semi-gloss finish. **Features:** Boxlock action, engraved case colored frame, auto selective ejectors, single selective trigger.
Price: . . . . **$1,050.00 to $1,069.00**

TRISTAR GENTRY SIDE-BY-SIDE SHOTGUN
Gauge: 12, 16, 20, 28, .410, 3" chambers (16 and 28-ga. @ 2 3/4"). **Barrel:** 12 ga., 27", 20 ga., 28"; 28 ga., 26", 410 ga., 26". All have CT-3 Chokes. **Weight:** 6.2 to 6.8 lbs. **Stock:** Walnut pistol grip stock, semi-beavertail forearm with cut checkering, standard semi-gloss finish. **Features:** Boxlock action, engraved antique silver frame, extractors, single selective trigger with top tang selector.
Price: . . . . **$929.00 to $945.00**

SHOTGUNS — Bolt Actions & Single Shot

Variety of designs for utility and sporting purposes, as well as for competitive shooting.

Browning BT-99 Trap

H&R Model 928
Ultra Slug Hunter Deluxe

H&R Tamer

H&R Topper

H&R Topper Deluxe

BERETTA DT10 TRIDENT TRAP TOP SINGLE SHOTGUN
Gauge: 12, 3" chamber. **Barrel:** 34"; five Optima Choke tubes (Full, Full, Imp. Modified, Mod. and Imp. Cyl.). **Weight:** 8.8 lbs. **Stock:** High-grade walnut; adjustable. **Features:** Detachable, adjustable trigger group; Optima Bore for improved shot pattern and reduced recoil; slim Optima Choke tubes; raised and thickened receiver for long life. Introduced 2000. Imported from Italy by Beretta USA.
Price: **$6,995.00**

BROWNING BT-99 TRAP O/U SHOTGUNS
Gauge: 12. **Barrel:** 30", 32", 34". **Stock:** Walnut; standard or adjustable. **Weight:** 7 lbs. 11 oz. to 9 lbs. **Features:** Back-bored single barrel; interchangeable chokes; beavertail forearm; extractor only; high rib.
Price: BT-99 w/conventional comb, 32" or 34" barrels **$1,396.00**
Price: BT-99 w/adjustable comb, 32" or 34" barrels **$1,584.00**
Price: BT-99 Golden Clays w/adjustable comb,
32" or 34" barrels **$3,509.00**
Price: BT-99 Micro w/conventional comb, 30" or 32" barrels **$1,396.00**

CHIPMUNK 410 YOUTH SHOTGUN
Gauge: .410. **Barrel:** 18-1/4" tapered, blue. **Weight:** 3.25 lbs. **Length:** 33".
Stock: Walnut. **Features:** Manually cocking single shot bolt, blued receiver.
Price: **$225.95**

HARRINGTON & RICHARDSON ULTRA SLUG HUNTER/TAMER SHOTGUNS
Gauge: 12, 20 ga., 3" chamber, .410. **Barrel:** 20" to 24" rifled. **Weight:** 6 to 9 lbs. **Length:** 34-1/2" to 40". **Stock:** Hardwood, laminate, or polymer with full pistol grip; semi-beavertail forend. **Sights:** Gold bead front. **Features:** Break-open action with side-lever release, automatic ejector. Introduced 1994. From H&R 1871, LLC.
Price: Ultra Slug Hunter, blued, hardwood **$273.00**
Price: Ultra Slug Hunter Youth, blued, hardwood, 13-1/8" LOP . . . **$273.00**
Price: Ultra Slug Hunter Deluxe, blued, laminated **$273.00**
Price: Tamer .410 bore, stainless barrel, black polymer stock **$173.00**

HARRINGTON & RICHARDSON TOPPER MODEL S
Gauge: 12, 16, 20, .410, up to 3.5" chamber. **Barrel:** 22 to 28". **Weight:** 5-7 lbs. **Stock:** Polymer, hardwood, or black walnut. **Features:** Satin nickel frame, blued barrel. Reintroduced 1992. From H&R 1871, LLC.
Price: Deluxe Classic, 12/20 ga., 28" barrel w/vent rib **$225.00**
Price: Topper Deluxe 12 ga., 28" barrel, black hardwood **$179.00**
Price: Topper 12, 16, 20 ga., .410, 26" to 28", black hardwood . . . **$153.00**
Price: Topper Junior 20 ga., .410, 22" barrel, hardwood **$160.00**
Price: Topper Junior Classic, 20 ga., .410, checkered hardwood . . **$160.00**

H&R Topper Junior

Ljutic Mono Gun

Mossberg SSi One

New England Firearms Standard Pardner

KRIEGHOFF K-80 SINGLE BARREL TRAP GUN
Gauge: 12, 2-3/4" chamber. **Barrel:** 32" or 34" Unsingle. Fixed Full or choke tubes. **Weight:** About 8-3/4 lbs. **Stock:** Four stock dimensions or adjustable stock available. All hand-checkered European walnut. **Features:** Satin nickel finish. Selective mechanical trigger adjustable for finger position. Tapered step vent rib. Adjustable point of impact.
Price: Standard grade Full Unsingle, from **$10,080.00**

KRIEGHOFF KX-5 TRAP GUN
Gauge: 12, 2-3/4" chamber. **Barrel:** 32", 34"; choke tubes. **Weight:** About 8-1/2 lbs. **Stock:** Factory adjustable stock. European walnut. **Features:** Ventilated tapered step rib. Adjustable position trigger, optional release trigger. Fully adjustable rib. Satin gray electroless nickel receiver. Fitted aluminum case. Imported from Germany by Krieghoff International, Inc.
Price: **$5,395.00**

LJUTIC MONO GUN SINGLE BARREL SHOTGUN
Gauge: 12 only. **Barrel:** 34", choked to customer specs; hollow-milled rib, 35-1/2" sight plane. **Weight:** Approx. 9 lbs. **Stock:** To customer specs. Oil finish, hand checkered. **Features:** Custom gun. Pull or release trigger; removable trigger guard contains trigger and hammer mechanism; Ljutic pushbutton opener on front of trigger guard. From Ljutic Industries.
Price: Std., med. or Olympic rib, custom bbls., fixed choke. **$6,995.00**
Price: As above with screw-in choke barrel **$7,395.00**
Price: Stainless steel mono gun **$7,995.00**

Ljutic LTX Pro 3 Deluxe Mono Gun
Deluxe, lightweight version of the Mono gun with high quality wood, upgrade checkering, special rib height, screw-in chokes, ported and cased.
Price: **$8,995.00**
Price: Stainless steel model **$9,995.00**

MOSSBERG SSi-ONE 12 GAUGE SLUG SHOTGUN
Gauge: 12, 3" chamber. **Barrel:** 24", fully rifled. **Weight:** 8 lbs. **Length:** 40" overall. **Stock:** Walnut, fluted and cut checkered; sling-swivel studs; drilled and tapped for scope base. **Sights:** None (scope base supplied). **Features:** Frame accepts interchangeable rifle barrels (see Mossberg SSi-One rifle listing); lever-opening, break-action design; ambidextrous, top-tang safety; internal eject/extract selector. Introduced 2000. From Mossberg.
Price: **$480.00**

Mossberg SSi-One Turkey Shotgun
Similar to SSi-One 12 gauge slug shotgun, but chambered for 12 ga., 3-1/2" loads. Includes Accu-Mag Turkey Tube. Introduced 2001. From Mossberg.
Price: **$459.00**

NEW ENGLAND FIREARMS PARDNER AND TRACKER II SHOTGUNS
Gauge: 10, 12, 16, 20, 28, .410, up to 3.5" chamber for 10 and 12 ga. 16, 28, 2-3/4" chamber. **Barrel:** 24" to 30". **Weight:** Varies from 5 to 9.5 lbs. **Length:** Varies from 36" to 48". **Stock:** Walnut-finished hardwood with full pistol grip, synthetic, or camo finish. **Sights:** Bead front on most. **Features:** Transfer bar ignition; break-open action with side-lever release. Introduced 1987. From New England Firearms.
Price: Pardner, all gauges, hardwood stock, 26" to 32" blued barrel,
    Mod. or Full choke **$140.00**
Price: Pardner Youth, hardwood stock, straight grip,
    22" blued barrel **$149.00**
Price: Pardner Screw-In Choke model, intr. 2006 . . . . **$164.00**
Price: Turkey model, 10/12 ga., camo finish or black . . **$192.00 to $259.00**
Price: Youth Turkey, 20 ga., camo finish or black **$192.00**
Price: Waterfowl, 10 ga., camo finish or hardwood **$227.00**
Price: Tracker II slug gun, 12/20 ga., hardwood **$196.00**

New England Firearms Tracker II

Rossi Single-Shot

Rossi Matched Pair

Savage 210F Slug Warrior

Stoeger Single-Shot

ROSSI SINGLE-SHOT SHOTGUNS

Gauge: 12, 20, .410. **Barrel:** 22" (Youth), 28". **Weight:** 3.75-5.25 lbs. **Stocks:** Wood. **Sights:** Bead front sight, fully adjustable fiber optic sight on Slug and Turkey. **Features:** Single-shot break open, 8 models available, positive ejection, internal transfer bar mechanism, trigger block system, Taurus Security System, blued finish, Rifle Slug has ported barrel.
Price: .... **$125.00 to $214.00**

ROSSI MATCHED PAIRS

Gauge/Caliber: 12, 20, .410, .22Mag, .22LR, .17HMR, .223Rem, .243Win, .270Win, .30-06, .308Win, .50 (black powder). **Barrel:** 23", 28". **Weight:** 5-6.3 lbs. **Stocks:** Wood or black synthetic. **Sights:** Bead front on shotgun barrel, fully adjustable front and rear on rifle barrel, drilled and tapped for scope, fully adjustable fiber optic sights (black powder). **Features:** Single-shot break open, 27 models available, internal transfer bar mechanism, manual external safety, blue finish, trigger block system, Taurus Security System, youth models available.
Price: Rimfire/Shotgun .... **$169.00 to $253.00**
Price: Centerfire/Shotgun **$297.00**
Price: Black Powder Matched Pair .... **$249.00 to $313.00**

ROSSI MATCHED SET

Gauge/Caliber: 12, 20, .22LR, .17HMR, .243Win, .270Win, .50 (black powder). **Barrel:** 33.5"–43". **Weight:** 6.25-6.3 lbs. **Stocks:** Wood. **Sights:** Bead front on shotgun barrel, fully adjustable front and rear on rifle barrel, drilled and tapped for scope, fully adjustable fiber optic sights (black powder). **Features:** Single-shot break open, 4 models available, internal transfer bar mechanism, manual external safety, blue finish, trigger block system, Taurus Security System, youth models available.
Price: .... **$319.00 to $398.00**

SAVAGE MODEL 210F SLUG WARRIOR SHOTGUN

Gauge: 12, 3" chamber; 2-shot magazine. **Barrel:** 24" 1:35" rifling twist. **Weight:** 7-1/2 lbs. **Length:** 43.5" overall. **Stock:** Glass-filled polymer with positive checkering. **Features:** Based on the Savage Model 110 action; 60-degree bolt lift; controlled round feed; comes with scope mount. Introduced 1996. Made in U.S. by Savage Arms.
Price: **$475.00**
Price: (Camo) **$513.00**

STOEGER SINGLE-SHOT SHOTGUN

Gauge: 12, 20, .410, 2-3/4", 3" chambers. **Barrel:** 26", 28". **Weight:** 5.4 lbs. **Length:** 40-1/2" to 42-1/2" overall. **Sights:** Brass bead. **Features:** .410, Full fixed choke tubes, screw-in. .410 12 ga. hardwood pistol-grip stock and forend. 20 ga. 26" bbl., hardwood forend.
Price: Blue; Youth **$109.00**
Price: Youth with English stock **$119.00**

Tar-Hunt RSG-20
Mountaineer

Thompson/Center Encore Rifled Slug

Thompson/Center
Encore Turkey

TAR-HUNT RSG-12 PROFESSIONAL RIFLED SLUG GUN
Gauge: 12, 2-3/4" or 3" chamber, 1-shot magazine. **Barrel:** 23", fully rifled with muzzle brake. **Weight:** 7-3/4 lbs. **Length:** 41-1/2" overall. **Stock:** Matte black McMillan fiberglass with Pachmayr Decelerator pad. **Sights:** None furnished; comes with Leupold windage or Weaver bases. **Features:** Uses rifle-style action with two locking lugs; two-position safety; Shaw barrel; single-stage, trigger; muzzle brake. Many options available. Right- and left-hand models at same prices. Introduced 1991. Made in U.S. by Tar-Hunt Custom Rifles, Inc.
Price: 12 ga. Professional model, right- or left-hand **$2,585.00**

Tar-Hunt RSG-16 Elite Shotgun
Similar to RSG-12 Professional except 16 gauge; right- or left-hand versions.
Price: **$2,585.00**

Tar-Hunt RSG-20 Mountaineer Slug Gun
Similar to the RSG-12 Professional except chambered for 20 gauge (2-3/4" and 3" shells); 23" Shaw rifled barrel, with muzzle brake; two-lug bolt; one-shot blind magazine; matte black finish; McMillan fiberglass stock with Pachmayr Decelerator pad; receiver drilled and tapped for Rem. 700 bases. Right- or left-hand versions. Weighs 6-1/2 lbs. Introduced 1997. Made in U.S. by Tar-Hunt Custom Rifles, Inc.
Price: **$2,585.00**

THOMPSON/CENTER ENCORE RIFLED SLUG GUN
Gauge: 20, 3" chamber. **Barrel:** 26", fully rifled. **Weight:** About 7 lbs. **Length:** 40-1/2" overall. **Stock:** Walnut with walnut forearm. **Sights:** Steel; click-adjustable rear and ramp-style front, both with fiber optics. **Features:** Encore system features a variety of rifle, shotgun and muzzle-loading rifle barrels interchangeable with the same frame. Break-open design operates by pulling up and back on trigger guard spur. Composite stock and forearm available. Introduced 2000.
Price: **$684.00**

THOMPSON/CENTER ENCORE TURKEY GUN
Gauge: 12 ga. **Barrel:** 24". **Features:** All-camo finish, high definition Realtree Hardwoods HD camo.
Price: **$763.00**

Designs for utility, suitable for and adaptable to competitions and other sporting purposes.

Benelli M3 Convertible

Fabarm FP6

Mossberg Model 500 Persuader

BENELLI M3 CONVERTIBLE SHOTGUN
Gauge: 12, 2-3/4", 3" chambers, 5-shot magazine. **Barrel:** 19-3/4" (Cyl.). **Weight:** 7 lbs., 4oz. **Length:** 41" overall. **Stock:** High-impact polymer with sling loop in side of butt; rubberized pistol grip on stock. **Sights:** Open rifle, fully adjustable. Ghost ring and rifle type. **Features:** Combination pump/auto action. Alloy receiver with inertia recoil rotating locking lug bolt; matte finish; automatic shell release lever. Introduced 1989. Imported by Benelli USA. Price with pistol grip, open rifle sights.
Price: With standard stock, open rifle sights **$1,255.00**
Price: With ghost ring sight system, standard stock **$1,335.00**
Price: With ghost ring sights, pistol grip stock **$1,335.00**

BENELLI M2 TACTICAL SHOTGUN
Gauge: 12, 2-3/4", 3" chambers, 5-shot magazine. **Barrel:** 18.5" IC, M, F choke tubes. **Weight:** 6.7 lbs. **Length:** 39.75" overall. **Stock:** Black polymer. **Sights:** Rifle type ghost ring system, tritium night sights optional. **Features:** Semi-auto intertia recoil action. Cross-bolt safety; bolt release button; matte-finish metal. Introduced 1993. Imported from Italy by Benelli USA.
Price: With rifle sights **$1,065.00**
Price: With ghost ring sights, standard stock **$1,175.00**
Price: With ghost ring sights, pistol grip stock **$1,175.00**
Price: With rifle sights, pistol grip stock **$1,065.00**
Price: ComforTech stock, rifle sights **$1,175.00**
Price: Comfortech Stock, Ghost Ring **$1,280.00**

CROSSFIRE SHOTGUN/RIFLE
Gauge/Caliber: 12, 2-3/4" Chamber: 4-shot/223 Rem. (5-shot). **Barrel:** 20" (shotgun), 18" (rifle). **Weight:** About 8.6 lbs. **Length:** 40" overall. **Stock:** Composite. **Sights:** Meprolight night sights. Integral Weaver-style scope rail. **Features:** Combination pump-action shotgun, rifle; single selector; single trigger; dual action bars for both upper and lower actions; ambidextrous selector and safety. Introduced 1997. Made in U.S. From Hesco.
Price: About **$1,895.00**
Price: With camo finish **$1,995.00**

E.M.F. OLD WEST PUMP (SLIDE ACTION) SHOTGUN
Gauge: 12. **Barrel:** 20". **Weight:** 7 lbs. **Length:** 39 1/2" overall. **Stock:** Smooth walnut with cushioned pad. **Sights:** Front bead. **Features:** Authentic reproduction of Winchester 1897 pump shotgun; blue receiver and barrel; standard modified choke. Introduced 2006. Imported from China for E.M.F. by TTN.
Price: **$474.90**

FABARM TACTICAL SEMI-AUTOMATIC SHOTGUN
Gauge: 12, 3" chamber. **Barrel:** 20". **Weight:** 6.6 lbs. **Length:** 41.2" overall. **Stock:** Polymer or folding. **Sights:** Ghost ring (tritium night sights optional). **Features:** Gas operated; matte receiver; twin action bars; over-sized bolt handle and safety button; Picatinny rail; includes cylinder bore choke tube. New features include polymer pistol grip stock. Introduced 2001. Imported from Italy by Heckler & Koch Inc.
Price: **$999.00**

FABARM FP6 PUMP SHOTGUN
Gauge: 12, 3" chamber. **Barrel:** 20" (Cyl.); accepts choke tubes. **Weight:** 6.6 lbs. **Length:** 41.25" overall. **Stock:** Black polymer with textured grip, grooved slide handle. **Sights:** Blade front. **Features:** Twin action bars; anodized finish; free carrier for smooth reloading. Introduced 1998. New features include ghost-ring sighting system, low profile Picatinny rail, and pistol grip stock. Imported from Italy by Heckler & Koch, Inc.
Price: (Carbon fiber finish) **$499.00**
Price: With flip-up front sight, Picatinny rail with rear sight, oversize safety button **$499.00**

MOSSBERG MODEL 500 PERSUADER SECURITY SHOTGUNS
Gauge: 12, 20, .410, 3" chamber. **Barrel:** 18-1/2", 20" (Cyl.). **Weight:** 7 lbs. **Stock:** Walnut-finished hardwood or black synthetic. **Sights:** Metal bead front. **Features:** Available in 6- or 8-shot models. Top-mounted safety, double action slide bars, swivel studs, rubber recoil pad. Blue, Parkerized, Marinecote finishes. Mossberg Cablelock included. From Mossberg.
Price: 12 ga., 18-1/2", blue, wood or synthetic stock, 6-shot **$353.00**
Price: Cruiser, 12 ga., 18-1/2", blue, pistol grip, heat shield **$357.00**
Price: As above, 20 ga. or .410 bore **$345.00**

Mossberg Ghost Ring

Mossberg Model HS410

Remington Model 870 Tactical

Tactical Response TR-870

Mossberg Model 500, 590 Mariner Pump Shotgun

Similar to the Model 500 or 590 Persuader except all metal parts finished with Marinecote metal finish to resist rust and corrosion. Synthetic field stock; pistol grip kit included. Mossberg Cablelock included.

Price: 6-shot, 18-1/2" barrel **$497.00**
Price: 9-shot, 20" barrel **$513.00**

Mossberg Model 500, 590 Ghost-Ring Shotgun

Similar to the Model 500 Persuader except has adjustable blade front, adjustable Ghost-Ring rear sight with protective "ears." Model 500 has 18.5" (Cyl.) barrel, 6-shot capacity; Model 590 has 20" (Cyl.) barrel, 9-shot capacity. Both have synthetic field stock. Mossberg Cablelock included. Introduced 1990. From Mossberg.

Price: 500 Parkerized **$468.00**
Price: 590 Parkerized **$543.00**
Price: 590 Parkerized Speedfeed stock **$586.00**

Mossberg Model HS410 Shotgun

Similar to the Model 500 Persuader pump except chambered for 20 gauge or .410 with 3" chamber; has pistol grip forend, thick recoil pad, muzzle brake and has special spreader choke on the 18.5" barrel. Overall length is 37.5", weight is 6.25 lbs. Blue finish; synthetic field stock. Mossberg Cablelock and video included. Introduced 1990.

Price: HS 410 . . . . **$355.00**

MOSSBERG MODEL 590 SHOTGUN

Gauge: 12, 3" chamber. **Barrel:** 20" (Cyl.). **Weight:** 7-1/4 lbs. **Stock:** Synthetic field or Speedfeed. **Sights:** Metal bead front. **Features:** Top-mounted safety, double slide action bars. Comes with heat shield, bayonet lug, swivel studs, rubber recoil pad. Blue, Parkerized or Marinecote finish. Mossberg Cablelock included. From Mossberg.

Price: Blue, synthetic stock **$417.00**
Price: Parkerized, synthetic stock **$476.00**
Price: Parkerized, Speedfeed stock **$519.00**

REMINGTON MODEL 870 AND MODEL 1100 TACTICAL SHOTGUNS

Gauge: 12, 2-3/4 or 3" chamber, 7-shot magazine. **Barrel:** 18", 20", 22" (Cyl or IC). **Weight:** 7.5-7.75 lbs. **Length:** 38.5-42.5" overall. **Stock:** Black synthetic, synthetic Speedfeed IV full pistol-grip stock, or Knoxx Industries SpecOps stock w/recoil-absorbing spring-loaded cam and adjustable length of pull (12" to 16", 870 only). **Sights:** Front post w/dot only on 870; rib and front dot on 1100. **Features:** R3 recoil pads, LimbSaver technology to reduce felt recoil, 2-, 3- or 4-shot extensions based on barrel length; matte-olive-drab barrels and receivers. Model 1100 Tactical is available with Speedfeed IV pistol grip stock or standard black synthetic stock and forend. Speedfeed IV model has an 18" barrel with two-shot extension. Standard synthetic-stocked version is equipped with 22" barrel and four-shot extension. Introduced 2006. From Remington Arms Co.

Price: 870, Speedfeed IV stock, 3" chamber, 38.5" overall **$599.00**
Price: 870, SpecOps stock, 3" chamber, 38.5" overall **$625.00**
Price: 1100, synthetic stock, 2-3/4" chamber, 42.5" overall **$759.00**

TACTICAL RESPONSE TR-870 STANDARD MODEL SHOTGUNS

Gauge: 12, 3" chamber, 7-shot magazine. **Barrel:** 18" (Cyl.). **Weight:** 9 lbs. **Length:** 38" overall. **Stock:** Fiberglass-filled polypropolene with non-snag recoil absorbing butt pad. Nylon tactical forend. **Sights:** Trak-Lock ghost ring sight system. Front sight has Tritium insert. **Features:** Highly modified Remington 870P with Parkerized finish. Comes with nylon three-way adjustable sling, high visibility non-binding follower, high performance magazine spring, Jumbo Head safety, and Side Saddle extended 6-shot shell carrier on left side of receiver. Introduced 1991. From Scattergun Technologies, Inc.

Price: Standard model **$815.00**
Price: FBI model **$770.00**
Price: Patrol model **$595.00**
Price: Border Patrol model **$605.00**
Price: K-9 model (Rem. 11-87 action) **$995.00**
Price: Urban Sniper, Rem. 11-87 action **$1,290.00**
Price: Louis Awerbuck model **$705.00**
Price: Practical Turkey model **$725.00**
Price: Expert model **$1,350.00**
Price: Professional model **$815.00**
Price: Entry model **$840.00**
Price: Compact model **$635.00**
Price: SWAT model **$1,195.00**

Dixie Pennsylvania   **Harper's Ferry**   **Kentucky**   **Le Page**   **Lyman Plains Pistol**

DIXIE KENTUCKY PISTOL
Caliber: 44 (.430" round ball). **Barrel:** 10", (7/8" octagon). **Weight:** 2-1/2 lbs. **Stocks:** Walnut-stained hardwood. **Sights:** Blade front, open rear drift-adjustable for windage; brass. **Features:** Flintlock only. Brass trigger guard, thimbles, instep, wedge plates; high- luster blue barrel. Imported from Italy by Dixie Gun Works.
Price: Finished flint $250.00
Price: Finished percussion $225.00
Price: Kit $195.00

FRENCH-STYLE DUELING PISTOL
Caliber: 44. **Barrel:** 10". **Weight:** 35 oz. **Length:** 15-3/4" overall. **Stocks:** Carved walnut. **Sights:** Fixed. **Features:** Comes with velvet-lined case and accessories. Imported by Mandall Shooting Supplies.
Price: $295.00

HARPER'S FERRY 1806 PISTOL
Caliber: 58 (.570" round ball). **Barrel:** 10". **Weight:** 40 oz. **Length:** 16" overall. **Stocks:** Walnut. **Sights:** Fixed. **Features:** Case- hardened lock, brass-mounted browned barrel. Replica of the first U.S. gov't.-made flintlock pistol. Imported by Navy Arms, Dixie Gun Works.
Price: Dixie Gun Works RH0225 . . . . $375.00
Price: Kit (Dixie) $295.00

KENTUCKY FLINTLOCK PISTOL
Caliber: 44, 45. **Barrel:** 10-1/8". **Weight:** 32 oz. **Length:** 15-1/2" overall. **Stocks:** Walnut. **Sights:** Fixed. **Features:** Specifications, including caliber, weight and length may vary with importer. Case-hardened lock, blued barrel; available also as brass barrel flintlock Model 1821. Imported by Navy Arms, The Armoury, Dixie Gun Works.
Price: $300.00
Price: In kit form. From . . . . $90.00 to $112.00
Price: Single cased set (Navy Arms) $360.00
Price: Double cased set (Navy Arms) $590.00

Kentucky Percussion Pistol
Similar to Flint version but percussion lock. Imported by The Armoury, Navy Arms, CVA (50-cal.).
Price: . . . . $129.95 to $225.00
Price: Steel barrel (Armoury) $179.00
Price: Single cased set (Navy Arms) $355.00
Price: Double cased set (Navy Arms) $600.00

Pedersoli Mang

LE PAGE PERCUSSION DUELING PISTOL
Caliber: 44. **Barrel:** 10", rifled. **Weight:** 40 oz. **Length:** 16" overall. **Stocks:** Walnut, fluted butt. **Sights:** Blade front, notch rear. **Features:** Single-set trigger. Blued barrel; trigger guard and buttcap are polished silver. Imported by Dixie Gun Works.
Price: PH0310 . . . . $470.00

LYMAN PLAINS PISTOL
Caliber: 50 or 54. **Barrel:** 8"; 1:30" twist, both calibers. **Weight:** 50 oz. **Length:** 15" overall. **Stocks:** Walnut half-stock. **Sights:** Blade front, square notch rear adjustable for windage. **Features:** Polished brass trigger guard and ramrod tip, color case-hardened coil spring lock, spring-loaded trigger, stainless steel nipple, blackened iron furniture. Hooked patent breech, detachable belt hook. Introduced 1981. From Lyman Products.
Price: Finished $244.95
Price: Kit $189.95

PEDERSOLI MANG TARGET PISTOL
Caliber: 38. **Barrel:** 10.5", octagonal; 1:15" twist, **Weight:** 2.5 lbs. **Length:** 17.25" overall. **Stocks:** Walnut with fluted grip. **Sights:** Blade front, open rear adjustable for windage. **Features:** Browned barrel, polished breech plug, remainder color case-hardened. Imported from Italy by Dixie Gun Works.
Price: PH0503 . . . . $1,100.00

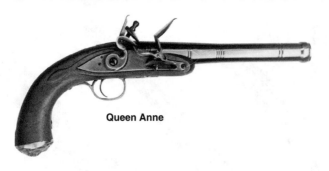

Queen Anne

Traditions Pioneer

Traditions William Parker

Traditions Buckhunter Pro

QUEEN ANNE FLINTLOCK PISTOL
Caliber: 50 (.490" round ball). **Barrel:** 7-1/2", smoothbore. **Stocks:** Walnut. **Sights:** None. **Features:** Browned steel barrel, fluted brass trigger guard, brass mask on butt. Lockplate left in the white. Made by Pedersoli in Italy. Introduced 1983. Imported by Dixie Gun Works.
Price: RH0211 . . . . **$290.00**
Price: Kit FH0421 . . . . **$225.00**

REPLICA ARMS "SEVEN SEAS" DERRINGER
Caliber: 36 cal., smoothbore percussion. **Barrel:** 4-5/8". **Weight:** 21 oz. **Length:** 11" overall. **Grips:** Walnut finished. **Features:** All steel barrel with brass accents. Introduced 2005. Imported by Navy Arms.
Price: **$99.95**

TRADITIONS BUCKHUNTER PRO IN-LINE PISTOL
Caliber: 50. **Barrel:** 9-1/2", round. **Weight:** 48 oz. **Length:** 14" overall. **Stocks:** Smooth walnut or black epoxy-coated hardwood grip and forend. **Sights:** Beaded blade front, folding adjustable rear. **Features:** Thumb safety; removable stainless steel breech plug; adjustable trigger, barrel drilled and tapped for scope mounting. From Traditions.
Price: With walnut grip **$229.00**
Price: Nickel with black grip **$239.00**
Price: With walnut grip and 12-1/2" barrel **$239.00**
Price: Nickel with black grip, muzzle brake and 14-3/4"
fluted barrel **$289.00**
Price: 45 cal. nickel w/bl. grip, muzzle brake and 14-3/4"
fluted bbl. **$289.00**

TRADITIONS KENTUCKY PISTOL
Caliber: 50. **Barrel:** 10"; octagon with 7/8" flats; 1:20" twist. **Weight:** 40 oz. **Length:** 15" overall. **Stocks:** Stained beech. **Sights:** Blade front, fixed rear. **Features:** Bird's-head grip; brass thimbles; color case-hardened lock. Percussion only. Introduced 1995. From Traditions.
Price: Finished **$139.00**
Price: Kit **$109.00**

TRADITIONS PIONEER PISTOL
Caliber: 45. **Barrel:** 9-5/8"; 13/16" flats, 1:16" twist. **Weight:** 31 oz. **Length:** 15" overall. **Stocks:** Beech. **Sights:** Blade front, fixed rear. **Features:** V-type mainspring. Single trigger. German silver furniture, blackened hardware. From Traditions.
Price: **$139.00**
Price: Kit **$119.00**

TRADITIONS TRAPPER PISTOL
Caliber: 50. **Barrel:** 9-3/4"; 7/8" flats; 1:20" twist. **Weight:** 2-3/4 lbs. **Length:** 16" overall. **Stocks:** Beech. **Sights:** Blade front, adjustable rear. **Features:** Double-set triggers; brass buttcap, trigger guard, wedge plate, forend tip, thimble. From Traditions.
Price: Percussion **$189.00**
Price: Flintlock **$209.00**
Price: Kit **$149.00**

TRADITIONS VEST-POCKET DERRINGER
Caliber: 31. **Barrel:** 2-1/4"; brass. **Weight:** 8 oz. **Length:** 4-3/4" overall. **Stocks:** Simulated ivory. **Sights:** Bead front. **Features:** Replica of riverboat gamblers' derringer; authentic spur trigger. From Traditions.
Price: **$109.00**

TRADITIONS WILLIAM PARKER PISTOL
Caliber: 50. **Barrel:** 10-3/8"; 15/16" flats; polished steel. **Weight:** 37 oz. **Length:** 17-1/2" overall. **Stocks:** Walnut with checkered grip. **Sights:** Brass blade front, fixed rear. **Features:** Replica dueling pistol with 1:20" twist, hooked breech. Brass wedge plate, trigger guard, cap guard; separate ramrod. Double-set triggers. Polished steel barrel, lock. Imported by Traditions.
Price: **$269.00**

Army 1860

Baby Dragoon 1848

Dixie Wyatt Earp

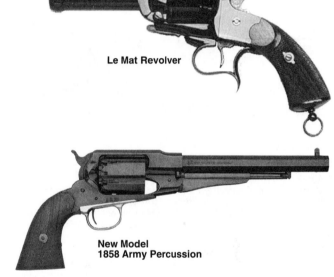

Le Mat Revolver

New Model
1858 Army Percussion

ARMY 1860 PERCUSSION REVOLVER
Caliber: 44, 6-shot. **Barrel:** 8". **Weight:** 40 oz. **Length:** 13-5/8" overall. **Stocks:** Walnut. **Sights:** Fixed. **Features:** Engraved Navy scene on cylinder; brass trigger guard; case-hardened frame, loading lever and hammer. Some importers supply pistol cut for detachable shoulder stock, have accessory stock available. Imported by Cabela's (1860 Lawman), E.M.F., Navy Arms, The Armoury, Cimarron, Dixie Gun Works (half-fluted cylinder, not roll engraved), Euroarms of America (brass or steel model), Armsport, Traditions (brass or steel), Uberti U.S.A. Inc., United States Patent Fire-Arms.
Price: Dixie Gun Works RH0125 . . . . **$232.00**
Price: Hartford model, steel frame, cartouches (E.M.F.) **$225.00**
Price: Single cased set (Navy Arms) **$300.00**
Price: Double cased set (Navy Arms) **$490.00**
Price: 1861 Navy: Same as Army except 36-cal., 7-1/2" bbl.,
weighs 41 oz., cut for shoulder stock; round cylinder
(fluted available), from Cabela's, CVA (brass frame, 44 cal.),
United States Patent Fire-Arms . . . . **$99.95 to $385.00**
Price: Steel frame kit (E.M.F., Euroarms) . . . . **$125.00 to $216.25**
Price: Colt Army Police, fluted cyl., 5-1/2", 36-cal. (Cabela's) . . . **$229.99**
Price: With nickeled frame, barrel and backstrap,
gold-tone fluted cylinder, trigger and hammer,
simulated ivory grips (Traditions) **$199.00**

BABY DRAGOON 1848, 1849 POCKET, WELLS FARGO
Caliber: 31. **Barrel:** 3", 4", 5", 6"; seven-groove; RH twist. **Weight:** About 21 oz. **Stocks:** Varnished walnut. **Sights:** Brass pin front, hammer notch rear. **Features:** No loading lever on Baby Dragoon or Wells Fargo models. Unfluted cylinder with stagecoach holdup scene; cupped cylinder pin; no grease grooves; one safety pin on cylinder and slot in hammer face; straight (flat) mainspring. From Armsport, Cimarron F.A. Co., Dixie Gun Works, E.M.F., Uberti U.S.A. Inc.
Price: 5.5" barrel, 1849 Pocket with loading lever (Dixie) **$232.00**
Price: 4" (Uberti USA Inc.) **$275.00**

DIXIE WYATT EARP REVOLVER
Caliber: 44. **Barrel:** 12", octagon. **Weight:** 46 oz. **Length:** 18" overall. **Stocks:** Two-piece walnut. **Sights:** Fixed. **Features:** Highly polished brass frame, backstrap and trigger guard; blued barrel and cylinder; case-hardened hammer, trigger and loading lever. Navy-size shoulder stock ($45) requires minor fitting. From Dixie Gun Works.
Price: RH0130 . . . . **$180.00**

LE MAT REVOLVER
Caliber: 44/65. **Barrel:** 6-3/4" (revolver); 4-7/8" (single shot). **Weight:** 3 lbs., 7 oz. **Stocks:** Hand-checkered walnut. **Sights:** Post front, hammer notch rear. **Features:** Exact reproduction with all-steel construction; 44-cal. 9-shot cylinder, 65-cal. single barrel; color case-hardened hammer with selector; spur trigger guard; ring at butt; lever-type barrel release. From Navy Arms and Dixie Gun Works.

Price: Cavalry model (lanyard ring, spur trigger guard) **$675.00**
Price: Army model (round trigger guard, pin-type barrel release) . **$675.00**
Price: Naval-style (thumb selector on hammer) **$675.00**

NEW MODEL 1858 ARMY PERCUSSION REVOLVER
Caliber: 36 or 44, 6-shot. **Barrel:** 6-1/2" or 8". **Weight:** 38 oz. **Length:** 13-1/2" overall. **Stocks:** Walnut. **Sights:** Blade front, groove- in-frame rear. **Features:** Replica of Remington Model 1858. Also available from some importers as Army Model Belt Revolver in 36- cal., a shortened and lightened version of the 44. Target Model (Uberti U.S.A. Inc., Navy Arms) has fully adjustable target rear sight, target front, 36 or 44. Imported by Cabela's, Cimarron F.A. Co., CVA (as 1858 Army, brass frame, 44 only), Dixie Gun Works, Navy Arms, The Armoury, E.M.F., Euroarms of America (engraved, stainless and plain), Armsport, Traditions (44 only), Uberti U.S.A. Inc.
Price: Steel frame, about . . . . **$99.95 to $280.00**
Price: Steel frame kit (Euroarms, Navy Arms) . . . . . **$115.95 to $150.00**
Price: Stainless steel Model 1858 (Euroarms,
Uberti U.S.A. Inc., Cabela's, Navy Arms,
Armsport, Traditions) . . . . **$169.95 to $380.00**
Price: Target Model, adjustable rear sight (Cabela's,
Euroarms, Uberti U.S.A. Inc., Stone Mountain
Arms) . . . . **$95.95 to $399.00**
Price: Brass frame (CVA, Cabela's, Traditions,
Navy Arms) . . . . **$79.95 to $199.99**
Price: As above, kit (Dixie Gun Works) . . . . **$145.00 to $188.95**
Price: Buffalo model, 44-cal. (Cabela's) **$119.99**
Price: Hartford model, steel frame, cartouche (E.M.F.) **$225.00**
Price: Improved Conversion (Cimarron) **$479.00**

Navy Arms 1836 Paterson

North American Companion

Rogers & Spencer

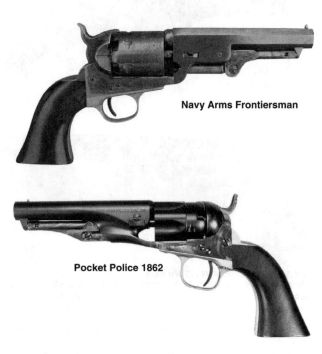

Navy Arms Frontiersman

Pocket Police 1862

NAVY ARMS NEW MODEL POCKET REVOLVER
Caliber: 31, 5-shot. **Barrel:** 3-1/2", octagon. **Weight:** 15 oz. **Length:** 7-3/4". **Stocks:** Two-piece walnut. **Sights:** Fixed. **Features:** Replica of the Remington New Model Pocket. Available with polished brass frame or nickel-plated finish. Introduced 2000. Imported by Navy Arms.
Price: **$300.00**

NAVY ARMS 1836 PATERSON REVOLVER
Caliber: 36. **Barrel:** 9". **Weight:** 2 lbs., 11 oz. **Length:** NA. **Stocks:** Walnut. **Sights:** NA. **Features:** Hidden trigger, blued barrel, replica of 5-shooter, roll-engraved with stagecoach holdup scene.
Price: . . . . **$425.00 to $461.00**

NAVY ARMS 1851 NAVY "FRONTIERSMAN" REVOLVER
Caliber: .36, 6-shot cylinder. **Barrel:** 5". **Weight:** 32 oz. **Length:** 10-1/2" overall. **Grips:** One piece walnut. **Sights:** Post front, notch rear. **Features:** Blued with color case-hardened receiver, trigger and hammer; German Silver backstrap and triggerguard. Introduced 2005. Imported by Navy Arms.
Price: **$315.00**

NAVY MODEL 1851 PERCUSSION REVOLVER
Caliber: 36, 44, 6-shot. **Barrel:** 7-1/2". **Weight:** 44 oz. **Length:** 13" overall. **Stocks:** Walnut finish. **Sights:** Post front, hammer notch rear. **Features:** Brass backstrap and trigger guard; some have 1st Model squareback trigger guard, engraved cylinder with navy battle scene; case-hardened frame, hammer, loading lever. Imported by The Armoury, Cabela's, Cimarron F.A. Co., Navy Arms, E.M.F., Dixie Gun Works, Euroarms of America, Armsport, CVA (44-cal. only), Traditions (44 only), Uberti U.S.A. Inc., United States Patent Fire-Arms.
Price: Brass frame . . . . **$99.95 to $385.00**
Price: Steel frame . . . . **$130.00 to $285.00**
Price: Kit form . . . . **$110.00 to $142.50**
Price: Engraved model (Dixie Gun Works) **$190.00**
Price: Single cased set, steel frame (Navy Arms) **$280.00**
Price: Double cased set, steel frame (Navy Arms) **$455.00**
Price: Confederate Navy (Cabela's) **$139.99**
Price: Hartford model, steel frame, German silver trim,
    cartouche (E.M.F.) **$190.00**
Price: Man With No Name Conversion (Cimarron, 2006) **$459.00**

NORTH AMERICAN COMPANION PERCUSSION REVOLVER
Caliber: 22. **Barrel:** 1-1/8". **Weight:** 5.1 oz. **Length:** 4-1/2" overall. **Stocks:** Laminated wood. **Sights:** Blade front, notch fixed rear. **Features:** All stainless steel construction. Uses standard #11 percussion caps. Comes with bullets, powder measure, bullet seater, leather clip holster, gun rag. Long Rifle or Magnum frame size. Introduced 1996. Made in U.S. by North American Arms.
Price: Long Rifle frame **$200.00**

North American Magnum Companion Percussion Revolver
Similar to the Companion except has larger frame. Weighs 7.2 oz., has 1-5/8" barrel, measures 5-7/16" overall. Comes with bullets, powder measure, bullet seater, leather clip holster, gun rag. Introduced 1996. Made in U.S. by North American Arms.
Price: **$215.00**

POCKET POLICE 1862 PERCUSSION REVOLVER
Caliber: 36, 5-shot. **Barrel:** 4-1/2", 5-1/2", 6-1/2", 7-1/2". **Weight:** 26 oz. **Length:** 12" overall (6-1/2" bbl.). **Stocks:** Walnut. **Sights:** Fixed. **Features:** Round tapered barrel; half-fluted and rebated cylinder; case-hardened frame, loading lever and hammer; silver or brass trigger guard and backstrap. Imported by Dixie Gun Works, Navy Arms (5-1/2" only), Uberti U.S.A. Inc. (5-1/2", 6-1/2" only), United States Patent Fire-Arms and Cimarron F.A. Co.
Price: About . . . . **$139.95 to $335.00**
Price: Single cased set with accessories (Navy Arms) **$365.00**
Price: Hartford model, steel frame, cartouche (E.M.F.) **$300.00**

ROGERS & SPENCER PERCUSSION REVOLVER
Caliber: 44. **Barrel:** 7-1/2". **Weight:** 47 oz. **Length:** 13-3/4" overall. **Stocks:** Walnut. **Sights:** Cone front, integral groove in frame for rear. **Features:** Accurate reproduction of a Civil War design. Solid frame; extra large nipple cut-out on rear of cylinder; loading lever and cylinder easily removed for cleaning. From Dixie Gun Works, Euroarms of America (standard blue, engraved, burnished, target models), Navy Arms.
Price: . . . . **$160.00 to 340.00**
Price: Nickel-plated **$215.00**
Price: Engraved (Euroarms) **$430.00**
Price: Kit version . . . . **$245.00 to $360.00**
Price: Target version (Euroarms) . . . . **$239.00 to $270.00**
Price: Burnished London Gray (Euroarms) . . . . **$245.00 to $370.00**

Ruger Old Army

3rd U.S. Model Dragoon

Spiller & Burr

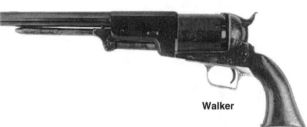

Walker

RUGER OLD ARMY PERCUSSION REVOLVER
Caliber: 45, 6-shot. Uses .457" dia. lead bullets or 454 conical. **Barrel:** 5-1/2", 7-1/2" (6-groove; 1:16" twist). **Weight:** 2-7/8 lbs. **Length:** 11-1/2" and 13-1/2" overall. **Stocks:** Rosewood, simulated ivory. **Sights:** Ramp front, rear adjustable for windage and elevation; or fixed (groove). **Features:** Stainless steel; standard size nipples, chrome-moly steel cylinder and frame, same lockwork as original Super Blackhawk. Also stainless steel. Includes hard case and lock. Introduced 1972.
Price: Blued steel, fixed sight (Model BP-5F) $595.00
Price: Stainless steel, fixed sight (Model KBP-5F-I) $685.00
Price: Stainless steel (Model KBP-7) $635.00

SHERIFF MODEL 1851 PERCUSSION REVOLVER
Caliber: 36, 44, 6-shot. **Barrel:** 5". **Weight:** 40 oz. **Length:** 10-1/2" overall. **Stocks:** Walnut. **Sights:** Fixed. **Features:** Brass backstrap and trigger guard; engraved navy scene; case-hardened frame, hammer, loading lever. Imported by E.M.F.
Price: Steel frame $169.95
Price: Brass frame $140.00

SPILLER & BURR REVOLVER
Caliber: 36 (.375" round ball). **Barrel:** 7", octagon. **Weight:** 2-1/2 lbs. **Length:** 12-1/2" overall. **Stocks:** Two-piece walnut. **Sights:** Fixed. **Features:** Reproduction of the C.S.A. revolver. Brass frame and trigger guard. Also available as a kit. From Dixie Gun Works, Navy Arms.
Price: $205.00
Price: Kit form (Dixie) $155.00
Price: Single cased set (Navy Arms) $270.00
Price: Double cased set (Navy Arms) $430.00

UBERTI 1847 WALKER REVOLVERS
Caliber: 36 (.375" round ball), 5-shot engraved cylinder. **Barrel:** 7-1/2" 11 grooves. **Weight:** 2.6 lbs. **Stocks:** One-piece walnut. **Sights:** Fixed. **Features:** Copy of Sam Colt's first commercially-made revolving pistol, loading lever available, no trigger guard. Made in Italy by Uberti, imported by Benelli USA.
Price: Walker with loading lever, 9" barrel, 6 shot $375.00

UBERTI 1848 DRAGOON AND POCKET REVOLVERS
Caliber: 44 6-shot engraved cylinder. **Barrel:** 7-1/2" 7 grooves. **Weight:** 4.1 lbs. **Stocks:** One-piece walnut. **Sights:** Fixed. **Features:** Copy of Eli Whitney's design for Colt using Walker parts. Blued barrel, backstrap, and trigger guard. Made in Italy by Uberti, imported by Benelli USA, E.M.F.

Price: 1848 Whitneyville Dragoon, 7-1/2" barrel $400.00
Price: 1848 Dragoon, 1st thru 3rd models, 7-1/2" barrel $350.00
Price: 1848 Baby Dragoon, 4" barrel $300.00

UBERTI 1858 NEW ARMY REVOLVERS
Caliber: 44 6-shot engraved cylinder. **Barrel:** 8" 7 grooves. **Weight:** 2.7 lbs. **Length:** 13.6". **Stocks:** Two-piece walnut. **Sights:** Fixed. **Features:** Blued or stainless barrel, backstrap; brass trigger guard. Made in Italy by Uberti, imported by Benelli USA.
Price: 1858 New Army Stainless 8" barrel $365.00
Price: 1858 New Army 8" barrel $300.00
Price: 1858 Target Carbine 18" barrel $475.00
Price: 1862 Pocket Navy 5.5" barrel, 36 caliber $300.00
Price: 1862 Police 5.5" barrel, 36 caliber $300.00

UBERTI 1861 NAVY PERCUSSION REVOLVER
Caliber: 36, 6-shot. **Barrel:** 7-1/2", 7-groove, round. **Weight:** 2 lbs., 6 oz. **Length:** 13". **Stocks:** One-piece walnut. **Sights:** German silver blade front sight. **Features:** Rounded trigger guard, "creeping" loading lever, fluted or round cylinder, steel backstrap, trigger guard, cut for stock. Imported by Cimarron F.A. Co., Uberti U.S.A. Inc., Dixie Gunworks.
Price: $300.00

1862 POCKET NAVY PERCUSSION REVOLVER
Caliber: 36, 5-shot. **Barrel:** 5-1/2", 6-1/2", octagonal, 7-groove, LH twist. **Weight:** 27 oz. (5-1/2" barrel). **Length:** 10-1/2" overall (5-1/2" bbl.). **Stocks:** One-piece varnished walnut. **Sights:** Brass pin front, hammer notch rear. **Features:** Rebated cylinder, hinged loading lever, brass or silver-plated backstrap and trigger guard, color-cased frame, hammer, loading lever, plunger and latch, rest blued. Has original-type markings. From Cimarron F.A. Co., Uberti U.S.A. Inc., Dixie Gunworks.
Price: With brass backstrap, trigger guard . . . . **$240.00 to $310.00**

WALKER 1847 PERCUSSION REVOLVER
Caliber: 44, 6-shot. **Barrel:** 9". **Weight:** 84 oz. **Length:** 15-1/2" overall. **Stocks:** Walnut. **Sights:** Fixed. **Features:** Case-hardened frame, loading lever and hammer; iron backstrap; brass trigger guard; engraved cylinder. Imported by Cabela's, Cimarron F.A. Co., Navy Arms, Dixie Gun Works, Uberti U.S.A. Inc., E.M.F., Cimarron, Traditions, United States Patent Fire-Arms.
Price: About . . . . **$225.00 to $445.00**
Price: Single cased set (Navy Arms) $405.00
Price: Deluxe Walker with French fitted case (Navy Arms) $540.00
Price: Hartford model, steel frame, cartouche (E.M.F.) $350.00

Cabela's Traditional Hawken

Dixie Sharps New Model 1859 Military

ARMOURY R140 HAWKEN RIFLE
Caliber: 45, 50 or 54.**Barrel:** 29". **Weight:** 8-3/4 to 9 lbs. **Length:** 45-3/4" overall. **Stock:** Walnut, with cheekpiece. **Sights:** Dovetailed front, fully adjustable rear. **Features:** Octagon barrel, removable breech plug; double set triggers; blued barrel, brass stock fittings, color case-hardened percussion lock. From Armsport, The Armoury.
Price: . . . . **$225.00 to $245.00**

BOSTONIAN PERCUSSION RIFLE
Caliber: 45. **Barrel:** 30", octagonal. **Weight:** 7-1/4 lbs. **Length:** 46" overall. **Stock:** Walnut. **Sights:** Blade front, fixed notch rear. **Features:** Color case-hardened lock, brass trigger guard, buttplate, patchbox. Imported from Italy by E.M.F.
Price: **$285.00**

CABELA'S BLUE RIDGE RIFLE
Caliber: 32, 36, 45, 50, .54. **Barrel:** 39", octagonal. **Weight:** About 7-3/4 lbs. **Length:** 55" overall. **Stock:** American black walnut. **Sights:** Blade front, rear drift adjustable for windage. **Features:** Color case-hardened lockplate and cock/hammer, brass trigger guard and buttplate, double set, double-phased triggers. From Cabela's.
Price: Percussion **$569.99**
Price: Flintlock **$599.99**

CABELA'S TRADITIONAL HAWKEN
Caliber: 50, 54. **Barrel:** 29". **Weight:** About 9 lbs. **Stock:** Walnut. **Sights:** Blade front, open adjustable rear. **Features:** Flintlock or percussion. Adjustable double-set triggers. Polished brass furniture, color case-hardened lock. Imported by Cabela's.
Price: Percussion, right-hand or left-hand **$339.99**
Price: Flintlock, right-hand **$379.99**

Cabela's Sporterized Hawken Hunter Rifle
Similar to the Traditional Hawken except has more modern stock style with rubber recoil pad, blued furniture, sling swivels. Percussion only, in 50- or 54-caliber.
Price: Carbine or rifle, right-hand **$399.99**

CABELA'S KODIAK EXPRESS DOUBLE RIFLE
Caliber: 50, 54, 58, 72. **Barrel:** Length NA; 1:48" twist. **Weight:** 9.3 lbs. **Length:** 45-1/4" overall. **Stock:** European walnut, oil finish. **Sights:** Fully adjustable double folding-leaf rear, ramp front. **Features:** Percussion. Barrels regulated to point of aim at 75 yards; polished and engraved lock, top tang and trigger guard. From Cabela's.
Price: 50, 54, 58 calibers **$929.99**
Price: 72 caliber **$959.99**

COOK & BROTHER CONFEDERATE CARBINE
Caliber: 58. **Barrel:** 24". **Weight:** 7-1/2 lbs. **Length:** 40-1/2" overall. **Stock:** Select walnut. **Features:** Re-creation of the 1861 New Orleans-made artillery carbine. Color case-hardened lock, browned barrel. Buttplate, trigger guard, barrel bands, sling swivels and nosecap of polished brass. From Euroarms of America.
Price: **$563.00**
Price: Cook & Brother rifle (33" barrel) **$606.00**

CVA OPTIMA PRO 209 BREAK-ACTION RIFLE
Caliber: 45, 50. **Barrel:** 29" fluted, blue or nickel. **Weight:** 8.8 lbs. **Stock:** Ambidextrous Mossy Oak® Camo or black FiberGrip. **Sights:** Adj. fiber-optic. **Features:** Break-action, stainless No. 209 breech plug, aluminum loading rod, cocking spur, lifetime warranty.
Price: Mossy Oak® Camo **$399.95**
Price: Camo, nickel bbl. **$379.95**
Price: Mossy Oak® Camo/blued **$349.95**
Price: Black/nickel **$329.95**
Price: Black/blued **$299.95**
Price: Blued fluted bbl. **$99.95**
Price: Nickel fluted bbl. **$115.95**

CVA Optima 209 Magnum Break-Action Rifle
Similar to Optima Pro but with 26" bbl., nickel or blue finish, 50 cal.
Price: Mossy Oak® Camo/nickel **$310.00**
Price: Mossy Oak® Camo/blue **$290.00**
Price: Black/blued **$235.00**

CVA Optima Elite
Similar to Optima Pro but chambered for 45, 50 black powder plus 243, 270, 30-06 centerfire cartridges.
Price: Hardwoods Green HD/blue **$415.00**
Price: Black Fleck/blue **$355.00**

CVA BUCKHORN 209 MAGNUM
Caliber: 50. **Barrel:** 24". **Weight:** 6.3 lbs. **Sights:** Illuminator fiber-optic. **Features:** Grip-dot stock, thumb-actuated safety; drilled and tapped for scope mounts.
Price: Black stock, blue barrel **$145.00**

CVA KODIAK MAGNUM RIFLE
Caliber: 50. No. 209 primer ignition. **Barrel:** 28"; 1:28" twist. **Stock:** Ambidextrous black or Mossy Oak® camo. **Sights:** Fiber-optic. **Features:** Blue or nickel finish, recoil pad, lifetime warranty. From CVA.
Price: Mossy Oak® camo; nickel barrel **$300.00**
Price: Black stock; nickel barrel **$255.00**
Price: Black stock; blued barrel **$225.00**

DIXIE EARLY AMERICAN JAEGER RIFLE
Caliber: 54. **Barrel:** 27-1/2" octagonal; 1:24" twist. **Weight:** 8-1/4 lbs. **Length:** 43-1/2" overall. **Stock:** American walnut; sliding wooden patchbox on butt. **Sights:** Notch rear, blade front. **Features:** Flintlock or percussion. Browned steel furniture. Imported from Italy by Dixie Gun Works.
Price: Flintlock FR0838 . . . . **$825.00**
Price: Percussion PR0835 . . . . **$825.00**

DIXIE DELUXE CUB RIFLE
Caliber: 40. **Barrel:** 28". **Weight:** 6-1/2 lbs. **Stock:** Walnut. **Sights:** Fixed. **Features:** Short rifle for small game and beginning shooters. Brass patchbox and furniture. Flint or percussion. From Dixie Gun Works.
Price: Finished FR0950 . . . . **$520.00**
Price: Kit PR0965 . . . . **$430.00**
Price: Super Cub (50-caliber percussion) PR0814 . . . . **$525.00**
Price: Super Cub (50-caliber flintlock) FR0803 . . . . **$550.00**

DIXIE PEDERSOLI 1857 MAUSER RIFLE
Caliber: 54. **Barrel:** 39-3/8". **Weight:** NA. **Length:** 52" overall. **Stock:** European walnut with oil finish, sling swivels. **Sights:** Fully adjustable rear, lug front. **Features:** Percussion (musket caps). Armory bright finish with color case-hardened lock and barrel tang, engraved lockplate, steel ramrod. Introduced 2000. Imported from Italy by Dixie Gun Works.
Price: PR1330 . . . . **$1,025.00**

Euroarms 1861 Springfield

Gonic Model 93 Thumbhole

Harper's Ferry 1803

DIXIE PEDERSOLI 1766 CHARLEVILLE MUSKET
Caliber: 69. **Barrel:** 44-3/4". **Weight:** 10-1/2 lbs. **Length:** 57-1/2" overall. **Stock:** European walnut with oil finish. **Sights:** Fixed rear, lug front. **Features:** Smoothbore flintlock. Armory bright finish with steel furniture and ramrod. Introduced 2000. Imported from Italy by Dixie Gun Works.
Price: PR1045 . . . . **$1,025.00**

DIXIE SHARPS NEW MODEL 1859 MILITARY RIFLE
Caliber: 54. **Barrel:** 30", 6-groove; 1:48" twist. **Weight:** 9 lbs. **Length:** 45-1/2" overall. **Stock:** Oiled walnut. **Sights:** Blade front, ladder-style rear. **Features:** Blued barrel, color case-hardened barrel bands, receiver, hammer, nosecap, lever, patchbox cover and buttplate. Introduced 1995. Imported from Italy by Dixie Gun Works.
Price: PR0862 . . . . **$1,025.00**

DIXIE U.S. MODEL 1816 FLINTLOCK MUSKET
Caliber: 69. **Barrel:** 42", smoothbore. **Weight:** 9.75 lbs. **Length:** 56.5" overall. **Stock:** Walnut with oil finish. **Sights:** Blade front. **Features:** All metal finished "National Armory Bright;" three barrel bands with springs; steel ramrod with button-shaped head. Imported by Dixie Gun Works.
Price: FR0305 . . . . **$1,025.00**

E.M.F. 1863 SHARPS MILITARY CARBINE
Caliber: 54. **Barrel:** 22", round. **Weight:** 8 lbs. **Length:** 39" overall. **Stock:** Oiled walnut. **Sights:** Blade front, military ladder-type rear. **Features:** Color case-hardened lock, rest blued. Imported by E.M.F.
Price: **$600.00**

EUROARMS VOLUNTEER TARGET RIFLE
Caliber: 451. **Barrel:** 33" (two-band), 36" (three-band). **Weight:** 11 lbs. (two-band). **Length:** 48.75" overall (two-band). **Stock:** European walnut with checkered wrist and forend. **Sights:** Hooded bead front, adjustable rear with interchangeable leaves. **Features:** Alexander Henry-type rifling with 1:20" twist. Color case-hardened hammer and lockplate, brass trigger guard and nosecap, remainder blued. Imported by Euroarms of America, Dixie Gun Works.
Price: Two-band. **$910.00**

EUROARMS 1861 SPRINGFIELD RIFLE
Caliber: 58. **Barrel:** 40". **Weight:** About 10 lbs. **Length:** 55.5" overall. **Stock:** European walnut. **Sights:** Blade front, three-leaf military rear. **Features:** Reproduction of the original three-band rifle. Lockplate marked "1861" with eagle and "U.S. Springfield." White metal. Imported by Euroarms of America.
Price: **$730.00**

EUROARMS ZOUAVE RIFLE
Caliber: 54, 58 percussion. **Barrel:** 33". **Weight:** 9-1/2 lbs. **Overall length:** 49". **Features:** One-piece solid barrel and bolster. For 54 caliber, .535 R.B., .540 minnie. For 58 caliber, .575 R.B., .577 minnie. 1863 issue. Made in Italy. Imported by Euroarms of America.
Price: **$469.00**

EUROARMS HARPERS FERRY RIFLE
Caliber: 58 flintlock. **Barrel:** 35". **Weight:** 9 lbs. **Overall length:** 59-1/2". **Features:** Antique browned barrel. Barrel .575 RB. .577 minnie. 1803 issue. Made in Italy. Imported by Euroarms of America.
Price: **$735.00**

GONIC MODEL 93 M/L RIFLE
Caliber: 45, 50. **Barrel:** 26"; 1:24" twist. **Weight:** 6-1/2 to 7 lbs. **Length:** 43" overall. **Stock:** American hardwood with black finish. **Sights:** Adjustable or aperture rear, hooded post front. **Features:** Adjustable trigger with side safety; unbreakable ramrod; comes with A. Z. scope bases installed. Introduced 1993. Made in U.S. by Gonic Arms, Inc.
Price: Model 93 Standard (blued barrel) **$720.00**
Price: Model 93 Standard (stainless brl., 50 cal. only) **$782.00**

Gonic Model 93 Deluxe M/L Rifle
Similar to the Model 93 except has classic-style walnut or gray laminated wood stock. Introduced 1998. Made in U.S. by Gonic Arms, Inc.
Price: Blue barrel, sights, scope base, choice of stock **$902.00**
Price: Stainless barrel, sights, scope base, choice of stock
(50 cal. only) **$964.00**

Gonic Model 93 Mountain Thumbhole M/L Rifles
Similar to the Model 93 except has high-grade walnut or gray laminate stock with extensive hand-checkered panels, Monte Carlo cheekpiece and beavertail forend; integral muzzle brake. Introduced 1998. Made in U.S. by Gonic Arms, Inc.
Price: Blued or stainless **$2,700.00**

HARPER'S FERRY 1803 FLINTLOCK RIFLE
Caliber: 54 or 58. **Barrel:** 35". **Weight:** 9 lbs. **Length:** 59-1/2" overall. **Stock:** Walnut with cheekpiece. **Sights:** Brass blade front, fixed steel rear. **Features:** Brass trigger guard, sideplate, buttplate; steel patchbox. Imported by Euroarms of America, Navy Arms (54- cal. only), Cabela's, and Dixie Gun Works.
Price: . . . . **$495.95 to $995.00**
Price: 54-cal. (Navy Arms) **$625.00**
Price: 54-cal. (Cabela's) **$599.99**
Price: 54-cal. (Dixie Gun Works), FR0171 . . . . **$995.00**
Price: 54-cal. (Euroarms) **$809.00**

HAWKEN RIFLE
Caliber: 45, 50, 54 or 58. **Barrel:** 28", blued, 6-groove rifling. **Weight:** 8-3/4 lbs. **Length:** 44" overall. **Stock:** Walnut with cheekpiece. **Sights:** Blade front, fully adjustable rear. **Features:** Coil mainspring, double-set triggers, polished brass furniture. From Armsport and E.M.F.
Price: . . . . **$220.00 to $345.00**

BLACKPOWDER MUSKETS & RIFLES

J.P. Murray

Kentucky Flintlock

Knight 50 Caliber DISC In-Line

Knight Master Hunter DISC Extreme

J.P. HENRY TRADE RIFLE
Caliber: 54. **Barrel:** 34"; 1" flats. **Weight:** 8-1/2 lbs. **Length:** 45" overall. **Stock:** Premium curly maple. **Sights:** Silver blade front, fixed buckhorn rear. **Features:** Brass buttplate, side plate, trigger guard and nosecap; browned barrel and lock; L&R Large English percussion lock; single trigger. Made in U.S. by J.P. Gunstocks, Inc.
Price: **$965.50**

J.P. MURRAY 1862-1864 CAVALRY CARBINE
Caliber: 58 (.577" Minie). **Barrel:** 23". **Weight:** 7 lbs., 9 oz. **Length:** 39" overall. **Stock:** Walnut. **Sights:** Blade front, rear drift adjustable for windage. **Features:** Browned barrel, color case-hardened lock, blued swivel and band springs, polished brass buttplate, trigger guard, barrel bands. From Euroarms of America.
Price: Dixie Gun Works PR0173 . . . . **$725.00**

KENTUCKY FLINTLOCK RIFLE
Caliber: 44, 45, or 50. **Barrel:** 35". **Weight:** 7 lbs. **Length:** 50" overall. **Stock:** Walnut stained, brass fittings. **Sights:** Fixed. **Features:** Available in carbine model also, 28" bbl. Some variations in detail, finish. Kits also available from some importers. Imported by The Armoury.
Price: About . . . . **$217.95 to $345.00**

Kentucky Percussion Rifle
Similar to Flintlock except percussion lock. Finish and features vary with importer. Imported by The Armoury and CVA.
Price: About **$259.95**
Price: 45 or 50 cal. (Navy Arms) **$425.00**
Price: Kit, 50 cal. (CVA) **$189.95**

KNIGHT 50 CALIBER DISC IN-LINE RIFLE
Caliber: 50. **Barrel:** 24", 26". **Weight:** 7 lbs., 14 oz. **Length:** 43" overall (24" barrel). **Stock:** Checkered synthetic with palm swell grip, rubber recoil pad, swivel studs; black, Advantage or Mossy Oak® Break-Up camouflage. **Sights:** Bead on ramp front, fully adjustable open rear. **Features:** Bolt-action in-line system uses #209 shotshell primer for ignition; primer is held in plastic drop-in Primer Disc. Available in blued or stainless steel. Made in U.S. by Knight Rifles (Modern Muzzleloading).
Price: . . . . **$439.95 to $632.45**

Knight Master Hunter II DISC In-Line Rifle
Similar to Knight 50 caliber DISC rifle except features premium, wood laminated two-tone stock, gold-plated trigger and engraved trigger guard, jeweled bolt and fluted, air-gauged Green Mountain 26" barrel. Length 45" overall, weighs 7 lbs., 7 oz. Includes black composite thumbhole stock. Introduced 2000. Made in U.S. by Knight Rifles (Modern Muzzleloading).
Price: **$1,099.95**

KNIGHT MUZZLELOADER DISC EXTREME
Caliber: 45 fluted, 50. **Barrel:** 26". **Stock:** Stainless steel laminate, blued walnut, black composite thumbhole with blued or SS. **Sights:** Fully adjustable metallic. **Features:** New full plastic jacket ignition system.
Price: 50 SS laminate **$703.95**
Price: 45 SS laminate **$769.95**
Price: 50 blue walnut **$626.95**
Price: 45 blue walnut **$703.95**
Price: 50 blue composite **$549.95**
Price: 45 blue composite **$632.45**
Price: 50 SS composite **$632.45**
Price: 45 SS composite **$703.95**

Knight Master Hunter DISC Extreme
Similar to DISC Extreme except fluted barrel, two-tone laminated thumbhole Monte Carlo-style stock, black composite thumbhole field stock included. Jeweled bolt, adjustable premium trigger.
Price: 50 . . . . **$1,044.95**

Knight American Knight

Knight Wolverine 209

London Armory 1861

Lyman Trade Percussion

KNIGHT AMERICAN KNIGHT M/L RIFLE
Caliber: 50. **Barrel:** 22"; 1:28" twist. **Weight:** 6 lbs. **Length:** 41" overall. **Stock:** Black composite. **Sights:** Bead on ramp front, open fully adjustable rear. **Features:** Double safety system; one-piece removable hammer assembly; drilled and tapped for scope mounting. Introduced 1998. Made in U.S. by Knight Rifles.
Price: Blued, black comp $197.95
Price: Blued, black comp VP $225.45

KNIGHT WOLVERINE 209
Caliber: 50. **Barrel:** 22". **Stock:** HD stock with SS barrel, break-up stock blued, black composite thumbhole with stainless steel, standard black composite with blued or SS. **Sights:** Metallic with fiber-optic. **Features:** Double safety system, adjustable match grade trigger; left-hand model available. Full plastic jacket ignition system.
Price: Starting at $302.45

KNIGHT REVOLUTION
Caliber: 50, 209 primer ignition. **Barrel:** Stainless, 27". **Weight:** 7 lbs., 14 oz. **Stock:** Walnut, laminated, black composite, Mossy Oak® Break-Up™ or Hardwoods Green finish. **Features:** Blued or stainless finish, adjustable trigger and sights.
Price: . . . . NA

LONDON ARMORY 1861 ENFIELD MUSKETOON
Caliber: 58, Minie ball. **Barrel:** 24", round. **Weight:** 7 to 7-1/2 lbs. **Length:** 40-1/2" overall. **Stock:** Walnut, with sling swivels. **Sights:** Blade front, graduated military-leaf rear. **Features:** Brass trigger guard, nosecap, buttplate; blued barrel, bands, lockplate, swivels. Imported by Euroarms of America, Navy Arms.
Price: . . . . $300.00 to $521.00
Price: Kit . . . . $365.00 to $402.00

LONDON ARMORY 2-BAND 1858 ENFIELD
Caliber: .577" Minie, .575" round ball. **Barrel:** 33". **Weight:** 10 lbs. **Length:** 49" overall. **Stock:** Walnut. **Sights:** Folding leaf rear adjustable for elevation. **Features:** Blued barrel, color case-hardened lock and hammer, polished brass buttplate, trigger guard, nosecap. From Navy Arms, Euroarms of America, Dixie Gun Works.
Price: . . . . $385.00 to $563.00

LONDON ARMORY 3-BAND 1853 ENFIELD
Caliber: 58 (.577" Minie, .575" round ball, .580" maxi ball). **Barrel:** 39". **Weight:** 9-1/2 lbs. **Length:** 54" overall. **Stock:** European walnut. **Sights:** Inverted "V" front, traditional Enfield folding ladder rear. **Features:** Re-creation of the famed London Armory Company Pattern 1853 Enfield Musket. One-piece walnut stock, brass buttplate, trigger guard and nosecap. Lockplate marked "London Armoury Co." and with a British crown. Blued Baddeley barrel bands. From Dixie Gun Works, Euroarms of America, Navy Arms.
Price: About . . . . $350.00 to $606.00
Price: Assembled kit (Dixie, Euroarms of America) $515.00

LYMAN TRADE RIFLE
Caliber: 50, 54. **Barrel:** 28" octagon;1:48" twist. **Weight:** 8-3/4 lbs. **Length:** 45" overall. **Stock:** European walnut. **Sights:** Blade front, open rear adjustable for windage or optional fixed sights. **Features:** Fast twist rifling for conical bullets. Polished brass furniture with blue steel parts, stainless steel nipple. Hook breech, single trigger, coil spring percussion lock. Steel barrel rib and ramrod ferrules. Introduced 1980. From Lyman.
Price: 50 cal. percussion $581.80
Price: 50 cal. flintlock $652.80
Price: 54 cal. percussion $581.80
Price: 54 cal. flintlock $652.80

LYMAN DEERSTALKER RIFLE
Caliber: 50, 54. **Barrel:** 24", octagonal; 1:48" rifling. **Weight:** 7-1/2 lbs. **Stock:** Walnut with black rubber buttpad. **Sights:** Lyman #37MA beaded front, fully adjustable fold-down Lyman #16A rear. **Features:** Stock has less drop for quick sighting. All metal parts are blackened, with color case-hardened lock; single trigger. Comes with sling and swivels. Available in flint or percussion. Introduced 1990. From Lyman.
Price: 50 cal. flintlock $652.80
Price: 50 or 54 cal., percussion, left-hand, carbine $695.40
Price: 50 or 54 cal., flintlock, left-hand $645.00
Price: 54 cal. flintlock $780.50
Price: 54 cal. percussion $821.80
Price: Stainless steel $959.80

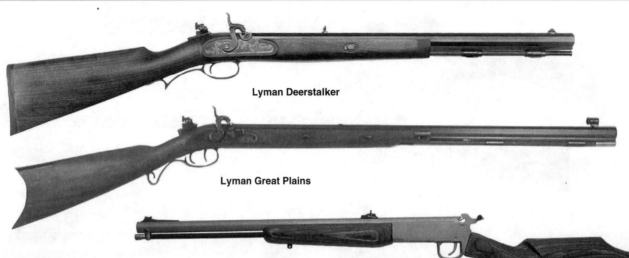

Lyman Deerstalker

Lyman Great Plains

Markesbery KM Colorado

LYMAN GREAT PLAINS RIFLE
Caliber: 50, 54. **Barrel:** 32"; 1:60" twist. **Weight:** 9 lbs. **Stock:** Walnut. **Sights:** Steel blade front, buckhorn rear adjustable for windage and elevation and fixed notch primitive sight included. **Features:** Blued steel furniture. Stainless steel nipple. Coil spring lock, Hawken-style trigger guard and double-set triggers. Round thimbles recessed and sweated into rib. Steel wedge plates and toe plate. Introduced 1979. From Lyman.
Price: Percussion $469.95
Price: Flintlock $494.95
Price: Percussion kit $359.95
Price: Flintlock kit $384.95
Price: Left-hand percussion $474.95
Price: Left-hand flintlock $499.95

Lyman Great Plains Hunter Model
Similar to Great Plains model except 1:32" twist shallow-groove barrel and comes drilled and tapped for Lyman 57GPR peep sight.
Price: $959.80

MARKESBERY KM BLACK BEAR M/L RIFLE
Caliber: 36, 45, 50, 54. **Barrel:** 24"; 1:26" twist. **Weight:** 6-1/2 lbs. **Length:** 38-1/2" overall. **Stock:** Two-piece American hardwood, walnut, black laminate, green laminate, black composition, X-Tra or Mossy Oak® Break-Up™ camouflage. **Sights:** Bead front, open fully adjustable rear. **Features:** Interchangeable barrels; exposed hammer; Outer-Line Magnum ignition system uses small rifle primer or standard No. 11 cap and nipple. Blue, black matte, or stainless. Made in U.S. by Markesbery Muzzle Loaders.
Price: American hardwood walnut, blue finish $536.63
Price: American hardwood walnut, stainless $553.09
Price: Black laminate, blue finish $539.67
Price: Black laminate, stainless $556.27
Price: Camouflage stock, blue finish $556.46
Price: Camouflage stock, stainless $573.73
Price: Black composite, blue finish $532.65
Price: Black composite, stainless $549.93
Price: Green laminate, blue finish $539.00
Price: Green laminate, stainless $556.27

Markesbery KM Brown Bear Rifle
Similar to KM Black Bear except one-piece thumbhole stock with Monte Carlo comb. Stock in Crotch Walnut composite, green or black laminate, black composite or X-Tra or Mossy Oak® Break-Up™ camouflage. Made in U.S. by Markesbery Muzzle Loaders, Inc.
Price: Black composite, blue finish $658.83
Price: Crotch Walnut, blue finish $658.83
Price: Camo composite, blue finish $682.64
Price: Walnut wood $662.81
Price: Black wood $662.81
Price: Black laminated wood $662.81
Price: Green laminated wood $662.81
Price: Camo wood $684.69
Price: Black composite, stainless $676.11
Price: Crotch Walnut composite, stainless $676.11

Price: Camo composite, stainless $697.69
Price: Walnut wood, stainless $680.07
Price: Black wood, stainless $680.07
Price: Black laminated wood, stainless $680.07
Price: Green laminate, stainless $680.07
Price: Camo wood, stainless $702.76

Markesbery KM Grizzly Bear Rifle
Similar to KM Black Bear except thumbhole buttstock with Monte Carlo comb. Stock in Crotch Walnut composite, green or black laminate, black composite or X-Tra or Mossy Oak® Break-Up camouflage. Made in U.S. by Markesbery Muzzle Loaders, Inc.
Price: Black composite, blue finish $642.96
Price: Crotch Walnut, blue finish $642.96
Price: Camo composite, blue finish $666.67
Price: Walnut wood $646.93
Price: Black wood $646.93
Price: Black laminate wood $646.93
Price: Green laminate wood $646.93
Price: Camo wood $670.74
Price: Black composite, stainless $660.98
Price: Crotch Walnut composite, stainless $660.98
Price: Black laminate wood, stainless $664.20
Price: Green laminate, stainless $664.20
Price: Camo wood, stainless $685.74
Price: Camo composite, stainless $684.04
Price: Walnut wood, stainless $664.20
Price: Black wood, stainless $664.20

Markesbery KM Polar Bear Rifle
Similar to KM Black Bear except one-piece stock with Monte Carlo comb. Stock in American Hardwood walnut, green or black laminate, black composite, or X-Tra or Mossy Oak® Break-Up™ camouflage. Interchangeable barrel system, Outer-Line ignition system, cross-bolt double safety. Available in 36, 45, 50, 54 caliber. Made in U.S. by Markesbery Muzzle Loaders, Inc.
Price: American Hardwood walnut, blue finish. $539.01
Price: Black composite, blue finish $536.63
Price: Black laminate, blue finish $541.17
Price: Green laminate, blue finish $541.17
Price: Camo, blue finish $560.43
Price: American Hardwood walnut, stainless $556.27
Price: Black composite, stainless $556.04
Price: Black laminate, stainless $570.56
Price: Green laminate, stainless $570.56
Price: Camo, stainless $573.94

Mississippi 1841

Navy Arms 1763 Charleville

Navy Arms Berdan

Navy Arms 1859 Sharps Cavalry Carbine

MARKESBERY KM COLORADO ROCKY MOUNTAIN RIFLE
Caliber: 36, 45, 50, 54. **Barrel:** 24"; 1:26" twist. **Weight:** 6-1/2 lbs. **Length:** 38-1/2" overall. **Stock:** American hardwood walnut, green or black laminate. **Sights:** Firesight bead on ramp front, fully adjustable open rear. **Features:** Replicates Reed/Watson rifle of 1851. Straight grip stock with or without two barrel bands, rubber recoil pad, large-spur hammer. Made in U.S. by Markesbery Muzzle Loaders, Inc.
Price: American hardwood walnut, blue finish **$545.92**
Price: Black or green laminate, blue finish **$548.30**
Price: American hardwood walnut, stainless **$563.17**
Price: Black or green laminate, stainless **$566.34**

MDM BUCKWACKA IN-LINE RIFLES
Caliber: 45, 50. **Barrel:** 23", 25". **Weight:** 7 to 7-3/4 lbs. **Stock:** Black, walnut, laminated and camouflage finishes. **Sights:** Williams Fire Sight blade front, Williams fully adjustable rear with ghost-ring peep aperture. **Features:** Break-open action; Incinerating Ignition System incorporates 209 shotshell primer directly into breech plug; 50-caliber models handle up to 150 grains of Pyrodex; synthetic ramrod; transfer bar safety; stainless or blued finish. Made in U.S. by Millennium Designed Muzzleloaders Ltd.
Price: 50 cal., blued finish **$309.95**
Price: 50 cal., stainless **$339.95**
Price: Camouflage stock . . . . **$359.95 to $389.95**

MDM M2K In-Line Rifle
Similar to Buckwacka except adjustable trigger and double-safety mechanism designed to prevent misfires. Made in U.S. by Millennium Designed Muzzleloaders Ltd.
Price: . . . . **$529.00 to $549.00**

MISSISSIPPI 1841 PERCUSSION RIFLE
Caliber: 54, 58. **Barrel:** 33". **Weight:** 9-1/2 lbs. **Length:** 48-5/8" overall. **Stock:** One-piece European walnut full stock with satin finish. **Sights:** Brass blade front, fixed steel rear. **Features:** Case-hardened lockplate marked "U.S." surmounted by American eagle. Two barrel bands, sling swivels. Steel ramrod with brass end, browned barrel. From Navy Arms, Dixie Gun Works, Cabela's, Euroarms of America.
Price: Dixie Gun Works PR0870 . . . . **$800.00**

NAVY ARMS 1763 CHARLEVILLE
Caliber: 69. **Barrel:** 44-5/8". **Weight:** 8 lbs., 12 oz. **Length:** 59-3/8" overall. **Stock:** Walnut. **Sights:** Brass blade front. **Features:** Replica of French musket used by American troops during the American Revolution. Imported by Navy Arms.
Price: **$1,020.00**

NAVY ARMS BERDAN 1859 SHARPS RIFLE
Caliber: 54. **Barrel:** 30". **Weight:** 8 lbs., 8 oz. **Length:** 46-3/4" overall. **Stock:** Walnut. **Sights:** Blade front, folding military ladder-type rear. **Features:** Replica of the Union sniper rifle used by Berdan's 1st and 2nd Sharpshooter regiments. Color case-hardened receiver, patchbox, furniture. Double-set triggers. Imported by Navy Arms.
Price: **$1,165.00**
Price: 1859 Sharps Infantry Rifle (three-band) **$1,100.00**

NAVY ARMS 1859 SHARPS CAVALRY CARBINE
Caliber: 54. **Barrel:** 22". **Weight:** 7-3/4 lbs. **Length:** 39" overall. **Stock:** Walnut. **Sights:** Blade front, military ladder-type rear. **Features:** Color case-hardened action, blued barrel. Has saddle ring. Introduced 1991. Imported from Navy Arms.
Price: **$1,000.00**

NAVY ARMS 1861 SPRINGFIELD RIFLE
Caliber: 58. **Barrel:** 40". **Weight:** 10 lbs., 4 oz. **Length:** 56" overall. **Stock:** Walnut. **Sights:** Blade front, military leaf rear. **Features:** Steel barrel, lock and all furniture have polished bright finish. Has 1855-style hammer. Imported by Navy Arms.
Price: **$590.00**

Navy Arms Whitworth

Navy Arms Smith Carbine

New England Firearms Sidekick

New England Firearms Huntsman

NAVY ARMS 1863 C.S. RICHMOND RIFLE
Caliber: 58. **Barrel:** 40". **Weight:** 10 lbs. **Length:** NA. **Stocks:** Walnut. **Sights:** Blade front, adjustable rear. **Features:** Copy of three- band rifle musket made at Richmond Armory for the Confederacy. All steel polished bright. Imported by Navy Arms.
Price: **$590.00**

NAVY ARMS 1863 SPRINGFIELD
Caliber: 58, uses .575 Minie. **Barrel:** 40", rifled. **Weight:** 9-1/2 lbs. **Length:** 56" overall. **Stock:** Walnut. **Sights:** Open rear adjustable for elevation. **Features:** Full-size, three-band musket. Polished bright metal, including lock. From Navy Arms.
Price: Finished rifle **$590.00**

NAVY ARMS PARKER-HALE VOLUNTEER RIFLE
Caliber: .451. **Barrel:** 32". **Weight:** 9-1/2 lbs. **Length:** 49" overall. **Stock:** Walnut, checkered wrist and forend. **Sights:** Globe front, adjustable ladder-type rear. **Features:** Recreation of the type of gun issued to volunteer regiments during the 1860s. Rigby-pattern rifling, patent breech, detented lock. Stock is glass bedded for accuracy. Imported by Navy Arms.
Price: **$905.00**

NAVY ARMS PARKER-HALE WHITWORTH MILITARY TARGET RIFLE
Caliber: 45. **Barrel:** 36". **Weight:** 9-1/4 lbs. **Length:** 52-1/2" overall. **Stock:** Walnut. Checkered at wrist and forend. **Sights:** Hooded post front, open step-adjustable rear. **Features:** Faithful reproduction of Whitworth rifle. Trigger has detented lock, capable of fine adjustments without risk of the sear nose catching on the half-cock notch and damaging both parts. Introduced 1978. Imported by Navy Arms.
Price: **$930.00**

NAVY ARMS SMITH CARBINE
Caliber: 50. **Barrel:** 21-1/2". **Weight:** 7-3/4 lbs. **Length:** 39" overall. **Stock:** American walnut. **Sights:** Brass blade front, folding ladder-type rear. **Features:** Replica of breech-loading Civil War carbine. Color case-hardened receiver, rest blued. Cavalry model has saddle ring and bar, Artillery model has sling swivels. Imported by Navy Arms.

Price: Cavalry model **$645.00**
Price: Artillery model **$645.00**

NEW ENGLAND FIREARMS SIDEKICK
Caliber: 50, 209 primer ignition. **Barrel:** 26" (magnum). **Weight:** 6.5 lbs. **Length:** 41.25". **Stock:** Black matte polymer or hardwood. **Sights:** Adjustable fiber-optic open, tapped for scope mounts. **Features:** Single-shot based on H&R break-open action. Uses No. 209 shotgun primer held in place by special primer carrier. Telescoping brass ramrod. Introduced 2004.
Price: Wood stock, blued frame, black-oxide barrel) **$216.00**
Price: Stainless barrel and frame, synthetic stock) **$310.00**

NEW ENGLAND FIREARMS HUNTSMAN
Caliber: 50, 209 primer ignition. **Barrel:** 22" to 26". **Weight:** 5.25 to 6.5 lbs. **Length:** 40" to 43". **Stock:** Black matte polymer or hardwood. **Sights:** Fiber-optic open sights, tapped for scope mounts. **Features:** Break-open action, transfer-bar safety system, breech plug removable for cleaning. Introduced 2004.
Price: Stainless Huntsman. **$306.00**
Price: Huntsman **$212.00**
Price: Pardner Combo 12 ga./50 cal muzzleloader **$259.00**
Price: Tracker II Combo 12 ga. rifled slug barrel /50 cal. **$288.00**
Price: Handi-Rifle Combo 243/50 cal. **$405.00**

New England Firearms Stainless Huntsman
Similar to Huntsman, but with matte nickel finish receiver and stainless bbl. Introduced 2003. From New England Firearms.
Price: **$81.00**

PACIFIC RIFLE MODEL 1837 ZEPHYR
Caliber: 62. **Barrel:** 30", tapered octagon. **Weight:** 7-3/4 lbs. **Length:** NA. **Stock:** Oil-finished fancy walnut. **Sights:** German silver blade front, semi-buckhorn rear. Options available. **Features:** Improved underhammer action. First production rifle to offer Forsyth rifle, with narrow lands and shallow rifling with 1:14" pitch for high-velocity round balls. Metal finish is slow rust brown with nitre blue accents. Optional sights, finishes and integral muzzle brake available. Introduced 1995. Made in U.S. by Pacific Rifle Co.
Price: From **$995.00**

BLACKPOWDER MUSKETS & RIFLES

Peifer TS-93

Prairie River Arms PRA Bullpup

Remington Genesis

C.S. Richmond 1863

Pacific Rifle Big Bore African Rifles
Similar to the 1837 Zephyr except in 72-caliber and 8-bore. The 72-caliber is available in standard form with 28" barrel, or as the African with flat buttplate, checkered upgraded wood; weight is 9 lbs. The 8-bore African has dual-cap ignition, 24" barrel, weighs 12 lbs., checkered English walnut, engraving, gold inlays. Introduced 1998. Made in U.S. by Pacific Rifle Co.
Price: 72-caliber, from **$1,150.00**
Price: 8-bore, from **$2,500.00**

PEIFER MODEL TS-93 RIFLE
Caliber: 45, 50. **Barrel:** 24" Douglas premium; 1:20" twist in 45; 1:28" in 50. **Weight:** 7 lbs. **Length:** 43-1/4" overall. **Stock:** Bell & Carlson solid composite, with recoil pad, swivel studs. **Sights:** Williams bead front on ramp, fully adjustable open rear. Drilled and tapped for Weaver scope mounts with dovetail for rear peep. **Features:** In-line ignition uses #209 shotshell primer; fast lock time; fully enclosed breech; adjustable trigger; automatic safety; removable primer holder. Blue or stainless. Made in U.S. by Peifer Rifle Co. Introduced 1996.
Price: Blue, black stock **$730.00**
Price: Blue, wood or camouflage composite stock,
    or stainless with black composite stock **$803.00**
Price: Stainless, wood or camouflage composite stock **$876.00**

PRAIRIE RIVER ARMS PRA BULLPUP RIFLE
Caliber: 50. **Barrel:** 28"; 1:28" twist. **Weight:** 7-1/2 lbs. **Length:** 31-1/2" overall. **Stock:** Hardwood or black all-weather. **Sights:** Blade front, open adjustable rear. **Features:** Bullpup design thumbhole stock. Patented internal percussion ignition system. Left-hand model available. Dovetailed for scope mount. Introduced 1995. Made in U.S. by Prairie River Arms, Ltd.
Price: 4140 alloy barrel, hardwood stock **$199.00**
Price: All Weather stock, alloy barrel **$205.00**

REMINGTON GENESIS MUZZLELOADER
Caliber: 50. **Barrel:** 28", 1-in-28" twist, blued or stainless fluted. **Weight:** 7.75 lbs. **Length:** NA. **Stock:** Black synthetic, Mossy Oak New Break-Up. **Sights:** Williams fiber-optic sights, drilled and tapped for scope mounts.

Features: TorchCam action, 209 primer, up to 150-grain charges. Over-travel hammer, crossbolt safety with ambidextrous HammerSpur (right- and left-handed operation). Buckmasters version has stainless fluted barrel with a Realtree Hardwoods HD camo stock, laser-engraved Buckmasters logo. Aluminum anodized ramrod with jag, front and rear swivel studs, removable 7/16" breech plug; optimized for use with Remington Kleanbore 209 Muzzleloading Primers. Introduced 2006. Made in U.S. by Remington Arms Co.
Price: Genesis ML, black synthetic, carbon matte blued **$293.00**
Price: Genesis MLS Overmold synthetic, tainless satin **$363.00**
Price: Genesis ML Camo Mossy Oak Break-Up,
    carbon matte blued (2007) **$405.00**
Price: Genesis ML SF Synthetic Thumbhole, stainless satin **$405.00**
Price: Genesis ML SF Buckmasters (2007) **$419.00**
Price: Genesis ML SF laminate thumbhole, stainless satin **$594.00**

REPLICA ARMS 1863 SHARPS SPORTING RIFLE
Caliber: .54 cal percussion. **Barrel:** 28" Octagonal. **Weight:** 8.82 lbs. **Length:** 45" overall. **Grips:** Walnut checkered at wrist and forend. **Sights:** Blade front, full buckhorn rear. **Features:** Color case-hardened receiver, trigger, hammer and lever. Double-set triggers.
Price: **$939.00**

RICHMOND, C.S., 1863 MUSKET
Caliber: 58. **Barrel:** 40". **Weight:** 11 lbs. **Length:** 56-1/4" overall. **Stock:** European walnut with oil finish. **Sights:** Blade front, adjustable folding leaf rear. **Features:** Reproduction of the three-band Civil War musket. Sling swivels attached to trigger guard and middle barrel band. Lockplate marked "1863" and "C.S. Richmond." All white metal. Brass buttplate and forend cap. Imported by Euroarms of America, Navy Arms, and Dixie Gun Works.
Price: Euroarms **$730.00**
Price: Dixie Gun Works PR0846 . . . . **$1,025.00**

ROSSI MUZZLELOADERS
Caliber: .50. **Barrel:** 20", 23". **Weight:** 5-6.3 lbs. **Stocks:** Wood. **Sights:** Fully adjustable fiber optic sights. **Features:** Black powder break open, 2 models available, manual external safety, Taurus Security System, blue or stainless finish, youth models available. From Rossi USA.
Price: **$199.00**
Price: MiniLoader **$256.00**

Savage 10MLSS-IIXP

Second Model Brown Bess

Thompson/Center Hawken

Thompson/Center Firestorm

SAVAGE MODEL 10ML MUZZLELOADER RIFLE SERIES
Caliber: 50. **Barrel:** 24", 1:24 twist, blue or stainless. **Weight:** 7.75 lbs. **Stock:** Black synthetic, Realtree Hardwood JD Camo, brown laminate. **Sights:** Green adjustable rear, Red FiberOptic front. **Features:** XP Models scoped, no sights, designed for smokeless powder, #209 primer ignition. Removeable breech plug and vent liner.

Price: Model 10ML-II **$531.00**
Price: Model 10ML-II Camo **$569.00**
Price: Model 10MLSS-II Camo **$628.00**
Price: Model 10MLBSS-II **$667.00**
Price: Model 10ML-IIXP **$569.00**
Price: Model 10MLSS-IIXP **$628.00**

SECOND MODEL BROWN BESS MUSKET
Caliber: 75, uses .735" round ball. **Barrel:** 42", smoothbore. **Weight:** 9-1/2 lbs. **Length:** 59" overall. **Stock:** Walnut (Navy); walnut-stained hardwood (Dixie). **Sights:** Fixed. **Features:** Polished barrel and lock with brass trigger guard and buttplate. Bayonet and scabbard available. From Navy Arms, Dixie Gun Works, Cabela's.

Price: Finished . . . . **$475.00 to $950.00**
Price: Kit Navy Arms, Dixie Gun Works, FR0825 . . . **$575.00 to $775.00**
Price: Carbine (Navy Arms) **$835.00**
Price: Dixie Gun Works FR0810 . . . . **$950.00**

THOMPSON/CENTER TRIUMPH MAGNUM MUZZLELOADER
Caliber: 50. **Barrel:** 28" Weather Shield coated. **Weight:** NA. **Length:** NA. **Stock:** Black composite or Realtree AP HD Camo. **Sights:** NA. **Features:** QLA 209 shotshell primer ignition. Introduced 2007. Made in U.S. by Thompson/Center Arms.

Price: . . . . **NA**

THOMPSON/CENTER ENCORE 209x50 MAGNUM
Caliber: 50. **Barrel:** 26"; interchangeable with centerfire calibers. **Weight:** 7 lbs. **Length:** 40-1/2" overall. **Stock:** American walnut butt and forend, or black composite. **Sights:** TruGlo fiber-optic front and rear. **Features:** Blue or stainless steel. Uses the stock, frame and forend of the Encore centerfire pistol; break-open design using trigger guard spur; stainless steel universal breech plug; uses #209 shotshell primers. Introduced 1998. Made in U.S. by Thompson/Center Arms.

Price: Stainless with camo stock **$772.00**
Price: Blue, walnut stock and forend **$678.00**
Price: Blue, composite stock and forend **$637.00**
Price: Stainless, composite stock and forend **$713.00**
Price: All camo Realtree Hardwoods **$729.00**

THOMPSON/CENTER FIRE STORM RIFLE
Caliber: 50. **Barrel:** 26"; 1:28" twist. **Weight:** 7 lbs. **Length:** 41-3/4" overall. **Stock:** Black synthetic with rubber recoil pad, swivel studs. **Sights:** Click-adjustable steel rear and ramp-style front, both with fiber-optic inserts. **Features:** Side hammer lock is the first designed for up to three 50-grain Pyrodex pellets; patented Pyrodex Pyramid breech directs ignition fire 360 degrees around base of pellet. Quick Load Accurizor Muzzle System; aluminum ramrod. Flintlock only. Introduced 2000. Made in U.S. by Thompson/ Center Arms.

Price: Blue finish, flintlock model with 1:48" twist for round balls, conicals **$436.00**
Price: SST, flintlock **$488.00**

THOMPSON/CENTER HAWKEN RIFLE
Caliber: 50. **Barrel:** 28" octagon, hooked breech. **Stock:** American walnut. **Sights:** Blade front, rear adjustable for windage and elevation. **Features:** Solid brass furniture, double-set triggers, button rifled barrel, coil-type mainspring. From Thompson/Center Arms.

Price: Percussion model **$590.00**
Price: Flintlock model **$615.00**

TRADITIONS BUCKSKINNER CARBINE
Caliber: 50. **Barrel:** 21"; 15/16" flats, half octagon, half round; 1:20" or 1:66" twist. **Weight:** 6 lbs. **Length:** 37" overall. **Stock:** Beech or black laminated. **Sights:** Beaded blade front, fiber-optic open rear click adjustable for windage and elevation or fiber-optics. **Features:** Uses V-type mainspring, single trigger. Non-glare hardware; sling swivels. From Traditions.

Price: Flintlock **$249.00**
Price: Flintlock, laminated stock **$303.00**

Traditions Deerhunter

Traditions Pursuit

Traditions PA Pellet

Traditions Shenandoah

TRADITIONS DEERHUNTER RIFLE SERIES

Caliber: 32, 50 or 54. **Barrel:** 24", octagonal; 15/16" flats; 1:48" or 1:66" twist. **Weight:** 6 lbs. **Length:** 40" overall. **Stock:** Stained hardwood or All-Weather composite with rubber buttpad, sling swivels. **Sights:** Lite Optic blade front, adjustable rear fiber-optics. **Features:** Flint or percussion with color case-hardened lock. Hooked breech, oversized trigger guard, blackened furniture, PVC ramrod. All-Weather has composite stock and C-nickel barrel. Drilled and tapped for scope mounting. Imported by Traditions, Inc.

Price: Percussion, 50; blued barrel; 1:48" twist **$189.00**
Price: Percussion, 54 . . . . **$169.00**
Price: Flintlock, 50 caliber only; 1:48" twist **$179.00**
Price: Flintlock, All-Weather, 50-cal. **$239.00**
Price: Redi-Pak, 50 cal. flintlock **$219.00**
Price: Flintlock, left-handed hardwood, 50 cal. **$209.00**
Price: Percussion, All-Weather, 50 or 54 cal. **$179.00**
Price: Percussion, 32 cal. **$199.00**

Traditions Panther Sidelock Rifle
Similar to Deerhunter rifle, but has blade front and windage-adjustable-only rear sights, black composite stock.
Price: **$129.00**

TRADITIONS PURSUIT BREAK-OPEN MUZZLELOADER

Caliber: 45, 54 and 12 gauge. **Barrel:** 28", tapered, fluted; blued, stainless or Hardwoods Green camo. **Weight:** 8-1/4 lbs. **Length:** 44" overall. **Stock:** Synthetic black or Hardwoods Green. **Sights:** Steel fiber-optic rear, bead front. Introduced 2004 by Traditions, Inc.

Price: Steel, blued, 45 or 50 cal., synthetic stock **$279.00**
Price: Steel, nickel, 45 or 50 cal., synthetic stock **$309.00**
Price: Steel, nickel w/Hardwoods Green stock **$359.00**
Price: Matte blued; 12 ga., synthetic stock **$369.00**
Price: Matte blued; 12 ga. w/Hardwoods Green stock **$439.00**
Price: Lightweight model, blued, synthetic stock **$199.00**
Price: Lightweight model, blued, Mossy Oak®
Break-Up™ Camo stock **$239.00**
Price: Lightweight model, nickel, Mossy Oak®
Break-Up™ Camo stock **$279.00**

TRADITIONS EVOLUTION BOLT-ACTION BLACKPOWDER RIFLE

Caliber: 50 percussion. **Barrel:** 26", fluted with porting. **Sights:** Steel fiber-optic. **Weight:** 7 to 7-1/4 lbs. **Length:** 45" overall. **Features:** Bolt-action, cocking indicator, thumb safety, aluminum ramrod, sling studs. Wide variety of stocks and metal finishes. Introduced 2004 by Traditions, Inc.

Price: Synthetic stock. **$279.00**

Price: Walnut X-wood **$349.00**
Price: Brown laminated **$469.00**
Price: Advantáge Timber **$369.00**
Price: Synthetic, TruGlo sights **$249.00**
Price: Mossy Oak® Break-up™ **$279.00**
Price: Nickel finish **$309.00**
Price: Beech/nickel, Advantage/nickel, Advantage 54 cal. **$289.00**

TRADITIONS PA PELLET FLINTLOCK

Caliber: 50. **Barrel:** 26", blued, nickel. **Weight:** 7 lbs. **Stock:** Hardwood, synthetic and synthetic break-up. **Sights:** Fiber-optic. **Features:** Removeable breech plug, left-hand model with hardwood stock. 1:48" twist.

Price: Hardwood, blued **$259.00**
Price: Hardwood left, blued **$269.00**

TRADITIONS HAWKEN WOODSMAN RIFLE

Caliber: 50 and 54. **Barrel:** 28"; 15/16" flats. **Weight:** 7 lbs., 11 oz. **Length:** 44-1/2" overall. **Stock:** Walnut-stained hardwood. **Sights:** Beaded blade front, hunting-style open rear adjustable for windage and elevation. **Features:** Percussion only. Brass patchbox and furniture. Double triggers. From Traditions.

Price: 50 or 54 . . . . **$299.00**
Price: 50-cal., left-hand **$279.00**
Price: 50-cal., flintlock **$299.00**

TRADITIONS KENTUCKY RIFLE

Caliber: 50. **Barrel:** 33-1/2"; 7/8" flats; 1:66" twist. **Weight:** 7 lbs. **Length:** 49" overall. **Stock:** Beech; inletted toe plate. **Sights:** Blade front, fixed rear. **Features:** Full-length, two-piece stock; brass furniture; color case-hardened lock. From Traditions.
Price: **$279.00**

TRADITIONS PENNSYLVANIA RIFLE

Caliber: 50. **Barrel:** 40-1/4"; 7/8" flats; 1:66" twist, octagon. **Weight:** 9 lbs. **Length:** 57-1/2" overall. **Stock:** Walnut. **Sights:** Blade front, adjustable rear. **Features:** Brass patchbox and ornamentation. Double-set triggers. From Traditions.
Price: Flintlock **$529.00**
Price: Percussion **$519.00**

TRADITIONS SHENANDOAH RIFLE

Caliber: 36, 50. **Barrel:** 33-1/2" octagon; 1:66" twist. **Weight:** 7 lbs., 3 oz. **Length:** 49-1/2" overall. **Stock:** Walnut. **Sights:** Blade front, buckhorn rear. **Features:** V-type mainspring; double-set trigger; solid brass buttplate, patchbox, nosecap, thimbles, trigger guard. Introduced 1996. From Traditions.
Price: Flintlock **$419.00**
Price: Percussion **$399.00**
Price: 36 cal. flintlock, 1:48" twist **$419.00**
Price: 36 cal. percussion, 1:48" twist **$449.00**

Traditions Tracker 209

Zouave Percussion

TRADITIONS TENNESSEE RIFLE
Caliber: 50. **Barrel:** 24", octagon; 15/16" flats; 1:66" twist. **Weight:** 6 lbs. **Length:** 40-1/2" overall. **Stock:** Stained beech. **Sights:** Blade front, fixed rear. **Features:** One-piece stock has inletted brass furniture, cheekpiece; double-set trigger; V-type mainspring. Flint or percussion. From Traditions.
Price: Flintlock **$339.00**
Price: Percussion **$329.00**

TRADITIONS TRACKER 209 IN-LINE RIFLES
Caliber: 45, 50. **Barrel:** 22" blued or C-nickel finish; 1:28" twist, 50 cal. 1:20" 45 cal. **Weight:** 6 lbs., 4 oz. **Length:** 41" overall. **Stock:** Black, Advantage Timber® composite, synthetic. **Sights:** Lite Optic blade front, adjustable rear. **Features:** Thumb safety; adjustable trigger; rubber butt pad and sling swivel studs; takes 150 grains of Pyrodex pellets; one-piece breech system takes 209 shotshell primers. Drilled and tapped for scope. From Traditions.
Price: (Black composite or synthetic stock, 22" blued barrel) **$129.00**
Price: (Black composite or synthetic stock, 22" C-nickel barrel) . . **$139.00**
Price: (Advantage Timber® stock, 22" C-nickel barrel) **$189.00**
Price: (Redi-Pak, black stock and blued barrel, powder flask,
    capper, ball starter, other accessories) **$179.00**
Price: (Redi-Pak, synthetic stock and blued barrel, with scope) . . **$229.00**

ULTRA LIGHT ARMS MODEL 209 MUZZLELOADER
Caliber: 45 or 50. **Barrel:** 24" button rifled; 1:32" twist. **Weight:** Under 5 lbs. **Stock:** Kevlar/Graphite. **Features:** Recoil pad, sling swivels included. Some color options available. Adj. Timney trigger, positive primer extraction.
Price: **$1,100.00**

WHITE MODEL 97 WHITETAIL HUNTER RIFLE
Caliber: 45, 50. **Barrel:** 22", 1:20 twist (45 cal.); 1:24 twist (50 cal.). **Weight:** 7.7 lbs. **Length:** 40" overall. **Stock:** Black laminated or black composite. **Sights:** Marble TruGlo fully adjustable, steel rear with white diamond, red bead front with high-visibility inserts. **Features:** In-line ignition with FlashFire one-piece nipple and breech plug that uses standard or magnum No. 11 caps, fully adjustable trigger, double safety system, aluminum ramrod, drilled and tapped for scope. Hard case. Made in U.S.A. by Split Fire Sporting Goods.
Price: Whitetail w/laminated or composite stock **$499.95**
Price: Adventurer w/26" stainless barrel & thumbhole stock) **$699.95**
Price: Odyssey w/24" carbon fiber wrapped
    barrel & thumbhole stock **$1,299.95**

WHITE MODEL 98 ELITE HUNTER RIFLE
Caliber: 45, 50. **Barrel:** 24", 1:24" twist (50 cal) **Weight:** 8.6 lbs. **Length:** 43-1/2" overall. **Stock:** Black laminate wtih swivel studs. **Sights:** TruGlo fully adjustable, steel rear with white diamond, red bead front with high-visibility inserts. **Features:** In-line ignition with FlashFire one-piece nipple and breech plug that uses standard or magnum No. 11 caps, fully adjustable trigger, double safety system, aluminum ramrod, drilled and tapped for scope, hard gun case. Made in U.S.A. by Split Fire Sporting Goods.
Price: Composite or laminate wood stock **$499.95**

White Thunderbolt Rifle
Similar to the Elite Hunter but is designed to handle 209 shotgun primers only. Has 26" stainless steel barrel, weighs 9.3 lbs. and is 45-1/2" long. Composite or laminate stock. Made in U.S.A. by Split Fire Sporting Goods.
Price: **$599.95**

WHITE MODEL 2000 BLACKTAIL HUNTER RIFLE
Caliber: 50. **Barrel:** 22", 1:24" twist (50 cal.). **Weight:** 7.6 lbs. **Length:** 39-7/8" overall. **Stock:** Black laminated with swivel studs with laser engraved deer or elk scene. **Sights:** TruGlo fully adjustable, steel rear with white diamond, red bead front with high-visibility inserts. **Features:** Teflon finished barrel, in-line ignition with FlashFire one-piece nipple and breech plug that uses standard or magnum No. 11 caps, fully adjustable trigger, double safety system, aluminum ramrod, drilled and tapped for scope. Hard gun case. Made in U.S.A. by Split Fire Sporting Goods.
Price: Laminate wood stock, w/laser engraved game scene **$599.95**

WHITE LIGHTNING II RIFLE
Caliber: 45 and 50 percussion. **Barrel:** 24", 1:32 twist. **Sights:** Adj. rear. **Stock:** Black polymer. **Weight:** 6 lbs. **Features:** In-line, 209 primer ignition system, blued or nickel-plated bbl., adj. trigger, Delrin ramrod, sling studs, recoil pad. Made in U.S.A. by Split Fire Sporting Goods.
Price: **$299.95**

WHITE ALPHA RIFLE
Caliber: 45, 50 percussion. **Barrel:** 27" tapered, stainless. **Sights:** Marble TruGlo rear, fiber-optic front. **Stock:** Laminated. **Features:** Lever action rotating block, hammerless; adj. trigger, positive safety. All stainless metal, including trigger. Made in U.S.A. by Split Fire Sporting Goods.
Price: **$449.95**

WINCHESTER APEX SWING-ACTION MAGNUM RIFLE
Caliber: 45, 50. **Barrel:** 28". **Stock:** Mossy Oak® Camo, Black Fleck. **Sights:** Adj. fiber-optic. **Weight:** 7 lbs., 12 oz. **Overall length:** 42". **Features:** Monte Carlo cheekpiece, swing-action design, external hammer.
Price: Mossy Oak®/stainless **$489.95**
Price: Black Fleck/stainless **$449.95**
Price: Full Mossy Oak® **$469.95**
Price: Black Fleck/blued **$364.95**

WINCHESTER X-150 BOLT-ACTION MAGNUM RIFLE
Caliber: 45, 50. **Barrel:** 26". **Stock:** Hardwoods or Timber HD, Black Fleck, Break-Up™. **Weight:** 8 lbs., 3 oz. **Sights:** Adj. fiber-optic. **Features:** No. 209 shotgun primer ignition, stainless steel bolt, stainless fluted bbl.
Price: Mossy Oak®, Timber, Hardwoods/stainless **$349.95**
Price: Black Fleck/stainless **$299.95**
Price: Mossy Oak®, Timber, Hardwoods/blued **$279.95**
Price: Black Fleck/blued **$229.95**

ZOUAVE PERCUSSION RIFLE
Caliber: 58, 59. **Barrel:** 32-1/2". **Weight:** 9-1/2 lbs. **Length:** 48-1/2" overall. **Stock:** Walnut finish, brass patchbox and buttplate. **Sights:** Fixed front, rear adjustable for elevation. **Features:** Color case-hardened lockplate, blued barrel. From Navy Arms, Dixie Gun Works, E.M.F., Cabela's, Euroarms of America.
Price: Dixie Gun Works PR0835 . . . . **$415.00 to $625.00**

Knight TK2000

CABELA'S BLACKPOWDER SHOTGUNS
Gauge: 10, 12, 20. **Barrel:** 10-ga., 30"; 12-ga., 28-1/2" (Extra-Full, Mod., Imp. Cyl. choke tubes); 20-ga., 27-1/2" (Imp. Cyl. & Mod. fixed chokes). **Weight:** 6-1/2 to 7 lbs. **Length:** 45" overall (28-1/2" barrel). **Stock:** American walnut with checkered grip; 12- and 20- gauge have straight stock, 10-gauge has pistol grip. **Features:** Blued barrels, engraved, color case-hardened locks and hammers, brass ramrod tip. From Cabela's.
Price: 10-gauge $849.99
Price: 12-gauge $719.99
Price: 20-gauge $659.99

DIXIE MAGNUM PERCUSSION SHOTGUN
Gauge: 10, 12, 20. **Barrel:** 30" (Imp. Cyl. & Mod.) in 10-gauge; 28" in 12-gauge. **Weight:** 6-1/4 lbs. **Length:** 45" overall. **Stock:** Hand- checkered walnut, 14" pull. **Features:** Double triggers; light hand engraving; case-hardened locks in 12-gauge, polished steel in 10- gauge; sling swivels. From Dixie Gun Works.
Price: 12 ga. PS0930 . . . . $685.00
Price: 12-ga. Kit PS0940 . . . . $500.00
Price: 20-ga. PS0334 . . . . $685.00
Price: 10-ga. PS1030 . . . . $685.00
Price: 10-ga. kit PS1040 . . . . $500.00
Price: Coach Gun, 12 ga. 20" bbl PS0914 . . . . $625.00

KNIGHT TK2000 MUZZLELOADING SHOTGUN (209)
Gauge: 12. **Barrel:** 26", extra-full choke tube. **Weight:** 7 lbs., 9 oz. **Length:** 45" overall. **Stock:** Synthetic black or Advantage Timber HD; recoil pad; swivel studs. **Sights:** Fully adjustable rear, blade front with fiber-optics. **Features:** Receiver drilled and tapped for scope mount; in-line ignition; adjustable trigger; removable breech plug; double safety system; Imp. Cyl. choke tube available. Made in U.S. by Knight Rifles.
Price: . . . . $349.95 to $399.95

KNIGHT VERSATILE TK2002
Gauge: 12. **Stock:** Black composite, blued, Advantage Timber HD finish. Both with sling swivel studs installed. **Sights:** Adjustable metallic TruGlo fiber-optic. **Features:** Full plastic jacket ignition system, screw-on choke tubes, load without removing choke tubes, jug-choked barrel design. Improved cylinder and modified choke tubes available.
Price: . . . . $349.95 to $399.95

NAVY ARMS STEEL SHOT MAGNUM SHOTGUN
Gauge: 10. **Barrel:** 28" (Cyl. & Cyl.). **Weight:** 7 lbs., 9 oz. **Length:** 45-1/2" overall. **Stock:** Walnut, with cheekpiece. **Features:** Designed specifically for steel shot. Engraved, polished locks; sling swivels; blued barrels. Imported by Navy Arms.
Price: $605.00

NAVY ARMS T&T SHOTGUN
Gauge: 12. **Barrel:** 28" (Full & Full). **Weight:** 7-1/2 lbs. **Stock:** Walnut. **Sights:** Bead front. **Features:** Color case-hardened locks, double triggers, blued steel furniture. From Navy Arms.
Price: $580.00

WHITE TOMINATOR SHOTGUN
Caliber: 12. **Barrel:** 25" blue, straight, tapered stainless steel. **Weight:** NA. **Length:** NA. **Stock:** Black laminated or black wood. **Sights:** Drilled and tapped for easy scope mounting. **Features:** Internchangeable choke tubes. Custom vent rib with high visibility front bead. Double safeties. Fully adjustable custom trigger. Recoil pad and sling swivel studs. Made in U.S.A. by Split Fire Sporting Goods.
Price: $349.95

ARS HUNTING MASTER AR6 AIR PISTOL
Caliber: 22 (177 +20 special order). **Barrel:** 12" rifled. **Weight:** 3 lbs. **Length:** 18.25 overall. **Power:** NA. **Grips:** Indonesian walnut with checkered grip. **Sights:** Adjustable rear, blade front. **Features:** 6 shot repeater with rotary magazine, single or double action, receiver grooved for scope, hammer block and trigger block safeties.
Price: .... **NA**

BEEMAN P1 MAGNUM AIR PISTOL
Caliber: 177, 20. **Barrel:** 8.4". **Weight:** 2.5 lbs. **Length:** 11" overall. **Power:** Top lever cocking; spring-piston. **Grips:** Checkered walnut. **Sights:** Blade front, square notch rear with click micrometer adjustments for windage and elevation. Grooved for scope mounting. **Features:** Dual power for 177 and 20 cal.: low setting gives 350-400 fps; high setting 500-600 fps. All Colt 45 auto grips fit gun. Dry-firing feature for practice. Optional wood shoulder stock. Imported by Beeman.
Price: **$450.00**

BEEMAN P3 PNEUMATIC AIR PISTOL
Caliber: 177. **Barrel:** NA. **Weight:** 1.7 lbs. **Length:** 9.6" overall. **Power:** Single-stroke pneumatic; overlever barrel cocking. **Grips:** Reinforced polymer. **Sights:** Front and rear fiber-optic sights. **Features:** Velocity 410 fps. Polymer frame; automatic safety; two-stage trigger; built-in muzzle brake.
Price: **$215.00**
Price: **$295.00**

BEEMAN/Feinwerkbau P44
Caliber: 177, single shot. **Barrel:** 9.17". **Weight:** 2.10 lbs. **Length:** 16.54" overall. **Power:** Pre-charged pneumatic. **Grips:** Walnut grip. **Sights:** front and rear sights. **Features:** 500 fps, sighting line adjustable from 360 to 395mm, adjustable 3-d grip in 3 sizes, adjustable match trigger, delivered in special transport case.
Price: **$1,890.00**

BEEMAN/Feinwerkbau P56
Caliber: 177, 5-shot magazine. **Barrel:** 8.81". **Weight:** 2.43 lbs. **Length:** 16.54" overall. **Power:** Pre-charged pneumatic. **Grips:** Walnut Morini grip. **Sights:** front and rear sights. **Features:** 500 fps, match-adjustable trigger, adjustable rear sight, front sight accepts interchangeable inserts, delivered in special transport case.
Price: **$2,280.00**

BEEMAN/FWB 103 AIR PISTOL
Caliber: 177. **Barrel:** 10.1", 12-groove rifling. **Weight:** 2.5 lbs. **Length:** 16.5" overall. **Power:** Single-stroke pneumatic, underlever cocking. **Grips:** Stippled walnut with adjustable palm shelf. **Sights:** Blade front, open rear adjustable for windage and elevation. Notch size adjustable for width. Interchangeable front blades. **Features:** Velocity 510 fps. Fully adjustable trigger. Cocking effort 2 lbs. Imported by Beeman.
Price: Right-hand **$1,805.00**
Price: Left-hand **$1,920.00**

BEEMAN HW70A AIR PISTOL
Caliber: 177. **Barrel:** 6-1/4", rifled. **Weight:** 38 oz. **Length:** 12-3/4" overall. **Power:** Spring, barrel cocking. **Grips:** Plastic, with thumbrest. **Sights:** Hooded post front, square notch rear adjustable for windage and elevation. Comes with scope base. **Features:** Adjustable trigger, 31-lb. cocking effort, 440 fps MV; automatic barrel safety. Imported by Beeman.
Price: **$240.00**

BENJAMIN & SHERIDAN CO2 PISTOLS
Caliber: 177, 22, single shot. **Barrel:** 6-3/8", brass. **Weight:** 1 lb. 12 oz. **Length:** 9" overall. **Power:** 12-gram CO2 cylinder. **Grips:** American Hardwood. **Sights:** High ramp front, fully adjustable notched rear. **Features:** Velocity to 500 fps. Turnbolt action with cross-bolt safety. Gives about 40 shots per CO2 cylinder. Black or nickel finish. Made in U.S. by Crosman Corp.
Price: EB17 (177), EB22 (22) **$185.00**

BENJAMIN & SHERIDAN PNEUMATIC PELLET PISTOLS
Caliber: 177, 22, single shot. **Barrel:** 9-3/8", rifled brass. **Weight:** 2 lbs., 8 oz. **Length:** 12.25" overall. **Power:** Underlever pnuematic, hand pumped. **Grips:** American Hardwood. **Sights:** High ramp front, fully adjustable notch rear. **Features:** Velocity to 525 fps (variable). Bolt action with cross-bolt safety. Choice of black or nickel finish. Made in U.S. by Crosman Corp.
Price: Black finish, HB17 (177), HB22 (22) **$115.00**

Benjamin & Sheridan EB17/EB22

COLT 1911 A1
Caliber: .177, 8-shot pellet. **Barrel:** 5" rifled. **Weight:** 2.4 lbs. **Length:** 9" overall. **Power:** 12g CO2. **Sights:** Fixed front, adjustable rear. **Features:** Velocity of 425 fps. 8-shot rotary clip. Double or single action. Replica of one of the most successful military designs ever developed.
Price: **$216.88**
Price: Nickel **$238.42**

COLT 1911 TACTICAL
Caliber: .177, 8-shot pellet. 5" rifled. **Weight:** 2.9 lbs. 13-3/4" overall. **Power:** 12g CO2. **Sights:** Fixed front, adjustable rear. Velocity of 425 fps. 8-shot rotary clip. Double or single action. Includes Walther Top Point Sight and compensator.
Price: **$320.00**

CROSMAN AUTO AIR II RED DOT PISTOLS
Caliber: BB, 17-shot magazine; 177 pellet, single shot. **Barrel:** 8-5/8" steel, smooth-bore. **Weight:** 13 oz. **Length:** 10-3/4" overall. **Power:** CO2 Powerlet. **Grips:** NA. **Sights:** Blade front, adjustable rear; highlighted system. **Features:** Velocity to 480 fps (BBs), 430 fps (pellets). Semi-automatic action with BBs, single shot with pellets. Black. From Crosman.
Price: AAIIB **$38.00**

CROSMAN MODEL 1008 REPEAT AIR PISTOL
Caliber: 177, 8-shot pellet clip. **Barrel:** 4.25", rifled steel. **Weight:** 17 oz. **Length:** 8.625" overall. **Power:** CO2 Powerlet. **Grips:** Checkered black plastic. **Sights:** Post front, adjustable rear. **Features:** Velocity about 430 fps. Break-open barrel for easy loading; single or double semi-automatic action; two 8-shot clips included. Optional carrying case available. From Crosman.
Price: **$60.00**

CROSMAN MAGNUM AIR PISTOLS
Caliber: 177, pellets. **Barrel:** Rifled steel. **Weight:** 2 lbs. **Length:** 9.38". **Power:** CO2. **Grips:** NA. **Sights:** Blade front, rear adjustable. **Features:** Single/double action accepts sights and scopes with standard 3/8" dovetail mount. Model 3576W features 6" barrel for increased accuracy. From Crosman.
Price: 3576W **$50.00**

DAISY/POWERLINE MODEL 15XT AIR PISTOL
Caliber: 177 BB, 15-shot built-in magazine. **Barrel:** NA. **Weight:** NA. **Length:** 7.21". **Power:** CO2. **Grips:** NA. **Sights:** NA. **Features:** Velocity 425 fps. Made in the U.S.A. by Daisy Mfg. Co.
Price: **$47.99**
Price: With electronic point sight **$57.99**

DAISY MODEL 717 AIR PISTOL
Caliber: 177, single shot. **Weight:** 2.25 lbs. **Length:** 13-1/2" overall. **Grips:** Molded checkered woodgrain with contoured thumbrest. **Sights:** Blade and ramp front, open rear with windage and elevation adjustments. **Features:** Single pump pneumatic pistol. Rifled steel barrel. Crossbolt trigger block. Muzzle velocity 360 fps. From Daisy Mfg. Co.
Price: **$152.99**

DAISY MODEL 747 TRIUMPH AIR PISTOL
Caliber: 177, single shot. **Weight:** 2.35 lbs. **Length:** 13-1/2" overall. **Grips:** Molded checkered woodgrain with contoured thumbrest. **Sights:** Blade and ramp front, open rear with windage and elevation adjustments. **Features:** Single pump pneumatic pistol. Lothar Walther rifled high-grade steel barrel; crowned 12 lands and grooves, right-hand twist. Precision bore sized for match pellets. Muzzle veocity 360 fps. From Daisy Mfg. Co.
Price: **$203.99**

AIRGUNS — Handguns

Daisy/Powerline 693

Gamo P-23

DAISY/POWERLINE 693 AIR PISTOL
Caliber: 177, single shot. **Weight:** 1.10 lbs. **Length:** 7.9" overall. **Grips:** Molded brown checkered. **Sights:** Blade and ramp front, fixed open rear. **Features:** Semi-automoatic BB pistol with a nickel finish and smooth bore steel barrel. Muzzle veocity 400 fps. From Daisy Mfg. Co.
Price: **$66.99**

EAA/BAIKAL IZH-M46 TARGET AIR PISTOL
Caliber: 177, single shot. **Barrel:** 10". **Weight:** 2.4 lbs. **Length:** 16.8" overall. **Power:** Underlever single-stroke pneumatic. **Grips:** Adjustable wooden target. **Sights:** Micrometer fully adjustable rear, blade front. **Features:** Velocity about 440 fps. Hammer-forged, rifled barrel. Imported from Russia by European American Armory.
Price: **$349.00**

GAMO P-23, P-23 LASER PISTOL
Caliber: 177, 12-shot. **Barrel:** 4.25". **Weight:** 1 lb. **Length:** 7.5". **Power:** CO2 cartridge, semi-automatic, 410 fps. **Grips:** Plastic. **Sights:** NA. **Features:** Walther PPK cartridge pistol copy, optional laser sight. Imported from Spain by Gamo.
Price: .... **$89.95**, (with laser) **$139.95**

GAMO PT-80, PT-80 LASER PISTOL
Caliber: 177, 8-shot. **Barrel:** 4.25". **Weight:** 1.2 lbs. **Length:** 7.2". **Power:** CO2 cartridge, semi-automatic, 410 fps. **Grips:** Plastic. **Sights:** 3-dot. **Features:** Optional laser sight and walnut grips available. Imported from Spain by Gamo.
Price: .... **$108.95**, (with laser) **$159.95**
Price: (with walnut grip) **$119.95**

HAMMERLI AP-40 AIR PISTOL
Caliber: 177. **Barrel:** 10". **Weight:** 2.2 lbs. **Length:** 15.5". **Power:** NA. **Grips:** Adjustable orthopedic. **Sights:** Fully adjustable micrometer. **Features:** Sleek, light, well balanced and accurate.
Price: **$1,400.00**

MAGNUM RESEARCH DESERT EAGLE
Caliber: .177, 8-shot pellet. 5.7" rifled. **Weight:** 2.5 lbs. 11" overall. **Power:** 12g CO2. **Sights:** Fixed front, adjustable rear. Velocity of 425 fps. 8-shot rotary clip. Double or single action. The first .177 caliber air pistol with BLOWBACK action. Big and weighty, designed in the likeness of the real Desert Eagle.
Price: **$172.31**

MAGNUM BABY DESERT
Caliber: .177, 15-shot BB. 4" **Weight:** 1.0 lbs. 8-1/4" overall. **Power:** 12g CO2. **Sights:** Fixed front and rear. Velocity of 420 fps. Double action BB repeater. Comes with bonus Picatinny top rail and built-in bottom rail.
Price: **$41.54**

MORINI CM 162 EL MATCH AIR PISTOLS
Caliber: 177, single shot. **Barrel:** 9.4". **Weight:** 32 oz. **Length:** 16.1" overall. **Power:** Scuba air. **Grips:** Adjustable match type. **Sights:** Interchangeable blade front, fully adjustable match-type rear. **Features:** Power mechanism shuts down when pressure drops to a preset level. Adjustable electronic trigger.
Price: **$1,075.00**

PARDINI K58 MATCH AIR PISTOLS
Caliber: 177, single shot. **Barrel:** 9". **Weight:** 37.7 oz. **Length:** 15.5" overall. **Power:** Precharged compressed air; single-stroke cocking. **Grips:** Adjustable match type; stippled walnut. **Sights:** Interchangeable post front, fully adjustable match rear. **Features:** Fully adjustable trigger. Short version K-2 available. Imported from Italy by Larry's Guns.
Price: **$819.00**

RWS 9B/9N AIR PISTOLS
Caliber: 177, single shot. **Barrel:** 8". **Weight:** 2.38 lbs. **Length:** 10.4". **Power:** 550 fps. **Grips:** Right hand with thumbrest. **Sights:** Adjustable. **Features:** Spring-piston powered. Black or nickel finish.
Price: 9B/9N **$150.00**

SMITH & WESSON 586
Caliber: .177, 10-shot pellet. Rifled. **Power:** 12g CO2. **Sights:** Fixed front, adjustable rear. 10-shot rotary clip. Double or single action. Replica revolvers that duplicate both weight and handling.
Price: 4" barrel, 2.5 lbs, 400 fps **$215.34**
Price: 6" barrel, 2.8 lbs, 425 fps **$231.49**
Price: 8" barrel, 3.0 lbs, 460 fps **$247.65**
Price: S&W 686 Nickel, 6" barrel, 2.8 lbs, 425 fps **$253.03**

STEYR LP10P MATCH AIR PISTOL
Caliber: 177, single shot. **Barrel:** 9". **Weight:** 38.7 oz. **Length:** 15.3" overall. **Power:** Scuba air. **Grips:** Adjustable Morini match, palm shelf, stippled walnut. **Sights:** Interchangeable blade in 4mm, 4.5mm or 5mm widths, adjustable open rear, interchangeable 3.5mm or 4mm leaves. **Features:** Velocity about 500 fps. Adjustable trigger, adjustable sight radius from 12.4" to 13.2". With compensator. Recoil elimination.
Price: **$1,400.00**

TECH FORCE SS2 OLYMPIC COMPETITION AIR PISTOL
Caliber: 177 pellet, single shot. **Barrel:** 7.4". **Weight:** 2.8 lbs. **Length:** 16.5" overall. **Power:** Spring piston, sidelever. **Grips:** Hardwood. **Sights:** Extended adjustable rear, blade front accepts inserts. **Features:** Velocity 520 fps. Recoilless design; adjustments allow duplication of a firearm's feel. Match-grade, adjustable trigger; includes carrying case. Imported from China by Compasseco, Inc.
Price: **$295.00**

TECH FORCE 35 AIR PISTOL
Caliber: 177 pellet, single shot. **Weight:** 2.86 lbs. **Length:** 14.9" overall. **Power:** Spring-piston, underlever. **Grips:** Hardwood. **Sights:** Micrometer adjustable rear, blade front. **Features:** Velocity 400 fps. Grooved for scope mount; trigger safety. Imported from China by Compasseco, Inc.
Price: **$39.95**

Tech Force S2-1 Air Pistol
Similar to Tech Force 8 except basic grips and sights for plinking.
Price: **$29.95**

WALTHER LP300 MATCH PISTOL
Caliber: 177. **Barrel:** 236mm. **Weight:** 1.018g. **Length:** NA. **Power:** NA. **Grips:** NA. **Sights:** Integrated front with three different widths, adjustable rear. **Features:** Adjustable grip and trigger.
Price: **$1,800.00**

WALTHER PPK/S
Caliber: .177, 15-shot steel BB. 3-1/2". **Weight:** 1.2 lbs. 6-1/4" overall. **Power:** 12g CO2. **Sights:** Fixed front and rear. Velocity of 295 fps. Lookalike of one of the world's most famous pistols. Realistic recoil. Heavyweight steel construction.
Price: **$71.92**
Price: With laser sight **$94.23**
Price: With BiColor pistol, CO2, targets, shooting glasses, BBs **$84.62**

WALTHER CP99 COMPACT
Caliber: .177, 17-shot steel BB semi-auto. 3". **Weight:** 1.7 lbs. 6-1/2" overall. **Power:** 12g CO2. **Sights:** Fixed front and rear. Velocity of 345 fps. Realistic recoil, blowback action. Heavyweight steel construction. Built-in Picatinny mount.
Price: **$83.08**

AIRFORCE CONDOR RIFLE
Caliber: .177, .22 single shot. **Barrel:** 24" rifled. **Weight:** 6.5 lbs. **Length:** 38.75" overall. **Power:** Pre-charged pneumatic. **Stock:** NA. **Sights:** Intended for scope use, fiber-optic open sights optional. **Features:** Lothar Walther match barrel, adjustable power levels from 600-1,300 fps. 3,000 psi fill pressure. Automatic safety. Air tank volume: 490cc. An integral extended scope rail allows easy mounting of the largest air-gun scopes. Operates on high-pressure air from scuba tank or hand pump. Manufactured in the U.S.A by AirForce Airguns
Price: Gun only (.22 or .177) **$589.95**

AIRFORCE TALON AIR RIFLE
Caliber: .177, .22, single-shot. **Barrel:** 18" rifled. **Weight:** 5.5 lbs. **Length:** 32.6". **Power:** Pre-charged pneumatic. **Stock:** NA. **Sights:** Intended for scope use, fiber-optic open sights optional. **Features:** Lothar Walther match barrel, adjustable power levels from 400-1,000 fps, 3,000 psi fill pressure. Automatic safety. Air tank volume: 490cc. Operates on high-pressure air from scuba tank or hand pump. Manufactured in the U.S.A. by AirForce Airguns.
Price: Gun only (.22 or .177) **$479.95**

AIRFORCE TALON SS AIR RIFLE
Caliber: .177, .22, single-shot. **Barrel:** 12" rifled. **Weight:** 5.25 lbs. **Length:** 32.75". **Power:** Pre-charged pneumatic. **Stock:** NA. **Sights:** Intended for scope use, fiber-optic open sights optional. **Features:** Lothar Walther match barrel, adjustable power levels from 400-1,000 fps. 3,000 psi fill pressure. Automatic safety. Chamber in front of barrel strips away air turbulence, protects muzzle and reduces firing report. Air tank volume: 490cc. Operates on high-pressure air from scuba tank or hand pump. Manufactured in the U.S.A. by AirForce Airguns.
Price: Gun only (.22 or .177) **$499.95**

AIRROW MODEL A-8SRB STEALTH AIR RIFLE
Caliber: 177, 22, 25, 9-shot. **Barrel:** 20"; rifled. **Weight:** 6 lbs. **Length:** 34" overall. **Power:** CO2 or compressed air; variable power. **Stock:** Telescoping CAR-15-type. **Sights:** Variable 3.5-10x scope. **Features:** Velocity 1100 fps in all calibers. Pneumatic air trigger. All aircraft aluminum and stainless steel construction. Mil-spec materials and finishes. From Swivel Machine Works, Inc.
Price: About **$2,299.00**

AIRROW MODEL A-8S1P STEALTH AIR RIFLE
Caliber: #2512 16" arrow. **Barrel:** 16". **Weight:** 4.4 lbs. **Length:** 30.1" overall. **Power:** CO2 or compressed air; variable power. **Stock:** Telescoping CAR-15-type. **Sights:** Scope rings only. 7 oz. rechargeable cylinder and valve. **Features:** Velocity to 650 fps with 260- grain arrow. Pneumatic air trigger. Broadhead guard. All aircraft aluminum and stainless steel construction. Mil-spec materials and finishes. A-8S Models perform to 2,000 PSIG above or below water levels. Waterproof case. From Swivel Machine Works, Inc.
Price: **$1,699.00**

ANSCHÜTZ 2002 MATCH AIR RIFLES
Caliber: .177, single shot. **Barrel:** 25.2". **Weight:** 10.8 lbs. **Length:** 42.5" overall. **Stock:** European walnut, blonde hardwood or colored laminated hardwood; stippled grip and forend. Also available with flat-forend walnut stock for benchrest shooting and aluminum. **Sights:** Optional sight set #6834. **Features:** Muzzle velocity 575 fps. Balance, weight match the 1907 ISU smallbore rifle. Uses #5021 match trigger. Recoil and vibration free. Fully adjustable cheekpiece and buttplate; accessory rail under forend. Available in pneumatic and compressed air versions. Imported from Germany by Gunsmithing, Inc., Accuracy International, Champion's Choice.
Price: Right-hand, blonde hardwood stock, with sights **$1,275.00**
Price: Right-hand, walnut stock **$1,275.00**
Price: Right-hand, color laminate stock **$1,300.00**
Price: Right-hand, aluminum stock, butt plate **$1,495.00**
Price: Left-hand, color laminate stock **$1,595.00**
Price: Model 2002D-RT Running Target, right-hand, no sights . . **$1,248.90**
Price: #6834 Sight Set **$227.10**

ARS HUNTING MASTER AR6 AIR RIFLE
Caliber: .22, 6-shot repeater. **Barrel:** 25-1/2". **Weight:** 7 lbs. **Length:** 41-1/4" overall. **Power:** Precompressed air from 3000 psi diving tank. **Stock:** Indonesian walnut with checkered grip; rubber buttpad. **Sights:** Blade front, adjustable peep rear. **Features:** Velocity over 1000 fps with 32-grain pellet. Receiver grooved for scope mounting. Has 6-shot rotary magazine. Imported by Air Rifle Specialists.
Price: **$580.00**

BEEMAN KODIAK AIR RIFLE
Caliber: .25, single shot. **Barrel:** 17.6". **Weight:** 9 lbs. **Length:** 45.6" overall. **Power:** Spring-piston, barrel cocking. **Stock:** Stained hardwood. **Sights:** Blade front, open fully adjustable rear. **Features:** Velocity to 820 fps. Up to 30 foot pounds muzzle energy. Imported by Beeman.
Price: **$725.00**

BEEMAN GH1050 AIR RIFLE
Caliber: .177 or .22, single shot. **Barrel:** NA. **Weight:** 6.4 lbs. **Length:** 45.67" overall. **Power:** Spring-piston. **Stock:** Anti-shock black synthetic stock w/recoil pad, checkered pistol grip and forend. **Sights:** Fiber optic front & rear sights. **Features:** Velocities 1000 fps in .177 or 812 fps in .22. Dovetail receiver, steel trigger blade, and automatic safety.
Price: .177 or .22 caliber air rifle **$235.00**
Price: .177 or .22 caliber air rile combo **$300.00**

BEEMAN HW100
Caliber: .177 or .22, 14-shot magazine. **Barrel:** 21-1/2". **Weight:** 9 lbs. **Length:** 42.13" overall. **Power:** Pre-charged. **Stock:** Walnut Sporter checkering on the pistol grip & forend; walnut thumbhose with lateral finger grooves on the forend & stippling on the pistol grip. **Sights:** None. Grooved for scope mounting. **Features:** 1140 fps .177 caliber; 945 fps .22 caliber. 14-shot magazine, quick-fill cylinder. Two-stage adjustable match trigger and manual safety.
Price: .177 or .22 caliber Sport Stock **$1,465.00**
Price: .177 or .22 caliber Thumbhole Stock **$1,465.00**

BEEMAN R1 AIR RIFLE
Caliber: .177, .20 or .22, single shot. **Barrel:** 19.6", 12-groove rifling. **Weight:** 8.5 lbs. **Length:** 45.2" overall. **Power:** Spring-piston, barrel cocking. **Stock:** Walnut-stained beech; cut-checkered pistol grip; Monte Carlo comb and cheekpiece; rubber buttpad. **Sights:** Tunnel front with interchangeable inserts, open rear click-adjustable for windage and elevation. Grooved for scope mounting. **Features:** Velocity 940-1000 fps (177), 860 fps (20), 800 fps (22). Non-drying nylon piston and breech seals. Adjustable metal trigger. Milled steel safety. Right- or left-hand stock. Adjustable cheekpiece and buttplate at extra cost. Custom and Super Laser versions available. Imported by Beeman.
Price: Right-hand **$665.00**
Price: Left-hand **$720.00**

BEEMAN R7 AIR RIFLE
Caliber: .177, .20, single shot. **Barrel:** 17". **Weight:** 6.1 lbs. **Length:** 40.2" overall. **Power:** Spring-piston. **Stock:** Stained beech. **Sights:** Hooded front, fully adjustable micrometer click open rear. **Features:** Velocity to 700 fps (177), 620 fps (20). Receiver grooved for scope mounting; double-jointed cocking lever; fully adjustable trigger; checkered grip. Imported by Beeman.
Price: **$370.00**

BEEMAN R9 AIR RIFLE
Caliber: .177, .20, single shot. **Barrel:** NA. **Weight:** 7.3 lbs. **Length:** 43" overall. **Power:** Spring-piston, barrel cocking. **Stock:** Stained hardwood. **Sights:** Tunnel post front, fully adjustable open rear. **Features:** Velocity to 1000 fps (177), 800 fps (20). Adjustable Rekord trigger; automatic safety; receiver dovetailed for scope mounting. Imported from Germany by Beeman Precision Airguns.
Price: **$440.00**

BEEMAN R11 MKII AIR RIFLE
Caliber: .177, single shot. **Barrel:** 19.6". **Weight:** 8.6 lbs. **Length:** 43.5" overall. **Power:** Spring-piston, barrel cocking. **Stock:** Walnut- stained beech; adjustable buttplate and cheekpiece. **Sights:** None furnished. Has dovetail for scope mounting. **Features:** Velocity 910-940 fps. All-steel barrel sleeve. Imported by Beeman.
Price: **$690.00**

AIRGUNS — Long Guns

BEEMAN RX-2 GAS-SPRING MAGNUM AIR RIFLE
Caliber: .177, .20, .22, single shot. **Barrel:** 19.6", 12-groove rifling. **Weight:** 8.8 lbs. **Power:** Gas-spring piston air; single stroke barrel cocking. **Stock:** Laminated wood stock. **Sights:** Tunnel front, click-adjustable rear. **Features:** Velocity adjustable to about 1200 fps. Imported by Beeman.
Price: .177, .20, .22 regular, right-hand **$798.00**

BEEMAN R1 CARBINE
Caliber: .177,. 20, .22 single shot. **Barrel:** 16.1". **Weight:** 8.6 lbs. **Length:** 41.7" overall. **Power:** Spring-piston, barrel cocking. **Stock:** Stained beech; Monte Carlo comb and checkpiece; cut checkered pistol grip; rubber buttpad. **Sights:** Tunnel front with interchangeable inserts, open adjustable rear; receiver grooved for scope mounting. **Features:** Velocity up to 1000 fps (177). Non- drying nylon piston and breech seals. Adjustable metal trigger. Machined steel receiver end cap and safety. Right- or left-hand stock. Imported by Beeman.
Price: 177, 20, 22, right-hand . . . . **$665.00;** left-hand **$720.00**

BEEMAN/FEINWERKBAU 603 AIR RIFLE
Caliber: .177, single shot. **Barrel:** 16.6". **Weight:** 10.8 lbs. **Length:** 43" overall. **Power:** Single stroke pneumatic. **Stock:** Special laminated hardwoods and hard rubber for stability. Multi-colored stock also available. **Sights:** Tunnel front sight with interchangeable inserts, click micrometer match aperture rear sight. **Features:** Velocity to 570 fps. Recoilless action; double supported barrel; special, short rifled area frees pellet from barrel faster. Fully adjustable match trigger with separately adjustable trigger and trigger slack weight. Trigger and sights blocked when loading latch is open. Imported by Beeman.
Price: Right-hand. **$2,445.00**
Price: Left-hand. **$2,625.00**
Price: Junior. **$2,170.00**

BEEMAN/FEINWERKBAU 700 – ALUMINUM OR WOOD STOCK
Caliber: .177, single shot. **Barrel:** 16.6". **Weight:** 10.8 lbs. Aluminum; 9.9 lbs. Wood. **Length:** 43.3-46.25" Aluminum; 43.7" Wood. **Power:** Pre-charged pneumatic. **Stock:** Aluminum stock – laminated hardwood. **Sights:** Tunnel front sight with interchangeable inserts, click micrometer match aperture rear sight. **Features:** Velocity 570 fps. Recoilless action. Anatomical grips can be tilted and pivoted to the barrel axis. Adjustable buttplate and cheekpiece.
Price: Aluminum 700, precharged, right **$3,000.00**
Price: Aluminum 700, precharged, left **$3,100.00**
Price: Laminated Wood Stock 700, precharged, right **$2,335.00**
Price: Laminated Wood Stock 700, precharged, left **$2,435.00**

BEEMAN/FEINWERKBAU P70 FIELD TARGET
Caliber: .177, single shot. **Barrel:** 24.6". **Weight:** 10.6 lbs. **Length:** 43.3" overall. **Power:** Pre-charged pneumatic. **Stock:** Aluminum stock (red or blue) anatomical grips, buttplate & cheekpiece. **Sights:** None, receiver grooved for scope mounting. **Features:** 870 fps velocity. At 50 yards, this air rifle is capable of achieving 1/2-inch groups. Match adjustable trigger. 2001 US Field Target National Champion.
Price: P70FT, precharged, right (red or blue) **$2,855.00**
Price: P70FT, precharged, left (red or blue) **$2,955.00**

BEEMAN/FEINWERKBAU P700 .177 BASIC AIR RIFLE
Caliber: .177, single shot. **Barrel:** 16.73". **Weight:** 9.04 lbs. **Length:** 43.31" overall. **Power:** Pre-charged pneumatic. **Stock:** Beech wood stock. **Sights:** Tunnel front sight with interchangeable inserts, click micrometer match aperture rear sight. **Features:** Velocity to 570 fps. Recoilless action; match adjustable trigger. Interior absorber.
Price: P700 Basic, .177. . . . . **$1,150.00**

BEEMAN/HW 97 AIR RIFLE
Caliber: .177, .20, single shot. **Barrel:** 17.75". **Weight:** 9.2 lbs. **Length:** 44.1" overall. **Power:** Spring-piston, underlever cocking. **Stock:** Walnut-stained beech; rubber buttpad. **Sights:** None. Receiver grooved for scope mounting. **Features:** Velocity 830 fps (177). Fixed barrel with fully opening, direct loading breech. Adjustable trigger. Imported by Beeman Precision Airguns.
Price: Right-hand only. **$625.00**

Beretta CX4 Storm

BENJAMIN & SHERIDAN PNEUMATIC (PUMP-UP) AIR RIFLE
Caliber: .177 or .22, single shot. **Barrel:** 19-3/8", rifled brass. **Weight:** 5-1/2 lbs. **Length:** 36-1/4" overall. **Power:** Underlever pneumatic, hand pumped. **Stock:** American walnut stock and forend. **Sights:** High ramp front, fully adjustable notched rear. **Features:** Variable velocity to 800 fps. Bolt action with ambidextrous push-pull safety. Black or nickel finish. Made in the U.S. by Benjamin Sheridan Co.
Price:. **$140.95**

BERETTA CX4 STORM
Caliber: .177, 30-shot semi auto. 17 1/2", rifled. **Weight:** 5.25 lbs. 30.75" overall. **Power:** 88g CO2. **Stock:** Replica style. **Sights:** Adjustable front and rear. Blowback action. Velocity of 600 fps. Accessory rails.
Price:. **$276.92**

BSA SUPERTEN MK3 AIR RIFLE
Caliber: .177, .22 10-shot repeater. **Barrel:** 17-1/2". **Weight:** 7 lbs., 8 oz. **Length:** 37" overall. **Power:** Precharged pneumatic via buddy bottle. **Stock:** Oil-finished hardwood; Monte Carlo with cheekpiece, cut checkered grip; adjustable recoil pad. **Sights:** No sights; intended for scope use. **Features:** Velocity 1000+ fps (177), 1000+ fps (22). Patented 10-shot indexing magazine, bolt-action loading. Left-hand version also available. Imported from U.K.
Price: **$599.95**

BSA SUPERTEN MK3 BULLBARREL
Caliber: .177,. 22, .25, single shot. **Barrel:** 18-1/2". **Weight:** 8 lbs., 8 oz. **Length:** 43" overall. **Power:** Spring-air, underlever cocking. **Stock:** Oil-finished hardwood; Monte Carlo with cheekpiece, checkered at grip; recoil pad. **Sights:** Ramp front, micrometer adjustable rear. Maxi-Grip scope rail. **Features:** Velocity 950 fps (177), 750 fps (22), 600 fps (25). Patented rotating breech design. Maxi-Grip scope rail protects optics from recoil; automatic anti-beartrap plus manual safety. Imported from U.K.
Price: Rifle, MKII Carbine (14" barrel, 39-1/2" overall) **$349.95**

BSA MAGNUM SUPERSPORT™ AIR RIFLE, CARBINE
Caliber: .177, .22, .25, single shot. **Barrel:** 18-1/2". **Weight:** 6 lbs., 8 oz. **Length:** 41" overall. **Power:** Spring-air, barrel cocking. **Stock:** Oil-finished hardwood; Monte Carlo with cheekpiece, recoil pad. **Sights:** Ramp front, micrometer adjustable rear. Maxi-Grip scope rail. **Features:** Velocity 950 fps (177), 750 fps (22), 600 fps (25). Patented Maxi-Grip scope rail protects optics from recoil; automatic anti-beartrap plus manual tang safety. Muzzle brake standard. Imported for U.K.
Price: **$194.95**
Price: Carbine, 14" barrel, muzzle brake **$214.95**

BSA METEOR AIR RIFLE
Caliber: .177, .22, single shot. **Barrel:** 18-1/2". **Weight:** 6 lbs. **Length:** 41" overall. **Power:** Spring-air, barrel cocking. **Stock:** Oil- finished hardwood. **Sights:** Ramp front, micrometer adjustable rear. **Features:** Velocity 650 fps (177), 500 fps (22). Automatic anti- beartrap; manual tang safety. Receiver grooved for scope mounting. Imported from U.K.
Price: Rifle **$144.95**
Price: Carbine **$164.95**

CROSMAN MODEL POWERMASTER 664SB AIR RIFLES
Caliber: .177 (single shot pellet) or BB, 200-shot reservoir. **Barrel:** 20", rifled steel. **Weight:** 2 lbs. 15 oz. **Length:** 38-1/2" overall. **Power:** Pneumatic; hand-pumped. **Stock:** Wood-grained ABS plastic; checkered pistol grip and forend. **Sights:** Fiber-optic front, fully adjustable open rear. **Features:** Velocity about 645 fps. Bolt action, cross-bolt safety. From Crosman.
Price:. **$65.00**

CROSMAN MODEL PUMPMASTER 760 AIR RIFLES

Caliber: .177 pellets (single shot) or BB (200-shot reservoir). **Barrel:** 19-1/2", rifled steel. **Weight:** 2 lbs., 12 oz. **Length:** 33.5" overall. **Power:** Pneumatic, hand-pump. **Stock:** Walnut-finished ABS plastic stock and forend. **Features:** Velocity to 590 fps (BBs, 10 pumps). Short stroke, power determined by number of strokes. Fiber-optic front sight and adjustable rear sight. Cross-bolt safety. From Crosman.
Price: Model 760 . . . . **$40.00**

CROSMAN MODEL REPEATAIR 1077 RIFLES

Caliber: .177 pellets, 12-shot clip. **Barrel:** 20.3", rifled steel. **Weight:** 3 lbs., 11 oz. **Length:** 38.8" overall. **Power:** CO2 Powerlet. **Stock:** Textured synthetic or hardwood. **Sights:** Blade front, fully adjustable rear. **Features:** Velocity 590 fps. Removable 12-shot clip. True semi-automatic action. From Crosman.
Price: **$68.00**
Price: 1077W (walnut stock) **$100.00**

CROSMAN 2260 AIR RIFLE

Caliber: .22, single shot. **Barrel:** 24". **Weight:** 4 lbs., 12 oz. **Length:** 39.75" overall. **Power:** CO2 Powerlet. **Stock:** Hardwood. **Sights:** Blade front, adjustable rear open or peep. **Features:** About 600 fps. Made in U.S. by Crosman Corp.
Price: **$80.00**

CROSMAN MODEL CLASSIC 2100 AIR RIFLE

Caliber: 177 pellets (single shot), or BB (200-shot BB reservoir). **Barrel:** 21", rifled. **Weight:** 4 lbs., 13 oz. **Length:** 39-3/4" overall. **Power:** Pump-up, pneumatic. **Stock:** Wood-grained checkered ABS plastic. **Features:** Three pumps give about 450 fps, 10 pumps about 755 fps (BBs). Cross-bolt safety; concealed reservoir holds over 200 BBs. From Crosman.
Price: Model 2100B **$55.00**

CROSMAN MODEL 2260 AIR RIFLE

Caliber: 22, single shot. **Barrel:** 19", rifled steel. **Weight:** 4 lbs., 12 oz. **Length:** 39.75" overall. **Stock:** Full-size, American hardwood. **Features:** Variable pump power; three pumps give 395 fps, six pumps 530 fps, 10 pumps 600 fps (average). Full-size adult air rifle. From Crosman.
Price: **$80.00**

DAISY 1938 RED RYDER AIR RIFLE

Caliber: BB, 650-shot repeating action. **Barrel:** Smoothbore steel with shroud. **Weight:** 2.2 lbs. **Length:** 35.4" overall. **Stock:** Walnut stock burned with Red Ryder lariat signature. **Sights:** Post front, adjustable V-slot rear. **Features:** Walnut forend. Saddle ring with leather thong. Lever cocking. Gravity feed. Controlled velocity. From Daisy Mfg. Co.
Price: **$44.95**

DAISY MODEL 840B GRIZZLY AIR RIFLE

Caliber: .177 pellet single shot; or BB 350-shot. **Barrel:** 19", smoothbore, steel. **Weight:** 2.25 lbs. **Length:** 36.8" overall. **Power:** Single pump pneumatic. **Stock:** Molded wood-grain stock and forend. **Sights:** Ramp front, open, adjustable rear. **Features:** Muzzle velocity 320 fps (BB), 300 fps (pellet). Steel buttplate; straight pull bolt action; cross-bolt safety. Forend forms pump lever. From Daisy Mfg. Co.
Price: **$47.99**
Price: (840C in Mossy Oak Breakup Camo) **$54.99**

DAISY MODEL 105 BUCK AIR RIFLE

Caliber: .177 or BB. **Barrel:** Smoothbore steel. **Weight:** 1.6 lbs. **Length:** 29.8" overall. **Power:** Lever cocking, spring air. **Stock:** Stained solid wood. **Sights:** TruGlo fiber-optic, open fixed rear. **Features:** Velocity to 275. Cross-bolt trigger block safety. From Daisy Mfg. Co.
Price: **$35.99**

DAISY/POWERLINE TARGET PRO 953 AIR RIFLE

Caliber: .177 pellets, single shot. **Weight:** 6.40 lbs. **Length:** 39.75" overall. **Power:** Pneumatic single-pump cocking lever; straight-pull bolt. **Stock:** Full-length, match-style black composite. **Sights:** Front and rear fiber optic. **Features:** Rifled high-grade steel barrel with 1:15 twist. Max. Muzzle Velocity of 560 fps. From Daisy Mfg. Co.
Price: **$89.99**

DAISY/POWERLINE 880 AIR RIFLE

Caliber: .177 pellet or BB, 50-shot BB magazine, single shot for pellets. **Barrel:** Rifled steel. **Weight:** 3.7 lbs. **Length:** 37.6" overall. **Power:** Multi-pump pneumatic. **Stock:** Molded wood grain; Monte Carlo comb. **Sights:** Hooded front, adjustable rear. **Features:** Velocity to 685 fps. (BB). Variable power (velocity, range) increase with pump strokes; resin receiver with dovetailed scope mount. Made in U.S.A. by Daisy Mfg. Co.
Price: **$60.99**

DAISY/POWERLINE 901 AIR RIFLE

Caliber: .177. **Barrel:** Rifled steel. **Weight:** 3.7 lbs. **Length:** 37.5" overall. **Power:** Multi-pump pneumatic. **Stock:** Advanced composite. **Sights:** Fiber-optic front, adjustable rear. **Features:** Velocity to 750 fps. (BB); advanced composite receiver with dovetailed mounts for optics. Made in U.S.A. by Daisy Mfg. Co.
Price: **$66.99**

EAA/BAIKAL MP-512 AIR RIFLE

Caliber: 177, single shot. **Barrel:** 17.7". **Weight:** 6.2 lbs. **Length:** 41.3" overall. **Power:** Spring-piston, single stroke. **Stock:** Black synthetic. **Sights:** Adjustable rear, hooded front. **Features:** Velocity 490 fps. Hammer-forged, rifled barrel; automatic safety; scope mount rail. Imported from Russia by European American Armory.
Price: 177 caliber **$49.00**

EAA/BAIKAL IZH-61 AIR RIFLE

Caliber: 177 pellet, 5-shot magazine. **Barrel:** 17.8". **Weight:** 6.4 lbs. **Length:** 31" overall. **Power:** Spring-piston, side-cocking lever. **Stock:** Black plastic. **Sights:** Adjustable rear, fully hooded front. **Features:** Velocity 490 fps. Futuristic design with adjustable stock. Imported from Russia by European American Armory.
Price: **$99.00**

EAA/BAIKAL IZHMP-532 AIR RIFLE

Caliber: 177 pellet, single shot. **Barrel:** 15.8". **Weight:** 9.3 lbs. **Length:** 46.1" overall. **Power:** Single-stroke pneumatic. **Stock:** One- or two-piece competition-style stock with adjustable buttpad, pistol grip. **Sights:** Fully adjustable rear, hooded front. **Features:** Velocity 460 fps. Five-way adjustable trigger. Imported from Russia by European American Armory.
Price: **$599.00**

GAMO VIPER AIR RIFLE

Caliber: 177. **Barrel:** NA. **Weight:** 7.25 lbs. **Length:** 43.5". **Power:** Single-stroke pneumatic, 1200 fps. **Stock:** Synthetic. **Sights:** 3-9x40IR scope. **Features:** 30-pound cocking effort. Imported from Spain by Gamo.
Price: **$299.95**

GAMO HUNTER AIR RIFLES

Caliber: 177. **Barrel:** NA. **Weight:** 6.5-10.5 lbs. **Length:** 43.5-48.5". **Power:** Single-stroke pneumatifc, 850-1,000 fps. **Stock:** Wood. **Sights:** Varies by model **Features:** Adjustable two-stage trigger, rifled barrel, raised scope ramp on receiver. Realtree camo model available.
Price: Sport **$219.95**
Price: Pro **$279.95**

HAMMERLI AR 50 AIR RIFLE

Caliber: 177. **Barrel:** 19.8". **Weight:** 10 lbs. **Length:** 43.2" overall. **Power:** Compressed-air. **Stock:** Anatomically-shaped universal and right-hand; match style; multi-colored laminated wood. **Sights:** Interchangeable element tunnel front, adjustable Hammerli peep rear. **Features:** Vibration-free firing release; adjustable match trigger and trigger stop; stainless air tank, built-in pressure gauge. Gives 270 shots per filling. Imported from Switzerland by SIGARMS, Inc.
Price: **$1,653.00**

HAMMERLI MODEL 450 MATCH AIR RIFLE

Caliber: 177, single shot. **Barrel:** 19.5". **Weight:** 9.8 lbs. **Length:** 43.3" overall. **Power:** Pneumatic. **Stock:** Match style with stippled grip, rubber buttpad. Beech or walnut. **Sights:** Match tunnel front, Hammerli diopter rear. **Features:** Velocity about 560 fps. Removable sights; forend sling rail; adjustable trigger; adjustable comb. Imported from Switzerland by SIGARMS, Inc.
Price: Beech stock **$1,355.00**
Price: Walnut stock **$1,395.00**

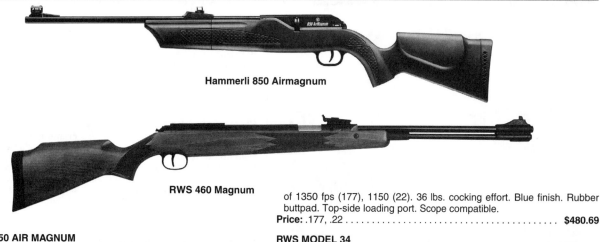

Hammerli 850 Airmagnum

RWS 460 Magnum

HAMMERLI 850 AIR MAGNUM
Caliber: .177, 22, 8-shot repeater. 23 1/2", rifled. **Weight:** 5.8 lbs. 41" overall. **Power:** 88g CO2. **Stock:** All-weather polymer, Monte Carlo, textured grip and forearm. **Sights:** Hooded fiber optic front, fiber optic adjustable rear. Velocity of 760 fps (177), 655 (22). Blue finish. Rubber buttpad. Bolt-Action. Scope compatible.
Price: .177, .22 . . . . **$248.08**

HAMMERLI STORM ELITE
Caliber: .177, single shot. 19 1/2", rifled. **Weight:** 6.8 lbs. 45 1/2" overall. **Power:** Spring-air, break-barrel cocking. **Stock:** Synthetic, burled wood look, checkered grip and forearm, cheekpiece. **Sights:** Hooded fiber optic front, fiber optic adjustable rear. Velocity of 1000 fps. 24 lbs. cocking effort. Nickel finish. Rubber buttpad. Scope compatible.
Price: **$222.31**

HAMMERLI RAZOR
Caliber: 177, 22, single shot. **Barrel:** 19", rifled. **Weight:** 17.5 lbs. **Length:** 45 1/2" overall. **Power:** Spring-air, break-barrel cocking. **Stock:** Vaporized beech wood, checkered grip and forearm, cheekpiece. Sleek curves. **Sights:** Hooded fiber optic front, fiber optic adjustable rear. **Features:** Velocity of 1000 fps (177), 820 (22). 35 lbs. cocking effort. Blued finish. Rubber buttpad. Scope compatible.
Price: **$309.23**

HAMMERLI NOVA
Caliber: .177, single shot. 18", rifled. **Weight:** 7.8 lbs. 45 1/2" overall. **Power:** Spring-air, under-lever cocking. **Stock:** Vaporized beech wood competition, checkered grip and forearm, cheekpiece. **Sights:** Hooded fiber optic front, fiber optic adjustable rear. Velocity of 1000 fps. 36 lbs. cocking effort. Blued finish. Rubber buttpad. Scope compatible.
Price: **$341.92**

HAMMERLI QUICK
Caliber: .177, single shot. 18 1/4", rifled. **Weight:** 5.5 lbs. 41" overall. **Power:** Spring-air, break-barrel cocking. **Stock:** Synthetic impact proof, checkered grip and forearm, cheekpiece. **Sights:** Hooded fiber optic front, fiber optic adjustable rear. Compact, light-weight. Velocity of 620 fps. 18 lbs. cocking effort. Blued finish. Rubber buttpad. Scope compatible. Automatic Safety.
Price: **$102.69**

RWS 460 MAGNUM
Caliber: .177, 22, single shot. 18 7/16", rifled. **Weight:** 8.3 lbs. 45" overall. **Power:** Spring-air, underlever cocking. **Stock:** American Sporter, checkered grip and forearm. **Sights:** Ramp front, adjustable rear. Velocity of 1350 fps (177), 1150 (22). 36 lbs. cocking effort. Blue finish. Rubber buttpad. Top-side loading port. Scope compatible.
Price: .177, .22 . . . . **$480.69**

RWS MODEL 34
Caliber: .177, .22, single shot. **Barrel:** 19 1/2", rifled. **Weight:** 7.3 lbs. Length: 45" overall. **Power:** Spring-air, break-barrel cocking. **Stock:** Wood. **Sights:** Hooded front, adjustable rear. **Features:** Velocity of 1000 fps (177), 800 (22). 33 lbs. cocking effort. Blued finish. Scope compatible.
Price: .177, .22 . . . . **$236.92**

RWS 34 PANTHER
Caliber: .177, .22, single shot. 19 3/4", rifled. **Weight:** 7.7 lbs. 46" overall. **Power:** Spring-air, break-barrel cocking. **Stock:** Synthetic black. **Sights:** Ramp fiber optic front, adjustable fiber optic rear. Velocity of 1000 fps (177), 800 (22). 33 lbs. cocking effort. Blued finish. Scope compatible. Automatic safety.
Price: .177, .22 . . . . **$236.92**

RWS 48
Caliber: 177, 22, single shot. 17", rifled, fixed. **Weight:** 9.0 lbs. 42 1/2" overall. **Power:** Spring-air, side-lever cocking. **Stock:** Wood stock. **Sights:** Adjustable front, adjustable rear. Velocity of 1100 fps (177), 900 (22). 39 lbs. cocking effort. Blued finish. Scope compatible. Automatic safety.
Price: .177, .22 . . . . **$409.23**

TECH FORCE 6 AIR RIFLE
Caliber: 177 pellet, single shot. **Barrel:** 14". **Weight:** 6 lbs. **Length:** 35.5" overall. **Power:** Spring-piston, sidelever action. **Stock:** Paratrooper-style folding, full pistol grip. **Sights:** Adjustable rear, hooded front. **Features:** Velocity 800 fps. All-metal construction; grooved for scope mounting. Imported from China by Compasseco, Inc.
Price: **$69.95**

TECH FORCE 25 AIR RIFLE
Caliber: 177, 22 pellet; single shot. **Barrel:** NA. **Weight:** 7.5 lbs. **Length:** 46.2" overall. **Power:** Spring piston, break-action barrel. **Stock:** Oil-finished wood; Monte Carlo stock with recoil pad. **Sights:** Adjustable rear, hooded front with insert. **Features:** Velocity 1,000 fps (177); grooved receiver and scope stop for scope mounting; adjustable trigger; trigger safety. Imported from China by Compasseco, Inc.
Price: 177 or 22 caliber **$125.00**
Price: Includes rifle and Tech Force 96 red dot point sight **$164.95**

WALTHER LEVER ACTION
Caliber: .177, 8-shot lever action. 18.9", rifled. **Weight:** 7.5 lbs. 38.3" overall. **Power:** two 12g CO2. **Stock:** Wood. **Sights:** Fixed front, adjustable rear. Classic design. Velocity of 630 fps. Scope compatible.
Price: **$269.18**

CH4D Heavyduty Champion

Frame: Cast iron
Die Thread: 7/8-14 or 1-14
Ram Stroke: 3-1/4"
Frame Type: O-frame
Avg. Rounds Per Hour: NA
Weight: 26 lbs.
Features: 1.185" diameter ram with 16 square inches of bearing surface; ram drilled to allow passage of spent primers; solid steel handle; toggle that slightly breaks over the top dead center. Includes universal primer arm with large and small punches. From CH Tool & Die/4D Custom Die.
Price:.. **$261.98**

CH4D No. 444 4-Station "H" Press

Frame: Aluminum alloy
Die Thread: 7/8-14
Ram Stroke: 3-3/4"
Frame Type: H-frame
Avg. Rounds Per Hour: 200
Weight: 21 lbs.
Features: Two 7/8" solid steel shaft "H" supports; platen rides on permanently lubed bronze bushings; loads smallest pistol to largest magnum rifle cases and has strength to full-length resize. Includes four rams, large and small primer arm and primer catcher. From CH Tool & Die/4D Custom Die, Co.
Price:.. **$235.46**

CH4D No. 444-X Pistol Champ

Frame: Aluminum alloy
Die Thread: 7/8-14
Ram Stroke: 3-3/4"
Frame Type: H-frame
Avg. Rounds Per Hour: 200
Weight: 12 lbs.
Features: Tungsten carbide sizing die; Speed Seater seating die with tapered entrance to automatically align bullet on case mouth; automatic primer feed for large or small primers; push-button powder measure with easily changed bushings for 215 powder/load combinations; taper crimp die. Conversion kit for caliber changeover available. From CH Tool & Die/4D Custom Die, Co.
Price:.............................. **$292.00 to $316.50**

CORBIN CSP-2 Mega Mite

Frame: Steel
Die Thread: 1.5x12
Ram Stroke: 6"
Frame Type: H-Frame
Avg. Rounds Per Hour: NA
Weight: 80 lbs.
Features: Handles 50 BMG and 20mm, smaller calibers with standard reloading adapter kit included. Die adapters for all threads available. Side-roller handle or extra long power handle, left- or right-hand operation. Ram is bearing guided. Uses standard Corbin-H swaging, drawing and jacket-making dies. Cold-forms lead bullets up to 12 gauge. Optional floor stand available.
Price:.. **$750.00**

CORBIN CSP-1H Hydro Mite Hydraulic Drawing/Swaging Press

Frame: Steel
Die Thread: 1.5x12
Ram Stroke: NA
Frame Type: Cabinet Mtg.
Avg. Rounds Per Hour: NA
Weight: 300 lbs.
Features: Reloads standard calibers, swages bullets up to 458 caliber, draws jackets and extrudes small diameter lead wire. Optional speed and thrust control unit available. Uses Corbin-S swaging and drawing dies. Comes with T-slot ram adapter for standard shell holders. Make free 22 and 6mm jackets from fired 22 cases using optional Corbin kit.
Price:...................................... **$2,995.00**

CORBIN Benchrest S-Press

Frame: All steel
Die Thread: 7/8-14 and T-slot adapter
Ram Stroke: 4" and 2"
Frame Type: O-Frame
Avg. Rounds Per Hour: NA
Weight: 22 lbs.
Features: Roller bearing linkage, removeable head, right- or left-hand mount.
Price:.. **$349.00**

FORSTER Co-Ax Press B-2

Frame: Cast iron
Die Thread: 7/8-14
Ram Stroke: 4"
Frame Type: Modified O-frame
Avg. Rounds Per Hour: 120
Weight: 18 lbs.
Features: Snap in/snap out die change; spent primer catcher with drop tube threaded into carrier below shellholder; automatic, handle-activated, cammed shellholder with opposing spring-loaded jaws to contact extractor groove; floating guide rods for alignment and reduced friction; no torque on the head due to design of linkage and pivots; shellholder jaws that float with die permitting case to center in the die; right- or left-hand operation; priming device for seating to factory specifications. "S" shellholder jaws included. From Forster Products.
Price:.. **$336.30**
Price: Extra LS shellholder jaws **$29.00**

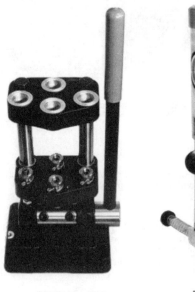

CH4D No. 444

CH4D 444-X Pistol Champ

Corbin CSP-1

Forster Co-Ax

METALLIC CARTRIDGE PRESSES

HOLLYWOOD Senior Press
Frame: Ductile iron
Die Thread: 7/8-14
Ram Stroke: 6-1/2"
Frame Type: O-frame
Avg. Rounds Per Hour: 50-100
Weight: 50 lbs.
Features: Leverage and bearing surfaces ample for reloading cartridges or swaging bullets. Precision ground one-piece 2-1/2" pillar with base; operating handle of 3/4" steel and 15" long; 5/8" steel tie-down rod for added strength when swaging; heavy steel toggle and camming arms held by 1/2" steel pins in reamed holes. The 1-1/2" steel die bushing takes standard threaded dies; removed, it allows use of Hollywood shotshell dies. From Hollywood Engineering.
Price: **$900.00**

HOLLYWOOD Senior Turret Press
Frame: Ductile iron
Die Thread: 7/8-14
Ram Stroke: 6-1/2"
Frame Type: H-frame
Avg. Rounds Per Hour: 50-100
Weight: 50 lbs.
Features: Same features as Senior press except has three-position turret head; holes in turret may be tapped 1-1/2" or 7/8" or four of each. Height 15". Comes complete with one turret indexing handle; one operating handle and three turret indexing handles; one 5/8" tie down bar for swaging. From Hollywood Engineering.
Price: **$1,000.00**

HORNADY Lock-N-Load Classic
Frame: Die cast heat-treated aluminum alloy
Die Thread: 7/8-14
Ram Stroke: 3-5/8"
Frame Type: O-frame
Avg. Rounds Per Hour: NA
Weight: 14 lbs.
Features: Features Lock-N-Load bushing system that allows instant die changeovers. Solid steel linkage arms that rotate on steel pins; 30° angled frame design for improved visibility and accessibility; primer arm automatically moves in and out of ram for primer pickup and solid seating; two primer arms for large and small primers; long offset handle for increased leverage and unobstructed reloading; lifetime warranty. Comes as a package with primer catcher, PPS automatic primer feed and three Lock-N-Load die bushings. Dies and shellholder available separately or as a kit with primer catcher, positive priming system, automatic primer feed, three die bushings and reloading accessories. From Hornady Mfg. Co.
Price: Press and Three Die Bushings **$129.44**
Price: Classic Reloading Kit **$347.06**

LEE Hand Press
Frame: ASTM 380 aluminum
Die Thread: 7/8-14
Ram Stroke: 3-1/4"
Frame Type: NA
Avg. Rounds Per Hour: 100
Weight: 1 lb., 8 oz.
Features: Small and lightweight for portability; compound linkage for handling up to 375 H&H and case forming. Dies and shellholder not included. From Lee Precision, Inc.
Price: **$29.98**

LEE Challenger Press
Frame: ASTM 380 aluminum
Die Thread: 7/8-14
Ram Stroke: 3-1/2"
Frame Type: O-frame
Avg. Rounds Per Hour: 100
Weight: 4 lbs., 1 oz.
Features: Larger than average opening with 30° offset for maximum hand clearance; steel connecting pins; spent primer catcher; handle adjustable for start and stop positions; handle repositions for left- or right-hand use; shortened handle travel to prevent springing the frame from alignment. Dies and shellholders not included. From Lee Precision, Inc.
Price: **$54.00**

LEE Classic Cast
Features: Cast iron, O-type. Adjustable handle moves from right to left, start and stop position is adjustable. Large 1-1/8" diameter hollow ram catches primers for disposal. Automatic primer arm with bottom of stroke priming. Two assembled primer arms included. From Lee Precision, Inc.
Price: **$115.00**

LEE Reloader Press
Frame: ASTM 380 aluminum
Die Thread: 7/8-14
Ram Stroke: 3"
Frame Type: C-frame
Avg. Rounds Per Hour: 100
Weight: 1 lb., 12 oz.
Features: Balanced lever to prevent pinching fingers; unlimited hand clearance; left- or right-hand use. Dies and shellholders not included. From Lee Precision, Inc.
Price: **$29.98**

Hollywood Senior Turret

Hornady Lock-N-Load Classic

Lee Hand Press

Lee Challenger

Lee Reloader

Lyman 310

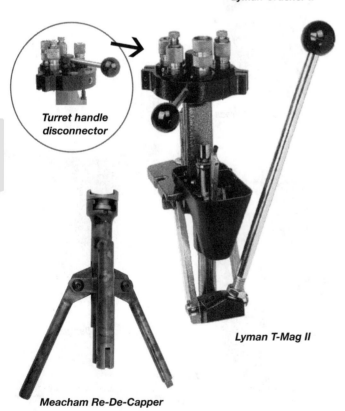

Lee Turret

Lyman Crusher II

Turret handle disconnector

Lyman T-Mag II

Meacham Re-De-Capper

LEE Turret Press

Frame: ASTM 380 aluminum
Die Thread: 7/8-14
Ram Stroke: 3"
Frame Type: O-frame
Avg. Rounds Per Hour: 300
Weight: 7 lbs., 2 oz.
Features: Replaceable turret lifts out by rotating 30°; T-primer arm reverses for large or small primers; built-in primer catcher; adjustable handle for right- or left-hand use or changing angle of down stroke; accessory mounting hole for Lee Auto-Disk powder measure. Optional Auto-Index rotates die turret to next station for semi-progressive use. Safety override prevents overstressing should turret not turn. From Lee Precision, Inc.
Price: **$79.98**
Price: Four-Hole Turret with Auto-Index **$89.98**
Price: Lee Classic Turret Press 90064 (2006) **$125.00**
Price: Lee Classic Cast 50 Cal BMG 90859 (2006) **$231.00**

LYMAN 310 Tool

Frame: Stainless steel
Die Thread: .609-30
Ram Stroke: NA
Frame Type: NA
Avg. Rounds Per Hour: NA
Weight: 10 oz.
Features: Compact, portable reloading tool for pistol or rifle cartridges. Adapter allows loading rimmed or rimless cases. Die set includes neck resizing/decapping die, primer seating chamber; neck expanding die; bullet seating die; and case head adapter. From Lyman Products Corp.
Price: Dies **$45.00**
Price: Handles **$47.50**
Price: Carrying pouch **$9.95**

LYMAN AccuPress

Frame: Die cast
Die Thread: 7/8-14
Ram Stroke: 3.4"
Frame Type: C-frame
Avg. Rounds Per Hour: 75
Weight: 4 lbs.
Features: Reversible, contoured handle for bench mount or hand-held use; for rifle or pistol; compound leverage; Delta frame design. Accepts all standard powder measures. From Lyman Products Corp.
Price: **$34.95**

LYMAN Crusher II

Frame: Cast iron
Die Thread: 7/8-14
Ram Stroke: 3-7/8"
Frame Type: O-frame
Avg. Rounds Per Hour: 75
Weight: 19 lbs.
Features: Reloads both pistol and rifle cartridges; 1" diameter ram; 4-1/2" press opening for loading magnum cartridges; direct torque design; right- or left-hand use. New base design with 14 square inches of flat mounting surface with three bolt holes. Comes with priming arm and primer catcher. Dies and shellholders not included. From Lyman Products Corp.
Price: **$116.50**

LYMAN T-Mag II

Frame: Cast iron with silver metalflake powder finish
Die Thread: 7/8-14
Ram Stroke: 3-13/16"
Frame Type: Turret
Avg. Rounds Per Hour: 125
Weight: 18 lbs.
Features: Re-engineered and upgraded with new turret system for ease of indexing and tool-free turret removal for caliber changeover; new flat machined base for bench mounting; new nickel-plated non-rust handle and links; and new silver hammertone powder coat finish for durability. Right- or left-hand operation; handles all rifle or pistol dies. Comes with priming arm and primer catcher. Dies and shellholders not included. From Lyman Products Corp.
Price: **$164.95**
Price: Extra turret **$37.50**

MEACHAM Anywhere Portable Reloading Press

Frame: Anodized 6061 T6 aircraft aluminum
Die Thread: 7/8-14
Ram Stroke: 2.7" (with docking kit)
Frame Type: Cylindrical
Avg. Rounds Per Hour: NA
Weight: 2 lbs. (hand held); 5 lbs.
Features: A lightweight portable press that can be used hand-held, or with a docking kit, can be clamped to a table top up to 9.75" thick. Docking kit includes a powder measure mount that clamps to the press body and a holder for the other die. Designed for neck sizing and bullet seating of short-action cartridges, it can be used for long-action cartridges with the addition of an Easy Seater straight line seating die. Dies not included.
Price: **$99.95**
Price: (with docking kit) **$144.95**
Price: Easy Seater **$114.95**
Price: Bushing type Neck Sizer **$74.95**
Price: Pope Style Re-De-Capper **$99.95**

METALLIC CARTRIDGE PRESSES

PONSNESS/WARREN Metal-Matic P-200
Frame: Die cast aluminum
Die Thread: 7/8-14
Frame Type: Unconventional
Avg. Rounds Per Hour: 200+
Weight: 18 lbs.
Features: Designed for straight-wall cartridges; die head with 10 tapped holes for holding dies and accessories for two calibers at one time; removable spent primer box; pivoting arm moves case from station to station. Comes with large and small primer tool. Optional accessories include primer feed, extra die head, primer speed feeder, powder measure extension and dust cover. Dies, powder measure and shellholder not included. From Ponsness/Warren.
Price: **$215.00**
Price: Extra die head **$44.95**
Price: Powder measure extension **$29.95**
Price: Primer feed **$44.95**
Price: Primer speed feed **$14.50**
Price: Dust cover **$21.95**

RCBS Partner
Frame: Aluminum
Die Thread: 7/8-14
Ram Stroke: 3-5/8"
Frame Type: O-frame
Avg. Rounds Per Hour: 50-60
Weight: 5 lbs.
Features: Designed for the beginning reloader. Comes with primer arm equipped with interchangeable primer plugs and sleeves for seating large and small primers. Shellholder and dies not included. Available in kit form (see Metallic Presses-Accessories). From RCBS.
Price: **$78.95**

RCBS AmmoMaster-2 Single Stage Press
Frame: Aluminum base; cast iron top plate connected by three steel posts
Die Thread: 1-1/4"-12 bushing; 7/8"-14 threads
Ram Stroke: 5-1/4"
Frame Type: NA
Avg. Rounds Per Hour: 50-60
Weight: 19 lbs.
Features: Single-stage press convertible to progressive. Will form cases or swage bullets. Case detection system to disengage powder measure when no case is present in powder charging station; five-station shellplate; Uniflow Powder measure with clear powder measure adaptor to make bridged powders visible and correctable. 50-cal. conversion kit allows reloading 50 BMG. Kit includes top plate to accommodate either 1-3/8" x 12 or 1-1/2" x 12 reloading dies. Piggyback die plate for quick caliber change-overs available. Reloading dies not included. From RCBS.
Price: AmmoMaster-2 No. 88703. .... **$292.95**
Price: 50 BMG 1-1/2" die kit No. 88705 .... **$417.95**
Price: 50 BMG 1-1/2" press conversion kit No. 88709 ...... **$137.95**
Price: Piggyback/AmmoMaster die plate **$34.95**
Price: Dust cover **$17.95**

RCBS Reloader Special-5
Frame: Aluminum
Die Thread: 1-1/4"-12 bushing; 7/8-14 threads
Ram Stroke: 3-1/16"
Frame Type: 30° offset O-frame
Avg. Rounds Per Hour: 50-60
Weight: 7.5 lbs.
Features: Single-stage press convertible to progressive with RCBS Piggyback II or 3. Primes cases during resizing operation. Will accept RCBS shotshell dies. From RCBS.
Price: **$139.95**

RCBS Rock Chucker Supreme
Frame: Cast iron
Die Thread: 1-1/4"-12 bushing; 7/8-14 threads
Ram Stroke: 4.25"
Frame Type: O-frame
Avg. Rounds Per Hour: 50-60
Weight: 17 lbs.
Features: Redesigned to allow loading of longer cartridge cases. Made for heavy-duty reloading, case forming and bullet swaging. Provides 4" of ram-bearing surface to support 1" ram and ensure alignment; ductile iron toggle blocks; hardened steel pins. Comes standard with Universal Primer Arm and primer catcher. Can be converted from single-stage to progressive with Piggyback II conversion unit. From RCBS.
Price: **$167.95**

REDDING T-7 Turret Press
Frame: Cast iron
Die Thread: 7/8-14
Ram Stroke: 3.4"
Frame Type: Turret
Avg. Rounds Per Hour: NA
Weight: 23 lbs., 2 oz.
Features: Strength to reload pistol and magnum rifle, linkage pins heat-treated, precision ground and in double shear; hollow ram to collect spent primers; removable turret head for caliber changes; progressive linkage for increased power as ram nears die; rear turret support for stability and precise alignment; 7-station turret head; priming arm for both large and small primers. Also available in kit form with shellholder and one die set. From Redding Reloading Equipment.
Price: **$357.00**
Price: Kit **$406.50**

REDDING Boss
Frame: Cast iron
Die Thread: 7/8-14
Ram Stroke: 3.4"
Frame Type: O-frame
Avg. Rounds Per Hour: NA
Weight: 11 lbs., 8 oz.
Features: 36° frame offset for visibility and accessibility; primer arm positioned at bottom ram travel; positive ram travel stop machined to hit exactly top-dead-center. Also available in kit form with shellholder and set of Redding A dies. From Redding Reloading Equipment.
Price: **$165.00**
Price: Kit **$214.50**
Price: Big Boss Press (heavier frame, longer stroke for mag. cartridges) .... **$205.50 to $255.50**

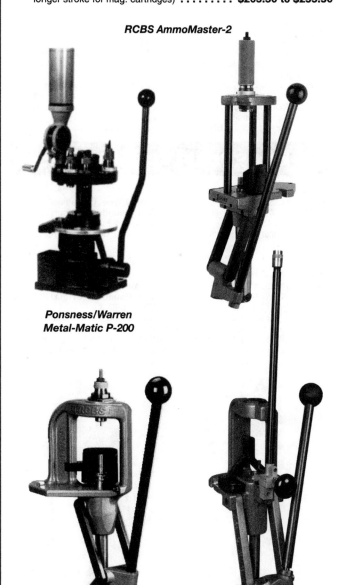

RCBS AmmoMaster-2

Ponsness/Warren Metal-Matic P-200

RCBS Reloader Special-5

RCBS Rock Crusher Supreme

METALLIC CARTRIDGE PRESSES

REDDING Ultramag

Frame: Cast iron
Die Thread: 7/8-14
Ram Stroke: 4-1/8"

Frame Type: Non-conventional
Avg. Rounds Per Hour: NA
Weight: 23 lbs., 6 oz.

Features: Unique compound leverage system connected to top of press for tons of ram pressure for case forming and bullet swaging; large 4-3/4" frame opening for loading oversized cartridges; hollow ram for spent primers. Kit available with shellholder and one set Redding A dies. From Redding Reloading Equipment.

Price: $372.00
Price: Kit $421.50

ROCK CRUSHER Press

Frame: Cast iron
Die Thread: 2-3/4"-12 with bushing reduced to 1-1/2"-12
Ram Stroke: 6"

Frame Type: O-frame
Avg. Rounds Per Hour: 50

Weight: 67 lbs.

Features: Designed to load and form ammunition from 50 BMG up to 23x115 Soviet. Frame opening of 8-1/2" x 3-1/2"; 1-1/2" x 12"; bushing can be removed and bushings of any size substituted; ram pressure can exceed 10,000 lbs. with normal body weight; 40mm diameter ram. Angle block for bench mounting and reduction bushing for RCBS dies available. Accessories for Rock Crusher include powder measure, dies, shellholder, bullet puller, priming tool, case gauge and others. From The Old Western Scrounger.

Price: $795.00
Price: Angle block $57.95
Price: Reduction bushing $21.00
Price: Shellholder $47.25
Price: Priming tool, 50 BMG, 20 Lahti $65.10

Progressive Presses

CORBIN Benchrest S-Press

Frame: All steel
Die Thread: 7/8-14 and T-slot adapter
Ram Stroke: 4" and 2"

Frame Type: O-Frame
Avg. Rounds Per Hour: NA
Weight: 22 lbs.

Features: Roller bearing linkage, removeable head, right- or left-hand mount.

Price: $329.00

DILLON RL 550B

Frame: Aluminum alloy
Die Thread: 7/8-14
Ram Stroke: 3-7/8"

Frame Type: NA
Avg. Rounds Per Hour: 500-600
Weight: 25 lbs.

Features: Four stations; removable tool head to hold dies in alignment and allow caliber changes without die adjustment; auto priming system that emits audible warning when primer tube is low; a 100-primer capacity magazine contained in DOM steel tube for protection; new auto powder measure system with simple mechanical connection between measure and loading platform for positive powder bar return; a separate station for crimping with star-indexing system; 220 ejected-round capacity bin; 3/4-lb. capacity powder measure. Height above bench, 35"; requires 3/4" bench overhang. Will reload 120 different rifle and pistol calibers. Comes with one caliber conversion kit. Dies not included. From Dillon Precision Products, Inc.

Price: $379.95

DILLON Super 1050

Frame: Ductile iron
Die Thread: 7/8-14

Frame Type: Platform type
Avg. Rounds Per Hour: 1000-1200

Ram Stroke: 2-5/16"
Weight: 62 lbs.

Features: Eight stations; auto case feed; primer pocket swager for military cartridge cases; auto indexing; removable tool head; auto prime system with 100-primer capacity; low primer supply alarm; positive powder bar return; auto powder measure; 515 ejected round bin capacity; 500-600 case feed capacity; 3/4-lb. capacity powder measure. Has lengthened frame and short-stroke crank to accommodate long calibers. Loads all pistol rounds as well as 30 M1 Carbine, 223, and 7.62x39 rifle rounds. Height above the bench, 43". Dies not included. From Dillon Precision Products, Inc.

Price: $1,499.95

DILLON Square Deal B

Frame: Zinc alloy
Die Thread: None (unique Dillon design)
Ram Stroke: 2-5/16"

Frame Type: NA
Avg. Rounds Per Hour: 400-500

Weight: 17 lbs.

Features: Four stations; auto indexing; removable tool head; auto prime system with 100-primer capacity; low primer supply alarm; auto powder measure; positive powder bar return; 170 ejected round capacity bin; 3/4-lb. capacity powder measure. Height above the bench, 34". Comes complete with factory adjusted carbide die set. From Dillon Precision Products, Inc.

Price: $319.95

DILLON XL 650

Frame: Aluminum alloy
Die Thread: 7/8-14

Frame Type: NA
Avg. Rounds Per Hour: 800-1000

Ram Stroke: 4-9/16"
Weight: 46 lbs.

Features: Five stations; auto indexing; auto case feed; removable tool head; auto prime system with 100-primer capacity; low primer supply alarm; auto powder measure; positive powder bar return; 220 ejected round capacity bin; 3/4-lb. capacity powder measure. 500-600 case feed capacity with optional auto case feed. Loads all pistol/rifle calibers less than 3-1/2" in length. Height above the bench, 44"; 3/4" bench overhang required. From Dillon Precision Products, Inc.

Price: Less dies $489.95

Redding Boss

Redding Turret Press

Redding Ultramag

Dillon RL 550B

METALLIC CARTRIDGE PRESSES

HORNADY Lock-N-Load AP
Frame: Die cast heat-treated aluminum alloy
Frame Type: O-frame
Die Thread: 7/8-14
Avg. Rounds Per Hour: NA
Ram Stroke: 3-3/4"
Weight: 26 lbs.
Features: Features Lock-N-Load bushing system that allows instant die changeovers; five-station die platform with option of seating and crimping separately or adding taper-crimp die; auto prime with large and small primer tubes with 100-primer capacity and protective housing; brass kicker to eject loaded rounds into 80-round capacity cartridge catcher; offset operating handle for leverage and unobstructed operation; 2" diameter ram driven by heavy-duty cast linkage arms rotating on steel pins. Comes with five Lock-N-Load die bushings, shellplate, deluxe powder measure, auto powder drop, and auto primer feed and shut-off, brass kicker and primer catcher. Lifetime warranty. From Hornady Mfg. Co.
Price: **$416.38**

LEE Load-Master
Frame: ASTM 380 aluminum
Frame Type: O-frame
Die Thread: 7/8-14
Avg. Rounds Per Hour: 600
Ram Stroke: 3-1/4"
Weight: 8 lbs., 4 oz.
Features: Available in kit form only. A 1-3/4" diameter hard chrome ram for han-dling largest magnum cases; loads rifle or pistol rounds; five station press to fac-tory crimp and post size; auto indexing with wedge lock mechanism to hold one ton; auto priming; removable turrets; four-tube case feeder with optional case collator and bullet feeder (late 1995); loaded round ejector with chute to optional loaded round catcher; quick change shellplate; primer catcher. Dies and shell-holder for one caliber included. From Lee Precision, Inc.
Price: Rifle **$320.00**
Price: Pistol **$330.00**
Price: Extra turret **$14.98**
Price: Adjustable charge bar **$9.98**

LEE Pro 1000
Frame: ASTM 380 aluminum and steel
Frame Type: O-frame
Die Thread: 7/8-14
Avg. Rounds Per Hour: 600
Ram Stroke: 3-1/4"
Weight: 8 lbs., 7 oz.
Features: Optional transparent large/small or rifle case feeder; deluxe auto-disk case-activated powder measure; case sensor for primer feed. Comes complete with carbide die set (steel dies for rifle) for one caliber. Optional accessories include: case feeder for large/small pistol cases or rifle cases; shell plate carrier with auto prime, case ejector, auto-index and spare parts; case collator for case feeder. From Lee Precision, Inc.
Price: **$215.98**

PONSNESS/WARREN Metallic II
Frame: Die cast aluminum
Frame Type: H-frame
Die Thread: 7/8-14
Avg. Rounds Per Hour: 150+
Ram Stroke: NA
Weight: 32 lbs.
Features: Die head with five tapped 7/8-14 holes for dies, powder measure or other accessories; pivoting die arm moves case from station to station; depriming tube for removal of spent primers; auto primer feed; interchangeable die head. Optional accessories include additional die heads, powder measure extension tube to accommodate any standard powder measure, primer speed feeder to feed press primer tube without disassembly. Comes with small and large primer seating tools. Dies, powder measure and shellholder not included. From Ponsness/ Warren.
Price: **$375.00**
Price: Extra die head **$56.95**
Price: Primer speed feeder **$14.50**
Price: Powder measure extension **$29.95**
Price: Dust cover **$27.95**

RCBS Pro 2000™
Frame: Cast iron
Frame Type: H-Frame
Die Thread: 7/8-14
Avg. Rounds Per Hour: 500-600
Ram Stroke: NA
Weight: NA
Features: Five-station manual indexing; full-length sizing; removable die plate; fast caliber conversion. Uses APS Priming System. From RCBS.
Price: **$616.95**

RCBS Turret Press
Frame: Cast iron
Frame Type: NA
Die Thread: 7/8-14
Avg. Rounds Per Hour: 50 to 200
Ram Stroke: NA
Weight: NA
Features: Six-station turret head; positive alignment; on-press priming.
Price: **$243.95**

STAR Universal Pistol Press
Frame: Cast iron w/aluminum base
Frame Type: Unconventional
Die Thread: 11/16-24 or 7/8-14
Avg. Rounds Per Hour: 300
Ram Stroke: NA
Weight: 27 lbs.
Features: Four or five-station press depending on need to taper crimp; handles all popular handgun calibers from 32 Long to 45 Colt. Comes completely assembled and adjusted with carbide dies (except 30 Carbine) and shellholder to load one caliber. Prices slightly higher for 9mm and 30 Carbine. From Star Machine Works.
Price: With taper crimp **$1,055.00**
Price: Without taper crimp **$1,025.00**
Price: Extra tool head, taper crimp **$425.00**
Price: Extra tool head, w/o taper crimp **$395.00**

Hornady Lock-N-Load

RCBS Pro 2000™

Lee Load-Master

Fully-automated Star Universal

DILLON SL 900

Press Type: Progressive
Avg. Rounds Per Hour: 700-900
Weight: 51 lbs.
Features: 12-ga. only; factory adjusted to load AA hulls; extra large 25-pound capacity shot hopper; fully-adjustable case-activated shot system; hardened steel starter crimp die; dual-action final crimp and taper die; tilt-out wad guide; auto prime; auto index; strong mount machine stand. From Dillon Precision Products.
Price: **$914.90**

Dillon SL 900

Hollywood Automatic

HOLLYWOOD Automatic Shotshell Press

Press Type: Progressive
Avg. Rounds Per Hour: 1,800
Weight: 100 lbs.
Features: Ductile iron frame; fully automated press with shell pickup and ejector; comes completely set up for one gauge; one crimps; one finish crimp; wad guide for plastic wads; decap and powder dispenser unit; one wrench for inside die lock screw; one medium and one large spanner wrench for spanner nuts; one shellholder; powder and shot measures. Available for 10, 12, 20, 28 or 410. From Hollywood Engineering.
Price: **$5,000.00**

HOLLYWOOD Senior Turret Press

Press Type: Turret
Avg. Rounds Per Hour: 200
Weight: 50 lbs.
Features: Multi-stage press constructed of ductile iron comes completely equipped to reload one gauge; one starter crimp; one finish crimp; wad guide for plastic wads; decap and powder dispenser unit; one wrench for inside die lock screw; one medium and one large spanner wrench for spanner nuts; one shellholder; powder and shot measures. Available for 10, 12, 16, 20, 28 or 410. From Hollywood Engineering.
Price: Press only **$1,000.00**
Price: Dies **$200.00**

Hollywood Senior Turret Press

Hornady 366 Auto

HORNADY 366 Auto

Press Type: Progressive
Avg. Rounds Per Hour: NA
Weight: 25 lbs.
Features: Heavy-duty die cast and machined steel body and components; auto primer feed system; large capacity shot and powder tubes; adjustable for right- or left-hand use; automatic charge bar with shutoff; swing-out wad guide; primer catcher at base of press; interchangeable shot and powder bushings; life-time warranty. Available for 12, 20, 28 2-3/4" and 410 2-1/2". From Hornady Mfg. Co.
Price: **$575.05**
Price: Die set, 12, 20, 28 .... **$202.77**
Price: Magnum conversion dies, 12, 20 .... **$43.25**

LEE Load-All

Press Type: Single stage
Avg. Rounds Per Hour: 100
Weight: 3 lbs. 3 oz.
Features: Loads steel or lead shot; built-in primer catcher at base with door in front for emptying; recesses at each station for shell positioning; optional primer feed. Comes with safety charge bar with 24 shot and powder bushings. Available for 12-, 16-or 20-gauge. From Lee Precision, Inc.
Price: **$52.98**

MEC 600 Jr. Mark V

Press Type: Single stage
Avg. Rounds Per Hour: 150
Weight: 16 lbs.
Features: Spindex crimp starter for shell alignment during crimping; a cam-action crimp die; Pro-Check to keep charge bar properly positioned; adjustable for three shells. Available in 10, 12, 16, 20, 28 gauges and 410 bore. Die set not included. From Mayville Engineering Company, Inc.
Price: **$120.32**
Price: Die set **$67.27**

Lee Load-All

MEC 600 Jr. Mark V

MEC 650N

Press Type: Progressive
Avg. Rounds Per Hour: 400
Weight: 19 lbs.
Features: Six-station press; does not resize except as separate operation; auto primer feed standard; three crimping stations for starting, closing and tapering crimp. Die sets not available. Available in 12, 16, 20, 28 and 410. From Mayville Engineering Company, Inc.
Price: **$240.00**

SHOTSHELL RELOADING PRESSES

MEC 8567N Grabber

Press Type: Progressive
Avg. Rounds Per Hour: 400
Weight: 22 lbs.
Features: Six-station press; auto primer feed; auto-cycle charging; three-stage crimp; power ring resizer returns base to factory specs; resizes high and low base shells; optional kits to reload three shells and steel shot. Available in 12, 16, 20, 28 gauge and 410 bore. From Mayville Engineering Company, Inc.
Price: $338.00
Price: 3" kit, 12-ga. $79.32
Price: 3" kit, 20-ga. $45.32
Price: Steel shot kit $39.65

MEC 9000GN

Press Type: Progressive
Avg. Rounds Per Hour: 400
Weight: 27 lbs.
Features: All same features as the MEC Grabber but with auto-indexing and auto-eject. Finished shells automatically ejected from shell carrier to drop chute for boxing. Available in 12, 16, 20, 28 and 410. From Mayville Engineering Company, Inc.
Price: $407.00

MEC 9000HN

Press Type: Progressive
Avg. Rounds Per Hour: 400
Weight: 31 lbs.
Features: Same features as 9000GN with addition of foot pedal-operated hydraulic system for complete automation. Operates on standard 110V household current. Comes with bushing-type charge bar and three bushings. Available in 12, 16, 20, 28 gauge and 410 bore. From Mayville Engineering Company, Inc.
Price: $958.00

MEC 8120 Sizemaster

Press Type: Single stage
Avg. Rounds Per Hour: 150
Weight: 20 lbs.
Features: Power ring eight-fingered collet resizer returns base to factory specs; handles brass or steel, high or low base heads; auto primer feed; adjustable for three shells. Available in 10, 12, 16, 20, 28 gauges and 410 bore. From Mayville Engineering Company, Inc.
Price: $182.18
Price: Die set, 12, 16, 20, 28, 410 . . . . $100.47
Price: Die set, 10-ga. $117.92

MEC Steelmaster

Press Type: Single stage
Avg. Rounds Per Hour: 150
Weight: 20 lbs.
Features: Same features as Sizemaster except can load steel shot. Press is available for 3-1/2" 10-ga. and 12-ga. 2-3/4", 3" or 3-1/2". For loading lead shot, die sets available in 10, 12, 16, 20, 28 and 410. From Mayville Engineering Company, Inc.
Price: $196.79
Price: 12 ga. 3-1/2" $220.41

PONSNESS/WARREN Du-O-Matic 375C

Press Type: Progressive
Avg. Rounds Per Hour: NA
Weight: 31 lbs.
Features: Steel or lead shot reloader; large shot and powder reservoirs; bushing access plug for dropping in shot buffer or buckshot; positive lock charging ring to prevent accidental flow of powder; double-post construction for greater leverage; removable spent primer box; spring-loaded ball check for centering size die at each station; tip-out wad guide; two-gauge capacity tool head. Available in 10 (extra charge), 12, 16, 20, 28 and 410 with case lengths of 2-1/2", 2-3/4", 3" and 3-1/2". From Ponsness/ Warren.
Price: 12-, 20-, and 28-ga., 2-3/4" and 410, 2-1/2" $289.00
Price: 12-ga. 3-1/2"; 3" 12, 20, 410 . . . . $305.00
Price: 12, 20 2-3/4" $383.95
Price: 10-ga. press $315.00

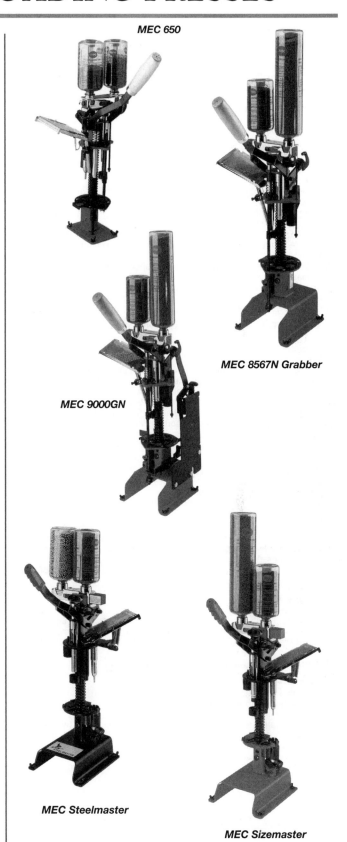

MEC 650

MEC 8567N Grabber

MEC 9000GN

MEC Steelmaster

MEC Sizemaster

PONSNESS/WARREN Hydro-Multispeed

Hydraulic system developed for Ponsness/Warren L/S-1000. Usable for the 950, 900 and 800 series presses. Three reloading speed settings operated with variable foot pedal control. Features stop/reverse at any station; automatic shutdown with pedal control release; fully adjustable hydraulic cylinder rod to prevent racking or bending of machine; quick disconnect hoses for ease of installation. Preassembled with step-by-step instructions. From Ponsness/Warren.
Price: **$879.00**
Price: Cylinder kit **$399.95**

PONSNESS/WARREN L/S-1000

Frame: Die cast aluminum
Avg. Rounds Per Hour: NA
Weight: 55 lbs.
Features: Fully progressive press to reload steel, bismuth or lead shot. Equipped with new Uni-Drop shot measuring and dispensing system which allows the use of all makes of shot in any size. Shells automatically resized and deprimed with new Auto-Size and De-Primer system. Loaded rounds drop out of shellholders when completed. Each shell pre-crimped and final crimped with Tru-Crimp system. Available in 10-gauge 3-1/2" or 12-gauge 2-3/4" and 3". 12-gauge 3-1/2" conversion kit also available. 20-gauge 2-3/4" and 3" special order only. From Ponsness/Warren.
Price: 12 ga. **$849.00**
Price: 10 ga. **$895.00**
Price: Conversion kit **$199.00**

PONSNESS/WARREN Size-O-Matic 900 Elite

Press Type: Progressive
Avg. Rounds Per Hour: 500-800
Weight: 49 lbs.
Features: Progressive eight-station press; frame of die-cast aluminum; center post design index system ensures positive indexing; timing factory set, drilled and pinned. Automatic features include index, deprime, reprime, powder and shot drop, crimp start, tapered final crimp, finished shell ejection. Available in 12, 20, 28 and 410. 16-ga. special order. Kit includes new shellholders, seating port, resize/primer knockout assembly, new crimp assembly. From Ponsness/Warren.
Price: **$749.00**
Price: Conversion tooling, 12, 20, 28, 410 . . . . **$189.00**

PONSNESS/WARREN Platinum 2000

Press Type: Progressive
Avg. Rounds Per Hour: 500-800
Weight: 52 lbs.
Features: Progressive eight-station press, similar to 900 and 950 except has die removal system that allows removal of any die component during reloading cycle. Comes standard with 25-lb. shot tube, 19" powder tube, brass adjustable priming feed allows adjustment of primer seating depth. From Ponsness/Warren.
Price: **$889.00**

RCBS The Grand

Press Type: Progressive
Avg. Rounds Per Hour: NA
Weight: NA
Features: Constructed from a high-grade aluminum casting, allows complete resizing of high and low base hulls. Available for 12 and 20 gauge.
Price: **$812.95**

RCBS Mini-Grand

Press Type: Progressive
Avg. Rounds Per Hour: 200
Weight: NA
Features: 7-station single-stage press, lead or steel reloading (with steel accessories). 12-gauge version loads 2-3/4" to 3-1/2" shells; 20-gauge product load 2-3/4" to 3" shotshells.
Price: **$147.95**

Ponsness/Warren Du-O-Matic 375C

Ponsness/Warren Size-O-Matic 900 Elite

RCBS The Grand

RCBS Mini-Grand

Maker and Model	Magn.	Field at 100 Yds. (feet)	Eye Relief (in.)	Length (in.)	Tube Dia. (in.)	W & E Adjustments	Weight (ozs.)	Price	Other Data
ADCO									[1]Multi-Color Dot system changes from red to green. [2]For airguns, paint ball, rimfires. Uses common lithium water battery. [3]Comes with standard dovetail mount. [4]10 MOA dot; black or nickel. [5]Square format; with mount battery. From ADCO Sales.
Magnum 50mm[5]	0			4.1	45 mm	Int.	6.8	$269.00	
MIRAGE Ranger 1"	0			5.2	1	Int.	3.9	159.00	
MIRAGE Ranger 30mm	0			5.5	30mm	Int.	5	159.00	
MIRAGE Competitor	0			5.5	30mm	Int.	5.5	229.00	
IMP Sight[2]	0			4.5		Int.	1.3	17.95	
Square Shooter 2[3]	0			5		Int.	5	99.00	
MIRAGE Eclipse[1]	0			5.5	30mm	Int.	5.5	229.00	
Champ Red Dot	0			4.5		Int.	2	33.95	
Vantage 1"	0			3.9	1	Int.	3.9	129.00	
Vantage 30mm	0			4.2	30mm	Int.	4.9	159.00	
Vision 2000[6]	0	60		4.7		Int.	6.2	79.00	
e-dot ESB[1]	0			4.12	1	Int.	3.7	139.00	
e-dot E1B	0			4.12	1	Int.	3.7	99.00	
e-dot ECB	0			3.8	30mm	Int.	6.4	99.00	
e-dot E30B	0			4.3	30mm	Int.	4.6	99.00	
AIMPOINT									Illuminates red dot in field of view. No parallax (dot does not need to be centered). Unlimited field of view and eye relief. On/off, adj. intensity. Comp M2 Series: Standard CQB sight for Special Forces. CET technology. Rings-SRP-L and QRP fit Picatinny rails. QRW fits Weaver mount. QR = Quick Release. Comp M3 Series: Compact for bows, pistols. Black matte and silver metallic finishes (SM). Rings SRW-L, SRP-M, SRW-M. 9000 Series: Matte black and camo finishes. ACET technology. 30mm rings fit on Weaver rail, No 11286. [1]Comes with 30mm rings, battery, lense cloth. [2]Requires 1" rings. Black finish. AP Comp avail. in black, blue, SS, camo.
Comp M2	0			5.1	30mm	Int.	7.8	471.00	
Comp ML2	0			5.1	30mm	Int.	7.8	422.00	
Comp ML2 2X	2			6.5	30mm	Int.	10.3	551.00	
Comp M3	0			5.1	30mm	Int.	7.8	535.00	
Comp ML3	0			5.1	30mm	Int.	7.8	480.00	
9000L	0			7.9	30mm	Int.	8.1	370.00	
9000L 2X	2			9.3	30mm	Int.	8.1	470.00	
9000SC	0			6.3	30mm	Int.	7.4	370.00	
9000SC Camo	0			6.3	30mm	Int.	7	390.00	
9000SC 2X	2			7.7	30mm	Int.	9.9	470.00	
Comp C3	0			4.9	30mm	Int.	7.1	399.00	
Comp C3 2X	2			6.1	30mm	Int.	9.5	507.00	
Comp SM	0			4.9	30mm	Int.	7.1	372.00	
Comp M[2]	0			5	30mm	Int.	6.1	409.00	
	0			6	30mm	Int.	6	297.00	
Series 3000 Universal[2]	0			6.25	1	Int.	6	232.00	
Series 5000/2x[1]	2			7	30mm	Int.	9	388.00	
APEX									
Model 4030		3-9x		40/14	42mm	Int.		250.00	
Model 4035		3.5-10x		28/10	50mm	Int.		285.00	
Model 4040		4-16x		23.6/6.2	50mm	Int.		300.00	
Model 4045		6-24x		15/4	50mm	Int.		310.00	
ARTEMIS 2000									Click-stop windage and elevation adjustments; constantly centered reticle; rubber eyepiece ring; nitrogen filled. Imported from the Czech Republic by CZ-USA.
4x32	4	34.4	3.15	10.7	1	Int.	17.5	215.00	
6x42	6	23	3.15	13.7	1	Int.	17.5	317.00	
7x50	7	18.7	3.15	13.9	1	Int.	17.5	329.00	
1.5-6x42	1.5-6	40-12.8	2.95	12.4	30mm	Int.	19.4	522.00	
2-8x42	2-8	31-9.5	2.95	13.1	30mm	Int.	21.1	525.00	
3-9x42	3-9	24.6-8.5	2.95	12.4	30mm	Int.	19.4	466.00	
3-12x50	3-12	20.6-6.2	2.95	14	30mm	Int.	22.9	574.00	
BEC									Black matte finish. Multi-coated lenses; 1/4-MOA click adjustments (1/2-MOA on EL4x25, AR4x22WA); fog and water-proof. [1]For AR-15; bullet drop compensator; q.d. mount. [2]Rubber armored. Imported by BEC Inc. Partial listing shown. Contact BEC for complete details. [3]All Goldlabel scopes feature lighted reticles and finger-adjustable windage and elevation adjustments. [4]Bullet-drop compensator system for Mini-14 and AR-15 rifles.
EuroLux									
EL2510x56	2.5-10	39.4-11.5	3.25-2	15.1	30mm	Int.	25.4	249.90	
EL39x42	3-9	34.1-13.2	3.5-3	12.3	30mm	Int.	17.7	99.80	
EL28x36	2-8	44.9-11.5	3.8-3	12.2	30mm	Int.	15.9	149.50	
ELA39x40RB[2]	3-9	39-13	3	12.7	30mm	Int.	14.3	95.95	
EL6x42	6	21	3	12.6	30mm	Int.	14.8	69.00	
EL4x42	4	29	3	12.6	30mm	Int.	14.8	59.60	
EL4x36	4	29	3	12	30mm	Int.	14	49.90	
EL4x25	4	26	3	7	30mm	Int.	7.6	37.00	
AR4x22WA[1]	4	24	3	7	34mm	Int.	13.6	109.97	
Goldlabel[3]									
GLI 624x50	6-24	16-4	3.5-3	15.3	1	Int.	22.5	139.00	
GLI 416x50	4-16	25-6	3.5-3	13.5	1	Int.	21.8	135.00	
GLI 39x40R[2]	3-9	39-13	3.5-3	12.7	28mm	Int.	18.5	99.00	
GLC 5x42BD[4]	5	24	3.5	8.7	1	Int.	16.5	79.00	

SCOPES / Hunting, Target & Varmint

Maker and Model	Magn.	Field at 100 Yds. (feet)	Eye Relief (in.)	Length (in.)	Tube Dia. (in.)	W & E Adjustments	Weight (ozs.)	Price	Other Data
BEEMAN									
Rifle Scopes									All scopes have 5 point reticle, all glass fully-coated lenses. [1]Parallel adjustable. Imported by Beeman.
5045[1]	4-12	26.9-9	3	13.2	1	Int.	15	**275.00**	
5046[1]	6-24	18-4.5	3	16.9	1	Int.	20.2	**395.00**	
5050[1]	4	26	3.5	11.7	1	Int.	11	**80.00**	
5055[1]	3-9	38-13	3.5	10.75	1	Int.	11.2	**90.00**	
5060[1]	4-12	30-10	3	12.5	1	Int.	16.2	**210.00**	
5065[1]	6-18	17-6	3	14.7	1	Int.	17.3	**265.00**	
Pistol Scopes									
5021	2	19	10-24	9.1	1	Int.	7.4	**85.50**	
5020	1.5	14	11-16	8.3	.75	Int.	3.6	**NA**	
BSA									
Catseye[1]									[1]Waterproof, fogproof; multi-coated lenses; finger-adjustable knobs. [2]Waterproof, fogproof; matte black finish. [3]With 4" sunshade; target knobs; 1/8-MOA click adjustments. [4]Adjustable for parallax; with sun shades; target knobs, 1/8-MOA adjustments. Imported by BSA. [5]Red dot sights also available in 42mm and 50mm versions. [6]Includes Universal Bow Mount. [7]Five other models offered. From BSA.
CE1545x32	1.5-4.5	78-23	4	11.25	1	Int.	12	**91.95**	
CE310x44	3-10	39-12	3.25	12.75	1	Int.	16	**151.95**	
CE3510x50	3.5-10	30-10.5	3.25	13.25	1	Int.	17.25	**171.95**	
CE416x50	4-16	25-6	3	15.25	1	Int.	22	**191.95**	
CE624x50	6-24	16-3	3	16	1	Int.	23	**222.95**	
CE1545x32IR	1.5-4.5	78-23	5	11.25	1	Int.	12	**121.95**	
Deer Hunter[2]									
DH25x20	2.5	72	6	7.5	1	Int.	7.5	**59.95**	
DH4x32	4	32	3	12	1	Int.	12.5	**49.95**	
DH39x32	3-9	39-13	3	12	1	Int.	11	**69.95**	
DH39x40	3-9	39-13	3	13	1	Int.	12.1	**89.95**	
DH39x50	3-9	41-15	3	12.75	1	Int.	13	**109.95**	
DH2510x44	2.5-10	42-12	3	13	1	Int.	12.5	**99.95**	
DH1545x32	1.5-4.5	78-23	5	11.25	1	Int.	12	**79.95**	
Contender[3]									
CT24x40TS	24	6	3	15	1	Int.	18	**129.95**	
CT36x40TS	36	3	3	15.25	1	Int.	19	**139.95**	
CT312x40TS	3-12	28-7	3	13	1	Int.	17.5	**129.95**	
CT416x40TS	4-16	21-5	3	13.5	1	Int.	18	**131.95**	
CT624x40TS	6-24	16-4	3	15.5	1	Int.	20	**149.95**	
CT832x40TS	8-32	11-3	3	15.5	1	Int.	20	**171.95**	
CT312x50TS	3-12	28-7	3	13.75	1	Int.	21	**131.95**	
CT416x50TS	4-16	21-5	3	15.25	1	Int.	22	**151.95**	
CT624x50TS	6-24	16-4	3	16	1	Int.	23	**171.95**	
CT832x50TS	8-32	11-3	3	16.5	1	Int.	24	**191.95**	
Pistol									
P52x20	2	NA	NA	NA	NA	Int.	NA	**89.95**	
Platinum[4]									
PT24x44TS	24	4.5	3	16.25	1	Int.	17.9	**189.55**	
PT36x44TS	36	3	3	14.9	1	Int.	17.9	**199.95**	
PT624x44TS	6-24	15-4.5	3	15.25	1	Int.	18.5	**221.95**	
PT832x44TS	8-32	11-3.5	3	17.25	1	Int.	19.5	**229.95**	
.22 Special									
S39x32WR	3-9	37.7-14.1	3	12	1	Int.	12.3	**89.95**	
S4x32WR	4	26	3	10.75	1	Int.	9	**39.95-44.95**	
Air Rifle									
AR4x32	4	33	3	13	1	Int.	14	**69.95**	
AR27x32	2-7	48	3	12.25	1	Int.	14	**79.95**	
AR312x44	3-12	36	3	12.25	1	Int.	15	**109.95**	
Red Dot									
RD30[5]	0			3.8	30mm	Int.	5	**59.95**	
PB30[5]	0			3.8	30mm	Int.	4.5	**79.95**	
Bow30[6]	0			NA	30mm	Int.	5	**89.95**	
Big Cat									
BlgCat[7]	3.5-10	30-11	5	9.7	1	Int.	16.8	**219.95**	
BURRIS									
Mr. T Black Diamond Titanium									
2.5-10x50A	2.5-10	4.25-4.75		13.6			29	**1,518.00**	
4-16x50	4-16	27-7.5	3.3-3.8	13.6	30mm	Int.	27	**1,594.00**	

Maker and Model	Magn.	Field at 100 Yds. (feet)	Eye Relief (in.)	Length (in.)	Tube Dia. (in.)	W & E Adjustments	Weight (ozs.)	Price	Other Data
BURRIS (cont.)									
Black Diamond									
3-12x50[3,4,6]	3.2-11.9	34-12	3.5-4	13.8	30mm	Int.	25	974.00	
6-24x50	6-24	18-6	3.5-4	16.2	30mm	Int.	25	1,046.00	
Fullfield II									
2.5x9	2.5	55	3.5-3.75	10.25	1	Int.	9	307.00	
1.75-5x[1,2,9,10]	1.7-4.6	66-25	3.5-3.75	10.875	1	Int.	13	400.00	
3-9x40[1,2,3,10]	3.3-8.7	38-15	3.5-3.75	12.625	1	Int.	15	336.00	
3-9x50	3-9	35-15	3.5-3.50	13	1	Int.	18	481.00	
3.5-10x50mm[3,5,10]	3.7-9.7	29.5-11	3.5-3.75	14	1	Int.	19	542.00	
4.5-14x[1,4,8,11]	4.4-11.8	27-10	3.5-3.75	15	1	Int.	18	585.00	
6.5-20x[1,3,4,6,7,8]	6.5-17.6	16.7	3.5-3.75	15.8	1	Int.	18.5	656.00	
Compact Scopes									
1x XER[3]	1	51	4.5-20	8.8	1	Int.	7.9	320.00	
4x[4,5]	3.6	24	3.75-5	8.25	1	Int.	7.8	397.00	
6x[1,4]	5.5	17	3.75-5	9	1	Int.	8.2	397.00	
6x HBR[1,5,8]	6	13	4.5	11.25	1	Int.	13	415.00	
1-4x XER[3]	1-3.8	53-15	4.25-30	8.8	1	Int.	10.3	467.00	
3-9x[4,5]	3.6-8.8	25-11	3.75-5	12.625	1	Int.	11.5	442.00	
4-12x[1,4,6]	4.5-11.6	19-8	3.75-4	15	1	Int.	15	534.00	
Signature Series									
1.5-6x[2,3,5,9,10]	1.7-5.8	70-20	3.5-4	10.8	1	Int.	13	601.00	
8x[2,5,11]	2.1-7.7	53-17	3.5-4	11.75	1	Int.	14	840.00	
3-10x[3,5,10,13]	3.3-8.8	36-14	3.5-4	12.875	1	Int.	15.5	665.00	
3-12x[3,10]	3.3-11.7	34-9	3.5-4	14.25	1	Int.	21	701.00	
4-16x[1,3,5,6,8,10]	4.3-15.7	33-9	3.5-4	15.4	1	Int.	23.7	760.00	
6-24x[1,3,5,6,8,10,13]	6.6-23.8	17-6	3.5-4	16	1	Int.	22.7	787.00	
8-32x[8,10,12]	8.6-31.4	13-3.8	3.5-4	17	1	Int.	24	840.00	
Speeddot 135[14]									
Red Dot	1			4.85	35mm	Int.	5	291.00	
Handgun									
1.50-4x LER[1,5,10]	1.6-3	16-11	11-25	10.25	1	Int.	11	411.00	
2-7x LER[3,4,5,10]	2-6.5	21-7	7-27	9.5	1	Int.	12.6	458.00	
2x LER[4,5,6]	1.7	21	10-24	8.75	1	Int.	6.8	286.00	
4x LER[1,4,5,6,10]	3.7	11	10-22	9.625	1	Int.	9	338.00	
3x12 LER[1,4,6]	9.5	4	8-12	13.5	1	Int.	14	558.00	
Scout Scope									
1xXER[3,9]	1.5	32	4-24	9	1	Int.	7.0	320.00	
2.75x[3,9]	2.7	15	7-14	9.375	1	Int.	7.0	356.00	
BUSHNELL (Bausch & Lomb Elite rifle scopes sold under Bushnell brand)									
Elite 4200 RainGuard									
426244M[1]	6-24	18-6	3	16.9	1	Int.	20.2	696.95	
422104G[2]	2.5-10	41.5-10.8	3	13.5	1	Int.	16	579.95	
422152	2.5-10	40.3-10.8	3.3	14.3	1	Int.	18	766.95	
424164M	4-16	26-7	3.5	18.6	1	Int.	18.6	614.95	
424165M	4-16	26-7	3	15.6	1	Int.	22	794.95	
428324M	8-32	14-3.75	3.3	18	1	Int.	22	766.95	
Elite 3200 RainGuard									
325155M	5-15	21-7	3	15.9	1	Int.	19	486.95	
324124A[1]	4-12	26.9-9	3	13.2	1	Int.	15	426.95	
321040M	10	11	3.5	11.7	1	Int.	15.5	290.95	
323940G[2]	3-9	33.8-11.5	3	12.6	1	Int.	13	279.95	
322732M	2-7	44.6-12.7	3	11.6	1	Int.	12	276.95	
3239544G[3]	3-9	31.5-10.5	3	15.7	1	Int.	19	348.95	
Elite 3200 Handgun RainGuard									
322632M7	2-6	10-4	20	9	1	Int.	10	404.95	
322636	2-6	10-4	20	9	1	Int.	10	448.95	
Holosight									
510021	1x	Unlimited	6"/10'	4.1	NA	Int.	6.4	450.95	
530021	1x	Unlimited	Unlimited	6	NA	Int.	12	350.95	
530027	1x	Unlimited	Unlimited	6	NA	Int.	12	370.95	

Available in Carbon Black, Titanium Gray and Autumn Gold finishes.
Black Diamond & Fullfield: All scopes avail. with Plex reticle. Steel-on-steel click adjustments. [1]Dot reticle on some models. [2]Post crosshair reticle extra. [3]Matte satin finish. [4]Available with parallax adjustment (standard on 10x, 12x, 4-12x, 6-12x, 6-18x, 6x HBR and 3-12x Signature). [5]Silver matte finish extra. [6]Target knobs extra, standard on silhouette models. LER and XER with P.A., 6x HBR. [7]Sunshade avail. [8]Avail. with Fine Plex reticle. [9]Available with Heavy Plex reticle. [10]Available with Posi-Lock. [11]Available with Peep Plex reticle. [12]Also avail. for rimfires, airguns. [13]Selected models available with camo finish.
Signature Series: LER=Long Eye Relief; IER=Intermediate Eye Relief; XER=Extra Eye Relief.
Speeddot 135: [14]Waterproof, fogproof, coated lenses, 11 bright ness set tings; 3-MOA or 11-MOA dot size; includes Weaver-style rings and battery. **Partial listing shown.** Contact Burris for complete details.

Plex   Fine Plex   Peep Plex

Target Dot   Heavy Plex & Electro-Dot Plex

Ballistic Mil-Dot   Mil-Dot

(Bushnell)
[1]Wide Angle. [2]Also silver finish.

(Bushnell Elite)
[1]Adj. objective, sunshade; with 1/4-MOA dot or Mil Dot reticle. [2]Also in matte and silver finish. [3]50mm objective; also in matte finish. [4]Also in silver finish. **Partial listings shown.** Contact Bushnell Performance Optics for details.

Maker and Model	Magn.	Field at 100 Yds. (feet)	Eye Relief (in.)	Length (in.)	Tube Dia. (in.)	W & E Adjustments	Weight (ozs.)	Price	Other Data
BUSHNELL (cont.)									
Legend									
752732M	2-7	56-16	3.5	11.6	1	Int.	11.6	194.95	
753940M	3-9	36-13	3.5	13.1	1	Int.	14.6	215.95	
753950M	3-9	36-13	3.5	13.1	1	Int.	16	236.95	
754124M	4-12	30.9-10.1	3.5	14.4	1	Int.	17.3	275.95	
755154M	5-15	23.8	3.5	14.6	1	Int.	17.7	287.95	
Trophy									
730134	1-2.8	68	Unlimited	5.5	1	Int.	6	124.95	
731500[1]	1.75-5	68-23	3.5	10.8	1	Int.	12.3	161.95	
734124[1]	4-12	32-11	3	12.5	1	Int.	16.1	273.95	
733940[2]	3-9	42-14	3	11.7	1	Int.	13.2	139.95	
736184	6-18	17.3-6	3	14.8	1	Int.	17.9	343.95	
Turkey & Brush									
731421	1.75-4	73-30	3.5	10.8	32mm	Int.	10.9	155.95	
Trophy Handgun									
732632	2-6	21-7	9-26	9.1	1	Int.	10.9	260.95	
Banner									
711545	1.5-4.5	67-23	3.5	10.5	1	Int.	10.5	105.95	
713944	3-9	36-13	4	11.5	1	Int.	12.5	113.95	
713950	3-9	26-10	3	16	1	Int.	19	169.95	
714124	4-12	29-11	3	12	1	Int.	15	142.95	
716185	6-18	17-6	3	16	1	Int.	18	190.95	
Sportsman									
720038	3-9	37-14	3.5	12	1	Int.	6	92.95	
720039	3-9	38-13	3.5	10.75	1	Int.	11.2	105.95	
720412[4]	4-12	27-9	3.2	13.1	1	Int.	14.6	128.95	
721393	3-9	35-12	3.5	11.75	1	Int.	10	62.95	
721548	1.5-4.5	71-25	3.5	10.4	1	Int.	11.8	99.95	
721403	4	29	4	11.75	1	Int.	9.2	51.80	
723940M	3-9	42-14	3	12.7	1	Int.	12.5	86.95	
22 Rimfire									
762239	3-9	40-13	3	11.75	1	Int.	11.2	55.95	
762243	4	30	3	11.5	1	Int.	10	47.95	
EUROPTIK SUPREME									
4x36K	4	39	3.5	11.6	26mm	Int.	14	795.00	[1]Military scope with adjustable parallax. Fixed powers have 26mm tubes, variables have 30mm tubes. Some models avail. with steel tubes. All lenses multi-coated. Dust and water tight. From Europtik.
6x42K	6	21	3.5	13	26mm	Int.	15	875.00	
8x56K	8	18	3.5	14.4	26mm	Int.	20	925.00	
1.5-6x42K	1.5-6	61.7-23	3.5	12.6	30mm	Int.	17	1,095.00	
2-8x42K	2-8	52-17	3.5	13.3	30mm	Int.	17	1,150.00	
2.5-10x56K	2.5-10	40-13.6	3.5	15	30mm	Int.	21	1,295.00	
3-12x56 Super	3-12	10.8-34.7	3.5-2.5	15.2	30mm	Int.	24	1,495.00	
4-16x56 Super	4-16	9.8-3.9	3.1	18	30mm	Int.	26	1,575.00	
3-9x40 Micro	3-9	3.2-12.1	2.7	13	1	Int.	14	1,450.00	
2.5-10x46 Micro	2.5-10	13.7-33.4	2.7	14	30mm	Int.	20	1,395.00	
4-16x56 EDP[1]	4-16	22.3-7.5	3.1	18	30mm	Int.	29	1,995.00	
7-12x50 Target	7-12	8.8-5.5	3.5	15	30mm	Int.	21	1,495.00	
JAEGER									
ST-10		10, 17	Varies	13	30mm, 35mm		34	895.00	All scopes available w/standard and extra-long eye relief eyepiece. Variable power military and police tactical scope systems are also available. Offers scope rings and bases. By U.S.O. Jaeger.
SN-1 Long Range		17, 22, 42	12.35 (10x)	Varies	30mm, 35mm, 40mm		36	2,395.00	
SN6 2d Perimeter		10, 17, 22	12.35 (10x)	Varies	30mm, 35mm, 40mm		34	1,295.00	
SN-9 Extreme Range		22, 42	6.2 (22x)	Varies			62.4	2,600.00	
SN-12 CQB		3, 4	38 (3x)	7.5	1		34	865.00	
USMC 10x Sniper		10	10.36	12.5	1		34	2,500.00	
USMC M40A3		10	10.36	12.5	1		34	NA	
JH-4 Safari		1-4	119-34	9.25	30mm		31	1,195.00	
JH-3 Denali		1.8-10x	48.7-12.35	13	30mm		32	1,695.00	
JH-3 Serengeti		3.2-17x		14.5	30mm		33	1,895.00	
JH-T-PAL Chucker		3.8-22x	30-6.2	17.5	30mm		34	1,995.00	

Multi-X

Circle-X

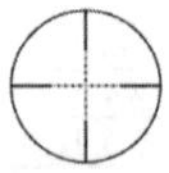

Mil-Dot

3-2-1 Low-Light

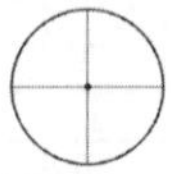

¼ M.O.A.

European

Maker and Model	Magn.	Field at 100 Yds. (feet)	Eye Relief (in.)	Length (in.)	Tube Dia. (in.)	W & E Adjustments	Weight (ozs.)	Price	Other Data
KAHLES									
C-1 Series									Aluminum tube. Multi-coated, waterproof. Imported from Austria by Swarovski Optik.
C1-4	1-1.4	108-31.8	3.55	10.83	30mm	Int.	14.6	943.33	
C5-6x42	1.5-6	72-21.3	3.55	12.01	30mm	Int.	16.4	1,043.33	
C2.5-10	2.5-10	43.5-12.9	3.55	12.8	30mm	Int.	17.3	1,187.76	
C3-12	3-12	37.5-10.8	3.55	13.98	30mm	Int.	19.4	1,332.22	
American Hunter Riflescopes									
2-7x36	2-7	48-27.3	3.35	11.06	1	Int.	12.2	621.11	
3-9	3-9	39-14.5	3.35	12.09	1	Int.	13.1	732.22	
Compact Fixed Power									
4x36	4	34.5	3.15	11.22	1	Int.	12.7	665.56	
6x42	6	23.4	3.15	12.4	1	Int.	14.5	854.44	
Compact 30mm Riflescopesw/Illuminated Reticle									
CSX 1-4x24	1.1-4	110.94-31.78	3.55	11.04	30mm	Int.	15.4	1,630.00	
CSX 1-6x42	1.5-6	74.96-21.29	3.55	12.2	30mm	Int.	17.15	1,808.00	
CSX 2.5-10x50	2.5-10	43.5-12.9	3.55	12.8	30mm	Int.	18.3	1,963.00	
Compact 30mm Riflescopes, Illuminated Reticle									
CBX 2.5-10x50	2.5-10'	43.5-12.9	3.55	12.8	30mm	Int.	17.3	1,832.00	
CBX 3-12x56	3-12	37.5-10.8	3.55	13.98	30mm	Int.	19.4	1,921.00	
CL 1" Riflescopes									
CL3-9x42	3-9	39-15	3.60	12.09	1	Int.	14.46	887.78	
CL3-10	3-10	34-12	3.60	12.59	1	Int.	16.4	1,108.00	
CL4-12	4-12	29-10	3.60	12.59	1	Int.	18.34	1,153.29	
CL 1" Riflescopes with Multizero									
CL3-9x42	3-9	39-15	3.60	12.09	1	Int.	14.99	1,242.67	
CL3-10x50	3-10	34-12	3.60	12.59	1	Int.	16.93	1,275.00	
CL4-12x52	4-12	29-10	3.60	12.59	1	Int.	18.87	1,353.67	
LEATHERWOOD									
Uni-Dial*									*Elevation adjustment is 1/8" and windage adjustment is 1/4". All air-glass surfaces are fully multi-coated to maximize light transmission.
U3510x50 3.5-10	50	36.7-12.8	3.25	13.11			18.7	335.50	
U412-50 4-12	50	30.6-10.2	3.25	14.53			22.1	385.00	
U618-50 6-18	50	20.4-7.5	3.25	15.35			22	418.50	
U6520x50 6.5-20	50	18.8-6.3	3.25	15.43			23.5	437.50	
U3501x50MD 3.5-10	50	36.7-12.8	3.25	13.11			18.7	475.00	
Distinguished									
D3510x50 3.5-10	50	36.7-12.8	3.25	13.11			17.2	199.00	
D412x50 4-12	50	30.6-10.2	3.25	14.53			20.6	239.00	
D618x5- 6-18	50	20.4-7.5	3.25	15.35			21.5	267.50	
D6520x50 6.5-20	50	18.8-6.3	3.35	15.43			22	275.00	
D3510x50MD 3.5-10	50	36.7-12.8	3.25	13.11			17.2	325.00	
Expert									
E412x44 4-12	44	30.6-10.7	3.25	14.53			19.7	149.00	
E618x44 6-18	44	20.4-6.8	3.25	15.35			20.2	159.00	
E6520x44 6.5-20	44	18.8-6.28	3.25	15.43			21.2	223.50	
Sharpshooter									
S39x40 3-9	40	41-15	3.25	13			13.5	95.00	
S39x40IR 3-9	40	39-13	3.25	12.75			14	105.00	
S39x50 3-9	50	41-13	3.25	12.75			14.5	112.00	
S3510x50 3.5-10	50	36.7-12.8	3.25	13.11			16.2	119.00	
S310x44IR	44	40.8-12.8	3.25	13.11			15.2	115.00	
S55-16x44 5.5-16	44	21.9-7.5	3.25	14.41			19.9	149.00	
S6520x44 6.5-20	44	18.8-6.28	3.25	15.43			21.7	145.00	
Long Eye Relief									
LER2732 2-7	32	18.88-6.28	11.2-8.7	11.08			11.57	185.00	
Double-Duce Rimfire									
RF4x32 4	32	26	3	12			11	49.50	
RF39x32 3-9	32	38.5-13	3	12.5			12	69.50	

SCOPES / Hunting, Target & Varmint

Maker and Model	Magn.	Field at 100 Yds. (feet)	Eye Relief (in.)	Length (in.)	Tube Dia. (in.)	W & E Adjustments	Weight (ozs.)	Price	Other Data
LEICA									
Ultravid 1.75-6x32	1.75-6	47-18	4.8-3.7	11.25	30mm	Int.	14	749.00	Aluminum tube with hard anodized matte black finish with titanium accents; finger-adjustable windage and elevation with 1/4-MOA clicks. Made in U.S. From Leica.
Ultravid 3.5-10x42	3.5-10	29.5-10.7	4.6-3.6	12.62	30mm	Int.	16	849.00	
Ultravid 4.5-14x42	4.5-14	20.5-7.4	5-3.7	12.28	30mm	Int.	18	949.00	

Leicaplex Standard

Leica Dot

Standard Dot

Crosshair

Euro

Post & Plex

Maker and Model	Magn.	Field at 100 Yds. (feet)	Eye Relief (in.)	Length (in.)	Tube Dia. (in.)	W & E Adjustments	Weight (ozs.)	Price	Other Data
LEUPOLD									
M8-3.5x10	3.2-9.5	29.9	4.7	13.5	30mm	Int.	19.5	1,124.99	Constantly centered reticles, choice of Duplex, tapered CPC, Leupold Dot, Crosshair and Dot. CPC and Dot reticles extra. [1]3x9 Compact, 6x Compact, 12x, 3x9, and 6.5x20 come with adjustable objective. Sunshade available for all adjustable objective scopes, $23.20-$41.10. Partial listing shown. **Contact Leupold for complete details.**
M8-2.7-28	2.66	41	3.8	9.9	1	Int.	8.2	299.99	
M8-4X Compact RF	3.6	25.5	4.5	9.2	1	Int.	7.5	289.99	
Vari-X 2-7x	2.5-6.5	41.7-17.3	4.2	10.8	1	Int.	10	299.99	
Vari-X 3-9x	3.3-8.5	32-13.1	4.2	12.2	1	Int.	12	314.99	
M8-4X	4	24	4	10.5	1	Int.	9.3	249.99	
M8-6x36mm	5.9	17.7	4.3	11.3	1	Int.	10	469.99	
M8-6x42mm	6	17	4.5	11.9	1	Int.	11.3	424.99	
M8-12x40	11.6	9.1	4.2	13	1	Int.	13.5	474.99	
Vari-X 3-9x	3.5-8.6	32.9-13.1	4-2	12.2	1	Int.	12	454.99	
Vari-X-III 1.5-5x20	1.5-4.5	65-17	4.4-3.6	9.4	1	Int.	9.7	499.99	
Vari-X-III 1.75-6x32	1.9-5.6	51	4.4-3.2	11.4	1	Int.	11.6	499.99	
Vari-X-III 2.5x8	2.6-7.8	37-13.5	4.4-3.6	11.4	1	Int.	11.6	499.99	
Vari-X-III 3.5-10x40	3.9-9.6	29.7-11	4.4-3.5	12.6	1	Int.	13	549.99	
Vari-X-III 3.5-10x50	3.3-9.5	29.8-11	4.4-3.5	12.2	1	Int.	15.1	624.99	
Vari-X-III 4.5-14x40	4.8-14.2	19.9	4.4-3.6	12.6	1	Int.	13.2	699.99	
Vari-X-III 4.5-14x50	4.9-14.4	19.1	4.4-3.6	12.6	1	Int.	16	789.99	
Vari-X 4.5-14x50 LRT	4.9-14.3	19-6	5-3.7	12.1	30mm	Int.	17.5	999.00	
Vari-X-III 6.5-20 A.O.	6.5-19.2	14.3-5.6	5-3.6	14.3	1	Int.	16	749.99	
Vari-X III 6.5-20xLRT	6.5-19.2	14.3-5.5	4.4	14.2	1	Int.	21	974.99	
Vari-X III 8.5-25x40 LRT	8.3-24.3	11.3-4.3	5.2	14.3	1	Int.	21	1,039.99	
Vari-X III 8.5-25x 50 LRT	8.3-24.3	11.3-4.3	5.2-7	14.4	30mm	Int.	21	1,149.99	
Mark 4 M1-10x40	10	11.1	3.6	13.125	30mm	Int.	21	1,124.99	
Mark 4 M1-16x40	16	6.6	4.1	12.875	30mm	Int.	22	1,509.99	
Mark 4 M3-10x40LRT	10	13.1	3.4	13.125	30mm	Int.	21	939.99	
Mark 4 6.5x20[1]	6.5-19.5	14.3-5.5	5.5-3.8	11.2	30mm	Int.	16	1,198.99	
LPS 1.5-6x42	1.5-6	58.7-15.7	4	11.2	30mm	Int.	16	1,198.99	
LPS 2.5-10x45	2.6-9.8	37.2	4.5-3.8		1	Int.	17.2	1,119.99	
LPS 3.5-14x52	3.5-14	28-7.2	4	13.1	30mm	Int.	22	1,249.99	
Rimfire									
Vari-X 2-7x RF Special	3.6	25.5	4.5	9.2	1	Int.	7.5	299.99	
Shotgun									
M8 2.5x20	2.3	39.5	4.9	8.4	1	Int.	6	249.99	

Duplex

CPC

Post & Duplex

Leupold Dot

Dot

Maker and Model	Magn.	Field at 100 Yds. (feet)	Eye Relief (in.)	Length (in.)	Tube Dia. (in.)	W & E Adjustments	Weight (ozs.)	Price	Other Data
LYMAN									
Super TargetSpot[1]	10, 12, 15, 20, 25, 30	5.5	2	24.3	.75	Int.	27.5	685.00	Made under license from Lyman to Lyman's orig. specs. Blue steel. Threepoint suspension rear mount with .25-min. click adj. Data listed for 20x model. [1]Price appx. Made in U.S. by Parsons Optical Mfg. Co.
McMILLAN									
Vision Master 2.5-10x	2.5-10	14.2-4.4	4.3-3.3	13.3	30mm	Int.	17	1,250.00	42mm obj. lens; .25-MOA clicks; nitrogen filled, fogproof, waterproof; etched duplex-type reticle. [1]Tactical Scope with external adj. knobs, military reticle; 60+ min. adj.
Vision Master Model 1[1]	2.5-10	14.2-4.4	4.3-3.3	13.3	30mm	Int.	17	1,250.00	
MEOPTA									
Artemis 2000 6x42	6	21	3.1	13.7	30mm	Int.	17.6	NA	Steel tubes are waterproof, dustproof, and shockproof; nitrogen filled. Anti-reflective coatings, protective rubber eye piece, clear caps. Made in Czech Replublic by Meopta.
R1 7x56RD	7	17.1	3.1	14.1	1	Int.	19/2	NA	
MEPROLIGHT									
Meprolight Reflex Sights 14-21 5.5 MOA 1x30[1]	1			4.4	30mm	Int.	5.2	335.00	[1]Also available with 4.2 MOA dot. Uses tritium and fiber-optics, no batteries required. From Hesco, Inc.

Maker and Model	Magn.	Field at 100 Yds. (feet)	Eye Relief (in.)	Length (in.)	Tube Dia. (in.)	W & E Adjustments	Weight (ozs.)	Price	Other Data
MILLETT									
Buck 3-9x44	3-9	38-14	3.25-4	13	1	Int.	16.2	249.65	13-MOA dot. 25-MOA dot. 33-, 5-, 8-, 10-MOA dots. 410-MOA dot. All have click adjustments; waterproof, shockproof; 11 dot intensity settings. All avail. in matte/black or silver finish. From Millett Sights.
Buck 3.5-10x50	3.5-10	NA	NA	NA	1	NA	NA	270.65	
Buck 3-12x44 A/O	3-12	NA	NA	NA	1	NA	NA	270.65	
Buck 4-16x44 A/O	4-16	NA	NA	NA	1	NA	NA	290.00	
Buck Varmint 4-16x56	4-16	NA	NA	NA	30mm	NA	NA	380.00	
Buck Varmint 6-25x56	6-25	NA	NA	NA	30mm	NA	NA	405.00	
Buck Varmint 6-25x56	6-25	NA	NA	NA	30mm	NA	NA	431.00	
Buck Lightning 1.5-6x44	1.5-6	NA	NA	NA	1	NA	NA	323.00	
Buck Lightning 3-9x44	3-9	NA	NA	NA	1	NA	NA	323.00	
Buck Silver 3-9x40	3-9	NA	NA	NA	1	NA	NA	135.95	
Buck Silver 4-12x40 A/O	4-12	NA	NA	NA	1	NA	NA	170.00	
Buck Silver 6-18x40 A/O	6-18	NA	NA	NA	1	NA	NA	170.00	
MultiDot SP[3]	1	50		4.8	30mm	Int.	5.3	205.90	
MIRADOR									
RXW 4x40[1]	4	37	3.8	12.4	1	Int.	12	179.95	[1]Wide angle scope. Multi-coated objective lens. Nitrogen filled; water proof; shockproof. From Mirador Optical Corp.
RXW 1.5-5x20[1]	1.5-5	46-17.4	4.3	11.1	1	Int.	10	188.95	
RXW 3-9x40	3-9	43-14.5	3.1	12.9	1	Int.	13.4	251.95	
NIGHTFORCE									
NXS 1-4X24	1.0-4	95-25	3.5	8.8	30mm		17	1,215	Lighted reticles with 11 intensity levels. Most scopes have choice of reticles. From Lightforce U.S.A. 11 custom reticles, illuminated reticles, 30mm tubes, Mil-Spec scratch resistant coatings. NXS models feature 1/4 MOA windage and elevation adjustments and incorporate a side focus/parallax adjustment except on the 1-4 and 2.5-10. Waterproof to 100 ft., function tested thermal stability from -80 F - +250 F. Recoil and impact tested at 1250 Gs for both positive and negative forces. BR models feature 1/8 MOA windage and elevation adjustment, adjustable objective for parallax correction.
NXS 2.5-10X24	2.5-10	44-11	3.7	9.9	30mm	Int.	17	1,256	
NXS 3.5-15X50	3.5-15	27.6-7.3	3.9	14.7	30mm	Int.	30	1,411	
NXS 3.5-15X56	3.5-15	27.6-7.3	3.8	14.8	30mm	Int.	31	1,517	
NXS 5.5-22X50	5.5-22	17.5-4.7	3.7	15.1	30mm	Int.	31	1,528	
NXS 5.5-22X56	5.5-22	17.5-4.7	3.9	15.2	30mm	Int.	32	1,544	
NXS 8-32X56	8.0-32	12.1-3.1	3.8	15.9	30mm	Int.	34	1,675	
NXS 12-42X56	12.0-42	8.2-2.4	3.8	16.1	30mm	Int.	34	1,817	
BR 8-32X56	8.0-32	9.4-3.1	2.9	16.6	30mm	Int.	36	1,271	
BR 12-42X56	12.0-42	6.7-2.3	2.9	17	30mm	Int.	36	1,342	
NIKON									
Buckmasters									
4x40	4	30.4	3.3	12.7	1	Int.	11.8	159.95	Super multi-coated lenses and blackening of all internal metal parts for maximum light gathering capability; positive .25-MOA; fogproof; waterproof; shockproof; luster and matte finish. [1]Also available in matte silver finish. [2]Available in silver matte finish. [3]Available with TurkeyPro or Nikoplex reticle. [4]Silver Shadow finish; black matte **$296.95**. Partial listing shown. From Nikon, Inc.
3-9x40[4]	3.3-8.6	33.8-11.3	3.5-3.4	12.7	1	Int.	13.4	209.95	
3-9x50	3.3-8.6	33.8-11.3	3.5-3.4	12.9	1	Int.	18.2	299.95	
4-12x50	4-12	24.3-8.0	3.7	13.9	1	Int.	20.6	349.95	
Monarch UCC									
4x40[2]	4	26.7	3.5	11.7	1	Int.	11.7	229.95	
1.5-4.5x20[3]	1.5-4.5	67.8-22.5	3.7-3.2	10.1	1	Int.	9.5	239.95	
2-7x32	2-7	46.7-13.7	3.9-3.3	11.3	1	Int.	11.3	269.95	
3-9x40[1]	3-9	33.8-11.3	3.6-3.2	12.5	1	Int.	12.5	299.95	
3.5-10x50	3.5-10	25.5-8.9	3.9-3.8	13.7	1	Int.	15.5	439.95	
4-12x40 A.O.	4-12	25.7-8.6	3.6-3.2	14	1	Int.	16.6	369.95	
6.5-20x44	6.5-19.4	16.2-5.4	3.5-3.1	14.8	1	Int.	19.6	469.95	
2x20 EER	2	22	26.4	8.1	1	Int.	6.3	169.95	
NORINCO									
N2520	2.5	44.1	4		1	Int.		52.28	Partial listing shown. Some with Ruby Lens coating, blue/black and matte finish. Imported by Nic Max, Inc.
N420	4	29.3	3.7		1	Int.		52.70	
N640	6	20	3.1		1	Int.		67.88	
N154520	1.5-4.5	63.9-23.6	4.1-3.2			Int.		80.14	
N251042	2.5-10	27-11	3.5-2.8		1	Int.		206.60	
N3956	3-9	35.1-6.3	3.7-2.6		1	Int.		231.88	
N31256	3-12	26-10	3.5-2.8		1	Int.		290.92	
NC2836M	2-8	50.8-14.8	3.6-2.7		1	Int.		255.60	
PARSONS									
Parsons Long Scope	6	10	2	28-34+	.75	Ext.	13	475.00-525.00	Adj. for parallax, focus. Micrometer rear mount with .25-min. click adjust ments. Price is approximate. Made in U.S. by Parsons Optical Mfg. Co.
PENTAX									
Lightseeker 1.75-6x[1]	1.75-6	71-20	3.5-4	10.8	1	Int.	13	546.00	
Lightseeker 2-8x[2]	2-8	53-17	3.5-4	11.7	1	Int.	14	594.00	
Lightseeker 3-9x[3, 4, 10, 11]	3-9	36-14	3.5-4	12.7	1	Int.	15	594.00	

SCOPES / Hunting, Target & Varmint

Maker and Model	Magn.	Field at 100 Yds. (feet)	Eye Relief (in.)	Length (in.)	Tube Dia. (in.)	W & E Adjustments	Weight (ozs.)	Price	Other Data
PENTAX *(cont.)*									
Lightseeker 3.5-10x[5]	3.5-10	29.5-11	3.5-4	14	1	Int.	19.5	630.00	[1]Glossy finish; Matte finish, Heavy Plex or Penta-Plex, **$546.00**. [2]Glossy finish; Matte finish, **$594.00**. [3]Glossy finish; Matte finish, **$628.00**; Heavy Plex, add **$20.00**. [4]Matte finish; Mil-Dot, **$798.00**. [5]Glossy finish; Matte finish, **$652.00**; Heavy Plex, add **$10.00**. [6]Glossy finish; Matte finish, **$816.00**; with Heavy Plex, **$830.00**; with Mil-Dot, **$978.00**. [7]Matte finish; with Mil-Dot, **$1,018.00**. [8]Matte finish; with Mil-Dot, **$1,098.00**. [9]Lightseeker II, Matte finish, **$844.00**. [10]Lightseeker II, Glossy finish, **$636.00**. [11]Lightseeker II, Matte finish, **$660.00**. [12]Lightseeker II, Matte finish, **$878.00**. [13]Matte finish; Advantage finish, Break-up Mossy Oak finish, Treestand Mossy Oak finish, **$364.00**. From Pentax Corp.
Lightseeker 4-16x[6, 9]	4-16	33-9	3.5-4	15.4	1	Int.	22.7	888.00	
Lightseeker 6-24x[7, 12]	6-24	18-5.5	3.5-4	16	1	Int.	23.7	1,028.00	
Lightseeker 8.5-32x[8]	8.5-32	13-3.8	3.5-4	17.2	1	Int.	24	968.00	
Shotgun									
Lightseeker 2.5x[13]	2.5	55	3.5-4	10	1	Int.	9	398.00	
Lightseeker Zero-X SG Plus	0	51	4.5-15	8.9	1	Int.	7.9	372.00	
Lightseeker Zero-X/ V Still-Target	0-4	53.8-15	3.5-7	8.9	1	Int.	10.3	476.00	
Lightseeker Zero X/ V	0-4	53.8-15	3.5-7	8.9	1	Int.	10.3	454.00	

Heavy Plex   Fine Plex   Penta-Plex   Deepwoods Plex   Comp-Plex   Mil-dot

Maker and Model	Magn.	Field at 100 Yds. (feet)	Eye Relief (in.)	Length (in.)	Tube Dia. (in.)	W & E Adjustments	Weight (ozs.)	Price	Other Data
RWS									
300	4	36	3.5	11.75	1	Int.	13.2	170.00	
450	3-9	43-14	3.5	12	1	Int.	14.3	215.00	
SCHMIDT & BENDER									
Fixed									
4x36	4	30	3.25	11	1	Int.	14	979.00	All scopes have 30-yr. warranty, click adjustments, centered reticles, rotation indicators. [1]Glass reticle; aluminum. Available in aluminum with mounting rail. [2]Aluminum only. [3]Parallax adjustment in third turret; extremely fine crosshairs. [4]Available with illuminated reticle that glows red; third turret houses on/off switch, dimmer and battery. [5]4-16x50/Long Range. From Schmidt & Bender, Inc. Available with illuminated crosshairs and parallax adjustment.
6x42	6	21	3.25	13	1	Int.	17	1,069.00	
8x56	8	16.5	3.25	14	1	Int.	22	1,229.00	
Variables									
2.5-10x56[1, 4]	2.5-10	37.5-12	3.90	14	30mm	Int.	24.6	1,659.00	
3-12x42[2]	3-12	34.5-11.5	3.90	13.5	30mm	Int.	19	2,059.00	
3-12x50[1, 4]	3-12	33.3-12.6	3.90	13.5	30mm	Int.	22.9	2,059.00	
4-16x50 Varmint[3, 5]	4-16	22.5-7.5	3.90	14	30mm	Int.	26	1,979.00	
Police/Marksman II									
3-12x50LP	3-12	33.3-12.6	3.74	13.9	34mm	Int.	18.5	2,849.00	
SCHMIDT & BENDER ZENITH SERIES									
3-12x50	3-12	33.3-11.4	3.70	13.71	NA	NA	23.4	1,795.00	
2.5-10x56	2.5-10	39.6-12	3.70	14.81	NA	NA	24	1,759.00	
1.1-4x24	1.1-4	96/30	3.70	11.2	30mm	Int.	16	1,439.00	

No. 1 (fixed)   No. 1 variable   No. 2   No. 3   No. 4   No. 6   No. 7   No. 8   No. 8 Dot   No. 9

Maker and Model	Magn.	Field at 100 Yds. (feet)	Eye Relief (in.)	Length (in.)	Tube Dia. (in.)	W & E Adjustments	Weight (ozs.)	Price	Other Data
SIGHTRON									
Variables									
SII 1.56x42	1.5-6	50-15	3.8-4	11.69	1	Int.	15.35	372.25	[1]Adjustable objective. [2]Satin black; also stainless. Electronic Red Dot scopes come with ring mount, front and rear extension tubes, polarizing filter, battery, haze filter caps, wrench. Rifle, pistol, shotgun scopes have aluminum tubes, Exac Trak adjustments. Lifetime warranty. From Sightron, Inc. [3]3" sun shade. [4]Mil-Dot or Plex reticle. [5]Dot or Plex reticle.
SII 2.58x42	2.5-8	36-12	3.6-4.2	11.89	1	Int.	12.82	338.40	
SII 39x42[2, 4, 5]	3-9	34-12	3.6-4.2	12.00	1	Int.	13.22	356.22	
SII 312x42[4]	3-12	32-9	3.6-4.2	11.89	1	Int.	12.99	421.55	
SII 3.510x42	3.5-10	32-11	3.6	11.89	1	Int.	13.16	421.01	
SII 4.514x42[1]	4.5-14	22-7.9	3.6	13.88	1	Int.	16.07	481.14	
Target									
SII 24x44	24	4.1	4.33	13.30	1	Int.	15.87	441.82	
SII 416x42[2, 3, 4, 5]	4-16	26-7	3.6	13.62	1	Int.	16	481.11	
SII 624-42[2, 3, 5]	6-24	16-5	3.6	14.6	1	Int.	18.7	562.96	
Compact									
SII 4x32	4	25	4.5	9.69	1	Int.	9.34	266.86	
SII 2.5-10x32	2.5-10	41-10.5	3.75-3.5	10.9	1	Int.	10.39	338.40	
Shotgun									
SII 2.5x20SG	2.5	41	4.3	10.28	1	Int.	8.46	266.88	
Pistol									
SII 1x28P[4]	1	30	9-24	9.49	1	Int.	8.46	314.79	
SII 2x28P[4]	2	16-10	9-24	9.49	1	Int.	8.28	314.79	

SCOPES / Hunting, Target & Varmint

Maker and Model	Magn.	Field at 100 Yds. (feet)	Eye Relief (in.)	Length (in.)	Tube Dia. (in.)	W & E Adjustments	Weight (ozs.)	Price	Other Data
SIMMONS									
22 Mag.									
80102[2]	4	29.5	3	11.75			11	49.99	
80103[1]	4	23.5	3	7.25			8.25	49.99	
80103[7]	3-9	29.5	3.3	11.5			10	59.99	
Aetec									
2100[8]	2.8-10	44-14	5	11.9	1	Int.	15.5	189.99	
21041[6]	3.8-12	33-11	4	13.5	1	Int.	20	199.99	
44 Mag									
M-1044[3]	3-10	34-10.5	3	12.75	1	Int.	15.5	149.99	
M-1045[3]	4-12	29.5-9.5	3	13.2	1	Int.	18.25	169.99	
M-1047[3]	6.5-20	14-.5	2.6-3.4	12.8	1	Int.	19.5	199.99	
1048[3, 14] (3)	6.5-20	16-5.5	2.6-3.4	14.5	1	Int.	20	219.99	
M-1050DM[3, 13]	3.8-12	26-9	3	13.08	1	Int.	16.75	189.99	
8-Point									
4-12x40mm AO[3]	4-12	29-10	3-2 7/8	13.5	1	Int.	15.75	99.99	
4x32mm[3]	4	28.75	3	11.625	1	Int.	14.25	34.99	
3-9x32mm[3]	3-9	37.5-13	3-2 7/8	11.875	1	Int.	11.5	39.99	
3-9x40mm[12]	3-9	37-13	3-2 7/8	12.25	1	Int.	12.25	49.99-79.99	
3-9x50mm[3]	3-9	32-11.75	3-2 7/8	13	1	Int.	15.25	79.99	
Prohunter									
7700	2-7	53-16.25	3	11.5	1	Int.	12.5	79.99	
7710[2]	3-9	36-13	3	12.6	1	Int.	13.5	89.99	
7716	4-12	26-9	3	12.6	1	Int.	16.75	129.99	
7721	6-18	18.5-6	3	13.75	1	Int.	16	144.99	
7740[3]	6	21.75	3	12.5	1	Int.	12	99.99	
Prohunter Handgun									
7732[12]	2	22	9-17	8.75	1	Int.	7	109.99	
7738[12]	4	15	11.8-17.6	8.5	1	Int.	8	129.99	
82200	2-6							159.99	
Whitetail Classic									
WTC 11[4]	1.5-5	75-23	3.4-3.2	9.3	1	Int.	9.7	184.99	
WTC 12[4]	2.5-8	45-14	3.2-3	11.3	1	Int.	13	199.99	
WTC 13[4]	3.5-10	30-10.5	3.2-3	12.4	1	Int.	13.5	209.99	
WTC 15[4]	3.5-10	29.5-11.5	3.2	12.75	1	Int.	13.5	289.99	
WTC 45[4]	4.5-14	22.5-8.6	3.2	13.2	1	Int.	14	265.99	
Whitetail Expedition									
1.5-6x32mm[3]	1.5-6	72-19	3	11.16	1	Int.	15	259.99	
3-9x42mm[3]	3-9	40-13.5	3	13.2	1	Int.	17.5	269.99	
4-12x42mm[3]	4-12	29-9.6	3	13.46	1	Int.	21.25	299.99	
6-18x42mm[3]	6-18	18.3-6.5	3	15.35	1	Int.	22.5	319.99	
Pro50									
8800[9]	4-12	27-9	3.5	13.2	1	Int.	18.25	179.99	
8810[9]	6-18	17-5.8	3.6	13.2	1	Int.	18.25	174.99	
808825	3.5-10	32-8.75	3.5	3.25	1	Int.	14.5	179.99	
808830	2.5-10	39-12.2	2.75	12.75	1	Int.	15.9	179.99	
Shotgun									
2100[4]	4	16	5.5	8.8	1	Int.	9.1	84.99	
2100[5]	2.5	24	6	7.4	1	Int.	7	59.99	
7789D	2	31	5.5	8.8	1	Int.	8.75	99.99	
7790D	4	17	5.5	8.5	1	Int.	8.75	114.99	
7791D	1.5-5	76-23.5	3.4	9.5	1	Int.	10.75	138.99	
Blackpowder									
BP0420M[11]	4	19.5	4	7.5	1	Int.	8.3	59.99	
BP2732M[10]	2-7	57.7-16.6	3	11.6	1	Int.	12.4	129.99	
Red Dot									
5100421	1			4.8	30mm	Int.	4.7	44.99	
5111222	1			5.25	42mm	Int.	6	49.99	
Pro Air Gun									
21608 A.O.	4	25	3.5	12	1	Int.	11.3	99.99	
21613 A.O.	4-12	25-9	3.1-2.9	13.1	1	Int.	15.8	179.99	
21619 A.O.	6-18	18-7	2.9-2.7	13.8	1	Int.	18.2	189.99	

[1]Matte; also polished finish. [2]Silver; also black matte or polished. [3]Black matte finish. [4]Granite finish. [5]Camouflage. [6]Black polish. [7]With ring mounts. [8]Silver; black polish avail. [9]50mm obj.; black matte. [10]75-yd. parallax; black or silver matte. [11]Octagon body; black matte or silver finish. [12]Black matte finish; also available in silver. [13]Smart reticle. [14]Target turrets. **Only selected models shown.** Contact Simmons Outdoor Corp. for complete details.

Truplex™

Smart

ProDiamond®

Crossbow

SCOPES / Hunting, Target & Varmint

Maker and Model	Magn.	Field at 100 Yds. (feet)	Eye Relief (in.)	Length (in.)	Tube Dia. (in.)	W & E Adjustments	Weight (ozs.)	Price	Other Data
SPRINGFIELD ARMORY									
	6		3.5	13	1	Int.	14.7	379.00	[1]Range finding reticle with automatic bullet drop compensator for 223 match ammo to 700 yds. [2]Also avail. as 2nd Gen. with target knobs and adj. obj., **$549.00**; as 3rd Gen. with illuminated reticle, **$749.00**; as Mil-Dot model with illuminated Target Tracking reticle, target knobs, adj. obj., **$698.00**. [3]Unlimited range finding, target knobs, adj. obj., illuminated Target Tracking green reticle. All scopes have matte black finish, internal bubble level, 1/4-MOA clicks. From Springfield, Inc.
4-14x70 Tactical Government Model[1]	4-14		3.5	14.25	1	Int.	15.8	395.00	
4-14x56 1st Gen. Government Model[2]	4-14		3.5	14.75	30mm	Int.	23	480.00	
10x56 Mil-Dot Government Model[3]	10		3.5	14.75	30mm	Int.	28	672.00	
6-20x56 Mil-Dot Government Model	6-20		3.5	18.25	30mm	Int.	33	899.00	
SWAROVSKI OPTIK									
PH Series									
1.25-4x24	1.25-4	98.4-31.2	3.15	10.63	30mm	Int.	16.2	**1,333.23**	
1.5-6x421	1.5-6	65.4-21	3.15	12.99	30mm	Int.	20.8	**1,483.34**	
2.5-10x42	2.5-10	39.6-12.6	3.15	13.23	30mm	Int.	19.8	**1,705.56**	
3-12x50	3-12	33-10.5	3.15	14.33	30mm	Int.	22.4	**1,727.78**	
4-16x50	4-16	30-8.5	3.15	14.22	30mm	Int.	22.3	**1,754.44**	
6-24x50	6-24	18.6-5.4	3.15	15.4	30mm	Int.	23.6	**1,976.67**	
AV Series									
3-9x36	3-9	39-13.5	3.35	11.8	1	Int.	11.7	**854.44**	
3-10x42AV	3-10	33-11.7	3.35	12.44	1	Int.	12.7	**943.33**	
4-12x50AV	4-12	29.1-9.9	3.35	13.5	1	Int.	13.9	**987.78**	
6-18x50	6-18	17.4-6.6	3.5	14.84	1	Int.	20.3	**1,065.56**	
SWIFT									
600 4x15	4	17	2.8	10.6	.75	Int.	3.5	**15.00**	All Swift scopes, with the exception of the 4x15, have Quadraplex reticles, are fogproof and waterproof. The 4x15 has crosshair reticle and is non-waterproof. [1]Available in regular matte black or silver finish. [2]Comes with ring mounts, wrench, lens caps, extension tubes, filter, battery. [3]Regular and matte black finish. [4]Speed Focus scopes. Partial listing shown. From Swift Instruments.
601 3-7x20	3-7	25-12	3-2.9	11	.75	Int.	5.6	**35.00**	
650 4x32	4	26	4	12	1	Int.	9.1	**75.00**	
653 4x40WA[1]	4	35	4	12.2	1	Int.	12.6	**125.00**	
654 3-9x32	3-9	35-12	3.4-2.9	12	1	Int.	9.8	**125.00**	
656 3-9x40WA[1]	3-9	40-14	3.4-2.8	12.6	1	Int.	12.3	**140.00**	
657 6x40	6	28	4	12.6	1	Int.	10.4	**125.00**	
658 2-7x40WA[3]	2-7	55-18	3.3-3	11.6	1	Int.	12.5	**160.00**	
659 3.5-10x44WA	3.5-10	34-12	3-2.8	12.8	1	Int.	13.5	**230.00**	
665 1.5-4.5x21	1.5-4.5	69-24.5	3.5-3	10.9	1	Int.	9.6	**125.00**	
665M 1.5-4.5x21	1.5-4.5	69-24.5	3.5-3	10.9	1	Int.	9.6	**125.00**	
666M Shotgun 1x20	1	113	3.2	7.5	1	Int.	9.6	**130.00**	
667 Fire-Fly[2]	1	40		5.4	30mm	Int.	5	**220.00**	
668M 4x32	4	25	4	10	1	Int.	8.9	**120.00**	
669M 6-18x44	6-18	18-6.5	2.8	14.5	1	Int.	17.6	**220.00**	
680M	3.9	43-14	4	18	40mm	Int.	17.5	**399.95**	
681M	1.5-6	56-13	4	11.8	40mm	Int.	17.5	**399.95**	
682M	4-12	33-11	4	15.4	50mm	Int.	21.7	**499.95**	
683M	2-7	55-17	3.3	11.6	32mm	Int.	10.6	**499.95**	
Premier Rifle Scopes									
648M[1] 1.5-4.5	32	71-25	3.05-3.27	10.41	1	Int.	12.7	**179.95**	
649R 4-12	50	29.5-9.5	3.3-3	13.8	1	Int.	15.8	**245.00**	
658M 2-7	40	55-18	3.3-3	11.6	1	Int.	12.5	**175.00**	
659S 3.5-10	44	34-12	3-2.8	12.8	1	Int.	13.5	**215.00**	
669M 6-18	44	18-6.5	2.8	14.5	1	Int.	17.6	**230.00**	
671M 3-9	50	35-25	3.24-3.12	15.5	1	Int.	18.2	**250.00**	
672M 6-18	50	19-6.7	3.25-3	15.8	1	Int.	20.9	**260.00**	
674M 3-9	40	40-14.2	3.6-2.9	12	1	Int.	13.1	**170.00**	
676S 4-12	40	29.3-10.5	3.15-2.9	12.4	1	Int.	15.4	**180.00**	
677M 6-24	50	18-5	3.1-3.2	15.9	1	Int.	20.8	**280.00**	
678M 8-32	50	13-3.5	3.13-2.94	16.9	1	Int.	21.5	**290.00**	
685M[3] 3-9	40	39-13.5	3.7-2.8	12.4	1	Int.	20.5	**189.95**	
686M[3] 6.5-20	44	19-6.5	2.7	15.6	1	Int.	23.6	**249.95**	
687M[2] 4.5-14	44	25.5-8.5	3.2	14.1	1	Int.	21.5	**220.00**	
688M[2] 6-18	44	19.597	2.8	15.4	1	Int.	22.6	**240.00**	
Standard Rifle Scopes									
587 4	32	25	3.1	11.7	1	Int.	13	**50.00**	
653M 4	40	35	4	12.2	1	Int.	12.6	**128.00**	
654M 3-9	32	35-12	3.4-2.9	12	1	Int.	9.8	**125.00**	

TDS   No. 4   No. 4A   No. 7A   Plex   No. 24

SCOPES / Hunting, Target & Varmint

Maker and Model	Magn.	Field at 100 Yds. (feet)	Eye Relief (in.)	Length (in.)	Tube Dia. (in.)	W & E Adjustments	Weight (ozs.)	Price	Other Data
SWIFT *(cont.)*									
656 3-9	40	40-14	3.4-2.8	12.6	1	Int.	12.3	**140.00**	
657M 6	40	28	4	12.6	1	Int.	10.4	**125.00**	
660M⁴ 2-6	32	14-4.5	20-12.6	5.5	1	Int.	10.6	**241.80**	
661M⁴ 4	32	6.6	13.8	9.4	1	Int.	9.9	**130.00**	
663S⁴ 4	32	9.8	7.3	7.2	1	Int.	8.5	**130.00**	
665M 1.5-4.5	21	69-24.5	3.5-3	10.8	1	Int.	9.6	**125.00**	
668M 4	32	25	4	10	1	Int.	8.9	**120.00**	
TASCO									
Target & Varmint									
VAR251042M	2.5-10	35.9	3	14	1	Int.	19.1	**89.95**	
MAG624X40	6-24	17-4	3	16	1	Int.	19.1	**113.95**	
VAR624X42M	6-24	13-3.7	7	16	1	Int.	19.6	**113.95**	
TG624X44DS	15-4.5	15-4.5	3	16.5	1	Int.	19.6	**199.95**	
World Class									
BA1545X32	1.5-4.5	77-23	4	11.25	1	Int.	12	**59.95**	
DWC39X40N	3-9	41-15	3.5	12.75	1	Int.	13	**73.95**	
WA39X40N	3-9	41-15	3.5	12.75	1	Int.	13	**73.95**	
WA39X40STN	3-9	41-15	3.5	12.75	1	Int.	13	**73.95**	
DWC39X50N	3-9	41-13	3	12.5	1	Int.	15.8	**87.95**	
DWC39X40M	3-9	41-15	3.5	12.75	1	Int.	13	**73.95**	
DWC416X40	4-16	22.5-5-9	3.7	14	1	Int.	16	**103.95**	
ProPoint									
PDP2	1	40	Un.	5	1	Int.	5.5	**117.95**	
PDP3	1	52	Un.	5	1	Int.	5.5	**137.95**	
PD3ST	1	52	Un.	5	1	Int.	5.5	**143.95**	
PDPRGD	1	60	Un.	5.4	1	Int.	5.7	**91.95**	
Golden Antler									
GA3940	3-9	41-15	3	12.75	1	Int.	13	**57.95**	
GA3932AGD	3-9	39	3	13.25	1	Int.	12	**43.95**	
Pronghhorn									
PH39X40D	3-9	39-13	3	13	1	Int.	12.1	**47.95**	
PH4X32D	4	32	3	12	1	Int.	11	**32.95**	
PH2533	2.5	43	3.2	11.4	1	Int.	10.1	**32.95**	
.22 Riflescopes									
MAG39X32D	3-9	17.75-6	3	12.75	1	Int.	11.3	**55.95**	
Rimfire									
RF37X20D	3-7	24	2.5	11.5	1	Int.	5.7	**23.95**	
RF4X15D	4	20.5	2.5	11	1	Int.	3.8	**7.95**	
Red Dot									
BKR30	1	57	Un.	3.75	1	Int.	6	**45.95**	
BKR3022* (22 rimfire)	1	57	Un.	3.75	1	Int.	6	**45.95**	
BKR42	1	62	Un.	3.75	1	Int.	6.7	**57.95**	
THOMPSON/CENTER RECOIL PROOF SERIES									
Pistol Scopes									
8315¹	2.5-7	15-5	8-21, 8-11	9.25	1	Int.	9.2	**364.00**	¹Black; lighted reticle. From Thompson/Center Arms.
8326	2.5-7	15-5	8-21, 8-11	9.25	1	Int.	10.5	**432.00**	
Muzzleloader Scopes									
8658	1	60	3.8	9.125	1	Int.	10.2	**146.00**	
8662	4	16	3	8.8	1	Int.	9.1	**141.00**	
TRIJICON									
Reflex II 1x24	1			4.25		Int.	4.3	**400.00**	¹Advanced Combat Optical Gunsight for AR-15, M16, with integral mount. Other mounts available. All models feature tritium and fiber optics dual-lighting system that requires no batteries. Other new products for 2007 include 3x30TA 33; 4x32 w BACTA31F, and 1x30TX30 Tripower. From Trijicon, Inc.
TA44 1.5x16¹	1.5	39	2.4	5.34		Int.	5.31	**990.00**	
TA45 1.5x24¹	1.5	25.6	3.6	5.76		Int.	5.92	**990.00**	
TA47 2x20¹	2	29.5	2.1	5.3		Int.	5.82	**990.00**	
TA50 3x24¹	3	25.6	1.4	5		Int.	5.89	**990.00**	
TA11 3.5x35¹	3.5	28.9	2.4	8		Int.	14	**1,295.00**	
TA01 4x32¹	4	36.8	1.5	5.8		Int.	9.9	**990.00**	
Variable AccuPoint									
3-9x40	3-9	33.8-11.3	3.6-3.2	12.2	1	Int.	12.8	**699.00**	
1.25-4x24	1.25-4	61.6-20.5	4.8-3.4	10.2	1	Int.	11.4	**650.00**	
2.5-10x56	2.5-10	37.6-10.1	4.1-2.8	13.8	30mm	Int.	22.1	**$899.00**	

SCOPES / Hunting, Target & Varmint

Maker and Model	Magn.	Field at 100 Yds. (feet)	Eye Relief (in.)	Length (in.)	Tube Dia. (in.)	W & E Adjustments	Weight (ozs.)	Price	Other Data
ULTRA DOT									
Micro-Dot Scopes[1]									[1]Brightness-adjustable fiber optic red dot reticle. Waterproof, nitro gen-filled one-piece tube. Tinted see-through lens covers and battery included. [2]Parallax adjustable. [3]Ultra Dot sights include rings, battery, polarized filter, and 5-year warranty. All models available in black or satin finish. [4]Illuminated red dot has 11 brightness settings. Shock-proof aluminum tube. From Ultra Dot Distribution.
1.5-4.5x20 Rifle	1.5-4.5	80-26	3	9.8	1	Int.	10.5	297.00	
2-7x32	2-7	54-18	3	11	1	Int.	12.1	308.00	
3-9x40	3-9	40-14	3	12.2	1	Int.	13.3	327.00	
4x-12x56[2]	4-12	30-10	3	14.3	1	Int.	18.3	417.00	
Ultra-Dot Sights[3]									
Ultra-Dot 25[4]	1			5.1	1	Int.	3.9	159.00	
Ultra-Dot 30[4]	1			5.1	30mm	Int.	4	179.00	
UNERTL									[1]Dural .25-MOA click mounts. Hard coated lenses. Non-rotating objective lens focusing. [2].25-MOA click mounts. [3]With target mounts. [4]With calibrated head. [5]Same as 1" Target but without objective lens focusing. [6]Range focus unit near rear of tube. Price is with Posa or standard mounts. Magnum clamp. From Unertl.
1" Target	6, 8, 10	16-10	2	21.5	.75	Ext.	21	675.00	
10X	10	10.3	3	12.5	1	Ext.	35	2,500.00	
1.25" Target[1]	8, 10, 12, 14	12-16	2	25	.75	Ext.	21	715.00	
1.5" Target	10, 12, 14, 16, 18, 20	11.5-3.2	2.25	25.5	.75	Ext.	31	753.50	
2" Target[2]	10, 12, 14, 16, 18, 24, 30, 32, 36	8	2.25	26.25	1	Ext.	44	918.50	
Varmint, 1.25"[3] 3" Ultra Varmint, 2"[4]	15	12.6-7	2.25	24	1	Ext.	34	918.50	
Small Game[5]	3, 4, 6	25-17	2.25	18	.75	Ext.	16	550.00	
Programmer 200[6]	10, 12, 14, 16, 18, 20, 24, 30, 36	11.3-4		26.5	1	Ext.	45	1,290.00	
B8									
Tube Sight				17		Ext.		420.00	
U.S. OPTICS									
SN-1/TAR Fixed Power System									Prices shown are estimates; scopes built to order; choice of reticles; choice of front or rear focal plane; extra-heavy MIL-SPEC construction; extra-long turrets; individual W&E rebound springs; up to 100mm dia. objectives; up to 50mm tubes; all lenses multi-coated. Other magnifications available. [1]Modular components allow a variety of fixed or variable magnifications, night vision, etc. Made in U.S. by U.S. Optics.
16.2x	15	8.6	4.3	16.5	30mm	Int.	27	1,700.00	
22.4x	20	5.8	3.8	18	30mm	Int.	29	1,800.00	
26x	24	5	3.4	18	30mm	Int.	31	1,900.00	
31x	30	4.6	3.5	18	30mm	Int.	32	2,100.00	
37x	36	4	3.6	18	30mm	Int.	32	2,300.00	
48x	50	3	3.8	18	30mm	Int.	32	2,500.00	
Variables									
SN-2	4-22	26.8-5.8	5.4-3.8	18	30mm	Int.	24	1,762.00	
SN-3	1.6-8		4.4-4.8	18.4	30mm	Int.	36	1,435.00	
SN-4	1-4	116-31.2	4.6-4.9	18	30mm	Int.	35	1,065.00	
Fixed Power									
SN-6	8, 10, 17, 22	14-8.5	3.8-4.8	9.2	30mm	Int.	18	1,195.00	
SN-8 Modular[1]	4, 10, 20, 40	32	3.3	7.5	30mm	Int.	11.1	890.00-4,000.00	
WEAVER									
Riflescopes									[1]Gloss black. [2]Matte black. [3]Silver. [4]Satin. All scopes are shock-proof, waterproof, and fogproof. Dual-X reticle available in all except V24 which has a fine X-hair and dot; T-Series in which certain models are available in fine X-hair and dots; Qwik-Point red dot scopes which are available in fixed 4 or 12 MOA, or variable 4-8-12 MOA. V16 also available with fine X-hair, dot or Dual-X reticle. T-Series scopes have Micro-Trac® adjustments. From Weaver Products.
K2.5[1]	2.5	35	3.7	9.5	1	Int.	7.3	132.86	
K4[1,2]	3.7	26.5	3.3	11.3	1	Int.	10	149.99	
K6[1]	5.7	18.5	3.3	11.4	1	Int.	10	154.99	
KT15[1]	14.6	7.5	3.2	12.9	1	Int.	14.7	281.43	
V3[1,2]	1.1-2.8	88-32	3.9-3.7	9.2	1	Int.	8.5	189.99	
V9[1,2]	2.8-8.7	33-11	3.5-3.4	12.1	1	Int.	11.1	249.99-299.99	
V9x50[1,2]	3-9	29.4-9.9	3.6-3	13.1	1	Int.	14.5	239.99	
V10[1-3]	2.2-9.6	38.5-9.9	3.4-3.3	12.2	1	Int.	11.2	259.99-269.99	
V10-50[1-3]	2.3-9.7	40.2-9.2	2.9-2.8	13.75	1	Int.	15.2	279.99	
V16 MDX[2,3]	3.8-15.5	26.8-6.8	3.1	13.9	1	Int.	16.5	329.99	
V16 MFC[2,3]	3.8-15.5	26.8-6.8	3.1	13.9	1	Int.	16.5	329.99	
V16 MDT[2,3]	3.8-15.5	26.8-6.8	3.1	13.9	1	Int.	16.5	329.99	
V24 Varmint[2]	6-24	15.3-4	3.15	14.3	1	Int.	17.5	379.99-399.99	
Handgun									
H2[1-3]	2	21	4-29	8.5	1	Int.	6.7	161.43	
H4[1-3]	4	18	11.5-18	8.5	1	Int.	6.7	175.00	
VH4[1-3]	1.5-4	13.6-5.8	11-17	8.6	1	Int.	8.1	215.71	
VH8[1-3]	2.5-8	8.5-3.7	12.16	9.3	1	Int.	8.3	228.57	
Rimfire									
RV7[2]	2.5-7	37-13	3.7-3.3	10.75	1	Int.	10.7	148.57	

SCOPES / Hunting, Target & Varmint

Maker and Model	Magn.	Field at 100 Yds. (feet)	Eye Relief (in.)	Length (in.)	Tube Dia. (in.)	W & E Adjustments	Weight (ozs.)	Price	Other Data
WEAVER *(cont.)*									
Grand Slam									
6-20x40mm Varminter Reticle[2]	6-20X	16.5-5.25	2.75-3	14.48	1	Int.	17.75	**419.99**	
6-20x40mm Fine Crosshairs w/Dot[2]	6-20X	16.5-5.25	2.75-3	14.48	1	Int.	17.75	**419.99**	
1.5-5x32mm[2]	1.5-5X	71-21	3.25	10.5	1	Int.	10.5	**349.99**	
4.75x40mm[2]	4.75X	14.75	3.25	11	1	Int.	10.75	**299.99**	
3-10x40mm[2]	3-10X	35-11.33	3.5-3	12.08	1	Int.	12.08	**329.99**	
3.5-10x50mm[2]	3.5-10X	30.5-10.8	3.5-3	12.96	1	Int.	16.25	**389.99**	
4.5-14x40mm	4.5-14X	22.5-10.5	3.5-3	14.48	1	Int.	17.5	**399.99**	
T-Series									
T-64	614	14	3.58	12.75	1	Int.	14.9	**424.95**	
T-36[3-4]	36	3	3	15.1	1	Int.	16.7	**489.99**	
ZEISS									
ZM/Z									**ZM/Z:** [1]Also avail. with illuminated reticle. All scopes have .25-min. click-stop adjustments. Choice of Z-Plex or fine crosshair reticles. Rubber armored objective bell, rubber eyepiece ring. Lenses have T-Star coating for highest light transmission. VM/V scopes avail. with rail mount. Partial listing shown. From Carl Zeiss Optical, Inc.
6x42MC	6	22.9	3.2	12.7	1	Int.	13.4	**749.00**	
8x56MC	8	18	3.2	13.8	1	Int.	17.6	**829.00**	
1.25-4x24MC	1.25-4	105-33	3.2	11.46	30mm	Int.	17.3	**779.00**	
1.5-6x42MC	1.5-6	65.5-22.9	3.2	12.4	30mm	Int.	18.5	**899.00**	
2.5-10x48MC[1]	2.5-10	33-11.7	3.2	14.5	30mm	Int.	24	**1,029.00**	
3-12x56MC[1]	3-12	27.6-9.9	3.2	15.3	30mm	Int.	25.8	**1,099.00**	
Conquest									**Conquest:** [1]Stainless. [2]Turkey reticle. [3]Black matte finish. All scopes have .25-min. click-stop adjustments. Choice of Z-Plex, Turkey or fine crosshair reticles. Coated lenses for highest light transmission. Partial listing shown. From Carl Zeiss Optical, Inc.
3-9x40MC[3]	3-9	37.5	3.34	12.36	1	Int.	17.28	**499.99**	
3-9x40MC[1]	3-9	37.5	3.34	12.36	1	Int.	17.28	**529.99**	
3-9x40S[3]	3-9	37.5	3.34	12.36	1	Int.	17.28	**499.99**	
3-9x40S[2,3]	3-9	37.5	3.34	12.36	1	Int.	17.28	**529.99**	
3-12x56MC[3]	2.5-10	27.6	3.2	15.3	30mm	Int.	25.8	**1,049.00**	
3-12x56MC[1]	3-12	27.6	3.2	15.3	30mm	Int.	25.8	**1,079.00**	
VM/V									
1.1-4x24 VariPoint T	1.1-4	120-34	3.5	11.8	30mm	Int.	15.8	**1,699.00**	
1.5-6x42T	1.5-6	65.5-22.9	3.2	12.4	30mm	Int.	18.5	**1,299.00**	
2.5-10x50T	2.5-10	47.1-13	3.5	12.5	30mm	Int.	16.25	**1,499.00**	
3-12x56T	3-12	37.5-10.5	3.5	13.5	30mm	Int.	19.5	**1,499.00**	
3-9x42T	3-9	42-15	3.74	13.3	1	Int.	15.3	**1,999.00**	
5-15x42T	5-15	25.7-8.5	3.74	13.3	1	Int.	15.4	**1,399.00**	

Hunting scopes in general are furnished with a choice of reticlecrosshairs, post with crosshairs, tapered or blunt post, or dot crosshairs, etc. The great majority of target and varmint scopes have medium or fine crosshairs but post or dot reticles may be ordered. W=windage; E=Elevation; MOA=Minute of Angle or 1" (approx.) at 100 yards.

Kahles CSX1-1-4

Schmidt & Bender 3-12x50

Burris SIG Select 8x32

Meopta Artemmis 6x42

Burris IXXER

Simmons Blackpowder

Weaver Grand Slam

Nikon Buckmaster 3-9x40 Silver

Swarovski PH 1.25-4x42

Sightron SII 39x42

LASER SIGHTS

Alpec Mini Shot

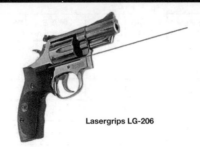

Lasergrips LG-206

Laser Devices ULS 2001
with TLS 8R light

Maker and Model	Wave length (nm)	Beam Color	Lens	Operating Temp. (degrees F.)	Weight (ozs.)	Price	Other Data
ALPEC							
Power Shot[1]	635	Red	Glass	NA	2.5	$199.95	[1]Range 1000 yards. [2]Range 300 yards. Mini Shot II range 500 yards, output 650mm, $129.95. [3]Range 300 yards; Laser Shot II 500 yards; Super Laser Shot 1000 yards. Black or stainless finish aluminum; removable pressure or push-button switch. Mounts for most hand guns, many rifles and shotguns. From Alpec Team, Inc.
Mini Shot[2]	670	Red	Glass	NA	2.5	$99.95	
Laser Shot[3]	670	Red	Glass	NA	3.0	$99.95	
BEAMSHOT							
1000[1]	670	Red	Glass	NA	3.8	NA	[1]Black or silver finish; adj. for windage and elevation; 300-yd. range; also M1000/S (500-yd. range), M1000/u (800-yd.). [2]Black finish; 300, 500-, 800-yd. models. All come with removable touch pad switch, 5" cable. Mounts to fit virtually any firearm. From Quarton USA Co.
3000[2]	635/670	Red	Glass	NA	2.0	NA	
1001/u	635	Red	Glass	NA	3.8	NA	
780	780	Red	Glass	NA	3.8	NA	
BSA							
LS650[1]	N/A	Red	NA	NA	NA	$49.95	[1]Comes with mounts for 22/air rifle and Weaver-style bases.
LASERAIM							
LRS-0650-SSW	650	Red	Glass	NA	1.2	$96.00	[1]Laser projects 2" dot at 100 yds.: with rotary switch; with Hotdot $237.00; with Hotdot touch switch $357.00. [2]For Glock 17-27; G1 Hotdot $299.00; price installed. 10Fits std. Weaver base, no rings required; 6-MOA dot; seven brightness settings. All have W&E adj.; black or satin silver finish. From Laseraim Technologies, Inc.
LRS-0650-SCS	650	Red	Glass	NA	1.2	$96.00	
LRS-0650-CCW	650	Red	Glass	NA	1.2	$96.00	
LRS-0635-SSW	635	Red	Glass	NA	1.2	$112.00	
LRS-0635-SCS	635	Red	Glass	NA	1.2	$112.00	
LRS-0635-CCW	635	Red	Glass	NA	1.2	$112.00	
QDL-65GB-730	650	Red	Glass	NA	1.8	$119.95	
QDL-65SW-730	650	Red	Glass	NA	1.8	$119.95	
QDL-63GB-730	635	Red	Glass	NA	1.8	$147.95	
QDL-63SW-730	635	Red	Glass	NA	1.8	$147.95	
PLR-0006-140	650	Red	Glass	NA	1.8	$78.95	
PLW-0006-140	635	Red	Glass	NA	1.8	$78.95	
BLS-0650/0635-140	650/635	Red	Glass	NA	NA	$78.95	
Lasers							
MA-35RB Mini Aimer[1]				NA	1.0	$129.00	
G1 Laser[2]				NA	2.0	$229.00	
LASER DEVICES							
BA-1[1]	632	Red	Glass	NA	2.4	$372.00	[1]For S&W P99 semi-auto pistols; also BA-2, 5 oz., $339.00. [2]For revolvers. [3]For HK, Walther P99. [4]For semi-autos. [5]For rifles; also FA- 4/ULS, 2.5 oz. $325.00. [6]For HK sub guns. [7]For military rifles. [8]For shotguns. [9]For SIG-Pro pistol. [10]Universal, semi-autos. From Laser Devices, Inc.
BA-3[2]	632	Red	Glass	NA	3.3	$332.50	
BA-5[3]	632	Red	Glass	NA	3.2	$372.00	
Duty-Grade[4]	632	Red	Glass	NA	3.5	$372.00	
FA-4[5]	632	Red	Glass	NA	2.6	$358.00	
LasTac[1]	632	Red	Glass	NA	5.5	$298.00 to 477.00	
MP-5[6]	632	Red	Glass	NA	2.2	$495.00	
MR-2[7]	632	Red	Glass	NA	6.3	$485.00	
SA-2[8]	632	Red	Glass	NA	3.0	$360.00	
SIG-Pro[9]	632	Red	Glass	NA	2.6	$372.00	
ULS-2001[10]	632	Red	Glass	NA	4.5	$210.95	
Universal AR-2A	632	Red	Glass	NA	4.5	$445.00	
LASERGRIPS							
LG-301/401/401-P1[1]	633	Red-Orange	Glass	NA		$299.00	Replaces existing grips with built-in laser high in the right grip panel. Integrated pressure sensi tive pad in grip activates the laser. Also has master on/off switch. [1]For Colt 1911/Commander. [2]For all Glock models. Option on/off switch. Requires factory installation. [3]For S&W K, L, N frames, round or square butt (LG-207); [4]For Taurus small-frame revolvers. [5]For Ruger SP-101. [6]For SIG Sauer P226. From Crimson Trace Corp. [7]For Beretta 92/96. [8]For Ruger MK II. [9]For S&W J-frame. [10]For Sig Sauer P228/229. [11]For Colt 1911 full size, wraparound. [12]For Beretta 92/96, wraparound. [13]For Colt 1911 compact, wraparound. [14]For S&W J-frame, rubber.
LG-304/404/404-P1[2]	633	Red-Orange	Glass	NA		$229.00	
LG-302/312[3]	633	Red-Orange	Glass	NA		$229.00	
LG-617[4]	633	Red-Orange	Glass	NA		$229.00	
LG-619[5]	633	Red-Orange	Glass	NA		$229.00	
LG-626[6]	633	Red-Orange	Glass	NA		$595.00	

LASER SIGHTS

Lasermax Glock 23 Lasers

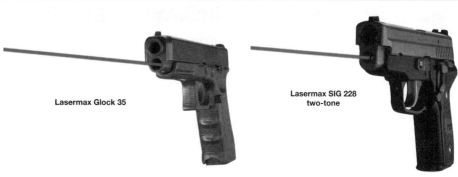

Lasermax Glock 35

Lasermax SIG 228
two-tone

Maker and Model	Wave length (nm)	Beam Color	Lens	Operating Temp. (degrees F.)	Weight (ozs.)	Price	Other Data
LG-629[7]	633	Red-Orange	Glass	NA		$299.00	
LG-203[8]	633	Red-Orange	Glass	NA		$299.00	
LG-389[9]	633	Red-Orange	Glass	NA		$299.00	
LG-320[10]	633	Red-Orange	Glass	NA		$299.00	
LG-326[11]	633	Red-Orange	Glass	NA		$329.00	
LG-329[12]	633	Red-Orange	Glass	NA		$329.00	
LG-359[13]	633	Red-Orange	Glass	NA		$329.00	
LG-101[14]	633	Red-Orange	Glass	NA		$299.00	

LASERLYTE

Maker and Model	Wave length (nm)	Beam Color	Lens	Operating Temp. (degrees F.)	Weight (ozs.)	Price	Other Data
LLX-0006-140/090[1]	635/645	Red		NA	1.4	$159.95	[1]Dot/circle or dot/crosshair projection; black or stainless. [2]Also 635/645mm model. From Tac Star Laserlyte. in grip activates the laser. Also has master on/off switch.
WPL-0004-140/090[2]	670	Red		NA	1.2	$109.95	
TPL-0004-140/090[2]	670	Red		NA	1.2	$109.95	
T7S-0004-140[2]	670	Red		NA	0.8	$109.95	

LASERMAX

Maker and Model	Wave length (nm)	Beam Color	Lens	Operating Temp. (degrees F.)	Weight (ozs.)	Price	Other Data
LMS-1131P[1]	635	Red-Orange	Glass	15° F - 120° F	.6	$339.00	Internal Laser Sights: Replace the recoil spring/guide rod assembly and include a customized takedown lever that serves as the laser on/off switch. For Glock, Sigarms, Beretta, Springfield and 1911 Gov't models and more. Easy installation - no gunsmithing necessary. Laser/Tactical Lights: LaserMax's distinctive pulsing beam combines with a 60 Lumen Tactical Light in the integrated LMS-1202 shotgun unit.
LMS-1141P[2]	635	Red-Orange	Glass	15° F - 120° F	.6	$339.00	
LMS-1141LP[3]	635	Red-Orange	Glass	15° F - 120° F	.6	$339.00	
LMS-1151P[4]	635	Red-Orange	Glass	15° F - 120° F	.6	$339.00	
LMS-1151PFGR[5]	635	Red-Orange	Glass	15° F - 120° F	.6	$339.00	
LMS-1161[6]	635	Red-Orange	Glass	15° F - 120° F	.6	$339.00	Compatability:
LMS-1171[7]	635	Red-Orange	Glass	15° F - 120° F	.6	$339.00	[1]Glock 19, 23, 32, 38
LMS-1181[8]	635	Red-Orange	Glass	15° F - 120° F	.6	$339.00	[2]Glock 17, 22, 31, 37
LMS-1191[9]	635	Red-Orange	Glass	15° F - 120° F	.6	$339.00	[3]Glock 34, 35, 17L, 24, 37L
LMS-2201[10]	635	Red-Orange	Glass	15° F - 120° F	.6	$399.00	[4]Glock 20, 21
LMS-2251[11]	635	Red-Orange	Glass	15° F - 120° F	.6	$399.00	[5]Glock 20, 21 FG/R
LMS-2261[12]	635	Red-Orange	Glass	15° F - 120° F	.6	$399.00	[6]Glock 26, 27, 33
LMS-2261S[13]	635	Red-Orange	Glass	15° F - 120° F	.6	$399.00	[7]Glock 39
LMS-2263[14]	635	Red-Orange	Glass	15° F - 120° F	.6	$399.00	[8]Glock 36
LMS-2281[15]	635	Red-Orange	Glass	15° F - 120° F	.6	$399.00	[9]Glock 29, 30
LMS-2291[16]	635	Red-Orange	Glass	15° F - 120° F	.6	$399.00	[10]SIG P220, .45 ACP
LMS-2391[17]	635	Red-Orange	Glass	15° F - 120° F	.6	$399.00	[11]SIG P225
LMS-2451[18]	635	Red-Orange	Glass	15° F - 120° F	.6	$399.00	[12]SIG P226, 9mm
LMS-1911M[19]	635	Red-Orange	Glass	15° F - 120° F	.6	$399.00	[13]SIG P226, 9mm*
LMS-1911S[20]	635	Red-Orange	Glass	15° F - 120° F	.6	$399.00	[14]SIG P226 .357/.40
LMS-1911B[21]	635	Red-Orange	Glass	15° F - 120° F	.6	$399.00	[15]SIG P228
LMS-PARA1911M[22]	635	Red-Orange	Glass	15° F - 120° F	.6	$399.00	[16]SIG P229
LMS-PARA1911S[23]	635	Red-Orange	Glass	15° F - 120° F	.6	$399.00	[17]SIG P239, .357, .40
LMS-PARA1911B[24]	635	Red-Orange	Glass	15° F - 120° F	.6	$399.00	[18]SIG P245
LMS-3XD[25]	635	Red-Orange	Glass	15° F - 120° F	.6	$399.00	[19]1911 Gov't, matte
LMS-4XD9/357[26]	635	Red-Orange	Glass	15° F - 120° F	.6	$399.00	[20]1911 Gov't, stainless
LMS-4XD40[27]	635	Red-Orange	Glass	15° F - 120° F	.6	$399.00	[21]1911 Gov't, blued
LMS-5XD[28]	635	Red-Orange	Glass	15° F - 120° F	.6	$399.00	[22]Para 1911, matte
LMS-1431[29]	635	Red-Orange	Glass	15° F - 120° F	.6	$399.00	[23]Para 1911, stainless
LMS-1441[30]	635	Red-Orange	Glass	15° F - 120° F	.6	$399.00	[24]Para 1911, blued
LMS-591S[31]	635	Red-Orange	Glass	15° F - 120° F	.6	$399.00	[25]Springfield XD, 3"
LMS-591B[32]	635	Red-Orange	Glass	15° F - 120° F	.6	$399.00	[26]Springfield XD, 4", 9mm, .357
LMS-1202[33]	635	Red-Orange	Glass	15° F - 120° F	.6	$399.00	[27]Springfield XD, 4", .40

[28]Springfield XD, 5"
[29]Beretta 92/96 Centurion
[30]Beretta 92/96 full-size
[31]S&W 5906-type, stainless
[32]S&W, full-size
[33]Remington 870, 1100, 11-87; Benelli M1014 12-gauge semi-auto combat shotgun

SCOPE RINGS & BASES

Maker, Model, Type	Adjust.	Scopes	Price
ADCO			
Std. Black or nickel		1"	$13.95
Std. Black or nickel		30mm	$13.95
Rings Black or nickel		30mm with 3/8" grv.	$13.95
Rings Black or nickel		1" raised 3/8" grv.	$13.95
AIMTECH			
AMT Auto Mag II .22 Mag.	No	Weaver rail	$56.99
Beretta/Taurus 92/99	No	Weaver rail	$63.25
Browning Buckmark/Challenger II	No	Weaver rail	$56.99
Browning Hi-Power	No	Weaver rail	$63.25
Glock 17, 17L, 19, 23, 24 etc. no rail	No	Weaver rail	$63.25
Glock 20, 21 no rail	No	Weaver rail	$63.25
Glock 9mm and .40 with access. rail	No	Weaver rail	$74.95
Govt. 45 Auto/.38 Super	No	Weaver rail	$63.25
Hi-Standard (Mitchell version) 107	No	Weaver rail	$63.25
H&K USP 9mm/40 rail mount	No	Weaver rail	$74.95
Ruger Mk I, Mk II	No	Weaver rail	$49.95
Ruger P85/P89	No	Weaver rail	$63.25
S&W K, L, N frames	No	Weaver rail	$63.25
S&W K, L, N with tapped top strap*	No	Weaver rail	$69.95
S&W Model 41 Target 22	No	Weaver rail	$63.25
S&W Model 52 Target 38	No	Weaver rail	$63.25
S&W Model 99 Walther frame rail mount	No	Weaver rail	$74.95
S&W 2nd Gen. 59/459/659 etc.	No	Weaver rail	$56.99
S&W 3rd Gen. full size 5906 etc.	No	Weaver rail	$69.95
S&W 422, 622, 2206	No	Weaver rail	$56.99
S&W 645/745	No	Weaver rail	$56.99
S&W Sigma	No	Weaver rail	$64.95
Taurus PT908	No	Weaver rail	$63.25
Taurus 44 6.5" bbl.	No	Weaver rail	$69.95
Walther 99	No	Weaver rail	$74.95
Shotguns			
Benelli M-1 Super 90	No	Weaver rail	$44.95
Benelli Montefeltro	No	Weaver rail	$44.95
Benelli Nova	No	Weaver rail	$69.95
Benelli Super Black Eagle	No	Weaver rail	$49.95
Browning A-5 12-ga.	No	Weaver rail	$40.95
Browning BPS 12-ga.	No	Weaver rail	$40.95
Browning Gold Hunter 12-ga.	No	Weaver rail	$44.95
Browning Gold Hunter 20-ga.	No	Weaver rail	$49.95
Browning Gold Hunter 10-ga.	No	Weaver rail	$49.95
Beretta 303 12-ga.	No	Weaver rail	$44.95
Beretta 390 12-ga.	No	Weaver rail	$44.95
Beretta Pintail	No	Weaver rail	$44.95
H&K Fabarms Gold/Silver Lion	No	Weaver rail	$49.95
Ithaca 37/87 12-ga.	No	Weaver rail	$40.95
Ithaca 37/87 20-ga.	No	Weaver rail	$40.95
Mossberg 500/Maverick 12-ga.	No	Weaver rail	$40.95
Mossberg 500/Maverick 20-ga.	No	Weaver rail	$40.95
Mossberg 835 3.5" Ulti-Mag	No	Weaver rail	$40.95
Mossberg 5500/9200	No	Weaver rail	$40.95
Remington 1100/1187 12-ga.	No	Weaver rail	$42.80
Remington 1100/1187 12-ga. LH	No	Weaver rail	$42.80
Remington 1100/1187 20-ga.	No	Weaver rail	$40.95
Remington 1100/1187 20-ga. LH	No	Weaver rail	$40.95
Remington 870 12-ga.	No	Weaver rail	$40.95
Remington 870 12-ga. LH	No	Weaver rail	$40.95
Remington 870 20-ga.	No	Weaver rail	$42.80
Remington 870 20-ga. LH	No	Weaver rail	$42.80
Remington 870 Express Magnum	No	Weaver rail	$40.95
Remington SP-10 10-ga.	No	Weaver rail	$49.95
Winchester 1300 12-ga.	No	Weaver rail	$40.95
Winchester 1400 12-ga.	No	Weaver rail	$40.95
Winchester Super X2	No	Weaver rail	$44.95
"Rib Rider" Ultra Low Profile Mounts Non See-Through 2-piece rib attached			
Mossberg 500/835/9200	No	Weaver rail	$29.95
Remington 1100/1187/870	No	Weaver rail	$29.95
Winchester 1300	No	Weaver rail	$29.95
1-Piece Rib Rider Low Rider Mounts			
Mossberg 500/835/9200	No	Weaver rail	$29.95
Remington 1100/1187/870	No	Weaver rail	$29.95
Winchester 1300	No	Weaver rail	$29.95

Maker, Model, Type	Adjust.	Scopes	Price
AIMTECH (cont.)			
2-Piece Rib Rider See-Through			
Mossberg 500/835/9200	No	Weaver rail	$29.95
Remington 1100/1187/870	No	Weaver rail	$29.95
Winchester 1300	No	Weaver rail	$29.95
1-Piece Rib Rider See-Through			
Mossberg 500/835/9200	No	Weaver rail	$29.95
Remington 1100/1187/870	No	Weaver rail	$29.95
Winchester 1300	No	Weaver rail	$29.95
Rifles			
AR-15/M16	No	Weaver rail	$21.95
Browning A-Bolt	No	Weaver rail	$21.95
Browning BAR	No	Weaver rail	$21.95
Browning BLR	No	Weaver rail	$21.95
Marlin 336	No	Weaver rail	$21.95
Mauser Mark X	No	Weaver rail	$21.95
Remington 700 Short Action	No	Weaver rail	$21.95
Remington 700 Long Action	No	Weaver rail	$21.95
Remington 7400/7600	No	Weaver rail	$21.95
Ruger 10/22	No	Weaver rail	$21.95
Ruger Mini 14 Scout Rail**	No	Weaver rail	$89.50
Savage 110, 111, 113, 114, 115, 116	No	Weaver rail	$21.95
Winchester Model 70	No	Weaver rail	$21.95
Winchester 94 AE	No	Weaver rail	$21.95

All mounts no-gunsmithing, iron sight usable. Rifle mounts are solid see-through bases. All mounts accommodate standard Weaver-style rings of all makers. From Aimtech division, L&S Technologies, Inc. *3-blade sight mount combination. **Replacement handguard and mounting rail.

Maker, Model, Type	Adjust.	Scopes	Price
A.R.M.S.			
M16A1, A2, AR-15	No	Weaver rail	$59.95
Multibase	No	Weaver rail	$59.95
#19 ACOG Throw Lever Mt.	No	Weaver rail	$160.00
#19 Weaver/STANAG Throw Lever Rail	No	Weaver rail	$150.00
STANAG Rings	No	30mm	$75.00
Throw Lever Rings	No	Weaver rail	$119.00
Ring Inserts	No	1", 30mm	$29.00
#22M68 Aimpoint Comp Ring Throw Lever	No	Weaver rail	$109.00
#38 Std. Swan Sleeve[1]	No		$180.00
#39 A2 Plus Mod. Mt.	No	#39T rail	$125.00

[1]Avail. in three lengths. From A.R.M.S., Inc.

Maker, Model, Type	Adjust.	Scopes	Price
AO			
AO/Lever Scout Scope	No	Weaver rail	$50.00

No gunsmithing required for lever-action rifles with 8" Weaver-style rails; surrounds barrel shank; 6" long; low profile. AO Sight Systems Inc.

Maker, Model, Type	Adjust.	Scopes	Price
B-SQUARE			
Pistols (centerfire)			
Colt M1911	E only	Weaver rail	$79.30
H&K USP, 9mm and 40 S&W	No	Weaver rail	$79.30
Pistols (rimfire)			
Browning Buck Mark	No	Weaver rail	$39.10
Ruger Mk I/II, bull or taper	No	Weaver rail	$44.56-48.02
Revolvers			
Colt Anaconda/Python/Taurus 689	No	Weaver rail	$70.36-79.30
Ruger Single-Six	No	Weaver rail	$66.50-74.94
Ruger GP-100	No	Weaver rail	$70.36-79.30
Ruger Blackhawk, Super	No	Weaver rail	$70.36-79.30
Ruger Redhawk, Super	No	Weaver rail	$70.36-79.30
Smith & Wesson K, L, N	No	Weaver rail	$66.50-74.94
Taurus 66, 669, 607, 608	No	Weaver rail	$66.50-74.94
InterLock Rings (sporting rifles)			
1" Standard Dovetail (w/recoil blade)	No	Weaver rail	$31.94-$36.34
30mm Stand. Dovetail (w/recoil blade)	No	Weaver rail	$36.34
1"x11mm Dovetail	No	Weaver rail	$34.14
1"x.22 Dovetail	No	Weaver rail	$31.94
InterLock Adjustable Rings (sporting rifles)			
1" Standard Dovetail (w/recoil blade)	Yes	Weaver rail	$60.55
30mm Stand. Dovetail (w/recoil blade)	Yes	Weaver rail	$64.96
1"x11mm Dovetail	Yes	Weaver rail	$60.56
1"x.22 Dovetail	Yes	Weaver rail	$64.96
InterLock One-Piece Bases			
Most models			$5.50

SCOPE RINGS & BASES

Maker, Model, Type	Adjust.	Scopes	Price
B-SQUARE *(cont.)*			
Modern Military (rings incl.)			
AK-47/MAC 90	No	Weaver rail	$70.36
Colt AR-15	No	Weaver rail	$72.60
FN/FAL/LAR (See-Thru rings)	No	Weaver rail	$99.40
Classic Military (rings incl.)			
H&K 91	No	Weaver rail	$110.56
Mauser 38, 94, 96, 98	E only	Weaver rail	$79.30
Mosin-Nagant (all)	E only	Weaver rail	$79.30
Air Rifles			
RWS, Diana, BSA, Gamo	W&E	11mm rail	$49.95-59.95
Weihrauch, Anschutz, Beeman, Webley	W&E	11mm rail	$59.95-69.95
Shotgun Saddle Mounts			
Benelli Super 90 (See-Thru)	No	Weaver rail	$61.86
Browning BPS, A-5 9 (See-Thru)	No	Weaver rail	$61.86
Browning Gold 10/12/20-ga. (See-Thru)	No	Weaver rail	$61.86
Ithaca 37, 87	No	Weaver rail	$61.86
Mossberg 500/Mav. 88	No	Weaver rail	$61.86
Mossberg 835/Mav. 91	No	Weaver rail	$61.86
Remington 870/1100/11-87	No	Weaver rail	$61.86
Remington SP10	No	Weaver rail	$61.86
Winchester 1200-1500	No	Weaver rail	$61.86

Prices shown for anodized black finish; add **$10** for stainless finish. Partial listing of mounts shown here. Contact B-Square for complete listing and details.

Maker, Model, Type	Adjust.	Scopes	Price
BEEMAN			
Two-Piece, Med.	No	1"	$36.65
Deluxe Two-Piece, High	No	1"	$38.00
Deluxe Two-Piece	No	30mm	$52.00
Deluxe One-Piece	No	1"	$69.35
Dampa Mount	No	1"	$153.35

All grooved receivers and scope bases on all known air rifles and 22-cal. rimfire rifles (1/2" to 5/8" 6mm to 15mm).

Maker, Model, Type	Adjust.	Scopes	Price
BOCK			
Swing ALK[1]	W&E	1", 26mm, 30mm	$349.00
Safari KEMEL[2]	W&E	1", 26mm, 30mm	$149.00
Claw KEMKA[3]	W&E	1", 26mm, 30mm	$224.00
ProHunter Fixed[4]	No	1", 26mm, 30mm	$95.00

[1]Q.D.: pivots right for removal. For Steyr-Mannlicher, Win. 70, Rem. 700, Mauser 98, Dakota, Sako, Sauer 80, 90. Magnum has extra-wide rings, same price. [2]Heavy-duty claw-type reversible for front or rear removal. For Steyr-Mannlicher rifles. [3]True claw mount for bolt-action rifles. Also in extended model. For Steyr-Mannlicher, Win. 70, Rem. 700. Also avail. as Gunsmith Bases, not drilled or contoured same price. [4]Extra-wide rings. Imported from Germany by GSI, Inc.

Maker, Model, Type	Adjust.	Scopes	Price
BSA			
AA Airguns	Yes	Super Ten, 240 Magnum, Maxi gripped scope rail equipped air rifles	$59.99 (adj.) $29.99 (fixed)

Maker, Model, Type	Adjust.	Scopes	Price
BURRIS			
Supreme (SU) One-Piece (T)[1]	W only	1" split rings, 3 heights	1-piece base - $23.00-27.00
Trumount (TU) Two-Piece (T)	W only	1" split rings, 3 heights	2-piece base - $21.00-30.00
Trumount (TU) Two-Piece Ext.	W only	1" split rings	$26.00
Browning 22-cal. Auto Mount[2]	No	1" split rings	$20.00
1" 22-cal. Ring Mounts[3]	No	1" split rings	$24.00-41.00
L.E.R. (LU) Mount Bases[4]	W only	1" split rings	$24.00-52.00
L.E.R. No Drill-No Tap Bases[4, 7, 8]	W only	1" split rings	$48.00-52.00
Extension Rings[5]	No	1" scopes	$28.00-46.00
Ruger Ring Mount[6, 9]	W only	1" split rings	$50.00-68.00
Std. 1" Rings[9]		Low, medium, high heights	$29.00-43.00
Zee Rings[9]		Fit Weaver bases; medium and high heights	$29.00-44.00
Signature Rings	No	30mm split rings	$68.00
Rimfire/Airgun Rings	W only	1" split rings, med. & high	$24.00-41.00
Double Dovetail (DD) Bases	No	30mm Signature	$23.00-26.00

[1]Most popular rifles. Universal rings, mounts fit Burris, Universal, Redfield, Leupold and Browning bases. Comparable prices. [2]Browning Standard 22 Auto rifle. [3]Grooved receivers. [4]Universal dovetail; accepts Burris, Universal, Redfield, Leupold rings. For Dan Wesson, S&W, Virginian, Ruger Blackhawk, Win. 94. [5]Medium standard front, extension rear, per pair. Low standard front, extension rear per pair. [6]Compact scopes, scopes with 2" bell for M77R. [7]Selected rings and bases available with matte Safari or silver finish. [8]For S&W K, L, N frames, Colt Python, Dan Wesson with 6" or longer barrels. [9]Also in 30mm.

Maker, Model, Type	Adjust.	Scopes	Price
BUSHNELL			
Centerfire rings, 2 piece, #763103	Integral 2 piece	1", matte black	$15.95
22 rings, 2 piece, #763022	Integral 2 piece	1", matte	$6.95

Maker, Model, Type	Adjust.	Scopes	Price
CATCO			
Enfield Drop-In	No	1"	$39.95

Uses Weaver-style rings (not incl.). No gunsmithing required. See-Thru design. From CATCO.

Maker, Model, Type	Adjust.	Scopes	Price
CLEAR VIEW			
Universal Rings, Mod. 101[1]	No	1" split rings	$21.95
Standard Model[2]	No	1" split rings	$21.95
Broad View[3]	No	1"	$21.95
22 Model[4]	No	3/4", 7/8", 1"	$13.95
SM-94 Winchester[5]	No	1" split rings	$23.95
94 EJ[6]	No	1" split rings	$21.95

[1]Most rifles by using Weaver-type base; allows use of iron sights. [2]Most popular rifles; allows use of iron sights. [3]Most popular rifles; low profile, wide field of view. [4]22 rifles with grooved receiver. [5]Side mount. [6]For Win. A.E. From Clear View Mfg.

Maker, Model, Type	Adjust.	Scopes	Price
CONETROL			
Huntur[1] (base & rings)	W only	1", split rings, 3 heights	$119.88
Gunnur[2] (base & rings)	W only	1", split rings, 3 heights	$149.88
Custum[3] (base & rings)	W only	1", split rings, 3 heights	$179.88
One-Piece Side Mount Base[4]	W only		
DapTar Bases[5]	W only		
Pistol Bases, 2- or 3-ring[6]	W only		
Fluted Bases[7]	W only		$179.88
Metric Rings[8]	W only	26mm, 26.5mm, 30mm	$119.96-179.88

[1]All popular rifles, including metric-drilled foreign guns. Price shown for base, two rings. Matte finish. [2]Gunnur grade has mirror-finished rings to match scopes. Satin-finish base to match guns. Price shown for base, two rings. [3]Custom grade has mirror-finished rings and mirror-finished, streamlined base. Price shown for base, two rings. [4]Win. 94, Krag, older split-bridge Mannlicher-Schoenauer, Mini-14, etc. Prices same as above. [5]For all popular guns with integral mounting provision, including Sako, BSA Ithacagun, Ruger, Tikka, H&K, BRNO and many others. Also for grooved-receiver rimfires and air rifles. Prices same as above. [6]For XP-100, T/C Contender, Colt SAA, Ruger Blackhawk, S&W and others. [7]Sculptured two-piece bases as found on fine custom rifles. Price shown is for base alone. Also available unfinished **$119.88**, or finished but unblued **$149.88**. [8]26mm, 26.5mm, and 30mm rings made in projectionless style, in three heights. Three-ring mount for T/C Contender and other pistols in Conetrol's three grades. Any Conetrol mount available in stainless steel add 50 percent. Adjust-Quik-Detach (AQD) mounting is now available from Conetrol. Jam screws return the horizontal-split rings to zero. Adjustable for windage. AQD bases **$99.96**. AQD rings **$99.96**. (Total cost of complete setup, rings and two-piece base, is **$199.92**).

Maker, Model, Type	Adjust.	Scopes	Price
EAW			
Quick-Loc Mount	W&E	1", 26mm	$345.00
	W&E	30mm	$360.00
Magnum Fixed Mount	W&E	1", 26mm	$305.00
	W&E	30mm	$320.00

Fit most popular rifles. Available in 4 heights, 4 extensions. Reliable return to zero. Stress-free mounting. Imported by New England Custom Gun Svc.

Maker, Model, Type	Adjust.	Scopes	Price
GENTRY			
Feather-Light Rings and Bases	No	1", 30mm	$90.00-125.00

Bases for Rem. Seven, 700, Mauser 98, Browning A-Bolt, Weatherby Mk. V, Win. 70, HVA, Dakota. Two-piece base for Rem. Seven, chrome-moly or stainless. Rings in matte, regular blue, or stainless gray; four heights. From David Gentry.

Maker, Model, Type	Adjust.	Scopes	Price
GRIFFIN & HOWE			
Topmount[1]	No	1", 30mm	$625.00
Sidemount[2]	No	1", 30mm	$255.00
Garand Mount[3]	No	1"	$255.00

[1]Quick-detachable, double-lever mount with 1" rings, installed; with 30mm rings **$875.00**. [2]Quick-detachable, double-lever mount; with 30mm rings **$375.00**; installed, 1" rings. **$405.00**; installed, 30mm rings **$525.00**. [3]Price installed, with 1" rings **$405.00**. From Griffin & Howe.

Maker, Model, Type	Adjust.	Scopes	Price
G. G. & G.			
Remington 700 Rail	No	Weaver base	$135.00
Sniper Grade Rings	No	30mm	$159.95
M16/AR15 F.I.R.E. Std.[1]	No	Weaver rail	$75.00
M16/AR15 F.I.R.E. Scout	No	Weaver rail	$82.95
Aimpoint Standard Ring	No		$164.95
Aimpoint Cantilever Ring	No	Weaver rail	$212.00

[1]For M16/A3, AR15 flat top receivers; also in extended length. From G. G. & G.

SCOPE RINGS & BASES

Maker, Model, Type	Adjust.	Scopes	Price
IRONSIGHTER			
Ironsighter See-Through Mounts[1]	No	1" split rings	$26.46
Ironsighter S-9[4]	No	1" split rings	$40.74
Ironsighter AR-15/M-16[6]	No	1", 30mm	$63.10
Ironsighter 22-Cal.Rimfire[2]	No	1"	$18.45
Model #570[7]	No	1" split rings	$26.46
Model #573[7]	No	30mm split rings	$40.74
Model #727[3]	No	.875" split rings	$16.60
Blackpowder Mount[5]	No	1"	$34.20-78.25

[1]Most popular rifles. Rings have oval holes to permit use of iron sights. [2]For 1" dia. scopes. [3]For .875 dia. scopes. [4]For 1" dia. extended eye relief scopes. [5]Fits most popular blackpowder rifles; two-piece (CVA, Knight, Marlin and Austin & Halleck) and one-piece integral (T/C). [6]Model 716 with 1" #540 rings; fits Weaver-style bases. Some models in stainless finish. [7]New detachable Weaver-style rings fit all Weaver-style bases. Price: **$26.95.** From Ironsighter Co.

Maker, Model, Type	Adjust.	Scopes	Price
K MOUNT by KENPATABLE			
Shotgun Mount	No	1", laser or red dot device	$49.95
SKS[1]	No	1"	$39.95

Wrap-around design; no gunsmithing required. Models for Browning BPS, A-5 12-ga., Sweet 16, 20, Rem. 870/1100 (LTW and L.H.), S&W 916, Mossberg 500, Ithaca 37 & 51 12-ga., S&W 1000/3000, Win. 1400. [1]Requires simple modification to gun. From KenPatable Ent.

Maker, Model, Type	Adjust.	Scopes	Price
KRIS MOUNTS			
Side-Saddle[1]	No	1", 26mm split rings	$12.98
Two-Piece (T)[2]	No	1", 26mm split rings	$8.98
One Piece (T)[3]	No	1", 26mm split rings	$12.98

[1]One-piece mount for Win. 94. [2]Most popular rifles and Ruger. [3]Blackhawk revolver. Mounts have oval hole to permit use of iron sights.

Maker, Model, Type	Adjust.	Scopes	Price
KWIK-SITE			
Adapter	No	1"	$13.50
KS-W2[2]	No	1"	$13.50
KS-W94[3]	No	1"	$42.95
KS-WEV (Weaver-style rings)	No	1"	$10.50
KS-WEV-HIGH	No	1"	$10.50
KS-T22 1"[4]	No	1"	$17.95
KS-FL Flashlite[5]	No	Mini or C cell flash light	$37.95
KS-T88[6]	No	1"	$11.84
KS-T89	No	30mm	$13.50
KSN 22 See-Thru	No	1", 7/8"	$17.95
KSN-T22	No	1", 7/8"	$17.95
KSN-M-16 See-Thru (for M16 + AR-15)	No	1"	$49.95
KS-202[1]	No	1"	$25.14
KS-203	No	30mm	$38.64
KSBP[7]	No	Integral	$76.95
KSB Base Set			$5.95
Combo Bases & Rings	No	1"	$19.84

Bases interchangeable with Weaver bases. [1]Most rifles. Allows use of iron sights. [2]22-cal. rifles with grooved receivers. Allows use of iron sights. [3]Model 94, 94 Big Bore. No drilling or tapping. Also in adjustable model **$57.95.** [4]Non-See-Thru model for grooved receivers. [5]Allows C-cell or Mini Mag Lites to be mounted atop See-Thru mounts. [6]Fits any Redfield, Tasco, Weaver or Universal-style Kwik-Site dovetail base. [7]Blackpowder mount with integral rings and sights.

Maker, Model, Type	Adjust.	Scopes	Price
LASER AIM	No	Laser Aim	$19.99-69.00

Mounts Laser Aim above or below barrel. Available for most popular hand guns, rifles, shotguns, including militaries. From Laser Aim Technologies, Inc.

Maker, Model, Type	Adjust.	Scopes	Price
LEUPOLD			
STD Bases[1]	W only	One- or two-piece bases	$25.40
STD Rings[2]		1" super low, low, medium, high	$33.60
DD RBH Handgun Mounts[2]	No		$34.00
Dual Dovetail Bases	No		$25.40
Dual Dovetail Rings[4]		1", low, med, high	$33.60
Ring Mounts	No	7/8", 1"	$102.80
22 Rimfire[4]	No	7/8", 1"	$73.60
Gunmaker Base[3]	W only	1"	$73.60
Quick Release Rings		1", low, med., high	$43.00-81.00
Quick Release Bases[5]	No	1", one- or two-piece	$73.60

[1]Base and two rings; Casull, Ruger, S&W, T/C; add **$5.00** for silver finish. [2]Rem. 700, Win. 70-type actions. For Ruger No. 1, 77, 77/22; interchangeable with Ruger units. For dovetailed rimfire rifles. Sako; high, medium, low. [3]Must be drilled, tapped for each action. [4]13mm dovetail receiver. [5]BSA Monarch, Rem. 40x, 700, 721, 725, Ruger M77, S&W 1500, Weatherby Mark V, Vanguard, Win. M70.

Maker, Model, Type	Adjust.	Scopes	Price
MARLIN			
One-Piece QD (T)	No	1" split rings	$10.10
Most Marlin lever actions.			

Maker, Model, Type	Adjust.	Scopes	Price
MILLETT RINGS			
One-Piece Bases[6]	Yes	1"	$26.41
Universal Two-Piece Bases			
700 Series	W only	Two-piece bases	$26.41
FN Series	W only	Two-piece bases	$26.41
70 Series[1]	W only	1", two-piece bases	$26.41
Angle-Loc Rings[2]	W only	1", low, medium, high	$35.49
Ruger 77 Rings[3]		1"	$38.14
Shotgun Rings[4]		1"	$32.55
Handgun Bases, Rings[5]		1"	$36.07-80.38
30mm Rings[7]		30mm	$20.95-41.63
Extension Rings[8]		1"	$40.43-56.44
See-Thru Mounts[9]	No	1"	$29.35-31.45
Shotgun Mounts[10]	No	1"	$52.45
Timber Mount	No	1"	$81.90

BRNO, Rem. 40x, 700, 722, 725, 7400 Ruger 77 (round top), Marlin, Weatherby, FN Mauser, FN Brownings, Colt 57, Interarms Mark X, Parker-Hale, Savage 110, Sako (round receiver), many others. [1]Fits Win. M70 70XTR, 670, Browning BBR, BAR, BLR, A-Bolt, Rem. 7400/7600, Four, Six, Marlin 336, Win. 94 A. E., Sav. 110. [2]To fit Weaver-type bases. [3]Engraved. Smooth **$34.60.** [4]For Rem. 870, 1100; smooth. [5]Two- and three-ring sets for Colt Python, Trooper, Diamondback, Peacekeeper, Dan Wesson, Ruger Redhawk, Super Redhawk. [6]Turn-in bases and Weaver-style for most popular rifles and T/C Contender, XP100 pistols. [7]Both Weaver and turn-in styles; three heights. [8]Med. or high; ext. front std. rear, ext. rear std. front, ext. front ext. rear; **$40.90** for double extension. [9]Many popular rifles, Knight MK-85, T/C Hawken, Renegade, Mossberg 500 Slugster, 835 slug. [10]For Rem. 879/1100, Win. 1200, 1300/1400, 1500, Mossberg 500. Some models available in nickel at extra cost. New Angle-Loc two-piece bases fit all Weaver-style rings. In smooth, matte and nickel finishes, they are available for Browning A-Bolt, Browning BAR/BLR, Interarms MK X, FN, Mauser 98, CVA rifles with octagon barrels, CVA rifles with round receiver, Knight MK-85, Knight Wolverine, Remington 700, Sauer SHR 970, Savage 110, Winchester 70 **$24.95** to **$28.95.** From Millett Sights.

Maker, Model, Type	Adjust.	Scopes	Price
MMC			
AK[1]	No		$39.95
FN FAL/LAR[2]	No		$59.95

[1]Fits all AK derivative receivers; Weaver-style base; low-profile scope position. [2]Fits all FAL versions; Weaver-style base. From MMC.

Maker, Model, Type	Adjust.	Scopes	Price
REDFIELD			
JR-SR (T)[1]. One/two-piece bases.	W only	3/4", 1", 26mm, 30mm	JR: $15.99-46.99 SR:$15.99-33.49
Ring (T)[2]	No	3/4" and 1"	$27.95-29.95
Widefield See-Thru Mounts	No	1"	$15.95
Ruger Rings[3]	No	1", med., high	$30.49-36.49
Ruger 30mm[4]	No	1"	$37.99-40.99

[1]Low, med. & high, split rings. Reversible extension front rings for 1". Two-piece bases for Sako. Colt Sauer bases **$39.95.** Med. Top Access JR rings nickel-plated **$28.95.** SR two-piece ABN mount nickel-plated **$22.95.** [2]Split rings for grooved 22s; 30mm, black matte **$42.95.** [3]For Ruger Model 77 rifles, medium and high; medium only for M77/22. [4]For Model 77. Also in matte finish **$45.95.** Scout mounts available for Mosin Nagant, Schmidt Rubin K-31, 98K Mauser, Husqvarna Mauser, Persian Mauser, Turkish Mauser.

Maker, Model, Type	Adjust.	Scopes	Price
S&K			
Insta-Mount (T) Bases and Rings[1]	W only	Weaver & S&K rings	$55.10-160.00
Insta-Mount (T) Scout Mounts[2]	W only	Weaver & S&K rings	From $51.00
Conventional Rings[3]	W only	1" horizontally split rings	From $40.00
Skulptured™ Bases, Rings[4]	W only	Uses only S&K rings	From $46.00
Smooth Kontoured™ Rings[5]	W only	1", 30mm vertically split	From $58.00

[1]1903, A3, M1 Carbine, #1 Lee Enfield. MkIII, #4, #5, M1917, M98 Mauser, AR-180, M-14, M-1, Mini-14, M1-A, Krag, Win. 94, SKS Type 56, Arasaka. [2]Mosin Nagant 91/30, 91/59 & M44, Schmidt Rubin K-31 &1911, M98 Mauser, Yugo 48, 24-47 & 48A, Carl Gustaf, Husqvarna, Persion, Turkish, Finnish, Czechoslovakian 24 & 98/22, Chilean, Arasaka. 3 horizontally split in low & high & supplied in matte & gloss. [4]For most popular rifles alredy drilled & tapped – also Sako, CZ, Tikka & 3/8 dovetail 22s in matte, gloss, mirror & stainless. Standard & extension bases available. Custom bases. [5]No projections; weigh 1/2 oz each; matte, gloss, mirror or stainless in low, med & high.

Maker, Model, Type	Adjust.	Scopes	Price
SAKO			
QD Dovetail	W only	1"	$70.00-155.00

Sako, or any rifle using Sako action, 3 heights available. Stoeger, importer.

Maker, Model, Type	Adjust.	Scopes	Price
SPRINGFIELD, INC.			
M1A Third Generation	No	1" or 30mm	$123.00
M1A Standard	No	1" or 30mm	$77.00
M6 Scout Mount	No		$29.00

Weaver-style bases. From Springfield, Inc.

SCOPE RINGS & BASES

Maker, Model, Type	Adjust.	Scopes	Price
TALBOT			
QD Bases	No		$180.00-190.00
Rings	No	1", 30mm	$50.00-70.00

Blue or stainless steel; standard or extended bases; rings in three heights. For most popular rifles. From Talbot QD Mounts.

Maker, Model, Type	Adjust.	Scopes	Price
TASCO			
Centerfire rings #791DSC	Integral	1", 30mm, matte black	$5.95
High centerfire rings #793DSC	Special high	1", matte black aluminum	$5.95
.22/airgun rings #797DSC	Yes	1", matte black aluminum	$5.95
.22/airgun "Quick Peep" rings #799DSC	Yes	1", matte black aluminum	$5.95

Maker, Model, Type	Adjust.	Scopes	Price
THOMPSON/CENTER			
Duo-Ring Mount[1]	No	1"	$78.00
Weaver-Style Bases	No		$14.00-28.50
Weaver-Style Rings[2]	No	1"	$36.00

[1]Attaches directly to T/C Contender bbl., no drilling/tapping; also for T/C M/L rifles, needs base adapter; blue or stainless. [2]Medium and high; blue or silver finish. From Thompson/Center.

Maker, Model, Type	Adjust.	Scopes	Price
UNERTL			
1/4 Click[1]	Yes	3/4", 1" target scopes	Per set $285.00

[1]Unertl target or varmint scopes. Posa or standard mounts, less bases. From Unertl.

Maker, Model, Type	Adjust.	Scopes	Price
WARNE			
Premier Series (all steel)			
T.P.A. (Permanently Attached)	No	1", 4 heights 30mm, 2 heights	$87.75-98.55
Premier Series Rings fit Premier Series Bases			
Premier Series (all-steel Q.D. rings)			
Premier Series (all steel) Quick detachable lever	No	1", 4 heights 26mm, 2 heights 30mm, 3 heights	$129.95-131.25 $142.00
BRNO 19mm	No	1", 3 heights 30mm, 2 heights	$125.00-136.70
BRNO 16mm	No	1", 2 heights	$125.00
Ruger	No	1", 4 heights 30mm, 3 heights	$125.00-136.70
Ruger M77	No	1", 3 heights 30mm, 2 heights	$125.00-136.70
Sako Medium & Long Action	No	1", 4 heights 30mm, 3 heights	$125.00-136.70
Sako Short Action	No	1", 3 heights	$125.00
All-Steel One-Piece Base, ea.			$38.50
All-Steel Two-Piece Base, ea.			$14.00
Maxima Series (fits all Weaver-style bases)			
Permanently Attached[1]	No	1", 3 heights 30mm, 3 heights	$25.50 $36.00
Adjustable Double Lever[2]	No	1", 3 heights 30mm, 3 heights	$72.60 $80.75
Thumb Knob	No	1", 3 heights 30mm, 3 heights	$59.95 $68.25
Stainless-Steel Two-Piece Base, ea.			$15.25

Vertically split rings with dovetail clamp, precise return to zero. Fit most popular rifles, handguns. Regular blue, matte blue, silver finish. [1]All-Steel, non-Q.D. rings. [2]All-steel, Q.D. rings. From Warne Mfg. Co.

Maker, Model, Type	Adjust.	Scopes	Price
WEAVER			
Top Mount	No	7/8", 1", 30mm, 33mm	$24.95-38.95
Side Mount	No	1", 1" long	$14.95-34.95
Tip-Off Rings	No	7/8", 1"	$24.95-32.95
Pivot Mounts	No	1"	$38.95
Complete Mount Systems			
Pistol	No	1"	$75.00-105.00
Rifle	No	1"	$32.95
SKS Mount System	No	1"	$49.95
Pro-View (no base required)	No	1"	$13.95-15.95
Converta-Mount, 12-ga. (Rem. 870, Moss. 500)	No	1", 30mm	$74.95

Maker, Model, Type	Adjust.	Scopes	Price
WEAVER (cont.)			
See-Thru Mounts			
Detachable	No	1"	$27.00-32.00
System (no base required)	No	1"	$15.00-35.00
Tip-Off	No	1"	$15.00

Nearly all modern rifles, pistols, and shotguns. Detachable rings in standard, See-Thru, and extension styles, in Low, Medium, High or X-High heights; gloss (blued), silver and matte finishes to match scopes. Extension rings are only available in 1" High style and See-Thru X-tensions only in gloss finish. Tip-Off rings only for 3/8" grooved receivers or 3/8" grooved adaptor bases; no base required. See-Thru & Pro-View mounts for most modern big bore rifles, some in silver. No Drill & Tap Pistol systems in gloss or silver for Colt Python, Trooper, 357, Officer's Model, Ruger Single-Six, Security-Six (gloss finish only), Blackhawk, Super Blackhawk, Blackhawk SRM 357, Redhawk, Mini-14 Series (not Ranch), Ruger 22 Auto Pistols, Mark II, Smith & Wesson I- and current K-frames with adj. rear sights. Converta-Mount Systems in Standard and See-Under for Mossberg 500 (12- and 20-ga.), Remington 870, 11-87 (12- and 20-ga. lightweight), Winchester 1200, 1300, 1400, 1500. Converta-Brackets, bases, rings also available for Beretta A303 and A390, Browning A-5, BPS Pump, Ithaca 37, 87. From Weaver.

Maker, Model, Type	Adjust.	Scopes	Price
WEIGAND			
Browning Buck Mark[1]	No		$29.95
Integra Mounts[2]	No		$39.95-69.00
S&W Revolver[3]	No		$29.95
Ruger 10/22[4]	No		$14.95-39.95
Ruger Revolver[5]	No		$29.95
Taurus Revolver[4]	No		$29.95-65.00
Lightweight Rings	No	1", 30mm	$29.95-39.95
1911			
SM3[6]	No	Weaver rail	$99.95
APCMNT[7]	No		$69.95

[1]No gunsmithing. [2]S&W K, L, N frames, Taurus vent rib models, Colt Anaconda/Python, Ruger Redhawk, Ruger 10/22. [3]K, L, N frames. [4]Three models. [5]Redhawk, Blackhawk, GP100. [6]3rd Gen., drill and tap, without slots $59.95. [7]For Aimpoint Comp. Red Dot scope, silver only. From Weigand Combat Handguns, Inc.

Maker, Model, Type	Adjust.	Scopes	Price
WIDEVIEW			
Premium 94 Angle Eject and side mount	No	1"	$22.44
Premium See-Thru	No	1"	$22.44
22 Premium See-Thru	No	3/4", 1"	$16.47
Universal Ring Angle Cut	No	1"	$31.28
Universal Ring Straight Cut	No	1"	$18.70
Solid Mounts			
Lo Ring Solid[1]	No	1"	$22.44
Hi Ring Solid[1]	No	1"	$18.14
SR Rings		1", 30mm	$16.32
22 Grooved Receiver	No	1"	$16.32
Blackpowder Mounts[2]	No	1"	$22.44
High, extra-high ring mounts with base	No	up to 60mm	$30.16
AR15 and M16	No		$33.92

[1]For Weaver-type base. Models for many popular rifles. Low ring, high ring and grooved receiver types. [2]No drilling, tapping, for T/C Renegade, Hawken, CVA, Knight Traditions guns. From Wideview Scope Mount Corp.

Maker, Model, Type	Adjust.	Scopes	Price
WILLIAMS			
Side Mount with HCO Rings[1]	No	1", split or extension rings	$74.35
Side Mount, Offset Rings[2]	No	Same	$61.45
Sight-Thru Mounts[3]	No	1", 7/8" sleeves	$19.50
Streamline Mounts	No	1" (bases form rings)	$26.50

[1]Most rifles, Br. S.M.L.E. (round rec.) $14.41 extra. [2]Most rifles including Win. 94 Big Bore. [3]Many modern rifles, including CVA Apollo, others with 1" octagon barrels.

Maker, Model, Type	Adjust.	Scopes	Price
YORK			
M-1 Garand	Yes	1"	$39.95

Centers scope over the action. No drilling, tapping or gunsmithing. Uses standard dovetail rings. From York M-1 Conversions.

NOTES

(S) Side Mount; (T) Top Mount; 22mm=.866"; 25.4mm=1.024"; 26.5mm=1.045"; 30mm=1.81".

METALLIC SIGHTS

Sporting Leaf and Open Sights

AUTOMATIC DRILLING REAR SIGHT Most German and Austrian drillings have this kind of rear sight. When rifle barrel is selected, the rear sight automatically comes to the upright position. Base length 2.165", width .472", folding leaf height .315". From New England Custom Gun Service.
Price: **$48.50**

CLASSIC MARBLE/WILLIAMS STYLE FULLY ADJUSTABLE REAR SPORTING SIGHTS Screw-on attachment. Dovetailed graduated windage and elevation adjustment. Elevation and windage lock with set screws. Available in steel or lightweight alloy construction. From Sarco, Inc.
Price: **$13.50**

ERA MASTERPIECE ADJUSTABLE REAR SIGHTS Precision-machined, all-steel, polished and blued. Attaches with 8-36 socket head screw. Use small screwdriver to adjust windage and elevation. Available for various barrel widths. From New England Custom Gun Service.
Price: **$95.00**

ERA CLASSIC ADJUSTABLE REAR SIGHT Similar to the Masterpiece unit except windage is adjusted by pushing sight sideways, then locking it with a reliable clamp. Precision machined all steel construction, polished, with 6-48 fastening screw and Allen wrench. Shallow "V" and "U" notch. Length 2.170", width .550". From New England Custom Gun Service.
Price: **$79.00**

ERA EXPRESS SIGHTS A wide variety of open sights and bases for custom installation. Partial listing shown. From New England Custom Gun Service.
Price: One-leaf express **$79.00**
Price: Two-leaf express **$89.00**
Price: Three-leaf express **$99.00**
Price: Bases for above .... **$48.00 to $53.00**
Price: Standing rear sight, straight **$19.00**
Price: Base for above **$30.00**

ERA CLASSIC EXPRESS SIGHTS Standing or folding leaf sights are securely locked to the base with the ERA Magnum Clamp, but can be loosened for sighting in. Base can be attached with two socket-head cap screws or soldered. Finished and blued. Barrel diameters from .600" to .930". From New England Custom Gun Service.
Price: One-leaf express **$125.00**
Price: Two-leaf express **$135.00**
Price: Three-leaf express **$145.00**

ERA MASTERPIECE REAR SIGHT Adjustable for windage and elevation, and adjusted and locked with a small screwdriver. Comes with 8-36 socket- head cap screw and wrench. Barrel diameters from .600" to .930".
Price: **$75.00**

G.G. & G. SAME PLANE APERTURE M-16/AR-15 A2-style dual aperture rear sight with both large and small apertures centered on the same plane.
Price: **$45.00**

LYMAN No.16 Middle sight for barrel dovetail slot mounting. Folds flat when scope or peep sight is used. Sight notch plate adjustable for elevation. White triangle for quick aiming. Designed to fit 3/8" dovetail slots. Three heights: A-.400" to .500", B-.345" to .445", C-.500" to .600". A slot blank designed to fill dovetail notch when sight is removed is available.
Price: **$5.00**
Price: **$13.25**

MARBLE FALSE BASE #76, #77, #78 New screw-on base for most rifles replaces factory base. 3/8" dovetail slot permits installation of any folding rear sight. Can be had in sweat-on models also.
Price: **$8.00**

MARBLE FOLDING LEAF Flattop or semi-buckhorn style. Folds down when scope or peep sights are used. Reversible plate gives choice of "U" or "V" notch. Adjustable for elevation.
Price: **$16.00**
Price: Also available with both windage and elevation adjustment ... **$18.00**

MARBLE SPORTING REAR With white enamel diamond, gives choice of two "U" and two "V" notches or different sizes. Adjustment in height by means of double step elevator and sliding notch piece. For all rifles; screw or dovetail installation.
Price: .... **$16.00 to $17.00**

MARBLE #20 UNIVERSAL New screw or sweat-on base. Both have .100" elevation adjustment. In five base sizes. Three styles of U-notch, square notch, peep. Adjustable for windage and elevation.
Price: Screw-on.. **$23.00**
Price: Sweat-on **$21.00**

MILLETT SPORTING & BLACKPOWDER RIFLE Open click adjustable rear fits 3/8" dovetail cut in barrel. Choice of white outline, target black or open express V rear blades. Also available is a replacement screw-on sight with express V, .562" hole centers. Dovetail fronts in white or blaze orange in seven heights (.157"-.540").
Price: Dovetail or screw-on rear................................... **$58.38**
Price: Front sight **$12.96**

MILLETT SCOPE-SITE Open, adjustable or fixed rear sights dovetail into a base integral with the top scope-mounting ring. Blaze orange front ramp sight is integral with the front ring half. Rear sights have white outline aperture. Provides fast, short-radius, Patridge-type open sights on the top of the scope. Can be used with all Millett rings, Weaver-style bases, Ruger 77 (also fits Redhawk), Ruger Ranch Rifle, No. 1, No. 3, Rem. 870, 1100; Burris, Leupold and Redfield bases.
Price: Scope-Site top only, windage only........................ **$31.15**
Price: As above, fully adjustable **$66.10**
Price: Scope-Site Hi-Turret, fully adjustable, low, medium, high ... **$66.10**

WHITWORTH STYLE ENGLISH 3 LEAF EXPRESS SIGHTS Folding leafs marked in 100, 200 and 300 yard increments. Slide assembly is dovetailed in base. Available in four different styles: 3 folding leaves, flat bottom; 1 fixed, 2 folding leaves, flat bottom; 3 folding leaves, round bottom; 1 fixed, 2 folding leaves, round bottom. Available from Sarco, Inc.
Price: **$49.95**

WICHITA MULTI RANGE SIGHT SYSTEM Designed for silhouette shooting. System allows you to adjust the rear sight to four repeatable range settings, once it is pre-set. Sight clicks to any of the settings by turning a serrated wheel. Front sight is adjustable for weather and light conditions with one adjustment. Specify gun when ordering.
Price: Rear sight... **$145.00**
Price: Front sight **$110.00**

WILLIAMS DOVETAIL OPEN SIGHT (WDOS) Open rear sight with windage and elevation adjustment. Furnished "U" notch or choice of blades. Slips into dovetail and locks with gib lock. Heights from .281" to .531".
Price: With blade... **$19.50**
Price:Less blade **$12.45**
Price:Rear sight blades, each **$7.05**

WILLIAMS GUIDE OPEN SIGHT (WGOS) Open rear sight with windage and elevation adjustment. Bases to fit most military and commercial barrels. Choice of square "U" or "V" notch blade, 3/16", 1/4", 5/16", or 3/8" high.
Price: Less blade.. **$19.50**
Price: Extra blades, each **$7.05**

WILLIAMS WGOS OCTAGON Open rear sight for 1" octagonal barrels. Installs with two 6-48 screws and uses same hole spacing as most T/C muzzleloading rifles. Four heights, choice of square, U, V, or B blade.
Price: **$26.55**

WILLIAMS WSKS, WAK47 Replaces original military-type rear sight. Adjustable for windage and elevation. No drilling or tapping. Peep aperture or open. For SKS carbines, AK-47-style rifles.
Price: Aperture.. **$25.95**
Price: Open **$24.95**

WILLIAMS WM-96 Fits Mauser 96-type military rifles. Replaces original rear sight with open blade or aperture. Fully adjustable for windage and elevation. No drilling or tapping.
Price: Aperture.. **$25.95**
Price: Open **$24.95**

WILLIAMS FIRE RIFLE SETS Replacement front and rear fiber optic sights. Red bead front, two green elements in the fully-adjustable rear. Made of CNC-machined metal.
Price: For Ruger 10/22.. **$24.95**
Price: For most Marlin and Win. (3/8" dovetail) **$34.95**
Price: For Remington (newer style sight base) **$28.95**

Aperture and Micrometer Receiver Sights

A2 REAR SIGHT KIT Featuring an exclusive numbered windage knob. For .223 AR-style rifles. From ArmaLite, Inc.
Price: **$55.00**

AO GHOST RING HUNTING SIGHT
Fully adjustable for windage and elevation. Available for most rifles, including blackpowder guns. Minimum gunsmithing required for most installations; matches most mounting holes. From AO Sight Systems, Inc.
Price: .. **$90.00**

AO Ghost Ring

AO AR-15/M-16 APERTURE Drop-in replacement of factory sights. Both apertures are on the same plane. Large ghost ring has .230" inside diameter; small ghost ring has .100" inside diameter. From AO Sight Systems, Inc.
Price: **$30.00**

METALLIC SIGHTS

AO BACKUP GHOST RING SIGHTS Mounts to scope base and retains zero when reinstalled in the field. Affords same elevation/windage adjustability as AO Hunting Ghost Rings. Included are both .191" and .230" apertures and test posts. Available for Ruger, Sako, Remington 700 and other rifles. From AO Sight Systems, Inc.
Price: **$65.00**

AO TACTICAL SIGHTS For HK UMP/USC/G36/SL8/MP5. The Big Dot Tritium or standard dot tritium is mated with a large .300" diameter rear ghost ring. The "same plane" rear aperture flips from the .300" to a .230" diameter ghost ring. From AO Sight Systems, Inc.
Price: .... **$90.00 to $120.00**

BEEMAN/FEINWERKBAU 5454 MATCH APERTURE SIGHT Small size, new-design sight uses constant-pressure flat springs to eliminate point of impact shifts.
Price: **$440.85**

BEEMAN SPORT APERTURE SIGHT Positive click micrometer adjustments. Deluxe version has target knobs. For air rifles with grooved receivers.
Price: Deluxe **$50.00**

BUSHMASTER COMPETITION A2 REAR SIGHT ASSEMBLY Elevation and windage mechanism feature either 1/2 or 1/4 minute of adjustment. Long distance aperture allows screw-in installation of any of four interchangeable micro-apertures.
Price: 1/2 M.O.A. **$109.95**
Price: 1/4 M.O.A. **$114.95**

DPMS NATIONAL MATCH Replaces the standard A2 rear sight on M16/AR-15 rifles. Has 1/4-minute windage and 1/2-minute elevation adjustments. Includes both a .052" and .200" diameter aperture.
Price: **$92.99**

ENFIELD NO. 4 TARGET/MATCH SIGHT Originally manufactured by Parker-Hale, has adjustments up to 1,300 meters. Micrometer click adjustments for windage. Adjustable aperture disc has six different openings from .030" to .053". From Sarco, Inc.
Price: **$49.95**

EAW RECEIVER SIGHT A fully adjustable aperture sight that locks securely into the EAW quick-detachable scope mount rear base. Made by New England Custom Gun Service.
Price: **$80.00**

ERA SEE-THRU Contains fiber optic center dot. Fits standard 3/8" American dovetails. Locks in place with set screw. Ideal for use on moving targets. Width 19.5mm. Available in low (.346", medium .425" and high .504" models. From New England Custom Gun Service.
Price: **$40.00**

G. G.& G. MAD IRIS Multiple Aperture Device is a four sight, rotating aperture disk with small and large apertures on the same plane. Mounts on M-16/ AR-15 flattop receiver. Fully adjustable.
Price: **$141.95**
Price: A2 IRIS, two apertures, full windage adjustments **$124.95**

KNIGHT'S ARMAMENT 600 METER FOLDING REAR SIGHT Click adjustable from 200 to 600 meters with clearly visible range markings. Intermediate clicks allows for precise zero at known ranges. Allows use of optical scopes by folding don. Mounts on rear of upper receiver rail on SR-25 and similar rifles. From Knight's Armament Co.
Price: **$181.00**

KNIGHT'S ARMAMENT FOLDING 300M SIGHT Mounts on flat-top upper receivers on SR-25 and similar rifles. May be used as a back-up iron sight for a scoped rifle/carbine or a primary sight. Peep insert may be removed to expose the 5mm diameter ghost ring aperture. From Knight's Armament Co.
Price: **$144.00**

LYMAN No. 2 Tang Sight Designed for the Winchester Model 94. Has high index marks on aperture post; comes with both .093" quick sighting aperture, .040" large disk aperture, and replacement mounting screws.
Price: **$76.00**
Price: For Marlin lever actions **$76.00**

LYMAN No. 57 1/4-minute clicks. Stayset knobs. Quick-release slide, adjustable zero scales. Made for almost all modern rifles.
Price: **$67.50**
Price: No. 57SME, 57SMET (for White Systems Model 91 and Whitetail rifles) **$62.50**

LYMAN 57GPR Designed especially for the Lyman Great Plains Rifle. Mounts directly onto the tang of the rifle and has 1/4-minute micrometer click adjustments.
Price: **$62.50**

LYMAN No. 66 Fits close to the rear of flat-sided receivers, furnished with Stayset knobs. Quick-release slide,

Lyman 57GPR

1/4-min. adjustments. For most lever or slide action or flat-sided automatic rifles.
Price: **$67.50**
Price: No. 66MK (for all current versions of the Knight MK-85 in-line rifle with flat-sided receiver) **$67.50**
Price: No. 66SKS fits Russian and Chinese SKS rifles; large and small apertures **$67.50**
Price: No. 66 WB for Model 1886 Winchester lever actions **$67.50**

LYMAN No. 66U Light weight, designed for most modern shotguns with a flat-sided, round-top receiver. 1/4-minute clicks. Requires drilling, tapping. Not for Browning A-5, Rem. M11.
Price: **$71.50**

LYMAN 90MJT RECEIVER SIGHT Mounts on standard Lyman and Williams FP bases. Has 1/4-minute audible micrometer click adjustments, target knobs with direction indicators. Adjustable zero scales, quick-release slide. Large 7/8" diameter aperture disk.
Price: Right- or left-hand **$74.95**

LYMAN RECEIVER SIGHT Audible-click adjustments for windage and elevation, coin-slotted "stayset" knobs and two interchangeable apertures. For Mauser, Springfield, Sako, T/C Hawken, Rem. 700, Win. 70, Savage 110, SKS, Win. 94, Marlin 336 and 1894.
Price: **$53.99**

LYMAN 1886 #2 TANG SIGHT Fits the Winchester 1886 lever action rifle and replicas thereof not containing a tang safety. Has height index marks on the aperture post and an .800" maximum elevation adjustment. Included is a .093" x 1/2" quick-sighting aperture and .040 x 5/8" target disk.
Price: **$76.00**

MARBLE PEEP TANG SIGHT All-steel construction. Micrometer-like click adjustments for windage and elevation. For most popular old and new lever-action rifles.
Price: **$125.00**

MILLETT PEEP RIFLE SIGHTS Fully adjustable, heat-treated nickel steel peep aperture receiver sight for the Mini-14. Has fine windage and elevation adjustments; replaces original.
Price: Rear sight, Mini-14 .... **$68.95**
Price: Front sight, Mini-14 .... **$37.95**
Price: Front and rear combo with hood **$89.95**

NATIONAL MATCH REAR SIGHT KIT For AR-15 style rifles. From Armalite, Inc.
Price: 1/2 W, 1/2E **$80.00**
Price: 1/4 W, 1/2 E **$80.00**

NECG PEEP SIGHT FOR WEAVER SCOPE MOUNT BASES Attaches to Weaver scope mount base. Windage adjusts with included Allen wrenches, elevation with a small screwdriver. Furnished with two apertures (.093" and .125" diameter hole) and two interchangeable elevation slides for high or low sight line. From New England Custom Gun Service.
Price: **$85.00**

NECG PEEP SIGHT FOR GROOVED MOUNT BASES Windage adjusts with included Allen wrenches, elevation with a small screwdriver. Furnished with two apertures (.093" and .125" diameter hole) and two interchangeable elevation slides for high or low sight line. From New England Custom Gun Service.
Price: **$85.00**

NECG RUGER PEEP SIGHT Made for Ruger M-77 and No. 1 rifles, it is furnished with .093" and .125" opening apertures. Can be installed on a standard Ruger rear mount base or quarter rib. Tightening the aperture disk will lock the elevation setting in place. From New England Custom Gun Service.
Price: **$85.00**

T/C HUNTING STYLE TANG PEEP SIGHT Compact, all steel construction, with locking windage and elevation adjustments. For use with "bead style" and fiber optic front sights. Models available to fit all traditional T/C muzzleloading rifles. From Thompson/Center Arms.
Price: **$58.00**

Lyman 66SKS

Lyman 90MJT

T/C CONTENDER CARBINE PEEP SIGHT All-steel, low profile, click-adjustable unit mounting on the pre-drilled tapped scope mount holes on the T/C Contender Carbine. From Thompson/Center Arms.
Price: $56.00

TRIJICON 3-DOT NIGHT SIGHTS Self-luminous and machined from steel. Available for the M16/AR-15, H&K rifles. Front and rear sets and front only.
Price: .... $50.00 to $99.00

WILLIAMS APERTURE SIGHT Made to fit SKS rifles.
Price: $19.95

WILLIAMS FIRE SIGHT PEEP SETS Combines the Fire Sight front bead with Williams fully adjustable metallic peep rear.
Price: For SKS $39.95
Price: For Ruger 10/22, 99/44, 96/22, 96/22 Mag. $48.95
Price: For Marlin or Winchester lever actions .... $50.95 to $80.95

WILLIAMS FP Internal click adjustments. Positive locks. For virtually all rifles, T/C Contender, Heckler & Koch HK-91, Ruger Mini-14, plus Win., Rem., and Ithaca shotguns.
Price: From $70.95
Price: With Target Knobs $82.50
Price: FP-GR (for dovetail-grooved receivers, .22s and air guns) $70.95

WILLIAMS TARGET FP Similar to the FP series but developed for most bolt-action rimfire rifles. Target FP High adjustable from 1.250" to 1.750" above centerline of bore; Target FP Low adjustable from .750" to 1.250". Attaching bases for Rem. 540X, 541-S, 580, 581, 582 (#540); Rem. 510, 511, 512, 513-T, 521-T (#510); Win. 75 (#75); Savage/ Anschutz 64 and Mark 12 (#64). Some rifles require drilling, tapping.

Williams Target FP

Price: High or Low ... $78.95
Price: Base only $20.95

WILLIAMS 5-D SIGHT Low cost sight for shotguns, 22s and the more popular big game rifles. Adjustment for windage and elevation. Fits most guns without drilling and tapping. Also for British SMLE, Winchester M94 Side Eject.
Price: From $38.95
Price: With Shotgun Aperture $38.95

WILLIAMS 5D RECEIVER SIGHT Alloy construction and similar design to the FP model except designed to fit Win. 94, Marlin 336, Marlin 1895, Mauser 98.
Price: $34.50

WILLIAMS GUIDE (WGRS) Receiver sight for 30 M1 Carbine, M1903A3 Springfield, Savage 24s, Savage-Anschutz and Weatherby XXII. Utilizes military dovetail; no drilling. Double-dovetail windage adjustment, sliding dovetail adjustment for elevation.
Price: .... $36.95 to $49.95

Vernier Tang Sights

BALLARD TANG SIGHTS Available in variety of models including short & long staff hunter, Pacific & Montana, custom units allowing windage & elevation adjustments. Uses 8x40 base screws with screw spacing of 1.120". From Axtell Rifle Co.
Price: .... $175.00 to $325.00

LYMAN TANG SIGHT Made for Win. 94, 1886, Marlin 30, 336 and 1895.
Price: .... $59.99 to $64.99

MARLIN TANG SIGHTS Available in short and long staff hunter models using 8x40 base screws and screw spacing of 1.120". From Axtell Rifle Co.
Price: .... $170.00 to $180.00

PEDERSOLI CREEDMORE Adjustable for windage and elevation, fits Traditions by Pedersoli rifles and other brands. From Dixie Gun Works.
Price: $110.00

REMINGTON TANG SIGHTS Available in short-range hunter and vernier, mid- and long-range vernier and custom models with windage and elevation adjustments. Uses 10x28 base screws, with screw spacing of 1.940". Eye disk has .052" hole with 10x40 thread. From Axtell Rifle Co.
Price: .... $175.00 to $325.00

SHARPS TANG SIGHTS Reproduction tang sights as manufactured for various Sharps rifles through the years 1859-1878. Wide variety of models available including Standard Issue Sporting Peep, Hartford Transition Mid and Long Range, and Custom Express Sights. From Axtell Rifle Co.
Price: .... $150.00 to $340.00

STEVENS CUSTOM Available in thin base short and long staff hunter, mid and long range sporting vernier, custom mid and long range (custom models allow windage and elevation adjustments) models. Uses 5x40 base screws with screw spacing of 1.485". From Axtell Rifle Co.
Price: .... $170.00 to $325.00

TAURUS TANG SIGHT Made of blue steel, available for Taurus Models 62, 72, 172, 63, 73 and 173. Folds down, aperture disk sight, height index marks on aperture post.
Price: $77.00

WINCHESTER & BROWNING TANG SIGHTS Available in variety of models, including thin & thick base short & long staff hunter, mid & long range sporting vernier and custom units. Screw spacing of 2.180" on all models. From Axtell Rifle Co.
Price: .... $170.00 to $325.00

Globe Target Front Sights

AXTELL CUSTOM GLOBE Designed similar to the original Winchester #35 sight, it contains five inserts. Also available with spirit level. From Axtell Rifle Co.
Price: .... $125.00 to $175.00

BALLARD FRONT SIGHTS Available in windgauge with spirit level, globe with clip, and globe with spirit level (all with five inserts) and beach combination with gold plated rocker models. Dovetail of .375" for all. From Axtell Rifle Co.
Price: .... $125.00 to $240.00

Lyman 20 LJT Globe Front

LYMAN 20 MJT TARGET FRONT Has 7/8" diameter, one-piece steel globe with 3/8" dovetail base. Height is .700" from bottom of dovetail to center of aperture; height on 20 LJT is .750". Comes with seven Anschutz-size steel inserts-two posts and five apertures .126" through .177".
Price: 20 MJT or 20 LJT $33.75

LYMAN NO. 17A TARGET Includes seven interchangeable inserts: four apertures, one transparent amber and two posts .50" and .100" in width.
Price: $28.25
Price: Insert set $13.25

LYMAN 17AEU Similar to the Lyman 17A except has a special dovetail design to mount easily onto European muzzleloaders such as CVA, Traditions and Investarm. All steel, comes with eight inserts.
Price: $26.00

LYMAN NO. 93 MATCH Has 7/8" diameter, fits any rifle with a standard dovetail mounting block. Comes with seven target inserts and accepts most Anschutz accessories. Hooked locking bolt and nut allows quick removal, installation. Base available in .860" (European) and .562" (American) hole spacing.
Price: $45.00

MAYNARD FRONT SIGHTS Custom globe with five inserts and clip. Also available with spirit level bracket and windgauge styles. From Axtell Rifle Co.
Price: .... $125.00 to $240.00

PEDERSOLI GLOBE A tunnel front sight with 12 interchangeable inserts for high precision target shooting. Fits Traditions by Pedersoli and other rifles.
Price: $69.95

REMINGTON FRONT SIGHTS Available in windgauge with spirit level, custom globe with clip and custom globe with spirit level (all with five inserts) and beach combination with gold plated rocker models. Dovetail .460". From Axtell Rifle Co.
Price: .... $125.00 to $250.00

SHARPS FRONT SIGHTS Original-style globe with non-moveable post and pinhead. Also available with windgauge and spirit level. From Axtell Rifle Co.
Price: .... $100.00 to $265.00

WILLIAMS TARGET GLOBE FRONT Adapts to many rifles. Mounts to the base with a knurled locking screw. Height is .545" from center, not including base. Comes with inserts.
Price: $49.95
Price: Dovetail base (low) .220" $19.95
Price: Dovetail base (high) .465" $19.95
Price: Screw-on base, .300" height, .300" radius $19.95
Price: Screw-on base, .450" height, .350" radius $19.95
Price: Screw-on base, .215" height, .400" radius $19.95

WINCHESTER & BROWNING FRONT SIGHTS Available in windgauge with spirit level, globe with clip, globe with spirit level (all with five inserts) and beach combination with gold plated rocker models. From Axtell Rifle Co.
Price: .... $125.00 to $240.00

METALLIC SIGHTS

Front Sights

AO TACTICAL SIGHTS Three types of drop-in replacement front posts–round top or square top night sight posts in standard and Big Dot sizes, or white stripe posts in .080 and .100 widths. For AR15 and M16 rifles. From AO Sight Systems, Inc.
Price: . . . . **$30.00 to $90.00**

AO RIFLE TEST POSTS Allows easy establishment of correct front post height. Provides dovetail post with .050" segments to allow shooter to "shoot-n-snip", watching point-of-impact walk into point of aim. Available for 3/8" standard dovetail, Ruger-style or Mauser. From AO Sight Systems, Inc.
Price: **$5.00**

AR-10 DETACHABLE FRONT SIGHT Allows use of the iron rear sight, but are removable for use of telescopic sights with no obstruction to the sight line, For AR-style rifles. From ArmaLite, Inc.
Price: . . . . **$50.00 to $70.00**
Price: Tritium Dot Express **$60.00**

BUSHMASTER FLIP-UP FRONT SIGHT Made for V Match AR-style rifles, this sight unit slips over milled front sight bases and clamps around barrel. Locks with the push of a button. For use with flip-up style rear sights or the A3 removable carry handle. From Bushmaster Firearms.
Price: **$99.95**

BUSHMASTER A2 COMPETITION FRONT SIGHT POST Surface ground on three sides for optimum visual clarity. Available in two widths: .052"; and .062". From Bushmaster Firearms.
Price: **$12.95**

CLASSIC STREAMLINED FRONT SPORTER RAMP SIGHT Comes with blade and sight cover. Serrated and contoured ramp. Screw-on attachment. Slide-on sight cover is easily detachable. Gold bead. From Sarco, inc.
Price: **$13.50**

ERA BEADS FOR RUGER RIFLES White bead and fiber optic front sights that replace the standard sights on M-77 and No. 1 Ruger rifles. Using 3/32" beads, they are available in heights of .330", .350", .375", .415" and .435". From New England Custom Gun Service.
Price: . . . . **$22.00 to $35.00**

ERA FRONT SIGHTS European-type front sights inserted from the front. Various heights available. From New England Custom Gun Service.
Price: 1/16" silver bead. **$18.00**
Price: 3/32" silver bead **$20.00**
Price: Sourdough bead **$20.00**
Price: Fiber optic **$35.00**
Price: Folding night sight with ivory bead **$49.00**

KNIGHT'S ARMAMENT FRONT STANDING/FOLDING SIGHT Mounts to the SR-25 rifle barrel gas block's MilStd top rail. Available in folding sight model. From Knight's Armament Co.
Price: . . . . **$145.00 to $175.00**

KNIGHT'S ARMAMENT CARRYING HANDLE SIGHT Rear sight and carry handle for the SR-25 rifle. Has fixed range and adjustable windage. From Knight's Armament Co.
Price: **$181.15**

KNIGHT'S ARMAMENT MK II FOLDING FRONT SIGHT For the SR-25 rifle. Requires modified handguard. From Knight's Armament Co.
Price: **$175.00**

KNIGHT'S ARMAMENT FOR FREE-FLOATING RAS Mounts to free-floating SR-25 and SR-15 RAS (rail adapter system) rifle forends. Adjustable for elevation. Made of aluminum. From Knight's Armament Co.
Price: **$155.25**

KNS PRECISION SYSTEMS SIGHT Screws into front base. Hooded for light consistency; precision machined with fine wire crosshairs measuring .010-inches thick. Aperture measures .240-inches diameter. Standard and duplex

reticles. Available for AK-47, MAK-90, AR-15, M16, FN-FAL, H&K 91, 93, 94, MP5, SP89, L1A1, M1 Garand.
Price: **$25.99**

LYMAN HUNTING SIGHTS Made with gold or white beads 1/16" to 3/32" wide and in varying heights for most military and commercial rifles. Dovetail bases.
Price: **$8.95**

MARBLE STANDARD Ivory, red, or gold bead. For all American-made rifles, 1/16" wide bead with semi-flat face that does not reflect light. Specify type of rifle when ordering.
Price: **$10.00**

MARBLE CONTOURED Has 3/8" dovetail base, .090" deep, is 5/8" long. Uses standard 1/16" or 3/32" bead, ivory, red, or gold. Specify rifle type.
Price: **$11.50**

NATIONAL MATCH FRONT SIGHT POST Has .050" blade. For AR-style rifle. From ArmaLite, Inc.
Price: **$12.00**

T/C FIBER OPTIC FRONT MUZZLELOADER SIGHT Ramp-style steel with fiber optic bead for all tradition cap locks, both octagonal and round barrels with dovetail, and most T/C rifles. From Thompson/Center Arms.
Price: . . . . **$16.95 to $36.00**

TRIJICON NIGHT SIGHT Self-luminous tritium gas-filled front sight for the M16/AR-15 series.
Price: **$85.00**

WILLIAMS GOLD BEAD Available in .312", .343", and .406" high models all with 3/32" bead.
Price: **$11.95**

WILLIAMS RISER BLOCKS For adding .250" height to front sights when using a receiver sight. Two widths available: .250" for Williams Streamlined Ramp or .340" on all standard ramps having this base width. Uses standard 3/8" dovetail.
Price: **$7.95**

WILLIAMS AR-15 FIRESIGHT Fiber optic unit attaches to any standard AR-15-style front sight assembly. From Williams Gun Sight Co.
Price: **$45.95**

Ramp Sights

ERA MASTERPIECE Banded ramps; 21 sizes; hand-detachable beads and hood; beads inserted from the front. Various heights available. From New England Custom Gun Service.
Price: Banded ramp **$54.00**
Price: Hood **$10.50**
Price: 1/16" silver bead **$11.50**
Price: 3/32" silver bead **$16.00**
Price: Sourdough bead **$14.50**
Price: Fiber optic **$22.00**
Price: Folding night sight with ivory bead **$39.50**

HOLLAND & HOLLAND STYLE FRONT SIGHT RAMPS Banded and screw-on models in the Holland & Holland-style night sight. Flips forward to expose a .0781" silver bead. Flip back for use of the .150" diameter ivory bead for poor light or close-up hunting. Band thickness .040", overall length 3.350", band length 1.180". From New England Custom Gun Service.
Price: . . . . **$90.00 to $115.00**

LYMAN NO. 18 SCREW-ON RAMP Used with 8-40 screws but may also be brazed on. Heights from .10" to .350". Ramp without sight.
Price: **$13.75**

MARBLE FRONT RAMPS Available in polished or dull matte finish or serrated style. Standard 3/8x.090" dovetail slot. Made for MR-width (.340") front sights. Can be used as screw-on or sweat-on. Heights: .100", .150", .300".
Price: Polished or matte **$14.00**
Price: Serrated **$10.00**

NECG UNIVERSAL FRONT SIGHTS Available in five ramp heights and three front sight heights. Sights can be adjusted up or down .030" with an Allen wrench. Slips into place and then locks into position with a set screw. Six different front sight shapes are offered, including extra large and fiber optic. All hoods except the extra low ramp slide on from the rear and click in place. Extra low ramp has spring-loaded balls to lock hood. Choose from three hood sizes. From New England Custom Gun Service.
Price: **$34.00**

T/C TARGET SIGHT FOR OCTAGON BARREL MUZZLELOADERS A precision rear sight with click adjustments (via knurled knobs) for windage and elevation. Available for 15/16-inch and 1-inch octagon barrels with a screw hole spacing of .836-inch between centers. From Thompson/Center Arms.
Price: **$56.00**

T/C FIBER OPTIC MUZZLELOADER SIGHT Click adjustable for windage and elevation. Steel construction fitted with Tru-Glo™ fiber optics. Models available for most T/C muzzleloading rifles. Fits others with 1-inch and 15/16-inch octagon barrels with a hole spacing of .836-inch between screws. From Thompson/Center Arms.
Price: **$36.00**

METALLIC SIGHTS

WILLIAMS SHORTY RAMP Companion to "Streamlined" ramp, about 1/2" shorter. Screw-on or sweat-on. It is furnished in 1/8", 3/16", 9/32", and 3/8" heights without hood only. Also for shotguns.
Price: **$20.95**
Price: With dovetail lock **$21.95**
WILLIAMS STREAMLINED RAMP Available in screw-on or sweat-on models. Furnished in 9/16", 7/16", 3/8", 5/16", 3/16" heights.
Price: **$24.95**
Price: Sight hood **$4.95**
WILLIAMS STREAMLINED FRONT SIGHTS Narrow (.250" width) for Williams Streamlined ramps and others with 1/4" top width; medium (.340" width) for all standard factory ramps. Available with white, gold or fluorescent beads, 1/16" or 3/32".
Price: .... **$10.95 to $11.95**

Handgun Sights

AO EXPRESS SIGHTS Low-profile, snag-free express-type sights. Shallow V rear with white vertical line, white dot front. All-steel, matte black finish. Rear is available in different heights. Made for most pistols, many with double set-screws. From AO Sight Systems, Inc.
Price: Standard Set, front and rear **$60.00**
Price: Big Dot Set, front and rear **$60.00**
Price: Tritium Set, Standard or Big Dot **$90.00**
Price: 24/7 Pro Express, Std. or Big Dot Tritium **$120.00**

BO-MAR DELUXE BMCS Gives 3/8" windage and elevation adjustment at 50 yards on Colt Gov't 45; sight radius under 7". For GM and Commander models only. Uses existing dovetail slot. Has shield-type rear blade.
Price: **$65.95**
Price: BMCS-2 (for GM and 9mm) **$68.95**
Price: Flat bottom ... **$65.95**
Price: BMGC (for Colt Gold Cup), angled serrated blade, rear ... **$68.95**
Price: BMGC front sight **$12.95**
Price: BMCZ-75 (for CZ-75,TZ-75, P-9 and most clones). Works with factory front ... **$68.95**

Bo-Mar BMGS

BO-MAR FRONT SIGHTS Dovetail style for S&W 4506, 4516, 1076; undercut style (.250", .280", 5/16" high); Fast Draw style (.210", .250", .230" high).
Price: **$12.95**

Bo-Mar BMU XP-100

BO-MAR BMU XP-100/ T/C CONTENDER No gunsmithing required; has .080" notch.
Price: **$77.00**
BO-MAR BMML For muzzleloaders; has .062" notch, flat bottom.
Price: **$65.95**
Price: With 3/8" dovetail **$65.95**

BO-MAR RUGER "P" ADJUSTABLE SIGHT Replaces factory front and rear sights.
Price: Rear sight **$65.95**
Price: Front sight **$12.00**
BO-MAR BMR Fully adjustable rear sight for Ruger MKI, MKII Bull barrel autos.
Price: Rear **$65.95**
Price: Undercut front sight **$12.00**
BO-MAR GLOCK Fully adjustable, all-steel replacement sights. Sight fits factory dovetail. Longer sight radius. Uses Novak Glock .275" high, .135" wide front, or similar.
Price: Rear sight **$68.95**
Price: Front sight **$20.95**
BO-MAR LOW PROFILE RIB & ACCURACY TUNER Streamlined rib with front and rear sights; 7 1/8" sight radius. Brings sight line closer to the bore than standard or extended sight and ramp. Weight 5 oz. Made for Colt Gov't 45, Super 38, and Gold Cup 45 and 38.
Price: **$140.00**
BO-MAR COMBAT RIB For S&W Model 19 revolver with 4" barrel. Sight radius 5 3/4", weight 5 1/2 oz.
Price: **$127.00**
BO-MAR WINGED RIB For S&W 4" and 6" length barrels-K-38, M10, HB 14 and 19. Weight for the 6" model is about 7 1/4 oz.
Price: **$140.00**

BO-MAR COVER-UP RIB Adjustable rear sight, winged front guards. Fits right over revolver's original front sight. For S&W 4" M-10HB, M-13, M-58, M- 64 & 65, Ruger 4" models SDA-34, SDA-84, SS-34, SS-84, GF-34, GF-84.
Price: **$130.00**

Chip McCormick "Drop-In"

CHIP MCCORMICK "DROP-IN" A low mount sight that fits any 1911-style slide with a standard military-type dovetail sight cut (60x.290"). Dovetail front sights also available. From Chip McCormick Corp.
Price: **$47.95**
CHIP MCCORMICK FIXED SIGHTS Same sight picture (.110" rear, 110" front) that's become the standard for pro combat shooters. Low mount design with rounded edges. For 1911-style pistols. May require slide machining for installation. From Chip McCormick Corp.
Price: **$24.95**
C-MORE SIGHTS Replacement front sight blades offered in two types and five styles. Made of Du Pont Acetal, they come in a set of five high-contrast colors: blue, green, pink, red and yellow. Easy to install. Patridge style for Colt Python (all barrels), Ruger Super Blackhawk (7 1/2"), Ruger Blackhawk (4 5/8"); ramp style for Python (all barrels), Blackhawk (4 5/8"), Super Blackhawk (7 1/2" and 10 1/2"). From C-More Systems.
Price: Per set **$19.95**
G.G. & G. GHOST RINGS Replaces the factory rear sight without gunsmithing. Black phosphate finish. Available for Colt M1911 and Commander, Beretta M92F, Glock, S&W, SIG Sauer.
Price: **$65.00**

Heinie Slant Pro

HEINIE SLANT PRO Made with a slight forward slant, the unique design of these rear sights is snag free for unimpeded draw from concealment. The combination of the slant and the rear serrations virtually eliminates glare. Made for most popular handguns. From Heinie Specialty Products.
Price: .... **$50.35 to $122.80**
HEINIE STRAIGHT EIGHT SIGHTS Consists of one tritium dot in the front sight and a slightly smaller Tritium dot in the rear sight. When aligned correctly, an elongated 'eight' is created. The Tritium dots are green in color. Designed with the belief that the human eye can correct vertical alignment faster than horizontal. Available for most popular handguns. From Heinie Specialty Products.
Price: .... **$104.95 to $122.80**
HEINIE CROSS DOVETAIL FRONT SIGHTS Made in a variety of heights, the standard dovetail is 60 degrees x .305" x .062" with a .002 taper. From Heinie Specialty Products.
Price: .... **$20.95 to $47.20**
JP GHOST RING Replacement bead front, ghost ring rear for Glock and M1911 pistols. From JP Enterprises.
Price: **$79.95**
Price: Bo-Mar replacement leaf with JP dovetail front bead **$99.95**
LES BAER CUSTOM ADJUSTABLE LOW MOUNT REAR SIGHT Considered one of the top adjustable sights in the world for target shooting with 1911- style pistols. Available with Tritium inserts. From Les Baer Custom.
Price: .... **$49.00 (standard); $99.00 (tritium)**

METALLIC SIGHTS

LES BAER DELUXE FIXED COMBAT SIGHT A tactical-style sight with a very low profile. Incorporates a no-snag design and has serrations on sides. For 1911-style pistols. Available with Tritium inserts for night shooting. From Les Baer Custom.
Price: .... **$26.00 (standard); $67.00 (with Tritium)**

LES BAER DOVETAIL FRONT SIGHT Blank dovetail sight machined from bar stock. Can be contoured to many different configurations to meet user's needs. Available with Tritium insert. From Les Baer Custom.
Price: .... **$17.00 (standard); $47.00 (with Tritium insert)**

LES BAER FIBER OPTIC FRONT SIGHT Dovetail .330x65 degrees, .125" wide post, .185" high, .060" diameter. Red and green fiber optic. From Les Baer Custom.
Price: **$24.00**

LES BAER PPC-STYLE ADJUSTABLE REAR SIGHT Made for use with custom built 1911-style pistols, allows the user to preset three elevation adjustments for PPC-style shooting. Milling required for installation. Made from 4140 steel. From Les Baer Custom.
Price: ... **$120.00**

LES BAER DOVETAIL FRONT SIGHT WITH TRITIUM INSERT This fully contoured and finished front sight comes ready for gunsmith installation. From Les Baer Custom.
Price: **$47.00**

Les Baer PPC-Style Adjustable Rear Sight

MMC TACTICAL GHOST RING SIGHT Click adjustable for elevation with 30 MOA total adjustment in 3 MOA increments. Click windage adjustment. Machined from solid steel and heat-treated. Front sights available in banded tactical or serrated ramp. Available with or without tritium and in three different finishes. Available for all shotgun makes and models.
Price: .... **$24.95-$149.95**

MEPROLIGHT TRITIUM NIGHT SIGHTS Replacement sight assemblies for low-light conditions. Available for pistols (fixed and adj.), rifles, shotguns. 12- year warranty for useable illumination, while non-TRU-DOT have a 5-year warranty. Distributed in America by Kimber.
Price: Kahr K9, K40, fixed, TRU-DOT **$100.00**
Price: Ruger P85, P89, P94, adjustable, TRU-DOT **$156.00**
Price: Ruger Mini-14R sights **$140.00**
Price: SIG Sauer P220, P225, P226, P228, adjustable, TRU-DOT ... **$156.00**
Price: Smith&Wesson autos, fixed or adjustable, TRU-DOT **$100.00**
Price: Taurus PT92, PT100, adjustable, TRU-DOT **$156.00**
Price: Walther P-99, fixed, TRU-DOT **$100.00**
Price: Shotgun bead **$32.00**
Price: Beretta M92, Cougar, Brigadier, fixed, TRU-DOT **$100.00**
Price: Browning Hi-Power, adjustable, TRU-DOT **$156.00**
Price: Colt M1911 Govt., adjustable, TRU-DOT **$156.00**

MILLETT SERIES 100 REAR SIGHTS All-steel highly visible, click adjustable. Blades in white outline, target black, silhouette, 3-dot. Fit most popular revolvers and autos.
Price: .... **$54.95 to $88.95**

MILLETT BAR/DOT Made with orange or white bar or dot for increased visibility. Available for Beretta 84, 85, 92S, 92SB, Browning, Colt Python & Trooper, Ruger GP 100, P85, Redhawk, Security Six.
Price: .... **$14.99 to $24.99**

MILLETT 3-DOT SYSTEM SIGHTS The 3-Dot System sights use a single white dot on the front blade and two dots flanking the rear notch. Fronts available in Dual-Crimp and Wide Stake-On styles, as well as special applications. Adjustable rear sight available for most popular auto pistols and revolvers including Browning Hi-Power, Colt 1911 Government and Ruger P85.
Price: Front, from **$18.00**
Price: Adjustable rear **$63.95**

MILLETT REVOLVER FRONT SIGHTS All-steel replacement front sights with either white or orange bar. Easy to install. For Ruger GP-100, Redhawk, Security-Six, Police-Six, Speed-Six, Colt Trooper, Diamondback, King Cobra, Peacemaker, Python, Dan Wesson 22 and 15-2.
Price: .... **$15.20 to $18.00**

MILLETT DUAL-CRIMP FRONT SIGHT Replacement front sight for automatic pistols. Dual-Crimp uses an all-steel two-point hollow rivet system. Available in eight heights and four styles. Has a skirted base that covers the front sight pad. Easily installed with the Millett Installation Tool Set. Available in Blaze Orange Bar, White Bar, Serrated Ramp, Plain Post. Available in heights of .185", .200", .225", .275", .312", .340" and .410".
Price: **$18.00**

MILLETT STAKE-ON FRONT SIGHT Replacement front sight for automatic pistols. Stake-On sights have skirted base that covers the front sight pad. Easily installed with the Millet Installation Tool Set. Available in seven heights and four styles-Blaze Orange Bar, White Bar, Serrated Ramp, Plain Post. Available for Glock 17L and 24, others.
Price: **$18.00**

MILLETT ADJUSTABLE TARGET Positive light-deflection serration and slant to eliminate glare and sharp edge sight notch. Audible "click" adjustments. For AMT Hardballer, Beretta 84, 85, 92S, 92SB, Browning Hi-Power, Colt 1911 Government and Gold Cup, Colt revolvers, Dan Wesson 15, 41, 44, Ruger revolvers, Glock 17, 17L, 19, 20, 21, 22, 23.
Price: **$63.95**

MILLETT ADJUSTABLE WHITE OUTLINE Similar to the Target sight, except has a white outline on the blade to increase visibility. Available for the same handguns as the Target model, plus BRNO CZ-75/TZ-75/TA-90 without pin on front sight, and Ruger P85.
Price: **$63.95**

OMEGA OUTLINE SIGHT BLADES Replacement rear sight blades for Colt and Ruger single action guns and the Interarms Virginian Dragoon. Standard Outline available in gold or white notch outline on blue metal. From Omega Sales, Inc.
Price: **$10.00**

OMEGA MAVERICK SIGHT BLADES Replacement "peep-sight" blades for Colt, Ruger SAs, Virginian Dragoon. Three models available-No. 1, Plain; No. 2, Single Bar; No. 3, Double Bar Rangefinder. From Omega Sales, Inc.
Price: Each. **$10.00**

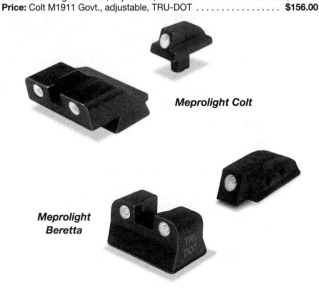

Meprolight Colt

Meprolight Beretta

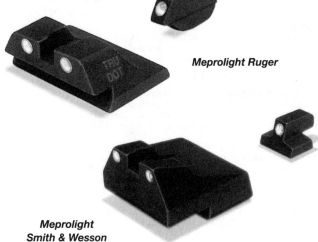

Meprolight Ruger

Meprolight Smith & Wesson

METALLIC SIGHTS

ONE RAGGED HOLE Replacement rear sight ghost ring sight for Ruger handguns. Fits Blackhawks, Redhawks, Super Blackhawks, GP series and Mk. II target pistols with adjustable sights. From One Ragged Hole, Tallahassee, Florida.
Price: **$24.95**
Price: Winchester Model 92s and Marlin 36/336/1894/ etc. **$34.95**

Pachmayr Accu-Set

PACHMAYR ACCU-SET Low-profile, fully adjustable rear sight to be used with existing front sight. Available with target, white outline or 3-dot blade. Blue finish. Uses factory dovetail and locking screw. For Browning, Colt, Glock, SIG Sauer, S&W and Ruger autos. From Pachmayr.
Price: **$59.98**

P-T TRITIUM NIGHT SIGHTS Self-luminous tritium sights available for virtually all makes and models of handguns, shotguns and rifles. Ten different configurations. Sights have lifetime guarantee, including tritium replacement. From Miniature Machine Corp. (MMC).
Price: .... **$45.00-$89.00**

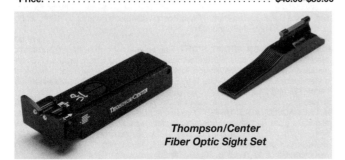

Thompson/Center Fiber Optic Sight Set

T/C ENCORE FIBER OPTIC SIGHT SETS Click adjustable, steel rear sight and ramp-style front sight, both fitted with Tru-Glo™ fiber optics. Specifically-designed for the T/C Encore pistol series. From Thompson/Center Arms.
Price: **$49.35**

T/C ENCORE TARGET REAR SIGHT Precision, steel construction with click adjustments (via knurled knobs) for windage and elevation. Models available with low, medium and high blades. From Thompson/Center Arms.
Price: **$54.00**

Thompson/Center Target Rear Sight

TRIJICON NIGHT SIGHTS Three-dot night sight system uses tritium lamps in the front and rear sights. Tritium "lamps" are mounted in silicone rubber inside a metal cylinder. A polished crystal sapphire provides protection and clarity. Inlaid white outlines provide 3-dot aiming in daylight also. Available for most popular handguns including Glock 17, 19, 20, 21, 23, 24, 25, 26, 29, 30, H&K USP, Ruger P94, SIG P220, P225, 226, Colt 1911. Front and rear sets available. From Trijicon, Inc.
Price: .... **$99.00-$175.00**

TRIJICON 3-DOT Self-luminous front iron night sight for the Ruger SP101.
Price: **$50.00**

WICHITA SERIES 70/80 SIGHT Provides click windage and elevation adjustments with precise repeatability of settings. Sight blade is grooved and angled back at the top to reduce glare. Available in Low Mount Combat or Low Mount Target styles for Colt 45s and their copies, S&W 645, Hi-Power, CZ 75 and others.
Price: Rear sight, target or combat **$80.70**
Price: Front sight, Patridge or ramp **$15.00**

WICHITA GRAND MASTER DELUXE RIBS Ventilated rib has wings machined into it for better sight acquisition and is relieved for Mag-Na-Porting. Milled to accept Weaver see-thru-style rings. Made of stainless; front and rear sights blued. Has Wichita Multi-Range rear sight system, adjustable front sight. Made for revolvers with 6" barrel.
Price: Model 301S, 301B (adj. sight K frames with custom bbl. of 1" to 1.032" dia. L and N frame with 1.062" to 1.100" dia. bbl.) **$265.00**
Price: Model 303S, 303B (adj. sight K, L, N frames with factory barrel) **$250.00**

Trijicon Night Sight

Wichita Series 70/80 Sight

WICHITA MULTI-RANGE QUICK CHANGE SIGHTING SYSTEM Multi-range rear sight can be pre-set to four positive repeatable range settings. Adjustable front sight allows compensation for changing lighting and weather conditions with just one front sight adjustment. Front sight comes with Lyman 17A Globe and set of apertures.
Price: Rear sight **$145.00**
Price: Front, sight **$110.00**

Williams Fire Sight Set

WILLIAMS FIRE SIGHT SETS Red fiber optic metallic sight replaces the original. Rear sight has two green fiber optic elements. Made of CNC-machined aluminum. Fits all Glocks, Ruger P-Series (except P-85), S&W 910, Colt Gov't. Model Series 80, Ruger GP 100 and Redhawk, and SIG Sauer (front only).
Price: Front and rear set **$46.95**
Price: SIG Sauer front **$23.95**
Price: Ruger P345/KP345 (2006) **$46.95**
Price: Taurus PT111, PT140, PT145, PT1232, PT138 .... **$46.95**

WILSON ADJUSTABLE REAR SIGHTS Machined from steel, the click adjustment design requires simple cuts and no dovetails for installation. Available in several configurations: matte black standard blade with .128" notch; with .110" notch; with Tritium dots and .128" square or "U" shaped notch; and Combat Pyramid. From Wilson Combat.
Price: .... **$24.95 to $69.95**

WILSON NITE-EYES SIGHTS Low-profile, snag free design with green and yellow Tritium inserts. For 1911-style pistols. From Wilson Combat.
Price: **$119.95**

WILSON TACTICAL COMBAT SIGHTS Low-profile and snag-free in design, the sight employs the Combat Pyramid shape. For many 1911-style pistols and some Glock models. From Wilson Combat.
Price: **$139.95**

Shotgun Sights

AO SHOTGUN SIGHTS 24/7 Pro Express sights fit Remington rifle sighted barrels. Front sight divetails into existing ramp, rear installs on Remington rear ramp. Available in Big Dot Tritium or Standard Dot Tritium. Three other styles (for pedestal base, beaded, and ribbed barrels) provide a Big Dot Tritium front that epoxies over the existing bead front sight. From AO Sight Systems, Inc.
Price: 24/7 Tritium Sets.......................... **$90.00 to $120.00**
Price: Big Dot Tritium (front only) **$60.00**

BRADLEY SHOTGUN SIGHTS Front beads available in sizes of 1/8" and 5/32" in thread sizes of #3-56, #6-48, and #8-40. From 100 Straight Products.
Price: **$5.00**

METALLIC SIGHTS

BRADLEY CENTER SIGHTS Available in 1/16" bead size and #3-56 thread or taper. Plain brass, bright silver and white finishes. From 100 Straight Products.
Price: . . . . **$2.50 to $6.00 each**

BRADLEY SHOTGUN SIGHT ASSORTMENT An assortment of the most frequently used sights including six each of 18-3, 18-6,532-3, 532-7, 532-9, MB-01 and MB-11. From 100 Straight Products.
Price: **$119.95**

CARLSON SHOTGUN SIGHT A brilliant orange bead securely held by two bands. Used for low light conditions. Bead size .150", thread size 6-48. From Carlson's and 100 Straight Products.
Price: **$7.50**

FIRE FLY EM-109 SL SHOTGUN SIGHT Made of aircraft-grade aluminum, this 1/4-oz. "channel" sight has a thick, sturdy hollowed post between the side rails to give a Patridge sight picture. All shooting is done with both eyes open, allowing the shooter to concentrate on the target, not the sights. The hole in the sight post gives reduced-light shooting capability and allows for fast, precise aiming. For sport or combat shooting. Model EM-109 fits all vent. rib and double barrel shotguns and muzzleloaders with octagon barrel. Model MOC-110 fits all plain barrel shotguns without screw-in chokes. From JAS, Inc.
Price: **$35.00**

LYMAN Three sights of over-sized ivory beads. No. 10 Front (press fit) for double barrel or ribbed single barrel guns $4.50; No. 10D Front (screw fit) for non-ribbed single barrel guns (comes with wrench) $5.50; No. 11 Middle (press fit) for double and ribbed single barrel guns.
Price: **$4.75**

MMC M&P COMBAT SHOTGUN SIGHT SET A durable, protected ghost ring aperture, combat sight made of steel. Fully adjustable for windage and elevation.
Price: M&P Sight Set (front and rear). **$73.45**
Price: As above, installed **$83.95**

MMC TACTICAL GHOST RING SIGHT Click adjustable for elevation with 30 MOA total adjustment in 3 MOA increments. Click windage adjustment. Machined from solid steel and heat-treated. Front sights available in banded tactical or serrated ramp. Available with or without tritium and in three different finishes. Available for all shotgun makes and models.
Price: . . . . **$24.95-$149.95**

MARBLE SHOTGUN BEAD SIGHTS No. 214-Ivory front bead, 11/64", tapered shank **$4.40**; No. 223-Ivory rear bead, .080", tapered shank **$4.40**; No. 217-Ivory front bead, 11/64", threaded shank **$4.75**; No. 223-T-Ivory rear bead, .080, threaded shank **$5.95**. Reamers, taps and wrenches available from Marble Arms.

MEPROLIGHT Ghost ring sight set for Benelli tactical shotguns. From Meprolight, Inc.
Price: **$100.00**

MILLETT SHURSHOT SHOTGUN SIGHT A sight system for shotguns with ventilated rib. Rear sight attaches to the rib, front sight replaces the front bead. Front has an orange face, rear has two orange bars. For 870, 1100 or other models.

Millett Shurshot

Price: Rear, fixed. **$14.95**
Price: Adjustable front and rear set. **$35.95**
Price: Front. **$14.95**

NECG IVORY SHOTGUN BEAD Genuine ivory shotgun beads with 6-48 thread. Available in heights of .157" and .197". From New England Custom Gun Service.
Price: **$9.00**

POLY-CHOKE Replacement front shotgun sights in four styles-Xpert, Poly Bead, Xpert Mid Rib sights, and Bev-L-Block. Xpert Front available in 3x56, 6x48 thread, 3/32" or 5/32" shank length, gold, ivory **$4.70**; or Sun Spot orange bead **$5.95**; Poly Bead is standard replacement 1/8" bead, 6x48 **$2.95**; Xpert Mid Rib in tapered carrier (ivory only) **$5.95**, or 3x56 threaded shank (gold only) $2.95; Hi and Lo Blok sights with 6x48 thread, gold or ivory **$5.25**. From Marble Arms.

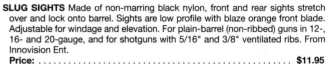

SLUG SIGHTS Made of non-marring black nylon, front and rear sights stretch over and lock onto barrel. Sights are low profile with blaze orange front blade. Adjustable for windage and elevation. For plain-barrel (non-ribbed) guns in 12-, 16- and 20-gauge, and for shotguns with 5/16" and 3/8" ventilated ribs. From Innovision Ent.
Price: **$11.95**

TRIJICON 3-DOT NIGHT SIGHTS Self-luminous and machined from steel. Available for Remington 870, 1100, 1187.
Price: . . . . **$75.00 to $175.00**

WILLIAMS GUIDE BEAD SIGHT Fits all shotguns, 1/8" ivory, red or gold bead. Screws into existing sight hole. Various thread sizes and shank lengths.
Price: **$8.50**

WILLIAMS UNIVERSAL SLUGGER shotgun fire sight set. Fiber optic, front and rear metallic sights attach to most vent ribs. Adjustable for windage and elevation. No gunsmithing required.
Price: **$39.95**

WILLIAMS FIRE SIGHTS Fiber optic light gathering front sights in red or yellow, glow with natural light. Fit 1/4", 5/16" or 3/8" vent. ribs, most popular shotguns.
Price: **$18.95**

Sight Attachments

MERIT ADJUSTABLE APERTURES Eleven clicks give 12 different apertures. No. 3 Disc and Master, primarily target types, 0.22" to .125"; No. 4, 1/2" dia. hunting type, .025" to .155". Available for all popular sights. The Master, with flexible rubber light shield, is particularly adapted to extension, scope height, and tang sights. All models have internal click springs; are hand fitted to minimum tolerance.
Price: No. 3 Master Disk. **$66.00**
Price: No. 3 Target Disc (Plain Face) **$56.00**
Price: No. 4 Hunting Disc **$48.00**

MERIT LENS DISC Similar to Merit Iris Shutter (Model 3 or Master) but incorporates provision for mounting prescription lens integrally. Lens may be obtained locally from your optician. Sight disc is 7/16" wide (Model 3), or 3/4" wide (Master).
Price: No. 3 Target Lens Disk. **$68.00**
Price: No. 3 Master Lens Disk **$78.00**

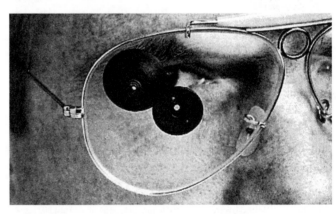

Merit Optical Attachment

MERIT OPTICAL ATTACHMENT For iron sight shooting with handgun or rifle. Instantly attached by rubber suction cup to prescription or shooting glasses. Swings aside. Aperture adjustable from .020" to .156".
Price: **$65.00**

WILLIAMS APERTURES Standard thread, fits most sights. Regular series 3/8" to 1/2" O.D., .050" to .125" hole. "Twilight" series has white reflector ring.
Price: Regular series. **$7.95**
Price: Twilight series **$9.95**
Price: Wide open 5/16" aperture for shotguns fits 5-D or Foolproof sights (specify model) **$10.95**

Simmons 1280

ALPEN MODEL 711 20x50 mini-scope, 20x, 50mm eyepiece, field of view at 1,000 yds. 147 ft., multi-coated lens, weighs 10 oz., waterproof.
Price: **$60.97**

ALPEN MODEL 722 12-36x compact, 50mm eyepiece, field of view at 1,000 yds: 115 ft. (12x); 59 ft. (36x); multi-coated lens, weighs 27 oz., waterproof.
Price: **$124.20**

ALPEN MODEL 725 and 728 Compact 15-45x60, 60mm obj., center focus, multi-coated lens, field of view at 1,000 yds: 136 ft. (15x); 107 ft. (45x); weighs 27 oz., waterproof.
Price: .... **$151.62 and $154.85**

ALPEN MODEL 730 15-30x50, 60mm obs., field of view at 1,000 yds: 136 ft. (15x); 99 ft. (50x); multi-coated lens, weighs 28 oz., waterproof.
Price: **$116.14**

ALPEN MODEL 788 20-60x80, 80mm obj., field of view at 1,000 yds: 93 ft. (20x); 47 ft. (60x); multi-coated lens, weighs 64 oz., waterproof.
Price: **$404.69**

BUSHNELL DISCOVERER, 15x to 60x zoom, 60mm objective. Constant focus throughout range. Field of view at 1,000 yds.: 38 ft. (60x), 150 ft. (15x). Comes with lens caps. Length: 17-1/2"; weighs 48.5 oz.
Price: **$342.95**

BUSHNELL ELITE 15x to 45x zoom, 60mm objective. Field of view at 1,000 yds.: 125 ft.@15X, 65 ft.@45X. Length: 12.2"; weighs 26.5 oz. Waterproof, armored. Tripod mount. Comes with black case and rainguard.
Price: **$586.95**

BUSHNELL ELITE ZOOM 20x-60x, 70mm objective. Roof prism. Field of view at 1,000 yds.: 90 ft.@20X, 50 ft.@60X. Length: 16"; weighs 40 oz. Waterproof, armored. Tripod mount. Comes with black case.
Price: **$806.95**

BUSHNELL 80MM ELITE 20x-60x zoom, 80mm objective. Field of view at 1,000 yds.: 98 ft.@20X, 50 ft.@60X. Weighs 53 oz. Length: 17". Interchangeable bayonet-style eyepieces. Built-in peep sight.
Price: With EDPrime Glass **$1,173.95**

BUSHNELL TROPHY 65mm objective, 20x-60x zoom. Field of view at 1,000 yds. 90 ft. (20x), 45 ft. (60x). Length: 12.7"; weighs 20 oz. Black rubber armored, waterproof. Case included.
Price: **$297.95**

BUSHNELL COMPACT TROPHY 50mm objective, 20x-50x zoom. Field of view at 1,000 yds. 92 ft. (20x), 52 ft. (50x). Length: 12.2"; weighs 17 oz. Black rubber armored, waterproof. Case included.
Price: **$257.95**

BUSHNELL COMPACT SENTRY 18-36x50mm objective. Field of view at 1,000 yds.: 15 ft.@18X, 75 ft.@36X. Length: 14.7"; weighs 31 oz. With tripod and hard case. Waterproof.
Price: **$157.95**

BUSHNELL SPACEMASTER 20x-45x zoom. Long eye relief. Rubber armored, prismatic. 60mm objective. Field of view at 1,000 yds.: 90 ft.@20X, 30 ft.@45X. Minimum focus 20 ft. Length: 12.7"; weighs 43 oz.
Price: With tripod, carrying case and 20x-45x LER eyepiece. **$502.95**

BUSHNELL SPACEMASTER COLLAPSIBLE 15-45x zoom, 50mm objective lens. Field of view at 1,000 yds., 113 ft. (15x), 52 ft. (45x). Length: 8". Weighs 22.8 oz. Comes with tripod, window mount and case.
Price: **$209.95**

BUSHNELL SPORTVIEW 15x-45x zoom, 50mm objective. Field of view at 1,000 yds. 103 ft. (15x), 35 ft. (45x). Length: 17.4"; weighs 34.4 oz.
Price: With tripod and carrying case **$91.95**

BUSHNELL LEGEND 20x-60x zoom, 60mm objective. Field of view at 1,000 yds. 138 ft. (20x), 68 ft. (60x). Length: 14.3"; weighs 34.3 oz.
Price: With carrying case **$398.95**

CELESTRON MINI 50MM ZOOM Offset 45° or straight body. Comes with 12x36x eyepiece. 50mm obj. Field of view at 1,000 yds. 160 (or 82), waterproof. Length: 8.5", weighs 1.4 lbs.
Price: .... **NA**

CELESTRON ULTIMA SERIES Offset 45° or straight body. 18x55, 20-60 zoom or 22- 60 zoom. Aperture: 65mm, 80mm or 100mm, field of view at 1,000 yds., 89' at 18x, 38' at 55x, 105' at 20x, 95' at 22x, 53' at 66x. Length: 13", 16" or 19". Weighs 2.3 to 4.5 lbs.
Price: Body . . . . **NA**

HERMES 1 70mm objective, 16x, 25x, 40x. Field of view at 1,000 meters 160 ft. (16x), 75 ft. (40x). Length: 12.2"; weighs 33 oz. From CZ-USA.
Price: Body **$359.00**
Price: 25x eyepiece **$86.00**
Price: 40x eyepiece **$128.00**

KOWA TS-500 SERIES Offset 45° or straight body. Comes with 20-40x zoom eyepiece or 20x fixed eyepiece. 50mm obj. Field of view at 1,000 yds.: 171 ft. (20x fixed), 132-74 ft. (20-40x zoom). Length: 8.9-10.4", weighs 13.4-14.8 oz.
Price: TS-501 (offset 45° body w/20x fixed eyepiece) **$258.00**
Price: TS-502 (straight body w/20x fixed eyepiece) **$231.00**
Price: TS-501Z (offset 45° body w/20-40x zoom eyepiece) **$321.00**
Price: TS-502Z (straight body w/20-40x zoom eyepiece) **$290.00**

KOWA TS-660 SERIES Offset 45° or straight body. Fully waterproof. Available with ED lens. Sunshade and rotating tripod mount. 66mm obj. Field of view at 1,000 yds.: 177 ft. (20xW), 154 ft. (27xW), 131 ft. (30xW), 102 ft. (25x), 92 ft. (25xLER), 108-79 ft. (20-40x multi-coated zoom), 98-62 ft. (20-60x high grade zoom). Length: 12.3"; weighs 34.9-36.7 oz.
Price: TSN-662 body (straight) **$610.00**
Price: TSN-663 body (45 offset, ED lens) **$1,070.00**
Price: TSN-664 body (straight, ED lens) **$1,010.00**
Price: TSE-Z6 (20-40x multi-coatedzoom eyepiece) **$378.00**
Price: TSE-17HB (25x long eye relief eyepiece) **$240.00**
Price: TSE-14W (30x wide angle high-grade eyepiece) **$288.00**
Price: TSE-21WB (20x wide-angle eyepiece) **$230.00**
Price: TSE-15 WM (27x wide-angle eyepiece) **$182.00**
Price: TSE-16 PM (25x eyepiece) **$108.00**
Price: TSN-DA1 digital photo adapter **$105.00**
Price: DA1 adapter rings **$43.00**
Price: TSN-PA2 (800mm photo adapter) **$269.00**
Price: TSN-PA4 (1200mm photo adapter) **$330.00**
Price: Camera mounts (for use with photo adapter) **$30.00**
Price: Eyepieces for TSN 77mm series,
TSN-660 series, 661 body (45° offset) **$660.00**

KOWA TSN-660 SERIES Offset 45° or straight body. Fully waterproof. Available with fluorite lens. Sunshade and rotating tripod mount. 66mm obj., field of view at 1,000 yds: 177 ft. (20x), 154 ft. (27xW), 131 ft. (30xW), 102 ft. (25x), 92 ft. (25xLER), 62 ft. (40x), 108-79 ft. (20-40x Multi-Coated Zoom), 102- 56 ft. (20-60x zoom), 98-62 ft. (20- 60x High Grade Zoom). Length: 12.3"; weighs 34.9-36.7 oz. Note: Eyepieces for TSN 77mm Series, TSN-660 Series, and TSN610 Series are interchangeable.
Price: TSN-661 body (45° offset) **$660.00**
Price: TSN-662 body (straight) **$610.00**
Price: TSN-663 body (45° offset, ED lens) **$1,070.00**
Price: TSN-664 body (straight, fluorite lens) **$1,010.00**
Price: TSE-Z4 (20-60x high-grade zoom eyepiece) **$378.00**
Price: TSE-Z6 (20-40x multi-coated zoom eyepiece) **$250.00**
Price: TSE-17HB (25x long eye relief eyepiece) **$240.00**
Price: TSE-14W (30x wide angle eyepiece) **$288.00**
Price: TSE-21WB (20x wide angle eyepiece) **$230.00**
Price: TSE-15PM (27x wide angle eyepiece) **$182.00**
Price: TSE-10PM (40x eyepiece) **$108.00**
Price: TSE-16PM (25x eyepiece) **$105.00**
Price: TSN-DA1 (digital photo adapter) **$105.00**
Price: Adapter rings for DA1 . . . . **$43.00**
Price: TSN-PA2 (800mm photo adapter) **$269.00**
Price: TSN-PA4 (1200mm photo adapter) **$330.00**
Price: Camera mounts (for use with photo adapter) **$30.00**

KOWA TSN-820M SERIES Offset 45° or straight body. Fully waterproof. Available with fluorite lens. Sunshade and rotating tripod mount. 82mm obj., field of view at 1,000 yds: 75 ft. (27xLER, 50xW), 126 ft. (32xW), 115-58 ft. (20-60xZoom). Length: 15"; weighs 49.4-52.2 oz.
Price: TSN-821M body (45° offset) **$850.00**
Price: TSN-822M body (straight) **$770.00**
Price: TSN-823M body (45° offset, fluorite lens) **$1,850.00**
Price: TSN-824M body (straight, fluorite lens) **$1,730.00**
Price: TSE-Z7 (20-60x zoom eyepiece) **$433.00**
Price: TSE-9W (50x wide angle eyepiece) **$345.00**
Price: TSE-14WB (32x wide angle eyepiece) **$366.00**
Price: TSE-17HC (27x long eye relief eyepiece) **$248.00**
Price: TSN-DA1 (digital photo adapter) **$105.00**
Price: Adapter rings for DA1 . . . . **$43.00**
Price: TSN-PA2C (850mm photo adapter) **$300.00**
Price: Camera mounts (for use with photo adapter) **$30.00**

LEUPOLD 10-20x40mm COMPACT 40mm objective, 10-20x. Field of view at 1,000 yds. 19.9-13.6 ft.; eye relief 18.5mm (10x). Overall length: 7.5", weighs 15.8 oz. Rubber armored.
Price: **$439.95**

LEUPOLD 55-30x50 COMPACT 50mm objective, 15-30x. Field of view at 100 yds. 13.6 ft.; eye relief 17.5mm; Overall length: 11"; weighs 1.5 oz.
Price: **$564.99**

LEUPOLD Wind River Sequoia 15-30x60mm, 60mm objective, 15-30x. Field of view at 100 yds.: 13.1 ft.; eye relief: 16.5mm. Overall length: 13". Weighs 35.1 oz.
Price: **$294.99**

LEUPOLD Wind River Sequoia 15-45x60mm Angled. Armored, 15-45x. Field of view at 100 yds.: 13.1-6.3 ft.; eye relief: 16.5-13.0. Overall length: 12.5". Weighs 35.1 oz.
Price: **$309.99**

LEUPOLD Golden Ring 12-40x60mm; 12.7x38.1x. Field of view at 100 yds.: 16.8-5.2 ft.; eye relief: 30.0; Overall length: 12.4". Weighs 37.0 oz.
Price: **$1,124.99**

SPOTTING SCOPES

LEUPOLD Golden Ring 15-30x50mm Compact Armored; 15.2-30.4x; field of view at 100 yds.: 13.6-8.9 ft.; eye relief: 17.5-17.1; overall length: 11.0". Weighs 21.5 oz.
Price: **$564.99**
MIRADOR TTB SERIES Draw tube armored spotting scopes. Available with 75mm or 80mm objective. Zoom model (28x-62x, 80mm) is 11-7/8" (closed), weighs 50 oz. Field of view at 1,000 yds. 70-42 ft. Comes with lens covers.
Price: 28-62x80mm **$1,133.95**
Price: 32x80mm **$971.95**
Price: 26-58x75mm **$989.95**
Price: 30x75mm **$827.95**
MIRADOR SSD SPOTTING SCOPES 60mm objective, 15x, 20x, 22x, 25x, 40x, 60x, 20-60x; field of view at 1,000 yds. 37 ft.; length: 10 1/4"; weighs 33 oz.
Price: 25x **$575.95**
Price: 22x Wide Angle **$593.95**
Price: 20-60x Zoom **$746.95**
Price: As above, with tripod, case **$944.95**
MIRADOR SIA SPOTTING SCOPES Similar to the SSD scopes except with 45° eyepiece. Length: 12-1/4"; weighs 39 oz.
Price: 25x **$809.95**
Price: 22x Wide Angle **$827.95**
Price: 20-60x Zoom **$980.95**
MIRADOR SSR SPOTTING SCOPES 50mm or 60mm objective. Similar to SSD except rubber armored in black or camouflage. Length: 11-1/8"; weighs 31 oz.
Price: Black, 20x. **$521.95**
Price: Black, 18x Wide Angle **$539.95**
Price: Black, 16-48x Zoom **$692.95**
Price: Black, 20x, 60mm, EER **$692.95**
Price: Black, 22x Wide Angle, 60mm **$701.95**
Price: Black, 20-60x Zoom **$854.95**
MIRADOR SSF FIELD SCOPES Fixed or variable power, choice of 50mm, 60mm, 75mm objective lens. Length: 9-3/4"; weighs 20 oz. (15-32x50).
Price: 20x50mm **$359.95**
Price: 25x60mm **$440.95**
Price: 30x75mm **$584.95**
Price: 15-32x50mm Zoom **$548.95**
Price: 18-40x60mm Zoom **$629.95**
Price: 22-47x75mm Zoom **$773.95**
MIRADOR SRA MULTI ANGLE SCOPES Similar to SSF Series except eyepiece head rotates for viewing from any angle.
Price: 20x50mm **$503.95**
Price: 25x60mm **$647.95**
Price: 30x75mm **$764.95**
Price: 15-32x50mm Zoom **$692.95**
Price: 18-40x60mm Zoom **$836.95**
Price: 22-47x75mm Zoom **$953.95**
MIRADOR SIB FIELD SCOPES Short-tube, 45° scopes with porro prism design. 50mm and 60mm objective. Length: 10 1/4"; weighs 18.5 oz. (15- 32x50mm); field of view at 1,000 yds. 129-81 ft.
Price: 20x50mm **$386.95**
Price: 25x60mm **$449.95**
Price: 15-32x50mm Zoom **$575.95**
Price: 18-40x60mm Zoom **$638.95**
NIKON FIELDSCOPES 60mm and 78mm lens. Field of view at 1,000 yds. 105 ft. (60mm, 20x), 126 ft. (78mm, 25x). Length: 12.8" (straight 60mm), 12.6" (straight 78mm); weighs 34.5 to 47.5 oz. Eyepieces available separately.
Price: 60mm straight body **$499.99**
Price: 60mm angled body **$519.99**
Price: 60mm straight ED body **$779.99**
Price: 60mm angled ED body **$849.99**
Price: 78mm straight ED body **$899.99**
Price: 78mm angled ED body **$999.99**
Price: Eyepieces (15x to 60x) . . . . **$146.95 to $324.95**
Price: 20-45x eyepiece (25-56x for 78mm) **$320.55**
NIKON 60mm objective, 20x fixed power or 15-45x zoom. Field of view at 1,000 yds. 145 ft. (20x). Gray rubber armored. Straight or angled eyepiece. Weighs 44.2 oz., length: 12.1" (20x).
Price: 20x60 fixed (with eyepiece) **$290.95**
Price: 15-45x zoom (with case, tripod, eyepiece) **$578.95**
PENTAX PF-80ED 80mm objective lens available in 18x, 24x, 36x, 48x, 72x and 20- 60x. Length: 15.6", weighs 11.9 to 19.2 oz.
Price: **$1,320.00**
SIGHTRON SII836x50 Kit 50mm objective lens, 18x-36x zoom. Field of view at 1,000 yds 105 ft. (18x), 73.5 ft. (36x). Length: 10.4"; weighs 20.1 oz. Black rubber finish. Kit comes with aluminum case and table-top tripod.
Price: **$235.28**
SIGHTRON SIIWP2050x65 65mm objective lens, 20x-50x zoom. Field of view at 1,000 yds 84 ft. (20x), 47 ft. (50x). Length: 13.4"; weighs 31.5 oz. Black rubber finish. Fanny-pack case. Also available in 80mm (13.8" length, 40.5 oz. weight).
Price: 65mm **$528.00**
Price: 80mm **$607.00**
SIGHTRON SIIWP2060x63 Multi-coated 63mm objective lens, 20x-60x and 25x wide-angle fully multi-coated eyepieces. Field of view at 1,000 yds 89 ft. (20x), 58 ft. (60x), 110 ft (25x). Length: 14.4"; weighs 32.7 oz. Black rubber finish. Custom Cordura Case.
Price: **$793.04**
SIMMONS 1280 50mm objective, 15-45x zoom. Black matte finish. Ocular focus. Peep finder sight. Waterproof. Field of view at 95-51 ft. 1,000 yds. Weights 33.5 oz., length: 12".
Price: With tripod **$189.99**
SIMMONS 1281 60mm objective, 20-60x zoom. Black matte finish. Ocular focus. Peep finder sight. Waterproof. Field of view at 78-43 ft. 1,000 yds. Weights 34.5 oz. Length: 12".
Price: With tripod **$209.99**
SIMMONS 77206 PROHUNTER 50mm objectives, 25x fixed power. Field of view at 1,000 yds. 113 ft.; length: 10.25"; weighs 33.25 oz. Black rubber armored.
Price: With tripod case **$160.60**
SIMMONS 41200 REDLINE 50mm objective, 15x-45x zoom. Field of view at 1,000 yds. 104-41 ft.; length: 16.75"; weighs 32.75 oz.
Price: With hard case and tripod **$74.99**
Price: 20-60x, 60mm objective **$99.99**
SWAROVSKI ATS-STS 65mm or 80mm objective, 20-60x zoom, or fixed 20x, 30x 45x eyepieces. Field of view at 1,000 yds. 180 ft. (20xSW), 126 ft. (30xSW), 84 ft. (45xSW), 108-60 ft. (20-60xS) for zoom. Length: 13.98" (ATS/STS 80), 12.8" (ATS/STS 65); weighs 45.93 oz. (ATS 80), 47.70 oz. (ATS 80HD), 45.23 oz. (STS 80), 46.91 oz. (STS 80 HD), 38.3 oz. (ATS 65), 39.9 oz. (ATS 65HD) 38.1 oz. (STS 65), 39.2 oz. (STS 65 HD).
Price: ATS 65 (angled eyepiece) **$1,254.45**
Price: STS 65 (straight eyepiece) **$1,254.45**
Price: ATS-80/STS 80 . . . . **$1,565.57**
Price: ATS/STS 80 (HD) **$2,110.01**
Price: 20xSW **$372.23**
Price: 30xSW **$388.90**
Price: 45xSW **$432.23**
SWIFT LYNX M836 15x-45x zoom, 60mm objective. Weighs 7 lbs., length: 14". Has 45° eyepiece, sunshade.
Price: **$315.00**
SWIFT NIGHTHAWK M849U 80mm objective, 20x-60x zoom, or fixed 19, 25x, 31x, 50x, 75x eyepieces. Has rubber armored body, 1.8x optical finder, retractable lens hood, 45° eyepiece. Field of view at 1,000 yds. 60 ft. (28x), 41 ft. (75x). Length: 13.4 oz.; weighs 39 oz.
Price: Body only **$870.00**
Price: 20-68x eyepiece **$370.00**
Price: Fixed eyepieces . . . . **$130.00 to $240.00**
Price: Model 849 (straight) body **$795.00**
SWIFT LYNX 60mm objective, 15-45x zoom, 45° inclined roof prism, magenta coated on all air-to-glass surfaces, rubber armored body, length: 14", weighs 30 oz. Equipped with sun shade, threaded dust covers and low level tripod.
Price: complete. **$330.00**
SWIFT TELEMASTER M841 60mm objective. 15x to 60x variable power. Field of view at 1,000 yds. 160 feet (15x) to 40 feet (60x). Weighs 3.25 lbs.; length: 18" overall.
Price: **$399.50**
SWIFT PANTHER M844 15x-45x zoom or 22x WA, 15x, 20x, 40x. 60mm objective. Field of view at 1,000 yds. 141 ft. (15x), 68 ft. (40x), 95-58 ft. (20x-45x).
Price: Body only **$380.00**
Price: 15x-45x zoom eyepiece **$120.00**
Price: 20x-45x zoom (long eye relief) eyepiece **$140.00**
Price: 15x, 40x eyepiece **$65.00**
Price: 22x WA eyepiece **$80.00**
SWIFT M700T 12x-36x, 50mm objective. Field of view at 100 yds. 16 ft. (12x), 9 ft. (36x). Length: 14"; weighs 3.22 lbs. (with tripod).
Price: **$30.00**
TASCO 15-45x zoom, 50mm objective lens, Field of view at 1000 yds: 115 ft. (15x), Length: 132". Weighs 24 oz. Matte black finish.
Price: **$128.95**
TASCO 20-50x zoom, 50mm objective. Field of view at 1000 yds: 147 ft. (20x). Length: 7.5". Weighs 10.6 oz. Black finish.
Price: **$80.95**
TASCO 20-60x zoom, 60mm objective. Field of view at 1000 yds: 91 ft. (20x). Length: 13.8". Weighs 30 oz. Black finish.
Price: **$138.95**
TASCO 12-36x zoom 50mm objective. Field of view at 1000 yds. 144 ft. (12x). Length: 7.8". Weighs 17 oz. Black rubber armor. Includes carrying case.
Price: **$118.95**
UNERTL "FORTY-FIVE" 54mm objective. 20x (single fixed power). Field of view at 100 yds. 10',10"; eye relief 1"; focusing range infinity to 33 ft. Weighs about 32 oz.; overall length: 15-3/4". With lens covers.
Price: With mono-layer magnesium coating. **$810.00**
UNERTL STRAIGHT PRISMATIC 24x63. 63.5mm objective, 24x. Field of view at 100 yds., 7 ft. Relative brightness, 6.96. Eye relief 1/2". Weighs 40 oz.; length: closed 19". Push-pull and screw-focus eyepiece. 16x and 32x eyepieces $125.00 each.
Price: **$786.00**
UNERTL 20x STRAIGHT PRISMATIC 54mm objective, 20x. Field of view at 100 yds. 8.5 ft. Relative brightness 6.1. Eye relief 1/2". Weighs 36 oz.; length: closed 13-1/2". Complete with lens covers.
Price: **$695.00**
UNERTL TEAM SCOPE 100mm objective. 15x, 24x, 32x eyepieces. Field of view at 100 yds. 13 to 7.5 ft. Relative brightness, 39.06 to 9.79. Eye relief 2" to 1-1/2". Weighs 13 lbs.; length: 29-7/8" overall. Metal tripod, yoke and wood carrying case furnished (total weighs 80 lbs.).
Price: **$3,624.50**
WEAVER 20x50 50mm objective. Field of view 124 ft. at 100 yds. Eye relief .85"; weighs 21 oz.; overall length: 10". Waterproof, armored.
Price: **$249.99**
WEAVER 15-40x60 ZOOM 60mm objective. 15x-40x zoom. Field of view at 100 yds. 119 ft. (15x), 66 ft. (60x). Overall length: 12.5", weighs 26 oz. Waterproof, armored.
Price: **$399.99**

Briley Screw-In Chokes

Installation of these choke tubes requires that all traces of the original choking be removed, the barrel threaded internally with square threads and then the tubes are custom fitted to the specific barrel diameter. The tubes are thin and, therefore, made of stainless steel. Cost of installation for single-barrel guns (pumps, autos), lead shot, 12-gauge, **$149.00**, 20-gauge **$159.00**; steel shot **$179.00** and **$189.00**, all with three chokes; un-single target guns run **$219.00**; over/unders and side-by-sides, lead shot, 12-gauge, **$369.00**; 20-gauge **$389.00**; steel shot **$469.00** and **$489.00**, all with five chokes. For 10-gauge auto or pump with two steel shot chokes, **$189.00**; over/unders, side-by-sides with three steel shot chokes, **$349.00**. For 16-gauge auto or pump, three lead shot chokes, **$179.00**; over/unders, side-by-sides with five lead shot chokes, **$449.00**. The 28 and 410-bore run **$179.00** for autos and pumps with three lead shot chokes, **$449.00** for over/unders and side-by-sides with five lead shot chokes.

Carlson's Choke Tubes

Manufactures choke tubes for Beretta, Benelli, Remington, Winchester, Browning Invector and Invector Plus, TruChokes, FranChokes, American Arms, Ruger and more. All choke tubes are manufactured from corrosion resistant stainless steel. Most tubes are compatible with lead, steel, Hevi-shot, etc. Available in flush mount, extended sporting clay and extended turkey designs, ported and non-ported. Also offers sights, rifled choke tubes and other accessories for most shotgun models. Prices range from **$16.95** to **$41.95**.

Cutts Compensator

The Cutts Compensator is one of the oldest variable choke devices available. Manufactured by Lyman Gunsight Corporation, it is available with a steel body. A series of vents allows gas to escape upward and downward. For the 12-ga. Comp body, six fixed-choke tubes are available: the Spreader–popular with skeet shooters; Improved Cylinder; Modified; Full; Superfull, and Magnum Full. Full, Modified and Spreader tubes are available for 12 or 20. Cutts Compensator, complete with wrench, adaptor and any single tube **$87.50**. All single choke tubes **$26.00** each. No factory installation available.

Dayson Automatic Brake System

This system fits most single barrel shotguns threaded for choke tubes, and cuts away 30 grooves on the exterior of a standard one-piece wad as it exits the muzzle. This slows the wad, allowing shot and wad to separate faster, reducing shot distortion and tightening patterns. The A.B.S. choke tube is claimed to reduce recoil by about 25 percent, and with the muzzle brake up to 60 percent. Ventilated choke tubes available from .685" to .725", in .005" increments. Model I ventilated choke tube for use with A.B.S. muzzle brake, **$49.95**; for use without muzzle brake, **$52.95**; A.B.S. muzzle brake, from **$69.95**. Contact Dayson Arms for more data.

Gentry Quiet Muzzle Brake

Developed by gunmaker David Gentry, the "Quiet Muzzle Brake" is said to reduce recoil by up to 85 percent with no loss of accuracy or velocity. There is no increase in noise level because the noise and gases are directed away from the shooter. The barrel is threaded for installation and the unit is blued to match the barrel finish. Price, installed, is **$150.00**. Add **$15.00** for stainless steel, **$45.00** for knurled cap to protect threads. Shipping extra.

JP Muzzle Brake

Designed for single shot handguns, AR-15, Ruger Mini-14, Ruger Mini Thirty and other sporting rifles, the JP muzzle brake redirects high pressure gases against a large frontal surface which applies forward thrust to the gun. All gases are directed up, rearward and to the sides. Priced at **$79.95** (AR-15 or sporting rifles), **$89.95** (bull barrel and SKS, AK models), **$89.95** (Ruger Minis), dual chamber model **$79.95**. From JP Enterprises, Inc.

KDF Slim Line Muzzle Brake

This threaded muzzle brake has 30 pressure ports that direct combustion gases in all directions to reduce felt recoil up to a claimed 80 percent without affecting accuracy or ballistics. Reduces felt recoil of a 30-06 to that of a 243. Price, installed, is **$199.00**. From KDF, Inc.

KDF Kick Arrestor

This mercury-filled, inertia-type recoil reducer is installed in the butt of a wood or synthetic stock (rifle or shotgun) to reduce recoil up to 20 percent. Adds 16 oz. ot the weight of the gun Measures 6.25; L x .75" in diameter. Price, installed, is **$165.00**. From KDF, Inc.

Laseraim

Simple, no-gunsmithing compensator reduces felt recoil and muzzle flip by up to 30 percent. Machined from single piece of stainless steel (Beretta/Taurus model made of aircraft aluminum). In black and polished finish. For Colt Government/Commander and Beretta/Taurus full-size pistols. Weighs 1 ounce. **$49.00**. From Laseraim Arms Inc.

Mag-Na-Port

Electrical Discharge Machining works on any firearm except those having non-conductive shrouded barrels. EDM is a metal erosion technique that uses carbon electrodes that control the area to be processed. The Mag-Na-Port venting process utilizes small trapezoidal openings to direct powder gases upward and outward to reduce recoil. No effect is had on bluing or nickeling outside the Mag-Na-Port area so no refinishing is needed. Rifle-style porting on single shot or large caliber handguns with barrels 7-1/2" or longer is **$115.00**; Dual Trapezoidal porting on most handguns with minimum barrel length of 3", **$115.00**; standard revolver porting, **$88.50**; Scandium/titanium-sleeved barrels **$139.50** (2 ports) or **$195.00** (4 ports); porting through the slide and barrel for semi-autos, **$129.50**; traditional rifle porting, **$135.00**. Prices do not include shipping, handling and insurance. From Mag-Na-Port International.

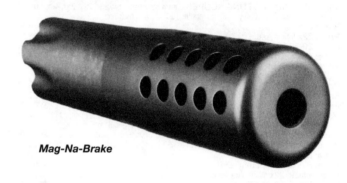

Mag-Na-Brake

Mag-Na-Brake

A screw-on brake under 2" long with progressive integrated exhaust chambers to neutralize expanding gases. Gases dissipate with an opposite twist to prevent the brake from unscrewing, and with a 5° forward angle to minimize sound pressure level. Available in blue, satin blue, bright or satin stainless. Standard and Light Contour installation cost **$195.00** for bolt-action rifles, many single action and single shot handguns. A knurled thread protector supplied at extra cost. Also available in Varmint-style with exhaust chambers covering 220° for prone-position shooters. From Mag-Na-Port International.

Poly-Choke

Marble Arms Corp., manufacturer of the Poly-Choke adjustable shotgun choke, now offers two models in 12-, 16-, 20-, and 28-gauge–the ventilated and standard-style chokes. Each provides nine choke settings including Xtra-Full and Slug. The ventilated model reduces 20 percent of a shotgun's recoil, the company claims, and is priced at **$135.00**. The standard model is **$125.00**. Postage not included. Contact Marble Arms for more data.

Pro-Port

Pro-port

A compound ellipsoid muzzle venting process similar to Mag-Na-Porting, only exclusively applied to shotguns. Like Mag-Na-Porting, this system reduces felt recoil, muzzle jump, and shooter fatigue. Pro-Port is a patented process and installation is available in both the U.S. and Canada. Cost for the Pro-Port process is **$139.00** for over/unders (both barrels); **$110.00** for only the top or bottom barrel; and **$88.50** for single-barrel shotguns. Optional pigeon porting costs **$25.00** extra per barrel. Prices do not include shipping and handling. From Mag-Na-Port International.

Que Industries Adjustable Muzzle Brake

The Que Brake allows for fine-tuning of a rifle's accuracy by rotating the brake to one of 100 indexed stops. Mounts in minutes without barrel modification with heat-activated tensioning ring. The slotted exhaust ports reduce recoil by venting gases sideways, away from rifle. **$189.50**. From Que Industries.

SSK Arrestor Brake

This is a true muzzle brake with an expansion chamber. It takes up about 1" of barrel and reduces velocity accordingly. Some Arrestors are added to a barrel, increasing its length. Said to reduce the felt recoil of a 458 to that approaching a 30-06. Can be set up to give zero muzzle rise in any caliber, and can be added to most guns. For handgun or rifle. Prices start at **$95.00**. Contact SSK Industries for full data.

THE 2008 GUN DIGEST WEB DIRECTORY

by Holt Bodinson

Roaming employees tote their laptops, BlackBerries and PDA's while our youth treasure their iPods, MP3 players and cell phone cameras. Hi-speed, Digital Subscriber Lines (DSL) are now available almost everywhere, and if there are no phone or cable lines, one can subscribe through a satellite service. Wi-Fi services, using Wireless Local Area Networks (WLAN), now cover entire cities and Wi-Fi free zones are common at airports, hotels, resorts and RV parks.

The latest statistics indicate that 73 percent of all adults and 83 percent of people between the ages of 18-49 use the Internet in the USA. Sixty-two percent of those have high-speed Internet access.

With the advent of e-mail, even our language is changing. "TTYL" means "Talk to you later;" "BCNU:" "Be seeing you;" "BTW:" "By the way;" "AFIK:" "As far as I know;" and "HRU?" "How are you?"

At last count, there were 13.7 billion web pages up-and-running and 56.4 percent of those were in English. It's a wired world.

The firearms industry has done a remarkably good job of adapting to e-commerce. More and more firearm-related businesses are striking out and creating their own discrete web pages. It's never been easier with the inexpensive software programs now available.

The GUN DIGEST Web Directory is now in its ninth year of publication. The Internet is a dynamic environment and, since our last edition, there have been numerous changes. Companies have consolidated and adopted a new owner's web site address. New companies have appeared and old companies and discussion groups have disappeared. Search engines are now more powerful than ever and seem to root out even the most obscure reference to a product name or manufacturer.

The following index of web addresses is offered to our readers as a convenient jumping-off point. Half the fun is just exploring what's out there. Considering that most of the web pages have hot links to other firearm-related web pages, the Internet trail just goes on-and-on once you've taken the initial step to go online.

Here are a few pointers:

If the web site you desire is not listed, try using the full name of the company or product, typed without spaces, between www.-and-.com, for example, www.krause.com. Probably 95 percent of current Web sites are based on this simple, self-explanatory format.

Try a variety of search engines like Microsoft Internet Explorer, Google, Yahoo, Ask.com, Dogpile.com, Metacrawler, GoTo.com, HotBot, AltaVista, Lycos, Excite, InfoSeek, Looksmart, and WebCrawler while using key words such as gun, firearm, rifle, pistol, blackpowder, shooting, hunting—frankly, any word that relates to the sport. Each search engine combs through their indices in a different fashion and produces different results. Google is currently the dominant, general search engine with a penetration of 45 percent. Accessing the various search engines is simple. Just type www.google.com for example, and you're on your way.

Welcome to the digital world of firearms. "A journey of a thousand sites begins with a single click, but don't byte off more than you can view."

WEB DIRECTORY

AMMUNITION AND COMPONENTS

A-Square Co. www.asquarecompany.com
3-D Ammunition www.3dammo.com
Accurate Arms Co. Inc www.accuratepowder.com
ADCO/Nobel Sport Powder www.adcosales.com
Aguila Ammunition www.aguilaammo.com
Alexander Arms www.alexanderarms.com
Alliant Powder www.alliantpowder.com
American Ammunition www.a-merc.com
American Derringer Co. www.amderringer.com
American Pioneer Powder
     www.americanpioneerpowder.com
Ammo Depot www.ammodepot.com
Arizona Ammunition, Inc. www.arizonaammunition.com
A-Zoom Ammo www.a-zoom.com
Ballistic Products,Inc. www.ballisticproducts.com
Barnaul Cartridge Plant www.ab.ru/~stanok
Barnes Bullets www.barnesbullets.com
Baschieri & Pellagri www.baschieri-pellagri.com
Beartooth Bullets www.beartoothbullets.com
Bell Brass www.bellbrass.com
Berger Bullets, Ltd. www.bergerbullets.com
Berry's Mfg., Inc. www.berrysmfg.com
Big Bore Bullets of Alaska
     www.awloo.com/bbb/index.htm
Big Bore Express www.powerbeltbullets.com
Bismuth Cartridge Co. www.bismuth-notox.com
Black Dawge Cartridge
     www.blackdawgecartridge.com
Black Hills Ammunition, Inc. www.black-hills.com
Brenneke of America Ltd. www.brennekeusa.com
Buffalo Arms www.buffaloarms.com
Calhoon, James, Bullets www.jamescalhoon.com
Cartuchos Saga www.saga.es
Cast Performance Bullet www.castperformance.com
CCI www.cci-ammunition.com
Century International Arms www.centuryarms.com
Cheaper Than Dirt www.cheaperthandirt.com
Cheddite France www.cheddite.com
Claybuster Wads www.claybusterwads.com
Clean Shot Powder www.cleanshot.com
Cole Distributing www.cole-distributing.com
Combined Tactical Systems www.less-lethal.com
Cor-Bon/Glaser www.cor-bon.com
Cowboy Bullets www.cowboybullets.com
Denver Bullet Co. denbullets@aol.com
Dillon Precision www.dillonprecision.com
Dionisi Cartridge www.dionisi.com
DKT, Inc. www.dktinc.com
Down Range Mfg. www.downrangemfg.com
Dynamit Nobel RWS Inc. www.dnrws.com
Elephant/Swiss Black Powder
     www.elephantblackpowder.com
Eley Ammunition www.eleyusa.com
Eley Hawk Ltd. www.eleyhawk.com
Environ-Metal www.hevishot.com
Estate Cartridge www.estatecartridge.com
Extreme Shock Munitions www.extremeshockusa.com
Federal Cartridge Co. www.federalpremium.com
Fiocchi of America www.fiocchiusa.com
Fowler Bullets www.benchrest.com/fowler
Garrett Cartridges www.garrettcartridges.com
Gentner Bullets www.benchrest.com/gentner/
Glaser Safety Slug, Inc. www.corbon.com
GOEX Inc. www.goexpowder.com
GPA www.cartouchegpa.com
Graf & Sons www.grafs.com
Hastings www.hastingsammunition.com
Hawk Bullets www.hawkbullets.com
Hevi.Shot www.hevishot.com
Hi-Tech Ammunition www.iidbs.com/hitech
Hodgdon Powder www.hodgdon.com
Hornady www.hornady.com
Hull Cartridge www.hullcartridge.com
Huntington Reloading Products www.huntingtons.com
Impact Bullets www.impactbullets.com
IMR Smokeless Powders www.imrpowder.com
International Cartridge Corp
     www.internationalcartridgecorp.com

Israel Military Industries www.imisammo.co.il
ITD Enterprise www.itdenterpriseinc.com
Kent Cartridge America www.kentgamebore.com
Knight Bullets www.benchrest.com/knight/
Kynoch Ammunition www.kynochammunition.com
Lapua www.lapua.com
Lawrence Brand Shot www.metalico.com
Lazzeroni Arms Co. www.lazzeroni.com
Leadheads Bullets www.proshootpro.com
Lightfield Ammunition Corp www.lightfieldslugs.com
Lomont Precision Bullets www.klomont.com/kent
Lost River Ballistic Technologies,Inc.
     www.lostriverballistic.com
Lyman www.lymanproducts.com
Magkor Industries. www.magkor.com
Magnum Muzzleloading Products www.mmpsabots.com
Magnus Bullets www.magnusbullets.com
MagSafe Ammunition
     www.realpages.com/magsafeammo
Magtech www.magtechammunition.com
Masterclass Bullet Co. www.mastercast.com
Meister Bullets www.meisterbullets.com
Midway USA www.midwayusa.com
Miltex,Inc. www.miltexusa.com
Mitchell Mfg. Co. www.mitchellsales.com
MK Ballistic Systems www.mkballistics.com
Mullins Ammunition www.mullinsammunition.com
National Bullet Co. www.nationalbullet.com
Navy Arms www.navyarms.com
Nobel Sport www.nobelsportammo.com
Norma www.norma.cc
North Fork Technologies www.northforkbullets.com
Nosler Bullets,Inc. www.nosler.com
Old Western Scrounger www.ows-ammunition.com
Oregon Trail/Trueshot Bullets www.trueshotbullets.com
Pattern Control www.patterncontrol.com
PMC-Eldorado Cartridge www.pmcammo.com
Polywad www.polywad.com
PowerBelt Bullets www.powerbeltbullets.com
PR Bullets www.prbullet.com
Precision Ammunition www.precisionammo.com
Precision Reloading www.precisionreloading.com
Pro Load Ammunition www.proload.com
Rainier Ballistics www.rainierballistics.com
Ram Shot Powder www.ramshot.com
Reloading Specialties Inc. www.reloadingspecialties.com
Remington www.remington.com
Rocky Mountain Cartridge
     www.rockymountaincartridge.com
RUAG Ammotec www.ruag.com
Samco Global Arms www.samcoglobal.com
Schuetzen Powder www.schuetzenpowder.com
Sellier & Bellot USA inc. www.sb-usa.com
Shilen www.shilen.com
Sierra www.sierrabullets.com
Simunition. www.simunition.com
SinterFire, Inc. www.sinterfire.com
Speer Bullets www.speer-bullets.com
Sporting Supplies Int'l Inc. www.ssiintl.com
Starline www.starlinebrass.com
Swift Bullets Co. www.swiftbullet.com
Ten-X Ammunition www.tenxammo.com
Top Brass www.top-brass.com
Triton Cartridge www.a-merc.com
Trueshot Bullets www.trueshotbullets.com
Tru-Tracer www.trutracer.com
Ultramax Ammunition www.ultramaxammunition.com
Vihtavuori Lapua www.vihtavuori-lapua.com
Weatherby www.weatherby.com
West Coast Bullets www.westcoastbullet.com
Western Powders Inc. www.westernpowders.com
Widener's Reloading & Shooters Supply
     www.wideners.com
Winchester Ammunition www.winchester.com
Windjammer Tournament Wads
     www.windjammer-wads.com
Wolf Ammunition www.wolfammo.com
Woodleigh Bullets www.woodleighbullets.com.au
Zanders Sporting Goods www.gzanders.com

CASES, SAFES, GUN LOCKS AND CABINETS

Ace Case Co. www.acecase.com
AG English Sales Co. www.agenglish.com
All Americas' Outdoors www.innernet.net/gunsafe
Alpine Cases www.alpinecases.com
Aluma Sport by Dee Zee www.deezee.com
American Security Products www.amsecusa.com
Americase www.americase.com
Avery Outdoors, Inc. www.averyoutdoors.com
Bear Track Cases www.beartrackcases.com
Boyt Harness Co. www.boytharness.com
Bulldog Gun Safe Co. www.gardall.com
Cannon Safe Co. www.cannonsafe.com
CCL Security Products www.cclsecurity.com
Concept Development Corp. www.saf-t-blok.com
Doskocil Mfg. Co. www.doskocilmfg.com
Fort Knox Safes www.ftknox.com
Franzen Security Products www.securecase.com
Frontier Safe Co. www.frontiersafe.com
Granite Security Products www.granitesafe.com
Gunlocker Phoenix USA Inc. www.gunlocker.com
GunVault www.gunvault.com
Hakuba USA Inc. www.hakubausa.com
Heritage Safe Co. www.heritagesafecompany.com
Hide-A-Gun www.hide-a-gun.com
Homak Safes www.homak.com
Hunter Company www.huntercompany.com
Kalispel Case Line www.kalispelcaseline.com
Knouff & Knouff, Inc. www.kkair.com
Knoxx Industries www.knoxx.com
Kolpin Mfg. Co. www.kolpin.com
Liberty Safe & Security www.libertysafe.com
New Innovative Products www.starlightcases
Noble Security Systems Inc. www.noble.co.ll
Phoenix USA Inc. www.gunlocker.com
Plano Molding Co. www.planomolding.com
Rhino Gun Cases www.rhinoguns.com
Rhino Safe www.rhinosafe.com
Safe Tech, Inc. www.safrgun.com
Saf-T-Hammer www.saf-t-hammer.com
Saf-T-Lok Corp. www.saf-t-lok.com
San Angelo All-Aluminum Products Inc.
     sasptuld@x.netcom.com
Securecase www.securecase.com
Shot Lock Corp. www.shotlock.com
Smart Lock Technology Inc. www.smartlock.com
Sportsmans Steel Safe Co.
     www.sportsmansteelsafes.com
Stack-On Products Co. www.stack-on.com
Sun Welding www.sunwelding.com
T.Z. Case Int'l www.tzcase.com
Versatile Rack Co. www.versatilegunrack.com
V-Line Industries www.vlineind.com
Winchester Safes www.fireking.com
Ziegel Engineering www.ziegeleng.com
Zonetti Armor www.zonettiarmor.com

CHOKE DEVICES, RECOIL REDUCERS, AND ACCURACY DEVICES

100 Straight Products www.100straight.com
Answer Products Co. www.answerrifles.com
Briley Mfg www.briley.com
Carlson's www.choketube.com
Colonial Arms www.colonialarms.com
Comp-N-Choke www.comp-n-choke.com
Hastings www.hastingsbarrels.com
Kick's Industries www.kicks-ind.com
Mag-Na-Port Int'l Inc. www.magnaport.com
Metro Gun www.metrogun.com
Patternmaster Chokes www.patternmaster.com
Poly-Choke www.poly-choke.com
Sims Vibration Laboratory www.limbsaver.com
Teague Precision Chokes www.teague.ca
Truglo www.truglo.com

WEB DIRECTORY

CHRONOGRAPHS AND BALLISTIC SOFTWARE

Barnes Ballistic Program www.barnesbullets.com
Ballisticard Systems www.ballisticards.com
Competition Electronics
   www.competitionelectronics.com
Competitive Edge Dynamics www.cedhk.com
Hodgdon Shotshell Program www.hodgdon.com
Lee Shooter Program www.leeprecision.com
Load From A Disk www.loadammo.com
Oehler Research Inc. www.oehler-research.com
PACT www.pact.com
ProChrony www.competitionelectronics.com
Quickload www.neconos.com
RCBS Load www.rcbs.com
Shooting Chrony Inc www.shootingchrony.com
Sierra Infinity Ballistics Program www.sierrabullets.com

CLEANING PRODUCTS

Accupro www.accupro.com
Ballistol USA www.ballistol.com
Battenfeld Technologies
   www.battenfeldtechnologies.com
Birchwood Casey www.birchwoodcasey.com
Blue Wonder www.bluewonder.com
Bore Tech www.boretech.com
Break-Free, Inc. www.break-free.com
Bruno Shooters Supply www.brunoshooters.com
Butch's Bore Shine www.lymanproducts.com
C.J. Weapons Accessories www.cjweapons.com
Clenzoil www.clenzoil.com
Corrosion Technologies www.corrosionx.com
Dewey Mfg. www.deweyrods.com
Eezox Inc. www.xmission.com
G 96 www.g96.com
Gunslick Gun Care www.gunslick.com
Gunzilla www.topduckproducts.com
Hollands Shooters Supply www.hollandgun.com
Hoppes www.hoppes.com
Hydrosorbent Products www.dehumidify.com
Inhibitor VCI Products www.theinhibitor.com
Iosso Products www.iosso.com
KG Industries www.kgcoatings.com
Kleen-Bore Inc. www.kleen-bore.com
L&R Mfg. www.lrultrasonics.com
Lyman www.lymanproducts.com
Mil-Comm Products www.mil-comm.com
Militec-1 www.militec-1.com
Mpro7 Gun Care www.mp7.com
Otis Technology, Inc. www.otisgun.com
Outers www.outers-guncare.com
Ox-Yoke Originals Inc. www.oxyoke.com
Parker-Hale Ltd. www.parker-hale.com
Prolix Lubricant www.prolixlubricant.com
ProShot Products www.proshotproducts.com
ProTec Lubricants www.proteclubricants.com
Rusteprufe Labs www.rusteprufe.com
Sagebrush Products www.sagebrushproducts.com
Sentry Solutions Ltd. www.sentrysolutions.com
Shooters Choice Gun Care www.shooters-choice.com
Silencio www.silencio.com
Slip 2000 www.slip2000.com
Stony Point Products www.uncle-mikes.com
Tetra Gun www.tetraproducts.com
The TM Solution thetmsolution@comsast.net
Top Duck Products www.topduckproducts.com
World's Fastest Gun Bore Cleaner
   www.michaels-oregon.com

FIREARM MANUFACTURERS AND IMPORTERS

AAR, Inc. www.iar-arms.com
Accuracy Int'l North America
   www.accuracyinternational.org
Accuracy Rifle Systems www.mini-14.net
Ace Custom 45's www.acecustom45.com

Advanced Weapons Technology www.AWT-Zastava.com
AIM www.aimsurplus.com
AirForce Airguns www.airforceairguns.com
Airguns of Arizona www.airgunsofarizona.com
Airgun Express www.airgunexpress.com
Alchemy Arms www.alchemyltd.com
Alexander Arms www.alexanderarms.com
American Derringer Corp. www.amderringer.com
American Spirit Arms Corp. www.gunkits.com
American Western Arms www.awaguns.com
Anics Corp. www.anics.com
Anschutz www.anschutz-sporters.com
Answer Products Co. www.answerrifles.com
AR-7 Industries, LLC www.ar-7.com
Ares Defense Systems www.aresdefense.com
Armalite www.armalite.com
Armi Sport www.armisport.com
Armory USA www.globaltraders.com
Armsco www.armsco.net
Armscorp USA Inc. www.armscorpusa.com
Arnold Arms www.arnoldarms.com
Arsenal Inc. www.arsenalinc.com
Arthur Brown Co. www.eabco.com
Auction Arms www.auctionarms.com
Autauga Arms, Inc. www.autaugaarms.com
Auto-Ordnance Corp. www.tommygun.com
AWA Int'l www.awaguns.com
Axtell Rifle Co. www.riflesmith.com
Aya www.aya-fineguns.com
Baikal www.baikalinc.ru/eng/
Ballard Rifles, LLC www.ballardrifles.com
Barrett Firearms Mfg. www.barrettrifles.com
Beeman Precision Airguns www.beeman.com
Benelli USA Corp. www.benelliusa.com
Benjamin Sheridan www.crosman.com
Beretta U.S.A. Corp. www.berettausa.com
Bernardelli www.bernardelli.com
Bersa www.bersa-llama.com
Bill Hanus Birdguns www.billhanusbirdguns.com
Bleiker www.bleiker.ch
Bluegrass Armory www.bluegrassarmory.com
Bond Arms www.bondarms.com
Borden's Rifles, Inc. www.bordensrifles.com
Boss & Co. www.bossguns.co.uk
Bowen Classic Arms www.bowenclassicarms.com
Briley Mfg www.briley.com
BRNO Arms www.zbrojovka.com
Brown, David McKay www.mckaybrown.com
Brown, Ed Products www.brownprecision.com
Browning www.browning.com
BSA Guns www.bsaguns.com
BUL Ltd. www.bultransmark.com
Bushmaster Firearms/Quality Parts www.bushmaster.com
BWE Firearms www.bwefirearms.com
Caesar Guerini USA www.gueriniusa.com
Cape Outfitters www.doublegun.com
Carbon 15 www.professional-ordnance.com
Caspian Arms, Ltd. www.caspianarmsltd.8m.com
Casull Arms Corp. www.casullarms.com
CDNN Investments, Inc. www.cdnninvestments.com
Century Arms www.centuryarms.com
Chadick's Ltd. www.chadicks-ltd.com
Champlin Firearms www.champlinarms.com
Chapuis Arms www.doubleguns.com/chapuis.htm
Charles Daly www.charlesdaly.com
Charter Arms www.charterfirearms.com
Christensen Arms www.christensenarms.com
Cimarron Firearms Co. www.cimarron-firearms.com
Clark Custom Guns www.clarkcustomguns.com
Cobra Enterprises www.cobrapistols.com
Cogswell & Harrison www.cogswell.co.uk/home.htm
Colt's Mfg. Co. www.colt.com
Compasseco, Inc. www.compasseco.com
Connecticut Valley Arms www.cva.com
Cooper Firearms www.cooperfirearms.com
Corner Shot www.cornershot.com
Crosman www.crosman.com
Crossfire, L.L.C. www.crossfirelle.com
C.Sharp Arms Co. www.csharparms.com
CZ USA www.cz-usa.com

Daisy Mfg Co. www.daisy.com
Dakota Arms Inc. www.dakotaarms.com
Dan Wesson Firearms www.danwessonfirearms.com
Davis Industries www.davisindguns.com
Detonics USA www.detonicsusa.com
Dixie Gun Works www.dixiegunworks.com
Dlask Arms Corp. www.dlask.com
D.P.M.S., Inc. www.dpmsinc.com
D.S.A, Inc. www.dsarms.com
Dumoulin www.dumoulin-herstal.com
Dynamit Noble www.dnrws.com
Eagle Imports, Inc. www.bersa-llama.com
EDM Arms www.edmarms.com
E.M.F. Co. www.emf-company.com
Enterprise Arms www.enterprise.com
European American Armory Corp. www.eaacorp.com
Evans, William www.williamevans.com
Excel Arms www.excelarms.com
Fabarm www.fabarm.com
FAC-Guns-N-Stuff www.gunsnstuff.com
Falcon Pneumatic Systems www.falcon-airguns.com
Fausti Stefano www.faustistefanoarms.com
Firestorm www.firestorm-sgs.com
Flodman Guns www.flodman.com
FN Herstal www.fnherstal.com
FNH USA www.fnhusa.com
Franchi www.franchiusa.com
Freedom Arms www.freedomarms.com
Galazan www.connecticutshotgun.com
Gambo Renato www.renatogamba.it
Gamo www.gamo.com
Gary Reeder Custom Guns www.reeder-customguns.com
Gazelle Arms www.gazellearms.com
Gibbs Rifle Company www.gibbsrifle.com
Glock www.glock.com
Griffin & Howe www.griffinhowe.com
Grizzly Big Boar Rifle www.largrizzly.com
GSI Inc. www.gsifirearms.com
Guerini www.gueriniusa.com
Gunbroker.Com www.gunbroker.com
Hammerli www.hammerli.com
Hatfield Gun Co. www.hatfield-usa.com
Hatsan Arms Co. www.hatsan.com.tr
Heckler and Koch www.hk-usa.com
Henry Repeating Arms Co. www.henryrepeating.com
Heritage Mfg. www.heritagemfg.com
Heym www.heym-waffenfabrik.de
High Standard Mfg. www.highstandard.com
Hi-Point Firearms www.hi-pointfirearms.com
Holland & Holland www.hollandandholland.com
H&R Firearms www.marlinfirearms.com
H-S Precision www.hsprecision.com
Hunters Lodge Corp. www.hunterslodge.com
IAR Inc. www.iar-arms.com
Imperial Miniature Armory www.1800miniature.com
Interarms www.interarms.com
International Military Antiques, Inc. www.ima-usa.com
Inter Ordnance www.interordnance.com
Intrac Arms International LLC www.hsarms.com
Israel Arms www.israelarms.com
Iver Johnson Arms www.iverjohnsonarms.com
Izhevsky Mekhanichesky Zavod www.baikalinc.ru
Jarrett Rifles, Inc. www.jarrettrifles.com
J&G Sales, Ltd. www.jgsales.com
Johannsen Express Rifle www.johannsen-jagd.de
Jonathan Arthur Ciener www.22lrconversions.com
JP Enterprises, Inc. www.jprifles.com
Kahr Arms/Auto-Ordnance www.kahr.com
K.B.I. www.kbi-inc.com
Kel-Tec CNC Ind., Inc. www.kel-tec.com
Kifaru www.kifaru.net
Kimber www.kimberamerica.com
Knight's Mfg. Co. www.knightsarmco.com
Knight Rifles www.knightrifles.com
Korth www.korthwaffen.de
Krieghoff GmbH www.krieghoff.de
KY Imports, Inc. www.kyimports.com
Krieghoff Int'l www.krieghoff.com
L.A.R Mfg www.largrizzly.com
Lazzeroni Arms Co. www.lazzeroni.com

Legacy Sports International www.legacysports.com
Les Baer Custom, Inc. www.lesbaer.com
Lewis Machine & Tool Co. www.lewismachine.net
Linebaugh Custom Sixguns
www.sixgunner.com/linebaugh
Ljutic www.ljuticgun.com
Llama www.bersa-llama.com
Lone Star Rifle Co. www.lonestarrifle.com
Magnum Research www.magnumresearch.com
Majestic Arms www.majesticarms.com
Markesbery Muzzleloaders www.markesbery.com
Marksman Products www.marksman.com
Marlin www.marlinfirearms.com
Mauser www.mauserwaffen.de
McMillan Bros Rifle Co. www.mcfamily.com
MDM www.mdm-muzzleloaders.com
Meacham Rifles www.meachamrifles.com
Merkel www.hk-usa.com
Miller Arms www.millerarms.com
Miltech www.miltecharms.com
Miltex, Inc. www.miltexusa.com
Mitchell's Mausers www.mitchellsales.com
MK Ballistic Systems www.mkballistics.com
M-Mag www.mmag.com
Montana Rifle Co. www.montanarifleman.com
Mossberg www.mossberg.com
Navy Arms www.navyarms.com
Nesika www.nesika.com
New England Arms Corp. www.newenglandarms.com
New England Custom Gun Svc, Ltd.
www.newenglandcustomgun.com
New England Firearms www.hr1871.com
New Ultra Light Arms www.newultralight.com
North American Arms www.northamericanarms.com
Nosler Bullets,Inc. www.nosler.com
Nowlin Mfg. Inc. www.nowlinguns.com
O.F. Mossberg & Sons www.mossberg.com
Ohio Ordnance Works www.ohioordnanceworks.com
Olympic Arms www.olyarms.com
Panther Arms www.dpmsinc.com
Para-Ordnance www.paraord.com
Pedersoli Davide & Co. www.davide-pedersoli.com
Perazzi www.perazzi.com
Pietta www.pietta.it
PKP Knife-Pistol www.sanjuanenterprise.com
Power Custom www.powercustom.com
PTR 91, Inc. www.ptr91.com
Purdey & Sons www.purdey.com
Remington www.remington.com
Republic Arms Inc. www.republicarmsinc.com
Rhineland Arms, Inc. www.rhinelandarms.com
Rigby www.johnrigbyandco.com
Rizzini USA www.rizziniusa.com
Robar Companies, Inc. www.robarguns.com
Robinson Armament Co. www.robarm.com
Rock River Arms, Inc. www.rockriverarms.com
Rogue Rifle Co. Inc. www.chipmunkrifle.com
Rohrbaugh Firearms www.rohrbaughfirearms.com
Rossi Arms www.rossiusa.com
RPM www.rpmxlpistols.com
Russian American Armory www.raacfirearms.com
RUAG Ammotec www.ruag.com
Sabatti SPA www.sabatti.com
Sabre Defense Industries www.sabredefense.com
Saco Defense www.sacoinc.com
Safari Arms www.olyarms.com
Sako www.berettausa.com
Samco Global Arms Inc. www.samcoglobal.com
Sarco Inc. www.sarcoinc.com
Savage Arms Inc. www.savagearms.com
Scattergun Technologies Inc. www.wilsoncombat.com
Searcy Enterprises www.searcyent.com
Shiloh Rifle Mfg. www.shilohrifle.com
SIGARMS,Inc. www.sigarms.com
Simpson Ltd. www.simpsonltd.com
SKB Shotguns www.skbshotguns.com
Smith & Wesson www.smith-wesson.com
SOG International, Inc. soginc@go-concepts.com
Sphinx System www.sphinxarms.com
Springfield Armory www.springfield-armory.com

SSK Industries www.sskindustries.com
Stag Arms www.stagarms.com
Steyr Arms, Inc. www.steyrarms.com
Stoeger Industries www.stoegerindustries.com
Strayer-Voigt Inc. www.sviguns.com
Sturm, Ruger & Company www.ruger-firearms.com
Tactical Solutions www.tacticalsol.com
Tar-Hunt Slug Guns, Inc. www.tar-hunt.com
Taser Int'l www.taser.com
Taurus www.taurususa.com
Taylor's & Co., Inc. www.taylorsfirearms.com
Tennessee Guns www.tennesseeguns.com
The 1877 Sharps Co. www.1877sharps.com
Thompson Center Arms www.tcarms.com
Tikka www.berettausa.com
TNW, Inc. tncorp@aol.com
Traditions www.traditionsfirearms.com
Tristar Sporting Arms www.tristarsportingarms.com
Uberti www.ubertireplicas.com
U.S. Firearms Mfg. Co. www.usfirearms.com
Ultra Light Arms www.newultralight.com
Valkyrie Arms www.valkyriearms.com
Vektor Arms www.vektorarms.com
Volquartsen Custom Ltd. www.volquartsen.com
Vulcan Armament www.vulcanarmament.com
Walther USA www.waltheramerica.com
Weatherby www.weatherby.com
Webley and Scott Ltd. www.webley.co.uk
Westley Richards www.westleyrichards.com
Widley www.widleyguns.com
Wild West Guns www.wildwestguns.com
William Larkin Moore & Co. www.doublegun.com
Wilson Combat www.wilsoncombat.com
Winchester Rifles and Shotguns
www.winchesterguns.com

GUN PARTS, BARRELS, AFTER-MARKET ACCESSORIES

300 Below www.300below.com
Accuracy International of North America
www.accuracyinternational.org
Accuracy Speaks, Inc. www.accuracyspeaks.com
Advanced Barrel Systems www.carbonbarrels.com
Advantage Arms www.advantagearms.com
Aim Surplus www.aimsurplus.com
AK-USA www.ak-103.com
American Spirit Arms Corp. www.gunkits.com
AMT Gun Parts www.amt-gunparts.com
Badger Barrels, Inc. www.badgerbarrels.com
Bar-Sto Precision Machine www.barsto.com
Battenfeld Technologies
www.battenfeldtechnologies.com
Bellm TC's www.bellmtcs.com
Belt Mountain Enterprises www.beltmountain.com
Briley www.briley.com
Brownells www.brownells.com
B-Square www.b-square.com
Buffer Technologies www.buffertech.com
Bullberry Barrel Works www.bullberry.com
Bushmaster Firearms/Quality Parts www.bushmaster.com
Butler Creek Corp www.butler-creek.com
Cape Outfitters Inc. www.capeoutfitters.com
Caspian Arms Ltd. www.caspianarms.com
Cheaper Than Dirt www.cheaperthandirt.com
Chesnut Ridge www.chestnutridge.com/
Chip McCormick Corp www.chipmccormickcorp.com
Choate Machine & Tool Co. www.riflestock.com
Cierner, Jonathan Arthur www.22lrconversions.com
CJ Weapons Accessories www.cjweapons.com
Clerke International Arms (Bo Clerke)
www.clerkebarrels.com
Colonial Arms www.colonialarms.com
Comp-N-Choke www.comp-n-choke.com
Cylinder & Slide Shop www.cylinder-slide.com
Digi-Twist www.fmtcorp.com
Dixie Gun Works www.dixiegun.com
Douglas Barrels www.benchrest.com/douglas/
DPMS www.dpmsinc.com

D.S.Arms, Inc. www.dsarms.com
eBay www.ebay.com
Ed Brown Products www.edbrown.com
EFK Marketing/Fire Dragon Pistol Accessories
www.flmfire.com
E.R. Shaw www.ershawbarrels.com
Federal Arms www.fedarms.com
Forrest Inc. www.gunmags.com
Fulton Armory www.fulton-armory.com
Galazan www.connecticutshotgun.com
Gemtech www.gem-tech.com
Gentry, David www.gentrycustom.com
GG&G www.gggaz.com
Green Mountain Rifle Barrels www.gmriflebarrel.com
Gun Parts Corp. www.e-gunparts.com
Harris Engineering www.harrisbipods.com
Hart Rifle Barrels www.hartbarrels.com
Hastings Barrels www.hastingsbarrels.com
Heinie Specialty Products www.heinie.com
Holland Shooters Supply www.hollandgun.com
H-S Precision www.hsprecision.com
100 Straight Products www.100straight.com
I.M.A. www.ima-usa.com
Jarvis, Inc. www.jarvis-custom.com
J&T Distributing www.jtdistributing.com
John's Guns www.johnsguns.com
John Masen Co. www.johnmasen.com
Jonathan Arthur Ciener, Inc. www.22lrconversions.com
JP Enterprises www.jpar15.com
Keng's Firearms Specialities www.versapod.com
KG Industries www.kgcoatings.com
Kick Eez www.kickeez.com
Kidd Triggers www.coolguyguns.com
King's Gunworks www.kingsgunworks.com
Knoxx Industries www.knoxx.com
Krieger Barrels www.kriegerbarrels.com
K-VAR Corp. www.k-var.com
Les Baer Custom, Inc. www.lesbaer.com
Lilja Barrels www.riflebarrels.com
Lone Star Rifle Co. www.lonestarrifles.com
Lone Wolf Dist. www.lonewolfdist.com
Lothar Walther Precision Tools Inc. www.lothar-walther.de
M&A Parts, Inc. www.m-aparts.com
MAB Barrels www.mab.com.au
Majestic Arms www.majesticarms.com
Marvel Products, Inc. www.marvelprod.com
MEC-GAR SrL www.mec-gar.com
Mesa Tactical www.mesatactical.com
Michaels of Oregon Co. www.michaels-oregon.com
North Mfg. Co. www.rifle-barrels.com
Numrich Gun Parts Corp. www.e-gunparts.com
Pachmayr www.pachmayr.com
Pac-Nor Barrels www.pac-nor.com
Para Ordinance Pro Shop www.ltms.com
Point Tech Inc. pointec@ibm.net
Promag Industries www.promagindustries.com
Power Custom, Inc. www.powercustom.com
Red Star Arms www.redstararms.com
Rocky Mountain Arms www.rockymountainarms.com
Royal Arms Int'l www.royalarms.com
R.W. Hart www.rwhart.com
Sarco Inc. www.sarcoinc.com
Scattergun Technologies Inc. www.wilsoncombat.com
Schuemann Barrels www.schuemann.com
Seminole Gunworks Chamber Mates
www.chambermates.com
Shilen www.shilen.com
Sims Vibration Laboratory www.limbsaver.com
Smith & Alexander Inc. www.smithandalexander.com
Speed Shooters Int'l www.shooternet.com/ssi
Sprinco USA Inc. sprinco@primenet.com
STI Int'l www.stiguns.com
S&S Firearms www.ssfirearms.com
SSK Industries www.sskindustries.com
Sunny Hill Enterprises www.sunny-hill.com
Tactical Innovations www.tacticalinc.com
Tapco www.tapco.com
Trapdoors Galore www.trapdoors.com
Triple K Manufacturing Co. Inc. www.triplek.com
U.S.A. Magazines Inc. www.usa-magazines.com

Verney-Carron SA www.verney-carron.com
Volquartsen Custom Ltd. www.volquartsen.com
W.C. Wolff Co. www.gunsprings.com
Waller & Son www.wallerandson.com
Weigand Combat Handguns www.weigandcombat.com
Western Gun Parts www.westerngunparts.com
Wilson Arms www.wilsonarms.com
Wilson Combat www.wilsoncombat.com
Wisner's Inc. www.gunpartsspecialist.com
Z-M Weapons www.zmweapons.com/home.htm

GUNSMITHING SUPPLIES AND INSTRUCTION

American Gunsmithing Institute
   www.americangunsmith.com
Battenfeld Technologies
   www.battenfeldtechnologies.com
Bellm TC's www.bellmtcs.com
Brownells, Inc. www.brownells.com
B-Square Co. www.b-square.com
Clymer Mfg. Co. www.clymertool.com
Craftguard Metal Finishing crftgrd@aol.com
Dem-Bart www.dembartco.com
Doug Turnbull Restoration www.turnbullrestoration.com
Du-Lite Corp. www.dulite.com
Dvorak Instruments www.dvorakinstruments.com
Gradiant Lens Corp. www.gradientlens.com
Grizzly Industrial www.grizzly.com
Gunline Tools www.gunline.com
Harbor Freight www.harborfreight.com
JGS Precision Tool Mfg. LLC www.jgstools.com
Mag-Na-Port International www.magnaport.com
Manson Precision Reamers www.mansonreamers.com
Midway www.midwayusa.com
Murray State College www.mscok.edu
Olympus America Inc. www.olympus.com
Pacific Tool & Gauge www.pacifictoolandgauge.com
Trinidad State Junior College www.trinidadstate.edu

HANDGUN GRIPS

Ajax Custom Grips, Inc. www.ajaxgrips.com
Altamont Co. www.altamontco.com
Aluma Grips www.alumagrips.com
Badger Grips www.pistolgrips.com
Barami Corp. www.hipgrip.com
Blu Magnum Grips www.blumagnum.com
Buffalo Brothers www.buffalobrothers.com
Crimson Trace Corp. www.crimsontrace.com
Eagle Grips www.eaglegrips.com
Falcon Industries www.ergogrips.net
Herrett's Stocks www.herrettstocks.com
Hogue Grips www.getgrip.com
Kirk Ratajesak www.kgratajesak.com
Lett Custom Grips www.lettgrips.com
N.C. Ordnance www.gungrip.com
Nill-Grips USA www.nill-grips.com
Pachmayr www.pachmayr.com
Pearce Grips www.pearcegrip.com
Trausch Grips Int.Co. www.trausch.com
Tyler-T Grips www.t-grips.com
Uncle Mike's: www.uncle-mikes.com

HOLSTERS AND LEATHER PRODUCTS

Akah www.akah.de
Aker Leather Products www.akerleather.com
Alessi Distributor R&F Inc. www.alessiholsters.com
Alfonso's of Hollywood www.alfonsogunleather.com
Armor Holdings www.holsters.com
Bagmaster www.bagmaster.com
Bianchi International www.bianchi-intl.com
Blackhills Leather www.blackhillsleather.com
BodyHugger Holsters www.nikolais.com
Boyt Harness Co. www.boytharness.com
Brigade Gun Leather www.brigadegunleather.com

Chimere www.chimere.com
Classic Old West Styles www.cows.com
Conceal It www.conceal-it.com
Concealment Shop Inc. www.theconcealmentshop.com
Coronado Leather Co. www.coronadoleather.com
Creedmoor Sports, Inc. www.creedmoorsports.com
Custom Leather Wear www.customleatherwear.com
Defense Security Products www.thunderwear.com
Dennis Yoder www.yodercustomleather.com
DeSantis Holster www.desantisholster.com
Dillon Precision www.dillonprecision.com
Don Hume Leathergoods, Inc. www.donhume.com
Ernie Hill International www.erniehill.com
Fist www.fist-inc.com
Fobus USA www.fobusholster.com
Front Line Ltd. frontlin@internet-zahav.net
Galco www.usgalco.com
Gilmore's Sports Concepts www.gilmoresports.com
Gould & Goodrich www.goulduse.com
Gunmate Products www.gun-mate.com
Hellweg Ltd. www.hellwegltd.com
Hide-A-Gun www.hide-a-gun.com
Holsters.Com www.holsters.com
Horseshoe Leather Products www.horseshoe.co.uk
Hunter Co. www.huntercompany.com
Kirkpatrick Leather Company
   www.kirkpatrickleather.com
KNJ www.knjmfg.com
Kramer Leather www.kramerleather.com
Law Concealment Systems
   www.handgunconcealment.com
Levy's Leathers Ltd. www.levysleathers.com
Michaels of Oregon Co. www.michaels-oregon.com
Milt Sparks Leather www.miltsparks.com
Mitch Rosen Extraordinary Gunleather
   www.mitchrosen.com
Old World Leather www.gun-mate.com
Pacific Canvas & Leather Co.
   paccanadleather@directway.com
Pager Pal www.pagerpal.com
Phalanx Corp. www.smartholster.com
PWL www.pwlusa.com
Rumanya Inc. www.rumanya.com
S.A. Gunleather www.elpasoleather.com
Safariland Ltd. Inc. www.safariland.com
Shooting Systems Group Inc. www.shootingsystems.com
Strictly Anything Inc. www.strictlyanything.com
Strong Holster Co. www.strong-holster.com
The Belt Co. www.conceal-it.com
The Leather Factory Inc. lflandry@flash.net
The Outdoor Connection www.outdoorconnection.com
Top-Line USA inc. www.toplineusa.com
Triple K Manufacturing Co. www.triplek.com
Wilson Combat www.wilsoncombat.com

MISCELLANEOUS SHOOTING PRODUCTS

10X Products Group www.10Xwear.com
Aero Peltor www.aearo.com
American Body Armor www.americanbodyarmor.com
Armor Holdings Products www.armorholdings.com
Battenfeld Technologies
   www.battenfeldtechnologies.com
Beamhit www.beamhit.com
Beartooth www.beartoothproducts.com
Bodyguard by S&W www.yourbodyguard.com
Burnham Brothers www.burnhambrothers.com
Collectors Armory www.collectorsarmory.com
Dalloz Safety www.cdalloz.com
Deben Group Industries Inc. www.deben.com
Decot Hy-Wyd Sport Glasses www.sportyglasses.com
E.A.R., Inc. www.earinc.com
First Choice Armor www.firstchoicearmor.com
Gunstands www.gunstands.com
Howard Leight Hearing Protectors www.howardleight.com
Hunters Specialities www.hunterspec.com
Johnny Stewart Wildlife Calls www.hunterspec.com
Merit Corporation www.meritcorporation.com

Michaels of Oregon www.michaels-oregon.com
MPI Outdoors www.mpioutdoors.com
MTM Case-Gard www.mtmcase-gard.com
North Safety Products www.northsafety-brea.com
Plano Molding www.planomolding.com
Pro-Ears www.pro-ears.com
Second Chance Body Armor Inc. www.secondchance.com
Silencio www.silencio.com
Smart Lock Technologies www.smartlock.com
Surefire www.surefire.com
Taser Int'l www.taser.com
Walker's Game Ear Inc. www.walkersgameear.com

MUZZLELOADING FIREARMS AND PRODUCTS

American Pioneer Powder
   www.americanpioneerpowder.com
Armi Sport www.armisport.com
Barnes Bullets www.barnesbullets.com
Black Powder Products www.bpiguns.com
Buckeye Barrels wwwbuckeyebarrels.com
CVA www.cva.com
Davide Perdsoli & co. www.davide-pedersoli.com
Dixie Gun Works, Inc. www.dixiegun.com
Elephant/Swiss Black Powder
   www.elephantblackpowder.com
Goex Black Powder www.goexpowder.com
Green Mountain Rifle Barrel Co. www.gmriflebarrel.com
Harvester Bullets www.harvesterbullets.com
Hornady www.hornady.com
Jedediah Starr Trading Co. www.jedediah-starr.com
Jim Chambers Flintlocks www.flintlocks.com
Kahnke Gunworks www.powderandbow.com/kahnke/
Knight Rifles www.knightrifles.com
L&R Lock Co. www.lr-rpl.com
Log Cabin Shop www.logcabinshop.com
Lyman www.lymanproducts.com
Magkor Industries www.magkor.com
MDM Muzzleloaders www.mdm-muzzleloaders.com
Millennium Designed Muzzleloaders
   www.mdm-muzzleloaders.com
MSM, Inc. www.msmfg.com
Muzzleload Magnum Products www.mmpsabots.com
Muzzleloading Technologies, Inc.
   www.mtimuzzleloading.com
Navy Arms www.navyarms.com
Northwest Trade Guns www.northstarwest.com
Nosler, Inc. www.nosler.com
October Country Muzzleloading www.oct-country.com
Ox-Yoke Originals Inc. www.oxyoke.com
Pacific Rifle Co. pacificrifle@aol.com
Palmetto Arms www.palmetto.it
Pietta www.pietta.it
Powerbelt Bullets www.powerbeltbullets.com
PR Bullets www.prbullets.com
Precision Rifle Dead Center Bullets www.prbullet.com
R.E. Davis CVo. www.redaviscompany.com
Remington www.remington.com
Rightnour Mfg. Co. Inc. www.rmcsports.com
The Rifle Shop trshoppe@aol.com
Savage Arms, Inc. www.savagearms.com
Schuetzen Powder www.schuetzenpowder.com
TDC www.tdcmfg.com
Thompson Center Arms www.tcarms.com
Traditions Performance Muzzleloading
   www.traditionsfirearms.com

PUBLICATIONS, VIDEOS, AND CD'S

A&J Arms Booksellers www.ajarmsbooksellers.com
Airgun Letter www.airgunletter.com
American Cop www.americancopmagazine.com
American Firearms Industry www.amfire.com
American Handgunner www.americanhandgunner.com
American Hunter www.nrapublications.org
American Rifleman www.nrapublications.org
American Shooting Magazine
   www.americanshooting.com

Blacksmith sales@blacksmithcorp.com
Black Powder Cartridge News www.blackpowderspg.com
Black Powder Journal www.blackpowderjournal.com
Blue Book Publications www.bluebookinc.com
Combat Handguns www.combathandguns.com
Concealed Carry www.uscca.us
Cornell Publications www.cornellpubs.com
Countrywide Press www.countrysport.com
DBI Books/Krause Publications www.krause.com
Delta Force www.infogo.com/delta
Gun List www.gunlist.com
Gun Video www.gunvideo.com
GUNS Magazine www.gunsmagazine.com
Guns & Ammo www.gunsandammomag.com
Gunweb Magazine WWW Links www.imags.com
Gun Week www.gunweek.com
Gun World www.gunworld.com
Harris Publications www.harrispublications.com
Heritage Gun Books www.gunbooks.com
Krause Publications www.krause.com
Law and Order www.hendonpub.com
Moose Lake Publishing MooselakeP@aol.com
Munden Enterprises Inc. www.bob-munden.com
Outdoor Videos www.outdoorvideos.com
Precision Shooting www.precisionshooting.com
Predator Extreme www.predatorextreme.com
Predator & Prey www.predatorandpreymag.com
Ray Riling Arms Books www.rayrilingarmsbooks.com
Rifle and Handloader Magazines www.riflemagazine.com
Safari Press Inc. www.safaripress.com
Shoot! Magazine www.shootmagazine.com
Shooters News www.shootersnews.com
Shooting Illustrated www.nrapublications.org
Shooting Industry www.shootingindustry.com
Shooting Sports Retailer
    www.shootingsportsretailer.com
Shooting Sports USA www.nrapublications.org
Shotgun News www.shotgunnews.com
Shotgun Report www.shotgunreport.com
Shotgun Sports Magazine www.shotgun-sports.com
Small Arms Review www.smallarmsreview.com
Small Caliber News www.smallcaliber.com
Sporting Clays Web Edition www.sportingclays.net
Sports Afield www.sportsafield.comm
Sports Trend www.sportstrend.com
Sportsmen on Film www.sportsmenonfilm.com
The Gun Journal www.shooters.com
The Shootin Iron www.off-road.com/4x4web/si/si.html
The Single Shot Exchange Magazine
    singleshot@earthlink.net
The Sixgunner www.sskindustries.com
Voyageur Press www.voyageurpress.com
VSP Publications www.gunbooks.com
Vulcan Outdoors Inc. www.vulcanpub.com

RELOADING TOOLS

Ballisti-Cast Mfg. www.ballisti-cast.com
Battenfeld Technologies
    www.battenfeldtechnologies.com
Bruno Shooters Supply www.brunoshooters.com
CH/4D Custom Die www.ch4d.com
Colorado Shooters Supply www.hochmoulds.com
Corbin Mfg & Supply Co. www.corbins.com
Dillon Precision www.dillonprecision.com
Forster Precision Products www.forsterproducts.com
Hanned Line www.hanned.com
Harrell's Precision www.harrellsprec.com
Holland's Shooting Supplies www.hollandgun.com
Hornady www.hornady.com
Huntington Reloading Products www.huntingtons.com
J & J Products Co. www.jandjproducts.com
Lead Bullet Technology LBTisaccuracy@lmbris.net
Lee Precision,Inc. www.leeprecision.com
Littleton Shotmaker www.leadshotmaker.com
Load Data www.loaddata.com
Lyman www.lymanproducts.com
Magma Engineering www.magmaengr.com
Mayville Engineering Co. (MEC) www.mecreloaders.com
Midway www.midwayusa.com

Moly-Bore www.molybore.com
MTM Case-Guard www.mtmcase-guard.com
NECO www.neconos.com
NEI www.neihandtools.com
Neil Jones Custom Products www.neiljones.com
Ponsness/Warren www.reloaders.com
Ranger Products
    www.pages.prodigy.com/rangerproducts.home.htm
Rapine Bullet Mold Mfg Co. www.bulletmoulds.com
RCBS www.rcbs.com
Redding Reloading Equipment
    www.redding-reloading.com
Russ Haydon's Shooting Supplies
    www.shooters-supply.com
Sinclair Int'l Inc. www.sinclairintl.com
Stoney Point Products Inc www.stoneypoint.com
Thompson Bullet Lube Co. www.thompsonbulletlube.com
Vickerman Seating Die www.castingstuff.com
Wilson (L.E. Wilson) www.lewilson.com

RESTS— BENCH, PORTABLE, ATTACHABLE

Battenfeld Technolgies www.battenfeldtechnologies.com
Bench Master www.bench-master.com
B-Square www.b-square.com
Bullshooter www.bullshooterssightingin.com
Desert Mountain Mfg. www.bench-master.com
Harris Engineering Inc. www.harrisbipods.com
Kramer Designs www.snipepod.com
L. Thomas Rifle Support www.ltsupport.com
Level-Lok www.levellok.com
Midway www.midwayusa.com
Predator Sniper Styx www.predatorsniperstyx.com
Ransom International www.ransom-intl.com
R.W. Hart www.rwhart.com
Sinclair Intl, Inc. www.sinclairintl.com
Stoney Point Products www.uncle-mikes.com
Target Shooting www.targetshooting.com
Varmint Masters www.varmintmasters.com
Versa-Pod www.versa-pod.com

SCOPES, SIGHTS, MOUNTS AND ACCESSORIES

Accumount www.accumounts.com
Accusight www.accusight.com
ADCO www.shooters.com/adco/index/htm
Adirondack Opitcs www.adkoptics.com
Aimpoint www.aimpoint.com
Aim Shot, Inc. www.miniosprey.com
Aimtech Mount Systems www.aimtech-mounts.com
Alpec Team, Inc. www.alpec.com
Alpen Outdoor Corp. www.alpenoutdoor.com
American Technologies Network, Corp. www.atncorp.com
AmeriGlo, LLC www.ameriglo.net
AO Sight Systems Inc. www.aosights.com
Ashley Outdoors, Inc. www.ashleyoutdoors.com
ATN www.atncorp.com
Badger Ordnance www.badgerordnance.com
Beamshot-Quarton www.beamshot.com
BSA Optics www.bsaoptics.com
B-Square Company, Inc. www.b-square.com
Burris www.burrisoptics.com
Bushnell Performance Optics www.bushnell.com
Carl Zeiss Optical Inc. www.zeiss.com
Carson Optical www.carson-optical.com
C-More Systems www.cmore.com
Conetrol Scope Mounts www.conetrol.com
Crimson Trace Corp. www.crimsontrace.com
Crossfire L.L.C. www.amfire.com/hesco/html
DCG Supply Inc. www.dcgsupply.com
D&L Sports www.dlsports.com
EasyHit, Inc. www.easyhit.com
EAW www.eaw.de
Elcan Optical Technologies
    www.armament.com, www.elcan.com
Electro-Optics Technologies
    www.eotechmdc.com/holosight

Europtik Ltd. www.europtik.com
Fujinon, Inc. www.fujinon.com
Gilmore Sports www.gilmoresports.com
Hakko Co. Ltd. www.hakko-japan.co.jp
Hesco www.hescosights.com
Hi-Lux Optics www.hi-luxoptics.com
Hitek Industries www.nightsight.com
HIVIZ www.hivizsights.com
Hollands Shooters Supply www.hollandguns.com
Horus Vision www.horusvision.com
Hunter Co. www.huntercompany.com
Innovative Weaponry, Inc. www.ptnightsights.com
Ironsighter Co. www.ironsighter.com
ITT Night Vision www.ittnightvision.com
Kahles www.kahlesoptik.com
Kowa Optimed Inc. www.kowascope.com
Kwik-Site Co. www.kwiksitecorp.com
Laser Bore Sight www.laserboresight.com
Laser Devices Inc. www.laserdevices.com
Lasergrips www.crimsontrace.com
LaserLyte www.laserlytesights.com
LaserMax Inc. www.lasermax.com
Laser Products www.surefire.com
Leapers, Inc. www.leapers.com
Leatherwood www.leatherwoodoptics.com
Leica Camera Inc. www.leica-camera.com/usa
Leupold www.leupold.com
LightForce/NightForce USA www.nightforcescopes.com
Lyman www.lymanproducts.com
Lynx www.b-square.com
Marble's Outdoors www.marblesoutdoors.com
MDS, Inc. www.mdsincorporated.com
Meopta www.meopta.com
Meprolight www.kimberamerica.com
Micro Sight Co. www.microsight.com
Millett www.millettsights.com
Miniature Machine Corp. www.mmcsight.com
Montana Vintage Arms www.montanavintagearms.com
Mounting Solutions Plus www.mountsplus.com
NAIT www.nait.com
Newcon International Ltd.
    newconsales@newcon-optik.com
Night Force Optics www.nightforcescopes.com
Night Owl Optics www.nightowloptics.com
Nikon Inc. www.nikonusa.com
North American Integrated Technologies www.nait.com
O.K. Weber, Inc. www.okweber.com
Optolyth-Optic www.optolyth.de
Pentax Corp. www.pentaxlightseeker.com
Premier Reticle www.premierreticles.com
Redfield www.redfieldoptics.com
R&R Int'l Trade www.nightoptic.com
Schmidt & Bender www.schmidt-bender.com
Scopecoat www.scopecoat.com
Scopelevel www.scopelevel.com
Segway Industries www.segway-industries.com
Shepherd Scope Ltd. www.shepherdscopes.com
Sightron www.sightron.com
Simmons www.simmonsoptics.com
S&K www.scopemounts.com
Springfield Armory www.springfield-armory.com
Sure-Fire www.surefire.com
Swarovski/Kahles www.swarovskioptik.com
Swift Optics www.swiftoptics.com
Talley Mfg. www.talleyrings.com
Tasco www.tascosales.com
Trijicon Inc. www.trijicon.com
Truglo Inc. www.truglo.com
UltraDot www.ultradotusa.com
Unertl Optical Co. www.unertloptics.com
US Night Vision www.usnightvision.com
U.S. Optics Technologies Inc. www.usoptics.com
Valdada-IOR Optics www.valdada.com
Warne www.warnescopemounts.com
Weaver Scopes www.weaveroptics.com
Wilcox Industries Corp www.wilcoxind.com
Williams Gun Sight Co. www.williamsgunsight.com
XS Sight Systems www.xssights.com
Zeiss www.zeiss.com

WEB DIRECTORY

SHOOTING ORGANIZATIONS, SCHOOLS AND RANGES

Amateur Trapshooting Assoc. www.shootata.com
American Custom Gunmakers Guild www.acgg.org
American Gunsmithing Institute
    www.americangunsmith.com
American Pistolsmiths Guild www.americanpistol.com
American Shooting Sports Council www.assc.com
American Single Shot Rifle Assoc. www.assra.com
Antique Shooting Tool Collector's Assoc.
    www.oldshootingtools.org
Assoc. of Firearm & Tool Mark Examiners www.afte.org
BATF www.atf.ustreas.gov
Blackwater Lodge and Training Center
    www.blackwaterlodge.com
Boone and Crockett Club www.boone-crockett.org
Buckmasters, Ltd. www.buckmasters.com
Cast Bullet Assoc. www.castbulletassoc.org
Citizens Committee for the Right to Keep & Bear Arms
    www.ccrkba.org
Civilian Marksmanship Program www.odcmp.com
Colorado School of Trades www.gunsmith-school.com
Ducks Unlimited www.ducks.org
4-H Shooting Sports Program
    www.4-hshootingsports.org
Fifty Caliber Institute www.fiftycal.org
Fifty Caliber Shooters Assoc. www.fcsa.org
Firearms Coalition www.nealknox.com
Front Sight Firearms Training Institute www.frontsight.com
German Gun Collectors Assoc. www.germanguns.com
Gun Clubs www.associatedgunclubs.org
Gun Owners' Action League www.goal.org
Gun Owners of America www.gunowners.org
Gun Trade Assoc. Ltd. www.brucepub.com/gta
Gunsite Training Center, Inc. www.gunsite.com
Handgun Hunters International www.sskindustries.com
Hunting and Shooting Sports Heritage Fund
    www.huntandshoot.org
International Defense Pistol Assoc. www.idpa.com
International Handgun Metallic Silhouette Assoc.
    www.ihmsa.org
International Hunter Education Assoc. www.ihea.com
International Single Shot Assoc. www.issa-schuetzen.org
Jews for the Preservation of Firearms Ownership
    www.jpfo.org
Mule Deer Foundation www.muledeer.org
Muzzle Loaders Assoc. of Great Britain www.mlagb.com
National 4-H Shooting Sports www.4-hshootingsports.org
National Association of Sporting Goods Wholesalers
    www.nasgw.org
National Benchrest Shooters Assoc. www.benchrest.com
National Muzzle Loading Rifle Assoc. www.nmlra.org
National Reloading Manufacturers Assoc
    www.reload-nrma.com
National Rifle Assoc. www.nra.org
National Rifle Assoc. ILA www.nraila.org
National Shooting Sports Foundation www.nssf.org
National Skeet Shooters Association www.nssa-nsca.com
National Sporting Clays Assoc. www.nssa-nsca.com
National Wild Turkey Federation www.nwtf.com
NICS/FBI www.fbi.gov
North American Hunting Club www.huntingclub.com
Order of Edwardian Gunners (Vintagers)
    www.vintagers.org
Outdoor Industry Foundation
    www.outdoorindustryfoundation.org
Pennsylvania Gunsmith School www.pagunsmith.com
Quail Unlimited www.qu.org
Right To Keep and Bear Arms www.rkba.org
Rocky Mountain Elk Foundation www.rmef.org
SAAMI www.saami.org
Safari Club International www.scifirstforhunters.org

Scholastic Clay Target Program www.nssf.org/sctp
Second Amendment Foundation www.saf.org
Second Amendment Sisters www.2asisters.org
Shooting Ranges Int'l www.shootingranges.com
Single Action Shooting Society www.sassnet.com
Students for Second Amendment www.sf2a.org
S&W Academy and Nat'l Firearms Trng. Center
    www.sw-academy.com
Tactical Defense Institute www.tdiohio.com
Ted Nugent United Sportsmen of America
    www.tnugent.com
Thunder Ranch www.thunderranchinc.com
Trapshooters Homepage www.trapshooters.com
Trinidad State Junior College www.trinidadstate.edu
U.S. Concealed Carry Association www.uscca.us
U.S. Int'l Clay Target Assoc. www.usicta.com
United States Fish and Wildlife Service www.fws.gov
U.S. Practical Shooting Assoc. www.uspsa.org
USA Shooting www.usashooting.com
Varmint Hunters Assoc. www.varminthunter.org
U.S. Sportsmen's Alliance www.ussportsmen.org
Women Hunters www.womanhunters.com
Women's Shooting Sports Foundation www.wssf.org

STOCKS

Advanced Technology www.atigunstocks.com
Battenfeld Technologies
    www.battenfeldtechnologies.com
Bell & Carlson, Inc. www.bellandcarlson.com
Boyd's Gunstock Industries, Inc.
    www.boydgunstocks.com
Butler Creek Corp www.butler-creek.com
Calico Hardwoods, Inc. www.calicohardwoods.com
Choate Machine www.riflestock.com
Elk Ridge Stocks
    www.reamerrentals.com/elk_ridge.htm
Fajen www.battenfeldtechnologies.com
Great American Gunstocks www.gunstocks.com
Herrett's Stocks www.herrettstocks.com
High Tech Specialties www.bansnersrifle.com/hightech
Holland's Shooting Supplies www.hollandgun.com
Knoxx Industries www.knoxx.com
Lone Wolf www.lonewolfriflestocks.com
McMillan Fiberglass Stocks www.mcmfamily.com
MPI Stocks www.mpistocks.com
Precision Gun Works www.precisiongunstocks.com
Ram-Line www.outers-guncare.com
Rimrock Rifle Stock www.rimrockstocks.com
Royal Arms Gunstocks www.imt.net/~royalarms
S&K Industries www.sandkgunstocks.com
Speedfeed, Inc. www.speedfeedinc.com
Tiger-Hunt Curly Maple Gunstocks
    www.gunstockwood.com
Wenig Custom Gunstocks Inc. www.wenig.com

TARGETS AND RANGE EQUIPMENT

Action Target Co. www.actiontarget.com
Advanced Interactive Systems www.ais-sim.com
Birchwood Casey www.birchwoodcasey.com
Caswell Meggitt Defense Systems www.mds-caswell.com
Champion Traps & Targets www.championtarget.com
Handloader/Victory Targets www.targetshandloader.com
Just Shoot Me Products www.ballistictec.com
Laser Shot www.lasershot.com
Mountain Plains Industries www.targetshandloader.com
MTM Products www.mtmcase-gard.com
Natiional Target Co. www.nationaltarget.com
Newbold Target Systems www.newboldtargets.com
Porta Target,Inc. www.portatarget.com
Range Management Services Inc. www.casewellintl.com
Range Systems www.shootingrangeproducts.com

Reactive Target Systems Inc. chrts@primenet.com
ShatterBlast Targets www.daisy.com
Super Trap Bullet Containment Systems
    www.supertrap.com
Thompson Target Technology www.thompsontarget.com
Tombstone Tactical Targets www.tttargets.com
Visible Impact Targets www.crosman.com
White Flyer www.whiteflyer.com

TRAP AND SKEET SHOOTING EQUIPMENT AND ACCESSORIES

Auto-Sporter Industries www.auto-sporter.com
10X Products Group www.10Xwear.com
Claymaster Traps www.claymaster.com
Do-All Traps, Inc. www.do-alltraps.com
Laporte USA www.laporte-shooting.com
Outers www.blount.com
Trius Products Inc. www.triustraps.com
White Flyer www.whiteflyer.com

TRIGGERS

Brownells www.brownells.com
Chip McCormick Corp. www.chipmccormickcorp.com
Huber Concepts www.huberconcepts.com
Kidd Triggers. www.coolguyguns.com
Shilen www.shilen.com
Timney Triggers www.timneytrigger.com

MAJOR SHOOTING WEB SITES AND LINKS

24 Hour Campfire www.24hourcampfire.com
Alphabetic Index of Links www.gunsgunsguns.com
Ammo Guide www.ammoguide.com
Auction Arms www.auctionarms.com
Benchrest Central www.benchrest.com
Big Game Hunt www.biggamehunt.net
Bullseye Pistol www.bullseyepistol.com
Firearms History www.researchpress.co.uk/firearms
Firearm News www.firearmnews.com
Gun Broker Auctions www.gunbroker.com
Gun Index www.gunindex.com
Gun Industry www.gunindustry.com
Gun Blast www.gunblast.com
Gun Boards www.gunboards.com
Gun Broker www.gunbroker.com
Gun Law www.gunlaw.com
Gun Manuals www.gunmanuals.ch/manuals.htm
Gun Nut www.gunnut.com
Gun Nuts Firearm Schematics www.gunuts.com
Guns For Sale www.gunsamerica.com
Guns Unified Nationally Endorsing Dignity www.guned.com
Gun Shop Finder www.gunshopfinder.com
Hunt and Shoot (NSSF) www.huntandshoot.org
Hunting Net www.hunting.net
Hunting Network www.huntingnetwork.com
Keep and Bear Arms www.keepandbeararms.com
Leverguns www.leverguns.com
Load Swap www.loadswap.com
Outdoor Press Room www.outdoorpressroom.com
Outdoor Yellow Pages www.outdoorsyp.com
Real Guns www.realguns.com
Rec.Guns www.recguns.com
Shooters Forum www.shootersforum.com
Shooter's Online Services www.shooters.com
Shotgun Sports Resource Guide www.shotgunsports.com
Sixgunner www.sixgunner.com
Sportsman's Web www.sportsmansweb.com
Surplus Rifles www.surplusrifle.com
Wing Shoooting USA www.wingshootingusa.org

PERIODICAL PUBLICATIONS

AAFTA News (M)
5911 Cherokee Ave., Tampa, FL 33604. Official newsletter of the American Airgun Field Target Assn.

Accurate Rifle, The
Precisions Shooting, Inc., 222 Mckee Street, Manchester CT 06040. $37/yr. Dedicated to the rifle accuracy enthusiast.

Action Pursuit Games Magazine (M)
CFW Enterprises, Inc., 4201 W. Vanowen Pl., Burbank, CA 91505 818-845-2656. $4.99 single copy U.S., $5.50 Canada. Editor: Dan Reeves. World's leading magazine of paintball sports.

Air Gunner Magazine
4 The Courtyard, Denmark St., Wokingham, Berkshire RG11 2AZ, England/011-44-734-771677. $U.S. $44/yr. Leading monthly airgun magazine in U.K.

Airgun Ads
Box 33, Hamilton, MT 59840/406-363-3805; Fax: 406-363-4117. $35/yr. (for first mailing; $20 for second mailing; $35 for Canada and foreign orders.) Monthly tabloid with extensive For Sale and Wanted airgun listings.

Airgun Letter, The
Gapp, Inc., 4614 Woodland Rd., Ellicott City, MD 21042-6329/410-730-5496; Fax: 410-730-9544; e-mail: staff@airgnltr.net; http://www.airgunletter.com. $21 U.S., $24 Canada, $27 Mexico and $33 other foreign orders, 1 yr. monthly newsletter for airgun users and collectors.

Airgun World
4 The Courtyard, Denmark St., Wokingham, Berkshire RG40 2AZ, England/011-44-734-771677. Call for subscription rates. Oldest monthly airgun magazine in U.K., sister publication to *Air Gunner.*

Alaska Magazine
Morris Communications, 735 Broad Street, Augusta, GA 30901/706-722-6060. Hunting, fishing and life on the Last Frontier articles of Alaska and western Canada.

American Firearms Industry
Nat'l. Assn. of Federally Licensed Firearms Dealers, 2455 E. Sunrise Blvd., Suite 916, Ft. Lauderdale, FL 33304. $35.00/yr. For firearms retailers, distributors and manufacturers.

American Guardian
NRA, 11250 Waples Mill Rd., Fairfax, VA 22030. Publications division. $15.00/yr. Magazine features personal protection; home-self-defense; family recreation shooting; women's issues; etc.

American Gunsmith
Belvoir Publications, Inc., 75 Holly Hill Lane, Greenwich, CT 06836-2626/203-661-6111. $49.00 (12 issues). Technical journal of firearms repair and maintenance.

American Handgunner*
Publisher's Development Corp., 12345 World Trade Drive, San Diego, CA 92128/800-537-3006 $16.95/yr. Articles for handgun enthusiasts, competitors, police and hunters.

American Hunter (M)
National Rifle Assn., 11250 Waples Mill Rd., Fairfax, VA 22030 (Same address for both.) Publications Div. $35.00/yr. Wide scope of hunting articles.

American Rifleman (M)
National Rifle Assn., 11250 Waples Mill Rd., Fairfax, VA 22030 (Same address for both). Publications Div. $35.00/yr. Firearms articles of all kinds.

American Survival Guide
McMullen Angus Publishing, Inc., 774 S. Placentia Ave., Placentia, CA 92670-6846. 12 issues $19.95/714-572-2255; FAX: 714-572-1864.

Armes & Tir*
c/o FABECO, 38, rue de Trévise 75009 Paris, France. Articles for hunters, collectors, and shooters. French text.

Arms Collecting (Q)
Museum Restoration Service, P.O. Box 70, Alexandria Bay, NY 13607-0070. $22.00/yr.; $62.00/3 yrs.; $112.00/5 yrs.

Australian Shooter (formerly Australian Shooters Journal)
Sporting Shooters' Assn. of Australia, Inc., P.O. Box 2066, Kent Town SA 5071, Australia. $60.00/yr. locally; $65.00/yr. overseas surface mail. Hunting and shooting articles.

Backwoodsman Magazine, The
P.O. Box 627, Westcliffe, CO 81252. $16.00/yr. 6 issues; $30.00/2 yrs.; sample copy $2.75. Subjects include muzzle-loading, woodslore, primitive survival, trapping, homesteading, blackpowder cartridge guns, 19th century how-to.

Black Powder Cartridge News (Q)
SPG, Inc., P.O. Box 761, Livingston, MT 59047/Phone/Fax: 406-222-8416. $17/yr. (4 issues) ($6 extra 1st class mailing).

Blackpowder Hunting (M)
Intl. Blackpowder Hunting Assn., P.O. Box 1180Z, Glenrock, WY 82637/307-436-9817. $20.00/yr., $36.00/2 yrs. How-to and where-to features by experts on hunting; shooting; ballistics; traditional and modern blackpowder rifles, shotguns, pistols and cartridges.

Black Powder Times
P.O. Box 234, Lake Stevens, WA 98258. $20.00/yr.; add $5/year for Canada, $10/year other foreign. Tabloid newspaper for blackpowder activities; test reports.

Blade Magazine
Krause Publications, 700 East State St., Iola, WI 54990-0001. $25.98 for 12 issues. Foreign price (including Canada-Mexico) $50.00. A magazine for all fans of handmade, factory and antique knives.

Caliber
GFI-Verlag, Theodor-Heuss Ring 62, 50668 Koln, Germany. For hunters, target shooters and reloaders.

Caller, The (Q) (M)
National Wild Turkey Federation, P.O. Box 530, Edgefield, SC 29824. Tabloid newspaper; 4 issues/yr. (membership fee $25.00)

Cartridge Journal (M)
Robert Mellichamp, 907 Shirkmere, Houston, TX 77008/713-869-0558. Dues $12 for U.S. and Canadian members (includes the newsletter); 6 issues.

Cast Bullet, The*(M)
Official journal of The Cast Bullet Assn., Dir. of Membership, 203 E. 2nd St., Muscatine, IA 52761. Membership $14/year, incl. 6 issues.

Cibles
14, rue du Patronage-Laique, BP 2057, 52902 Chaumont, cedex 9, France. French-language magazine also carries small amount of arms-related and historical content. 12 issues/year. Tel/03-25-03-87-47/Email: cibeles@graphycom.com; Web: www.graphycom

COLTELLI, che Passione (Q)
Casella postale N.519, 20101 Milano, Italy/Fax: 02-48402857. $15/yr., $27/2 yrs. Covers all types of knives—collecting, combat, historical. Italian text.

Combat Handguns*
Harris Publications, Inc., 1115 Broadway, New York, NY 10010.

Deer & Deer Hunting Magazine
Krause Publications, 700 E. State St., Iola, WI 54990-0001. $19.95/yr. (9 issues). For the serious deer hunter. Web: www.krause.com

Derringer Peanut, The (M)
The National Association of Derringer Collectors, P.O. Box 20572, San Jose, CA 95160. A newsletter dedicated to developing the best derringer information. Write for details.

Deutsches Waffen Journal
Journal-Verlag Schwend GmbH, Postfach 100340, D-74503 Schwäbisch Hall, Germany/0791-404-500; FAX:0791-404-505 and 404-424. DM102/yr. (interior); DM125.30 (abroad), postage included. Antique and modern arms and equipment. German text.

Double Gun Journal
P.O. Box 550, East Jordan, MI 49727/800-447-1658. $35/4 issues.

Ducks Unlimited, Inc. (M)
1 Waterfowl Way, Memphis, TN 38120

Engraver, The (M) (Q)
P.O. Box 4365, Estes Park, CO 80517/970-586-2388; Fax: 970-586-0394. Mike Dubber, editor. The journal of firearms engraving.

Field, The
King's Reach Tower, Stamford St., London SE1 9LS England. £36.40 U.K./yr.; 49.90 (overseas, surface mail) yr.; £82.00 (overseas, air mail)/yr. Hunting and shooting articles, and all country sports.

Field & Stream
Time4 Media, Two Park Ave., New York, NY 10016/212-779-5000. 12 issues/$19.97. Monthly shooting column. Articles on hunting and fishing.

Field Tests
Belvoir Publications, Inc., 75 Holly Hill Lane; P.O. Box 2626, Greenwich, CT 06836-2626/203-661-6111; 800-829-3361 (subscription line). U.S. & Canada $29/yr., $58/2 yrs.; all other countries $45/yr., $90/2 yrs. (air).

Fur-Fish-Game
A.R. Harding Pub. Co., 2878 E. Main St., Columbus, OH 43209. $15.95/yr. Practical guidance for trapping, fishing and hunting.

Gottlieb-Tartaro Report, The
Second Amendment Foundation, James Madison Bldg., 12500 NE 10th Pl., Bellevue, WA 98005/206-454-7012; Fax:206-451-3959. $30/12 issues. An insider's guide for gun owners.

Gray's Sporting Journal
P.O. Box 1207, Augusta, GA 30903. $36.95/6 issues. Hunting and fishing. Expeditions and Guides Book (Annual Travel Guide).

Gun Digest, The Magazine (formerly Gun List)†
700 E. State St., Iola, WI 54990. $37.98/yr. (26 issues); $66.98 (52 issues). Indexed market publication for firearms collectors and active shooters; guns, supplies and services. Web: www.krause.com

Gun News Digest (Q)
Second Amendment Fdn., P.O. Box 488, Station C, Buffalo, NY 14209/716-885-6408; Fax:716-884-4471. $10 U.S.; $20 foreign.

Gun Report, The
World Wide Gun Report, Inc., Box 38, Aledo, IL 61231-0038. $33.00/yr. For the antique and collectable gun dealer and collector.

Gunmaker (M) (Q)
ACGG, P.O. Box 812, Burlington, IA 52601-0812. The journal of custom gunmaking.

Gunrunner, The
Div. of Kexco Publ. Co. Ltd., Box 565G, Lethbridge, Alb., Canada T1J 3Z4. $23.00/yr., sample $2.00. Monthly newspaper, listing everything from antiques to artillery.

Gun Show Calendar (Q)
700 E. State St., Iola, WI 54990. $14.95/yr. (4 issues). Gun shows listed; chronologically and by state. Web: www.krause.com

Gun Tests
11 Commerce Blvd., Palm Coast, FL 32142. The consumer resource for the serious shooter. Write for information.

Gun Trade News
Bruce Publishing Ltd., P.O. Box 82, Wantage, Ozon OX12 7A8, England/44-1-235-771770; Fax: 44-1-235-771848. Britain's only "trade only" magazine exclusive to the gun trade.

Gun Week†
Second Amendment Foundation, P.O. Box 488, Station C, Buffalo, NY 14209. $35.00/yr. U.S. and possessions; $45.00/yr. other countries. Tabloid paper on guns, hunting, shooting and collecting (36 issues).

Gun World
Y-Visionary Publishing, LP 265 South Anita Drive, Ste. 120, Orange, CA 92868. $21.97/yr.; $34.97/2 yrs. For the hunting, reloading and shooting enthusiast.

Guns & Ammo
Intermedia, 6420 Wilshire Blvd., Los Angeles, CA 90048/213-782-2780. $23.94/yr. Guns, shooting, and technical articles.

Guns
Publishers Development Corporation, 12345 World Trade Drive, San Diego, CA 92128/800-537-3006. $19.95/yr. In-depth articles on guns, shooting equipment and accessories for collectors, hunters and shooters.

Guns Review
Ravenhill Publishing Co. Ltd., Box 35, Standard House, Bonhill St., London EC 2A 4DA, England. £20.00 sterling (approx. U.S. $38 USA & Canada)/yr. For collectors and shooters.

H.A.C.S. Newsletter (M)
Harry Moon, Pres., P.O. Box 50117, South Slope RPO, Burnaby BC, V5J 5G3, Canada/604-438-0950; Fax:604-277-3646. $25/yr. U.S. and Canada. Official newsletter of The Historical Arms Collectors of B.C. (Canada).

Handgunner*
Richard A.J. Munday, Seychelles house, Brightlingsen, Essex CO7 ONN, England/012063-305201. £18.00 (sterling).

Handguns*
Intermedia, 6420 Wilshire Blvd., Los Angeles, CA 90048/323-782-2868. For the handgunning and shooting enthusiast.

Handloader*
Wolfe Publishing Co., 2626 Stearman Road, Ste. A, Prescott, AZ 86301/520-445-7810; Fax: 520-778-5124. $22.00/yr. The journal of ammunition reloading.

INSIGHTS*
NRA, 11250 Waples Mill Rd., Fairfax, VA 22030. $15.00/yr., includes NRA jr. membership; $10.00 adult subscriptions (12 issues). Details for the young hunter and target shooter; emphasizes gun safety, marksmanship training, hunting skills.

International Arms & Militaria Collector (Q)
Arms & Militaria Press, P.O. Box 80, Labrador, Qld. 4215, Australia. $39.50/yr. (U.S. & Canada), 2 yrs./$77.50; A$37.50 (others)/yr., 2 yrs./$73.50 air express mail; surface mail is less.

International Shooting Sport*/UIT Journal
International Shooting Union (UIT), Bavariaring 21, D-80336 Munich, Germany. Europe: (Deutsche Mark) DM44.00/yr., DM83.00/2 yrs.; outside Europe: DM50.00/yr., DM95.00/2 yrs. (air mail postage included.) For international sport shooting.

Internationales Waffen-Magazin
Habegger-Verlag Zürich, Postfach 9230, CH-8036 Zürich, Switzerland. SF 105.00 (U.S. $73.00) surface mail/10 issues. Modern and antique arms, self-defense. German text; English summary of contents.

Journal of the Arms & Armour Society, The (M)
A. Dove, P.O. Box 10232, London, SW19 2ZD England. £15.00 surface mail; £20.00 airmail sterling only yr. Articles for the historian and collector.

Journal of the Historical Breechloading Smallarms Assn.
Published annually. P.O. Box 12778, London, SE1 6XB, England. $21.00/yr. Articles for the collector plus mailings of short articles on specific arms, reprints, newsletters, etc.

Knife World
Knife World Publications, P.O. Box 3395, Knoxville, TN 37927. $15.00/yr.; $25.00/2 yrs. Published monthly for knife enthusiasts and collectors. Articles on custom and factory knives; other knife-related interests, monthly column on knife identification, military knives.

Man At Arms*
P.O. Box 460, Lincoln, RI 02865. $27.00/yr., $52.00 2 yrs. plus $8.00 for foreign subscribers. The N.R.A. magazine of arms collecting-investing, with articles for the collector of antique arms and militaria.

Mannlicher Collector, The (Q)(M)
Mannlicher Collectors Assn., Inc., P.O. Box 7144, Salem Oregon 97303. $20/yr. subscription included in membership.

MAGNUM
Rua Madre Rita Amada de Jesus, 182, Granja Julieta, Sao Paulo – SP – 04721-050 Brazil. No details.

---

* Published bi-monthly
† Published weekly
‡ Published three times per month
All others are published monthly
M Membership requirements; write for details
Q Published Quarterly

PERIODICAL PUBLICATIONS

MAN/MAGNUM
S.A. Man (Pty) Ltd., P.O. Box 35204, Northway, Durban 4065, Republic of South Africa. SA Rand 200.00 for 12 issues. Africa's only publication on hunting, shooting, firearms, bushcraft, knives, etc.

Marlin Collector, The (M)
R.W. Paterson, 407 Lincoln Bldg., 44 Main St., Champaign, IL 61820.

Muzzle Blasts (M)
National Muzzle Loading Rifle Assn., P.O. Box 67, Friendship, IN 47021/812-667-5131. $35.00/yr. membership. For the blackpowder shooter.

Muzzleloader Magazine*
Scurlock Publishing Co., Inc., Dept. Gun, Route 5, Box 347-M, Texarkana, TX 75501. $18.00 U.S.; $22.50 U.S./yr. for foreign subscribers. The publication for blackpowder shooters.

National Defense (M)*
American Defense Preparedness Assn., Two Colonial Place, Suite 400, 2101 Wilson Blvd., Arlington, VA 22201-3061/703-522-1820; FAX: 703-522-1885. $35.00/yr. Articles on both military and civil defense field, including weapons, materials technology, management.

National Knife Magazine (M)
Natl. Knife Coll. Assn., 7201 Shallowford Rd., P.O. Box 21070, Chattanooga, TN 37424-0070. Membership $35/yr.; $65/Int'l yr.

National Rifle Assn. Journal (British) (Q)
Natl. Rifle Assn. (BR.), Bisley Camp, Brookwood, Woking, Surrey, England. GU24, OPB. £24.00 Sterling including postage.

National Wildlife*
Natl. Wildlife Fed., 1400 16th St. NW, Washington, DC 20036, $16.00/yr. (6 issues); *International Wildlife*, 6 issues, $16.00/yr. Both, $22.00/yr., includes all membership benefits. Write attn.: Membership Services Dept., for more information.

New Zealand GUNS*
Waitekauri Publishing, P.O. 45, Waikino 3060, New Zealand. $NZ90.00 (6 issues)/yr. Hunting and firearms in New Zealand.

New Zealand Wildlife (Q)
New Zealand Deerstalkers Assoc., Inc., P.O. Box 6514, Wellington, N.Z. $30.00 (N.Z.). Hunting, shooting and firearms/game research articles.

North American Hunter* (M)
P.O. Box 3401, Minnetonka, MN 55343/612-936-9333; e-mail: huntingclub@pclink.com. $18.00/yr. (7 issues). Articles on all types of North American hunting.

Outdoor Life
Time4 Media, Two Park Ave., New York, NY 10016. $14.97/10 issues. Extensive coverage of hunting and shooting. Shooting column by Jim Carmichel.

La Passion des Courteaux (Q)
Phenix Editions, 25 rue Mademoiselle, 75015 Paris, France. French text.

Paintball Games International Magazine
Aceville Publications, Castle House, 97 High St., Colchester, Essex, England CO1 1TH/011-44-206-564840. Write for subscription rates. Leading magazine in the U.K. covering competitive paintball activities.

Paintball News
PBN Publishing, P.O. Box 1608, 24 Henniker St., Hillsboro, NH 03244/603-464-6080. $35 U.S./yr. Bi-weekly. Newspaper covering the sport of paintball, new product reviews and industry features.

Paintball Sports (Q)
Paintball Publications, Inc., 540 Main St., Mount Kisco, NY 10549/941-241-7400. $24.75 U.S./yr., $32.75 foreign. Covering the competitive paintball scene.

Performance Shooter
Belvoir Publications, Inc., 75 Holly Hill Lane, Greenwich, CT 06836-2626/203-661-6111. $45.00/yr. (12 issues). Techniques and technology for improved rifle and pistol accuracy.

Petersen's HUNTING Magazine
Primedia, 6420 Wilshire Blvd., Los Angeles, CA 90048. $19.94/yr.; Canada $29.34/yr.; foreign countries $29.94/yr. Hunting articles for all game; test reports.

P.I. Magazine
America's Private Investigation Journal, 755 Bronx Dr., Toledo, OH 43609. Chuck Klein, firearms editor with column about handguns.

Pirsch
BLV Verlagsgesellschaft GmbH, Postfach 400320, 80703 Munich, Germany/089-12704-0;Fax:089-12705-354. German text.

Point Blank
Citizens Committee for the Right to Keep and Bear Arms (sent to contributors), Liberty Park, 12500 NE 10th Pl., Bellevue, WA 98005

POINTBLANK (M)
Natl. Firearms Assn., Box 4384 Stn. C, Calgary, AB T2T 5N2, Canada. Official publication of the NFA.

Police Marksman, The*
6000 E. Shirley Lane, Montgomery, AL 36117. $17.95/yr. For law enforcement personnel.

Police Times (M)
3801 Biscayne Blvd., Miami, FL 33137/305-573-0070.

Popular Mechanics
Hearst Corp., 224 W. 57th St., New York, NY 10019. Firearms, camping, outdoor oriented articles.

Precision Shooting
Precision Shooting, Inc., 222 McKee St., Manchester, CT 06040. $37.00/yr. U.S. Journal of the International Benchrest Shooters, and target shooting. Considerable coverage of varmint shooting, big bore, small bore, schuetzen, lead bullet, wildcats and precision reloading.

Rifle*
Wolfe Publishing Co., 2626 Stearman Road, Ste. A, Prescott, AZ 86301/520-445-7810; Fax: 520-778-5124. $19.00/yr. The sporting firearms journal.

Rifle's Hunting Annual
Wolfe Publishing Co., 2626 Stearman Road, Ste. A, Prescott, AZ 86301/520-445-7810; Fax: 520-778-5124. $4.99/yr.. Dedicated to the finest pursuit of the hunt.

Rod & Rifle Magazine
Lithographic Serv. Ltd., P.O. Box 38-138, Wellington, New Zealand. $50.00/yr. (6 issues). Hunting, shooting and fishing articles.

Safari* (M)
Safari Magazine, 4800 W. Gates Pass Rd., Tucson, AZ 85745/602-620-1220. $55.00 (6 times). Journal of big game hunting, published by Safari Club International. Also publish *Safari Times*, a monthly newspaper, included in price of $55.00 national membership.

Second Amendment Reporter
Second Amendment Foundation, James Madison Bldg., 12500 NE 10th Pl., Bellevue, WA 98005. $15.00/yr. (non-contributors).

Shoot! Magazine*
Shoot! Magazine Corp., 1770 West State Stret PMB 340, Boise ID 83702/208-368-9920; Fax: 208-338-8428. Web: www.shootmagazine.com; $32.95 (6 times/yr.). Cowboy action shooting and the Western-era firearms and ammunition.

Shooter's News
23146 Lorain Rd., Box 349, North Olmsted, OH 44070/216-979-5258; Fax: 216-979-5259. $29 U.S./yr., $54/2 yrs.; $52 foreign surface. A journal dedicated to precision riflery.

Shooting Industry
Publisher's Dev. Corp., 12345 World Trade Drive, San Diego, CA 92128. $50.00/yr. To the trade. $25.00.

Shooting Sports USA
NRA of America, 11250 Waples Mill Road, Fairfax, VA 22030. Subscriptions for NRA members are $5/yr. for classified shooters and $10 for non-classified shooters. $15/non-NRA members. Covering events, techniques and personalities in competitive shooting.

Shooting Sportsman*
P.O. Box 11282, Des Moines, IA 50340/800-666-4955 (for subscriptions). Editorial: P.O. Box 1357, Camden, ME 04843. $19.95 for six issues. The magazine of wingshooting and fine guns.

Shooting Times & Country Magazine, The (England)†
IPC Magazines Ltd., King's Reach Tower, Stamford St, 1 London SE1 9LS, England/0171-261-6180; Fax: 0171-261-7179. £65 (approx. $98.00)/yr.; £79/yr. overseas (52 issues). Game shooting, wild fowling, hunting, game fishing and firearms articles. Britain's best selling field sports magazine.

Shooting Times
Intermedia, 2 News Plaza, P.O. Box 1790, Peoria, IL 61656/309-682-6626. $16.97/yr. Guns and shooting articles on every gun activity.

Shotgun News, The‡
Intermedia, 2 News Plaza, P.O. Box 1790, Peoria, IL 61656/800-495-8362. 36 issues/yr. @ $28.95; 12 issues/yr. @ $19.95. foreign subscription call for rates. Sample copy $4.00. Gun ads of all kinds.

SHOT Business
National Shooting Sports Foundation, Flintlock Ridge Office Center, 11 Mile Hill Rd., Newtown, CT 06470-2359/203-426-1320; FAX: 203-426-1087. For the shooting, hunting and outdoor trade retailer.

Shotgun Sports
PO Box 6810, Auburn, CA 95604/916-889-2220; FAX: 916-889-9106. $31.00/yr. Trapshooting how-to's, shotshell reloading, patterning, tests and evaluations, sporting clays action, waterfowl/upland hunting. Call 1-800-676-8920 for a free sample copy.

Single Shot Exhange Magazine, The
PO Box 1055, York SC 29745/803-628-5326. $31.50/yr., monthly. Articles for blackpowder shooters and antique arms collectors.

Single Shot Rifle Journal* (M)
Editor John Campbell, PO Box 595, Bloomfield Hills, MI 48303/248-458-8415. Email: jcampbel@dmbb.com Annual dues $35 for 6 issues. Journal of the American Single Shot Rifle Assn.

Sixgunner, The (M)
Handgun Hunters International, P.O. Box 357, MAG, Bloomingdale, OH 43910

Skeet Shooting Review, The
National Skeet Shooting Assn., 5931 Roft Rd., San Antonio, TX 78253. $20.00/yr. (Membership incl. mag.) Competition results, personality profiles of top shooters, how-to articles, technical, reloading information.

Soldier of Fortune
Subscription Dept., P.O. Box 348, Mt. Morris, IL 61054. $29.95/yr.; $39.95 Canada; $50.95 foreign.

Sporting Classics
Sporting Classics, Inc., P.O. Box 23707, Columbia, SC 29223/1-800-849-1004. 1 yr. 6 issues/$23.95; 2 yrs. 12 issues/$38.95; 3 yrs. 18 issues/$47.95. Firearms & outdoor articles and columns.

Sporting Clays Magazine
Patch Communications, 5211 South Washington Ave., Titusville, FL 32780/407-268-5010; FAX: 407-267-7216. $29.95/yr. (12 issues). Official publication of the National Sporting Clays Association.

Sporting Goods Business
Miller Freeman, Inc., One Penn Plaza, 10th Fl., New York, NY 10119-0004. Trade journal.

Sporting Goods Dealer
Two Park Ave., New York, NY 10016. $100.00/yr. Sporting goods trade journal.

Sporting Gun
Bretton Court, Bretton, Peterborough PE3 8DZ, England. £27.00 (U.S. $36.00), airmail £35.50/yr. For the game and clay enthusiasts.

Sports Afield
15621 Chemical Lane, Huntington Beach CA 92648. U.S./800-234-3537. International/714-894-9080. Web: www.sportsafield.com. $29.97/9 issues. America's oldest outdoor publication devoted to high-end sporting pursuits, especially in North America and Africa.

Squirrel Hunter, The
P.O. Box 368, Chireno, TX 75937. $14.00/yr.

Stott's Creek Calendar
Stott's Creek Printers, 2526 S 475 W, Morgantown, IN 46160/317-878-5489. (3 issues) $11.50/yr.; (6 issues) $20.00/2 yrs. Lists all gun shows everywhere in convenient calendar form.

Super Outdoors
2695 Aiken Road, Shelbyville, KY 40065/502-722-9463; 800-404-6064; Fax: 502-722-8093. Mark Edwards, publisher.

TACARMI
Via E. De Amicis, 25; 20123 Milano, Italy. $100.00/yr. approx. Antique and modern guns. (Italian text.)

Territorial Dispatch—1800s Historical Publication (M)
National Assn. of Buckskinners, 4701 Marion St., Suite 324, Livestock Exchange Bldg., Denver, CO 80216. Michael A. Nester & Barbara Wyckoff, editors. 303-297-9671.

Trap & Field
1000 Waterway Blvd., Indianapolis, IN 46202. $25.00/yr. Official publ. Amateur Trapshooting Assn. Scores, averages, articles.

Turkey Call* (M)
Natl. Wild Turkey Federation, Inc., P.O. Box 530, Edgefield, SC 29824. $25.00 with membership (6 issues/yr.)

Turkey & Turkey Hunting*
Krause Publications, 700 E. State St., Iola, WI 54990-0001. $13.95 (6 issue/yr.). Magazine with leading-edge articles on all aspects of wild turkey behavior, biology and successful ways to hunt better. Learn the proper techniques to calling, the right equipment, and more.

U.S. Handgunner, The* (M)
U.S. Revolver Assn., 40 Larchmont Ave., Taunton, MA 02780. $10.00/yr. General handgun and competition articles. Bi-monthly.

U.S. Airgun Magazine
P.O. Box 2021, Benton, AR 72018/800-247-4867; Fax: 501-316-8549. 10 issues/yr. Cover the sport from hunting, 10-meter, field target and collecting.

Varmint Hunter Magazine, The (Q)
The Varmint Hunters Assn., Box 759, Pierre, SD 57501/800-528-4868. $24.00/yr.

Waffenmarkt-Intern
GFI-Verlag, Theodor-Heuss Ring 62, 50668 K'ln, Germany. Only for gunsmiths, licensed firearms dealers and their suppliers in Germany, Austria and Switzerland.

Wild Sheep (M) (Q)
Foundation for North American Wild Sheep, 720 Allen Ave., Cody, WY 82414. Web: http://iigi.com/os/non/fnaws/fnaws.htm; e-mail: fnaws@wyoming.com. Official journal of the foundation.

Wisconsin Outdoor Journal
Krause Publications, 700 E. State St., Iola, WI 54990-0001. $17.97/yr. (8 issues). Web: www.krause.com. For Wisconsin's avid hunters and fishermen, with features from all over that state with regional reports, legislative updates, etc.

Women & Guns
P.O. Box 488, Sta. C, Buffalo, NY 14209. $24.00/yr. U.S.; $72.00 foreign (12 issues). Only magazine edited by and for women gun owners.

World War II*
Cowles History Group, 741 Miller Dr. SE, Suite D-2, Leesburg, VA 20175-8920. Annual subscriptions $19.95 U.S.; $25.95 Canada; 43.95 foreign. The title says it—WWII; good articles, ads, etc.

* Published bi-monthly
† Published weekly
‡ Published three times per month
All others are published monthly
M Membership requirements; write for details
Q Published Quarterly

ARMS LIBRARY

FOR COLLECTOR ✸ HUNTER ✸ SHOOTER ✸ OUTDOORSMAN
IMPORTANT NOTICE TO BOOK BUYERS

Books listed here may be bought from **Ray Riling Arms Books Co.**, 6844 Gorsten St., Philadelphia, PA 19119, Phone 215-438-2456; FAX: 215-438-5395. E-mail: sales@rayrilingarmsbooks.com. Larry Riling is the researcher and compiler of "The Arms Library" and a seller of gun books for over 65 years. The Riling stock includes books classic and modern, many hard-to-find items, and many not obtainable elsewhere. These pages list a portion of the current stock. They offer prompt, complete service, with delayed shipments occurring only on out-of-print or out-of-stock books.

Visit our Web site at **www.rayrilingarmsbooks.com** and order all of your favorite titles online from our secure site.

NOTICE FOR ALL CUSTOMERS: Remittance in U.S. funds must accompany all orders. For your convenience we accept VISA, MasterCard, Discover & American Express. For shipments in the U.S., add $7.00 for the 1st book and $2.00 for each additional book

for postage and insurance. Minimum order $10.00. International Orders add $13.00 for the 1st book and $5.00 for each additional book. All International orders are shipped at the buyer's risk unless an additional $5 for insurance is included. USPS does not offer insurance to all countries unless shipped Air-Mail. Please e-mail or call for pricing.

Payments in excess of order or for "Backorders" are credited or fully refunded at request. Books "As-Ordered" are not returnable except by permission and a handling charge on these of 10% or $2.00 per book, whichever is greater, is deducted from refund or credit. Only Pennsylvania customers must include current sales tax.

A full variety of arms books also available from **Rutgers Book Center**, 127 Raritan Ave., Highland Park, NJ 08904/732-545-4344; FAX: 732-545-6686 or **I.D.S.A. Books**, 3220 E. Galbraith Rd., Cincinnati, OH 45236. Email IDSABooks@IDSABooks.com; www.IDSABooks.com.

BALLISTICS AND HANDLOADING

ABC's of Reloading, 7th Edition, by Bill Chevalier, Iola, WI, Krause Publications, 2005. 288 pp., illustrated with 550 b&w photos. Softcover. NEW. $21.95

American Cartridge, The, by Charles Suydam, Borden Publishing Co. Alhambra, CA, 1986. 184 pp., illus. Softcover $24.95
An illustrated study of the rimfire cartridge in the United States.

Ammo and Ballistics II, by Robert W. Forker, Safari Press, Inc., Huntington Beach, CA, 2002. 298 pp., illus. Paper covers. $19.95
Ballistic data on 125 calibers and 1,400 loads out to 500 yards.

Barnes Bullets Reloading Manual Number 3, Barnes Bullets, American Fork, UT, 2003. 668 pp., illus. $29.95
Features data and trajectories on the new weight X, XBT and Solids in calibers from .22 to .50 BMG.

Black Powder, Pig Lead and Steel Silhouettes, by Paul A. Matthews, Prescott, AZ, Wolfe Publishing, 2002. 132 pp., illustrated with b&w photographs and detailed drawings and diagrams. Softcover. NEW. $16.95

Cartridge Reloading Tools of the Past, by R.H. Chamberlain, and Tom Quigley, Castle Rock, WA, 1998. 167 pp., illus. Paper covers. $25.00
A detailed treatment of the extensive Winchester and ideal line of handloading tools and bullet molds, plus Remington, Marlin, Ballard, Browning, Maynard, and many others.

Cast Bullets for the Black Powder Rifle, by Paul A. Matthews, Wolfe Publishing Co., Prescott, AZ, 1996. 133 pp., illus. Paper covers. $22.50
The tools and techniques used to make your cast bullet shooting a success.

Complete Blackpowder Handbook, 5th Edition, by Sam Fadala, DBI Books, a division of Krause Publications, Iola, WI, 2006. 448 pages, with over 650 b&w photos. Paper covers. $26.95
More than 650 detailed photos illustrating new gear and demonstrating effective techniques. Written for every blackpowder enthusiast-hunters, war re-enactors, collectors, cowboy action shooters, target shooters and DIY blackpowder hobbyists.

Complete Reloading Manual, One Book / One Caliber, CA, Load Books USA, 2000. $7.95 each
Contains unabridged information from U.S. bullet and powder makers. With thousands of proven and tested loads, plus dozens of various bullet designs and different powders. Spiral bound. Available in all calibers.

Designing and Forming Custom Cartridges for Rifles and Handguns, by Ken Howell. Precision Shooting, Manchester, CT. 2002. 600 pp., illus. $59.95
The classic work in its field, out of print for the last few years and virtually unobtainable on the used book market, now returns in an exact reprint of the original. Full size (8½" x 11"), hardcovers. Dozens of cartridge drawings never published anywhere before–dozens you've never heard of (guaranteed!). Precisely drawn to the dimensions specified by the men who designed them, the factories that made them, and the authorities that set the standards. All drawn to the same format and scale (1.5x) for most, how to form them from brass. Other practical information included.

Early Gunpowder Artillery 1300-1600 by John Norris, London, The Crowood Press, 2003. 1st edition. 141 pp., with 160 b&w photos. Hardcover. New in new dust jacket. $34.95

Early Loading Tools & Bullet Molds, Pioneer Press, 1988. 88 pp., illus. Softcover. $7.50

Handbook for Shooters and Reloaders, by P.O. Ackley, Salt Lake City, UT, 1998, (Vol. I), 567 pp., illus. Includes a separate exterior ballistics chart. $24.95; (Vol. II), a new printing with specific new material. 495 pp., illus. $21.95

Handgun Stopping Power; The Definitive Study, by Marshall & Sandow. Boulder, CO, Paladin Press, 1992. 240 pp. $45.00
Offers accurate predictions of the stopping power of specific loads in calibers from 380 Auto to 45 ACP, as well as such specialty rounds as the Glaser Safety Slug, Federal Hydra-Shok, MagSafe, etc. This is the definitive methodology for predicting the stopping power of handgun loads, the first to take into account what really happens when a bullet meets a man.

Handloader's Digest: 18th Edition edited by Ken Ramage, Iola, WI, Krause Publications, 2003. 300 b&w photos, 256 pp. Softcover. NEW. $19.95

Handloader's Manual of Cartridge Conversions, Revised 3rd edition, by John Donnelly, and Bryce Towsley, Accokeek, MD, Stoeger Publications, 2004. 609pp, Hardcover. NEW $39.95
Over 900 cartridges described in detail, complete with dimensions, and accurate drawings. Includes case capacities and all physical data.

Hatcher's Notebook, by S. Julian Hatcher, Stackpole Books, Harrisburg, PA, 1992. 488 pp., illus. $39.95
A reference work for shooters, gunsmiths, ballisticians, historians, hunters and collectors.

Headstamped Cartridges and Their Variations; Volume 1, by Daniel L. Shuey, W.R.A. Co., Rockford, IL, WCF Publications, 2003. 351 pp. illustrated with b&w photos. Hardcover. NEW. $55.00

Headstamped Cartridges and Their Variations; Volume 2, by Daniel L. Shuey, W.R.A. Co., Rockford, IL, WCF Publications, 2003. 351 pp. illustrated with b&w photos. Hardcover. NEW. $55.00

History & Development of Small Arms Ammunition, Volume 1, Second Edition–With A Value Guide, Martial Long Arms, Flintlock through Rimfire, by George A. Hoyem, Missoula, MI, Armory Publications, 2005. Hardcover. New in new dust jacket. $60.00

Hornady Handbook of Cartridge Reloading, 7th Edition, edited by Larry Steadman, Hornady Mfg. Co., Grand Island, NE, 2007, 978 pages, illus. $44.95
This completely revised and updated manual contains load data for almost every cartridge available, including the latest developments like the 204 Ruger and 500 S&W. Includes tips on basic reloading, rifle and handgun load data and an illustrated glossary.

How-To's for the Black Powder Cartridge Rifle Shooter, by Paul A. Matthews, Wolfe Publishing Co., Prescott, AZ, 1995. 45 pp. Paper covers. $22.50
Covers lube recipes, good bore cleaners and over-powder wads. Tips include compressing powder charges, combating wind resistance, improving ignition and much more.

Loading the Black Powder Rifle Cartridge, by Paul A. Matthews, Wolfe Publishing Co., Prescott, AZ, 1993. 121 pp., illus. Paper covers. $22.50
Author Matthews brings the blackpowder cartridge shooter valuable information on the basics, including cartridge care, lubes and moulds, powder charges and developing and testing loads in his usual authoritative style.

Lyman 48th Reloading Handbook, No. 48. Connecticut, Lan Publishing Corporation, 2003. 48th edition. 480 pp. Softcover. NEW. $26.95

Lyman Cast Bullet Handbook, 3rd Edition, edited by C. Kenneth Ramage, Lyman Publications, Middlefield, CT, 1980. 416 pp., illus. Paper covers. $19.95
Information on more than 5000 tested cast bullet loads and 19 pages of trajectory and wind drift tables for cast bullets.

Lyman Black Powder Handbook, 2nd Edition, edited by Sam Fadala, Lyman Products for Shooters, Middlefield, CT, 2000. 239 pp., illus. Paper covers. $19.95
Comprehensive load information for the modern blackpowder shooter.

Lyman Shotshell Handbook, 5th Edition, edited by Edward A. Matunas, Lyman Products Co., Middlefield, CT, 2007. 330 pp., illus. Paper covers. $25.95
This new 5th edition covers cases, wads and primers currently offered by all leading manufacturers in all gauges from .410 to 10 gauge. In addition, the latest and also the most popular powders from Alliant, Hodgdon, Accurate, IMR, VihtaVuori, Ramshot, Winchester are included.

Make It Accurate-Get the Maximum Performance from Your Hunting Rifle, by Craig Boddington, Long Beach, CA, Safari Press, 1999. Hardcover. New in new dust jacket. $24.95

Metallic Cartridge Conversions: The History of the Guns and Modern Reproductions, by Dennis Adler, Foreword by R. L. Wilson, Iola, WI, Krause Publications, 2003. 1st edition. 208 pp. 250 color photos. Hardcover. New in new dust jacket. $39.95

Modern Exterior Ballistics, by Robert L. McCoy, Schiffer Publishing Co., Atglen, PA, 1999. 128 pp. $95.00
Advanced students of exterior ballistics and flight dynamics will find this comprehensive textbook on the subject a useful addition to their libraries.

ARMS LIBRARY

Modern Reloading 2nd Edition, by Richard Lee, Inland Press, 2003. 623 pp., illus. $29.95

The how-to's of rifle, pistol and shotgun reloading plus load data for rifle and pistol calibers.

Mr. Single Shot's Cartridge Handbook, by Frank de Haas, Mark de Haas, Orange City, IA, 1996. 116 pp., illus. Paper covers. $22.50

This book covers most of the cartridges, both commercial and wildcat, that the author has known and used.

Norma Reloading Manual, by Norma Precision AB, 2004, 1st edition. Data for over 2,000 loads in 73 calibers. 432pp, hardcover, NEW. $34.95

Nosler Reloading Manual #5, edited by Gail Root, Nosler Bullets, Inc., Bend, OR, 2002. 516 pp., illus. $29.99

Combines information on their ballistic tip, partition and handgun bullets with traditional powders and new powders never before used, plus trajectory information from 100 to 500 yards.

Reloading for Shotgunners, 4th Edition, by Kurt D. Fackler, and M.L. McPherson, DBI Books, a division of Krause Publications, Iola, WI, 1997. 320 pp., illus. Paper covers. $19.95

Expanded reloading tables with over 11,000 loads. Bushing charts for every major press and component maker. All new presentation on all aspects of shotshell reloading by two of the top experts in the field.

Reloading Tools, Sights and Telescopes for S/S Rifles, by Gerald O. Kelver, Brighton, CO, 1982. 163 pp., illus. Softcover. $15.00

A listing of most of the famous makers of reloading tools, sights and telescopes with a brief description of the products they manufactured.

Rimfire Cartridge in the United States and Canada, Illustrated History of Rimfire Cartridges, Manufacturers, and the Products Made from 1857-1984, by John L. Barber, Thomas Publications, Gettysburg, PA 2000. 1st edition. Profusely illus. 221 pp. $50.00

The author has written an encyclopedia of rimfire cartridges from the 22 to the massive 1.00 in. Gatling. Fourteen chapters, six appendices and an excellent bibliography.

Round Ball to Rimfire: Civil War Small Arms Ammunition, Vol. 1, by Dean S. Thomas, Gettysburg, PA, Thomas Publications, 2003. 344 pp. Hardcover. $40.00

Federal Ordnance Dept., Arsenals, Smoothbores & Rifle Muskets. Detailed information on the Ordnance Department, Northern arsenals, patents, designers, & manufacturers of Federal musket ammunition.

Round Ball to Rimfire: Civil War Small Arms Ammunition, Vol. 2, by Dean S. Thomas, Gettysburg, PA, Thomas Publications, 2004. 528 pp. Hardcover. NEW. $49.95

Federal Breechloading Carbines and Rifles. Federal carbine and rifle ammunition. Detailed information on patents, designers, & manufacturers of Federal breechloaders and their ammunition.

Round Ball to Rimfire: Civil War Small Arms Ammunition, Vol. 3, by Dean S. Thomas, Gettysburg, PA, Thomas Publications, 2005. 488 pp. Hardcover. $49.95

Federal pistols, revolvers and miscellaneous essays. Detailed information on patents, designers, & manufacturers. Miscellaneous essays wrap-up the Northern side of the story.

Shotshells & Ballistics, Safari Press, 2002. 275 pp., photos. Softcover, $19.95

Accentuated with photos from the field and the range, this is a reference book unlike any other.

Sierra Reloading Manual, 5th Edition: Rifle and Handgun Manual of Reloading Data. Sedalia, MO, Sierra Bullets, 2003. Hardcover. NEW. $39.95

Speer Reloading Manual No. 13, edited by members of the Speer research staff, Omark Industries, Lewiston, ID, 1999. 621 pp., illus. $29.95

With 13 new sections containing the latest technical information and reloading trends for both novice and expert in this latest edition. More than 9,300 loads are listed, including new propellant powders from Accurate Arms, Alliant, Hodgdon and Vihtavuori.

Stopping Power: A Practical Analysis of the Latest Handgun Ammunition, by Marshall & Sanow, Paladin Press, 2002. 600+ photos, 360 pp. Softcover. $49.95

Stopping Power bases its conclusions on real-world facts from real-world gunfights. It provides the latest street results of actual police and civilian shootings in all of the major handgun calibers, from 22 LR to 45 ACP, plus more than 30 chapters of vital interest to all gun owners.

Street Stoppers, The Latest Handgun Stopping Power Street Results, by Marshall & Lanow, Boulder, CO, Paladin Press, 1996. 374 pp., illus. Softcover. $42.95

Street Stoppers is the long-awaited sequel to *Handgun Stopping Power*. It provides the latest results of real-life shootings in all of the major handgun calibers, plus more than 25 thought-provoking chapters that are vital to anyone interested in firearms, wound ballistics, and combat shooting. This book also covers the street results of the hottest new caliber to hit the shooting world in years, the 40 Smith & Wesson, plus updated street results of the latest exotic ammunition.

Understanding Firearm Ballistics, 6th Edition, by Robert A. Rinker, Mulberry House Corydon, IN, 2005. 437 pp., illus. Paper covers. New, revised and expanded. $24.95

Explains basic to advanced firearm ballistics in understandable terms.

Why Not Load Your Own?, by Col. T. Whelen, Gun Room Press, Highland Park, NJ 1996, 4th ed., rev. 237 pp., illus. $20.00

A basic reference on handloading, describing each step, materials and equipment. Includes loads for popular cartridges.

Wildcat Cartridges, "Reloader's Handbook of Wildcat Cartridge Design", by Fred Zeglin, privately printed, 2005. 1st edition. 287 Pages, Hard back book. Forward by Wayne van Zwoll. Pictorial Hardcover. NEW. $39.95

Twenty-two chapters cover wildcatting from every possible angle. History, dimensions, load data, and how to make or use reloading tool and reamers. If you're interested in reloading or wildcatting this is a must have book.

Wildcat Cartridges Volumes 1 & 2 Combination, by the editors of *Handloaders* magazine, Wolfe Publishing Co., Prescott, AZ, 1997. 350 pp., illus. Paper covers. $39.95

A profile of the most popular information on wildcat cartridges that appeared in the *Handloaders* magazine.

W.R.A. Co.; Headstamped Cartridges and their Variations; Volume 1, by Daniel Shuey, Rockford, IL, WCF Publications, 2001. 298pp illustrated with b&w photos, Hardcover, NEW. $55.00

W.R.A. Co.; Headstamped Cartridges and their Variations; Volume 2, by Daniel Shuey, Rockford, IL, WCF Publications, 2003. 351pp illustrated with b&w photos, Hardcover, NEW. $50.00

COLLECTORS

1 October 1934 SS Dienstalterliste, by the Ulric of England Research Unit San Jose, CA, R. James Bender Publishing, 1994. Reprint softcover. NEW. $29.95

10. Panzer Division: In Action in the East, West and North Africa 1939-1943, by Jean Resta and N. Moller, Canada, J.J. Fedorowicz Publishing Inc., 2003. 1st edition. Hardcover. NEW. $89.95

18th Century Weapons of the Royal Welsh Fuziliers from Flixton Hall, by Erik Goldstein, Thomas Publications, Gettysburg, PA, 2002. 1st edition. 126 pp., illustrated with b&w photos. Softcover. $19.95

.45-70 Springfield Book I, by Albert Frasca and Robert Hill, Frasca Publishing, 2000. Memorial edition. Hardback with gold embossed cover and spine. $95.00

The Memorial edition reprint of the .45-70 Springfield was done to honor Robert H. Hill who was an outstanding Springfield collector, historian, researcher, and gunsmith. Only 1,000 of these highly regarded books were printed, using the same binding and cover material as the original 1980 edition. The book is considered the bible for 45-70 Springfield Trapdoor collectors.

.45-70 Springfield Book II 1865-1893, by Albert Frasca, Frasca Publishing, Springfield, Ohio 1997, 400+ pp. and 400+ photographs which cover ALL the trapdoor Springfield models. Hardback with gold embossed cover and spine. A MUST for the trapdoor collector! $85.00

.45-70 Springfield 4th Ed. Revised & Expanded, The, by Joe Poyer and Craig Riesch, North Cape Publications, Tustin, CA, 2006. 274 pp., illus. Paper covers. $19.95

Every part and every change to that part made by the Ordnance Department is described in photos and drawings. Dimensions and finishes are listed for each part in both the text and tables.

'51 Colt Navies, by Nathan L. Swayze, The Gun Room Press, Highland Park, NJ, 1993. 243 pp., illus. $59.95

The Model 1851 Colt Navy, its variations and markings.

1862 U.S. Cavalry Tactics, by Philip St. George Cooke, Mechanicsburg, PA, Stackpole Books, 2004. 416 pp. Hardcover. New in new dust jacket. $19.89

A Collector's Guide to the '03 Springfield, by Bruce N. Canfield, Andrew Mowbray Inc., Lincoln, RI, 2004. 160 pp., illus. Paper covers. $22.00

A comprehensive guide follows the '03 through its unparalleled tenure of service. Covers all of the interesting variations, modifications and accessories of this highly collectible military rifle.

An Illustrated Guide To The '03 Springfield Service Rifle, by Bruce N. Canfield Andrew Mowbray, Inc., Pictorial Hardcover 2005. $49.95

Your ultimate guide to the military '03 Springfield! Three times as large as the author's previous best selling book on this topic. Covers all models, all manufacturers and all conflicts, including WWI, WWII and beyond. Heavily illustrated. Serial number tables, combat photos, sniper rifles and more! 240 pages, illustrated with over 450 photos.

Complete Guide To The United States Military Combat Shotguns, by Bruce N. Canfield Andrew Mowbray, Inc., 2007. 1st edition. 312 Pages. $49.95

From the famed Winchester M97 to the Mossberg and beyond! Expanded and updated covereage of American combat shotguns with three times the information found in the author's pervious best-selling book on this topic. Hundreds of detailed photographs show you the specific features that you need to recognize in order to identify fakes and assembled guns. Special, in-depth historical coverage of WWI, WWII, Korea, Vietnam and Iraq!

A Collector's Guide to United States Combat Shotguns, by Bruce N. Canfield, Andrew Mowbray Inc., Lincoln, RI, 1992. 184 pp., illus. Paper covers. $24.00

This book provides full coverage of combat shotguns, from the earliest examples right up to the Gulf War and beyond.

A Collector's Guide to Winchester in the Service, by Bruce N. Canfield, Andrew Mowbray, Inc., Lincoln, RI, 1991. 192 pp., illus. Paper covers. $24.00

The firearms produced by Winchester for the national defense. From Hotchkiss to the M14, each firearm is examined and illustrated.

A Concise Guide to the Artillery at Gettysburg, by Gregory Coco, Thomas Publications, Gettysburg, PA, 1998. 96 pp., illus. Paper covers. $10.00

Coco's book on Gettysburg is a beginner's guide to artillery and its use at the battle. It covers the artillery batteries, describing the types of cannons, shells, fuses, etc. using interesting narrative and human interest stories.

A Glossary of the Construction, Decoration and Use of Arms and Armor in All Countries and in All Times, by George Cameron Stone, Dover Publishing, New York 1999. Softcover. $39.95

An exhaustive study of arms and armor in all countries through recorded history-from the Stone Age up to WWII. With over 4,500 b&w illustrations, this Dover edition is an unabridged republication of the work originally published in 1934 by the Southworth Press, Portland, MA. A new Introduction has been specially prepared for this edition.

A Guide to American Trade Catalogs 1744-1900, by Lawrence B. Romaine, Dover Publications, New York, NY. 422 pp., illus. Paper covers. $12.95

A Guide to Ballard Breechloaders, by George J. Layman, Pioneer Press, Union City, TN, 1997. 261 pp., illus. Paper covers. $19.95

Documents the saga of this fine rifle from the first models made by Ball & Williams of Worchester, to its production by the Marlin Firearms Co., to the cessation of 19th century manufacture in 1891, and finally to the modern reproductions made in the 1990s.

A Guide to the Maynard Breechloader, by George J. Layman, George J. Layman, Ayer, MA, 1993. 125 pp., illus. Paper covers. $14.95

The first book dedicated entirely to the Maynard family of breech-loading firearms. Coverage of the arms is given from the 1850s through the 1880s.

ARMS LIBRARY

A Guide to U.S. Army Dress Helmets 1872-1904, by Kasal and Moore, North Cape Publications, 2000. 88 pp., illus. Paper covers. $15.95

This thorough study provides a complete description of the Model 1872 and 1881 dress helmets worn by the U.S. Army.

A Study of Remington's Smoot Patent and Number Four Revolvers, by Parker Harry, Parker Ora Lee, and Joan Reisch, Foreword by Roy M. Marcot, Santa Ana, CA, Armslore Press, Graphic Publishers, 2003. 1st edition. 120 pp., profusely illus., plus 8-page color section. Softcover. $17.95

A detailed, pictorial essay on Remington's early metallic cartridge-era pocket revolvers: their design, development, patents, models, identification and variations. Includes the biography of arms inventor Wm. S. Smoot, as well as a mini-history of the Remington Arms Company.

Accoutrements of the United States Infantry, Riflemen, and Dragoons 1834-1839, by R.T. Huntington, Historical Arms Series No. 20. Canada, Museum Restoration. 58 pp. illus. Softcover. $8.95

Although the 1841 edition of the U.S. Ordnance Manual provides ample information on the equipment that was in use during the 1840s, it is evident that the patterns of equipment that it describes were not introduced until 1838 or 1839. This guide is intended to fill this gap in our knowledge by providing an overview of what we now know about the accoutrements that were issued to the regular infantryman, rifleman, and dragoon, in the 1830s with excursions into earlier and later years.

Ackermann Military Prints: Uniforms of the British and Indian Armies 1840-1855, by William Y. Carman with Robert W. Kenny Jr., Schiffer Publications, Atglen, PA, 2002. 1st edition. 176 pp., with over 160 color images. $69.95

Afrikakorps: Rommel's Tropical Army in Original Color, by Bernd Peitz, Gary Wilkins. Atglen, PA, Schiffer Publications, 2004. 1st edition. 192 pp., with over 200 color and b&w photographs. Hardcover. New in new dust jacket. $59.95

Air Guns, by Eldon G. Wolff, Duckett's Publishing Co., Tempe, AZ, 1997. 204 pp., illus. Paper covers. $35.00

Historical reference covering many makers, European and American guns, canes and more.

All About Southerners, by Lionel J. Bogut, White Star, Inc., 2002. A limited edition of 1,000 copies. Signed and numbered. 114 pp., including bibliography, and plenty of b&w photographs and detailed drawings. Hardcover. $29.95

Detailed look at the characteristics and design of the "Best Little Pistol in the World."

Allgemeine-SS The Commands, Units and Leaders of the General SS, by Mark C. Yerger, Atglen, PA, Schiffer Publications, 1997. 1st edition. Hardcover. New in new dust jacket. $49.95

Allied and Enemy Aircraft: May 1918; Not to be Taken from the Front Lines, Historical Arms Series No. 27. Canada, Museum Restoration. Softcover. $8.95

The basis for this title is a very rare identification manual published by the French government in 1918 that illustrated 60 aircraft with three or more views: French, English American, German, Italian, and Belgian, which might have been seen over the trenches of France. Each is described in a text translated from the original French. This is probably the most complete collection of illustrations of WWI aircraft that has survived.

American Beauty; The Prewar Colt National Match Government Model Pistol, by Timothy J. Mullin, Collector Grade Publications, Cobourg, Ontario, Canada. 72 pp., illus. $34.95

Includes over 150 serial numbers, and 20 spectacular color photos of factory engraved guns and other authenticated upgrades, including rare "double-carved" ivory grips.

American Civil War Artillery 1861-65: Field Artillery, by Philip Oxford Katcher, United Kingdom, Osprey Publishing, 2001. 1st edition. 48 pp. Softcover. $14.95

Perhaps the most influential arm of either army in the prosecution of the American Civil War, the artillery of both sides grew to be highly professional organizations. This book covers all the major artillery pieces employed, including the Napoleon, Parrott Rifle and Mountain Howitzer.

American Military and Naval Belts, 1812-1902, by R. Stephen Dorsey, Eugene, OR, Collectors Library, 2002. 1st edition. Hardcover. $80.00

With introduction by Norm Flayderman, this massive work is the NEW key reference on sword belts, waist belts, sabre belts, shoulder belts and cartridge belts (looped and non-looped). At over 460 pp., this 8½" x 11" book offers over 840 photos (primarily in color) and original period drawings. In addition, this work offers the first, comprehensive research on the Anson Mills woven cartridge belts, the belt-related patents and the government contracts from 1880 through 1902. This book is a "must" for all accoutrements collectors, military historians and museums.

American Military Headgear Insignia, by Michael J. O'Donnell and J. Duncan, Campbell, Alexandria, VA, O'Donnell Publishing, 2004. 1st edition. 311 pp., 703 photo figures, 4 sketches. Hardcover. New in new dust jacket. $89.95

American Military Saddle, 1776-1945, The, by R. Stephen Dorsey and Kenneth L. McPheeters, Collector's Library, Eugene, OR, 1999. 400 pp., illus. $67.00

The most complete coverage of the subject ever written on the American Military Saddle. Nearly 1,000 actual photos and official drawings, from the major public and private collections in the U.S. and Great Britain.

American Police Collectibles; Dark Lanterns and Other Curious Devices, by Matthew G. Forte, Turn of the Century Publishers, Upper Montclair, NJ, 1999. 248 pp., illus. $24.95

For collectors of police memorabilia (handcuffs, police dark lanterns, mechanical and chain nippers, rattles, billy clubs and nightsticks) and police historians.

American Thunder II: The Military Thompson Submachine Guns, by Frank Iannamico, Harmony, ME, Moose Lake Publishing, 2004, 2nd edition. Many great photographs that show detail markings and features of the various models, as well as vintage WW11 photographs showing the Thompson in action. 536 pages, Soft cover, NEW. $29.95

An Introduction to the Civil War Small Arms, by Earl J. Coates and Dean S. Thomas, Thomas Publishing Co., Gettysburg, PA, 1990. 96 pp., illus. Paper covers. $10.00

The small arms carried by the individual soldier during the Civil War.

Arming the Glorious Cause; Weapons of the Second War for Independence, by James B. Whisker, Daniel D. Hartzler and Larry W. Tantz, Old Bedford Village Press, Bedford, PA., 1998. 175 pp., illus. $45.00

A photographic study of Confederate weapons.

Arms & Accoutrements of the Mounted Police 1873-1973, by Roger F. Phillips, and Donald J. Klancher, Museum Restoration Service, Ont., Canada, 1982. 224 pp., illus. $49.95 Also, available in paperback, $29.95

A definitive history of the revolvers, rifles, machine guns, cannons, ammunition, swords, etc. used by the NWMP, the RNWMP and the RCMP during the first 100 years of the Force.

Arms and Armor in Colonial America 1526-1783, by Harold Peterson, Dover Publishing, New York, 2000. 350 pp. with over 300 illustrations, index, bibliography and appendix. Softcover. $34.95

Over 200 years of firearms, ammunition, equipment and edged weapons.

Arms and Armor in the Art Institute of Chicago, by Waltler J. Karcheski, Bulfinch, New York 1999. 128 pp., 103 color photos, 12 b&w illustrations. $50.00

The George F. Harding Collection of arms and armor is the most visited installation at the Art Institute of Chicago–a testament to the enduring appeal of swords, muskets and the other paraphernalia of medieval and early modern war. Organized both chronologically and by type of weapon, this book captures the best of this astonishing collection in 115 striking photographs-most in color–accompanied by illuminating text.

Arms Makers of Western Pennsylvania, by James B. Whisker, Old Bedford Village Press. 1st edition. Deluxe hardbound edition, 176 pp., $50.00

Printed on fine coated paper with many large photographs and detailed text describing the period, lives, tools, and artistry of the Arms Makers of Western Pennsylvania.

Arsenal of Freedom: The Springfield Armory 1890-1948, by Lt. Col. William Brophy, Andrew Mowbray, Inc., Lincoln, RI,1997. 20 pgs. of photos. 400 pp. As new, Softcover. $29.95

A year-by-year account drawn from offical records. Packed with reports, charts, tables and line drawings.

Art of Remington Arms, by Tom Davis, Sporting Classics, 2004, 1st edition. Large format book, featuring 200 paintings by Remington Arms over the years on it's calendars, posters, shell boxes, etc. 50 full-color by Bob Kuhn alone. Hardcover. NEW $54.95

Astra Automatic Pistols, by Leonardo M. Antaris, FIRAC Publishing Co., Sterling, CO, 1989. 248 pp., illus. $55.00

Charts, tables, serial ranges, etc. The definitive work on Astra pistols.

Ballard: The Great American Single Shot Rifle, by John T. Dutcher. Denver, CO, privately printed, 2002. 1st edition. 380 pp., illustrated with b&w photos, with 8-page color insert. Hardcover. New in new dust jacket. $79.95

Basic Documents on U.S. Martial Arms, commentary by Col. B.R. Lewis, reissue by Ray Riling, Phila., PA, 1956 and 1960. Rifle Musket Model 1855. Each $10.00

The first issue rifle of musket caliber, a muzzleloader equipped with the Maynard Primer, 32 pp. Rifle Musket Model 1863. The typical Union muzzleloader of the Civil War, 26 pp. Breech-Loading Rifle Musket Model 1866. The first of our 50-caliber breechloading rifles, 12 pp. Remington Navy Rifle Model 1870. A commercial type breech-loader made at Springfield, 16 pp. Lee Straight Pull Navy Rifle Model 1895. A magazine cartridge arm of 6mm caliber, 23 pp. Breech-Loading Arms (five models) 27 pp. Ward-Burton Rifle Musket 1871, 16 pp.

Battle Colors: Insignia and Aircraft Markings of the Eighth Air Force in World War II, by Robert A. Watkins, Atglen, PA, Schiffer Publications, 2004. Hardcover. $45.00

This book is an invaluable tool for anyone with an interest in the history of the U.S. Eighth Air Force in World War II. 128 pages, with over 500 color illustrations.

Battle Colors: Insignia and Aircraft Markings of the Eighth Air Force in World War II, Vol. 2, by Robert A. Watkins, Atglen, PA, Schiffer Publications, 2006. $45.00

This work includes diagrams showing approved specifications for the size and placement of all versions of the U.S. insignia as applied to USAAF P-38, P-47 and P-51 fighter aircraft. Also included are all unit airfield location maps and order-of-battle charts for all combat air elements assigned to the 8th AAF from June 1942 through June 1945. 144 pages, with over 600 color profiles, insignia, photographs, and maps. Hardcover

Battle Weapons of the American Revolution, by George C. Neuman, Scurlock Publishing Co., Texarkana, TX, 2001. 400 pp. Illus. Softcovers. $44.95

The most extensive photographic collection of Revolutionary War weapons ever in one volume. More than 1,600 photos of over 500 muskets, rifles, swords, bayonets, knives and other arms used by both sides in America's War for Independence.

Bedford County Rifle and Its Makers, by Calvin Hetrick, Introduction by George Shumway, George Shumway Pub., 1975. 40 pp. illus. Softcover. $10.00

The author's study of the graceful and distinctive muzzle-loading rifles made in Bedford County, Pennsylvania, stands as a milestone on the long path to the understanding of America's longrifles.

Belgian Rattlesnake; The Lewis Automatic Machine Gun, by William M. Easterly, Collector Grade Publications, Cobourg, Ontario, Canada, 1998. 584 pp., illus. $79.95

The most complete account ever published on the life and times of Colonel Isaac Newton Lewis and his crowning invention, the Lewis Automatic machine gun.

Best of Holland & Holland, England's Premier Gunmaker, by Michael McIntosh and Jan G. Roosenburg. Safari Press, Inc., Long Beach, CA, 2002. 1st edition. 298 pp. Profuse color illustrations. $69.95

Holland & Holland has had a long history of not only building London's "best" guns but also providing superior guns–the ultimate gun in finish, engraving, and embellishment.

Big Guns, Civil War Siege, Seacoast, and Naval Cannon, by Edwin Olmstead, Wayne E. Stark, and Spencer C. Tucker, Museum Restoration Service, Bloomfield, Ontario, Canada, 1997. 360 pp., illus. $80.00

This book is designed to identify and record the heavy guns available to both sides by the end of the Civil War.

Blue Book of Air Guns, 6th Edition, edited by S.P. Fjestad, Blue Book Publications, Inc. Minneapolis, MN 2007. $29.95

It contains most of the popular 2007 and vintage makes and models with detailed descriptions and up-to-date pricing! There are also hundreds of b&w images, and the Color Photo Grading System™ allows readers to stop guessing at airgun condition factors.

ARMS LIBRARY

Blue Book of Gun Values, 28th Edition, edited by S.P. Fjestad, Blue Book Publications, Inc. Minneapolis, MN 2007. $39.95

This new edition simply contains more firearm values and information than any other single publication. Expanded to 2,080 pages featuring over 100,000 firearms prices, up-to-date pricing and information on thousands of firearms, including new 2007 makes/models. Completely revised 80 page color Photo Percentage Grading System.

Blue Book of Modern Black Powder Values, 4th Edtion, by Dennis Adler, Blue Book Publications, Inc. Minneapolis, MN 2005. 271 pp., illus. 41 color photos. $24.95

This new title contains more up-to-date blackpowder values and related information than any other single publication and will keep you up-to-date on modern blackpowder models and prices, including most makes and models introduced by 2005!

Blunderbuss 1500-1900, The, by James D. Forman, Historical Arms Series No. 32. Canada, Museum Restoration, 1994. 40 pp., illus. Softcover. $8.95

An excellent and authoritative booklet giving tons of information on the Blunderbuss, a very neglected subject.

Boarders Away Volume I: With Steel-Edged Weapons & Polearms, by William Gilkerson, Andrew Mowbray, Inc. Publishers, Lincoln, RI, 1993. 331 pp. $48.00

Contains the essential 24-page chapter "War at Sea" which sets the historical and practical context for the arms discussed. Includes chapters on Early Naval Weapons, Boarding Axes, Cutlasses, Officers Fighting Swords and Dirks, and weapons at hand of Random Mayhem.

Boarders Away, Volume II: Firearms of the Age of Fighting Sail, by William Gilkerson, Andrew Mowbray, Inc. Publishers, Lincoln, RI, 1993. 331 pp., illus. $65.00

Covers the pistols, muskets, combustibles and small cannons used aboard American and European fighting ships, 1626-1826.

Boston's Gun Bible, by Boston T. Party, Ignacio, CO, Javelin Press, August 2000. Expanded edition. Softcover. $28.00

This mammoth guide for gun owners everywhere is a completely updated and expanded edition (more than 500 new pages!) of Boston T. Party's classic Boston on Guns and Courage. Boston gives new advice on which shoulder weapons and handguns to buy and why, before exploring such topics as why you should consider not getting a concealed carry permit, what guns and gear will likely be outlawed next and much more.

Bren Gun Saga, by Thomas B. Dugelby, Collector Grade Publications, Cobourg, Ontario, Canada, 1999, revised and expanded edition. 406 pp., illus. $65.95

A modern, definitive book on the Bren in this revised expanded edition, which in terms of numbers of pages and illustrations is nearly twice the size of the original.

British Board of Ordnance Small Arms Contractors 1689-1840, by De Witt Bailey, Rhyl, England, W. S. Curtis, 2000. 150 pp. $18.00

Thirty years of research in the Archives of the Ordnance Board in London has identified more than 600 of these suppliers. The names of many can be found marking the regulation firearms of the period. In the study, the contractors are identified both alphabetically and under a combination of their date period together with their specialist trade.

British Enfield Rifles, Volume 1, The SMLE MK I and MK III Rifles, by Charles R. Stratton, North Cape Pub., Tustin, CA, 1997. 150 pp., illus. Paper covers. $16.95

A systematic and thorough examination on a part-by-part basis of the famous British battle rifle that endured for nearly 70 years as the British Army's number one battle rifle.

British Enfield Rifles, Volume 2, No. 4 and No. 5 Rifles, by Charles R. Stratton, North Cape Publications, Tustin, CA, 1999. 150 pp., illus. Paper covers. $16.95

The historical background for the development of both rifles describing each variation and an explanation of all the marks, numbers and codes found on most parts.

British Enfield Rifles, Volume 4, The Pattern 1914 and U. S. Model 1917 Rifles, by Charles R. Stratton, North Cape Publications, Tustin, CA, 2000. Paper covers. $16.95

One of the least known American and British collectible military rifles is analyzed on a part by part basis. All markings and codes, refurbishment procedures and WWII upgrade are included as are the various sniper rifle versions.

British Falling Block Breechloading Rifle from 1865, by Jonathan Kirton, Tom Rowe Books, Maynardsville, TN, 2nd edition, 1997. 380 pp., illus. $70.00

Expanded edition of a comprehensive work on the British falling block rifle.

British Gun Engraving, by Douglas Tate, Safari Press, Inc., Huntington Beach, CA, 1999. 240 pp., illus. Limited, signed and numbered edition, in a slipcase. $80.00

A historic and photographic record of the last two centuries.

British Gunmakers: Volume One – London, by Nigel Brown, London, Quiller, 2004. 280 pp., 33 colour, 43 b&w photographs, line drawings. Hardcover. $99.95

British Gunmakers: Volume Two-Birmingham, Scotland, And the Regions, by Nigel Brown, London, Quiller, 2005. 1st edition. 439pp, hardcover. $99.95

With this book, read in conjunction with Volume One, the reader or scholar should be able to trace the history and likely age of any shotgun or rifle made in this region since 1800.

British Military Flintlock Rifles 1740-1840, With a Remarkable Wealth of Data about the Riflemen and Regiments that Carried These Weapons, by De Witt Bailey, Andrew Mowbray, Inc. Lincoln, RI, 2002. 1st edition. 264 pp. with over 320 photographs. Hardcover. $47.95

Pattern 1776 Rifles, the Ferguson Breechloader, the famous Baker Rifle, rifles of the Hessians and other German Mercenaries, American Loyalist rifles, rifles given to Indians, Cavalry rifles and rifled carbines, bayonets, accoutrements, ammunition and more.

British Service Rifles and Carbines 1888-1900, by Alan M. Petrillo, Excaliber Publications, Latham, NY, 1994. 72 pp., illus, Paper covers. $11.95

A complete review of the Lee-Metford and Lee-Enfield rifles and carbines.

British Single Shot Rifles, Volume 1, Alexander Henry, by Wal Winfer, Tom Rowe, Maynardsville, TN, 1998, 200 pp., illus. $50.00

Detailed study of the single shot rifles made by Henry. Illustrated with hundreds of photographs and drawings.

British Single Shot Rifles, Volume 3, Jeffery, by Wal Winfer, Rowe Publications, Rochester, N.Y., 1999. 260 pp., illus. $60.00

The Farquharsen as made by Jeffery and his competitors, Holland & Holland, Bland, Westley, Manton. Large section on the development of nitro cartridges including the 600.

British Single Shot Rifles, Volume 4; Westley Richards, by Wal Winfer, Rowe Publications, Rochester, N.Y., 2000. 265 pp., illus., photos. $60.00

In this 4th volume, Winfer covers a detailed study of the Westley Richards single shot rifles, including Monkey Tails, Improved Martini, 1872,1873, 1878,1881, 1897 Falling Blocks. He also covers Westley Richards cartridges, history and reloading information.

British Single Shot Rifles, Volume 5; Holland & Holland, by Winfer, Wal, Rochester, NY: Rowe Publications, 2004. 1st edition. ISBN: 097076085X. 218 pages. Hardcover. New in new dust jacket. (12063)

Volume 5 of the never ending study of the British single shot. One of the rarest and finest quality single shots made by any British firm is described. A large section is devoted to the cartridge developments carried on by Hollands with a large section on their Paradox cartridges.

Broad Arrow: British & Empire Factory Production, Proof, Inspection, Armourers, Unit & Issue Markings, by Ian Skennerton. Australia, Arms & Militaria Press, 2001. 140 pp., circa 80 illus. Stiff paper covers. $29.95

Thousands of service markings are illustrated and their applications described. Invaluable reference on units, also ideal for medal collectors.

Browning Dates of Manufacture, compiled by George Madis, Art and Reference House, Brownsboro, TX, 1989. 48 pp. $8.00

Gives the date codes and product codes for all models from 1824 to the present.

Browning Sporting Firearms: Dates of Manufacture, by D. R. Morse. Phoenix, AZ, Firing Pin Enterprizes, 2003. 37 pp. Softcover. New. $6.95

Covers their pistols, revolvers, rifles, shotguns and commemoratives, plus, models and serial numbers.

Browning Machine Gun Volume 1-Rifle Caliber Brownings in U.S. Service, by Dolf Goldsmith, Canada: Collector Grade Publications, 2005. 1st Edition, 552 pages, 568 illustrations. Hardcover. $79.95

This profusely illustrated history covers all models of the U.S. Browning, from the first "gas hammer" Model 1895 and the initial recoil-operated Models of 1901 and 1910, through the adoption and manufacture of the famous water-cooled heavy Model 1917 during World War I and the numerous Interwar experimental tank and aircraft guns, most of which were built up on surplus M1917 receivers.

Browning Machine Gun Volume 2-Rifle Caliber Brownings Abroad, by Dolf Goldsmith, Canada: Collector Grade Publications, 2006. 1st Edition, 392 pages, with over 486 illustrations. Hardcover, $69.95

This second volume of Dolf Goldsmith's series on Browning machine guns proves beyond doubt that the rifle-caliber Browning was simply the most popular and most-used machine gun ever designed. In some ways this book is even more engrossing than Volume I, as it describes and illustrates in considerable detail the many variations on the basic Browning which were manufactured and/or used by over twenty countries, in virtually every corner of the world, in both World Wars, in Korea and in Vietnam.

Browning–Sporting Arms of Distinction 1903-1992, by Matt Eastman, Long Beach, CA, Safari Press, 2004. 428 pp., profuse illus. Hardcover. $50.00

Bullard Firearms, by G. Scott Jamieson, Schiffer Publications, Atglen, PA 2002. 400 pp., with over 1100 color and b&w photos, charts, diagrams. Hardcover. $100.00

Bullard Firearms is the story of a mechanical genius whose rifles and cartridges were the equal of any made in America in the 1880s, yet little of substance had been written about James H. Bullard or his arms prior to 1988 when the first edition, called *Bullard Arms*, was published. This greatly expanded volume, with over 1,000 b&w and 150 color plates, most not previously published, answers many of the questions posed in the first edition. The final chapter outlines, in chart form, almost 500 Bullard rifles by serial number, caliber and type. Quick and easy to use, this book is a real benefit for collectors and dealers alike.

Burning Powder, compiled by Major D.B. Wesson, Wolfe Publishing Company, Prescott, AZ, 1992. 110 pp. Soft cover. $10.95

A rare booklet from 1932 for Smith & Wesson collectors.

Burnside Breech Loading Carbines, The, by Edward A. Hull, Andrew Mowbray, Inc., Lincoln, RI, 1986. 95 pp., illus. $16.00

No. 1 in the "Man at Arms Monograph Series." A model-by-model historical/technical examination of one of the most widely used cavalry weapons of the American Civil War based upon important and previously unpublished research.

C.S. Armory Richmond: History of the Confederate States Armory, Richmond, VA and the Stock Shop at the C.S. Armory, Macon, GA., by Paul Davies, privately printed, 2000. 368 pp., illustrated with b&w photos. Hardcover. $75.00

The American Society of Arms Collectors is pleased to recommend C.S. Armory Richmond as a useful and valuable reference for collectors and scholars in the field of antique firearms. Gives fantastic explanations of machinery, stocks, barrels, and every facet of the production process during the timeframe covered in this book.

Cacciare A Palla: Uso E Tecnologia Dell'arma Rigata, by Marco E. Nobili, Italy, Il Volo Srl, 1994. 4th Edition-1st printing. 397 pp., illustrated with b&w photographs. Hardcover. New in new dust jacket. $75.00

Call of Duty; Military Awards and Decorations of the United States of America, by John E. Strandberg, LTC and Roger James Bender, San Jose, CA, R. James Bender Publishing, 2005. (New expanded edition). 559 pp. illustrated with 1,293 photos (most in color). Hardcover. NEW. $67.95

Camouflage Uniforms of European and NATO Armies; 1945 to the Present, by J. F. Borsarello, Atglen, PA, Schiffer Publications. Over 290 color and b&w photographs, 120 pp. Softcover. $29.95

This full-color book covers nearly all of the NATO, and other European armies' camouflaged uniforms, and not only shows and explains the many patterns, but also their efficacy of design. Described and illustrated are the variety of materials tested in over 40 different armies, and includes the history of obsolete trial tests from 1945 to the present time. This book provides a superb reference for the historian, reenactor, designer, and modeler.

ARMS LIBRARY

Camouflage Uniforms of the Waffen-SS A Photographic Reference, by Michael Beaver, Schiffer Publishing, Atglen, PA. Over 1,000 color and b&w photographs and illustrations, 296 pp. $69.95

Finally a book that unveils the shroud of mystery surrounding Waffen-SS camouflage clothing. Illustrated here, both in full color and in contemporary b&w photographs, this unparalleled look at Waffen-SS combat troops and their camouflage clothing will benefit both the historian and collector.

Canadian Colts for the Boer War, by Col. Robert D. Whittington III. Hooks, TX, Brownlee Books, 2003. A limited edition of 1,000 copies. Numbered. 5 pp. Paper covers. New. $15.00

A study of Colt Revolvers issued to the First and Second Canadian Contingents Special Service Force.

Canadian Colts for the Boer War, Part 2, Col. Robert D. by Whittington III, Hooks, TX, Brownlee Books, 2005. A limited edition of 1,000 copies. Numbered. 5 pp. Paper covers, NEW. $5.00

Canadian Gunsmiths from 1608: A Checklist of Tradesmen, by John Belton, Historical Arms Series No. 29. Canada, Museum Restoration, 1992. 40 pp., 17 illustrations. Softcover. $8.95

This checklist is a greatly expanded version of HAS No. 14, listing the names, occupation, location, and dates of more than 1,500 men and women who worked as gunmakers, gunsmiths, armorers, gun merchants, gun patent holders, and a few other gun related trades.

Canadian Miliitaria Directory & Sourcebook Second Edition, by Clive M. Law, Ont. Canada, Service Publications, 1998. pp. 90. Softcover. NEW. $14.95

Cap Guns, by James Dundas, Schiffer Publishing, Atglen, PA, 1996. 160 pp., illus. Paper covers. $29.95

Over 600 full-color photos of cap guns and gun accessories with a current value guide.

Carbines of the Civil War, by John D. McAulay, Pioneer Press, Union City, TN, 1981. 123 pp., illus. Paper covers. $12.95

A guide for the student and collector of the colorful arms used by the Federal cavalry.

Carbines of the U.S. Cavalry 1861-1905, by John D. McAulay, Andrew Mowbray Publishers, Lincoln, RI, 1996. $35.00

Covers the crucial use of carbines from the beginning of the Civil War to the end of the cavalry carbine era in 1905.

Cartridge Carbines of the British Army, by Alan M. Petrillo, Excalibur Publications, Latham, NY, 1998. 72 pp., illus. Paper covers. $11.95

Begins with the Snider-Enfield which was the first regulation cartridge carbine introduced in 1866 and ends with the 303 caliber No.5, Mark 1 Enfield.

Cartridges for Collectors, by Fred Datig, Pioneer Press, Union City, TN, 1999. Three volumes of 176 pp. each. Vol. 1 (Centerfire); Vol. 2 (Rimfire and Misc.) types. Volume 1, softcover only, $19.95. Volumes 2 and 3, hardcover. $19.95

Vol. 3 (Additional Rimfire, Centerfire, and Plastic). All illustrations are shown in full-scale drawings.

Civil War Arms Makers and Their Contracts, edited by Stuart C. Mowbray and Jennifer Heroux, Andrew Mowbray Publishing, Lincoln, RI, 1998. 595 pp. $39.50

A facsimile reprint of the Report by the Commissioner of Ordnance and Ordnance Stores, 1862.

Civil War Arms Purchases and Deliveries, edited by Stuart C. Mowbray, Andrew Mowbray Publishing, Lincoln, RI, 1998. 300pp., illus. $39.50

A facsimile reprint of the master list of Civil War weapons purchases and deliveries including Small Arms, Cannon, Ordnance and Projectiles.

Civil War Cartridge Boxes of the Union Infantryman, by Paul Johnson, Andrew Mowbray, Inc., Lincoln, RI, 1998. 352 pp., illus. $45.00

There were four patterns of infantry cartridge boxes used by Union forces during the Civil War. The author describes the development and subsequent pattern changes to these cartridge boxes. All updated prices, scores of new listings, and hundreds of new pictures! It's the one reference work no collector should be without. An absolute must.

Civil War Collector's Price Guide; 11th Edition, Orange, VA, Publisher's Press, 2006. 300 pps., softbound, heavily illustrated, full color cover. $37.95

Our newly released 11th edition of the popular Civil War Collector's Price Guide! Expanded to include new images and new listings.

Civil War Commanders, by Dean Thomas, Thomas Publications, Gettysburg, PA. 1998. 72 pp., illus., photos. Paper covers. $9.95

138 photographs and capsule biographies of Union and Confederate officers. A convenient personalities reference guide.

Civil War Heavy Explosive Ordnance: A Guide to Large Artillery Projectiles, Torpedoes, and Mines, by Jack Bell, Denton, TX, University of North Texas Press, 2003. 1,016 b&w photos. 537 pp. Hardcover. New in new dust jacket. $50.00

Civil War Infantryman: In Camp, on the March, and in Battle, by Dean Thomas, Thomas Publications, Gettysburg, PA. 1998. 72 pp., illus. Softcovers. $12.95

Uses first-hand accounts to shed some light on the "common soldier" of the Civil War from enlistment to muster-out, including camp, marching, rations, equipment, fighting, and more.

Civil War Pistols, by John D. McAulay, Andrew Mowbray Inc., Lincoln, RI, 1992. 166 pp., illus. $38.50

A survey of the handguns used during the American Civil War.

Civil War Relic Hunting A to Z, by Robert Buttafuso, Sheridan Books, 2000. 1st edition. illus., 91 pp., b&w illustrations. Softcover. NEW. $21.95

Civil War Sharps Carbines and Rifles, by Earl J. Coates and John D. McAulay, Thomas Publications, Gettysburg, PA, 1996. 108 pp., illus. Paper covers. $12.95

Traces the history and development of the firearms including short histories of specific serial numbers and the soldiers who received them.

Civil War Small Arms of the U.S. Navy and Marine Corps, by John D. McAulay, Mowbray Publishing, Lincoln, RI, 1999. 186 pp., illus. $39.00

The first reliable and comprehensive guide to the firearms and edged weapons of the Civil War Navy and Marine Corps.

Collecting Military Headgear; A Guide to 5000 Years of Helmet History, by Robert Atglen Attard, PA, Schiffer Publications, 2004. 1st edition. Hardcover. New in new dust jacket. $69.95

Collecting Third Reich Recordings, by Stuart McKenzie, San Jose, CA, R. James Bender Publishing, 2001. 1st edition. Softcover. NEW. $29.95

Collector's Illustrated Encyclopedia of the American Revolution, by George C. Neumann and Frank J. Kravic, Rebel Publishing Co., Inc., Texarkana, TX, 1989. 286 pp., illus. $42.95

A showcase of more than 2,300 artifacts made, worn, and used by those who fought in the War for Independence.

Colonel Thomas Claiborne Jr. and the Colt Whitneyville-Walker Pistol, by Col. Robert D. Whittington III, Hooks, TX, Brownlee Books, 2005. A limited edition of 1,000 copies. Numbered. 8 pp. Paper covers, NEW. $7.50

Colonels in Blue: Union Army Colonels of the Civil War, by Roger Hunt, New York, Atglen, PA, Schiffer Publications, 2003. 1st edition. 288 pp., with over 640 b&w photographs. Hardcover. New in new dust jacket. $59.95

Colonial Frontier Guns, by T.M. Hamilton, Pioneer Press, Union City, TN, 1988. 176 pp., illus. Paper covers. $17.50

A complete study of early flint muskets of this country.

Colt 1909 Military Revolvers; The 1904 Thompson-Lagarde Report, and General John J. Pershing, by Col. Robert D. Whittington III. Hooks, TX, Brownlee Books, 2003. A limited edition of 1,000 copies. Numbered. 10 pp. Paper covers. New. $10.00

The 1904 Thompson-Lagarde Report, and General John J. Pershing.

Colt and Its Collectors Exhibition Catalog for Colt: The Legacy of A Legend, Buffalo Bill Historical Center, Cody, Wyoming. Colt Collectors Association, 2003. 1st edition. Hardcover. New in new dust jacket. $125.00

Colt and Its Collectors accompanies the upcoming special exhibition, Colt: The Legacy of a Legend, opening at the Buffalo Bill Historical Center in May 2003. Numerous essays, over 750 color photographs by Paul Goodwin.

Colt Armory, by Ellsworth Grant, Man-at-Arms Bookshelf, Lincoln, RI, 1996. 232 pp., illus. $35.00

A history of Colt's Manufacturing Company.

Colt Engraving Book, Volumes I & II, by R. L. Wilson. Privately printed, 2001. Each volume is appx. 500 pp., with 650 illustrations, most in color. $390.00

This third edition from the original texts of 1974 and 1982 has been fine-tuned and dramatically expanded, and is by far the most illuminating and complete. With over 1,200 illustrations, more than 2/3 of which are in color, this book joins the author's The Book of Colt Firearms, and Fine Colts as companion volumes. Approximately 1,000 pages in two volumes, each signed by the author, serial numbered, and strictly limited to 3000 copies. Volume I covers from the Paterson and pre-Paterson period through c.1921 (end of the Helfricht period). Volume II commences with Kornbrath, and Glahn, and covers Colt embellished arms from c.1919 through 2000.

Colt Model 1905 Automatic Pistol, by John Potocki, Andrew Mowbray Publishing, Lincoln, RI, 1998. 191 pp., illus. $28.00

Covers all aspects of the Colt Model 1905 Automatic Pistol, from its invention by the legendary John Browning to its numerous production variations.

Colt Peacemaker British Model, by Keith Cochran, Cochran Publishing Co., Rapid City, SD, 1989. 160 pp., illus. $35.00

Covers those revolvers Colt squeezed in while completing a large order of revolvers for the U.S. Cavalry in early 1874, to those magnificent cased target revolvers used in the pistol competitions at Bisley Commons in the 1890s.

Colt Peacemaker Encyclopedia, by Keith Cochran, Cochran Publishing Co., Rapid City, SD, 1986. 434 pp., illus. $60.00

A must-have book for the Peacemaker collector.

Colt Peacemaker Encyclopedia, Volume 2, by Keith Cochran, Cochran Publishing Co., SD, 1992. 416 pp., illus. $60.00

Included in this volume are extensive notes on engraved, inscribed, historical and noted revolvers, as well as those revolvers used by outlaws, lawmen, movie and television stars.

Colt Pistols, Texas, And The U.S. Army 1847-1861, by Col. Robert D. Whittington III. Hooks, TX, Brownlee Books, 2003. A limited edition of 1,000 copies. Numbered. 8 pp. Paper covers. New. $7.50

A study of the Colt pistols used in Texas by the U.S. Army between 1847-1861. A remarkable detailed report.

Colt Presentations: From the Factory Ledgers 1856-1869, by Herbert G. Houze. Lincoln, RI, Andrew Mowbray, Inc., 2003. 112 pp., 45 b&w photos. Softcover. $21.95

Samuel Colt was a generous man. He also used gifts to influence government decision makers. But after Congress investigated him in 1854, Colt needed to hide the gifts from prying eyes, which makes it very difficult for today's collectors to document the many revolvers presented by Colt and the factory. Using the original account journals of the Colt's Patent Fire Arms Manufacturing Co., renowned arms authority Herbert G. Houze finally gives us the full details behind hundreds of the most exciting Colts ever made.

Colt Single Action Army Revolver Study: New Discoveries, by Kenneth Moore, Lincoln, RI, Andrew Mowbray, Inc., 2003. 1st edition. 200 pp., with 77 photos and illustrations. Hardcover. New. $49.95

Twenty-five years after co-authoring the classic Study of the Colt Single Action Army Revolver, Ken fills in the gaps and sets the record straight. The serial number data alone will astound you. Includes, ejector models, special section on low serial numbers, U.S. Army testing data, new details about militia S.A.A.'s plus a true wealth of cartridge info.

Colt Single Action Army Revolvers: The Legend, the Romance and the Rivals, by "Doc" O'Meara, Krause Publications, Iola, WI, 2000. 160 pp., illustrated with 250 photos in b&w and a 16-page color section. $22.95

Production figures, serial numbers by year, and rarities.

Colt Single Action Army Revolvers and Alterations, by C. Kenneth Moore, Mowbray Publishers, Lincoln, RI, 1999. 112 pp., illus. $35.00

A comprehensive history of the revolvers that collectors call "Artillery Models." These are the most historical of all S.A.A. Colts, and this new book covers all the details.

ARMS LIBRARY

Colt Single Action Army Revolvers and the London Agency, by C. Kenneth Moore, Andrew Mowbray Publishers, Lincoln, RI, 1990. 144 pp., illus. $35.00

Drawing on vast documentary sources, this work chronicles the relationship between the London Agency and the Hartford home office.

Colt Sporting Firearms: Dates of Manufacture, by D.R. Morse, Phoenix, AZ, Firing Pin Enterprizes, 2003. 82 pp. Softcover. New. $6.95

Covers their pistols, revolvers, rifles, shotguns and commemoratives, plus models and serial numbers.

Colt U.S. General Officers' Pistols, by Horace Greeley IV, Andrew Mowbray Inc., Lincoln, RI, 1990. 199 pp., illus. $38.00

These unique weapons, issued as a badge of rank to General Officers in the U.S. Army from WWII onward, remain highly personal artifacts of the military leaders who carried them. Includes serial numbers and dates of issue.

Colt Walker's, Walkers Controversy is Solved, by Col. Robert D. Whittington III. Hooks, TX, Brownlee Books, 2005. A limited edition of 1,000 copies. Numbered. 17 pp. Paper covers. New. $15.00

The truth about serial numbers on the Colt Whitneyville-Walker Pistols presented to Captain Samuel Hamilton Walker by Sam Colt and J. B. Colt on July 28th, 1847.

Colts from the William M. Locke Collection, by Frank Sellers, Andrew Mowbray Publishers, Lincoln, RI, 1996. 192 pp., illus. $55.00

This important book illustrates all of the famous Locke Colts, with captions by arms authority Frank Sellers.

Colt's Dates of Manufacture 1837-1978, by R.L. Wilson, published by Maurie Albert, Coburg, Australia; N.A. distributor Madis Books, TX, 1997. 61 pp. $8.50

An invaluable pocket guide to the dates of manufacture of Colt firearms up to 1978.

Colt's Pocket '49: Its Evolution Including the Baby Dragoon and Wells Fargo, by Robert Jordan and Darrow Watt, privately printed, Loma Mar, CA 2000. 304 pp., with 984 color photos, illus. Beautifully bound in a deep blue leather-like case. $125.00

Detailed information on all models and covers engaving, cases, accoutrements, holsters, fakes, and much more. Included is a summary booklet containing information such as serial numbers, production ranges and identifing photos. This book is a masterpiece on its subject.

Colt's SAA Post War Models, by George Garton, The Gun Room Press, Highland Park, NJ, 1995. 166 pp., illus. $39.95

Complete facts on the post-war Single Action Army revolvers. Information on calibers, production numbers and variations taken from factory records.

Combat Helmets of the Third Reich: A Study in Photographs, by Thomas Kibler, Pottsboro, TX, Reddick Enterprises, 2003. 1st edition. 96 pp., illustrated in full color. Pictorial softcover. NEW. $19.95

Combat Perspective The Thinking Man's Guide to Self-Defense, by Gabriel Suarez, Boulder, CO, Paladin Press, 2003. 1st edition. 112 pp. Softcover. NEW. $15.00

Complete Guide to United States Military Medals 1939 to Present, 6th Edition, by Colonel Frank C. Foster, Medals of America Press, Fountain Inn, SC, 2006. 168 pp., illus., photos. $29.95

Complete criteria for every Army, Navy, Marine, Air Force, Coast Guard, and Merchant Marine award since 1939. All decorations, service medals, and ribbons shown in full color and accompanied by dates and campaigns, as well as detailed descriptions on proper wear and display.

Complete Guide to the M1 Garand and the M1 Carbine, by Bruce N. Canfield, 2nd printing, Andrew Mowbray Inc., Lincoln, RI, 1999. 296 pp., illus. $39.50

Expanded and updated coverage of both the M1 Garand and the M1 Carbine, with more than twice as much information as the author's previous book on this topic.

Complete Guide to U.S. Infantry Weapons of the First War, by Bruce Canfield, Andrew Mowbray, Publisher, Lincoln, RI, 2000. 304 pp., illus. $39.95

The definitive study of the U.S. Infantry weapons used in WWI.

Complete Guide to U.S. Infantry Weapons of World War Two, by Bruce Canfield, Andrew Mowbray, Publisher, Lincoln, RI, 1995. 303 pp., illus. $39.95

A definitive work on the weapons used by the United States Armed Forces in WWII.

Confederate Belt Buckles & Plates, by Steve E. Mullinax, O'Donnell Publishing, Alexandria, VA, 1999. Expanded edition. 247 pp., illus. Hardcover. $34.00

Hundreds of crisp photographs augment this classic study of Confederate accoutrement plates.

Confederate Carbines & Musketoons Cavalry Small Arms Manufactured in and for the Southern Confederacy 1861-1865, by John M. Murphy, Santa Ana, CA, privately printed, 2002. Reprint. Hardcover. New in new dust jacket. $79.95

Confederate Rifles & Muskets: Infantry Small Arms Manufactured in the Southern Confederacy 1861-1865, by John M. Murphy. Santa Ana, CA, privately printed, 1996. Reprint. 768 pp., 8 pp. color plates, profusely illustrated. Hardcover. $119.95

The first in-depth and academic analysis and discussion of the "long" longarms produced in the South by and for the Confederacy during the American Civil War. The collection of Dr. Murphy is doubtless the largest and finest grouping of Confederate longarms in private hands today.

Confederate Saddles & Horse Equipment, by Ken R. Knopp, Orange, VA, Publisher's Press, 2002. 194 pps., illus. Hardcover. $39.95

A pioneer work on the subject. After 10 years of research Ken Knopp has compiled a thorough and fascinating study of the little-known field of Confederate saddlery and equipment. An indispensable source for collectors and historians.

Cooey Firearms, Made in Canada 1919-1979, by John A. Belton, Museum Restoration, Canada, 1998. 36pp., with 46 illus. Paper covers. $8.95

More than 6 million rifles and at least 67 models were made by this small Canadian riflemaker. They have been identified from the first 'Cooey Canuck' through the last variations made by the 'Winchester-Cooey'. Each is descibed and most are illustrated in this first book on the Cooey.

Cowboy and Gunfighter Collectible, by Bill Mackin, Mountain Press Publishing Co., Missoula, MT, 1995. 178 pp., illus. Paper covers. $25.00

A photographic encyclopedia with price guide and makers' index.

Cowboy Collectibles and Western Memorabilia, by Bob Bell and Edward Vebell, Schiffer Publishing, Atglen, PA, 1992. 160 pp., illus. Paper covers. $29.95

The exciting era of the cowboy and the wild west collectibles including rifles, pistols, gun rigs, etc.

Cowboy Culture: The Last Frontier of American Antiques, by Michael Friedman, Schiffer Publishing, Ltd., West Chester, PA, 2002. 300 pp., illus. $89.95

Covers the artful aspects of the old west, the antiques and collectibles. Illustrated with clear color plates of over 1,000 items such as spurs, boots, guns, saddles, etc.

Cowboys and the Trappings of the Old West, by William Manns and Elizabeth Clair Flood, Zon International Publishing Co., Santa Fe, NM, 1997, 1st edition. 224 pp., illus. $45.00

A pictorial celebration of the cowboy dress and trappings.

Custom Firearms Engraving, by Tom Turpin, Krause Publications, Iola, WI, 1999. 208 pp., illus. $49.95

Over 200 four-color photos with more than 75 master engravers profiled. Engravers directory with addresses in the U.S. and abroad.

Daisy Air Rifles & BB Guns: The First 100 Years, by Neal Punchard. St. Paul, MN, Motorbooks, 2002. 1st edition. 10" x 10", 156 pp., 300 color. Hardcover. $29.95

Flash back to the days of your youth and recall fond memories of your Daisy. Daisy Air Rifles and BB Guns looks back fondly on the first 100 years of Daisy BB rifles and pistols, toy and cork guns, accessories, packaging, period advertising and literature.

Death From Above: The German FG42 Paratrooper Rifle, New Expanded Edition, by Blake Stevens, Collector Grade Publications, Canada, 2007. 228 pages, 278 illustrations. $59.95

This book depicts and describes seven basic models of the FG42, from the earliest prototype (the Type 'A') through the first or 'early' production series (the Type 'E') with its distinctively swept-back handgrip and intricately machined receiver, then the initial Rheinmetall redesign utilizing a stamped receiver (the Type 'F'), followed by the ultimate if extremely short-lived final series-production model, the Type 'G'. Amazingly, virtually none of the Type 'G' components will interchange with their lookalike Type 'F' counterparts. This includes magazines.

Decorations, Medals, Ribbons, Badges and Insignia of the United States Navy; World War II to Present, by James G. Thompson, Medals of America Press, Fountain Inn, SC. 2005. 124 pp., illus. $29.95

The most complete guide to United States Army medals, ribbons, rank, insignia and patches from WWII to the present day. Each medal and insignia shown in full color. Includes listing of respective criteria and campaigns.

Defending the Dominion, Canadian Military Rifles, 1855-1955, by David Edgecombe. Service Publications, Ont., Canada, 2003. 168 pp., with 60+ illustrations. Hardcover. $39.95

This book contains much new information on the Canadian acquisition, use and disposal of military rifles during the most significant century in the development of small arms. In addition to the venerable Martini-Henry, there are chapters on the Winchester, Snider, Starr, Spencer, Peabody, Enfield rifles and others.

Derringer in America, Volume 1, The Percussion Period, by R.L. Wilson and L.D. Eberhart, Andrew Mowbray Inc., Lincoln, RI, 1985. 271 pp., illus. $48.00

A long awaited book on the American percussion derringer.

Derringer in America, Volume 2, the Cartridge Period, by L.D. Eberhart and R.L. Wilson, Andrew Mowbray Inc., Publishers, Lincoln, RI, 1993. 284 pp., illus. $65.00

Comprehensive coverage of cartridge derringers organized alphabetically by maker. Includes all types of derringers known by the authors to have been offered in the American market.

Devil's Paintbrush: Sir Hiram Maxim's Gun, by Dolf Goldsmith, 3rd Edition, expanded and revised, Collector Grade Publications, Toronto, Canada, 2002. 384 pp., illus. $79.95

The classic work on the world's first true automatic machine gun.

Dressed For Duty: America's Women in Uniform, 1898-1973 Volume I, by Jill Halcomb Smith, San Nose, CA, Bender Publishing, 2002. 1st edition. 480 pages-1,089 photos & illustrations (many in color), deluxe binding. Hardcover. NEW. $54.95

Dressed For Duty: America's Women in Uniform, 1898-1973 Volume II, by Jill Halcomb Smith, San Nose, CA, Bender Publishing, 2004. 1st edition. 544 pages-1,300 photos & illustrations (many in color), deluxe binding. Hardcover. NEW. $59.95

Dr. Josephus Requa Civil War Dentist and the Billinghurst-Requa Volley Gun, by John M. Hyson Jr., and Margaret Requa DeFrancisco, Museum Restoration Service, Bloomfield, Ont., Canada, 1999. 36 pp., illus. Paper covers. $8.95

The story of the inventor of the first practical rapid-fire gun to be used during the American Civil War.

Dutch Luger (Parabellum) A Complete History, by Bas J. Martens and Guus de Vries, Ironside International, Alexandria, VA, 1995. 268 pp., illus. $49.95

The history of the Luger in the Netherlands. An extensive description of the Dutch pistol and trials and the different models of the Luger in the Dutch service.

E.C. Prudhomme's Gun Engraving Review, by E. C. Prudhomme, R&R Books, Livonia, NY, 1994. 164 pp., illus. $60.00

As a source for engravers and collectors, this book is an indispensable guide to styles and techniques of the world's foremost engravers.

Eagle on U.S. Firearms, by John W. Jordan, Pioneer Press, Union City, TN, 1992. 140 pp., illus. Paper covers. $17.50

Stylized eagles have been stamped on government owned or manufactured firearms in the U.S. since the beginning of our country. This book lists and illustrates these various eagles in an informative and refreshing manner.

Emblems of Honor; Patches and Insignia of the U.S. Army from the Great War to the Early Cold War Vol. IV Armor-Cavalry-Tank Destroyer, by Kurt Keller, Constabulary, PA, privately printed, 2005. 1st edition, signed. 232 pp., with over 600 color photos. Hardcover. New in new dust jacket. $59.95

Emma Gees, by Capt. Herbert W. McBride, Mt. Ida, AR, Lancer Publishing, 2003. 224 pp., b&w photos. Softcover. NEW. $19.95

Encyclopedia of Rifles & Handguns; A Comprehensive Guide to Firearms, edited by Sean Connolly, Chartwell Books, Inc., Edison, NJ., 1996. 160 pp., illus. $26.00

ARMS LIBRARY

Encyclopedia of United States Army Insignia and Uniforms, by William Emerson, OK, University of Oklahoma Press, 1996. Hardcover. NEW. $134.95

Enemies Foreign and Domestic, by Matthew Bracken, San Diego, CA, Steelcutter Publishing, 2003. Softcover. NEW. $19.89

Eprouvettes: A Comprehensive Study of Early Devices for the Testing of Gunpowder, by R.T.W. Kempers, Royal Armouries Museum, Leeds, England, 1999. 352 pp., illustrated with 240 b&w and 28 color plates. $125.00

Equipment of the WWII Tommy, by David Gordon, Missoula, MT, Pictorial Histories Publishing, 2004. 1st edition. Softcover. NEW. $24.95

Fifteen Years in the Hawken Lode, by John D. Baird, The Gun Room Press, Highland Park, NJ, 1976. 120 pp., illus. $24.95

A collection of thoughts and observations gained from many years of intensive study of the guns from the shop of the Hawken brothers.

Fighting Colors: The Creation of Military Aircraft Nose Art, by Gary Velasco, Paducah, KY, Turner Publishing, 2005. 1st edition. Hardcover. New in new dust jacket. $57.95

Fighting Iron, by Art Gogan, Andrew Mowbray, Inc., Lincoln, R.I., 2002. 176 pp., illus. $28.00

It doesn't matter whether you collect guns, swords, bayonets or accoutrement–sooner or later you realize that it all comes down to the metal. If you don't understand the metal, you don't understand your collection.

Fine Art of the West, by Byron Price, New York, Abbeville Press, 2004, 2nd revised edition. $75.00

A glossary and bibliography complete this first comprehensive look at one of America's most fascinating forms of artistic expression. 276 pages illustrated with color photos.

Firearm Suppressor Patents; Volume 1: United States Patents, by N.R. Parker, Foreword by Alan C. Paulson, Boulder, CO, Paladin Press, 2004. 392 pp., illus. Softcover. $45.00

Firearms from Europe, 2nd Edition, by David Noe, Larry W. Yantz, Dr. James B. Whisker, Rowe Publications, Rochester, N.Y., 2002. 192 pp., illus. $45.00

A history and description of firearms imported during the American Civil War by the United States of America and the Confederate States of America.

Firearms of the American West 1803-1865, Volume 1, by Louis A. Garavaglia and Charles Worman, University of Colorado Press, Niwot, CO, 1998. 402 pp., illus. $79.95

Traces the development and uses of firearms on the frontier during this period.

Firearms of the American West 1866-1894, Volume 2, by Louis A. Garavaglia and Charles G. Worman, University of Colorado Press, Niwot, CO, 1998. 416 pp., illus. $79.95

A monumental work that offers both technical information on all of the important firearms used in the West during this period and a highly entertaining history of how they were used, who used them, and why.

Firepower from Abroad, by Wiley Sword, Andrew Mowbray Publishing, Lincoln, R.I., 2000. 120 pp., illus. $23.00

The Confederate Enfield and the LeMat revolver and how they reached the Confederate market.

Flayderman's Guide to Antique American Firearms and Their Values, 8th Edition, edited by Norm Flayderman, Krause Publications, Iola, WI, 2001. 692 pp., illus. Paper covers. $34.95

A completely updated and new edition with more than 3,600 models and variants extensively described with all marks and specifications necessary for quick identification.

Flintlock Fowlers: The First Guns Made in America, by Tom Grinslade, Texarkana, TX: Scurlock Publishing Co., 2005. 1st edition. 248 pages. Hardcover. New in new dust jacket. $75.00 Paperback $38.00

The most complete compilation of fowlers ever in one book. Essential resource for collectors, builders and flintlock enthusiasts!

F.N. F.A.L. Assembly, Disassembly Manual 7.62mm, by Skennerton & Riling, Ray Riling Arms Books Co. Philadelphia, PA 2004. 36 pages, $5.00

Over 60 photos & line drawings. Ideal workshop reference for stripping & assembly with exploded parts drawings, specifications, service accessories, historical information and recommended reading references. Triple saddle-stitched binding with durable plastic laminated cover makes this an ideal workshop guide.

FN-FAL Rifle, et al, by Duncan Long, Paladin Press, Boulder, CO, 1999. 144 pp., illus. Paper covers. $18.95

Detailed descriptions of the basic models produced by Fabrique Nationale and the myriad variants that evolved as a result of the firearms' universal acceptance.

Freund & Bro. Pioneer Gunmakers to the West, by F.J. Pablo Balentine, Graphic Publishers, Newport Beach, CA, 1997. 380 pp., illus. $69.95

The story of Frank W. and George Freund, skilled German gunsmiths who plied their trade on the Western American frontier during the final three decades of the nineteenth century.

Full Circle: A Treatise On Roller Locking, by Blake Stevens, Collector Grade Publications, Toronto, Canada, 2006. 536 pages, with over 737 illustrations. $79.95

After the war the roller lock was taken from Germany first to France; then to Spain, and Switzerland; through Holland; and finally back "Full Circle" to Germany again, where it was used in the G3, the service rifle of the Bundeswehr, from 1959 through to the adoption of the 5.56mm G36 in 1995. The classic work on the world's first true automatic machine gun.

Fusil de Tulole in New France, 1691-1741, by Russel Bouchard, Museum Restorations Service, Bloomfield, Ontario, Canada, 1997. 36 pp., illus. Paper covers. $8.95

The development of the company and the identification of their arms.

Gas Trap Garand, by Billy Pyle, Collector Grade Publications, Cobourg, Ontario, Canada, 1999 316 pp., illus. $59.95

The in-depth story of the rarest Garands of them all, the initial 80 Model Shop rifles made under the personal supervision of John Garand himself in 1934 and 1935, and the first 50,000 plus production "gas trap" M1's manufactured at Springfield Armory between August, 1937 and August, 1940.

George Schreyer, Sr. and Jr., Gunmakers of Hanover, Pennsylvania, by George Shumway, George Shumway Publishers, York, PA, 1990. 160pp., illus. $50.00

This monograph is a detailed photographic study of almost all known surviving longrifles and smoothbore guns made by highly regarded gunsmiths George Schreyer, Sr. and George Schreyer Jr.

German and Austrian Gunmakers Trade Catalogs, by George Hoyem, Jaeger Press, 2002. This is a 252 page 11" x 8.5" case bound book with a four color dust jacket, compiled by Hans E. Pfingsten and George A. Hoyem, containing five illustrated gunmakers trade catalogues dating from 1914 to 1935, three of them export issues in German, English, French and Spanish. Hardcover. New in new dust jacket. $60.00

German Anti-Tank Weapons-Panzerbuchse, Panzerfaust and Panzerschrek: Propaganda Series Volume 5, by DeVries and Martens. Alexandria,VA, Ironside Intl., 2005. 1st edition. 152pp, illustrated with 200 high quality b&w photos, most never published before. Hardcover, NEW. $38.95

German Assault Rifle 1935-1945, The, by Peter R. Senich, Paladin Press, Boulder, CO, 1987. 328 pp., illus. $60.00

A complete review of machine carbines, machine pistols and assault rifles employed by Hitler's Wehrmacht during WWII.

German Belt Buckles 1845-1945: Buckles of the Enlisted Soldiers, by Peter Nash Atglen, PA, Schiffer Publications, 2003. 1st edition. Hardcover. New in new dust jacket. $59.95

German Camouflaged Helmets of the Second World War; Volume 1: Painted and Textured Camouflage, by Branislav Atglen Radovic, PA, Schiffer Publications, 2004. 1st edition. Hardcover. New in new dust jacket. $79.95

German Camouflaged Helmets of the Second World War; Volume 2: Wire, Netting, Covers, Straps, Interiors, Miscellaneous, by Branislav Atglen Radovic, PA, Schiffer Publications, 2004. 1st edition. Hardcover. New in new dust jacket. $79.95

German Cross in Gold-Holders of the SS and Police, by Mark Yerger, San Jose, CA, Bender Publishing, 2004. 1st edition. 432 pp., 295 photos and illustrations, deluxe binding. Hardcover. NEW. $44.95

German Cross in Gold-Holders of the SS and Police Volume 2-"Das Reich", by Mark Yerger, San Jose, CA, Bender Publishing, 2005. 1st edition. 432 pp., 295 photos and illustrations, deluxe binding. Hardcover. NEW. $44.95

German K98k Rifle, 1934-1945: The Backbone of the Wehrmacht, by Richard D. Law, Collector Grade Publications, Toronto, Canada, 1993. 336 pp., illus. $69.95

The most comprehensive study ever published on the 14,000,000 bolt-action K98k rifles produced in Germany between 1934 and 1945.

German Machine Guns, by Daniel D. Musgrave, revised edition, Ironside International Publishers, Inc. Alexandria, VA, 1992. 586 pp., 650 illus. $49.95

The most definitive book ever written on German machine guns. Covers the introduction and development of machine guns in Germany from 1899 to the rearmament period after WWII.

German Military Abbreviations, by Military Intelligence Service, Canada, Service Publications. 268 pp. Stiff paper covers. NEW. $16.95

German Paratroops: Uniforms, Insignia & Equipment of the Fallschirmjager in World War II, by Robert Atglen Kurtz, PA, Schiffer Publications, 2003. 1st edition. Hardcover. New in new dust jacket. $59.95

German Tanks of World War II in Color, by Michael Green; Thomas Anderson; Frank Schultz, St. Paul, MN, MBI Publishing Company, 2000. 1st edition. Softcover. NEW. $14.95

Government Issue: U.S. Army European Theater of Operations Collector Guide, by Henry-Paul Enjames, Philippe Charbonnier, France, Histoire & Collections, 2004. Hardcover, NEW. $49.89

Government Models, by William H.D. Goddard, Andrew Mowbray Publishing, Lincoln, RI, 1998. 296 pp., illus. $58.50

The most authoritative source on the development of the Colt model of 1911.

Grasshoppers and Butterflies, by Adrian B. Caruana, Museum Restoration Service, Alexandria Bay, N.Y., 1999. 32 pp., illus. Paper covers. $8.95

No.39 in the Historical Arms Series. The light 3 pounders of Pattison and Townsend.

Greenhill Dictionary of Guns and Gunmakers: From Colt's First Patent to the Present Day, 1836-2001, by John Walter, Greenhill Publishing, 2001 $59.95

1st edition, 576 pp., illustrated with 200 photos, 190 trademarks and 40 line drawings, Hardcover. $59.95

Covers military small arms, sporting guns and rifles, air and gas guns, designers, inventors, patentees, trademarks, brand names and monograms. A famed book of great value, truly encyclopedic in scope and sought after by firearms collectors.

Gun Powder Cans & Kegs, by Ted and David Bacyk and Tom Rowe, Rowe Publications, Rochester, NY, 1999. 150 pp., illus. $65.00

The first book devoted to powder tins and kegs. All cans and kegs in full color. With a price guide and rarity scale.

Gun Tools, Their History and Identification, by James B. Shaffer, Lee A. Rutledge and R. Stephen Dorsey, Collector's Library, Eugene, OR, 1992. 375 pp., illus. $30.00

Written history of foreign and domestic gun tools from the flintlock period to WWII.

Gun Tools, Their History and Identifications, Volume 2, by Stephen Dorsey and James B. Shaffer, Collectors' Library, OR, 1997. 396 pp., illus. Paper covers. $30.00

Gun tools from the Royal Armouries Museum in England, Pattern Room, Royal Ordnance Reference Collection in Nottingham and from major private collections.

Gunmakers of London 1350-1850 with Supplement, by Howard L. Blackmore, Museum Restoration Service, Alexandria Bay, NY, 1999. 222 pp., illus. Two volumes. Slipcased. $135.00

A listing of all the known workmen of gunmaking in the first 500 years, plus a history of the guilds, cutlers, armourers, founders, blacksmiths, etc. 260 gunmarks are illustrated. Supplement is 156 pages, and begins with an introductory chapter on "foreign" gunmakers followed by records of all the new information found about previously unidentified armourers, gunmakers and gunsmiths.

Guns of Dagenham: Lanchester, Patchett, Sterling, by Peter Laidler and David Howroyd, Collector Grade Publications, Inc., Canada, 1995. 310 pp. illus. $39.95

An in-depth history of small arms made by the Sterling Company of Dagenham, England, from 1940 until Sterling was purchased by British Aerospace in 1989 and closed.

ARMS LIBRARY

Guns of Remington: Historic Firearms Spanning Two Centuries, compiled by Howard M. Madaus, Biplane Productions, Publisher, in cooperation with Buffalo Bill Historical Center, Cody, WY, 1998. 352 pp., illustrated with over 800 color photos. $79.95

A complete catalog of the firearms in the exhibition, "It Never Failed Me: The Arms & Art of Remington Arms Company" at the Buffalo Bill Historical Center, Cody, Wyoming.

Guns of the Third Reich, by John Walter, Pennsylvania, Stackpole Books, 2004. 1st edition. 256pp, 60 illust. Hardcover. $34.95

John Walter examines the full range of guns used by the Third Reich from the commercially successful Walter PP and PPK, to the double-action, personal defense pistols Mauser HSc and Sauer M38.

Guns of the Western Indian War, by R. Stephen Dorsey, Collector's Library, Eugene, OR, 1997. 220 pp., illus. Paper covers. $30.00

The full story of the guns and ammunition that made western history in the turbulent period of 1865-1890.

Gunsmiths of Illinois, by Curtis L. Johnson, George Shumway Publishers, York, PA, 1995. 160 pp., illus. $50.00

Genealogical information is provided for nearly 1,000 gunsmiths. Contains hundreds of illustrations of rifles and other guns, of handmade origin, from Illinois.

Gunsmiths of Manhattan, 1625-1900: A Checklist of Tradesmen, by Michael H. Lewis, Museum Restoration Service, Bloomfield, Ont., Canada, 1991. 40 pp., illus. Paper covers. $8.95

This listing of more than 700 men in the arms trade in New York City prior to about the end of the 19th century will provide a guide for identification and further research.

Gunsmiths of Maryland, by Daniel D. Hartzler and James B. Whisker, Old Bedford Village Press, Bedford, PA, 1998. 208 pp., illus. $45.00

Covers firelock Colonial period through the breech-loading patent models. Featuring longrifles.

Gunsmiths of Virginia, by Daniel D. Hartzler and James B. Whisker, Old Bedford Village Press, Bedford, PA, 1992. 206 pp., illus. $40.00

A photographic study of American longrifles.

Gunsmiths of West Virginia, by Daniel D. Hartzler and James B. Whisker, Old Bedford Village Press, Bedford, PA, 1998. 176 pp., illus. $40.00

A photographic study of American longrifles.

Gunsmiths of York County, Pennsylvania, by Daniel D. Hartzler and James B. Whisker, Old Bedford Village Press, Bedford, PA, 1998. 160 pp., illus. $40.00

Photographs and research notes on the longrifles and gunsmiths of York County, Pennsylvania.

Hand Forged for Texas Cowboys, by Kurt House, an Antonio, TX, Three Rivers Publishing, 2005. This beautifully illustrated book features color photos as well as b&w period photos, and will be a welcome addition to the library of any reader. 160 pages. Hardcover. New in new dust jacket. $69.95

Harrington & Richardson Sporting Firearms: Dates of Manufacture 1871-1991, by D.R. Morse. Phoenix, AZ, Firing Pin Enterprizes, 2003. 14 pp. Softcover. NEW. $6.95

Covers their pistols, revolvers, rifles, shotguns and commemoratives, plus models.

Hawken Rifle: Its Place in History, by Charles E. Hanson Jr., The Fur Press, Chadron, NE, 1979. 104 pp., illus. Paper covers. $15.00

A definitive work on this famous rifle.

Hi-Standard Sporting Firearms: Dates of Manufacture, by D.R. Morse. 1926-1992. Phoenix, AZ, Firing Pin Enterprizes, 2003. 22 pp. Softcover. New. $6.95

Covers their pistols, revolvers, rifles, shotguns and commemoratives, plus models and serial numbers.

High Standard: A Collector's Guide to the Hamden & Hartford Target Pistols, by Tom Dance, Andrew Mowbray, Inc., Lincoln, RI, 1991. 192 pp. Paper covers. $24.00

From Citation to Supermatic, all of the production models and specials made from 1951 to 1984 are covered according to model number or series.

History of Modern U.S. Military Small Arms Ammunition, Volume 1, 1880-1939, revised by F.W. Hackley, W.H. Woodin and E.L. Scranton, Thomas Publications, Gettysburg, PA, 1998. 328 pp., illus. $49.95

This revised edition incorporates all publicly available information concerning military small arms ammunition for the period 1880 through 1939 in a single volume.

History of Modern U.S. Military Small Arms Ammunition, Volume 2, 1940-1945, by F.W. Hackley, W.H. Woodin and E.L. Scranton, Gun Room Press, Highland Park, NJ, 1998. 297 pages, illustrated. $49.95

Based on decades of original research conducted at the National Archives, numerous military, public and private museums and libraries, as well as individual collections, this edition incorporates all publicly available information concerning military small arms ammunition for the period 1940 through 1945.

History of Smith & Wesson Firearms, by Dean Boorman, Lyons Press, New York, NY, 2002. 44 pp., illustrated in full color. Hardcover. $29.95

The definitive guide to one of the world's best-known firearms makers. Takes the story through the years of the Military and Police 38 and of the Magnum cartridge, to today's wide range of products for law-enforcement customers.

History of Winchester Rifles, by Dean Boorman, Lyons Press, New York, NY, 2001. 144 pp., illus. 150 full-color photos. $29.95

A captivating and wonderfully photographed history of one of the most legendary names in gun lore.

History of Colt Firearms, by Dean Boorman, Lyons Press, New York, NY, 2001. 144 pp., illus. $29.95

Discover the fascinating story of the world's most famous revolver, complete with more than 150 stunning full-color photographs.

Holsters and Shoulder Stocks of the World, by Anthony Vanderlinden, Greensboro, NC, Wet Dog Publications, 2005. 1st edition. Hardcover $45.95

About 500 holsters and shoulder-stocks will be documented in this first edition. Pistols are listed by make and model. The user guide references the countries that used the holsters so that collectors can instantly refer to either a pistol model or country or use. 204 pages, with over 1000 b& w photos.

Honour Bound: The Chauchat Machine Rifle, by Gerard Demaison and Yves Buffetaut, Collector Grade Publications, Inc., Cobourg, Ont., Canada, 1995. $39.95

The story of the CSRG (Chauchat) machine rifle, the most manufactured automatic weapon of WWI.

Hunting Weapons from the Middle Ages to the Twentieth Century, by Howard L. Blackmore, Dover Publications, Meneola, NY, 2000. 480 pp., illus. Paper covers. $16.95

Dealing mainly with the different classes of weapons used in sport: swords, spears, crossbows, guns, and rifles, from the Middle Ages until the present day.

Illustrations of United States Military Arms 1776-1903 and Their Inspector's Marks, compiled by Turner Kirkland, Pioneer Press, Union City, TN, 1988. 37 pp., illus. Paper covers. $7.00

Reprinted from the 1949 Bannerman catalog. Valuable information for both the advanced and beginning collector.

Imperial German Military Officers' Helmets and Headdress 1871-1918, by Thomas N.G. Stubbs, Atglen, PA, Schiffer Publications, 2003. 1st edition. Hardcover. New in new dust jacket. $79.95

Imperial Japanese Grenade Rifles and Launchers, by Gregory A. Babich and Thomas A. Keep Lemont, PA, Dutch Harlow Publishing, 2004. 1st edition. Hardcover. New in new dust jacket. $75.00

Indian Trade Relics, by Lar Hothem, Paducah, KY, Collector Books, 2003. 1st edition. 320pp. Pictorial Hardcover. NEW. $29.95

Indian War Cartridge Pouches, Boxes and Carbine Boots, by R. Stephen Dorsey, Collector's Library, Eugene, OR, 1993. 156 pp., illus. Paper covers. $20.00

The key reference work to the cartridge pouches, boxes, carbine sockets and boots of the Indian War period 1865-1890.

Individual Gear and Personal Items of the GI in Europe 1942-1945; From Pro-Kits to Pin-Up, by James Klokner, Atglen., PA, Schiffer Publications, 2005. 224 pages with over 470 color and b&w photographs. Hardcover. $59.95

This book is by far the best and most complete study available of personal items of the American soldier during World War II and truly an indispensable resource.

International Armament, with History, Data, Technical Information and Photographs of Over 800 Weapons, 2nd edition, new printing, by George B. Johnson, Alexandria, VA, Ironside International, 2002. Hardcover. New in new dust jacket. $59.95

The development and progression of modern military small arms. Over 800 photographs and illustrations with both historical and technical data. Two volumes are now bound into one book.

Jaeger Rifles, collected articles published in Muzzle Blasts, by George Shumway, York PA, 2003. Reprint. 108 pp., illus. Stiff paper covers. New. $30.00

Thirty-six articles previously published in *Muzzle Blasts* are reproduced here.

Japanese Rifles of World War Two, by Duncan O. McCollum, Excalibur Publications, Latham, NY, 1996. 64 pp., illus. Paper covers. $18.95

A sweeping view of the rifles and carbines that made up Japan's arsenal during the conflict.

Kentucky Rifle, by Captain John G.W. Dillin, George Shumway Publisher, York, PA, 1993. 221 pp., illus. $50.00

This well-known book was the first attempt to tell the story of the American longrifle. This edition retains the original text and illustrations with supplemental footnotes provided by Dr. George Shumway.

Legends and Reality of the AK, by Val Shilin and Charlie Cutshaw, Paladen Press, Boulder, CO, 2000. 192 pp., illus. Paper covers. $35.00

A behind-the-scenes look at history, design and impact of the Kalashnikov family of weapons.

Light 6-Pounder Battalion Gun of 1776, by Adrian Caruana, Museum Restoration Service, Bloomfield, Ontario, Canada, 2001. 76 pp., illus. Paper covers. $8.95

London Gun Trade, 1850-1920, by Joyce E. Gooding, Museum Restoration Service, Bloomfield, Ontario, Canada, 2001. 48 pp., illus. Paper covers. $8.95

Names, dates and locations of London gunmakers working between 1850 and 1920 are listed. Compiled from the original Kelly's post office directories of the City of London.

London Gunmakers and the English Duelling Pistol, 1770-1830, by Keith R. Dill, Museum Restoration Service, Bloomfield, Ontario, Canada, 1997. 36 pp., illus. Paper covers. $8.95

Ten gunmakers made London one of the major gunmaking centers of the world. This book examines how the design and construction of their pistols contributed to that reputation and how these characteristics may be used to date flintlock arms.

Longrifles of Pennsylvania, Volume 1, Jefferson, Clarion & Elk Counties, by Russel H. Harringer, George Shumway Publisher, York, PA, 1984. 200 pp., illus. $50.00

First in series that will treat in great detail the longrifles and gunsmiths of Pennsylvania.

M1 Garand .30 Assembly, Disassembly Manual, by Skennerton & Riling, Ray Riling Arms Books Co. Philadelphia, PA 2004. 36 pages, $5.00

With over 60 photos & line drawings. Ideal workshop reference for stripping & assembly with exploded parts drawings, specifications, service accessories, historical information and recommended reading references.

M1 Carbine .30 M1, M1A1, M2 & M3 Assembly, Disassembly Manual, by Skennerton & Riling, Ray Riling Arms Books Co. Philadelphia, PA 2004. 36 pages, $5.00

With over 60 photos & line drawings. Ideal workshop reference for stripping & assembly with exploded parts drawings, specifications, service accessories, historical information and recommended reading references.

M1 Carbine: A Revolution in Gun-Stocking, by Grafton H. Cook II and Barbara W. Cook, Lincoln, RI, Andrew Mowbray, Inc., 2002. 1st edition. 208 pp., heavily illustrated with 157 rare photographs of the guns and the men and women who made them. Softcover. $29.95

Shows you, step by step, how M1 carbine stocks were made, right through to assembly with the hardware. Also contains lots of detailed information about other military weapons, like the M1A1, the M1 Garand, the M14 and much, much more.

M1 Carbine: Design, Development, and Production, by Larry Ruth, Gun Room Press, Highland Park, NJ, 1987. 291 pp., illus. Paper $19.95

The origin, development, manufacture and use of this famous carbine of WWII.

M1 Carbine Owner's Guide, by Larry Ruth and Scott A. Duff, Scott A. Duff Publications, Export, PA, 1997. 126 pp., illus. Paper covers. $21.95

This book answers the questions M1 owners most often ask concerning maintenance activities not encounted by military users.

ARMS LIBRARY

M1 Garand: Owner's Guide, by Scott A. Duff, Scott A. Duff Publications, Export, PA, 1998. 132 pp., illus. Paper covers. $21.95

This book answers the questions M1 owners most often ask concerning maintenance activities not encounted by military users.

M1 Garand Complete Assembly Guide, Vol 2, by Scott A. Duff, Scott A. Duff Publications, Export, PA, 2006. 162 pp., illus. Paper covers. $20.95

This book goes beyond the military manuals in depth and scope, using words It won't make you an Garand armorer, but it will make you a more knowledgeable owner.

M1 Garand: Post World War, by Scott A. Duff, Scott A. Duff Publications, Export, PA, 1990. 139 pp., illus. Softcover. $21.95

A detailed account of the activities at Springfield Armory through this period. International Harvester, H&R, Korean War production and quantities delivered. Serial numbers.

M1 Garand: World War II, by Scott A. Duff, Scott A. Duff Publications, Export, PA, 2001. 210 pp., illus. Paper covers. $34.95

The most comprehensive study available to the collector and historian on the M1 Garand of WWII.

M1 Garand 1936 to 1957, 4th Edition, Revised & Expanded, by Joe Poyer and Craig Riesch, North Cape Publications, Tustin, CA, 2006. 232 pp., illus. PC. $19.95

Describes the entire range of M1 Garand production in text and quick-scan charts.

M1 Garand Serial Numbers and Data Sheets, by Scott A. Duff, Scott A. Duff Publications, Export, PA, 1995. 101 pp., illus. Paper covers. $11.95

Provides the reader with serial numbers related to dates of manufacture and a large sampling of data sheets to aid in identification or restoration.

Machine Guns, by Ian V. Hogg, Iola, WI, Krause Publications, 2002. 1st edition. 336 pp., illustrated with b&w photos with a 16-page color section. Softcover. $29.95

A detailed history of the rapid-fire gun, 14th Century to present. Covers the development, history and specifications.

Made in the C.S.A.: Saddle Makers of the Confederacy, by Ken R. Knopp, Hattiesburg, MS, privately printed, 2003. 1st edition signed. 205 pp., illus., signed by the author. Softcover. NEW. $30.00

Maine Made Guns and Their Makers, by Dwight B. Demeritt Jr., Maine State Museum, Augusta, ME, 1998. 209 pp., illus. $55.00

An authoritative, biographical study of Maine gunsmiths.

Marksmanship in the U.S. Army, by William Emerson, Oklahoma, Univ. of Oklahoma Press, 2004 256 pages Illustrated with b&w photos. Hardcover. NEW $64.95

Marlin Firearms: A History of the Guns and the Company That Made Them, by Lt. Col. William S. Brophy, USAR, Ret., Stackpole Books, Harrisburg, PA, 1989. 672 pp., illus. $89.95

The definitive book on the Marlin Firearms Co. and their products.

Martini-Henry .450 Rifles & Carbines, by Dennis Lewis, Excalibur Publications, Latham, NY, 1996. 72 pp., illus. Paper covers. $11.95

The stories of the rifles and carbines that were the mainstay of the British soldier through the Victorian wars.

Mauser Bolt Rifles, by Ludwig Olson, F. Brownell & Son, Inc., Montezuma, IA, 1999. 364 pp., illus. $64.95

The most complete, detailed, authoritative and comprehensive work ever done on Mauser bolt rifles. Completely revised deluxe 3rd edition.

Mauser Military Rifle Markings, by Terence W. Lapin, Arlington, VA, Hyrax Publishers, LLC, 2001. 167 pp., illus. 2nd edition. Revised and expanded. Softcover. $22.95

A general guide to reading and understanding the often mystifying markings found on military Mauser rifles. Includes German Regimental markings as well as German police markings and WWII German Mauser subcontractor codes. A handy reference to take to gun shows.

Military Holsters of World War II, by Eugene J. Bender, Rowe Publications, Rochester, NY, 1998. 200 pp., illus. $49.95

A revised edition with a new price guide of the most definitive book on this subject.

Military Remington Rolling Block Rifle, The, by George Layman, Pioneer Press, TN, 1998. 146 pp., illus. Paper covers. $24.95

A standard reference for those with an interest in the Remington rolling block family of firearms.

Mortimer, the Gunmakers, 1753-1923, by H. Lee Munson, Andrew Mowbray Inc., Lincoln, RI, 1992. 320 pp., illus. $65.00

Seen through a single, dominant, English gunmaking dynasty, this fascinating study provides a window into the classical era of firearms artistry.

Mossberg Sporting Firearms: Dates of Manufacture, by D.R. Morse, Phoenix, AZ, Firing Pin Enterprizes, 2003. Softcover. NEW. $6.95

Covers their pistols, revolvers, rifles, shotguns and commemoratives, plus models and serial numbers.

MP38, 40, 40/1 & 41 Submachine Gun, by de Vries & Martens. Propaganda Photo Series, Volume II. Alexandria, VA, Ironside International, 2001. 1st edition. 150 pp., illustrated with 200 high quality b&w photos. Hardcover. $34.95

Covers all essential information on history and development, ammunition and accessories, codes and markings, and contains photos of nearly every model and accessory. Includes a unique selection of original German WWII propaganda photos, most never published before.

Navy Luger, by Joachim Gortz and John Walter, Handgun Press, Glenview, IL, 1988. 128 pp., illus. $24.95

The 9mm Pistole 1904 and the Imperial German Navy. A concise illustrated history.

New World of Russian Small Arms and Ammunition, by Charlie Cutshaw, Paladin Press, Boulder, CO, 1998. 160 pp., illus. $42.95

Detailed descriptions, specifications and first-class illustrations of the AN-94, PSS silent pistol, Bizon SMG, Saifa-12 tactical shotgun, the GP-25 grenade launcher and more cutting edge Russian weapons.

Number 5 Jungle Carbine, by Alan M. Petrillo, Excalibur Publications, Latham, NY, 1994. 32 pp., illus. Paper covers. $7.95

A comprehensive treatment of the rifle that collectors have come to call the "Jungle Carbine"– the Lee-Enfield Number 5, Mark 1.

Observations on Colt's Second Contract, November 2, 1847, by G. Maxwell Longfield and David T. Basnett, Museum Restoration Service, Bloomfield, Ontario, Canada, 1997. 36 pp., illus. Paper covers. $6.95

This study traces the history and the construction of the Second Model Colt Dragoon supplied in 1848 to the U.S. Cavalry.

Official Soviet SVD Manual, The, by Major James F. Gebhardt (Ret.), Paladin Press, Boulder, CO, 1999. 112 pp., illus. Paper covers. $22.00

Operating instructions for the 7.62mm Dragunov, the first Russian rifle developed from scratch specifically for sniping.

Ordnance Tools, Accessories & Appendages of the M1 Rifle, by Billy Pyle. Houston, TX, privately printed, 2002. 2nd edition. 206 pp., illustrated with b&w photos. Softcover $40.00

OSS Special Weapons II, by John Brunner, Williamstown, NJ, Phillips Publications, 2005, 2nd edition. 276pp. profusely illustrated with photos, some in color. Hardcover, New in New DJ. $59.95

P-08 Parabellum Luger Automatic Pistol, The, edited by J. David McFarland, Desert Publications, Cornville, AZ, 1982. 20 pp., illus. Paper covers. $11.95

Covers every facet of the Luger, plus a listing of all known Luger models.

Packing Iron, by Richard C. Rattenbury, Zon International Publishing, Millwood, NY, 1993. 216 pp., illus. $45.00

The best book yet produced on pistol holsters and rifle scabbards. Over 300 variations of holster and scabbards are illustrated in large, clear plates.

Painted Steel, Steel Pots Volume 2, by Chris Armold, Bender Publishing, San Jose, CA, 2001. 384 pp.-1,053 photos, hundreds in color. $57.95

From the author of *Steel Pots: The History of America's Steel Combat Helmets* comes *Painted Steel: Steel Pots, Vol. II.* This companion volume features detailed chapters on painted and unit marked helmets of WWI and WWII, plus a variety of divisional, regimental and subordinate markings. Special full-color plates detail subordinate unit markings such as the tactical markings used by the U.S. 2nd Division in WWI.

Parker Gun Catalog 1900, by Parker Brothers, Davis, IL: Old Reliable Publishing, 1996. Reprint. One of the most attractive and sought-after of the Parker gun catalogs, this one shows the complete Parker line circa 1900. This is the only catalog which pictures EH and NH grades, and is the first to picture $50.00 VH grade. A deluxe reprint, 15pp., illustrated. Stiff Paper Covers. Fine. $10.00

Parker Gun Catalog 1910, by Parker Brothers, Davis, IL: Old Reliable Publishing, 1996. Reprint. One of the most attractive and sought-after of the Parker gun catalogs, this one shows the complete Parker line circa 1910. A deluxe reprint, 20pp., illustrated. Stiff Paper Covers. Fine. $10.00

Parker Gun Catalog 1913 (Flying Ducks), by Parker Brothers, Davis, IL: Old Reliable Publishing, 1996. 36pp., illustrated. Stiff Paper Covers. Fine. $20.00

One of the most attractive and sought-after of the Parker gun catalogs, this one shows the complete Parker line circa 1913. A deluxe reprint, it has the same embossed cover as the original "Flying Ducks" catalog.

Pattern Dates for British Ordnance Small Arms, 1718-1783, by DeWitt Bailey, Thomas Publications, Gettysburg, PA, 1997. 116 pp., illus. Paper covers. $20.00

The weapons discussed in this work are those carried by troops sent to North America between 1737 and 1783, or shipped to them as replacement arms while in America.

Percussion Ammunition Packets 1845-1888 Union, Confederate & European, by John J. Malloy, Dean S. Thomas and Terry A. White with Foreward by Norm Flayderman. Gettysburg, PA, Thomas Publications, 2003. 1st edition. 134 pp., illustrated with color photos. Hardcover. New. $75.00

Finally a means to recognize the untold variety of labeled types of ammunition box labels.

Peters & King, by Thomas D. Schiffer. Krause Publications, Iola, WI 2002. 1st edition. 256 pp., 200+ b&w photos with a 32-page color section. Hardcover. $44.95

Discover the history behind Peters Cartridge and King Powder and see how they shaped the arms industry into what it is today and why their products fetch hundreds, even thousands of dollars at auctions. Current values are provided for their highly collectible product packaging and promotional advertising premiums such as powder kegs, tins, cartridge boxes, and calendars.

Presentation and Commercial Colt Walker Pistols, by Col. Robert D. Whittington III. Hooks, TX, Brownlee Books, 2005. A limited edition of 1,000 copies. Numbered. 21 pp. Paper covers. New. $15.00

A study of events at the Whitneyville Armoury and Samuel Colt's Hartford Factory from 1 June 1847 to 29 November 1848.

Presentation and Commercial Colt Walker Pistols, 2nd Revision, by Col. Robert D. Whittington III. Hooks, TX, Brownlee Books, 2006. A limited edition of 1,000 copies. Numbered. 26 pp. Paper covers. New. $20.00

A study of events at the Whitneyville Armoury and Samuel Colt's Hartford Factory from 1 June 1847 to 29 November 1848. Updated.

Price Guide: Orders and Decorations Germany, 1871-1945, Second Edition, by Klaus Lubbe, Germany, Niemann,2004. 2nd edition. German and English text. 817 pages, over 2,000 photos. Hardcover. NEW. $104.95

It is a reference for prices as well as on the differences between the various orders, decorations, award documents, award cases of issue, and miniatures. No fantasy pieces are included, or projected orders which were never realized.

Proud Promise: French Autoloading Rifles, 1898-1979, by Jean Huon, Collector Grade Publications, Inc., Cobourg, Ont., Canada, 1995. 216 pp., illus. $39.95

The author has finally set the record straight about the importance of French contributions to modern arms design.

Purdey Gun and Rifle Makers: The Definitive History, by Donald Dallas, Quiller Press, London, 2000. 245 pp., illus. Color throughout. A limited edition of 3,000 copies. Signed and numbered. With a PURDEY book plate. $99.95

Queen Anne Pistol, 1660-1780: A History of the Turn-Off Pistol, by John W. Burgoyne, Bloomfield, Ont., Canada, Museum Restoration Service, 2002. 1st edition-Historical Arms New Series No. 1. 120 pp. Pictorial hardcover. $35.00

A detailed, fast moving, thoroughly researched text and almost 200 cross-referenced illustrations.

ARMS LIBRARY

Recreating the 18th Century Powder Horn, by Scott and Cathy Sibley, Texarkana, TX, Scurlock Publishing, 2005. 1st edition. 91 pages. Softcover. NEW. $19.95

Scott and Cathy Sibley demonstrates every detail and secret of recreating an 18th century powder horn. New and experienced horn makers will enjoy this how-to book. Lavishly illustrated wtih full-color photos and step-by-step illustrations.

Red Shines The Sun: A Pictorial History of the Fallschirm-Infantrie, by Eric Queen. San Jose, CA, R. James Bender Publishing, 2003. 1st edition. Hardcover. $69.95

A culmination of 12 years of research, this reference work traces the history of the Army paratroopers of the Fallschirm-Infanterie from their origins in 1937, to the expansion to battalion strength in 1938, then on through operations at Wola Gulowska (Poland) and Moerdijk (Holland). This 240-page comprehensive look at their history is supported by 600 images, many of which are in full color, and nearly 90% are previously unpublished.

Reloading Tools, Sights and Telescopes for Single Shot Rifles, by Gerald O. Kelver, Brighton, CO, 1982. 163 pp., illus. Paper covers. $13.95

A listing of most of the famous makers of reloading tools, sights and telescopes with a brief description of the products they manufactured.

Remington-Lee Rifle, by Eugene F. Myszkowski, Excalibur Publications, Latham, NY, 1995. 100 pp., illus. Paper covers. $22.50

Features detailed descriptions, including serial number ranges, of each model from the first Lee magazine rifle produced for the U.S. Navy to the last Remington-Lee small bore shipped to the Cuban Rural Guard.

Remington 'America's Oldest Gunmaker', The Official Authorized History of the Remington Arms Company, by Roy Marcot. Madison, NC, Remington Arms Company, 1999. 1st edition. 312 pp., with 167 b&w illustrations, plus 291 color plates. $79.95

This is without a doubt the finest history of that firm ever to have been compiled. Based on firsthand research in the Remington company archives, it is extremely well written.

Remington Sporting Firearms: Dates of Manufacture, by D.R. Morse, Phoenix, AZ, Firing Pin Enterprizes, 2003. 43 pp. Softcover. New. $6.95

Covers their pistols, revolvers, rifles, shotguns and commemoratives, plus models and serial numbers.

Remington's Vest Pocket Pistols, by Robert E. Hatfield, Lincoln, RI, Andrew Mowbray, Inc., 2002. 117 pp. Hardcover. $29.95

While Remington Vest Pocket pistols have always been popular with collectors, very little solid information has been available about them. Inside you will find 100+ photographs, serial number data, exploded views of all four Remington Vest Pocket pistol sizes, component parts lists and a guide to disassembly and reassembly. Also includes a discussion of Vest Pocket Wire-Stocked Buggy/Bicycle rifles, plus the documented serial number story.

Revolvers of the British Services 1854-1954, by W.H.J. Chamberlain and A.W.F. Taylerson, Museum Restoration Service, Ottawa, Canada, 1989. 80 pp., illus. $27.50

Covers the types issued among many of the United Kingdom's naval, land or air services.

Rifles of the U.S. Army 1861-1906, by John D. McAulay, Andrew Mowbray, Inc., Lincoln, RI, 2003. 1st edition. Over 40 rifles covered, 278 pp., illus. Hardcover. New. $47.95

This exciting new book by renowned authority John McAulay gives the reader detailed coverage of the issue and actual field service of America's fighting rifles, both in peacetime and in war, including their military service with the infantry, artillery, cavalry and engineers. One feature that all readers will value is the impressive number of historical photos, taken during the Civil War, the Mexican War, the Indian Wars, the Spanish-American War, the Philippine Insurrection and more. Procurement information, issue details and historical background.

Ruger and his Guns, by R.L. Wilson, Book Sales, New York, NY, 2006. 358 pp., illus. $24.95

A history of the man, the company and their firearms.

Running Recon: A photo Jorney with SOG Special Ops Along the Ho Chi Minh Trail, by Frank Grecco. Boulder, CO: Paladin Press, 2006. Softcover. NEW. $50.00

Running Recon is a combination of military memoir and combat photography book. It reflects both the author's experience in Kontum, Vietnam, from April 1969 to April 1970 as part of the top-secret Studies and Observation Group (SOG) and the collective experience of SOG veterans in general.

Russell M. Catron and His Pistols, by Warren H. Buxton, Ucross Books, Los Alamos, NM, 1998. 224 pp., illus. Paper covers. $49.50

An unknown American firearms inventor and manufacturer of the mid-twentieth century. Military, commerical, ammunition.

SAFN-49 and the FAL, by Joe Poyer and Dr. Richard Feirman, North Cape Publications, Tustin, CA, 1998. 160 pp., illus. Paper covers. $14.95

The first complete overview of the SAFN-49 battle rifle, from its pre-WWII beginnings to its military service in countries as diverse as the Belgian Congo and Argentina. The FAL was a "light" version of the SAFN-49 and it became the Free World's most adopted battle rifle.

Sash Hook Smith & Wesson Revolvers, The, by Col. Robert D. Whittington III. & and Kolman A. Gabel, Hooks, TX, Brownlee Books, 2003. A limited edition of 1,000 copies. Numbered. 10 pp. Paper covers. New. $10.00

The true story of the Sash Hook Smith & Wesson Revolvers and how they came to be.

Savage Sporting Firearms: Dates of Manufacture 1907-1997, by D.R. Morse. Phoenix, AZ, Firing Pin Enterprizes, 2003. 22 pp. Softcover. New. $6.95

Covers their pistols, revolvers, rifles, shotguns and commemoratives, plus models and serial numbers.

Scottish Firearms, by Claude Blair and Robert Woosnam-Savage, Museum Restoration Service, Bloomfield, Ont., Canada, 1995. 52 pp., illus. Paper covers. $8.95

This revision of the first book devoted entirely to Scottish firearms is supplemented by a register of surviving Scottish long guns.

Sharps Firearms, by Frank Seller, Denver, CO, 1998. 358 pp., illus. $65.00

Traces the development of Sharps firearms with full range of guns made including all martial variations.

Sight Book; Winchester, Lyman, Marble, and Other Companies, by George Madis, Borwsboro,TX, Art & Reference House, 2005. 1st edition. 183 pages, with over 350 illustrations. Hardcover. NEW. $26.95

Silk and Steel: Women at Arms, by R. L. Wilson, New York, Random House, 2003. 1st edition. 300+ Striking four-color images; 8½" x 11", 320 pgs. Hardcover. New in new dust jacket. (9775). $65.00

Beginning with Artemis and Diana, goddesses of hunting, evolving through modern times, here is the first comprehensive presentation on the subject of women and firearms. No object has had a greater impact on world history over the past 650 years than the firearm, and a surprising number of women have been keen on the subject, as shooters, hunters, collectors, engravers, and even gunmakers.

SKS Carbine, by Steve Kehaya and Joe Poyer, North Cape Publications, Tustin, CA, 1997. 150 pp., illus. Paper covers $16.95

The first comprehensive examination of a major historical firearm used through the Vietnam conflict to the diamond fields of Angola.

SKS Type 45 Carbines, by Duncan Long, Desert Publications, El Dorado, AZ, 1992. 110 pp., illus. Paper covers. $19.95

Covers the history and practical aspects of operating, maintaining and modifying this abundantly available rifle.

Slave Badges and the Slave-Hire System in Charleston, South Carolina, 1783-1865, by Harlan Greene, Harry S. Hutchins Jr., Brian E. Hutchins. Jefferson, NC, McFarland & Company, 2004. 152 pp. Hardcover, NEW. $35.00

Smith & Wesson 1857-1945, by Robert J. Neal and Roy G. Jinks, R&R Books, Livonia, NY, 1996. 434 pp., illus. $50.00

The bible for all existing and aspiring Smith & Wesson collectors.

Smith & Wesson Sporting Firearms: Dates of Manufacture, by D.R. Morse, Phoenix, AZ, Firing Pin Enterprizes, 2003. 76 pp. Softcover. NEW. $6.95

Covers their pistols, revolvers, rifles, shotguns and commemoratives, plus models and serial numbers.

Sniper Variations of the German K98k Rifle, by Richard D. Law, Collector Grade Publications, Ontario, Canada, 1997. 240 pp., illus. $47.50

Volume 2 of "Backbone of the Wehrmacht" the author's in-depth study of the German K98k rifle. This volume concentrates on the telescopic-sighted rifle of choice for most German snipers during WWII.

Southern Derringers of the Mississippi Valley, by Turner Kirkland, Pioneer Press, Tenn., 1971. 80 pp., illus., paper covers. $10.00

A guide for the collector and a much-needed study.

Soviet Russian Tokarev "TT" Pistols and Cartridges 1929-1953, by Fred Datig, Graphic Publishers, Santa Ana, CA, 1993. 168 pp., illus. $39.95

Details of rare arms and their accessories are shown in hundreds of photos. It also contains a complete bibliography and index.

Spencer Repeating Firearms, by Roy M. Marcot, New York, Rowe Publications, 2002. 316 pp.; numerous b&w photos and illustrations. Hardcover. $65.00

Springfield 1903 Rifles, by Lt. Col. William S. Brophy, USAR, Ret., Stackpole Books Inc., Harrisburg, PA, 1985. 608 pp., illus. $75.00

The illustrated, documented story of the design, development, and production of all the models, appendages, and accessories.

SS Headgear, by Kit Wilson. Johnson Reference Books, Fredericksburg, VA. 72 pp., 15 full-color plates and over 70 b&w photos. $16.50

An excellent source of information concerning all types of SS headgear, to include Allgemeine-SS, Waffen-SS, visor caps, helmets, overseas caps, M-43's and miscellaneous headgear. Also includes a guide on the availability and current values of SS headgear. This guide was compiled from auction catalogs, dealer price lists, and input from advanced collectors in the field.

SS Helmets: A Collector's Guide, Vol 1, by Kelly Hicks, Johnson Reference Books, Fredericksburg, VA. 96 pp., illus. $17.50

Deals only with SS helmets and features some very nice color close-up shots of the different SS decals used. Over 85 photographs, 27 in color. The author has documented most of the known types of SS helmets, and describes in detail all of the vital things to look for in determining the originality, style type, and finish.

SS Helmets: A Collector's Guide, Vol 2, by Kelly Hicks. Johnson Reference Books, Fredericksburg, VA. 2000. 128 pp. 107 full-color photos, 14 period photos. $25.00

Volume II contains dozen of highly detailed, full-color photos of rare and original SS and Field Police helmets, featuring both sides as well as interior view. The outstanding decal section offers detailed close-ups of original SS and Police decals and, in conjunction with Volume I, completes the documentation of virtually all types of original decal variations used between 1934 and 1945.

SS Uniforms, Insignia and Accoutrements, by A. Hayes. Schiffer Publications, Atglen, PA. 1996. 248 pp., with over 800 color and b&w photographs. $69.95

This new work explores in detailed color the complex subject of Allgemeine and Waffen-SS uniforms, insignia, and accoutrements. Hundreds of authentic items are extensively photographed in close-up to enable the reader to examine and study.

Sturmgewehr! From Firepower to Striking Power, by Hans-Dieter Handrich. Canada, Collector Grade, 2004. 1st edition. 600pp., 392 illustrations. Hardcover $79.95

Hans-Dieter spent years researching original documentation held in the military archives of Germany and elsewhere to produce the entire technical and tactical history of the design, development and fielding of the world's first mass-produced assault rifle and the revolutionary 7.92x33mm Kurz cartridge.

Sturm Ruger Sporting Firearms: Dates of Manufacture, by D.R. Morse, Phoenix, AZ, Firing Pin Enterprizes, 2003. 22 pp. Softcover. NEW. $6.95

Covers their pistols, revolvers, rifles, shotguns and commemoratives, plus models and serial numbers.

Sumptuous Flaske, by Herbert G. Houze, Andrew Mowbray, Inc., Lincoln, RI, 1989. 158 pp., illus. Softcover. $35.00

Catalog of a recent show at the Buffalo Bill Historical Center bringing together some of the finest European and American powder flasks of the 16th to 19th centuries.

Swedish Mauser Rifles, The, by Steve Kehaya and Joe Poyer, North Cape Publications, Tustin, CA, 1999. 267 pp., illus. Paper covers. $19.95

Every known variation of the Swedish Mauser carbine and rifle is described, all match and target rifles and all sniper versions. Includes serial number and production data.

ARMS LIBRARY

System Lefaucheaux: Continuing the Study of Pinfire Cartridge Arms Including Their Role in the American Civil War, by Chris C. Curtis, Foreword by Norm Flayderman, Armslore Press, 2002. 1st edition. 312 pp., heavily illustrated with b&w photos. Hardcover. New in new dust jacket. $44.95

Thoughts on the Kentucky Rifle in its Golden Age, by Joe K. Kindig, Ill. York, PA, George Shumway Publisher, 2002. Annotated second edition. 561 pp.; Illustrated. This scarce title, long out of print, is once again available. Hardcover. $85.00

The definitive book on the Kentucky Rifle, illustrating 266 of these guns in 856 detailed photographs.

Tin Lids–Canadian Combat Helmets, #2 in "Up Close" Series, by Roger V. Lucy, Ottawa, Ontario, Service Publications, 2000. 2nd edition. 48 pp. Softcover. NEW. $17.95

Toys That Shoot and Other Neat Stuff, by James Dundas, Schiffer Books, Atglen, PA, 1999. 112 pp., illus. Paper covers. $24.95

Shooting toys from the twentieth century, especially 1920s to 1960s, in over 420 color photographs of BB guns, cap shooters, marble shooters, squirt guns and more. Complete with a price guide.

Trade Guns of the Hudson's Bay Company 1670-1970, Historical Arms New Series No. 2, by S. James Gooding, Bloomfield, Ont. Canada, Museum Restoration Service, 2003. 1st edition. 158 pp., thoroughly researched text. Includes bibliographical references. Pictorial hardcover. NEW. $35.00

Trapdoor Springfield, by M.D. Waite and B.D. Ernst, The Gun Room Press, Highland Park, NJ, 1983. 250 pp., illus. $39.95

The first comprehensive book on the famous standard military rifle of the 1873-92 period.

Treasures of the Moscow Kremlin: Arsenal of the Russian Tsars, A Royal Armories and the Moscow Kremlin exhibition, HM Tower of London 13, June 1998 to 11 September, 1998, BAS Printers, Over Wallop, Hampshire, England. XXII plus 192 pp. over 180 color illustrations. Text in English and Russian. $65.00

For this exhibition catalog, each of the 94 objects on display are photographed and described in detail to provide the most informative record of this important exhibition.

U.S. Army Headgear 1812-1872, by John P. Langellier and C. Paul Loane. Atglen, PA, Schiffer Publications, 2002. 167 pp., with over 350 color and b&w photos. Hardcover. $69.95

This profusely illustrated volume represents more than three decades of research in public and private collections by military historian John P. Langellier and Civil War authority C. Paul Loane.

U.S. Army Rangers & Special Forces of World War II Their War in Photographs, by Robert Todd Ross, Atglen, PA, Schiffer Publications, 2002. 216 pp., over 250 b&w and color photographs. Hardcover. $59.95

Never before has such an expansive view of WWII elite forces been offered in one volume. An extensive search of public and private archives unearthed an astonishing number of rare and never before seen images, including color. Most notable are the nearly 20 exemplary photographs of Lieutenant Colonel William O. Darby's Ranger Force in Italy, taken by Robert Capa, considered by many to be the greatest combat photographer of all time.

U.S. Guns of World War II, by Paul Davies, Gettysburg, PA, Thomas Publications, 2004. 1st edition. A record of army ordnance research and the development of small arms. Hundreds of photos. 144pp, Softcover. NEW. $17.95

U.S. Handguns of World War II: The Secondary Pistols and Revolvers, by Charles W. Pate, Andrew Mowbray, Inc., Lincoln, RI, 1998. 515 pp., illus. $39.00

This indispensable new book covers all of the American military handguns of WWII except for the M1911A1 Colt automatic.

U.S. Martial Single Shot Pistols, by Daniel D. Hartzler and James B. Whisker, Old Bedford Village Press, Bedford, PA, 1998. 128 pp., illus. $45.00

A photographic chronicle of military and semi-martial pistols supplied to the U.S. Government and the several States.

U.S. Military Arms Dates of Manufacture from 1795, by George Madis, Dallas, TX, 1995. 64 pp. Softcover. $9.95

Lists all U.S. military arms of collector interest alphabetically, covering about 250 models.

U.S. Naval Handguns, 1808-1911, by Fredrick R. Winter, Andrew Mowbray Publishers, Lincoln, RI, 1990. 128 pp., illus. $26.00

The story of U.S. Naval handguns spans an entire century–included are sections on each of the important naval handguns within the period.

U.S. Silent Service-Dolphins & Combat Insignia 1924-1945, by David Jones. Bender Publishing, San Jose, CA, 2001. 224 pp., 532 photos (most in full color). $39.95

This beautiful full-color book chronicles, with period letters and sketches, the developmental history of U.S. submarine insignia prior to 1945. It also contains many rare and never before published photographs, plus interviews with WWII submarine veterans, from enlisted men to famous skippers. All known contractors are covered plus embroidered versions, mess dress variations, the Roll of Honor, submarine combat insignia, battleflags, launch memorabilia and related submarine collectibles (postal covers, match book covers, jewelry, posters, advertising art, postcards).

Uniform and Dress Army and Navy of the Confederate States of America (Official Regulations), by Confederate States of America, Ray Riling Arms Books, Philadelphia, PA, 1960. $20.00

A portfolio containing a complete set of nine color plates especially prepared for framing, reproduced in exactly 200 sets from the very rare Richmond, VA., 1861 regulations.

Uniforms & Equipment of the Austro-Hungarian Army in World War One, by Spencer A. Coil, Atglen, PA, Schiffer Publications, 2003. 1st edition. 352 pp., with over 550 b&w and color photographs. Hardcover. New in new dust jacket. $69.95

Uniforms and Insignia of the Cossacks in the German Wehrmacht in World War II, by Peter Schuster and Harald Tiede, Atglen, PA, Schiffer Publications, 2003. 1st edition. 160 pp., illustrated with over 420 b&w and color photographs. Hardcover. New in new dust jacket. $49.95

Uniforms & Equipment of the Imperial German Army 1900-1918: A Study in Period Photographs, by Charles Woolley, Schiffer Publications, Atglen, PA, 2000. 375 pp., over 500 b&w photographs and 50 color drawings. Fully illustrated. $69.95

Features formal studio portraits of pre-war dress and wartime uniforms of all arms. Includes a 60-page full-color uniform section reproduced from rare 1914 plates.

Uniforms of the Third Reich: A Study in Photographs, by Maguire Hayes, Schiffer Publications, Atglen, PA, 1997. 200 pp., with over 400 color photographs. $69.95

This new book takes a close look at a variety of authentic WWII era German uniforms including examples from the Army, Luftwaffe, Kriegsmarine, Waffen-SS, Allgemeine-SS, Hitler youth and political leaders. Various accoutrements worn with the uniforms are also included to aid the collector.

Uniforms of the United States Army, 1774-1889, by Henry Alexander Ogden, Dover Publishing, Mineola, NY. 1998. 48 pp. of text plus 44 color plates. Softcover. $9.95

A republication of the work published by the quarter-master general, United States army in 1890. A striking collection of lithographs and a marvelous archive of military, social, and costume history portraying the gamut of U.S. Army uniforms from fatigues to full dress, between 1774 and 1889.

Uniforms of the Waffen-SS; Black Service Uniform-LAH Guard Uniform-SS Earth-Grey Service Uniform-Model 1936 Field Service Uniform-1939-1940-1941 Volume 1, by Michael D. Beaver, Schiffer Publications, Atglen, PA, 2002. 272 pp., with 500 color, and b&w photos. $79.95

This spectacular work is a heavily documented record of all major clothing articles of the Waffen-SS. Hundreds of unpublished photographs were used in production. This book is indispensable and an absolute must-have for any serious historian of WWII German uniforms.

Uniforms of the Waffen-SS; Sports and Drill Uniforms-Black Panzer Uniform-Camouflage-Concentration Camp Personnel-SD-SS Female Auxiliaries, Volume 3, by Michael D. Beaver, Schiffer Publications, Atglen, PA, 2002. 272 pp., with 500 color, and b&w photos. $79.95

Uniforms of the Waffen-SS; 1942-1943-1944-1945-Ski Uniforms-Overcoats-White Service Uniforms-Tropical Clothing, Volume 2, by Michael D. Beaver, Schiffer Publications, Atglen, PA, 2002. 272 pp., with 500 color, and b&w photos. $79.95

Uniforms, Organization, and History of the German Police, Volume I, by John R. Angolia and Hugh Page Taylor, San Jose, CA, R. James Bender Publishing, 2004. 704 pp. illustrated with b&w and color photos. Hardcover. NEW. $59.95

United States Marine Corps Uniforms, Insignia, and Personal Items of World War II, by Harlan Glenn Atglen, PA: Schiffer Publications, 2005. 1st edition. 272pp. Hardcover. NEW $79.95

Covering in detail the combat and dress uniforms of the United States Marine in World War II, this new volume is destined to become the World War II Marine Corps collector's reference! Shown in detail are the herringbone utilities that Marines wore from Guadalcanal to Okinawa, as well as Summer Service, Winter Service and Dress (Blues) uniforms.

United States Martial Flintlocks, by Robert M. Reilly, Mowbray Publishing Co., Lincoln, RI, 1997. 264 pp., illus. $40.00

A comprehensive history of American flintlock longarms and handguns (mostly military) c. 1775 to c. 1840.

United States Submachine Guns: From the American 180 to the ZX-7, by Frank Iannamico, Harmony, ME, Moose Lake Publishing, 2004. 1st edition. This profusely illustrated new book covers the research and development of the submachine gun in the U.S. from World War I to the present. to1943. Many photos and charts, nearly 500 pages! Soft cover. NEW. $29.95

Variations of Colt's New Model Police and Pocket Breech Loading Pistols, by John D. Breslin, William Q. Pirie and David E. Price, Lincoln, RI, Andrew Mowbray Publishers, 2002. 1st edition. 158 pp., heavily illustrated with over 160 photographs and superb technical detailed drawings and diagrams. Pictorial hardcover. $37.95

A type-by-type guide to what collectors call small frame conversions.

Vietnam Order of Battle, by Shelby L. Stanton, William C. Westmoreland. Mechanicsburg, PA, Stackpole Books, 2003. 1st edition. 416 pp., 32 in full color, 101 pp. halftones. Hardcover. New in new dust jacket. $69.95

Visor Hats of the United States Armed Forces 1930-1950, by Joe Tonelli, Atglen, PA, Schiffer Publications, 2003. 1st edition. Hardcover. New in new dust jacket. $79.95

W.F. Cody Buffalo Bill Collector's Guide with Values, The, by James W. Wojtowicz, Collector Books, Paducah, KY, 1998. 271 pp., illus. $24.95

A profusion of colorful collectibles including lithographs, programs, photographs, books, medals, sheet music, guns, etc. and today's values.

Walther: A German Legend, by Manfred Kersten, Safari Press, Inc., Huntington Beach, CA, 2000. 400 pp., illus. $85.00

This comprehensive book covers, in rich detail, all aspects of the company and its guns, including an illustrious and rich history, the WWII years, all the pistols (models 1 through 9), the P-38, P-88, the long guns, 22 rifles, centerfires, Wehrmacht guns, and even a gun that could shoot around a corner.

Walther P-38 Pistol, by Maj. George Nonte, Desert Publications, Cornville, AZ, 1982. 100 pp., illus. Paper covers. $12.95

Complete volume on one of the most famous handguns to come out of WWII. All models covered.

Walther Pistols: Models 1 Through P99, Factory Variations and Copies, by Dieter H. Marschall, Ucross Books, Los Alamos, NM. 2000. 140 pp., with 140 b&w illustrations, index. Paper covers. $19.95

This is the English translation, revised and updated, of the highly successful and widely acclaimed German language edition. This book provides the collector with a reference guide and overview of the entire line of the Walther military, police, and self-defense pistols from the very first to the very latest. Models 1-9, PP, PPK, MP, AP, HP, P.38, P1, P4, P38K, P5, P88, P99 and the Manurhin models. Variations, where issued, serial ranges, calibers, marks, proofs, logos, and design aspects in an astonishing quantity and variety are crammed into this very well researched and highly regarded work.

Walther Models PP & PPK, 1929-1945 – Volume 1, by James L. Rankin, Coral Gables, FL, 1974. 142 pp., illus. $40.00

Complete coverage on the subject as to finish, proofmarks and Nazi Party inscriptions.

Walther Volume II, Engraved, Presentation and Standard Models, by James L. Rankin, J.L. Rankin, Coral Gables, FL, 1977. 112 pp., illus. $40.00

The new Walther book on embellished versions and standard models. Has 88 photographs, including many color plates.

Walther, Volume III, 1908-1980, by James L. Rankin, Coral Gables, FL, 1981. 226 pp., illus. $40.00
Covers all models of Walther handguns from 1908 to date, includes holsters, grips and magazines.

Winchester an American Legend, by R.L. Wilson, New York, Book Sales, 2004. Reprint. Hardcover. New in new dust jacket. $24.95

Winchester Bolt Action Military & Sporting Rifles 1877 to 1937, by Herbert G. Houze, Andrew Mowbray Publishing, Lincoln, RI, 1998. 295 pp., illus. $45.00
Winchester was the first American arms maker to commercially manufacture a bolt action repeating rifle, and this book tells the exciting story of these Winchester bolt actions.

Winchester Book, by George Madis, David Madis Gun Book Distributor, Dallas, TX, 2000. 650 pp., illus. $54.50
A new, revised 25th anniversary edition of this classic book on Winchester firearms. Complete serial ranges have been added.

Winchester Dates of Manufacture 1849-1984, by George Madis, Art & Reference House, Brownsboro, TX, 1984. 59 pp. $8.50
A most useful work, compiled from records of the Winchester factory.

Winchester Engraving, by R.L. Wilson, Beinfeld Books, Springs, CA, 1989. 500 pp., illus. $185.00
A classic reference work of value to all arms collectors.

Winchester Handbook, The, by George Madis, Art & Reference House, Lancaster, TX, 1982. 287 pp., illus. $26.95
The complete line of Winchester guns, with dates of manufacture, serial numbers, etc.

Winchester Lever Action Repeating Firearms, Vol. 1, The Models of 1866, 1873 and 1876, by Arthur Pirkle, North Cape Publications, Tustin, CA, 1995. 112 pp., illus. Paper covers. $19.95
Complete, part-by-part description, including dimensions, finishes, markings and variations throughout the production run of these fine, collectible guns.

Winchester Lever Action Repeating Rifles, Vol. 2, The Models of 1886 and 1892, by Arthur Pirkle, North Cape Publications, Tustin, CA, 1996. 150 pp., illus. Paper covers. $19.95
Describes each model on a part-by-part basis by serial number range complete with finishes, markings and changes.

Winchester Lever Action Repeating Rifles, Vol. 3, The Model of 1894, by Arthur Pirkle, North Cape Publications, Tustin, CA, 1998. 150 pp., illus. Paper covers. $19.95
The first book ever to provide a detailed description of the Model 1894 rifle and carbine.

Winchester Lever Legacy, The, by Clyde "Snooky" Williamson, Buffalo Press, Zachary, LA, 1988. 664 pp., illus. $75.00
A book on reloading for the different calibers of the Winchester lever action rifle.

Winchester Model 1876 "Centennial" Rifle, The, by Herbert G. Houze. Lincoln, RI, Andrew Mowbray, Inc., 2001. Illustrated with over 180 b&w photographs. 192 pp. Hardcover. $45.00
The first authoritative study of the Winchester Model 1876 written using the company's own records. This book dispels the myth that the Model 1876 was merely a larger version of the Winchester company's famous Model 1873 and instead traces its true origins to designs developed immediately after the American Civil War. For Winchester collectors, and those interested in the mechanics of the 19th-century arms industry, this book provides a wealth of previously unpublished information.

Winchester Pocket Guide: Identification & Pricing for 50 Collectible Rifles and Shotguns, by Ned Schwing, Iola, WI, Krause Publications, 2004. 1st edition. 224 pp., illus. Softcover. NEW. $12.95

Winchester Repeating Arms Company Its History & Development from 1865 to 1981, by Herbert G. Houze, Iola, WI, Krause Publications, 2004. 1st edition. Softcover. NEW. $34.98

Winchester Single-Shot, Volume 1; A History and Analysis, The, by John Campbell, Andrew Mowbray, Inc., Lincoln, RI, 1995. 272 pp., illus. $55.00
Covers every important aspect of this highly-collectible firearm.

Winchester Single-Shot, Volume 2; Old Secrets and New Discoveries, The, by John Campbell, Andrew Mowbray, Inc., Lincoln, RI, 2000. 280 pp., illus. $55.00
An exciting follow-up to the classic first volume.

Winchester Sporting Firearms: Dates of Manufacture, by D.R. Morse, Phoenix, AZ, Firing Pin Enterprizes, 2003. 45 pp. Softcover. NEW. $6.95
Covers their pistols, revolvers, rifles, shotguns and commemoratives, plus models and serial numbers.

Winchester-Lee Rifle, The, by Eugene Myszkowski, Excalibur Publications, Tucson, AZ 2000. 96 pp., illus. Paper covers. $22.95
The development of the Lee Straight Pull, the cartridge and the approval for military use. Covers details of the inventor and memorabilia of Winchester-Lee related material.

World War One Collectors Handbook Volumes 1 and 2, by Paul Schulz, Hayes Otoupalik and Dennis Gordon, Missoula, MT, privately printed, 2002. Two volumes in one edition. 110 pp., loaded with b&w photos. Softcover. NEW. $21.95
Covers, uniforms, insignia, equipment, weapons, souvenirs and miscellaneous. Includes price guide. For all of you Doughboy collectors, this is a must.

World War II German War Booty, A Study in Photographs, by Thomas M. Johnson, Atglen, PA, Schiffer Publications, 2003. 1st edition. 368 pp. Hardcover. New in new dust jacket. $79.95

Worldwide Webley and the Harrington and Richardson Connection, by Stephen Cuthbertson, Ballista Publishing and Distributing Ltd., Gabriola Island, Canada, 1999. 259 pp., illus. $50.00
A masterpiece of scholarship. Over 350 photographs plus 75 original documents, patent drawings, and advertisements accompany the text.

World's Great Handguns: From 1450 to the Present Day, The, by Roger Ford, Secaucus, NJ, Chartwell Books, Inc., 1997. 1st edition. 176 pp. Hardcover. New in new dust jacket. $19.95

EDGED WEAPONS

A Photographic Supplement of Confederate Swords, with addendum, by William A. Albaugh III, Broadfoot Publishing, Wilmington, NC. 1999. 205 plus 54 pp. of the addendum, illustrated with b&w photos. $45.00

Advanced Bowie Techniques: The Finer Points of Fighting with a Large Knife, by Dwight McLemore, Boulder, CO, Paladin Press, 2005. 1st edition. 248 pp. Soft cover. NEW. $35.00
Progressive drills combine techniques into sequences designed to show you how to maximize time, distance and movement to create openings for attacking or defending yourself against one or more opponents.

Advertising Cutlery; With Values, by Richard White, Schiffer Publishing, Ltd., Atglen, PA, 176 pp., with over 400 color photos. Softcover. $29.95
Advertising Cutlery is the first-ever publication to deal exclusively with the subject of promotional knives. Containing over 400 detailed color photographs, this book explores over 100 years of advertisements stamped into the sides of knives.

Allied Military Fighting Knives; And the Men Who Made Them Famous, by Robert A. Buerlein, Paladin Press, Boulder, CO, 2001. 185 pp., illustrated with b&w photos. Softcover. $35.00

American Eagle Pommel Sword: The Early Years 1794-1830, The, by Andrew Mowbray, Manrat Arms Publications, Lincoln, RI, 1997. 244 pp., illus. $65.00
The standard guide to the most popular style of American sword.

American Military Bayonets of the 20th Century, by Gary M. Cunningham, Scott A. Duff Publications, Export, PA, 1997. 116 pp., illus. Paper covers. $21.95
A guide for collectors, including notes on makers, markings, finishes, variations, scabbards, and production data.

American Premium Guide To Knives & Razors; Identification and Value Guide 6th Edition, by Jim Sargent, Iola, WI, Krause Publications, 2004. 504 pp. plus 2,500 b&w photos. Softcover. NEW. $24.99

American Primitive Knives 1770-1870, by G.B. Minnes, Museum Restoration Service, Ottawa, Canada, 1983. 112 pp., illus. $24.95
Origins of the knives, outstanding specimens, structural details, etc.

American Socket Bayonets and Scabbards, by Robert M. Reilly, 2nd printing, Andrew Mowbray, Inc., Lincoln, RI, 1998. 208 pp., illus. $45.00
Full coverage of the socket bayonet in America, from Colonial times through the post-Civil War.

American Sword, 1775-1945, The, by Harold L. Peterson, Ray Riling Arms Books, Co., Phila., PA, 2001. 286 pp. plus 60 pp. of illus. $49.95
1977 reprint of a survey of swords worn by U.S. uniformed forces, plus the rare "American Silver Mounted Swords, (1700-1815)."

American Swords and Sword Makers, by Richard H. Bezdek, Paladin Press, Boulder, CO, 1994. 648 pp., illus. $79.95
The long-awaited definitive reference volume to American swords, sword makers and sword dealers from Colonial times to the present.

American Swords & Sword Makers Volume 2, by Richard H. Bezdek, Paladin Press, Boulder, CO, 1999. 376 pp., illus. $69.95
More than 400 stunning photographs of rare, unusual and one-of-a-kind swords from the top collections in the country.

American Swords from the Philip Medicus Collection, edited by Stuart C. Mowbray, with photographs and an introduction by Norm Flayderman, Andrew Mowbray Publishers, Lincoln, RI, 1998. 272 pp., with 604 swords illustrated. $55.00
Covers all areas of American sword collecting.

Ames Sword Company Catalog: An Exact Reprint of the Original 19th Century Military and Fraternal Sword Catalog, by Stuart C. Mowbray, Lincoln, RI, Andrew Mowbray, Inc., 2003. 1st edition. 200 pp., 541 swords illustrated with original prices and descriptions. Pictorial hardcover. $37.50
The level of detail in these original catalog images will surprise you. Dealers who sold Ames swords used this catalog in their stores, and every feature is clearly shown. Reproduced directly from the incredibly rare originals, military, fraternal and more! Shows the whole Ames line, including swords from the Civil War and even earlier. Lots of related military items like belts, bayonets, etc.

Ames Sword Company, 1829-1935, by John D. Hamilton, Andrew Mowbray Publisher, Lincoln, RI, 1995. 255 pp., illus. $45.00
An exhaustively researched and comprehensive history of America's foremost sword manufacturer and arms supplier during the Civil War.

Antique American Switchblades; Identification & Value Guide, by Mark Erickson, Iola, WI, Krause Publications, 2004. 1st edition. Softcover. NEW. $19.95

Antlers & Iron II, by Krause Publications, Iola, WI, 1999. 40 pp., illustrated with 100 photos. Paper cover. $12.00
Lays out actual plans so you can build your mountain man folding knife using ordinary hand tools. Step-by-step instructions, with photos, design, antler slotting and springs.

Art of Throwing Weapons, by James W. Madden, Paladin Press, Boulder, CO, 1993. 102 pp., illus. $14.00
This comprehensive manual covers everything from the history and development of the five most common throwing weapons—spears, knives, tomahawks, shurikens and boomerangs—to their selection or manufacture, grip, distances, throwing motions and advanced combat methods.

Arte of Defence an Introduction to the Use of the Rapier, by William E. Wilson, Union City, CA, Chivalry Bookshelf, 2002. 1st edition. 167 pp., illustrated with over 300 photographs. Softcover $24.95

Battle Blades: A Professional's Guide to Combat Fighting Knives, by Greg Walker; Foreword by Al Mar, Paladin Press, Boulder, CO, 1993. 168 pp., illus. $40.95
The author evaluates daggers, Bowies, switchblades and utility blades according to their design, performance, reliability and cost.

ARMS LIBRARY

Bayonet in New France, 1665-1760, by Erik Goldstein, Museum Restoration Service, Bloomfield, Ontario, Canada, 1997. 36 pp., illus. Paper covers. $8.95

Traces bayonets from the recently developed plug bayonet, through the regulation socket bayonets, which saw service in North America.

Bayonets from Janzen's Notebook, by Jerry Jansen, Cedar Ridge Publications, Tulsa, OK, 2000. 6th printing. 258 pp., illus. Hardcover. $45.00

This collection of over 1,000 pieces is one of the largest in the U.S.

Bayonets: An Illustrated History, by Martin J. Brayley, Iola, WI, Krause Publications, 2004. 1st edition 256 pp., illus. Softcover. NEW. $29.95

Bayonets, Knives & Scabbards; United States Army Weapons Report 1917 Thru 1945, edited by Frank Trzaska, Knife Books, Deptford, NJ, 1999. 80 pp., illus. Paper covers. $15.95

Follows the United States edged weapons from the close of WWI through the end of WWII. Manufacturers involved, dates, numbers produced, problems encountered, and production data.

Best of U.S. Military Knives, Bayonets & Machetes, by M.H. Cole, edited by Michael W. Silvey. Privately printed, 2002. Hardcover. New in new dust jacket. $59.95

Blade's Guide to Making Knives, by Joe Kertzman, Iola,WI, Krause Publications,2005. 1st edition. Soft cover. $24.89

Techniques for everything from forging steel to making a tomahawk are covered for the diverse population of knife makers. 160 pages, 250 color illustrations demonstrate expert techniques.

Book of the Sword, The, by Richard F. Burton, Dover Publications, New York, NY, 1987. 199 pp., illus. Paper covers. $12.95

Traces the sword's origin from its birth as a charged and sharpened stick through diverse stages of development.

Borders Away, Volume 1: With Steel, by William Gilkerson, Andrew Mowbray, Inc., Lincoln, RI, 1991. 184 pp., illus. $48.00

A comprehensive study of naval armament under fighting sail. This first volume covers axes, pikes and fighting blades in use from 1626 to 1826.

Borders Away, Volume 2: Firearms of the Age of Fighting Sail, by William Gilkerson, Andrew Mowbray, Inc., Lincoln, RI, 1999. 331 pp., illus. with 200 photos, 16-color plates. $65.00

Completing a two-volume set, this impressive work covers the pistols, muskets, combustibles, and small cannons once employed aboard American and European fighting ships.

Bowie and Big-Knife Fighting System, by Dwight C. McLemore, Boulder, CO, Paladin Press, 2003. 240 pp., illus. Softcover. NEW. $35.00

Bowie Knife: Unsheathing an American Legend, by Norm Flayderman, Lincoln, RI, Andrew Mowbray, Inc., 2004. 1st edition. New in new dust jacket. $79.95

Bowie Knives and Bayonets of the Ben Palmer Collection, 2nd Edition, by Ben Palmer, Bill Moran and Jim Phillips. Williamstown, NJ, Phillips Publications, 2002. 224 pp. Illustrated with photos. Hardcover. $49.95

Vastly expanded with more than 300 makers, distributors and dealers added to the makers list; chapter on the Bowie knife photograph with 50 image photo gallery of knife holders from the Mexican War, Civil War, and the West; contains a chapter on Bowie Law; includes several unpublished Bowie documents, including the first account of the Alamo.

Bowies, Big Knives, and the Best of Battle Blades, by Bill Bagwell, Paladin Press, Boulder, CO. 2001. 184 pp., illus. Paper covers. $30.00

This book binds the timeless observations and invaluable advice of master bladesmith and blade combat expert Bill Bagwell under one cover for the first time. Here, you'll find all of Bagwell's classic SOF columns, plus all-new material linking his early insights with his latest conclusions.

British & Commonwealth Bayonets, by Ian D. Skennerton and Robert Richardson, I.D.S.A. Books, Piqua, OH, 1986. 404 pp., 1300 illus. $40.00

Case Cutler Dynasty, The, by Brad Lockwood, Paducah,KY, Collector Books, 2005. 1st edition. 320 pages. Pictorial hardcover. NEW. $19.95

The Case Cutlery Dynasty shows how history becomes mythology over time, money is sometimes thicker than blood, and how a single family from humble beginnings came to dominate an important American industry.

Civil War Cavalry & Artillery Sabers, 1833-1865, by John H. Thillmann, Andrew Mowbray, Inc. Lincoln, RI, 2002. 1st edition. 500+ pp., over 50 color photographs, 1,373 b&w illustrations, coated paper, dust jacket, premium hardcover binding. Hardcover. $79.95

Clandestine Edged Weapons, by William Windrum, Phillips Publications, Williamstown, NJ, 2001. 74 pp., illustrated with b&w photographs. Pictorial softcover. $9.95

Collecting the Edged Weapons of Imperial Germany, by Johnson & Wittmann, Johnson Reference Books, Fredericksburg, VA, 1989. 363 pp., illus. $39.50

An in-depth study of the many ornate military, civilian, and government daggers and swords of the Imperial era.

Collector's Guide to Ames U.S. Contract Military Edged Weapons: 1832-1906, by Ron G. Hickox, Pioneer Press, Union City, IN, 1993. 70 pp., illus. Paper covers. $17.50

While this book deals primarily with edged weapons made by the Ames Manufacturing Company, this guide refers to other manufacturers of United States swords.

Collector's Guide to E.C. Simmons Keen Kutter Cutlery Tools, by Jerry and Elaine Heuring, Paducah, KY, Collector Books, 2000. 1st edition. 192 pp. Softcover. $19.95

Collector's Guide to Switchblade Knives, an Illustrated Historical and Price Reference, by Richard V. Langston, Paladin Press, Boulder, CO. 2001. 224 pp., illus. $49.95

It has been more than 20 years since a major work on switchblades has been published, and never has one showcased as many different types as Rich Langston's new book. It contains a history of the early cutlery industry in America; the evolution of switchblades; and an illustrated reference section that helps collectors and novices alike identify all kinds of knives.

Complete Bladesmith: Forging Your Way to Perfection, by Jim Hrisoulas, Paladin Press, Boulder, CO, 1987. 192 pp., illus. $42.95

Novices as well as the experienced bladesmith will benefit from this definitive guide to smithing world-class blades.

Complete Book of Pocketknife Repair, by Ben Kelly Jr., Krause Publications, Iola, WI, 1995. 130 pp., illus. Paper covers. $10.95

Everything you need to know about repairing knives can be found in this step-by-step guide to knife repair.

Complete Enclyclopedia to Knives, by A.E. Hartink, NJ, Chartwell, 2005. More than 600 superb illustrations. 448 pages. Hardcover. New in new Dust Jacket. $19.95

Confederate Edged Weapons, by W.A. Albaugh, R&R Books, Lavonia, NY, 1994. 198 pp., illus. $40.00

The master reference to edged weapons of the Confederate forces. Features precise line drawings and an extensive text.

Connoisseur's Book of Japanese Swords, The, by Kodauska Nagayama, International, Tokyo, Japan, 1997. 348 pp., illus. $75.00

Translated by Kenji Mishina. A comprehensive guide to the appreciation and appraisal of the blades of Japanese swords. The most informative guide to the blades of Japanese swords ever to appear in English.

Counterfeiting Antique Cutlery, by Gerald Witcher, National Brokerage and Sales, Inc., Brentwood, TN. 1997. 512 pp., illustrated with 1,500-2,000 b&w photographs. $24.95

Cutting Edge: Japanese Swords in the British Museum, by Victor Harris, VT, Tuttle Publishing, 2005. 1st edition. It includes hundreds of photos, with 16 pages in full color. 160 pages, illustrated with 320 b&w photos; 34 color photos; and a 2-page spread of line art. Hardcover. New in new Dust Jacket. $40.00

Daggers and Fighting Knives of the Western World: From the Stone Age til 1900, by Harold Peterson, Dover Publishing, Mineola, NY, 2001. 96 pp., plus 32 pp. of matte stock. Over 100 illustrations. Softcover. $9.95

The only full-scale reference book devoted entirely to the subject of fighting knives, flint knives, daggers of all sorts, scramasaxes, hauswehren, dirks and more. 108 plates, bibliography and Index.

Earliest Commando Knives, by William Windrum. Phillips Publications, Williamstown, NJ. 2001. 74 pp., illus. Softcover. $9.95

Edged Weapon Accouterments of Germany 1800-1945, Kreutz, Hofmann, Johnson, Reddick, Pottsboro, TX, Reddick Enterprises, 2002. 1st edition. Hardcover. NEW. $49.00

Eickhorn Edged Weapons Exports, Vol. 1: Latin America, by A.M. de Quesada Jr. and Ron G. Hicock, Pioneer Press, Union City, TN, 1996. 120 pp., illus. Softcovers. $15.00

This research studies the various Eickhorn edged weapons and accessories manufactured for various countries outside of Germany.

Exploring the Dress Daggers and Swords of the SS, by Thomas T. Wittmann, Johnson Reference Books, Fredericksburg, VA, 2003. 1st edition. 750 pp., illustrated with nearly 1000 photographs, many in color. $150.00

Profusely illustrated with historically important period in-wear photographs. Most artifacts appearing for the first time in reference.

Exploring the Dress Daggers of the German Army, by Thomas T. Wittmann, Johnson Reference Books, Fredericksburg, VA, 1995. 350 pp., illus. $69.95

The first in-depth analysis of the dress daggers worn by the German Army.

Exploring the Dress Daggers of the German Luftwaffe, by Thomas T. Wittmann, Johnson Reference Books, Fredericksburg, VA, 1998. 350 pp., illus. $79.95

Examines the dress daggers and swords of the German Luftwaffe. The designs covered include the long DLV patterns, the Glider Pilot designs of the NSFK and DLV, 1st and 2nd model Luftwaffe patterns, the Luftwaffe sword and the General Officer Degen. Many are pictured for the first time in color.

Exploring The Dress Daggers of the German Navy, by Thomas T. Wittmann, Johnson Reference Books, Fredericksburg, VA, 2000. 560 pp., illus. $89.95

Explores the dress daggers and swords of the Imperial, Weimar, and Third Reich eras, from 1844-1945. Provides detailed information, as well as many superb b&w and color photographs of individual edged weapons. Many are pictured for the first time in full color.

Fighting Tomahawk: An Illustrated Guide to Using the Tomahawk and Long Knife as Weapons, by Dwight C. McLemore, Boulder, CO, Paladin Press, 2004. 1st edition. 296 pp. Softcover. NEW. $39.95

First Commando Knives, by Prof. Kelly Yeaton and Col. Rex Applegate, Phillips Publications, Williamstown, NJ, 1996. 115 pp., illus. Paper covers. $12.95

Here is the full story of the Shanghai origins of the world's best known dagger.

George Schrade and His Accomplishments, by George Schrade, privately printed, 2004. 84 pp. Softcover. NEW. $25.00

German Clamshells and Other Bayonets, by G. Walker and R.J. Weinard, Johnson Reference Books, Fredericksburg, VA, 1994. 157 pp., illus. $22.95

Includes unusual bayonets, many of which are shown for the first time. Current market values are listed.

German Etched Dress Bayonets (Extra-Seitengewehr) 1933-1945, by Wayne H. Techet. Printed by the author, Las Vegas, NV. 2002. Color section and value guide. 262 pp. Limited edition of 1,300 copies. Signed and numbered. $55.00

Photographs of over 200 obverse and reverse motifs. Rare SS and Panzer patterns pictured for the first time, with an extensive chapter on reproductions and Red Flags.

German Swords and Sword Makers: Edged Weapons Makers from the 14th to the 20th Centuries, by Richard H. Bezdek, Paladin Press, Boulder, CO, 2000. 248 pp., illus. Paper covers $40.00

This book contains the most information ever published on German swords and edged weapons makers from the Middle Ages to the present.

Halberd and other European Polearms 1300-1650, by George Snook, Museum Restoration Service, Bloomfield, Ontario, Canada, 1998. 40 pp., illus. Paper covers. $8.95

A comprehensive introduction to the history, use, and identification of the staff weapons of Europe.

Highland Swordsmanship: Techniques of the Scottish Swordmasters, edited by Mark Rector. Chivalry Bookshelf, Union City, CA, 2001. 208 pp., Includes more than 100 illustrative photographs. Softcover $29.95

Rector has done a superb job at bringing together two influential yet completely different 18th century fencing manuals from Scotland. Adding new interpretive plates, Mark offers new insights and clear presentations of many useful techniques.

ARMS LIBRARY

How to Make a Tactical Folder, by Bob Tetzuola, Krause Publications, Iola, WI, 2000. 160 pp., illus. Paper covers. $16.95
Step-by-step instructions and outstanding photography guide the knifemaker from start to finish.

How to Make Folding Knives, by Ron Lake, Frank Centofante and Wayne Clay, Krause Publications, Iola, WI, 1995. 193 pp., illus. Paper covers. $13.95
With step-by-step instructions, learn how to make your own folding knife from three top custom makers.

How to Make Knives, by Richard W. Barney and Robert W. Loveless, Krause Publications, Iola, WI, 1995. 182 pp., illus. Paper covers. $13.95
Complete instructions from two premier knife makers on making high-quality, handmade knives.

How to Make Multi-Blade Folding Knives, by Eugene Shadley & Terry Davis, Krause Publications, Iola, WI, 1997. 192 pp., illus. Paper covers. $19.95
This step-by-step instructional guide teaches knifemakers how to craft these complex folding knives.

KA-BAR: The Next Generation of the Ultimate Fighting Knife, by Greg Walker, Paladin Press, Boulder, CO, 2001. 88 pp., illus. Softcover. $16.00
The KA-BAR fighting/utility knife is the most widely recognized and popular combat knife ever to be produced in the United States. Since its introduction on 23 November 1942, the KA-BAR has performed brilliantly on the battlefields of Europe, the South Pacific, Korea, Southeast Asia, Central America and the Middle East, earning its moniker as the "ultimate fighting knife."

Kalashnikov Bayonets: The Collector's Guide to Bayonets for the AK and its Variations, by Martin D. Ivie, Texas, Diamond Eye Publications, 2002. 1st edition. 220 pp., with over 250 color photos and illustrations. Hardcover. $59.95

Knife and Tomahawk Throwing: The Art of the Experts, by Harry K. McEvoy, Charles E. Tuttle, Rutland, VT, 1989. 150 pp., illus. Softcover. $8.95
The first book to employ side-by-side the fascinating art and science of knives and tomahawks.

Knife in Homespun America and Related Items: Its Construction and Material, as used by Woodsmen, Farmers, Soldiers, Indians and General Population, by Madison Grant, York, PA, privately printed, 1984. 1st edition. 187 pp., profusely illustrated. $45.00
Shows over 300 examples of knives and related items made and used by woodsmen, farmers, soldiers, Indians and the general frontier population.

Knife Talk, The Art and Science of Knifemaking, by Ed Fowler, Krause Publications, Iola, WI, 1998. 158 pp., illus. Paper covers. $14.95
Valuable how-to advice on knife design and construction plus 20 years of memorable articles from the pages of "Blade" Magazine.

Knifemakers of Old San Francisco, by Bernard Levine, 2nd edition, Paladin Press, Boulder, CO, 1998. 150 pp., illus. $39.95
The definitive history of the knives and knife-makers of 19th century San Francisco.

Knives 2007 27th Anniversary Edition, edited by Joe Kertzman, Iola, WI, Krause Publications, 2006. Softcover. NEW. $27.99

Knives of the United States Military-World War II, by Michael W. Silvey, privately printed, Sacramento, CA 1999. 250 pp., illustrated with full color photos. $60.00
240 full-page color plates depicting the knives of WWII displayed against a background of wartime accoutrements and memorabilia. The book focuses on knives and their background.

Knives of the United States Military in Vietnam: 1961-1975, by Michael W. Silvey, privately printed, Sacramento, CA., 139 pp. Hardcover. $45.00
A beautiful color celebration of the most interesting and rarest knives of the Vietnam War, emphasizing SOG knives, Randalls, Gerbers, Eks, and other knives of this era. Shown with these knives are the patches and berets of the elite units who used them.

Master Bladesmith: Advanced Studies in Steel, by Jim Hrisoulas, Paladin Press, Boulder, CO, 1990. 296 pp., illus. Paper Covers $46.00
The author reveals the forging secrets that for centuries have been protected by guilds.

Medieval Swordsmanship, Illustrated Methods and Techniques, by John Clements, Paladin Press, Boulder, CO, 1998. 344 pp., illus. $40.00
The most comprehensive and historically accurate view ever written of the lost fighting arts of Medieval knights.

Military Knife & Bayonet Book, by Homer Brett, World Photo Press, Japan. 2001. 392 pp., illus. $69.95
Professional studio color photographs with more than 1,000 military knives and knife-bayonets illustrated. Both the U.S. and foreign sections are extensive, and includes standard models, prototypes and experimental models. Many of the knives and bayonets photographed have never been previously illustrated in any other book. The U.S. section also includes the latest developments in military Special Operations designs. Written in Japanese and English.

Military Knives: A Reference Book, by Frank Trzaska (editor), Knife Books, Deptford, NJ, 2001. 255 pp., illus. Softcover. $17.95
A collection of your favorite Military Knife articles from the pages of Knife World magazine. 67 articles ranging from the Indian Wars to the present day modern military knives.

Modern Combat Blades, by Duncan Long, Paladin Press, Boulder, CO, 1993. 128 pp., illus. $30.00
Long discusses the pros and cons of bowies, bayonets, commando daggers, kukris, switchblades, butterfly knives, belt-buckle blades and many more.

Modern Fencing: A Comprehensive Manual for the Foil, The Epee, The Sabre, by Clovis Deladrier, Boulder, CO, Paladin Press, 2005. 312pp. Soft cover. NEW. $35.00
Though long out of print, Modern Fencing is still considered one of the best fencing manuals ever written and is often cited by modern fencing masters for its concise lessons and excellent photos.

Modern Swordsman, The, by Fred Hutchinson, Paladin Press, Boulder, CO, 1999. 80 pp., illus. Paper covers. $22.00
Realistic training for serious self-defense.

Moran, 50 Years Anniversary Knives: The Complete History of Their Making, by Dominique Beaucant, Privately Printed, 1998, Signed by the publisher. Soft cover, 108 pp. Soft cover. NEW. $20.00
Includes photos and descriptions of the 50 knives Moran made to celebrate his golden anniversary as a knife maker, and much more.

Officer Swords of the German Navy 1806-1945, by Claus P. Stefanski & Dirk, Schiffer Publications, Atglen, PA, 2002. 1st edition. 176 pp., with over 250 b&w and color photos. Hardcover. $59.95

Official Price Guide to Collector Knives; 14th Edition, by C. Houston Price, New York, House of Collectibles, 2004. 500 photos, 8 pp. in color. 497 pp. Softcover. NEW. $17.95

Official Scout Blades with Prices, by Ed Holbrook, privately printed, 2004. Softcover. NEW. $25.00

On Damascus Steel, by Dr. Leo S. Figiel, Atlantis Arts Press, Atlantis, FL, 1991. 145 pp., illus. $65.00
The historic, technical and artistic aspects of Oriental and mechanical Damascus. Persian and Indian sword blades, from 1600-1800, which have never been published, are illustrated.

Pattern-Welded Blade: Artistry in Iron, The, by Jim Hrisoulas, Paladin Press, Boulder, CO, 1994. 120 pp., illus. Paper Covers $30.00
Reveals the secrets of this craft–from the welding of the starting billet to the final assembly of the complete blade.

Pocket Knives of the United States Military, by Michael W. Silvey, Sacramento, CA, privately printed, 2002. 135 pp. Hardcover. $34.95
This beautiful new full color book is the definitive reference on U.S. military folders. Pocket Knives of the United States Military is organized into the following sections: Introduction, The First Folders, WWI, WWII, and Postwar (which covers knives up through the late 1980s). Essential reading for pocketknife and military knife collectors alike!

Randall Chronicles, The, by Pete Hamilton, privately printed, 2002. 160 pp., profusely illustrated in color. Hardcover in dust jacket. $79.95

Randall Fighting Knives In Wartime: WWII, Korea, and Vietnam, by Robert E. Hunt. Paducah, Ky, Turner Publishing Company, 2002. 192 pp. Hardcover. $44.95
While other books on Randall knives have been published, this new title is the first to focus specifically on Randalls with military ties. There are three main sections, containing more than 80 knives from the WWII, Korea, and Vietnam War periods. Each knife is featured in a high quality, full page, full color photograph, with the opposing page carrying a detailed description of the knife and its history or other related information.

Randall Made Knives, by Robert L. Gaddis, Paladin Press, Boulder, CO, 2000. 292 pp., illus. $59.95
Plots the designs of all 24 of Randall's unique knives. This step-by-step book, seven years in the making, is worth every penny and moment of your time.

Randall Made Knives-A Timeline, The Quick Reference Guide, by Edna and Sheldon Wickersham, privatey printed, 2005. $20.00
This 12" x 25" two-sided laminated reference sheet folds neatly into a back pants pocket, and allows you to date any given Randall knife with a good degree of confidence, wherever you need it. A great resource for all Randall fans! Stiff Paper Covers.

Randall Military Models; Fighters, Bowies and Tang Knives, by Robert E. Hunt, Paducah, Ky, Turner Publishing Company, 2004. 304 pages (including 150 full color photos) Hardcover. $74.95
This new volume provides a vast amount of material, carefully organized & presented to enable the reader to further his own research in the areas most interesting to him.

Randall Fighting Knives: Rare, Unique & Experimental Knives, by Robert E. Hunt, Paducah, Ky, Turner Publishing Company, 2006. 176 pages. Hardcover. $59.95
Many of the knives featured in this new compilation have been held in private collections and museums, and demonstrate the continuous design innovation that remains a hallmark of Randall Made Knives.

Remington Knives–Past & Present, by Ron Stewart and Roy Ritchie, Paducah, KY, Collector Books, 2005. 1st edition. 288 pp. Softcover. NEW. $16.95

Renaissance Swordsmanship, by John Clements, Paladin Press, Boulder, CO, 1997. 152 pp., illus. Paper covers. $25.00
The illustrated use of rapiers and cut-and-thrust swords.

Rice's Trowel Bayonet, reprinted by Ray Riling Arms Books Co., Philadelphia, PA, 1968. 8 pp., illus. Paper covers. $3.00
A facsimile reprint of a rare circular originally published by the U.S. government in 1875 for the information of U.S. troops.

Scottish Dirk, The, by James D. Forman, Museum Restoration Service, Bloomfield, Ont., Canada, 1991. 60 pp., illus. Paper covers. $8.95
More than 100 dirks are illustrated with a text that sets the dirk and Sgian Dubh in their socio-historic content following design changes through more than 300 years of evolution.

Seitengewehr: History of the German Bayonet, 1919-1945, by George T. Wheeler, Johnson Reference Books, Fredericksburg, VA, 2000. 320 pp., illus. $44.95
Provides complete information on Weimar and Third Reich bayonets, as well as their accompanying knots and frogs. Illustrates re-issued German and foreign bayonets utilized by both the Reichswehr and the Wehrmacht, and details the progression of newly manufactured bayonets produced after Hitler's rise to power. Book contains an up-to-date price guide including current valuations.

Silver Mounted Swords: The Lattimer Family Collection; Featuring Silver Hilts Through the Golden Age, by Daniel Hartzler, Rowe Publications, New York, 2000. 300 pp., with over 1,000 illustrations and 1,350 photos. Oversize 9" x12". $75.00
The world's largest Silver Hilt collection.

Small Arms Identification Series, No. 6. British Service Sword & Lance Patterns, by Ian Skennerton, I.D.S.A. Books, Piqua, OH, 1994. 48 pp. $12.50

Small Arms Series, No. 2. The British Spike Bayonet, by Ian Skennerton, I.D.S.A. Books, Piqua, OH, 1982. 32 pp., 30 illus. $9.95

Socket Bayonets of the Great Powers, by Robert W. Shuey, Excalibur Publications, Tucson, AZ, 2000 96 pp., illus. Paper covers $22.95
With 175 illustrations, the author brings together, in one place, many of the standard socket arrangements used by some of the " Great Powers." With an illustrated glossary of blade shape and socket design.

ARMS LIBRARY

Socket in the British Army 1667-1783, The, by Erik Goldstein, Andrew Mowbray, Inc., Lincoln, RI, 2001. 136 pp., illus. $23.00

The spectacle of English "redcoats" on the attack, relentlessly descending upon enemy lines with fixed bayonets, is one of the most chilling images from European history and the American Revolution. Drawing upon new information from archaeological digs and archival records, the author explains how to identify each type of bayonet and shows which bayonets were used where and with which guns.

Switchblade: The Ace of Blades, Revised and Updated, by Ragnar Benson and edited by Michael D. Janich, Boulder, CO, Paladin Press, 2004. 104 pp. Softcover. $16.00

Switchblades of Italy, by Tim Zinser, Dan Fuller and Neal Punchard. Paducah, KY, Turner Publishing, 2002. 128 pp. Hardcover. New in new dust jacket. $44.95

The first ever comprehensive publication about Italian switchblade knives, featuring knives and history from the late 1700s to the 1970s.

Swords and Blades of the American Revolution, by George C. Neumann, Rebel Publishing Co., Inc., Texarkana, TX, 1991. 288 pp., illus. $36.95

The encyclopedia of bladed weapons–swords, bayonets, spontoons, halberds, pikes, knives, daggers, axes–used by both sides, on land and sea, in America's struggle for independence.

Swords and Sabers of the Armory at Springfield, by Burton A. Kellerstedt, New Britain, CT, 1998. 121 pp., illus. Softcover. $29.95

The basic and most important reference for its subject, and one that is unlikely to be surpassed for comprehensiveness and accuracy.

Swords and Sword Makers of England and Scotland, by Richard H. Bezdek, Boulder, CO, Paladin Press, 2003. 1st edition. 424 pp., illus. Hardcover. New in new dust jacket. $69.95

Covers English sword makers from the 14th century and Scottish makers from the 16th century all the way through the renowned Wilkinson Sword Company and other major sword manufacturers of today. Also, the important early English sword- and blade-making communities of Hounslow Heath and Shotley Bridge, and the influential Cutlers Company of London. Includes more than 450 spectacular photographs of English and Scottish swords of every type and era from some of the world's major collections.

Tactical Folding Knife; A Study of the Anatomy and Construction of the Liner-Locked Folder, by Bob Terzuola, Krause Publications, Iola, WI. 2000. 160 pp., 200 b&w photos, illus. Paper covers. $16.00

Step-by-step instructions and outstanding photography guide the knifemaker from start to finish. This book details everything from the basic definition of a tactical folder to the final polishing as the knife is finished.

Tactical Knives, by Dietmar Pohl, Iola, WI, Krause Publications, 2003. 191 Pages, illustrated with 170 color photos. Softcover. $24.95

Dozens of knife styles are identified and showcased, including survival knives, multi-tool, tantos, Bowie, machetes, and other trench, commando, boot, and neck knives. Special attention is given to knives that served troops in WWII and Vietnam, as well as those carried by today's Special Forces.

Travels for Daggers, Historic Edged Weaponry, by Eiler R. Cook, Hendersonville, NC, 2004. 1st edition. Hardcover. 288 illustrations $50.00

An indispensable guide for all collectors, historians, military members, travelers, and the intellectually curious interested in the edged weaponry of the world.

U.S. M-3 Trench Knife of World War Two, The, by Vincent J. Coniglio and Robert S. Laden. Matamoras, PA, privately printed, 2003. 2nd printing. Softcover. NEW. $18.00

U.S. Military Knives, Bayonets and Machetes Price Guide, 5th Edition, by Frank Trzaska (editor), Knife Books, Deptford, NJ, 2006. 80 pp., illus. Softcover. $9.95

This volume follows in the tradition of the previous three versions of using major works on the subject as a reference to keep the price low to you.

U.S. Naval Officers; Their Swords and Dirks Featuring the Collection of the United States Naval Academy Museum, by Peter Tuite, Lincoln, RI, Andrew Mowbray, Inc., 2005. 1st edition. 240 pp., illustrated with over 500 color photos. Pictorial hardcover. NEW. $75.00

Wayne Goddards $50 Knife Shop: Getting Started Without Investing a Fortune, by Wayne Goddard, Krause Publications, Iola, WI, 2006. 160 pp., illus. Softcover. $19.95

This book expands on information from Goddard's popular column in *Blade* magazine to show knifemakers of all skill levels how to create helpful gadgets and supply their shop on a shoestring. The easiest guide to making knives is Wayne Goddard's $50 Knife Shop, Revised. 200+ color photos demonstrate basic knife making techniques.

Wittmann German Dagger Price Guide for 2004, The, by David Hohaus and Thomas Wittmann, Moorestown, NJ, 2004. 1st edition. Stiff paper covers. NEW. $11.95

Wonder of Knifemaking, by Wayne Goddard, Krause Publications, Iola, WI. 2000. 160 pp., illustrated with 150 b&w photos and 16-page color section. Softcover. $19.95

Master bladesmith Wayne Goddard draws on his decades of experience to answer questions of knifemakers at all levels. As a columnist for *Blade* magazine, Goddard has been answering real questions from real knifemakers for the past eight years. Now, all the details are compiled in one place as a handy reference for every knifemaker, amateur or professional.

GENERAL

331+ Essential Tips and Tricks; A How-To Guide for the Gun Collector, by Stuart Mowbray, Lincoln, RI, 2006. 1st edition, photographs. Full color, 272 pp., 357 photographs. Soft cover. NEW. $35.99

Everything from gun photography to detecting refinishes can be found in this comprehensive new reference book.

A Rifleman Went to War, by H. W. McBride, Lancer Militaria, Mt. Ida, AR, 1987. 398 pp., illus. $29.95

The classic account of practical marksmanship on the battlefields of WWI.

Action Shooting: Cowboy Style, by John Taffin, Krause Publications, Iola, WI, 1999. 320 pp., illus. $39.95

Details on the guns and ammunition. Explanations of the rules used for many events.

Advanced Muzzleloader's Guide, by Toby Bridges, Stoeger Publishing Co., So. Hackensack, NJ, 1985. 256 pp., illus. Paper covers. $14.95

The complete guide to muzzle-loading rifles, pistols and shotguns–flintlock and percussion.

Aids to Musketry for Officers & NCOs, by Capt. B.J. Friend, Excalibur Publications, Latham, NY, 1996. 40 pp., illus. Paper covers. $7.95

A facsimile edition of a pre-WWI British manual filled with useful information for training the common soldier.

Airgun Odyssey, by Steve Hanson, Manchester, CT, Precision Shooting, Inc., 2004. 1st edition. 175 pp. Pictorial softcover. $27.95

America's Great Gunmakers, by Wayne van Zwoll, Stoeger Publishing Co., So. Hackensack, NJ, 1992. 288 pp., illus. Paper covers. $16.95

This book traces in great detail the evolution of guns and ammunition in America and the men who formed the companies that produced them.

American Air Rifles, by James E. House, Krause Publications, Iola, WI, 2002. 1st edition. 208 pp., with 198 b&w photos. Softcover. $22.95

Air rifle ballistics, sights, pellets, games, and hunting caliber recommendations are thoroughly explained to help shooters get the most out of their American air rifles. Evaluation of more than a dozen American-made and American-imported air rifle models.

American and Imported Arms, Ammunition and Shooting Accessories, Catalog No. 18 of the Shooter's Bible, Stoeger, Inc., reprinted by Fayette Arsenal, Fayetteville, NC, 1988. 142 pp., illus. Paper covers. $10.95

A facsimile reprint of the 1932 Stoeger's Shooter's Bible.

American B.B. Gun: A Collector's Guide, by Arni T. Dunathan. A.S. Barnes and Co., Inc., South Brunswick, 2001. 154 pp., illustrated with nearly 200 photographs, drawings and detailed diagrams. Hardcover. $35.00

Annie Oakley of the Wild West, by Walter Havighurst, New York, Castle Books, 2000. 246 pp. Hardcover. New in new dust jacket. $10.00

Antique Guns; The Collector's Guide, by Steve Carpenteri, Accokeek, MD: Stoeger Publications, 2005. Revised edition. 260 pages, illus. plus a 32 page color section. Soft cover. New. $22.95

Covers a vast spectrum of pre-1900 firearms: those manufactured by U.S. gun makers as well as Canadian, French, German, Belgian, Spanish and other foreign firms.

Armed Response, by Massad Ayoob, and David Kenik, NY, Merril Press, 2005. These are valuable real-life lessons about preparing to face a lethal threat, winning a gunfight, and surviving the ensuing court battle that can not be found outside of expensive tactical schools. 179 pages, with b&w photos. Foreword by Massad Ayoob. Soft cover. NEW. $19.95

Arming & Equipping the United States Cavalry 1865-1902, by Dusan Farrington, Lincoln, RI: Andrew Mowbray, Inc., 2005. 1st edition. $68.95

775 photos!!! Simply packed with serial numbers, issue information, reports from the field and more! Meticulously researched and absolutely up-to-date. A complete reference to all the arms and accoutrements. And at a bargain price to boot! Hardcover. New in new dust jacket. $68.95

Arming the Glorious Cause: Weapons of the Second War for Independence, by James B. Whisker, Daniel D. Hartzler and Larry W. Yantz, R & R Books, Livonia, NY, 1998. 175 pp., illus. $45.00

A photographic study of Confederate weapons.

Arms & Armor in the Art Institute of Chicago, by Walter J. Karcheski Jr., Bulfinch Press, Boston, MA, 1995. 128 pp., illus. $35.00

Now, for the first time, the Art Institute of Chicago's arms and armor collection is presented in the visual delight of 103 color illustrations.

Arms for the Nation: Springfield Longarms, edited by David C. Clark, Scott A. Duff, Export, PA, 1994. 73 pp., illus. Paper covers. $9.95

A brief history of the Springfield Armory and the arms made there.

Arrowmaker Frontier Series Volume 1, by Roy Chandler, Jacksonville, NC, Ron Brigade Armory, 2000. 390 pp. Hardcover. New in new dust jacket. $38.95

Arsenal of Freedom, The Springfield Armory, 1890-1948: A Year-by-Year Account Drawn from Official Records, compiled and edited by Lt. Col. William S. Brophy, USAR Ret., Andrew Mowbray, Inc., Lincoln, RI, 1991. 400 pp., illus. Softcover. $29.95

A "must buy" for all students of American military weapons, equipment and accoutrements.

Art of American Arms Makers Marketing Guns, Ammunition, and Western Adventure During the Golden Age of Illustration, by Richard C., Rattenbury, Oklahoma City, OK, National Cowboy Museum, 2004. 132 pp. of color photos. Softcover. NEW. $29.95

Art of American Game Calls, by Russell E. Lewis, Paducah, KY, Collector Books, 2005. 1st edition. 176 pp. Pictorial hardcover. NEW. $24.95

Art of Blacksmithing, by Alex W. Bealer, New York, Book Sales, 1996. Revised edition. 440 pp. Hardcover. New in new dust jacket. $10.00

Art of Remington Arms, Sporting Classics, 2004, by Tom Davis. 1st edition. Hardcover. NEW. $60.00

Battle of the Bulge: Hitler's Alternate Scenarios, by Peter Tsouras, Mechanicsburg, PA, Stackpole Books, 2004. 1st edition. 256 pp., 24 b&w photos, 10 maps. Hardcover. NEW. $34.95

Belgian Rattlesnake: The Lewis Automatic Machine Gun, The, by William M. Easterly, Collector Grade Publications, Inc., Cobourg, Ont. Canada, 1998. 542 pp., illus. $79.95

A social and technical biography of the Lewis automatic machine gun and its inventors.

Benchrest Shooting Primer, The, edited by Dave Brennan, Precision Shooting, Inc., Manchester, CT, 2000. 2nd edition. 420 pp., illustrated with b&w photographs, drawings and detailed diagrams. Pictorial softcover. $24.95

The very best articles on shooting and reloading for the most challenging of all the rifle accuracy disciplines…benchrest shooting.

Black Rifle Frontier Series Volume 2, The, by Roy Chandler, Jacksonville, NC, Iron Brigade Armory, 2002. 226 pp. Hardcover. New in new dust jacket. $42.95

In 1760, inexperienced Jack Elan settles in Sherman's Valley, suffers tragedy, is captured by hostiles, escapes, and fights on. This is the "2nd" book in the Frontier Series.

ARMS LIBRARY

Blue Book of Airguns 6th Edition, by Robert Beeman and John Allen, Minneapolis, MN, Blue Book Publications, Inc., 2007. Softcover. NEW. $29.95

Blue Book of Gun Values, 28th Edition (2007 Edition), by S.P. Fjestad, Minneapolis, MN, Blue Book Publications, Inc., 2080 pp., illus. Paper covers. $39.95

Blue Book of Modern Black Powder Values, 4th Edition, by Dennis Adler, John Allen, Minneapolis, MN, Blue Book Publications, Inc., 2004. Softcover. NEW. $24.95

Bodyguard Manual, by Leroy Thompson, Mechanicsburg,PA. Greehnill Books, 2005. 208 pages, 16 pages of plates. Soft cover. NEW. $23.95
Bodyguard Manual details the steps a protective team takes to prevent attack as well as the tactics employed when it is necessary to counter one.

British Small Arms of World War II, by Ian D. Skennerton, Arms & Militaria Press, Australia, 1988. 110 pp., 37 illus. $25.00

C Stories, by Jeff Cooper, Sycamore Island Books, 2005. 1st edition. Quite simply, CStories is Jeff Cooper at his best. illus., 316 pp. Hardcover. New in new dust jacket. $49.95

Carbine and Shotgun Speed Shooting: How to Hit Hard and Fast in Combat, by Steve Moses. Paladin Press, Boulder, CO. 2002. 96 pp., illus. Softcover $18.00
In this groundbreaking book, he breaks down the mechanics of speed shooting these weapons, from stance and grip to sighting, trigger control and more, presenting them in a concise and easily understood manner.

Cavalry Raids of the Civil War, by Col. Robert W. Black, Mechanicsburg, PA, Stackpole Books, 2004. 1st edition. 288 pp., 30 b&w drawings. Softcover. NEW. $17.95

CO2 Pistols and Rifles, by James E. House, Iola, WI, Krause Publications, 2004. 1st edition 240 pp., with 198 b&w photos. Softcover. NEW. $24.95

Combatives FM-3-25.150, by U.S. Army, Boulder, CO, Paladin Press, 2004. Photos, illus., 272 pp. Softcover. NEW. $19.95
This exact reprint of the U.S. Army's most current field manual on hand-to-hand combat (FM 3-25.150) reflects the first major revision to the Army's close-quarters combat program in a decade. This field manual shows them how.

Complete .50-caliber Sniper Course, The, by Dean Michaelis, Paladin Press, Boulder, CO, 2000. 576 pp., illus.. $60.00
The history from German Mauser T-Gewehr of WWI to the Soviet PTRD and beyond. Includes the author's Program of Instruction for Special Operations Hard-Target Interdiction Course.

Complete Guide to Game Care and Cookery, 4th Edition, The, by Sam Fadala, Krause Publications, Iola, WI, 2003. 320 pp., illus. Paper covers. $21.95
Over 500 photos illustrating the care of wild game in the field and at home with a separate recipe section providing over 400 tested recipes.

Concealed Handgun Manual, 4th Edition, The, by Chris Bird, San Antonio, TX, Privateer Publications, 2004. 332 pp., illus. Softcover, NEW. $21.95

Cowboys & the Trappings of the Old West, by William Manns & Elizabeth Clair Flood, Santa Fe, NM, ZON International Publishing Company, 1997. 224 pp., 550 colorful photos. Foreword by Roy Rogers. Hardcover. $45.00
Big & beautiful book covering: Hats, boots, spurs, chaps, guns, holsters, saddles and more. It's really a pictorial cele bration of the old time buckaroo. This exceptional book presents all the accoutrements of the cowboy life in a comprehensive tribute to the makers. The history of the craftsmen and the evolution of the gear are lavishly illustrated.

Cowgirls, Revised and Expanded 2nd Edition Early Images and Collectibles Price Guide, by Judy Crandall, Atglen, PA, Schiffer Publications, 2005. 2nd edition. Soft cover. NEW. $24.95
The First Ladies from the Great American West live again in this comprehensive pictorial chronicle.

Cowgirls: Women of the Wild West, by Elizabeth Clair Flood and William Maims, edited by Helene Helene, Santa Fe, NM, ZON International Publishing Company, 2000. 1st edition. Hardcover. New in new dust jacket. $45.00

Custom Firearms Engraving, by Tom Turpin, Krause Publications, Iola, WI, 1999. 208 pp., illus. $49.95
Provides a broad and comprehensive look at the world of firearms engraving. The exquisite styles of more than 75 master engravers are shown on beautiful examples of handguns, rifles, shotguns, and other firearms, as well as knives.

Custom Gunmakers of the 20th Century, by Michael Pretov, Manchester, CT, Precision Shooting, 2005. 168 pages, illustrated with Photos. Hardcover. $24.95 NEW.

Daisy Air Rifles & BB Guns: The First 100 Years, by Neal Punchard, St. Paul, MN, Motorbooks, 2002. 1st edition. Hardcover, 10" x 10", 156 pp., 300 color. Hardcover. $29.95

Dead On, by Tony Noblitt and Warren Gabrilska, Paladin Press, Boulder, CO, 1998. 176 pp., illus. Paper covers. $22.00
The long-range marksman's guide to extreme accuracy. *Defensive Use of Firearms*, by Stephen Wenger, Boulder,CO, Paladin Press, 2005. 5½" x 8½", soft cover, illus., 120 pp. Soft cover. NEW. $20.00
This concise and affordable handbook offers the reader a set of common-sense principles, tactics and techniques distilled from hundreds of hours of the author's training, which includes certification as a law-enforcement handgun, shotgun, patrol rifle and tactical shooting instructor.

Do or Die A Supplementary Manual on Individual Combat, by Lieut. Col. A.J. Drexel Biddle, U.S.M.C.R., Boulder, CO, Paladin Press, 2004. 80 pp., illus. Softcover, $15.00

Down to Earth: The 507th Parachute Infantry Regiment in Normandy: June 6-july 11 1944, by Martin Morgan ICA, Atglen, PA, Schiffer Publishing, 2004. 1st edition. 304 pp., color and b&w photos. Hardcover. New in new dust jacket. $69.95

Effective Defense: The Woman, the Plan, the Gun, by Gila Hayes, Onalaska, WA, Police Bookshelf, 2000. 2nd edition. Photos, 264 pp. Softcover. NEW. $16.95

Elmer Keith: The Other Side of a Western Legend, by Gene Brown, Precision Shooting, Inc., Manchester, CT 2002. 1st edition. 168 pp., illustrated with b&w photos. Softcover $19.95
An updated and expanded edition of his original work, incorporating new tales and information that have come to light in the past six years. Gene Brown was a long time friend of Keith, and today is unquestionably the leading authority on Keith's books.

Encyclopedia of Native American Bows, Arrows and Quivers, by Steve Allely and Jim Hamm, The Lyons Press, N.Y., 1999. 160 pp., illus. $29.95
A landmark book for anyone interested in archery history, or Native Americans.

Exercise of Armes, The, by Jacob de Gheyn, Dover Publications, Inc., Mineola, NY, 1999. 144 pp., illus. Paper covers. $14.95
Republications of all 117 engravings from the 1607 classic military manual. A meticulously accurate portrait of uniforms and weapons of the 17th century Netherlands.

Fighting Iron: A Metals Handbook for Arms Collectors, by Art Gogan, Mowbray Publishers, Inc., Lincoln, RI, 2002. 176 pp., illus. $28.00
A guide that is easy to use, explains things in simple English and covers all of the different historical periods that we are interested in.

FBI Guide to Concealable Weapons, by the FBI, Boulder, Co, Paladin Press, 2005. As citizens responsible for our own safety, we must know everything possible about the dangers that face us, and awareness is the first, vital step in this direction. Photos, 88 pp. Soft cover. NEW. $15.00

Filipino Fighting Whip: Advanced Training Methods and Combat Applications, The, by Tom Meadows, Boulder, CO, Paladin Press, 2005. This book is a comprehensive guide for advanced training methods and combat applications as practiced and taught by the best fighters and whip practitioners in the world. 216 pp. Soft cover. NEW. $20.00

Fine Art of the West, by Byron B. Price and Christopher Lyon, New York, Abbeville Press, 2004. Hardcover. NEW. $75.00

Firearm Suppressor Patents, Volume One: United States Patents, by N.R. Parker, Boulder, CO, Paladin Press, 2004. 392 pages, illustrated. Soft cover. NEW. $45.00
This book provides never-before-published interviews with three of today's top designers as well as a special section on the evolution of cutting-edge silencer mounting systems.

Firearms Assembly Disassembly; Part 4: Centerfire Rifles (2nd Edition), by J. B. Wood, Iola, WI, Krause Publications, 2004. 2nd edition. 576 pp., 1,750 b&w photos. Softcover. NEW. $24.95

Fireworks: A Gunsight Anthology, by Jeff Cooper, Paladin Press, Boulder, CO, 1998. 192 pp., illus. Paper cover. $27.00
A collection of wild, hilarious, shocking and always meaningful tales from the remarkable life of an American firearms legend.

Force-On-Force Gunfight Training: The Interactive, Reality Based Solution, by Gabriel Suarez, Boulder,CO, Paladin Press, 2005. 105 pages, illustrated with photos. Soft cover. NEW. $15.00

Fort Robinson, Frontier Series, Volume 4, by Roy Chandler, Jacksonville, NC, Ron Brigade Armory, 2003. 1st edition. 560 pp. Hardcover. New in new dust jacket. $39.95

Frederic Remington: The Color of Night, by Nancy Anderson, Princeton University Press, 2003. 1st edition. 136 color illus, 24 halftones; 10" x 11", 208 pgs. Hardcover, New in new dust jacket. $49.95; UK $52.49

From a Stranger's Doorstep to the Kremlin Gate, by Mikhail Kalashnikov, Ironside International Publishers, Inc., Alexandria, VA, 1999. 460 pp., illus. $34.95
A biography of the most influential rifle designer of the 20th century. His AK-47 assault rifle has become the most widely used (and copied) assault rifle of this century.

Frontier Rifleman, The, by H.B. LaCrosse Jr., Pioneer Press, Union City, TN, 1989. 183 pp., illus. Softcover. $17.50
The Frontier rifleman's clothing and equipment during the era of the American Revolution, 1760-1800.

Galloping Thunder: The Stuart Horse Artillery Battalion, by Robert Trout, Mechanicsburg, PA, Stackpole Books, 2002. 1st edition. Hardcover, NEW. $39.95

Gatling Gun: 19th Century Machine Gun to 21st Century Vulcan, The, by Joseph Berk, Paladin Press, Boulder, CO, 1991. 136 pp., illus. $34.95
Here is the fascinating on-going story of a truly timeless weapon, from its beginnings during the Civil War to its current role as a state-of-the-art modern combat system.

German Artillery of World War Two, by Ian V. Hogg, Stackpole Books, Mechanicsburg, PA, 1997, 304 pp., illus. $44.95
Complete details of German artillery use in WWII.

Gone Diggin: Memoirs of a Civil War Relic Hunter, by Toby Law, Orange, VA, Publisher's Press, 2002. 1st edition signed. 151 pp., illustrated with b&w photos. $24.95
The true story of one relic hunter's life-The author kept exacting records of every relic hunt and every relic hunter he was with working with.

Gun Digest 2007, 61st Annual Edition, edited by Ken Ramage, Iola, WI, Krause Publications, 2006. Softcover. NEW. $27.95
This all new 61st edition continues the editorial excellence, quality, content and comprehensive cataloguing that firearms enthusiasts have come to know and expect. The most read gun book in the world for the last half century.

Gun Digest Book of Cowboy Action Shooting: Gear, Guns, Tactics, The, edited by Kevin Michalowski, Iola, WI, Krause Publications, 2005. Softcover. 288 pages, plus 200 b&w photos! $24.99
This one-of-a-kind guide offers complete coverage of the sport from the top experts and personalities in the field.

Gun Digest Book of Exploded Firearms Drawings: 975 Isometric Views, The, by Harold Murtz, Iola,WI, Krause Publications, 2005, 3rd edition. 1032pp, 975 photos. Soft cover. $34.95
This book is sure to become a must-have for gunsmiths, shooters and law enforcement officials!

Gun Digest Blackpowder Loading Manual New Expanded 4th Edition, by Sam Fadala, Iola, WI, Krause Publications, 2006. 352 pp., illus. Softcover. NEW. $27.95
All blackpowder rifle, pistol, and shotgun users should be equipped with the new information supplied in this seminal reference--complete with loading tutorial and instructive articles expertly written by author Sam Fadala. Loading techniques are covered for more than 250 different modern blackpowder firearms--the illustrations are clear and the text is expertly laid out--easily understandable to even the most novice shooter. Experts will also benefit from the tips and techniques of Sam Fadala. This is the must-have book blackpowder shooters have been craving.

ARMS LIBRARY

Gun Digest Book of Deer Guns, The, edited by Dan Shideler, Iola, WI, Krause Publications, 2004. 1st edition Softcover, NEW. 160pp, 225 b&w photos. $14.99

An illustrated catalog section details deer rifles, shotguns, handguns and muzzleloaders, complete with current pricing information from "Modern Gun Values." A special reference section includes selected portions of the Arms Library, as well as a website directory of state game and fish departments. This practical guide is a must for any deer hunter!

Gun Digest Book of Guns for Personal Defense Arms & Accessories for Self-Defense, The, edited by Kevin Michalowski, Iola, WI, Krause Publications, 2004. 1st edition Softcover. NEW. 160pp plus 200 b&w photos! $14.99

Handgun enthusiasts or anyone looking to find out about handguns for personal defense will find everything they need to know in the pages of this comprehensive guide and reference. Readers will learn the basics of selection and use of handguns for personal defense. The book covers uses of revolvers, semi-automatic pistols, ammunition, holsters, firearms training options, buying a used gun and much more. A catalog section contains listings of currently available pistols and revolvers suitable for personal defense, complete with pricing for each.

Gun Digest Book of Sporting Clays, 3rd Edition, The, edited by Rick Sapp, Iola, WI, Krause Publications, 2005. 1st edition Softcover, NEW. 288 pages, illustrated. $19.95

New articles cover equipment selection, strategies, technical issues and more. Features a review of the 50 best clay ranges in the country -Includes a fully illustrated catalog of currently available sporting clays shotguns showing complete specifications and retail prices.

Gun Digest Book of Trap & Skeet Shooting, 4th Edition, The, edited by Rick Sapp, Iola, WI, Krause Publications, 2004. 1st edition Softcover, NEW. 256 pages, illustrated. $22.95

The book includes comprehensive coverage on choosing and fitting the right shotgun for each sport, explains the hows and whys of chokes in plain language, and provides an in-depth review of shells, loads and reloading. Valuable reference tools include the official rules for each game as well as a manufacturer's directory for guns, ammunition, clothing and accessories.

Gun Engraving, by C. Austyn, Safari Press Publication, Huntington Beach, CA, 1998. 128 pp., plus 24 pp. of color photos. $50.00

A well-illustrated book on fine English and European gun engravers. Includes a fantastic pictorial section that lists types of engravings and prices.

Gun Notes, Volume 1, by Elmer Keith, Safari Press, Huntington Beach, CA, 2002. 219 pp., illus. Softcover. $24.95

A collection of Elmer Keith's most interesting columns and feature stories that appeared in *"Guns & Ammo"* magazine from 1961 to the late 1970s.

Gun Notes, Volume 2, by Elmer Keith, Safari Press, Huntington Beach, CA, 2002. 292 pp., illus. Softcover. $24.95

Covers articles from Keith's monthly column in *"Guns & Ammo"* magazine during the period from 1971 through Keith's passing in 1982.

Guns & Shooting: A Selected Bibliography, by Ray Riling, Ray Riling Arms Books Co., Phila., PA, 1982. 434 pp., illus. Limited, numbered edition. $75.00

A limited edition of this superb bibliographical work, the only modern listing of books devoted to guns and shooting.

Guns Illustrated 2007: 39th Edition, edited by Ken Ramage, Iola, WI, Krause Publications, 2006. Softcover. NEW. $21.95

Highly informative, technical articles on a wide range of shooting topics by some of the top writers in the industry. A catalog section lists more than 3,000 firearms currently manufactured in or imported to the U.S.

Guns of the Gunfighters: Lawmen, Outlaws & TV Cowboys, by Doc O'Meara, Iola, WI, Krause Publications, 2003. 1st edition. 16-page color section, 225 b&w photos. Hardcover. $34.95

Explores the romance of the Old West, focusing on the guns that the good guys & bad guys, real & fictional characters, carried with them. Profiles of more than 50 gunslingers, half from the Old West and half from Hollywood, include a brief biography of each gunfighter, along with the guns they carried. Fascinating stories about the TV and movie celebrities of the 1950s and 1960s detail their guns and the skill–or lack thereof–they displayed.

Guns, Bullets, and Gunfighters, by Jim Cirillo, Paladin Press, Boulder, CO, 1996. 119 pp., illus. Paper covers. $16.00

Lessons and tales from a modern-day gunfighter.

Gunstock Carving: A Step-by-Step Guide to Engraving Rifles and Shotguns, by Bill Janney, East Pertsburg, PA, Fox Chapel Publishing, October 2002. 89 pp., illustrated in color. Softcover. $19.95

Learn gunstock carving from an expert. Includes step-by-step projects and instructions, patterns, tips and techniques.

Hands Off! Self Defense for Women, by Maj. Fairbairn, Boulder, CO: Paladin Press, 2004. 56 pages. Soft cover. NEW. $15.00

Paladin Press is proud to bring back a work by the inimitable self-defense master W.E. Fairbairn so that a new generation of Americans can enjoy his teachings.

Hand-To-Hand Combat: United States Naval Institute, by U.S. Navy, Boulder, CO, Paladin Press, 2003. 1st edition. 240 pp. Softcover. $25.00

Now you can own one of the classic publications in the history of U.S. military close-quarters combat training. In 11 photo-heavy chapters, Hand-to-Hand Combat covers training tips; vulnerable targets; the brutal fundamentals of close-in fighting; frontal and rear attacks; prisoner search and control techniques; disarming pistols, rifles, clubs and knives; offensive means of "liquidating an enemy"; and much more. After reading this book (originally published by the United States Naval Institute in 1943), you will see why it has long been sought by collectors and historians of hand-to-hand combat.

Hidden in Plain Sight, "A Practical Guide to Concealed Handgun Carry" (Revised 2nd Edition), by Trey Bloodworth and Mike Raley, Paladin Press, Boulder, CO, 1997, softcover, photos, 176 pp. $20.00

This invaluable guide offers the latest advice on what to look for when choosing a CCW, how to dress for comfortable, effective concealed carry, traditional and more unconventional carry modes, accessory holsters, customized clothing and accessories, accessibility data based on draw-time comparisons and new holsters on the market. Includes 40 new manufacturer listings.

HK Assault Rifle Systems, by Duncan Long, Paladin Press, Boulder, CO, 1995. 110 pp., illus. Paper covers. $27.95

The little known history behind this fascinating family of weapons tracing its beginnings from the ashes of WWII to the present time.

Holsters for Combat and Concealed Carry, by R.K. Campbell, Boulder, CO, Paladin Press, 2004. 1st edition. 144 pp. Softcover. NEW. $22.00

Hostage Rescue Manual; Tactics of the Counter-Terrorist Professionals, by Leroy Thompson, Mechanicsburg, PA. Greehnill Books, 2005. 208 pages, with 16 pages of photos. Soft cover. $23.95

Incorporating vivid photographs and diagrams of rescue units in action, the Hostage Rescue Manual is the complete reference work on counter-terrorist procedures all over the world.

Hunter's Guide to Accurate Shooting, by Wayne van Zwoll, Guilford, CT, Lyons Press, 2002. 1st edition. 288 pp. Hardcover. $29.95

Firearms expert van Zwoll explains exactly how to shoot the big-game rifle accurately. Taking into consideration every pertinent factor, he shows a step-by-step analysis of shooting and hunting with the big-game rifle.

Hunting Time: Adventures in Pursuit of North American Big Game: A Forty-Year Chronicle, The, by John E. Howard, Deforest, WI, Saint Huberts Press, 2002. 1st edition. 537 pp., illustrated with drawings. Hardcover. $29.95

From a novice's first hunt for whitetailed deer in his native Wisconsin, to a seasoned hunter's pursuit of a Boone and Crockett Club record book caribou in the northwest territories, the author carries the reader along on his forty year journey through the big game fields of North America.

Instinct Combat Shooting; Defensive Handgunning for Police, by Chuck Klein, Flushing, NY, Looseleaf Law, 2004. 54 pages. Soft cover. NEW. $22.95

Tactical tips for effective armed defense, helpful definitions and court-ready statements that help you clearly articulate and competently justify your deadly force decision-making.

Jack O'Connor Catalogue of Letters, by Ellen Enzler Herring, Agoura, CA, Trophy Room Books, 2002. 1st edition. Hardcover. NEW. 262 pages, 18 illustrations. $55.00

During a sixteen year period beginning in 1960, O'Connor exchanged many letters with his pal, John Jobson. Material from nearly three hundred of these has been assembled and edited by Ellen Enzler Herring and published in chronological order. A number of the letters have been reproduced in full or part. They offer considerable insight into the beloved gun editor and "Dean of Outdoor Writers"over and beyond what we know about him from his books.

Jane's Guns Recognition Guide: 4th Edition, by Ian Hogg, Terry Gander, NY, Harper Collins, 2005. 464 pages, illustrated. Soft cover. NEW. $24.95

This book will help you identify them all. Jane's, always known for meticulous detail in the information of military equipment, aircraft, ships and much more!

Kill or Get Killed, by Col. Rex Applegate, Paladin Press, Boulder, CO, 1996. 400 pp., illus. $49.95

The best and longest-selling book on close combat in history.

Living With Terrorism; Survival Lessons from the Streets of Jerusalem, by Howard Linett, Boulder, CO, Paladin Press, 2005. 277 pages, illustrated with photos. Soft cover. NEW. $20.00

Before these dangers become a reality in your life, read this book.

Lost Classics of Jack O'Connor, The, edited by Jim Casada, Columbia, SC, Live Oak Press, 2004. 1st edition. Hardcover. New in new dust jacket. 33 photos, 40 illus by Dan Burr; 376 pages, with illustrations and photos. $35.00

You'll find 40 of O'Connor's most fascinating stories in the Trade Edition of Lost Classics. Exciting tales with a twist of humor.

Manual for H&R Reising Submachine Gun and Semi-Auto Rifle, edited by George P. Dillman, Desert Publications, El Dorado, AZ, 1994. 81 pp., illus. Paper covers. $14.95

A reprint of the Harrington & Richardson 1943 factory manual and the rare military manual on the H&R submachine gun and semi-auto rifle.

Manufacture of Gunflints, The, by Sydney B.J. Skertchly, facsimile reprint with new introduction by Seymour de Lotbiniere, Museum Restoration Service, Ontario, Canada, 1984. 90 pp., illus. $24.50

Limited edition reprinting of the very scarce London edition of 1879.

Master Tips, by J. Winokur, Potshot Press, Pacific Palisades, CA, 1985. 96 pp., illus. Paper covers. $11.95

Basics of practical shooting.

Military and Police Sniper, The, by Mike R. Lau, Precision Shooting, Inc., Manchester, CT, 1998. 352 pp., illus. Paper covers. $34.95

Advanced precision shooting for combat and law enforcement.

Military Small Arms of the 20th Century, 7th Edition, by Ian V. Hogg and John Weeks, DBI Books, a division of Krause Publications, Iola, WI, 2000. 416 pp., illus. Paper covers. Over 800 photographs and illustrations. $24.95

Covers small arms of 46 countries.

Modern Guns Identification and Values, 16th Edition, by Steve and Russell Quertermous, Paducah, KY, Collector's Books, 2006. 1800+ illus; 8.5"x11", 575 pgs. Soft cover. NEW. $18.95

Updated edition features current market values for over 2,500 models of rifles, shotguns, & handguns. Contains model name, gauge or caliber, action, finish or stock & forearm, barrel, cylinder or magazine, sights, weight & length, & comments.

Modern Gun Values: 13th Edition, edited by Dan Shideler, Krause Publications, Iola, WI, 2006. Softcover. NEW. 680 Pages, 3,000+ b&w photos. $24.95

This all-new expanded edition helps collectors identify the firearm, evaluate condition and determine value. Detailed specifications—and current values from specialized experts—are provided for domestic and imported handguns, rifles, shotguns and commemorative firearms. Heavily illustrated. Over 7,500 arms described and valued, in three grades of condition, according to the NRA's Modern standards.

Modern Law Enforcement Weapons & Tactics, 3rd edition, by Patrick Sweeney, Iola, WI, Krause Publications, 2004. Illustrated, b&w photos, 256 pages. $22.99

Sweeney walks you through the latest gear and tactics employed by American law enforcement officers.

ARMS LIBRARY

Modern Sporting Guns, by Christopher Austyn, Safari Press, Huntington Beach, CA, 1994. 128 pp., illus. $40.00
A discussion of the "best" English guns; round action, over-and-under, boxlocks, hammer guns, bolt action and double rifles as well as accessories.

More Tactical Reality; Why There's No Such Thing as an Advanced Gunfight, by Louis Awerbuck, Boulder, CO, Paladin Press, 2004. 144 pp. Softcover. $25.00

MP-40 Machine Gun, The, Desert Publications, El Dorado, AZ, 1995. 32 pp., illus. Paper covers. $11.95
A reprint of the hard-to-find operating and maintenance manual for one of the most famous machine guns of WWII.

Naval Percussion Locks and Primers, by Lt. J. A. Dahlgren, Museum Restoration Service, Bloomfield, Canada, 1996. 140 pp., illus. $35.00
First published as an Ordnance Memoranda in 1853, this is the finest existing study of percussion locks and primers origin and development.

Official Soviet AKM Manual, translated by Maj. James F. Gebhardt (Ret.), Paladin Press, Boulder, CO, 1999. 120 pp., illus. Paper covers. $18.00
This official military manual, available in English for the first time, was originally published by the Soviet Ministry of Defence. Covers the history, function, maintenance, assembly and disassembly, etc. of the 7.62mm AKM assault rifle.

One-Round War: U.S.M.C. Scout-Snipers in Vietnam, by Peter Senich, Paladin Press, Boulder, CO, 1996. 384 pp., illus. Paper covers $59.95
Sniping in Vietnam focusing specifically on the Marine Corps program.

Optics Digest: Scopes, Binoculars, Rangefinders, and Spotting Scopes, by Clair Rees, Long Beach, CA, Safari Press, 2005. 189 pp. Softcover. NEW. $24.95

OSS Special Operations in China, by Col. F. Mills and John W. Brunner, Williamstown, NJ, Phillips Publications, 2003. 1st edition. 550 pp., illustrated with photos. Hardcover. New in new dust jacket. $34.95

Paintball Digest The Complete Guide to Games, Gear, and Tactics, by Richard Sapp, Iola, WI, Krause Publications, 2004. 1st edition. 272 pp. Softcover. NEW. $19.99

Paleo-Indian Artifacts: Identification & Value Guide, by Lar Hothem, Paducah, KY, Collector Books, 2005. 1st edition. 379 pp. Pictorial hardcover. NEW. $29.95

Panzer Aces German Tank Commanders of WWII, by Franz Kurowski, translated by David Johnston, Mechanicsburg, PA, Stackpole Books, 2004. 1st edition. 448 pp., 50 b&w photos Softcover. NEW. $19.95

Parker Brothers: Knight of the Trigger, by Ed Muderlak, Davis, IL, Old Reliable Publishing, 2002. 223 pp. $25.00
Knight of the Trigger tells the story of the Old West when Parker's most famous gun saleman traveled the country by rail, competing in the pigeon ring, hunting with the rich and famous, and selling the "Old Reliable" Parker shotgun. The life and times of Captain Arthur William du Bray, Parker Brothers' on-the-road sales agent from 1884 to 1926, is described in a novelized version of his interesting life.

Peril in the Powder Mills: Gunpowder & Its Men, by David McMahon & Anne Kelly Lane, West Conshohocken, PA, privately printed, 2004. 1st edition. 118 pp. Softcover. NEW. $18.95

Powder Horns and their Architecture; And Decoration as Used by the Soldier, Indian, Sailor and Traders of the Era, by Madison Grant, York, PA, privately printed, 1987. 165 pp., profusely illustrated. Hardcover. $45.00
Covers homemade pieces from the late eighteenth and early nineteenth centuries.

Practically Speaking: An Illustrated Guide-The Game, Guns and Gear of the International Defensive Pistol Association, by Walt Rauch, Lafayette Hills, PA, privately printed, 2002. 1st edition. 79 pp., illustrated with drawings and color photos. Softcover. $24.95
The game, guns and gear of the International Defensive Pistol Association with real-world applications.

Present Sabers: A Popular History of the U.S. Horse Cavalry, by Allan T. Heninger, Tucson, AZ, Excalibur Publications, 2002. 1st edition. 160 pp., with 148 photographs, 45 illustrations and 4 charts. Softcover. $24.95
An illustrated history of America's involvement with the horse cavalry, from its earliest beginnings during the Revolutionary War through its demise in WWII. The book also contains several appendices, as well as depictions of the regular insignia of all the U.S. Cavalry units.

Principles of Personal Defense, by Jeff Cooper, Paladin Press, Boulder, CO, 2006. 80 pp., illus. Paper covers. $14.00
This revised edition of Jeff Cooper's classic on personal defense offers great new illustrations and a new preface while retaining the theory of individual defense behavior presented in the original book.

Queen's Rook: A Soldier's Story, by Croft Barker, Flatonia,TX, Cistern Publishing, 2004. Limited edition of 500 copies. 177 pages, with 50 never before published photographs. Soft cover. NEW. $35.00
Men of the U.S. Army were assigned to South Vietnamese Infantry companies and platoons. Many of these men were lost in a war that is still misunderstood. This is their story, written in their own words. These Americans, and the units they lived with, engaged in savage fights against Viet Cong guerillas and North Vietnamese Army Regulars in the dark, deadly jungles north of Saigon.

Quotable Hunter, The, edited by Jay Cassell and Peter Fiduccia, The Lyons Press, N.Y., 1999. 224 pp., illus. $20.00
This collection of more than three hundred memorable quotes from hunters through the ages captures the essence of the sport, with all its joys idiosyncrasies, and challenges.

Real World Self-Defense by Jerry Vancook, Boulder, CO, Paladin Press, 1999. 224 pp. Soft cover. NEW. $20.00
Presenting tactics and techniques that are basic, easy to learn and proven effective under the stress of combat, he covers unarmed defense, improvised weapons, edged weapons, firearms and more, photos, illus.

Renaissance Drill Book, by Jacob de Gheyn, edited by David J. Blackmore, Mechanicsburg, PA, Greenhill Books, 2003. 1st edition. 248 pp., 117 illustrations. Hardcover. $24.95
Jacob de Gheyn's Exercise of Armes was an immense success when first published in 1607. It is a fascinating 17th-century military manual, designed to instruct contemporary soldiers how to handle arms effectively, and correctly, and it makes for a unique glimpse into warfare as waged in the Thirty Years War and the English Civil War. In addition, detailed illustrations show the various movements and postures to be adopted during use of the pike.

Running Recon, A Photo Journey with SOG Special Ops Along the Ho Chi Minh Trail, by Frank Greco, Boulder, CO, Paladin Press, 2004. Paper covers. $50.00
Running Recon is a combination of military memoir and combat photography book. It reflects both the author's experience in Kontum, Vietnam, from April 1969 to April 1970 as part of the top-secret Studies and Observation Group (SOG) and the collective experience of SOG veterans in general. What sets it apart from other Vietnam books is its wealth of more than 700 photographs, many never before published, from the author's personal collection and those of his fellow SOG veterans.

Sharpshooting for Sport and War, by W.W. Greener, Wolfe Publishing Co., Prescott, AZ, 1995. 192 pp., illus. $30.00
This classic reprint explores the *first* expanding bullet; service rifles; shooting positions; trajectories; recoil; external ballistics; and other valuable information.

Shooter's Bible 2007 No. 98, by Wayne Van Zwoll, Stoeger Publishing, 2006. New for this edition is a special Web Directory designed to complement the regular Reference section, including the popular Gun finder index. 576 pages. Pictorial Soft cover. NEW. $24.95

Shooting Buffalo Rifles of the Old West, by Mike Venturino, MLV Enterprises, Livingston, MT, 2002. 278 pp., illustrated with b&w photos. Softcover. $30.00
This tome will take you through the history, the usage, the many models, and the actual shooting (and how to's) of the many guns that saw service on the Frontier and are lovingly called "Buffalo Rifles" today. If you love to shoot your Sharps, Ballards, Remingtons, or Springfield "Trapdoors" for hunting or competition, or simply love Old West history, your library WILL NOT be complete without this latest book from Mike Venturino!

Shooting Colt Single Actions, by Mike Venturino, MLV Enterprises, Livingston, MT, 1997. 205 pp., illus. Softcover. $25.00
A complete examination of the Colt Single Action including styles, calibers and generations, b&w photos throughout.

Shooting Lever Guns of the Old West, by Mike Venturino, MLV Enterprises, Livingston, MT, 1999. 300 pp., illus. Softcover. $27.95
Shooting the lever action type repeating rifles of our American West.

Shooting Sixguns of the Old West, by Mike Venturino, MLV Enterprises, Livingston, MT, 1997. 221 pp., illus. Paper covers. $26.50
A comprehensive look at the guns of the early West: Colts, Smith & Wesson and Remingtons, plus blackpowder and reloading specs.

Shooting to Live, by Capt. W.E. Fairbairn and Capt. E.A. Sykes, Paladin Press, Boulder, CO, 1997, 4½" x 7", soft cover, illus., 112 pp. $14.00
Shooting to Live is the product of Fairbairn's and Sykes' practical experience with the handgun. Hundreds of incidents provided the basis for the first true book on life-or-death shootouts with the pistol. Shooting to Live teaches all concepts, considerations and applications of combat pistol craft.

Small Arms of World War II, by Chris Chant, St. Paul, MN, MBI Publishing Company, 2001. 1st edition. 96 pp., single page on each weapon with photograph, description, and a specifications table. Hardcover. New. $13.95
Detailing the design and development of each weapon, this book covers the most important infantry weapons used by both Allied and Axis soldiers between 1939 and 1945. These include both standard infantry bolt-action rifles, such as the German Kar 98 and the British Lee-Enfield, plus the automatic rifles that entered service toward the end of the war, such as the Stg 43. As well as rifles, this book also features submachine guns, machine guns and handguns and a specifications table for each weapon.

Sniper Training, FM 23-10, Reprint of the U.S. Army field manual of August, 1994, Paladin Press, Boulder, CO, 1995. 352 pp., illus. Paper covers. $30.00
The most up-to-date U.S. military sniping information and doctrine.

Song of Blue Moccasin, by Roy Chandler, Jacksonville, NC, Ron Brigade Armory, 2004. 231 pp. Hardcover. New in new dust jacket. $45.00

Speak Like a Native; Professional Secrets for Mastering Foreign Languages, by Michael Janich, Boulder CO, Paladin Press, 2005. 136 pages. Soft cover. NEW. $19.00
No matter what language you wish to learn or the level of fluency you need to attain, this book can help you learn to speak like a native.

Special Operations: Weapons and Tactics, by Timothy Mullin, London, Greenhill Press, 2003. 1st edition. 176 pp., with 189 illustrations. $39.95
The tactics and equipment of Special Forces explained in full, Contains 200 images of weaponry and training. This highly illustrated guide covers the full experience of special operations training from every possible angle. There is also considerable information on nonfirearm usage, such as specialized armor and ammunition.

Standard Catalog of Firearms 2007, 17th Edition, by Dan Shideler, Iola, WI, Krause Publications, 2006. 1504 pages, 7,100+ b&w photos, plus a 16-page color section. Paper covers. $34.95
Now in its 17th year and completely updated for 2007, this edition of the world famous Standard Catalog of Firearms is bigger and better than ever. With entries for virtually all of the world's commercial firearms from the percussion era to the present day, Standard Catalog of Firearms is the only book you need to identify and price collectible rifles, handguns and shotguns. New for 2007: "Sleepers": Collectible firearms that are outperforming the market. Value Trends: Real-Life auction reports showing value ranges. How to buy and sell on the Internet.

Standard Catalog of Military Firearms 3rd Edition: The Collector's Price & Reference Guide, by Ned Schwing, Iola, WI, Krause Publications, 2005. 480 pp. Softcover. $29.99
A companion volume to Standard Catalog of Firearms, this revised and expanded second edition comes complete with all the detailed information readers found useful and more. Listings beginning with the early cartridge models of the 1870s to the latest high-tech sniper rifles have been expanded to include more models, variations, historical information, and data, offering more detail for the military firearms collector, shooter, and history buff. Identification of specific firearms is easier with nearly 250 additional photographs. Plus, readers will enjoy "snap shots," small personal articles from experts relating real-life experiences with exclusive models. Revised to include every known military firearm available to the U.S. collector. Special feature articles on focused aspects of collecting and shooting.

ARMS LIBRARY

Street Tough, Hard Core, Anything Goes, Street Fighting Fundamentals, by Phil Giles, Boulder, CO, Paladin Press, 2004. 176 pages. Soft cover. NEW. $25.00
A series of intense training drills performed at full power and full speed sets the Street Tough program apart from all other self-defense regimens.

Stress Fire, Vol. 1: Stress Fighting for Police, by Massad Ayoob, Police Bookshelf, Concord, NH, 1984. 149 pp., illus. Paper covers. $11.95
Gunfighting for police, advanced tactics and techniques.

Stress Fire Gunfighting for Police Vol. 2; Advanced Combat Shotgun, by Massad Ayoob, Police Bookshelf, Concord, NH, 1997. 212 pp., illus. Paper covers. $12.95
The long-awaited second volume in Massad Ayoob's series on Advanced Gunfighting for Police. Learn to control the 12-gauge shotgun in the most rapid fire, pain-free aimed fire from the shoulder, Speed reloads that don't fail under stress, proven jam-response techniques, keys to selecting a good shotgun.

Tactical Advantage, The, by Gabriel Suarez, Paladin Press, Boulder, CO, 1998. 216 pp., illus. Paper covers. $22.00
Learn combat tactics that have been tested in the world's toughest schools.

Tactical Marksman, by Dave M. Lauch, Paladin Press, Boulder, CO, 1996. 165 pp., illus. Paper covers. $35.00
A complete training manual for police and practical shooters.

Tim Murphy Rifleman Frontier Series Volume 3, by Roy Chandler, Jacksonville, NC, Iron Brigade Armory, 2003. 1st edition. 396 pp. Hardcover. $39.95
Tim Murphy may be our young nation's earliest recognized hero. Murphy was seized by Seneca Tribesmen during his infancy. Traded to the Huron, he was renamed and educated by Sir William Johnson, a British colonial officer. Freed during the prisoner exchange of 1764, Murphy discovered his superior ability with a Pennsylvania longrifle. An early volunteer in the Pennsylvania militia, Tim Murphy served valiantly in rifle companies including the justly famed Daniel Morgan's Riflemen. This is Murphy's story.

To Ride, Shoot Straight, and Speak the Truth, by Jeff Cooper, Paladin Press, Boulder, CO, 1997, 5½" x 8½", soft-cover, illus., 384 pp. $32.00
Combat mind-set, proper sighting, tactical residential architecture, nuclear war-these are some of the many subjects explored by Jeff Cooper in this illustrated anthology. The author discusses various arms, fighting skills and the importance of knowing how to defend oneself, and one's honor, in our rapidly changing world.

Trailriders Guide to Cowboy Action Shooting, by James W. Barnard, Pioneer Press, Union City, TN, 1998. 134 pp., plus 91 photos, drawings and charts. Paper covers. $24.95
Covers the complete spectrum of this shooting discipline, from how to dress to authentic leather goods, which guns are legal, calibers, loads and ballistics.

Traveler's Guide to the Firearms Laws of the Fifty States, 2007 Edition, by Scott Kappas, KY, Traveler's Guide, 2007, 64pp,. Softcover. $12.95

U.S. Army Hand-to-Hand Combat: FM 21-150, 1954 Edition, Boulder,CO, Paladin Press, 2005. 192 pp. illus. Soft cover. $20.00

U.S. Infantry Weapons in Combat: Personal Experiences from Woird War II and Korea, by Mark Goodwin w/ forward by Scott Duff, Export, PA, Scott Duff Pub., 2005. 237pp, over 50 photos and drawings. Soft cover. $23.50
The stories about U.S. infantry weapons contained in this book are the real hands-on experiences of the men who actually used them for their intended purposes.

U.S. Marine Corp Rifle and Pistol Marksmanship, 1935, reprinting of a government publication, Lancer Militaria, Mt. Ida, AR, 1991. 99 pp., illus. Paper covers. $11.95
The old corps method of precision shooting.

U.S. Marine Corps Scout/Sniper Training Manual, Lancer Militaria, Mt. Ida, AR, 1989. Softcover. $27.95
Reprint of the original sniper training manual used by the Marksmanship Training Unit of the Marine Corps Development and Education Command in Quantico, **Virginia.**

U.S. Marine Corps Scout-Sniper, World War II and Korea, by Peter R. Senich, Paladin Press, Boulder, CO, 1994. 236 pp., illus. $44.95
The most thorough and accurate account ever printed on the training, equipment and combat experiences of the U.S. Marine Corps Scout-Snipers.

U.S. Marine Corps Sniping, Lancer Militaria, Mt. Ida, AR, 1989. Irregular pagination. Softcover. $18.95
A reprint of the official Marine Corps FMFM1-3B.

U.S. Military Uniforms-1912-1940, by Jim Moran, Williamstown, NJ, Phillips Publications, 2001. 174 pp., illustrated with b&w photographs. Hardcover. $49.95

Ultimate Sniper: An Advanced Training Manual for Military and Police Snipers, Updated and Expanded Edition, by Major John L. Plaster, Paladin Press, Boulder, CO, 2006. 584 pp., illus. Paper covers. $49.95
Now this revolutionary book has been completely updated and expanded for the 21st century. Through revised text, new photos, specialized illustrations, updated charts and additional information sidebars, The Ultimate Sniper once again thoroughly details the three great skill areas of sniping – marksmanship, fieldcraft and tactics.

Uniforms And Equipment of the Imperial Japanese Army in World War II, by Mike Hewitt, Atglen, PA, Schiffer Publications, 2002. 176 pp., with over 520 color and b&w photos. Hardcover. $59.95

Unrepentant Sinner, by Col. Charles Askins, Paladin Press, Boulder, CO, 2000. 322 pp., illus. $29.95
The autobiography of Colonel Charles Askins.

Vietnam Order of Battle, by Shelby L. Stanton, William C. Westmoreland, Mechanicsburg, PA, Stackpole Books, 2003. 1st edition. 416 pp., 32 in full color, 101 halftones. Hardcover. $69.95
A monumental, encyclopedic work of immense detail concerning U.S. Army and allied forces that fought in the Vietnam War from 1962 through 1973. Extensive lists of units providing a record of every Army unit that served in Vietnam, down to and including separate companies, and also including U.S. Army aviation and riverine units. Shoulder patches and distinctive unit insignia of all divisions and battalions. Extensive maps portraying unit locations at each six-month interval. Photographs and descriptions of all major types of equipment employed in the conflict. Plus much more!

Warriors; On llving with Courage, Discipline, and Honor, by Loren Christensen, Boulder, CO, Paladin Press, 2004. 376 pages. Soft cover. NEW. $20.00
The writers who contributed to this work are a diverse mix, from soldiers, cops and SWAT officers to martial art masters to experts in the fields of workplace violence, theology and school safety. They are some of the finest warrior authors, warrior trainers and warrior scholars today. Many have faced death, survived and now teach others to do the same. Here they speak candidly on what it's like to sacrifice, to train, to protect.

"Walking Stick" Method of Self-Defence, The, by an officer of the Indian police, Boulder, CO: Paladin Press, 2004. 1st edition. 112 pages. Soft cover. NEW. $15.00
The entire range of defensive and offensive skills is discussed and demonstrated, including guards, strikes, combinations, counterattacks, feints and tricks, double-handed techniques and training drills.

Weapons of Delta Force, by Fred Pushies, St. Paul, MN, MBI Publishing Company, 2002. 1st edition. 128 pgs., 100 b&w and 100 color illustrated. Hardcover. $24.95
America's elite counter-terrorist organization, Delta Force, is a handpicked group of the U.S. Army's finest soldiers. Delta uses some of the most sophisticated weapons in the field today, and all are detailed in this book. Pistols, sniper rifles, special mission aircraft, fast attack vehicles, SCUBA and paratrooper gear, and more are presented in this fully illustrated account of our country's heroes and their tools of the trade.

Weapons of the Waffen-SS, by Bruce Quarrie, Sterling Publishing Co., Inc., 1991. 168 pp., illus. $24.95
An in-depth look at the weapons that made Hitler's Waffen-SS the fearsome fighting machine it was.

Weatherby: The Man, The Gun, The Legend, by Grits and Tom Gresham, Cane River Publishing Co., Natchitoches, LA, 1992. 290 pp., illus. $34.95
A fascinating look at the life of the man who changed the course of firearms development in America.

Winchester Era, The, by David Madis, Art & Reference House, Brownsville, TX, 1984. 100 pp., illus. $19.95
Story of the Winchester company, management, employees, etc.

Winchester Pocket Guide; Identification and Pricing for 50 Collectible Rifles and Shotguns, by Ned Schwing, Iola,WI, Krause Publications, 2004. 224 pages, illustrated. Soft cover. NEW. $12.95
The Winchester Pocket Guide also features advice on collecting, grading and pricing the collectible firearms.

With British Snipers to the Reich, by Capt. C. Shore, Lander Militaria, Mt. Ida, AR, 1988. 420 pp., illus. $29.95
One of the greatest books ever written on the art of combat sniping.

World's Machine Pistols and Submachine Guns-Vol. 2a 1964 to 1980, The, by Nelson & Musgrave, Ironside International, Alexandria, VA, 2000. 673 pp. $69.95
Containing data, history and photographs of over 200 weapons. With a special section covering shoulder stocked automatic pistols, 100 additional photos.

Wyatt Earp: A Biography of the Legend: Volume 1: The Cowtown Years, by Lee A. Silva, Santa Ana, CA, privately printed, 2002. 1st edition signed. Hardcover. New in new dust jacket. $86.95

GUNSMITHING

Accurizing the Factory Rifle, by M.L. McPhereson, Precision Shooting, Inc., Manchester, CT, 1999. 335 pp., illus. Paper covers. $44.95
A long-awaiting book, which bridges the gap between the rudimentary (mounting sling swivels, scope blocks and that general level of accomplishment) and the advanced (precision chambering, barrel fluting, and that general level of accomplishment) books that are currently available today.

Antique Firearms Assembly Disassembly: The Comprehensive Guide to Pistols, Rifles, & Shotguns, by David Chicoine, Iola, WI, Krause Publications, 2005. 528 pages, 600 b&w photos & illus. Soft cover. NEW. $29.95
Create a resource unequaled by any. Features over 600 photos of antique and rare firearms for quick identification.

Art of Engraving, The, by James B. Meek, F. Brownell & Son, Montezuma, IA, 1973. 196 pp., illus. $47.95
A complete, authoritative, imaginative and detailed study in training for gun engraving. The first book of its kind–and a great one.

Checkering and Carving of Gun Stocks, by Monte Kennedy, Stackpole Books, Harrisburg, PA, 1962. 175 pp., illus. $39.95
Revised, enlarged cloth-bound edition of a much sought-after, dependable work.

Firearms Assembly/Disassembly, Part I: Automatic Pistols, 2nd Revised Edition, The Gun Digest Book of, by J.B. Wood, DBI Books, a division of Krause Publications, Iola, WI, 1999. 480 pp., illus. Paper covers. $24.95
Covers 58 popular autoloading pistols plus nearly 200 variants of those models integrated into the text and completely cross-referenced in the index.

Firearms Assembly/Disassembly Part II: Revolvers, Revised Edition, The Gun Digest Book of, by J.B. Wood, DBI Books, a division of Krause Publications, Iola, WI, 1997. 480 pp., illus. Paper covers. $27.95
Covers 49 popular revolvers plus 130 variants. The most comprehensive and professional presentation available to either hobbyist or gunsmith.

Firearms Assembly/Disassembly Part III: Rimfire Rifles 3rd Edition, The Gun Digest Book of, by J. B. Wood, Krause Publications, Iola, WI, 2006. Softcover. 576 Pages, 1,590 b&w photos. $27.95
This redesigned volume provides comprehensive step-by-step disassembly instruction patterns for 74 rifles-nearly 200 firearms when combined with variations. All the hands-on information you need to increase accuracy and speed.

ARMS LIBRARY

Firearms Assembly/Disassembly Part IV: Centerfire Rifles, 3rd Revised Edition, The Gun Digest Book of, by J.B. Wood, Krause Publications, Iola, WI, 2004. 480 pp., illus. Paper covers. $24.95
Covers 54 popular centerfire rifles plus 300 variants. The most comprehensive and professional presentation available to either hobbyist or gunsmith.

Firearms Assembly/Disassembly, Part V: Shotguns, Revised Edition, The Gun Digest Book of, by J.B. Wood, Krause Publications, Iola, WI, 2002. 480 pp., illus. Paper covers. $24.95
Covers 46 popular shotguns plus over 250 variants with step-by-step instructions on how to dismantle and reassemble each. The most comprehensive and professional presentation available to either hobbyist or gunsmith.

Firearms Assembly: The NRA Guide to Rifle and Shotguns, NRA Books, Wash., DC, 1980. 264 pp., illus. Paper covers. $14.95
Text and illustrations explaining the takedown of 125 rifles and shotguns, domestic and foreign.

Firearms Assembly: The NRA Guide to Pistols and Revolvers, NRA Books, Wash., DC, 1980. 253 pp., illus. Paper covers. $14.95
Text and illustrations explaining the takedown of 124 pistol and revolver models, domestic and foreign.

Firearms Bluing and Browning, by R.H. Angier, Stackpole Books, Harrisburg, PA. 151 pp., illus. $19.95
A world master gunsmith reveals his secrets of building, repairing and renewing a gun, quite literally, lock, stock and barrel. A useful, concise text on chemical coloring methods for the gunsmith and mechanic.

Guns and Gunmaking Tools of Southern Appalachia, by John Rice Irwin, Schiffer Publishing Ltd., 1983. 118 pp., illus. Paper covers. $9.95
The story of the Kentucky rifle.

Gunsmith Kinks, by F.R. (Bob) Brownell, F. Brownell & Son, Montezuma, IA, 1st ed., 1969. 496 pp., well illus. $22.98
A widely useful accumulation of shop kinks, short cuts, techniques and pertinent comments by practicing gunsmiths from all over the world.

Gunsmith Kinks 2, by Bob Brownell, F. Brownell & Son, Publishers, Montezuma, IA, 1983. 496 pp., illus. $22.95
A collection of gunsmithing knowledge, shop kinks, new and old techniques, shortcuts and general know-how straight from those who do them best–the gunsmiths.

Gunsmith Kinks 3, edited by Frank Brownell, Brownells Inc., Montezuma, IA, 1993. 504 pp., illus. $24.95
Tricks, knacks and "kinks" by professional gunsmiths and gun tinkerers. Hundreds of valuable ideas are given in this volume.

Gunsmith Kinks 4, edited by Frank Brownell, Brownells Inc., Montezuma, IA, 2001. 564 pp., illus. 332 detailed illustrations. 560+ pages with 706 separate subject headings and over 5000 cross-indexed entries. $27.75
An incredible gold mine of information.

Gunsmith Machinist, The, by Steve Acker, Village Press Publications Inc, Michigan. 2001. Hardcover, New in new dust jacket. $69.95

Gunsmith of Grenville County: Building the American Longrifle, The, by Peter Alexander, Texarkana, TX, Scurlock Publishing Co., 2002. 400 pp.in, with hundreds of illustrations, and six color photos of original rifles. Stiff paper covers. $45.00
The most extensive how-to book on building longrifles ever published. Takes you through every step of building your own longrifle, from shop set up and tools to engraving, carving and finishing.

Gunsmithing, by Roy F. Dunlap, Stackpole Books, Harrisburg, PA, 1990. 742 pp., illus. $44.95
A manual of firearm design, construction, alteration and remodeling. For amateur and professional gunsmiths and users of modern firearms.

Gunsmithing at Home: Lock, Stock and Barrel, by John Traister, Stoeger Publishing Co., Wayne, NJ, 1997. 320 pp., illus. Paper covers. $19.95
A complete step-by-step fully illustrated guide to the art of gunsmithing.

Gunsmithing Shotguns: The Complete Guide to Care & Repair, by David Henderson, New York, Globe Pequot, 2003. 1st edition. Hardcover. NEW. $24.95

Gunsmithing: Guns of the Old West: Expanded 2nd Edition, by David Chicoine, Iola, WI, Krause Publications, 2004. 446 pp.in, illus. Softcover. NEW. $29.95
This updated second edition guides collectors, cowboy action shooters, hobbyists and Old West re-enactors through repairing and improving Old West firearms. New additions include 125 high-resolution diagrams and illustrations, five new handgun models, four new long gun models, and an expanded and illustrated glossary. The book offers expanded coverage of the first edition's featured guns (over 40 original and replica models), as well as updated gunsmithing tips and advice. The step-by-step, detailed illustrations demonstrate to both amateur and advanced gunsmiths how to repair and upgrade Old West firearms.

Gunsmithing: Pistols & Revolvers: Expanded 2nd Edition, by Patrick Sweeney, Iola, WI, Krause Publications, 2004. 384 Pages, illustrated, 850 b&w photos. $24.99
Set up an efficient and organized workplace and learn what tools are needed. Then, tackle projects like installing new grips, adjusting trigger pull and sight replacement. Includes a troubleshooting guide, glossary terms and a directory of suppliers and services for most brands of handguns.

Gunsmithing: Rifles, by Patrick Sweeney, Krause Publications, Iola, WI, 1999. 352 pp., illus. Paper covers. $24.95
Tips for lever-action rifles. Building a custom Ruger 10/22. Building a better hunting rifle.

Home Gunsmithing the Colt Single Action Revolvers, by Loren W. Smith, Ray Riling Arms Books, Co., Phila., PA, 2001. 119 pp., illus. $24.95
Affords the Colt Single Action owner detailed, pertinent information on the operating and servicing of this famous and historic handgun.

How to Convert Military Rifles, Williams Gun Sight Co., Davision, MI, new and enlarged seventh edition, 1997. 76 pp., illus. Paper covers. $13.95
This latest edition updated the changes that have occured over the past thirty years. Tips, instructions and illustratons on how to convert popular military rifles as the Enfield, Mauser 96 and SKS just to name a few are presented.

Mauser M98 & M96, by R.A. Walsh, Wolfe Publishing Co., Prescott, AR, 1998. 123 pp., illus. Paper covers. $32.50
How to build your own favorite custom Mauser rifle from two of the best bolt action rifle designs ever produced–the military Mauser Model 1898 and Model 1896 bolt rifles.

Mr. Single Shot's Gunsmithing-Idea-Book, by Frank de Haas, Mark de Haas, Orange City, IA, 1996. 168 pp., illus. Paper covers. $22.50
Offers easy to follow, step-by-step instructions for a wide variety of gunsmithing procedures all reinforced by plenty of photos.

Recreating the American Longrifle, by William Buchele, et al, George Shumway Publisher, York, Pa, 5th edition, 1999. 175 pp., illus. $40.00
Includes full size plans for building a Kentucky rifle.

Story of Pope's Barrels, The, by Ray M. Smith, R&R Books, Livonia, NY, 1993. 203 pp., illus. $39.00
A reissue of a 1960 book whose author knew Pope personally. It will be of special interest to Schuetzen rifle fans, since Pope's greatest days were at the height of the Schuetzen-era before WWI.

Survival Gunsmithing, by J.B. Wood, Desert Publications, Cornville, AZ, 1986. 92 pp., illus. Paper covers. $11.95
A guide to repair and maintenance of the most popular rifles, shotguns and handguns.

Tactical 1911, The, by Dave Lauck, Paladin Press, Boulder, CO, 1998. 137 pp., illus. Paper covers. $20.00
Here is the only book you will ever need to teach you how to select, modify, employ and maintain your Colt.

HANDGUNS

.22 Caliber Handguns; A Shooter's Guide, by D.F. Geiger, Lincoln, RI, Andrew Mowbray, Inc., 2003. 1st edition. Softcover. $21.95

.380 Enfield No. 2 Revolver, The, by Mark Stamps and Ian Skennerton, I.D.S.A. Books, Piqua, OH, 1993. 124 pp., 80 illus. Paper covers. $19.95

9mm Parabellum; The History & Development of the World's 9mm Pistols & Ammunition, by Klaus-Peter Konig and Martin Hugo, Schiffer Publishing Ltd., Atglen, PA, 1993. 304 pp., illus. $39.95
Detailed history of 9mm weapons from Belguim, Italy, Germany, Israel, France, U.S.A., Czechoslovakia, Hungary, Poland, Brazil, Finland and Spain.

A Study of Colt New Army and Navy Pattern Double action Revolvers 1889-1908, by Robert Best. Privately Printed, 2005, 2nd Printing. 276 pages. Hardcover $62.00
A Study…" is a detailed look into Colt's development and production of the Double Action Swing Out Cylinder New Army and Navy series revolvers. Civilian model production, U.S. Army and Navy models and contracts, and other Government organizations using these revolvers are all covered in this book. There are over 150 photographs with 24 pages of color photos to show specific markings and manufacturing changes. Fully documented.

Advanced Master Handgunning, by Charles Stephens, Paladin Press, Boulder, CO, 1994. 72 pp., illus. Paper covers. $14.00
Secrets and surefire techniques for winning handgun competitions.

Advanced Tactical Marksman More High Performance Techniques for Police, Military, and Practical Shooters, by Dave M. Lauck. Paladin Press, Boulder, CO, 2002. 1st edition. 232 pp., photos, illus. Softcover $35.00
Lauck, one of the most respected names in high-performance shooting and gunsmithing, refines and updates his 1st book. Dispensing with overcomplicated mil-dot formulas and minute-of-angle calculations, Lauck shows you how to achieve superior accuracy and figure out angle shots, train for real-world scenarios, choose optics and accessories.

American Beauty: The Prewar Colt National Match Government Model Pistol, by Timothy Mullin, Collector Grade Publications, Canada, 1999. 72 pp., 69 illus. $34.95
69 illustrations, 20 in full color photos of factory engraved guns and other authenticated upgrades, including rare 'double-carved' ivory grips.

Automatic Pistol, The, by J.B.L. Noel, Foreword by Timothy J. Mullin, Boulder, CO, Paladin Press, 2004. 128 pp., illus. Softcover. NEW. $14.00

Ayoob Files: The Book, The, by Massad Ayoob, Police Bookshelf, Concord, NH, 1995. 223 pp., illus. Paper covers. $14.95
The best of Massad Ayoob's acclaimed series in *American Handgunner* magazine.

Big Bore Handguns, by John Taffin, Krause Publications, Iola, WI, 2002. 1st edition. 352 pp., 320 b&w photos with a 16-page color section. Hardcover. $39.95
Gives honest reviews and an inside look at shooting, hunting, and competing with the biggest handguns around. Covers handguns from major gunmakers, as well as handgun customizing, accessories, reloading, and cowboy activities. Significant coverage is also given to handgun customizing, accessories, reloading, and popular shooting hobbies including hunting and cowboy activities.

Bill Ruger's .22 Pistol: A Photographic Essay of the Ruger Rimfire Pistol, by Don Findlay, New York, Simon & Schuster, 2000. 2nd printing. Limited edition of 100 copies, signed and numbered. Hardcover, NEW. $100.00

Browning High Power Automatic Pistol (Expanded Edition), by Blake R. Stevens, Collector Grade Publications, Canada, 1996. 310 pp., with 313 illus. $49.95
An in-depth chronicle of seventy years of High Power history, from John M. Browning's original 16-shot prototypes to the present. Profusely illustrated with rare original photos and drawings from the FN Archive to describe virtually every sporting and military version of the High Power. The Expanded Edition contains 30 new pages on the interesting Argentine full-auto High Power, the latest FN 'MK3' and BDA9 pistols, plus FN's revolutionary P90 5.7x28mm Personal Defense Weapon, and more!

Browning Hi-Power Assembly, Disassembly Manual 9mm, by Skennerton & Riling, Ray Riling Arms Books Co. Philadelphia, PA, 2005. 36 pages, illustrated. $5.00
Ideal workshop reference for stripping & assembly with exploded parts drawings, specifications, service accessories, historical information and recommended reading references. Ideal workbook for shooters and collectors alike. The binding is triple saddle-stitched with a durable plastic laminated cover.

ARMS LIBRARY

Browning Hi-Power Pistols, Desert Publications, Cornville, AZ, 1982. 20 pp., illus. Paper covers. $13.95

Covers all facets of the various military and civilian models of the Browning Hi-Power pistol.

Canadian Military Handguns 1855-1985, by Clive M. Law, Museum Restoration Service, Bloomfield, Ont., Canada, 1994. 130pp., illus. $40.00

A long-awaited and important history for arms historians and pistol collectors.

Classic Handguns of the 20th Century, by David Arnold. Iola, WI, Krause Publications, 2004. 144 pages, color photos. Softcover. $24.99

You'll need this book to find out what qualities, contributions and characteristics made each of the twenty handguns found within a "classic" in the eyes of noted gun historian and author, David W. Arnold. Join him on this most fascinating visual walk through the most significant and prolific handguns of the 20th century. From the Colt Single-Action Army Revolver and the German P08 Luger to the Walther P-38 and Beretta Model 92.

Collecting U. S. Pistols & Revolvers, 1909-1945, by J. C. Harrison. The Arms Chest, Oklahoma City, OK, 1999. 2nd edition (revised). 185 pp., illus. Spiral bound. $35.00

Valuable and detailed reference book for the collector of U.S. pistols & revolvers. Identifies standard issue original military models of the M1911, M1911A1 and M1917 Cal .45 pistols and revolvers as produced by all manufacturers from 1911 through 1945. Plus .22 Ace models, National Match models, and similar foreign military models produced by Colt or manufactured under Colt license, plus arsenal repair, refinish and lend-lease models.

Colt .45 Pistol M1911A1 Assembly, Disassembly Manual, by Skennerton & Riling, Ray Riling Arms Books Co. Philadelphia, PA, 2005. 36 pages, illustrated. $5.00

Ideal workshop reference for stripping & assembly with exploded parts drawings, specifications, service accessories, historical information and recommended reading references. Ideal workbook for shooters and collectors alike. The binding is triple saddle-stitched with a durable plastic laminated cover.

Colt .45 Auto Pistol, compiled from U.S. War Dept. Technical Manuals, and reprinted by Desert Publications, Cornville, AZ, 1978. 80 pp., illus. Paper covers. $14.95

Covers every facet of this famous pistol from mechanical training, manual of arms, disassembly, repair and replacement of parts.

Colt Single Action Army Revolver Study: New Discoveries, by Kenneth Moore, Lincoln, RI, Andrew Mowbray, Inc., 2003. 1st edition. Hardcover. NEW. $47.95

Combat Perspective; The Thinking Man's Guide to Self-Defense, by Gabriel Suarez, Boulder, CO, Paladin Press, 2003. 1st edition. 112 pp. Softcover. $15.00

In the Combat Perspective, Suarez keys in on developing your knowledge about and properly organizing your mental attitude toward combat to improve your odds of winning – not just surviving – such a fight. In this book he examines each in a logical and scientific manner, demonstrating why, when it comes to defending your life, the mental edge is at least as critical to victory as the tactical advantage.

Complete Encyclopedia of Pistols & Revolvers, by A.E. Hartnik, Knickerbocker Press, New York, NY, 2003. 272 pp., illus. $19.95

A comprehensive encyclopedia specially written for collectors and owners of pistols and revolvers.

Concealable Pocket Pistols: How to Choose and Use Small-Caliber Handguns, by Terence McLeod, Paladin Press, 2001. 1st edition. 80 pp. Softcover. $14.00

Small-caliber handguns are often maligned as too puny for serious self-defense, but millions of Americans own and carry these guns and have used them successfully to stop violent assaults. Find out what millions of Americans already know about these practical self-defense tools.

Concelealed Handgun Manual, The, 4th Edition, by Chris Bird. San Antonio, Privateer Publications, 2004. 332 pages, illus. Softcover. NEW. $21.95

If you carry a gun for personal protection, or plan to, you need to read this book. You will learn whether carrying a gun is for you, what gun to choose and how to carry it, how to stay out of trouble, when to shoot and how to shoot, gunfighting tactics, what to expect after you have shot someone, and how to apply for a concealed-carry license in 30 states, plus never-before published details of actual shooting incidents.

Confederate Lemat Revolver; Secret Weapon of the Confederacy?, The, by Doug Adams, Lincoln, RI, Andrew Mowbray, Inc.,2005. 1st edition. Nearly 200 spectacular full-color illustrations and over 70 b&w period photos, illustrations and patent drawings. 112 pages. Softcover. NEW. $29.95

This exciting new book describes LeMat's wartime adventures aboard blockade runners and alongside the famous leaders of the Confederacy, as well as exploring, as never before, the unique revolvers that he manufactured for the Southern Cause.

Darling Pepperbox: The Story of Samuel Colt's Forgotten Competitors in Bellingham, The, Mass. and Woonsocket, RI, by Stuart C. Mowbray, Lincoln, RI, Andrew Mowbray, Inc., 2004. 1st edition. 104 pp. Softcover. NEW. $19.95

Developmental Cartridge Handguns of .22 Calibre, as Produced in the United States & Abroad from 1855 to 1875, by John S. Laidacker, Atglen, PA, Schiffer Publications, 2003. Reprint. 597 pp., with over 860 b&w photos, drawings, and charts. Hardcover. $100.00

This book is a reprint edition of the late John Laidacker's personal study of early .22 Cartridge Handguns from 1855-1875. Laidacker's primary aim was to offer a quick reference to the collector, and his commentary on the wide variety of types, variations and makers, as well as detailed photography, make this a superb addition to any firearm library.

Effective Handgun Defense, by Frank James, Iola, WI, Krause Publications, 2004. 1st edition. 223 pp, illustated, softcover. NEW $19.95

Effective Handgun Defense, it's readily apparent that he'd have had no problem making his way in an urban environment either. He has a keen mind for the requirements and nuances for "concealed carry" and personal defense, and a fluid style of presenting his material that is neither awkward nor "precious."

Engraved Handguns of .22 Calibre, by John S. Laidacker, Atglen, PA, Schiffer Publications, 2003. 1st edition. 192 pp., with over 400 color and b&w photos. $69.95

Essential Guide to Handguns: Firearms Instruction for Personal Defense and Protection, by Stephen Rementer and Brian Eimer, Phd., Flushing, NY, Looseleaf law Publications, 2005. 1st edition. Over 300 pages plus illustrations. Softcover. NEW. $24.89

Farnam Method of Defensive Handgunning, The, by John S. Farnam, Police Bookshelf, 1999. 191 pp., illus. Paper covers. $24.00

A book intended to not only educate the new shooter, but also to serve as a guide and textbook for his and his instructor's training courses.

Fast and Fancy Revolver Shooting, by Ed McGivern, Anniversary Edition, Winchester Press, Piscataway, NJ, 1984. 484 pp., illus. $19.95

A fascinating volume, packed with handgun lore and solid information by the acknowledged dean of revolver shooters.

French Service Handguns: 1858-2004, by Eugene Medlin & Jean Huon, Tommy Gun Publications, 2004. 1st edition. Over 200 pages and more than 125 photographs. Hardcover, NEW. $44.95

Over 10 years in the making, this long awaited volume on French handguns is finally here. this book offers in depth coverage on everything from the 11mm Pinfire to the 9mm Parabellum-including various Lefaucheux revolvers, MAB's, Spanish pistols, and revolvers used in WWI, Uniques, plus, many photos of one-of-a-kind prototypes of the French contract Browning, Model 1935s, and 35a pistols used in WWII.

German Handguns: The Complete Book of the Pistols and Revolvers of Germany, 1869 to the Present, by Ian Hogg, Greenhill Publishing, 2001. 320 pp., 270 illustrations. Hardcover. $49.95

Ian Hogg examines the full range of handguns produced in Germany from such classics as the Luger M1908, Mauser HsC and Walther PPK, to more unusual types such as the Reichsrevolver M1879 and the Dreyse 9mm. He presents the key data (length, weight, muzzle velocity, and range) for each weapon discussed and also gives its date of introduction and service record, evaluates and discusses peculiarities, and examines in detail particular strengths and weaknesses.

Glock in Competition, by Robin Taylor, Spokane, WA, Taylor Press, 2006, 2nd edition. 248pp, Softcover. NEW $19.95

Covered topics include reloading, trigger configurations, recalls, and refits, magazine problems, modifying the Glock, choosing factory ammo, and a host of others.

Glock: The New Wave in Combat Handguns, by Peter Alan Kasler, Paladin Press, Boulder, CO, 1993. 304 pp., illus. $27.00

Kasler debunks the myths that surround what is the most innovative handgun to be introduced in some time.

Glock's Handguns, by Duncan Long, Desert Publications, El Dorado, AR, 1996. 180 pp., illus. Paper covers. $19.95

An outstanding volume on one of the world's newest and most successful firearms of the century.

Gun Digest Book of Beretta Pistols, The, by Massad Ayoob, Iola, WI, Krause Publications, 2005. 288 pages, 300+ photos help with identification. Softcover. $27.99

This new release from the publishers of Gun Digest, readers get information including caliber,weight and barrel lengths for modern pistols. A review of the accuracy and function of all models of modern Beretta pistols give active shooters details needed to make the most of this popular firearm. More than 300 photographs, coupled with articles detailing the development of design and style of these handguns, create a comprehensive must-have resource.

Gun Digest Book of Combat Handgunnery 5th Edition, The, Complete Guide to Combat Shooting, by Massad Ayoob, Iola, WI, Krause Publications, 2002. $22.95

Tap into the knowledge of an international combat handgun expert for the latest in combat handgun designs, strengths and limitations; caliber, size, power and ability; training and technique; cover, concealment and hostage situations. Unparalleled!

Gun Digest Book of the 1911, The, by Patrick Sweeney, Krause Publications, Iola, WI, 2002. 336 pp., with 700 b&w photos. Softcover. $27.95

Complete guide of all models and variations of the Model 1911. The author also includes repair tips and information on buying a used 1911.

Gun Digest Book of the 1911 2nd Edition, The, by Patrick Sweeney, Krause Publications, Iola, WI, 2006. 336 pp., with 700 b&w photos. Softcover. $27.95

Complete guide of all models and variations of the Model 1911. The author also includes repair tips and information on buying a used 1911.

Gun Digest Book of the Glock; A Comprehensive Review, Design, History and Use, The, Iola, WI, Krause Publications, 2003. 303 pp., with 500 b&w photos. Softcover. 27.95

Examine the rich history and unique elements of the most important and influential firearms design of the past 50 years, the Glock autoloading pistol. This comprehensive review of the revolutionary pistol analyzes the performance of the various models and chamberings and features a complete guide to available accessories and little-known factory options. You'll see why it's the preferred pistol for law enforcement use and personal protection.

Gun Digest Book of the SIG-Sauer, The, by Massad Ayoob, Iola, WI, Krause Publications, 2005. 1st edition 304pp. Softcover. NEW. $27.99

Noted firearms training expert Massad Ayoob takes an in-depth look at some of the finest pistols on the market. If you own a SIG-Sauer pistol, have consdered buying one or just appreciate the fine quality of these pistols, this is the book for you. Ayoob takes a practical look at each of the SIG-Sauer pistols including handling characteristics, and design and performance. Each gun in every caliber is tested and evaluated, giving you all the details you need as you choose and use your SIG-Sauer pistol.

Gun Digest Book of Smith & Wesson, The, by Patrick Sweeney, Iola, WI, Krause Publications, 2005. 1st edition. Covers all categories of Smith & Wesson Guns in both competition and law enforcement. 312pp, 500 b&w photos. Softcover, NEW. $27.99

Hand Cannons: The World's Most Powerful Handguns, by Duncan Long, Paladin Press, Boulder, CO, 1995. 208 pp., illus. Paper covers. $22.00

Long describes and evaluates each powerful gun according to their features.

Handgun Combatives, by Dave Spaulding, Flushing, NY, Looseleaf Law Publications,2005. 212pp, with 60 plus photos, softcover. NEW $22.95

Handgun Stopping Power "The Definitive Study," by Evan P. Marshall & Edwin J. Sanow, Paladin Press, Boulder, CO, 1997. 240 pp. photos. Softcover. $45.00

Dramatic first-hand accounts of the results of handgun rounds fired into criminals by cops, storeowners, cabbies and others are the heart and soul of this long-awaited book. This is the definitive methodology for predicting the stopping power of handgun loads, the first to take into account what really happens when a bullet meets a man.

ARMS LIBRARY

Handguns 2007, 19th Edition, Ken Ramage, Iola WI, Gun Digest Books, 2006, 320pp, 500 b&w photos, Softcover. NEW. $24.99
 Target shooters, handgun hunters, collectors and those who rely upon handguns for self-defense will want to pack this value-loaded and entertaining volume in their home libraries. Shooters will find the latest pistol and revolver designs and accessories, plus test reports on several models. The handgun becomes an artist's canvas in a showcase of engraving talents. The catalog section–with comprehensive specs on every known handgun in production–includes a new display of semi-custom handguns, plus an expanded, illustrated section on the latest grips, sights, scopes and other aiming devices. Offer easy access to products, services and manufacturers.

Handguns of the Armed Organizations of the Soviet Occupation Zone and German Democratic Republic, by Dieter H. Marschall, Los Alamos, NM, Ucross Books, 2000. Softcover. NEW. $29.95
 Translated from German this groundbreaking treatise covers the period from May 1945 through 1996. The organizations that used these pistols are described along with the guns and holsters. Included are the P08, P38, PP, PPK, P1001, PSM, Tokarev, Makarov, (including .22 LR, cutaway, silenced, Suhl marked), Stechlin, plus Hungarian, Romanian and Czech pistols.

Heckler & Koch's Handguns, by Duncan Long, Desert Publications, El Dorado, AR, 1996. 142 pp., illus. Paper covers. $19.95
 Traces the history and the evolution of H&K's pistols from the company's beginning at the end of WWII to the present.

Hidden in Plain Sight, by Trey Bloodworth & Mike Raley, Paladin Press, Boulder, CO, 2003. Paper covers. $20.00
 A practical guide to concealed handgun carry.

High Standard: A Collectors Guide to the Hamden & Hartford Target Pistols, by Tom Dance, Andrew Mowbray, Inc., Lincoln, RI, 1999. 192 pp., heavily illustrated with b&w photographs and technical drawings. $24.00
 From Citation to Supermatic, all of the production models and specials made from 1951 to 1984 are covered according to model number or series, making it easy to understand the evolution to this favorite of shooters and collectors.

High Standard Automatic Pistols 1932-1950, by Charles E. Petty, The Gun Room Press, Highland Park, NJ, 1989. 124 pp., illus. $19.95
 A definitive source of information for the collector of High Standard arms.

Hi-Standard Pistols and Revolvers, 1951-1984, by James Spacek, Chesire, CT, 1998. 128 pp., illus. Paper covers. $14.95
 Technical details, marketing features and instruction/parts manual of every model High Standard pistol and revolver made between 1951 and 1984. Most accurate serial number information available.

History of Smith & Wesson Firearms, by Dean Boorman, New York, Lyons Press, 2002. 1st edition. 144 pp., illustrated in full color. Hardcover. $29.95
 The definitive guide to one of the world's best-known firearms makers. Takes the story through the years of the Military & Police .38 & of the Magnum cartridge, to today's wide range of products for law-enforcement customers.

How to Become a Master Handgunner: The Mechanics of X-Count Shooting, by Charles Stephens, Paladin Press, Boulder, CO, 1993. 64 pp., illus. Paper covers. $14.00
 Offers a simple formula for success to the handgunner who strives to master the technique of shooting accurately.

How to Customize Your Glock: Step-By-Step Modifications You Can Do at Little Cost, by Robert and Morgan Boatman, Paladin Press, Boulder, CO, 2005, 1st edition. 8½" x 11", photos, 72 pp. Softcover. NEW. $20.00
 This mini-"Glocksmithing" course by Glock enthusiasts Robert and Morgan Boatman first explains why you would make a specific modification and what you gain in terms of improved performance. The workbook format makes the manual simple to follow as you work on your Glock, andhigh-resolution photos illustrate each part and step precisely. Make your Glock work even more effectively for you bythinking outside the box.

Inglis Diamond: The Canadian High Power Pistol, by Clive M. Law, Collector Grade Publications, Canada, 2001. 312 pp., illus. $49.95
 This definitive work on Canada's first and indeed only mass produced handgun, in production for a very brief span of time and consequently made in relatively few numbers, the venerable Inglis-made Browning High Power covers the pistol's initial history, the story of Chinese and British adoption, use post-war by Holland, Australia, Greece, Belgium, New Zealand, Peru, Brasil and other countries. All new information on the famous light-weights and the Inglis Diamond variations. Completely researched through official archives in a dozen countries. Many of the bewildering variety of markings have never been satisfactorily explained until now

Japanese Military Cartridge Handguns 1893-1945, A Revised and Expanded Edition of Hand Cannons of Imperial Japan, by Harry L. Derby III and James D. Brown, Atglen, PA, Schiffer Publications, 2003. 1st edition. Hardcover. New in new dust jacket. $79.95
 When originally published in 1981, *The Hand Cannons of Imperial Japan* was heralded as one of the most readable works on firearms ever produced. To arms collectors and scholars, it remains a prized source of information on Japanese handguns, their development, and their history. In this new revised and expanded edition, original author Harry Derby has teamed with Jim Brown to provide a thorough update reflecting twenty years of additional research. An appendix on valuation has also been added, using a relative scale that should remain relevant despite inflationary pressures. For the firearms collector, enthusiast, historian or dealer, this is the most complete and up-to-date work on Japanese military handguns ever written.

Living with Glocks: The Complete Guide to the New Standard in Combat Handguns, by Robert H. Boatman, Boulder, CO, Paladin Press, 2002. 1st edition. 184 pp., illus. Hardcover. $29.95
 In addition to demystifying the enigmatic Glock trigger, Boatman describes and critiques each Glock model in production. Separate chapters on the G36, the enhanced G20 and the full-auto G18 emphasize the job-specific talents of these standout models for those seeking insight on which Glock pistol might best meet their needs. And for those interested in optimizing their Glock's capabilities, this book addresses all the peripherals–holsters, ammo, accessories, silencers, modifications and conversions, training programs and more.

Living With the 1911, by Robert Boatman, Boulder, CO, Paladin Press, 2005. 144pp, softcover. NEW $25.00

Luger P'08 Pistol, 9mm Assembly, Disassembly Manual, by Skennerton & Riling, Ray Riling Arms Books Co. Philadelphia, PA, 2005. 36 pages, illustrated. $5.00
 Ideal workshop reference for stripping & assembly with exploded parts drawings, specifications, service accessories, historical information and recommended reading references. The binding is triple saddle-stitched with a durable plastic laminated cover.

Luger Handbook, by Aarron Davis, Krause Publications, Iola, WI, 1997. 112 pp., illus. Paper covers. $9.95
 Now you can identify any of the legendary Luger variations using a simple decision tree. Each model and variation includes pricing information, proof marks and detailed attributes in a handy, user-friendly format. Plus, it's fully indexed. Instantly identify that Luger!

Lyman Pistol and Revolver Handbook, 3rd edition, by Lyman. Middletown, CT, Lyman Products Corp, 2005. 3rd edition. 272pp, Softcover. NEW $22.95

Makarov Pistol Assembly, Disassembly Manual 9mm, by Skennerton & Riling, Ray Riling Arms Books Co. Philadelphia, PA, 2005. 36 pages, illustrated. $5.00
 Ideal workshop reference for stripping & assembly with exploded parts drawings, specifications, ervice accessories, historical information and recommended reading references. The binding is triple saddle-stitched with a durable plastic laminated cover.

Mauser Self-Loading Pistol, by Belford & Dunlap, Borden Publishing Co., Alhambra, CA. Over 200 pp., 300 illus., large format. $29.95
 The long-awaited book on the "Broom Handles," covering their inception in 1894 to the end of production. Complete and in detail: pocket pistols, Chinese and Spanish copies.

Mauser Broomhandle Model 1896 Pistol Assembly, Disassembly Manual, by Skennerton & Riling, Ray Riling Arms Books Co. Philadelphia, PA, 2005. 36 pages, illustrated. $5.00
 Ideal workshop reference for stripping & assembly with exploded parts drawings, specifications, service accessories, historical information and recommended reading references.

Mental Mechanics of Shooting: How to Stay Calm at the Center, by Vishnu Karmakar and Thomas Whitney, Littleton, CO, Center Vision, Inc., 2001. 144 pp. Softcover. $19.95
 Not only will this book help you stay free of trigger jerk, it will help you in all areas of your shooting.

Model 35 Radom Pistol, The, by Terence Lapin, Hyrax Publishers, 2004. 95 pages with b&w photos, Stiff paper covers. NEW. $18.95

Model 1911 Automatic Pistol, by Robert Campbell, Accokeek, Maryland, Stoeger Publications, 2004. Hardcover. NEW. $24.95

Modern Law Enforcement Weapons & Tactics, 3rd Edition, by Patrick Sweeney, Iola, WI, Krause Publications, 2004. 256 pp. Softcover. NEW. $22.99

Official 9mm Markarov Pistol Manual, translated into English by Major James Gebhardt, U.S. Army (Ret.), Desert Publications, El Dorado, AR, 1996. 84 pp., illus. Paper covers. $14.95
 The information found in this book will be of enormous benefit and interest to the owner or a prospective owner of one of these pistols.

Operator's Tactical Pistol Shooting Manual; A Practical Guide to Combat Marksmanship, by Erik Lawrence, Linesville, PA, Blackheart Publishing, 2003. 1st edition. 233 pp. Softcover. $24.50
 This manual-type book begins with the basics of safety with a pistol and progresses into advanced pistol handling. A self-help guide for improving your capabilities with a pistol at your own pace.

P08 Luger Pistol, by de Vries & Martens, Alexandria, VA, Ironside International, 2002. 152 pp., illustrated with 200 high quality b&w photos. Hardcover. $34.95
 Covers all essential information on history and development, ammunition and accessories, codes and markings, and contains photos of nearly every model and accessory. Includes a unique selection of original German WWII propaganda photos, most never published before.

P-08 Parabellum Luger Automatic Pistol, edited by J. David McFarland, Desert Publications, Cornville, AZ, 1982. 20 pp., illus. Paper covers. $14.95
 Covers every facet of the Luger, plus a listing of all known Luger models.

P-38 Pistol: Postwar Distributions, 1945-1990, Volume 3, by Warren Buxton, Ucross Books, Los Alamos, MN 1999, plus an addendum to Volumes 1 & 2: 272 pp. with 342 illustrations. $75.00

P-38 Pistol: The Contract Pistols, 1940-1945, Volume 2, by Warren Buxton, Ucross Books, Los Alamos, MN 1999. 256 pp. with 237 illustrations. $75.00

P-38 Pistol: The Walther Pistols, 1930-1945, Volume 1, by Warren Buxton, Ucross Books, Los Alamos, MN 1999. 328 pp. with 160 illustrations. $75.00
 A limited run reprint of this scarce and sought-after work on the P-38 Pistol.

Peacemakers: Arms and Adventure in the American West, by RL Wilson. New York, Book Sales, 2004. reprint. 392pp. colored endpapers, 320 full color illustrations. Hardcover in New DJ, NEW. $24.89

Percussion Pistols and Revolvers: History, Performance and Practical Use, by Mike Cumpston and Johnny Bates, Texas, Iunivers, Inc, 2005. 1st edition. 208 pages. Softcover. $19.95
 With the advent of the revolving pistols came patents that created monopolies in revolver production and the through-bored cylinder necessary for self-contained metallic cartridges. The caplock revolvers took on a separate evolution and remained state of the art long after the widespread appearance of cartridge-firing rifles and shotguns.

Pistol as a Weapon of Defence in the House and on the Road, by Jeff Cooper, Boulder, CO, Paladin Press, 2004. 1st edition. 48pp. Softcover. NEW. $9.00
 Penned in 1875 and recently discovered collecting dust on a library bookshelf, this primer for the pistol is remarkably timely in its insights and observations. From a historical perspective, it contains striking parallels to the thinking and controversy that swirl about the practical use of the pistol today.

Pistols of the World; Fully Revised, 4th Edition, Iola, WI, Krause Publications, 2005. 432pp, chronicles 2,500 handguns made from 1887-2004. Stiff paper covers, NEW. $22.95
 More than 1,000 listings and 20 years of coverage were added since the previous edition.

Pistols of World War I, by Robert J. Adamek, Pittsburgh, Pentagon Press, 2001. 1st edition signed and numbered. 296 pp. with illustrations and photos. Softcover. $45.00
 Over 90 pistols illustrated, technical data, designers, history, proof marks. Over 25 pistol magazines illustrated with dimensions, serial number ranges. Over 35 cartridges illustrated with dimensions, manufactures, year of introduction. Weapons from 16 countries involved in WWI, statistics, quantities made, identification.

ARMS LIBRARY

Remington Large-Bore Conversion Revolvers, by R. Phillips. Canada, Prately printed, 2005. Limited printing of 250 signed and numbered copies in leather hardcover. 126pp, with 200 illustrations. NEW $55.00

Ruger .22 Automatic Pistol, Standard/Mark I/Mark II Series, by Duncan Long, Paladin Press, Boulder, CO, 1989. 168 pp., illus. Paper covers. $16.00
The definitive book about the pistol that has served more than 1 million owners so well.

Ruger .22 Automatic Pistols: The Complete Guide for all Models from 1947 to 2003, Grand Rapids, MI, The Ruger Store, 2004. 74 pp., 66 high-resolution grayscale images. Printed in the U.S.A. with card stock cover and bright white paper. Softcover. NEW. $12.95
Includes 'rare' complete serial numbers and manufacturing dates from 1949-2004.

Ruger "P" Family of Handguns, by Duncan Long, Desert Publications, El Dorado, AZ, 1993. 128 pp., illus. Paper covers. $14.95
A full-fledged documentary on a remarkable series of Sturm Ruger handguns.

Ruger Pistol Reference Booklet 1949-1982 (Pocket Guide to Ruger Rimfire Pistols Standard and Mark I), by Don Findlay. Lubbock Tx, 2005. Softcover. 24 pages, illustrated with b&w photos. $9.95
Designed for the professional un dealer as well as the collector. Complete list of serial numbers as well as production dates. Also, includes photos of the original boxes the guns came in.

Semi-automatic Pistols in Police Service and Self Defense, by Massad Ayoob, Police Bookshelf, Concord, NH, 1990. 25 pp., illus. Softcover. $11.95
First quantitative, documented look at actual police experience with 9mm and 45 police service automatics.

Shooting Colt Single Actions, by Mike Venturino, Livingston, MT, 1997. 205 pp., illus. Paper covers. $25.00
A definitive work on the famous Colt SAA and the ammunition it shoots.

SIG Handguns, by Duncan Long, Desert Publications, El Dorado, AZ, 1995. 150 pp., illus. Paper covers. $19.95
The history of SIG/Sauer handguns, including Sig, Sig-Hammerli and Sig/Sauer variants.

Smith & Wesson's Automatics, by Larry Combs, Desert Publications, El Dorado, AZ, 1994. 143 pp., illus. Paper covers. $19.95
A must for every S&W auto owner or prospective owner.

Smith & Wesson: Sixguns of the Old West, by David Chicoine. Lincoln, RI., Andrew Mowbray, Inc., 2004. 1st edition. 480 pages, countless photos and detailed technical drawings. Hardcover. New in new dust jacket. $69.49
The Schofields, The Americans, The Russians, The New Model #3s, and The DAs.

Smith & Wesson American Model; In U.S. And Foreign Service, by Charles W. Pate, Mowbray Publishers, Lincoln, RI, 2006. 408 pp., illus. $65.00
This new book is an awesome new collector's guide to the S&W American. A huge resource on the military and western use of this classic large frame revolver.

Spanish Handguns: The History of Spanish Pistols and Revolvers, by Gene Gangarosa Jr., Stoeger Publishing Co., Accokeek, MD, 2001. 320 pp., illustrated, b&w photos. Paper covers. $21.95

Standard Catalog Of Luger, by Aarron Davis, Gun Digest Books, Iola WI, 2006. 256 pages, illustrated with photos. Paper Covers $29.99
This comprehensive identification and price guide goes a long way to giving Luger enthusiasts information to enjoy and be successful in an extremely active collector market. With Standard Catalog of Luger, firearms enthusiasts receive an unrivaled reference that includes: Reproductions of symbols and makers' marks from every model of Luger for use in accurately identifying the hundreds of Luger variations, More than 1,000 detailed photos and line illustrations demonstrating design and performance of Luger pistols, Manufacturing data and model rarity information to aid collectors when buying Lugers as an investment. Perfect for firearms collectors, gun shop owners, auction houses, museums, and appraisers.

Standard Catalog Of Smith & Wesson; 3rd Edition, by Jim Supica, & Richard Nahas, Gun Digest Books, Iola WI, 2006 384 pages, with photos, Hardcover. $39.99
Definitive Smith & Wesson identification and pricing reference, includes 350+ full-color photos for improved identification. Smith & Wesson is one of the hottest manufacturers of handguns, offering more new models than any other maker-39 new products in 2005 alone. Comprehensive coverage of Smith & Wesson firearm line including the only handgun in the world in continuous production since 1899. The 3rd Edition combines full color photos with details collectors need to identify and better appreciate all Smith & Wesson firearms.

Star Firearms, by Leonardo M. Antaris, Davenport, TA, Firac Publications Co., 2002. 1st edition. Hardcover. New in new dust jacket. $119.95

Tactical 1911, by Dave Lauck, Paladin Press, Boulder, CO, 1999. 152 pp., illus. Paper covers. $22.00
The cop's and SWAT operator's guide to employment and maintenance.

Tactical Pistol, by Gabriel Suarez, Foreword by Jeff Cooper, Paladin Press, Boulder, CO, 1996. 216 pp., illus. Paper covers. $25.00
Advanced gunfighting concepts and techniques.

Tactical Pistol Shooting; Your Guide to Tactics that Work, by Erik Lawrence. Iola, WI, Krause Publications, 2005. 1st edition. More than 250 step-by-step photos to illustrate techniques. 233pp, Softcover. NEW $18.95

Thompson/Center Contender Pistol, by Charles Tephens, Paladin Press, Boulder, CO, 1997. 58 pp., illus. Paper covers. $14.00
How to tune and time, load and shoot accurately with the Contender pistol.

U.S. Handguns of World War II, The Secondary Pistols and Revolvers, by Charles W. Pate, Mowbray Publishers, Lincoln, RI, 1997. 368 pp., illus. $39.00
This indispensable new book covers all of the American military handguns of WWII except for the M1911A1.

Walther P-38 Assembly, Disassembly Manual 9mm, by Skennerton & Riling, Ray Riling Arms Books Co. Philadelphia, PA, 2005. 36 pages, illustrated. $5.00

Ideal workshop reference for stripping & assembly with exploded parts drawings, specifications, service accessories, historical information and recommended reading references. The binding is triple saddle-stitched with a durable plastic laminated cover.

Walther Pistols: Models 1 Through P99, Factory Variations and Copies, by Dieter H. Marschall, Ucross Books, Los Alamos, NM. 2000. 140 pp., with 140 b&w illustrations, index. Paper covers. $21.95
This is the English translation, revised and updated, of the highly successful and widely acclaimed German language edition. This book provides the collector with a reference guide and overview of the entire line of the Walther military, police, and self-defense pistols from the very first to the very latest Variations, where issued, serial ranges, calibers, marks, proofs, logos, and design aspects in an astonishing quantity and variety are crammed into this very well researched and highly regarded work.

HUNTING

NORTH AMERICA

A Varmint Hunter's Odyssey, by Steve Hanson with guest chapter by Mike Johnson, Precision Shooting, Inc. Manchester, CT, 1999. 279 pp., illus. Paper covers. $39.95
A new classic by a writer who eats, drinks and sleeps varmint hunting and varmint rifles.

Advanced Black Powder Hunting, by Toby Bridges, Stoeger Publishing Co., Wayne, NJ, 1998. 288 pp., illus. Paper covers. $21.95
The first modern day publication to be filled from cover to cover with guns, loads, projectiles, accessories and the techniques to get the most from today's front loading guns.

Adventures of an Alaskan–You Can Do, by Dennis W. Confer, Foreword by Craig Boddington. Anchorage, AK, Wiley Ventures, 2003. 1st edition. 279 pp., illus. Softcover. $24.95
This book is about 45% fishing, 45% hunting, & 10% related adventures; travel, camping and boating. It is written to stimulate, encourage and motivate readers to make happy memories that they can do on an average income and to entertain, educate and inform readers of outdoor opportunities.

Aggressive Whitetail Hunting, by Greg Miller, Krause Publications, Iola, WI, 1995. 208 pp., illus. Paper covers. $14.95
Learn how to hunt trophy bucks in public forests, private farmlands and exclusive hunting grounds from one of America's foremost hunters.

Alaska Safari, by Harold Schetzle & Sam Fadala, Anchorage, AK, Great Northwest Publishing, 2002. Revised 2nd edition. 366 pp., illus. with b&w photos. Softcover. $29.95
The author has brought a wealth of information to the hunter and anyone interested in Alaska. Harold Schetzle is a great guide and has also written another book of stories of Alaska hunting taken from many, many years of hunting and guiding. The most comprehensive guide to Alaska hunting.

Alaskan Adventures-Volume I-The Early Years, by Russell Annabel, Long Beach, CA, Safari Press,2005, 2nd printing. 453pp. illus. Hardcover. New in new dust jacket. $35.00
No other writer has ever been able to capture the spirit of adventure and hunting in Alaska like Russell Annabel.

Alaskan Yukon Trophies Won and Lost, by G.O. Young, Wolfe Publishing, Prescott, AZ, 2002. Softcover. $35.00
.A classic big game hunting tale with 273 pages b&w photographs and a five-page epilogue by the publisher.

American Duck Shooting, by George Bird Grinnell, Stackpole Books, Harrisburg, PA, 1991. 640 pp., illus. Paper covers. $19.95
First published in 1901 at the height of the author's career. Describes 50 species of waterfowl, and discusses hunting methods common at the turn of the century.

Bear Hunting in Alaska: How to Hunt Brown and Grizzly Bears, by Tony Russ, Northern Publishing, 2004. 116 b&w photos, illus. 256 pgs. Soft cover. Excellent. $22.95
Teaches every skill you will need to prepare for, scout, find, select, stalk, shoot and care for one of the most sought-after trophies on earth – the Alaskan brown bear and the Alaskan Grizzly.

Bears of Alaska, by Erwin Bauer, Sasquatch Books, 2002. Soft cover. Excellent . $15.95

Best of Babcock, The, by Havilah Babcock, Introduction by Hugh Grey, The Gunnerman Press, Auburn Hills, MI, 1985. 262 pp., illus. $19.95
A treasury of memorable pieces, 21 of which have never before appeared in book form.

Blacktail Trophy Tactics, by Boyd Iverson, Stoneydale Press, Stevensville, MI, 1992. 166 pp., illus. Paper covers. $14.95
A comprehensive analysis of blacktail deer habits, describing a deer's and man's use of scents, still hunting, tree techniques, etc.

Bowhunter's Handbook, Expert Strategies and Techniques, by M.R. James with Fred Asbell, Dave Holt, Dwight Schuh and Dave Samuel, DBI Books, a division of Krause Publications, Iola, WI, 1997. 256 pp., illus. Paper covers. $19.95
Tips from the top on taking your bowhunting skills to the next level.

Buffalo Harvest, The, by Frank Mayer as told to Charles Roth, Pioneer Press, Union City, TN, 1995. 96 pp., illus. Paper covers. $12.50
The story of a hide hunter during his buffalo hunting days on the plains.

Call of the Quail: A Tribute to the Gentleman Game Bird, by Michael McIntosh, et al., Countrysport Press, Traverse City, MI, 1990. 175 pp., illus. $35.00
A new anthology on quail hunting.

Calling All Elk, by Jim Zumbo, Cody, WY, 1989. 169 pp., illus. Paper covers. $14.95
The only book on the subject of elk hunting that covers every aspect of elk vocalization.

Complete Book of Grouse Hunting, The, by Frank Woolner, The Lyons Press, New York, NY, 2000. 192 pp., illus. Paper covers. $24.95
The history, habits, and habitat of one of America's great game birds–and the methods used to hunt it.

Complete Book of Mule Deer Hunting, The, by Walt Prothero, The Lyons Press, New York, NY, 2000. 192 pp., illus. Paper covers. $24.95
Field-tested practical advice on how to bag the trophy buck of a lifetime.

ARMS LIBRARY

Complete Book of Wild Turkey Hunting, The, by John Trout Jr., The Lyons Press, New York, NY, 2000. 192 pp., illus. Paper covers. $24.95
An illustrated guide to hunting for one of America's most popular game birds.

Complete Book of Woodcock Hunting, The, by Frank Woolner, The Lyons Press, New York, NY, 2000. 192 pp., illus. Paper covers. $24.95
A thorough, practical guide to the American woodcock and to woodcock hunting.

Complete Guide To Hunting Wild Boar in California, The, by Gary Kramer, Safari Press, 2002. 1st edition. 127 pp., 37 photos. Softcover. $15.95
Gary Kramer takes the hunter all over California, from north to south and east to west. He discusses natural history, calibers, bullets, rifles, pistols, shotguns, black powder, and bow and arrows—even recipes.

Complete Venison Cookbook from Field to Table, The, by Jim & Ann Casada, Krause Publications, Iola, WI, 1996. 208 pp., Comb-bound. $12.95
More than 200 kitchen-tested recipes make this book the answer to a table full of hungry hunters or guests.

Cougar Attacks: Encounters of the Worst Kind, by Kathy Etling, NY, Lyons Press, 2004. 1st edition. 256 pages, illustrated with b&w photos. Soft cover. NEW. $14.95
Blood-curdling encounters between the big cats of North America and their most reluctant prey, humans.

Coyote Hunting, by Phil Simonski, Stoneydale Press, Stevensville, MT, 1994. 126 pp., illus. Paper covers. $12.95
Probably the most thorough "how-to-do-it" book on coyote hunting ever written.

Dabblers & Divers: A Duck Hunter's Book, compiled by the editors of *Ducks Unlimited* magazine, Willow Creek Press, Minocqua, WI, 1997. 160 pp., illus. $39.95
A word-and-photographic portrayal of waterfowl hunter's singular intimacy with, and passion for, watery haunts and wildfowl.

Deer & Deer Hunting, by Al Hofacker, Krause Publications, Iola, WI, 1993. 208 pp., illus. $34.95
Coffee-table volume packed full of how-to-information that will guide hunts for years to come.

Dreaming the Lion, by Thomas McIntyre, Countrysport Press, Traverse City, MI, 1994. 309 pp., illus. $35.00
Reflections on hunting, fishing and a search for the wild. Twenty-three stories by *Sports Afield* editor, Tom McIntyre.

Eastern Cougar: Historic Accounts, Scientific Investigations, and New Evidence, by Chris Bolgiano, Mechanicsburg,PA, Stackpole Books, 2005. Soft cover. NEW. $19.95
This fascinating anthology probes America's troubled history with large predators and makes a vital contribution to the wildlife management debates of today.

Elk and Elk Hunting, by Hart Wixom, Stackpole Books, Harrisburg, PA, 1986. 288 pp., illus. $34.95
Your practical guide to fundamentals and fine points of elk hunting.

Elk Hunting Guide: Skills, Gear, and Insight, by Tom Airhart, Stackpole Books,2005. A thorough, informative guide to the growing sport of elk hunting with in-depth coverage of current equipment and gear, techniques for tracking elk and staying safe in the wilderness and advice on choosing guides and outfitters. 432pp, 71 b&w photos, 38 illus. $19.95

Elk Hunting in the Northern Rockies, by Ed Wolff, Stoneydale Press, Stevensville, MT, 1984. 162 pp., illus. $18.95
Helpful information about hunting the premier elk country of the northern Rocky Mountain states–Wyoming, Montana and Idaho.

Elk Hunting with the Experts, by Bob Robb, Stoneydale Press, Stevensville, MT, 1992. 176 pp., illus. $15.95
A complete guide to elk hunting in North America by America's top elk hunting expert.

Encyclopedia of Buffalo Hunters and Skinners Volume 1 A-D, by Gilbert Reminger, Pioneer Press, 2003. The first volume in the series. 286 pages, acknowledgements, introduction, preface, illustrated, maps, plates, portraits, appendices, bibliography, index. Hardcover. NEW. $35.00

Encyclopedia of Buffalo Hunters and Skinners Volume 2 E-K, by Gilbert Reminger, Pioneer Press, 2006. The 2nd volume in the series. 285 pages, 115 photos, 15 drawings/newspaper items, and 6 maps. Index, Bibliography. Hardcover. NEW. $35.00
Vol. II covers hunters and skinners, that have so far surfaced, with surnames that begin with E-K, beginning with skinner William Earl and runs through the Kuykendall brothers, Judge and John, who hunted late (1886-1888) in southeastern New Mexico.

Fair Chase in North America, by Craig Boddington, Long Beach, CA, Safari Press, 2004. 1st edition. Hardcover. New in new dust jacket. $39.95

Getting a Stand, by Miles Gilbert, Pioneer Press, Union City, TN, 1993. 204 pp., illus. Paper covers. $13.95
An anthology of 18 short personal experiences by buffalo hunters of the late 1800s, specifically from 1870-1882.

Greatest Elk; The Complete Historical and Illustrated Record of North America's Biggest Elk, by R. Selner, Safari Press, Huntington Beach, CA, 2000. 209 pp., profuse color illus. $39.95
Here is the book all elk hunters have been waiting for! This oversized book holds the stories and statistics of the biggest bulls ever killed in North America. Stunning, full-color photographs highlight over 40 world-class heads, including the old world records!

Grouse and Woodcock, A Gunner's Guide, by Don Johnson, Krause Publications, Iola, WI, 1995. 256 pp., illus. Paper covers. $14.95
Find out what you need in guns, ammo, equipment, dogs and terrain.

Gunning for Sea Ducks, by George Howard Gillelan, Tidewater Publishers, Centreville, MD, 1988. 144 pp., illus. $14.95
A book that introduces you to a practically untouched arena of waterfowling.

Head Fer the Hills-Volume VI (1934-1960), by Russell Annabel, Long Beach, CA, Safari Press, 2005, Deluxe, Limited, Signed edition. 312pp., photos, drawings. Hardcover in a Slipcase. NEW. $60.00
As Tex Cobb, Russell Annabel's famous mentor and eternal companion, was famous for saying, "Head fer the hills," which is exactly what Rusty did.

Heck with Moose Hunting, The, by Jim Zumbo, Wapiti Valley Publishing Co., Cody, WY, 1996. 199 pp., illus. $17.95
Jim's hunts around the continent including encounters with moose, caribou, sheep, antelope and mountain goats.

High Pressure Elk Hunting, by Mike Lapinski, Stoneydale Press Publishing Co., Stevensville, MT, 1996. 192 pp., illus. $19.95
The secrets of hunting educated elk revealed.

Horns in the High Country, by Andy Russell, Alfred A. Knopf, NY, 1973. 259 pp., illus. Paper covers. $12.95
A many-sided view of wild sheep and their natural world.

How to Hunt, by Dave Bowring, Winchester Press, Piscataway, NJ, 1982. 208 pp., illus. Hardcover $15.00
A basic guide to hunting big game, small game, upland birds, and waterfowl.

Hunt High for Rocky Mountain Goats, Bighorn Sheep, Chamois & Tahr, by Duncan Gilchrist, Stoneydale Press, Stevensville, MT, 1992. 192 pp., illus. Paper covers. $19.95
The source book for hunting mountain goats.

Hunter's Alaska, The, by Roy F. Chandler, Iron Brigade, 2005. Hardcover. NEW. $49.95
This is a book written by Roy F. Chandler (Rocky). Rocky's Alaskan travels span half a century. Hunters hoping to hunt the "Great Land" will read exactly how it is done and what they can hope for if they ever make it into the Alaskan wilderness. This is a new publication of 2500 signed and numbered copies. Previous books, written by Rocky, about hunting Alaska have become collectors items. This book has some information from the prior books and much more "added" information.

Hunting Adventure of Me and Joe, by Walt Prothero, Safari Press, Huntington Beach, CA, 1995. 220 pp., illus. $22.50
A collection of the author's best and favorite stories.

Hunting America's Wild Turkey, by Toby Bridges, Stoeger Publishing Company, Pocomoke, MD, 2001. 256 pp., illus. $16.95
The techniques and tactics of hunting North America's largest, and most popular, woodland game bird.

Hunting Hard in Alaska, by Marc Taylor, Anchorage, AK, Biblio Distribution, 2003 Softcover. $19.95

Hunting In Alaska: A Comprehensive Guide, by Christopher Batin, Alaska Angler Pubs., 2002. 430 pages. Soft cover. NEW. $29.95

Hunting the Land of the Midnight Sun, by Alaska Professional Hunters Assoc., Safari Press, 2005. Hardcover. New in new dust jacket. $29.95
Contains contributions by Rob Holt, Gary King, Gary LaRose, Garth Larsen, Jim Shockey, Jeff Davis, and many others.

Hunting Mature Bucks, by Larry L. Weishuhn, Krause Publications, Iola, WI, 1995. 256 pp., illus. Paper covers. $14.95
One of North America's top white-tailed deer authorities shares his expertise on hunting those big, smart and elusive bucks.

Hunting Open-Country Mule Deer, by Dwight Schuh, Sage Press, Nampa, ID, 1989. 180 pp., illus. $18.95
A guide taking Western bucks with rifle and bow.

Hunting the Rockies, Home of the Giants, by Kirk Darner, Marceline, MO, 1996. 291 pp., illus. $25.00
Understand how and where to hunt Western game in the Rockies.

Hunting Western Deer, by Jim and Wes Brown, Stoneydale Press, Stevensville, MT, 1994. 174 pp., illus. Paper covers. $14.95
A pair of expert Oregon hunters provide insight into hunting mule deer and blacktail deer in the western states.

Hunting Wild Turkeys in the West, by John Higley, Stoneydale Press, Stevensville, MT, 1992. 154 pp., illus. Paper covers. $12.95
Covers the basics of calling, locating and hunting turkeys in the western states.

Hunting with the Twenty-Two, by Charles Singer Landis, R&R Books, Livonia, NY, 1994. 429 pp., illus. $35.00
A miscellany of articles touching on the hunting and shooting of small game.

In Search of the Buffalo, by Charles G. Anderson, Pioneer Press, Union City, TN, 1996. 144 pp., illus. Paper covers. $13.95
The primary study of the life of J. Wright Mooar, one of the few hunters fortunate enough to kill a white buffalo.

In the Turkey Woods, by Jerome B. Robinson, The Lyons Press, N.Y., 1998. 207 pp., illus. $24.95
Practical expert advice on all aspects of turkey hunting–from calls to decoys to guns.

Kodiak Island and its Bears, by Harry Dodge, Anchorage, Great Northwest Publishing, 2004. 364 pages, carefully indexed, thoughtfully footnoted, and lavishly illustrated. $27.50
This is the most significant volume about Kodiak Island and its bears that has been published in at least 20 years. This book now stands to become a new classic for all time.

Lost Classics of Jack O'Connor, by Jim Casada, Live Oak Press, 2004. Exciting tales with a twist of humor. 33 photos, 40 illus. by Dan Burr; 376 pages, with illustrations and photos. Hardcover. New in new dust jacket. $35.00

Montana–Land of Giant Rams, Volume 2, by Duncan Gilchrist, Outdoor Expeditions and Books, Corvallis, MT, 1992. 208 pp., illus. $34.95
The reader will find stories of how many of the top-scoring trophies were taken.

Montana–Land of Giant Rams, Volume 3, by Duncan Gilchrist, Outdoor Expeditions and Books, Corvallis, MT, 1999. 224 pp., illus. Paper covers. $19.95
All new sheep information including over 70 photos. Learn about how Montana became the "Land of Giant Rams" and what the prospects of the future are.

More Tracks: 78 Years of Mountains, People & Happiness, by Howard Copenhaver, Stoneydale Press, Stevensville, MT, 1992. 150 pp., illus. $18.95
A collection of stories by one of the back country's best storytellers about the people who shared with Howard his great adventure in the high places and wild Montana country.

Mostly Huntin', by Bill Jordan, Everett Publishing Co., Bossier City, LA, 1987. 254 pp., illus. $21.95
Jordan's hunting adventures in North America, Africa, Australia, South America and Mexico.

Mule Deer: Hunting Today's Trophies, by Tom Carpenter and Jim Van Norman, Krause Publications, Iola, WI, 1998. 256 pp., illus. Paper covers. $19.95
A tribute to both the deer and the people who hunt them. Includes info on where to look for big deer, prime mule deer habitat and effective weapons for the hunt.

Muzzleloading for Deer and Turkey, by Dave Ehrig, Stackpole Books,2005. 475 pages, 293 b&w photos. Hardcover. New in new dust jacket. $29.95

My Health is Better in November, by Havilah Babcock, University of S. Carolina Press, Columbia, SC, 1985. 284 pp., illus. $24.95
Adventures in the field set in the plantation country and backwater streams of SC.

North American Waterfowler, The, by Paul S. Bernsen, Superior Publ. Co., Seattle, WA, 1972. 206 pp. Paper covers. $9.95
The complete inside and outside story of duck and goose shooting. Big and colorful, illustrations by Les Kouba.

Old Man and the Boy, The, by Robert Ruark, Henry Holt & Co., New York, NY, 303 pp., illus. $24.95
A timeless classic, telling the story of a remarkable friendship between a young boy and his grandfather as they hunt and fish together.

Old Man's Boy Grows Older, The, by Robert Ruark, Henry Holt & Co., Inc., New York, NY, 1993. 300 pp., illus. $24.95
The heartwarming sequel to the best-selling The Old Man and the Boy.

One Man, One Rifle, One Land; Hunting all Species of Big Game in North America, by J.Y. Jones, Safari Press, Huntington Beach, CA, 2000. 400 pp., illus. $59.95
Journey with J.Y. Jones as he hunts each of the big-game animals of North America–from the polar bear of the high Arctic to the jaguar of the low-lands of Mexico–with just one rifle.

Outdoor Pastimes of an American Hunter, by Theodore Roosevelt, Stackpole Books, Mechanicsburg, PA, 1994. 480 pp., illus. Paper covers. $18.95
Stories of hunting big game in the West and notes about animals pursued and observed.

Outlaw Gunner, The, by Harry M. Walsh, Tidewater Publishers, Cambridge, MD, 1973. 178 pp., illus. $22.95
A colorful story of market gunning in both its legal and illegal phases.

Pheasant Days, by Chris Dorsey, Voyageur Press, Stillwater, MN, 1992. 233 pp., illus. $24.95
The definitive resource on ringnecks. Includes everything from basic hunting techniques to the life cycle of the bird.

Pheasant Hunter's Harvest, by Steve Grooms, Lyons & Burford Publishers, New York, NY, 1990. 180 pp. $22.95
A celebration of pheasant, pheasant dogs and pheasant hunting. Practical advice from a passionate hunter.

Pheasant Tales, by Gene Hill et al, Countrysport Press, Traverse City, MI, 1996. 202 pp., illus. $39.00
Charley Waterman, Michael McIntosh and Phil Bourjaily join the author to tell some of the stories that illustrate why the pheasant is America's favorite game bird.

Pheasants of the Mind, by Datus Proper, Wilderness Adventures Press, Bozeman, MT, 1994. 154 pp., illus. $25.00
No single title sums up the life of the solitary pheasant hunter like this masterful work.

Portraits of Elk Hunting, by Jim Zumbo, Safari Press, Huntington Beach, CA, 2001. 222 pp. illus. $39.95
Zumbo has captured in photos as well as in words the essence, charisma, and wonderful components of elk hunting: back-country wilderness camps, sweaty guides, happy hunters, favorite companions, elk woods, and, of course, the majestic elk. Join Zumbo in the uniqueness of the pursuit of the magnificent and noble elk.

Precision Bowhunting: A Year-Round approach to taking Mature Whitetails, by John and Chrs Eberhart, Stackpole Books, 2005. 214pp, b&w photos. Soft cover. NEW. $16.95
Packed with vital information and fresh insights, Precision Bow hunting belongs on the bookshelf of every serious bow hunter.

Proven Whitetail Tactics, by Greg Miller, Krause Publications, Iola, WI, 1997. 224 pp., illus. Paper covers. $19.95
Proven tactics for scouting, calling and still-hunting whitetail.

Quest for Dall Rams, by Duncan Gilchrist, Duncan Gilchrist Outdoor Expeditions and Books, Corvallis, MT, 1997. 224 pp., illus. Paper covers. $19.95
The most complete book of Dall sheep ever written. Covers information on Alaska and provinces with Dall sheep and explains hunting techniques, equipment, etc.

Quest for Giant Bighorns, by Duncan Gilchrist, Outdoor Expeditions and Books, Corvallis, MT, 1994. 224 pp., illus. Paper covers. $19.95
How some of the most successful sheep hunters hunt and how some of the best bighorns were taken.

Radical Elk Hunting Strategies, by Mike Lapinski, Stoneydale Press Publishing Co., Stevensville, MT, 1988. 161 pp., illus. $18.95
Secrets of calling elk in close.

Rattling, Calling & Decoying Whitetails, by Gary Clancy, edited by Patrick Durkin, Krause Publications, Iola, WI, 2000. 208 pp., illus. Paper covers. $19.95
How to consistently coax big bucks into range.

Records of North American Caribou and Moose, Craig Boddington et al, The Boone & Crockett Club, Missoula, MT, 1997. 250 pp., illus. $24.95
More than 1,800 caribou listings and more than 1,500 moose listings, organized by the state or Canadian province where they were taken.

Records of North American Elk and Mule Deer, 2nd Edition, edited by Jack and Susan Reneau, The Boone & Crockett Club, Missoula, MT, 1996. 360 pp., illus. Paper cover, $18.95; hardcover $24.95
Updated and expanded edition featuring more than 150 trophy, field and historical photos of the finest elk and mule deer trophies ever recorded.

Records of North American Sheep, Rocky Mountain Goats and Pronghorn, edited by Jack and Susan Reneau, The Boone & Crockett Club, Missoula, MT, 1996. 400 pp., illus. Paper cover, $18.95; hardcover, $24.95
The first B&C Club records book featuring all 3941 accepted wild sheep, Rocky Mountain goats and pronghorn trophies.

Reflections on Snipe, by Worth Mathewson, illustrated by Eldridge Hardie, Camden, ME, Country Sport Press, 2003. Hardcover. 144 pp. $25.00
Reflections on Snipe is a delightful compendium of information on snipe behavior and habitats; gunning history; stories from the field; and the pleasures of hunting with good companions, whether human or canine.

Ringneck; A Tribute to Pheasants and Pheasant Hunting, by Steve Grooms, Russ Sewell and Dave Nomsen, The Lyons Press, New York, NY, 2000. 120 pp., illus. $40.00
A glorious full-color coffee-table tribute to the pheasant and those who hunt them.

Rooster! A Tribute to Pheasant Hunting, by Dale C. Spartas, Riverbend Publishing, 2003. 1st edition. 150+ glorious photos of pheasants, hunting dogs and hunting trips with family and friends. 128 pgs. Hardcover. $39.95
A very special, must-have book for the 2.3 million pheasant hunters across the country!

Rub-Line Secrets, by Greg Miller, edited by Patrick Durkin, Krause Publications, Iola, WI, 1999. 208 pp., illus. Paper covers. $19.95
Based on nearly 30 years' experience. Proven tactics for finding, analyzing and hunting big bucks' rub-lines.

Season, The, by Tom Kelly, Lyons & Burford, New York, NY, 1997. 160 pp., illus. $22.95
The delight and challenges of a turkey hunter's spring season.

Secret Strategies from North America's Top Whitetail Hunters, compiled by Nick Sisley, Krause Publications, Iola, WI, 1995. 256 pp., illus. Paper covers. $14.95
Bow and gun hunters share their success stories.

Sheep Hunting in Alaska–The Dall Sheep Hunter's Guide, by Tony Russ, Outdoor Expeditions and Books, Corvallis, MT, 1994. 160 pp., illus. Paper covers. $19.95
A how-to guide for the Dall sheep hunter.

Southern Deer & Deer Hunting, by Larry Weishuhn and Bill Bynum, Krause Publications, Iola, WI, 1995. 256 pp., illus. Paper covers. $14.95
Mount a trophy southern whitetail on your wall with this firsthand account of stalking big bucks below the Mason-Dixon line.

Spring Gobbler Fever, by Michael Hanback, Krause Publications, Iola, WI, 1996. 256 pp., illus. Paper covers. $15.95
Your complete guide to spring turkey hunting.

Stand Hunting for Whitetails, by Richard P. Smith, Krause Publications, Iola, WI, 1996. 256 pp., illus. Paper covers. $14.95
The author explains the tricks and strategies for successful stand hunting.

Successful Black Bear Hunting, by Bill Vaznis, Iola,WI, Krause Publications, 2004. 144 pages, illustrated with full color photographs and drawings. Pictorial Soft cover. $23.99

Sultan of Spring: A Hunter's Odyssey Through the World of the Wild Turkey, The, by Bob Saile, The Lyons Press, New York, NY, 1998. 176 pp., illus. $22.95
A literary salute to the magic and mysticism of spring turkey hunting.

Taking Big Bucks, by Ed Wolff, Stoneydale Press, Stevensville, MT, 1987. 169 pp., illus. $18.95
Solving the whitetail riddle.

Tales of Quails 'n Such, by Havilah Babcock, University of S. Carolina Press, Columbia, SC, 1985. 237 pp. $19.95
A group of hunting stories, told in informal style, on field experiences in the South in quest of small game.

They Left Their Tracks, by Howard Coperhaver, Stoneydale Press Publishing Co., Stevensville, MT, 1990. 190 pp., illus. $18.95
Recollections of 60 years as an outfitter in the Bob Marshall Wilderness.

To Heck with Moose Hunting, by Jim Zumbo, Wapiti Publishing Co., Cody, WY, 1996. 199 pp., illus. $17.95
Jim's hunts around the continent and even an African adventure.

Track Pack: Animal Tracks In Full Life Size, by Ed Gray, Mechanicsburg, PA, Stackpole Books, 2003. 1st edition. Spiral-bound, 34 pp. $7.95
An indispensable reference for hunters, trackers, and outdoor enthusiasts. This handy guide features the tracks of 38 common North American animals, from squirrels to grizzlies.

Trickiest Thing in Feathers, The, by Corey Ford, compiled and edited by Laurie Morrow, illustrated by Christopher Smith, Wilderness Adventures, Gallatin Gateway, MT, 1998. 208 pp., illus. $29.95
Here is a collection of Corey Ford's best wing-shooting stories, many of them previously unpublished.

Upland Equation: A Modern Bird-Hunter's Code, The, by Charles Fergus, Lyons & Burford Publishers, New York, NY, 1996. 86 pp. $18.00
A book that deserves space in every sportsman's library. Observations based on firsthand experience.

Upland Tales, edited by Worth Mathewson, Sand Lake Press, Amity, OR, 1996. 271 pp., illus. $29.95
A collection of articles on grouse, snipe and quail.

Waterfowler's World, by Bill Buckley, Ducks Unlimited, Inc., Memphis, TN, 1999. 192 pp., illustrated in color. $37.50
An unprecedented pictorial book on waterfowl and waterfowlers.

When the Duck Were Plenty, by Ed Muderlak, Safari Press, Inc., Huntington Beach, CA, 2000. 300 pp., illus. $29.95
The golden age of waterfowling and duck hunting from 1840 until 1920. An anthology.

Whitetail: Behavior Through the Seasons, by Charles J. Alsheimer, Krause Publications, Iola, WI, 1996. 208 pp., illus. $34.95
In-depth coverage of whitetail behavior presented through striking portraits of the whitetail in every season.

ARMS LIBRARY

Whitetail: The Ultimate Challenge, by Charles J. Alsheimer, Krause Publications, Iola, WI, 1995. 228 pp., illus. Paper covers. $14.95
Learn deer hunting's most intriguing secrets—fooling deer using decoys, scents and calls—from America's premier authority.

Whitetails by the Moon, by Charles J. Alsheimer, edited by Patrick Durkin, Krause Publications, Iola, WI, 1999. 208 pp., illus. Paper covers. $19.95
Predict peak times to hunt whitetails. Learn what triggers the rut.

Wildfowler's Season, by Chris Dorsey, Lyons & Burford Publishers, New York, NY, 1998. 224 pp., illus. $37.95
Modern methods for a classic sport.

Wildfowling Tales, by William C. Hazelton, Wilderness Adventures Press, Belgrade, MT, 1999. 117 pp., illustrated with etchings by Brett Smith. In a slipcase. $50.00
Tales from the great ducking resorts of the continent.

Windward Crossings: A Treasury of Original Waterfowling Tales, by Chuck Petrie et al, Willow Creek Press, Minocqua, WI, 1999. 144 pp., 48 color art and etching reproductions. $35.00
An illustrated, modern anthology of previously unpublished waterfowl hunting (fiction and creative nonfiction) stories by America's finest outdoor journalists.

Wings of Thunder: New Grouse Hunting Revisited, by Steven Mulak, Countrysport Books, Selma, AL, 1998. 168 pp. illus. $30.00
The author examines every aspect of New England grouse hunting as it is today—the bird and its habits, the hunter and his dog, guns and loads, shooting and hunting techniques, practice on clay targets, clothing and equipment.

Woodchuck Hunter, The, by Paul C. Estey, R&R Books, Livonia, NY, 1994. 135 pp., illus. $25.00
This book contains information on woodchuck equipment, the rifle, telescopic sights and includes interesting stories.

AFRICA/ASIA/ELSEWHERE

A Bullet Well Placed; One Hunter's Adventures Around the World, by Johnny Chilton, Safari Press, 2004. 245 pages. Hardcover. New in new dust jacket. $34.95
Painting a picture of what it is actually like to be there and do it, this well-written book captures the excitement and emotions of each journey.

A Country Boy in Africa, by George Hoffman, Trophy Room Books, Agoura, CA, 1998. 267 pp., illustrated with over 100 photos. Limited, numbered edition signed by the author. $85.00
In addition to the author's long and successful hunting career, he is known for developing a most effective big game cartridge, the .416 Hoffman.

A Hunter's Africa, by Gordon Cundill, Trophy Room Books, Agoura, CA, 1998. 298 pp., over 125 photographic illustrations. Limited numbered edition signed by the author. $125.00
A good look by the author at the African safari experience-elephant, lion, spiral-horned antelope, firearms, people and events, as well as the clients that make it worthwhile.

A Hunter's Wanderings in Africa, by Frederick Courteney Selous, Alexanders Books, Alexander, NC, 2003. 504 pp., illus. $28.50
A reprinting of the 1920 London edition. A narrative of nine years spent amongst the game of the far interior of South Africa.

A Pioneering Hunter, by B Marsh, Safari Press, 2006. A limited edition of 1,000 copies. Signed and Numbered. 107. 247pp. color photos. Hardcover in a Slipcase. NEW. $65.00
Elephant cropping, buffalo tales, and colorful characters—this book has it all.

A Professional Hunter's Journey of Discovery, by Alec McCallum, Agoura, CA, Trophy Room Books, 2003. Limited of 1,000. Signed and numbered. 132 pp. Hardcover. New in new dust jacket. $125.00

A View From A Tall Hill: Robert Ruark in Africa, by Terry Wieland, Bristol, CT, Country Sport Press, 2004. Reprint. 432 pp., Hardcover New in new dust jacket $45.00

African Adventures and Misadventures: Escapades in East Africa with Mau Mau and Giant Forest Hogs, by William York, Long Beach, CA, Safari Press, 2003. A limited edition of 1,000 copies. Signed and numbered. 250 pp., color and b&w photos. Hardcover in a slipcase. $70.00
From his early days in Kenya when he and a companion trekked alone through the desert of the NFD and had to fend off marauding lions that ate his caravan ponies to encountering a Mau Mau terrorist who took potshots at his victims with a stolen elephant gun, the late Bill York gives an entertaining account of his life that will keep you turning the pages. As with York's previous book, the pages are loaded with interesting anecdotes, fascinating tales, and well-written prose that give insight into East Africa and its more famous characters.

African Game Trails, by Theodore Roosevelt, Peter Capstick, Series Editor, St. Martin's Press, New York, NY 1988. 583 pp., illus. $26.95
The famed safari of the noted sportsman, conservationist, and president.

African Hunter II, edited by Craig Boddington and Peter Flack, Foreword by Robin Hurt, Introduction by James Mellon, Long Beach, CA, Safari Press, 2004. 606 pp., profuse color and b&w photos. $135.00
James Mellon spent five years hunting in every African country open to hunting during the late 1960s and early 1970s, making him uniquely qualified to write a book of such scope and breadth. Because so much has changed in today's Africa, however, it was necessary to update the original. With over 500 full-color pages, hundreds of photographs, and updated tables on animals and where they are available, this is THE book to consult for the information on Africa today.

African Rifles & Cartridges, by John Taylor, The Gun Room Press, Highland Park, NJ, 1977. 431 pp., illus. $35.00
Experiences and opinions of a professional ivory hunter in Africa describing his knowledge of numerous arms and cartridges for big game. A reprint.

African Twilight, by Robert F. Jones, Wilderness Adventure Press, Bozeman, MT, 1994. 208 pp., illus. $36.00
Details the hunt, danger and changing face of Africa over a span of three decades.

Atkin, Grant & Lang: A Detailed History of Enduring Gunmakers (trade edition), by Don Masters, Safari Press, 2005. 316pp., color and b&w photos. Hardcover. New in new dust jacket. $69.89
The history of three makers and their several relatives making guns under their own names. In the pages of this book you can learn all the details of the gun makers: dates, premises, main employees, rises and declines in sales fortunes, as well as the many interesting historical anecdotes and insights we have come to expect from Don Masters.

Baron in Africa; The Remarkable Adventures of Werner von Alvensleben, by Brian Marsh, Foreword by Ian Player, Safari Press, Huntington Beach, CA, 2001. 288 pp., illus. $35.00
Follow his career as he hunts lion, goes after large kudu, kills a full-grown buffalo with a spear, and hunts for elephant and ivory in some of the densest brush in Africa. The adventure and the experience were what counted to this fascinating character, not the money or fame; indeed, in the end he left Mozambique with barely more than the clothes on his back. This is a must-read adventure story of one of the most interesting characters to have come out of Africa after WWII.

Buffalo!, by Craig Boddington, Safari Books, 2006. 256pp, color photos, Hardcover. NEW. $39.95
Craig tells his readers where to hunt, how and when to hunt, and what will happen when they do hunt. He describes what it means to rush the herd, one of his favorite methods of hunting these worthy opponents. He tells of the great bull in Masailand that he almost got, of the perfect hunt he had in Zambia, and of the charge he experienced in Tanzania.

Buffalo, Elephant, & Bongo (trade edition): Alone in the Savannas and Rain Forests of the Cameroon, by Reinald Von Meurers, Long Beach, CA, Safari Press, 2004. Hardcover. New in new dust jacket. $39.50

Cottar: The Exception was the Rule, by Pat Cottar, Trophy Room Books, Agoura, CA, 1999. 350 pp., illus. Limited, numbered and signed edition. $135.00
The remarkable big game hunting stories of one of Kenya's most remarkable pioneers.

Dangerous Game, True Stories of Dangerous Hunting on Three Continents, The, Safari Press, 2006. A limited edition of 500 copies. Signed and Numbered. 225pp, photos. Hardcover in a Slipcase. NEW. $70.00

Death and Double Rifles, by Mark Sullivan, Nitro Express Safaris, Phoenix, AZ, 2000. 295 pp., illus. $85.00
Sullivan has captured every thrilling detail of hunting dangerous game in this lavishly illustrated book. Full of color pictures of African hunts & rifles.

Death in a Lonely Land, by Peter Capstick, St. Martin's Press, New York, NY, 1990. 284 pp., illus. $22.95
Twenty-three stories of hunting as only the master can tell them.

Death in the Dark Continent, by Peter Capstick, St. Martin's Press, New York, NY, 1983. 238 pp., illus. $22.95
A book that brings to life the suspense, fear and exhilaration of stalking ferocious killers under primitive, savage conditions, with the ever present threat of death.

Death in the Long Grass, by Peter Hathaway Capstick, St. Martin's Press, New York, NY, 1977. 297 pp., illus. $22.95
A big game hunter's adventures in the African bush.

Death in the Silent Places, by Peter Capstick, St. Martin's Press, New York, NY, 1981. 243 pp., illus. $23.95
The author recalls the extraordinary careers of legendary hunters such as Corbett, Karamojo Bell, Stigand and others.

Elephant Hunters, Men of Legend, by Tony Sanchez-Arino, Safari Press, 2005. A limited edition of 1,000 copies. Signed and Numbered. 240 pages. Hardcover in a Slipcase. NEW. $100.00
This newest book from Tony Sanchez is the most interesting ever to emerge on that intrepid and now finished breed of man: Elephant Hunters, Men of Legend.

Encounters with Lions, by Jan Hemsing, Trophy Room Books, Agoura, CA, 1995. 302 pp., illus. $75.00
Some stories fierce, fatal, frightening and even humorous of when man and lion meet.

Fodor's African Safari, From Budget to Big Spending Where and How to Find the Best Big Game Adventure in Southern and Eastern Africa, by David Bristow, Julian Harrison, Chris Swiac, New York, Fodor's, 2004. 1st edition. 190 pp. Softcover. NEW. $9.95

Frederick Selous: A Hunting Legend-Recollections By and About the Great Hunter (trade edition), by F.C. Selous (edited by James Casada), Safari Press, 2005. 187pp., illus. Hardcover. $34.95
This second book on Selous, edited by Africana expert Dr. James Casada, completes the work on the lost writings by Selous begun in Africa's Greatest Hunter.

From Mt. Kenya to the Cape: Ten Years of African Hunting, by Craig Boddington, Long Beach, CA, Safari Press, 2005. Hardcover. New in new dust jacket. $39.95
This wealth of information makes not only great reading, but the appendixes also provide tips on rifles, cartridges, equipment, and how to plan a safari.

From Sailor to Professional Hunter: The Autobiography of John Northcote, Trophy Room Books, Agoura, CA, 1997. 400 pp., illus. Limited edition, signed and numbered. $125.00
Only a handful of men can boast of having a 50-year professional hunting career throughout Africa as John Northcote has had.

Gone are the Days; Jungle Hunting for Tiger and other Game in India and Nepal 1953-1969, by Peter Byrne, Safari Press, Inc., Huntington Beach, CA, 2001. 225 pp., illus. Limited signed, numbered, slipcased. $70.00

Great Hunters: Their Trophy Rooms and Collections, Volume 1, compiled and published by Safari Press, Inc., Huntington Beach, CA, 1997. 312 pp., illustrated in color. $60.00
A rare glimpse into the trophy rooms of top international hunters. A few of these trophy rooms are museums.

Great Hunters: Their Trophy Rooms & Collections, Volume 2, compiled and published by Safari Press, Inc., Huntington Beach, CA, 1998. 224 pp., illustrated with 260 full-color photographs. $60.00
Volume Two of the world's finest, best produced series of books on trophy rooms and game collections. 46 sportsmen sharing sights you'll never forget on this guided tour.

ARMS LIBRARY

Great Hunters: Their Trophy Rooms & Collections, Volume 3, compiled and published by Safari Press, Inc., Huntington Beach, CA, 2000. 204 pp., illustrated with 260 full-color photographs. $60.00

At last, the long-awaited third volume in the best photographic series ever published of trophy room collections is finally available. As before, each trophy room is accompanied by an informative text explaining the collection and giving you insights into the hunters who went to such great efforts to create their trophy rooms. All professionally photographed in the highest quality possible.

Great Hunters: Their Trophy Rooms & Collections, Volume 4, compiled and published by Safari Press, Inc., Huntington Beach, CA, 2005. 204 pp., illustrated with 260 full-color photographs. $60.00

At last, the long-awaited fourth volume in the best photographic series ever published of trophy room collections is finally available. Each trophy room is accompanied by an informative text explaining the collection and giving you insights into the hunters who went to such great efforts to create their trophy rooms. All professionally photographed in the highest quality possible.

Heart of an African Hunter, by Peter Flack, Long Beach, CA, Safari Press, 2005. 266 pp. illustrated with b&w photos. Hardcover. NEW. $35.00

Hemingway in Africa: The Last Safari, by Christopher Ondaatje, Overlook Press, 2004. 1st edition. 240 pp. Hardcover. New in new dust jacket. $37.50

Horn of the Hunter, by Robert Ruark, Safari Press, Long Beach, CA, 1987. 315 pp., illus. $35.00

Ruark's most sought-after title on African hunting, here in reprint.

Hunter's Tracks, by J.A. Hunter, Safari Press Publications, Huntington Beach, CA, 1999. 240 pp., illus. $24.95

This is the exciting story of John Hunter's efforts to capture the shady head man of a gang of ivory poachers and smugglers. The story is interwoven with the tale of one of East Africa's most grandiose safaris taken with an Indian maharaja.

Hunting in Ethiopia, An Anthology, by Tony Sanchez-Arino, Safari Press, Huntington Beach, CA, 1996. 350 pp., illus. Limited, signed and numbered edition. $135.00

The finest selection of hunting stories ever compiled on hunting in this great game country.

Hunting in Kenya, by Tony Sanchez-Arino, Safari Press, Inc., Huntington Beach, CA, 2000. 350 pp., illus. Limited, signed and numbered edition in a slipcase. $135.00

The finest selection of hunting stories ever compiled on hunting in this great game country make up this anthology.

Hunting in the Sudan, An Anthology, compiled by Tony Sanchez-Arino, Safari Press, Huntington Beach, CA, 1992. 350 pp., illus. Limited, signed and numbered edition in a slipcase. $125.00

The finest selection of hunting stories ever compiled on hunting in this great game country.

Hunting Instinct, The, by Phillip D. Rowter, Safari Press, Inc., Huntington Beach, CA, 2005, trade edition. Hardcover. New in new dust jacket. $29.95

Safari chronicles from the Republic of South Africa and Namibia 1990-1998.

Hunting the Dangerous Game of Africa, by John Kingsley-Heath, Sycamore Island Books, Boulder, CO, 1998. 477 pp., illus. $95.00

Written by one of the most respected, successful, and ethical P.H.'s to trek the sunlit plains of Botswana, Kenya, Uganda, Tanganyika, Somaliland, Eritrea, Ethiopia, and Mozambique. Filled with some of the most gripping and terrifying tales ever to come out of Africa.

Hunting, Settling and Remembering, by Philip H. Percival, Trophy Room Books, Agoura, CA, 1997. 230 pp., illus. Limited, numbered and signed edition. $85.00

If Philip Percival is to come alive again, it will be through this, the first edition of his easy, intricate and magical book illustrated with some of the best historical big game hunting photos ever taken.

Hunting Trips in The Land of the Dragon; Anglo and American Sportsmen in Old China, 1870-1940, by Kenneth Czech, Safari Press, 2005. Hardcover. New in new dust jacket. $34.95

The first part of this anthology takes the reader after duck, pheasant, and other upland game while the second part focuses on the large game of China and the border regions. The latter includes hunts for Manchurian tiger, tufted deer, goral, wild goat, wild yak, antelope, takin, wild sheep in the Mongolian Altai, wapiti, blue sheep, ibex, Ovis poli of the Pamir, wild sheep of the Tian Shan, brown bear, and panda--all written by such famous names as Major General Kinloch, St. George Littledale, Kermit Roosevelt, and Roy Chapman Andrews.

In the Salt, by Lou Hallamore, Trophy Room Books, Agoura, CA, 1999. 227 pp., illustrated in b&w and full color. Limited, numbered and signed edition. $125.00

A book about people, animals and the big game hunt, about being outwitted and outmaneuvered. It is about knowing that sooner or later your luck will change and your trophy will be "in the salt."

International Hunter 1945-1999, Hunting's Greatest Era, by Bert Klineburger, Sportsmen on Film, Kerrville, TX, 1999. 400 pp., illus. A limited, numbered and signed edition. $125.00

The most important book of the greatest hunting era by the world's preeminent international hunter.

Jim Corbett Collection, by Jim Corbett, Safari press, 2005. 1124 pages, illus, 5 volumes. Hardcover in a Slipcase. NEW. $100.00

The complete set of Jim Corbett's works, housed in a printed slipcase and feature the work of the internationally famous wildlife artist Guy Coheleach.

King of the Wa-Kikuyu, by John Boyes, St. Martin Press, New York, NY, 1993. 240 pp., illus. $19.95

In the 19th and 20th centuries, Africa drew to it a large number of great hunters, explorers, adventurers and rogues. Many have become legendary, but John Boyes (1874-1951) was the most legendary of them all.

Kwaheri! On the Spoor of Big Game in East Africa, by Robert von Reitnauer, Long beach, CA, Safari Press, 2005. A limited edition of 1,000 copies. Signed and Numbered. 285 pages, illustrated with photos. Hardcover in a Slipcase. NEW. $75.00

This is the story of an immense land in the days before the truly big tuskers all but disappeared. A very good read.

Last Horizons: Hunting, Fishing and Shooting on Five Continents, by Peter Capstick, St. Martin's Press, New York, NY, 1989. 288 pp., illus. $19.95

The first in a two-volume collection of hunting, fishing and shooting tales from the selected pages of *The American Hunter*, *Guns & Ammo* and *Outdoor Life*.

Last of the Ivory Hunters, by John Taylor, Safari Press, Long Beach, CA, 1990. 354 pp., illus. $29.95

Reprint of the classic book "Pondoro" by one of the most famous elephant hunters of all time.

Legends of the Field: More Early Hunters in Africa, by W.R. Foran, Trophy Room Press, Agoura, CA, 1997. 319 pp., illus. Limited edition. $100.00

This book contains the biographies of some very famous hunters: William Cotton Oswell, F.C. Selous, Sir Samuel Baker, Arthur Neumann, Jim Sutherland, W.D.M. Bell and others.

Lives of A Professional Hunting Family, by Gerard Agoura Miller, Trophy Room Books, 2003. A limited edition of 1,000 copies. Signed and numbered. 303 pp., 230 b&w photographic illustrations. Hardcover. $135.00

Lost Classics, by Robert Ruark, Safari Press, Huntington Beach, CA, 1996. 260 pp., illus. $35.00

The magazine stories that Ruark wrote in the 1950s and 1960s finally in print in book form.

Lost Wilderness; True Accounts of Hunters and Animals in East Africa, by Mohamed Ismail and Alice Pianfetti, Safari Press, Inc., Huntington Beach, CA, 2000. 216 pp., photos, illus. Limited edition signed, numbered and slipcased. $60.00

Mahonhboh, by Ron Thomson, Hartbeesport, South Africa, 1997. 312 pp., illus. Limited signed and numbered edition. $50.00

Elephants and elephant hunting in South Central Africa.

Man-Eaters of Tsavo, The, by Lt. Colonel J.H. Patterson, Peter Capstick, series editor, St. Martin's Press, New York, NY, 1986, 5th printing. 346 pp., illus. $22.95

Maneaters and Marauders, by John "Pondoro" Taylor, Long Beach, CA, Safari Press, 2005. 1st edition, Safari edition. Hardcover. New in new dust jacket. $29.95

McElroy Hunts Asia, by C.J. McElroy, Safari Press, Inc., Huntington Beach, CA, 1989. 272 pp., illus. $50.00

From the founder of SCI comes a book on hunting the great continent of Asia for big game: tiger, bear, sheep and ibex. Includes the story of the all-time record Altai Argali as well as several markhor hunts in Pakistan.

Memoirs of A Sheep Hunter, by Rashid Jamsheed, Safari Press, Inc., Huntington Beach, CA, 1996. 330 pp., illus. $70.00

The author reveals his exciting accounts of obtaining world-record heads from his native Iran, and his eventual move to the U.S. where he procured a grand-slam of North American sheep.

Memoirs of An African Hunter (Trade Edition), by Terry Irwin, Safari Press, 2005. 411pp, 95 color and 20 b&w photos, large format. Hardcover $70.00

Memories of Africa; Hunting in Zambia and Sudan, by W. Brach, Safari Press, 2005. 2005. A limited edition of 1,000 copies. Signed and Numbered. Written with an interesting flair and a true graphic perspective of the animals, people, and the hunt, this is a realistic portrayal, not Hollywood-style swaggering and gun-slinging, of hunting the magnificent wildlife of Zambia and Sudan over the last three decades. 285 pages, illustrated with photos. Hardcover in a Slipcase. NEW. $85.00

Mundjamba: The Life Story of an African Hunter, by Hugo Seia, Trophy Room Books, Agoura, CA, 1996. 400 pp., illus. Limited, numbered and signed by the author. $125.00

An autobiography of one of the most respected and appreciated professional African hunters.

My Africa: A Professional Hunter's Journey of Discovery, by Alec McCallum, Trouphy Room Books, 2003. Limited Edition: 1000. Signed and numbered. hunting. 232pp. Hardcover. New in new dust jacket. $125.00

My Wanderings Though Africa: The Life and Times of a Professional Hunter, by Mike and James Cameron, Safari Press, 2004. Deluxe, Limited, Signed edition. 208pp, b&w photos. Hardcover in a Slipcase. NEW. $75.00

This is a book for readers whose imagination carries them into a world where reality means starry skies, the call of a jackal and the moan of a lion, the smell of gun oil, and smoke from a cooking fire rising into the African night.

On Target, by Christian Le Noel, Trophy Room Books, Agoura, CA, 1999. 275 pp., illus. Limited, numbered and signed edition. $85.00

History and hunting in Central Africa.

One Long Safari, by Peter Hay, Trophy Room Books, Agoura, CA, 1998. 350 pp., with over 200 photographic illustrations and 7 maps. Limited numbered edition signed by the author. $100.00

Contains hunts for leopards, sitatunga, hippo, rhino, snakes and, of course, the general African big game bag.

Optics for the Hunter, by John Barsness, Safari Press, Inc., Huntington Beach, CA, 1999. 236 pp., illus. $24.95

An evaluation of binoculars, scopes, range finders, spotting scopes for use in the field.

Out in the Midday Shade, by William York, Safari Press, Inc., Huntington Beach, CA, 2005. Trade Edition. Hardcover. New in new dust jacket. $35.00

Path of a Hunter, The, by Gilles Tre-Hardy, Trophy Room Books, Agoura, CA, 1997. 318 pp., illus. Limited Edition, signed and numbered. $85.00

A most unusual hunting autobiography with much about elephant hunting in Africa.

Perfect Shot: Mini Edition for Africa, The, by Kevin Robertson, Long Beach, CA, Safari Press, 2004. 2nd printing Softcover. NEW. $17.95

Perfect Shot: Shot Placement for African Big Game, The, by Kevin "Doctari" Robertson, Safari Press, Inc., Huntington Beach, CA, 1999. 230 pp., illus. $65.00

The most comprehensive work ever undertaken to show the anatomical features for all classes of African game. Includes caliber and bullet selection, rifle selection and trophy handling.

Peter Capstick's Africa: A Return to the Long Grass, by Peter Hathaway Capstick, St. Martin's Press, N. Y., NY, 1987. 213 pp., illus. $35.00

A first-person adventure in which the author returns to the long grass for his own dangerous and very personal excursion.

Pondoro, by John Taylor, Safari Press, Inc., Huntington Beach, CA, 1999. 354 pp., illus. $39.95

The author is considered one of the best storytellers in the hunting book world, and Pondoro is highly entertaining. A classic African big-game hunting title.

Quotable Hunter, The, by Jay Cassell and Peter Fiduccia, The Lyons Press, N.Y., 1999. 288 pp., illus. $20.00

This collection of more than three hundred quotes from hunters through the ages captures the essence of the sport, with all its joys, idosyncrasies, and challenges.

ARMS LIBRARY

Return to Toonaklut–The Russell Annabel Story, by Jeff Davis, Long Beach, CA, Safari Press, 2002. 248 pp., photos, illus. $34.95

Those of us who grew up after WW II cannot imagine the Alaskan frontier that Rusty Annabel walked into early in the twentieth century. The hardships, the resourcefulness, the natural beauty, not knowing what lay beyond the next horizon, all were a part of his existence. This is the story of the man behind the legend, and it is as fascinating as any of the tales Rusty Annabel ever spun for the sporting magazines.

Rifles and Cartridges for Large Game–From Deer to Bear–Advice on the Choice of A Rifle, by Layne Simpson, Long Beach, CA, Safari Press, 2002. Illustrated with 100 color photos, oversize book. 225 pp., color illus. $39.95

Layne Simpson, who has been field editor for *Shooting Times* magazine for 20 years, draws from his hunting experiences on five continents to tell you what rifles, cartridges, bullets, loads, and scopes are best for various applications, and he explains why in plain English. Developer of the popular 7mm STW cartridge, Simpson has taken big game with rifle cartridges ranging in power from the .220 Swift to the .460 Weatherby Magnum, and he pulls no punches when describing their effectiveness in the field.

Rifles for Africa; Practical Advice on Rifles and Ammunition for an African Safari, by Gregor Woods, Long Beach, CA, Safari Press, 2002. 1st edition. 430 pp., illus., photos. $39.95

Invaluable to the person who seeks advice and information on what rifles, calibers, and bullets work on African big game, be they the largest land mammals on earth or an antelope barely weighing in at 20 lbs.!

Robert Ruark's Africa, by Robert Ruark, edited by Michael McIntosh, Countrysport Press, Selma, AL, 1999. 256 pp. illustrated with 19 original etchings by Bruce Langton. $32.00

These previously uncollected works of Robert Ruark make this a classic big-game hunting book.

Safari: The Last Adventure, by Peter Capstick, St. Martin's Press, New York, NY, 1984. 291 pp., illus. $22.95

A modern comprehensive guide to the African Safari.

Safari Rifles: Double, Magazine Rifles and Cartridges for African Hunting, by Craig Boddington, Safari Press, Huntington Beach, CA, 1990. 416 pp., illus. $37.50

A wealth of knowledge on the safari rifle. Historical and present double-rifle makers, ballistics for the large bores, and much, much more.

Sands of Silence, by Peter H. Capstick, Saint Martin's Press, New York, NY, 1991. 224 pp., illus. $35.00

Join the author on safari in Nambia for his latest big-game hunting adventures.

Song of the Summits–Hunting Sheep, Ibex, and Markhor in Asia, Europe, and North America, by Jesus Yurén, Long Beach, CA, Safari Press, 2003. Limited edition. Hardcover in a slipcase. NEW. $75.00

Sunset Tales of Safariland, by Stan Bleazard, Trophy Room Books, 2006. Deluxe, Limited, Signed edition. Large 8½" x11" format, bound in sumptuous forest green gilt stamped suede binding. 274 pages. 113 b&w photographic illustrations and index. NEW. $125.00

Sunset Tales of Safariland will be of considerable interest to anyone interested in big game hunting.

Tales of the African Frontier, by J.A. Hunter, Safari Press Publications, Huntington Beach, CA, 1999. 308 pp., illus. $24.95

The early days of East Africa is the subject of this powerful John Hunter book.

Tanzania Safari: Hei Safari, by Robert DePole, Trophy Room Books, 2004. Sumptuous Burgundy gilt stamped faux suede binding, 343 pages plus 12 page index of people and places. 32 pages of black & white photographic illustrations. The reader will "see" the animals on the pages long enough to remember them forever. Hardcover. NEW. $125.00

To Heck With It–I'm Going Hunting–My First Eighteen Years as an International Big-Game Hunter–Limited Edition, by Arnold Alward with Bill Quimby, Long Beach, CA, Safari Press, 2003. Deluxe, 1st edition, limited to 1,000 signed copies. NEW. $80.00

Uganda Safaris, by Brian Herne, Winchester Press, Piscataway, NJ, 1979. 236 pp., illus. $24.95

The chronicle of a professional hunter's adventures in Africa.

Under the African Sun, by Dr. Frank Hibben, Safari Press, Inc., Huntington Beach, CA, 1999. Limited edition signed, numbered and in a slipcase. $85.00

Forty-eight years of hunting the African continent.

Under the African Sun, by Dr. Frank Hibben, Safari Press, Inc., Huntington Beach, CA, 2005. Trade edition. 305 pages illustrated with b&w and color photos. Hardcover. New in new dust jacket. $39.95

Under the Shadow of Man Eaters, by Jerry Jaleel, The Jim Corbett Foundation, Edmonton, Alberta, Canada, 1997. 152 pp., illus. A limited, numbered and signed edition. Paper covers. $35.00

The life and legend of Jim Corbett of Kumaon.

Use Enough Gun, by Robert Ruark, Safari Press, Huntington Beach, CA, 1997. 333 pp., illus. $35.00

Robert Ruark on big game hunting.

Warrior: The Legend of Col. Richard Meinertzhagen, by Peter H. Capstick, St. Martins Press, New York, NY, 1998. 320 pp., illus. $23.95

A stirring and vivid biography of the famous British colonial officer Richard Meinertzhagen, whose exploits earned him fame and notoriety as one of the most daring and ruthless men to serve during the glory days of the British Empire.

Waterfowler's World, The, by Bill Buckley, Willow Creek Press, Minocqua, WI, 1999. 176 pp., 225 color photographs. $37.50

Waterfowl hunting from Canadian prairies, across the U.S. heartland, to the wilds of Mexico, from the Atlantic to the Pacific coasts and the Gulf of Mexico.

Weatherby: Stories From the Premier Big-Game Hunters of the World, 1956-2002, The, edited by Nancy Vokins, Long Beach, CA, Safari Press, 2004. Deluxe, limited, signed edition. 434 pp., profuse color and b&w illus. Hardcover in a slipcase. $200.00

Wheel of Life–Bunny Allen, A Life of Safaris and Sex, The, by Bunny Allen, Long Beach, CA, Safari Press, 2004. 1st edition. 300 pp., illus, photos. Hardcover. $34.95

Wind, Dust & Snow-Great Rams of Asia, by Robert M. Anderson, Collectors Covey, 1997. Deluxe Limited edition of 500 copies. Signed and Numbered. 240pp profuse illus. More than 200 photos some on the greatest Asian rams ever taken by sportsmen. $150.00

A complete chronology of modern exploratory and pioneering Asian sheep-hunting expeditions from 1960 until 1996, with wonderful background history and previously untold stories.

With a Gun in Good Country, by Ian Manning, Trophy Room Books, Agoura, CA, 1996. Limited, numbered and signed by the author. $85.00

A book written about that splendid period before the poaching onslaught which almost closed Zambia and continues to the granting of her independence. It then goes on to recount Manning's experiences in Botswana, Congo, and briefly in South Africa.

Yoshi–The Life and Travels of an International Trophy Hunter, by W. Yoshimoto with Bill Quimby, Long Beach, CA, Safari Press, Inc., 2002. A limited edition of 1,000 copies, signed and numbered. 298 pp., color and b&w photos. Hardcover in a slipcase. $85.00

Watson T. Yoshimoto, a native Hawaiian, collected all 16 major varieties of the world's wild sheep and most of the many types of goats, ibex, bears, antelopes, and antlered game of Asia, Europe, North America, South America, and the South Pacific...as well as the African Big Five. Along the way he earned the respect of his peers and was awarded hunting's highest achievement, the coveted Weatherby Award.

RIFLES

'03 Springfield Rifles Era, by Clark S. Campbell, Richmond, VA, privately printed, 2003. 1st edition. 368 pp., 146 illustrations, drawn to scale by author. Hardcover. $58.00

A much-expanded version of this author's famous The '03 Springfield (1957) and The '03 Springfields (1971), representing 40 years of research into all things '03. Part I is a complete and verifiably correct study of all standardized and special-purpose models of the U.S. M1903 Springfield rifle, in both .22 and .30 calibers, including those prototypes which led to standard models, and also all standardized .30 caliber cartridges, including National and International Match, and caliber .22. Part II is the result of the author's five years as a Research and Development Engineer with Remington Arms Co., and will be of inestimable value to anyone planning a custom sporter, whether or not based on the '03.

.303 SMLE Rifle No. 1 Assembly, Disassembly Manual, by Skennerton & Riling, Ray Riling Arms Books Co. Philadelphia, PA 2004. 36 pages, $5.00

With over 60 photos & line drawings. Ideal workshop reference for stripping & assembly with exploded parts drawings, specifications, service accessories, historical information and recommended reading references.

.303 British Rifle No. 4 Assembly, Disassembly Manual, by Skennerton & Riling, Ray Riling Arms Books Co. Philadelphia, PA 2004. 36 pages, $5.00

With over 60 photos & line drawings. Ideal workshop reference for stripping & assembly with exploded parts drawings, specifications, service accessories, historical information and recommended reading references.

.577 Snider-Enfield Rifles & Carbines; British Service Longarms, by Ian Skennerton. 1866-C.1880. Australia, Arms & Militaria Press, 2003. 1st edition. 240 pp. plus 8 color plates, 100 illustrations. Marking Ribbon. Hardcover. $39.50

The definitive study of Britain's first breech-loading rifle, at first converted from Enfield muskets, then newly made with Mk III breech. The trials, development, rifle and carbine models are detailed; new information along with descriptions of the cartridges.

1903 Springfield Assembly, Disassembly Manual .30 Model, by Skennerton & Riling, Ray Riling Arms Books Co. Philadelphia, PA 2004. 36 pages, $5.00

With over 60 photos & line drawings. Ideal workshop reference for stripping & assembly with exploded parts drawings, specifications, service accessories, historical information and recommended reading references.

1903 Springfield Rifle and Its Variations, by Joe Poyer, Tustin, CA, North Cape Publications, 2004. 466 pages, illustrated with hundreds of color and b& drawings and photos. Soft cover. NEW. $22.95

It covers the entire spectrum of the Model 1903 rifle from the rod bayonet to the M1903A4 sniper rifle.

A Master Gunmaker's Guide to Building Bolt-Action Rifles, by Bill Holmes, Boulder, CO, Paladin Press, 2003. Photos, illus., 152 pp. Softcover. $25.00

Many people today call themselves gunmakers, but very few have actually made a gun. Most buy parts wherever available and simply assemble them. During the past 50 years Bill Holmes has built from scratch countless rifles, shotguns and pistols of amazing artistry, ranging in caliber from .17 to .50.

A Potpourri of Single Shot Rifles and Actions, by Frank de Haas and Mark de Haas, Ridgeway, MO, 1993. 153 pp., illus. Paper covers. $22.50

The author's 6th book on non-bolt-action single shots. Covers more than 40 single-shot rifles in historical and technical detail.

Accurizing & Shooting Lee-Enfields, by Ian Skennerton, Australia, Arms & Militaria Press, 2005. 35pp, saddle-stitched laminated covers. ALL color photos and illustrations. Stiff paper covers. NEW. $15.00

This new full color heavily illustrated work by Ian Skennerton answers all those questions regarding the use of the Lee Enfield Rifles. Packed with detailed information covering the guns, the armourer's tools, and the sighting options for this fascinating series.

AK-47 and AK-74 Kalashnikov Rifles and Their Variations, by Joe Poyer, Tustin, CA, North Cape Publications, 2004. 1st edition. Softcover, NEW. 188 pages, illustrated. $22.95

This is the newest book in the "Shooter's and Collector's Guide" series. Prepared with the help of members of the Kalashnikov Collectors Association, this 188 page book surveys every variation of the 7.62 AK-47 and the 5.45 AK-74 developed in the old Soviet Union on a part-to-part basis to permit easy identification of original rifles and those made from kits available from various manufacturers in different countries.

ARMS LIBRARY

AK-47 Assembly, Disassembly Manual 7.62 X 39mm, by Skennerton & Riling, Ray Riling Arms Books Co. Philadelphia, PA 2004. 36 pages, $5.00

With over 60 photos & line drawings. Ideal workshop reference for stripping & assembly with exploded parts drawings, specifications, service accessories, historical information and recommended reading references. Ideal workbook for shooters and collectors alike. Triple saddle-stitched binding with durable plastic laminated cover makes this an ideal workshop guide.

AK-47 Assault Rifle, Desert Publications, Cornville, AZ, 1981. 150 pp., illus. Paper covers. $15.95

Complete and practical technical information on the only weapon in history to be produced in an estimated 30,000,000 units.

American Hunting Rifles: Their Application in the Field for Practical Shooting, by Craig Boddington, Safari Press, Huntington Beach, CA, 1996. 446 pp., illus. Second printing trade edition. Softcover $24.95

Covers all the hunting rifles and calibers that are needed for North America's diverse game.

American Krag Rifle and Carbine, by Joe Poyer, North Cape Publications, Tustin, CA, 2002. 1st edition. 317 pp., illustrated with hundreds of b&w drawings and photos. Softcover. $19.95

Provides the arms collector, historian and target shooter with a part by part analysis of what has been called the rifle with the smoothest bolt action ever designed. All changes to all parts are analyzed in detail and matched to serial number ranges. A monthly serial number chart by production year has been devised that will provide the collector with the year and month in which his gun was manufactured. A new and complete exploded view was produced for this book.

American Percussion Schuetzen Rifle, by J. Hamilton and T. Rowe, Rochester, NY, Rowe Publications, 2005. 1st edition. 388 pp. Hardcover. New in new dust jacket. $98.00

An Illustrated Guide to the '03 Springfield Service Rifle, by Bruce Canfield, Lincoln, RI, Andrew Mowbray, 2005. 240 pages, illustrated with over 450 photos. Pictorial Hardcover. NEW. $49.95

Your ultimate guide to the military '03 Springfield! Covers all models, all manufacturers and all conflicts, including WWI, WWII and beyond. Heavily illustrated with professional photography showing the details that separate a great collectible rifle from the rest. Serial number tables, combat photos, sniper rifles and more!

AR-15 & M-16 5.56mm Assembly, Disassembly Manual, by Skennerton & Riling, Ray Riling Arms Books Co. Philadelphia, PA 2004. 36 pages, $5.00

With over 60 photos & line drawings. Ideal workshop reference for stripping & assembly with exploded parts drawings, specifications, service accessories, historical information and recommended reading references.

AR-15 Complete Owner's Guide, Volume 1, 2nd Edition, by Walt Kuleck and Scott Duff, Export, PA, Scott A. Duff Publications, 2002. 224 pp., 164 photographs & line drawings. Softcover. $21.95

This book provides the prospective, new or experienced AR-15 owner with the in-depth knowledge he or she needs to select, configure, operate, maintain and troubleshoot his or her rifle. The Guide covers history, applications, details of components and subassemblies, operating, cleaning, maintenance, and future of perhaps the most versatile rifle system ever produced. A comprehensive Colt model number table and pre-/post-ban serial number information are included.

AR-15 Complete Assembly Guide, Volume 2, by Walt Kuleck and Clint McKee. Export, PA, Scott A. Duff Publications, 2002. 1st edition. 155 pp., 164 photographs & line drawings. Softcover. $19.95

This book goes beyond the military manuals in depth and scope, using words and pictures to clearly guide the reader through every operation required to assemble their AR-15-type rifle. You'll learn the best and easiest ways to build your rifle. It won't make you an AR-15 armorer, but it will make you a more knowledgeable owner. In short, if you build it, you'll know how to repair it.

AR-15/M16, A Practical Guide, by Duncan Long, Paladin Press, Boulder, CO, 1985. 168 pp., illus. Paper covers. $22.00

The definitive book on the rifle that has been the inspiration for so many modern assault rifles.

Argentine Mauser Rifles 1871-1959, by Colin Atglen, Webster, PA, Schiffer Publications, 2003. 1st edition. 304 pp., over 400 b&w and color photographs, drawings, and charts. Hardcover. $79.95

This is the complete story of Argentina's contract Mauser rifles from the purchase of their first Model 1871s to the disposal of the last shipment of surplus rifles received in the United States in May 2002. The Argentine Commission's relentless pursuit of tactical superiority resulted in a major contribution to the development of Mauser's now famous bolt-action system.

Art of Shooting with the Rifle, by Col. Sir H. St. John Halford, Excalibur Publications, Latham, NY, 1996. 96 pp., illus. Paper covers. $12.95

A facsimile edition of the 1888 book by a respected rifleman providing a wealth of detailed information.

Art of the Rifle, by Jeff Cooper, Paladin Press, Boulder, CO, 1997. 104 pp., illus. Paper covers $22.00

Everything you need to know about the rifle whether you use it for security, meat or target shooting.

Assault Rifle, by Maxim Popenker, and Anthony Williams, London, Crowood Press, 2005. 224 pages. Hardcover. New in new dust jacket. $34.95

Includes brief historical summary of the assault rifle, its origins and development; gun design including operating mechanisms and weapon configuration, and more. The second part includes: national military rifle programs since the end of WWII; history of developments in each country including experimental programs; and detailed descriptions of the principal service and experimental weapons.

Ballard: The Great American Single Shot Rifle, by John T. Dutcher, Denver, CO, privately printed, 2002. 1st edition. 380 pp., illustrated with b&w photos, with an 8-page color insert. Hardcover. $79.95

Benchrest Actions and Triggers, by Stuart Otteson. Rohnert Park, CA, Adams-Kane Press, July 2003. Limited edition. 64 pp. Softcover $27.95

Stuart Otteson's *Benchrest Actions and Triggers* is truly a lost classic. Benchrest Actions and Triggers is a compilation of 17 articles Mr. Otteson wrote. The articles contained are of particular interest to the benchrest crowd. Reprinted by permission of Wolfe Publishing.

Black Magic: The Ultra Accurate AR-15, by John Feamster, Precision Shooting, Manchester, CT, 1998. 300 pp., illus. $29.95

The author has compiled his experiences pushing the accuracy envelope of the AR-15 to its maximum potential. A wealth of advice on AR-15 loads, modifications and accessories for everything from NRA Highpower and Service Rifle competitions to benchrest and varmint shooting.

Black Rifle, M16 Retrospective, by R. Blake Stevens and Edward C. Ezell, Collector Grade Publications, Toronto, Canada, 1987. 416 pp., 441 illustrations and photos. $59.95

At the time of this writing, the 5.56mm NATO M16A2 rifle is heir to world wide acceptance after a quarter-century of U.S. service, longer than any other U.S. rifle in this century except the 1903 bolt-action Springfield. Its history has been far from one of calm acceptance.

Black Rifle II: The M16 into the 21st Century, by Christopher R. Bartocci, Canada, Collector Grade Publications, 2004. 408 pages, 626 illustrations. $69.95

This book chronicles all the new third- and fourth-generation rifle and carbine models which have been introduced by Colt and Diemaco since *The Black Rifle* was originally published, and describes and depicts the myriad of enhanced sights and rails systems which help make the M16s of today the most versatile, modular and effective combat weapons in the world. Includes an in-depth reference compendium of all Colt military and civilian models and components.

Blitzkrieg!–The MP40 Maschinenpistole of WWII, by Frank Iannamico, Harmony, ME, Moose Lake Publishing, 2003. 1st edition. Over 275 pp., 280 photos and documents. Softcover. $29.95

It's back, now in a new larger 8" x11" format. Lots of new information and many unpublished photos. This book includes the history and development of the German machine pistol from the MP18.I to the MP40.

Bolt Action Rifles, Expanded 4th Edition, by Frank de Haas and Wayne van Zwoll, Krause Publications, Iola, WI 2003. 696 pp., illustrated with 615 b&w photos. Softcover. $29.95

British .22RF Training Rifles, by Dennis Lewis and Robert Washburn, Excaliber Publications, Latham, NY, 1993. 64 pp., illus. Paper covers. $10.95

The story of Britain's training rifles from the early Aiming Tube models to the post-WWII trainers.

Building Double Rifles on Shotgun Actions, by W. Ellis Brown, Ft. Collins, CO, Bunduki Publishing, 2001. 1st edition. 187 pp., including index and b&w photographs. Hardcover. $55.00

Carbine .30 M1, M1A1, M2 & M3 Assembly, Disassembly Manual, by Skennerton & Riling, Ray Riling Arms Books Co. Philadelphia, PA 2004. 36 pages, over 60 photos & line drawings. $5.00

Ideal workshop reference for stripping & assembly with exploded parts drawings, specifications, service accessories, historical information and recommended reading references.

Classic Sporting Rifles, by Christopher Austyn, Safari Press, Huntington Beach, CA, 1997. 128 pp., illus. $50.00

As the head of the gun department at Christie's Auction House the author examines the "best" rifles built over the last 150 years.

Collectable '03, by J.C. Harrison, The Arms Chest, Oklahoma City, OK. 1999. 2nd edition (revised). 234 pp., illustrated with drawings, Spiral bound. $35.00

Valuable and detailed reference book for the collector of the Model 1903 Springfield rifle.

Collecting Classic Bolt Action Military Rifles, by Paul S. Scarlata, Andrew Mowbray, Inc., Lincoln, RI, 2001. 280 pp., illus. $39.95

Over 400 large photographs detail key features you will need to recognize in order to identify guns for your collection. Learn the original military configurations of these service rifles so you can tell them apart from altered guns and bad restorations. The historical sections are particularly strong, giving readers a clear understanding of how and why these rifles were developed, and which troops used them.

Collecting the Garand, by J.C. Harrison, The Arms Chest, Oklahoma City, OK. 2001. 2nd edition (revised). 198 pp., illus. with pictures and drawings. Spiral bound. $35.00

Valuable and detailed reference book for the collector of the Garand.

Collecting the M1 Carbine, by J.C. Harrison, The Arms Chest, Oklahoma City, OK. 2000. 2nd edition (revised). 247 pp., illustrated with pictures and drawings. Spiral bound. $35.00

Valuable and detailed reference book for the collector of the M1 Carbine. Identifies standard issue original military models of M1 and M1A1 Models of 1942, '43, '44, and '45 carbines as produced by each manufacturer, plus arsenal repair, refinish and lend-lease.

Competitive AR15: The Mouse That Roared, by Glenn Zediker, Zediker Publishing, Oxford, MS, 1999. 286 pp., illus. Paper covers. $29.95

A thorough and detailed study of the newest precision rifle sensation.

Complete AR15/M16 Sourcebook, Revised and Updated Edition, by Duncan Long, Paladin Press, Boulder, CO, 2002. 336 pp., illus. Paper covers. $39.95

The latest development of the AR15/M16 and the many spin-offs now available, selective-fire conversion systems for the 1990s, the vast selection of new accessories.

Complete Book of the .22: A Guide to the World's Most Popular Guns, by Wayne van Zwoll, Lyons Press, 2004. 1st edition. 336 pgs. Hardcover. NEW. $26.95

Complete Guide to the M1 Garand and the M1 Carbine, by Bruce Canfield, Andrew Mowbray, Inc., Lincoln, RI, 1999. 296 pp., illus. $39.50

Covers all of the manufacturers of components, parts, variations and markings. The total story behind these guns, from their invention through WWII, Korea, Vietnam and beyond! 300+ photos show you features, markings, overall views and action shots. Thirty-three tables and charts give instant reference to serial numbers, markings, dates of issue and proper configurations. Special sections on sniper guns, National Match rifles, exotic variations, and more!

Complete M1 Garand, by Jim Thompson, Paladin Press, Boulder, CO, 1998. 160 pp., illus. Paper cover. $24.00

A guide for the shooter and collector, heavily illustrated.

Crown Jewels: The Mauser In Sweden; A Century of Accuracy and Precision, by Dana Jones, Canada, Collector Grade Publications, 2003. 1st edition. 312 pp., 691 illustrations. Hardcover. $49.95

Here is the first in-depth study of all the Swedish Mausers: the 6.5mm M/94 carbines, M/96 long rifles, M/38 short rifles, Swedish K98Ks (called the M/39 in 7.92x57mm, then, after rechambering to fire the 8x63mm machine un cartridge, the M/40); sniper rifles, and other military adaptations such as grenade launchers and artillery simulators. Also covers a wide variety of the micrometer-adjustment rear sight inserts and "diopter" receiver sights produced for the Swedish Mauser. Full chapters on bayonets and the many accessories, both military and civilian.

ARMS LIBRARY

Defending the Dominion, Canadian Military Rifles, 1855-1955, by David Edgecombe, Ont. Canada, Service Publications, 2003. 1st edition. 168 pp., with 60+ illustrations. Hardcover. NEW. $39.95

Desperate Measures-The Last Ditch Weapons of the Nazi Voksstrurm, by Darrin Weaver, Canada, Collector Grade Publications, 2005. 424 pages, 558 illustrations. $69.50
   All are covered in detail, and the book includes many previously unpublished photographs of original Volkssturm weapons, including prototypes and rare presentation examples.

F.N.-F.A.L. Auto Rifles, Desert Publications, Cornville, AZ, 1981. 130 pp., illus. Paper covers. $18.95
   A definitive study of one of the free world's finest combat rifles.

FAL Rifle, by R. Blake Stevens and Jean van Rutten, Collector Grade Publications, Cobourg, Canada, 1993. 848 pp., illus. $129.95
   Originally published in three volumes, this classic edition covers North American, UK and Commonwealth and the metric FAL's.

Fighting Rifle, by Chuck Taylor, Paladin Press, Boulder, CO, 1983. 184 pp., illus. Paper covers. $25.00
   The difference between assault and battle rifles and auto and light machine guns.

FN-49; Last Elegant Old-World Military Rifle, by Wayne Johnson., Greensboro, NC, Wet Dog Pub. 2004. 200 pages with Over 300 quality b&w photographs. $45.95
   The FN-49 The Last Elegant old World Military Rifle book contains both information on the SAFN as well as the AFN rifle.

FN-FAL Rifle, The, et al, by Duncan Long, Delta Press, El Dorado, AR, 1998. 148 pp., illus. Paper covers. $18.95
   A comprehensive study of one of the classic assault weapons of all times. Detailed descriptions of the basic models plus the myriad of variants that evolved as a result of its universal acceptance.

Forty Years with the .45-70, 2nd Edition, Revised and Expanded, by Paul A. Matthews, Wolfe Publishing Co., Prescott, AZ, 1997. 184 pp., illus. Paper covers. $17.95
   This book is pure gun lore of the .45-70. It not only contains a history of the cartridge, but also years of the author's personal experiences.

Garand .30 Assembly, Disassembly Manual, by Skennerton & Riling, Ray Riling Arms Books Co. Philadelphia, PA 2004. 36 pages, $5.00
   With over 60 photos & line drawings. Ideal workshop reference for stripping & assembly with exploded parts drawings, specifications, service accessories, historical information and recommended reading references.

German Sniper 1914-1945, by Peter R. Senich, Paladin Press, Boulder, CO, 1997 8½" x 11", hardcover, photos, 468 pp. $79.95
   The complete story of Germany's sniping arms development through both world wars. Presents more than 600 photos of Mauser 98's, Selbstladegewehr 41s and 43s, optical sights by Goerz, Zeiss, etc., plus German snipers in action. An exceptional hardcover collector's edition for serious military historians everywhere.

Great Remington 8 and Model 81 Autoloading Rifles, by John Henwood, Canada, Collector Grade Publications, 2003. 1st edition. 304 pp., 291 illustrations, 31 in color. Hardcover. $59.95

Gun Digest Book of the.22 Rimfire, by James House, Iola,WI, Krause Publications, 2005. 288pgs. Soft cover. 250 b&w photos. NEW. $24.99
   The most comprehensive guide to rimfire weapons & ammo. Info on current & vintage models. Covers the history, sights & sighting, techniques for testing accuracy, options for enhancing models, & more.

Gun-Guides, AK-47 AKM All Variants, Disassembly and Reassembly Guide, by Gun Guides, 2005. 16pp, illustrations, cardstock cover. Bright white paper. Soft cover. NEW. $6.99
   The complete guide for ALL models.

Gun-Guides, Colt AR15 and All Variants, Disassembly and Reassembly Guide, by Gun Guides, 2005. 16pp, illustrations, cardstock cover. Bright white paper. Soft cover. NEW. $6.99
   The complete guide for ALL models.

Gun-Guides, 1911 Pistols & All Variants-Disassembly & Reassembly, by Gun Guides, 2006. 16pp, illustrations, cardstock cover. Bright white paper. Soft cover. NEW. $6.99
   The complete guide for ALL models.

Gun-Guides, Glock, Disassembly and Reassembly for All Models, by Gun Guides, 2005. 16pp, illustrations, cardstock cover. Bright white paper. Soft cover. NEW. $6.99
   The complete guide for ALL models.

Gun-Guides, Remington 1100, 11-87 Shotguns, Disassembly and Reassembly Guides, by Gun Guides, 2005. The complete guide for ALL models, 16pp, illustrations, Cardstock cover. Bright white paper. Soft cover. NEW. $6.99

Gun-Guides, Remington 870 Shotguns, Disassembly and Reassembly Guides, by Gun Guides, 2005. The complete guide for ALL models, 16pp, illustrations, Cardstock cover. Bright white paper. Soft cover. NEW. $6.99

Gun-Guides, Ruger .22 Automatic Pistols: The Complete Guide for All Models from 1947 to 2003, by Gun Guides, 2005. 74 pages, 66 high-resolution grayscale images. Cardstock cover. Bright white paper. $11.95
   The complete guide for ALL models. Includes "rare" complete serial numbers and manufacturing dates from 1949-2004.

Gun-Guides, Ruger Single Action Revolvers, Blackhawk, Super Blackhawk, Vaquero and Bisley Models Disassembly and Reassembly Guide for All Models, 1955-2005, by Gun Guides, 2005. 16pp, illustrations, cardstock cover. Bright white paper. $6.99
   The complete guide for ALL models.

Gun-Guides, Ruger 10/22 & 10/17 Carbines Complete Guide to All Models from 1964-2004, by Gun Guides, 2005. 55 pages & 66 high-resolution grayscale images. Bright white paper. Soft cover. NEW. $11.95
   Easy to use: Comb binding lies open and flat on your work surface. Includes all serial numbers and manufacture dates for all models from 1964-2004!

Gun-Guides, Ruger Mini-14 Complete Guide to All Models from 1972-2003, by Gun Guides, 2005. 52pp, illustrations, cardstock cover. Bright white paper. Soft cover. NEW. $11.95
   The complete guide for ALL models.

Gun-Guides, SKS Semi-Automatic Rifles, Disassembly and Reassembly Guide, by Gun Guides, 2005. 16pp, illustrations, cardstock cover. Bright white paper. Soft cover. NEW. $6.99
   The complete guide for ALL models.

Handbook of Military Rifle Marks 1866-1950 (third edition), by Richard Hoffman, and Noel Schott, Maple leaf Militaria Publications, 2002. 66 pp, with illustrations, signed by the authors. Stiff paper covers. NEW. $20.00
   An illustrated military rifles and marks. Officially being used as a reference tool by many law enforcement agencies including BATF, the St. Louis and Philadelphia Police Departments and the Illinois State Police.

High Performance Muzzle Loading Big Game Rifles, by Toby Bridges, Maryland, Stoeger Publications, 2004. 160 pages. Pictorial Hardcover. NEW. $24.95
   Covers all aspects of in-lines including getting top performance, working up loads, choosing projectiles, scope selection, coping with muzzleloader trajectory, tips for maintaining accuracy, plus much, much more.

Historic Henry Rifle: Oliver Winchester's Famous Civil War Repeater, by Wiley Sword, Andrew Mowbray, Inc., Lincoln, RI. 2002. Softcover. $29.95
   It was perhaps the most important firearm of its era. Tested and proved in the fiery crucible of the Civil War, the Henry Rifle became the forerunner of the famous line of Winchester Repeating Rifles that "Won the West." Here is the fascinating story from the frustrations of early sales efforts aimed at the government to the inspired purchase of the Henry Rifle by veteran soldiers who wanted the best weapon.

Hitler's Garands: German Self-Loading Rifles of World War II, by Darrin W. Weaver, Collector Grade Publications, Canada, 2001. 392 pp., 590 illustrations. $69.95
   Hitler's Wehrmacht began WWII armed with the bolt-action K98k, a rifle only cosmetically different from that with which Imperial Germany had fought the Great War a quarter-century earlier. Then in 1940, the Heereswaffenamt (HWaA, the Army Weapons Office) issued a requirement for a new self-loading rifle.

How-To's for the Black Powder Cartridge Rifle Shooter, by Paul A. Matthews, Wolfe Publishing Co., Prescott, AZ, 1996. 136 pp., illus. Paper covers. $22.50
   Practices and procedures used in the reloading and shooting of blackpowder cartridges.

Imperial Japanese Grenade Rifles and Launchers, by Greg Babisch and Thomas Keep, Lemont, PA, Dutch Harlow Publishing, 2004. 247 pages, illustrated with numerous b&w and color photos throughout. Hardcover. New in new dust jacket. $75.00
   This book is a must for museums, military historians, and collectors of Imperial Japanese rifles, rifle cartridges, and ordnance.

Jaeger Rifles Collected Articles Published in Muzzle Blasts, by George Shumway, York, PA, George Shumway, 2003. 108 pp., illus. Hardcover. $30.00

Johnson Rifles and Machine Guns: The Story of Melvin Maynard Johnson Jr. and his Guns, by Bruce N. Canfield, Lincoln, RI, Andrew Mowbray, Inc., 2002. 1st edition. 272 pp. with over 285 photographs. Hardcover. $49.95
   The M1941 Johnson rifle is the hottest WWII rifle on the collector's market today. From invention and manufacture through issue to the troops, this book covers them all!

Kalashnikov: The Arms and the Man, A Revised and Expanded Edition of the AK47 Story, by Edward C. Ezell, Canada, Collector Grade Publications, 2002. 312 pp., 356 illustrations. Hardcover. $59.95
   The original edition of The AK47 Story was published in 1986, and the events of the intervening fifteen years have provided much fresh new material. Beginning with an introduction by Dr. Kalashnikov himself, this is a most comprehensive study of the "life and times" of the AK, starting with the early history of small arms manufacture in Czarist Russia and then the Soviet Union.

Last Enfield: SA80–The Reluctant Rifle, by Steve Raw, Collector Grade Publications, Canada 2003. 1st edition. 360 pp., with 382 illustrations. Hardcover. $49.95
   This book presents the entire, in-depth story of its subject firearm, in this case the controversial British SA80, right from the founding of what became the Royal Small Arms Factory (RSAF) Enfield in the early 1800s; briefly through two world wars with Enfield at the forefront of small arms production for British forces; and covering the adoption of the 7.62mm NATO cartridge in 1954 and the L1A1 rifle in 1957.

Last Steel Warrior: The U.S. M14 Rifle, by Frank Iannamico, Moose Lake Pub., 2006. With over 400 pages and 537 photos and illustrations. Soft cover. NEW. $29.95
   Acclaimed gun author Frank Iannamico's latest book covers history, development and deployment of the influential M14 rifle.

Lee Enfield No. 1 Rifles, by Alan M. Petrillo, Excaliber Publications, Latham, NY, 1992. 64 pp., illus. Paper covers. $10.95
   Highlights the SMLE rifles from the Mark 1-VI.

Lee Enfield Number 4 Rifles, by Alan M. Petrillo, Excalibur Publications, Latham, NY, 1992. 64 pp., illus. Paper covers. $10.95
   A pocket-sized, bare-bones reference devoted entirely to the .303 WWII and Korean War vintage service rifle.

Legendary Sporting Rifles, by Sam Fadala, Stoeger Publishing Co., So. Hackensack, NJ, 1992. 288 pp., illus. Paper covers. $16.95
   Covers a vast span of time and technology beginning with the Kentucky longrifle.

Li'l M1 .30 Cal. Carbine, by Duncan Long, Desert Publications, El Dorado, AZ, 1995. 203 pp., illus. Paper covers. $19.95
   Traces the history of this little giant from its original creation.

Living With the Big .50, The Shooter's Guide to the World's Most Powerful Rifle, Robert Boatman, Boulder, CO, Paladin Press, 2004. 176 pp. Soft cover. NEW. $29.00
   Living with the Big .50 is the most thorough book ever written on this powerhouse rifle.

M1 Carbine Owner's Manual, M1, M2 & M3 .30 Caliber Carbines, Firepower Publications, Cornville, AZ, 1984. 102 pp., illus. Paper covers. $9.95
   The complete book for the owner of an M1 carbine.

ARMS LIBRARY

M1 Carbine Owner's Guide, by Scott A. Duff, Export, PA, Scott Duff Publications, 2002. 144 pages, illustrated. $21.95
  Tells you what to look for before you choose a Carbine for collecting or shooting. Identification guide with serial numbers by production quarter for approximate date of manufacture. Illustrated, complete guide to markings, nomenclature of parts, assembly, disassembly and special tools. History and identification guide with serial numbers by production quarter for approximate date of manufacture. Includes troubleshooting, maintenance, cleaning and lubrication guide.

M1 Garand .30 Assembly, Disassembly Manual, by Skennerton & Riling, Ray Riling Arms Books Co. Philadelphia, PA 2004. 36 pages, over 60 photos & line drawings. $5.00
  Ideal workshop reference for stripping & assembly with exploded parts drawings, specifications, service accessories, historical information and recommended reading references.

M1 Garand Owners Guide, Vol 1, by Scott A. Duff, Export, PA, Scott Duff Publications, 2002. 126 pages, illustrated. $21.95
  Makes shooting, disassembly and maintenance work easier. Contains a brief history as well as production dates and other information to help identify who made it and when. Line drawings identify the components and show their position and relationships plainly.

M1 Garand Complete Assembly Guide, Vol. 2, by Walt Kuleck, and Clint McKee, Export, PA, Scott Duff Publications, 2004. 162 pp. $21.95
  You'll learn the best and easiest ways to build your rifle. It won't make you a Garand armorer, but it will make you a more knowledgeable owner. You'll be able to do more with (and to) your rifle.

M1 Garand Serial Numbers & Data Sheets, by Scott A. Duff, Scott A. Duff, Export, PA, 1995. 101 pp. Paper covers. $11.95
  This pocket reference book includes serial number tables and data sheets on the Springfield Armory, gas trap rifles, gas port rifles, Winchester Repeating Arms, International Harvester and H&R Arms Co. and more.

M1 Garand: Post World War, by Scott A. Duff, Scott A. Duff Publications, Export, PA, 1990. 139 pp., illus. Softcover. $21.95
  A detailed account of the activities at Springfield Armory through this period. International Harvester, H&R, Korean War production and quantities delivered. Serial numbers.

M1 Garand: World War 2, by Scott A. Duff, Scott A. Duff Publications, Export, PA, 1993. 210 pp., illus. Paper covers. $34.95
  The most comprehensive study available to the collector and historian on the M1 Garand of WWII.

M14 Rifle Assembly, Disassembly Manual 7.62mm, by Skennerton & Riling, Ray Riling Arms Books Co. Philadelphia, PA 2004. 36 pages, over 60 photos & line drawings. $5.00
  Ideal workshop reference for stripping & assembly with exploded parts drawings, specifications, service accessories, historical information and recommended reading references.

M14 Owner's Guide and Match Conditioning Instructions, by Scott A. Duff and John M. Miller, Duff Publications, Export, PA, 1996. 180 pp., illus. Paper covers. $19.95
  Traces the history and development from the T44 through the adoption and production of the M14 rifle.

M14 Complete Assembly Guide; Vol. 2, by Walt Kuleck, and Clint McKee, Duff Publications, Export, PA, 1996. 180 pp., illus. Paper covers. $24.95
  You'll learn the best and easiest ways to enhance, disassemble and assemble your rifle. It won't make you an M14/M1A armorer, but it will make you a knowledgeable owner. You'll be able to do more with (and to) your rifle.

M14 Rifle, facsimile reprint of FM 23-8, Desert Publications, Cornville, AZ, 50 pp., illus. Paper $11.95
  Well illustrated and informative reprint covering the M-14 and M-14E2.

M14-Type Rifle: A Shooter's And Collector's Guide; 3rd Edition Revised and Expanded edition, by Joe Poyer, North Cape Publications, Tustin, CA, 2007. 104 pp., illus. Paper covers. $19.95
  This new revised and expanded edition examines the M14 rifle and its two sniper variations on a part-by-part basis but surveys all current civilian semiautomatic M14-type rifles and components available today. It also provides as a guide for shooters who want to restore an M14 to original condition or build a superb match rifle. Included are the Chinese variations of the M14. The history of the development and use of the M14 in Vietnam, and now in Iraq and Afghanistan, is detailed. The book is fully illustrated with photos and drawings that clarify the text. Appendices provide up-to-date information on parts and supplies and gunsmithing services.

M14/M14A1 Rifles and Rifle Marksmanship, Desert Publications, El Dorado, AZ, 1995. 236 pp., illus. Paper covers. $19.95
  Contains a detailed description of the M14 and M14A1 rifles and their general characteristics, procedures for disassembly & assembly, operating and functioning of the rifles.

M16/AR15 Rifle, by Joe Poyer, North Cape Publications, Tustin, CA, 1998. 150 pp., illus. Paper covers. $19.95
  From its inception as the first American assault battle rifle to the firing lines of the National Matches, the M16/AR15 rifle in all its various models and guises has made a significant impact on the American rifleman.

Major Ned H. Roberts and the Schuetzen Rifle, edited by Gerald O. Kelver, Brighton, CO, 1998. 3rd edition. 122 pp., illus. $13.95
  A compilation of the writings of Major Ned H. Roberts which appeared in various gun magazines.

Mannlicher Military Rifles: Straight Pull and Turn Bolt Designs, Paul Scarlata, Lincoln, RI, Andrew Mowbray, 2004. Hardcover, 168 pages 8.5 x 11, filled with black & white photos. Hardcover. NEW $32.49
  Profusely illustrated with close-up photos, drawings and diagrams, this book is the most detailed examination of Mannlicher military rifles ever produced in the English language.

Mauser Military Rifles Of The World, 4th Edition, by Robert Ball, Iola, WI, Krause Publications, 2006. 448 pp., with historical data, coupled with detailed color photos. $49.95
  The ultimate Mauser military rifle reference, this superior guide is packed with more models, all-color photos and Mauser history tailored to the interests and needs of firearms collectors. With more than 50 countries represented, 75 years of Mauser military rifle production is meticulously cataloged with descriptions, historical details, model specifications and markings, for easy identification by collectors.

Mauser Military Rifle Markings, 2nd Edition, Revised and Expanded, by Terence Lapin, Hyrax Publishers, Arlington, VA. 2005, 167 pages, illustrated. Softcover. $22.95
  A general guide to reading and understanding the often mystifying markings found on military Mauser Rifles. Includes German Regimental markings as well as German police markings and W.W. 2 German Mauser subcontractor codes. A handy reference to take to gun shows.

Mauser Rifles & Carbines Assembly, Disassembly Manual, by Skennerton & Riling, Ray Riling Arms Books Co. Philadelphia, PA 2004. 36 pages, over 60 photos & line drawings. $5.00
  Ideal workshop reference for stripping & assembly with exploded parts drawings, specifications, service accessories, historical information and recommended reading references.

Mauser Smallbore Sporting, Target and Training Rifles, by Jon Speed, Collector Grade Publications, Inc., Cobourg, Ont., Canada, 1998. 372 pp., illus. $67.50
  The history of all the smallbore sporting, target and training rifles produced by the legendary Mauser-Werke of Obendorf am Neckar.

Mauser: Original-Oberndorf Sporting Rifles, by Jon Speed, Collector Grade Publications, Inc., Cobourg, Ont., Canada, 1997. 508 pp., illus. $89.95
  The most exhaustive study ever published of the design origins and manufacturing history of the original Oberndorf Mauser Sporter.

MG34-MG42 German Universal Machineguns, by Folke Myrvang, Collector Grade Publications, Canada. 2002. 496 pp., 646 illustrations. $79.95
  This is the first-ever COMPETE study of the MG34 & MG42. Here the author presents in-depth coverage of the historical development, fielding, tactical use of and modifications made to these remarkable guns and their myriad accessories and ancillaries, plus authoritative tips on troubleshooting.

Military Bolt Action Rifles, 1841-1918, by Donald B. Webster, Museum Restoration Service, Alexander Bay, NY, 1993. 150 pp., illus. $34.50
  A photographic survey of the principal rifles and carbines of the European and Asiatic powers of the last half of the 19th century and the first years of the 20th century.

Military Rifles of Japan, 5th Edition, by F.L. Honeycutt, Julin Books, Lake Park, FL, 1999. 208 pp., illus. $42.00
  A new revised and updated edition. Includes the early Murata-period markings, etc.

Mini-14, by Duncan Long, Paladin Press, Boulder, CO, 1987. 120 pp., illus. Paper covers. $17.00
  History of the Mini-14, the factory-produced models, specifications, accessories, suppliers, and much more.

MKB 42, MP43, MP44 and the Sturmgewehr 44, by de Vries & Martens. Alexandria, VA, Ironside International, 2003. 1st edition. 152 pp., illustrated with 200 high quality b&w photos. Hardcover. $39.95
  Covers all essential information on history and development, ammunition and accessories, codes and markings, and contains photos of nearly every model and accessory. Includes a unique selection of original German WWII propaganda photos, most never published before.

Modern Guns: Fred Adolph Genoa, by Fred Adolph, Oceanside, CA, Armory Publications, 2003. One of only a few catalogs that list 2, 3 and 4 barrel guns. 68 pages, illustrated. Stiff Paper Covers. New. $19.95

Modern Sniper Rifles, by Duncan Long, Paladin Press, Boulder, CO, 1997, 8½" x 11", soft cover, photos, illus., 120 pp. $20.00
  Noted weapons expert Duncan Long describes the .22 LR, single-shot, bolt-action, semiautomatic and large-caliber rifles that can be used for sniping purposes, including the U.S. M21, Ruger Mini-14, AUG and HK-94SG1. These and other models are evaluated on the basis of their features, accuracy, reliability and handiness in the field. The author also looks at the best scopes, ammunition and accessories.

More Single Shot Rifles and Actions, by Frank de Haas and Mark de Haas, Orange City, IA, 1996. 146 pp., illus. Paper covers. $22.50
  Covers 45 different single shot rifles. Includes the history plus photos, drawings and personal comments.

Mosin-Nagant Assembly, Disassembly Manual 7.62mmR, by Skennerton & Riling, Ray Riling Arms Books Co. Philadelphia, PA 2004. 36 pages, $5.00
  With over 60 photos & line drawings. Ideal workshop reference for stripping & assembly with exploded parts drawings, specifications, service accessories, historical information and recommended reading references.

Mosin-Nagant Rifle, by Terence W. Lapin, North Cape Publications, Tustin, CA, 1998. 30 pp., illus. Paper covers. $19.95
  The first ever complete book on the Mosin-Nagant rifle written in English. Covers every variation.

Mr. Single Shot's Book of Rifle Plans, by Frank de Haas and Mark de Haas, Orange City, IA, 1996. 85 pp., illus. Paper covers. $22.50
  Contains complete and detailed drawings, plans and instructions on how to build four different and unique breech-loading single shot rifles of the author's own proven design.

Muskets of the Revolution and the French & Indian Wars; The Smoothbore Longarm in Early America, Including British, French, Dutch, German, Spanish, and American Weapons, by Bill Ahearn, Lincoln, RI, Andrew Mowbray, 2005. 248 pages, illustrated. Pictorial hardcover. NEW. $49.95
  Not just a technical study of old firearms, this is a tribute to the bravery of the men who fought on both sides of that epic conflict and a celebration of the tools of freedom that have become so much a part of our national character. Includes many never-before published photos!

Neutrality Through Marksmanship: A Collector's and Shooter's Guide to Swedish Army Rifles 1867-1942, by Doug Bowser, Camellia City Military Publications, 1996. 1st edition. Stiff paper covers. NEW. $20.00

No. 4 (T) Sniper Rifle: An Armourer's Perspective, The, by Peter Laidler with Ian Skennerton, I.D.S.A. Books, Piqua, OH, 1993. 125 pp., 75 illus. Paper covers. $19.95
  A reprint of the 1864 London edition. Captain Heaton was one of the great rifle shots from the earliest days of the Volunteer Movement.

Official SKS Manual, Translation by Major James F. Gebhardt (Ret.), Paladin Press, Boulder, CO, 1997. 96 pp., illus. Paper covers. $16.00
  This Soviet military manual covering the widely distributed SKS is now available in English.

ARMS LIBRARY

Official Soviet AK-47 Manual: Operating Instructions for the 5.45mm Kalashnikov Assault Rifle, and Kalashnikov Light Machine Gun, by James Gebhardt, Boulder, CO, Paladin Press, 2006. 8½" x 11", illus., 150 pp. Soft cover. NEW. $25.00

Written to teach Russian soldiers every detail of the operation and maintenance of the Kalashnikov Assault Rifle (AK-74) and Kalashnikov Light Machine Gun (RPK-74), this manual includes ballistic tables, zeroing information, combat firing instructions, data for the 5.45mm service cartridge and more.

Old German Target Arms: Alte Schiebenwaffen, by Jesse Thompson, C. Ron Dillon, Allen Hallock and Bill Loos, Rochester, NY, Tom Rowe Publications, 2003. 1st edition. 392 pp. Hardcover. $98.00

History of Schueten shooting from the middle ages through WWII. Hundreds of illustrations, most in color. History & memorabilia of the Bundesschiessen (State or National Shoots), bird target rifles, American shooters in Germany. Schutzen rifles such as matchlocks, wheellocks, flintlocks, percussion, bader, bornmuller, rifles by Buchel and more.

Old German Target Arms: Alte Schiebenwaffen Volume 2, by Jesse Thompson, C. Ron Dillon, Allen Hallock and Bill Loos, Rochester, NY, Tom Rowe Publications, 2004. 1st edition. 392 pp. Hardcover. $98.00

Old German Target Arms: Alte Schiebenwaffen Volume 3, by Jesse Thompson, C. Ron Dillon, Allen Hallock and Bill Loos, Rochester, NY, Tom Rowe Publications, 2005. 1st edition. 392 pp. Hardcover. $98.00

Ordnance Tools, Accessories & Appendages of the M1 Rifle, by Billy Pyle, Houston, TX, privately printed, 2002. 2nd edition. 206 pp., illustrated with b&w photos. Softcover. $40.00

This is the new updated second edition with over 350 pictures and drawings, of which 30 are new. Part I contains accessories, appendages, and equipment. Part II covers ammunition, grenades, and pyrotechnics. Part III shows the inspection gages. Part IV presents the ordnance tools, fixtures, and assemblies. Part V contains miscellaneous items related to the M1.

Police Rifles, by Richard Fairburn, Paladin Press, Boulder, CO, 1994. 248 pp., illus. Paper covers. $35.00

Selecting the right rifle for street patrol and special tactical situations.

Poor Man's Sniper Rifle, by D. Boone, Paladin Press, Boulder, CO, 1995. 152 pp., illus. Paper covers. $18.95

Here is a complete plan for converting readily available surplus military rifles to high-performance sniper weapons.

Precision Shooting with the M1 Garand, by Roy Baumgardner, Precision Shooting, Inc., Manchester, CT, 1999. 142 pp., illus. Paper covers. $12.95

Starts off with the ever popular ten-article series on accurizing the M1 that originally appeared in Precision Shooting in the 1993-95 era. There follows nine more Baumgardner-authored articles on the M1 Garand and finally a 1999 updating chapter.

Remington 700, by John F. Lacy, Taylor Publishing Co., Dallas, TX, 2002. 208 pp., illus. $54.95

Covers the different models, limited editions, chamberings, proofmarks, serial numbers, military models, and much more.

Remington Autoloading and Pump Action Rifles, by Eugene Myszkowski, Tucson, AZ, Excalibur Publications, 2002. 132 pp., with 162 photographs, 6 illustrations and 18 charts. Softcover. $20.95

An illustrated history of Remington's centerfire Models 760, 740, 742, 7400 and 7600. The book is thoroughly researched and features many previously unpublished photos of the rifles, their accessories and accoutrements. Also covers high grade, unusual and experimental rifles. Contains information on collecting, serial numbers and barrel codes.

Rifle Rules: Magic for the Ultimate Rifleman, by Don Paul, Kaua'i, HI, Pathfinder Publications, 2003. 1st edition. 116 pp., illus. Softcover. $14.95

A new method that shows you how to add hundreds of yards to your effective shooting ability. Ways for you to improve your rifle's accuracy which no factory can do. Illustrations & photos added to make new concepts easy.

Rifle Shooter, by G. David Tubb, Oxford, MS, Zediker Publishing, 2004. 1st edition. 416 pp softcover, 7" x 10" size, 400 photos and illustrations, very high quality printing. Softcover. $34.95

This is not just a revision of his landmark "Highpower Rifle" but an all-new, greatly expanded work that reveals David's thoughts and recommendations on all aspects of precision rifle shooting. Each shooting position and event is dissected and taken to extreme detail, as are the topics of ammunition, training, rifle design, event strategies, and wind shooting. You will learn the secrets of perhaps the greatest rifleman ever, and you'll learn how to put them to work for you!

Rifles of the U.S. Army 1861-1906, by John D. McAulay, Lincoln, RI, Andrew Mowbray, Inc., 2003. 1st edition. 278 pp., illus. Hardcover. NEW. $45.89

Rifles of the White Death (Valkoisen Kuoleman Kivaarit) A Collector's and Shooter's Guide to Finnish Military Rifles 1918-1944, by Doug Bowser, MS, Camellia City Military Publications, 1998. 1st edition. Stiff paper covers. NEW. $35.00

Rock In A Hard Place The Browning Automatic Rifle, by James L. Ballou. Collector Grade, Canada, 2004. 1st edition. 500 pages, with 751 illustrations. Hardcover $79.95

This first-ever in-depth study of the popular BAR includes clear photos of all U.S.-made military and commercial models, experimental models from Britain and France, plus offshore copies and clones from Belgium, Poland and Sweden.

Rock Island Rifle Model 1903, by C.S. Ferris, Export, PA, Scott A. Duff Publications, 2002. 177 pp., illustrated with b&w photographs. Foreword by Scott A. Duff. Softcover. $22.95

S.L.R.–Australia's F.N. F.A.L., by Ian Skennerton and David Balmer, Arms & Militaria Press, 1989. 124 pp., 100 illus. Paper covers. $24.50

Schuetzen Rifles, History and Loading, by Gerald O. Kelver, Pioneer Press, Union City, TN, 1998. 3rd edition. Illus. $13.95

Reference work on these rifles, their bullets, loading, telescopic sights, accuracy, etc. A limited, numbered ed.

Serbian and Yugoslav Mauser Rifles, by Banko Bogdanovich, Tustin, CA, North Cape Publications, 2005. 278pp. Soft cover. NEW. $19.95

In Serbian and Yugoslav Mauser Rifles, each model is discussed in its own chapter. All serial numbers are presented by year. All markings are presented and translated and all finishes and changes to all models are described in text and charts and well illustrated with both photographs and excellent drawings for clarity.

Shooting Lever Guns of the Old West, by Mike Venturino, MLV Enterprises, Livingston, MT, 1999. 300 pp., illus. Paper covers. $27.95

Shooting the lever action type repeating rifles of our American west.

Shooting the .43 Spanish Rolling Block, by Croft Barker, Flatonia, TX, Cistern Publishing, 2003. 1st edition. 137 pp. Softcover. $25.50

The source for information on .43 caliber rolling blocks. Lots of photos and text covering Remington & Oveido actions, antique cartridges, etc. Features smokless & black powder loads, rifle disassembly and maintenance, 11mm bullets. Required reading for the rolling block owner.

Shooting the Blackpowder Cartridge Rifle, by Paul A. Matthews, Wolfe Publishing Co., Prescott, AZ, 1994. 129 pp., illus. Paper covers. $22.50

A general discourse on shooting the blackpowder cartridge rifle and the procedure required to make a particular rifle perform.

Single Shot Military Rifle Handbook, by Croft Barker, Flatonia, TX, Cistern Publishing, 2005. Includes over 40 new high quality photos of vintage rifles, antique cartridges and related equipment. 130pp., many b&w photos. Soft cover. NEW. $25.50

Contains instruction on preparing authentic ammunition, shooting techniques, the uses of vintage military sights, rifle refurbishing, etc. Evolution of the single shot military rifle and the center fire cartridge is described.

Single Shot Rifles and Actions, by Frank de Haas, Orange City, IA, 1990. 352 pp., illus. Softcover. $27.00

The definitive book on over 60 single shot rifles and actions.

SKS Carbine 7.62 x 39mm Assembly, Disassembly Manual, by Skennerton & Riling, Ray Riling Arms Books Co. Philadelphia, PA 2004. 36 pages, over 60 photos & line drawings. $5.00

Ideal workshop reference for stripping & assembly with exploded parts drawings, specifications, service accessories, historical information and recommended reading references.

Small Arms Identification Series, No. 1–.303 Rifle, No. 1 S.M.L.E. Marks III and III*, by Ian Skennerton, I.D.S.A. Books, Piqua, OH, 1981. 48 pp. $10.50

Small Arms Identification Series, No. 2–.303 Rifle, No. 4 Marks I, & I*, Marks 1/2, 1/3 & 2, by Ian Skennerton, I.D.S.A. Books, Piqua, OH, 1994. 48 pp. $10.50

Small Arms Identification Series, No. 3–9mm Austen Mk I & 9mm Owen Mk I Sub-Machine Guns, by Ian Skennerton, I.D.S.A. Books, Piqua, OH, 1994. 48 pp. $10.50

Small Arms Identification Series, No. 4–.303 Rifle, No. 5 Mk I, by Ian Skennerton, I.D.S.A. Books, Piqua, OH, 1994. 48 pp. $10.50

Small Arms Identification Series, No. 5–.303-in. Bren Light Machine Gun, by Ian Skennerton, I.D.S.A. Books, Piqua, OH, 1994. 48 pp. $10.50

Springfield Rifle M1903, M1903A1, M1903A3, M1903A4, Desert Publications, Cornville, AZ, 1982. 100 pp., illus. Paper covers. $14.95

Covers every aspect of disassembly and assembly, inspection, repair and maintenance.

Still More Single Shot Rifles, by James J. Grant, Pioneer Press, Union City, TN, 1995. 211 pp., illus. $29.95

This is Volume Four in a series of single-shot rifles by America's foremost authority. It gives more in-depth information on those single-shot rifles that were presented in the first three books.

Sturm, Ruger 10/22 Rifle and .44 Magnum Carbine, by Duncan Long, Paladin Press, Boulder, CO, 1988. 108 pp., illus. Paper covers. $15.00

An in-depth look at both weapons detailing the elegant simplicity of the Ruger design. Offers specifications, troubleshooting procedures and ammunition recommendations.

Swedish Mauser Rifles, by Steve Kehaya and Joe Poyer, Tustin, CA, North Cape Publications, 2004. 2nd edition, revised. 267 pp., illus. Softcover. $19.95

Every known variation of the Swedish Mauser carbine and rifle is described including all match and target rifles and all sniper versions. Includes serial number and production data.

Swiss Magazine Loading Rifles 1869 to 1958, by Joe Poyer, Tustin, CA, North Cape Publications, 2003. 1st edition. 317 pp., illustrated with hundreds of b&w drawings and photos. Softcover. $19.95

It covers the K-31 on a part-by-part basis, as well as its predecessor models of 1889 and 1911, and the first repeating magazine rifle ever adopted by a military, the Model 1869 Vetterli rifle and its successor models. Also includes a history of the development and use of these fine rifles. Details regarding their ammunition, complete assembly/disassembly instructions as well as sections on cleaning, maintenance and trouble shooting.

Tactical Rifle, by Gabriel Suarez, Paladin Press, Boulder, CO, 1999. 264 pp., illus. Paper covers. $25.00

The precision tool for urban police operations.

Target Rifle in Australia, by J.E. Corcoran, R&R, Livonia, NY, 1996. 160 pp., illus. $40.00

A most interesting study of the evolution of these rifles from 1860-1900. British rifles from the percussion period through the early smokeless era are discussed.

Total Airguns; The Complete Guide to Huting with Air Rifles, by Peter Wadeson, London, Swan Hill Press, 2005. 300 pages, illustrated with b&w photos. Hardcover. NEW. $29.95

This book covers every aspect from choosing a rifle and scope to field craft and hunting techniques, camouflage, decoys, night shooting, and equipment maintenance. Extensive details on all air gun shooting techniques.

U.S. M1 Carbine: Wartime Production, 5th Edition, Revised and Expanded! by Craig Riesch, North Cape Publications, Tustin, CA 2007 237 pages. $19.95

The book contains 38 charts and 212 photographs, and 14 drawings. The book provides a history of the M1 Carbine's development, manufacture and use during World War II, as well as through the Korean War and the war in Vietnam. All variations of the M1 Carbine are discussed – M1, M1A1, and M2 – by manufacturer. Serial number ranges for original manufacture are included.

ARMS LIBRARY

U.S. Rifle .30 Model 1917 and .303 BRITISH Pattern 1914 Assembly, Disassembly Manual, by Skennerton & Riling, Ray Riling Arms Books Co. Philadelphia, PA 2004. 36 pages, over 60 photos & line drawings. $5.00

Ideal workshop reference for stripping & assembly with exploded parts drawings, specifications, service accessories, historical information and recommended reading references. Ideal workbook for shooters and collectors alike. Triple saddle-stitched binding with durable plastic laminated cover makes this an ideal workshop guide.

U.S. Marine Corps AR15/M16 A2 Manual, reprinted by Desert Publications, El Dorado, AZ, 1993. 262 pp., illus. Paper covers. $16.95

A reprint of TM05538C-23&P/2, August, 1987. The A-2 manual for the Colt AR15/M16.

U.S. Marine Corps Rifle Marksmanship, by U.S. Marine Corps, Boulder, CO, Paladin Press, 2002. Photos, illus., 120 pp. Softcover. $20.00

This manual is the very latest Marine doctrine on the art and science of shooting effectively in battle. Its 10 chapters teach the versatility, flexibility and skills needed to deal with a situation at any level of intensity across the entire range of military operations. Topics covered include the proper combat mindset; cleaning your rifle under all weather conditions; rifle handling and marksmanship the Marine way; engaging targets from behind cover; obtaining a battlefield zero; engaging immediate threat, multiple and moving targets; shooting at night and at unknown distances; and much more.

U.S. Rifle M14–From John Garand to the M21, by R. Blake Stevens, Collector Grade Publications, Inc., Toronto, Canada, revised 2nd edition, 1991. 350 pp., illus. $49.50

A classic, in-depth examination of the development, manufacture and fielding of the last wood-and-metal ("lock, stock, and barrel") battle rifle to be issued to U.S. troops.

United States Rifle Model of 1917, by CS Ferris, Export, PA, Scott Duff Pubs., 2004. 213 pages, illustrated with b&w photographs. Foreword by Scott A. Duff. Soft cover. NEW. $23.95

If you are interested in the study of the United States Rifle Model of 1917 and have been disappointed by the lack of information available, then this book is for you!

Ultimate in Rifle Accuracy, by Glenn Newick, Stoeger Publishing Co., Wayne, NJ, 1999. 205 pp., illus. Paper covers. $11.95

This handbook contains the information you need to extract the best performance from your rifle.

War Baby! The U.S. Caliber 30 Carbine, Volume 1, by Larry Ruth, Collector Grade Publications, Toronto, Canada, 1992. 512 pp., illus. $69.95

Volume 1 of the in-depth story of the phenomenally popular U.S. caliber 30 carbine. Concentrates on design and production of the military 30 carbine during WWII.

War Baby Comes Home: The U.S. Caliber 30 Carbine, Volume 2, by Larry Ruth, Collector Grade Publications, Toronto, Canada, 1993. 386 pp., illus. $49.95

The triumphant completion of Larry Ruth's two-volume, in-depth series on the most popular U.S. military small arm in history.

Winchester: An American Legend, by R.L. Wilson, NY, Book Sales, 2004, reprint. 404 pages, illustrated with color and b&w photographs. Hardcover. New in new dust jacket. $29.95

Winchester Model 52: Perfection in Design, by Herbert Houze, Iola, WI, Krause Publications, 2006. Soft cover. NEW. $22.95

Herbert Houze unravels the mysteries surrounding the development of what many consider the most perfect rifle ever made. The book covers the rifle's improvements through five modifications. Users, collectors and marksmen will appreciate each variation's history, serial number sequences and authentic photos.

Winchester Model 61 Assembly, Disassembly Manual, by Skennerton & Riling, Ray Riling Arms Books Co. Philadelphia, PA 2004. 36 pages, over 60 photos & line drawings. $5.00

Ideal workshop reference for stripping & assembly with exploded parts drawings, specifications, service accessories, historical information and recommended reading references.

Winchester Model 70 Assembly, Disassembly Manual, by Skennerton & Riling, Ray Riling Arms Books Co. Philadelphia, PA 2004. 36 pages, over 60 photos & line drawings. $5.00

Ideal workshop reference for stripping & assembly with exploded parts drawings, specifications, service accessories, historical information and recommended reading references.

Winchester Model 94 Assembly, Disassembly Manual, by Skennerton & Riling, Ray Riling Arms Books Co. Philadelphia, PA 2004. 36 pages, over 60 photos & line drawings. $5.00

Ideal workshop reference for stripping & assembly with exploded parts drawings, specifications, service accessories, historical information and recommended reading references.

Winchester Slide-Action Rifles, Models 61, 62, 1890 & 1906, by Ned Schwing, Iola, WI, Krause Publications, 2004. 456 Pages, illustrated, 300 b&w photos. Soft cover. NEW. $39.95

Take a complete historical look at the favorite slide-action guns of America through Ned Schwing's eyes. Explore receivers, barrels, markings, stocks, stampings and engraving in complete detail.

Workbench AR-15 Project; A Step by Step Guide to Building Your Own Legal AR-15 Without Paperwork, The, by D.A. Hanks, Boulder, CO, Paladin Press, 2004. 80 pages, photos. Soft cover. NEW. $19.89

Hanks walks you through the entire process with clear text and detailed photos—staying legal, finishing the lower receiver, assembling all the parts and test-firing your completed rifle. For academic study only.

SHOTGUNS

A Collector's Guide to United States Combat Shotguns, by Bruce N. Canfield, Andrew Mowbray Inc., Publishers, Lincoln, RI, 1993. 184 pp., illus. Paper covers. $24.00

Full coverage of the combat shotgun, from the earliest examples to the Gulf War and beyond.

A.H. Fox: "The Finest Gun in the World," revised and enlarged edition, by Michael McIntosh, Countrysport, Inc., New Albany, OH, 1995. 408 pp., illus. $60.00

The first detailed history of one of America's finest shotguns.

Advanced Combat Shotgun: Stress Fire 2, by Massad Ayoob, Police Bookshelf, Concord, NH, 1993. 197 pp., illus. Paper covers. $14.95

Advanced combat shotgun fighting for police.

Best Guns, by Michael McIntosh, Countrysport Press, Selma, AL, 1999, revised edition. 418 pp. $45.00

Combines the best shotguns ever made in America with information on British and Continental makers.

Best of Holland & Holland, England's Premier Gunmaker, by Michael McIntosh and Jan G. Roosenburg. Long Beach, CA, Safari Press, Inc., 2002. 1st edition. 298 pp., profuse color illustrations. Hardcover. $69.95

Holland & Holland has had a long history of not only building London's "best" guns but also providing superior guns–the ultimate gun in finish, engraving, and embellishment. From the days of old in which a maharaja would order 100 fancifully engraved H&H shotguns for his guests to use at his duck shoot to the recent elaborately decorated sets depicting the Apollo 11 moon landing or the history of the British Empire, all of these guns represent the zenith in the art and craft of gunmaking and engraving. Never before have so many superlative guns from H&H– or any other maker for that matter–been displayed in one book.

Better Shot, by Ken Davies, Quiller Press, London, England, 1992. 136 pp., illus. $39.95

Step-by-step shotgun techniques with Holland and Holland.

Black's Buyer's Directory 2007 Wing & Clay, by James Black, Grand View Media, 2006. Soft cover. NEW. $17.95

1,637 companies in 62 sections providing shotgun related products and services worldwide. Destinations: 1,412 hunting destinations, 1,279 sporting clays, trap and skeet clubs state by state.

Breaking Clays, by Chris Batha, Stackpole Books, Mechanicsburg, PA, 2005. Hardcover. $29.95

This clear and concise book offers a distillation of the best tips and techniques that really work to improve your scores and give you the knowledge to develop to your full shooting potential

Browning Auto-5 Shotguns: The Belgian FN Production, by H. M. Shirley Jr. and Anthony Vanderlinden, Geensboro, NC, Wet Dog Publications, 2003. Limited edition of 2,000 copies, signed by the author. 233 pp., plus index. Over 400 quality b&w photographs and 24 color photographs. Hardcover $59.95

This is the first book devoted to the history, model variations, accessories and production dates of this legendary gun. This publication is to date the only reference book on the Auto-5 (A-5) shotgun prepared entirely with the extensive cooperation and support of Browning, FN Herstal, the Browning Firearms Museum and the Liege Firearms Museum.

Browning-Sporting Arms of Distinction 1903-1992, by Matt Eastman, Safari Press, 2005. Hardcover. $50.00

Finally, the history of the Browning family, the inventions, the company, and Browning's association with Colt, Winchester, Savage, and others is detailed in this all-inclusive book, which is profusely illustrated with hundreds of pictures and charts.

Cogswell & Harrison; Two Centuries of Gunmaking, by G. Cooley and J. Newton, Safari Press, Long Beach, CA, 2000. 128 pp., 30 color photos, 100 b&w photos. $39.95

The authors have gathered a wealth of fascinating historical and technical material that will make the book indispensable, not only to many thousands of "Coggie" owners worldwide, but also to anyone interested in the general history of British gunmaking.

Defensive Shotgun, The, by Louis Awerbuck, S.W.A.T. Publications, Cornville, AZ, 1989. 77 pp., illus. Softcover. $14.95

Cuts through the myths concerning the shotgun and its attendant ballistic effects.

Ducks Unlimited Guide to Shotgunning, The, by Don Zutz, Willow Creek Press, Minocqua, WI, 2000. 166 pg. Illustrated. $24.50

This book covers everything from the grand old guns of yesterday to today's best shotguns and loads, from the basic shotgun fit and function to expert advice on ballistics, chocks, and shooting techniques.

Fine European Gunmakers: Best Continental European Gunmakers & Engravers, by M. Nobili, Long Beach, CA, Safari Press, 2002. 250 pp., illustated in color. $69.95

Many experts argue that Continental gunmakers produce guns equally as good or better than British makers. Marco Nobili's new work showcases the skills of the best craftsmen from continental Europe. The book covers the histories of the individual firms and looks at the guns they currently build, tracing the developments of their most influential models.

Firearms Assembly/Disassembly, Part V: Shotguns, 2nd Edition, The Gun Digest Book of, by J.B. Wood, Krause Publications, Iola, WI, 2002. 560 pp., illus. $24.95

Covers 54 popular shotguns plus over 250 variants. The most comprehensive and professional presentation available to either hobbyist or gunsmith.

Game Shooting, by Robert Churchill, Countrysport Press, Selma, AL, 1998. 258 pp., illus. $30.00

The basis for every shotgun instructional technique devised and the foundation for all wingshooting and the game of sporting clays.

Greatest Hammerless Repeating Shotgun Ever Built: The Model 12 Winchester 1912-1964 by David Riffle, 1995. Color illustrations. 195 large detailed b&w photos, 298 pgs. Pictorial hardcover. NEW. $54.95

This offers an extremely well written and detailed year-by-year study of the gun, its details, inventors, makers, engravers, and star shooters.

Greener Story, by Graham Greener, Safari Press, Long Beach, CA, 2000. 231 pp., color and b&w illustrations. $69.95

The history of the Greener gunmakers and their guns.

Gunsmithing Shotguns: The Complete Guide to Care & Repair, by David Henderson, New York, Globe Pequot, 2003. 1st edition, b&w photos & illus; 6" x 9", 256 pp., illus. Hardcover. $24.95

An overview designed to provide insight, ideas and techniques that will give the amateur gunsmith the confidence and skill to work on his own guns. General troubleshooting, common problems, stocks and woodworking, soldering and brazing, barrel work and more.

Heyday of the Shotgun, by David Baker, Safari Press, Inc., Huntington Beach, CA, 2000. 160 pp., illus. $39.95

The art of the gunmaker at the turn of the last century when British craftsmen brought forth the finest guns ever made.

ARMS LIBRARY

Holland & Holland: The "Royal" Gunmaker, by Donald Dallas, London, Safari Press, 2004. 1st edition. 311 pp. Hardcover. $75.00
Donald Dallas tells the fascinating story of Holland & Holland from its very beginnings, and the history of the family is revealed for the first time. The terrific variety of the firm's guns and rifles is described in great detail and set within the historical context of their eras. The book is profusely illustrated with 112 color and 355 b&w photographs, mostly unpublished. In addition many rare guns and rifles are described and illustrated.

House of Churchill, by Don Masters, Safari Press, Long Beach, CA, 2002. 512 pp., profuse color and b&w illustrations. $79.95
This marvelous work on the house of Churchill contains serial numbers and dates of manufacture of its guns from 1891 forward, price lists from 1895 onward, a complete listing of all craftsmen employed at the company, as well as the prices realized at the famous Dallas auction where the "last" production guns were sold. It was written by Don Masters, a long-time Churchill employee, who is keeping the flame of Churchill alive.

Italian Gun, by Steve Smith and Laurie Morrow, Wilderness Adventures, Gallatin Gateway, MT, 1997. 325 pp., illus. $49.95
The first book ever written entirely in English for American enthusiasts who own, aspire to own, or simply admire Italian guns.

Ithaca Featherlight Repeater; The Best Gun Going, by Walter C. Snyder, Southern Pines, NC, 1998. 300 pp., illus. $89.95
Describes the complete history of each model of the legendary Ithaca Model 37 and Model 87 Repeaters from their conception in 1930 throught 1997.

Ithaca Gun Company from the Beginning, by Walter C. Snyder, Cook & Uline Publishing Co., Southern Pines, NC, 2nd edition, 1999. 384 pp., illustrated in color and b&w. $90.00
The entire family of Ithaca Gun Company products is described along with new historical information and the serial number/date of manufacturing listing has been improved.

Little Trapshooting Book, by Frank Little, Shotgun Sports Magazine, Auburn, CA, 1994. 168 pp., illus. Paper covers. $19.95
Packed with know-how from one of the greatest trapshooters of all time.

Mental Training for the Shotgun Sports, by Michael J. Keyes, Shotgun Sports, Auburn, CA, 1996. 160 pp., illus. Paper covers. $29.95
The most comprehensive book ever published on what it takes to shoot winning scores at trap, skeet and sporting clays.

More Shotguns and Shooting, by Michael McIntosh, Countrysport Books, Selma, AL, 1998. 256 pp., illus. $30.00
From specifics of shotguns to shooting your way out of a slump, it's McIntosh at his best.

Mossberg Shotguns, by Duncan Long, Delta Press, El Dorado, AR, 2000. 120 pp., illus. $24.95
This book contains a brief history of the company and its founder, full coverage of the pump and semiautomatic shotguns, rare products and a care and maintenance section.

Mysteries of Shotgun Patterns, by George G. Oberfell and Charles E. Thompson, Ray Riling Arms Books, Philadelphia, PA, 2005. 164 pp., illus. Paper covers. $25.00
Shotgun ballistics for the hunter in non-technical language.

Parker Gun, by Larry Baer, Gun Room Press, Highland Park, NJ, 1993. 195 pp., illustrated with b&w and color photos. $35.00
Covers in detail, production of all models on this classic gun. Many fine specimens from great collections are illustrated.

Parker Guns 'The Old Reliable'-A Concise HIsory of the Famous American Shotgun Manufacturing Co., by Ed Muderlak, Long Beach, CA, Safari Press, 2004. results. A must-have for the American shotgun enthusiast. Hardcover. New in new dust jacket. $48.50

Parker Gun Identification & Serialization, by S.P. Fjestad, Minneapolis, MN, Blue Book Publications, 2002. 1st edition. Softcover. $34.95
This new 608-page publication is the only book that provides an easy reference for Parker shotguns manufactured between 1866-1942. Included is a comprehensive 46-page section on Parker identification, with over 100 detailed images depicting serialization location and explanation, various Parker grades, extra features, stock configurations, action types, and barrel identification.

Parker Story: Volumes 1 & 2, by Bill Mullins, "et al." The Double Gun Journal, East Jordan, MI, 2000. 1,025 pp. of text and 1,500 color and monochrome illustrations. Hardbound in a gold-embossed cover. $295.00
The most complete and attractive "last word" on America's preeminent double gun maker. Includes tables showing the number of guns made by gauge, barrel length and special features for each grade.

Pigeon Shooter: The Complete Guide to Modern Pigeon Shooting, by Jon Batley, London, Swan Hill press, 2005. Hardcover. NEW. $29.95
Covering everything from techniques to where and when to shoot. This updated edition contains all the latest information on decoys, hides, and the new pigeon magnets as well as details on the guns and equipment required and invaluable hands-on instruction.

Purdey Gun and Rifle Makers: The Definitive History, by Donald Dallas, Quiller Press, London 2000. 245 pp., illus. Signed and numbered. Limited edition of 3,000 copies. With a PURDEY bookplate. $100.00

Re-Creating the Double Barrel Muzzle Loading Shotgun, by William R. Brockway, York, PA, George Shumway, 2003. Revised 2nd edition. 175 pp., illus. Includes full size drawings. Softcover. $40.00
This popular book, first published in 1985 and out of print for over a decade, has been updated by the author. This book treats the making of double guns of classic style, and is profusely illustrated, showing how to do it all. Many photos of old and contemporary shotguns.

Reloading for Shotgunners, 4th Edition, by Kurt D. Fackler and M.L. McPherson, DBI Books, a division of Krause Publications, Iola, WI, 1997. 320 pp., illus. Paper covers. $19.95

Expanded reloading tables with over 11,000 loads. Bushing charts for every major press and component maker. All new presentation on all aspects of shotshell reloading by two of the top experts in the field.

Remington Double Shotguns, by Charles G. Semer, Denver, CO, 1997. 617 pp., illus. $60.00
This book deals with the entire production and all grades of double shotguns made by Remington during the period of their production 1873-1910.

Shotgun Encyclopedia, The, by John Taylor, Safari Press, Inc., Huntington Beach, CA, 2000. 260 pp., illus. $34.95
A comprehensive reference work on all aspects of shotguns and shotgun shooting.

Shotgun Technicana, by Michael McIntosh and David Trevallion, Camden, ME, Down East Books, 2002. 272 pp., with 100 illustrations. Hardcover $28.00
Everything you wanted to know about fine double shotguns by the nation's foremost experts.

Shotgun–A Shooting Instructor's Handbook, by Michael Yardley, Long Beach, CA, Safari Press, 2002. 272 pp., b&w photos, line drawings. Hardcover. $29.95
This is one of the very few books intended to be read by shooting instructors and other advanced shooters. There is practical advice on gun fit, and on gun and cartridge selection.

Shotgunning: The Art and the Science, by Bob Brister, Winchester Press, Piscataway, NJ, 1976. 321 pp., illus. $18.95
Hundreds of specific tips and truly novel techniques to improve the field and target shooting of every shotgunner.

Shotguns and Shooting, by Michael McIntosh, Countrysport Press, New Albany, OH, 1995. 258 pp., illus. $30.00
The art of guns and gunmaking, this book is a celebration no lover of fine doubles should miss.

Shotguns & Shotgunning, by Layne Simpson, Iola, WI, Krause Publications, 2003. 1st edition. High-quality color photography 224 pp., color illus. Hardcover. $36.95
This is the most comprehensive and valuable guide on the market devoted exclusively to shotguns. Part buyer's guide, part technical manual, and part loving tribute, shooters and hunters of all skill levels will enjoy this comprehensive reference tool.

Spanish Best: The Fine Shotguns of Spain, 2nd Edition, by Terry Wieland, Down East Books, Traverse City, MI, 2001. 364 pp., illus. $60.00
A practical source of information for owners of Spanish shotguns and a guide for those considering buying a used shotgun.

Streetsweepers: The Complete Book of Combat Shotguns, Revised and Updated Edition, by Duncan Long, Boulder Co, Paladin Press, 2004. illus., 224 pp. Soft cover. NEW. $35.00
Including how to choose the right gauge and shot, decipher the terminology and use special-purpose rounds such as flechettes and tear-gas projectiles; and gives expert instruction on customizing shotguns, telling you what you must know about the assault weapon ban before you choose or modify your gun.

Successful Shotgunning; How to Build Skill in the Field and Take More Birds in Competition, by Peter F. Blakeley, Mechanicsburg, PA, Stackpole Books, 2003. 1st edition. 305 pp., illustrated with 119 b&w photos & 4-page color section with 8 photos. Hardcover. $24.95
Successful Shotgunning focuses on wing-shooting and sporting clays techniques.

Tactical Shotgun, The, by Gabriel Suzrez, Paladin Press, Boulder, CO, 1996. 232 pp., illus. Paper covers. $25.00
The best techniques and tactics for employing the shotgun in personal combat.

Trapshooting is a Game of Opposites, by Dick Bennett, Shotgun Sports, Inc., Auburn, CA, 1996. 129 pp., illus. Paper covers. $19.95
Discover everything you need to know about shooting trap like the pros.

U.S. Winchester Trench and Riot Guns and Other U.S. Military Combat Shotguns, by Joe Poyer, North Cape Publications, Tustin, CA, 1992. 124 pp., illus. Paper covers. $15.95
A detailed history of the use of military shotguns, and the acquisition procedures used by the U.S. Army's Ordnance Department in both world wars.

Uncle Dan Lefever, Master Gunmaker: Guns of Lasting Fame, by Robert W. Elliott, privately printed, 2002. Profusely illustrated with b&w photos, with a 45-page color section. 239 pp. Handsomely bound, with gilt titled spine and top cover. Hardcover. $60.00

Winchester Model 12 Assembly, Disassembly Manual, by Skennerton & Riling, Ray Riling Arms Books Co. Philadelphia, PA 2004. 36 pages, over 60 photos & line drawings. $5.00
Ideal workshop reference for stripping & assembly with exploded parts drawings, specifications, service accessories, historical information and recommended reading references. Ideal workbook for shooters and collectors alike. Triple saddle-stitched binding with durable plastic laminated cover makes this an ideal workshop guide.

Winchester Model Twelve, by George Madis, Art and Reference House, Dallas, TX, 1982. 176 pp., illus. $26.95
A definitive work on this famous American shotgun.

Winchester Model 97 Assembly, Disassembly Manual, by Skennerton & Riling, Ray Riling Arms Books Co. Philadelphia, PA 2004. 36 pages, over 60 photos & line drawings. $5.00
Ideal workshop reference for stripping & assembly with exploded parts drawings, specifications, service accessories, historical information and recommended reading references. Ideal workbook for shooters and collectors alike. Triple saddle-stitched binding with durable plastic laminated cover makes this an ideal workshop guide.

World's Fighting Shotguns, by Thomas F. Swearengen, T.B.N. Enterprises, Alexandria, VA, 1998. 500 pp., illus. $59.95
The complete military and police reference work from the shotgun's inception to date, with up-to-date developments.

ARMS ASSOCIATIONS

UNITED STATES

ALABAMA

Alabama Gun Collectors Assn.
Secretary, P.O. Box 70965,
Tuscaloosa, AL 35407

ALASKA

Alaska Gun Collectors Assn., Inc.
C.W. Floyd, Pres., 5240 Little Tree,
Anchorage, AK 99507

ARIZONA

Arizona Arms Assn.
Don DeBusk, President, 4837 Bryce
Ave., Glendale, AZ 85301

CALIFORNIA

California Cartridge Collectors Assn.
Rick Montgomery, 1729 Christina,
Stockton, CA 95204 209-463-7216
eves.

California Waterfowl Assn.
4630 Northgate Blvd., #150,
Sacramento, CA 95834

Greater Calif. Arms & Collectors Assn.
Donald L. Bullock, 8291 Carburton
St., Long Beach, CA 90808-3302

Los Angeles Gun Ctg. Collectors Assn.
F.H. Ruffra, 20810 Amie Ave., Apt.
#9, Torrance, CA 90503

Stock Gun Players Assn.
6038 Appian Way, Long Beach, CA,
90803

COLORADO

Colorado Gun Collectors Assn.
L.E.(Bud) Greenwald, 2553
S. Quitman St., Denver, CO
80219/303-935-3850

Rocky Mountain Cartridge Collectors Assn.
John Roth, P.O. Box 757, Conifer,
CO 80433

CONNECTICUT

Ye Connecticut Gun Guild, Inc.
Dick Fraser, P.O. Box 425, Windsor,
CT 06095

FLORIDA

Unified Sportsmen of Florida
P.O. Box 6565, Tallahassee, FL
32314

GEORGIA

Georgia Arms Collectors Assn., Inc.
Michael Kindberg, President, P.O.
Box 277, Alpharetta, GA 30239-
0277

ILLINOIS

Illinois State Rifle Assn.
P.O. Box 637, Chatsworth, IL 60921

Mississippi Valley Gun & Cartridge Coll. Assn.
Bob Filbert, P.O. Box 61, Port Byron,
IL 61275/309-523-2593

Sauk Trail Gun Collectors
Gordell M. Matson, P.O. Box 1113,
Milan, IL 61264

Wabash Valley Gun Collectors Assn., Inc.
Roger L. Dorsett, 2601 Willow Rd.,
Urbana, IL 61801 217-384-7302

INDIANA

Indiana State Rifle & Pistol Assn.
Thos. Glancy, P.O. Box 552,
Chesterton, IN 46304

Southern Indiana Gun Collectors Assn., Inc.
Sheila McClary, 309 W. Monroe St.,
Boonville, IN 47601/812-897-3742

IOWA

Beaver Creek Plainsmen Inc.
Steve Murphy, Secy., P.O. Box 298,
Bondurant, IA 50035

Central States Gun Collectors Assn.
Dennis Greischar, Box 841, Mason
City, IA 50402-0841

KANSAS

Kansas Cartridge Collectors Assn.
Bob Linder, Box 84, Plainville, KS
67663

KENTUCKY

Kentuckiana Arms Collectors Assn.
Charles Billips, President, Box 1776,
Louisville, KY 40201

Kentucky Gun Collectors Assn., Inc.
Ruth Johnson, Box 64, Owensboro,
KY 42302/502-729-4197

LOUISIANA

Washitaw River Renegades
Sandra Rushing, P.O. Box 256,
Main St., Grayson, LA 71435

MARYLAND

Baltimore Antique Arms Assn.
Mr. Cillo, 1034 Main St., Darlington,
MD 21304

MASSACHUSETTS

Bay Colony Weapons Collectors, Inc.
John Brandt, Box 111, Hingham,
MA 02043

Massachusetts Arms Collectors
Bruce E. Skinner, P.O. Box 31, No.
Carver, MA 02355/508-866-5259

MICHIGAN

Association for the Study and Research of .22 Caliber Rimfire Cartridges
George Kass, 4512 Nakoma Dr.,
Okemos, MI 48864

MINNESOTA

Sioux Empire Cartridge Collectors Assn.
Bob Cameron, 14597 Glendale Ave.
SE, Prior Lake, MN 55372

MISSISSIPPI

Mississippi Gun Collectors Assn.
Jack E. Swinney, P.O. Box 16323,
Hattiesburg, MS 39402

MISSOURI

Greater St. Louis Cartridge Collectors Assn.
Don MacChesney, 634 Scottsdale
Rd., Kirkwood, MO 63122-1109

Mineral Belt Gun Collectors Assn.
D.F. Saunders, 1110 Cleveland
Ave., Monett, MO 65708

Missouri Valley Arms Collectors Assn., Inc.
L.P Brammer II, Membership Secy.,
P.O. Box 33033, Kansas City, MO
64114

MONTANA

Montana Arms Collectors Assn.
Dean E. Yearout, Sr., Exec. Secy.,
1516 21st Ave. S., Great Falls, MT
59405

Weapons Collectors Society of Montana
R.G. Schipf, Ex. Secy., 3100
Bancroft St., Missoula, MT 59801
406-728-2995

NEBRASKA

Nebraska Cartridge Collectors Club
Gary Muckel, P.O. Box 84442,
Lincoln, NE 68501

NEW HAMPSHIRE

New Hampshire Arms Collectors, Inc.
James Stamatelos, Secy., P.O. Box
5, Cambridge, MA 02139

NEW JERSEY

Englishtown Benchrest Shooters Assn.
Michael Toth, 64 Cooke Ave.,
Carteret, NJ 07008

Jersey Shore Antique Arms Collectors
Joe Sisia, P.O. Box 100, Bayville, NJ
08721-0100

New Jersey Arms Collectors Club, Inc.
Angus Laidlaw, Vice President, 230
Valley Rd., Montclair, NJ 07042/201-
746-0939; e-mail: acclaidlaw@juno.
com

NEW YORK

Iroquois Arms Collectors Assn.
Bonnie Robinson, Show Secy.,
P.O. Box 142, Ransomville, NY
14131/716-791-4096

Mid-State Arms Coll. & Shooters Club
Jack Ackerman, 24 S. Mountain
Terr., Binghamton, NY 13903

NORTH CAROLINA

North Carolina Gun Collectors Assn.
Jerry Ledford, 3231-7th St. Dr. NE,
Hickory, NC 28601

OHIO

Ohio Gun Collectors Assn.
P.O. Box 9007, Maumee, OH
43537-9007/419-897-0861; Fax:
419-897-0860

Shotshell Historical and Collectors Society
Madeline Bruemmer, 3886 Dawley
Rd., Ravenna, OH 44266

The Stark Gun Collectors, Inc.
William I. Gann, 5666 Waynesburg
Dr., Waynesburg, OH 44688

OREGON

Oregon Arms Collectors Assn., Inc.
Phil Bailey, P.O. Box 13000-A,
Portland, OR 97213-0017 503-281-
6864; off.: 503-281-0918

Oregon Cartridge Collectors Assn.
Boyd Northrup, P.O. Box 285,
Rhododendron, OR 97049

PENNSYLVANIA

Presque Isle Gun Collectors Assn.
James Welch, 156 E. 37 St., Erie,
PA 16504

SOUTH CAROLINA

Belton Gun Club, Inc.
Attn. Secretary, P.O. Box 126,
Belton, SC 29627/864-369-6767

Gun Owners of South Carolina
Membership Div.: William Strozier,
Secretary, P.O. Box 70, Johns
Island, SC 29457-0070/803-762-
3240; Fax: 803-795-0711; e-mail:
76053.222@compuserve. com

SOUTH DAKOTA

Dakota Territory Gun Coll. Assn., Inc.
Curt Carter, Castlewood, SD 57223

TENNESSEE

Smoky Mountain Gun Coll. Assn., Inc.
Hugh W. Yabro, President, P.O. Box
23225, Knoxville, TN 37933

Tennessee Gun Collectors Assn., Inc.
M.H. Parks, 3556 Pleasant Valley
Rd., Nashville, TN 37204-3419

TEXAS

Houston Gun Collectors Assn., Inc.
P.O. Box 741429, Houston, TX
77274-1429

Texas Gun Collectors Assn.
Bob Eder, Pres., P.O. Box 12067, El
Paso, TX 79913/915-584-8183

Texas State Rifle Assn.
1131 Rockingham Dr., Suite 101,
Richardson, TX 75080-4326

VIRGINIA

Virginia Gun Collectors Assn., Inc.
Addison Hurst, Secy., 38802
Charlestown Height, Waterford, VA
20197/540-882-3543

ARMS ASSOCIATIONS

WASHINGTON

Association of Cartridge Collectors on the Pacific Northwest
Robert Jardin, 14214 Meadowlark Drive KPN, Gig Harbor, WA 98329

Washington Arms Collectors, Inc.
Joyce Boss, P.O. Box 389, Renton, WA, 98057-0389/206-255-8410

WISCONSIN

Great Lakes Arms Collectors Assn., Inc.
Edward C. Warnke, 2913 Woodridge Lane, Waukesha, WI 53188

Wisconsin Gun Collectors Assn., Inc.
Lulita Zellmer, P.O. Box 181, Sussex, WI 53089

WYOMING

Wyoming Weapons Collectors
P.O. Box 284, Laramie, WY 82073/307-745-4652 or 745-9530

NATIONAL ORGANIZATIONS

Amateur Trapshooting Assn.
David D. Bopp, Exec. Director, 601 W. National Rd., Vandalia, OH 45377/937-898-4638; Fax: 937-898-5472

American Airgun Field Target Assn.
5911 Cherokee Ave., Tampa, FL 33604

American Coon Hunters Assn.
Opal Johnston, P.O. Cadet, Route 1, Box 492, Old Mines, MO 63630

American Custom Gunmakers Guild
Jan Billeb, Exec. Director, 22 Vista View Drive, Cody, WY 82414-9606 (307) 587-4297 (phone/fax) Email: acgg@acgg.org Web: www.acgg.org

American Defense Preparedness Assn.
Two Colonial Place, 2101 Wilson Blvd., Suite 400, Arlington, VA 22201-3061

American Paintball League
P.O. Box 3561, Johnson City, TN 37602/800-541-9169

American Pistolsmiths Guild
Alex B. Hamilton, Pres., 1449 Blue Crest Lane, San Antonio, TX 78232/210-494-3063

American Police Pistol & Rifle Assn.
3801 Biscayne Blvd., Miami, FL 33137

American Single Shot Rifle Assn.
Gary Staup, Secy., 709 Carolyn Dr., Delphos, OH 45833 419-692-3866. Web: www.assra.com

American Society of Arms Collectors
George E. Weatherly, P.O. Box 2567, Waxahachie, TX 75165

American Tactical Shooting Assn. (A.T.S.A.)
c/o Skip Gochenour, 2600 N. Third St., Harrisburg, PA 17110 717-233-0402; Fax: 717-233-5340

Association of Firearm and Tool Mark Examiners
Lannie G. Emanuel, Secy., Southwest Institute of Forensic Sciences, P.O. Box 35728, Dallas, TX 75235/214-920-5979; Fax: 214-920-5928; Membership Secy., Ann D. Jones, VA Div. of Forensic Science, P.O. Box 999, Richmond, VA 23208 804-786-4706; Fax: 804-371-8328

Boone & Crockett Club
250 Station Dr., Missoula, MT 59801-2753

Browning Collectors Assn.
Secretary: Scherrie L. Brennac, 2749 Keith Dr., Villa Ridge, MO 63089/314-742-0571

The Cast Bullet Assn., Inc.
Ralland J. Fortier, Editor, 4103 Foxcraft Dr., Traverse City, MI 49684

Citizens Committee for the Right to Keep and Bear Arms
Natl. Hq., Liberty Park, 12500 NE Tenth Pl., Bellevue, WA 98005

Colt Collectors Assn.
25000 Highland Way, Los Gatos, CA 95030/408-353-2658

Contemporary Longrifle Association
P.O. Box 2097, Staunton, VA 24402/540-886-6189 Web: www.CLA@longrifle.ws

Ducks Unlimited, Inc.
Natl. Headquarters, One Waterfowl Way, Memphis, TN 38120 901-758-3937

Fifty Caliber Shooters Assn.
PO Box 111, Monroe UT 84754-0111

Firearms Coalition/Neal Knox Associates
Box 6537, Silver Spring, MD 20906 301-871-3006

Firearms Engravers Guild of America
Rex C. Pedersen, Secy., 511 N. Rath Ave., Lundington, MI 49431 616-845-7695 (Phone/Fax)

Foundation for North American Wild Sheep
720 Allen Ave., Cody, WY 82414-3402; web site: iigi.com/os/non/fnaws/fnaws.htm; e-mail: fnaws@wyoming.com

Freedom Arms Collectors Assn.
P.O. Box 160302, Miami, FL 33116-0302

Garand Collectors Assn.
P.O. Box 181, Richmond, KY 40475

Glock Collectors Association
P.O. Box 1063, Maryland Heights, MO 63043 314-878-2061 Phone/Fax

Glock Shooting Sports Foundation
BO Box 309, Smyrna GA 30081 770-432-1202; Web: www.gssfonline.com

Golden Eagle Collectors Assn. (G.E.C.A.)
Chris Showler, 11144 Slate Creek Rd., Grass Valley, CA 95945

Gun Owners of America
8001 Forbes Place, Suite 102, Springfield, VA 22151/703-321-8585

Handgun Hunters International
J.D. Jones, Director, P.O. Box 357 MAG, Bloomingdale, OH 43910

Harrington & Richardson Gun Coll. Assn.
George L. Cardet, 330 S.W. 27th Ave., Suite 603, Miami, FL 33135

High Standard Collectors' Assn.
John J. Stimson, Jr., Pres., 540 W. 92nd St., Indianapolis, IN 46260 Web: www.highstandard.org

Hopkins & Allen Arms & Memorabilia Society (HAAMS)
P.O. Box 187, 1309 Pamela Circle, Delphos, OH 45833

International Ammunition Association, Inc.
C.R. Punnett, Secy., 8 Hillock Lane, Chadds Ford, PA 19317 610-358-1285; Fax: 610-358-1560

International Benchrest Shooters
Joan Borden, RR1, Box 250BB, Springville, PA 18844 717-965-2366

International Blackpowder Hunting Assn.
P.O. Box 1180, Glenrock, WY 82637/307-436-9817

IHMSA (Intl. Handgun Metallic Silhouette Assn.)
PO Box 368, Burlington, IA 52601 Web: www.ihmsa.org

International Society of Mauser Arms Collectors
Michael Kindberg, Pres., P.O. Box 277, Alpharetta, GA 30239-0277

Jews for the Preservation of Firearms Ownership (JPFO) 501(c)(3)
2872 S. Wentworth Ave., Milwaukee, WI 53207 414-769-0760; Fax: 414-483-8435

The Mannlicher Collectors Assn.
Membership Office: P.O. Box 1249, The Dalles, Oregon 97058

Marlin Firearms Collectors Assn., Ltd.
Dick Paterson, Secy., 407 Lincoln Bldg., 44 Main St., Champaign, IL 61820

Merwin Hulbert Association,
2503 Kentwood Ct., High Point, NC 27265

Miniature Arms Collectors/Makers Society, Ltd.
Ralph Koebbeman, Pres., 4910 Kilburn Ave., Rockford, IL 61101 815-964-2569

M1 Carbine Collectors Assn. (M1-CCA)
623 Apaloosa Ln., Gardnerville, NV 89410-7840

National Association of Buckskinners (NAB)
Territorial Dispatch—1800s Historical Publication, 4701 Marion St., Suite 324, Livestock Exchange Bldg., Denver, CO 80216 303-297-9671

The National Association of Derringer Collectors
P.O. Box 20572, San Jose, CA 95160

National Assn. of Federally Licensed Firearms Dealers
Andrew Molchan, 2455 E. Sunrise, Ft. Lauderdale, FL 33304

National Association to Keep and Bear Arms
P.O. Box 78336, Seattle, WA 98178

National Automatic Pistol Collectors Assn.
Tom Knox, P.O. Box 15738, Tower Grove Station, St. Louis, MO 63163

National Bench Rest Shooters Assn., Inc.
Pat Ferrell, 2835 Guilford Lane, Oklahoma City, OK 73120-4404 405-842-9585; Fax: 405-842-9575

National Muzzle Loading Rifle Assn.
Box 67, Friendship, IN 47021 812-667-5131 Web: www.nmlra@nmlra.org

National Professional Paintball League (NPPL)
540 Main St., Mount Kisco, NY 10549/914-241-7400

National Reloading Manufacturers Assn.
One Centerpointe Dr., Suite 300, Lake Oswego, OR 97035

National Rifle Assn. of America
11250 Waples Mill Rd., Fairfax, VA 22030/703-267-1000 Web: www.nra.org

National Shooting Sports Foundation, Inc.
Doug Painter, President, Flintlock Ridge Office Center, 11 Mile Hill Rd., Newtown, CT 06470-2359 203-426-1320; Fax: 203-426-1087

National Skeet Shooting Assn.
Dan Snyuder, Director, 5931 Roft Road, San Antonio, TX 78253-9261/800-877-5338 Web: nssa-nsca.com

National Sporting Clays Assn.
Ann Myers, Director, 5931 Roft Road, San Antonio, TX 78253-9261/800-877-5338 Web: nssa-nsca.com

National Wild Turkey Federation, Inc.
P.O. Box 530, 770 Augusta Rd., Edgefield, SC 29824

North American Hunting Club
P.O. Box 3401, Minnetonka, MN 55343/612-936-9333; Fax: 612-936-9755

ARMS ASSOCIATIONS

North American Paintball Referees Association (NAPRA)
584 Cestaric Dr., Milpitas, CA 95035

North-South Skirmish Assn., Inc.
Stevan F. Meserve, Exec. Secretary, 507 N. Brighton Court, Sterling, VA 20164-3919

Old West Shooter's Association
712 James Street, Hazel TX 76020
817-444-2049

Remington Society of America
Gordon Fosburg, Secretary, 11900 North Brinton Road, Lake, MI 48623

Rocky Mountain Elk Foundation
P.O. Box 8249, Missoula, MT 59807-8249/406-523-4500; Fax: 406-523-4581; Web: www.rmef.org

Ruger Collector's Assn., Inc.
P.O. Box 240, Greens Farms, CT 06436

Safari Club International
4800 W. Gates Pass Rd., Tucson, AZ 85745/520-620-1220

Sako Collectors Assn., Inc.
Jim Lutes, 202 N. Locust, Whitewater, KS 67154

Second Amendment Foundation
James Madison Building, 12500 NE 10th Pl., Bellevue, WA 98005

Single Action Shooting Society (SASS)
23255-A La Palma Avenue, Yorba Linda, CA 92887/714-694-1800; Fax: 714-694-1815 email: sasseot@aol.com Web: www.sassnet.com

Smith & Wesson Collectors Assn.
Cally Pletl, Admin. Asst.,PO Box 444, Afton, NY 13730

The Society of American Bayonet Collectors
P.O. Box 234, East Islip, NY 11730-0234

Southern California Schuetzen Society
Dean Lillard, 34657 Ave. E., Yucaipa, CA 92399

Sporting Arms and Ammunition Manufacturers' Institute (SAAMI)
Flintlock Ridge Office Center, 11 Mile Hill Rd., Newtown, CT 06470-2359/203-426-4358; Fax: 203-426-1087

Sporting Clays of America (SCA)
Ron L. Blosser, Pres., 9257 Buckeye Rd., Sugar Grove, OH 43155-9632/614-746-8334; Fax: 614-746-8605

Steel Challenge
23234 Via Barra, Valencia CA 91355
Web: www.steelchallenge.com

The Thompson/Center Assn.
Joe Wright, President, Box 792, Northboro, MA 01532/508-845-6960

U.S. Practical Shooting Association/IPSC
Dave Thomas, P.O. Box 811, Sedro Woolley, WA 98284/360-855-2245
Web: www.uspsa.org

U.S. Revolver Assn.
Brian J. Barer, 40 Larchmont Ave., Taunton, MA 02780/508-824-4836

U.S.A. Shooting
U.S. Olympic Shooting Center, One Olympic Plaza, Colorado Springs, CO 80909/719-578-4670; Web: wwwusashooting.org

The Varmint Hunters Assn., Inc.
Box 759, Pierre, SD 57501 Member Services 800-528-4868

Weatherby Collectors Assn., Inc.
P.O. Box 478, Pacific, MO 63069
Web: www.weatherbycollectors.com
Email: WCAsecretary@aol.com

The Wildcatters
P.O. Box 170, Greenville, WI 54942

Winchester Arms Collectors Assn.
P.O. Box 230, Brownsboro, TX 75756/903-852-4027

The Women's Shooting Sports Foundation (WSSF)
4620 Edison Avenue, Ste. C, Colorado Springs, CO 80915 719-638-1299; Fax: 719-638-1271 email: wssf@worldnet.att.net

ARGENTINA

Asociacion Argentina de Coleccionistas de Armes y Municiones
Castilla de Correos No. 28, Succursal I B, 1401 Buenos Aires, Republica Argentina

AUSTRALIA

Antique & Historical Arms Collectors of Australia
P.O. Box 5654, GCMC Queensland 9726, Australia

The Arms Collector's Guild of Queensland, Inc.
Ian Skennerton, P.O. Box 433, Ashmore City 4214, Queensland, Australia

Australian Cartridge Collectors Assn., Inc.
Bob Bennett, 126 Landscape Dr., E. Doncaster 3109, Victoria, Australia

Sporting Shooters Assn. of Australia, Inc.
P.O. Box 2066, Kent Town, SA 5071, Australia

BRAZIL

Associaçao de Armaria Coleçao e Tiro (ACOLTI)
Rua do Senado, 258 - 2 andar, Centro, Rio de Janeiro - RJ - 20231-002 Brazil / tel: 0055-21-31817989

CANADA

ALBERTA

Canadian Historical Arms Society
P.O. Box 901, Edmonton, Alb., Canada T5J 2L8

National Firearms Assn.
Natl. Hq: P.O. Box 1779, Edmonton, Alb., Canada T5J 2P1

BRITISH COLUMBIA

The Historical Arms Collectors of B.C. (Canada)
Harry Moon, Pres., P.O. Box 50117, South Slope RPO, Burnaby, BC V5J 5G3, Canada 604-438-0950; Fax: 604-277-3646

ONTARIO

Association of Canadian Cartridge Collectors
Monica Wright, RR 1, Millgrove, ON, LOR IVO, Canada

Tri-County Antique Arms Fair
P.O. Box 122, RR #1, North Lancaster, Ont., Canada K0C 1Z0

EUROPE

BELGIUM

European Cartridge Research Association
Graham Irving, 21 Rue Schaltin, 4900 Spa, Belgium 32.87.77.43.40; Fax: 32.87.77.27.51

CZECHOSLOVAKIA

Spolecnost Pro Studium Naboju (Czech Cartridge Research Association)
JUDr. Jaroslav Bubak, Pod Homolko 1439, 26601 Beroun 2, Czech Republic

DENMARK

Aquila Dansk Jagtpatron Historic Forening (Danish Historical Cartridge Collectors Club)
Steen Elgaard Møller, Ulriksdalsvej 7, 4840 Nr. Alslev, Denmark 10045-53846218; Fax: 00455384 6209

ENGLAND

Arms and Armour Society
Hon. Secretary A. Dove, P.O. Box 10232, London, 5W19 2ZD, England

Dutch Paintball Federation
Aceville Publ., Castle House 97 High Street, Colchester, Essex C01 1TH, England/011-44-206-564840

European Paintball Sports Foundation
c/o Aceville Publ., Castle House 97 High St., Colchester, Essex, C01 1TH, England

Historical Breechloading Smallarms Assn.
D.J. Penn M.A., Secy., P.O. Box 12778, London SE1 6BX, England

National Rifle Assn.
(Great Britain) Bisley Camp, Brookwood, Woking Surrey GU24 OPB, England/01483.797777; Fax: 014730686275

United Kingdom Cartridge Club
Ian Southgate, 20 Millfield, Elmley Castle, Nr. Pershore, Worcestershire, WR10 3HR, England

FRANCE

STAC-Western Co.
3 Ave. Paul Doumer (N.311); 78360 Montesson, France 01.30.53-43-65; Fax: 01.30.53.19.10

GERMANY

Bund Deutscher Sportschützen e.v. (BDS)
Borsigallee 10, 53125 Bonn 1, Germany

Deutscher Schützenbund
Lahnstrasse 120, 65195 Wiesbaden, Germany

NORWAY

Scandinavian Ammunition Research Association
c/o Morten Stoen, Annerudstubben 3, N-1383 Asker, Norway

NEW ZEALAND

New Zealand Cartridge Collectors Club
Terry Castle, 70 Tiraumea Dr., Pakuranga, Auckland, New Zealand

New Zealand Deerstalkers Association
P.O. Box 6514 TE ARO, Wellington, New Zealand

SOUTH AFRICA

Historical Firearms Soc. of South Africa
P.O. Box 145, 7725 Newlands, Republic of South Africa

Republic of South Africa Cartridge Collectors Assn.
Arno Klee, 20 Eugene St., Malanshof Randburg, Gauteng 2194, Republic of South Africa

S.A.A.C.A. (Southern Africa Arms and Ammunition Assn.)
Gauteng office: P.O. Box 7597, Weltevreden Park, 1715, Republic of South Africa/ 011-679-1151; Fax: 011-679-1131; e-mail: saaaca@iafrica.com
Kwa-Zulu Natal office: P.O. Box 4065, Northway, Kwazulu-Natal 4065, Republic of South Africa

SAGA (S.A. Gunowners' Assn.)
P.O. Box 35203, Northway, Kwazulu-Natal 4065, Republic of South Africa

SPAIN

Asociacion Espanola de Collectionistas de Cartuchos (A.E.C.C.)
Secretary: Apdo. Correos No. 1086, 2880-Alcala de Henares (Madrid), Spain. President: Apdo. Correos No. 682, 50080 Zaragoza, Spain

2008
GUN DIGEST
DIRECTORY OF THE
ARMS TRADE

The **Product Directory** contains 84 product categories. The **Manufacturer's Directory** alphabetically lists the manufacturer's work with their addresses, phone numbers, FAX numbers and internet addresses, if available.

DIRECTORY OF THE ARMS TRADE INDEX

PRODUCT & SERVICE DIRECTORY

AMMUNITION COMPONENTS, SHOTSHELL

A.W. Peterson Gun Shop, Inc., The
Ballistic Products, Inc.
Blount, Inc., Sporting Equipment Div.
CCI/Speer Div of ATK
Cheddite, France S.A.
Dina Arms Corp.
Gentner Bullets
Guncrafter Industries
Magtech Ammunition Co. Inc.
National Gun, Inc.
Peterson Gun Shop, Inc., A.W.
Precision Reloading, Inc.
Ravell Ltd.
Tar-Hunt Custom Rifles, Inc.
Vitt/Boos

AMMUNITION COMPONENTS- BULLETS, POWDER, PRIMERS, CASES

A.W. Peterson Gun Shop, Inc., The
Acadian Ballistic Specialties
Accuracy Unlimited
Accurate Arms Co., Inc.
Action Bullets & Alloy Inc.
ADCO Sales, Inc.
Alaska Bullet Works, Inc.
Alex, Inc.
Alliant Techsystems, Smokeless Powder Group
Allred Bullet Co.
Alpha LaFranck Enterprises
American Products, Inc.
Armfield Custom Bullets
A-Square Co.
Austin Sheridan USA, Inc.
Baer's Hollows
Ballard Rifle & Cartridge Co., LLC
Barnes Bullets, Inc.
BC-Handmade Bullets
Beartooth Bullets
Bell Reloading, Inc.
Berger Bullets Ltd.
Berry's Mfg., Inc.
Big Bore Bullets of Alaska
Big Bore Express
Bitterroot Bullet Co.
Black Belt Bullets (See Big Bore Express)
Black Hills Shooters Supply
Black Powder Products
Blount, Inc., Sporting Equipment Div.
Blue Mountain Bullets
Brenneke GmbH
Briese Bullet Co., Inc.
BRP, Inc. High Performance Cast Bullets
Buck Stix-SOS Products Co.
Buckeye Custom Bullets
Buckskin Bullet Co.
Buffalo Arms Co.
Buffalo Bullet Co., Inc.
Buffalo Rock Shooters Supply
Bull-X, Inc.
Butler Enterprises
C. Sharps Arms Co. Inc./ Montana Armory
Cain's Outdoors, Inc.
Canyon Cartridge Corp.
Cast Performance Bullet Co.

Casull Arms Corp.
CCI/Speer Div of ATK
Champion's Choice, Inc.
Cheddite, France S.A.
CheVron Bullets
Chuck's Gun Shop
Clean Shot Technologies
Competitor Corp., Inc.
Cook Engineering Service
Cummings Bullets
Curtis Cast Bullets
Curtis Gun Shop (See Curtis Cast Bullets)
Custom Bullets by Hoffman
D.L. Unmussig Bullets
Dakota Arms, Inc.
Davide Pedersoli and Co.
Dina Arms Corp.
DKT, Inc.
Dohring Bullets
Eichelberger Bullets, Wm.
Federal Cartridge Co.
Fiocchi of America, Inc.
Firearm Brokers
Forkin Custom Classics
Fowler, Bob (See Black Powder Products)
Freedom Arms, Inc.
Gehmann, Walter (See Huntington Die Specialties)
GOEX, Inc.
Golden Bear Bullets
Gotz Bullets
Grayback Wildcats
Gun City
Gun Works, The
Harris Enterprises
Harrison Bullets
Hart & Son, Inc.
Hawk Laboratories, Inc. (See Hawk, Inc.)
Hawk, Inc.
Heidenstrom Bullets
Hercules, Inc. (See Alliant Techsystems Smokeless Powder Group)
Hi-Performance Ammunition Co.
Hirtenberger AG
Hobson Precision Mfg. Co.
Hodgdon Powder Co.
Hornady Mfg. Co.
HT Bullets
Hunters Supply, Inc.
Huntington Die Specialties
Impact Case & Container, Inc.
Imperial Magnum Corp.
IMR Powder Co.
Intercontinental Distributors, Ltd.
J R Guns
J&D Components
J&L Superior Bullets (See Huntington Die Specialties)
J.R. Williams Bullet Co.
James Calhoon Mfg.
Jamison International
Jensen Bullets
Jensen's Firearms Academy
Jericho Tool & Die Co., Inc.
Jester Bullets
JLK Bullets
JRP Custom Bullets
Kaswer Custom, Inc.
Keith's Bullets
Ken's Kustom Kartridges
Knight Rifles
Knight Rifles (See Modern Muzzleloading, Inc.)
Lawrence Brand Shot (See Precision Reloading, Inc.)

Liberty Shooting Supplies
Lightning Performance Innovations, Inc.
Lindsley Arms Cartridge Co.
Littleton, J. F.
Lomont Precision Bullets
Lyman Products Corp.
Magnus Bullets
MagSafe Ammo, Inc.
Magtech Ammunition Co. Inc.
Markesbery Muzzle Loaders, Inc.
McMurdo, Lynn
Meister Bullets (See Gander Mountain)
Men-Metallwerk Elisenhuette GmbH
Midway Arms, Inc.
MI-TE Bullets
Montana Precision Swaging
Mulhern, Rick
Murmur Corp.
Nagel's Custom Bullets
Nammo Lapua Oy
National Bullet Co.
National Gun, Inc.
Naval Ordnance Works
North American Shooting Systems
North Devon Firearms Services
Northern Precision
Northwest Custom Projectile
Nosler, Inc.
OK Weber, Inc.
Oklahoma Ammunition Co.
Old Wagon Bullets
Old Western Scrounger LLC
Ordnance Works, The
Oregon Trail Bullet Co.
Pacific Rifle Co.
Page Custom Bullets
Penn Bullets
Peterson Gun Shop, Inc., A.W.
Petro-Explo Inc.
Phillippi Custom Bullets, Justin
Pinetree Bullets
PMC/Eldorado Cartridge Corp.
Polywad, Inc.
Pony Express Reloaders
Power Plus Enterprises, Inc.
Precision Delta Corp.
Price Bullets, Patrick W.
PRL Bullets, c/o Blackburn Enterprises
Professional Hunter Supplies
Proofmark Corp.
PWM Sales Ltd.
Quality Cartridge
Quarton Beamshot
Rainier Ballistics
Ravell Ltd.
Redwood Bullet Works
Reloading Specialties, Inc.
Remington Arms Co., Inc.
Rhino
Robinson H.V. Bullets
Rubright Bullets
Russ Haydon's Shooters' Supply
SAECO (See Redding Reloading Equipment)
Scharch Mfg., Inc.-Top Brass
Schneider Bullets
Schroeder Bullets
Schumakers Gun Shop
Seebeck Assoc., R.E.
Shappy Bullets
Sharps Arms Co., Inc., C.
Shilen, Inc.
Sierra Bullets
SOS Products Co. (See Buck Stix-SOS Products Co.)

Southern Ammunition Co., Inc.
Specialty Gunsmithing
Speer Bullets
Spencer's Rifle Barrels, Inc.
SSK Industries
Star Ammunition, Inc.
Star Custom Bullets
Starke Bullet Co.
Starline, Inc.
Stewart's Gunsmithing
Swift Bullet Co.
T.F.C. S.p.A.
Taracorp Industries, Inc.
Tar-Hunt Custom Rifles, Inc.
TCCI
TCSR
Thompson Bullet Lube Co.
Thompson Precision
Traditions Performance Firearms
True Flight Bullet Co.
Tucson Mold, Inc.
USAC
Vann Custom Bullets
Vihtavuori Oy/Kaltron-Pettibone
Vincent's Shop
Viper Bullet and Brass Works
Walters Wads
Watson Bullets
Western Nevada West Coast Bullets
Widener's Reloading & Shooting Supply, Inc.
Wildey F. A., Inc.
Winchester Div. Olin Corp.
Woodleigh (See Huntington Die Specialties)
Wyant Bullets
Wyoming Custom Bullets
Zero Ammunition Co., Inc.

AMMUNITION, COMMERCIAL

3-Ten Corp.
A.W. Peterson Gun Shop, Inc., The
Ad Hominem
Air Arms
American Ammunition
Arms Corp. of the Philippines
A-Square Co.
Austin Sheridan USA, Inc.
Ballistic Products, Inc.
Benjamin/Sheridan Co., Crosman
Black Hills Ammunition, Inc.
Blount, Inc., Sporting Equipment Div.
Brenneke GmbH
Buchsenmachermeister
Buffalo Arms Co.
Buffalo Bullet Co., Inc.
Bull-X, Inc.
Cabela's
Casull Arms Corp.
CBC
CCI/Speer Div of ATK
Champion's Choice, Inc.
Cleland's Outdoor World, Inc.
Cor-Bon Inc./Glaser LLC
Crosman Airguns
Cubic Shot Shell Co., Inc.
Dan Wesson Firearms
Dead Eye's Sport Center
Delta Arms Ltd.
Dynamit Nobel-RWS, Inc.
Effebi SNC-Dr. Franco Beretta
Eley Ltd.
Ellett Bros.

Estate Cartridge, Inc.
Federal Cartridge Co.
Fiocchi of America, Inc.
Firearm Brokers
Garrett Cartridges, Inc.
Garthwaite Pistolsmith, Inc., Jim
Gibbs Rifle Co., Inc.
Gil Hebard Guns, Inc.
Glaser LLC
Glaser Safety Slug, Inc. (see CorBon/Glaser
GOEX, Inc.
Goodwin's Guns
Grayback Wildcats
Gun City
Gun Room Press, The
Gun Works, The
Guncrafter Industries
Hansen & Co.
Hart & Son, Inc.
Hastings
Hi-Performance Ammunition Co.
Hirtenberger AG
Hofer Jagdwaffen, P.
Hornady Mfg. Co.
Hunters Supply, Inc.
Intercontinental Distributors, Ltd.
Ion Industries, Inc.
Keng's Firearms Specialty, Inc.
Kent Cartridge America, Inc.
Knight Rifles
Lethal Force Institute (See Police Bookshelf)
Lock's Philadelphia Gun Exchange
Lomont Precision Bullets
Magnum Research, Inc.
MagSafe Ammo, Inc.
Magtech Ammunition Co. Inc.
Markell, Inc.
Men-Metallwerk Elisenhuette GmbH
Mullins Ammunition
Nammo Lapua Oy
National Gun, Inc.
New England Ammunition Co.
Oklahoma Ammunition Co.
Old Western Scrounger LLC
Outdoor Sports Headquarters, Inc.
P.S.M.G. Gun Co.
Paragon Sales & Services, Inc.
Parker & Sons Shooting Supply
Peterson Gun Shop, Inc., A.W.
PMC/Eldorado Cartridge Corp.
Police Bookshelf
Polywad, Inc.
Pony Express Reloaders
Precision Delta Corp.
Quality Cartridge
R.E.I.
Ravell Ltd.
Remington Arms Co., Inc.
Rucker Dist. Inc.
RWS (See U.S. Importer-Dynamit Nobel-RWS, Inc.)
Sellier & Bellot, USA, Inc.
Southern Ammunition Co., Inc.
Speer Bullets
Starr Trading Co., Jedediah
TCCI
Thompson Bullet Lube Co.
USAC
VAM Distribution Co. LLC
Vihtavuori Oy/Kaltron-Pettibone
Voere-KGH GmbH

PRODUCT & SERVICE DIRECTORY

Weatherby, Inc.
Westley Richards & Co. Ltd.
Whitestone Lumber Corp.
Widener's Reloading & Shooting Supply, Inc.
Wildey F. A., Inc.
William E. Phillips Firearms
Winchester Div. Olin Corp.
Zero Ammunition Co., Inc.

AMMUNITION, CUSTOM

3-Ten Corp.
A.W. Peterson Gun Shop, Inc., The
Accuracy Unlimited
AFSCO Ammunition
Allred Bullet Co.
American Derringer Corp.
American Products, Inc.
Arms Corp. of the Philippines
Ballard Rifle & Cartridge Co., LLC
Bear Arms
Berger Bullets Ltd.
Big Bore Bullets of Alaska
Black Hills Ammunition, Inc.
Blue Mountain Bullets
Brynin, Milton
Buckskin Bullet Co.
Buffalo Arms Co.
CBC
CFVentures
Champlin Firearms, Inc.
Country Armourer, The
Cubic Shot Shell Co., Inc.
Custom Tackle and Ammo
D.L. Unmussig Bullets
Dakota Arms, Inc.
Dead Eye's Sport Center
DKT, Inc.
Estate Cartridge, Inc.
GDL Enterprises
Gentner Bullets
GOEX, Inc.
Grayback Wildcats
Hawk, Inc.
Hirtenberger AG
Hobson Precision Mfg. Co.
Horizons Unlimited
Hornady Mfg. Co.
Hunters Supply, Inc.
J R Guns
Jensen Bullets
Jensen's Arizona Sportsman
Jensen's Firearms Academy
Kaswer Custom, Inc.
L. E. Jurras & Assoc.
L.A.R. Mfg., Inc.
Lethal Force Institute (See Police Bookshelf)
Lindsley Arms Cartridge Co.
Linebaugh Custom Sixguns
MagSafe Ammo, Inc.
Magtech Ammunition Co. Inc.
McMurdo, Lynn
Men-Metallwerk Elisenhuette GmbH
Mullins Ammunition
Oklahoma Ammunition Co.
P.S.M.G. Gun Co.
Peterson Gun Shop, Inc., A.W.
Phillippi Custom Bullets, Justin
Power Plus Enterprises, Inc.
Precision Delta Corp.
Professional Hunter Supplies
Quality Cartridge
R.E.I.
Sandia Die & Cartridge Co.
SOS Products Co. (See Buck Stix-SOS Products Co.)

Specialty Gunsmithing
Spencer's Rifle Barrels, Inc.
SSK Industries
Star Custom Bullets
Stewart's Gunsmithing
TCCI
Vitt/Boos
Vulpes Ventures, Inc., Fox Cartridge Division
Watson Bullets
Zero Ammunition Co., Inc.

AMMUNITION, FOREIGN

A.W. Peterson Gun Shop, Inc., The
Ad Hominem
AFSCO Ammunition
Air Arms
Armscorp USA, Inc.
B&P America
Cape Outfitters
CBC
Cheddite, France S.A.
Cubic Shot Shell Co., Inc.
Dead Eye's Sport Center
DKT, Inc.
Dynamit Nobel-RWS, Inc.
E. Arthur Brown Co. Inc.
Fiocchi of America, Inc.
Gamebore Division, Polywad, Inc.
Gibbs Rifle Co., Inc.
GOEX, Inc.
Gunsmithing, Inc.
Hansen & Co.
Heidenstrom Bullets
Hirtenberger AG
Hornady Mfg. Co.
International Shooters Service
Intrac Arms International
J R Guns
Jack First, Inc.
K.B.I. Inc.
MagSafe Ammo, Inc.
Magtech Ammunition Co. Inc.
Marksman Products
Mullins Ammunition
Navy Arms Co.
Oklahoma Ammunition Co.
P.S.M.G. Gun Co.
Paragon Sales & Services, Inc.
Paul Co., The
Peterson Gun Shop, Inc., A.W.
Petro-Explo Inc.
Precision Delta Corp.
R.E.T. Enterprises
RWS (See U.S. Importer-Dynamit Nobel-RWS, Inc.)
Samco Global Arms, Inc.
Southern Ammunition Co., Inc.
Speer Bullets
Stratco, Inc.
T.F.C. S.p.A.
Vector Arms, Inc.
Victory Ammunition
Vihtavuori Oy/Kaltron-Pettibone
Wolf Performance Ammunition

ANTIQUE ARMS DEALER

Ackerman & Co.
Ad Hominem
Antique American Firearms
Antique Arms Co.
Aplan Antiques & Art
Ballard Rifle & Cartridge Co., LLC

Bear Mountain Gun & Tool
Bob's Tactical Indoor Shooting Range & Gun Shop
Buffalo Arms Co.
C. Sharps Arms Co. Inc./ Montana Armory
Cape Outfitters
CBC-BRAZIL
Chadick's Ltd.
Chambers Flintlocks Ltd., Jim
Champlin Firearms, Inc.
Chuck's Gun Shop
Clements' Custom Leathercraft, Chas
Cousin Bob's Mountain Products
D&D Gunsmiths, Ltd.
David R. Chicoine
Dixie Gun Works
Dixon Muzzleloading Shop, Inc.
Duffy, Charles E. (See Guns Antique & Modern DBA)
Ed's Gun House
Enguix Import-Export
Fagan Arms
Flayderman & Co., Inc.
Getz Barrel Co.
Glass, Herb
Goergen's Gun Shop, Inc.
Golden Age Arms Co.
Goodwin's Guns
Gun Hunter Books (See Gun Hunter Trading Co.)
Gun Hunter Trading Co.
Gun Room Press, The
Gun Room, The
Gun Works, The
Guns Antique & Modern DBA / Charles E. Duffy
Hallowell & Co.
Hammans, Charles E.
HandCrafts Unltd. (See Clements' Custom Leathercraft)
Handgun Press
Hansen & Co.
Imperial Miniature Armory
James Wayne Firearms for Collectors and Investors
Kelley's
Knight's Manufacturing Co.
Ledbetter Airguns, Riley
LeFever Arms Co., Inc.
Lever Arms Service Ltd.
Lock's Philadelphia Gun Exchange
Log Cabin Sport Shop
Logdewood Mfg.
Martin B. Retting Inc.
Martin's Gun Shop
Michael's Antiques
Mid-America Recreation, Inc.
Montana Outfitters, Lewis E. Yearout
Muzzleloaders Etcetera, Inc.
Navy Arms Co.
New England Arms Co.
Olathe Gun Shop
P.S.M.G. Gun Co.
Peter Dyson & Son Ltd.
Pony Express Sport Shop
Powder Horn Ltd.
Ravell Ltd.
Reno, Wayne
Retting, Inc., Martin B.
Robert Valade Engraving
Rutgers Book Center
Samco Global Arms, Inc.
Sarco, Inc.
Scott Fine Guns Inc., Thad

Shootin' Shack
Sportsmen's Exchange & Western Gun Traders, Inc.
State Line Gun Shop
Steves House of Guns
Stott's Creek Armory, Inc.
Track of the Wolf, Inc.
Turnbull Restoration, Doug
Vic's Gun Refinishing
Wallace, Terry
Westley Richards & Co. Ltd.
Wild West Guns
Winchester Consultants
Winchester Sutler, Inc., The
Yearout, Lewis E. (See Montana Outfitters)

APPRAISER - GUNS, ETC.

A.W. Peterson Gun Shop, Inc., The
Ackerman & Co.
Antique Arms Co.
Barta's Gunsmithing
Beitzinger, George
Blue Book Publications, Inc.
Bob's Tactical Indoor Shooting Range & Gun Shop
Bonham's & Butterfields
Cape Outfitters
Chadick's Ltd.
Champlin Firearms, Inc.
Christie's East
Clark Firearms Engraving
Cleland's Outdoor World, Inc.
Clements' Custom Leathercraft, Chas
Colonial Arms, Inc.
Colonial Repair
Corry, John
Custom Tackle and Ammo
D&D Gunsmiths, Ltd.
David R. Chicoine
DGR Custom Rifles
Dietz Gun Shop & Range, Inc.
Dixie Gun Works
Dixon Muzzleloading Shop, Inc.
Duane's Gun Repair (See DGR Custom Rifles)
Ed's Gun House
Eversull Co., Inc.
Fagan Arms
Ferris Firearms
Firearm Brokers
Flayderman & Co., Inc.
Frontier Arms Co., Inc.
Gene's Custom Guns
Getz Barrel Co.
Gillmann, Edwin
Goergen's Gun Shop, Inc.
Golden Age Arms Co.
Griffin & Howe, Inc.
Gun City
Gun Hunter Books (See Gun Hunter Trading Co.)
Gun Hunter Trading Co.
Gun Room Press, The
Gun Shop, The
Gun Works, The
Guncraft Books (See Guncraft Sports, Inc.)
Guncraft Sports, Inc.
Gunsmithing, Inc.
Hallowell & Co.
Hammans, Charles E.
HandCrafts Unltd. (See Clements' Custom Leathercraft)
Handgun Press

Hank's Gun Shop
Hansen & Co.
Irwin, Campbell H.
Ithaca Classic Doubles
J R Guns
J.W. Wasmundt-Gunsmith
Jackalope Gun Shop
James Wayne Firearms for Collectors and Investors
Jensen's Arizona Sportsman
JG Airguns, LLC
Kelley's
Ken Eyster Heritage Gunsmiths, Inc.
L.L. Bean, Inc.
Lampert, Ron
LaRocca Gun Works
Ledbetter Airguns, Riley
LeFever Arms Co., Inc.
Lock's Philadelphia Gun Exchange
Log Cabin Sport Shop
Logdewood Mfg.
Long, George F.
Martin B. Retting Inc.
Martin's Gun Shop
Mathews Gun Shop & Gunsmithing, Inc.
McCann Industries
Mercer Custom Guns
Montana Outfitters, Lewis E. Yearout
Muzzleloaders Etcetera, Inc.
Navy Arms Co.
New England Arms Co.
Nu Line Guns, Inc.
Olathe Gun Shop
Orvis Co., The
P&M Sales & Services, LLC
P.S.M.G. Gun Co.
Pasadena Gun Center
Pentheny de Pentheny
Perazone-Gunsmith, Brian
Peterson Gun Shop, Inc., A.W.
Pettinger Books, Gerald
Pony Express Sport Shop
Powder Horn Ltd.
R.A. Wells Custom Gunsmith
R.E.T. Enterprises
Retting, Inc., Martin B.
Robert Valade Engraving
Russ Haydon's Shooters' Supply
Rutgers Book Center
Scott Fine Guns Inc., Thad
Shootin' Shack
Sportsmen's Exchange & Western Gun Traders, Inc.
State Line Gun Shop
Steven Dodd Hughes
Stott's Creek Armory, Inc.
Stratco, Inc.
Swampfire Shop, The (See Peterson Gun Shop, Inc., A.W.)
Ten-Ring Precision, Inc.
Vic's Gun Refinishing
Walker Arms Co., Inc.
Wallace, Terry
Weber & Markin Custom Gunsmiths
Werth, T. W.
Whitestone Lumber Corp.
Wild West Guns
Williams Shootin' Iron Service, The Lynx-Line
Winchester Consultants
Winchester Sutler, Inc., The
Yearout, Lewis E. (See Montana Outfitters)

PRODUCT & SERVICE DIRECTORY

AUCTIONEER - GUNS, ETC.

"Little John's" Antique Arms
Bonham's & Butterfields
Buck Stix-SOS Products Co.
Christie's East
Fagan Arms
Pete de Coux Auction House
Sotheby's

BOOKS & MANUALS (PUBLISHERS & DEALERS)

A.W. Peterson Gun Shop, Inc., The
Alpha 1 Drop Zone
American Gunsmithing Institute
American Handgunner Magazine
Armory Publications
Arms & Armour Press
Austin Sheridan USA, Inc.
Ballistic Products, Inc.
Barnes Bullets, Inc.
Beartooth Bullets
Beeman Precision Airguns
Blacksmith Corp.
Blacktail Mountain Books
Blue Book Publications, Inc.
Blue Ridge Machinery & Tools, Inc.
Boone's Custom Ivory Grips, Inc.
Brownells, Inc.
Buchsenmachermeister
C. Sharps Arms Co. Inc./ Montana Armory
Cain's Outdoors, Inc.
Cape Outfitters
Cheyenne Pioneer Products
Collector's Armoury, Ltd.
Colonial Repair
Crit' R Calls
David R. Chicoine
deHaas Barrels
Dixon Muzzleloading Shop, Inc.
Excalibur Publications
Executive Protection Institute
F+W Publications, Inc.
Fulton Armory
Galati International
GAR
Golden Age Arms Co.
Gun City
Gun Digest (See F+W Publications)
Gun Hunter Books (See Gun Hunter Trading Co.)
Gun Hunter Trading Co.
Gun Room Press, The
Gun Works, The
Guncraft Books (See Guncraft Sports, Inc.)
Guncraft Sports, Inc.
Gunnerman Books
GUNS Magazine
Gunsmithing, Inc.
H&P Publishing
Handgun Press
Harris Publications
Hawk Laboratories, Inc. (See Hawk, Inc.)
Hawk, Inc.
Heritage/VSP Gun Books
Hodgdon Powder Co.
Hofer Jagdwaffen, P.
Hornady Mfg. Co.
Huntington Die Specialties

I.D.S.A. Books
Info-Arm
Ironside International Publishers, Inc.
Jantz Supply, Inc.
Jeff's Outfitters
JG Airguns, LLC
Kelley's
King & Co.
Koval Knives
L.B.T.
Lebeau-Courally
Lethal Force Institute (See Police Bookshelf)
Log Cabin Sport Shop
Lyman Products Corp.
Machinist's Workshop-Village Press
Madis Books
Magma Engineering Co.
Midwest Shooting School, The
Montana Armory, Inc.
Montana Precision Swaging
Mulberry House Publishing
Nammo Lapua Oy
Navy Arms Co.
NgraveR Co., The
Numrich Gun Parts Corp.
OK Weber, Inc.
Outdoor Sports Headquarters, Inc.
Paintball Games International Magazine Aceville
Pansch, Robert F
Pejsa Ballistics
Pete Rickard Co.
Pettinger Books, Gerald
PFRB Co.
Police Bookshelf
Precision Reloading, Inc.
Precision Shooting, Inc.
Primedia Publishing Co.
Professional Hunter Supplies
Ravell Ltd.
Ray Riling Arms Books Co.
Remington Double Shotguns
Russ Haydon's Shooters' Supply
Rutgers Book Center
S&S Firearms
Safari Press, Inc.
Saunders Gun & Machine Shop
Scharch Mfg., Inc.-Top Brass
Semmer, Charles (See Remington Double Shotguns)
Sharps Arms Co., Inc., C.
Shotgun Sports Magazine, dba Shootin' Accessories Ltd.
Sierra Bullets
Speer Bullets
SPG, Inc.
Stackpole Books
Star Custom Bullets
Stoeger Industries
Stoeger Publishing Co. (See Stoeger Industries)
Swift Bullet Co.
Thomas, Charles C.
Track of the Wolf, Inc.
Trafalgar Square
Trotman, Ken
Tru-Balance Knife Co.
Vega Tool Co.
VSP Publishers (See Heritage/ VSP Gun Books)
W.E. Brownell Checkering Tools
WAMCO-New Mexico
Wells Creek Knife & Gun Works

Wilderness Sound Products Ltd.
Williams Gun Sight Co.
Winchester Consultants
Winfield Galleries LLC
Wolfe Publishing Co.

BULLET CASTING, ACCESSORIES

A.W. Peterson Gun Shop, Inc., The
Ballisti-Cast, Inc.
Buffalo Arms Co.
Bullet Metals
Cast Performance Bullet Co.
CFVentures
Cooper-Woodward Perfect Lube
Davide Pedersoli and Co.
Ferguson, Bill
Fluoramics, Inc.
Hanned Line, The
Huntington Die Specialties
L.B.T.
Lee Precision, Inc.
Lithi Bee Bullet Lube
Lyman Products Corp.
MA Systems, Inc.
Magma Engineering Co.
Rapine Bullet Mould Mfg. Co.
Redding Reloading Equipment
SPG, Inc.

BULLET CASTING, FURNACES & POTS

A.W. Peterson Gun Shop, Inc., The
Ballisti-Cast, Inc.
Buffalo Arms Co.
Bullet Metals
Ferguson, Bill
GAR
Gun Works, The
Lee Precision, Inc.
Lyman Products Corp.
Magma Engineering Co.
Rapine Bullet Mould Mfg. Co.
Thompson Bullet Lube Co.

BULLET CASTING, LEAD

A.W. Peterson Gun Shop, Inc., The
Action Bullets & Alloy Inc.
Ames Metal Products Co.
Buckskin Bullet Co.
Buffalo Arms Co.
Bullet Metals
Gun Works, The
Hunters Supply, Inc.
Jericho Tool & Die Co., Inc.
Lee Precision, Inc.
Lithi Bee Bullet Lube
Magma Engineering Co.
Montana Precision Swaging
Penn Bullets
Proofmark Corp.
SPG, Inc.
Splitfire Sporting Goods, L.L.C.
Walters Wads

BULLET PULLERS

A.W. Peterson Gun Shop, Inc., The
Battenfeld Technologies, Inc.
Davide Pedersoli and Co.
Gun Works, The

Howell Machine, Inc.
Huntington Die Specialties
Royal Arms Gunstocks

BULLET TOOLS

A.W. Peterson Gun Shop, Inc., The
Brynin, Milton
Camdex, Inc.
Corbin Mfg. & Supply, Inc.
Eagan Gunsmiths
Hanned Line, The
Lee Precision, Inc.
Niemi Engineering, W. B.
North Devon Firearms Services
Rorschach Precision Products
Sport Flite Manufacturing Co.
WTA Manufacturing

BULLET, CASE & DIE LUBRICANTS

Beartooth Bullets
Bonanza (See Forster Products)
Buckskin Bullet Co.
Buffalo Arms Co.
Camp-Cap Products
CFVentures
Cooper-Woodward Perfect Lube
CVA
Ferguson, Bill
Forster Products, Inc.
GAR
Guardsman Products
Hanned Line, The
Heidenstrom Bullets
Hornady Mfg. Co.
Javelina Lube Products
Knoell, Doug
L.B.T.
Lee Precision, Inc.
Lithi Bee Bullet Lube
MI-TE Bullets
RCBS Operations/ATK
Reardon Products
Rooster Laboratories
Shay's Gunsmithing
Uncle Mike's (See Michaels of Oregon, Co.)
Widener's Reloading & Shooting Supply, Inc.
Young Country Arms

CARTRIDGES FOR COLLECTORS

Ackerman & Co.
Ad Hominem
Armory Publications
Cameron's
Campbell, Dick
Colonial Repair
Country Armourer, The
Cubic Shot Shell Co., Inc.
Duane's Gun Repair (See DGR Custom Rifles)
Ed's Gun House
Enguix Import-Export
Goergen's Gun Shop, Inc.
Gun City
Gun Hunter Books (See Gun Hunter Trading Co.)
Gun Hunter Trading Co.
Gun Room Press, The
Jack First, Inc.
Kelley's
Liberty Shooting Supplies
Michael's Antiques

Montana Outfitters, Lewis E. Yearout
Numrich Gun Parts Corp.
Pasadena Gun Center
Pete de Coux Auction House
Samco Global Arms, Inc.
SOS Products Co. (See Buck Stix-SOS Products Co.)
Stone Enterprises Ltd.
Ward & Van Valkenburg
Winchester Consultants
Yearout, Lewis E. (See Montana Outfitters)

CASE & AMMUNITION PROCESSORS, INSPECTORS, BOXERS

A.W. Peterson Gun Shop, Inc., The
Ammo Load Worldwide, Inc.
Hafner World Wide, Inc.
Scharch Mfg., Inc.-Top Brass

CASE CLEANERS & POLISHING MEDIA

A.W. Peterson Gun Shop, Inc., The
Battenfeld Technologies, Inc.
Buffalo Arms Co.
G96 Products Co., Inc.
Gun Works, The
Huntington Die Specialties
Lee Precision, Inc.
Penn Bullets
Tru-Square Metal Products, Inc.
VibraShine, Inc.

CASE PREPARATION TOOLS

A.W. Peterson Gun Shop, Inc., The
Battenfeld Technologies, Inc.
Forster Products, Inc.
High Precision
Huntington Die Specialties
J. Dewey Mfg. Co., Inc.
K&M Services
Lee Precision, Inc.
Match Prep-Doyle Gracey
Plum City Ballistic Range
PWM Sales Ltd.
RCBS Operations/ATK
Redding Reloading Equipment
Russ Haydon's Shooters' Supply
Sinclair International, Inc.
Six Enterprises
Stoney Point Products, Inc.

CASE TRIMMERS, TRIM DIES & ACCESSORIES

A.W. Peterson Gun Shop, Inc., The
Buffalo Arms Co.
Creedmoor Sports, Inc.
Forster Products, Inc.
Fremont Tool Works
K&M Services
Lyman Products Corp.
Match Prep-Doyle Gracey
OK Weber, Inc.
PWM Sales Ltd.
Redding Reloading Equipment

PRODUCT & SERVICE DIRECTORY

CASE TUMBLERS, VIBRATORS, MEDIA & ACCESSORIES

A.W. Peterson Gun Shop, Inc., The
Battenfeld Technologies, Inc.
Berry's Mfg., Inc.
CH Tool & Die/4-D Custom Die Co.
Dillon Precision Products, Inc.
Penn Bullets
Raytech Div. of Lyman Products Corp.
Tru-Square Metal Products, Inc.
VibraShine, Inc.

CASES, CABINETS, RACKS & SAFES - GUN

All Rite Products, Inc.
Allen Co., Inc.
Alumna Sport by Dee Zee
American Display Co.
American Security Products Co.
Americase
Art Jewel Enterprises Ltd.
Bagmaster Mfg., Inc.
Barramundi Corp.
Berry's Mfg., Inc.
Big Spring Enterprises "Bore Stores"
Bison Studios
Black Sheep Brand
Brauer Bros.
Browning Arms Co.
Bushmaster Hunting & Fishing
Cannon Safe, Inc.
Chipmunk (See Oregon Arms, Inc.)
Connecticut Shotgun Mfg. Co.
D&L Industries (See D.J. Marketing)
D.J. Marketing
Dara-Nes, Inc. (See Nesci Enterprises, Inc.)
Deepeeka Exports Pvt. Ltd.
Doskocil Mfg. Co., Inc.
DTM International, Inc.
EMF Co. Inc.
English, Inc., A.G.
Enhanced Presentations, Inc.
Eversull Co., Inc.
Flambeau, Inc.
Fort Knox Security Products
Freedom Arms, Inc.
Galati International
GALCO International Ltd.
Gun-Ho Sports Cases
Hall Plastics, Inc., John
Homak
Hoppe's Div. Penguin Industries, Inc.
Hunter Co., Inc.
Hydrosorbent Dehumidifiers
Impact Case & Container, Inc.
Jeff's Outfitters
Johanssons Vapentillbehor, Bert
Kalispel Case Line
KK Air International (See Impact Case & Container Co., Inc.)
Knock on Wood Antiques
Kolpin Outdoors, Inc.
Lakewood Products Div of Midwest Textile
Liberty Safe

Marsh, Mike
McWelco Products
Morton Booth Co.
MPC
MTM Molded Products Co., Inc.
Nalpak
Necessary Concepts, Inc.
Nesci Enterprises Inc.
Oregon Arms, Inc. (See Rogue Rifle Co., Inc.)
Outa-Site Gun Carriers
Outdoor Connection, Inc., The
Pflumm Mfg. Co.
Poburka, Philip (See Bison Studios)
Powell & Son (Gunmakers) Ltd., William
Prototech Industries, Inc.
Rogue Rifle Co., Inc./Chipmunk Rifles
S.A.R.L. G. Granger
Schulz Industries
Silhouette Leathers
Southern Security
Sportsman's Communicators
Sun Welding Safe Co.
Surecase Co., The
Sweet Home, Inc.
Tinks & Ben Lee Hunting Products (See Wellington Outdoors)
Trulock Tool
Universal Sports
W. Waller & Son, Inc.
Whitestone Lumber Corp.
Wilson Case, Inc.
Woodstream
Zanotti Armor, Inc.
Ziegel Engineering

CHOKE DEVICES, RECOIL ABSORBERS & RECOIL PADS

3-Ten Corp.
A.W. Peterson Gun Shop, Inc., The
Action Products, Inc.
Bansner's Ultimate Rifles, LLC
Bartlett Engineering
Battenfeld Technologies, Inc.
Bob Allen Sportswear
Briley Mfg. Inc.
Brooks Tactical Systems-Agrip
Brownells, Inc.
Buffer Technologies
Bull Mountain Rifle Co.
C&H Research
Cation
Chicasaw Gun Works
Clearview Products
Colonial Arms, Inc.
Connecticut Shotgun Mfg. Co.
CRR, Inc./Marble's Inc.
Danuser Machine Co.
Dina Arms Corp.
Gentry Custom LLC
Gruning Precision, Inc.
Harry Lawson LLC
Hastings
Haydel's Game Calls, Inc.
Hogue Grips
Holland's Shooters Supply, Inc.
I.N.C. Inc. (See Kickeez I.N.C., Inc.)
Jackalope Gun Shop
Jenkins Recoil Pads
JP Enterprises, Inc.
KDF, Inc.
Kickeez, I.N.C., Inc.

London Guns Ltd.
Lyman Products Corp.
Mag-Na-Port International, Inc.
Marble Arms (See CRR, Inc./Marble's Inc.)
Middlebrooks Custom Shop
Mobile Area Networks, Inc.
Morrow, Bud
Nu Line Guns, Inc.
One Of A Kind
P.S.M.G. Gun Co.
Palsa Outdoor Products
Parker & Sons Shooting Supply
Pro-Port Ltd.
Que Industries, Inc.
RPM
Shotguns Unlimited
Simmons Gun Repair, Inc.
Stan Baker Sports
Stone Enterprises Ltd.
Time Precision
Truglo, Inc.
Trulock Tool
Uncle Mike's (See Michaels of Oregon, Co.)
Universal Sports
Virgin Valley Custom Guns
Williams Gun Sight Co.
Wilsom Combat
Wise Guns, Dale

CHRONOGRAPHS & PRESSURE TOOLS

C.W. Erickson's Mfg., L.L.C.
Clearview Products
Competition Electronics, Inc.
Hege Jagd-u. Sporthandels GmbH
Mac-1 Airgun Distributors
Oehler Research, Inc.
PACT, Inc.
Romain's Custom Guns, Inc.
Savage Arms, Inc.
Stratco, Inc.
Tepeco

CLEANERS & DEGREASERS

A.W. Peterson Gun Shop, Inc., The
Barnes Bullets, Inc.
Camp-Cap Products
G96 Products Co., Inc.
Gun Works, The
Hafner World Wide, Inc.
Half Moon Rifle Shop
Kleen-Bore, Inc.
Modern Muzzleloading, Inc.
Northern Precision
Parker & Sons Shooting Supply
Parker Gun Finishes
PrOlixr Lubricants
R&S Industries Corp.
Rusteprufe Laboratories
Sheffield Knifemakers Supply, Inc.
Shooter's Choice Gun Care
Sierra Specialty Prod. Co.
Spencer's Rifle Barrels, Inc.
United States Products Co.

CLEANING & REFINISHING SUPPLIES

A.W. Peterson Gun Shop, Inc., The

AC Dyna-tite Corp.
Alpha 1 Drop Zone
American Gas & Chemical Co., Ltd.
Armite Laboratories Inc.
Atlantic Mills, Inc.
Atsko/Sno-Seal, Inc.
Barnes Bullets, Inc.
Battenfeld Technologies, Inc.
Beeman Precision Airguns
Bill's Gun Repair
Birchwood Casey
Blount, Inc., Sporting Equipment Div.
Blount/Outers ATK
Blue and Gray Products Inc. (See Ox-Yoke Originals)
Break-Free, Inc.
Brownells, Inc.
C.S. Van Gorden & Son, Inc.
Cain's Outdoors, Inc.
Camp-Cap Products
CCI/Speer Div of ATK
Cleland's Outdoor World, Inc.
Connecticut Shotgun Mfg. Co.
Creedmoor Sports, Inc.
CRR, Inc./Marble's Inc.
Custom Products (See Jones Custom Products)
Cylinder & Slide, Inc., William R. Laughridge
Dara-Nes, Inc. (See Nesci Enterprises, Inc.)
Deepeeka Exports Pvt. Ltd.
Dem-Bart Checkering Tools, Inc.
Desert Mountain Mfg.
Du-Lite Corp.
Dykstra, Doug
E&L Mfg., Inc.
Effebi SNC-Dr. Franco Beretta
Faith Associates
Flitz International Ltd.
Fluoramics, Inc.
Frontier Products Co.
G96 Products Co., Inc.
Golden Age Arms Co.
Guardsman Products
Gunsmithing, Inc.
Hafner World Wide, Inc.
Half Moon Rifle Shop
Hammans, Charles E.
Hoppe's Div. Penguin Industries, Inc.
Hornady Mfg. Co.
Hydra-Tone Chemicals, Inc.
Hydrosorbent Dehumidifiers
Iosso Products
J. Dewey Mfg. Co., Inc.
Jantz Supply, Inc.
Jonad Corp.
K&M Industries, Inc.
Kellogg's Professional Products
Kesselring Gun Shop
Kleen-Bore, Inc.
Knight Rifles
Laurel Mountain Forge
Lee Supplies, Mark
Lewis Lead Remover, The (See Brownells, Inc.)
List Precision Engineering
LPS Laboratories, Inc.
Lyman Products Corp.
Mac-1 Airgun Distributors
Marble Arms (See CRR, Inc./Marble's Inc.)
Mark Lee Supplies
Micro Sight Co.
Minute Man High Tech Industries

MTM Molded Products Co., Inc.
Muscle Products Corp.
Nesci Enterprises Inc.
Northern Precision
October Country Muzzleloading
Otis Technology, Inc.
Outers Laboratories Div. of ATK
Parker & Sons Shooting Supply
Parker Gun Finishes
Paul Co., The
Pete Rickard Co.
Precision Airgun Sales, Inc.
Precision Reloading, Inc.
PrOlixr Lubricants
Pro-Shot Products, Inc.
R&S Industries Corp.
Radiator Specialty Co.
Richards MicroFit Stocks, Inc.
Rooster Laboratories
Saunders Gun & Machine Shop
Schumakers Gun Shop
Shooter's Choice Gun Care
Shotgun Sports Magazine, dba Shootin' Accessories Ltd.
Silencio/Safety Direct
Sinclair International, Inc.
Sno-Seal, Inc. (See Atsko/Sno-Seal, Inc.)
Southern Bloomer Mfg. Co.
Splitfire Sporting Goods, L.L.C.
Stoney Point Products, Inc.
Svon Corp.
T.F.C. S.p.A.
Tennessee Valley Mfg.
Tetra Gun Care
Texas Platers Supply Co.
Tru-Square Metal Products, Inc.
United States Products Co.
Van Gorden & Son Inc., C. S.
Venco Industries, Inc. (See Shooter's Choice Gun Care)
VibraShine, Inc.
Watson Bullets
WD-40 Co.
Wick, David E.
Willow Bend
Young Country Arms

COMPUTER SOFTWARE - BALLISTICS

Action Target, Inc.
AmBr Software Group Ltd.
Arms, Programming Solutions (See Arms Software)
Ballistic Program Co., Inc., The
Barnes Bullets, Inc.
Corbin Mfg. & Supply, Inc.
Country Armourer, The
Data Tech Software Systems
Gun Works, The
Hodgdon Powder Co.
Jensen Bullets
Oehler Research, Inc.
Outdoor Sports Headquarters, Inc.
PACT, Inc.
Pejsa Ballistics
Powley Computer (See Hutton Rifle Ranch)
RCBS Operations/ATK
Sierra Bullets
Tioga Engineering Co., Inc.
W. Square Enterprises

CUSTOM GUNSMITH

A&W Repair

PRODUCT & SERVICE DIRECTORY

A.A. Arms, Inc.
A.W. Peterson Gun Shop, Inc., The
Acadian Ballistic Specialties
Accuracy Unlimited
Acra-Bond Laminates
Actions by "T" Teddy Jacobson
Adair Custom Shop, Bill
Ahlman Guns
Aldis Gunsmithing & Shooting Supply
Alpha Precision, Inc.
Alpine Indoor Shooting Range
Amrine's Gun Shop
Antique Arms Co.
Armament Gunsmithing Co., Inc.
Arms Craft Gunsmithing
Armscorp USA, Inc.
Artistry in Wood
Art's Gun & Sport Shop, Inc.
Baelder, Harry
Bain & Davis, Inc.
Bansner's Ultimate Rifles, LLC
Barnes Bullets, Inc.
Baron Technology
Barrel & Gunworks
Barta's Gunsmithing
Bauska Barrels
Bear Arms
Bear Mountain Gun & Tool
Beitzinger, George
Bengtson Arms Co., L.
Bill Adair Custom Shop
Billings Gunsmiths
BlackStar AccuMax Barrels
BlackStar Barrel Accurizing (See BlackStar AccuMax)
Bob Rogers Gunsmithing
Bond Custom Firearms
Borden Ridges Rimrock Stocks
Borovnik K.G., Ludwig
Bowen Classic Arms Corp.
Brace, Larry D.
Briese Bullet Co., Inc.
Briganti Custom Gunsmith
Briley Mfg. Inc.
Broad Creek Rifle Works, Ltd.
Brockman's Custom Gunsmithing
Broken Gun Ranch
Brown Precision, Inc.
Buchsenmachermeister
Buckhorn Gun Works
Buehler Custom Sporting Arms
Bull Mountain Rifle Co.
Bullberry Barrel Works, Ltd.
Burkhart Gunsmithing, Don
Campbell, Dick
Carolina Precision Rifles
Carter's Gun Shop
Caywood, Shane J.
CBC-BRAZIL
Chambers Flintlocks Ltd., Jim
Champlin Firearms, Inc.
Chicasaw Gun Works
Chuck's Gun Shop
Clark Custom Guns, Inc.
Clark Firearms Engraving
Classic Arms Co.
Classic Arms Corp.
Clearview Products
Cleland's Outdoor World, Inc.
Coffin, Charles H.
Cogar's Gunsmithing
Colonial Arms, Inc.
Colonial Repair
Colorado Gunsmithing Academy
Colorado School of Trades
Colt's Mfg. Co., Inc.

Competitive Pistol Shop, The
Conrad, C. A.
Corkys Gun Clinic
Cullity Restoration
Custom Shop, The
Custom Single Shot Rifles
D&D Gunsmiths, Ltd.
D.L. Unmussig Bullets
Dangler's Custom Flint Rifles
D'Arcy Echols & Co.
Darlington Gun Works, Inc.
Dave's Gun Shop
David Miller Co.
David R. Chicoine
David W. Schwartz Custom Guns
Davis, Don
Delorge, Ed
Del-Sports, Inc.
DGR Custom Rifles
DGS, Inc., Dale A. Storey
Dietz Gun Shop & Range, Inc.
Dilliott Gunsmithing, Inc.
Don Klein Custom Guns
Donnelly, C. P.
Duane A. Hobbie Gunsmithing
Duane's Gun Repair (See DGR Custom Rifles)
Duffy, Charles E. (See Guns Antique & Modern DBA)
Duncan's Gun Works, Inc.
E. Arthur Brown Co. Inc.
Ed Brown Products, Inc.
Eggleston, Jere D.
Entreprise Arms, Inc.
Erhardt, Dennis
Eversull Co., Inc.
Evolution Gun Works, Inc.
FERLIB
Ferris Firearms
Fisher, Jerry A.
Fisher Custom Firearms
Fleming Firearms
Flynn's Custom Guns
Forkin Custom Classics
Forster, Kathy (See Custom Checkering)
Forster, Larry L.
Forthofer's Gunsmithing & Knifemaking
Frontier Arms Co., Inc.
Fullmer, Geo. M.
Fulton Armory
G.G. & G.
Galaxy Imports Ltd., Inc.
Garthwaite Pistolsmith, Inc., Jim
Gary Reeder Custom Guns
Gator Guns & Repair
Genecco Gun Works
Gene's Custom Guns
Gentry Custom LLC
George Hoenig, Inc.
Gillmann, Edwin
Gilmore Sports Concepts, Inc.
Goens, Dale W.
Goodling's Gunsmithing
Grace, Charles E.
Greg Gunsmithing Repair
Gre-Tan Rifles
Griffin & Howe, Inc.
Gruning Precision, Inc.
Gun Doc, Inc.
Gun Shop, The
Gun Works, The
Guncraft Books (See Guncraft Sports, Inc.)
Guncraft Sports, Inc.
Guns Antique & Modern DBA / Charles E. Duffy
Gunsite Training Center

Gunsmithing Ltd.
Hamilton, Alex B. (See Ten-Ring Precision, Inc.)
Hammans, Charles E.
Hammerli Service-Precision Mac
Hammond Custom Guns Ltd.
Hank's Gun Shop
Hanson's Gun Center, Dick
Harry Lawson LLC
Hart & Son, Inc.
Hart Rifle Barrels, Inc.
Hartmann & Weiss GmbH
Hawken Shop, The (See Dayton Traister)
Hecht, Hubert J., Waffen-Hecht
Heilmann, Stephen
Heinie Specialty Products
Hensley, Gunmaker, Darwin
High Bridge Arms, Inc.
High Performance International
High Precision
High Standard Mfg. Co./F.I., Inc.
Hill, Loring F.
Hiptmayer, Armurier
Hiptmayer, Klaus
Hoag, James W.
Hodgson, Richard
Hoehn Sales, Inc.
Hofer Jagdwaffen, P.
Holland's Shooters Supply, Inc.
Huebner, Corey O.
Imperial Magnum Corp.
Irwin, Campbell H.
Israel Arms Inc.
Ivanoff, Thomas G. (See Tom's Gun Repair)
J R Guns
J&S Heat Treat
J.J. Roberts / Engraver
J.W. Wasmundt-Gunsmith
Jack Dever Co.
Jackalope Gun Shop
James Calhoon Mfg.
Jamison's Forge Works
Jarrett Rifles, Inc.
Jarvis, Inc.
Jay McCament Custom Gunmaker
Jensen's Arizona Sportsman
Jim Norman Custom Gunstocks
Jim's Precision, Jim Ketchum
John Rigby & Co.
John's Custom Leather
Jones Custom Products, Neil A.
Juenke, Vern
K. Eversull Co., Inc.
KDF, Inc.
Keith's Custom Gunstocks
Ken Eyster Heritage Gunsmiths, Inc.
Ken Starnes Gunmaker
Ketchum, Jim (See Jim's Precision)
Kilham & Co.
King's Gun Works
Kleinendorst, K. W.
KOGOT
Korzinek Riflesmith, J.
L. E. Jurras & Assoc.
LaFrance Specialties
Lampert, Ron
LaRocca Gun Works
Larry Lyons Gunworks
Lathrop's, Inc.
Laughridge, William R. (See Cylinder & Slide, Inc.)
Lazzeroni Arms Co.

LeFever Arms Co., Inc.
Les Baer Custom, Inc.
Linebaugh Custom Sixguns
List Precision Engineering
Lock's Philadelphia Gun Exchange
Lone Star Rifle Co.
Long, George F.
Mag-Na-Port International, Inc.
Mahovsky's Metalife
Makinson, Nicholas
Martini & Hagn, Ltd.
Martin's Gun Shop
Martz, John V.
Mathews Gun Shop & Gunsmithing, Inc.
Mazur Restoration, Pete
McCann, Tom
McCluskey Precision Rifles
McGowen Rifle Barrels
McMillan Rifle Barrels
MCS, Inc.
Mercer Custom Guns
Michael's Antiques
Mid-America Recreation, Inc.
Middlebrooks Custom Shop
Miller Arms, Inc.
Miller Custom
Mills Jr., Hugh B.
Moeller, Steve
Monell Custom Guns
Morrison Custom Rifles, J. W.
Morrow, Bud
Mo's Competitor Supplies (See MCS, Inc.)
Mowrey's Guns & Gunsmithing
Mullis Guncraft
Muzzleloaders Etcetera, Inc.
NCP Products, Inc.
Neil A. Jones Custom Products
Nelson's Custom Guns, Inc.
Nettestad Gun Works
New England Arms Co.
New England Custom Gun Service
Newman Gunshop
Nicholson Custom
Nickels, Paul R.
North American Shooting Systems
Nu Line Guns, Inc.
Olson, Vic
Orvis Co., The
Ottmar, Maurice
Ozark Gun Works
P&M Sales & Services, LLC
P.S.M.G. Gun Co.
PAC-NOR Barreling, Inc.
Pagel Gun Works, Inc.
Parker & Sons Shooting Supply
Parker Gun Finishes
Pasadena Gun Center
Paterson Gunsmithing
Paulsen Gunstocks
Peacemaker Specialists
Pence Precision Barrels
Pennsylvania Gunsmith School
Penrod Precision
Pentheny de Pentheny
Perazone-Gunsmith, Brian
Performance Specialists
Pete Mazur Restoration
Peterson Gun Shop, Inc., A.W.
Piquette's Custom Engraving
Plum City Ballistic Range
Powell & Son (Gunmakers) Ltd., William
Power Custom, Inc.
Professional Hunter Supplies
Quality Custom Firearms

R&J Gun Shop
R.A. Wells Custom Gunsmith
Ray's Gunsmith Shop
Renfrew Guns & Supplies
Ridgetop Sporting Goods
Ries, Chuck
RMS Custom Gunsmithing
Robar Co., Inc., The
Robert Valade Engraving
Robinson, Don
Romain's Custom Guns, Inc.
Ron Frank Custom
Royal Arms Gunstocks
Ruger's Custom Guns
Rupert's Gun Shop
Savage Arms, Inc.
Schiffman, Mike
Schumakers Gun Shop
Score High Gunsmithing
Sharp Shooter Supply
Shaw, Inc., E. R. (See Small Arms Mfg. Co.)
Shay's Gunsmithing
Shooters Supply
Shootin' Shack
Shotguns Unlimited
Silver Ridge Gun Shop (See Goodwin Guns)
Simmons Gun Repair, Inc.
Singletary, Kent
Siskiyou Gun Works (See Donnelly, C. P.)
Skeoch, Brian R.
Sklany's Machine Shop
Small Arms Mfg. Co.
Smith, Art
Snapp's Gunshop
Speiser, Fred D.
Spencer Reblue Service
Spencer's Rifle Barrels, Inc.
Splitfire Sporting Goods, L.L.C.
Sportsmen's Exchange & Western Gun Traders, Inc.
Spradlin's
Springfield Armory
Springfield, Inc.
SSK Industries
Star Custom Bullets
State Line Gun Shop
Steelman's Gun Shop
Steffens, Ron
Steven Dodd Hughes
Stiles Custom Guns
Stott's Creek Armory, Inc.
Sturgeon Valley Sporters
Sullivan, David S. (See Westwind Rifles, Inc.)
Swampfire Shop, The (See Peterson Gun Shop, Inc., A.W.)
Swann, D. J.
Swenson's 45 Shop, A. D.
Swift River Gunworks
Szweda, Robert (See RMS Custom Gunsmithing)
Taconic Firearms Ltd., Perry Lane
Tank's Rifle Shop
Tar-Hunt Custom Rifles, Inc.
Tarnhelm Supply Co., Inc.
Taylor & Robbins
Tennessee Valley Mfg.
Ten-Ring Precision, Inc.
Terry K. Kopp Professional Gunsmithing
Terry Theis-Engraver
Time Precision
Tom's Gun Repair, Thomas G. Ivanoff
Tom's Gunshop
Trevallion Gunstocks

Trulock Tool
Tucker, James C.
Turnbull Restoration, Doug
Upper Missouri Trading Co.
Van Horn, Gil
Van Patten, J. W.
Vest, John
Vic's Gun Refinishing
Virgin Valley Custom Guns
Walker Arms Co., Inc.
Wallace, Terry
Wardell Precision
Weatherby, Inc.
Weber & Markin Custom
  Gunsmiths
Wells Sport Store
Werth, T. W.
Wessinger Custom Guns &
  Engraving
Westley Richards & Co. Ltd.
Westwind Rifles, Inc., David S.
  Sullivan
White Barn Wor
White Rifles, Inc.
Wichita Arms, Inc.
Wiebe, Duane
Wild West Guns
William E. Phillips Firearms
Williams Gun Sight Co.
Williams Shootin' Iron Service,
  The Lynx-Line
Williamson Precision
  Gunsmithing
Wilsom Combat
Winter, Robert M.
Wise Guns, Dale
Wiseman and Co., Bill
Wright's Gunstock Blanks
Zeeryp, Russ

CUSTOM METALSMITH

A&W Repair
A.W. Peterson Gun Shop,
  Inc., The
Ackerman & Co.
Ahlman Guns
Alaskan Silversmith, The
Aldis Gunsmithing & Shooting
  Supply
Alpha Precision, Inc.
Amrine's Gun Shop
Antique Arms Co.
Artistry in Wood
Baron Technology
Barrel & Gunworks
Bauska Barrels
Bear Mountain Gun & Tool
Beitzinger, George
Bengtson Arms Co., L.
Bill Adair Custom Shop
Billings Gunsmiths
Billingsley & Brownell
Bob Rogers Gunsmithing
Bowen Classic Arms Corp.
Brace, Larry D.
Briganti Custom Gunsmith
Broad Creek Rifle Works, Ltd.
Brown Precision, Inc.
Buckhorn Gun Works
Buehler Custom Sporting Arms
Bull Mountain Rifle Co.
Bullberry Barrel Works, Ltd.
Campbell, Dick
Carter's Gun Shop
Caywood, Shane J.
Checkmate Refinishing
Colonial Repair
Colorado Gunsmithing
  Academy

Craftguard
Crandall Tool & Machine Co.
Cullity Restoration
Custom Shop, The
Custom Single Shot Rifles
D&D Gunsmiths, Ltd.
D'Arcy Echols & Co.
Dave's Gun Shop
Delorge, Ed
DGS, Inc., Dale A. Storey
Dietz Gun Shop & Range, Inc.
Dilliott Gunsmithing, Inc.
Don Klein Custom Guns
Duane's Gun Repair (See DGR
  Custom Rifles)
Erhardt, Dennis
Eversull Co., Inc.
Ferris Firearms
Fisher, Jerry A.
Forster, Larry L.
Forthofer's Gunsmithing &
  Knifemaking
Fullmer, Geo. M.
Genecco Gun Works
Gentry Custom LLC
Grace, Charles E.
Gun Shop, The
Gunsmithing Ltd.
Hamilton, Alex B. (See Ten-
  Ring Precision, Inc.)
Harry Lawson LLC
Hartmann & Weiss GmbH
Hecht, Hubert J., Waffen-Hecht
Heilmann, Stephen
High Precision
Hiptmayer, Armurier
Hiptmayer, Klaus
Hoag, James W.
Holland's Shooters Supply, Inc.
Ivanoff, Thomas G. (See Tom's
  Gun Repair)
J J Roberts Firearm Engraver
J&S Heat Treat
J.J. Roberts / Engraver
Jackalope Gun Shop
Jamison's Forge Works
Jay McCament Custom
  Gunmaker
KDF, Inc.
Ken Eyster Heritage
  Gunsmiths, Inc.
Ken Starnes Gunmaker
Kilham & Co.
Kleinendorst, K. W.
Lampert, Ron
LaRocca Gun Works
Larry Lyons Gunworks
Les Baer Custom, Inc.
List Precision Engineering
Lock's Philadelphia Gun
  Exchange
Mahovsky's Metalife
Makinson, Nicholas
Martini & Hagn, Ltd.
Mazur Restoration, Pete
McFarland, Stan
Mid-America Recreation, Inc.
Miller Arms, Inc.
Morrison Custom Rifles, J. W.
Morrow, Bud
Mullis Guncraft
Nelson's Custom Guns, Inc.
Nettestad Gun Works
New England Custom Gun
  Service
Nicholson Custom
Noreen, Peter H.
Nu Line Guns, Inc.
Olson, Vic
Ozark Gun Works
P.S.M.G. Gun Co.

Pagel Gun Works, Inc.
Parker & Sons Shooting
  Supply
Parker Gun Finishes
Pasadena Gun Center
Penrod Precision
Pete Mazur Restoration
Precision Specialties
Quality Custom Firearms
R.A. Wells Custom Gunsmith
Rice, Keith (See White Rock
  Tool & Die)
Robar Co., Inc., The
Robinson, Don
Romain's Custom Guns, Inc.
Ron Frank Custom
Score High Gunsmithing
Simmons Gun Repair, Inc.
Singletary, Kent
Skeoch, Brian R.
Sklany's Machine Shop
Smith, Art
Smith, Sharmon
Snapp's Gunshop
Spencer Reblue Service
Spencer's Rifle Barrels, Inc.
Sportsmen's Exchange &
  Western Gun Traders, Inc.
Spradlin's
SSK Industries
State Line Gun Shop
Steffens, Ron
Stiles Custom Guns
Taylor & Robbins
Ten-Ring Precision, Inc.
Time Precision
Tom's Gun Repair, Thomas G.
  Ivanoff
Turnbull Restoration, Doug
Van Horn, Gil
Van Patten, J. W.
Vic's Gun Refinishing
Waldron, Herman
Wallace, Terry
Weber & Markin Custom
  Gunsmiths
Wells Sport Store
Werth, T. W.
Wessinger Custom Guns &
  Engraving
White Rock Tool & Die
Wiebe, Duane
Wild West Guns
Williams Shootin' Iron Service,
  The Lynx-Line
Williamson Precision
  Gunsmithing
Winter, Robert M.
Wise Guns, Dale
Wright's Gunstock Blanks

DECOYS

A.W. Peterson Gun Shop,
  Inc., The
Ad Hominem
Bill Russ Trading Post
Carry-Lite, Inc.
Farm Form Decoys, Inc.
Feather, Flex Decoys
Flambeau, Inc.
G&H Decoys, Inc.
Grand Slam Hunting Products
Klingler Woodcarving
Kolpin Outdoors, Inc.
L.L. Bean, Inc.
Murphy, R.R. Co., Inc.
Original Deer Formula Co., The
Quack Decoy & Sporting Clays
Tanglefree Industries
Tru-Nord Compass
Woods Wise Products

DIE ACCESSORIES, METALLIC

A.W. Peterson Gun Shop,
  Inc., The
High Precision
Howell Machine, Inc.
King & Co.
Rapine Bullet Mould Mfg. Co.
Redding Reloading Equipment
Sinclair International, Inc.
Sport Flite Manufacturing Co.

DIES, METALLIC

A.W. Peterson Gun Shop,
  Inc., The
Austin Sheridan USA, Inc.
Bald Eagle Precision Machine
  Co.
Buffalo Arms Co.
CH Tool & Die/4-D Custom
  Die Co.
Competitor Corp., Inc.
Dakota Arms, Inc.
Dillon Precision Products, Inc.
Dixie Gun Works
Fremont Tool Works
Gruning Precision, Inc.
Hollywood Engineering
Jones Custom Products,
  Neil A.
King & Co.
Lee Precision, Inc.
MEC-Gar S.R.L.
Montana Precision Swaging
Neil A. Jones Custom Products
Ozark Gun Works
PWM Sales Ltd.
Rapine Bullet Mould Mfg. Co.
RCBS Operations/ATK
Romain's Custom Guns, Inc.
Sinclair International, Inc.
Six Enterprises
Spencer's Rifle Barrels, Inc.
Sport Flite Manufacturing Co.
SSK Industries
Vega Tool Co.

DIES, SHOTSHELL

A.W. Peterson Gun Shop,
  Inc., The
Hollywood Engineering
Lee Precision, Inc.
MEC, Inc.

DIES, SWAGE

A.W. Peterson Gun Shop,
  Inc., The
Bullet Swaging Supply, Inc.
CH Tool & Die/4-D Custom
  Die Co.
Competitor Corp., Inc.
Corbin Mfg. & Supply, Inc.
D.L. Unmussig Bullets
Hollywood Engineering
Howell Machine, Inc.
Montana Precision Swaging
Sport Flite Manufacturing Co.

ENGRAVER, ENGRAVING TOOLS

Ackerman & Co.
Adair Custom Shop, Bill
Ahlman Guns
Alaskan Silversmith, The
Allard, Gary/Creek Side Metal
  & Woodcrafters
Allen Firearm Engraving
Altamont Co.

American Pioneer Video
Baron Technology
Barraclough, John K.
Bates Engraving, Billy
Bill Adair Custom Shop
Billy Bates Engraving
Boessler, Erich
Brooker, Dennis
Buchsenmachermeister
Churchill, Winston G.
Clark Firearms Engraving
Collings, Ronald
Cullity Restoration
Cupp, Alana, Custom Engraver
Dayton Traister
Delorge, Ed
Dolbare, Elizabeth
Dremel Mfg. Co.
Dubber, Michael W.
Engraving Artistry
Eversull Co., Inc.
Firearms Engraver's Guild of
  America
Fountain Products
Frank Knives
Gary Reeder Custom Guns
Gene's Custom Guns
Glimm's Custom Gun
  Engraving
Golden Age Arms Co.
Gournet Artistic Engraving
Grant, Howard V.
GRS/Glendo Corp.
Gun Room, The
Gurney, F. R.
Half Moon Rifle Shop
Harris Hand Engraving, Paul A.
Hawken Shop, The (See
  Dayton Traister)
Hiptmayer, Armurier
Hiptmayer, Heidemarie
Hofer Jagdwaffen, P.
J J Roberts Firearm Engraver
Jeff Flannery Engraving
Jim Blair Engraving
John J. Adams & Son
  Engravers
Kehr, Roger
Kelly, Lance
Ken Eyster Heritage
  Gunsmiths, Inc.
Kenneth W. Warren Engraver
Klingler Woodcarving
Koevenig's Engraving Service
Larry Lyons Gunworks
LeFever Arms Co., Inc.
Lindsay Engraving & Tools
McCombs, Leo
McDonald, Dennis
McKenzie, Lynton
Mele, Frank
Mid-America Recreation, Inc.
Nelson, Gary K.
New Orleans Jewelers Supply
  Co.
NgraveR Co., The
Oker's Engraving
Pedersen, C. R.
Pedersen, Rex C.
Peter Hale/Engraver
Piquette's Custom Engraving
Quality Custom Firearms
Rabeno, Martin
Reed, Dave
Reno, Wayne
Riggs, Jim
Robert Evans Engraving
Robert Valade Engraving
Robinson, Don
Rohner, Hans
Rohner, John
Rosser, Bob

Rundell's Gun Shop
Sam Welch Gun Engraving
Sampson, Roger
Schiffman, Mike
Sheffield Knifemakers Supply, Inc.
Sherwood, George
Singletary, Kent
Smith, Mark A.
Smith, Ron
Smokey Valley Rifles
SSK Industries
Steve Kamyk Engraver
Swanson, Mark
Terry Theis-Engraver
Thiewes, George W.
Thirion Gun Engraving, Denise
Viramontez Engraving
Vorhes, David
W.E. Brownell Checkering Tools
Wagoner, Vernon G.
Wallace, Terry
Weber & Markin Custom Gunsmiths
Wells, Rachel
Wells Sport Store
Wessinger Custom Guns & Engraving
Winchester Consultants

GAME CALLS

A.W. Peterson Gun Shop, Inc., The
African Import Co.
Bill Russ Trading Post
Bostick Wildlife Calls, Inc.
Cedar Hill Game Calls, LLC
Crit' R Calls
Crit'R Call (See Rocky Mountain Wildlife Products)
Custom Calls
D-Boone Ent., Inc.
Deepeeka Exports Pvt. Ltd.
DJ Illinois River Valley Calls, Inc.
Dr. O's Products Ltd.
Faulhaber Wildlocker
Faulk's Game Call Co., Inc.
Flambeau, Inc.
Glynn Scobey Duck & Goose Calls
Grand Slam Hunting Products
Green Head Game Call Co.
Hally Caller
Haydel's Game Calls, Inc.
Hunter's Specialties Inc.
Keowee Game Calls
Kolpin Outdoors, Inc.
Lohman Mfg. Co., Inc.
Mallardtone Game Calls
Moss Double Tone, Inc.
Oakman Turkey Calls
Original Deer Formula Co., The
Outdoor Sports Headquarters, Inc.
Pete Rickard Co.
Primos Hunting Calls
Protektor Model
Quaker Boy, Inc.
Sceery Game Calls
Sure-Shot Game Calls, Inc.
Tanglefree Industries
Tinks & Ben Lee Hunting Products (See Wellington Outdoors)
Tink's Safariland Hunting Corp.
Wellington Outdoors
Wilderness Sound Products Ltd.
Woods Wise Products

GAUGES, CALIPERS & MICROMETERS

Blue Ridge Machinery & Tools, Inc.
Gruning Precision, Inc.
Huntington Die Specialties
JGS Precision Tool Mfg., LLC
K&M Services
King & Co.
Spencer's Rifle Barrels, Inc.
Starrett Co., L. S.
Stoney Point Products, Inc.

GUN PARTS, U.S. & FOREIGN

A.A. Arms, Inc.
A.W. Peterson Gun Shop, Inc., The
Advantage Arms, Inc.
Ahlman Guns
Amherst Arms
Antique Arms Co.
Armscorp USA, Inc.
Auto-Ordnance Corp.
B.A.C.
Ballard Rifle & Cartridge Co., LLC
Bar-Sto Precision Machine
Bear Mountain Gun & Tool
Billings Gunsmiths
Bill's Gun Repair
Bob's Gun Shop
Briese Bullet Co., Inc.
Brownells, Inc.
Bryan & Assoc.
Buffer Technologies
Cape Outfitters
Caspian Arms, Ltd.
CBC-BRAZIL
Century International Arms, Inc.
Chicasaw Gun Works
Chip McCormick Corp.
Colonial Arms, Inc.
Colonial Repair
Colt's Mfg. Co., Inc.
Cylinder & Slide, Inc., William R. Laughridge
David R. Chicoine
Delta Arms Ltd.
DGR Custom Rifles
Dibble, Derek A.
Dixie Gun Works
Duane's Gun Repair (See DGR Custom Rifles)
Duffy, Charles E. (See Guns Antique & Modern DBA)
E.A.A. Corp.
Ed Brown Products, Inc.
EMF Co. Inc.
Enguix Import-Export
Entreprise Arms, Inc.
European American Armory Corp. (See E.A.A. Corp.)
Evolution Gun Works, Inc.
Falcon Industries, Inc.
Fleming Firearms
Fulton Armory
Gentry Custom LLC
Glimm's Custom Gun Engraving
Granite Mountain Arms, Inc.
Greider Precision
Gre-Tan Rifles
Gun Doc, Inc.
Gun Hunter Books (See Gun Hunter Trading Co.)
Gun Hunter Trading Co.
Gun Room Press, The

Gun Shop, The
Gun Works, The
Guns Antique & Modern DBA / Charles E. Duffy
Gunsmithing, Inc.
Hawken Shop, The (See Dayton Traister)
High Performance International
High Standard Mfg. Co./F.I., Inc.
Irwin, Campbell H.
Jack First, Inc.
Jamison's Forge Works
JG Airguns, LLC
Jonathan Arthur Ciener, Inc.
Kimber of America, Inc.
Knight's Manufacturing Co.
Krico Deutschland GmbH
LaFrance Specialties
Lampert, Ron
LaPrade
Laughridge, William R. (See Cylinder & Slide, Inc.)
Leapers, Inc.
List Precision Engineering
Lodewick, Walter H.
Logdewood Mfg.
Lomont Precision Bullets
Long, George F.
Markell, Inc.
Martin's Gun Shop
MCS, Inc.
Mid-America Recreation, Inc.
Mobile Area Networks, Inc.
Morrow, Bud
Mo's Competitor Supplies (See MCS, Inc.)
North Star West, Inc.
Nu Line Guns, Inc.
Numrich Gun Parts Corp.
Olathe Gun Shop
Olympic Arms Inc.
P.S.M.G. Gun Co.
Pacific Armament Corp
Peacemaker Specialists
Perazone-Gunsmith, Brian
Performance Specialists
Peter Dyson & Son Ltd.
Peterson Gun Shop, Inc., A.W.
Ranch Products
Randco UK
Ravell Ltd.
Retting, Inc., Martin B.
Romain's Custom Guns, Inc.
Ruger (See Sturm Ruger & Co., Inc.)
Rutgers Book Center
S&S Firearms
Sabatti SPA
Samco Global Arms, Inc.
Sarco, Inc.
Scherer Supplies, Inc.
Shootin' Shack
Silver Ridge Gun Shop (See Goodwin Guns)
Simmons Gun Repair, Inc.
Smires, C. L.
Smith & Wesson
Southern Ammunition Co., Inc.
Southern Armory, The
Sportsmen's Exchange & Western Gun Traders, Inc.
Springfield Sporters, Inc.
Springfield, Inc.
Steyr Mannlicher GmbH & Co. KG
STI International
Strayer-Voigt, Inc.
Sturm Ruger & Co. Inc.
"Su-Press-On", Inc.
Sunny Hill Enterprises, Inc.

Swampfire Shop, The (See Peterson Gun Shop, Inc., A.W.)
T&S Industries, Inc.
Tank's Rifle Shop
Tarnhelm Supply Co., Inc.
Taylor's & Co., Inc.
Terry K. Kopp Professional Gunsmithing
Tom Forrest, Inc.
VAM Distribution Co. LLC
W. Waller & Son, Inc.
W.C. Wolff Co.
Walker Arms Co., Inc.
Wescombe, Bill (See North Star West)
Wild West Guns
Williams Mfg. of Oregon
Wilsom Combat
Winchester Sutler, Inc., The
Wise Guns, Dale
Wisners, Inc.

GUNS & GUN PARTS, REPLICA & ANTIQUE

A.W. Peterson Gun Shop, Inc., The
Ackerman & Co.
Ahlman Guns
Armi San Paolo
Auto-Ordnance Corp.
Ballard Rifle & Cartridge Co., LLC
Bear Mountain Gun & Tool
Billings Gunsmiths
Bob's Gun Shop
Buffalo Arms Co.
Cash Mfg. Co./ TDC
CBC-BRAZIL
CCL Security Products
Chambers Flintlocks Ltd., Jim
Chicasaw Gun Works
Cimarron F.A. Co.
Cogar's Gunsmithing
Colonial Repair
Colt Blackpowder Arms Co.
Colt's Mfg. Co., Inc.
Custom Single Shot Rifles
Delhi Gun House
Delta Arms Ltd.
Dilliott Gunsmithing, Inc.
Dixie Gun Works
Dixon Muzzleloading Shop, Inc.
Duncan's Gun Works, Inc.
Ed's Gun House
Euroarms of America, Inc.
Flintlocks, Etc.
Getz Barrel Co.
Golden Age Arms Co.
Gun Doc, Inc.
Gun Hunter Books (See Gun Hunter Trading Co.)
Gun Hunter Trading Co.
Gun Room Press, The
Gun Works, The
Hastings
Heidenstrom Bullets
IAR Inc.
Imperial Miniature Armory
Ithaca Classic Doubles
Jack First, Inc.
JG Airguns, LLC
Ken Starnes Gunmaker
L&R Lock Co.
Leonard Day
List Precision Engineering
Lock's Philadelphia Gun Exchange
Log Cabin Sport Shop

Logdewood Mfg.
Lone Star Rifle Co.
Lucas, Edward E
Martin's Gun Shop
Mathews Gun Shop & Gunsmithing, Inc.
McCann Industries
Mid-America Recreation, Inc.
Mowrey Gun Works
Navy Arms Co.
North Star West, Inc.
Nu Line Guns, Inc.
Numrich Gun Parts Corp.
Olathe Gun Shop
Parker & Sons Shooting Supply
Pasadena Gun Center
Peacemaker Specialists
Peter Dyson & Son Ltd.
Pony Express Sport Shop
R.A. Wells Custom Gunsmith
Randco UK
Ravell Ltd.
Retting, Inc., Martin B.
Rutgers Book Center
S&S Firearms
Samco Global Arms, Inc.
Sarco, Inc.
Shootin' Shack
Silver Ridge Gun Shop (See Goodwin Guns)
Simmons Gun Repair, Inc.
Sklany's Machine Shop
Southern Ammunition Co., Inc.
Starr Trading Co., Jedediah
Stott's Creek Armory
Taylor's & Co., Inc.
Tennessee Valley Mfg.
Tristar Sporting Arms, Ltd.
Turnbull Restoration, Doug
Upper Missouri Trading Co.
VTI Gun Parts
Weber & Markin Custom Gunsmiths
Wescombe, Bill (See North Star West)
Whitestone Lumber Corp.
Winchester Sutler, Inc., The

GUNS, AIR

A.W. Peterson Gun Shop, Inc., The
Air Arms
Air Venture Airguns
AirForce Airguns
Airrow
Allred Bullet Co.
Arms Corp. of the Philippines
BEC, Inc.
Beeman Precision Airguns
Benjamin/Sheridan Co., Crosman
Bryan & Assoc.
BSA Guns Ltd.
Compasseco, Ltd.
Component Concepts, Inc.
Crosman Airguns
Daisy Outdoor Products
Daystate Ltd.
Domino
Dynamit Nobel-RWS, Inc.
Effebi SNC-Dr. Franco Beretta
European American Armory Corp. (See E.A.A. Corp.)
Feinwerkbau Westinger & Altenburger
Gamo USA, Inc.
Gun Room Press, The
Hammerli Service-Precision Mac

IAR Inc.
International Shooters Service
J.G. Anschutz GmbH & Co. KG
JG Airguns, LLC
Labanu Inc.
Leapers, Inc.
List Precision Engineering
Mac-1 Airgun Distributors
Marksman Products
Maryland Paintball Supply
Nationwide Airgun Repair
Olympic Arms Inc.
Pardini Armi Srl
Park Rifle Co., Ltd., The
Precision Airgun Sales, Inc.
Ripley Rifles
Robinson, Don
RWS (See U.S. Importer-
 Dynamit Nobel-RWS, Inc.)
Safari Arms/Schuetzen Pistol
 Works
Savage Arms, Inc.
Smith & Wesson
Steyr Mannlicher GmbH &
 Co. KG
Stone Enterprises Ltd.
Tippman Sports, LLC
Tristar Sporting Arms, Ltd.
Trooper Walsh
Walther GmbH, Carl
Webley and Scott Ltd.
Weihrauch KG, Hermann

GUNS, FOREIGN
MANUFACTURER U.S.
IMPORTER

A.W. Peterson Gun Shop,
 Inc., The
Accuracy International
 Precision Rifles (See U.S.)
Accuracy Int'l. North America,
 Inc.
Ad Hominem
Air Arms
Armas Garbi, S.A.
Armas Kemen S. A. (See U.S.
 Importers)
Armi Perazzi S.P.A.
Armi San Marco (See Taylor's
 & Co.)
Armi Sport (See Cimarron
 Firearms, E.M.F., KBI &
 Taylor's & Co.)
Arms Corp. of the Philippines
Armscorp USA, Inc.
Arrieta S.L.
Astra Sport, S.A.
Atamec-Bretton
AyA (See U.S. Importer-New
 England Custom Gun Serv
B.A.C.
B.C. Outdoors
BEC, Inc.
Benelli Armi S.P.A.
Benelli USA Corp.
Beretta Pietro S.P.A.
Beretta U.S.A. Corp.
Bernardelli, Vincenzo
Bersa S.A.
Bertuzzi (See U.S. Importer-
 New England Arms Co.)
Bill Hanus Birdguns, LLC
Blaser Jagdwaffen GmbH
Borovnik K.G., Ludwig
Bosis (See U.S. Importer-New
 England Arms Co.)
Brenneke GmbH
Browning Arms Co.
Bryan & Assoc.
BSA Guns Ltd.

Buchsenmachermeister
Cabanas (See U.S. Importer-
 Mandall Shooting Supply
Cabela's
Cape Outfitters
CBC
Century International Arms,
 Inc.
Champlin Firearms, Inc.
Chapuis Armes
Churchill (See U.S. Importer-
 Ellett Bros.)
Collector's Armoury, Ltd.
Cosmi Americo & Figlio S.N.C.
Crucelegui, Hermanos (See
 U.S. Importer-Mandall)
Dakota (See U.S. Importer-EMF
 Co., Inc.)
Dakota Arms, Inc.
Daly, Charles/KBI
Davide Pedersoli and Co.
Domino
Dumoulin, Ernest
Eagle Imports, Inc.
EAW (See U.S. Importer-New
 England Custom Gun Serv
Ed's Gun House
Effebi SNC-Dr. Franco Beretta
EMF Co. Inc.
Euro-Imports
Eversull Co., Inc.
F.A.I.R., S.R.L.
Fabarm S.p.A.
FEG
Feinwerkbau Westinger &
 Altenburger
FERLIB
Fiocchi Munizioni S.A. (See
 U.S. Importer-Fiocch
Firearms Co. Ltd. / Alpine (See
 U.S. Importer-Mandall
Flintlocks, Etc.
Galaxy Imports Ltd., Inc.
Gamba Renato Bremec Srl
Gamo (See U.S. Importers-
 Arms United Corp., Daisy M
Gibbs Rifle Co., Inc.
Glock GmbH
Goergen's Gun Shop, Inc.
Griffin & Howe, Inc.
Grulla Armes
Hammerli AG
Hammerli USA
Hartford (See U.S. Importer-
 EMF Co. Inc.)
Hartmann & Weiss GmbH
Heckler & Koch, Inc.
Hege Jagd-u. Sporthandels
 GmbH
Helwan (See U.S. Importer-
 Interarms)
Hofer Jagdwaffen, P.
Holland & Holland Ltd.
Howa Machinery, Ltd.
I.A.B. (See U.S. Importer-
 Taylor's & Co., Inc.)
IAR Inc.
IGA (See U.S. Importer-
 Stoeger Industries)
Imperial Magnum Corp.
Imperial Miniature Armory
Inter Ordnance of America LP
International Shooters Service
Intrac Arms International
J.G. Anschutz GmbH & Co. KG
JSL Ltd. (See U.S. Importer-
 Specialty Shooters Supply)
K. Eversull Co., Inc.
Kimar (See U.S. Importer-IAR,
 Inc.)
Korth Germany GmbH

Krico Deutschland GmbH
Krieghoff Gun Co., H.
Lakefield Arms Ltd. (See
 Savage Arms, Inc.)
Laurona Armas Eibar, S.A.L.
Lebeau-Courally
Lever Arms Service Ltd.
Lomont Precision Bullets
London Guns Ltd.
Marocchi F.lli S.p.A
Mauser Werke Oberndorf
 Waffensysteme GmbH
McCann Industries
MEC-Gar S.R.L.
Merkel
Mitchell's Mauser
Morini (See U.S. Importers-
 Mandall Shooting Supplies,
 Inc.)
Nammo Lapua Oy
New England Custom Gun
 Service
New SKB Arms Co.
Norica, Avnda Otaola
Norinco
Norma Precision AB (See U.S.
 Importers-Dynamit)
OK Weber, Inc.
Para-Ordnance Mfg., Inc.
Pardini Armi Srl
Perugini Visini & Co. SAS
Peters Stahl GmbH
Pietta (See U.S. Importers-
 Navy Arms Co, Taylor's
Piotti (See U.S. Importer-
 Moore & Co., Wm. Larkin)
PMC/Eldorado Cartridge Corp.
Powell & Son (Gunmakers)
 Ltd., William
Prairie Gun Works
Rizzini F.lli (See U.S.
 Importers-Wm. Larkin Moore
 & Co., N.E. Arms Corp.)
Rizzini SNC
Robinson Armament Co.
Rossi Firearms
Rottweil Compe
Rutten (See U.S. Importer-
 Labanu Inc.)
RWS (See U.S. Importer-
 Dynamit Nobel-RWS, Inc.)
S.A.R.L. G. Granger
S.I.A.C.E. (See U.S. Importer-
 IAR Inc.)
Sabatti SPA
Sako Ltd. (See U.S. Importer-
 Stoeger Industries)
San Marco (See U.S.
 Importers-Cape Outfitters-
 EMF Co., Inc.
Sarsilmaz Shotguns-Turkey
 (see B.C. Outdoors)
Sauer (See U.S. Importers-
 Paul Co., The Sigarms Inc.)
Savage Arms (Canada), Inc.
SGS Importer's International,
 Inc.
SIG
SIG-Sauer (See U.S. Importer-
 Sigarms, Inc.)
SKB Shotguns
Societa Armi Bresciane Srl
 (See U.S. Importer-Jeff's
 Outfitters)
Sphinx Systems Ltd.
Springfield Armory
Springfield, Inc.
State Line Gun Shop
Steyr Mannlicher GmbH &
 Co. KG
T.F.C. S.p.A.

Tanfoglio Fratelli S.r.l.
Tanner (See U.S. Importer-
 Mandall Shooting Supplies,
 Inc.)
Taurus International Firearms
 (See U.S. Importer Taurus
 Firearms, Inc.)
Taurus S.A. Forjas
Techno Arms (See U.S.
 Importer- Auto-Ordnance
 Corp.)
Tikka (See U.S. Importer-
 Stoeger Industries)
TOZ (See U.S. Importer-
 Nygord Precision Products,
 Inc.)
Ugartechea S. A., Ignacio
Ultralux (See U.S. Importer-
 Keng's Firearms Specialty,
 Inc.)
Valtro USA, Inc.
Verney-Carron
Voere-KGH GmbH
Walther GmbH, Carl
Webley and Scott Ltd.
Weihrauch KG, Hermann
Westley Richards & Co. Ltd.
Yankee Gunsmith "Just
 Glocks"
Zabala Hermanos S.A.

GUNS, FOREIGN-
IMPORTER

A.W. Peterson Gun Shop,
 Inc., The
Accuracy International
AcuSport Corp.
Armscor Precision
Auto-Ordnance Corp.
B.A.C.
B.C. Outdoors
Bell's Legendary Country Wear
Benelli USA Corp.
Bill Hanus Birdguns, LLC
Bridgeman Products
British Sporting Arms
Browning Arms Co.
Caesar Guerini USA, Inc.
Cape Outfitters
Century International Arms,
 Inc.
Champion Shooters' Supply
Champion's Choice, Inc.
Cimarron F.A. Co.
CVA
CZ USA
Daly, Charles/KBI
Dixie Gun Works
Dynamit Nobel-RWS, Inc.
E&L Mfg., Inc.
E.A.A. Corp.
Eagle Imports, Inc.
Ellett Bros.
EMF Co. Inc.
Euroarms of America, Inc.
Eversull Co., Inc.
Fiocchi of America, Inc.
Flintlocks, Etc.
Franzen International, Inc. (See
 U.S. Importer-Importer Co.)
G.U., Inc. (See U.S. Importer-
 New SKB Arms Co.)
Galaxy Imports Ltd., Inc.
Gamo USA, Inc.
Giacomo Sporting USA
Glock, Inc.
GSI, Inc.
Gun Shop, The
Guncraft Books (See Guncraft
 Sports, Inc.)

Guncraft Sports, Inc.
Gunsite Training Center
Hammerli USA
IAR Inc.
Imperial Magnum Corp.
Imperial Miniature Armory
Intrac Arms International
K. Eversull Co., Inc.
K.B.I. Inc.
Keng's Firearms Specialty, Inc.
Krieghoff International, Inc.
Labanu Inc.
Legacy Sports International
Lion Country Supply
London Guns Ltd.
Magnum Research, Inc.
Marlin Firearms Co.
Marx, Harry (See U.S. Importer
 for FERLIB)
MCS, Inc.
MEC-Gar U.S.A., Inc.
Mitchell Mfg. Corp.
Navy Arms Co.
New England Arms Co.
OK Weber, Inc.
Orvis Co., The
P.S.M.G. Gun Co.
Para-Ordnance, Inc.
Paul Co., The
Perazone-Gunsmith, Brian
Perazzi U.S.A. Inc.
Powell Agency, William
Quality Arms, Inc.
Rocky Mountain Armoury
S.D. Meacham
Safari Arms/Schuetzen Pistol
 Works
Samco Global Arms, Inc.
Savage Arms, Inc.
Scott Fine Guns Inc., Thad
SGS Importer's International,
 Inc.
SKB Shotguns
Southern Ammunition Co., Inc.
Specialty Shooters Supply, Inc.
Springfield, Inc.
State Line Gun Shop
Stoeger Industries
Stone Enterprises Ltd.
Swarovski Optik North America
 Ltd.
Taurus Firearms, Inc.
Taylor's & Co., Inc.
Track of the Wolf, Inc.
Traditions Performance
 Firearms
Tristar Sporting Arms, Ltd.
Trooper Walsh
U.S. Importer-Wm. Larkin
 Moore
VAM Distribution Co. LLC
Vector Arms, Inc.
VTI Gun Parts
Westley Richards Agency USA
 (See U.S. Importer
Wingshooting Adventures
Yankee Gunsmith "Just
 Glocks"

GUNS, SURPLUS,
PARTS &
AMMUNITION

A.W. Peterson Gun Shop,
 Inc., The
Ahlman Guns
Alpha 1 Drop Zone
Armscorp USA, Inc.
B.A.C.
Bob's Gun Shop
Century International Arms,
 Inc.

Delta Arms Ltd.
Duncan's Gun Works, Inc.
Ed's Gun House
Firearm Brokers
Fleming Firearms
Fulton Armory
Gun City
Gun Hunter Books (See Gun
　Hunter Trading Co.)
Gun Hunter Trading Co.
Gun Room Press, The
Hank's Gun Shop
Hege Jagd-u. Sporthandels
　GmbH
Ken Starnes Gunmaker
LaRocca Gun Works
Lever Arms Service Ltd.
Martin B. Retting Inc.
Martin's Gun Shop
National Gun, Inc.
Navy Arms Co.
Numrich Gun Parts Corp.
Oil Rod and Gun Shop
Olathe Gun Shop
Paragon Sales & Services, Inc.
Pasadena Gun Center
Power Plus Enterprises, Inc.
Ravell Ltd.
Retting, Inc., Martin B.
Rutgers Book Center
Samco Global Arms, Inc.
Sarco, Inc.
Shootin' Shack
Silver Ridge Gun Shop (See
　Goodwin Guns)
Simmons Gun Repair, Inc.
Sportsmen's Exchange &
　Western Gun Traders, Inc.
Springfield Sporters, Inc.
T.F.C. S.p.A.
Tarnhelm Supply Co., Inc.
Taylor's & Co., Inc.
Whitestone Lumber Corp.
Williams Shootin' Iron Service,
　The Lynx-Line

GUNS, U.S. MADE

3-Ten Corp.
A.A. Arms, Inc.
A.W. Peterson Gun Shop,
　Inc., The
Accu-Tek
Acra-Bond Laminates
Ad Hominem
Airrow
Allred Bullet Co.
American Derringer Corp.
AR-7 Industries, LLC
ArmaLite, Inc.
Armscorp USA, Inc.
A-Square Co.
Austin & Halleck, Inc.
Auto-Ordnance Corp.
Ballard Rifle & Cartridge Co.,
　LLC
Barrett Firearms Manufacturer,
　Inc.
Bar-Sto Precision Machine
Benjamin/Sheridan Co.,
　Crosman
Beretta Pietro S.P.A.
Beretta U.S.A. Corp.
Bill Hanus Birdguns, LLC
Bill Russ Trading Post
Bond Arms, Inc.
Borden Ridges Rimrock Stocks
Borden Rifles Inc.
Brockman's Custom
　Gunsmithing
Browning Arms Co.

Bryan & Assoc.
Bushmaster Firearms, Inc.
C. Sharps Arms Co. Inc./
　Montana Armory
Cabela's
Cape Outfitters
Casull Arms Corp.
CCL Security Products
Century International Arms,
　Inc.
Champlin Firearms, Inc.
Charter 2000
Cleland's Outdoor World, Inc.
Cobra Enterprises, Inc.
Colt's Mfg. Co., Inc.
Competitor Corp., Inc.
Conetrol Scope Mounts
Connecticut Shotgun Mfg. Co.
Connecticut Valley Classics
　(See CVC, BPI)
Cooper Arms
Crosman Airguns
CVA
CZ USA
Dakota Arms, Inc.
Dan Wesson Firearms
Dayton Traister
Detonics USA
Dixie Gun Works
Downsizer Corp.
DS Arms, Inc.
DunLyon R&D, Inc.
E&L Mfg., Inc.
E. Arthur Brown Co. Inc.
Eagle Arms, Inc. (See
　ArmaLite, Inc.)
Ed Brown Products, Inc.
Ellett Bros.
Emerging Technologies, Inc.
　(See Laseraim Technologies,
　Inc.)
Empire Rifles
Entreprise Arms, Inc.
Essex Arms
Excel Industries, Inc.
Firearm Brokers
Fletcher-Bidwell, LLC
FN Manufacturing
Freedom Arms, Inc.
Fulton Armory
Galena Industries AMT
Gary Reeder Custom Guns
Genecco Gun Works
Gentry Custom LLC
George Hoenig, Inc.
Gibbs Rifle Co., Inc.
Gil Hebard Guns, Inc.
Gilbert Equipment Co., Inc.
Goergen's Gun Shop, Inc.
Granite Mountain Arms, Inc.
Gun Room Press, The
Gun Works, The
Guncrafter Industries
H&R 1871, LLC
Hammans, Charles E.
Hammerli USA
Harrington & Richardson (See
　H&R 1871, Inc.)
Hart & Son, Inc.
Hatfield Gun
Hawken Shop, The (See
　Dayton Traister)
Heritage Firearms (See
　Heritage Mfg., Inc.)
Heritage Manufacturing, Inc.
High Precision
High Standard Mfg. Co./F.I.,
　Inc.
Hi-Point Firearms/MKS Supply
HJS Arms, Inc.
Hoehn Sales, Inc.

H-S Precision, Inc.
IAR Inc.
Imperial Miniature Armory
Israel Arms Inc.
Ithaca Classic Doubles
Ithaca Guns, LLC
J R Guns
Jim Norman Custom
　Gunstocks
John Rigby & Co.
John's Custom Leather
JP Enterprises, Inc.
K.B.I. Inc.
Kahr Arms
Kehr, Roger
Kelbly, Inc.
Kel-Tec CNC Industries, Inc.
Keystone Sporting Arms, Inc.
　(Crickett Rifles)
Kimber of America, Inc.
Knight Rifles
Knight's Manufacturing Co.
Kolar
L.A.R. Mfg., Inc.
LaFrance Specialties
Lakefield Arms Ltd. (See
　Savage Arms, Inc.)
Laseraim Technologies, Inc.
Les Baer Custom, Inc.
Lever Arms Service Ltd.
Ljutic Industries, Inc.
Lock's Philadelphia Gun
　Exchange
Lomont Precision Bullets
Lone Star Rifle Co.
Mag-Na-Port International, Inc.
Magnum Research, Inc.
Marlin Firearms Co.
Mathews Gun Shop &
　Gunsmithing, Inc.
Maverick Arms, Inc.
McCann Industries
Meacham Tool & Hardware
　Co., Inc.
Mid-America Recreation, Inc.
Miller Arms, Inc.
MKS Supply, Inc. (See Hi-Point
　Firearms)
MOA Corp.
Montana Armory, Inc.
MPI Stocks
National Gun, Inc.
Navy Arms Co.
NCP Products, Inc.
New Ultra Light Arms, LLC
Noreen, Peter H.
North American Arms, Inc.
North Star West, Inc.
Nowlin Mfg. Co.
Olympic Arms Inc.
Oregon Arms, Inc. (See Rogue
　Rifle Co., Inc.)
P&M Sales & Services, LLC
Parker & Sons Shooting
　Supply
Parker Gun Finishes
Phoenix Arms
Police Bookshelf
Precision Small Arms Inc.
Rapine Bullet Mould Mfg. Co.
Remington Arms Co., Inc.
Rifles, Inc.
Robinson Armament Co.
Rock River Arms
Rogue Rifle Co., Inc./Chipmunk
　Rifles
Rogue River Rifleworks
Rohrbaugh
Romain's Custom Guns, Inc.
RPM
Ruger (See Sturm Ruger &
　Co., Inc.)

Safari Arms/Schuetzen Pistol
　Works
Savage Arms (Canada), Inc.
Schumakers Gun Shop
Searcy Enterprises
Sharps Arms Co., Inc., C.
Sigarms Inc.
Sklany's Machine Shop
Smith & Wesson
Sound Tech
Spencer's Rifle Barrels, Inc.
Springfield Armory
Springfield, Inc.
SSK Industries
State Line Gun Shop
STI International
Stoeger Industries
Strayer-Voigt, Inc.
Sturm Ruger & Co. Inc.
Sunny Hill Enterprises, Inc.
T&S Industries, Inc.
Taconic Firearms Ltd., Perry
　Lane
Tank's Rifle Shop
Tar-Hunt Custom Rifles, Inc.
Taurus Firearms, Inc.
Taylor's & Co., Inc.
Texas Armory (See Bond Arms,
　Inc.)
Thompson/Center Arms
Tippmann Sports, LLC
Tristar Sporting Arms, Ltd.
U.S. Repeating Arms Co., Inc.
Uselton/Arms, Inc.
Vector Arms, Inc.
Volquartsen Custom Ltd.
Wallace, Terry
Weatherby, Inc.
Wescombe, Bill (See North
　Star West)
Wessinger Custom Guns &
　Engraving
Whitestone Lumber Corp.
Wichita Arms, Inc.
Wildey F. A., Inc.
Wilsom Combat
Winchester Consultants
Z-M Weapons

GUNSMITH SCHOOL

American Gunsmithing
　Institute
Colorado Gunsmithing
　Academy
Colorado School of Trades
Cylinder & Slide, Inc., William
　R. Laughridge
Gun Doc, Inc.
Lassen Community College,
　Gunsmithing Dept.
Laughridge, William R. (See
　Cylinder & Slide, Inc.)
Modern Gun Repair School
Murray State College
North American
　Correspondence Schools,
　The Gun Pro
Nowlin Mfg. Co.
NRI Gunsmith School
Pennsylvania Gunsmith School
Piedmont Community College
Pine Technical College
Professional Gunsmiths of
　America
Smith & Wesson
Southeastern Community
　College
Spencer's Rifle Barrels, Inc.
Trinidad St. Jr. Col. Gunsmith
　Dept.

Wright's Gunstock Blanks
Yavapai College

GUNSMITH SUPPLIES, TOOLS & SERVICES

A.W. Peterson Gun Shop,
　Inc., The
Alaskan Silversmith, The
Aldis Gunsmithing & Shooting
　Supply
Alley Supply Co.
Allred Bullet Co.
Alpec Team, Inc.
American Gunsmithing
　Institute
Ballard Rifle & Cartridge Co.,
　LLC
Bar-Sto Precision Machine
Battenfeld Technologies, Inc.
Bauska Barrels
Bear Mountain Gun & Tool
Bengtson Arms Co., L.
Bill's Gun Repair
Blue Ridge Machinery & Tools,
　Inc.
Boyds' Gunstock Industries,
　Inc.
Briley Mfg. Inc.
Brockman's Custom
　Gunsmithing
Brownells, Inc.
Bryan & Assoc.
B-Square Co., Inc.
Buffer Technologies
Bushmaster Firearms, Inc.
C.S. Van Gorden & Son, Inc.
Cain's Outdoors, Inc.
Carbide Checkering Tools (See
　J&R Engineering)
Caywood, Shane J.
CBC-BRAZIL
Chapman Manufacturing Co.
Chicasaw Gun Works
Chip McCormick Corp.
Choate Machine & Tool Co.,
　Inc.
Colonial Arms, Inc.
Colorado School of Trades
Colt's Mfg. Co., Inc.
Conetrol Scope Mounts
Cousin Bob's Mountain
　Products
CRR, Inc./Marble's Inc.
Custom Checkering Service,
　Kathy Forster
Dan's Whetstone Co., Inc.
D'Arcy Echols & Co.
Dem-Bart Checkering Tools,
　Inc.
Dixie Gun Works
Dremel Mfg. Co.
Du-Lite Corp.
Ed Brown Products, Inc.
Entreprise Arms, Inc.
Evolution Gun Works, Inc.
Faith Associates
FERLIB
Fisher, Jerry A.
Forgreens Tool & Mfg., Inc.
Forster, Kathy (See Custom
　Checkering)
Forster Products, Inc.
Gentry Custom LLC
Gilmore Sports Concepts, Inc.
Grace Metal Products
Gre-Tan Rifles
Gruning Precision, Inc.
Gun Works, The
Gunline Tools
Half Moon Rifle Shop

PRODUCT & SERVICE DIRECTORY

Hammond Custom Guns Ltd.
Hastings
Henriksen Tool Co., Inc.
High Performance International
High Precision
Holland's Shooters Supply, Inc.
Ironsighter Co.
Israel Arms Inc.
Ivanoff, Thomas G. (See Tom's Gun Repair)
J&R Engineering
J&S Heat Treat
J. Dewey Mfg. Co., Inc.
Jack First, Inc.
Jantz Supply, Inc.
Jenkins Recoil Pads
JGS Precision Tool Mfg., LLC
Jonathan Arthur Ciener, Inc.
Jones Custom Products, Neil A.
Kailua Custom Guns Inc.
Kasenit Co., Inc.
Kleinendorst, K. W.
Korzinek Riflesmith, J.
L. E. Jurras & Assoc.
LaBounty Precision Reboring, Inc
LaFrance Specialties
Laurel Mountain Forge
Lee Supplies, Mark
List Precision Engineering
Lock's Philadelphia Gun Exchange
London Guns Ltd.
Mahovsky's Metalife
Marble Arms (See CRR, Inc./ Marble's Inc.)
Mark Lee Supplies
Marsh, Mike
Martin's Gun Shop
McFarland, Stan
Menck, Gunsmith Inc., T.W.
Metalife Industries (See Mahovsky's Metalife)
Micro Sight Co.
Midway Arms, Inc.
MMC
Mo's Competitor Supplies (See MCS, Inc.)
Mowrey's Guns & Gunsmithing
Neil A. Jones Custom Products
New England Custom Gun Service
NgraveR Co., The
Nu Line Guns, Inc.
Ole Frontier Gunsmith Shop
Olympic Arms Inc.
Parker & Sons Shooting Supply
Parker Gun Finishes
Parker Gun Finishes
Paulsen Gunstocks
Perazone-Gunsmith, Brian
Peter Dyson & Son Ltd.
Power Custom, Inc.
Practical Tools, Inc.
Precision Specialties
R.A. Wells Custom Gunsmith
Ranch Products
Ransom International Corp.
Reardon Products
Rice, Keith (See White Rock Tool & Die)
Richards MicroFit Stocks, Inc.
Robar Co., Inc., The
Romain's Custom Guns, Inc.
Royal Arms Gunstocks
Score High Gunsmithing
SGS Importer's International, Inc.
Sharp Shooter Supply

Shooter's Choice Gun Care
Simmons Gun Repair, Inc.
Smith Abrasives, Inc.
Southern Bloomer Mfg. Co.
Spencer's Rifle Barrels, Inc.
Spradlin's
Starrett Co., L. S.
Stiles Custom Guns
Stoney Point Products, Inc.
Sullivan, David S. (See Westwind Rifles, Inc.)
Sunny Hill Enterprises, Inc.
T&S Industries, Inc.
T.W. Mench Gunsmith, Inc.
Tank's Rifle Shop
Tar-Hunt Custom Rifles, Inc.
Terry Theis-Engraver
Texas Platers Supply Co.
Tiger-Hunt Longrifle Gunstocks
Tom's Gun Repair, Thomas G. Ivanoff
Track of the Wolf, Inc.
Trinidad St. Jr. Col. Gunsmith Dept.
Trulock Tool
Turnbull Restoration, Doug
United States Products Co.
Van Gorden & Son Inc., C. S.
Venco Industries, Inc. (See Shooter's Choice Gun Care)
Volquartsen Custom Ltd.
W.C. Wolff Co.
Washita Mountain Whetstone Co.
Weigand Combat Handguns, Inc.
Wessinger Custom Guns & Engraving
White Rock Tool & Die
Wilcox All-Pro Tools & Supply
Wild West Guns
Will-Burt Co.
Williams Gun Sight Co.
Williams Shootin' Iron Service, The Lynx-Line
Willow Bend
Windish, Jim
Wise Guns, Dale
Wright's Gunstock Blanks
Yavapai College
Ziegel Engineering

HANDGUN ACCESSORIES

A.A. Arms, Inc.
A.W. Peterson Gun Shop, Inc., The
Action Direct, Inc.
ADCO Sales, Inc.
Advantage Arms, Inc.
Aimtech Mount Systems
Ajax Custom Grips, Inc.
Alpha 1 Drop Zone
American Derringer Corp.
Arms Corp. of the Philippines
Astra Sport, S.A.
Bagmaster Mfg., Inc.
Bar-Sto Precision Machine
Berry's Mfg., Inc.
Blue and Gray Products Inc. (See Ox-Yoke Originals)
Bond Custom Firearms
Bowen Classic Arms Corp.
Bridgeman Products
Broken Gun Ranch
Brooks Tactical Systems-Agrip
Bushmaster Hunting & Fishing
Butler Creek Corp.
Cannon Safe, Inc.
Centaur Systems, Inc.

Central Specialties Ltd. (See Trigger Lock Division)
Charter 2000
Cheyenne Pioneer Products
Chicasaw Gun Works
Clark Custom Guns, Inc.
Classic Arms Co.
Concealment Shop, Inc., The
Conetrol Scope Mounts
Crimson Trace Lasers
CRR, Inc./Marble's Inc.
Cylinder & Slide, Inc., William R. Laughridge
D&L Industries (See D.J. Marketing)
D.J. Marketing
Dan Wesson Firearms
Delhi Gun House
DeSantis Holster & Leather Goods, Inc.
Dina Arms Corp.
Dixie Gun Works
Don Hume Leathergoods
Doskocil Mfg. Co., Inc.
E&L Mfg., Inc.
E. Arthur Brown Co. Inc.
E.A.A. Corp.
Eagle Imports, Inc.
Ed Brown Products, Inc.
Essex Arms
European American Armory Corp. (See E.A.A. Corp.)
Evolution Gun Works, Inc.
Falcon Industries, Inc.
Feinwerkbau Westinger & Altenburger
Fisher Custom Firearms
Fleming Firearms
Freedom Arms, Inc.
G.G. & G.
Galati International
GALCO International Ltd.
Garthwaite Pistolsmith, Inc., Jim
Gil Hebard Guns, Inc.
Gilmore Sports Concepts, Inc.
Glock, Inc.
Gould & Goodrich Leather, Inc.
Gun Works, The
Gun-Alert
Gun-Ho Sports Cases
H.K.S. Products
Hafner World Wide, Inc.
Hammerli USA
Heinie Specialty Products
Henigson & Associates, Steve
High Standard Mfg. Co./F.I., Inc.
Hill Speed Leather, Ernie
HIP-GRIP Barami Corp.
Hi-Point Firearms/MKS Supply
Hobson Precision Mfg. Co.
Hoppe's Div. Penguin Industries, Inc.
H-S Precision, Inc.
Hunter Co., Inc.
Impact Case & Container, Inc.
Jarvis, Inc.
JB Custom
Jim Noble Co.
John's Custom Leather
Jonathan Arthur Ciener, Inc.
JP Enterprises, Inc.
Kalispel Case Line
KeeCo Impressions, Inc.
King's Gun Works
KK Air International (See Impact Case & Container Co., Inc.)
Kolpin Outdoors, Inc.
L&S Technologies Inc. (See Aimtech Mount Systems)

Lakewood Products Div of Midwest Textile
LaserMax
Les Baer Custom, Inc.
Lock's Philadelphia Gun Exchange
Lohman Mfg. Co., Inc.
Mag-Na-Port International, Inc.
Marble Arms (See CRR, Inc./ Marble's Inc.)
Markell, Inc.
MEC-Gar S.R.L.
Middlebrooks Custom Shop
Millett Sights
Mogul Co./Life Jacket
MTM Molded Products Co., Inc.
National Gun, Inc.
No-Sho Mfg. Co.
Numrich Gun Parts Corp.
Outdoor Sports Headquarters, Inc.
Pachmayr Div. Lyman Products
Pager Pal
Parker & Sons Shooting Supply
Pearce Grip, Inc.
Phoenix Arms
Police Bookshelf
Practical Tools, Inc.
Precision Small Arms Inc.
Protector Mfg. Co., Inc., The
Ram-Line ATK
Ranch Products
Ransom International Corp.
RPM
Scherer Supplies, Inc.
SGS Importer's International, Inc.
Simmons Gun Repair, Inc.
Southern Bloomer Mfg. Co.
Springfield Armory
Springfield, Inc.
SSK Industries
Sturm Ruger & Co. Inc.
T.F.C. S.p.A.
Tactical Defense Institute
Tanfoglio Fratelli S.r.l.
Thompson/Center Arms
Trigger Lock Division / Central Specialties Ltd.
Trijicon, Inc.
Triple-K Mfg. Co., Inc.
Truglo, Inc.
United States Products Co.
Universal Sports
Volquartsen Custom Ltd.
W. Waller & Son, Inc.
W.C. Wolff Co.
Weigand Combat Handguns, Inc.
Wessinger Custom Guns & Engraving
Whitestone Lumber Corp.
Wichita Arms, Inc.
Wild West Guns
Williams Gun Sight Co.
Wilsom Combat
Yankee Gunsmith "Just Glocks"
Ziegel Engineering

HANDGUN GRIPS

A.A. Arms, Inc.
A.W. Peterson Gun Shop, Inc., The
African Import Co.
Ahrends Grips
Ajax Custom Grips, Inc.
Altamont Co.

American Derringer Corp.
Arms Corp. of the Philippines
Art Jewel Enterprises Ltd.
Baelder, Harry
Bob's Gun Shop
Boone Trading Co., Inc.
Boone's Custom Ivory Grips, Inc.
Boyds' Gunstock Industries, Inc.
Brooks Tactical Systems-Agrip
Clark Custom Guns, Inc.
Claro Walnut Gunstock Co.
Cole-Grip
Colonial Repair
Crimson Trace Lasers
Cylinder & Slide, Inc., William R. Laughridge
Dan Wesson Firearms
Dixie Gun Works
Dolbare, Elizabeth
E.A.A. Corp.
Eagle Imports, Inc.
Ed Brown Products, Inc.
EMF Co. Inc.
Essex Arms
European American Armory Corp. (See E.A.A. Corp.)
Falcon Industries, Inc.
Feinwerkbau Westinger & Altenburger
Fisher Custom Firearms
Garthwaite Pistolsmith, Inc., Jim
Goodwin's Guns
Herrett's Stocks, Inc.
High Standard Mfg. Co./F.I., Inc.
HIP-GRIP Barami Corp.
Hogue Grips
H-S Precision, Inc.
Huebner, Corey O.
International Shooters Service
Israel Arms Inc.
John Masen Co. Inc.
KeeCo Impressions, Inc.
Keng's Firearms Specialty, Inc.
Korth Germany GmbH
Les Baer Custom, Inc.
Lett Custom Grips
Linebaugh Custom Sixguns
Lyman Products Corp.
Michaels of Oregon Co.
Mobile Area Networks, Inc.
N.C. Ordnance Co.
Newell, Robert H.
Northern Precision
Pachmayr Div. Lyman Products
Pardini Armi Srl
Parker & Sons Shooting Supply
Pearce Grip, Inc.
Precision Small Arms Inc.
Radical Concepts
Robinson, Don
Rosenberg & Son, Jack A.
Roy's Custom Grips
Spegel, Craig
Stoeger Industries
Sturm Ruger & Co. Inc.
Sunny Hill Enterprises, Inc.
Tactical Defense Institute
Taurus Firearms, Inc.
Tirelli
Tom Forrest, Inc.
Triple-K Mfg. Co., Inc.
Uncle Mike's (See Michaels of Oregon, Co.)
Volquartsen Custom Ltd.
Western Mfg. Co.
Whitestone Lumber Corp.
Wright's Gunstock Blanks

PRODUCT & SERVICE DIRECTORY

HEARING PROTECTORS

A.W. Peterson Gun Shop, Inc., The
Aero Peltor
Ajax Custom Grips, Inc.
Browning Arms Co.
Creedmoor Sports, Inc.
David Clark Co., Inc.
Dillon Precision Products, Inc.
Dixie Gun Works
E-A-R, Inc.
Electronic Shooters Protection, Inc.
Gentex Corp.
Gun Room Press, The Gunsmithing, Inc.
Hoppe's Div. Penguin Industries, Inc.
Kesselring Gun Shop
Parker & Sons Shooting Supply
Paterson Gunsmithing
Peltor, Inc. (See Aero Peltor)
Police Bookshelf
R.E.T. Enterprises
Ridgeline, Inc.
Rucker Dist. Inc.
Silencio/Safety Direct
Tactical Defense Institute
Triple-K Mfg. Co., Inc.
Watson Bullets
Whitestone Lumber Corp.

HOLSTERS & LEATHER GOODS

A.A. Arms, Inc.
A.W. Peterson Gun Shop, Inc., The
Action Direct, Inc.
Action Products, Inc.
Aker International, Inc.
AKJ Concealco
Alessi Holsters, Inc.
Arratoonian, Andy (See Horseshoe Leather Products)
Bagmaster Mfg., Inc.
Bang-Bang Boutique (See Holster Shop, The)
Beretta Pietro S.P.A.
Bianchi International, Inc.
Bond Arms, Inc.
Brooks Tactical Systems-Agrip
Browning Arms Co.
Bull-X, Inc.
Camp-Cap Products
Cape Outfitters
Cathey Enterprises, Inc.
Chace Leather Products
Churchill Glove Co., James
Cimarron F.A. Co.
Classic Old West Styles
Clements' Custom Leathercraft, Chas
Cobra Sport S.R.I.
Collector's Armoury, Ltd.
Colonial Repair
Counter Assault
Delhi Gun House
DeSantis Holster & Leather Goods, Inc.
Dillon Precision Products, Inc.
Dixie Gun Works
Don Hume Leathergoods
Eagle Imports, Inc.
El Paso Saddlery Co.
Ellett Bros.
EMF Co. Inc.
Faust Inc., T. G.

Freedom Arms, Inc.
Gage Manufacturing
GALCO International Ltd.
Gil Hebard Guns, Inc.
Gilmore Sports Concepts, Inc.
GML Products, Inc.
Gould & Goodrich Leather, Inc.
Gun Leather Limited
Gun Works, The
Hafner World Wide, Inc.
HandCrafts Unltd. (See Clements' Custom Leathercraft)
Hank's Gun Shop
Heinie Specialty Products
Henigson & Associates, Steve
Hill Speed Leather, Ernie
HIP-GRIP Barami Corp.
Hobson Precision Mfg. Co.
Hogue Grips
Horseshoe Leather Products
Hunter Co., Inc.
Jeff's Outfitters
Jim Noble Co.
John's Custom Leather
Kirkpatrick Leather Co.
Kolpin Outdoors, Inc.
Korth Germany GmbH
Kramer Handgun Leather
L.A.R. Mfg., Inc.
Lawrence Leather Co.
Lock's Philadelphia Gun Exchange
Lone Star Gunleather
Markell, Inc.
Marksman Products
Michaels of Oregon Co.
Minute Man High Tech Industries
National Gun, Inc.
Navy Arms Co.
No-Sho Mfg. Co.
Null Holsters Ltd. K.L.
October Country Muzzleloading
Oklahoma Leather Products, Inc.
Old West Reproductions, Inc. R.M. Bachman
Outdoor Connection, Inc., The
Pager Pal
Parker & Sons Shooting Supply
Pathfinder Sports Leather
Police Bookshelf
Protektor Model
PWL Gunleather
Renegade
Ringler Custom Leather Co.
Rogue Rifle Co., Inc./Chipmunk Rifles
S&S Firearms
Safariland Ltd., Inc.
Scharch Mfg., Inc.-Top Brass
Schulz Industries
Second Chance Body Armor
SGS Importer's International, Inc.
Silhouette Leathers
Smith Saddlery, Jesse W.
Sparks, Milt
Stalker, Inc.
Starr Trading Co., Jedediah
Strong Holster Co.
Stuart, V. Pat
Tabler Marketing
Tactical Defense Institute
Ted Blocker Holsters
Tex Shoemaker & Sons, Inc.
Thad Rybka Custom Leather Equipment
Torel, Inc./Tandy Brands Outdoors/AA & E

Triple-K Mfg. Co., Inc.
Tristar Sporting Arms, Ltd.
Uncle Mike's (See Michaels of Oregon, Co.)
Venus Industries
W. Waller & Son, Inc.
Walt's Custom Leather, Walt Whinnery
Watson Bullets
Westley Richards & Co. Ltd.
Whinnery, Walt (See Walt's Custom Leather)
Wild Bill's Originals
Wilsom Combat

HUNTING & CAMP GEAR, CLOTHING, ETC.

A.W. Peterson Gun Shop, Inc., The
Action Direct, Inc.
Action Products, Inc.
Adventure 16, Inc.
All Rite Products, Inc.
Alpha 1 Drop Zone
Armor (See Buck Stop Lure Co., Inc.)
Atlanta Cutlery Corp.
Atsko/Sno-Seal, Inc.
Bagmaster Mfg., Inc.
Barbour, Inc.
Bauer, Eddie
Bear Archery
Beaver Park Product, Inc.
Beretta Pietro S.P.A.
Better Concepts Co.
Bill Russ Trading Post
Bob Allen Sportswear
Boonie Packer Products
Boss Manufacturing Co.
Browning Arms Co.
Buck Stop Lure Co., Inc.
Bushmaster Hunting & Fishing
Camp-Cap Products
Carhartt, Inc.
Case & Sons Cutlery Co., W R
Churchill Glove Co., James
Clarkfield Enterprises, Inc.
Classic Old West Styles
Clements' Custom Leathercraft, Chas
Coghlan's Ltd.
Cold Steel Inc.
Coleman Co., Inc.
Coulston Products, Inc.
Counter Assault
Dakota Corp.
Danner Shoe Mfg. Co.
Deepeeka Exports Pvt. Ltd.
Dr. O's Products Ltd.
Duofold, Inc.
Dynalite Products, Inc.
E-A-R, Inc.
Flambeau, Inc.
Forrest Tool Co.
Fox River Mills, Inc.
Frontier
G&H Decoys, Inc.
Gerber Legendary Blades
Glacier Glove
Grand Slam Hunting Products
HandCrafts Unltd. (See Clements' Custom Leathercraft)
High North Products, Inc.
Hinman Outfitters, Bob
Hodgman, Inc.
Houtz & Barwick
Hunter's Specialties Inc.
James Churchill Glove Co.

John's Custom Leather
K&M Industries, Inc.
Kamik Outdoor Footwear
Kolpin Outdoors, Inc.
L.L. Bean, Inc.
LaCrosse Footwear, Inc.
Leapers, Inc.
MAG Instrument, Inc.
Mag-Na-Port International, Inc.
McCann Industries
Murphy, R.R. Co., Inc.
Original Deer Formula Co., The
Orvis Co., The
Palsa Outdoor Products
Partridge Sales Ltd., John
Pointing Dog Journal, Village Press Publications
Powell & Son (Gunmakers) Ltd., William
Pro-Mark Div. of Wells Lamont
Ringler Custom Leather Co.
Rocky Shoes & Boots
Scansport, Inc.
Sceery Game Calls
Schaefer Shooting Sports
Servus Footwear Co.
Simmons Outdoor Corp.
Sno-Seal, Inc. (See Atsko/Sno-Seal, Inc.)
TEN-X Products Group
Tink's Safariland Hunting Corp.
Torel, Inc./Tandy Brands Outdoors/AA & E
Triple-K Mfg. Co., Inc.
Tru-Nord Compass
United Cutlery Corp.
Venus Industries
Walls Industries, Inc.
Wideview Scope Mount Corp.
Wilderness Sound Products Ltd.
Winchester Sutler, Inc., The
Wolverine Footwear Group
Woolrich, Inc.
Wyoming Knife Corp.

KNIVES & KNIFEMAKER'S SUPPLIES

A.G. Russell Knives, Inc.
A.W. Peterson Gun Shop, Inc., The
Action Direct, Inc.
Adventure 16, Inc.
African Import Co.
Aitor-Berrizargo S.L.
American Target Knives
Art Jewel Enterprises Ltd.
Atlanta Cutlery Corp.
B&D Trading Co., Inc.
Barteaux Machete
Beitzinger, George
Benchmark Knives (See Gerber Legendary Blades)
Beretta Pietro S.P.A.
Beretta U.S.A. Corp.
Bill Russ Trading Post
Boker USA, Inc.
Boone Trading Co., Inc.
Boone's Custom Ivory Grips, Inc.
Bowen Knife Co., Inc.
Brooks Tactical Systems-Agrip
Browning Arms Co.
Buck Knives, Inc.
Buster's Custom Knives
Cain's Outdoors, Inc.
Camillus Cutlery Co.
Campbell, Dick
Case & Sons Cutlery Co., W R

Chicago Cutlery Co.
Claro Walnut Gunstock Co.
Clements' Custom Leathercraft, Chas
Cold Steel Inc.
Coleman Co., Inc.
Collector's Armoury, Ltd.
Compass Industries, Inc.
Creative Craftsman, Inc., The
Crosman Blades (See Coleman Co., Inc.)
CRR, Inc./Marble's Inc.
Cutco Cutlery
damascususa@inteliport.com
Dan's Whetstone Co., Inc.
Deepeeka Exports Pvt. Ltd.
Delhi Gun House
DeSantis Holster & Leather Goods, Inc.
Diamond Machining Technology Inc. (See DMT)
Dixie Gun Works
Dolbare, Elizabeth
EdgeCraft Corp., S. Weiner
Empire Cutlery Corp.
Eze-Lap Diamond Prods.
Flitz International Ltd.
Forrest Tool Co.
Forthofer's Gunsmithing & Knifemaking
Fortune Products, Inc.
Frank Knives
Frost Cutlery Co.
Galati International
George Ibberson (Sheffield) Ltd.
Gerber Legendary Blades
Glock, Inc.
Golden Age Arms Co.
Gun Room, The
Gun Works, The
H&B Forge Co.
Hafner World Wide, Inc.
Hammans, Charles E.
HandCrafts Unltd. (See Clements' Custom Leathercraft)
Harris Publications
High North Products, Inc.
Hoppe's Div. Penguin Industries, Inc.
Hunter Co., Inc.
J.A. Blades, Inc. (See Christopher Firearms Co.)
J.A. Henckels Zwillingswerk Inc.
Jantz Supply, Inc.
Jenco Sales, Inc.
Jim Blair Engraving
Johnson Wood Products
KA-BAR Knives
Kasenit Co., Inc.
Kershaw Knives
Knifeware, Inc.
Koval Knives
Lamson & Goodnow Mfg. Co.
Lansky Sharpeners
Leapers, Inc.
Leatherman Tool Group, Inc.
Lethal Force Institute (See Police Bookshelf)
Marble Arms (See CRR, Inc./ Marble's Inc.)
McCann Industries
Normark Corp.
North Star West, Inc.
October Country Muzzleloading
Outdoor Edge Cutlery Corp.
Plaza Cutlery, Inc.
Police Bookshelf
Queen Cutlery Co.

PRODUCT & SERVICE DIRECTORY

R&C Knives & Such
R. Murphy Co., Inc.
Randall-Made Knives
Robert Valade Engraving
Scansport, Inc.
Schiffman, Mike
Sheffield Knifemakers Supply, Inc.
Sigarms Inc.
Smith Saddlery, Jesse W.
Springfield Armory
Spyderco, Inc.
Starr Trading Co., Jedediah
T.F.C. S.p.A.
Terry Theis-Engraver
Traditions Performance Firearms
Tru-Balance Knife Co.
Tru-Nord Compass
United Cutlery Corp.
Utica Cutlery Co.
Venus Industries
W.R. Case & Sons Cutlery Co.
Washita Mountain Whetstone Co.
Wells Creek Knife & Gun Works
Wenger North America/Precise Int'l.
Western Cutlery (See Camillus Cutlery Co.)
Whinnery, Walt (See Walt's Custom Leather)
Wideview Scope Mount Corp.
Wyoming Knife Corp.

LABELS, BOXES & CARTRIDGE HOLDERS

Ballistic Products, Inc.
Berry's Mfg., Inc.
Cabinet Mtn. Outfitters Scents & Lures
Cheyenne Pioneer Products
Del Rey Products
DeSantis Holster & Leather Goods, Inc.
Flambeau, Inc.
Hafner World Wide, Inc.
J&J Products, Inc.
Kolpin Outdoors, Inc.
Liberty Shooting Supplies
Midway Arms, Inc.
MTM Molded Products Co., Inc.
Outdoor Connection, Inc., The
Walt's Custom Leather, Walt Whinnery
Ziegel Engineering

LEAD WIRES & WIRE CUTTERS

Ames Metal Products Co.
Big Bore Express
Bullet Swaging Supply, Inc.
Corbin Mfg. & Supply, Inc.
D.L. Unmussig Bullets
Liberty Mfg., Inc.
Lightning Performance Innovations, Inc.
Montana Precision Swaging
Northern Precision
Sport Flite Manufacturing Co.
Star Ammunition, Inc.

LOAD TESTING & PRODUCT TESTING

Ballistic Research
Bridgeman Products

Briese Bullet Co., Inc.
Buckskin Bullet Co.
Clearview Products
Dead Eye's Sport Center
Defense Training International, Inc.
Duane's Gun Repair (See DGR Custom Rifles)
Gruning Precision, Inc.
H.P. White Laboratory, Inc.
Hank's Gun Shop
Henigson & Associates, Steve
J&J Sales
Jensen Bullets
Jonathan Arthur Ciener, Inc.
L. E. Jurras & Assoc.
L.B.T.
Liberty Shooting Supplies
Linebaugh Custom Sixguns
Lomont Precision Bullets
McMurdo, Lynn
Middlebrooks Custom Shop
Modern Gun Repair School
Multiplex International
Oil Rod and Gun Shop
Plum City Ballistic Range
R.A. Wells Custom Gunsmith
Rupert's Gun Shop
SOS Products Co. (See Buck Stix-SOS Products Co.)
Spencer's Rifle Barrels, Inc.
Tar-Hunt Custom Rifles, Inc.
Trinidad St. Jr. Col. Gunsmith Dept.
Vulpes Ventures, Inc., Fox Cartridge Division
W. Square Enterprises
X-Spand Target Systems

LOADING BLOCKS, METALLIC & SHOTSHELL

A.W. Peterson Gun Shop, Inc., The
Battenfeld Technologies, Inc.
Buffalo Arms Co.
Huntington Die Specialties
Jericho Tool & Die Co., Inc.
Sinclair International, Inc.

LUBRISIZERS, DIES & ACCESSORIES

A.W. Peterson Gun Shop, Inc., The
Ballisti-Cast, Inc.
Buffalo Arms Co.
Cast Performance Bullet Co.
Cooper-Woodward Perfect Lube
Eagan Gunsmiths
GAR
Hart & Son, Inc.
Javelina Lube Products
Lee Precision, Inc.
Lithi Bee Bullet Lube
Lyman Products Corp.
Magma Engineering Co.
PWM Sales Ltd.
RCBS Operations/ATK
S&S Firearms
SPG, Inc.
Thompson Bullet Lube Co.
United States Products Co.
WTA Manufacturing

MOULDS & MOULD ACCESSORIES

A.W. Peterson Gun Shop, Inc., The

Ad Hominem
American Products, Inc.
Ballisti-Cast, Inc.
Buffalo Arms Co.
Bullet Swaging Supply, Inc.
Cast Performance Bullet Co.
Davide Pedersoli and Co.
Eagan Gunsmiths
GAR
Gun Works, The
Huntington Die Specialties
L.B.T.
Lee Precision, Inc.
Lyman Products Corp.
Magma Engineering Co.
MEC-Gar S.R.L.
North Star West, Inc.
Old West Bullet Moulds
Pacific Rifle Co.
Penn Bullets
Peter Dyson & Son Ltd.
Rapine Bullet Mould Mfg. Co.
RCBS Operations/ATK
S&S Firearms

MUZZLE-LOADING GUNS, BARRELS & EQUIPMENT

A.W. Peterson Gun Shop, Inc., The
Accuracy Unlimited
Ackerman & Co.
Allen Mfg.
Armi San Paolo
Austin & Halleck, Inc.
Bentley, John
Big Bore Express
Birdsong & Assoc., W. E.
Black Powder Products
Blount/Outers ATK
Blue and Gray Products Inc. (See Ox-Yoke Originals)
Buckskin Bullet Co.
Bullberry Barrel Works, Ltd.
Butler Creek Corp.
Cabela's
Cain's Outdoors, Inc.
California Sights (See Fautheree, Andy)
Cash Mfg. Co./ TDC
Caywood Gunmakers
CBC-BRAZIL
Chambers Flintlocks Ltd., Jim
Chicasaw Gun Works
Cimarron F.A. Co.
Cogar's Gunsmithing
Colonial Repair
Colt Blackpowder Arms Co.
Cousin Bob's Mountain Products
Curly Maple Stock Blanks (See Tiger-Hunt)
CVA
Dangler's Custom Flint Rifles
Davide Pedersoli and Co.
Dayton Traister
deHaas Barrels
Delhi Gun House
Dixie Gun Works
Dixon Muzzleloading Shop, Inc.
Dolbare, Elizabeth
Ellett Bros.
EMF Co. Inc.
Euroarms of America, Inc.
Flintlocks, Etc.
Fort Hill Gunstocks
Fowler, Bob (See Black Powder Products)
Frontier

Getz Barrel Co.
Goergen's Gun Shop, Inc.
Golden Age Arms Co.
Green Mountain Rifle Barrel Co., Inc.
Gun Works, The
H&R 1871, LLC
Hastings
Hawken Shop, The
Hawken Shop, The (See Dayton Traister)
Hege Jagd-u. Sporthandels GmbH
Hodgdon Powder Co.
Hoppe's Div. Penguin Industries, Inc.
Hornady Mfg. Co.
House of Muskets, Inc., The
Hydra-Tone Chemicals, Inc.
IAR Inc.
Impact Case & Container, Inc.
Ironsighter Co.
J. Dewey Mfg. Co., Inc.
Jamison's Forge Works
K&M Industries, Inc.
Kalispel Case Line
Kennedy Firearms
Knight Rifles
Knight Rifles (See Modern Muzzleloading, Inc.)
Kolar
L&R Lock Co.
L&S Technologies Inc. (See Aimtech Mount Systems)
Lakewood Products Div of Midwest Textile
Lodgewood Mfg.
Log Cabin Sport Shop
Lothar Walther Precision Tool Inc.
Lyman Products Corp.
Markesbery Muzzle Loaders, Inc.
Mathews Gun Shop & Gunsmithing, Inc.
McCann, Tom
Michaels of Oregon Co.
Millennium Designed Muzzleloaders
Modern Muzzleloading, Inc.
Mowrey Gun Works
Navy Arms Co.
Newman Gunshop
North Star West, Inc.
October Country Muzzleloading
Oklahoma Leather Products, Inc.
Olson, Myron
Orion Rifle Barrel Co.
Pacific Rifle Co.
Parker & Sons Shooting Supply
Parker Gun Finishes
Pecatonica River Longrifle
Peter Dyson & Son Ltd.
Pioneer Arms Co.
Rossi Firearms
S&S Firearms
Selsi Co., Inc.
Simmons Gun Repair, Inc.
Sklany's Machine Shop
Smokey Valley Rifles
South Bend Replicas, Inc.
Southern Bloomer Mfg. Co.
Splitfire Sporting Goods, L.L.C.
Starr Trading Co., Jedediah
Stone Mountain Arms
Sturm Ruger & Co. Inc.
Taylor's & Co., Inc.
Tennessee Valley Mfg.
Thompson Bullet Lube Co.

Thompson/Center Arms
Tiger-Hunt Longrifle Gunstocks
Track of the Wolf, Inc.
Traditions Performance Firearms
Truglo, Inc.
Uncle Mike's (See Michaels of Oregon, Co.)
Universal Sports
Upper Missouri Trading Co.
Venco Industries, Inc. (See Shooter's Choice Gun Care)
Village Restorations & Consulting, Inc.
Virgin Valley Custom Guns
Voere-KGH GmbH
W.E. Birdsong & Assoc.
Wescombe, Bill (See North Star West)
White Rifles, Inc.
William E. Phillips Firearms
Woodworker's Supply
Wright's Gunstock Blanks
Young Country Arms
Ziegel Engineering

PISTOLSMITH

A.W. Peterson Gun Shop, Inc., The
Acadian Ballistic Specialties
Accuracy Unlimited
Actions by "T" Teddy Jacobson
Adair Custom Shop, Bill
Ahlman Guns
Aldis Gunsmithing & Shooting Supply
Alpha Precision, Inc.
Alpine Indoor Shooting Range
Armament Gunsmithing Co., Inc.
Bain & Davis, Inc.
Bar-Sto Precision Machine
Bengtson Arms Co., L.
Bill Adair Custom Shop
Billings Gunsmiths
Bowen Classic Arms Corp.
Broken Gun Ranch
Caraville Manufacturing
Chicasaw Gun Works
Chip McCormick Corp.
Clark Custom Guns, Inc.
Colonial Repair
Colorado School of Trades
Colt's Mfg. Co., Inc.
Corkys Gun Clinic
Cylinder & Slide, Inc., William R. Laughridge
D&D Gunsmiths, Ltd.
D&L Sports
David R. Chicoine
Dayton Traister
Dilliott Gunsmithing, Inc.
Duncan's Gun Works, Inc.
Ellicott Arms, Inc. / Woods Pistolsmithing
Evolution Gun Works, Inc.
Ferris Firearms
Firearm Brokers
Fisher Custom Firearms
Forkin Custom Classics
G.G. & G.
Garthwaite Pistolsmith, Inc., Jim
Gary Reeder Custom Guns
Genecco Gun Works
Gentry Custom LLC
Greider Precision
Gun Doc, Inc.
Gun Works, The
Guncraft Sports, Inc.
Gunsite Training Center

Hamilton, Alex B. (See Ten-Ring Precision, Inc.)
Hammerli Service-Precision Mac
Hammond Custom Guns Ltd.
Hank's Gun Shop
Hanson's Gun Center, Dick
Hawken Shop, The (See Dayton Traister)
Heinie Specialty Products
High Bridge Arms, Inc.
High Standard Mfg. Co./F.I., Inc.
Hoag, James W.
Irwin, Campbell H.
Ivanoff, Thomas G. (See Tom's Gun Repair)
J R Guns
J&S Heat Treat
Jackalope Gun Shop
Jarvis, Inc.
Jensen's Arizona Sportsman
Jungkind, Reeves C.
Kaswer Custom, Inc.
Ken Starnes Gunmaker
Kilham & Co.
King's Gun Works
La Clinique du .45
LaFrance Specialties
LaRocca Gun Works
Lathrop's, Inc.
Lawson, John G. (See Sight Shop, The)
Leckie Professional Gunsmithing
Les Baer Custom, Inc.
Linebaugh Custom Sixguns
List Precision Engineering
Long, George F.
Mag-Na-Port International, Inc.
Mahovsky's Metalife
Marvel, Alan
Mathews Gun Shop & Gunsmithing, Inc.
MCS, Inc.
Middlebrooks Custom Shop
Miller Custom
Mitchell's Accuracy Shop
MJK Gunsmithing, Inc.
Modern Gun Repair School
Mo's Competitor Supplies (See MCS, Inc.)
Mowrey's Guns & Gunsmithing
Mullis Guncraft
NCP Products, Inc.
Novak's, Inc.
Nowlin Mfg. Co.
Olathe Gun Shop
Paris, Frank J.
Pasadena Gun Center
Peacemaker Specialists
Performance Specialists
Peterson Gun Shop, Inc., A.W.
Piquette's Custom Engraving
Power Custom, Inc.
Precision Specialties
Randco UK
Ries, Chuck
Rim Pac Sports, Inc.
Robar Co., Inc., The
RPM
Ruger's Custom Guns
Score High Gunsmithing
Shooters Supply
Shootin' Shack
Sight Shop, The
Singletary, Kent
Spradlin's
Springfield, Inc.
SSK Industries
State Line Gun Shop

Swenson's 45 Shop, A. D.
Swift River Gunworks
Ten-Ring Precision, Inc.
Terry K. Kopp Professional Gunsmithing
Time Precision
Tom's Gun Repair, Thomas G. Ivanoff
Turnbull Restoration, Doug
Vic's Gun Refinishing
Volquartsen Custom Ltd.
Walker Arms Co., Inc.
Walters Industries
Wardell Precision
Wessinger Custom Guns & Engraving
White Barn Wor
Wichita Arms, Inc.
Wild West Guns
Williams Gun Sight Co.
Williamson Precision Gunsmithing
Wilsom Combat
Wright's Gunstock Blanks

POWDER MEASURES, SCALES, FUNNELS & ACCESSORIES

A.W. Peterson Gun Shop, Inc., The
Battenfeld Technologies, Inc.
Buffalo Arms Co.
Cain's Outdoors, Inc.
CH Tool & Die/4-D Custom Die Co.
Davide Pedersoli and Co.
Dillon Precision Products, Inc.
Fremont Tool Works
Frontier
GAR
High Precision
Hoehn Sales, Inc.
J R Guns
Jones Custom Products, Neil A.
Modern Muzzleloading, Inc.
Neil A. Jones Custom Products
Pacific Rifle Co.
Precision Reloading, Inc.
RCBS Operations/ATK
Redding Reloading Equipment
Saunders Gun & Machine Shop
Schumakers Gun Shop
Spencer's Rifle Barrels, Inc.
Vega Tool Co.
VibraShine, Inc.
VTI Gun Parts

PRESS ACCESSORIES, METALLIC

A.W. Peterson Gun Shop, Inc., The
Buffalo Arms Co.
Hollywood Engineering
Huntington Die Specialties
MA Systems, Inc.
R.E.I.
Redding Reloading Equipment
Thompson Tool Mount
Vega Tool Co.

PRESS ACCESSORIES, SHOTSHELL

A.W. Peterson Gun Shop, Inc., The
Hollywood Engineering

Lee Precision, Inc.
MEC, Inc.
Precision Reloading, Inc.
R.E.I.

PRESSES, ARBOR

A.W. Peterson Gun Shop, Inc., The
Blue Ridge Machinery & Tools, Inc.
Hoehn Sales, Inc.
K&M Services
RCBS Operations/ATK
Spencer's Rifle Barrels, Inc.

PRESSES, METALLIC

A.W. Peterson Gun Shop, Inc., The
Austin Sheridan USA, Inc.
Battenfeld Technologies, Inc.
CH Tool & Die/4-D Custom Die Co.
Dillon Precision Products, Inc.
Fremont Tool Works
Hornady Mfg. Co.
Huntington Die Specialties
Lee Precision, Inc.
Meacham Tool & Hardware Co., Inc.
Midway Arms, Inc.
R.E.I.
RCBS Operations/ATK
Spencer's Rifle Barrels, Inc.

PRESSES, SHOTSHELL

A.W. Peterson Gun Shop, Inc., The
Ballistic Products, Inc.
Dillon Precision Products, Inc.
Hornady Mfg. Co.
MEC, Inc.
Precision Reloading, Inc.
Spolar Power Load, Inc.

PRESSES, SWAGE

A.W. Peterson Gun Shop, Inc., The
Bullet Swaging Supply, Inc.
Corbin Mfg. & Supply, Inc.
Howell Machine, Inc.

PRIMING TOOLS & ACCESSORIES

A.W. Peterson Gun Shop, Inc., The
Bald Eagle Precision Machine Co.
GAR
Hart & Son, Inc.
Huntington Die Specialties
K&M Services
RCBS Operations/ATK
Simmons, Jerry
Sinclair International, Inc.

REBORING & RERIFLING

Ahlman Guns
Barrel & Gunworks
Bauska Barrels
BlackStar AccuMax Barrels
BlackStar Barrel Accurizing (See BlackStar AccuMax)
Buffalo Arms Co.
Champlin Firearms, Inc.
Ed's Gun House

Ivanoff, Thomas G. (See Tom's Gun Repair)
Jonathan Arthur Ciener, Inc.
LaBounty Precision Reboring, Inc
NCP Products, Inc.
Pence Precision Barrels
Redman's Rifling & Reboring
Rice, Keith (See White Rock Tool & Die)
Ridgetop Sporting Goods
Savage Arms, Inc.
Shaw, Inc., E. R. (See Small Arms Mfg. Co.)
Siegrist Gun Shop
Simmons Gun Repair, Inc.
Stratco, Inc.
Terry K. Kopp Professional Gunsmithing
Time Precision
Tom's Gun Repair, Thomas G. Ivanoff
Turnbull Restoration, Doug
Van Patten, J. W.
Wells Sport Store
White Rock Tool & Die

RELOADING TOOLS AND ACCESSORIES

Advance Car Mover Co., Rowell Div.
American Products, Inc.
Ammo Load Worldwide, Inc.
Armfield Custom Bullets
Armite Laboratories Inc.
Arms Corp. of the Philippines
Atsko/Sno-Seal, Inc.
Bald Eagle Precision Machine Co.
Ballistic Products, Inc.
BC-Handmade Bullets
Berger Bullets Ltd.
Berry's Mfg., Inc.
Blount, Inc., Sporting Equipment Div.
Blue Mountain Bullets
Blue Ridge Machinery & Tools, Inc.
Bonanza (See Forster Products)
BRP, Inc. High Performance Cast Bullets
Brynin, Milton
Buck Stix-SOS Products Co.
Buffalo Arms Co.
C&D Special Products (See Claybuster Wads & Harvester Bullets)
Camdex, Inc.
Canyon Cartridge Corp.
Case Sorting System
CCI/Speer Div of ATK
CH Tool & Die/4-D Custom Die Co.
CheVron Bullets
Cook Engineering Service
Curtis Cast Bullets
Custom Products (See Jones Custom Products)
CVA
D.C.C. Enterprises
Davide Pedersoli and Co.
Davis, Don
Davis Products, Mike
Denver Instrument Co.
Dillon Precision Products, Inc.
Dropkick
E&L Mfg., Inc.
Eagan Gunsmiths
Eichelberger Bullets, Wm.

Enguix Import-Export
Euroarms of America, Inc.
Federated-Fry (See Fry Metals)
Ferguson, Bill
Fisher Custom Firearms
Flambeau, Inc.
Flitz International Ltd.
Forster Products, Inc.
Fremont Tool Works
Fry Metals
Gehmann, Walter (See Huntington Die Specialties)
Graf & Sons
Graphics Direct
Graves Co.
Green, Arthur S.
Gun City
Hanned Line, The
Hanned Precision (See The Hanned Line)
Harrell's Precision
Harris Enterprises
Harrison Bullets
Heidenstrom Bullets
High Precision
Hirtenberger AG
Hodgdon Powder Co.
Holland's Shooters Supply, Inc.
Hornady Mfg. Co.
Howell Machine, Inc.
Hunters Supply, Inc.
Image Ind. Inc.
Imperial Magnum Corp.
INTEC International, Inc.
Iosso Products
J&L Superior Bullets (See Huntington Die Specialties)
Jack First, Inc.
Javelina Lube Products
JLK Bullets
Jonad Corp.
Jones Custom Products, Neil A.
Jones Moulds, Paul
K&M Services
Kapro Mfg. Co. Inc. (See R.E.I.)
Knoell, Doug
Korzinek Riflesmith, J.
L.A.R. Mfg., Inc.
L.E. Wilson, Inc.
Lee Precision, Inc.
Liberty Mfg., Inc.
Liberty Shooting Supplies
Lightning Performance Innovations, Inc.
Lithi Bee Bullet Lube
Littleton, J. F.
Lock's Philadelphia Gun Exchange
Lyman Instant Targets, Inc. (See Lyman Products Corp.)
Lyman Products Corp.
MA Systems, Inc.
Magma Engineering Co.
Match Prep-Doyle Gracey
Mayville Engineering Co. (See MEC, Inc.)
MCS, Inc.
MEC, Inc.
Midway Arms, Inc.
MI-TE Bullets
Montana Armory, Inc.
Mo's Competitor Supplies (See MCS, Inc.)
MTM Molded Products Co., Inc.
MWG Co.
Nammo Lapua Oy
Navy Arms Co.
Newman Gunshop

PRODUCT & SERVICE DIRECTORY

North Devon Firearms Services
Old West Bullet Moulds
Outdoor Sports Headquarters, Inc.
Paragon Sales & Services, Inc.
Pinetree Bullets
Ponsness, Warren
Professional Hunter Supplies
Protector Mfg. Co., Inc., The
R.A. Wells Custom Gunsmith
R.E.I.
Rapine Bullet Mould Mfg. Co.
Redding Reloading Equipment
Reloading Specialties, Inc.
Rice, Keith (See White Rock Tool & Die)
Rochester Lead Works
Rooster Laboratories
Rorschach Precision Products
SAECO (See Redding Reloading Equipment)
Sandia Die & Cartridge Co.
Saunders Gun & Machine Shop
Saville Iron Co. (See Greenwood Precision)
Seebeck Assoc., R.E.
Sharp Shooter Supply
Sharps Arms Co., Inc., C.
Sierra Specialty Prod. Co.
Silver Eagle Machining
Skip's Machine
Sno-Seal, Inc. (See Atsko/Sno-Seal, Inc.)
SOS Products Co. (See Buck Stix-SOS Products Co.)
Spencer's Rifle Barrels, Inc.
SPG, Inc.
SSK Industries
Stalwart Corp.
Star Custom Bullets
Stoney Point Products, Inc.
Stratco, Inc.
Taracorp Industries, Inc.
TCCI
TCSR
Tetra Gun Care
Thompson/Center Arms
Vega Tool Co.
Venco Industries, Inc. (See Shooter's Choice Gun Care)
VibraShine, Inc.
Vibra-Tek Co.
Vihtavuori Oy/Kaltron-Pettibone
Vitt/Boos
W.B. Niemi Engineering
W.J. Riebe Co.
WD-40 Co.
Webster Scale Mfg. Co.
White Rock Tool & Die
Widener's Reloading & Shooting Supply, Inc.
Wise Custom Guns
Woodleigh (See Huntington Die Specialties)
Young Country Arms

RESTS BENCH, PORTABLE AND ACCESSORIES

A.W. Peterson Gun Shop, Inc., The
Adventure 16, Inc.
Armor Metal Products
B.M.F. Activator, Inc.
Bald Eagle Precision Machine Co.
Bartlett Engineering
Battenfeld Technologies, Inc.
Blount/Outers ATK

Browning Arms Co.
B-Square Co., Inc.
Clift Mfg., L.R.
Desert Mountain Mfg.
Harris Engineering Inc.
Hart & Son, Inc.
Hidalgo, Tony
Hoehn Sales, Inc.
Hoppe's Div. Penguin Industries, Inc.
J&J Sales
Keng's Firearms Specialty, Inc.
Kolpin Outdoors, Inc.
Kramer Designs
Midway Arms, Inc.
Millett Sights
Outdoor Connection, Inc., The
Protektor Model
Ransom International Corp.
Russ Haydon's Shooters' Supply
Saville Iron Co. (See Greenwood Precision)
Sinclair International, Inc.
Six Enterprises
Stoney Point Products, Inc.
Tonoloway Tack Drives
Torel, Inc./Tandy Brands Outdoors/AA & E
Varmint Masters, LLC
Wichita Arms, Inc.
York M-1 Conversion
Zanotti Armor, Inc.
Ziegel Engineering

RIFLE BARREL MAKER

Airrow
American Safe Arms, Inc.
Barrel & Gunworks
Bauska Barrels
BlackStar AccuMax Barrels
BlackStar Barrel Accurizing (See BlackStar AccuMax)
Border Barrels Ltd.
Buchsenmachermeister
Bullberry Barrel Works, Ltd.
Bushmaster Firearms, Inc.
Carter's Gun Shop
Christensen Arms
Cincinnati Swaging
D.L. Unmussig Bullets
deHaas Barrels
Dilliott Gunsmithing, Inc.
Dina Arms Corp.
DKT, Inc.
Donnelly, C. P.
Douglas Barrels, Inc.
Gaillard Barrels
Getz Barrel Co.
Granite Mountain Arms, Inc.
Green Mountain Rifle Barrel Co., Inc.
Gruning Precision, Inc.
Gun Works, The
Half Moon Rifle Shop
Hart Rifle Barrels, Inc.
Hastings
Hofer Jagdwaffen, P.
H-S Precision, Inc.
Krieger Barrels, Inc.
Les Baer Custom, Inc.
Lilja Precision Rifle Barrels
Lothar Walther Precision Tool Inc.
Martini & Hagn, Ltd.
McGowen Rifle Barrels
McMillan Rifle Barrels
Mid-America Recreation, Inc.
Modern Gun Repair School

Morrison Precision
Obermeyer Rifled Barrels
Olympic Arms Inc.
Orion Rifle Barrel Co.
PAC-NOR Barreling, Inc.
Pence Precision Barrels
Perazone-Gunsmith, Brian
Rogue Rifle Co., Inc./Chipmunk Rifles
Sabatti SPA
Savage Arms, Inc.
Schneider Rifle Barrels, Inc.
Shaw, Inc., E. R. (See Small Arms Mfg. Co.)
Shilen, Inc.
Siskiyou Gun Works (See Donnelly, C. P.)
Small Arms Mfg. Co.
Specialty Shooters Supply, Inc.
Spencer's Rifle Barrels, Inc.
Steyr Mannlicher GmbH & Co. KG
Strutz Rifle Barrels, Inc., W. C.
Swift River Gunworks
Terry K. Kopp Professional Gunsmithing
Turnbull Restoration, Doug
Verney-Carron
Virgin Valley Custom Guns
Wells Sport Store
William E. Phillips Firearms
Wilson Arms Co., The
Wiseman and Co., Bill

SCOPES, MOUNTS, ACCESSORIES, OPTICAL EQUIPMENT

A.R.M.S., Inc.
A.W. Peterson Gun Shop, Inc., The
Accu-Tek
Ackerman, Bill (See Optical Services Co.)
Action Direct, Inc.
ADCO Sales, Inc.
Aimpoint, Inc.
Aimtech Mount Systems
Air Venture Airguns
All Rite Products, Inc.
Alley Supply Co.
Alpec Team, Inc.
Apel GmbH, Ernst
ArmaLite, Inc.
B.A.C.
B.M.F. Activator, Inc.
Bansner's Ultimate Rifles, LLC
Barrett Firearms Manufacturer, Inc.
Beaver Park Product, Inc.
BEC, Inc.
Beeman Precision Airguns
Benjamin/Sheridan Co., Crosman
Bill Russ Trading Post
BKL Technologies
Blount, Inc., Sporting Equipment Div.
Blount/Outers ATK
Borden Rifles Inc.
Broad Creek Rifle Works, Ltd.
Brockman's Custom Gunsmithing
Brownells, Inc.
Brunton U.S.A.
BSA Optics
B-Square Co., Inc.
Bull Mountain Rifle Co.
Burris Co., Inc.
Bushmaster Firearms, Inc.
Bushnell Outdoor Products

Butler Creek Corp.
Cabela's
Carl Zeiss Inc.
Center Lock Scope Rings
Chuck's Gun Shop
Clark Custom Guns, Inc.
Clearview Mfg. Co., Inc.
Compass Industries, Inc.
Compasseco, Ltd.
Concept Development Corp.
Conetrol Scope Mounts
Creedmoor Sports, Inc.
Crimson Trace Lasers
Crosman Airguns
D.C. Engineering, Inc.
D.C.C. Enterprises
D.L. Unmussig Bullets
Daisy Outdoor Products
Del-Sports, Inc.
DHB Products
Dolbare, Elizabeth
E. Arthur Brown Co. Inc.
Eagle Imports, Inc.
Edmund Scientific Co.
Eggleston, Jere D.
Ellett Bros.
Emerging Technologies, Inc. (See Laseraim Technologies, Inc.)
Entreprise Arms, Inc.
Evolution Gun Works, Inc.
Excalibur Electro Optics, Inc.
Excel Industries, Inc.
Falcon Industries, Inc.
Farr Studio, Inc.
Freedom Arms, Inc.
Fujinon, Inc.
G.G. & G.
Galati International
Gentry Custom LLC
Gil Hebard Guns, Inc.
Gilmore Sports Concepts, Inc.
Goodwin's Guns
GSI, Inc.
Gun South, Inc. (See GSI, Inc.)
Gunsmithing, Inc.
Hammerli USA
Hart & Son, Inc.
Harvey, Frank
Highwood Special Products
Hiptmayer, Armurier
Hiptmayer, Klaus
Hoehn Sales, Inc.
Holland's Shooters Supply, Inc.
Hunter Co., Inc.
Impact Case & Container, Inc.
Ironsighter Co.
J R Guns
Jantz Supply, Inc.
Jena Eur
Jerry Phillips Optics
Jewell Triggers, Inc.
John Masen Co. Inc.
John's Custom Leather
Kahles A. Swarovski Co.
Kalispel Case Line
KDF, Inc.
Keng's Firearms Specialty, Inc.
Kesselring Gun Shop
Kimber of America, Inc.
Knight's Manufacturing Co.
Kowa Optimed, Inc.
KVH Industries, Inc.
Kwik-Site Co.
L&S Technologies Inc. (See Aimtech Mount Systems)
L.A.R. Mfg., Inc.
Laser Devices, Inc.
Laseraim Technologies, Inc.
LaserMax
Leapers, Inc.

Leica Sport Optics
Les Baer Custom, Inc.
Leupold & Stevens, Inc.
List Precision Engineering
Lohman Mfg. Co., Inc.
Lomont Precision Bullets
London Guns Ltd.
Mac-1 Airgun Distributors
Mag-Na-Port International, Inc.
Marksman Products
Maxi-Mount Inc.
McMillan Optical Gunsight Co.
MCS, Inc.
MDS
Meopta USA, LLC
Merit Corp.
Military Armament Corp.
Millett Sights
Mirador Optical Corp.
Mitchell Optics, Inc.
MMC
Monell Custom Guns
Mo's Competitor Supplies (See MCS, Inc.)
MWG Co.
Navy Arms Co.
New England Custom Gun Service
Nikon, Inc.
Norincoptics (See BEC, Inc.)
Olympic Optical Co.
Op-Tec
Optical Services Co.
Orchard Park Enterprise
Oregon Arms, Inc. (See Rogue Rifle Co., Inc.)
Outdoor Connection, Inc., The
Parker & Sons Shooting Supply
Parsons Optical Mfg. Co.
PECAR Herbert Schwarz GmbH
Pentax U.S.A., Inc.
PMC/Eldorado Cartridge Corp.
Precision Sport Optics
Quarton Beamshot
R.A. Wells Custom Gunsmith
Ram-Line ATK
Ranch Products
Randolph Engineering, Inc.
Rice, Keith (See White Rock Tool & Die)
Robinson Armament Co.
Rogue Rifle Co., Inc./Chipmunk Rifles
Romain's Custom Guns, Inc.
RPM
S&K Scope Mounts
Saunders Gun & Machine Shop
Schmidt & Bender, Inc.
Schumakers Gun Shop
Scope Control, Inc.
Score High Gunsmithing
Segway Industries
Selsi Co., Inc.
Sharp Shooter Supply
Shepherd Enterprises, Inc.
Sightron, Inc.
Simmons Outdoor Corp.
Six Enterprises
Southern Bloomer Mfg. Co.
Spencer's Rifle Barrels, Inc.
Splitfire Sporting Goods, L.L.C.
Sportsmatch U.K. Ltd.
Spradlin's
Springfield Armory
Springfield, Inc.
SSK Industries
Stiles Custom Guns
Stoeger Industries
Stoney Point Products, Inc.
Sturm Ruger & Co. Inc.

Sunny Hill Enterprises, Inc.
Swarovski Optik North America Ltd.
Swift Instruments
T.K. Lee Co.
Talley, Dave
Tasco Sales, Inc.
Tele-Optics
Thompson/Center Arms
Traditions Performance Firearms
Trijicon, Inc.
Truglo, Inc.
U.S. Optics, A Division of Zeitz Optics U.S.A.
Ultra Dot Distribution
Uncle Mike's (See Michaels of Oregon, Co.)
Unertl Optical Co., Inc.
United Binocular Co.
Virgin Valley Custom Guns
Voere-KGH GmbH
Watson Bullets
Weaver Products ATK
Weaver Scope Repair Service
Webley and Scott Ltd.
Weigand Combat Handguns, Inc.
Wessinger Custom Guns & Engraving
Westley Richards & Co. Ltd.
White Rifles, Inc.
White Rock Tool & Die
Whitestone Lumber Corp.
Wideview Scope Mount Corp.
Wilcox Industries Corp.
Wild West Guns
Williams Gun Sight Co.
York M-1 Conversion
Zanotti Armor, Inc.

SHELLHOLDERS

A.W. Peterson Gun Shop, Inc., The
CH Tool & Die/4-D Custom Die Co.
Fremont Tool Works
GAR
Hart & Son, Inc.
Huntington Die Specialties
K&M Services
King & Co.
Protektor Model
PWM Sales Ltd.
RCBS Operations/ATK
Redding Reloading Equipment
Vega Tool Co.

SHOOTING/TRAINING SCHOOL

Alpine Indoor Shooting Range
American Gunsmithing Institute
American Small Arms Academy
Auto Arms
Beretta U.S.A. Corp.
Bob's Tactical Indoor Shooting Range & Gun Shop
Bridgeman Products
Chapman Academy of Practical Shooting
Chelsea Gun Club of New York City, Inc.
CQB Training
Defense Training International, Inc.
Executive Protection Institute
Ferris Firearms
Front Sight Firearms Training Institute

Gene's Custom Guns
Gentner Bullets
Gilmore Sports Concepts, Inc.
Griffin & Howe, Inc.
Gun Doc, Inc.
Guncraft Books (See Guncraft Sports, Inc.)
Guncraft Sports, Inc.
Gunsite Training Center
Henigson & Associates, Steve
High North Products, Inc.
Jensen's Arizona Sportsman
Jensen's Firearms Academy
L.L. Bean, Inc.
Lethal Force Institute (See Police Bookshelf)
Long, George F.
McMurdo, Lynn
Mendez, John A.
Midwest Shooting School, The
NCP Products, Inc.
North American Shooting Systems
North Mountain Pine Training Center (See Executive Protection Institute)
Nowlin Mfg. Co.
Paxton Quigley's Personal Protection Strategies
Pentheny de Pentheny
Performance Specialists
Protektor Model
SAFE
Shoot Where You Look
Shooter's World
Shooters, Inc.
SIGARMS Inc.
Smith & Wesson
Specialty Gunsmithing
Starlight Training Center, Inc.
Tactical Defense Institute
The Midwest Shooting School
Thunder Ranch
Western Missouri Shooters Alliance
Yankee Gunsmith "Just Glocks"
Yavapai Firearms Academy Ltd.

SHOTSHELL MISCELLANY

A.W. Peterson Gun Shop, Inc., The
American Products, Inc.
Ballistic Products, Inc.
Bridgeman Products
Gun Works, The
Lee Precision, Inc.
MEC, Inc.
Precision Reloading, Inc.
R.E.I.
RCBS Operations/ATK
T&S Industries, Inc.
Vitt/Boos
Ziegel Engineering

SIGHTS, METALLIC

100 Straight Products, Inc.
A.W. Peterson Gun Shop, Inc., The
Accura-Site (See All's, The Jim Tembelis Co., Inc.)
Ad Hominem
Alley Supply Co.
Alpec Team, Inc.
Andela Tool & Machine, Inc.
AO Sight Systems
ArmaLite, Inc.
Aspen Outfitting Co.
Axtell Rifle Co.

B.A.C.
Ballard Rifle & Cartridge Co., LLC
BEC, Inc.
Bob's Gun Shop
Bo-Mar Tool & Mfg. Co.
Bond Custom Firearms
Bowen Classic Arms Corp.
Brockman's Custom Gunsmithing
Brooks Tactical Systems-Agrip
Brownells, Inc.
Buffalo Arms Co.
Bushmaster Firearms, Inc.
California Sights (See Fautheree, Andy)
Cape Outfitters
Cash Mfg. Co./ TDC
Center Lock Scope Rings
Champion's Choice, Inc.
Chip McCormick Corp.
C-More Systems
Colonial Repair
CRR, Inc./Marble's Inc.
D.C. Engineering, Inc.
Davide Pedersoli and Co.
DHB Products
Dixie Gun Works
DPMS (Defense Procurement Manufacturing Services, Inc.)
Duffy, Charles E. (See Guns Antique & Modern DBA)
E. Arthur Brown Co. Inc.
Effebi SNC-Dr. Franco Beretta
Evolution Gun Works, Inc.
Farr Studio, Inc.
G.G. & G.
Garthwaite Pistolsmith, Inc., Jim
Goergen's Gun Shop, Inc.
Gun Doctor, The
Guns Antique & Modern DBA / Charles E. Duffy
Gunsmithing, Inc.
Hank's Gun Shop
Heidenstrom Bullets
Heinie Specialty Products
Hiptmayer, Armurier
Hiptmayer, Klaus
Innovative Weaponry Inc.
International Shooters Service
J.G. Anschutz GmbH & Co. KG
Jeff's Outfitters
JP Enterprises, Inc.
Keng's Firearms Specialty, Inc.
Knight Rifles
Knight's Manufacturing Co.
L.P.A. Inc.
Leapers, Inc.
Les Baer Custom, Inc.
List Precision Engineering
London Guns Ltd.
Lyman Instant Targets, Inc. (See Lyman Products Corp.)
Marble Arms (See CRR, Inc./ Marble's Inc.)
MCS, Inc.
MEC-Gar S.R.L.
Merit Corp.
Mid-America Recreation, Inc.
Middlebrooks Custom Shop
Millett Sights
MMC
Modern Muzzleloading, Inc.
Montana Armory, Inc.
Montana Vintage Arms
Mo's Competitor Supplies (See MCS, Inc.)
Navy Arms Co.
New England Custom Gun Service

Newman Gunshop
Novak's, Inc.
OK Weber, Inc.
One Ragged Hole
Parker & Sons Shooting Supply
Perazone-Gunsmith, Brian
RPM
Sharps Arms Co., Inc., C.
Slug Site
STI International
T.F.C. S.p.A.
Talley, Dave
Tank's Rifle Shop
Trijicon, Inc.
Truglo, Inc.
U.S. Optics, A Division of Zeitz Optics U.S.A.
Weigand Combat Handguns, Inc.
Wichita Arms, Inc.
Wild West Guns
Williams Gun Sight Co.
Wilsom Combat
XS Sight Systems

STOCK MAKER

Acra-Bond Laminates
Amrine's Gun Shop
Antique Arms Co.
Artistry in Wood
Aspen Outfitting Co.
Bain & Davis, Inc.
Bansner's Ultimate Rifles, LLC
Baron Technology
Billings Gunsmiths
Boltin, John M.
Borden Ridges Rimrock Stocks
Bowerly, Kent
Boyds' Gunstock Industries, Inc.
Brace, Larry D.
Briganti Custom Gunsmith
Broad Creek Rifle Works, Ltd.
Brown Precision, Inc.
Buehler Custom Sporting Arms
Bullberry Barrel Works, Ltd.
Burkhart Gunsmithing, Don
Campbell, Dick
Caywood, Shane J.
Chicasaw Gun Works
Chuck's Gun Shop
Claro Walnut Gunstock Co.
Coffin, Charles H.
Colorado Gunsmithing Academy
Custom Shop, The
Custom Single Shot Rifles
D&D Gunsmiths, Ltd.
Dangler's Custom Flint Rifles
D'Arcy Echols & Co.
David W. Schwartz Custom Guns
DGR Custom Rifles
DGS, Inc., Dale A. Storey
Don Klein Custom Guns
Duncan's Gun Works, Inc.
Erhardt, Dennis
Eversull Co., Inc.
Fieldsport Ltd.
Fisher, Jerry A.
Forster, Larry L.
Gary Goudy Classic Stocks
Genecco Gun Works
Gene's Custom Guns
Gillmann, Edwin
Grace, Charles E.
Great American Gunstock Co.
Gruning Precision, Inc.
Gunsmithing Ltd.
Hank's Gun Shop

Harry Lawson LLC
Heilmann, Stephen
Hensley, Gunmaker, Darwin
Heydenberk, Warren R.
High Tech Specialties, Inc.
Huebner, Corey O.
Jack Dever Co.
Jackalope Gun Shop
Jamison's Forge Works
Jay McCament Custom Gunmaker
Jim Norman Custom Gunstocks
John Rigby & Co.
K. Eversull Co., Inc.
Keith's Custom Gunstocks
Ken Eyster Heritage Gunsmiths, Inc.
Larry Lyons Gunworks
Martini & Hagn, Ltd.
Mathews Gun Shop & Gunsmithing, Inc.
McFarland, Stan
McGowen Rifle Barrels
Mercer Custom Guns
Mid-America Recreation, Inc.
Mike Yee Custom Stocking
Mitchell, Jack
Mobile Area Networks, Inc.
Modern Gun Repair School
Morrow, Bud
Nelson's Custom Guns, Inc.
Nettestad Gun Works
Nickels, Paul R.
Paul and Sharon Dressel
Paul D. Hillmer Custom Gunstocks
Paulsen Gunstocks
Pawling Mountain Club
Pecatonica River Longrifle
Pentheny de Pentheny
Quality Custom Firearms
R&J Gun Shop
R.A. Wells Custom Gunsmith
Richards MicroFit Stocks, Inc.
RMS Custom Gunsmithing
Robinson, Don
Ron Frank Custom
Royal Arms Gunstocks
Ruger's Custom Guns
Skeoch, Brian R.
Smith, Art
Smith, Sharmon
Speiser, Fred D.
Steven Dodd Hughes
Stott's Creek Armory, Inc.
Sturgeon Valley Sporters
Taylor & Robbins
Tennessee Valley Mfg.
Tiger-Hunt Longrifle Gunstocks
Treebone Carving
Tucker, James C.
Turnbull Restoration, Doug
Vest, John
Walker Arms Co., Inc.
Weber & Markin Custom Gunsmiths
Wells Sport Store
Wenig Custom Gunstocks
Werth, T. W.
Wiebe, Duane
Wild West Guns
Williamson Precision Gunsmithing
Winter, Robert M.

STOCKS (COMMERCIAL)

A.W. Peterson Gun Shop, Inc., The

PRODUCT & SERVICE DIRECTORY

Accuracy Unlimited
Acra-Bond Laminates
African Import Co.
Ahlman Guns
Aspen Outfitting Co.
B.A.C.
Baelder, Harry
Bansner's Ultimate Rifles, LLC
Barnes Bullets, Inc.
Battenfeld Technologies, Inc.
Beitzinger, George
Bell & Carlson, Inc.
Blount, Inc., Sporting
  Equipment Div.
Blount/Outers ATK
Bob's Gun Shop
Borden Ridges Rimrock Stocks
Borden Rifles Inc.
Bowerly, Kent
Boyds' Gunstock Industries,
  Inc.
Brockman's Custom
  Gunsmithing
Buckhorn Gun Works
Bull Mountain Rifle Co.
Butler Creek Corp.
Cali'co Hardwoods, Inc.
Cape Outfitters
Caywood, Shane J.
Chambers Flintlocks Ltd., Jim
Chicasaw Gun Works
Claro Walnut Gunstock Co.
Coffin, Charles H.
Colonial Repair
Colorado Gunsmithing
  Academy
Colorado School of Trades
Conrad, C. A.
Curly Maple Stock Blanks (See
  Tiger-Hunt)
Custom Checkering Service,
  Kathy Forster
D&D Gunsmiths, Ltd.
D&G Precision Duplicators
  (See Greenwood Precision)
D.C. Engineering, Inc.
Davide Pedersoli and Co.
DGR Custom Rifles
Duane's Gun Repair (See DGR
  Custom Rifles)
Effebi SNC-Dr. Franco Beretta
Eggleston, Jere D.
Eversull Co., Inc.
Falcon Industries, Inc.
Fieldsport Ltd.
Fisher, Jerry A.
Folks, Donald E.
Forster, Kathy (See Custom
  Checkering)
Forthofer's Gunsmithing &
  Knifemaking
Game Haven Gunstocks
George Hoenig, Inc.
Gervais, Mike
Gillmann, Edwin
Goens, Dale W.
Golden Age Arms Co.
Great American Gunstock Co.
Gun Shop, The
Hammerli USA
Hanson's Gun Center, Dick
Harry Lawson LLC
Hecht, Hubert J., Waffen-Hecht
Hensley, Gunmaker, Darwin
High Tech Specialties, Inc.
Hiptmayer, Armurier
Hiptmayer, Klaus

Hogue Grips
H-S Precision, Inc.
Huebner, Corey O.
Israel Arms Inc.
Ivanoff, Thomas G. (See Tom's
  Gun Repair)
Jarrett Rifles, Inc.
Jeff's Outfitters
Jim Norman Custom
  Gunstocks
John Masen Co. Inc.
Johnson Wood Products
KDF, Inc.
Keith's Custom Gunstocks
Kelbly, Inc.
Kilham & Co.
Klingler Woodcarving
McDonald, Dennis
McMillan Fiberglass Stocks,
  Inc.
Michaels of Oregon Co.
Mid-America Recreation, Inc.
Miller Arms, Inc.
Mitchell, Jack
Mobile Area Networks, Inc.
Morrison Custom Rifles, J. W.
MPI Stocks
MWG Co.
NCP Products, Inc.
Nelson's Custom Guns, Inc.
New England Arms Co.
New England Custom Gun
  Service
Newman Gunshop
Oil Rod and Gun Shop
One Of A Kind
Orvis Co., The
Ottmar, Maurice
Pagel Gun Works, Inc.
Paragon Sales & Services, Inc.
Parker & Sons Shooting
  Supply
Paul and Sharon Dressel
Paul D. Hillmer Custom
  Gunstocks
Paulsen Gunstocks
Pawling Mountain Club
Pecatonica River Longrifle
Perazone-Gunsmith, Brian
Powell & Son (Gunmakers)
  Ltd., William
Precision Gun Works
R&J Gun Shop
R.A. Wells Custom Gunsmith
Ram-Line ATK
Rampart International
Richards MicroFit Stocks, Inc.
RMS Custom Gunsmithing
Robinson, Don
Robinson Armament Co.
Robinson Firearms Mfg. Ltd.
Romain's Custom Guns, Inc.
Ron Frank Custom
Saville Iron Co. (See
  Greenwood Precision)
Schiffman, Mike
Score High Gunsmithing
Simmons Gun Repair, Inc.
Six Enterprises
Speiser, Fred D.
Stan De Treville & Co.
Stiles Custom Guns
Swann, D. J.
Swift River Gunworks
Szweda, Robert (See RMS
  Custom Gunsmithing)
T.F.C. S.p.A.

Tecnolegno S.p.A.
Tiger-Hunt Longrifle Gunstocks
Tirelli
Tom's Gun Repair, Thomas G.
  Ivanoff
Track of the Wolf, Inc.
Treebone Carving
Trevallion Gunstocks
Tuttle, Dale
Vic's Gun Refinishing
Virgin Valley Custom Guns
Volquartsen Custom Ltd.
Walker Arms Co., Inc.
Weber & Markin Custom
  Gunsmiths
Wenig Custom Gunstocks
Werth, T. W.
Western Mfg. Co.
Wild West Guns
Williams Gun Sight Co.
Windish, Jim
Wright's Gunstock Blanks
Zeeryp, Russ

STUCK CASE REMOVERS

A.W. Peterson Gun Shop,
  Inc., The
GAR
Huntington Die Specialties
Redding Reloading Equipment
Tom's Gun Repair, Thomas G.
  Ivanoff

TARGETS, BULLET & CLAYBIRD TRAPS

A.W. Peterson Gun Shop,
  Inc., The
Action Target, Inc.
Air Arms
American Target
Beeman Precision Airguns
Benjamin/Sheridan Co.,
  Crosman
Birchwood Casey
Blount, Inc., Sporting
  Equipment Div.
Blount/Outers ATK
Blue and Gray Products Inc.
  (See Ox-Yoke Originals)
Brown Precision, Inc.
Bull-X, Inc.
Caswell Inc.
Champion Target Co.
Creedmoor Sports, Inc.
Crosman Airguns
D.C.C. Enterprises
Daisy Outdoor Products
Diamond Mfg. Co.
Federal Champion Target Co.
H-S Precision, Inc.
Hunterjohn
J.G. Dapkus Co., Inc.
Kennebec Journal
Kleen-Bore, Inc.
Lakefield Arms Ltd. (See
  Savage Arms, Inc.)
Leapers, Inc.
Lyman Instant Targets, Inc.
  (See Lyman Products Corp.)
Marksman Products
Mendez, John A.
Mountain Plains Industries
MSR Targets
N.B.B., Inc.

National Target Co.
North American Shooting
  Systems
Outers Laboratories Div. of ATK
Palsa Outdoor Products
Passive Bullet Traps, Inc. (See
  Savage Range Systems, Inc.)
PlumFire Press, Inc.
Precision Airgun Sales, Inc.
Protektor Model
Quack Decoy & Sporting Clays
Remington Arms Co., Inc.
Rockwood Corp.
Rocky Mountain Target Co.
Savage Range Systems, Inc.
Schaefer Shooting Sports
Seligman Shooting Products
Shooters Supply
Shoot-N-C Targets (See
  Birchwood Casey)
SPG, Inc.
Sun Welding Safe Co.
Target Shooting, Inc.
Thompson Target Technology
Trius Traps, Inc.
Universal Sports
Watson Bullets
Woods Wise Products
World of Targets (See
  Birchwood Casey)
X-Spand Target Systems

TAXIDERMY

African Import Co.
Bill Russ Trading Post
Kulis Freeze Dry Taxidermy
World Trek, Inc.

TRAP & SKEET SHOOTER'S EQUIPMENT

American Products, Inc.
Bagmaster Mfg., Inc.
Ballistic Products, Inc.
Beretta Pietro S.P.A.
Blount/Outers ATK
Bob Allen Sportswear
Bridgeman Products
C&H Research
Campbell, Dick
Cape Outfitters
Danuser Machine Co.
Fiocchi of America, Inc.
Gun Works, The
Hoppe's Div. Penguin
  Industries, Inc.
Jamison's Forge Works
Jenkins Recoil Pads
Jim Noble Co.
Kalispel Case Line
Kolar
Lakewood Products Div of
  Midwest Textile
Ljutic Industries, Inc.
Mag-Na-Port International, Inc.
MEC, Inc.
Moneymaker Guncraft Corp.
MTM Molded Products Co.,
  Inc.
NCP Products, Inc.
Pachmayr Div. Lyman Products
Palsa Outdoor Products
Pro-Port Ltd.
Protektor Model
Quack Decoy & Sporting Clays

Remington Arms Co., Inc.
Rhodeside, Inc.
Shotgun Sports Magazine, dba
  Shootin' Accessories Ltd.
Stan Baker Sports
T&S Industries, Inc.
TEN-X Products Group
Torel, Inc./Tandy Brands
  Outdoors/AA & E
Trius Traps, Inc.
Truglo, Inc.
Universal Sports
Weber & Markin Custom
  Gunsmiths
X-Spand Target Systems
Ziegel Engineering

TRIGGERS, RELATED EQUIPMENT

A.W. Peterson Gun Shop,
  Inc., The
B&D Trading Co., Inc.
B.M.F. Activator, Inc.
Bond Custom Firearms
Boyds' Gunstock Industries,
  Inc.
Broad Creek Rifle Works, Ltd.
Bull Mountain Rifle Co.
Chicasaw Gun Works
Dayton Traister
Dolbare, Elizabeth
Eversull Co., Inc.
Feinwerkbau Westinger &
  Altenburger
Gentry Custom LLC
Gun Works, The
Hart & Son, Inc.
Hastings
Hawken Shop, The (See
  Dayton Traister)
High Performance International
Holland's Shooters Supply, Inc.
Impact Case & Container, Inc.
Jewell Triggers, Inc.
John Masen Co. Inc.
Jones Custom Products,
  Neil A.
JP Enterprises, Inc.
K. Eversull Co., Inc.
Kelbly, Inc.
KK Air International (See
  Impact Case & Container
  Co., Inc.)
Knight's Manufacturing Co.
L&R Lock Co.
Les Baer Custom, Inc.
List Precision Engineering
London Guns Ltd.
M.H. Canjar Co.
Master Lock Co.
Miller Single Trigger Mfg. Co.
NCP Products, Inc.
Neil A. Jones Custom Products
Nowlin Mfg. Co.
Penrod Precision
Perazone-Gunsmith, Brian
Robinson Armament Co.
Sharp Shooter Supply
Shilen, Inc.
Simmons Gun Repair, Inc.
Spencer's Rifle Barrels, Inc.
Tank's Rifle Shop
Target Shooting, Inc.
Time Precision
Watson Bullets
York M-1 Conversion

A

A Zone Bullets, 2039 Walter Rd., Billings, MT 59105 / 800-252-3111; FAX: 406-248-1961

A&W Repair, 2930 Schneider Dr., Arnold, MO 63010 / 617-287-3725

A.A. Arms, Inc., 4811 Persimmont Ct., Monroe, NC 28110 / 704-289-5356 or 800-935-1119; FAX: 704-289-5859

A.B.S. III, 9238 St. Morritz Dr., Fern Creek, KY 40291

A.G. Russell Knives, Inc., 2900 S. 26th St., Rogers, AR 72758 / 800-255-9034; FAX: 479-636-8493 ag@agrussell.com agrussell.com

A.R.M.S., Inc., 230 W. Center St., West Bridgewater, MA 02379-1620 / 508-584-7816; FAX: 508-588-8045

A.W. Peterson Gun Shop, Inc., The, 4255 West Old U.S. 441, Mount Dora, FL 32757-3299 / 352-383-4258; FAX: 352-735-1001

AC Dyna-tite Corp., 155 Kelly St., P.O. Box 0984, Elk Grove Village, IL 60007 / 847-593-5566; FAX: 847-593-1304

Acadian Ballistic Specialties, P.O. Box 787, Folsom, LA 70437 / 504-796-0078 gunsmith@neasoft.com

Accuracy Den, The, 25 Bitterbrush Rd., Reno, NV 89523 / 702-345-0225

Accuracy International Precision Rifles (See U.S.)

Accuracy International, Foster, P.O. Box 111, Wilsall, MT 59086 / 406-587-7922; FAX: 406-585-9434

Accuracy Int'l. North America, Inc., P.O. Box 5267, Oak Ridge, TN 37831 / 423-482-0330; FAX: 423-482-0336

Accuracy Unlimited, 7479 S. DePew St., Littleton, CO 80123

Accuracy Unlimited, 16036 N. 49 Ave., Glendale, AZ 85306 / 602-978-9089; FAX: 602-978-9089 fglenn@cox.net www.glenncustom.com

Accura-Site (See All's, The Jim Tembelis Co., Inc.)

Accurate Arms Co., Inc., 5891 Hwy. 230 West, McEwen, TN 37101 / 931-729-4207; FAX: 931-729-4211 burrensburg@aac-ca.com www.accuratepowder.com

Accu-Tek, 4510 Carter Ct., Chino, CA 91710

Ackerman & Co., Box 133 U.S. Highway Rt. 7, Pownal, VT 05261 / 802-823-9874 muskets@togsther.net

Ackerman, Bill (See Optical Services Co.)

Acra-Bond Laminates, 134 Zimmerman Rd., Kalispell, MT 59901 / 406-257-9003; FAX: 406-257-9003 merlins@digisys.net www.acrabondlaminates.com

Action Bullets & Alloy Inc., RR 1, P.O. Box 189, Quinter, KS 67752 / 785-754-3609; FAX: 785-754-3629 bullets@ruraltel.net

Action Direct, Inc., 14285 SW 142nd St., Miami, FL 33186-6720 / 800-472-2388; FAX: 305-256-3541 info@action-direct.com www.action-direct.com

Action Products, Inc., 954 Sweeney Dr., Hagerstown, MD 21740 / 301-797-1414; FAX: 301-733-2073

Action Target, Inc., P.O. Box 636, Provo, UT 84603 / 801-377-8033; FAX: 801-377-8096 www.actiontarget.com

Actions by "T" Teddy Jacobson, 16315 Redwood Forest Ct., Sugar Land, TX 77478 / 281-565-6977 tjacobson@houston.rr.com www.actionsbyt.com

AcuSport Corporation, William L. Fraim, One Hunter Place, Bellefontaine, OH 43311-3001 / 937-593-7010; FAX: 937-592-5625 www.acusport.com

Ad Hominem, 3130 Gun Club Lane, RR #3, Orillia, ON L3V 6H3 CANADA / 705-689-5303; FAX: 705-689-5303

Adair Custom Shop, Bill, 2886 Westridge, Carrollton, TX 75006

ADCO Sales, Inc., 4 Draper St. #A, Woburn, MA 01801 / 781-935-1799; FAX: 781-935-1011

Advance Car Mover Co., Rowell Div., P.O. Box 1, 240 N. Depot St., Juneau, WI 53039 / 414-386-4464; FAX: 414-386-4416

Advantage Arms, Inc., 25163 W. Ave. Stanford, Valencia, CA 91355 / 661-257-2290

Adventure 16, Inc., 4620 Alvarado Canyon Rd., San Diego, CA 92120 / 619-283-6314

Aero Peltor, 90 Mechanic St., Southbridge, MA 01550 / 508-764-5500; FAX: 508-764-0188

African Import Co., 22 Goodwin Rd., Plymouth, MA 02360 / 508-746-8552; FAX: 508-746-0404 africanimport@aol.com

AFSCO Ammunition, 731 W. Third St., P.O. Box L, Owen, WI 54460 / 715-229-2516 sailers@webtv.net

Ahlman Guns, 9525 W. 230th St., Morristown, MN 55052 / 507-685-4243; FAX: 507-685-4280 www.ahlmans.com

Ahrends Grips, Box 203, Clarion, IA 50525 / 515-532-3449; FAX: 515-532-3926 ahrends@goldfieldaccess.net www.ahrendsgripsusa.com

Aimpoint, Inc., 14103 Mariah Ct., Chantilly, VA 20151-2113 / 877-246-7668; FAX: 703-263-9463 info@aimpoint.com www.aimpoint.com

Aimtech Mount Systems, P.O. Box 223, Thomasville, GA 31799 / 229-226-4313; FAX: 229-227-0222 mail@aimtech-mounts.com www.aimtech-mounts.com

Air Arms, Hailsham Industrial Park, Diplocks Way, Hailsham, E. Sussex, BN27 3JF ENGLAND / 011-0323-845853; FAX: 1323 440573 general.air-arms.co.uk. www.air-arms.co.uk.

Air Venture Airguns, 9752 E. Flower St., Bellflower, CA 90706 / 562-867-6355

AirForce Airguns, P.O. Box 2478, Fort Worth, TX 76113 / 817-451-8966; FAX: 817-451-1613 www.airforceairguns.com

Airrow, 11 Monitor Hill Rd., Newtown, CT 06470 / 203-270-6343

Aitor-Berrizargo S.L., Eitua 15 P.O. Box 26, 48240, Berriz (Viscaya), SPAIN / 43-17-08-50 info@aitor.com www.ailor.com

Ajax Custom Grips, Inc., 9130 Viscount Row, Dallas, TX 75247 / 214-630-8893; FAX: 214-630-4942

Aker International, Inc., 2248 Main St., Suite 6, Chula Vista, CA 91911 / 619-423-5182; FAX: 619-423-1363 aker@akerleather.com www.akerleather.com

AKJ Concealco, P.O. Box 871596, Vancouver, WA 98687-1596 / 360-891-8222; FAX: 360-891-8221 Concealco@aol.com www.greatholsters.com

Alana Cupp Custom Engraver, P.O. Box 207, Annabella, UT 84711 / 801-896-4834

Alaska Bullet Works, Inc., 9978 Crazy Horse Drive, Juneau, AK 99801 / 907-789-3834; FAX: 907-789-3433

Alaskan Silversmith, The, 2145 Wagner Hollow Rd., Fort Plain, NY 13339 / 518-993-3983 sidbell@capital.net www.sidbell.cizland.com

Aldis Gunsmithing & Shooting Supply, 502 S. Montezuma St., Prescott, AZ 86303 / 602-445-6723; FAX: 602-445-6763

Alessi Holsters, Inc., 2465 Niagara Falls Blvd., Amherst, NY 14228-3527 / 716-691-5615

Alex, Inc., 3420 Cameron Bridge Rd., Manhattan, MT 59741-8523 / 406-282-7396; FAX: 406-282-7396

All American Lead Shot Corp., P.O. Box 224566, Dallas, TX 75062

All Rite Products, Inc., 9554 Wells Circle, Suite D, West Jordan, UT 84088-6226 / 800-771-8471; FAX: 801-280-8302 info@allriteproducts.com www.allriteproducts.com

Allard, Gary/Creek Side Metal & Woodcrafters, Fishers Hill, VA 22626 / 540-465-3903

Allen Co., Inc., 525 Burbank St., Broomfield, CO 80020 / 303-469-1857 or 800-876-8600; FAX: 303-466-7437

Allen Firearm Engraving, P.O. Box 155, Camp Verde, AZ 86322 / 928-567-6711 rosebudmulgco@netzero.com rosebudmulgco@netzero.com

Allen Mfg., 2784 Highway 23, Brook Park, MN 55007

Alley Supply Co., P.O. Box 848, Gardnerville, NV 89410 / 775-782-3800; FAX: 775-782-3827 jetalley@aol.com www.alleysupplyco.com

Alliant Techsystems, Smokeless Powder Group, P.O. Box 6, Rt. 114, Bldg. 229, Radford, VA 24141-0096 www.alliantpowder.com

Allred Bullet Co., 932 Evergreen Drive, Logan, UT 84321 / 435-752-6983; FAX: 435-752-6983

Alpec Team, Inc., 1231 Midas Way, Sunnyvale, CA 94085 / 510-606-8245; FAX: 510-606-4279

Alpha 1 Drop Zone, 2121 N. Tyler, Wichita, KS 67212 / 316-729-0800; FAX: 316-729-4262 www.alpha1dropzone.com

Alpha LaFranck Enterprises, P.O. Box 81072, Lincoln, NE 68501 / 402-466-3193

Alpha Precision, Inc., 3238 Della Slaton Rd., Comer, GA 30629-2212 / 706-783-2131 jim@alphaprecisioninc.com www.alphaprecisioninc.com

Alpine Indoor Shooting Range, 2401 Government Way, Coeur d'Alene, ID 83814 / 208-676-8824; FAX: 208-676-8824

Altamont Co., 901 N. Church St., P.O. Box 309, Thomasboro, IL 61878 / 217-643-3125 or 800-626-5774; FAX: 217-643-7973

Alumna Sport by Dee Zee, 1572 NE 58th Ave., P.O. Box 3090, Des Moines, IA 50316 / 800-798-9899

Amadeo Rossi S.A., Rua: Amadeo Rossi, 143, Sao Leopoldo, RS 93030-220 BRAZIL / 051-592-5566 rossi.firearms@pnet.com.br

Amato, Jeff. See: J&M PRECISION MACHINING

AmBr Software Group Ltd., P.O. Box 301, Reisterstown, MD 21136-0301 / 800-888-1917; FAX: 410-526-7212

American Ammunition, 3545 NW 71st St., Miami, FL 33147 / 305-835-7400; FAX: 305-694-0037

American Derringer Corp., 127 N. Lacy Dr., Waco, TX 76705 / 800-642-7817 or 254-799-9111; FAX: 254-799-7935

American Display Co., 55 Cromwell St., Providence, RI 02907 / 401-331-2464; FAX: 401-421-1264

American Gas & Chemical Co., Ltd., 220 Pegasus Ave., Northvale, NJ 07647 / 201-767-7300

American Gunsmithing Institute, 1325 Imola Ave. #504, Napa, CA 94559 / 707-253-0462; FAX: 707-253-7149 www.americangunsmith.com

American Handgunner Magazine, 12345 World Trade Dr., San Diego, CA 92128 / 800-537-3006; FAX: 858-605-0204 www.americanhandgunner.com

American Pioneer Video, P.O. Box 50049, Bowling Green, KY 42102-2649 / 800-743-4675

American Products, Inc., 14729 Spring Valley Road, Morrison, IL 61270 / 815-772-3336; FAX: 815-772-8046

American Safe Arms, Inc., 1240 Riverview Dr., Garland, UT 84312 / 801-257-7472; FAX: 801-785-8156

American Security Products Co., 11925 Pacific Ave., Fontana, CA 92337 / 909-685-9680 or 800-421-6142; FAX: 909-685-9685

American Small Arms Academy, P.O. Box 12111, Prescott, AZ 86304 / 602-778-5623

American Target, 1328 S. Jason St., Denver, CO 80223 / 303-733-0433; FAX: 303-777-0311

American Target Knives, 1030 Brownwood NW, Grand Rapids, MI 49504 / 616-453-1998

Americase, P.O. Box 271, 1610 E. Main, Waxahachie, TX 75165 / 800-880-3629; FAX: 214-937-8373

Ames Metal Products Co., 4323 S. Western Blvd., Chicago, IL 60609 / 773-523-3230 or 800-255-6937; FAX: 773-523-3854 amesmetal@webtv.net

Amherst Arms, P.O. Box 1457, Englewood, FL 34295 / 941-475-2020; FAX: 941-473-1212

Ammo Load Worldwide, Inc., 815 D St., Lewiston, ID 83501 / 800-528-5610; FAX: 208-746-1730 info@ammoload.com www.ammoload.com

Amrine's Gun Shop, 937 La Luna, Ojai, CA 93023 / 805-646-2376

Amsec, 11925 Pacific Ave., Fontana, CA 92337

AMT/Crusader Arms, 5200 Mitchelldale, Ste. E17, Houston, TX 77092 / 800-272-7816 www.highstandard.com

Analog Devices, Box 9106, Norwood, MA 02062

Andela Tool & Machine, Inc., RD3, Box 246, Richfield Springs, NY 13439

Anderson Manufacturing Co., Inc., 22602 53rd Ave. SE, Bothell, WA 98021 / 206-481-1858; FAX: 206-481-7839

Andres & Dworsky KG, Bergstrasse 18, A-3822 Karlstein, Thaya, AUSTRIA / 0 28 44-285; FAX: 0 28 44-28619 andres.dnorsky@wvnet.as

Angelo & Little Custom Gun Stock Blanks, P.O. Box 240046, Dell, MT 59724-0046

Antique American Firearms, Douglas Carlson, P.O. Box 71035, Dept. GD, Des Moines, IA 50325 / 515-224-6552 drearlson@mailstation.com

Antique Arms Co., 1110 Cleveland Ave., Monett, MO 65708 / 417-235-6501

AO Sight Systems, 2401 Ludelle St., Fort Worth, TX 76105 / 888-744-4880; or 817-536-0136; FAX: 817-536-3517

Apel GmbH, Ernst, Am Kirschberg 3, D-97218, Gerbrunn, GERMANY / 0 (931) 707192 info@eaw.de www.eaw.de

Aplan Antiques & Art, James O., HC 80, Box 793-25, Piedmont, SD 57769 / 605-347-5016

AR-7 Industries, LLC, 998 N. Colony Rd., Meriden, CT 06450 / 203-630-3536; FAX: 203-630-3637

ArmaLite, Inc., P.O. Box 299, Geneseo, IL 61254 / 800-336-0184 or 309-944-6939; FAX: 309-944-6949

Armament Gunsmithing Co., Inc., 525 Rt. 22, Hillside, NJ 07205 / 908-686-0960; FAX: 718-738-5019 armamentgunsmithing@worldnet.att.net

MANUFACTURER'S DIRECTORY

Armas Garbi, S.A., 12-14 20.600 Urki, 12, Eibar (Guipuzcoa), SPAIN / 943 20 3873; FAX: 943 20 3873 armosgarbi@euskalnet.n

Armas Kemen S. A. (See U.S. Importers)

Armfield Custom Bullets, 10584 County Road 100, Carthage, MO 64836 / 417-359-8480; FAX: 417-359-8497

Armi Perazzi S.P.A., Via Fontanelle 1/3, 1-25080, Botticino Mattina, ITALY / 030-2692591; FAX: 030-2692594

Armi San Marco (See Taylor's & Co.)

Armi San Paolo, 172-A, I-25062, via Europa, ITALY / 030-2751725

Armi Sport (See Cimarron Firearms, E.M.F., KBI & Taylor's & Co.)

Armite Laboratories Inc., 1560 Superior Ave., Costa Mesa, CA 92627 / 949-646-9035; FAX: 949-646-8319 armite@pacbell.net www.armitelahs.com

Armoloy Co. of Ft. Worth, 204 E. Daggett St., Fort Worth, TX 76104 / 817-332-5604; FAX: 817-335-6517 info@armoloyftworth.com www.armoloyftworth.com

Armor (See Buck Stop Lure Co., Inc.)

Armor Metal Products, P.O. Box 4609, Helena, MT 59604 / 406-442-5560; FAX: 406-442-5650

Armory Publications, 2120 S. Reserve St., PMB 253, Missoula, MT 59801 / 406-549-7670; FAX: 406-728-0597 armorypub@aol.com www.armorypub.com

Arms & Armour Press, Wellington House, 125 Strand, London, WC2R 0BB ENGLAND / 0171-420-5555; FAX: 0171-240-7265

Arms Corporation of the Philippines, Armscor Ave. Brgy. Fortune, Marikina City, PHILIPPINES / 632-941-6243 or 632-941-6244; FAX: 632-942-0682 info@armscor.com.ph www.armscor.com.ph

Arms Craft Gunsmithing, 1106 Linda Dr., Arroyo Grande, CA 93420 / 805-481-2830

Arms, Programming Solutions (See Arms Software)

Armscor Precision, 5740 S. Arville St. #219, Las Vegas, NV 89118 / 702-362-7750

Armscorp USA, Inc., 4424 John Ave., Baltimore, MD 21227 / 301-775-8134 info@armscorpusa.com www.armscorpusa.com

Arratoonian, Andy (See Horseshoe Leather Products)

Arrieta S.L., Morkaiko 5, 20870, Elgoibar, SPAIN / 34-43-743150; FAX: 34-43-743154

Art Jewel Enterprises Ltd., Eagle Business Ctr., 460 Randy Rd., Carol Stream, IL 60188 / 708-260-0400

Artistry in Wood, 134 Zimmerman Rd., Kalispell, MT 59901 / 406-257-9003; FAX: 406-257-9167 merlins@digisys.net www.acrabondlaminates.com

Art's Gun & Sport Shop, Inc., 6008 Hwy. Y, Hillsboro, MO 63050

Aspen Outfitting Co., Jon Hollinger, 9 Dean St., Aspen, CO 81611 / 970-925-3406

A-Square Co., 205 Fairfield Ave., Jeffersonville, IN 47130 / 812-283-0577; FAX: 812-283-0375

Astra Sport, S.A., Apartado 3, 48300 Guernica, Espagne, SPAIN / 34-4-6250100; FAX: 34-4-6255186

Atamec-Bretton, 19 rue Victor Grignard, F-42026, St.-Etienne (Cedex 1, FRANCE / 33-77-93-54-69; FAX: 33-77-93-57-98

Atlanta Cutlery Corp., 2143 Gees Mill Rd., Box 839 CIS, Conyers, GA 30207 / 800-883-0300; FAX: 404-388-0246

Atlantic Mills, Inc., 1295 Towbin Ave., Lakewood, NJ 08701-5934 / 800-242-7374

Atsko/Sno-Seal, Inc., 2664 Russell St., Orangeburg, SC 29115 / 803-531-1820; FAX: 803-531-2139 info@atsko.com www.atsko.com

Austin & Halleck, Inc., 2150 South 950 East, Provo, UT 84606-6285 / 877-543-3256 or 801-374-9990; FAX: 801-374-9998 www.austinhallek.com

Austin Sheridan USA, Inc., 89 Broad St., Middlefield, CT 06455 / 860-346-2500; FAX: 860-346-2510 asusa@sbcglobal.net www.austinsheridanusa.com

Auto Arms, 738 Clearview, San Antonio, TX 78228 / 512-434-5450

Auto-Ordnance Corp., P.O. Box 220, Blauvelt, NY 10913 / 914-353-7770

Autumn Sales, Inc. (Blaser), 1320 Lake St., Fort Worth, TX 76102 / 817-335-1634; FAX: 817-338-0119

Avnda Otaola Norica, 16 Apartado 68, 20600, Eibar, SPAIN

AWC Systems Technology, P.O. Box 41938, Phoenix, AZ 85080-1938 / 623-780-1050; FAX: 623-780-2967 awc@awcsystech.com www.awcsystech.com

Axtell Rifle Co., 353 Mill Creek Road, Sheridan, MT 59749 / 406-842-5814

AYA (See U.S. Importer-New England Custom Gun Serv

B

B&D Trading Co., Inc., 3935 Fair Hill Rd., Fair Oaks, CA 95628 / 800-334-3790 or 916-967-9366; FAX: 916-967-4873

B&P America, 12321 Brittany Cir., Dallas, TX 75230 / 972-726-9069

B.A.C., 17101 Los Modelos St., Fountain Valley, CA 92708 / 435-586-3286

B.C. Outdoors, Larry McGhee, PO Box 61497, Boulder City, NV 89006 / 702-294-3056; FAX: 702-294-0413 jdalton@pmcammo.com www.pmcammo.com

B.M.F. Activator, Inc., 12145 Mill Creek Run, Plantersville, TX 77363 / 936-894-2397; FAX: 936-894-2397 bmf25years@aol.com

Baelder, Harry, Alte Goennebeker Strasse 5, 24635, Rickling, GERMANY / 04328-722732; FAX: 04328-722733

Baer's Hollows, P.O. Box 603, Taft, CA 93268 / 719-438-5718

Bagmaster Mfg., Inc., 2731 Sutton Ave., St. Louis, MO 63143 / 314-781-8002; FAX: 314-781-3363 sales@bagmaster.com www.bagmaster.com

Bain & Davis, Inc., 307 E. Valley Blvd., San Gabriel, CA 91776-3522 / 626-573-4241; FAX: 626-573-8102 baindavis@aol.com

Baker, Stan. See: STAN BAKER SPORTS

Bald Eagle Precision Machine Co., 101-A Allison St., Lock Haven, PA 17745 / 570-748-6772; FAX: 570-748-4443 bepmachine@aol.com www.baldeaglemachine.com

Ballard, Donald. See: BALLARD INDUSTRIES

Ballard Industries, Donald Ballard Sr., P.O. Box 2035, Arnold, CA 95223 / 408-996-0957; FAX: 408-257-6828

Ballard Rifle & Cartridge Co., LLC, 113 W. Yellowstone Ave., Cody, WY 82414 / 307-587-4914; FAX: 307-527-6097 ballard@wyoming.com www.ballardrifles.com

Ballistic Products, Inc., 20015 75th Ave. North, Corcoran, MN 55340-9456 / 763-494-9237; FAX: 763-494-9236 info@ballisticproducts.com www.ballisticproducts.com

Ballistic Program Co., Inc., The, 2417 N. Patterson St., Thomasville, GA 31792 / 912-228-5739 or 800-368-0835

Ballistic Research, 1108 W. May Ave., McHenry, IL 60050 / 815-385-0037

Ballisti-Cast, Inc., P.O. Box 1057, Minot, ND 58702-1057 / 701-497-3333; FAX: 701-497-3335

Bang-Bang Boutique (See Holster Shop, The)

Bansner's Ultimate Rifles, LLC, P.O. Box 839, 261 E. Main St., Adamstown, PA 19501 / 717-484-2370; FAX: 717-484-0523 bansner@aol.com www.bansnersrifle.com

Barbour, Inc., 55 Meadowbrook Dr., Milford, NH 03055 / 603-673-1313; FAX: 603-673-6510

Barnes Bullets, Inc., P.O. Box 215, American Fork, UT 84003 / 801-756-4222 or 800-574-9200; FAX: 801-756-2465 email@barnesbullets.com www.barnesbullets.com

Baron Technology, 62 Spring Hill Rd., Trumbull, CT 06611 / 203-452-0515; FAX: 203-452-0663 dbaron@baronengraving.com www.baronengraving.com

Barraclough, John K., 55 Merit Park Dr., Gardena, CA 90247 / 310-324-2574 jbarraclough@sbcglobal.net

Barramundi Corp., P.O. Drawer 4259, Homosassa Springs, FL 32687 / 904-628-0200

Barrel & Gunworks, 2601 Lake Valley Rd., Prescott Valley, AZ 86314 / 928-772-4060 www.cutrifle.com

Barrett Firearms Manufacturer, Inc., P.O. Box 1077, Murfreesboro, TN 37133 / 615-896-2938; FAX: 615-896-7313

Bar-Sto Precision Machine, 73377 Sullivan Rd., P.O. Box 1838, Twentynine Palms, CA 92277 / 760-367-2747; FAX: 760-367-2407 barsto@eee.org www.barsto.com

Barta's Gunsmithing, 10231 U.S. Hwy. 10, Cato, WI 54230 / 920-732-4472

Barteaux Machete, 1916 SE 50th Ave., Portland, OR 97215-3238 / 503-233-5880

Bartlett Engineering, 40 South 200 East, Smithfield, UT 84335-1645 / 801-563-5910

Bates Engraving, Billy, 2302 Winthrop Dr. SW, Decatur, AL 35603 / 256-355-3690 bbrn@aol.com www.angelfire.com/al/billybates

Battenfeld Technologies, Inc., 5885 W. Van Horn Tavern Rd., Columbia, MO 65203 / 573-445-9200; FAX: 573-447-4158 battenfeldtechnologies.com

Bauer, Eddie, 15010 NE 36th St., Redmond, WA 98052

Baumgartner Bullets, 3011 S. Alane St., W. Valley City, UT 84120

Bauska Barrels, 105 9th Ave. W., Kalispell, MT 59901 / 406-752-7706

BC-Handmade Bullets, 482 Comerwood Court, S. San Francisco, CA 94080 / 650-583-1550; FAX: 650-583-1550

Bear Archery, RR 4, 4600 Southwest 41st Blvd., Gainesville, FL 32601 / 904-376-2327

Bear Arms, 374-A Carson Rd., St. Mathews, SC 29135

Bear Mountain Gun & Tool, 120 N. Plymouth, New Plymouth, ID 83655 / 208-278-5221; FAX: 208-278-5221

Beartooth Bullets, P.O. Box 491, Dept. HLD, Dover, ID 83825-0491 / 208-448-1865 bullets@beartoothbullets.com beartoothbullets.com

Beaver Park Product, Inc., 840 J St., Penrose, CO 81240 / 719-372-6744

BEC, Inc., 1227 W. Valley Blvd., Suite 204, Alhambra, CA 91803 / 626-281-5751; FAX: 626-293-7073

Beeks, Mike. See: GRAYBACK WILDCATS

Beeman Precision Airguns, 5454 Argosy Dr., Huntington Beach, CA 92649 / 714-890-4808; FAX: 714-890-4808

Beitzinger, George, 116-20 Atlantic Ave., Richmond Hill, NY 11419 / 718-847-7661

Bell & Carlson, Inc., Dodge City Industrial Park, 101 Allen Rd., Dodge City, KS 67801 / 800-634-8586 or 620-225-6688; FAX: 620-225-6688 email@bellandcarlson.com www.bellandcarlson.com

Bell Reloading, Inc., 1725 Harlin Lane Rd., Villa Rica, GA 30180

Bell's Gun & Sport Shop, 3309-19 Mannheim Rd., Franklin Park, IL 60131

Bell's Legendary Country Wear, 22 Circle Dr., Bellmore, NY 11710 / 516-679-1158

Benchmark Knives (See Gerber Legendary Blades)

Benelli Armi S.P.A., Via della Stazione, 61029, Urbino, ITALY / 39-722-307-1; FAX: 39-722-327427

Benelli USA Corp., 17603 Indian Head Hwy., Accokeek, MD 20607 / 301-283-6981; FAX: 301-283-6988 benelliusa.com

Bengtson Arms Co., L., 6345-B E. Akron St., Mesa, AZ 85205 / 602-981-6375

Benjamin/Sheridan Co., Crosman, Rts. 5 and 20, E. Bloomfield, NY 14443 / 716-657-6161; FAX: 716-657-5405 www.crosman.com

Bentley, John, 128-D Watson Dr., Turtle Creek, PA 15145

Beretta Pietro S.P.A., Via Beretta, 18, 25063, Gardone Valtrompia, ITALY / 39-30-8341-1 www.beretta.com

Beretta U.S.A. Corp., 17601 Beretta Dr., Accokeek, MD 20607 / 301-283-2191; FAX: 301-283-0435

Berger Bullets Ltd., 5443 W. Westwind Dr., Glendale, AZ 85310 / 602-842-4001; FAX: 602-934-9083

Bernardelli, Vincenzo, P.O. Box 460243, Houston, TX 77056-8243 www.bernardelli.com

Bernardelli, Vincenzo, Via Grande, 10, Sede Legale Torbole Casaglia, Brescia, ITALY / 39-30-8912851-2-3; FAX: 39-030-2150963 bernardelli@bernardelli.com www.bernardelli.com

Berry's Mfg., Inc., 401 North 3050 East St., St. George, UT 84770 / 435-634-1682; FAX: 435-634-1683 sales@berrysmfg.com www.berrysmfg.com

Bersa S.A., Benso Bonadimani, Magallanes 775 B1704 FLC, Ramos Mejia, ARGENTINA / 011-4656-2377; FAX: 011-4656-2093+ info@bersa-sa.com.dr www.bersa-sa.com.ar

Bert Johanssons Vapentillbehor, S-430 20 Veddige, SWEDEN,

Bertuzzi (See U.S. Importer-New England Arms Co.)

Better Concepts Co., 663 New Castle Rd., Butler, PA 16001 / 412-285-9000

Beverly, Mary, 3969 102nd Pl. N., Clearwater, FL 33762

Bianchi International, Inc., 27969 Jefferson Ave., Temecula, CA 92590 / 951-676-5621; FAX: 951-676-6777 www.customerservice@bianchi-intl.com www.bianchi-intl.com

Big Bore Bullets of Alaska, P.O. Box 521455, Big Lake, AK 99652 / 907-373-2673; FAX: 907-373-2673 doug@mtaonline.net ww.awloo.com/bbb/index.

Big Bore Express, 2316 E. Railroad St., Nampa, ID 83651 / 800-376-4010 FAX: 208-466-6927 info@powerbeltbullets.com bigbore.com

MANUFACTURER'S DIRECTORY

Big Spring Enterprises "Bore Stores", P.O. Box 1115, Big Spring Rd., Yellville, AR 72687 / 870-449-5297; FAX: 870-449-4446

Bilal, Mustafa. See: TURK'S HEAD PRODUCTIONS

Bilinski, Bryan. See: FIELDSPORT LTD.

Bill Adair Custom Shop, 2886 Westridge, Carrollton, TX 75006 / 972-418-0950

Bill Austin's Calls, Box 284, Kaycee, WY 82639 / 307-738-2552

Bill Hanus Birdguns, LLC, P.O. Box 533, Newport, OR 97365 / 541-265-7433; FAX: 541-265-7400 www. billhanusbirdguns.com

Bill Russ Trading Post, William A. Russ, 25 William St., Addison, NY 14801-1326 / 607-359-3896

Bill Wiseman and Co., P.O. Box 3427, Bryan, TX 77805 / 409-690-3456; FAX: 409-690-0156

Billeb, Stephen. See: QUALITY CUSTOM FIREARMS

Billings Gunsmiths, 1841 Grand Ave., Billings, MT 59102 / 406-256-8390; FAX: 406-256-6530 blgsgunsmiths@msn.com

Billingsley & Brownell, P.O. Box 25, Dayton, WY 82836 / 307-655-9344

Bill's Gun Repair, 1007 Burlington St., Mendota, IL 61342 / 815-539-5786

Billy Bates Engraving, 2302 Winthrop Dr. SW, Decatur, AL 35603 / 256-355-3690 bbrn@aol.com www.angelfire. com/al/billybates

Birchwood Casey, 7900 Fuller Rd., Eden Prairie, MN 55344 / 800-328-6156 or 612-937-7933; FAX: 612-937-7979

Birdsong & Assoc., W. E., 1435 Monterey Rd., Florence, MS 39073-9748 / 601-366-8270

Bismuth Cartridge Co., 3500 Maple Ave., Suite 1650, Dallas, TX 75219 / 214-521-5880; FAX: 214-521-9035

Bison Studios, 1409 South Commerce St., Las Vegas, NV 89102 / 702-388-2891; FAX: 702-383-9967

Bitterroot Bullet Co., 2001 Cedar Ave., Lewiston, ID 83501-0412 / 208-743-5635 brootbil@lewiston.com

BKL Technologies, P.O. Box 5237, Brownsville, TX 78523

Black Belt Bullets (See Big Bore Express)

Black Hills Ammunition, Inc., P.O. Box 3090, Rapid City, SD 57709-3090 / 605-348-5150; FAX: 605-348-9827

Black Hills Shooters Supply, P.O. Box 4220, Rapid City, SD 57709 / 800-289-2506

Black Powder Products, 67 Township Rd. 1411, Chesapeake, OH 45619 / 614-867-8047

Black Sheep Brand, 3220 W. Gentry Pkwy., Tyler, TX 75702 / 903-592-3853; FAX: 903-592-0527

Blacksmith Corp., P.O. Box 280, North Hampton, OH 45349 / 937-969-8389; FAX: 937-969-8399 sales@blacksmithcorp.com www.blacksmithcorp.com

BlackStar AccuMax Barrels, 11501 Brittmoore Park Drive, Houston, TX 77041 / 281-721-6040; FAX: 281-721-6041

BlackStar Barrel Accurizing (See BlackStar AccuMax)

Blacktail Mountain Books, 42 First Ave. W., Kalispell, MT 59901 / 406-257-5573

Blaser Jagdwaffen GmbH, D-88316, Isny Im Allgau, GERMANY

Blount, Inc., Sporting Equipment Div., 2299 Snake River Ave., P.O. Box 856, Lewiston, ID 83501 / 800-627-3640 or 208-746-2351; FAX: 208-799-3904

Blount/Outers ATK, P.O. Box 39, Onalaska, WI 54650 / 608-781-5800; FAX: 608-781-0368

Blue and Gray Products Inc. (See Ox-Yoke Originals)

Blue Book Publications, Inc., 8009 34th Ave. S., Ste. 175, Minneapolis, MN 55425 / 952-854-5229; FAX: 952-853-1486 bluebook@bluebookinc.com www.bluebookinc.com

Blue Mountain Bullets, 64146 Quail Ln., Box 231, John Day, OR 97845 / 541-820-4594; FAX: 541-820-4594

Blue Ridge Machinery & Tools, Inc., P.O. Box 536-GD, Hurricane, WV 25526 / 800-872-6500; FAX: 304-562-5311 blueridgemachine@worldnet.att.net www. blueridgemachinery.com

BMC Supply, Inc., 26051 - 179th Ave. SE, Kent, WA 98042

Bob Allen Sportswear, One Bort Dr., Osceola, IA 50213 / 210-344-8531; FAX: 210-342-2703 sales@bob-allen.com www.bob-allen.com

Bob Rogers Gunsmithing, P.O. Box 305, 344 S. Walnut St., Franklin Grove, IL 61031 / 815-456-2685; FAX: 815-456-2685 3006bud@netscape.comm

Bob's Gun Shop, P.O. Box 200, Royal, AR 71968 / 501-767-1970; FAX: 501-767-1970 gunparts@hsnp.com www. gun-parts.com

Bob's Tactical Indoor Shooting Range & Gun Shop, 90 Lafayette Rd., Salisbury, MA 01952 / 508-465-5561

Boessler, Erich, Am Vogeltal 3, 97702, Munnerstadt, GERMANY

Boker USA, Inc., 1550 Balsam Street, Lakewood, CO 80214 / 303-462-0662; FAX: 303-462-0668 sales@bokerusa. com bokerusa.com

Boltin, John M., P.O. Box 644, Estill, SC 29918 / 803-625-2185

Bo-Mar Tool & Mfg. Co., 6136 State Hwy. 300, Longview, TX 75604 / 903-759-4784; FAX: 903-759-9141 marykor@earthlink.net bo-mar.com

Bonadimani, Benso. See: BERSA S.A.

Bonanza (See Forster Products), 310 E. Lanark Ave., Lanark, IL 61046 / 815-493-6360; FAX: 815-493-2371

Bond Arms, Inc., P.O. Box 1296, Granbury, TX 76048 / 817-573-4445; FAX: 817-573-5636 www.bondarms.com

Bond Custom Firearms, 8954 N. Lewis Ln., Bloomington, IN 47408 / 812-332-4519

Bonham's & Butterfields, 220 San Bruno Ave., San Francisco, CA 94103 / 415-861-7500; FAX: 415-861-0183 arms@butterfields.com www.butterfields.com

Boone Trading Co., Inc., P.O. Box 669, Brinnon, WA 98320 / 800-423-1945 or 360-796-4330; FAX: 360-796-4511 sales@boonetrading.com boonetrading.com

Boone's Custom Ivory Grips, Inc., 562 Coyote Rd., Brinnon, WA 98320 / 206-796-4330

Boonie Packer Products, P.O. Box 12517, Salem, OR 97309-0517 / 800-477-3244 or 503-581-3244; FAX: 503-581-3191 customerservice@booniepacker.com www. booniepacker.com

Borden Ridges Rimrock Stocks, RR 1 Box 250 BC, Springville, PA 18844 / 570-965-2505; FAX: 570-965-2328

Borden Rifles Inc., RD 1, Box 250 #BC, Springville, PA 18844 / 717-965-2505; FAX: 717-965-2328

Border Barrels Ltd., Riccarton Farm, Newcastleton, SCOTLAND UK

Borovnik K.G., Ludwig, 9170 Ferlach, Bahnhofstrasse 7, AUSTRIA / 042 27 24 42; FAX: 042 26 43 49

Bosis (See U.S. Importer-New England Arms Co.)

Boss Manufacturing Co., 221 W. First St., Kewanee, IL 61443 / 309-852-2131 or 800-447-4581; FAX: 309-852-0848

Bostick Wildlife Calls, Inc., P.O. Box 728, Estill, SC 29918 / 803-625-2210; or 803-625-4512

Bowen Classic Arms Corp., P.O. Box 67, Louisville, TN 37777 / 865-984-3583 bcacorp@aks.net www. bowenclassicarms.com

Bowen Knife Co., Inc., P.O. Box 802, Magnolia, AR 71754 / 800-397-4794; FAX: 870-234-9005 info@bowen.com www.bowenknife.com

Bowerly, Kent, 9104 Golden Pheasant Dr., Redmond, OR 97756 / 541-923-3501 bowerly@bendbroadband.com

Boyds' Gunstock Industries, Inc., 25376 403 Rd. Ave., Mitchell, SD 57301 / 605-996-5011; FAX: 605-996-9878 www.boydsgunstocks.com

Brace, Larry D., 771 Blackfoot Ave., Eugene, OR 97404 / 541-688-1278; FAX: 541-607-5833

Brauer Bros., P.O. Box 2485, McKinney, TX 75070 / 976-548-8881; FAX: 972-548-8886 www.brauerbros.com

Break-Free, Inc., 13386 International Pkwy., Jacksonville, FL 32218 / 800-428-0588; FAX: 904-741-5407 contactus@armorholdings.com www. break-free.com

Brenneke GmbH, P.O. Box 1646, 30837, Langenhagen, GERMANY / +49-511-97262-0; FAX: +49-511-97262-62 info@brenneke.de brenneke.com

Bridgeman Products, Harry Jaffin, 153 B Cross Slope Ct., Englishtown, NJ 07726 / 732-536-3604; FAX: 732-972-1004

Briese Bullet Co., Inc., 3442 42nd Ave. SE, Tappen, ND 58487 / 701-327-4578; FAX: 701-327-4579

Brigade Quartermasters, 1025 Cobb International Blvd., Dept. VH, Kennesaw, GA 30144-4300 / 404-428-1248 or 800-241-3125; FAX: 404-426-7726

Briganti, A.J. See: BRIGANTI CUSTOM GUNSMITH

Briganti Custom Gunsmith, A.J. Briganti, 512 Rt. 32, Highland Mills, NY 10930 / 845-928-9573

Briley Mfg. Inc., 1230 Lumpkin, Houston, TX 77043 / 800-331-5718 or 713-932-6995; FAX: 713-932-1043

Brill, R. See: ROYAL ARMS INTERNATIONAL

British Sporting Arms, RR 1, Box 193A, Millbrook, NY 12545 / 845-677-8303; FAX: 845-677-5756 info@bsaltd. com www.bsaltd.com

Broad Creek Rifle Works, Ltd., 120 Horsey Ave., Laurel, DE 19956 / 302-875-5446; FAX: 302-875-1448 bcrw4guns@aol.com

Brockman's Custom Gunsmithing, 445 Idaho St., Gooding, ID 83330 / 208-934-5050 brockman@brockmansrifles. com www.brockmansrifles.com

Broken Gun Ranch, 10739 126 Rd., Spearville, KS 67876 / 316-385-2587; FAX: 316-385-2597 nbowlin@ucom.net www.brokengunranch

Brooker, Dennis, Rt. 1, Box 12A, Derby, IA 50068 / 515-533-2103

Brooks Tactical Systems-Agrip, 279-C Shorewood Ct., Fox Island, WA 98333 / 253-549-2866; FAX: 253-549-2703 brooks@brookstactical.com www.brookstactical.com

Brown Precision, Inc., 7786 Molinos Ave., Los Molinos, CA 96055 / 530-384-2506; FAX: 916-384-1638 www. brownprecision.com

Brownells, Inc., 200 S. Front St., Montezuma, IA 50171 / 800-741-0015; FAX: 800-264-3068 orderdesk@brownells.com www.brownells.com

Browning Arms Co., One Browning Place, Morgan, UT 84050 / 801-876-2711; FAX: 801-876-3331 www. browning.com

Browning Arms Co. (Parts & Service), 3005 Arnold Tenbrook Rd., Arnold, MO 63010 / 617-287-6800; FAX: 617-287-9751

BRP, Inc. High Performance Cast Bullets, 1210 Alexander Rd., Colorado Springs, CO 80909 / 719-633-0658

Brunton U.S.A., 2255 Brunton Ct., Riverton, WY 82501 info@brunton.com www.brunton.com

Bryan & Assoc., R. D. Sauls, P.O. Box 5772, Anderson, SC 29623-5772 / 864-261-6810 bryanandac@aol.com www. huntersweb.com/bryanandac

Brynin, Milton, P.O. Box 383, Yonkers, NY 10710 / 914-779-4333

BSA Guns Ltd., Armoury Rd. Small Heath, Birmingham B11 2PP, ENGLAND / 011-021-772-8543; FAX: 011-021-773-0845 sales@bsagun.com www.bsagun.com

BSA Optics, 3911 SW 47th Ave., Ste. 914, Ft. Lauderdale, FL 33314 / 954-581-2144; FAX: 954-581-3165 4info@basaoptics.com www.bsaoptics.com

B-Square Company, Inc., 8909 Forum Way, Ft. Worth, TX 76140 / 800-433-2909; FAX: 817-926-7012 bsquare@b-square.com www.b-square.com

Buchsenmachermeister, Peter Hofer Jagdwaffen, A-9170 Ferlach, Kirchgasse 24, Kirchgasse, AUSTRIA / 43 4227 3683; or 43 664 3200216; FAX: 43 4227 368330 peterhofer@hoferwaffen.com www.hoferwaffen.com

Buck Knives, Inc., 660 Lochsa St., Post Falls, ID 83854 / 208-262-0500; FAX: 800-326-2825 www.buckknives.com

Buck Stix-SOS Products Co., Box 3, Neenah, WI 54956

Buck Stop Lure Co., Inc., 3600 Grow Rd. NW, P.O. Box 636, Stanton, MI 48888 / 989-762-5091; FAX: 989-762-5124 buckstop@nethawk.com www.buckstopscents.com

Buckeye Custom Bullets, 6490 Stewart Rd., Elida, OH 45807 / 419-641-4463

Buckhorn Gun Works, 8109 Woodland Dr., Black Hawk, SD 57718 / 605-787-6472

Buckskin Bullet Co., P.O. Box 1893, Cedar City, UT 84721 / 435-586-3286

Budin, Dave. See: DEL-SPORTS, INC.

Buehler Custom Sporting Arms, P.O. Box 4096, Medford, OR 97501 / 541-664-9109 rbrifle@earthlink.net

Buenger Enterprises/Goldenrod Dehumidifier, 3600 S. Harbor Blvd., Oxnard, CA 93035 / 800-451-6797 or 805-985-5828; FAX: 805-985-1534

Buffalo Arms Co., 660 Vermeer Ct., Ponderay, ID 83852 / 208-263-6953; FAX: 208-265-2096 www.buffaloarms. com

Buffalo Bullet Co., Inc., 12637 Los Nietos Rd., Unit A, Santa Fe Springs, CA 90670 / 800-423-8069; FAX: 562-944-5054 rdanlitz@verizon.net

Buffalo Gun Center, 3385 Harlem Rd., Buffalo, NY 14225 / 716-833-2581; FAX: 716-833-2265 www. buffaloguncenter.com

Buffalo Rock Shooters Supply, R.R. 1, Ottawa, IL 61350 / 815-433-2471

Buffer Technologies, P.O. Box 105047, Jefferson City, MO 65110 / 573-634-8529; FAX: 573-634-8522 sales@buffertech.com buffertech.com

MANUFACTURER'S DIRECTORY

Bull Mountain Rifle Co., 6327 Golden West Terrace, Billings, MT 59106 / 406-656-0778

Bullberry Barrel Works, Ltd., 2430 W. Bullberry Ln., Hurricane, UT 84737 / 435-635-9866; FAX: 435-635-0348 fred@bullberry.com www.bullberry.com

Bullet Metals, Bill Ferguson, P.O. Box 1238, Sierra Vista, AZ 85636 / 520-458-5321; FAX: 520-458-1421 info@ theantimonyman.com www.bullet-metals.com

Bullet Swaging Supply, Inc., P.O. Box 1056, 303 McMillan Rd., West Monroe, LA 71291 / 318-387-3266; FAX: 318-387-7779 leblackmon@colla.com

Bull-X, Inc., 411 E. Water St., Farmer City, IL 61842-1556 / 309-928-2574 or 800-248-3845; FAX: 309-928-2130

Burkhart Gunsmithing, Don, P.O. Box 852, Rawlins, WY 82301 / 307-324-6007

Burnham Bros., P.O. Box 1148, Menard, TX 78659 / 915-396-4572; FAX: 915-396-4574

Burris Co., Inc., P.O. Box 1747, 331 E. 8th St., Greeley, CO 80631 / 970-356-1670; FAX: 970-356-8702

Bushmaster Firearms, Inc., 999 Roosevelt Trail, Windham, ME 04062 / 800-998-7928; FAX: 207-892-8068 info@ bushmaster.com www.bushmaster.com

Bushmaster Hunting & Fishing, 451 Alliance Ave., Toronto, ON M6N 2J1 CANADA / 416-763-4040; FAX: 416-763-0623

Bushnell Outdoor Products, 9200 Cody, Overland Park, KS 66214 / 913-752-3400 or 800-423-3537; FAX: 913-752-3550

Buster's Custom Knives, P.O. Box 214, Richfield, UT 84701 / 435-896-5319; FAX: 435-896-8333 www. warenskiknives.com

Butler Creek Corp., 9200 Cody St., Overland Park, KS 66214 / 800-845-2444 or 406-388-1356; FAX: 406-388-7204

Butler Enterprises, 834 Oberting Rd., Lawrenceburg, IN 47025 / 812-537-3584

Buzz Fletcher Custom Stockmaker, 117 Silver Road, P.O. Box 189, Taos, NM 87571 / 505-758-3486

C

C&D Special Products (See Claybuster Wads & Harvester Bullets)

C&H Research, 115 Sunnyside Dr., Box 351, Lewis, KS 67552 / 316-324-5445 or 888-324-5445; FAX: 620-324-5984 info@mercuryrecoil.com www.mercuryrecoil.com

C. Sharps Arms Co. Inc./Montana Armory, 100 Centennial Dr., P.O. Box 885, Big Timber, MT 59011 / 406-932-4353; FAX: 406-932-4443 www.csharpsarms.com

C.S. Van Gorden & Son, Inc., 1815 Main St., Bloomer, WI 54724 / 715-568-2612 vangorden@bloomer.net

C.W. Erickson's Mfg., L.L.C., P.O. Box 522, Buffalo, MN 55313 / 763-682-3665; FAX: 763-682-4328 cwerickson@ archerhunter.com www.archerhunter.com

Cabanas (See U.S. Importer-Mandall Shooting Supply

Cabela's, One Cabela Drive, Sidney, NE 69160 / 308-254-5505; FAX: 308-254-8420

Cabinet Mtn. Outfitters Scents & Lures, P.O. Box 766, Plains, MT 59859 / 406-826-3970

Caesar Guerini USA, Inc., 700 Lake St., Cambridge, MD 21613 / 410-901-1131; FAX: 410-901-1137 info@ gueriniusa.com www.gueriniusa.com

Cain's Outdoors, Inc., 1832 Williams Hwy., Williamstown, WV 26187 / 304-375-7842; FAX: 304-375-7842 muzzleloading@cainsoutdoor.com www.cainsoutdoor. com

Cali'co Hardwoods, Inc., 3580 Westwind Blvd., Santa Rosa, CA 95403 / 707-546-4045; FAX: 707-546-4027 calicohardwoods@msn.com

California Sights (See Fautheree, Andy)

Camdex, Inc., 2330 Alger, Troy, MI 48083 / 810-528-2300; FAX: 810-528-0989

Cameron's, 16690 W. 11th Ave., Golden, CO 80401 / 303-279-7365; FAX: 303-568-1009 ncnoremac@aol.com

Camillus Cutlery Co., 54 Main St., Camillus, NY 13031 / 315-672-8111; FAX: 315-672-8832

Campbell, Dick, 196 Garden Homes Dr., Colville, WA 99114 / 509-684-6080; FAX: 509-684-6080 dicksknives@aol. com

Camp-Cap Products, P.O. Box 3805, Chesterfield, MO 63006 / 866-212-4639; FAX: 636-536-6320 mandrytrc@ sbcglobal.net www.langenberghats.com

Cannon Safe, Inc., 216 S. 2nd Ave. #BLD-932, San Bernardino, CA 92400 / 800-242-1055; FAX: 909-382-0707 info@cannonsafe.com www.cannonsafe.com

Canyon Cartridge Corp., P.O. Box 152, Albertson, NY 11507 FAX: 516-294-8946

Cape Outfitters, 599 County Rd. 206, Cape Girardeau, MO 63701 / 573-335-4103; FAX: 573-335-1555

Caraville Manufacturing, P.O. Box 4545, Thousand Oaks, CA 91359 / 805-499-1234

Carbide Checkering Tools (See J&R Engineering)

Carhartt, Inc., 5750 Mercury Dr., Dearborn, MI 48126 / 800-833-3118 www.carhartt.com

Carl Walther GmbH, B.P. 4325, D-89033, Ulm, GERMANY

Carl Zeiss Inc., 13005 N. Kingston Ave., Chester, VA 23836 / 800-441-3005; FAX: 804-530-8481

Carlson, Douglas. See: ANTIQUE AMERICAN FIREARMS

Carolina Precision Rifles, 1200 Old Jackson Hwy., Jackson, SC 29831 / 803-827-2069

Carrell, William. See: CARRELL'S PRECISION FIREARMS

Carrell's Precision Firearms, William Carrell, 1952 W. Silver Falls Ct., Meridian, ID 83642-3837

Carry-Lite, Inc., P.O. Box 1587, Fort Smith, AR 72902 / 479-782-8971; FAX: 479-783-0234

Carter's Gun Shop, 225 G St., Penrose, CO 81240 / 719-372-6240 rlewiscarter@msn.com

Case & Sons Cutlery Co., W R, Owens Way, Bradford, PA 16701 / 814-368-4123 or 800-523-6350; FAX: 814-768-5369 info@wrcase.com www.wrcase.com

Case Sorting System, 12695 Cobblestone Creek Rd., Poway, CA 92064 / 619-486-9340

Cash Mfg. Co./ TDC, P.O. Box 130, 201 S. Klein Dr., Waunakee, WI 53597-0130 / 608-849-5664; FAX: 608-849-5664 office@tdcmfg.com www.tdcmfg.com

Caspian Arms, Ltd., 14 North Main St., Hardwick, VT 05843 / 802-472-6454; FAX: 802-472-6709

Cast Bullet Association, The, 12857 S. Road, Hoyt, KS 66440-9116 cbamemdir@castbulletassoc.org www. castbulletassoc.org

Cast Performance Bullet Company, P.O. Box 1466, Rainier, OR 97048 / 503-556-3006; FAX: 503-556-8037 info@ bornhunter.com www.bornhunter.com

Casull Arms Corp., P.O. Box 1629, Afton, WY 83110 / 307-886-0200

Caswell Inc., 2540 2nd St. NE, Minneapolis, MN 55410 / 847-639-7666; FAX: 847-639-7694 www.caswellintl.com

Cathey Enterprises, Inc., P.O. Box 2202, Brownwood, TX 76804 / 915-643-2553; FAX: 915-643-3653

Cation, 2341 Alger St., Troy, MI 48083 / 810-689-0658; FAX: 810-689-7558

Caywood, Shane J., P.O. Box 321, Minocqua, WI 54548 / 715-277-3866

Caywood Gunmakers, 18 Kings Hill Estates, Berryville, AR 72616 / 870-423-4741 www.caywoodguns.com

CBC, Avenida Humberto de Campos 3220, 09400-000, Ribeirao Pires, SP, BRAZIL / 55 11 4822 8378; FAX: 55 11 4822 8323 export@cbc.com.bc www.cbc.com.bc

CBC-BRAZIL, 3 Cuckoo Lane, Honley, Yorkshire HD7 2BR, ENGLAND / 44-1484-661062; FAX: 44-1484-663709

CCG Enterprises, 5217 E. Belknap St., Halton City, TX 76117 / 800-819-7464

CCI/Speer Div of ATK, P.O. Box 856, 2299 Snake River Ave., Lewiston, ID 83501 / 800-627-3640 or 208-746-2351

CCL Security Products, 199 Whiting St., New Britain, CT 06051 / 800-733-8588

Cedar Hill Game Calls, LLC, 238 Vic Allen Rd., Downsville, LA 71234 / 318-982-5632; FAX: 318-982-2031

Centaur Systems, Inc., 1602 Foothill Rd., Kalispell, MT 59901 / 406-755-8609; FAX: 406-755-8609

Center Lock Scope Rings, 9901 France Ct., Lakeville, MN 55044 / 952-461-2114; FAX: 952-461-2194 marklee55044@usfamily.net

Central Specialties Ltd. (See Trigger Lock Division)

Century International Arms, Inc., 430 S. Congress Ave. Ste. 1, Delray Beach, FL 33445-4701 / 800-527-1252; FAX: 561-265-4520 support@centuryarms.com www. centuryarms.com

CFVentures, 509 Harvey Dr., Bloomington, IN 47403-1715 paladinwilltravel@yahoo.com www.caversam16. freeserve.co.uk

CH Tool & Die/4-D Custom Die Co., 711 N. Sandusky St., P.O. Box 889, Mt. Vernon, OH 43050-0889 / 740-397-7214; FAX: 740-397-6600 info@ch4d.com ch4d.com

Chace Leather Products, 507 Alden St., Fall River, MA 02722 / 508-678-7556; FAX: 508-675-9666 chacelea@ aol.com www.chaceleather.com

Chadick's Ltd., P.O. Box 100, Terrell, TX 75160 / 214-563-7577

Chambers Flintlocks Ltd., Jim, 116 Sams Branch Rd., Candler, NC 28715 / 828-667-8361; FAX: 828-665-0852 www.flintlocks.com

Champion Shooters' Supply, P.O. Box 303, New Albany, OH 43054 / 614-855-1603; FAX: 614-855-1209

Champion Target Co., 232 Industrial Parkway, Richmond, IN 47374 / 800-441-4971

Champion's Choice, Inc., 201 International Blvd., LaVergne, TN 37086 / 615-793-4066; FAX: 615-793-4070 champ. choice@earthlink.net www.champchoice.com

Champlin Firearms, Inc., P.O. Box 3191, Woodring Airport, Enid, OK 73701 / 580-237-7388; FAX: 580-242-6922 info@champlinarms.com www.champlinarms.com

Chapman Academy of Practical Shooting, 4350 Academy Rd., Hallsville, MO 65255 / 573-696-5544; FAX: 573-696-2266 hq@chapmanacademy.com www.chapmanacademy.com

Chapman, J. Ken. See: OLD WEST BULLET MOULDS

Chapman Manufacturing Co., 471 New Haven Rd., Durham, CT 06422 / 860-349-9228; FAX: 860-349-0084 sales@ chapmanmfg.com www.chapmanmfg.com

Chapuis Armes, Z1 La Gravoux, BP15, 42380 P.O. Box 15, St. Bonnet-le-Chatea, FRANCE / (33)477.50.06.96; FAX: (33)477 50 10 70 info@chapuis.armes.com www. chapuis-armes.com

Charter 2000, 273 Canal St., Shelton, CT 06484 / 203-922-1652

Checkmate Refinishing, 370 Champion Dr., Brooksville, FL 34601 / 352-799-5774; FAX: 352-799-2986 checkmatecustom.com

Cheddite, France S.A., 99 Route de Lyon, F-26501, Bourg-les-Valence, FRANCE / 33-75-56-4545; FAX: 33-75-56-3587 info@cheddite.com www.cheddite.com

Chelsea Gun Club of New York City, Inc., 237 Ovington Ave., Apt. D53, Brooklyn, NY 11209 / 718-836-9422 or 718-833-2704

CheVron Bullets, RR1, Ottawa, IL 61350 / 815-433-2471

Cheyenne Pioneer Products, P.O. Box 28425, Kansas City, MO 64188 / 816-413-9196; FAX: 816-455-2859 cheyennepp@aol.com www.cartridgeboxes.com

Chicago Cutlery Co., 5500 N. Pearl St., Ste. 400, Rosemont, IL 60018 / 847-678-8600 www.chicagocutlery.com

Chicasaw Gun Works, 4 Mi. Mkr., 322 Willow Br. Pluto Rd., Shady Spring, WV 25918-0868 / 304-763-2848; FAX: 304-763-3725

Chip McCormick Corp., P.O. Box 694, Spicewood, TX 78669 / 800-328-2447; FAX: 830-693-4975 www. chipmccormickcorp.com

Chipmunk (See Oregon Arms, Inc.)

Choate Machine & Tool Co., P.O. Box 218, 116 Lovers Ln., Bald Knob, AR 72010 / 501-724-6193; or 800-972-6390; FAX: 501-724-5873

Christensen Arms, 192 East 100 North, Fayette, UT 84630 / 435-528-7999; FAX: 435-528-7494 www. christensenarms.com

Christie's East, 20 Rockefeller Plz., New York, NY 10020-1902 / 212-606-0406 christics.com

Chu Tani Ind., Inc., P.O. Box 2064, Cody, WY 82414-2064

Chuck's Gun Shop, P.O. Box 597, Waldo, FL 32694 / 904-468-2264

Churchill (See U.S. Importer-Ellett Bros.)

Churchill, Winston G., 2838 20 Mile Stream Rd., Proctorville, VT 05153 / 802-226-7772

Churchill Glove Co., James, P.O. Box 298, Centralia, WA 98531 / 360-736-2816; FAX: 360-330-0151

Cimarron F.A. Co., P.O. Box 906, Fredericksburg, TX 78624-0906 / 830-997-9090; FAX: 830-997-0802 cimgraph@ koc.com www.cimarron-firearms.com

Cincinnati Swaging, 2605 Marlington Ave., Cincinnati, OH 45208

Clark Custom Guns, Inc., 336 Shootout Lane, Princeton, LA 71067 / 318-949-9884; FAX: 318-949-9829

Clark Firearms Engraving, 6347 Avon Ave., San Gabriel, CA 91775-1801 / 818-287-1652

Clarkfield Enterprises, Inc., 1032 10th Ave., Clarkfield, MN 56223 / 612-669-7140

Claro Walnut Gunstock Co., 1235 Stanley Ave., Chico, CA 95928 / 530-342-5188; FAX: 530-342-5199 wally@ clarowalnutgunstocks.com www.clarowalnutgunstocks. com

Classic Arms Company, Rt 1 Box 120F, Burnet, TX 78611 / 512-756-4001

Classic Arms Corp., P.O. Box 106, Dunsmuir, CA 96025-0106 / 530-235-2000

Classic Old West Styles, 1060 Doniphan Park Circle C, El Paso, TX 79936 / 915-587-0684

Clean Shot Technologies, 21218 St. Andrews Blvd. Ste 504, Boca Raton, FL 33433 / 888-866-2532

Clearview Mfg. Co., Inc., 413 S. Oakley St., Fordyce, AR 71742 / 870-352-8557; FAX: 870-352-7120

Clearview Products, 3021 N. Portland, Oklahoma City, OK 73107

Cleland's Outdoor World, Inc., 10306 Airport Hwy., Swanton, OH 43558 / 419-865-4713; FAX: 419-865-5865 mail@clelands.com www.clelands.com

Clements' Custom Leathercraft, Chas, 1741 Dallas St., Aurora, CO 80010-2018 / 303-364-0403; FAX: 303-739-9824 gryphons@home.com kuntaoslcat.com

Clenzoil Worldwide Corp., Jack Fitzgerald, 25670 1st St., Westlake, OH 44145-1430 / 440-899-0482; FAX: 440-899-0483

Clift Mfg., L.R., 3821 Hammonton Rd., Marysville, CA 95901 / 916-755-3390; FAX: 916-755-3393

Clymer Mfg. Co., 1645 W. Hamlin Rd., Rochester Hills, MI 48309-3312 / 248-853-5555; FAX: 248-853-1530

C-More Systems, P.O. Box 1750, 7553 Gary Rd., Manassas, VA 20108 / 703-361-2663; FAX: 703-361-5881

Cobra Enterprises, Inc., 1960 S. Milestone Drive, Suite F, Salt Lake City, UT 84104 FAX: 801-908-8301 www.cobrapistols@networld.com

Cobra Sport S.R.I., Via Caduti Nei Lager No. 1, 56020 San Romano, Montopoli v/Arno Pi, ITALY / 0039-571-450490; FAX: 0039-571-450492

Coffin, Charles H., 3719 Scarlet Ave., Odessa, TX 79762 / 915-366-4729; FAX: 915-366-4729

Cogar's Gunsmithing, 206 Redwine Dr., Houghton Lake, MI 48629 / 517-422-4591 ecogar@peoplepc.com

Coghlan's Ltd., 121 Irene St., Winnipeg, MB R3T 4C7 CANADA / 204-284-9550; FAX: 204-475-4127

Cold Steel Inc., 3036 Seaborg Ave. Ste. A, Ventura, CA 93003 / 800-255-4716; or 800-624-2363; FAX: 805-642-9727

Cole-Grip, 16135 Cohasset St., Van Nuys, CA 91406 / 818-782-4424

Coleman Co., Inc., 3600 N. Hydraulic, Wichita, KS 67219 / 800-835-3278 www.coleman.com

Collector's Armoury, Ltd., Tom Nelson, 9404 Gunston Cove Rd., Lorton, VA 22079 / 703-493-9120; FAX: 703-493-9424 www.collectorsarmoury.com

Collings, Ronald, 1006 Cielta Linda, Vista, CA 92083

Colonial Arms, Inc., P.O. Box 636, Selma, AL 36702-0636 / 334-872-9455; FAX: 334-872-9540 colonialarms@mindspring.com www.colonialarms.com

Colonial Repair, 47 Navarre St., Roslindale, MA 02131-4725 / 617-469-4951

Colorado Gunsmithing Academy, RR 3 Box 79B, El Campo, TX 77437 / 719-336-4099 or 800-754-2046; FAX: 719-336-9642

Colorado School of Trades, 1575 Hoyt St., Lakewood, CO 80215 / 800-234-4594; FAX: 303-233-4723

Colt Blackpowder Arms Co., 110 8th Street, Brooklyn, NY 11215 / 718-499-4678; FAX: 718-768-8056

Colt's Mfg. Co., Inc., P.O. Box 1868, Hartford, CT 06144-1868 / 800-962-COLT or 860-236-6311; FAX: 860-244-1449

Compass Industries, Inc., 104 East 25th St., New York, NY 10010 / 212-473-2614 or 800-221-9904; FAX: 212-353-0826

Compasseco, Ltd., 151 Atkinson Hill Ave., Bardstown, KY 40004 / 502-349-0910

Competition Electronics, Inc., 3469 Precision Dr., Rockford, IL 61109 / 815-874-8001; FAX: 815-874-8181

Competitive Pistol Shop, The, 5233 Palmer Dr., Fort Worth, TX 76117-2433 / 817-834-8479

Competitor Corp., Inc., 26 Knight St. Unit 3, P.O. Box 352, Jaffrey, NH 03452 / 603-532-9483; FAX: 603-532-8209 competitorcorp@aol.com competitor-pistol.com

Component Concepts, Inc., 530 S. Springbrook Road, Newberg, OR 97132 / 503-554-8095; FAX: 503-554-9370 cci@cybcon.com www.phantomonline.com

Concealment Shop, Inc., The, 3550 E. Hwy. 80, Mesquite, TX 75149 / 972-289-8997 or 800-444-7090; FAX: 972-289-4410 theconcealmentshop@msn.com www.theconcealmentshop.com

Concept Development Corp., 16610 E. Laser Drive, Suite 5, Fountain Hills, AZ 85268-6644

Conetrol Scope Mounts, 10225 Hwy. 123 S., Seguin, TX 78155 / 830-379-3030 or 800-CONETROL; FAX: 830-379-3030 email@conetrol.com www.conetrol.com

Connecticut Shotgun Mfg. Co., P.O. Box 1692, 35 Woodland St., New Britain, CT 06051 / 860-225-6581; FAX: 860-832-8707

Connecticut Valley Classics (See CVC, BPI)

Conrad, C. A., 3964 Ebert St., Winston-Salem, NC 27127 / 919-788-5469

Cook Engineering Service, 891 Highbury Rd., Vict 3133, 3133 AUSTRALIA

Cooper Arms, P.O. Box 114, Stevensville, MT 59870 / 406-777-0373; FAX: 406-777-5228

Cooper-Woodward Perfect Lube, 4120 Oesterle Rd., Helena, MT 59602 / 406-459-2287 cwperfectlube@mt.net cwperfectlube.com

Corbin Mfg. & Supply, Inc., 600 Industrial Circle, P.O. Box 2659, White City, OR 97503 / 541-826-5211; FAX: 541-826-8669 sales@corbins.com www.corbins.com

Cor-Bon Inc./Glaser LLC, P.O. Box 173, 1311 Industry Rd., Sturgis, SD 57785 / 605-347-4544 or 800-221-3489; FAX: 605-347-5055 email@corbon.com www.corbon.com

Corkys Gun Clinic, 4401 Hot Springs Dr., Greeley, CO 80634-9226 / 970-330-0516

Corry, John, 861 Princeton Ct., Neshanic Station, NJ 08853 / 908-369-8019

Cosmi Americo & Figlio S.N.C., Via Flaminia 307, Ancona, ITALY / 071-888208; FAX: 39-071-887008

Coulston Products, Inc., P.O. Box 30, 201 Ferry St. Suite 212, Easton, PA 18044-0030 / 215-253-0167 or 800-445-9927; FAX: 215-252-1511

Counter Assault, 120 Industrial Court, Kalispell, MT 59901 / 406-257-4740; FAX: 406-257-6674

Country Armourer, The, P.O. Box 308, Ashby, MA 01431-0308 / 508-827-6797; FAX: 508-827-4845

Cousin Bob's Mountain Products, 7119 Ohio River Blvd., Ben Avon, PA 15202 / 412-766-5114; FAX: 412-766-9354

CP Bullets, 1310 Industrial Hwy #5-6, Southhampton, PA 18966 / 215-953-7264; FAX: 215-953-7275

CQB Training, P.O. Box 1739, Manchester, MO 63011

Craftguard, 3624 Logan Ave., Waterloo, IA 50703 / 319-232-2959; FAX: 319-234-0804

Crandall Tool & Machine Co., 19163 21 Mile Rd., Tustin, MI 49688 / 616-829-4430

Creative Craftsman, Inc., The, 95 Highway 29 N., P.O. Box 331, Lawrenceville, GA 30246 / 404-963-2112; FAX: 404-513-9488

Creedmoor Sports, Inc., 1405 South Coast Hwy., Oceanside, CA 92054 / 800-273-3366; FAX: 760-757-5558 shoot@creedmoorsports.com www.creedmoorsports.com

Creighton Audette, 19 Highland Circle, Springfield, VT 05156 / 802-885-2331

Crimson Trace Lasers, 8090 S.W. Cirrus Dr., Beverton, OR 97008 / 800-442-2406; FAX: 503-627-0166 travis@crimsontrace.com www.crimsontrace.com

Crit' R Calls, P.O. Box 999, La Porte, CO 80535 / 970-484-2768; FAX: 970-484-0807 critrcall@larinet.net www.critrcall.com

Crit'R Call (See Rocky Mountain Wildlife Products)

Crosman Airguns, Rts. 5 and 20, E. Bloomfield, NY 14443 / 716-657-6161; FAX: 716-657-5405

Crosman Blades (See Coleman Co., Inc.)

CRR, Inc./Marble's Inc., 420 Industrial Park, P.O. Box 111, Gladstone, MI 49837 / 906-428-3710; FAX: 906-428-3711

Crucelegui, Hermanos (See U.S. Importer-Mandall)

Cubic Shot Shell Co., Inc., 98 Fatima Dr., Campbell, OH 44405 / 330-755-0349

Cullity Restoration, 209 Old Country Rd., East Sandwich, MA 02537 / 508-888-1147

Cummings Bullets, 1417 Esperanza Way, Escondido, CA 92027

Cunningham, Jerry. See: ORION RIFLE BARREL CO.

Cupp, Alana, Custom Engraver, P.O. Box 207, Annabella, UT 84711 / 801-896-4834

Curly Maple Stock Blanks (See Tiger-Hunt)

Curtis Cast Bullets, 527 W. Babcock St., Bozeman, MT 59715 / 406-587-8117; FAX: 406-587-8117

Curtis Gun Shop (See Curtis Cast Bullets)

Custom Bullets by Hoffman, 2604 Peconic Ave., Seaford, NY 11783

Custom Calls, 607 N. 5th St., Burlington, IA 52601 / 319-752-4465

Custom Checkering Service, Kathy Forster, 2124 S.E. Yamhill St., Portland, OR 97214 / 503-236-5874

Custom Products (See Jones Custom Products)

Custom Shop, The, 890 Cochrane Crescent, Peterborough, ON K9H 5N3 CANADA / 705-742-6693

Custom Single Shot Rifles, 9651 Meadows Lane, Guthrie, OK 73044 / 405-282-3634

Custom Tackle and Ammo, P.O. Box 1886, Farmington, NM 87499 / 505-632-3539

Cutco Cutlery, P.O. Box 810, Olean, NY 14760 / 716-372-3111

CVA, 5988 Peachtree Corners East, Norcross, GA 30071 / 770-449-4687; FAX: 770-242-8546 info@cva.com www.cva.com

Cylinder & Slide, Inc., William R. Laughridge, 245 E. 4th St., Fremont, NE 68025 / 402-721-4277; FAX: 402-721-0263 bill@cylinder-slide.com www.cylinder-slide.com

CZ USA, P.O. Box 171073, Kansas City, KS 66117 / 913-321-1811; FAX: 913-321-4901

D

D&D Gunsmiths, Ltd., 363 E. Elmwood, Troy, MI 48083 / 248-583-1512; FAX: 248-583-1524

D&G Precision Duplicators (See Greenwood Precision)

D&L Industries (See D.J. Marketing)

D&L Sports, P.O. Box 651, Gillette, WY 82717 / 307-686-4008

D.C. Engineering, Inc., 17195 Silver Parkway, Ste. 135, Fenton, MI 48430 / 248-382-1210 guns@rifletech.com www.rifletech.com

D.C.C. Enterprises, 259 Wynburn Ave., Athens, GA 30601

D.J. Marketing, 10602 Horton Ave., Downey, CA 90241 / 310-806-0891; FAX: 310-806-6231

D.L. Unmussig Bullets, 7862 Brentford Dr., Richmond, VA 23225 / 804-320-1165; FAX: 804-320-4587

Daisy Outdoor Products, P.O. Box 220, Rogers, AR 72757 / 479-636-1200; FAX: 479-636-0573 www.daisy.com

Dakota (See U.S. Importer-EMF Co., Inc.)

Dakota Arms, Inc., 130 Industry Road, Sturgis, SD 57785 / 605-347-4686; FAX: 605-347-4459 info@dakotaarms.com www.dakotaarms.com

Dakota Corp., 77 Wales St., P.O. Box 543, Rutland, VT 05701 / 802-775-6062 or 800-451-4167; FAX: 802-773-3919

Daly, Charles/KBI, P.O. Box 6625, Harrisburg, PA 17112 / 866-DALY GUN

Da-Mar Gunsmith's, Inc., 102 1st St., Solvay, NY 13209 damascususa@inteliport.com, 149 Deans Farm Rd., Tyner, NC 27980 / 252-221-2010 damascususa@inteliport.com www.damascususa.com

Dan Wesson Firearms, 5169 Rt. 12 South, Norwich, NY 13815 / 607-336-1174; FAX: 607-336-2730 dwservice@cz-usa.com dz-usa.com

Dangler, Homer. See: DANGLER'S CUSTOM FLINT RIFLES

Dangler's Custom Flint Rifles, Homer L. Dangler, 2870 Lee Marie Dr., Adrian, MI 49221 / 517-266-1997 homerdangler@yahoo.com

Danner Shoe Mfg. Co., 12722 N.E. Airport Way, Portland, OR 97230 / 503-251-1100 or 800-345-0430; FAX: 503-251-1119

Dan's Whetstone Co., Inc., 418 Hilltop Rd., Pearcy, AR 71964 / 501-767-1616; FAX: 501-767-9598 questions@danswhetstone.com www.danswhetstone.com

Danuser Machine Co., 550 E. Third St., P.O. Box 368, Fulton, MO 65251 / 573-642-2246; FAX: 573-642-2240 sales@danuser.com www.danuser.com

Dara-Nes, Inc. (See Nesci Enterprises, Inc.)

D'Arcy Echols & Co., P.O. Box 421, Millville, UT 84326 / 435-755-6842

Darlington Gun Works, Inc., P.O. Box 698, 516 S. 52 Bypass, Darlington, SC 29532 / 803-393-3931

Darwin Hensley Gunmaker, P.O. Box 329, Brightwood, OR 97011 / 503-622-5411

Data Tech Software Systems, 19312 East Eldorado Drive, Aurora, CO 80013

Dave Norin Schrank's Smoke & Gun, 2010 Washington St., Waukegan, IL 60085 / 708-662-4034

Dave's Gun Shop, P.O. Box 2824, Casper, WY 82602-2824 / 307-754-9724

David Clark Co., Inc., P.O. Box 15054, Worcester, MA 01615 / 508-756-6216; FAX: 508-753-5827 sales@davidclark.com www.davidclark.com

David Condon, Inc., 109 E. Washington St., Middleburg, VA 22117 / 703-687-5642

David Miller Co., 3131 E. Greenlee Rd., Tucson, AZ 85716 / 520-326-3117

David R. Chicoine, PO Box 635, Gastonia, NC 28053 / 704-853-0265 bnpress@quik.com www.oldwestgunsmith.com

David W. Schwartz Custom Guns, 2505 Waller St., Eau Claire, WI 54703 / 715-832-1735

Davide Pedersoli and Co., Via Artigiani 57, Gardone VT, Brescia 25063, ITALY / 030-8915000; FAX: 030-8911019 info@davidepedersoli.com www.davide_pedersoli.com

Davis, Don, 1619 Heights, Katy, TX 77493 / 713-391-3090

Davis Industries (See Cobra Enterprises, Inc.)

Davis Products, Mike, 643 Loop Dr., Moses Lake, WA 98837 / 509-765-6178 or 509-766-7281

Daystate Ltd., Birch House Lanee, Cotes Heath Staffs, ST15.022, ENGLAND / 01782-791755; FAX: 01782-791617

Dayton Traister, 4778 N. Monkey Hill Rd., P.O. Box 593, Oak Harbor, WA 98277 / 360-679-4657; FAX: 360-675-1114

D-Boone Ent., Inc., 5900 Colwyn Dr., Harrisburg, PA 17109

Dead Eye's Sport Center, 76 Baer Rd., Shickshinny, PA 18655 / 570-256-7432 deadeyeprizz@aol.com

Deepeeka Exports Pvt. Ltd., D-78, Saket, Meerut-250-006, INDIA / 011-91-121-640363 or ; FAX: 011-91-121-640988 deepeeka@poboxes.com www.deepeeka.com

Defense Training International, Inc., 749 S. Lemay, Ste. A3-337, Ft. Collins, CO 80524 / 303-482-2520; FAX: 303-482-0548 www.defense_training.com

deHaas Barrels, 20049 W. State Hwy. Z, Ridgeway, MO 64481 / 660-872-6308 dehaas@grm.net

Del Rey Products, P.O. Box 5134, Playa Del Rey, CA 90296-5134 / 213-823-0494

Delhi Gun House, 1374 Kashmere Gate, New Delhi 110 006, INDIA / 2940974 or 394-0974; FAX: 2917344 dgh@vsnl.com www.dgh@vsnl.com

Delorge, Ed, 6734 W. Main, Houma, LA 70360 / 985-223-0206 delorge@triparish.net www.eddelorge.com

Del-Sports, Inc., Dave Budin, P.O. Box 685, 817 Main St., Margaretville, NY 12455 / 845-586-4103; FAX: 845-586-4105

Delta Arms Ltd., P.O. Box 1000, Delta, VT 84624-1000

Delta Enterprises, 284 Hagemann Drive, Livermore, CA 94550

Dem-Bart Checkering Tools, Inc., 1825 Bickford Ave., Snohomish, WA 98290 / 360-568-7356 walt@dembartco.com www.dembartco.com

Denver Instrument Co., 6542 Fig St., Arvada, CO 80004 / 800-321-1135 or 303-431-7255; FAX: 303-423-4831

DeSantis Holster & Leather Goods, Inc., 431 Bayview Ave., Amityville, NY 11701 / 631-841-6300; FAX: 631-841-6320 www.desantisholster.com

Desert Mountain Mfg., P.O. Box 130184, Coram, MT 59913 / 800-477-0762 or 406-387-5361; FAX: 406-387-5361

Detonics USA, 53 Perimeter Center East #200, Atlanta, GA 30346 / 866-759-1169

DGR Custom Rifles, 4191 37th Ave. SE, Tappen, ND 58487 / 701-327-8135

DGS, Inc., Dale A. Storey, 1117 E. 12th, Casper, WY 82601 / 307-237-2414; FAX: 307-237-2414 dalest@trib.com www.dgsrifle.com

DHB Products, 336 River View Dr., Verona, VA 24482-2547 / 703-836-2648

Diamond Machining Technology Inc. (See DMT)

Diamond Mfg. Co., P.O. Box 174, Wyoming, PA 18644 / 800-233-9601

Dibble, Derek A., 555 John Downey Dr., New Britain, CT 06051 / 203-224-2630

Dietz Gun Shop & Range, Inc., 421 Range Rd., New Braunfels, TX 78132 / 830-885-4662

Dilliott Gunsmithing, Inc., 657 Scarlett Rd., Dandridge, TN 37725 / 865-397-9204 gunsmithd@aol.com dilliottgunsmithing.com

Dillon Precision Products, Inc., 8009 East Dillon's Way, Scottsdale, AZ 85260 / 480-948-8009 or 800-762-3845; FAX: 480-998-2786 sales@dillonprecision.com www.dillonprecision.com

Dina Arms Corporation, P.O. Box 46, Royersford, PA 19468 / 610-287-0266; FAX: 610-287-0266 dinaarms@erols.com www.users.erds.com/dinarms

Dixie Gun Works, P.O. Box 130, Union City, TN 38281 / 731-885-0700; FAX: 731-885-0440 info@dixiegunworks.com www.dixiegunworks.com

Dixon Muzzleloading Shop, Inc., 9952 Kunkels Mill Rd., Kempton, PA 19529 / 610-756-6271 dixonmuzzleloading.com

DJ Illinois River Valley Calls, Inc., P.O. Box 370, S. Pekin, IL 61564-0370 / 866-352-2557; FAX: 309-348-3987 djcalls@grics.net www.djcalls.com

DKT, Inc., 14623 Vera Dr., Union, MI 49130-9744 / 800-741-7083 orders; FAX: 616-641-2015

DLO Mfg., 10807 SE Foster Ave., Arcadia, FL 33821-7304

DMT-Diamond Machining Technology, Inc., 85 Hayes Memorial Dr., Marlborough, MA 01752 FAX: 508-485-3924

Dohring Bullets, 100 W. 8 Mile Rd., Ferndale, MI 48220

Dolbare, Elizabeth, P.O. Box 502, Dubois, WY 82513-0502 / 307-450-7500 edolbare@hotmail.com www.scrimshaw-engraving.com

Domino, P.O. Box 108, 20019 Settimo Milanese, Milano, ITALY / 1-39-2-33512040; FAX: 1-39-2-33511587

Don Hume Leathergoods, Don Hume, 500 26th Ave. NW, Miami, OK 74354 / 800-331-2686; FAX: 918-542-4340 info@donhume.com www.donhume.com

Don Klein Custom Guns, 433 Murray Park Dr., Ripon, WI 54971 / 920-748-2931 daklein@charter.net www.donkleincustomguns.com

Donnelly, C. P., 405 Kubli Rd., Grants Pass, OR 97527 / 541-846-6604

Doskocil Mfg. Co., Inc., P.O. Box 1246, 4209 Barnett, Arlington, TX 76017 / 817-467-5116; FAX: 817-472-9810

Douglas Barrels, Inc., 5504 Big Tyler Rd., Charleston, WV 25313-1398 / 304-776-1341; FAX: 304-776-8560 www.benchrest.com/douglas

Downsizer Corp., P.O. Box 710316, Santee, CA 92072-0316 / 619-448-5510 www.downsizer.com

DPMS (Defense Procurement Manufacturing Services, Inc.), 13983 Industry Ave., Becker, MN 55308 / 800-578-DPMS or 763-261-5600; FAX: 763-261-5599

Dr. O's Products Ltd., 1177 US Route SW, Selkirk, NY 12150

Dremel Mfg. Co., 4915-21st St., Racine, WI 53406

Dri-Slide, Inc., 411 N. Darling, Fremont, MI 49412 / 616-924-3950

Dropkick, 1460 Washington Blvd., Williamsport, PA 17701 / 717-326-6561; FAX: 717-326-4950

DS Arms, Inc., P.O. Box 370, 27 West 990 Industrial Ave., Barrington, IL 60010 / 847-277-7258; FAX: 847-277-7259 www.dsarms.com

DTM International, Inc., 40 Joslyn Rd., P.O. Box 5, Lake Orion, MI 48362 / 313-693-6670

Duane A. Hobbie Gunsmithing, 2412 Pattie Ave., Wichita, KS 67216 / 316-264-8266

Duane's Gun Repair (See DGR Custom Rifles)

Dubber, Michael W., P.O. Box 312, Evansville, IN 47702 / 812-424-9000; FAX: 812-424-6551

Duffy, Charles E. (See Guns Antique & Modern DBA), 224 Williams Ln., P.O. Box 2, West Hurley, NY 12491 / 845-679-2997 ceo1923@prodigy.net

Du-Lite Corp., 171 River Rd., Middletown, CT 06457 / 203-347-2505; FAX: 203-347-9404

Dumoulin, Ernest, Rue Florent Boclinville 8-10, 13-4041, Votten, BELGIUM / 41 27 78 92

Duncan's Gun Works, Inc., 1619 Grand Ave., San Marcos, CA 92078 / 760-727-0515; FAX: 760-591-9245

DunLyon R&D, Inc., 52151 E. U.S. Hwy. 60, Miami, AZ 85539 / 928-473-9027

Duofold, Inc., RD 3 Rt. 309, Valley Square Mall, Tamaqua, PA 18252 / 717-386-2666; FAX: 717-386-3652

Dybala Gun Shop, P.O. Box 1024, FM 3156, Bay City, TX 77414 / 409-245-0866

Dykstra, Doug, 411 N. Darling, Fremont, MI 49412 / 616-924-3950

Dynalite Products, Inc., 215 S. Washington St., Greenfield, OH 45123 / 513-981-2124

Dynamit Nobel-RWS, Inc., 6007 S. 29th St., Fort Smith, AR 72908

E

E&L Mfg., Inc., 4177 Riddle Bypass Rd., Riddle, OR 97469 / 541-874-2137; FAX: 541-874-3107

E. Arthur Brown Co. Inc., 4353 Hwy. 27 E., Alexandria, MN 56308 / 320-762-8847; FAX: 320-763-4310 www.eabco.com

E.A.A. Corp., P.O. Box 1299, Sharpes, FL 32959 / 407-639-4842 or 800-536-4442; FAX: 407-639-7006

Eagan, Donald. See: EAGAN GUNSMITHS

Eagan Gunsmiths, Donald V. Eagan, P.O. Box 196, Benton, PA 17814 / 570-925-6134

Eagle Arms, Inc. (See ArmaLite, Inc.)

Eagle Grips, Eagle Business Center, 460 Randy Rd., Carol Stream, IL 60188 / 800-323-6144 or 708-260-0400; FAX: 708-260-0486

Eagle Imports, Inc., 1750 Brielle Ave., Unit B1, Wanamassa, NJ 07712 / 732-493-0333; FAX: 732-493-0301 gsodini@aol.com www.bersafirearmsusa.com

E-A-R, Inc., Div. of Cabot Safety Corp., 5457 W. 79th St., Indianapolis, IN 46268 / 800-327-3431; FAX: 800-488-8007

EAW (See U.S. Importer-New England Custom Gun Serv

Ed Brown Products, Inc., P.O. Box 492, Perry, MO 63462 / 573-565-3261; FAX: 573-565-2791 edbrown@edbrown.com www.edbrown.com

Ed Brown Products, Inc., 43825 Muldrow Trl., P.O. Box 492, Perry, MO 63462 / 573-565-3261; FAX: 573-565-2791 edbrown@edbrown.com www.edbrown.com

Edenpine, Inc. c/o Six Enterprises, Inc., 320 D Turtle Creek Ct., San Jose, CA 95125 / 408-999-0201; FAX: 408-999-0216

EdgeCraft Corp., S. Weiner, 825 Southwood Rd., Avondale, PA 19311 / 610-268-0500 or 800-342-3255; FAX: 610-268-3545 www.edgecraft.com

Edmisten Co., P.O. Box 1293, Boone, NC 28607

Edmund Scientific Co., 101 E. Gloucester Pike, Barrington, NJ 08033 / 609-543-6250

Ed's Gun House, Ed Kukowski, P.O. Box 62, Minnesota City, MN 55959 / 507-689-2925

Effebi SNC-Dr. Franco Beretta, via Rossa, 4, 25062, ITALY / 030-2751955; FAX: 030-2180414

Eggleston, Jere D., 400 Saluda Ave., Columbia, SC 29205 / 803-799-3402

Eichelberger Bullets, Wm., 158 Crossfield Rd., King Of Prussia, PA 19406

El Paso Saddlery Co., P.O. Box 27194, El Paso, TX 79926 / 915-544-2233; FAX: 915-544-2535 info@epsaddlery.com www.epsaddlery.com

Electro Prismatic Collimators, Inc., 1441 Manatt St., Lincoln, NE 68521

Electronic Shooters Protection, Inc., 15290 Gadsden Ct., Brighton, CO 80603 / 800-797-7791; FAX: 303-659-8668 esp@usa.net www.espamerica.com

Eley Ltd., Selco Way Minworth Industrial Estate, Minworth Sutton Coldfield, West Midlands, B76 1BA ENGLAND / 44 0 121-313-4567; FAX: 44 0 121-313-4568 www.eley.co.uk

Ellett Bros., 267 Columbia Ave., P.O. Box 128, Chapin, SC 29036 / 803-345-3751 or 800-845-3711; FAX: 803-345-1820 www.ellettbrothers.com

Ellicott Arms, Inc. / Woods Pistolsmithing, 8390 Sunset Dr., Ellicott City, MD 21043 / 410-465-7979

EMAP USA, 6420 Wilshire Blvd., Los Angeles, CA 90048 / 213-782-2000; FAX: 213-782-2867

Emerging Technologies, Inc. (See Laseraim Technologies, Inc.)

EMF Co. Inc., 1900 E. Warner Ave., Suite 1-D, Santa Ana, CA 92705 / 949-261-6611; FAX: 949-756-0133

Empire Cutlery Corp., 12 Kruger Ct., Clifton, NJ 07013 / 201-472-5155; FAX: 201-779-0759

Empire Rifles, P.O. Box 406, Meriden, NH 03770 info@empirerifles.com www.empirerifles.com

English, Inc., A.G., 708 S. 12th St., Broken Arrow, OK 74012 / 918-251-3399 info@agenglish.com www.agenglish.com

Engraving Artistry, 36 Alto Rd., Burlington, CT 06013 / 860-673-6837

Enguix Import-Export, Alpujarras 58, Alzira, Valencia, SPAIN / (96) 241 43 95; FAX: (96) 241 43 95

Enhanced Presentations, Inc., 3504 Iris St., Wilmington, NC 28409 / 910-799-1622; FAX: 910-799-5004

Ensign-Bickford Co., The, 660 Hopmeadow St., Simsbury, CT 06070

Entreprise Arms, Inc., 5321 Irwindale Ave., Irwindale, CA 91706-2025 / 626-962-8712; FAX: 626-962-4692 www.entreprise.com

EPC, 1441 Manatt St., Lincoln, NE 68521 / 402-476-3946

Erhardt, Dennis, 4508 N. Montana Ave., Helena, MT 59602 / 406-442-4533

MANUFACTURER'S DIRECTORY

Essex Arms, P.O. Box 363, Island Pond, VT 05846 / 802-723-6203; FAX: 802-723-6203

Estate Cartridge, Inc., 900 Bob Ehlen Dr., Anoka, MN 55303-7502 / 409-856-7277; FAX: 409-856-5486

Euber Bullets, No. Orwell Rd., Orwell, VT 05760 / 802-948-2621

Euroarms of America, Inc., P.O. Box 3277, Winchester, VA 22604 / 540-662-1863; FAX: 540-662-4464 mail@euroarms.net www.euroarms.net

Euro-Imports, George Tripes, 412 Slayden St., Yoakum, TX 77995 / 361-293-9353; FAX: 361-293-9353 mrbrno@yahoo.com

European American Armory Corp. (See E.A.A. Corp.)

Eversull Co., Inc., 1 Tracemont, Boyce, LA 71409 / 318-793-8728; FAX: 318-793-5483 bestguns@aol.com

Evolution Gun Works, Inc., 48 Belmont Ave., Quakertown, PA 18951-1347 www.egw-guns.com

Excalibur Electro Optics, Inc., P.O. Box 400, Fogelsville, PA 18051-0400 / 610-391-9105; FAX: 610-391-9220

Excalibur Publications, P.O. Box 89667, Tucson, AZ 85752 / 520-575-9057 excalibureditor@earthlink.net

Excel Industries, Inc., 4510 Carter Ct., Chino, CA 91710 / 909-627-2404; FAX: 909-627-7817 www.excelarms.com or accu-tekfirearms.com

Executive Protection Institute, P.O. Box 802, Berryville, VA 22611 / 540-554-2540; FAX: 540-554-2558 ruk@crosslink.net www.personalprotecion.com

Eze-Lap Diamond Prods., P.O. Box 2229, 15164 W. State St., Westminster, CA 92683 / 714-847-1555; FAX: 714-897-0280

F

F.A.I.R., S.R.L., Via Gitti, 41, 25060 Marcheno (BS), 25060 Marcheno Bresc, ITALY / 030 861162-8610344; FAX: 030 8610179 info@fair.it www.fair.it

F+W Publications, Inc., 700 E. State St., Iola, WI 54990 / 715-445-2214; FAX: 715-445-4087

Fabarm S.p.A., Via Averolda 31, 25039 Travagliato, Brescia, ITALY / 030-6863629; FAX: 030-6863684 info@fabarm.com www.fabarm.com

Fagan Arms, 22952 15 Mile Rd., Clinton Township, MI 48035 / 810-465-4637; FAX: 810-792-6996

Faith Associates, P.O. Box 549, Flat Rock, NC 28731-0549 FAX: 828-697-6827

Falcon Industries, Inc., P.O. Box 1690, Edgewood, NM 87015 / 505-281-3783; FAX: 505-281-3991 shines@ergogrips.com www.ergogrips.com

Farm Form Decoys, Inc., 1602 Biovu, P.O. Box 748, Galveston, TX 77553 / 409-744-0762 or 409-765-6361; FAX: 409-765-8513

Farr Studio, Inc., 17149 Bournbrook Ln., Jeffersonton, VA 22724-1796 / 615-638-8825

Farrar Tool Co., Inc., 11855 Cog Hill Dr., Whittier, CA 90601-1902 / 310-863-4367; FAX: 310-863-5123

Faulhaber Wildlocker, Dipl.-Ing. Norbert Wittasek, Seilergasse 2, A-1010 Wien, AUSTRIA / 43-1-5137001; FAX: 43-1-5137001 faulhaber1@utanet.at

Faulk's Game Call Co., Inc., 616 18th St., Lake Charles, LA 70601 / 337-436-9726; FAX: 337-494-7205 www.faulkcalls.com

Faust Inc., T. G., 544 Minor St., Reading, PA 19602 / 610-375-8549; FAX: 610-375-4488

Fautheree, Andy, P.O. Box 4607, Pagosa Springs, CO 81157 / 970-731-5003; FAX: 970-731-5009

Feather, Flex Decoys, 4500 Doniphan Dr., Neosho, MO 64850 / 318-746-8596; FAX: 318-742-4815

Federal Cartridge Co., 900 Ehlen Dr., Anoka, MN 55303 / 612-323-2300; FAX: 612-323-2506

Federal Champion Target Co., 232 Industrial Pkwy., Richmond, IN 47374 / 800-441-4971; FAX: 317-966-7747

Federated-Fry (See Fry Metals)

FEG, Budapest, Soroksariut 158, H-1095, HUNGARY

Feinwerkbau Westinger & Altenburger, Neckarstrasse 43, 78727, Oberndorf a. N., GERMANY / 07423-814-0; FAX: 07423-814-200 info@feinwerkbau.de www.feinwerkbau.de

Ferguson, Bill, P.O. Box 1238, Sierra Vista, AZ 85636 / 520-458-5321; FAX: 520-458-9125

Ferguson, Bill. See: BULLET METALS

FERLIB, Via Parte 33 Marcheno/BS, Marcheno/BS, ITALY / 00390308610191; FAX: 00390308966682 info@ferlib.com www.ferlib.com

Ferris Firearms, 7110 F.M. 1863, Bulverde, TX 78163 / 210-980-4424

Fieldsport Ltd., Bryan Bilinski, 3313 W. South Airport Rd., Traverse City, MI 49684 / 616-933-0767

Fiocchi Munizioni S.A. (See U.S. Importer-Fiocch

Fiocchi of America, Inc., 5030 Fremont Rd., Ozark, MO 65721 / 417-725-4118 or 800-721-2666; FAX: 417-725-1039

Firearm Brokers, PO Box 91787, Louisville, KY 40291 firearmbrokers@aol.com www.firearmbrokers.com

Firearms Co. Ltd. / Alpine (See U.S. Importer-Mandall

Firearms Engraver's Guild of America, 3011 E. Pine Dr., Flagstaff, AZ 86004 / 928-527-8427 fegainfo@fega.com

Fisher, Jerry A., 631 Crane Mt. Rd., Big Fork, MT 59911 / 406-837-2722

Fisher Custom Firearms, 2199 S. Kittredge Way, Aurora, CO 80013 / 303-755-3710

Fitzgerald, Jack. See: CLENZOIL WORLDWIDE CORP.

Flambeau, Inc., 15981 Valplast Rd., Middlefield, OH 44062 / 216-632-1631; FAX: 216-632-1581 www.flambeau.com

Flayderman & Co., Inc., P.O. Box 2446, Fort Lauderdale, FL 33303 / 954-761-8855 www.flayderman.com

Fleming Firearms, 7720 E. 126th St. N., Collinsville, OK 74021-7016 / 918-665-3624

Fletcher-Bidwell, LLC, 305 E. Terhune St., Viroqua, WI 54665-1631 / 866-637-1860 fbguns@netscape.net

Flintlocks, Etc., 160 Rossiter Rd., P.O. Box 181, Richmond, MA 01254 / 413-698-3822; FAX: 413-698-3866 flintetc@berkshire.rr.com

Flitz International Ltd., 821 Mohr Ave., Waterford, WI 53185 / 414-534-5898; FAX: 414-534-2991

Fluoramics, Inc., 18 Industrial Ave., Mahwah, NJ 07430 / 800-922-0075; FAX: 201-825-7035 pdouglas@fluoramics.com www.tufoil.com

Flynn's Custom Guns, P.O. Box 7461, Alexandria, LA 71306 / 318-455-7130

FN Manufacturing, P.O. Box 24257, Columbia, SC 29224 / 803-736-0522

Folks, Donald E., 205 W. Lincoln St., Pontiac, IL 61764 / 815-844-7901

Foredom Electric Co., Rt. 6, 16 Stony Hill Rd., Bethel, CT 06801 / 203-792-8622

Forgreens Tool & Mfg., Inc., P.O. Box 955, Robert Lee, TX 76945 / 915-453-2800; FAX: 915-453-2460

Forkin Custom Classics, 205 10th Ave. S.W., White Sulphur Spring, MT 59645 / 406-547-2344

Forrest Tool Co., P.O. Box 768, 44380 Gordon Ln., Mendocino, CA 95460 / 707-937-2141; FAX: 717-937-1817

Forster, Kathy (See Custom Checkering)

Forster, Larry L., Box 212, 216 Hwy. 13 E., Gwinner, ND 58040-0212 / 701-678-2475

Forster Products, Inc., 310 E. Lanark Ave., Lanark, IL 61046 / 815-493-6360; FAX: 815-493-2371 info@forsterproducts.com www.forsterproducts.com

Fort Hill Gunstocks, 12807 Fort Hill Rd., Hillsboro, OH 45133 / 513-466-2763

Fort Knox Security Products, 1051 N. Industrial Park Rd., Orem, UT 84057 / 801-224-7233 or 800-821-5216; FAX: 801-226-5493

Forthofer's Gunsmithing & Knifemaking, 5535 U.S. Hwy. 93S, Whitefish, MT 59937-8411 / 406-862-2674

Fortune Products, Inc., 205 Hickory Creek Rd., Marble Falls, TX 78654 / 210-693-6111; FAX: 210-693-6394 randy@accusharp.com

Foster, . See: ACCURACY INTERNATIONAL

Fountain Products, 492 Prospect Ave., West Springfield, MA 01089 / 413-781-4651; FAX: 413-733-8217

Fowler, Bob (See Black Powder Products)

Fox River Mills, Inc., P.O. Box 298, 227 Poplar St., Osage, IA 50461 / 515-732-3798; FAX: 515-732-5128

Fraim, William. See: ACUSPORT CORPORATION

Frank Knives, 1147 SW Bryson St. 1, Dallas, OR 97338 / 503-831-1489; FAX: 541-563-3041

Frank Mittermeier, Inc., P.O. Box 1, Bronx, NY 10465

Franzen International, Inc (See U.S. Importer-Importer Co.)

Freedom Arms, Inc., P.O. Box 150, Freedom, WY 83120 / 307-883-2468; FAX: 307-883-2005

Fremont Tool Works, 1214 Prairie, Ford, KS 67842 / 316-369-2327

Front Sight Firearms Training Institute, P.O. Box 2619, Aptos, CA 95001 / 800-987-7719; FAX: 408-684-2137

Frontier, 2910 San Bernardo, Laredo, TX 78040 / 956-723-5409; FAX: 956-723-1774

Frontier Arms Co., Inc., 401 W. Rio Santa Cruz, Green Valley, AZ 85614-3932

Frontier Products Co., 2401 Walker Rd., Roswell, NM 88201-8950 / 505-627-0763

Frost Cutlery Co., P.O. Box 22636, Chattanooga, TN 37422 / 615-894-6079; FAX: 615-894-9576

Fry Metals, 4100 6th Ave., Altoona, PA 16602 / 814-946-1611

Fujinon, Inc., 10 High Point Dr., Wayne, NJ 07470 / 201-633-5600; FAX: 201-633-5216

Fullmer, Geo. M., 2499 Mavis St., Oakland, CA 94601 / 510-533-4193

Fulton Armory, 8725 Bollman Place No. 1, Savage, MD 20763 / 301-490-9485; FAX: 301-490-9547 www.fulton-armory.com

Furr Arms, 91 N. 970 West, Orem, UT 84057 / 801-226-3877; FAX: 801-226-3877

G

G&H Decoys, Inc., P.O. Box 1208, Hwy. 75 North, Henryetta, OK 74437 / 918-652-3314; FAX: 918-652-3400

G.C. Bullet Co., Inc., 40 Mokelumne River Dr., Lodi, CA 95240

G.G. & G., 3602 E. 42nd Stravenue, Tucson, AZ 85713 / 520-748-7167; FAX: 520-748-7583 ggg&3@aol.com www.ggg&3.com

G.U., Inc. (See U.S. Importer-New SKB Arms Co.)

G96 Products Co., Inc., 85 5th Ave., Bldg. #6, Paterson, NJ 07544 / 973-684-4050; FAX: 973-684-3848 g96prod@aol

Gage Manufacturing, 20820 W. Kaibab Rd., Buckeye, AZ 85326 / 310-832-3546

Gaillard Barrels, Box 68, St. Brieux, SK S0K 3V0 CANADA / 306-752-3769; FAX: 306-752-5969

Galati International, P.O. Box 10, 616 Burley Ridge Rd., Wesco, MO 65586 / 636-584-0785; FAX: 573-775-4308 support@galatiinternational.com www.galatiinternational.com

Galaxy Imports Ltd., Inc., P.O. Box 3361, Victoria, TX 77903 / 361-573-4867 galaxy06@suddenlink.net

GALCO International Ltd., 2019 W. Quail Ave., Phoenix, AZ 85027 / 623-474-7070; FAX: 623-582-6854 customerservice@usgalco.com www.usgalco.com

Galena Industries AMT, 5463 Diaz St., Irwindale, CA 91706 / 626-856-8883; FAX: 626-856-8878

Gamba Renato Bremec Srl, Via Artigiani 93, 25063 Gardone V.T. BS, ITALY / 30-8910264-5; FAX: 30-8912180 infocomm@renatogamba.it www.renatogamba.it

Game Haven Gunstocks, 13750 Shire Rd., Wolverine, MI 49799 / 616-525-8257

Gamebore Division, Polywad, Inc., P.O. Box 7916, Macon, GA 31209 / 478-477-0669 or 800-998-0669

Gamo (See U.S. Importers-Arms United Corp., Daisy M

Gamo USA, Inc., 3911 SW 47th Ave., Suite 914, Fort Lauderdale, FL 33314 / 954-581-5822; FAX: 954-581-3165 gamousa@gate.net www.gamo.com

Gander Mountain, Inc., 12400 Fox River Rd., Wilmont, WI 53192 / 414-862-6848

GAR, 590 McBride Ave., West Paterson, NJ 07424 / 973-754-1114; FAX: 973-754-1114 garreloading@aol.com www.garreloading.com

Garrett Cartridges, Inc., P.O. Box 178, Chehalis, WA 98532 / 360-736-0702 www.garrettcartridges.com

Garthwaite Pistolsmith, Inc., Jim, 12130 State Route 405, Watsontown, PA 17777 / 570-538-1566 www.garthwaite.com

Gary Goudy Classic Stocks, 1512 S. 5th St., Dayton, WA 99328 / 509-382-2726 goudy@icehouse.net

Gary Reeder Custom Guns, 2601 7th Ave. E., Flagstaff, AZ 86004 / 928-526-3313; FAX: 928-527-0840 gary@reedercustomguns.com www.reedercustomguns.com

Gator Guns & Repair, 7952 Kenai Spur Hwy., Kenai, AK 99611-8311

GDL Enterprises, 409 Le Gardeur, Slidell, LA 70460 / 504-649-0693

Gehmann, Walter (See Huntington Die Specialties)

Genco, P.O. Box 5704, Asheville, NC 28803

Genecco Gun Works, 10512 Lower Sacramento Rd., Stockton, CA 95210 / 209-951-0706; FAX: 209-931-3872

Gene's Custom Guns, P.O. Box 10534, White Bear Lake, MN 55110 / 651-429-5105; FAX: 651-429-7365

Gentex Corp., 5 Tinkham Ave., Derry, NH 03038 / 603-434-0311; FAX: 603-434-3002 sales@derry.gentexcorp.com www.derry.gentexcorp.com

Gentner Bullets, 109 Woodlawn Ave., Upper Darby, PA 19082 / 610-352-9396 dongentner@rcn.com www.gentnerbullets.com

Gentry Custom LLC, 314 N. Hoffman, Belgrade, MT 59714 / 406-388-GUNS gentryshop@earthlink.net www.gentrycustom.com

George & Roy's, P.O. Box 2125, Sisters, OR 97759-2125 / 503-228-5424 or 800-553-3022; FAX: 503-225-9409

George Hoenig, Inc., 4357 Frozen Dog Rd., Emmett, ID 83617 / 208-365-7716; FAX: 208-365-3472 gnhoenig@msn.com

George Ibberson (Sheffield) Ltd., 25-31 Allen St., Sheffield, S3 7AW ENGLAND / 0114-2766123; FAX: 0114-2738465 sales@eggintongroup.co.uk www.eggintongroup.co.uk

Gerber Legendary Blades, 14200 SW 72nd Ave., Portland, OR 97223 / 503-639-6161 or 800-950-6161; FAX: 503-684-7008

Gervais, Mike, 3804 S. Cruise Dr., Salt Lake City, UT 84109 / 801-277-7729

Getz Barrel Company, P.O. Box 88, 426 E. Market St., Beavertown, PA 17813 / 570-658-7263; FAX: 570-658-4110 www.getzbrl.com

Giacomo Sporting USA, 6234 Stokes Lee Center Rd., Lee Center, NY 13363

Gibbs Rifle Co., Inc., 219 Lawn St., Martinsburg, WV 25401 / 304-262-1651; FAX: 304-262-1658 support@gibbsrifle.com www.gibbsrifle.com

Gil Hebard Guns, Inc., 125 Public Square, P.O. Box 3, Knoxville, IL 61448-0003 / 309-289-2700; FAX: 309-289-2233

Gilbert Equipment Co., Inc., 960 Downtowner Rd., Mobile, AL 36609 / 205-344-3322

Gillmann, Edwin, 33 Valley View Dr., Hanover, PA 17331 / 717-632-1662 gillmaned@superpa.net

Gilmore Sports Concepts, Inc., 5949 S. Garnett Rd., Tulsa, OK 74146 / 918-250-3810; FAX: 918-250-3845 info@gilmoresports.com www.gilmoresports.com

Glacier Glove, 4890 Aircenter Circle, Suite 210, Reno, NV 89502 / 702-825-8225; FAX: 702-825-6544

Glaser LLC, P.O. Box 173, Sturgis, SD 57785 / 605-347-4544 or 800-221-3489; FAX: 605-347-5055 email@corbon.com www.safetyslug.com

Glaser Safety Slug, Inc. (see CorBon/Glaser safetyslug.com

Glass, Herb, P.O. Box 25, Bullville, NY 10915 / 914-361-3021

Glimm, Jerome. See: GLIMM'S CUSTOM GUN ENGRAVING

Glimm's Custom Gun Engraving, Jerome C. Glimm, 19 S. Maryland, Conrad, MT 59425 / 406-278-3574 lag@mcn.net www.gunengraver.biz

Glock GmbH, P.O. Box 50, A-2232, Deutsch, Wagram, AUSTRIA

Glock, Inc., P.O. Box 369, Smyrna, GA 30081 / 770-432-1202; FAX: 770-433-8719

Glynn Scobey Duck & Goose Calls, Rt. 3, Box 37, Newbern, TN 38059 / 731-643-6128

GML Products, Inc., 394 Laredo Dr., Birmingham, AL 35226 / 205-979-4867

Goens, Dale W., P.O. Box 224, Cedar Crest, NM 87008 / 505-281-5419

Goergen's Gun Shop, Inc., 17985 538th Ave., Austin, MN 55912 / 507-433-9280; FAX: 507-433-9280 jim_debgoergen@msn.com

GOEX, Inc., P.O. Box 659, Doyline, LA 71023-0659 / 318-382-9300; FAX: 318-382-9303 mfahringer@goexpowder.com www.goexpowder.com

Golden Age Arms Co., 115 E. High St., Ashley, OH 43003 / 614-747-2488

Golden Bear Bullets, 3065 Fairfax Ave., San Jose, CA 95148 / 408-238-9515

Goodling's Gunsmithing, 1950 Stoverstown Rd., Spring Grove, PA 17362 / 717-225-3350

Goodwin, Fred. See: GOODWIN'S GUNS

Goodwin's Guns, Fred Goodwin, 1028 Silver Ridge Rd., Silver Ridge, ME 04776 / 207-365-4451

Gotz Bullets, 11426 Edgemere Ter., Roscoe, IL 61073-8232

Gould & Goodrich Leather, Inc., 709 E. McNeil St., Lillington, NC 27546 / 910-893-2071; FAX: 910-893-4742 info@gouldusa.com www.gouldusa.com

Gournet Artistic Engraving, Geoffroy Gournet, 820 Paxinosa Ave., Easton, PA 18042 / 610-559-0710 ggournet@yahoo.com www.gournetusa.com

Gournet, Geoffroy. See: GOURNET ARTISTIC ENGRAVING

Grace, Charles E., 718 E. 2nd, Trinidad, CO 81082 / 719-846-9435 riflemakerone@yahoo.com

Grace Metal Products, P.O. Box 67, Elk Rapids, MI 49629 / 616-264-8133

Graf & Sons, 4050 S. Clark St., Mexico, MO 65265 / 573-581-2266; FAX: 573-581-2875 customerservice@grafs.com www.grafs.com

Grand Slam Hunting Products, Box 121, 25454 Military Rd., Cascade, MD 21719 / 301-241-4900; FAX: 301-241-4900 rlj6call@aol.com

Granite Mountain Arms, Inc., 3145 W. Hidden Acres Trail, Prescott, AZ 86305 / 520-541-9758; FAX: 520-445-6826

Grant, Howard V., Hiawatha 15, Woodruff, WI 54568 / 715-356-7146

Graphics Direct, P.O. Box 372421, Reseda, CA 91337-2421 / 818-344-9002

Graves Co., 1800 Andrews Ave., Pompano Beach, FL 33069 / 800-327-9103; FAX: 305-960-0301

Grayback Wildcats, Mike Beeks, 5306 Bryant Ave., Klamath Falls, OR 97603 / 541-884-1072; FAX: 541-884-1072 graybackwildcats@aol.com

Great American Gunstock Co., 3420 Industrial Drive, Yuba City, CA 95993 / 800-784-4867; FAX: 530-671-3906 gunstox@hotmail.com www.gunstocks.com

Green, Arthur S., 485 S. Robertson Blvd., Beverly Hills, CA 90211 / 310-274-1283

Green Head Game Call Co., RR 1, Box 33, Lacon, IL 61540 / 309-246-2155

Green Mountain Rifle Barrel Co., Inc., P.O. Box 2670, 153 W. Main St., Conway, NH 03818 / 603-447-1095; FAX: 603-447-1099 info@gmriflebarrel.com www.gmriflebarrel.com

Greg Gunsmithing Repair, 3732 26th Ave. N., Robbinsdale, MN 55422 / 612-529-8103

Greg's Superior Products, P.O. Box 46219, Seattle, WA 98146

Greider Precision, 431 Santa Marina Ct., Escondido, CA 92029 / 760-480-8892; FAX: 760-480-9800 greider@msn.com

Gre-Tan Rifles, 29742 W.C.R. 50, Kersey, CO 80644 / 970-353-6176; FAX: 970-356-5940 www.gtrtooling.com

Griffin & Howe, Inc., 340 W. Putnam Ave., Greenwich, CT 06830 / 203-618-0270 info@griffinhowe.com www.griffinhowe.com

Griffin & Howe, Inc., 33 Claremont Rd., Bernardsville, NJ 07924 / 908-766-2287; FAX: 908-766-1068 info@griffinhowe.com www.griffinhowe.com

Groenewold, John. See: JG AIRGUNS, LLC

GRS/Glendo Corp., P.O. Box 1153, 900 Overlander St., Emporia, KS 66801 / 620-343-1084 or 800-836-3519; FAX: 620-343-9640 glendo@glendo.com www.glendo.com

Grulla Armes, Apartado 453, Avda Otaloa 12, Eiber, SPAIN

Gruning Precision, Inc., 7101 Jurupa Ave., No. 12, Riverside, CA 92504 / 909-289-4371; FAX: 909-689-7791 gruningprecision@earthlink.net www.gruningprecision.com

GSI, Inc., 7661 Commerce Ln., Trussville, AL 35173 / 205-655-8299

Guarasi, Robert. See: WILCOX INDUSTRIES CORP.

Guardsman Products, 411 N. Darling, Fremont, MI 49412 / 616-924-3950

Gun City, 212 W. Main Ave., Bismarck, ND 58501 / 701-223-2304

Gun Digest (See F+W Publications), 700 E. State St., Iola, WI 54990 / 715-445-2214; FAX: 715-445-4087 www.gundigestmagazine.com

Gun Doc, Inc., 5405 NW 82nd Ave., Miami, FL 33166 / 305-477-2777; FAX: 305-477-2778 www.gundoc.com

Gun Doctor, The, P.O. Box 72817, Roselle, IL 60172 / 708-894-0668

Gun Hunter Books (See Gun Hunter Trading Co.), 5075 Heisig St., Beaumont, TX 77705 / 409-835-3006; FAX: 409-838-2266 gunhuntertrading@hotmail.com

Gun Hunter Trading Co., 5075 Heisig St., Beaumont, TX 77705 / 409-835-3006; FAX: 409-838-2266 gunhuntertrading@hotmail.com

Gun Leather Limited, 116 Lipscomb, Fort Worth, TX 76104 / 817-334-0225; FAX: 800-247-0609

Gun Room Press, The, 127 Raritan Ave., Highland Park, NJ 08904 / 732-545-4344; FAX: 732-545-6686 gunbooks@rutgersgunbooks.com www.rutgersgunbooks.com

Gun Room, The, 1121 Burlington, Muncie, IN 47302 / 765-282-9073; FAX: 765-282-5270 bshstleguns@aol.com

Gun Shop, The, 5550 S. 900 East, Salt Lake City, UT 84117 / 801-263-3633

Gun South, Inc. (See GSI, Inc.)

Gun Vault, 7339 E. Acoma Dr., Ste. 7, Scottsdale, AZ 85260 / 602-951-6855

Gun Works, The, 247 S. 2nd St., Springfield, OR 97477 / 541-741-4118; FAX: 541-988-1097 info@thegunworks.com www.thegunworks.com

Gun-Alert, 1010 N. Maclay Ave., San Fernando, CA 91340 / 818-365-0864; FAX: 818-365-1308

Guncraft Books (See Guncraft Sports, Inc.), 10737 Dutchtown Rd., Knoxville, TN 37932 / 865-966-4545; FAX: 865-966-4500 findit@guncraft.com www.guncraft.com

Guncraft Sports, Inc., 10737 Dutchtown Rd., Knoxville, TN 37932 / 865-966-4545; FAX: 865-966-4500 findit@guncraft.com www.usit.net/guncraft

Guncraft Sports, Inc., Marie C. Wiest, 10737 Dutchtown Rd., Knoxville, TN 37932 / 865-966-4545; FAX: 865-966-4500 findit@guncraft.com www.guncraft.com

Guncrafter Industries, 171 Madison 1510, Huntsville, AR 72740 / 479-665-2466 www.guncrafterindustries.com

Gun-Ho Sports Cases, 110 E. 10th St., St. Paul, MN 55101 / 612-224-9491

Gunline Tools, 2950 Saturn St., "O", Brea, CA 92821 / 714-993-5100; FAX: 714-572-4128

Gunnerman Books, P.O. Box 81697, Rochester Hills, MI 48308 / 248-608-2856 gunnermanbks@att.net

Guns Antique & Modern DBA / Charles E. Duffy, 224 Williams Lane, P.O. Box 2, West Hurley, NY 12491 / 845-679-2997 ceo1923@prodigy.net

GUNS Magazine, 12345 World Trade Dr., San Diego, CA 92128-3743 / 619-297-5350; FAX: 619-297-5353

Gunsight, The, 5292 Kentwater Pl., Yorba Linda, CA 92886

Gunsite Training Center, P.O. Box 700, Paulden, AZ 86334 / 520-636-4565; FAX: 520-636-1236

Gunsmithing Ltd., 3 Lacey Place, 2530 Post Rd., Southport, CT 06890 / 203-254-0436; FAX: 203-254-1535

Gunsmithing, Inc., 30 W. Buchanan St., Colorado Springs, CO 80907 / 719-632-3795; FAX: 719-632-3493 www.nealsguns.com

Gurney, F. R., Box 13, Sooke, BC V0S 1N0 CANADA / 604-642-5282; FAX: 604-642-7859

H

H&B Forge Co., Rt. 2, Geisinger Rd., Shiloh, OH 44878 / 419-895-1856

H&P Publishing, 7174 Hoffman Rd., San Angelo, TX 76905 / 915-655-5953

H&R 1871, LLC, 60 Industrial Rowe, Gardner, MA 01440 / 508-632-9393; FAX: 508-632-2300 hr1871@hr1871.com www.hr1871.com

H. Krieghoff Gun Co., Boschstrasse 22, D-89079, Ulm, GERMANY / 731-401820; FAX: 731-4018270

H.K.S. Products, 7841 Founion Dr., Florence, KY 41042 / 606-342-7841 or 800-354-9814; FAX: 606-342-5865

H.P. White Laboratory, Inc., 3114 Scarboro Rd., Street, MD 21154 / 410-838-6550; FAX: 410-838-2802 info@hpwhite.com www.hpwhite.com

Hafner World Wide, Inc., P.O. Box 1987, Lake City, FL 32055 / 904-755-6481; FAX: 904-755-6595 hafner@isgroupe.net

Half Moon Rifle Shop, 490 Halfmoon Rd., Columbia Falls, MT 59912 / 406-892-4409 halfmoonrs@centurytel.net

Hall Plastics, Inc., John, P.O. Box 1526, Alvin, TX 77512 / 713-489-8709

Hallowell & Co., P.O. Box 1445, Livingston, MT 59047 / 406-222-4770; FAX: 406-222-4792 morris@hallowellco.com www.hallowellco.com

Hally Caller, 443 Wells Rd., Doylestown, PA 18901 / 215-345-6354; FAX: 215-345-6354 info@hallycaller.com www.hallycaller.com

Hamilton, Alex B. (See Ten-Ring Precision, Inc.)

Hammans, Charles E., P.O. Box 788, 2022 McCracken, Stuttgart, AR 72160-0788 / 870-673-1388

Hammerli AG, Industrieplaz, a/Rheinpall, CH-8212 Neuhausen, SWITZERLAND info@hammerli.com www.haemmerliich.com

Hammerli Service-Precision Mac, Rudolf Marent, 9711 Tiltree St., Houston, TX 77075 / 713-946-7028 rmarent@webtv.net

Hammerli USA, 19296 Oak Grove Circle, Groveland, CA 95321 FAX: 209-962-5311

Hammond Custom Guns Ltd., 619 S. Pandora, Gilbert, AZ 85234 / 602-892-3437

HandCrafts Unltd. (See Clements' Custom Leathercraft), 1741 Dallas St., Aurora, CO 80010-2018 / 303-364-0403; FAX: 303-739-9824 gryphons@home.com kuntaoslcat.com

Handgun Press, P.O. Box 406, Glenview, IL 60025 / 847-657-6500; FAX: 847-724-8831 handgunpress@comcast.net

Hank's Gun Shop, Box 370, 50 W. 100 South, Monroe, UT 84754 / 435-527-4456 hanksgs@altazip.com

Hanned Line, The, 4463 Madoc Way, San Jose, CA 95130 smith@hanned.com www.hanned.com

Hanned Precision (See The Hanned Line)

Hansen & Co., 244-246 Old Post Rd., Southport, CT 06490 / 203-259-6222; FAX: 203-254-3832

Hanson's Gun Center, Dick, 233 Everett Dr., Colorado Springs, CO 80911

Harford (See U.S. Importer-EMF Co., Inc.)

Harrell's Precision, 5756 Hickory Dr., Salem, VA 24153 / 540-380-2683

Harrington & Richardson (See H&R 1871, Inc.)

Harris Engineering Inc., Dept. GD54, 999 Broadway, Barlow, KY 42024 / 270-334-3633; FAX: 270-334-3000

Harris Enterprises, P.O. Box 105, Bly, OR 97622 / 503-353-2625

Harris Hand Engraving, Paul A., 113 Rusty Ln., Boerne, TX 78006-5746 / 512-391-5121

Harris Publications, 1115 Broadway, New York, NY 10010 / 212-807-7100; FAX: 212-627-4678

Harrison Bullets, 6437 E. Hobart St., Mesa, AZ 85205

Harry Lawson LLC, 3328 N. Richey Blvd., Tucson, AZ 85716 / 520-326-1117; FAX: 520-326-1117

Hart & Son, Inc., Robert W., 401 Montgomery St., Nescopeck, PA 18635 / 717-752-3655; FAX: 717-752-1088

Hart Rifle Barrels, Inc., P.O. Box 182, 1690 Apulia Rd., Lafayette, NY 13084 / 315-677-9841; FAX: 315-677-9610 hartriflebarrels@sbcglobal.net hartbarrels.com

Hartford (See U.S. Importer-EMF Co. Inc.)

Hartmann & Weiss GmbH, Rahlstedter Bahnhofstr. 47, 22143, Hamburg, GERMANY / (40) 677 55 85; FAX: (40) 677 55 92 hartmannundweiss@t-online.de

Harvey, Frank, 218 Nightfall, Terrace, NV 89015 / 702-558-6998

Hastings, P.O. Box 135, Clay Center, KS 67432 / 785-632-3169; FAX: 785-632-6554

Hatfield Gun, 224 N. 4th St., St. Joseph, MO 64501

Hawk Laboratories, Inc. (See Hawk, Inc.), 849 Hawks Bridge Rd., Salem, NJ 08079 / 609-299-2700; FAX: 609-299-2800

Hawk, Inc., 849 Hawks Bridge Rd., Salem, NJ 08079 / 609-299-2700; FAX: 609-299-2800 info@hawkbullets.com www.hawkbullets.com

Hawken Shop, The, P.O. Box 593, Oak Harbor, WA 98277 / 206-679-4657; FAX: 206-675-1114

Hawken Shop, The (See Dayton Traister)

Haydel's Game Calls, Inc., 5018 Hazel Jones Rd., Bossier City, LA 71111 / 318-746-3586; FAX: 318-746-3711 www.haydels.com

Hecht, Hubert J., Waffen-Hecht, P.O. Box 2635, Fair Oaks, CA 95628 / 916-966-1020

Heckler & Koch GmbH, P.O. Box 1329, 78722 Oberndorf, Neckar, GERMANY / 49-7423179-0; FAX: 49-7423179-2406

Heckler & Koch, Inc., 21480 Pacific Blvd., Sterling, VA 20166-8900 / 703-450-1900; FAX: 703-450-8160 www.hecklerkoch-usa.com

Hege Jagd-u. Sporthandels GmbH, P.O. Box 101461, W-7770, Ueberlingen a. Boden, GERMANY

Heidenstrom Bullets, Dalghte 86-3660 Rjukan, 35091818, NORWAY, olau.joh@online.tuo

Heilmann, Stephen, P.O. Box 657, Grass Valley, CA 95945 / 530-272-8758; FAX: 530-274-0285 sheilmann@jps.net www.metalwood.com

Heinie Specialty Products, 301 Oak St., Quincy, IL 62301-2500 / 217-228-9500; FAX: 217-228-9502 rheinie@heinie.com www.heinie.com

Helwan (See U.S. Importer-Interarms)

Henigson & Associates, Steve, P.O. Box 2726, Culver City, CA 90231 / 310-305-8288; FAX: 310-305-1905

Henriksen Tool Co., Inc., 8515 Wagner Creek Rd., Talent, OR 97540 / 541-535-2309; FAX: 541-535-2309

Henry Repeating Arms Co., 110 8th St., Brooklyn, NY 11215 / 718-499-5600; FAX: 718-768-8056 info@henryrepeating.com www.henryrepeating.com

Hensley, Gunmaker, Darwin, P.O. Box 329, Brightwood, OR 97011 / 503-622-5411

Heppler, Keith. See: KEITH'S CUSTOM GUNSTOCKS

Hercules, Inc. (See Alliant Techsystems Smokeless Powder Group)

Heritage Firearms (See Heritage Mfg., Inc.)

Heritage Manufacturing, Inc., 4600 NW 135th St., Opa Locka, FL 33054 / 305-685-5966; FAX: 305-687-6721 infohmi@heritagemfg.com www.heritagemfg.com

Heritage/VSP Gun Books, P.O. Box 887, McCall, ID 83638 / 208-634-4104; FAX: 208-634-3101 heritage@gunbooks.com www.gunbooks.com

Herrett's Stocks, Inc., P.O. Box 741, Twin Falls, ID 83303 / 208-733-1498

Hesse Arms, Robert Hesse, 1126 70th St. E., Inver Grove Heights, MN 55077-2416 / 651-455-5760; FAX: 612-455-5760

Hesse, Robert. See: HESSE ARMS

Heydenberk, Warren R., 1059 W. Sawmill Rd., Quakertown, PA 18951 / 215-538-2682

Hidalgo, Tony, 12701 SW 9th Pl., Davie, FL 33325 / 954-476-7645

High Bridge Arms, Inc., 3185 Mission St., San Francisco, CA 94110 / 415-282-8358

High North Products, Inc., P.O. Box 2, Antigo, WI 54409 / 715-627-2331; FAX: 715-623-5451

High Performance International, 5734 W. Florist Ave., Milwaukee, WI 53218 / 414-466-9040; FAX: 414-466-7050 mike@hpirifles.com hpirifles.com

High Precision, Bud Welsh, 80 New Road, E. Amherst, NY 14051 / 716-688-6344; FAX: 716-688-0425 welsh5168@aol.com www.high-precision.com

High Standard Mfg. Co./F.I., Inc., 5200 Mitchelldale St., Ste. E17, Houston, TX 77092-7222 / 713-462-4200 or 800-272-7816; FAX: 713-681-5665 info@highstandard.com www.highstandard.com

High Tech Specialties, Inc., P.O. Box 839, 293 E Main St., Rear, Adamstown, PA 19501 / 717-484-0405; FAX: 717-484-0523 bansner@aol.com www.hightech-specialties.com

Highwood Special Products, 1531 E. Highwood, Pontiac, MI 48340

Hill, Loring F., 304 Cedar Rd., Elkins Park, PA 19027

Hill Speed Leather, Ernie, 4507 N 195th Ave., Litchfield Park, AZ 85340 / 602-853-9222; FAX: 602-853-9235

Hinman Outfitters, Bob, 107 N Sanderson Ave., Bartonville, IL 61607-1839 / 309-691-8132

Hi-Performance Ammunition Company, 5231 Greensburg Rd., Apollo, PA 15613 / 304-674-9000; FAX: 304-675-6700 gjrahiperwvo@yahoo.com

HIP-GRIP Barami Corp., P.O. Box 252224, West Bloomfield, MI 48325-2224 / 248-738-0462; FAX: 248-738-2542 hipgripja@aol.com www.hipgrip.com

Hi-Point Firearms/MKS Supply, 8611-A North Dixie Dr., Dayton, OH 45414 / 877-425-4867; FAX: 937-454-0503 www.hi-pointfirearms.com

Hiptmayer, Armurier, RR 112 750, P.O. Box 136, Eastman, PQ J0E 1P0 CANADA / 514-297-2492

Hiptmayer, Heidemarie, RR 112 750, P.O. Box 136, Eastman, PQ J0E 1P0 CANADA / 514-297-2492

Hiptmayer, Klaus, RR 112 750, P.O. Box 136, Eastman, PQ J0E 1P0 CANADA / 514-297-2492

Hirtenberger AG, Leobersdorferstrasse 31, A-2552, Hirtenberg, AUSTRIA / 43(0)2256 81184; FAX: 43(0)2256 81808 www.hirtenberger.ot

HJS Arms, Inc., P.O. Box 3711, Brownsville, TX 78523-3711 / 956-542-2767; FAX: 956-542-2767

Hoag, James W., 8523 Canoga Ave., Suite C, Canoga Park, CA 91304 / 818-998-1510

Hobson Precision Mfg. Co., 210 Big Oak Ln., Brent, AL 35034 / 205-926-4662; FAX: 205-926-3193 cahobbob@dbtech.net

Hodgdon Powder Co., 6231 Robinson, Shawnee Mission, KS 66202 / 913-362-9455; FAX: 913-362-1307

Hodgman, Inc., 1100 Stearns Dr., Sauk Rapids, MN 56379

Hodgson, Richard, 9081 Tahoe Lane, Boulder, CO 80301

Hoehn Sales, Inc., 2045 Kohn Road, Wright City, MO 63390 / 636-745-8144; FAX: 636-745-7868 ron@hoehnsales.com

Hofer Jagdwaffen, P., A9170 Ferlach, Kirchgasse 24, Kirchgasse, AUSTRIA / 43 4227 3683; FAX: 43 4227 368330 peterhofer@hoferwaffen.com www.hoferwaffen.com

Hoffman New Ideas, 821 Northmoor Rd., Lake Forest, IL 60045 / 312-234-4075

Hogue Grips, P.O. Box 1138, Paso Robles, CA 93447 / 800-438-4747 or 805-239-1440; FAX: 805-239-2553

Holland & Holland Ltd., 33 Bruton St., London, ENGLAND / 44-171-499-4411; FAX: 44-171-408-7962

Holland's Shooters Supply, Inc., P.O. Box 69, Powers, OR 97466 / 541-439-5155; FAX: 541-439-2105 bestrifles@aol.com www.hollandguns.com

Hollinger, Jon. See: ASPEN OUTFITTING CO.

Hollywood Engineering, 10642 Arminta St., Sun Valley, CA 91352 / 818-842-8376; FAX: 818-504-4168 cadqueenel1@aol.com

Homak, 350 N. La Salle Dr. Ste. 1100, Chicago, IL 60610-4731 / 312-523-3100; FAX: 312-523-9455

Hoppe's Div. Penguin Industries, Inc., 9200 Cody St., Overland Park, KS 66214 / 800-845-2444

Horizons Unlimited, P.O. Box 426, Warm Springs, GA 31830 / 706-655-3603; FAX: 706-655-3603

Hornady Mfg. Co., P.O. Box 1848, Grand Island, NE 68802 / 800-338-3220 or 308-382-1390; FAX: 308-382-5761

Horseshoe Leather Products, Andy Arratoonian, The Cottage Sharow, Ripon, ENGLAND U.K. / 44-1765-605858 andy@horseshoe.co.uk www.holsters.org

House of Muskets, Inc., The, PO Box 4640, Pagosa Springs, CO 81157 / 970-731-2295

Houtz & Barwick, P.O. Box 435, W. Church St., Elizabeth City, NC 27909 / 800-775-0337 or 919-335-4191; FAX: 919-335-1152

Howa Machinery, Ltd., 1900-1 Sukaguchi Kiyosu, Aichi 452-8601, JAPAN / 81-52-408-1231; FAX: 81-52-401-4999 howa@howa.co.jp http://www.howa.cojpl

Howell Machine, Inc., 815 D St., Lewiston, ID 83501 / 208-743-7418; FAX: 208-746-1703 ammoload@microwavedsl.com www.ammoload.com

H-S Precision, Inc., 1301 Turbine Dr., Rapid City, SD 57701 / 605-341-3006; FAX: 605-342-8964

HT Bullets, 244 Belleville Rd., New Bedford, MA 02745 / 508-999-3338

Hubert J. Hecht Waffen-Hecht, P.O. Box 2635, Fair Oaks, CA 95628 / 916-966-1020

Huebner, Corey O., P.O. Box 564, Frenchtown, MT 59834 / 406-721-7168 bugsboys@hotmail.com

Huey Gun Cases, 820 Indiana St., Lawrence, KS 66044-2645 / 785-842-0062; FAX: 785-842-0062 ketchsailor27@aol.com www.hueycases.com

Hume, Don. See: DON HUME LEATHERGOODS

Hunter Co., Inc., 3300 W. 71st Ave., Westminster, CO 80030 / 303-427-4626; FAX: 303-428-3980 debbiet@huntercompany.com www.huntercompany.com

Hunterjohn, P.O. Box 771457, St. Louis, MO 63177 / 314-531-7250 www.hunterjohn.com

Hunter's Specialties Inc., 6000 Huntington Ct. NE, Cedar Rapids, IA 52402-1268 / 319-395-0321; FAX: 319-395-0326

Hunters Supply, Inc., 1177 Hwy. 96, Regina, NM 87046 / 940-437-2458; FAX: 940-437-2228 hunterssupply@hotmail.com www.hunterssupply.net

Huntington Die Specialties, 601 Oro Dam Blvd., Oroville, CA 95965 / 530-534-1210 or 866-735-6237; FAX: 530-534-1212 buy@huntingtons.com www.huntingtons.com

Hydra-Tone Chemicals, Inc., 7065 Production Coast, Florence, KY 41042 / 859-534-5630; FAX: 859-594-3312 graff-off@hydra-tone.com www.hydra-tone.com

Hydrosorbent Dehumidifiers, P.O. Box 437, Ashley Falls, MA 01222 / 800-448-7903; FAX: 413-229-8743 orders@dehumidify.com www.dehumidify.com

I

I.A.B. (See U.S. Importer-Taylor's & Co., Inc.)

I.D.S.A. Books, 3220 E. Galbraith Rd., Cincinnati, OH 45236 / 513-985-9112; FAX: 513-985-9116 idsabooks@idsabooks.com www.idsabooks.com

I.N.C. Inc. (See Kickeez I.N.C., Inc.)

I.S.W., 106 E. Cairo Dr., Tempe, AZ 85282

MANUFACTURER'S DIRECTORY

IAR Inc., 33171 Camino Capistrano, San Juan Capistrano, CA 92675 / 949-443-3642; FAX: 949-443-3647 sales@iar-arms.com iar-arms.com

Ide, Ken. See: STURGEON VALLEY SPORTERS

IGA (See U.S. Importer-Stoeger Industries)

Image Ind. Inc., 11220 E. Main St., Huntley, IL 60142-7369 / 630-766-2402; FAX: 630-766-7373

Impact Case & Container, Inc., P.O. Box 1129, Rathdrum, ID 83858 / 877-687-2452; FAX: 208-687-0632 bradk@icc-case.com www.icc-case.com

Imperial Magnum Corp., P.O. Box 249, Oroville, WA 98844 / 604-495-3131; FAX: 604-495-2816

Imperial Miniature Armory, 1115 FM 359, Richland, TX 77449 / 800-646-4288; FAX: 832-595-8787 miniguns@houston.rr.com www.1800miniature.com

IMR Powder Co., 1080 Military Turnpike, Suite 2, Plattsburgh, NY 12901 / 518-563-2253; FAX: 518-563-6916

Info-Arm, P.O. Box 1262, Champlain, NY 12919 / 514-955-0355; FAX: 514-955-0357 infoarm@qc.aira.com

Innovative Weaponry Inc., 2513 E. Loop 820 N., Fort Worth, TX 76118 / 817-284-0099 or 800-334-3573

INTEC International, Inc., P.O. Box 5708, Scottsdale, AZ 85261 / 602-483-1708

Inter Ordnance of America LP, 3305 Westwood Industrial Dr., Monroe, NC 28110-5204 / 704-821-8337; FAX: 704-821-8523

Intercontinental Distributors, Ltd., P.O. Box 815, Beulah, ND 58523

International Shooters Service, P.O. Box 185234, Ft. Worth, TX 76181 / 817-595-2090; FAX: 817-595-2090 is_s_@sbcglobal.net www.iss-internationalshootersservice.com

Intrac Arms International, 5005 Chapman Hwy., Knoxville, TN 37920

Ion Industries, Inc., 3508 E Allerton Ave., Cudahy, WI 53110 / 414-486-2007; FAX: 414-486-2017

Iosso Products, 1485 Lively Blvd., Elk Grove Village, IL 60007 / 847-437-8400; FAX: 847-437-8478

Iron Bench, 12619 Bailey Rd., Redding, CA 96003 / 916-241-4623

Ironside International Publishers, Inc., P.O. Box 1050, Lorton, VA 22199 / 703-493-9120; FAX: 703-493-9424

Ironsighter Co., P.O. Box 85070, Westland, MI 48185 / 734-326-8731; FAX: 734-326-3378 www.ironsighter.com

Irwin, Campbell H., 140 Hartland Blvd., East Hartland, CT 06027 / 203-653-3901

Israel Arms Inc., 5625 Star Ln. #B, Houston, TX 77057 / 713-789-0745; FAX: 713-914-9515 www.israelarms.com

Ithaca Classic Doubles, Stephen Lamboy, No. 5 Railroad St., Victor, NY 14564 / 716-924-2710; FAX: 716-924-2737 ithacadoubles.com

Ithaca Guns LLC, 420 N. Walpole St., Upper Sandusky, OH 43351 / 419-294-4113; FAX: 419-294-9433 service@ithacaguns.com www.ithacaguns-usa.com

Ivanoff, Thomas G. (See Tom's Gun Repair)

J

J J Roberts Firearm Engraver, 7808 Lake Dr., Manassas, VA 20111 / 703-330-0448; FAX: 703-264-8600 james.roberts@angelfire.com www.angelfire.com/va2/engraver

J R Guns, P.O. Box 370, Monticello, NY 12701 / 845-794-2510

J&D Components, 75 East 350 North, Orem, UT 84057-4719 / 801-225-7007 www.jdcomponents.com

J&J Products, Inc., 9240 Whitmore, El Monte, CA 91731 / 818-571-5228; FAX: 800-927-8361

J&J Sales, 1501 21st Ave. S., Great Falls, MT 59405 / 406-727-9789 mtshootingbench@yahoo.com www.j&jsales.us

J&L Superior Bullets (See Huntington Die Specialties)

J&M Precision Machining, Jeff Amato, RR 1 Box 91, Bloomfield, IN 47424

J&R Engineering, P.O. Box 77, 200 Lyons Hill Rd., Athol, MA 01331 / 508-249-9241

J&R Enterprises, 4550 Scotts Valley Rd., Lakeport, CA 95453

J&S Heat Treat, 803 S. 16th St., Blue Springs, MO 64015 / 816-229-2149; FAX: 816-228-1135

J. Dewey Mfg. Co., Inc., P.O. Box 2014, Southbury, CT 06488 / 203-264-3064; FAX: 203-262-6907 deweyrods@att.net www.deweyrods.com

J. Korzinek Riflesmith, RD 2, Box 73D, Canton, PA 17724 / 717-673-8512

J.A. Blades, Inc. (See Christopher Firearms Co.)

J.A. Henckels Zwillingswerk Inc., 9 Skyline Dr., Hawthorne, NY 10532 / 914-592-7370

J.G. Anschutz GmbH & Co. KG, Daimlerstr. 12, D-89079 Ulm, Ulm, GERMANY / 49 731 40120; FAX: 49 731 4012700 JGA-info@anschuetz-sport.com www.anschuetz-sport.com

J.G. Dapkus Co., Inc., Commerce Circle, P.O. Box 293, Durham, CT 06422 www.explodingtargets.com

J.J. Roberts / Engraver, 7808 Lake Dr., Manassas, VA 20111 / 703-330-0448 jjrengraver@aol.com www.angelfire.com/va2/engraver

J.R. Williams Bullet Co., 2008 Tucker Rd., Perry, GA 31069 / 912-987-0274

J.W. Morrison Custom Rifles, 4015 W. Sharon, Phoenix, AZ 85029 / 602-978-3754

J.W. Wasmundt-Gunsmith, Jim Wasmundt, P.O. Box 130, 140 Alder St., Powers, OR 97466-0130 / 541-439-2044 jwasm@juno.com

Jack A. Rosenberg & Sons, 12229 Cox Ln., Dallas, TX 75234 / 214-241-6302

Jack Dever Co., 8520 NW 90th St., Oklahoma City, OK 73132 / 405-721-6393 jbdever1@home.com

Jack First, Inc., 1201 Turbine Dr., Rapid City, SD 57703 / 605-343-9544; FAX: 605-343-9420

Jack Jonas Appraisals & Taki, 13952 E. Marina Dr., #604, Aurora, CO 80014

Jackalope Gun Shop, 1048 S. 5th St., Douglas, WY 82633 / 307-358-3441 wildcatoutfitters@msn.com www.jackalopegunshop.com

Jaffin, Harry. See: BRIDGEMAN PRODUCTS

Jagdwaffen, Peter. See: BUCHSENMACHERMEISTER

James Calhoon Mfg., 4343 U.S. Highway 87, Havre, MT 59501 / 406-395-4079 www.jamescalhoon.com

James Churchill Glove Co., PO Box 298, Centralia, WA 98531 / 360-736-2816; FAX: 360-330-0151 churchillglove@localaccess.com

James Wayne Firearms for Collectors and Investors, 2608 N. Laurent, Victoria, TX 77901 / 361-578-1258; FAX: 361-578-3559

Jamison International, Marc Jamison, 3551 Mayer Ave., Sturgis, SD 57785 / 605-347-5090; FAX: 605-347-4704 jbell2@masttechnology.com

Jamison, Marc. See: JAMISON INTERNATIONAL

Jamison's Forge Works, 4527 Rd. 6.5 NE, Moses Lake, WA 98837 / 509-762-2659

Jantz Supply, Inc., 309 West Main Dept HD, Davis, OK 73030-0584 / 580-369-2316; FAX: 580-369-3082 jantz@jantzusa.com www.knifemaking.com

Jarrett Rifles, Inc., 383 Brown Rd., Jackson, SC 29831 / 803-471-3616 www.jarrettrifles.com

Jarvis, Inc., 1123 Cherry Orchard Lane, Hamilton, MT 59840 / 406-961-4392

Javelina Lube Products, P.O. Box 337, San Bernardino, CA 92402 / 909-350-9556; FAX: 909-429-1211

Jay McCament Custom Gunmaker, Jay McCament, 1730-134th St. Ct. S., Tacoma, WA 98444 / 253-531-8832

JB Custom, P.O. Box 6912, Leawood, KS 66206 / 913-381-2329

Jeff Flannery Engraving, 11034 Riddles Run Rd., Union, KY 41091 / 859-384-3127; FAX: 859-384-2222 engraving@fuse.net www.flannerygunengraving.com

Jeff's Outfitters, 63F Sena Fawn, Cape Girardeau, MO 63701 / 573-651-3200; FAX: 573-651-3207 info@jeffsoutfitters.com www.jeffsoutfitters.com

Jena Eur, P.O. Box 319, Dunmore, PA 18512

Jenco Sales, Inc., P.O. Box 1000, Manchaca, TX 78652 / 800-531-5301; FAX: 800-266-2373 jencosales@sbcglobal.net

Jenkins Recoil Pads, 5438 E. Frontage Ln., Olney, IL 62450 / 618-395-3416

Jensen Bullets, RR 1 Box 187, Arco, ID 83213 / 208-785-5590

Jensen's Arizona Sportsman, 1325 W. Silverlake Rd. Unit 144, Tucson, AZ 85713 / 602-325-3346; FAX: 602-322-5704

Jensen's Firearms Academy, 3975 E. Dripping Springs Rd., Winkelman, AZ 85292 / 602-293-8516

Jericho Tool & Die Co., Inc., 121 W. Keech Rd., Bainbridge, NY 13733-3248 / 607-563-8222; FAX: 607-563-8560 jerichotool.com www.jerichotool.com

Jerry Phillips Optics, P.O. Box L632, Langhorne, PA 19047 / 215-757-5037; FAX: 215-757-7097

Jesse W. Smith Saddlery, 0499 County Road J, Pritchett, CO 81064 / 509-325-0622

Jester Bullets, Rt. 1 Box 27, Orienta, OK 73737

Jewell Triggers, Inc., 3620 Hwy. 123, San Marcos, TX 78666 / 512-353-2999; FAX: 512-392-0543

JG Airguns, LLC, John Groenewold, P.O. Box 830, Mundelein, IL 60060 / 847-566-2365; FAX: 847-566-4065 john@jgairguns.biz www.jgairguns.biz

JGS Precision Tool Mfg., LLC, 60819 Selander Rd., Coos Bay, OR 97420 / 541-267-4331; FAX: 541-267-5996 jgstools@harborside.com www.jgstools.com

Jim Blair Engraving, P.O. Box 64, Glenrock, WY 82637 / 307-436-8115 jblairengrav@msn.com

Jim Noble Co., 204 W. 5th St., Vancouver, WA 98660 / 360-695-1309; FAX: 360-695-6835 jnobleco@aol.com

Jim Norman Custom Gunstocks, 14281 Cane Rd., Valley Center, CA 92082 / 619-749-6252

Jim's Precision, Jim Ketchum, 1725 Moclips Dr., Petaluma, CA 94952 / 707-762-3014

JLK Bullets, 414 Turner Rd., Dover, AR 72837 / 501-331-4194

Johanssons Vapentillbehor, Bert, S-430 20, Veddige, SWEDEN

John Hall Plastics, Inc., P.O. Box 1526, Alvin, TX 77512 / 713-489-8709

John J. Adams & Son Engravers, 7040 VT Rt 113, Vershire, VT 05079 / 802-685-0019

John Masen Co. Inc., 1305 Jelmak, Grand Prairie, TX 75050 / 817-430-8732; FAX: 817-430-1715

John Partridge Sales Ltd., Trent Meadows Rugeley, Staffordshire, WS15 2HS ENGLAND

John Rigby & Co., 500 Linne Rd. Ste. D, Paso Robles, CA 93446 / 805-227-4236; FAX: 805-227-4723 jrigby@calinet www.johnrigbyandco.com

John's Custom Leather, 523 S. Liberty St., Blairsville, PA 15717 / 724-459-6802; FAX: 724-459-5996 john'scustomleather@verizon.net www.jclleather.com

Johnson Wood Products, 34897 Crystal Road, Strawberry Point, IA 52076 / 563-933-6504 johnsonwoodproducts@yahoo.com

Jonad Corp., 2091 Lakeland Ave., Lakewood, OH 44107 / 216-226-3161

Jonathan Arthur Ciener, Inc., 8700 Commerce St., Cape Canaveral, FL 32920 / 321-868-2200; FAX: 321-868-2201 www.22lrconversions.com

Jones Custom Products, Neil A., 17217 Brookhouser Rd., Saegertown, PA 16433 / 814-763-2769; FAX: 814-763-4228 njones@mdvl.net neiljones.com

Jones, J. See: SSK INDUSTRIES

Jones Moulds, Paul, 4901 Telegraph Rd., Los Angeles, CA 90022 / 213-262-1510

JP Enterprises, Inc., P.O. Box 378, Hugo, MN 55038 / 651-426-9196; FAX: 651-426-2472 www.jprifles.com

JP Sales, Box 307, Anderson, TX 77830

JRP Custom Bullets, RR2 2233 Carlton Rd., Whitehall, NY 12887 / 518-282-0084 or 802-438-5548

JSL Ltd. (See U.S. Importer-Specialty Shooters Supply)

Juenke, Vern, 25 Bitterbush Rd., Reno, NV 89523 / 702-345-0225

Jungkind, Reeves C., 509 E. Granite St., Llano, TX 78643-3055 / 325-247-1151

Jurras, L. See: L. E. JURRAS & ASSOC.

Justin Phillippi Custom Bullets, P.O. Box 773, Ligonier, PA 15658 / 412-238-9671

K

K&M Industries, Inc., Box 66, 510 S. Main, Troy, ID 83871 / 208-835-2281; FAX: 208-835-5211

K&M Services, 5430 Salmon Run Rd., Dover, PA 17315 / 717-292-3175; FAX: 717-292-3175

K. Eversull Co., Inc., 1 Tracemont, Boyce, LA 71409 / 318-793-8728; FAX: 318-793-5483 bestguns@aol.com

K.B.I. Inc., P.O. Box 6625, Harrisburg, PA 17112 / 717-540-8518; FAX: 717-540-8567

KA-BAR Knives, 200 Homer St., Olean, NY 14760 / 800-282-0130; FAX: 716-790-7188 info@ka-bar.com www.ka-bar.com

Kahles A. Swarovski Company, 2 Slater Rd., Cranston, RI 02920 / 401-946-2220; FAX: 401-946-2587

MANUFACTURER'S DIRECTORY

Kahr Arms, P.O. Box 220, 630 Route 303, Blauvelt, NY 10913 / 845-353-7770; FAX: 845-353-7833 www.kahr.com

Kailua Custom Guns Inc., 51 N. Dean Street, Coquille, OR 97423 / 541-396-5413 kailuacustom@aol.com www.kailuacustom.com

Kalispel Case Line, P.O. Box 267, Cusick, WA 99119 / 509-445-1121

Kamik Outdoor Footwear, 554 Montee de Liesse, Montreal, PQ H4T 1P1 CANADA / 514-341-3950; FAX: 514-341-1861

Kapro Mfg. Co. Inc. (See R.E.I.)

Kasenit Co., Inc., 39 Park Ave., Highland Mills, NY 10930 / 845-928-9595; FAX: 845-986-8038

Kaswer Custom, Inc., 13 Surrey Drive, Brookfield, CT 06804 / 203-775-0564; FAX: 203-775-6872

KDF, Inc., 2485 Hwy. 46 N., Seguin, TX 78155 / 830-379-8141; FAX: 830-379-5420

KeeCo Impressions, Inc., 346 Wood Ave., North Brunswick, NJ 08902 / 800-468-0546

Kehr, Roger, 2131 Agate Ct. SE, Lacy, WA 98503 / 360-491-0691

Keith's Bullets, 942 Twisted Oak, Algonquin, IL 60102 / 708-658-3520

Keith's Custom Gunstocks, Keith M. Heppler, 540 Banyan Circle, Walnut Creek, CA 94598 / 925-934-3509; FAX: 925-934-3143 kmheppler@hotmail.com

Kelbly, Inc., 7222 Dalton Fox Lake Rd., North Lawrence, OH 44666 / 216-683-4674; FAX: 216-683-7349

Kelley's, P.O. Box 125, Woburn, MA 01801-0125 / 800-879-7273; FAX: 781-272-7077 kels@star.net www.kelsmilitary.com

Kellogg's Professional Products, 325 Pearl St., Sandusky, OH 44870 / 419-625-6551; FAX: 419-625-6167 skwigton@sbcglobal.net

Kelly, Lance, 1723 Willow Oak Dr., Edgewater, FL 32132 / 904-423-4933

Kel-Tec CNC Industries, Inc., P.O. Box 236009, Cocoa, FL 32923 / 321-631-0068; FAX: 321-631-1169 www.kel-tec.com

Ken Eyster Heritage Gunsmiths, Inc., 6441 Bisop Rd., Centerburg, OH 43011 / 740-625-6131; FAX: 740-625-7811

Ken Starnes Gunmaker, 15617 NE 324th Circle, Battle Ground, WA 98604 / 360-666-5025; FAX: 360-666-5024 kstarnes@kdsa.com

Keng's Firearms Specialty, Inc., 875 Wharton Dr., P.O. Box 44405, Atlanta, GA 30336-1405 / 404-691-7611; FAX: 404-505-8445 kfs@bellsouth.net www.versa-pod.com

Kennebec Journal, 274 Western Ave., Augusta, ME 04330 / 207-622-6288

Kennedy Firearms, 10 N. Market St., Muncy, PA 17756 / 717-546-6695

Kenneth W. Warren Engraver, P.O. Box 2842, Wenatchee, WA 98807 / 509-663-6123; FAX: 509-665-6123

Ken's Kustom Kartridges, 331 Jacobs Rd., Hubbard, OH 44425 / 216-534-4595

Kent Cartridge America, Inc., P.O. Box 849, 1000 Zigor Rd., Kearneysville, WV 25430

Keowee Game Calls, 608 Hwy. 25 North, Travelers Rest, SC 29690 / 864-834-7204; FAX: 864-834-7831

Kershaw Knives, 18600 SW Teton Ave., Tualatin, OR 97062 / 503-682-1966 or 800-325-2891; FAX: 503-682-7168

Kesselring Gun Shop, 4024 Old Hwy. 99N, Burlington, WA 98233 / 360-724-3113; FAX: 360-724-7003 info@kesselrings.com www.kesselrings.com

Ketchum, Jim (See Jim's Precision)

Keystone Sporting Arms, Inc. (Crickett Rifles), 8920 State Route 405, Milton, PA 17847 / 800-742-2777; FAX: 570-742-1455

Kickeez, I.N.C., Inc., 13715 NE 384th St., La Center, WA 98629 / 877-542-5339; FAX: 954-656-4527 info@kickeezproducts www.kickeez.products.com

Kilham & Co., Main St., P.O. Box 37, Lyme, NH 03768 / 603-795-4112

Kimar (See U.S. Importer-IAR, Inc.)

Kimber of America, Inc., 1 Lawton St., Yonkers, NY 10705 / 800-880-2418; FAX: 914-964-9340

King & Co., P.O. Box 1242, Bloomington, IL 61702 / 309-473-3964 or 800-914-5464; FAX: 309-473-2161

King's Gun Works, 1837 W. Glenoaks Blvd., Glendale, CA 91201 / 818-956-6010; FAX: 818-548-8606

Kirkpatrick Leather Co., P.O. Box 677, Laredo, TX 78040 / 956-723-6631; FAX: 956-725-0672 mike@kirkpatrickleather.com www.kirkpatrickleather.com

KK Air International (See Impact Case & Container Co., Inc.)

Kleen-Bore, Inc., 8909 Forum Way, Ft. Worth, TX 76140 / 413-527-0300; FAX: 817-926-7012 info@kleen-bore.com www.kleen-bore.com

Kleinendorst, K. W., RR 1, Box 1500, Hop Bottom, PA 18824 / 570-289-4687; FAX: 570-289-8673

Klingler Woodcarving, P.O. Box 141, Thistle Hill, Cabot, VT 05647 / 802-426-3811 www.vermartcrafts.com

Knifeware, Inc., P.O. Box 3, Greenville, WV 24945 / 304-832-6878

Knight Rifles, 21852 Hwy. J46, P.O. Box 130, Centerville, IA 52544 / 515-856-2626; FAX: 515-856-2628 www.knightrifles.com

Knight Rifles (See Modern Muzzleloading, Inc.)

Knight's Manufacturing Co., 701 Columbia Blvd., Titusville, FL 32780 / 321-607-9900; FAX: 321-268-1498 civiliansales@knightarmco.com www.knightarmco.com

Knock on Wood Antiques, 355 Post Rd., Darien, CT 06820 / 203-655-9031

Knoell, Doug, 9737 McCardle Way, Santee, CA 92071 / 619-449-5189

Knopp, Gary. See: SUPER 6 LLC

Koevenig's Engraving Service, Box 55 Rabbit Gulch, Hill City, SD 57745 / 605-574-2239 ekoevenig@msn.com

KOGOT, 410 College, Trinidad, CO 81082 / 719-846-9406; FAX: 719-846-9406

Kolar, 1925 Roosevelt Ave., Racine, WI 53406 / 414-554-0800; FAX: 414-554-9093

Kolpin Outdoors, Inc., P.O. Box 107, 205 Depot St., Fox Lake, WI 53933 / 414-928-3118; FAX: 414-928-3687 cdutton@kolpin.com www.kolpin.com

Korth Germany GmbH, Robert Bosch Strasse, 11, D-23909, 23909 Ratzeburg, GERMANY / 4541-84 03 63; FAX: 4541-84 05 35 info@korthwaffen.de www.korthwaffen.com

Korth USA, 437R Chandler St., Tewksbury, MA 01876 / 978-851-8656; FAX: 978-851-9462 info@kortusa.com www.korthusa.com

Korzinek Riflesmith, J., RD 2 Box 73D, Canton, PA 17724 / 717-673-8512

Koval Knives, 5819 Zarley St., Suite A, New Albany, OH 43054 / 614-855-0777; FAX: 614-855-0945 koval@kovalknives.com www.kovalknives.com

Kowa Optimed, Inc., 20001 S. Vermont Ave., Torrance, CA 90502 / 310-327-1913; FAX: 310-327-4177 scopekowa@kowa.com www.kowascope.com

KP Books Division of F+W Publications, 700 E. State St., Iola, WI 54990-0001 / 715-445-2214

Kramer Designs, P.O. Box 129, Clancy, MT 59634 / 406-933-8658; FAX: 406-933-8658

Kramer Handgun Leather, P.O. Box 112154, Tacoma, WA 98411 / 800-510-2666; FAX: 253-564-1214 www.kramerleather.com

Krico Deutschland GmbH, Nurnbergerstrasse 6, D-90602, Pyrbaum, GERMANY / 09180-2780; FAX: 09180-2661

Krieger Barrels, Inc., 2024 Mayfield Rd, Richfield, WI 53076 / 262-628-8558; FAX: 262-628-8748

Krieghoff Gun Co., H., Boschstrasse 22, D-89079 Elm, GERMANY / 731-4018270

Krieghoff International, Inc., 7528 Easton Rd., Ottsville, PA 18942 / 610-847-5173; FAX: 610-847-8691 info@krieghoff.com www.krieghoff.com

Kukowski, Ed. See: ED'S GUN HOUSE

Kulis Freeze Dry Taxidermy, 725 Broadway Ave., Bedford, OH 44146 / 440-232-8352; FAX: 440-232-7305 jkulis@kastaway.com kastaway.com

KVH Industries, Inc., 110 Enterprise Center, Middletown, RI 02842 / 401-847-3327; FAX: 401-849-0045

Kwik-Site Co., 5555 Treadwell St., Wayne, MI 48184 / 734-326-1500; FAX: 734-326-4120 kwiksitecorp@aol.com www.kwiksiteco.com

L

L&R Lock Co., 2328 Cains Mill Rd., Sumter, SC 29154 / 803-481-5790; FAX: 803-481-5795

L&S Technologies Inc. (See Aimtech Mount Systems)

L. Bengtson Arms Co., 6345-B E. Akron St., Mesa, AZ 85205 / 602-981-6375

L. E. Jurras & Assoc., L. E. Jurras, P.O. Box 680, Washington, IN 47501 / 812-254-6170; FAX: 812-254-6170 jurras@sbcglobal.net www.leejurras.com

L.A.R. Mfg., Inc., 4133 W. Farm Rd., West Jordan, UT 84088 / 801-280-3505; FAX: 801-280-1972

L.B.T., Judy Smith, HCR 62, Box 145, Moyie Springs, ID 83845 / 208-267-3588 lbtisaccuracy@imbris.net

L.E. Wilson, Inc., Box 324, 404 Pioneer Ave., Cashmere, WA 98815 / 509-782-1328; FAX: 509-782-7200

L.L. Bean, Inc., Freeport, ME 04032 / 207-865-4761; FAX: 207-552-2802

L.P.A. Inc., Via Alfieri 26, Gardone V.T., Brescia, ITALY / 30-891-14-81; FAX: 30-891-09-51

L.R. Clift Mfg., 3821 Hammonton Rd., Marysville, CA 95901 / 916-755-3390; FAX: 916-755-3393

La Clinique du .45, 1432 Rougemont, Chambly, PQ J3L 2L8 CANADA / 514-658-1144

Labanu Inc., 2201-F Fifth Ave., Ronkonkoma, NY 11779 / 516-467-6197; FAX: 516-981-4112

LaBoone, Pat. See: MIDWEST SHOOTING SCHOOL, THE

LaBounty Precision Reboring, Inc, 7968 Silver Lake Rd., PO Box 186, Maple Falls, WA 98266 / 360-599-2047; FAX: 360-599-3018

LaCrosse Footwear, Inc., 18550 NE Riverside Parkway, Portland, OR 97230 / 503-766-1010 or 800-323-2668; FAX: 503-766-1015 customerservice@lacrossefootwear.com www.lacrossefootwear.com

LaFrance Specialties, P.O. Box 87933, San Diego, CA 92138 / 619-293-3373; FAX: 619-293-0819 timlafrance@att.net lafrancespecialties.com

Lake Center Marina, P.O. Box 670, St. Charles, MO 63302 / 314-946-7500

Lakefield Arms Ltd. (See Savage Arms, Inc.)

Lakewood Products Div of Midwest Textile, PO Box 342, Suamico, WI 54173 / 800-872-8458; FAX: 877-676-3559 info@lakewoodproduct.com www.lakewoodproducts.com

Lamboy, Stephen. See: ITHACA CLASSIC DOUBLES

Lampert, Ron, Rt. 1, 44857 Schoolcraft Trl., Guthrie, MN 56461 / 218-854-7345

Lamson & Goodnow Mfg. Co., 15 Greenfield St., Greenfield, MA 01301 / 800-872-6564; FAX: 413-774-7776 info@lamsonsharp.com www.lamsonsharp.com

Lansky Levine, Arthur. See: LANSKY SHARPENERS

Lansky Sharpeners, Arthur Lansky Levine, P.O. Box 50830, Las Vegas, NV 89016 / 702-361-7511; FAX: 702-896-9511

LaPrade, P.O. Box 250, Ewing, VA 24248 / 423-733-2615

LaRocca Gun Works, 51 Union Place, Worcester, MA 01608 / 508-754-2887; FAX: 508-754-2887 www.laroccagunworks.com

Larry Lyons Gunworks, 29994 M 62 W., Dowagiac, MI 49047 / 616-782-9478

Laser Devices, Inc., 2 Harris Ct. A-4, Monterey, CA 93940 / 831-373-0701; FAX: 831-373-0903 sales@laserdevices.com www.laserdevices.com

Laseraim Technologies, Inc., P.O. Box 3548, Little Rock, AR 72203 / 501-375-2227

Laserlyte, 2201 Amapola Ct., Torrance, CA 90501

LaserMax, 3495 Winton Place, Rochester, NY 14623-2807 / 800-527-3703; FAX: 585-272-5427 customerservice@lasermax-inc.com www.lasermax.com

Lassen Community College, Gunsmithing Dept., P.O. Box 3000, Hwy. 139, Susanville, CA 96130 / 916-251-8800; FAX: 916-251-8838 staylor@lassencollege.edu www.lassencommunitycollege.edu

Lathrop's, Inc., 5146 E. Pima, Tucson, AZ 85712 / 520-881-0266 or 800-875-4867; FAX: 520-322-5704

Laughridge, William R. (See Cylinder & Slide, Inc.)

Laurel Mountain Forge, P.O. Box 52, Crown Point, IN 46308 / 219-548-2950; FAX: 219-548-2950

Laurona Armas Eibar, S.A.L., Avenida de Otaola 25, P.O. Box 260, Eibar 20600, SPAIN / 34-43-700600; FAX: 34-43-700616

Lawrence Brand Shot (See Precision Reloading, Inc.)

Lawrence Leather Co., P.O. Box 1479, Lillington, NC 27546 / 910-893-2071; FAX: 910-893-4742

Lawson, John. See: SIGHT SHOP, THE

Lawson, John G. (See Sight Shop, The)

Lazzeroni Arms Co., P.O. Box 26696, Tucson, AZ 85726 / 888-492-7247; FAX: 520-624-4250

Leapers, Inc., 7675 Five Mile Rd., Northville, MI 48167 / 248-486-1231; FAX: 248-486-1430

Leatherman Tool Group, Inc., 12106 NE Ainsworth Cir., P.O. Box 20595, Portland, OR 97294 / 503-253-7826; FAX: 503-253-7830

Lebeau-Courally, Rue St. Gilles, 386 4000, Liege, BELGIUM / 042-52-48-43; FAX: 32-4-252-2008 info@lebeau-courally.com www.lebeau-courally.com

Leckie Professional Gunsmithing, 546 Quarry Rd., Ottsville, PA 18942 / 215-847-8594

Ledbetter Airguns, Riley, 1804 E Sprague St., Winston Salem, NC 27107-3521 / 919-784-0676

Lee Precision, Inc., 4275 Hwy. U, Hartford, WI 53027 / 262-673-3075; FAX: 262-673-9273 info@leeprecision.com www.leeprecision.com

Lee Supplies, Mark, 9901 France Ct., Lakeville, MN 55044 / 612-461-2114

LeFever Arms Co., Inc., 6234 Stokes, Lee Center Rd., Lee Center, NY 13363 / 315-337-6722; FAX: 315-337-1543

Legacy Sports International, 206 S. Union St., Alexandria, VA 22314 / 703-548-4837 www.legacysports.com

Leica Sport Optics, 1 Pearl Ct., Ste. A, Allendale, NJ 07401 / 201-995-1686 www.leica-camera.com/usa

Leonard Day, 3 Kings Hwy., West Hatfield, MA 01027-9506 / 413-337-8369

Les Baer Custom, Inc., 29601 34th Ave., Hillsdale, IL 61257 / 309-658-2716; FAX: 309-658-2610 www.lesbaer.com

LesMerises, Felix. See: ROCKY MOUNTAIN ARMOURY

Lethal Force Institute (See Police Bookshelf), P.O. Box 122, Concord, NH 03301 / 603-224-6814; FAX: 603-226-3554 ayoob@attglobal.net www.ayoob.com

Lett Custom Grips, 672 Currier Rd., Hopkinton, NH 03229-2652 / 800-421-5388; FAX: 603-226-4580 info@lettgrips.com www.lettgrips.com

Leupold & Stevens, Inc., 14400 NW Greenbrier Pky., Beaverton, OR 97006 / 503-646-9171; FAX: 503-526-1455

Lever Arms Service Ltd., 2131 Burrard St., Vancouver, BC V6J 3H7 CANADA / 604-736-2711; FAX: 604-738-3503 leverarms@leverarms.com www.leverarms.com

Lew Horton Dist. Co., Inc., 15 Walkup Dr., Westboro, MA 01581 / 508-366-7400; FAX: 508-366-5332

Lewis Lead Remover, The (See Brownells, Inc.)

Liberty Mfg., Inc., 2233 East 16th St., Los Angeles, CA 90021 / 323-581-9171; FAX: 323-581-9351 libertymfginc@aol.com

Liberty Safe, 999 W. Utah Ave., Payson, UT 84651-1744 / 800-247-5625; FAX: 801-489-6409

Liberty Shooting Supplies, P.O. Box 357, Hillsboro, OR 97123 / 503-640-5518; FAX: 503-640-5518 info@libertyshootingsupplies.com www.libertyshootingsupplies.com

Lightning Performance Innovations, Inc., RD1 Box 555, Mohawk, NY 13407 / 315-866-8819; FAX: 315-867-5701

Lilja Precision Rifle Barrels, P.O. Box 372, Plains, MT 59859 / 406-826-3084; FAX: 406-826-3083 lilja@riflebarrels.com www.riflebarrels.com

Lincoln, Dean, Box 1886, Farmington, NM 87401

Lindsay Engraving & Tools, Steve Lindsay, 3714 W. Cedar Hills, Kearney, NE 68845 / 308-236-7885 steve@lindsayengraving.com www.handgravers.com

Lindsay, Steve. See: LINDSAY ENGRAVING & TOOLS

Lindsley Arms Cartridge Co., P.O. Box 757, 20 College Hill Rd., Henniker, NH 03242 / 603-995-1267

Linebaugh Custom Sixguns, P.O. Box 455, Cody, WY 82414 / 307-645-3332 www.sixgunner.com

Lion Country Supply, P.O. Box 480, Port Matilda, PA 16870

List Precision Engineering, Unit 1 Ingley Works, 13 River Road, Barking, ENGLAND / 011-081-594-1686

Lithi Bee Bullet Lube, 1728 Carr Rd., Muskegon, MI 49442 / 616-788-4479 lithibee@att.net

"Little John's" Antique Arms, 1740 W. Laveta, Orange, CA 92668

Littleton, J. F., 275 Pinedale Ave., Oroville, CA 95966 / 916-533-6084

Ljutic Industries, Inc., 732 N. 16th Ave., Suite 22, Yakima, WA 98902 / 509-248-0476; FAX: 509-576-8233 ljuticgun@earthlink.net www.ljuticgun.com

Lock's Philadelphia Gun Exchange, 6700 Rowland Ave., Philadelphia, PA 19149 / 215-332-6225; FAX: 215-332-4800 locks.gunshop@verizon.net

Lodewick, Walter H., 2816 NE Halsey St., Portland, OR 97232 / 503-284-2554 wlodewick@aol.com

Lodgewood Mfg., P.O. Box 611, Whitewater, WI 53190 / 262-473-5444; FAX: 262-473-6448 lodgewd@idcnet.com lodgewood.com

Log Cabin Sport Shop, 8010 Lafayette Rd., Lodi, OH 44254 / 330-948-1082; FAX: 330-948-4307 logcabin@logcabinshop.com www.logcabinshop.com

Logdewood Mfg., P.O. Box 611, Whitewater, WI 53190 / 262-473-5444; FAX: 262-473-6448 lodgewd@idcnet.com www.lodgewood.com

Lohman Mfg. Co., Inc., 4500 Doniphan Dr., P.O. Box 220, Neosho, MO 64850 / 417-451-4438; FAX: 417-451-2576

Lomont Precision Bullets, 278 Sandy Creek Rd., Salmon, ID 83467 / 208-756-6819; FAX: 208-756-6824 www.klomont.com

London Guns Ltd., Box 3750, Santa Barbara, CA 93130 / 805-683-4141; FAX: 805-683-1712

Lone Star Gunleather, 1301 Brushy Bend Dr., Round Rock, TX 78681 / 512-255-1805

Lone Star Rifle Company, 11231 Rose Road, Conroe, TX 77303 / 936-856-3363; FAX: 936-856-3363 dave@lonestar.com

Long, George F., 1402 Kokanee Ln., Grants Pass, OR 97527 / 541-476-0836

Lothar Walther Precision Tool Inc., 3425 Hutchinson Rd., Cumming, GA 30040 / 770-889-9998; FAX: 770-889-4919 lotharwalther@mindspring.com www.lothar-walther.com

LPS Laboratories, Inc., 4647 Hugh Howell Rd., P.O. Box 3050, Tucker, GA 30084 / 404-934-7800

Lucas, Edward E, 32 Garfield Ave., East Brunswick, NJ 08816 / 201-251-5526

Lupton, Keith. See: PAWLING MOUNTAIN CLUB

Lyman Instant Targets, Inc. (See Lyman Products Corp.)

Lyman Products Corp., 475 Smith St., Middletown, CT 06457-1541 / 800-423-9704; FAX: 860-632-1699 lymansales@cshore.com www.lymanproducts.com

M

M.H. Canjar Co., 6510 Raleigh St., Arvada, CO 80003 / 303-295-2638; FAX: 303-295-2638

MA Systems, Inc., P.O. Box 894, Pryor, OK 74362-0894 / 918-824-3705; FAX: 918-824-3710

Mac-1 Airgun Distributors, 13974 Van Ness Ave., Gardena, CA 90249-2900 / 310-327-3581; FAX: 310-327-0238 mac1@mac1airgun.com www.mac1airgun.com

Machinist's Workshop-Village Press, P.O. Box 1810, Traverse City, MI 49685 / 800-447-7367; FAX: 231-946-6180

Madis Books, 2453 West Five Mile Pkwy., Dallas, TX 75233 / 214-330-7168

Madis, George. See: WINCHESTER CONSULTANTS

MAG Instrument, Inc., 1635 S. Sacramento Ave., Ontario, CA 91761 / 909-947-1006; FAX: 909-947-3116

Magma Engineering Co., P.O. Box 161, 20955 E. Ocotillo Rd., Queen Creek, AZ 85242 / 602-987-9008; FAX: 602-987-0148

Mag-Na-Port International, Inc., 41302 Executive Dr., Harrison Twp., MI 48045-1306 / 586-469-6727; FAX: 586-469-0425 email@magnaport.com www.magnaport.com

Magnum Power Products, Inc., P.O. Box 17768, Fountain Hills, AZ 85268

Magnum Research, Inc., 7110 University Ave. NE, Minneapolis, MN 55432 / 800-772-6168 or 763-574-1868; FAX: 763-574-0109 info@magnumresearch.com

Magnus Bullets, P.O. Box 239, Toney, AL 35773 / 256-420-8359; FAX: 256-420-8360 bulletman@mchsi.com www.magnusbullets.com

MagSafe Ammo, Inc., 4700 S. US Highway 17/92, Casselberry, FL 32707-3814 / 407-834-9966; FAX: 407-834-8185 www.magsafeammo.com

Magtech Ammunition Co. Inc., 248 Apollo Dr. Ste. 180, Linolakes, MN 55014 / 800-466-7191; FAX: 763-235-4004 www.magtechammunition.com

Mahovsky's Metalife, R.D. 1, Box 149a Eureka Road, Grand Valley, PA 16420 / 814-436-7747

Makinson, Nicholas, RR 3, Komoka, ON N0L 1R0 CANADA / 519-471-5462

Mallardtone Game Calls, 10406 96th St., Court West, Taylor Ridge, IL 61284 / 309-798-2481; FAX: 309-798-2501

Marble Arms (See CRR, Inc./Marble's Inc.)

Marent, Rudolf. See: HAMMERLI SERVICE-PRECISION MAC

Mark Lee Supplies, 9901 France Ct., Lakeville, MN 55044 / 952-461-2114; FAX: 952-461-2194 marklee55044@usfamily.net

Markell, Inc., 422 Larkfield Center 235, Santa Rosa, CA 95403 / 707-573-0792; FAX: 707-573-9867

Markesbery Muzzle Loaders, Inc., 7065 Production Ct., Florence, KY 41042 / 859-342-5553; FAX: 859-342-2380 www.markesbery.com

Marksman Products, 5482 Argosy Dr., Huntington Beach, CA 92649 / 714-898-7535 or 800-822-8005; FAX: 714-891-0782

Marlin Firearms Co., 100 Kenna Dr., North Haven, CT 06473 / 203-239-5621; FAX: 203-234-7991 www.marlinfirearms.com

Marocchi F.lli S.p.A, Via Galileo Galilei 8, I-25068 Zanano, ITALY

Marsh, Mike, Croft Cottage, Main St., Derbyshire, DE4 2BY ENGLAND / 01629 650 669

Marshall Enterprises, 792 Canyon Rd., Redwood City, CA 94062

Martin B. Retting Inc., 11029 Washington, Culver City, CA 90232 / 213-837-2412 retting@retting.com

Martini & Hagn, Ltd., 1264 Jimsmith Lake Rd., Cranbrook, BC V1C 6V6 CANADA / 250-417-2926; FAX: 250-417-2928 martini-hagn@shaw.ca www.martiniandhagngunmakers.com

Martin's Gun Shop, 937 S. Sheridan Blvd., Lakewood, CO 80226 / 303-922-2184 rdrnnr74479@peoplepc.com

Martz, John V., 8060 Lakeview Lane, Lincoln, CA 95648 FAX: 916-645-3815

Marvel, Alan, 3922 Madonna Rd., Jarretsville, MD 21084 / 301-557-6545

Marx, Harry (See U.S. Importer for FERLIB)

Maryland Paintball Supply, 8507 Harford Rd., Parkville, MD 21234 / 410-882-5607

Master Lock Co., 2600 N. 32nd St., Milwaukee, WI 53245 / 414-444-2800

Match Prep-Doyle Gracey, P.O. Box 155, Tehachapi, CA 93581 / 661-822-5383; FAX: 661-823-8680 gracenotes@as.net www.matchprep.com

Mathews Gun Shop & Gunsmithing, Inc., 2791 S. Gaffey St., San Pedro, CA 90731-6515 / 562-928-2129; FAX: 562-928-8629

Mauser Werke Oberndorf Waffensysteme GmbH, Postfach 1349, 78722, Oberndorf/N., GERMANY

Maverick Arms, Inc., 7 Grasso Ave., P.O. Box 497, North Haven, CT 06473 / 203-230-5300; FAX: 203-230-5420

Maxi-Mount Inc., P.O. Box 291, Willoughby Hills, OH 44096-0291 / 440-944-9456; FAX: 440-944-9456 maximount454@yahoo.com

Mayville Engineering Co. (See MEC, Inc.)

Mazur Restoration, Pete, 13083 Drummer Way, Grass Valley, CA 95949 / 530-268-2412

McCament, Jay. See: JAY MCCAMENT CUSTOM GUNMAKER

McCann, Tom, 14 Walton Dr., New Hope, PA 18938 / 215-862-2728

McCann Industries, P.O. Box 641, Spanaway, WA 98387 / 253-537-6919; FAX: 253-537-6919 mccann.machine@worldnet.att.net www.mccannindustries.com

McCluskey Precision Rifles, 10502 14th Ave. NW, Seattle, WA 98177 / 206-781-2776

McCombs, Leo, 1862 White Cemetery Rd., Patriot, OH 45658 / 740-256-1714

McDonald, Dennis, 8359 Brady St., Peosta, IA 52068 / 319-556-7940

McFarland, Stan, 2221 Idella Ct., Grand Junction, CO 81505 / 970-243-4704

McGhee, Larry. See: B.C. OUTDOORS

McGowen Rifle Barrels, 5961 Spruce Lane, St. Anne, IL 60964 / 815-937-9816; FAX: 815-937-4024

Mchalik, Gary. See: ROSSI FIREARMS

McKenzie, Lynton, 6940 N. Alvernon Way, Tucson, AZ 85718 / 520-299-5090

McMillan Fiberglass Stocks, Inc., 1638 W. Knudsen Dr. #101, Phoenix, AZ 85027 / 623-582-9635; FAX: 623-581-3825 mfsinc@mcmfamily.com www.mcmfamily.com

McMillan Optical Gunsight Co., 28638 N. 42nd St., Cave Creek, AZ 85331 / 602-585-7868; FAX: 602-585-7872

McMillan Rifle Barrels, P.O. Box 3427, Bryan, TX 77805 / 409-690-3456; FAX: 409-690-0156

MANUFACTURER'S DIRECTORY

McMurdo, Lynn, P.O. Box 404, Afton, WY 83110 / 307-886-5535

MCS, Inc., 166 Pocono Rd., Brookfield, CT 06804-2023 / 203-775-1013; FAX: 203-775-9462

McWelco Products, 6730 Santa Fe Ave., Hesperia, CA 92345 / 619-244-8876; FAX: 619-244-9398 products@mcwelco.com www.mcwelco.com

MDS, P.O. Box 1441, Brandon, FL 33509-1441 / 813-653-1180; FAX: 813-684-5953

Meacham Tool & Hardware Co., Inc., 37052 Eberhardt Rd., Peck, ID 83545 / 208-486-7171 smeacham@clearwater.net www.meachamrifles.com

Measures, Leon. See: SHOOT WHERE YOU LOOK

MEC, Inc., 715 South St., Mayville, WI 53050 reloaders@mayvl.com www.mecreloaders.com

MEC-Gar S.R.L., Via Madonnina 64, Gardone V.T. Brescia, ITALY / 39-030-3733668; FAX: 39-030-3733687 info@mec-gar.it www.mec-gar.it

MEC-Gar U.S.A., Inc., Hurley Farms Industr. Park, 905 Middle St., Middletown, CT 06457 / 203-262-1525; FAX: 203-262-1719 mecgar@aol.com www.mec-gar.com

Mech-Tech Systems, Inc., 1602 Foothill Rd., Kalispell, MT 59901 / 406-755-8055

Meister Bullets (See Gander Mountain)

Mele, Frank, 201 S. Wellow Ave., Cookeville, TN 38501 / 615-526-4860

Menck, Gunsmith Inc., T.W., 5703 S 77th St., Ralston, NE 68127

Mendez, John A., 1309 Continental Dr., Daytona Beach, FL 32117-3807 / 407-344-2791

Men-Metallwerk Elisenhuette GmbH, P.O. Box 1263, Nassau/Lahn, D-56372 GERMANY / 2604-7819

Meopta USA, LLC, 50 Davids Dr., Hauppauge, NY 11788 / 631-436-5900 ussales@meopta.com www.meopta.com

Mercer Custom Guns, 216 S. Whitewater Ave., Jefferson, WI 53549 / 920-674-3839

Merit Corp., P.O. Box 9044, Schenectady, NY 12309 / 518-346-1420 sales@meritcorporation.com www.meritcorporation.com

Merkel, Schutzenstrasse 26, D-98527 Suhl, Suhl, GERMANY FAX: 011-49-3681-854-203 www.merkel-waffen.de

Metal Merchants, P.O. Box 186, Walled Lake, MI 48390-0186

Metalife Industries (See Mahovsky's Metalife)

Michael's Antiques, Box 591, Waldoboro, ME 04572

Michaels of Oregon Co., 9200 Cody St., Overland Park, KS 66214 / 800-845-2444 www.michaels-oregon.com

Micro Sight Co., 502 May St., Arroyo Grande, CA 93420-2832

Microfusion Alfa S.A., Paseo San Andres N8, P.O. Box 271, Eibar 20600, 20600 SPAIN / 34-43-11-89-16; FAX: 34-43-11-40-38

Mid-America Recreation, Inc., 1328 5th Ave., Moline, IL 61265 / 309-764-5089; FAX: 309-764-5089 fmilcusguns@aol.com www.midamericarecreation.com

Middlebrooks Custom Shop, 7366 Colonial Trail East, Surry, VA 23883 / 757-357-0881; FAX: 757-365-0442

Midway Arms, Inc., 5875 W. Van Horn Tavern Rd., Columbia, MO 65203 / 800-243-3220; FAX: 800-992-8312 www.midwayusa.com

Midwest Gun Sport, 1108 Herbert Dr., Zebulon, NC 27597 / 919-269-5570

Midwest Shooting School, The, Pat LaBoone, 2550 Hwy. 23, Wrenshall, MN 55797 / 218-384-3670 shootingschool@starband.net

Midwest Sport Distributors, Box 129, Fayette, MO 65248

Mike Davis Products, 643 Loop Dr., Moses Lake, WA 98837 / 509-765-6178; or 509-766-7281

Mike Yee Custom Stocking, 29927 56 Pl. S., Auburn, WA 98001 / 253-839-3991 miknadyee@comcast.net

Military Armament Corp., P.O. Box 120, Mt. Zion Rd., Lingleville, TX 76461 / 817-965-3253

Millennium Designed Muzzleloaders, P.O. Box 536, Routes 11 & 25, Limington, ME 04049 / 207-637-2316

Miller Arms, Inc., 1310 Industry Rd., Sturgis, SD 57785-9129 / 605-642-5160; FAX: 605-642-5160

Miller Custom, 210 E. Julia, Clinton, IL 61727 / 217-935-9362

Miller Single Trigger Mfg. Co., 6680 Rt. 5-20, P.O. Box 471, Bloomfield, NY 14469 / 585-657-6338; FAX: 585-657-7743 info@turnbullrestoration.com turnbullrestoration.com

Millett Sights, 16131 Gothard St., Huntington Beach, CA 92647 / 714-842-5575 or 800-645-5388; FAX: 714-843-5707 sales@millettsights.com www.millettsights.com

Mills Jr., Hugh B., 3615 Canterbury Rd., New Bern, NC 28560 / 919-637-4631

Minute Man High Tech Industries, 10611 Canyon Rd. E., Suite 151, Puyallup, WA 98373 / 800-233-2734

Mirador Optical Corp., P.O. Box 11614, Marina Del Rey, CA 90295-7614 / 310-821-5587; FAX: 310-305-0386

Mitchell, Jack, c/o Geoff Gaebe, Addieville East Farm, 200 Pheasant Dr., Mapleville, RI 02839 / 401-568-3185

Mitchell Mfg. Corp., P.O. Box 9295, Fountain Valley, CA 92728 / 714-444-2220

Mitchell Optics, Inc., 2072 CR 1100 N, Sidney, IL 61877 / 217-688-2219 or 217-621-3018; FAX: 217-688-2505 mitchell@attglobal.net

Mitchell's Accuracy Shop, 68 Greenridge Dr., Stafford, VA 22554 / 703-659-0165

Mitchell's Mauser, P.O. Box 9295, Fountain Valley, CA 92728 / 714-979-7663; FAX: 714-899-3660

MI-TE Bullets, 1396 Ave. K, Ellsworth, KS 67439 / 785-472-4575; FAX: 785-472-5579

MJK Gunsmithing, Inc., 417 N. Huber Ct., E. Wenatchee, WA 98802 / 509-884-7683

MKS Supply, Inc. (See Hi-Point Firearms)

MMC, 4430 Mitchell St., North Las Vegas, NV 89081 / 800-998-7483; FAX: 702-267-9463 info@mmcsight.com www.mmcsight.com

MOA Corporation, 285 Government Valley Rd., Sundance, WY 82729 / 307-283-3030 www.moaguns.com

Mobile Area Networks, Inc., 2772 Depot St., Sanford, FL 32773 / 407-333-2350; FAX: 407-333-9903 georgew@mobilan.com www.mobilan.com

Modern Gun Repair School, P.O. Box 846, Saint Albans, VT 05478 / 802-524-2223; FAX: 802-524-2053 jfwp@dlilearn.com www.mgsinfoadlifearn.com

Modern Muzzleloading, Inc., P.O. Box 130, Centerville, IA 52544 / 515-856-2626

Moeller, Steve, 1213 4th St., Fulton, IL 61252 / 815-589-2300

Mogul Co./Life Jacket, 500 N. Kimball Rd., Ste. 109, South Lake, TX 76092

Monell Custom Guns, 228 Red Mills Rd., Pine Bush, NY 12566 / 845-744-3021

Moneymaker Guncraft Corp., 1420 Military Ave., Omaha, NE 68131 / 402-556-0226

Montana Armory, Inc., 100 Centennial Dr., P.O. Box 885, Big Timber, MT 59011 / 406-932-4353; FAX: 406-932-4443

Montana Outfitters, Lewis E. Yearout, 308 Riverview Dr. E., Great Falls, MT 59404 / 406-761-0859; or 406-727-4560

Montana Precision Swaging, P.O. Box 4746, Butte, MT 59702 / 406-494-0600; FAX: 406-494-0600

Montana Rifleman, Inc., 2593A Hwy. 2 East, Kalispell, MT 59901 / 406-755-4867

Montana Vintage Arms, 2354 Bear Canyon Rd., Bozeman, MT 59715

Morini (See U.S. Importers-Mandall Shooting Supplies, Inc.)

Morrison Custom Rifles, J. W., 4015 W Sharon, Phoenix, AZ 85029 / 602-978-3754

Morrison Precision, 6719 Calle Mango, Hereford, AZ 85615 / 520-378-6207 morprec@c2i2.com

Morrow, Bud, 11 Hillside Lane, Sheridan, WY 82801-9729 / 307-674-8360

Morton Booth Co., P.O. Box 123, Joplin, MO 64802 / 417-673-1962; FAX: 417-673-3642

Mo's Competitor Supplies (See MCS, Inc.)

Moss Double Tone, Inc., P.O. Box 1112, 2101 S. Kentucky, Sedalia, MO 65301 / 816-827-0827

Mountain Plains Industries, 3720 Otter Place, Lynchburg, VA 24503 / 800-687-3000; FAX: 434-386-6217 MPI_targets@adelphia.net www.targetshandloader.com

Mowrey Gun Works, P.O. Box 246, Waldron, IN 46182 / 317-525-6181; FAX: 317-525-9595

Mowrey's Guns & Gunsmithing, 119 Fredericks St., Canajoharie, NY 13317 / 518-673-3483

MPC, P.O. Box 450, McMinnville, TN 37110-0450 / 615-473-5513; FAX: 615-473-5516 thebox@blomand.net www.mpc-thebox.com

MPI Stocks, P.O. Box 83266, Portland, OR 97283 / 503-226-1215; FAX: 503-226-2661

MSR Targets, P.O. Box 1042, West Covina, CA 91793 / 818-331-7840

MTM Molded Products Co., Inc., 3370 Obco Ct., Dayton, OH 45414 / 937-890-7461; FAX: 937-890-1747

Mulberry House Publishing, P.O. Box 2180, Apache Junction, AZ 85217 / 888-738-1567; FAX: 480-671-1015

Mulhern, Rick, Rt. 5, Box 152, Rayville, LA 71269 / 318-728-2688

Mullins Ammunition, Rt. 2 Box 304N, Clintwood, VA 24228 / 276-926-6772; FAX: 276-926-6092 mammo@extremeshockusa.com www.extremeshockusa.com

Mullis Guncraft, 3523 Lawyers Road E., Monroe, NC 28110 / 704-283-6683

Multiplex International, 26 S. Main St., Concord, NH 03301 FAX: 603-796-2223

Multipropulseurs, La Bertrandiere, 42580, FRANCE / 77 74 01 30; FAX: 77 93 19 34

Mundy, Thomas A., 69 Robbins Road, Somerville, NJ 08876 / 201-722-2199

Murmur Corp., RR 2, Dallas, TX 75241 / 214-630-5400

Murphy, R.R. Murphy Co., Inc. See: MURPHY, R.R. CO., INC.

Murphy, R.R. Co., Inc., R.R. Murphy Co., Inc. Murphy, P.O. Box 102, Ripley, TN 38063 / 901-635-4003; FAX: 901-635-2320

Murray State College, 1 Murray Campus St., Tishomingo, OK 73460 / 508-371-2371 darnold@mscol.edu

Muscle Products Corp., 112 Fennell Dr., Butler, PA 16002 / 800-227-7049 or 724-283-0567; FAX: 724-283-8310 mpc@mpc_home.com www.mpc_home.com

Muzzleloaders Etcetera, Inc., 9901 Lyndale Ave. S., Bloomington, MN 55420 / 952-884-1161 www.muzzleloaders-etcetera.com

MWG Co., P.O. Box 971202, Miami, FL 33197 / 800-428-9394 or 305-253-8393; FAX: 305-232-1247

N

N.B.B., Inc., 24 Elliot Rd., Sterling, MA 01564 / 508-422-7538 or 800-942-9444

N.C. Ordnance Co., P.O. Box 3254, Wilson, NC 27895 / 919-237-2440; FAX: 919-243-9845 bharvey@nc.rr.com www.gungrip.com

Nagel's Custom Bullets, 100 Scott St., Baytown, TX 77520-2849

Nalpak, 1267 Vernon Way, El Cajon, CA 92020

Nammo Lapua Oy, P.O. Box 5, Lapua, FINLAND / 358-6-4310111; FAX: 358-6-4310317 info@nammo.ti www.lapua.com

Nastoff, Steve. See: NASTOFFS 45 SHOP, INC.

Nastoffs 45 Shop, Inc., Steve Nastoff, 1057 Laverne Dr., Youngstown, OH 44511

National Bullet Co., 1585 E. 361 St., Eastlake, OH 44095 / 216-951-1854; FAX: 216-951-7761

National Gun, Inc., 3709 W. Flagler St., Coral Gables, FL 33134 / 305-642-2355

National Target Co., 3958-D Dartmouth Ct., Frederick, MD 21703 / 800-827-7060; FAX: 301-874-4764 www.nationaltarget.com

Nationwide Airgun Repair, 2310 Windsor Forest Dr., Louisville, KY 40272 / 502-937-2614 shortshoestring@insightbb.com

Naval Ordnance Works, 467 Knott Rd., Sheperdstown, WV 25443 / 304-876-0998; FAX: 304-876-0998 nvordfdy@earthlink.net

Navy Arms Company, 219 Lawn St., Martinsburg, WV 25401 / 304-262-9870; FAX: 304-262-1658 info@navyarms.com www.navyarms.com

NCP Products, Inc., 3500 12th St. N.W., Canton, OH 44708 / 330-456-5130; FAX: 330-456-5234

Necessary Concepts, Inc., P.O. Box 571, Deer Park, NY 11729 / 516-667-8509; FAX: 516-667-8588

NEI Handtools, Inc., 10960 Gary Player Dr., El Paso, TX 79935

Neil A. Jones Custom Products, 17217 Brookhouser Road, Saegertown, PA 16433 / 814-763-2769; FAX: 814-763-4228

Nelson, Gary K., 975 Terrace Dr., Oakdale, CA 95361 / 209-847-4590

Nelson, Stephen. See: NELSON'S CUSTOM GUNS, INC.

Nelson's Custom Guns, Inc., Stephen Nelson, 7430 Valley View Dr. N.W., Corvallis, OR 97330 / 541-745-5232 nelsons-custom@attbi.com

MANUFACTURER'S DIRECTORY

Nesci Enterprises Inc., P.O. Box 119, Summit St., East Hampton, CT 06424 / 203-267-2588

Nesika Bay Precision, 22239 Big Valley Rd., Poulsbo, WA 98370 / 206-697-3830

Nettestad Gun Works, 38962 160th Avenue, Pelican Rapids, MN 56572 / 218-863-1338

New England Ammunition Co., 1771 Post Rd. East, Suite 223, Westport, CT 06880 / 203-254-8048

New England Arms Co., Box 278, Lawrence Lane, Kittery Point, ME 03905 / 207-439-0593; FAX: 207-439-0525 info@newenglandarms.com www.newenglandarms.com

New England Custom Gun Service, 438 Willow Brook Rd., Plainfield, NH 03781 / 603-469-3450; FAX: 603-469-3471 bestguns@adelphia.net www.newenglandcustom.com

New Orleans Jewelers Supply Co., 206 Charters St., New Orleans, LA 70130 / 504-523-3839; FAX: 504-523-3836

New SKB Arms Co., C.P.O. Box 1401, Tokyo, JAPAN / 81-3-3943-9550; FAX: 81-3-3943-0695

New Ultra Light Arms, LLC, P.O. Box 340, Granville, WV 26534

Newark Electronics, 4801 N. Ravenswood Ave., Chicago, IL 60640

Newell, Robert H., 55 Coyote, Los Alamos, NM 87544 / 505-662-7135

Newman Gunshop, 2035 Chester Ave. #411, Ottumwa, IA 52501-3715 / 515-937-5775

NgraveR Co., The, 67 Wawecus Hill Rd., Bozrah, CT 06334 / 860-823-1533; FAX: 860-887-6252 ngraver98@aol.com www.ngraver.com

Nicholson Custom, 17285 Thornlay Road, Hughesville, MO 65334 / 816-826-8746

Nickels, Paul R., 2216 Jacob Dr., Santa Clara, UT 84765-5399 / 435-652-1959

Niemi Engineering, W. B., Box 126 Center Rd., Greensboro, VT 05841 / 802-533-7180; FAX: 802-533-7141

Nighthawk Custom, 1306 W. Trimble, Berryville, AR 72616 / 877-268-GUNS; (4867) or 870-423-GUNS; FAX: 870-423-4230 www.nighthawkcustom.com

Nikon, Inc., 1300 Walt Whitman Rd., Melville, NY 11747 / 516-547-8623; FAX: 516-547-0309

Noreen, Peter H., 5075 Buena Vista Dr., Belgrade, MT 59714 / 406-586-7383

Norica, Avnda Otaola, 16 Apartado 68, Eibar, SPAIN

Norinco, 7A Yun Tan N, Beijing, CHINA

Norincoptics (See BEC, Inc.)

Norma Precision AB (See U.S. Importers-Dynamit)

Normark Corp., 10395 Yellow Circle Dr., Minnetonka, MN 55343-9101 / 612-933-7060; FAX: 612-933-0046

North American Arms, Inc., 2150 South 950 East, Provo, UT 84606-6285 / 800-821-5783 or 801-374-9990; FAX: 801-374-9998

North American Correspondence Schools, The Gun Pro, Oak & Pawney St., Scranton, PA 18515 / 717-342-7701

North American Shooting Systems, P.O. Box 306, Osoyoos, BC V0H 1V0 CANADA / 250-495-3131; FAX: 250-495-3131 rifle@cablerocket.com

North Devon Firearms Services, 3 North St., Braunton, EX33 1AJ ENGLAND / 01271 813624; FAX: 01271 813624

North Mountain Pine Training Center (See Executive Protection Institute)

North Star West, Inc., P.O. Box 487, 57 Terrace Ct., Superior, MT 59872 / 406-822-8778 laffindog@msn.com www.northstarwest.com

Northern Precision, 329 S. James St., Carthage, NY 13619 / 315-493-1711

Northside Gun Shop, 2725 NW 109th, Oklahoma City, OK 73120 / 405-840-2353

Northwest Custom Projectile, P.O. Box 127, Butte, MT 59703-0127 www.customprojectile.com

No-Sho Mfg. Co., 10727 Glenfield Ct., Houston, TX 77096 / 713-723-5332

Nosler, Inc., P.O. Box 671, Bend, OR 97709 / 800-285-3701 or 541-382-3921; FAX: 541-388-4667 www.nosler.com

Novak's, Inc., 1206 1/2 30th St., P.O. Box 4045, Parkersburg, WV 26101 / 304-485-9295; FAX: 304-428-6722 www.novaksights.com

Nowlin Mfg. Co., 20622 S 4092 Rd., Claremore, OK 74017 / 918-342-0689; FAX: 918-342-0624 nowlinguns@msn. com www.nowlinguns.com

NRI Gunsmith School, P.O. Box 182968, Columbus, OH 43218-2968

Nu Line Guns, Inc., 8150 CR 4055, Rhineland, MO 65069 / 573-676-5500; FAX: 573-676-3400 nlg@ktis.net

Null Holsters Ltd. K.L., 161 School St. N.W., Resaca, GA 30735 / 706-625-5643; FAX: 706-625-9392 ken@klnullholsters.com www.klnullholsters.com

Numrich Gun Parts Corporation, 226 Williams Lane, P.O. Box 299, West Hurley, NY 12491 / 866-686-7424; FAX: 877-GUNPART info@gunpartscorp.com www.@ e-gunparts.com

O

O.F. Mossberg & Sons, Inc., 7 Grasso Ave., North Haven, CT 06473 / 203-230-5300; FAX: 203-230-5420

Oakman Turkey Calls, RD 1, Box 825, Harrisonville, PA 17228 / 717-485-4620

Obermeyer Rifled Barrels, 23122 60th St., Bristol, WI 53104 / 262-843-3537; FAX: 262-843-2129 www.obermeyerbarrels.com

October Country Muzzleloading, P.O. Box 969, Dept. GD, Hayden, ID 83835 / 208-772-2068; FAX: 208-772-9230 ocinfo@octobercountry.com www.octobercountry.com

Oehler Research, Inc., P.O. Box 9135, Austin, TX 78766 / 512-327-6900 or 800-531-5125; FAX: 512-327-6903 www.oehler-research.com

Oil Rod and Gun Shop, 69 Oak St., East Douglas, MA 01516 / 508-476-3687

OK Weber, Inc., P.O. Box 7485, Eugene, OR 97401 / 541-747-0458; FAX: 541-747-5927 okweber@pacinfo www.okweber.com

Oker's Engraving, P.O. Box 126, Shawnee, CO 80475 / 303-838-6042 engraver@netscape.com

Oklahoma Ammunition Co., 3701A S. Harvard Ave., No. 367, Tulsa, OK 74135-2265 / 918-396-3187; FAX: 918-396-4270

Oklahoma Leather Products, Inc., 500 26th NW, Miami, OK 74354 / 918-542-6651; FAX: 918-542-6653

Olathe Gun Shop, 716-A South Rogers Road, Olathe, KS 66062 / 913-782-6900; FAX: 913-782-6902 info@olathegunshop.com www.olathegunshop.com

Old Wagon Bullets, 32 Old Wagon Rd., Wilton, CT 06897

Old West Bullet Moulds, J. Ken Chapman, P.O. Box 519, Flora Vista, NM 87415 / 505-334-6970

Old West Reproductions, Inc. R.M. Bachman, 446 Florence S. Loop, Florence, MT 59833 / 406-273-2615; FAX: 406-273-2615 rick@oldwestreproductions.com www.oldwestreproductions.com

Old Western Scrounger LLC, 219 Lawn St., Martinsburg, NV 25401 / 304-262-9870; FAX: 304-262-1658 www.ows-ammo.com

Ole Frontier Gunsmith Shop, 2617 Hwy. 29 S., Cantonment, FL 32533 / 904-477-8074

Olson, Myron, 989 W. Kemp, Watertown, SD 57201 / 605-886-9787

Olson, Vic, 5002 Countryside Dr., Imperial, MO 63052 / 314-296-8086

Olympic Arms Inc., 620-626 Old Pacific Hwy. SE, Olympia, WA 98513 / 360-456-3471; FAX: 360-491-3447 info@olyarms.com www.olyarms.com

Olympic Optical Co., P.O. Box 752377, Memphis, TN 38175-2377 / 901-794-3890 or 800-238-7120; FAX: 901-794-0676

One Of A Kind, 15610 Purple Sage, San Antonio, TX 78255 / 512-695-3364

One Ragged Hole, P.O. Box 13624, Tallahassee, FL 32317-3624

Op-Tec, P.O. Box L632, Langhorn, PA 19047 / 215-757-5037; FAX: 215-757-7097

Optical Services Co., P.O. Box 1174, Santa Teresa, NM 88008-1174 / 505-589-3833

Orchard Park Enterprise, P.O. Box 563, Orchard Park, NY 14127 / 616-656-0356

Ordnance Works, The, 2969 Pigeon Point Rd., Eureka, CA 95501 / 707-443-3252

Oregon Arms, Inc. (See Rogue Rifle Co., Inc.)

Oregon Trail Bullet Company, P.O. Box 529, Dept. P, Baker City, OR 97814 / 800-811-0548; FAX: 514-523-1803

Original Deer Formula Co., The, P.O. Box 1705, Dickson, TN 37056 / 800-874-6965; FAX: 615-446-0646 deerformula1@aol.com www.deerformula.com

Orion Rifle Barrel Co., Jerry Cunningham, P.O. Box 130192, Coram, MT 59913 / 406-257-5649

Orvis Co., The, Rt. 7, Manchester, VT 05254 / 802-362-3622; FAX: 802-362-3525

Otis Technology, Inc., RR 1 Box 84, Boonville, NY 13309 / 315-942-3320

Ottmar, Maurice, 920 Timber Trl, Cedar Park, TX 78613

Outa-Site Gun Carriers, 219 Market St., Laredo, TX 78040 / 210-722-4678 or 800-880-9715; FAX: 210-726-4858

Outdoor Connection, Inc., The, 7901 Panther Way, Waco, TX 76712-6556 / 800-533-6076; FAX: 254-776-3553 info@outdoorconnection.com www.outdoorconnection.com

Outdoor Edge Cutlery Corp., 4699 Nautilus Ct. S. Ste. 503, Boulder, CO 80301-5310 / 303-530-7667; FAX: 303-530-7020 www.outdooredge.com

Outdoor Enthusiast, 3784 W. Woodland, Springfield, MO 65807 / 417-883-9841

Outdoor Sports Headquarters, Inc., 967 Watertower Ln., West Carrollton, OH 45449 / 513-865-5855; FAX: 513-865-5962

Outers Laboratories Div. of ATK, Route 2, P.O. Box 39, Onalaska, WI 54650 / 608-781-5800; FAX: 608-781-0368

Ozark Gun Works, 11830 Cemetery Rd., Rogers, AR 72756 / 479-631-1024; FAX: 479-631-1024 ozarkgunworks@cox.net www.geocities.com

P

P&M Sales & Services, LLC, 4697 Tote Rd. Bldg. H-B, Comins, MI 48619 / 989-848-8364; FAX: 989-848-8364 info@pmsales-online.com

P.S.M.G. Gun Co., 10 Park Ave., Arlington, MA 02174 / 781-646-1699; FAX: 781-643-7212 psmg2@aol.com

Pachmayr Div. Lyman Products, 475 Smith St., Middletown, CT 06457 / 860-632-2020 or 800-225-9626; FAX: 860-632-1699 lymansales@cshore.com www.pachmayr.com

Pacific Armament Corp, 4813 Enterprise Way, Unit K, Modesto, CA 95356 / 209-545-2800 gunsparts@att.net

Pacific Rifle Co., P.O. Box 841, Carlton, OR 97111 / 503-852-6276 pacificrifle@aol.com

PAC-NOR Barreling, Inc., 99299 Overlook Rd., P.O. Box 6188, Brookings, OR 97415 / 541-469-7330; FAX: 541-469-7331 chris@pac-nor.com www.pac-nor.com

PACT, Inc., P.O. Box 535025, Grand Prairie, TX 75053 / 972-641-0049; FAX: 972-641-2641

Page Custom Bullets, P.O. Box 25, Port Moresby, NEW GUINEA

Pagel Gun Works, Inc., 2 SE 1st St., Grand Rapids, MN 55744

Pager Pal, P.O. Box 54864, Hurst, TX 76054-4864 / 800-561-1603; FAX: 817-285-8769 info@pagerpal.com www.pagerpal.com

Paintball Games International Magazine Aceville, Castle House 97 High St., Essex, ENGLAND / 011-44-206-564840

Palsa Outdoor Products, P.O. Box 81336, Lincoln, NE 68501 / 402-488-5288; FAX: 402-488-2321

Pansch, Robert F, 1004 Main St. #10, Neenah, WI 54956 / 920-725-8175

Paragon Sales & Services, Inc., 2501 Theodore St., Crest Hill, IL 60435-1613 / 815-725-9212; FAX: 815-725-8974

Para-Ordnance Mfg., Inc., 980 Tapscott Rd., Scarborough, ON M1X 1E7 CANADA / 416-297-7855; FAX: 416-297-1289

Para-Ordnance, Inc., 1919 NE 45th St., Ste 215, Ft. Lauderdale, FL 33308 / 416-297-7855; FAX: 416-297-1289 info@paraord.com www.paraord.com

Pardini Armi Srl, Via Italica 154, 55043, Lido Di Camaiore Lu, ITALY / 584-90121; FAX: 584-90122

Paris, Frank J., 17417 Pershing St., Livonia, MI 48152-3822

Park Rifle Co., Ltd., The, Unit 6a Dartford Trade Park, Power Mill Lane, Dartford DA7 7NX, ENGLAND / 011-0322-222512

Parker & Sons Shooting Supply, 9337 Smoky Row Road, Strawberry Plains, TN 37871 / 865-933-3286; FAX: 865-932-8586

Parker Gun Finishes, 9337 Smokey Row Rd., Strawberry Plains, TN 37871 / 865-933-3286; FAX: 865-932-8586 parcraft7838@netzero.com

Parsons Optical Mfg. Co., PO Box 192, Ross, OH 45061 / 513-867-0820; FAX: 513-867-8380 psscopes@concentric.net

MANUFACTURER'S DIRECTORY

Partridge Sales Ltd., John, Trent Meadows, Rugeley, ENGLAND

Pasadena Gun Center, 206 E. Shaw, Pasadena, TX 77506 / 713-472-0417; FAX: 713-472-1322

Passive Bullet Traps, Inc. (See Savage Range Systems, Inc.)

Paterson Gunsmithing, 438 Main St., Paterson, NJ 07502 / 201-345-4100

Pathfinder Sports Leather, 2920 E. Chambers St., Phoenix, AZ 85040 / 602-276-0016

Patrick W. Price Bullets, 16520 Worthley Drive, San Lorenzo, CA 94580 / 510-278-1547

Pattern Control, 114 N. Third St., P.O. Box 462105, Garland, TX 75046 / 214-494-3551; FAX: 214-272-8447

Paul A. Harris Hand Engraving, 113 Rusty Lane, Boerne, TX 78006-5746 / 512-391-5121

Paul and Sharon Dressel, 209 N. 92nd Ave., Yakima, WA 98908 / 509-966-9233; FAX: 509-966-3365 dressels@ nwinfo.net www.dressels.com

Paul Co., The, 27385 Pressonville Rd., Wellsville, KS 66092 / 785-883-4444; FAX: 785-883-2525

Paul D. Hillmer Custom Gunstocks, 7251 Hudson Heights, Hudson, IA 50643 / 319-988-3941

Paul Jones Moulds, 4901 Telegraph Rd., Los Angeles, CA 90022 / 213-262-1510

Paulsen Gunstocks, Rt. 71, Box 11, Chinook, MT 59523 / 406-357-3403

Pawling Mountain Club, Keith Lupton, P.O. Box 573, Pawling, NY 12564 / 914-855-3825

Paxton Quigley's Personal Protection Strategies, 9903 Santa Monica Blvd., 300, Beverly Hills, CA 90212 / 310-281-1762 www.defend-net.com/paxton

Payne Photography, Robert, Robert, P.O. Box 141471, Austin, TX 78714 / 512-272-4554

Peacemaker Specialists, 144 Via Fuchsia, Paso Robles, CA 93446 / 805-238-9100; FAX: 805-238-9100 www. peacemakerspecialists.com

Pearce Grip, Inc., P.O. Box 40367, Fort Worth, TX 76140 / 817-568-9704; FAX: 817-568-9707 info@pearcegrip.com www.pearcegrip.com

PECAR Herbert Schwarz GmbH, Kreuzbergstrasse 6, 10965, Berlin, GERMANY / 004930-785-7383; FAX: 004930-785-1934 michael.schwarz@pecar-berlin.de www.pecar-berlin.de

Pecatonica River Longrifle, 5205 Nottingham Dr., Rockford, IL 61111 / 815-968-1995; FAX: 815-968-1996

Pedersen, C. R., 2717 S. Pere Marquette Hwy., Ludington, MI 49431 / 231-843-2061; FAX: 231-845-7695 fega@ fega.com

Pedersen, Rex C., 2717 S. Pere Marquette Hwy., Ludington, MI 49431 / 231-843-2061; FAX: 231-845-7695 fega@ fega.com

Peifer Rifle Co., P.O. Box 220, Nokomis, IL 62075

Pejsa Ballistics, 1314 Marquette Ave., Apt 906, Minneapolis, MN 55403 / 612-332-5073; FAX: 612-332-5204 pejsa@sprintmail.com pejsa.com

Peltor, Inc. (See Aero Peltor)

Pence Precision Barrels, 7567 E. 900 S., S. Whitley, IN 46787 / 219-839-4745

Pendleton Woolen Mills, P.O. Box 3030, 220 N.W. Broadway, Portland, OR 97208 / 503-226-4801

Penn Bullets, P.O. Box 756, Indianola, PA 15051

Pennsylvania Gun Parts Inc., RR 7 Box 150, Mount Pleasant, PA 15666

Pennsylvania Gunsmith School, 812 Ohio River Blvd., Avalon, Pittsburgh, PA 15202 / 412-766-1812; FAX: 412-766-0855 pgs@pagunsmith.edu www.pagunsmith.edu

Penrod, Mark. See: PENROD PRECISION

Penrod Precision, Mark Penrod, 312 College Ave., P.O. Box 307, N. Manchester, IN 46962 / 260-982-8385; FAX: 260-982-1819 markpenrod@kconline.com

Pentax U.S.A., Inc., 600 12th St. Ste. 300, Golden, CO 80401 / 303-799-8000; FAX: 303-460-1628 www. pentaxlightseeker.com

Pentheny de Pentheny, c/o H.P. Okelly, 321 S. Main St., Sebastopol, CA 95472 / 707-824-1637; FAX: 707-824-1637

Perazone-Gunsmith, Brian, Cold Spring Rd., Roxbury, NY 12474 / 607-326-4088; FAX: 607-326-3140 bpgunsmith@catskill.net www.bpgunsmith@catskill.net

Perazzi U.S.A. Inc., 1010 West Tenth, Azusa, CA 91702 / 626-334-1234; FAX: 626-334-0344 perazziusa@aol.com

Performance Specialists, 308 Eanes School Rd., Austin, TX 78746 / 512-327-0119

Perugini Visini & Co. SAS, Via Camprelle, 126, 25080 Nuvolera, ITALY / 30-6897535; FAX: 30-6897821 info@ peruvisi@visini.com

Pete de Coux Auction House, 14940 Brenda Dr., Prescott, AZ 86305-7447 / 928-776-8285; FAX: 928-776-8276 pdbullets@commspeed.net

Pete Mazur Restoration, 13083 Drummer Way, Grass Valley, CA 95949 / 530-268-2412; FAX: 530-268-2412

Pete Rickard Co., 115 Roy Walsh Rd., Cobleskill, NY 12043 / 518-234-2731; FAX: 518-234-2454 rickard@telenet.net www.peterickard.com

Peter Dyson & Son Ltd., 3 Cuckoo Lane, Honley, Holmfirth, West Yorkshire, HD9 6AS ENGLAND / 44-1484-661062; FAX: 44-1484-663709 peter@peterdyson.co.uk www. peterdyson.co.uk

Peter Hale/Engraver, 997 Maple Dr., Spanish Fork, UT 84660-2524 / 801-798-8215

Peters Stahl GmbH, Stettiner Strasse 42, D-33106, Paderborn, GERMANY / 05251-750025; FAX: 05251-75611 info@peters-stahl.com www.peters-stahl.com

Peterson Gun Shop, Inc., A.W., 4255 W. Old U.S. 441, Mt. Dora, FL 32757-3299 / 352-383-4258; FAX: 352-735-1001

Petro-Explo Inc., 7650 U.S. Hwy. 287, Suite 100, Arlington, TX 76017 / 817-478-8888

Pettinger Books, Gerald, 47827 300th Ave., Russell, IA 50238 / 641-535-2239 gpettinger@lisco.com

Pflumm Mfg. Co., 10662 Widmer Rd., Lenexa, KS 66215 / 800-888-4867; FAX: 913-451-7857

PFRB Co., P.O. Box 1242, Bloomington, IL 61702 / 800-914-5464; FAX: 888-554-8369

Phillippi Custom Bullets, Justin, P.O. Box 773, Ligonier, PA 15658 / 724-238-2962; FAX: 724-238-9671 jrp@wpa.net http://www.wpa.net~jrphil

Phoenix Arms, 4231 Brickell St., Ontario, CA 91761 / 909-937-6900; FAX: 909-937-0060

Piedmont Community College, P.O. Box 1197, Roxboro, NC 27573 / 336-599-1181; FAX: 336-597-3817 www. piedmont.cc.nc.us

Pietta (See U.S. Importers-Navy Arms Co, Taylor's

Pine Technical College, 1100 4th St., Pine City, MN 55063 / 800-521-7463; FAX: 612-629-6766

Pinetree Bullets, 133 Skeena St., Kitimat, BC V8C 1Z1 CANADA / 604-632-3768; FAX: 604-632-3768

Pioneer Arms Co., 355 Lawrence Rd., Broomall, PA 19008 / 215-356-5203

Piotti (See U.S. Importer-Moore & Co., Wm. Larkin)

Piquette, Paul. See: PIQUETTE'S CUSTOM ENGRAVING

Piquette's Custom Engraving, Paul R. Piquette, 511 Southwick St., Feeding Hills, MA 01030 / 413-789-4582 ppiquette@comcast.net www.pistoldynamics.com

Plaza Cutlery, Inc., 3333 Bristol, 161 South Coast Plaza, Costa Mesa, CA 92626 / 714-549-3932

Plum City Ballistic Range, N2162 80th St., Plum City, WI 54761 / 715-647-2539

PlumFire Press, Inc., 30-A Grove Ave., Patchogue, NY 11772-4112 / 800-695-7246; FAX: 516-758-4071

PMC/Eldorado Cartridge Corp., P.O. Box 62508, 12801 U.S. Hwy. 95 S., Boulder City, NV 89005 / 702-294-0025; FAX: 702-294-0121 kbauer@pmcammo.com www.pmcammo.com

Poburka, Philip (See Bison Studios)

Pointing Dog Journal, Village Press Publications, P.O. Box 968, Dept. PGD, Traverse City, MI 49685 / 800-272-3246; FAX: 616-946-3289

Police Bookshelf, P.O. Box 122, Concord, NH 03301 / 603-224-6814; FAX: 603-226-3554 ayoob@attglobal.net www.ayoob.com

Polywad, Inc., P.O. Box 7916, Macon, GA 31209 / 478-477-0669 or 800-998-0669 FAX: 478-477-0666 polywadmpb@aol.com www.polywad.com

Ponsness, Warren, 7634 W. Ohio St., Rathdrum, ID 83858 / 800-732-0706; FAX: 208-687-2233 www.reloaders.com

Pony Express Reloaders, 608 E. Co. Rd. D, Suite 3, St. Paul, MN 55117 / 612-483-9406; FAX: 612-483-9884

Pony Express Sport Shop, 23404 Lyons Ave., PMB 448, Newhall, CA 91321-2511 / 818-895-1231

Powder Horn Ltd., P.O. Box 565, Glenview, IL 60025 / 305-565-6060

Powell & Son (Gunmakers) Ltd., William, 35-37 Carrs Lane, Birmingham, B4 7SX ENGLAND / 121-643-0689; FAX: 121-631-3504 sales@william-powell.co.uk www.william-powell.co.uk

Powell Agency, William, 22 Circle Dr., Bellmore, NY 11710 / 516-679-1158

Power Custom, Inc., 29739 Hwy. J, Gravois Mills, MO 65037 / 573-372-5684; FAX: 573-372-5799 rwpowers@ laurie.net www.powercustom.com

Power Plus Enterprises, Inc., P.O. Box 38, Warm Springs, GA 31830 / 706-655-2132

Powley Computer (See Hutton Rifle Ranch)

Practical Tools, Inc., 7067 Easton Rd., P.O. Box 133, Pipersville, PA 18947 / 215-766-7301; FAX: 215-766-8681

Prairie Gun Works, 1-761 Marion St., Winnipeg, MB R2J 0K6 CANADA / 204-231-2976; FAX: 204-231-8566

Pranger, Ed G., 1414 7th St., Anacortes, WA 98221 / 206-293-3488

Precision Airgun Sales, Inc., 5247 Warrensville Ctr. Rd., Maple Hts., OH 44137 / 216-587-5005; FAX: 216-587-5005

Precision Cast Bullets, 101 Mud Creek Lane, Ronan, MT 59864 / 406-676-5135

Precision Delta Corp., P.O. Box 128, Ruleville, MS 38771 / 662-756-2810; FAX: 662-756-2590

Precision Firearm Finishing, 25 N.W. 44th Avenue, Des Moines, IA 50313 / 515-288-8680; FAX: 515-244-3925

Precision Gun Works, 104 Sierra Rd., Dept. GD, Kerrville, TX 78028 / 830-367-4587

Precision Reloading, 124 S. Main St., Mitchell, SD 57301 / 605-996-9984

Precision Reloading, Inc., 124 S. Main St., Mitchell, SD 57301 / 800-223-0900; FAX: 605-996-9987 info@ precisionreloading.com www.precisionreloading.com

Precision Shooting, Inc., 222 McKee St., Manchester, CT 06040 / 860-645-8776; FAX: 860-643-8215 www.precisionshooting.com

Precision Small Arms Inc., 9272 Jeronimo Rd., Ste. 121, Irvine, CA 92618 / 800-554-5515 or 949-768-3530; FAX: 949-768-4808 www.tcbebe.com

Precision Specialties, 131 Hendom Dr., Feeding Hills, MA 01030 / 413-786-3365; FAX: 413-786-3365

Precision Sport Optics, 15571 Producer Lane, Unit G, Huntington Beach, CA 92649 / 714-891-1309; FAX: 714-892-6920

Preslik's Gunstocks, 4245 Keith Ln., Chico, CA 95926 / 916-891-8236

Price Bullets, Patrick W., 16520 Worthley Dr., San Lorenzo, CA 94580 / 510-278-1547

Primedia Publishing Co., 6420 Wilshire Blvd., Los Angeles, CA 90048 / 213-782-2000; FAX: 213-782-2867

Primos Hunting Calls, 604 First St., Flora, MS 39071 / 601-879-9323; FAX: 601-879-9324 www.primos.com

PRL Bullets, c/o Blackburn Enterprises, 114 Stuart Rd., Ste. 110, Cleveland, TN 37312 / 423-559-0340

Professional Gunsmiths of America, 1209 South 13 Hwy., Lexington, MO 64067 / 816-529-1337

Professional Hunter Supplies, P.O. Box 608, 468 Main St., Ferndale, WA 95536 / 707-786-9140; FAX: 707-786-9117 wmebride@humboldt.com

ProLixr;lubricants, P.O. Box 1466, West Jordan, UT 84084-1466 / 801-569-2763; FAX: 801-569-8225 prolix@ prolixlubricant.com www.prolixlubricant.com

Pro-Mark Div. of Wells Lamont, 6640 W. Touhy, Chicago, IL 60648 / 312-647-8200

Proofmark Corp., P.O. Box 357, Burgess, VA 22432 / 804-453-4337; FAX: 804-453-4337 proofmark@direcway.com www.proofmarkbullets.com

Pro-Port Ltd., 41302 Executive Dr., Harrison Twp., MI 48045-1306 / 586-469-6727; FAX: 586-469-0425 e-mail@magnaport.com www.magnaport.com

Pro-Shot Products, Inc., P.O. Box 763, Taylorville, IL 62568 / 217-824-9133; FAX: 217-824-8861 www.proshotproducts.com

Protector Mfg. Co., Inc., The, 443 Ashwood Pl., Boca Raton, FL 33431 / 407-394-6011

Protektor Model, 1-11 Bridge St., Galeton, PA 16922 / 814-435-2442 mail@protektormodel.com www.protektormodel.com

Prototech Industries, Inc., 10532 E Road, Delia, KS 66418 / 785-771-3571 prototec@grapevine.net

MANUFACTURER'S DIRECTORY

PWL Gunleather, P.O. Box 450432, Atlanta, GA 31145 / 800-960-4072; FAX: 770-822-1704 covert@pwlusa.com www.pwlusa.com

PWM Sales Ltd., N.D.F.S., Gowdall Lane, Pollington DN14 0AU, ENGLAND / 01405862688; FAX: 01405862622 Paulwelburn9@aol.com

Pyramyd Stone Inter. Corp., 2447 Suffolk Lane, Pepper Pike, OH 44124-4540

Q

Quack Decoy & Sporting Clays, 4 Ann & Hope Way, P.O. Box 98, Cumberland, RI 02864 / 401-723-8202; FAX: 401-722-5910

Quaker Boy, Inc., 5455 Webster Rd., Orchard Parks, NY 14127 / 716-662-3979; FAX: 716-662-9426

Quality Arms, Inc., Box 19477, Dept. GD, Houston, TX 77224 / 281-870-8377 arrieta2@excite.com www.arrieta.com

Quality Cartridge, P.O. Box 445, Hollywood, MD 20636 / 301-373-3719 www.qual-cart.com

Quality Custom Firearms, Stephen Billeb, 22 Vista View Dr., Cody, WY 82414 / 307-587-4278; FAX: 307-587-4297 stevebilleb@wyoming.com

Quarton Beamshot, 4538 Centerview Dr., Ste. 149, San Antonio, TX 78228 / 800-520-8435; FAX: 210-735-1326 www.beamshot.com

Que Industries, Inc., P.O. Box 2471, Everett, WA 98203 / 425-303-9088; FAX: 206-514-3266 queinfo@queindustries.com

Queen Cutlery Co., P.O. Box 500, Franklinville, NY 14737 / 800-222-5233; FAX: 800-299-2618

R

R&C Knives & Such, 2136 Candy Cane Walk, Manteca, CA 95336-9501 / 209-239-3722; FAX: 209-825-6947

R&D Gun Repair, Kenny Howell, RR1 Box 283, Beloit, WI 53511

R&J Gun Shop, 337 S. Humbolt St., Canyon City, OR 97820 / 541-575-2130 rjgunshop@highdesertnet.com

R&S Industries Corp., 8255 Brentwood Industrial Dr., St. Louis, MO 63144 / 314-781-5169 ron@miraclepolishingcloth.com www.miraclepolishingcloth.com

R. Murphy Co., Inc., 13 Groton-Harvard Rd., P.O. Box 376, Ayer, MA 01432 / 617-772-3481 www.r.murphyknives.com

R.A. Wells Custom Gunsmith, 3452 1st Ave., Racine, WI 53402 / 414-639-5223

R.E. Seebeck Assoc., P.O. Box 59752, Dallas, TX 75229

R.E.I., P.O. Box 88, Tallevast, FL 34270 / 813-755-0085

R.E.T. Enterprises, 2608 S. Chestnut, Broken Arrow, OK 74012 / 918-251-GUNS; (4867) FAX: 918-251-0587

R.T. Eastman Products, P.O. Box 1531, Jackson, WY 83001 / 307-733-3217; or 800-624-4311

Rabeno, Martin, 530 The Eagle Pass, Durango, CO 81301 / 970-382-0353 fancygun@aol.com

Radack Photography, Lauren, 21140 Jib Court L-12, Aventura, FL 33180 / 305-931-3110

Radiator Specialty Co., 1900 Wilkinson Blvd., P.O. Box 34689, Charlotte, NC 28234 / 800-438-6947; FAX: 800-421-9525 tkrossell@gunk.com www.gunk.com

Radical Concepts, P.O. Box 1473, Lake Grove, OR 97035 / 503-538-7437

Rainier Ballistics, 4500 15th St. East, Tacoma, WA 98424 / 800-638-8722; FAX: 253-922-7854 sales@rainierballistics.com www.rainierballistics.com

Ram-Line ATK, P.O. Box 39, Onalaska, WI 54650

Rampart International, 2781 W. MacArthur Blvd., B-283, Santa Ana, CA 92704 / 800-976-7240 or 714-557-6405

Ranch Products, P.O. Box 145, Malinta, OH 43535 / 313-277-3118; FAX: 313-565-8536 stevenacrawford@msn.com ranchproducts.com

Randall-Made Knives, P.O. Box 1988, Orlando, FL 32802 / 407-855-8075

Randco UK, 286 Gipsy Rd., Welling, DA16 1JJ ENGLAND / 44 81 303 4118

Randolph Engineering, Inc., Ranger Shooting Glasses, 26 Thomas Patten Dr., Randolph, MA 02368 / 800-541-1405; FAX: 781-986-0337 sales@randolphusa.com www.randolphusa.com

Range Brass Products Company, P.O. Box 218, Rockport, TX 78381

Ransom International Corp., P.O. Box 3845, Prescott, AZ 86302 / 928-778-7899; FAX: 928-778-7993 ransom@cableone.net www.ransomrest.com

Rapine Bullet Mould Mfg. Co., 9503 Landis Lane, East Greenville, PA 18041 / 215-679-5413; FAX: 215-679-9795

Ravell Ltd., 289 Diputacion St., 08009, Barcelona, SPAIN / 34(3) 4874486; FAX: 34(3) 4881394

Ray Riling Arms Books Co., 6844 Gorsten St., Philadelphia, PA 19119 / 215-438-2456; FAX: 215-438-5395 sales@rayrilingarmsbooks.com www.rayrilingarmsbooks.com

Ray's Gunsmith Shop, 3199 Elm Ave., Grand Junction, CO 81504 / 970-434-6162; FAX: 970-434-3452

Raytech Div. of Lyman Products Corp., 475 Smith Street, Middletown, CT 06457-1541 / 860-632-2020 or 800-225-9626; FAX: 860-632-1699 raysales@cshore.com www.raytech-ind.com

RCBS Operations/ATK, 605 Oro Dam Blvd., Oroville, CA 95965 / 800-533-5000; FAX: 530-533-1647 www.rcbs.com

Reardon Products, P.O. Box 126, Morrison, IL 61270 / 815-772-3155

Recoilless Technologies, Inc. (RTI), RTI/High-Low, 2141 E. Cedar #2, Tempe, AZ 85281 / 480-966-7051

Red Diamond Dist. Co., 1304 Snowdon Dr., Knoxville, TN 37912

Redding Reloading Equipment, 1089 Starr Rd., Cortland, NY 13045 / 607-753-3331; FAX: 607-756-8445 techline@redding-reloading.com www.redding-reloading.com

Redfield Media Resource Center, 4607 N.E. Cedar Creek Rd., Woodland, WA 98674 / 360-225-5000; FAX: 360-225-7616

Redman's Rifling & Reboring, 189 Nichols Rd., Omak, WA 98841 / 509-826-5512

Redwood Bullet Works, 3559 Bay Rd., Redwood City, CA 94063 / 415-367-6741

Reed, Dave, Rt. 1, Box 374, Minnesota City, MN 55959 / 507-689-2944

Reimer Johannsen, Inc., 438 Willow Brook Rd., Plainfield, NH 03781 / 603-469-3450; FAX: 603-469-3471

Reloaders Equipment Co., 4680 High St., Ecorse, MI 48229

Reloading Specialties, Inc., Box 1130, Pine Island, MN 55463 / 507-356-8500; FAX: 507-356-8800

Remington Arms Co., Inc., 870 Remington Drive, P.O. Box 700, Madison, NC 27025-0700 / 800-243-9700; FAX: 336-548-8700 info@remington.com www.remington.com

Remington Double Shotguns, 7885 Cyd Dr., Denver, CO 80221 / 303-429-6947

Renegade, P.O. Box 31546, Phoenix, AZ 85046 / 602-482-6777; FAX: 602-482-1952

Renfrew Guns & Supplies, R.R. 4, Renfrew, ON K7V 3Z7 CANADA / 613-432-7080

Reno, Wayne, 2808 Stagestop Road, Jefferson, CO 80456

Republic Arms, Inc. (See Cobra Enterprises, Inc.)

Retting, Inc., Martin B., 11029 Washington, Culver City, CA 90232 / 213-837-2412

RG-G, Inc., P.O. Box 935, Trinidad, CO 81082 / 719-845-1436

RH Machine & Consulting Inc., P.O. Box 394, Pacific, MO 63069 / 314-271-8465

Rhino, P.O. Box 787, Locust, NC 28097 / 704-753-2198

Rhodeside, Inc., 1704 Commerce Dr., Piqua, OH 45356 / 513-773-5781

Rice, Keith (See White Rock Tool & Die)

Richards MicroFit Stocks, Inc., P.O. Box 1066, Sun Valley, CA 91352 / 800-895-7420; FAX: 818-771-1242 sales@rifle-stocks.com www.rifle-stocks.com

Ridgeline, Inc., Bruce Sheldon, P.O. Box 930, Dewey, AZ 86327-0930 / 800-632-5900; FAX: 520-632-5900

Ridgetop Sporting Goods, P.O. Box 306, 42907 Hilligoss Ln. East, Eatonville, WA 98328 / 360-832-6422; FAX: 360-832-6422

Ries, Chuck, 415 Ridgecrest Dr., Grants Pass, OR 97527 / 503-476-5623

Rifles, Inc., 3580 Leal Rd., Pleasanton, TX 78064 / 830-569-2055; FAX: 830-569-2297

Riggs, Jim, 206 Azalea, Boerne, TX 78006 / 210-249-8567

Riley Ledbetter Airguns, 1804 E. Sprague St., Winston Salem, NC 27107-3521 / 919-784-0676

Rim Pac Sports, Inc., 1034 N. Soldano Ave., Azusa, CA 91702-2135

Ringler Custom Leather Co., 31 Shining Mtn. Rd., Powell, WY 82435 / 307-645-3255

Ripley Rifles, 42 Fletcher Street, Ripley, Derbyshire, DE5 3LP ENGLAND / 011-0773-748353

Rizzini F.lli (See U.S. Importers-Wm. Larkin Moore & Co., N.E. Arms Corp.)

Rizzini SNC, Via 2 Giugno, 7/7Bis-25060, Marcheno (Brescia), ITALY

RLCM Enterprises, 110 Hill Crest Drive, Burleson, TX 76028

RMS Custom Gunsmithing, 4120 N. Bitterwell, Prescott Valley, AZ 86314 / 520-772-7626 www.customstockmaker.com

Robar Co., Inc., The, 21438 N. 7th Ave., Suite B, Phoenix, AZ 85027 / 623-581-2648; FAX: 623-582-0059 info@robarguns.com www.robarguns.com

Robert Evans Engraving, 332 Vine St., Oregon City, OR 97045 / 503-656-5693

Robert Valade Engraving, 931 3rd Ave., Seaside, OR 97138 / 503-738-7672

Robinett, R. G., P.O. Box 72, Madrid, IA 50156 / 515-795-2906

Robinson, Don, Pennsylvania Hse, 36 Fairfax Crescent, W Yorkshire, ENGLAND / 01484-421-362 donrobinsonuk@yahoo.co.uk www.guns4u2.co.uk

Robinson Armament Co., P.O. Box 16776, Salt Lake City, UT 84116 / 801-355-0401; FAX: 801-355-0402 zdf@robarm.com www.robarm.com

Robinson Firearms Mfg. Ltd., 1699 Blondeaux Crescent, Kelowna, BC V1Y 4J8 CANADA / 604-868-9596

Robinson H.V. Bullets, 3145 Church St., Zachary, LA 70791 / 504-654-4029

Rochester Lead Works, 76 Anderson Ave., Rochester, NY 14607 / 716-442-8500; FAX: 716-442-4712

Rock River Arms, 101 Noble St., Cleveland, IL 61241

Rockwood Corp., Speedwell Division, 136 Lincoln Blvd., Middlesex, NJ 08846 / 800-243-8274; FAX: 980-560-7475

Rocky Mountain Armoury, Mr. Felix LesMerises, 610 Main Street, P.O. Box 691, Frisco, CO 80443-0691 / 970-668-0136; FAX: 970-668-4484 felix@rockymountainarmoury.com

Rocky Mountain Target Co., 3 Aloe Way, Leesburg, FL 34788 / 352-365-9598

Rocky Shoes & Boots, 294 Harper St., Nelsonville, OH 45764 / 800-848-9452 or 614-753-1951; FAX: 614-753-4024

Rogue Rifle Co., Inc./Chipmunk Rifles, 1140 36th St. N., Ste. B, Lewiston, ID 83501 / 208-743-4355; FAX: 208-743-4163 customerservice@roguerifle.com www.roguerifle.com

Rogue River Rifleworks, 500 Linne Road #D, Paso Robles, CA 93446 / 805-227-4706; FAX: 805-227-4723 rrrifles@calinet.com

Rohner, Hans, 1148 Twin Sisters Ranch Rd., Nederland, CO 80466-9600

Rohner, John, 186 Virginia Ave., Asheville, NC 28806 / 828-281-3704

Rohrbaugh, P.O. Box 785, Bayport, NY 11705 / 631-363-2843; FAX: 631-363-2681 API380@aol.com

Romain's Custom Guns, Inc., RD 1, Whetstone Rd., Brockport, PA 15823 / 814-265-1948 romwhetstone@penn.com

Ron Frank Custom, 7131 Richland Rd., Ft. Worth, TX 76118 / 817-284-9300; FAX: 817-284-9300 rfrank3974@aol.com

Rooster Laboratories, P.O. Box 414605, Kansas City, MO 64141 / 816-474-1622; FAX: 816-474-7622

Rorschach Precision Products, 417 Keats Cir., Irving, TX 75061 / 214-790-3487

Rosenberg & Son, Jack A., 12229 Cox Ln., Dallas, TX 75234 / 214-241-6302

Ross, Don, 12813 West 83 Terrace, Lenexa, KS 66215 / 913-492-6982

Rosser, Bob, 2809 Crescent Ave., Suite 20, Homewood, AL 35209 / 205-870-4422; FAX: 205-870-4421 www.hand-engravers.com

Rossi Firearms, Gary Mchalik, 16175 NW 49th Ave., Miami, FL 33014-6314 / 305-474-0401; FAX: 305-623-7506

Rottweil Compe, 1330 Glassell, Orange, CA 92667

Royal Arms Gunstocks, 919 8th Ave. NW, Great Falls, MT 59404 / 406-453-1149; FAX: 406-453-1149 royalarms@bresnar.net www.lmt.net/~royalarms

Royal Arms International, R J Brill, P.O. Box 6083, Woodland Hills, CA 91365 / 818-704-5110; FAX: 818-887-2059 royalarms.com

Roy's Custom Grips, 793 Mt. Olivet Church Rd., Lynchburg, VA 24504 / 434-993-3470

RPM, 15481 N. Twin Lakes Dr., Tucson, AZ 85739 / 520-825-1233; FAX: 520-825-3333

Rubright Bullets, 1008 S. Quince Rd., Walnutport, PA 18088 / 215-767-1339

Rucker Dist. Inc., P.O. Box 479, Terrell, TX 75160 / 214-563-2094

Ruger (See Sturm Ruger & Co., Inc.)

Ruger, Chris. See: RUGER'S CUSTOM GUNS

Ruger's Custom Guns, Chris Ruger, 1050 Morton Blvd., Kingston, NY 12401 / 845-336-7106; FAX: 845-336-7106 rugerscustom@outdrs.net rugergunsmith.com

Rundell's Gun Shop, 6198 Frances Rd., Clio, MI 48420 / 313-687-0559

Rupert's Gun Shop, 2202 Dick Rd., Suite B, Fenwick, MI 48834 / 517-248-3252 17rupert@pathwaynet.com

Russ Haydon's Shooters' Supply, 15018 Goodrich Dr. NW, Gig Harbor, WA 98329 / 877-663-6249; FAX: 253-857-7884 info@shooters-supply.com www.shooters-supply.com

Russ, William. See: BILL RUSS TRADING POST

Rusteprufe Laboratories, 1319 Jefferson Ave., Sparta, WI 54656 / 608-269-4144; FAX: 608-366-1972 rusteprufe@centurytel.net www.rusteprufe.com

Rutgers Book Center, 127 Raritan Ave., Highland Park, NJ 08904 / 732-545-4344; FAX: 732-545-6686 gunbooks@rutgersgunbooks.com www.rutgersgunbooks.com

Rutten (See U.S. Importer-Labanu Inc.)

RWS (See U.S. Importer-Dynamit Nobel-RWS, Inc.), 6007 S. 29th St., Fort Smith, AR 72908

S

S&K Scope Mounts, RD 2 Box 21C, Sugar Grove, PA 16350 / 814-489-3091 or 800-578-9862; FAX: 814-489-5466 comments@scopemounts.com www.scopemounts.com

S&S Firearms, 74-11 Myrtle Ave., Glendale, NY 11385 / 718-497-1100; FAX: 718-497-1105 info@ssfirearms.com ssfirearms.com

S.A.R.L. G. Granger, 66 Cours Fauriel, 42100, Saint Etienne, FRANCE / 04 77 25 14 73; FAX: 04 77 38 66 99

S.D. Meacham, 1070 Angel Ridge, Peck, ID 83545

S.I.A.C.E. (See U.S. Importer-IAR Inc.)

Sabatti SPA, Via A Volta 90, 25063 Gandome V.T.(BS), Brescia, ITALY / 030-8912207-831312; FAX: 030-8912059 info@sabatti.it www.sabatti.com

SAECO (See Redding Reloading Equipment)

Safari Arms/Schuetzen Pistol Works, 620-626 Old Pacific Hwy. SE, Olympia, WA 98513 / 360-459-3471; FAX: 360-491-3447 info@olyarms.com www.olyarms.com

Safari Press, Inc., 15621 Chemical Lane B, Huntington Beach, CA 92649 / 714-894-9080; FAX: 714-894-4949 info@safaripress.com www.safaripress.com

Safariland Ltd., Inc., 3120 E. Mission Blvd., P.O. Box 51478, Ontario, CA 91761 / 909-923-7300; FAX: 909-923-7400

SAFE, P.O. Box 864, Post Falls, ID 83877 / 208-773-3624; FAX: 208-773-6819 staysafe@safe-llc.com www.safe-llc.com

Sako Ltd. (See U.S. Importer-Stoeger Industries)

Sam Welch Gun Engraving, Sam Welch, HC 64 Box 2110, Moab, UT 84532 / 435-259-8131

Samco Global Arms, Inc., 6995 NW 43rd St., Miami, FL 33166 / 305-593-9782; FAX: 305-593-1014 samco@samcoglobal.com www.samcoglobal.com

Sampson, Roger, 2316 Mahogany St., Mora, MN 55051 / 320-679-4868

San Marco (See U.S. Importers-Cape Outfitters-EMF Co., Inc.

Sandia Die & Cartridge Co., 37 Atancacio Rd. NE, Albuquerque, NM 87123 / 505-298-5729

Sarco, Inc., 323 Union St., Stirling, NJ 07980 / 908-647-3800; FAX: 908-647-9413

Sarsilmaz Shotguns-Turkey (see B.C. Outdoors)

Sauer (See U.S. Importers-Paul Co., The Sigarms Inc.)

Sauls, R. See: BRYAN & ASSOC.

Saunders Gun & Machine Shop, 145 Delhi Rd., Manchester, IA 52057 / 563-927-4026

Savage Arms (Canada), Inc., 248 Water St., P.O. Box 1240, Lakefield, ON K0L 2H0 CANADA / 705-652-8000; FAX: 705-652-8431 www.savagearms.com

Savage Arms, Inc., 100 Springdale Rd., Westfield, MA 01085 / 413-568-7001; FAX: 413-562-7764

Savage Range Systems, Inc., 100 Springdale Rd., Westfield, MA 01085 / 413-568-7001; FAX: 413-562-1152 snailtraps@savagearms.com www.snailtraps.com

Saville Iron Co. (See Greenwood Precision)

Scansport, Inc., P.O. Box 700, Enfield, NH 03748 / 603-632-7654

Sceery Game Calls, P.O. Box 6520, Sante Fe, NM 87502 / 505-471-9110; FAX: 505-471-3476

Schaefer Shooting Sports, P.O. Box 1515, Melville, NY 11747-0515 / 516-643-5466; FAX: 516-643-2426 robert@robertschaefer.com www.schaefershooting.com

Scharch Mfg., Inc.-Top Brass, 10325 Co. Rd. 120, Salida, CO 81201 / 800-836-4683; FAX: 719-539-3021 topbrass@scharch.com www.handgun-brass.com

Scherer, Liz. See: SCHERER SUPPLIES, INC.

Scherer Supplies, Inc., Liz Scherer, Box 250, Ewing, VA 24248 FAX: 423-733-2073

Schiffman, Mike, 8233 S. Crystal Springs, McCammon, ID 83250 / 208-254-9114

Schmidt & Bender, Inc., P.O. Box 134, Meriden, NH 03770 / 603-469-3565; FAX: 603-469-3471 info@schmidtbender.com www.schmidtbender.com

Schneider Bullets, 3655 West 214th St., Fairview Park, OH 44126

Schneider Rifle Barrels, Inc., 1403 W. Red Baron Rd., Payson, AZ 85541 / 602-948-2525

School of Gunsmithing, The, 6065 Roswell Rd., Atlanta, GA 30328 / 800-223-4542

Schroeder Bullets, 1421 Thermal Ave., San Diego, CA 92154 / 619-423-3523; FAX: 619-423-8124

Schulz Industries, 16247 Minnesota Ave., Paramount, CA 90723 / 213-439-5903

Schumakers Gun Shop, 512 Prouty Corner Lp. A, Colville, WA 99114 / 509-684-4848

Scope Control, Inc., 5775 Co. Rd. 23 SE, Alexandria, MN 56308 / 612-762-7295

Score High Gunsmithing, 9812-A, Cochiti SE, Albuquerque, NM 87123 / 800-326-5632 or 505-292-5532; FAX: 505-292-2592 scorehi@scorehi.com www.probed2000.com

Scott Fine Guns Inc., Thad, P.O. Box 412, Indianola, MS 38751 / 601-887-5929

Searcy Enterprises, P.O. Box 584, Boron, CA 93596 / 760-762-6771; FAX: 760-762-0191

Second Chance Body Armor, P.O. Box 578, Central Lake, MI 49622 / 616-544-5721; FAX: 616-544-9824

Seebeck Assoc., R.E., P.O. Box 59752, Dallas, TX 75229

Segway Industries, P.O. Box 783, Suffern, NY 10901-0783 / 914-357-5510

Seligman Shooting Products, Box 133, Seligman, AZ 86337 / 602-422-3607 shootssp@yahoo.com

Sellier & Bellot, USA, Inc., P.O. Box 27006, Shawnee Mission, KS 66225 / 913-685-0916; FAX: 913-685-0917

Selsi Co., Inc., P.O. Box 10, Midland Park, NJ 07432-0010 / 201-935-0388; FAX: 201-935-5851

Semmer, Charles (See Remington Double Shotguns), 7885 Cyd Dr., Denver, CO 80221 / 303-429-6947

Servus Footwear Co., 1136 2nd St., Rock Island, IL 61204 / 309-786-7741; FAX: 309-786-9808

SGS Importer's International, Inc., 1750 Brielle Ave., Unit B1, Wanamassa, NJ 07712 / 732-493-0302; FAX: 732-493-0301 sgodini@aol.com www.firestorm-sgs.com

Shappy Bullets, 76 Milldale Ave., Plantsville, CT 06479 / 203-621-3704

Sharp Shooter Supply, 4970 Lehman Road, Delphos, OH 45833 / 419-695-3179

Sharps Arms Co., Inc., C., 100 Centennial, Box 885, Big Timber, MT 59011 / 406-932-4353

Shaw, Inc., E. R. (See Small Arms Mfg. Co.)

Shay's Gunsmithing, 931 Marvin Ave., Lebanon, PA 17042

Sheffield Knifemakers Supply, Inc., P.O. Box 741107, Orange City, FL 32774-1107 / 386-775-6453; FAX: 386-774-5754

Sheldon, Bruce. See: RIDGELINE, INC.

Shepherd Enterprises, Inc., Box 189, Waterloo, NE 68069 / 402-779-2424; FAX: 402-779-4010 sshepherd@shepherdscopes.com www.shepherdscopes.com

Sherwood, George, 46 N. River Dr., Roseburg, OR 97470 / 541-672-3159

Shilen, Inc., 205 Metro Park Blvd., Ennis, TX 75119 / 972-875-5318; FAX: 972-875-5402

Shiloh Rifle Mfg., P.O. Box 279, Big Timber, MT 59011

Shoot Where You Look, Leon Measures, Dept GD, 408 Fair, Livingston, TX 77351

Shooters Arms Manufacturing, Inc., Rivergate Mall, Gen. Maxilom Ave., Cebu City 6000, PHILIPPINES / 6332-254-8478 www.shootersarms.com.ph

Shooter's Choice Gun Care, 15050 Berkshire Ind. Pkwy., Middlefield, OH 44062 / 440-834-8888; FAX: 440-834-3388 www.shooterschoice.com

Shooter's Edge Inc., 3313 Creekstone Dr., Fort Collins, CO 80525

Shooters Supply, 1120 Tieton Dr., Yakima, WA 98902 / 509-452-1181

Shooter's World, 3828 N. 28th Ave., Phoenix, AZ 85017 / 602-266-0170

Shooters, Inc., 5139 Stanart St., Norfolk, VA 23502 / 757-461-9152; FAX: 757-461-9155 gflocker@aol.com

Shootin' Shack, 357 Cypress Drive, No. 10, Tequesta, FL 33469 / 561-746-2731; FAX: 561-545-4861

Shoot-N-C Targets (See Birchwood Casey)

Shotgun Sports, P.O. Box 6810, Auburn, CA 95604 / 530-889-2220; FAX: 530-889-9106 custsrv@shotgunsportsmagazine.com shotgunsportsmagazine.com

Shotgun Sports Magazine, dba Shootin' Accessories Ltd., P.O. Box 6810, Auburn, CA 95604 / 916-889-2220 custsrv@shotgunsportsmagazine.com shotgunspotsmagazine.com

Shotguns Unlimited, 2307 Fon Du Lac Rd., Richmond, VA 23229 / 804-752-7115

Siegrist Gun Shop, 8752 Turtle Road, Whittemore, MI 48770 / 989-873-3929

Sierra Bullets, 1400 W. Henry St., Sedalia, MO 65301 / 816-827-6300; FAX: 816-827-6300 www.sierrabullets.com

Sierra Specialty Prod. Co., 1344 Oakhurst Ave., Los Altos, CA 94024 FAX: 415-965-1536

SIG, CH-8212 Neuhausen, SWITZERLAND

Sigarms Inc., 18 Industrial Dr., Exeter, NH 03833 / 603-772-2302; FAX: 603-772-9082 customerservice@sigarms.com www.sigarms.com

SIG-Sauer (See U.S. Importer-Sigarms, Inc.)

Silencio/Safety Direct, 3975 Vantech Dr 2, Memphis, TN 38115 / 800-648-1812 or 702-354-4451; FAX: 702-359-1074

Silent Hunter, 1100 Newton Ave., W. Collingswood, NJ 08107 / 609-854-3276

Silhouette Leathers, 8598 Hwy. 51 N. #4, Millington, TN 38053 silhouetteleathers@yahoo.com silhouetteleathers.com

Silver Eagle Machining, 18007 N. 69th Ave., Glendale, AZ 85308

Silver Ridge Gun Shop (See Goodwin Guns)

Simmons, Jerry, 715 Middlebury St., Goshen, IN 46528-2717 / 574-533-8546

Simmons Gun Repair, Inc., 700 S. Rogers Rd., Olathe, KS 66062 / 913-782-3131; FAX: 913-782-4189

Simmons Outdoor Corp., 6001 Oak Canyon, Irvine, CA 92618 / 949-451-1450; FAX: 949-451-1460 www.meade.com

Sinclair International, Inc., 2330 Wayne Haven St., Fort Wayne, IN 46803 / 260-493-1858 or 800-717-8211; FAX: 260-493-2530 sales@sinclairintl.com www.sinclairintl.com

Singletary, Kent, 4538 W. Carol Ave., Glendale, AZ 85302 / 602-526-6836 kent@kscustom.com www.kscustom.com

Siskiyou Gun Works (See Donnelly, C. P.)

Six Enterprises, 320-D Turtle Creek Ct., San Jose, CA 95125 / 408-999-0201; FAX: 408-999-0216

SKB Shotguns, 4325 S. 120th St., Omaha, NE 68137 / 800-752-2767; FAX: 402-330-8040 skb@skbshotguns.com www.skbshotguns.com

Skeoch, Brian R., P.O. Box 279, Glenrock, WY 82637 / 307-436-9655 skeochbrian@netzero.com

Skip's Machine, 364 29 Road, Grand Junction, CO 81501 / 303-245-5417

Sklany's Machine Shop, 566 Birch Grove Dr., Kalispell, MT 59901 / 406-755-4257

Slug Site, Ozark Wilds, 21300 Hwy. 5, Versailles, MO 65084 / 573-378-6430 john@ebeling.com john.ebeling.com

Small Arms Mfg. Co., 5312 Thoms Run Rd., Bridgeville, PA 15017 / 412-221-4343; FAX: 412-221-4303 www.ershawbarrels.com

Smires, C. L., 5222 Windmill Lane, Columbia, MD 21044-1328

Smith & Wesson, 2100 Roosevelt Ave., Springfield, MA 01104 / 413-781-8300; FAX: 413-731-8980 qa@smith-wesson.com www.smith-wesson.com

Smith, Art, P.O. Box 645, Park Rapids, MN 56470 / 218-732-5333

Smith, Mark A., P.O. Box 182, Sinclair, WY 82334 / 307-324-7929

Smith, Michael, 2612 Ashmore Ave., Red Bank, TN 37415 / 615-267-8341

Smith, Ron, 5869 Straley, Fort Worth, TX 76114 / 817-732-6768

Smith, Sharmon, 4545 Speas Rd., Fruitland, ID 83619 / 208-452-6329 sharmon@fmtc.com

Smith Abrasives, Inc., 1700 Sleepy Valley Rd., Hot Springs, AR 71902-5095 / 501-321-2244; FAX: 501-321-9232 www.smithabrasives.com

Smith, Judy. See: L.B.T.

Smith Saddlery, Jesse W., 0499 County Road J, Pritchett, CO 81064 / 509-325-0622

Smokey Valley Rifles, E1976 Smokey Valley Rd., Scandinavia, WI 54977 / 715-467-2674

Snapp's Gunshop, 6911 E. Washington Rd., Clare, MI 48617 / 989-386-9226 snapp@glccomputers.com

Sno-Seal, Inc. (See Atsko/Sno-Seal, Inc.)

Societa Armi Bresciane Srl (See U.S. Importer-Jeff's Outfitters)

SOS Products Co. (See Buck Stix-SOS Products Co.), Box 3, Neenah, WI 54956

Sotheby's, 1334 York Ave. at 72nd St., New York, NY 10021 / 212-606-7260

Sound Tech, Box 738, Logan, NM 88426 / 205-999-0416; or 505-487-2277 silenceio@wmconnect.com www.soundtechsilencers.com

South Bend Replicas, Inc., 61650 Oak Rd., South Bend, IN 46614 / 574-289-4500

Southeastern Community College, 1015 S. Gear Ave., West Burlington, IA 52655 / 319-752-2731

Southern Ammunition Co., Inc., 4232 Meadow St., Loris, SC 29569-3124 / 803-756-3262; FAX: 803-756-3583

Southern Armory, The, 25 Millstone Rd., Woodlawn, VA 24381 / 703-238-1343; FAX: 703-238-1453

Southern Bloomer Mfg. Co., P.O. Box 1621, Bristol, TN 37620 / 423-878-6660; FAX: 423-878-8761 southernbloomer@earthlink.net www.southernbloomer.com

Southern Security, 1700 Oak Hills Dr., Kingston, TN 37763 / 423-376-6297; FAX: 800-251-9992

Sparks, Milt, 605 E. 44th St. No. 2, Boise, ID 83714-4800

Spartan-Realtree Products, Inc., 1390 Box Circle, Columbus, GA 31907 / 706-569-9101; FAX: 706-569-0042

Specialty Gunsmithing, Lynn McMurdo, P.O. Box 404, Afton, WY 83110 / 307-886-5535

Specialty Shooters Supply, Inc., 3325 Griffin Rd., Suite 9mm, Fort Lauderdale, FL 33317

Speer Bullets, P.O. Box 856, Lewiston, ID 83501 / 208-746-2351 www.speer-bullets.com

Spegel, Craig, P.O. Box 387, Nehalem, OR 97131 / 503-368-5653

Speiser, Fred D., 2229 Dearborn, Missoula, MT 59801 / 406-549-8133

Spencer Reblue Service, 1820 Tupelo Trail, Holt, MI 48842 / 517-694-7474

Spencer's Rifle Barrels, Inc., 4107 Jacobs Creek Dr., Scottsville, VA 24590 / 804-293-6836; FAX: 804-293-6836 www.spencersriflebarrels.com

SPG, Inc., P.O. Box 1625, Cody, WY 82414 / 307-587-7621; FAX: 307-587-7695 spg@cody.wtp.net www.blackpowderspg.com

Sphinx Systems Ltd., Gesteigtstrasse 12, CH-3800, Matten, BRNE, SWITZERLAND

Splitfire Sporting Goods, L.L.C., P.O. Box 1044, Orem, UT 84059-1044 / 801-932-7950; FAX: 801-932-7959 www.splitfireguns.com

Spolar Power Load, Inc., 17376 Filbert, Fontana, CA 92335 / 800-227-9667

Sport Flite Manufacturing Co., 637 Kingsley Trl., Bloomfield Hills, MI 48304-2320 / 248-647-3747

Sporting Clays Of America, 9257 Buckeye Rd., Sugar Grove, OH 43155-9632 / 740-746-8334 FAX: 740-746-8605

Sports Afield Magazine, 15621 Chemical Lane B, Huntington Beach, CA 92649 / 714-894-9080; FAX: 714-894-4949 info@sportsafield.com www.sportsafield.com

Sportsman Safe Mfg. Co., 6309-6311 Paramount Blvd., Long Beach, CA 90805 / 800-266-7150; or 310-984-5445

Sportsman's Communicators, 588 Radcliffe Ave., Pacific Palisades, CA 90272 / 800-538-3752

Sportsmatch U.K. Ltd., 16 Summer St. Leighton,, Buzzard Beds, Bedfordshire, LU7 1HT ENGLAND / 4401525-381638; FAX: 4401525-851236 info@sportsmatch-uk.com www.sportsmatch-uk.com

Sportsmen's Exchange & Western Gun Traders, Inc., 813 Doris Ave., Oxnard, CA 93030 / 805-483-1917

Spradlin's, 457 Shannon Rd., Texas Creek Cotopaxi, CO 81223 / 719-275-7105; FAX: 719-275-3852 spradlins@prodigy.net www.spradlins.net

Springfield Armory, 420 W. Main St., Geneseo, IL 61254 / 309-944-5631; FAX: 309-944-3676 sales@springfield-armory.com www.springfieldarmory.com

Springfield Sporters, Inc., RD 1, Penn Run, PA 15765 / 412-254-2626; FAX: 412-254-9173

Springfield, Inc., 420 W. Main St., Geneseo, IL 61254 / 309-944-5631; FAX: 309-944-3676

Spyderco, Inc., 820 Spyderco Way, Golden, CO 80403 / 800-525-7770; FAX: 303-278-2229 sales@spyderco.com www.spyderco.com

SSK Industries, J. D. Jones, 590 Woodvue Lane, Wintersville, OH 43953 / 740-264-0176; FAX: 740-264-2257 www.sskindustries.com

Stackpole Books, 5067 Ritter Rd., Mechanicsburg, PA 17055-6921 / 717-796-0411 FAX: 717-796-0412 tmanney@stackpolebooks.com www.stackpolebooks.com

Stalker, Inc., P.O. Box 21, Fishermans Wharf Rd., Malakoff, TX 75148 / 903-489-1010

Stalwart Corporation, P.O. Box 46, Evanston, WY 82931 / 307-789-7687; FAX: 307-789-7688

Stan Baker Sports, Stan Baker, 10000 Lake City Way, Seattle, WA 98125 / 206-522-4575

Stan De Treville & Co., 4129 Normal St., San Diego, CA 92103 / 619-298-3393

Star Ammunition, Inc., 5520 Rock Hampton Ct., Indianapolis, IN 46268 / 800-221-5927; FAX: 317-872-5847

Star Custom Bullets, P.O. Box 608, 468 Main St., Ferndale, CA 95536 / 707-786-9140; FAX: 707-786-9117 wmebridge@humboldt.com

Star Machine Works, P.O. Box 1872, Pioneer, CA 95666 / 209-295-5000

Starke Bullet Company, P.O. Box 400, 605 6th St. NW, Cooperstown, ND 58425 / 888-797-3431

Starkey Labs, 6700 Washington Ave. S., Eden Prairie, MN 55344

Starkey's Gun Shop, 9430 McCombs, El Paso, TX 79924 / 915-751-3030

Starlight Training Center, Inc., Rt. 1, P.O. Box 88, Bronaugh, MO 64728 / 417-843-3555

Starline, Inc., 1300 W. Henry St., Sedalia, MO 65301 / 660-827-6640; FAX: 660-827-6650 info@starlinebrass.com http://www.starlinebrass.com

Starr Trading Co., Jedediah, P.O. Box 2007, Farmington Hills, MI 48333 / 877-857-8277; FAX: 248-683-3282 mtman1849@aol.com www.jedediah-starr.com

Starrett Co., L. S., 121 Crescent St., Athol, MA 01331 / 978-249-3551; FAX: 978-249-8495

State Line Gun Shop, 443 Firchburg Rd., Mason, NH 03048 / 603-878-2854; FAX: 603-878-3905 miniguns@empire.net www.statelinegunshop.com

Steelman's Gun Shop, 10465 Beers Rd., Swartz Creek, MI 48473 / 810-735-4884

Steffens, Ron, 18396 Mariposa Creek Rd., Willits, CA 95490 / 707-485-0873

Stegall, James B., 26 Forest Rd., Wallkill, NY 12589

Steve Henigson & Associates, P.O. Box 2726, Culver City, CA 90231 / 310-305-8288; FAX: 310-305-1905

Steve Kamyk Engraver, 9 Grandview Dr., Westfield, MA 01085-1810 / 413-568-0457 stevek201@comcast.net

Steven Dodd Hughes, P.O. Box 545, Livingston, MT 59047 / 406-222-9377; FAX: 406-222-9377

Steves House of Guns, Rt. 1, Minnesota City, MN 55959 / 507-689-2573

Stewart's Gunsmithing, P.O. Box 5854, Pietersburg North 0750, Transvaal, SOUTH AFRICA / 01521-89401

Steyr Arms, P.O. Box 2609, Cumming, GA 30028 / 770-888-4201 www.steyrarms.com

Steyr Mannlicher GmbH & Co. KG, Ramingtal 46, A-4442 Kleinraming, Steyr, AUSTRIA / 0043-7252-896-0; FAX: 0043-7252-78620 office@steyr-mannlicher.com www.steyr-mannlicher.com

STI International, 114 Halmar Cove, Georgetown, TX 78628 / 800-959-8201; FAX: 512-819-0465 www.stiguns.com

Stiles Custom Guns, 76 Cherry Run Rd., Box 1605, Homer City, PA 15748 / 712-479-9945 glstiles@yourinter.net www.yourinter.net/glstiles

Stoeger Industries, 17603 Indian Head Hwy., Suite 200, Accokeek, MD 20607-2501 / 301-283-6300; FAX: 301-283-6986 www.stoegerindustries.com

Stoeger Publishing Co. (See Stoeger Industries)

Stone Enterprises Ltd., 426 Harveys Neck Rd., P.O. Box 335, Wicomico Church, VA 22579 / 804-580-5114; FAX: 804-580-8421

Stone Mountain Arms, 5988 Peachtree Corners E., Norcross, GA 30071 / 800-251-9412

Stoney Point Products, Inc., 9200 Cody St., Overland Park, KS 66214 / 800-845-2444; FAX: 507-354-7236 stoney@newulmtel.net www.stoneypoint.com

Storm, Gary, P.O. Box 5211, Richardson, TX 75083 / 214-385-0862

Stott's Creek Armory, Inc., 2526 S. 475W, Morgantown, IN 46160 / 317-878-5489 stottscrk@aol.com www.Sccalendar.aol.com

Stratco, Inc., P.O. Box 2270, Kalispell, MT 59901 / 406-755-1221; FAX: 406-755-1226

Strayer, Sandy. See: STRAYER-VOIGT, INC.

Strayer-Voigt, Inc., Sandy Strayer, 3435 Ray Orr Blvd., Grand Prairie, TX 75050 / 972-513-0575

Strong Holster Co., 39 Grove St., Gloucester, MA 01930 / 508-281-3300; FAX: 508-281-6321

Strutz Rifle Barrels, Inc., W. C., P.O. Box 611, Eagle River, WI 54521 / 715-479-4766

Stuart, V. Pat, 279 Pilson, Greenville, VA 24440 / 540-377-6187

Sturgeon Valley Sporters, Ken Ide, P.O. Box 283, Vanderbilt, MI 49795 / 989-983-4338 k.ide@mail.com

Sturm Ruger & Co. Inc., 200 Ruger Rd., Prescott, AZ 86301 / 928-541-8820; FAX: 520-541-8850 www.ruger.com

"Su-Press-On," Inc., P.O. Box 09161, Detroit, MI 48209 / 313-842-4222

Sullivan, David S. (See Westwind Rifles, Inc.)

Sun Welding Safe Co., 290 Easy St. No. 3, Simi Valley, CA 93065 / 805-584-6678; or 800-729-SAFE; (7233) FAX: 805-584-6169 sun-welding@sbcglobal.net www.sunwelding.com

Sunny Hill Enterprises, Inc., W1790 Cty. HHH, Malone, WI 53049 / 920-418-3906; FAX: 920-795-4822 triggerguard@sunny-hill.com www.sunny-hill.com

Super 6 LLC, Gary Knopp, 3806 W. Lisbon Ave., Milwaukee, WI 53208 / 414-344-3343; FAX: 414-344-0304

Surecase Co., The, 233 Wilshire Blvd., Ste. 900, Santa Monica, CA 90401 / 800-92ARMLOC

Sure-Shot Game Calls, Inc., P.O. Box 816, 6835 Capitol, Groves, TX 77619 / 409-962-1636; FAX: 409-962-5465

Svon Corp., 2107 W. Blue Heron Blvd., Riviera Beach, FL 33404 / 508-881-8852

Swampfire Shop, The (See Peterson Gun Shop, Inc., A.W.)

Swann, D. J., 5 Orsova Close, Eltham North Vic., 3095 AUSTRALIA / 03-431-0323

Swanson, Mark, 975 Heap Avenue, Prescott, AZ 86301 / 928-778-4423

Swarovski Optik North America Ltd., 2 Slater Rd., Cranston, RI 02920 / 401-946-2220 or 800-426-3089; FAX: 401-946-2587

Sweet Home, Inc., P.O. Box 900, Orrville, OH 44667-0900

Swenson's 45 Shop, A. D., 3839 Ladera Vista Rd., Fallbrook, CA 92028-9431

Swift Bullet Co., P.O. Box 27, 201 Main St., Quinter, KS 67752 / 913-754-3959; FAX: 913-754-2359

Swift Instruments, 2055 Gateway Place, Ste. 500, San Jose, CA 95110 / 800-523-4544; FAX: 408-292-7967 www.swiftoptics.com

Swift River Gunworks, 450 State St., Belchertown, MA 01007 / 413-323-4052

Szweda, Robert (See RMS Custom Gunsmithing)

T

T&S Industries, Inc., 1027 Skyview Dr., W. Carrollton, OH 45449 / 513-859-8414; FAX: 937-859-8404 keith.tomlinson@tandsshellcatcher.com www.tandsshellcatcher.com

T.F.C. S.p.A., Via G. Marconi 118, B, Villa Carcina 25069, ITALY / 030-881271; FAX: 030-881826

T.G. Faust, Inc., 544 Minor St., Reading, PA 19602 / 610-375-8549; FAX: 610-375-4488

T.K. Lee Co., 1282 Branchwater Ln., Birmingham, AL 35216 / 205-913-5222 odonmich@aol.com www.scopedot.com

T.W. Mench Gunsmith, Inc., 5703 S. 77th St., Ralston, NE 68127 guntools@cox.net http://llwww.members.cox.net/guntools

Tabler Marketing, 2554 Lincoln Blvd., Suite 555, Marina Del Rey, CA 90291 / 818-386-0373; FAX: 818-386-0373

Taconic Firearms Ltd., Perry Lane, P.O. Box 553, Cambridge, NY 12816 / 518-677-2704; FAX: 518-677-5974

Tactical Defense Institute, 2174 Bethany Ridges, West Union, OH 45693 / 937-544-7228; FAX: 937-544-2887 tdiohio@dragonbbs.com www.tdiohio.com

Talley, Dave, P.O. Box 369, Santee, SC 29142 / 803-854-5700 or 307-436-9315; FAX: 803-854-9315 talley@diretway www.talleyrings.com

Talon Industries Inc. (See Cobra Enterprises, Inc.)

Tanfoglio Fratelli S.r.l., via Valtrompia 39, 41, Brescia, ITALY / 011-39-030-8910361; FAX: 011-39-030-8910183 info@tanfoglio.it www.tanfoglio.it

Tanglefree Industries, 1261 Heavenly Dr., Martinez, CA 94553 / 800-982-4868; FAX: 510-825-3874

Tank's Rifle Shop, P.O. Box 474, Fremont, NE 68026-0474 / 402-727-1317 jtank@tanksrifleshop.com www.tanksrifleshop.com

Tanner (See U.S. Importer-Mandall Shooting Supplies, Inc.)

Taracorp Industries, Inc., 1200 Sixteenth St., Granite City, IL 62040 / 618-451-4400

Target Shooting, Inc., P.O. Box 773, Watertown, SD 57201 / 605-882-6955; FAX: 605-882-8840

Tar-Hunt Custom Rifles, Inc., 101 Dogtown Rd., Bloomsburg, PA 17815 / 570-784-6368; FAX: 570-389-9150 www.tar-hunt.com

Tarnhelm Supply Co., Inc., 431 High St., Boscawen, NH 03303 / 603-796-2551; FAX: 603-796-2918 info@tarnhelm.com www.tarnhelm.com

Tasco Sales, Inc., 2889 Commerce Pkwy., Miramar, FL 33025

Taurus Firearms, Inc., 16175 NW 49th Ave., Miami, FL 33014 / 305-624-1115; FAX: 305-623-7506

Taurus International Firearms (See U.S. Importer Taurus Firearms, Inc.)

Taurus S.A. Forjas, Avenida Do Forte 511, Porto Alegre, RS BRAZIL 91360 / 55-51-347-4050; FAX: 55-51-347-3065

Taylor & Robbins, P.O. Box 164, Rixford, PA 16745 / 814-966-3233

Taylor's & Co., Inc., 304 Lenoir Dr., Winchester, VA 22603 / 540-722-2017; FAX: 540-722-2018 info@taylorsfirearms.com www.taylorsfirearms.com

TCCI, P.O. Box 302, Phoenix, AZ 85001 / 602-237-3823; FAX: 602-237-3858

TCSR, 3998 Hoffman Rd., White Bear Lake, MN 55110-4626 / 800-328-5323; FAX: 612-429-0526

Techno Arms (See U.S. Importer- Auto-Ordnance Corp.)

Tecnolegno S.p.A., Via A. Locatelli, 6 10, 24019 Zogno, ITALY / 0345-55111; FAX: 0345-55155

Ted Blocker Holsters, 9438 SW Tigard St., Tigard, OR 97223 / 800-650-9742; FAX: 503-670-9692 www.tedblockerholsters.com

Tele-Optics, 630 E. Rockland Rd., P.O. Box 6313, Libertyville, IL 60048 / 847-362-7757; FAX: 847-362-7757

Tennessee Valley Mfg., 14 County Road 521, Corinth, MS 38834 / 601-286-5014 tvm@avsia.com www.avsia.com/tvm

Ten-Ring Precision, Inc., Alex B. Hamilton, 1449 Blue Crest Lane, San Antonio, TX 78232 / 210-494-3063; FAX: 210-494-3066

TEN-X Products Group, 1905 N. Main St., Suite 133, Cleburne, TX 76031-1305 / 972-243-4016 or 800-433-2225; FAX: 972-243-4112

Tepeco, P.O. Box 342, Friendswood, TX 77546 / 713-482-2702

Terry K. Kopp Professional Gunsmithing, 1209 South 13 Hwy., Lexington, MO 64067 / 816-529-1337 tkkopp@earthlink.net

Terry Theis-Engraver, Terry Theis, 21452 FM 2093, Harper, TX 78631 / 830-864-4438

Testing Systems, Inc., 220 Pegasus Ave., Northvale, NJ 07647

Tetra Gun Care, 8 Vreeland Rd., Florham Park, NJ 07932 / 973-443-0004; FAX: 973-443-0263

Tex Shoemaker & Sons, Inc., 714 W. Cienega Ave., San Dimas, CA 91773 / 909-592-2071; FAX: 909-592-2378 texshoemaker@texshoemaker.com www.texshoemaker.com

Texas Armory (See Bond Arms, Inc.)

Texas Platers Supply Co., 2453 W. Five Mile Parkway, Dallas, TX 75233 / 214-330-7168

Thad Rybka Custom Leather Equipment, 2050 Canoe Creek Rd., Springvale, AL 35146-6709

Thad Scott Fine Guns, Inc., P.O. Box 412, Indianola, MS 38751 / 601-887-5929

The Midwest Shooting School, 2550 Hwy. 23, Wrenshall, MN 55797 / 218-384-3670 patrick@midwestshootingschool.com www.midwestshootingschool.com

Theis, Terry. See: TERRY THEIS-ENGRAVER

Thiewes, George W., 14329 W. Parada Dr., Sun City West, AZ 85375

Things Unlimited, 235 N. Kimbau, Casper, WY 82601 / 307-234-5277

Thirion Gun Engraving, Denise, P.O. Box 408, Graton, CA 95444 / 707-829-1876

Thomas, Charles C., 2600 S. First St., Springfield, IL 62704 / 217-789-8980; FAX: 217-789-9130 books@ccthomas.com ccthomas.com

Thompson Bullet Lube Co., 6341 FM 2965, Wills Point, TX 75169 / 866-476-1500; FAX: 866-476-1500 thompsonbulletlube.com www.thompsonbulletlube.com

Thompson Precision, 110 Mary St., P.O. Box 251, Warren, IL 61087 / 815-745-3625

Thompson Target Technology, 4804 Sherman Church Ave. S.W., Canton, OH 44710 / 330-484-6480; FAX: 330-491-1087 www.thompsontarget.com

Thompson Tool Mount, 1550 Solomon Rd., Santa Maria, CA 93455 / 805-934-1281 ttm@pronet.net www.thompsontoolmount.com

Thompson/Center Arms, P.O. Box 5002, Rochester, NH 03866 / 603-332-2394; FAX: 603-332-5133 tech@tcarms.com www.tcarms.com

Thunder Ranch, 96747 Hwy. 140 East, Lakeview, OR 97630 / 541-947-4104; FAX: 541-947-4105 troregon@centurytel.net www.thunderranchinc.com

Tiger-Hunt Longrifle Gunstocks, Box 379, Beaverdale, PA 15921 / 814-472-5161 tigerhunt4@aol.com www.gunstockwood.com

Tikka (See U.S. Importer-Stoeger Industries)

Time Precision, 4 Nicholas Sq., New Milford, CT 06776-3506 / 860-350-8343; FAX: 860-350-6343 timeprecision@aol.com www.benchrest.com/timeprecision

Tinks & Ben Lee Hunting Products (See Wellington Outdoors)

Tink's Safariland Hunting Corp., P.O. Box 244, 1140 Monticello Rd., Madison, GA 30650 / 706-342-4915; FAX: 706-342-7568

Tioga Engineering Co., Inc., P.O. Box 913, 13 Cone St., Wellsboro, PA 16901 / 570-724-3533; FAX: 570-724-3895 tiogaeng@epix.net

Tippman Sports, LLC, 2955 Adams Center Rd., Fort Wayne, IN 46803 / 260-749-6022; FAX: 260-441-8504 www.tippmann.com

Tirelli, Snc Di Tirelli Primo E.C., Via Matteotti No. 359, Gardone V.T. Brescia, ITALY / 0039-030-8912819; FAX: 0039-030-832240 tirelli@tirelli.it www.tirelli.it

TM Stockworks, 6355 Maplecrest Rd., Fort Wayne, IN 46835 / 219-485-5389

Tom Forrest, Inc., P.O. Box 326, Lakeside, CA 92040 / 619-561-5800; FAX: 888-GUN-CLIP info@gunmag.com www.gunmags.com

Tombstone Smoken' Deals, 4038 E. Taro Ln., Phoenix, AZ 85050

Tom's Gun Repair, Thomas G. Ivanoff, 76-6 Rt. Southfork Rd., Cody, WY 82414 / 307-587-6949

Tom's Gunshop, 3601 Central Ave., Hot Springs, AR 71913 / 501-624-3856

Tonoloway Tack Drives, HCR 81, Box 100, Needmore, PA 17238

Torel, Inc./Tandy Brands Outdoors/AA & E, 208 Industrial Loop, Yoakum, TX 77995 / 361-293-6366; FAX: 361-293-9127

TOZ (See U.S. Importer-Nygord Precision Products, Inc.)

Track of the Wolf, Inc., 18308 Joplin St. NW, Elk River, MN 55330-1773 / 763-633-2500; FAX: 763-633-2550 sales@trackofthewolf.com www.trackofthewolf.com

Traditions Performance Firearms, P.O. Box 776, 1375 Boston Post Rd., Old Saybrook, CT 06475 / 860-388-4656; FAX: 860-388-4657 info@traditionsfirearms.com www.traditionsfirearms.com

Trafalgar Square, P.O. Box 257, N. Pomfret, VT 05053 / 802-457-1911

Trail Visions, 5800 N. Ames Terrace, Glendale, WI 53209 / 414-228-1328

Treebone Carving, P.O. Box 551, Cimarron, NJ 87714 / 505-376-2145 treebonecarving.com

Treemaster, P.O. Box 247, Guntersville, AL 35976 / 205-878-3597

Trevallion Gunstocks, 9 Old Mountain Rd., Cape Neddick, ME 03902 / 207-361-1130

Trigger Lock Division / Central Specialties Ltd., 220-D Exchange Dr., Crystal Lake, IL 60014 / 847-639-3900; FAX: 847-639-3972

Trijicon, Inc., 49385 Shafer Ave., P.O. Box 930059, Wixom, MI 48393-0059 / 248-960-7700 or 800-338-0563

Trilby Sport Shop, 1623 Hagley Rd., Toledo, OH 43612-2024 / 419-472-6222

Trilux, Inc., P.O. Box 24608, Winston-Salem, NC 27114 / 910-659-9438; FAX: 910-768-7720

Trinidad St. Jr. Col. Gunsmith Dept., 600 Prospect St., Trinidad, CO 81082 / 719-846-5631; FAX: 719-846-5667

Tripes, George. See: EURO-IMPORTS

Triple-K Mfg. Co., Inc., 2222 Commercial St., San Diego, CA 92113 / 619-232-2066; FAX: 619-232-7675 sales@triplek.com www.triplek.com

Tristar Sporting Arms, Ltd., 1816 Linn St. #16, N. Kansas City, MO 64116-3627 / 816-421-1400; FAX: 816-421-4182 tristarsporting@sbcglobal.net www.tristarsportingarms

Trius Traps, Inc., P.O. Box 25, 221 S. Miami Ave., Cleves, OH 45002 / 513-941-5682; FAX: 513-941-7970 triustraps@fuse.net www.triustraps.com

Trooper Walsh, 2393 N. Edgewood St., Arlington, VA 22207

Trotman, Ken, P.O. Box 505, Huntingdon, PE 29 2XW ENGLAND / 01480 454292; FAX: 01480 384651 enquiries@kentrotman.com www.kentrotman.com

Tru-Balance Knife Co., P.O. Box 140555, Grand Rapids, MI 49514 / 616-647-1215

True Flight Bullet Co., 5581 Roosevelt St., Whitehall, PA 18052 / 610-262-7630; FAX: 610-262-7806

Truglo, Inc., P.O. Box 1612, McKinna, TX 75070 / 972-774-0300; FAX: 972-774-0323 www.truglosights.com

Trulock Tool, P.O. Box 530, Whigham, GA 31797 / 229-762-4678; FAX: 229-762-4050 trulockchokes@hotmail.com trulockchokes.com

Tru-Nord Compass, 1504 Erick Lane, Brainerd, MN 56401 / 218-829-2870; FAX: 218-829-2870 www.trunord.com

Tru-Square Metal Products, Inc., 640 First St. SW, P.O. Box 585, Auburn, WA 98071 / 253-833-2310 or 800-225-1017; FAX: 253-833-2349 t-tumbler@qwest.net

Tucker, James C., P.O. Box 366, Medford, OR 97501 / 541-664-9160 jctstocker@yahoo.com

Tucson Mold, Inc., 930 S. Plumer Ave., Tucson, AZ 85719 / 520-792-1075; FAX: 520-792-1075

MANUFACTURER'S DIRECTORY

Turk's Head Productions, Mustafa Bilal, 13545 Erickson Pl. NE, Seattle, WA 98125-3794 / 206-782-4164; FAX: 206-783-5677 info@turkshead.com www.turkshead.com

Turnbull Restoration, Doug, 6680 Rts. 5 & 20, P.O. Box 471, Bloomfield, NY 14469 / 585-657-6338; FAX: 585-657-7743 info@turnbullrestoration.com www.turnbullrestoration.com

Tuttle, Dale, 4046 Russell Rd., Muskegon, MI 49445 / 616-766-2250

U

U.S. Importer-Wm. Larkin Moore, 8430 E. Raintree Ste. B-7, Scottsdale, AZ 85260

U.S. Optics, A Division of Zeitz Optics U.S.A., 5900 Dale St., Buena Park, CA 90621 / 714-994-4901; FAX: 714-994-4904 www.usoptics.com

U.S. Repeating Arms Co., Inc., 275 Winchester Ave., Morgan, UT 84050-9333 / 801-876-3440; FAX: 801-876-3737 www.winchester-guns.com

U.S. Tactical Systems (See Keng's Firearms Specialty, Inc.)

Ugartechea S. A., Ignacio, Chonta 26, Eibar, SPAIN / 43-121257; FAX: 43-121669

Ultra Dot Distribution, P.O. Box 362, 6304 Riverside Dr., Yankeetown, FL 34498 / 352-447-2255; FAX: 352-447-2266

Ultralux (See U.S. Importer-Keng's Firearms Specialty, Inc.)

Uncle Bud's, HCR 81, Box 100, Needmore, PA 17238 / 717-294-6000; FAX: 717-294-6005

Uncle Mike's (See Michaels of Oregon, Co.)

Unertl Optical Co., Inc., 103 Grand Avenue, P.O. Box 895, Mars, PA 16046-0895 / 724-625-3810; FAX: 724-625-3819 unertl@nauticom.net www.unertloptics.net

UniTec, 1250 Bedford SW, Canton, OH 44710 / 216-452-4017

United Binocular Co., 9043 S. Western Ave., Chicago, IL 60620

United Cutlery Corp., 1425 United Blvd., Sevierville, TN 37876 / 865-428-2532 or 800-548-0835; FAX: 865-428-2267 www.unitedcutlery.com

United States Products Co., 518 Melwood Ave., Pittsburgh, PA 15213-1136 / 412-621-2130; FAX: 412-621-8740 sales@us-products.com www.usporepaste.com

Universal Sports, P.O. Box 532, Vincennes, IN 47591 / 812-882-8680; FAX: 812-882-8680

Upper Missouri Trading Co., P.O. Box 100, 304 Harold St., Crofton, NE 68730-0100 / 402-388-4844 www.uppermotradingco.com

USAC, 4500-15th St. East, Tacoma, WA 98424 / 206-922-7589

Uselton/Arms, Inc., 842 Conference Dr., Goodlettsville, TN 37072 / 615-851-4919

Utica Cutlery Co., 820 Noyes St., Utica, NY 13503 / 315-733-4663; FAX: 315-733-6602

V

V. H. Blackinton & Co., Inc., 221 John L. Dietsch, Attleboro Falls, MA 02763-0300 / 508-699-4436; FAX: 508-695-5349

Valdada Enterprises, P.O. Box 773122, 31733 County Road 35, Steamboat Springs, CO 80477 / 970-879-2983; FAX: 970-879-0851 www.valdada.com

Valtro USA, Inc., 1281 Andersen Dr., San Rafael, CA 94901 / 415-256-2575; FAX: 415-256-2576

VAM Distribution Co. LLC, 1141-B Mechanicsburg Rd., Wooster, OH 44691 www.rex10.com

Van Gorden & Son Inc., C. S., 1815 Main St., Bloomer, WI 54724 / 715-568-2612

Van Horn, Gil, P.O. Box 207, Llano, CA 93544

Van Patten, J. W., 214 Christian Hill Rd., Milford, PA 18337 / 717-296-7069

Vann Custom Bullets, 2766 N. Willowside Way, Meridian, ID 83642

Varmint Masters, LLC, Rick Vecqueray, P.O. Box 6724, Bend, OR 97708 / 541-318-7306; FAX: 541-318-7306 varmintmasters@bendcable.com www.varmintmasters.net

Vecqueray, Rick. See: VARMINT MASTERS, LLC

Vector Arms, Inc., 270 W. 500 N., North Salt Lake, UT 84054 / 801-295-1917; FAX: 801-295-9316 vectorarms@bbscmail.com www.vectorarms.com

Vega Tool Co., c/o T. R. Ross, 4865 Tanglewood Ct., Boulder, CO 80301 / 303-530-0174 clanlaird@aol.com www.vegatool.com

Venco Industries, Inc. (See Shooter's Choice Gun Care)

Venus Industries, P.O. Box 246, Sialkot-1, PAKISTAN FAX: 92 432 85579

Verney-Carron, 54 Boulevard Thiers-B.P. 72, 42002 St. Etienne Cedex 1, St. Etienne Cedex 1, FRANCE / 33-477791500; FAX: 33-477790702 email@verney-carron.com www.verney-carron.com

Vest, John, 1923 NE 7th St., Redmond, OR 97756 / 541-923-8898

VibraShine, Inc., P.O. Box 577, Taylorsville, MS 39168 / 601-785-9854; FAX: 601-785-9874 rdbeke@vibrashine.com www.vibrashine.com

Vibra-Tek Co., 1844 Arroya Rd., Colorado Springs, CO 80906 / 719-634-8611; FAX: 719-634-6886

Vic's Gun Refinishing, 6 Pineview Dr., Dover, NH 03820-6422 / 603-742-0013

Victory Ammunition, P.O. Box 1022, Milford, PA 18337 / 717-296-5768; FAX: 717-296-9298

Vihtavuori Oy, FIN-41330 Vihtavuori, FINLAND, / 358-41-3779211; FAX: 358-41-3771643

Vihtavuori Oy/Kaltron-Pettibone, 1241 Ellis St., Bensenville, IL 60106 / 708-350-1116; FAX: 708-350-1606

Village Restorations & Consulting, Inc., P.O. Box 569, Claysburg, PA 16625 / 814-239-8200; FAX: 814-239-2165 www.villagerestoration@yahoo.com

Vincent's Shop, 210 Antoinette, Fairbanks, AK 99701

Viper Bullet and Brass Works, 11 Brock St., Box 582, Norwich, ON N0J 1P0 CANADA

Viramontez Engraving, Ray Viramontez, 601 Springfield Dr., Albany, GA 31721 / 229-432-9683 sgtvira@aol.com

Viramontez, Ray. See: VIRAMONTEZ ENGRAVING

Virgin Valley Custom Guns, 450 E 800 N. #20, Hurricane, UT 84737 / 435-635-8941; FAX: 435-635-8943 vvcguns@infowest.com www.virginvalleyguns.com

Vitt/Boos, 1195 Buck Hill Rd., Townshend, VT 05353 / 802-365-9232

Voere-KGH GmbH, Untere Sparchen 56, A-6330 Kufstein, Tirol, AUSTRIA / 0043-5372-62547; FAX: 0043-5372-65752 voere@aon.com www.voere.com

Volquartsen Custom Ltd., 24276 240th Street, P.O. Box 397, Carroll, IA 51401 / 712-792-4238; FAX: 712-792-2542 info@volquartsen.com www.volquartsen.com

Vorhes, David, 3042 Beecham St., Napa, CA 94558 / 707-226-9116; FAX: 707-253-7334

VSP Publishers (See Heritage/VSP Gun Books), P.O. Box 887, McCall, ID 83638 / 208-634-4104; FAX: 208-634-3101 heritage@gunbooks.com www.gunbooks.com

VTI Gun Parts, P.O. Box 509, Lakeville, CT 06039 / 860-435-8068; FAX: 860-435-8146 mail@vtigunparts.com www.vtigunparts.com

Vulpes Ventures, Inc., Fox Cartridge Division, P.O. Box 1363, Bolingbrook, IL 60440-7363 / 630-759-1229

W

W. Square Enterprises, 9826 Sagedale Dr., Houston, TX 77089 / 281-484-0935; FAX: 281-464-9940 lfdw@pdq.net www.loadammo.com

W. Waller & Son, Inc., 52 Coventry Dr., Sunapee, NH 03782 / 603-763-3320 or 800-874-2247 FAX: 603-763-3225; waller@wallerandson.com www.wallerandson.com

W.B. Niemi Engineering, Box 126 Center Road, Greensboro, VT 05841 / 802-533-7180 or 802-533-7141

W.C. Wolff Co., P.O. Box 458, Newtown Square, PA 19073 / 610-359-9600 or 800-545-0077 mail@gunsprings.com www.gunsprings.com

W.E. Birdsong & Assoc., 1435 Monterey Rd., Florence, MS 39073-9748 / 601-366-8270

W.E. Brownell Checkering Tools, 9390 Twin Mountain Cir., San Diego, CA 92126 / 858-695-2479; FAX: 858-695-2479

W.J. Riebe Co., 3434 Tucker Rd., Boise, ID 83703

W.R. Case & Sons Cutlery Co., Owens Way, Bradford, PA 16701 / 814-368-4123 or 800-523-6350; FAX: 814-368-1736 jsullivan@wrcase.com www.wrcase.com

Wagoner, Vernon G., 2325 E. Encanto St., Mesa, AZ 85213-5917 / 480-835-1307

Waldron, Herman, Box 475, 80 N. 17th St., Pomeroy, WA 99347 / 509-843-1404

Walker Arms Co., Inc., 499 County Rd. 820, Selma, AL 36701 / 334-872-6231; FAX: 334-872-6262

Wallace, Terry, 385 San Marino, Vallejo, CA 94589 / 707-642-7041

Walls Industries, Inc., P.O. Box 98, 1905 N. Main, Cleburne, TX 76033 / 817-645-4366; FAX: 817-645-7946 www.wallsoutdoors.com

Walters Industries, 6226 Park Lane, Dallas, TX 75225 / 214-691-6973

Walters, John. See: WALTERS WADS

Walters Wads, John Walters, 500 N. Avery Dr., Moore, OK 73160 / 405-799-0376; FAX: 405-799-7727 www.tinwadman@cs.com

Walther America, P.O. Box 22, Springfield, MA 01102 / 413-747-3443 www.walther-usa.com

Walther GmbH, Carl, B.P. 4325, D-89033 Ulm, GERMANY

Walt's Custom Leather, Walt Whinnery, 1947 Meadow Creek Dr., Louisville, KY 40218 / 502-458-4361

WAMCO-New Mexico, P.O. Box 205, Peralta, NM 87042-0205 / 505-869-0826

Ward & Van Valkenburg, 114 32nd Ave. N., Fargo, ND 58102 / 701-232-2351

Ward Machine, 5620 Lexington Rd., Corpus Christi, TX 78412 / 512-992-1221

Wardell Precision, P.O. Box 391, Clyde, TX 79510-0391 / 325-893-3763 fwardell@valornet.com

Washita Mountain Whetstone Co., 418 Hilltop Rd., Pearcy, AR 71964 / 501-767-1616; FAX: 501-767-9598 www.@hsnp.com

Wasmundt, Jim. See: J.W. WASMUNDT-GUNSMITH

Watson Bros., 39 Redcross Way, London Bridge SE1 1H6, London, ENGLAND FAX: 44-171-403-336

Watson Bullets, 231 Allies Pass, Frostproof, FL 33843 / 863-635-7948 cbestbullet@aol.com

Wayne Specialty Services, 260 Waterford Drive, Florissant, MO 63033 / 413-831-7083

WD-40 Co., 1061 Cudahy Pl., San Diego, CA 92110 / 619-275-1400; FAX: 619-275-5823

Weatherby, Inc., 3100 El Camino Real, Atascadero, CA 93422 / 805-466-1767; FAX: 805-466-2527 www.weatherby.com

Weaver Products ATK, P.O. Box 39, Onalaska, WI 54650 / 800-648-9624 or 608-781-5800; FAX: 608-781-0368

Weaver Scope Repair Service, 1121 Larry Mahan Dr., Suite B, El Paso, TX 79925 / 915-593-1005 frank@weaver-scope-repair.com www.weaver-scope-repair.com

Webb, Bill, 6504 North Bellefontaine, Kansas City, MO 64119 / 816-453-7431

Weber & Markin Custom Gunsmiths, 4-1691 Powick Rd., Kelowna, BC V1X 4L1 CANADA / 250-762-7575; FAX: 250-861-3655 www.weberandmarkinguns.com

Webley and Scott Ltd., Frankley Industrial Park, Tay Rd., Birmingham, B45 0PA ENGLAND / 011-021-453-1864; FAX: 0121-457-7846 guns@webley.co.uk www.webley.co.uk

Webster Scale Mfg. Co., P.O. Box 188, Sebring, FL 33870 / 813-385-6362

Weigand Combat Handguns, Inc., 1057 South Main Rd., Mountain Top, PA 18707 / 570-868-8358; FAX: 570-868-5218 sales@jackweigand.com www.jackweigand.com

Weihrauch KG, Hermann, Industriestrasse 11, 8744 Mellrichstadt, Mellrichstadt, GERMANY

Welch, Sam. See: SAM WELCH GUN ENGRAVING

Wellington Outdoors, P.O. Box 244, 1140 Monticello Rd., Madison, GA 30650 / 706-342-4915; FAX: 706-342-7568

Wells, Rachel, 110 N. Summit St., Prescott, AZ 86301 / 928-445-3655 wellssportstore@cableone.net

Wells Creek Knife & Gun Works, 32956 State Hwy. 38, Scottsburg, OR 97473 / 541-587-4202; FAX: 541-587-4223

Wells, Margaret. See: WELLS SPORT STORE

Wells Sport Store, Margaret R Wells, 110 N. Summit St., Prescott, AZ 86301 / 928-445-3655 www.wellssportstore@cableone.net

Welsh, Bud. See: HIGH PRECISION

Wenger North America/Precise Int'l., 15 Corporate Dr., Orangeburg, NY 10962 / 800-431-2996; FAX: 914-425-4700

Wenig Custom Gunstocks, 103 N. Market St., P.O. Box 249, Lincoln, MO 65338 / 660-547-3334; FAX: 660-547-2881 gustock@wenig.com www.wenig.com

Werth, T. W., 1203 Woodlawn Rd., Lincoln, IL 62656 / 217-732-1300; FAX: 217-735-5106

Wescombe, Bill (See North Star West)

Wessinger Custom Guns & Engraving, 268 Limestone Rd., Chapin, SC 29036 / 803-345-5677

West, Jack L., 1220 W. Fifth, P.O. Box 427, Arlington, OR 97812

Western Cutlery (See Camillus Cutlery Co.)

Western Mfg. Co., 550 Valencia School Rd., Aptos, CA 95003 / 831-688-5884 lotsabears@eathlink.net

Western Missouri Shooters Alliance, P.O. Box 11144, Kansas City, MO 64119 / 816-597-3950; FAX: 816-229-7350

Western Nevada West Coast Bullets, P.O. Box 2270, Dayton, NV 89403-2270 / 702-246-3941; FAX: 702-246-0836

Westley Richards & Co. Ltd., 40 Grange Rd., Birmingham, ENGLAND / 010-214722953; FAX: 010-214141138 sales@westleyrichards.com www.westleyrichards.com

Westley Richards Agency USA (See U.S. Importer

Westwind Rifles, Inc., David S. Sullivan, P.O. Box 261, 640 Briggs St., Erie, CO 80516 / 303-828-3823

Weyer International, 2740 Nebraska Ave., Toledo, OH 43607 / 419-534-2020; FAX: 419-534-2697

Whinnery, Walt (See Walt's Custom Leather)

White Barn Wor, 431 County Road, Broadlands, IL 61816

White Pine Photographic Services, Hwy. 60, General Delivery, Wilno, ON K0J 2N0 CANADA / 613-756-3452

White Rifles, Inc., 234 S. 1250 W., Linden, UT 84042 / 801-932-7950 www.whiterifles.com

White Rock Tool & Die, 6400 N. Brighton Ave., Kansas City, MO 64119 / 816-454-0478

Whitestone Lumber Corp., 148-02 14th Ave., Whitestone, NY 11357 / 718-746-4400; FAX: 718-767-1748 whstco@aol.com

Wichita Arms, Inc., 923 E. Gilbert, Wichita, KS 67211 / 316-265-0661; FAX: 316-265-0760 sales@wichitaarms.com www.wichitaarms.com

Wick, David E., 1504 Michigan Ave., Columbus, IN 47201 / 812-376-6960

Widener's Reloading & Shooting Supply, Inc., P.O. Box 3009 CRS, Johnson City, TN 37602 / 615-282-6786; FAX: 615-282-6651

Wideview Scope Mount Corp., 13535 S. Hwy. 16, Rapid City, SD 57702 / 605-341-3220; FAX: 605-341-9142 wvdon@rapidnet.com www.wideviewscopemount.com

Wiebe, Duane, 1111 157th St. Ct. E., Tacoma, WA 98445 / 253-535-0066; FAX: 253-535-0066 duane@directcom.net

Wiest, Marie. See: GUNCRAFT SPORTS, INC.

Wilcox All-Pro Tools & Supply, 4880 147th St., Montezuma, IA 50171 / 515-623-3138; FAX: 515-623-3104

Wilcox Industries Corp., Robert F. Guarasi, 53 Durham St., Portsmouth, NH 03801 / 603-431-1331; FAX: 603-431-1221

Wild Bill's Originals, P.O. Box 13037, Burton, WA 98013 / 206-463-5738; FAX: 206-465-5925 billcleaver@centurytel.net billcleaver@centurytel.net

Wild West Guns, 7100 Homer Dr., Anchorage, AK 99518 / 800-992-4570 or 907-344-4500; FAX: 907-344-4005 wwguns@ak.net www.wildwestguns.alaska.net

Wilderness Sound Products Ltd., 4015 Main St. A, Springfield, OR 97478

Wildey F. A., Inc., 45 Angevin Rd., Warren, CT 06754-1818 / 860-355-9000; FAX: 860-354-7759 wildeyfa@optonline.net www.wildeyguns.com

Wildlife Research Center, Inc., 1050 McKinley St., Anoka, MN 55303 / 763-427-3350 or 800-USE-LURE; (873-5873) FAX: 763-427-8354 www.wildlife.com

Will-Burt Co., 169 S. Main, Orrville, OH 44667

William E. Phillips Firearms, 38 Avondale Rd., Wigston, Leicester, ENGLAND / 0116 2886334; FAX: 0116 2810644 william.phillips2@tesco.net

William Powell Agency, 22 Circle Dr., Bellmore, NY 11710 / 516-679-1158

Williams Gun Sight Co., 7389 Lapeer Rd., Box 329, Davison, MI 48423 / 810-653-2131 or 800-530-9028; FAX: 810-658-2140 williamsgunsight.com

Williams Mfg. of Oregon, 110 East B St., Drain, OR 97435 / 503-836-7461; FAX: 503-836-7245

Williams Shootin' Iron Service, The Lynx-Line, Rt. 2 Box 223A, Mountain Grove, MO 65711 / 417-948-0902; FAX: 417-948-0902

Williamson Precision Gunsmithing, 117 W. Pipeline, Hurst, TX 76053 / 817-285-0064; FAX: 817-280-0044

Willow Bend, P.O. Box 203, Chelmsford, MA 01824 / 978-256-8508; FAX: 978-256-8508

Wilson Combat, 2234 CR 719, Berryville, AR 72616-4573 / 800-955-4856; FAX: 870-545-3310 info@wilsoncombat.com www.wilsoncombat.com

Wilson Arms Co., The, 63 Leetes Island Rd., Branford, CT 06405 / 203-488-7297; FAX: 203-488-0135

Wilson Case, Inc., P.O. Box 1106, Hastings, NE 68902-1106 / 800-322-5493; FAX: 402-463-5276 sales@wilsoncase.com www.wilsoncase.com

Wilson Combat, 2234 CR 719, Berryville, AR 72616-4573 / 800-955-4856

Winchester Consultants, George Madis, P.O. Box 545, Brownsboro, TX 75756 / 903-852-6480; FAX: 903-852-5486 gmadis@earthlink.com www.georgemadis.com

Winchester Div. Olin Corp., 427 N. Shamrock, E. Alton, IL 62024 / 618-258-3566; FAX: 618-258-3599

Winchester Sutler, Inc., The, 270 Shadow Brook Lane, Winchester, VA 22603 / 540-888-3595; FAX: 540-888-4632

Windish, Jim, 2510 Dawn Dr., Alexandria, VA 22306 / 703-765-1994

Winfield Galleries LLC, 748 Hanley Industrial Ct., St. Louis, MO 63144 / 314-645-7636; FAX: 314-781-0224 info@winfieldgalleries.com www.winfieldgalleries.com

Wingshooting Adventures, 0-1845 W. Leonard, Grand Rapids, MI 49544 / 616-677-1980; FAX: 616-677-1986

Winter, Robert M., P.O. Box 484, 42975-287th St., Menno, SD 57045 / 605-387-5322

Wise Custom Guns, 1402 Blanco Rd., San Antonio, TX 78212-2716 / 210-828-3388

Wise Guns, Dale, 1402 Blanco Rd., San Antonio, TX 78212 / 210-734-9999

Wiseman and Co., Bill, P.O. Box 3427, Bryan, TX 77805 / 409-690-3456; FAX: 409-690-0156

Wisners, Inc., P.O. Box 58, Adna, WA 98522 / 360-748-4590; FAX: 360-748-6028 parts@wisnersinc.com www.wisnersinc.com

Wolf Performance Ammunition, 2201 E. Winston Rd., Ste. K, Anaheim, CA 92806-5537 / 702-837-8506; FAX: 702-837-9250

Wolfe Publishing Co., 2625 Stearman Rd., Ste. A, Prescott, AZ 86301 / 928-445-7810 or 800-899-7810; FAX: 928-778-5124 wolfepub@riflemag.com www.riflemagazine.com

Wolverine Footwear Group, 9341 Courtland Dr. NE, Rockford, MI 49351 / 616-866-5500; FAX: 616-866-5658

Woodleigh (See Huntington Die Specialties)

Woods Wise Products, P.O. Box 681552, Franklin, TN 37068 / 800-735-8182; FAX: 615-726-2637

Woodstream, P.O. Box 327, Lititz, PA 17543 / 717-626-2125; FAX: 717-626-1912

Woodworker's Supply, 1108 North Glenn Rd., Casper, WY 82601 / 307-237-5354

Woolrich, Inc., Mill St., Woolrich, PA 17701 / 800-995-1299; FAX: 717-769-6234/6259

World of Targets (See Birchwood Casey)

World Trek, Inc., 7170 Turkey Creek Rd., Pueblo, CO 81007-1046 / 719-546-2121; FAX: 719-543-6886

Wright's Gunstock Blanks, 8540 SE Kane Rd., Gresham, OR 97080 / 503-666-1705 doyal@wrightsguns.com www.wrightsguns.com

WTA Manufacturing, P.O. Box 164, Kit Carson, CO 80825 / 719-962-3570 or 719-962-3570 wta@rebeltec.net http://www.members.aol.com/ductman249/wta.html

Wyant Bullets, Gen. Del., Swan Lake, MT 59911

Wyoming Custom Bullets, 1626 21st St., Cody, WY 82414

Wyoming Knife Corp., 101 Commerce Dr., Fort Collins, CO 80524 / 303-224-3454

X

XS Sight Systems, 2401 Ludelle St., Fort Worth, TX 76105 / 888-744-4880; FAX: 800-734-7939

X-Spand Target Systems, 26-10th St. SE, Medicine Hat, AB T1A 1P7 CANADA / 403-526-7997; FAX: 403-528-2362

Y

Yankee Gunsmith "Just Glocks", 2901 Deer Flat Dr., Copperas Cove, TX 76522 / 817-547-8433; FAX: 254-547-8887 ed@justglocks.com www.justglocks.com

Yavapai College, 1100 E. Sheldon St., Prescott, AZ 86301 / 520-776-2353; FAX: 520-776-2355

Yavapai Firearms Academy Ltd., P.O. Box 27290, Prescott Valley, AZ 86312 / 928-772-8262; FAX: 928-772-0062 info@yfainc.com www.yfainc.com

Yearout, Lewis E. (See Montana Outfitters)

York M-1 Conversion, 12145 Mill Creek Run, Plantersville, TX 77363 / 936-894-2397; FAX: 936-894-2397 bmf25years@aol.com

Young Country Arms, William, 1409 Kuehner Dr. #13, Simi Valley, CA 93063-4478

Z

Zabala Hermanos S.A., P.O. Box 97, Elbar Lasao, 6, Elgueta, Guipuzcoa, 20600 SPAIN / 34-943-768076; FAX: 34-943-768201 imanol@zabalahermanos.com www.zabalahermanos.com

Zander's Sporting Goods, 7525 Hwy. 154 West, Baldwin, IL 62217-9706 / 800-851-4373; FAX: 618-785-2320

Zanotti Armor, Inc., 123 W. Lone Tree Rd., Cedar Falls, IA 50613 / 319-232-9650 www.zanottiarmor.com

Zeeryp, Russ, 1601 Foard Dr., Lynn Ross Manor, Morristown, TN 37814 / 615-586-2357

Zero Ammunition Co., Inc., 1601 22nd St. SE, P.O. Box 1188, Cullman, AL 35056-1188 / 800-545-9376; FAX: 205-739-4683 zerobulletco@aoz.com www.zerobullets.com

Ziegel Engineering, 1390 E. Bunnett St. "F", Signal Hill, CA 90755 / 562-596-9481; FAX: 562-598-4734 ziegel@aol.com www.ziegeleng.com

Zim's, Inc., 4370 S. 3rd West, Salt Lake City, UT 84107 / 801-268-2505

Z-M Weapons, 203 South St., Bernardston, MA 01337 / 413-648-9501; FAX: 413-648-0219

NUMBERS

100 Straight Products, Inc., P.O. Box 6148, Omaha, NE 68106 / 402-556-1055; FAX: 402-556-1055

3-Ten Corp., P.O. Box 269, Feeding Hills, MA 01030 / 413-789-2086; FAX: 413-789-1549 www.3-ten.com

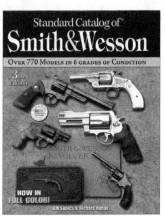
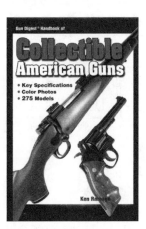
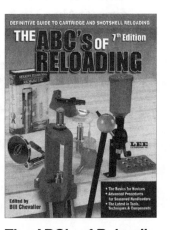